CONTRACTS:
LAW IN ACTION

CONTRACTS: LAW IN ACTION

Volume II
The Advanced Course

Fourth Edition

Stewart Macaulay
Professor of Law Emeritus
University of Wisconsin Law School

William Whitford
Professor of Law Emeritus
University of Wisconsin Law School

Kathryn Hendley
William Voss-Bascom Professor of Law and Political Science
University of Wisconsin Law School

Jonathan Lipson
Harold E. Kohn Chair and Professor of Law
Temple University Beasley School of Law

CAROLINA ACADEMIC PRESS
Durham, North Carolina

ISBN: 978-1-5221-0407-0
e-ISBN: 978-1-5221-0408-7
LCCN: 2016939504

Carolina Academic Press, LLC
700 Kent Street Durham, NC 27701
Telephone (919) 489-7486
Fax (919) 493-5668
www.caplaw.com

Printed in the United States of America

Table of Contents

Preface to the Fourth Edition

New editions of *Contracts: Law in Action* allow us to offer new cases and statutes to keep our materials up to date. In this edition, we continue the philosophy and the coverage of the first three editions; once again, we are republishing the preface to the second edition, in which that philosophy is described.

As in previous editions, the cases have been edited to make them easier to read. We have used ellipses whenever substantive text has been omitted from the body of an opinion, but some case citations and many footnotes have been omitted without indication. The footnote numbers in our text do not match the footnote numbers in the cases, since we number our footnotes sequentially by chapter. When we reproduce footnotes from cases, we have indicated the original footnote number by putting it in brackets: [ ]. When we have added our own footnote to a case, it is indicated by an "Eds. note," also in brackets.

The list of authors has changed; we have added Kathryn Hendley and Jonathan Lipson to our group. Each of them brings something new to the enterprise. Professor Hendley is one of the foremost scholars of law in the transition from socialism to capitalism in Russia. Professor Lipson has long experience as a corporate lawyer and transaction planner. Each has used earlier editions of *Contracts: Law in Action* for a number of years.

Sadly, two of the authors of our third edition have died since it was published. John Kidwell's participation in the creation and development of the book dates back to its earliest days. First and foremost, John was a great and award-winning teacher, and he insisted that the materials had to work in class. We knew that if John had a problem teaching something in the book, it had to be fixed.

John also wrote bar exam questions, and he insisted that our course had to play a real part in transforming beginners into skilled lawyers. John was sympathetic to the goal of fashioning a modern contracts course that emphasized law in action, but he worried about losing something important if and when we abandoned what had long been in the traditional course.

He was a wonderful colleague, always prepared to go above and beyond any possible call of duty to get the manuscript to the publisher in a timely manner, to get a jointly composed exam completed, or to help newly minted law school professors cope with their first classes. John wrote the following about himself for his law school profile:

"He enjoys reading, listening to music,[1] idle conversation, and the game of poker. His favorite composer is J.S. Bach, and his favorite writer is John McPhee. He subscribes to too many magazines."

Jean Braucher first used a photocopied version of *Contracts: Law in Action* in 1992 at the University of Cincinnati Law School, and she continued teaching from it when she moved to the University of Arizona in 1998. We appreciated her kind words about the book when it was first published:[2]

> [*Contracts: Law in Action*] weaves the history, philosophy, sociology, and doctrine of contract into a vibrant if troubling picture, confronting students with the conflicts, complexities, and above all, the limits of the subject. [The authors] challenge students to become "skeptical idealists" in the practice of law. Their approach is both theoretically sophisticated and thoroughly practical.

Jean had done empirical research on the practices of lawyers in consumer bankruptcy,[3] and she worked on law reform in many places, including the American Law Institute and the Uniform Law Commission (formerly known as the National Conference of Commissioners on Uniform State Laws).

In November 2007, Jean accepted our offer to become an author and editor for the third, and all subsequent, editions of *Contracts: Law in Action*. The publisher had insisted that the new edition of the book not be any longer than the previous one: if we added anything, we had to take something out. Jean enforced this rule, pushed us to bring the book up to date, and was always on the lookout for ways in which new statutes, new standard contracts clauses—and especially recent advances in technology—presented new settings for the classic problems dealt with in traditional contracts courses.

Jean used these materials for 22 years and edited them for seven. She concluded from this and other experiences: "The law does not march forward so much as stumble on ... Law is about social struggle, and we never get neat, perfect conclusions."[4]

We have missed, and will continue to miss, John and Jean. Both contributed so much to this project. In the preparation of both this edition and the third edition, we also had the extraordinary assistance of Ellen Vinz (J.D., University of Wisconsin Law School, 2011), a professional copyeditor as well as a former lawyer. We were also assisted by Erica Maier at Temple University Beasley School of Law and the following student research assistants: Andrew Brehm (J.D., University of Wisconsin Law School,

---

1. John often opened class by playing a song that fit one or more of the cases for that day. For example, when he taught *Vokes v. Arthur Murray*, he treated students raised on rock and roll to an ancient Jimmy Dorsey big band recording of "Arthur Murray Taught Me Dancing in a Hurry."

Jonathan Lipson carries on John's tradition, albeit with a lower brow. He opens the class on *Hadley v. Baxendale* with the "Theme from Shaft," for example.

2. Jean Braucher, *The Afterlife of Contract*, 90 Nw. U.L. Rev. 49, 52–53 (1995).

3. *See* Jean Braucher, *Lawyers and Consumer Bankruptcy: One Code, Many Cultures*, 67 Am. Bankr. L.J. 501 (1993).

4. *See* William Whitford, *Jean Braucher's Contracts World View*, 58 Ariz. L. Rev. 13, 31 (2016).

2015); Miranda Bullard (J.D., Temple University Beasley School of Law, 2017); Nicholas Zuiker (J.D., University of Wisconsin Law School, 2015); Nicholas Korger (J.D. University of Wisconsin Law School, 2017); and Chelsea Zielke (J.D. University of Wisconsin Law School, 2018).

Stewart Macaulay

William Whitford

Kathryn Hendley

Jonathan Lipson

November 9, 2016

Preface to the Second Edition

We revised our book for a number of reasons. Most importantly, our original book and this revision reject the idea that contract law is no more than a small collection of timeless principles. Contracts problems change as the society changes. Corporate lawyers also have been busy, seeking ways to use the form of contract to ward off liability to employees and consumers. Fashions in scholarly work reflect changes in the academy as we move through cycles of classical contract; realist judging in the grand style; dedication to the consumer movement; reductionist pursuits of efficiency, default rules, and formalism; and, perhaps, the coming new realism that reflects a law and society perspective. We have reviewed the entire book to see where we should reflect these changes and new developments, but the major effort has been devoted to bringing up to date our materials on such matters as unconscionability, form contracts printed in fine print or hidden in other ways (particularly in the area of computer programs), and the growing uses of arbitration to repeal the reform statutes of earlier decades. These are the interesting and important matters coming before the courts when this revision was prepared, and we expect these topics to have a fairly long shelf life.

At the same time, those who have used *Contracts: Law in Action* in the past will find much of the book unchanged or only slightly modified. After teaching *Contracts: Law in Action* and earlier photocopied versions for about 20 years, the authors think that the book works. Moreover, it has worked for instructors who emphasize very different approaches in their teaching. The original book and the revision both take the "Law in Action" part of the title seriously. Putting contract problems in context makes the course both more theoretical and more practical at the same time. Whatever a person's theoretical outlook, there is a high price to be paid if he or she forgets such things as that law is not free; most disputes end in settlement; crafting nice-sounding legal standards is one thing but finding evidence to establish a cause of action is another; and that all institutions, including the market, are flawed. American contract law is messy and often contradictory. Even when the form of the rules stay more or less the same, their application varies from court to court over time. Yet the flaws in our contract law have not blocked great economic progress or caused recessions. We quote Wittgenstein near the beginning of the course: "Is it even always an advantage to replace an indistinct picture by a sharp one? Isn't the indistinct one often exactly what we need?" At the very least, the answer to this question cannot just be assumed away. We also have been pleased to discover that many of our former students find that our course prepares them to hit the ground running when they begin practice.

We have tried to focus on live contracts problems that our students will face when they become lawyers.

We are heavily in debt to contracts teachers at schools other than Wisconsin who have used *CLA*. We have had an e-mail list for those interested in the book. Our friends at other schools have contributed ideas and suggestions, and they have asked us to explain why we did certain things. Sometimes we have been able to explain choices we made long ago, and when we could not we rethought what we had done. We have learned a great deal from these friends. While we risk leaving out people who deserve mention, we wish to thank particularly Tom Russell, Tom Stipanowich, Bill Woodward, Sandy Meiklejohn, Alan Hunt, Jean Braucher, Peter Linzer, and Carolyn Brown. In addition, we staged a conference in the fall of 2001. We gathered many who had used the book and other friends whose contributions we wanted to hear. The papers were later published in 2001 *Wisconsin Law Review* 525–1006. The papers, discussions, and final articles helped us in the revision process.

The authors are not the only people at Wisconsin who have taught from the book. We have a small-group program in which each first-year student gets one class of around 20 students, and Contracts 1 often has been that class. This means that we have many contracts teachers at Wisconsin. Those teaching the course have met for lunch once a week during the semester. The authors have been challenged by the experiences and questions of their colleagues. In addition to Joe Thome, who was thanked in our original preface and who continued to teach from the materials until recently, we should acknowledge the many contributions of Kathryn Hendley, Lawrence Bugge, Gordon Smith, and Lori Ringhand (now at the University of Kentucky Law School). Lori was a beginning law teacher when she joined us, and she helped us rewrite the employment-at-will material and paid particular attention to the teaching notes that we have made available to those who use the book. She has revised them, pulling together the one set created by John Kidwell and the other by Stewart Macaulay. Our colleague Marc Galanter decided not to participate in the second edition of *Contracts: Law in Action*. He has not taught contracts for some time. However, he did present a paper at our 2001 contracts conference, and the revision still reflects his many contributions to the original version of the book. Also, Nicole Denow (J.D., Wisconsin, 2001) was a talented and hard-working research assistant in the revision of the materials dealing with policing contracts, and Nora Kersten (J.D., Wisconsin, 2002) did many memos that were helpful in expanding some of the notes, or in verifying that no changes were required.

We also owe a debt to the thousands of law students who have worked their way through *Contracts: Law in Action* and its photocopied predecessors. For example, Donovan Bezer, then a student at Rutgers Law School, sent us his reactions, which we found provocative. Other students have known one or more of the parties who appear in the cases in the book, or they have known much about the kinds of transactions involved. We have been reassured that the book has prompted students to see the hard choices lurking behind what seem to be the simple rules of contract law.

Americans, of course, always want to have their cake and eat it too. One student, who identified herself as a liberal, sent us an e-mail saying, "This class has put me in touch with my inner Republican, and I am not sure that I like *him.*" Students have also reminded us that most of them are twenty-something, and what we see as things "everyone knows" are but ancient history to them. Students stay about the same age while authors age. Thus, we have tried to change examples so that they will not date too fast and explain a little about such "commonplace things" as the Vietnam conflict, OPEC, the consumer movement, and other manifestations of pre-Reagan politics — as well as what were ice houses, dial telephones, and typewriters. While we find it hard to believe, many of our students have never heard of Shirley MacLaine, Lee Marvin, or Bette Davis. We, on the other hand, are not great followers of River Phoenix. All of these stars, of course, play the parts of litigants in contracts cases.

During the past decade or so, the National Conference of Commissioners on Uniform State Law and the American Law Institute have attempted to revise Article 2 of the Uniform Commercial Code. We debated what to do with the proposed revisions. Then our friend Richard Speidel found the process intolerable and felt that he had to resign as the Reporter after twelve years of work. At the time this is being written, it seems unlikely that there will be ambitious changes to Article 2, with the possible exception of the addition of a highly controversial separate statute dealing with computer-related transactions. There is a risk that states may end up moving in the direction of creating "Un-Uniform Commercial Codes." As a result, we decided not to include material on the proposed revisions. Instructors, of course, may want to offer their classes particular proposals as a way to raise policy questions about the current law. However, we think that it is hard enough finding your way around Article 2 without having to navigate two or more versions.

Chapter 1

FORMATION OF CONTRACT

The major focus of the following chapters is the performance of contracts. We consider questions such as the effect of a seller's only slightly defective performance. Must the buyer accept it with, perhaps, an offset for its flaws? Or does close count only in horseshoes and hand grenades? Suppose a seller tenders defective goods. Can it have a second chance and cure its performance, or can the buyer call off the deal? Should courts consider whether the buyer really was hurt by the defective tender or wants out only because it can get the goods more cheaply elsewhere? Suppose a seller is almost certain that buyer will not be able to pay for the goods when the day for performance comes. Must seller continue performance, or can seller stop unless buyer can offer assurances that it will pay when the time comes?

Before we reach these questions, we need to establish familiarity with two opposed models of the contracting process; judicial answers to questions of performance often reflect assumptions about how deals are made. The first model sees the parties' contract as a blueprint for performance. It assumes buyers and sellers can and should specify obligations very precisely and allocate all the risks of possible contingencies. Contract drafters bring the future back to the present, dealing with the possibility of a war, a depression, a strike, and so on. If something goes wrong in performance, ideally all that the parties, lawyers, and judges need do is read a written document and discover what is to happen in this event.

The second model acknowledges that many contracts reflect long-term, continuing relationships within rich business and social contexts. Instead of a magic moment when everything is defined, the contours of the parties' bargain emerge as they perform through time. While they may have agreed to terms at the outset, everything is always subject to formal or tacit renegotiation. Moreover, those accepting this second model of bargaining processes understand that a written document signed by the parties is not necessarily their bargain-in-fact. For example, the contract may be drafted by elite lawyers at the home office, but the actual agreement is negotiated and performed by people in the field. In this world, it is unsurprising that there are gaps between the real deal and the paper deal.[1]

Those who feel more comfortable with the first image of bargaining are likely to solve questions concerning performance by looking to what the parties agreed at the

---

1. Some might opt for a third model, in which it is acknowledged that people don't really thoroughly embody their intentions in advance of an exchange, but which nevertheless endorses the appealing fiction that they do, in order to increase predictability and social order.

point they made their deal. They will be uneasy when the parties left too much un-specified. Those who are more comfortable with relational contracts will view written documents signed by the parties as but one factor to consider in solving problems. They will seek fair results in light of the way things turned out, with risk assumption just one factor among many that are relevant to what is fair.

Because questions of performance often turn on whether the parties made a deal and what its terms were, we must begin with some of the classic dilemmas concerning how courts know whether the parties closed a deal and how they discover what the bargain means. People often communicate sloppily. They sign documents that say things they don't mean. While every bargain rests on what the parties assume about the world, at times they assume very different things or make assumptions that turn out to be wrong. Courts must respond to all these situations.

Thus, we begin with questions that involve the formation and interpretation of contracts. Then we consider performance questions. As we do, we discover that for-mation and interpretation issues influence the solutions. Finally, we return to un-pleasant surprises in a different context. One party discovers she has made a very bad deal and seeks relief, arguing that she shouldn't be required to absorb the losses as-sociated with what has happened.

We begin by considering how the American legal system legitimates holding people bound to what judges, lawyers, and scholars call contracts. Why do we care? The rea-sons judges accept as common sense may influence how they decide cases. Judges and lawyers form a community with a common language. Judges try to explain their decisions so that lawyers will understand and accept them. Sometimes other audiences respond to a judge's explanations. For example, newspapers, television, or websites may attack a decision. Judges are like the rest of us; they do not like to appear foolish or stupid before any audience.

The relationship between law and legitimacy is unclear. Law contributes something to our view that we live in a just, decent, or tolerable society. Americans tend to regard their legal system as at least acceptable, particularly when they compare it with those found in authoritarian states. It is less clear that Americans honor the results in par-ticular cases. Nonetheless, the legal system itself may have enough prestige so that any norms applied by legal officials seem just. In part, this claim rests on our assumption that the legal system is autonomous enough from other centers of power so that it can apply its procedures, make decisions, and enforce them impartially. Both the President and Bank of America operate under the law. Moreover, legal officials are selected in ways Americans find acceptable. They are experts, selected by presidents or governors in recognition of their skill or, alternatively, elected on the basis of their probity and wisdom. This view suggests that politics should play no role in judicial selection.

Finally, some see particular norms of the law as naturally flowing from legal science, reflecting common sense, and dictated by wise policy. We should not, under this view, question the result in a particular case. Experts, far removed from power and politics, have decided. Their decisions reflect legitimate rules.

You probably noticed a few problems with this account. Many, if not most, Americans understand that the legal system is not autonomous and free from the influence of those who hold power in society. On one hand, some think that legal officials use their power to favor the wealthy and influential. On the other hand, some think those with wealth can play the legal game better, even if the rules are applied evenly and fairly by officials. Then, too, some think that a judge is a lawyer who knew the governor. Judges may be picked in part to achieve diversity, a way of symbolizing that a particular group is both worthy and powerful.

Many challenge the idea that law reflects common sense. Any book of quotations will offer classics, such as: " 'If the law supposes that,' said Mr. Bumble, 'the law is a ass, a idiot.'" (Dickens, *Oliver Twist*, ch. 51); "In a thousand pounds of law there is not an ounce of love." (John Ray, English Proverbs); "The law is a sort of hocus-pocus science, that smiles in yer face while it picks yer pocket; the glorious uncertainty of it is of main use to the professors than the justice of it." (Charles Macklin, *Love a la Mode*, Act ii, scene 1 (1759)); "Laws are spiders' webs, which stand firm when any light and yielding object falls upon them, while a larger thing breaks through them and escapes." (Solon).

We face a major problem in specifying the link between a claim to legitimacy and the attitude of a particular audience. Most people, after all, know very little about particular laws or the legal system. We can wonder whether those who lose when they come before the courts are impressed by the majesty of the law. Few convicted murderers, for example, comment favorably on the skill with which the judge instructed the jury. Indeed, perhaps the major audience for the law's claims to legitimacy is lawyers. Whatever the impact of law on our views about legitimacy, do these attitudes affect our behavior? Do people obey or disobey law because they think it just or unjust?

Having said all this, we can observe that lawyers and judges do make legitimacy claims. Much of the business of law school consists of studying this rhetoric. Although the legitimacy claim is often assumed, law professors, lawyers, and judges exert great effort to show that a rule or procedure reflects some version of the good, the true, and the beautiful. The problem comes when we recognize that each side can usually make a plausible claim that a decision in its favor will serve an important value. If this is true, how do we persuade judges and legislators? How do we predict what they will do? How much do litigation results depend on the ability of lawyers?

In the pages that follow, we will first look at explanations offered for holding or refusing to hold people to obligations that might be called contracts. We have attempted to select problems important to modern business. We also set the stage for the following chapters, which deal with problems in the performance of contracts. We will see that questions about formation and performance are closely related. Whether or not I have performed my promise often turns on what, if anything, the courts will say that I promised to do.

A. CHOICE, FAULT, OR SOMETHING ELSE?

EMBRY v. HARGADINE, MCKITTRICK DRY GOODS CO.

Missouri Court of Appeals
127 Mo. App. 383, 105 S.W. 777 (1907)

GOODE, J.

The appellant was an employee of the respondent company under a written contract to expire December 15, 1903, at a salary of $2,000 per annum. His duties were to attend to the sample department of respondent, of which he was given complete charge. It was his business to select samples for the traveling salesmen of the company, which is a wholesale dry goods concern, to use in selling goods to retail merchants. Appellant contends that on December 23, 1903, he was re-engaged by respondent, through its president, Thos. H. McKittrick, for another year at the same compensation and for the same duties stipulated in his previous written contract. On March 1, 1904, he was discharged, having been notified in February that, on account of the necessity of retrenching expenses, his services and that of some other employees would no longer be required. The respondent company contends that its president never re-employed appellant after the termination of his written contract, and hence that it had a right to discharge him when it chose. The point with which we are concerned requires an epitome of the testimony of appellant and the counter-testimony of McKittrick, the president of the company, in reference to the alleged re-employment. Appellant testified that several times prior to the termination of his written contract on December 15, 1903, he had endeavored to get an understanding with McKittrick for another year, but had been put off from time to time; that on December 23d, eight days after the expiration of said contract, he called on McKittrick, in the latter's office, and said to him that as appellant's written employment had lapsed eight days before, and as there were only a few days between then and the first of January in which to seek employment with other firms, if respondent wished to retain his services longer he must have a contract for another year, or he would quit respondent's service then and there; that he had been put off twice before and wanted an understanding or contract at once so that he could go ahead without worry; that McKittrick asked him how he was getting along in his department, and appellant said he was very busy, as they were in the height of the season getting men out—had about 110 salesmen on the line and others in preparation; that McKittrick then said: "Go ahead, you're all right; get your men out and don't let that worry you," that appellant took McKittrick at his word and worked until February 15th without any question in his mind. It was on February 15th that he was notified his services would be discontinued on March 1st. McKittrick denied this conversation as related by appellant and said that, when accosted by the latter on December 23d, he (McKittrick) was working on his books in order to get out a report for a stockholders' meeting, and, when appellant said if he did not get a contract he would leave, that he (McKittrick) said:

> "Mr. Embry, I am just getting ready for the stockholders' meeting tomorrow,
> I have no time to take it up now; I have told you before I would not take it

up until I had these matters out of the way; you will have to see me at a later time. I said: 'Go back upstairs and get your men out on the road.' I may have asked him one or two other questions relative to the department; I don't remember. The whole conversation did not take more than a minute."

Embry also swore that when he was notified he would be discharged, he complained to McKittrick about it, as being a violation of their contract, and McKittrick said it was due to the action of the board of directors, and not to any personal action of his, and that others would suffer by what the board had done as well as Embry. Appellant requested an instruction to the jury setting out, in substance, the conversation between him and McKittrick according to his version, and declaring that those facts, if found to be true, constituted a contract between the parties that defendant would pay plaintiff the sum of $2,000 for another year, provided the jury believed from the evidence that plaintiff commenced said work believing he was to have $2,000 for the year's work. This instruction was refused, but the court gave another embodying in substance appellant's version of the conversation, and declaring it made a contract "if you (the jury) find both parties thereby intended and did contract with each other for plaintiff's employment for one year from and including December 23, 1903, at a salary of $2,000 per annum." Embry swore that on several occasions when he spoke to McKittrick about employment for the ensuing year, he asked for a renewal of his former contract, and that on December 23d, the date of the alleged renewal, he went into Mr. McKittrick's office and told him his contract had expired and he wanted to renew it for a year, having always worked under year contracts. Neither the refused instruction nor the one given by the court embodied facts quite as strong as appellant's testimony, because neither referred to appellant's alleged statement to McKittrick that unless he was re-employed he would stop work for respondent then and there.

It is assigned for error that the court required the jury, in order to return a verdict for appellant, not only to find the conversation occurred as appellant swore, but that both parties intended by such conversation to contract with each other for plaintiff's employment for the year from December, 1903, at a salary of $2,000. If it appeared from the record that there was a dispute between the parties as to the terms on which appellant wanted re-employment, there might have been sound reason for inserting this clause in the instruction; but no issue was made that they split on terms; the testimony of McKittrick tending to prove only that he refused to enter into a contract with appellant regarding another year's employment until the annual meeting of stockholders was out of the way. Indeed, as to the proposed terms McKittrick agrees with Embry; for the former swore as follows: "Mr. Embry said he wanted to know *about the renewal of his contract*; said if he did not have the contract made he would leave." As the two witnesses coincided as to the terms of the proposed re-employment, there was no reason for inserting the above-mentioned clause in the instruction in order that it might be settled by the jury whether or not plaintiff, if employed for one year from December 23, 1903, was to be paid $2,000 a year. Therefore it remains to determine whether or not this part of the instruction was a correct statement of the law in regard to what was necessary to constitute a contract between the parties;

that is to say, whether the formation of a contract by what, according to Embry, was said, depended on the intention of both Embry and McKittrick. Or, to put the question more precisely, did what was said constitute a contract of re-employment on the previous terms irrespective of the intention or purpose of McKittrick?

Judicial opinion and elementary treatises abound in statements of the rule that to constitute a contract there must be a meeting of the minds of the parties, and both must agree to the same thing in the same sense. Generally speaking this may be true; but it is not literally or universally true. That is to say, the inner intention of parties to a conversation subsequently alleged to create a contract cannot either make a contract of what transpired, or prevent one from arising, if the words used were sufficient to constitute a contract. In so far as their intention is an influential element, it is only such intention as the words or acts of the parties indicate; not one secretly cherished which is inconsistent with those words or acts....

In *Smith v. Hughes*, L.R. 6 Q.B. 597, 607, it was said:

> If, whatever a man's real intention may be, he so conducts himself that a reasonable man would believe that he was assenting to the terms proposed by the other party, and that other party upon that belief enters into the contract with him, the man thus conducting himself would be equally bound as if he intended to agree to the other party's terms.

In view of those authorities we hold that, though McKittrick may not have intended to employ Embry by what transpired between them according to the latter's testimony, yet if what McKittrick said would have been taken by a reasonable man to be an employment, and Embry so understood it, it constituted a valid contract of employment for the ensuing year.

The next question is whether or not the language used was of that character; namely, was such that Embry, as a reasonable man, might consider he was re-employed for the ensuing year on the previous terms, and act accordingly. We do not say that in every instance it would be for the court to pronounce on this question, because, peradventure, instances might arise in which there would be such an ambiguity in the language relied on to show an assent by the obligor to the proposal of the obligee, that it would be for the jury to say whether a reasonable mind would take it to signify acceptance of the proposal.... In *Lancaster v. Elliott*, 28 Mo. App. 86, 92, the opinion, as to the immediate point, reads:

> The interpretation of a contract in writing is always a matter of law for determination by the court, and equally so, upon like principles, is the question what acts and words, in nearly every case, will suffice to constitute an acceptance by one party, of a proposal submitted by the other, so that a contract or agreement thereby becomes matured.

The general rule is that it is for the court to construe the effect of writings relied on to make a contract, and also the effect of unambiguous oral words.... However, if the words are in dispute, the question of whether they were used or not is for the jury.... With these rules of law in mind, let us recur to the conversation of December

23d between Embry and McKittrick as related by the former. Embry was demanding a renewal of his contract, saying he had been put off from time to time, and that he had only a few days before the end of the year in which to seek employment from other houses, and that he would quit then and there unless he was re-employed. McKittrick inquired how he was getting along with the department and Embry said they (*i.e.*, the employees of the department) were very busy getting out salesmen. Whereupon McKittrick said: "Go ahead, you are all right. Get your men out, and do not let that worry you." We think no reasonable man would construe that answer to Embry's demand that he be employed for another year, otherwise than as an assent to the demand, and that Embry had the right to rely on it as an assent. The natural inference is, though we do not find it testified to, that Embry was at work getting samples ready for the salesmen to use during the ensuing season. Now, when he was complaining of the worry and mental distress he was under because of his uncertainty about the future, and his urgent need, either of an immediate contract with respondent, or a refusal by it to make one, leaving him free to seek employment elsewhere, McKittrick must have answered as he did for the purpose of assuring appellant that any apprehension was needless, as appellant's services would be retained by the respondent. The answer was unambiguous, and we rule that if the conversation was according to appellant's version, and he understood he was employed, it constituted in law a valid contract of re-employment, and the court erred in making the formation of a contract depend on a finding that both parties intended to make one. It was only necessary that Embry, as a reasonable man, had a right to and did so understand....

The judgment is reversed, and the cause remanded. All concur.

NOTES AND QUESTIONS

1. *"Don't worry ... be happy"*: *Embry* was decided more than a hundred years ago, but it continues to be cited as authority. In *Townsend v. Daniel, Mann, Johnson & Mendenhall*, 196 F.3d 1140 (10th Cir. 1999), an employer raised an issue about the vagueness of language its agent used to assent to an agreement for a longtime employee to go on disability, work part-time, and retain his insurance benefits until death or age 65. Daniel Townsend, a vice president in an engineering and architectural firm, entered into negotiations for an arrangement that would protect his insurance but allow him to reduce his hours after he was diagnosed with leukemia. He ultimately wrote a memo summarizing the terms of a deal, which involved him going on disability but continuing to work one day a week until age 65 or his death. William Cavanagh, another vice president, responded with a memo proposing deletion of the section on employment until death or retirement on the grounds that the company never guaranteed future employment. Townsend then called Gerald Seelman, the number two person in the firm and his personal friend, and told him that without the duration term there was no agreement and he would not go on disability. Townsend testified that Seelman responded, "Don't worry about it ... [w]e have the agreement we talked about ... [g]o ahead and go on disability and be happy." According to Townsend, Seelman added, "If you can't trust your friends, who can you

trust?" Seelman later terminated Townsend's employment. The court held that Seelman's words were not too vague to constitute assent in the circumstances and cited *Embry*, particularly the use of the employer's statement "Go ahead, you're all right."

2. *Individual choice and freedom:* Some see the legitimacy of contract resting on its connection with individual choice. People have rights, and they do not lose them unless they freely choose to do so. However, the court in the *Embry* case abridges Thos. H. McKittrick's freedom. It exposes his business to liability even if, upon retrial, a jury were to find he did not intend to make a contract. Does this mean that assertions about contract and free choice are largely mystification?

3. *Generational differences:* Professor David Hoffman explored how online contracting has changed attitudes towards contracts more generally. His results, which were obtained through experimental methods, suggest that younger consumers are different. "They are more likely to breach contracts; are less likely to see oral contracts as binding; are more likely to see contracts formed online as binding and legitimizing; are (naively) less attentive to the fairness of bargains than older subjects, but, when informed of the law, more likely to excuse obligation; and are less fearful of being bound to 'contracts' than older consumers, who are especially disposed to find 'no contract' clauses attractive."[2] He refrains from speculating as to whether these attitudes will persist as millennials grow older, but he wonders what will become of contract law if they do.

4. *Protecting the reasonable reliance of the promisee:* Professor Melvin Eisenberg explains the objective approach to contract formation as "promisee-based," stating that "it is fair to say that American contract law ... tends to focus on compensating injured promisees and facilitating commerce rather than on promise-keeping as an end in itself."[3] Eisenberg cites *Embry* for the point that in determining whether a promise was made, the issue is normally not whether one party intended to make a promise but rather whether the other party "reasonably understood the expression to be a promise."[4]

Another way to look at objectivism is as a theory that deals with a subset of the more difficult formation cases, while most contracts involve actual subjective agreement. Professor Lawrence Solan argues that "when both parties agree that a commitment has been made, the promisor is bound, and when neither believes that a promise has been made, the promisor is not bound." He adds: "Promises are enforced when the parties have reached an agreement, and are not enforced when the parties have not actually reached an agreement, unless the promisee actually and reasonably believes that a promise was made even though none was intended.... [W]hat is called an objective theory is better seen as a rule designed to handle a particular set of cases,

---

2. David A. Hoffman, *From Promise to Form: How Contracting Online Changes Consumers*, 91 N.Y.U. L. Rev. ___ (forthcoming 2017), http://papers.ssrn.com/sol3/papers.cfm?abstract_id=2724661, at 35.

3. Melvin A. Eisenberg, *The World of Contract and the World of Gift*, 85 Cal. L. Rev. 821, 839 (1997).

4. *Id.* at 840, n.49.

embedded in a larger theory whose basic organizing principle is the actual mutual assent of the parties."[5]

5. *A consent theory of contract:* Professor Randy Barnett advocates what he calls a consent theory of contract.[6] He says consent is a "moral prerequisite" to contractual obligation, but on the other hand, courts must protect the reliance of others. However, he continues: "The consent that is required is a *manifestation of an intention* to alienate rights.... [A]ny such manifestation necessarily implies that one intends to be 'legally bound,' to adhere to one's commitment. Therefore, the phrase 'a manifestation of an intention to be legally bound' neatly captures what a court should seek to find before holding that a contractual obligation has been created."[7]

Under Barnett's theory, would the *Embry* case be decided differently? Would a reasonable person in the employee's position have understood that his boss intended to be legally bound to the employee? Suppose that I manifest intent to be legally bound to a contract, but, in fact, I do not intend subjectively to be legally bound. If a court holds me to what a reasonable person can take as my intention, in what sense does liability rest on consent?

Peter Meijes Tiersma[8] relies on speech act theory, a widely used approach to the philosophy of language, for a different view of intention. Offer and acceptance are not matters of expression or manifestation of intent. They are acts that commit a speaker. Thus, "[l]oosely stated, the speaker must intend to create in the hearer the perception that in saying the words, the speaker is committing himself to a particular proposal." Under this theory, would the *Embry* case be decided differently? Tiersma asserts it would not. He bases this on the conversational maxims of Paul Grice, a British philosopher of language. Most parties will interpret an utterance as being relevant to what went before. Considering the *Embry* case, Tiersma says:

> The primary reason that "Don't worry about it" can constitute acceptance of the employee's implicit offer has to do with Grice's conversational maxim of relevance. A literal interpretation of the employer's statement would not be a relevant answer to the employee's concern. Therefore, this possible interpretation can be eliminated. All that remains is the more idiomatic meaning of the phrase as a promise to dispose of the employee's concern. The employer's response was relevant only as an acceptance.[9]

---

5. Lawrence M. Solan, *Contract as Agreement*, 83 Notre Dame L. Rev. 353, 357 (2007).

6. Randy E. Barnett, *A Consent Theory of Contract*, 86 Colum. L. Rev. 269, 297 (1986).

7. *Id.* at 304. Section 22 of the Restatement (Second) of Contracts (1981) specifically rejects the idea that formation of a contract requires a real or apparent intention to be *legally* bound and requires only a manifestation of assent, without reference to legal consequences. *Id.* § 18. *See also* Jean Braucher, *Contract versus Contractarianism: The Regulatory Role of Contract Law*, 47 Wash. & Lee L. Rev. 697, 704–05 (1990) (noting that Barnett adopts an objective approach in his consent theory but does not address the difficulty that interpretation of what has been manifested can be difficult and that using an objective test introduces inevitable social control).

8. Peter Meijes Tiersma, Comment, *The Language of Offer and Acceptance: Speech Acts and the Question of Intent*, 74 Cal. L. Rev. 189, 189 (1986).

9. *Id.* at 210.

Does Tiersma's analysis just quoted establish that the employer intended to create in the employee the perception that the employer was committing himself to a year's renewal of the contract?

How likely is it that either Embry's or McKittrick's recollection of the December 23, 1903, conversation was entirely accurate? How should the reliability of the evidence affect the legal rule, if at all?

6. *Committing contracts (or contract as a type of tort)*: In *Hotchkiss v. National City Bank of New York*,[10] Judge Learned Hand gave a robust statement of the objective theory of contract:

> A contract has, strictly speaking, nothing to do with the personal, or individual, intent of the parties. A contract is an obligation attached by the mere force of law to certain acts of the parties, usually words, which ordinarily accompany and represent a known intent. If, however, it were proved by twenty bishops that either party, when he used the words, intended something else than the usual meaning which the law imposes upon them, he would still be held, unless there were some mutual mistake, or something else of the sort. Of course, if it appear by other words, or acts, of the parties, that they attribute a peculiar meaning to such words as they use in the contract, that meaning will prevail, but only by virtue of the other words, and not because of their unexpressed intent.

In *Kabil Developments Corp. v. Mignot*,[11] Justice Hans Linde of the Oregon Supreme Court quoted the passage above and then said, "It is not clear from Judge Hand's words in *Hotchkiss, supra,* whether he would have admitted the testimony of the twenty bishops at all." *Kabil* held that although the standard of formation is objective, testimony of a party about his feelings that both parties were bound was admissible because a party's subjective state of mind is probative of objective appearances.

In *Hotchkiss*, Hand is expressing what Professor Grant Gilmore called the Holmes-Williston construct. Holmes offered the idea in the late 19th century and Williston developed it in the early 20th century. It certainly had great influence on the vocabulary of generations of law students who have learned about the objective theory of contracts.[12]

---

10. 200 F. 287, 293 (S.D.N.Y. 1911).

11. 279 Or. 151, 566 P.2d 505, 157 (1977).

12. In contrast, a subjective theory of contract would require that both offeror and offeree actually intend to make a bargain. The classic way of putting this is that there must be a "meeting of the minds." Judges and lawyers still use the phrase. For example, it appears in well over a thousand cases reported by LEXIS from January 1, 2014, to December 31, 2014. Of course, many of these decisions could be explained on the basis of an objective theory as well. An advocate must watch for misleading dicta selected from only part of an opinion. For example, in Midway Airlines, Inc. v. Northwest Airlines, Inc., 180 B.R. 851 (N.D. Ill. 1995), the court says: "[I]t is essential that the parties to the agreement have a meeting of the minds, and that they truly assent to the same things in the same sense on all of the [agreement's] essential terms and conditions." But then, several pages later, the court comments: "A literal meeting of the minds, however, is not required for an enforceable contract.... In determining the intent of the parties, the Court focuses on the parties' objective mani-

[T]he "objective theory of contract" became the great metaphysical solvent—the critical test for distinguishing between the false and the true.... [T]he post-Holmesian "objectivists," led by Williston, made no attempt to argue that their principle had any common law past. Perhaps the attempt would have overtaxed even their own very considerable ingenuity. On the contrary, the emergence and triumph of the "objective theory" was put forward as one of the great accomplishments of recent times—the apprehension of a fundamental truth which had long been hidden in a deep morass of error....

The effect of the application of the objective theory to such areas of law as mistake was of course to narrow the range within which mistake could be successfully pleaded as a defense. That is, it is no longer enough that I was subjectively mistaken, even with respect to a fundamental term of the contract.... With the narrowing of the range of availability of such excuses as mistake, we move toward the ideal of absolute liability which ... was one of the basic ideas of the great theory.[13]

7. *A theory about the rise of objective theory:* Holmes's lectures on the common law were first published in 1881; Williston's great treatise on the American law of contracts was first published in 1920. Why did an objective theory of contracts appeal to men such as Holmes and Williston? Why were they able to sell it to the elite of the American bar at this period? Professor Morton Horwitz, a legal historian, argues that Holmes and Williston merely reflected a battle that had largely been won earlier. This battle served distinct social ends. Horwitz tells us:

For seventy or eighty years after the American Revolution the major direction of common law policy reflected the overthrow of eighteenth-century pre-commercial and anti-developmental common law values. As political and economic power shifted to merchant and entrepreneurial groups in the post-revolutionary period, they began to forge an alliance with the legal profession to advance their own interests through a transformation of the legal system.

By around 1850, that transformation was largely complete. Legal rules providing for the subsidization of enterprise and permitting the legal destruction of old forms of property for the benefit of more recent entrants had triumphed. Anti-commercial legal doctrines had been destroyed or undermined and the legal system had almost completely shed its eighteenth-

---

festations of intent and not on their subjective beliefs." Can an advocate arguing for a "meeting of the minds" standard ethically quote the first statement to a court without quoting the second?

Whenever the law makes a state of mind relevant, someone must prove it. Almost always we infer a state of mind from external manifestations. Thus, even if courts adopted a true "meeting of the minds" standard, they would look to objective manifestations of intent. *See* Joseph M. Perillo, *The Origins of the Objective Theory of Contract Formation and Interpretation*, 69 FORDHAM L. REV. 427 (2000).

13. GRANT GILMORE, THE DEATH OF CONTRACT 42–44 (1974).

century commitment to regulating the substantive fairness of economic exchange. Legal relations that had once been conceived of as deriving from natural law or custom were increasingly subordinated to the disproportionate economic power of individuals or corporations that were allowed the right to "contract out" of many existing legal obligations. Law, once conceived of as protective, regulative, paternalistic, and, above all, a paramount expression of the moral sense of the community, had come to be thought of as facilitative of individual desires and as simply reflective of the existing organization of economic and political power.

This transformation in American law both aided and ratified a major shift in power in an increasingly market-oriented society. By the middle of the nineteenth century the legal system had been reshaped to the advantage of men of commerce and industry at the expense of farmers, workers, consumers, and other less powerful groups within the society. Not only had the law come to establish legal doctrines that maintained the new distribution of economic and political power, but, wherever it could, it actively promoted a legal redistribution of wealth against the weakest groups in the society.

The rise of legal formalism can be fully correlated with the attainment of these substantive legal changes. If a flexible, instrumental conception of law was necessary to promote the transformation of the post-revolutionary American legal system, it was no longer needed once the major beneficiaries of that transformation had obtained the bulk of their objectives. Indeed, once successful, those groups could only benefit if both the recent origins and the foundations in policy and group self-interest of all newly established legal doctrines could be disguised. There were, in short, major advantages in creating an intellectual system that gave common law rules the appearance of being self-contained, apolitical, and inexorable, and which, by making "legal reasoning seem like mathematics," conveyed "an air ... of ... inevitability" about legal decisions....

Contract law provides another excellent illustration of the deep pressure towards formalism in nineteenth-century law.... As a result, one of the central problems of the "new" contract law was the development of supposedly "non-political" criteria for distinguishing between "free" and "unfree" wills, while at the same time barring any substantive inquiry into the equivalency of an exchange, which now had come to be regarded as "subjective" and "political." This proscription against examining "consequences" or "outcomes" eventually led to the creation of a disembodied conception of "unfree" states of mind which measured the impairment of "will" by criteria entirely detached from concrete social or economic forms of coercion....

These efforts during the first half of the nineteenth century to disengage the contract system from substantive criteria of fairness produced internal pressures to generate "objective" and "non-political" doctrinal measures of "free will" and "meeting of the minds." These pressures were generalized still further beginning in the 1850s into an "objective" theory of contract. What most distinguished the "objective" theory was its insistence upon establishing uniform and general rules of law with reference to which contracting parties would be required to shape their conduct....

[E]conomic pressures towards uniformity and predictability, as well as the efforts to restrict the scope of jury discretion, also ultimately contributed to this shift toward formal and objective legal rules. But it is important to see as well that this trend towards uniformity necessarily required doctrines of greater abstraction and generality, which in turn had the effect of detaching contract doctrine from the particularities of individual cases and of creating internal logical pressure to conceive of the law of contract as a system of disembodied logical interrelationships. This tendency throughout the second half of the nineteenth century to seek higher levels of generality and inclusiveness of legal doctrine is one of the more important characteristics associated with the development of legal formalism. One of the most important results of this trend in thought was to prevent particularized equitable inquiries into the circumstances of individual cases and to destroy more particular legal rules in the name of promoting the "rule of law." ...

There were, in short, extremely deep and powerful currents which moved American law to formalism after 1850.... For the paramount social condition that is necessary for legal formalism to flourish in a society is for the powerful groups in that society to have a great interest in disguising and suppressing the inevitably political and redistributive functions of law.[14]

Horwitz's positions on many issues have been criticized sharply. For example, Professor A.W.B. Simpson responds:

No doubt certain aspects of contract law pressed on the poor — imprisonment for debt is surely the principal villain here. But ... it was their misfortune to be outside the world in which such luxuries as legal actions at common law or bills in equity much mattered.[15]

Professor Harry Scheiber also questions interpretations that ignore what he sees as the complexities of American history:

[T]he courts *did not* inexorably devolve advantage upon industrial interests at the expense of agrarian interests (the very dichotomy is inapplicable in the West except on fundamentally different terms). Nor did the courts predictably mobilize either "instrumentalist" or "formalist" doctrine to defend and advance large-scale industrial aggregates. Both judicial defenses of "rights of the public" and judicial surprises, in choosing between contending economic interests, are prominent enough to cast doubt on any simplistic model

---

14. Morton J. Horwitz, *The Rise of Legal Formalism*, 19 Am. J. Legal Hist. 251, 251–52, 259, 261–62, 264 (1975). Reprinted by permission.

15. A.W.B. Simpson, *The Horwitz Thesis and the History of Contracts*, 46 U. Chi. L. Rev. 533, 601 (1979).

of unilinear and monolithic doctrinal innovation. There is ample room for agreement that law was often, if not to say usually, mobilized to provide effective subsidies and immunities to heavily capitalized special interests without leaping to the simplistic corollaries that some scholars have advanced.[16]

Notably, an application of the objective theory in the *Embry* case favors an employee, albeit a department head working under a contract for a term rather than the more common "at will" employee without job security. Can the positions of Simpson, Scheiber, and Horwitz be reconciled when we consider the *Embry* case?

8. *Value conflict in contract law:* Modern contract law contains many inconsistent goals. If we accept Horwitz's explanation for the appeal of the objective theory, we must also explain legal realism and its attacks on formalism beginning in the 1920s. We then would have to turn to reactions to realism. Scholars searched for neutral principles for decision in the early 1960s. Law and economics offered another attack on appeals to fairness and case-by-case reactions to situations in the 1970s, while behavioral law and economics has more recently again raised questions about fairness in light of cognitive biases and the ability of businesses to frame marketing efforts to take advantage of them. Critical theories continue to emphasize power imbalances as formally left out of formation doctrines.[17]

The following excerpts from Professor Stewart Macaulay's article attempt to sketch some of the conflicting goals of contract law. Notice that Macaulay's discussion is empirical and descriptive. Unlike Horwitz, Macaulay does not link any of the approaches he identifies with the interests of particular classes or groups. Nonetheless, do some of the approaches he identifies seem to serve some interests more than others? Might an approach serve manufacturers at one time but, say, consumers at another?

Stewart Macaulay, *Private Legislation and the Duty to Read— Business Run by IBM Machine, the Law of Contracts, and Credit Cards*
19 Vand. L. Rev. 1051, 1056–65 (1966)[18]

An analytical scheme I find helpful calls for first separating out the substantive policies that contract and restitution may serve and then identifying at least some of the goals related to the proper or efficient operation of the legal system. For example, we might want our legal system to aid the operation of the insurance industry in order to minimize premium costs (a substantive policy), but we also might want our

16. Harry N. Scheiber, *Regulation, Property Rights, and Definition of "The Market": Law and the American Economy*, 41 J. Econ. Hist. 103, 109 (1981). Published by Cambridge University Press.

17. Danielle K. Hart, *Contract Formation and the Entrenchment of Power*, 41 Loy. U. Chi. L.J. 175, 216–17 (2009) (arguing that contract formation doctrine immunizes coercion by the more powerful with a presumption of contract validity, leaving it to weaker doctrines to compensate).

18. Reprinted with permission.

legal system, insofar as reasonably possible, to reflect the policy choices of a community consensus or those made by an elected legislature rather than those of an appointed judge (a system policy).

Substantive policies can be classified into two primary dimensions. The first concerns a choice of a market or non-market orientation, in which contract law and restitution can either (a) be tools to facilitate the operation of a market economy—focusing on the needs of those exchanging goods, services, labor, and capital or (b) serve to blunt the impact of the unregulated market by refusing to recognize some socially undesirable business practices or by giving aid to people or groups seeking to get out from under onerous contracts. The second dimension concerns the approaches by which contract law and restitution can proceed, tending *toward* either (a) relatively precise general rules or (b) a case-by-case approach.[19] This classification yields four primary categories, which must be explained in some detail. The categories, and their somewhat arbitrary names, can be represented as follows:

	Market Goals	Other-than-Market Goals
Generalizing approach ("rules")	a. market functioning policy	c. social (or economic) planning policy
Particularistic approach ("case-by-case")	b. transactional policy	d. relief-of-hardship policy

a. *Market functioning policy* calls for rules of general application in relatively specific terms that minimize (but never eliminate) the creative role of judge and jury or administrators. Predictable law is to be preferred to results that satisfy in particular cases. Thus the parties can consider the impact of contract law both in planning their bargains and in settling disputes. Legal results will not turn on vague abstractions such as "good faith" but on specific conduct such as signing a contract. In addition to certainty, the rules should tend to reward rational assessment of risks in the market and penalize un-businesslike conduct. One can usefully identify at least three products

---

19. Of course, my transactional and market functioning categories differ from the orthodox learning about the meeting of the minds (subjective theory) and the objective theory of contracts. I would view a "meeting of the minds" approach as entirely a non-market approach; it usually operates as a rationalization for relief-of-hardship. Moreover, there are many kinds of objective theories that fall on the scale that ranges from transactional to market functioning. At one extreme, an objective theory can mean that a contract neither party intended but both appear to have made will be enforced. At the other extreme, transactional policy can call for imposing liability on one who has, without using due care, misled another by his language and conduct, even though the careless person did not "intend" to make a contract. As is apparent from this discussion, my categories are not dichotomies but extreme points on a range: a given rule or standard is *more or less*, say, transactional or market functional, or *more or less*, say, transactional or based on relief-of-hardship.

of market functioning policy: increased self-reliance, rewards to the crafty, and advantages to the operation of bureaucratic organizations.

The duty to read in a fairly strict form carries out the substantive goal. The legal system should enforce contracts "as written" and ignore pleas that one party did not read or understand, that the parties agreed that some of the written terms would not apply or that additional ones which were never reduced to writing would apply, and that the words used should be read in some unusual fashion, or in light of some general abstraction such as "reasonableness." On the basis of common sense but not much evidence, some have assumed that this tack will promote self-reliance. If one knows he will be legally bound to what he signs, he will take care to protect himself (or so it is said). And this would be a good thing. People will recognize risks, allocate them in their bargains, and plan to deal with them rationally. As a result, more bargains will approach the economists' ideal where both leave the bargaining table in a better position than when the negotiations began. Moreover, disputes during the life of the transaction should tend to be minimized since the process of reading and understanding should make clear who is to do what and who is to take what loss if a particular risk occurs. Also where the legal result is clearly that documents will mean what they say, there is less chance that in settlement negotiations one party's rights must be discounted because of the risk of what a jury might do or because of delay.

Such rules reward those who plan and are careful. In one view those who can drive the best bargains, short of gross fraud, are entitled to their winnings. Perhaps one who can slip into a contract with terms highly favorable to himself that are undetected by the other party, is to be praised for his skill rather than censured. This is just good salesmanship. In this view, a bargain is not an exchange of mutual advantage but a game where each party is to maximize his own gains at the expense of the other. Some may feel that the ability to do well in this game is a skill to be rewarded. A strict duty-to-read rule often will help supply this reward.

Another product of market functioning policy—advantages to the operation of bureaucratic organizations—often derives from people being treated as if they had read and understood a written contract even when it is probable they have not done so. Large economic organizations frequently promulgate rules to govern their exchanges with other organizations and individuals. Typically, these rules are cast, or can be cast, in the form of a contract. The other unit's representative or the other individual signs a printed form document or accepts a contractual symbol (say, delivery of a document or goods) although he has little chance or incentive to read, understand, bargain to change the rules, or do any or all of these things. Larger firms operate this way for a number of reasons. They must deal through a corps of agents in a myriad of transactions. As a result, there is a need to standardize and formalize procedures. On one hand, the large organization must control its agents who deal with the outside world and limit their power to "give the company away." These agents are under many pressures to treat their customers as individuals and tailor the particular deal to suit their customers' needs; most obvious is the pressure to make sales to earn commissions or promotions. Also, "the customer is always right" in the salesman's world. A rigid form contract that the customer must sign without alteration often is thought to be an efficient way to exercise control over salesmen. The customer is "on notice" of the salesman's limited authority, and the firm wants to avoid being legally bound to expectations its salesman has created by his conduct that are inconsistent with company policy. On the other hand, the written document signed by the customer becomes the obligation within the larger organization because of the problems of internal communication. It specifies what must be produced or shipped, and it indicates the full extent of future payments to be received and contingent obligations assumed. If a salesman has made a promise inconsistent with the formal written contract which is highly standardized, it is difficult to communicate this to those who must perform and to those who must make plans based on cash flow and risk assumption. Even if the inconsistent promise is communicated, it poses a problem for a rational bureaucratic organization that tends to thrive on routine. Large organizations are helped if they can control and plan their exposure to risks; if they can do so, their accounting and pricing will be more accurate, and they will not have to set up large reserves to cover a host of unpredictable contingencies. Arguably, this kind of certainty will foster their activities in the market, which in turn should yield more jobs and more products at lower prices. A rather strict duty to read, rather than attacking the balance of economic power in the society, supports the operations of large organizations that have this power. This tends to promote rational business affairs, whatever the impact on the individual who assumed he could rely on what he was told rather than what he signed....

Usually these bureaucratic considerations are coupled with the self-reliance idea—the large organization can deal through standardized forms and the prudent individual will protect himself by reading and taking appropriate action—although at times the likelihood of self-protection is slim indeed. Occasionally, bureaucratic policy is coupled with a requirement designed to help self-reliance. For example, a Virginia statute demands that a written contract be set in a certain size type to be legally enforceable, and the Uniform Commercial Code requires some warranty disclaimers to be conspicuous to be effective.

b. *Transactional policy*, the second policy category, also seeks to aid the operation of the market, but with a case-by-case strategy rather than by rules that ignore particular circumstances. The courts ought to take steps to carry out the particular transaction brought before them—they should discover the bargain-in-fact and enforce it with appropriate remedies cut to fit the facts of the case. If this discovery is not possible, the court should work out a result involving the least disruption of plans and causing the least amount of reliance loss in light of the situation at the time of the dispute. In short, courts should seek to implement the "sense of the transaction," and thus solve the problem in the particular case in market terms—assumption of the risk, reasonable reliance, and so on.

Transactional policy calls for a duty to read and understand only where the one who has failed to do this is responsible for misleading the other into believing that the document has been read and approved or that the careless one is willing to sign and assume the risk of whatever might be found in the document. Suppose seller sends buyer an offer quoting a price in a letter that also very clearly spells out a number of conditions the seller says are most important to him. The buyer reads the first few sentences of the letter and the price quoted but not the seller's important conditions. The buyer writes on the bottom margin of the seller's letter, "We accept your offer," and signs it; he then mails this back to the seller, who begins production of the items in question. The buyer later wants to back out and asserts he did not read the seller's conditions and would not have agreed to them if he had. The buyer has been negligent in conveying his agreement, resulting in disappointed plans and at least the probability of a good deal of reliance loss. A court following a transactional approach would treat the buyer *as if* he had read and understood the seller's letter. But the decision would turn on the rather extreme facts of the case—the buyer's communication was careless and caused either very probable or actual injury.

Perhaps more often transactional policy will call for overturning or modifying a written document (by reforming or construing it) in light of the bargain-in-fact of the parties. While a case can be made for self-reliance, part of decent social and business conduct is trust. In many negotiation situations all of the pressures push for friendly gestures rather than a suspicious line-by-line analysis of the writing. The buyer of home siding can believe the president of the home remodeling company when he says his siding will not rust or crack; the buyer does not have to parse the text of the lengthy and technical printed form and spot the integration clause at his peril. In cases such as this, the writing was drafted to run counter to the likely agreement-in-fact. If a court is seeking the actual sense of the transaction, it will not let such a writing get in its way....

c. *Social planning policies* can be reflected in contracts and restitution, as well. In one sense, rather than enforcing the bargain that was made, in this third type of policy the courts will enforce the bargain which the parties should have made. Conversely, the courts may refuse to take any action when the actual bargain is found offensive. This policy is something of a catchall, as social planning can call for a variety of things ranging from wealth redistribution to the regulation, or even promotion, of particular types of people, industries, or transactions. The most obvious examples involve a change in the market context by removing certain types of bargains from the kinds that will be enforced by the legal system or by requiring or prohibiting particular terms in some bargains. Again, this is a generalizing approach stressing specific rules, so it parallels market functioning policy in strategy—but the goals of the two are very different since social planning policies, by definition, seek to blunt the impact of the market.

A social planning rule relevant to our topic would be one that said certain classes of people could not be held to contracts they signed or accepted, despite their careless failure to read and protect themselves. One could conceive of a rule protecting such people as consumers, illiterates, those of limited mental ability, or minors. In effect, the power of a minor to disaffirm even contracts that he has read and understood is such a rule. Since, in theory, the minor cannot guard his own interests, the legal system protects him from his own carelessness and improvident bargains. Consumers may get some of the same treatment under Uniform Commercial Code § 2-719's provisions on limiting remedies for breach of warranty; perhaps consumers need not read and protect themselves since limitations of liability for personal injury caused by a breach of warranty are *prima facie* unconscionable. It is difficult to offer many examples of this kind of social planning rule since the legal system has preferred a more case-by-case (relief of hardship) approach, rather than letting a whole class of people out of certain kinds of contracts. On the other hand, social planning goals often enter as the price for following the bureaucratic type of market functioning policy. For example, the standard fire insurance policy is set by statute in many states. One side of the coin involves the setting of terms deemed fair to the consumer by the legislature—removing the insurance contract from the area of self-reliance and the exercise of market power. The other side of the coin, however, involves telling insurance companies that if they follow the statute, certain practices have been validated. An insurance company can know where it stands, and this certainty may be extremely important to it. The insurers get certainty at the cost of following fair terms imposed by the legal system.

d. *Relief-of-hardship* is the fourth policy. It calls for the legal system to let one party out of his bargain in exceptional cases where enforcement would be unduly harsh, or, where the content of the bargain is in doubt, to place the burden on the party best able to spread the loss or absorb it.[20] This case-by-case approach is based not upon considerations of market functioning or protecting actual expectations but upon ethical ideals and emotional reactions to the plight of the underdog, to pressing an advantage too far, to making too much profit, or to inequality of resources. To a great extent, this is the policy that is not expressed openly in contract doctrine, but courts can construe language and stretch the innocent misrepresentation or mistake doctrines to help out when the facts are particularly appealing. When done with a deft hand, a relief-of-hardship approach will leave little trace of a precedent to embarrass the court in the next case, where the facts are not quite so appealing.

It is hard to offer a pure example of this policy in operation, but it can be suggested that a good deal of it lurks in the insurance release cases where a duty to read and understand sometimes is and sometimes is not applied. Also, the Supreme Court of Wisconsin in several cases has stressed the lack of education of the person seeking to be relieved from a written contract he signed or accepted. On one hand, this factor tracks with transactional policy and the degree of care one could expect from a particular individual. Arguably, an illiterate person is not responsible for misleading

---

20. Eds. note: As an example, in an exception to the tendency of courts to enforce arbitration clauses, a Massachusetts court invalidated such a clause in a contract signed by the son of a nursing home resident. Although he had his mother's health care proxy, the court found that he did not have the authority to bind his mother to arbitration. Michael Corkery & Jessica Silver-Greenberg, *A Nursing Home Murder and a Family's Arbitration Fight*, N.Y. TIMES, February 22, 2016, at A1. Along similar lines, some courts questioned the validity of mortgages and other documents generated by banks in the wake of the massive foreclosures after the 2008 financial crisis. Marian Wang, *Who's Who in the Foreclosure Scandal: A Primer on the Players*, PROPUBLICA, Oct. 18, 2010.

someone who knows the illiterate person cannot read the document. But on the other hand, the party seeking to uphold the contract, especially the home office of a corporation that deals through a sales force in the field, may have no way accurately to gauge the education and literacy of a person who signed the printed form. Its expectations and potential reliance remain despite the illiteracy of the person it dealt with. We can speculate that the inability to read and understand is correlated with a generally low socio-economic status, and such people may be the best candidates for relief-of-hardship in the eyes of many.

_____

Appearing at an American Constitution Society conference in 2010, Judge Richard Posner, a former University of Chicago law professor and a major figure in the law and economics movement, got a big laugh when he admitted that he had signed for a home equity loan without reading the hundreds of pages of boilerplate language in the loan documents.[21] Was Judge Posner a "rational actor" in choosing not to read the contract terms?

B. THE RISK OF AMBIGUITY OR MISUNDERSTANDING

People make many different kinds of mistakes in entering contracts. Sometimes the law lets a mistaken party back out. Sometimes it doesn't. A true Holmes-Williston objective theory draws sharp lines, but the cases are blurred.

Suppose I write a letter saying that I will sell my house to you for $400,000. You accept my offer. However, I own two houses. One is located in the city where I work. The other is located about 100 miles away in a resort area. I always refer to the house in the city as "my house." I call the one in the resort area "my cottage." However, the cottage is an architect-designed large house built on the shore of a beautiful lake. I thought I was selling my house in the city. You, however, thought you were buying my house in the resort area. You did not know that I usually called one the house and the other the cottage. If courts are concerned with my free choice, they will hesitate before deciding that I sold a house I did not want to sell. Of course, I did use language that could refer to two different structures, but this is not the same thing as choosing to sell my house. Nonetheless, you also made a choice, and my letter prompted you to create certain expectations. A court cannot protect both my choice and yours.

Suppose, to change the case, both of us correctly understand my letter to refer to my house in the city. You accept my offer to sell the house for $400,000. Later you

_____

21. David Lat, *Do Lawyers Actually Read Boilerplate Contracts? Richard Posner and Evan Chesler Don't; Do You?* ABOVE THE LAW, (June 22, 2010), http://abovethelaw.com/2010/06/do-lawyers-actually-read-boilerplate-contracts-judge-richard-posner-doesnt-do-you/?utm_source=feedburner&utm_medium=feed&utm_campaign=Feed%3A+abovethelaw+%28Above+the+Law%29.

discover that the house is worth no more than $350,000. If you had known this, you would not have bought it. Is this kind of error different from that suggested by our conflicting interpretations of the term "house"?

Suppose, instead, I submit a bid to you. I propose to do all the electrical work involved in constructing a large building that you are erecting. When I was compiling the information needed to make my bid, the piece of paper on which my assistant had calculated the cost of wiring the third floor fell into my wastebasket. I did not notice this. As a result, I neglected to take the cost of the work on the third floor into my calculations. My bid is much lower than it would have been had I not made a mistake. Is this a kind of mistake different from those involved in the examples about ambiguity and value of an asset?

Suppose we applied an objective theory of contract to all of these cases. A reasonable person hearing or reading the offer and acceptance would assume a deal had been closed. The outward manifestations are that a deal has been made. All of the mistakes are subjective. To recognize them, a court would have to look past the form of the bargain to the actual situation. We can defend holding seller and buyer to a contract in all three cases. Such a rule promotes reliance, protects reasonable expectations, and offers an incentive for taking care to avoid mistakes. The person making an error will be taught a lesson. Moreover, others learning of the result will shape up or face the consequences. Not insignificantly, this rule makes the court's job much easier too. We will often hear this song played loudly in the cases. However, there is also a powerful countertheme that we cannot ignore, reflecting our sensitivity to the harsh consequences of applying such an approach.

1. Choice and the Careless Use of Language

Frank Chapman Sharp and Philip G. Fox offer an ethical analysis of the problem of mistake:

> The rule for interpretation of ambiguous promises and contracts was laid down by William Paley in the classical discussion of the subject.... It will be found in his *Moral Philosophy* (1785), Book III, Part I, Chapters 5 and 6, and reads as follows: "Where the terms of the promise admit of more senses than one, the promise is to be performed in that sense in which the promiser apprehended at the time that the promisee received it." ... [M]orality is a matter of intent. My obligations to the promisee accordingly depend on the answer to this question: What expectations did I intend to arouse in him? And since ... desired results may sometimes be obtained by silence as effectively as by any other means, we must go farther and say: I am responsible not merely for those expectations which I actively strove to create, but also for those which I knowingly allowed the promisee to entertain at the time of the promise. And this is precisely what Paley's definition means....
>
> Where, as the result of my negligence in formulating or accepting a contract, the words in which it is incorporated misrepresent my intention, and

where at the same time its provisions affect my interests adversely, then, according to what we have termed Paley's principle, I am not morally bound to perform. But this does not mean that I am released from all obligations to my co-contractor.... An honorable man will pay for all losses which are due to his negligence in formulating or accepting a contract; he should not be expected to do more....

What ought to be done when both parties are negligent? Where the negligence is, as far as can be judged, equal, the loss should be equally divided; otherwise, in proportion to the amount of fault, insofar as this proportion can be estimated....

The principle that in negligence the damages are to be paid by the party through whose negligence the loss takes place ought to be tempered in morals—whatever may be true in law—by another principle. This is that burdens should be carried by those who can bear them most easily.[22]

To what extent, if at all, does the law reach the same conclusions as Sharp and Fox? Insofar as it does not, does this mean that the law is immoral or amoral, that Sharp and Fox have overlooked something, or that what is moral and what is legal are two distinct questions with little or no connection? Keep these questions in mind as you consider the legal rules in the materials that follow. We begin with one of the classics of contracts folklore. Remember, as you read this opinion, that at the time this case was decided, the objective theory of contracts was still largely in the future.

RAFFLES v. WICHELHAUS[23]
Court of the Exchequer
2 Hurl. & C. 906, 159 Eng. Rep. 375 (1864)

[The plaintiff sued the defendant for failing to accept delivery of 125 bales of Surat cotton, pursuant to a contract which specified that defendant was to buy cotton "to arrive ex 'Peerless' from Bombay." Defendant argued for dismissal of the claim on the ground that there were two ships named "Peerless," both bringing cotton from Bombay, and that it appeared that the plaintiff intended to *sell* the cotton which was on a "Peerless" which was to leave Bombay in December, while the defendant intended to *buy* cotton on a "Peerless" which was to sail in October. The defendant had refused to accept the cotton tendered by the plaintiff.]

[The report of the case begins with Milward arguing for the plaintiff.]

The contract was for the sale of a number of bales of cotton of a particular description, which the plaintiff was ready to deliver. It is immaterial by what ship the cotton was to arrive, so that it was a ship called the "Peerless." The words "to arrive

---

22. Frank Chapman Sharp & Philip G. Fox, Business Ethics 110, 116, 117 (1937).

23. Eds. note: English opinions can be difficult to read. In order to focus your attention on the substantive issue, we offer an edited version of the opinion, with some clarifications noted by brackets ([ ]), which don't appear in the original report. This kind of editing occurs frequently throughout this edition. Purists may consult the original.

ex 'Peerless,'" only mean that if the vessel is lost on the voyage, the contract is to be at an end. [At this point, Lord Chief Baron Pollock interrupted: "It would be a question for the jury whether both parties meant the same ship called the 'Peerless.'"] That would be so if the contract was for the sale of a ship called the "Peerless"; but it is for the sale of cotton on board a ship of that name. [Pollock interrupted again: "The defendant only bought that cotton which was to arrive by a particular ship. It may as well be said, that if there is a contract for the purchase of certain goods in warehouse A, that is satisfied by the delivery of goods of the same description in warehouse B.] In that case there would be goods in both warehouses; here it does not appear that the plaintiff had any goods on board the other "Peerless." [At this point, Baron Martin chimed in: "It is imposing on the defendant a contract different from that which he entered into." Baron Pollock added: "It is like a contract for the purchase of wine coming from a particular estate in France or Spain, where there are two estates of that name."] The defendant has no right to contradict by parol evidence a written contract good upon the face of it. He does not impute misrepresentation or fraud, but only says that he fancied the ship was a different one. Intention is of no avail, unless stated at the time of the contract. [Baron Pollock again: "One vessel sailed in October and the other in December."] The time of sailing is no part of the contract.

[Mellish, who was presenting the case for the defendant, then began to make arguments for defendant's position.]

There is nothing on the face of the contract to shew that any particular ship called the "Peerless" was meant; but the moment it appears that two ships called the "Peerless" were about to sail from Bombay there is a latent ambiguity, and parol evidence may be given for the purpose of shewing that the defendant meant one "Peerless" and the plaintiff another. That being so, there was no *consensus ad idem*, and therefore no binding contract.

[At this point, apparently the Court had heard enough, and Mellish was instructed he need not continue.]

PER CURIAM. There must be judgment for the defendants.

NOTES AND QUESTIONS

1. *Legal history:* Professor A.W.B. Simpson, in his article *Contracts for Cotton to Arrive: The Case of the Two Ships Peerless*,[24] concluded that traditional contracts scholarship has misinterpreted the *Raffles* case.[25] Accepting Simpson's research and con-

---

24. A.W.B. Simpson, *Contracts for Cotton to Arrive: The Case of the Two Ships Peerless*, 11 CARDOZO L. REV. 287 (1989).

25. The *Raffles* case has been read by almost every American first-year contracts student for more than a century. The case was decided without opinion but is usually read, and taught, as if it had to do with the parties' misunderstanding of which ship Peerless was to carry the cotton for which they contracted a sale. In fact, as Simpson's elaborate historical research revealed, the case is a rare glimpse into the dawn of the market in cotton futures and of judicial acceptance of arbitration. Through examination of shipping records in England and the United States, Simpson demonstrated that the transaction was one that Liverpool cotton merchants of the time would have understood well.

clusions, the conventional interpretation of the case has a life of its own (as is also true of *Hadley v. Baxendale*). It is a part of American, and probably common law, legal culture. You can talk to most lawyers and judges about the two ships named *Peerless*, and they will know what you are talking about; most would not remember that there was no opinion in the case. The case is interesting for its schematic "facts" suggesting that the parties misunderstood each other because each was talking about a different ship *Peerless*.

2. *The Restatement (Second) of Contracts and the* **Raffles** *case:* The modern statement of the rule follows neither the 1864 opinion nor the pure objective theory of Holmes, discussed in Notes 5 and 6 after the *Embry* case, *supra*. You should consult, at this point, § 20 (Effect of Misunderstanding) and § 201 (Whose Meaning Prevails) of the Restatement (Second) of Contracts.

In *Lamb Plumbing & Heating Co. v. Kraus-Anderson of Minneapolis, Inc.*,[26] Lamb sued a general contractor for the value of work done on a large project that Lamb said was not covered by its bid but that the general contractor had demanded Lamb do. The general contractor learned of a problem in the specifications before bids were submitted. Another subcontractor pointed out that different interpretations of the specifications were possible concerning whether the subcontractor was to furnish and install certain valves. The general contractor notified several mechanical subcontractors it knew were likely to bid on the job that the mechanical subcontractor must supply and install the valves. Plaintiff had obtained the plans and specifications on its own, and the general contractor did not know it would bid. Plaintiff reasonably interpreted the contract documents as not requiring it to supply and install the valves. Its officials did not see the ambiguity in the contract documents. It submitted a bid on this basis, and the general awarded it the contract. The general demanded Lamb install the valves, Lamb did this, and sued for extra compensation for work beyond that required by the contract. Under the Restatement (Second) of Contracts §§ 20, 201, how should a court decide this case? What more, if anything, do you need to know to answer this question?

3. *Professor Sharp and carelessness in communication:* Professor Malcolm Sharp offered an explanation for the position later taken in the Restatement (Second) of Contracts. Essentially, he argued that a promise is a dependable statement about the statement maker's future behavior that may predictably lead to reliance by the person to whom it is made. The actual intentions of the maker are not important. What is important is that language be used carefully, and that losses resulting from the careless use (or understanding) of language be shifted to the person who has

---

While the volume in such "contracts for cotton to arrive" was large, *Raffles* was one of the only judicial cases to arise from trading in them. The plaintiff was a relative outsider to the closely knit group of cotton brokers and not a regular trader in the contracts. His lawsuit was a breach of the uniformly observed custom of broker arbitration over failures of such contracts. The judgment for the defendant may thus reflect an equally rare common law decision enforcing, if without opinion, a customary requirement of resort to arbitration (Cornell Law Forum, Feb. 1986, at 16.).

26. 296 N.W.2d 859 (Minn. 1980).

been careless. Since our social system is largely built on the protection of private property interests, one must protect those whose business interests suffer as the result of the carelessness of others. Analogizing losses arising from confusion in business situations to losses arising from automobile accidents, Sharp suggests that loss can intelligibly be allocated in terms of fault.[27] That is, one can analyze contractual liability in terms of fault rather than consent. One can rely on an analysis of the meaning of the language used, measured against what is "more or less normal in the business community," rather than against the actual intentions of either party to the communication. Professor Sharp added:

> It will be noted that we have now said that care must be used by both parties to communications. If the promisor is careful and the promisee careless, the promisor's understanding will control, in the event of misunderstanding. If both are careful or both careless, neither understanding will control, and there will be no effective communication in the event of misunderstanding.[28]

Does Professor Sharp's explanation of promissory liability support Professor Horwitz's position? Does it make a substantial change in the claim for legitimacy one puts forward for contract law?[29] Sharp's fault theory of contract analogizes contract to tort, in that it recognizes liability for the negligent use of language.[30]

Part of Sharp's position is that a person relying on what she thinks is a promise must be justified or reasonable in her reliance. Randy Barnett asserts that this does no more than pose the crucial question it is supposed to answer.[31] He says:

> [W]hether a person has "reasonably" relied on a promise depends on what most people would (or ought to) do. We cannot make this assessment independently of the legal rule in effect in the relevant community, because what many people would do in reliance on a promise is crucially affected by their perception of whether or not the promise is enforceable.... A prediction that a promise can reasonably be expected to induce reliance by a promisee or third party will unavoidably depend upon whether the promisee or third party believes that reliance will be legally protected. The legal rule itself cannot be formulated based on such a prediction, however, without introducing a practical circularity into the analysis....

In short, a person, rather than being entitled to legal enforcement because reliance is justified, is justified in relying on those commitments that will be legally enforced.

---

27. How successful is the system for allocating accident costs on the basis of fault? Would the same problems bedevil a contract model based on fault?

28. Malcolm Pitman Sharp, *Promissory Liability I*, 7 U. CHI. L. REV. 1, 7 (1939).

29. *See* William C. Whitford, *The Role of the Jury (and the Fact/Law Distinction) in the Interpretation of Written Contracts*, 2001 WIS. L. REV. 931, 947 n.38 (noting that Professor Sharp was strongly individualistic in his basic philosophy and believed that the autonomy policy of self-determination was not in conflict with protection of reasonable reliance).

30. *See id.* (stating that the "so-called 'fault' theory of contract law, analogizing contractual liability to tort liability, is often associated with Malcolm Sharp.").

31. Barnett, *supra* note 6, at 275–76.

Does Barnett's objection require us to disregard Sharp's position? What does Barnett assume about bargaining? Where does he get his data?

4. *Other theories of liability:* Choice and fault are not the only possible principles for decision in contracts cases. We could frame rules designed to support the market or the process of contracting. Is the following case an illustration of such a rule? Why does Barnett find Sharp's position troubling? Note that the title of his article is *A Consent Theory of Contract.*

2. Flat Rules to Allocate Losses

WPC ENTERPRISES, INC. v. UNITED STATES

United States Court of Claims
323 F.2d 874 (1964)

DAVIS, J.

This is a study in the toils of ambiguity. The parties put their names to a contract which, on the point crucial to this lawsuit, could reasonably be read in two conflicting fashions. Each signatory seized in its own mind upon a different one of these contradictory versions. Compounding that confusion, they discussed the issue with each other in such a way that each thought, but this time without good reason, it had obtained the other's acquiescence in its chosen reading. The impasse became unmistakably plain when it was too late. Our task is to determine on whom should fall the risk of such mutually reinforced obscurity.

The Government set out to procure, through bids, a large number of complex generator sets—called the MD-3 set—used to calibrate the electronic systems of the B-47 and other aircraft and to start the engines when an electric starter is required. Beech Aircraft Corporation, which had previously made these elaborate devices for the Air Force on a negotiated basis, had prepared specifications and drawings of various of the component parts which the Government acquired and incorporated in the bid invitations. Plaintiff was the low bidder, lower than Beech and another company which had also provided the sets under a negotiated contract. After a period of consideration and some discussion, the award was made to plaintiff and it performed the contract as required by the Government.

The only dispute now before us is whether five components of these generator sets had to be manufactured by (or with the authorization of) certain named companies, as the Government urges, or whether plaintiff was entitled under the contract to furnish identical components made by other firms (presumably at lower prices). After the award, defendant insisted that the products of the specified companies had to be furnished. Plaintiff complied but, claiming that this directive constituted a contractual change, sought review by the Board of Contract Appeals under the Changes and Disputes articles. The Board turned down the appeal on the ground that plaintiff had been told before the award of the defendant's position and had acquiesced.

For the five components now involved, the textual provisions of the specifications (borrowed from Beech) gave general descriptions, without naming any manufacturer; however, the drawings (also from Beech) listed the part numbers given to the item by a particular firm and declared that that manufacturer was the "approved source," or that the component "may be purchased" from that company, or indicated "make from" a part furnished by a particular company, or simply said that the component was a certain part number of a specific firm. There are also other, slighter, indications of contractual meaning on which the parties rely; the details are set forth in the findings.

Each side urges that its position is sustained by the invitation as a whole—without any need to go beyond the bounds of the contractual instruments. The defendant stresses the references to specific part numbers, designated by particular fabricators, as necessarily showing that only parts made under the aegis of that manufacturer would be acceptable; this use of exact part numbers is said to be equivalent to a mandatory direction to incorporate only those very items. Defendant also points out that: (i) the drawings and specifications for the five components were not adequate for a new manufacturer to make those articles in the relatively short time allotted for completion of the procurement; (ii) the defendant was satisfied with components made from parts supplied by the named manufacturers (because they had been fully tested in the past), but would be required before acceptance to test components made by others; and (iii) this burdensome and time-consuming testing would not be practicable within the scheduled period of delivery. It should have been clear, defendant concludes, that the contract called for items supplied by or through the specific companies named in the drawings. (Defendant's witnesses testified to this effect before the Board and at the trial in this court.)

The plaintiff, on the other hand, emphasizes the lack of express mandatory language in the references to particular manufacturers for the five disputed components—in contrast to certain other components which the specifications very plainly declared "shall be" or "shall consist of" an identified part made by a named manufacturer. A command to use only materials or elements made by a specific firm is not frequent in government procurement; it can be expected to be phrased explicitly and not left to inference. Moreover, the references to particular part numbers are not read as mandatory because of a specification provision (labeled "Identification of Parts") which stated:

> "Beech and vendor part numbers will be shown on all items except those items supplied by other than Beech Aircraft Corporation or vendors to Beech. On items supplied by other than present sources Beech part numbers will be used with a suffix to indicate a different supplier."

To plaintiff, this clause implicitly authorized the use of identical components made by other companies than those named in the Beech drawings. It thought that it could obtain such qualified substitutes by combining the knowledge gained from three sources: the drawings and specifications (insufficient though they might be); a careful breakdown of the sample models supplied plaintiff by the defendant; and general engineering competence. Plaintiff was satisfied that the proper components could be produced in this way within the time allowed. (The contractor's position was likewise supported by evidence before the Board of Contract Appeals.)

This summary of the opposing contentions is enough to show that no sure guide to the solution of the problem can be found within the four corners of the contractual documents. As with so many other agreements, there is something for each party and no ready answer can be drawn from the texts alone. Both plaintiff's and defendant's interpretations lie within the zone of reasonableness; neither appears to rest on an obvious error in drafting, a gross discrepancy, or an inadvertent but glaring gap; the arguments, rather, are quite closely in balance. It is precisely to this type of contract that this court has applied the rule that if some substantive provision of a government-drawn agreement is fairly susceptible of a certain construction and the contractor actually and reasonably so construes it, in the course of bidding or performance, that is the interpretation which will be adopted—unless the parties' intention is otherwise affirmatively revealed.... This rule is fair both to the drafters and to those who are required to accept or reject the contract as proffered, without haggling. Although the potential contractor may have some duty to inquire about a major patent discrepancy, or obvious omission, or a drastic conflict in provisions ... he is not normally required (absent a clear warning in the contract) to seek clarification of any and all ambiguities, doubts, or possible differences in interpretation. The Government, as the author, has to shoulder the major task of seeing that within the zone of reasonableness the words of the agreement communicate the proper notions—as well as the main risk of a failure to carry that responsibility. If the defendant chafes under the continued application of this check, it can obtain a looser rein by a more meticulous writing of its contracts and especially of the specifications.[32] Or it can shift the burden of ambiguity (to some extent) by inserting provisions in the contract clearly calling upon possible contractors aware of a problem interpretation to seek an explanation before bidding....

If there were nothing more, the case would end here with a ruling for the plaintiff. But the defendant argues, and the Board of Contract Appeals found, that before the award was made or the contract signed the plaintiff learned the Government's view of the disputed point and accepted that position....

At the trial in this court, Commissioner McConnaughey had the benefit, with respect to the pre-award meetings between the parties, of testimony by Sugarman[33] (who did not appear before the Board) and of other representatives of both sides, as well as of certain documentary materials (notably an internal memorandum by a

_____

32. [2] It was a clear mistake to borrow the Beech specifications and drawings for the Government's procurement without more editorial revision and adaptation. Those specifications and drawings were tailored to manufacture and procurement by Beech, a private concern—not by the United States. The trouble came about because the defendant's contracting officials failed to modify the documents, which may have been adequate for a private procurement, so as to make them entirely suitable for a public procurement through bidding.

33. Eds. note: Cecil Sugarman was WPC's sales manager.

Government contracting official made after the December 19, 1956, meeting with Sugarman). He also had the evidence before the Board....

[W]e agree with the Trial Commissioner that (i) both parties became aware of the other's interpretation; (ii) neither acquiesced knowingly in the other's interpretation; (iii) both thought, however, that the other had acquiesced; (iv) without either having reasonable grounds for so thinking; and, finally, that (v) neither took the proper steps to clarify the pertinent terms of the transaction until after the award was made. On both sides ambiguous utterance was piled on unwarranted assumption and laced together by unspoken premise. In the end, the Government officials thought they had made it quite clear that the named manufacturers would have to be used for all components, while the plaintiff's people felt that they had successfully stood their ground at least as to these five components. Both were wholly wrong in their understanding of the other's understanding. The discussions had been one prolonged minuet of cross-purposes.

In these circumstances should the onus of the original ambiguity in the specifications still rest on the defendant? We can see no other conclusion. As the author of the defect in the drafting which led plaintiff to the reasonable supposition that it could obtain the five components elsewhere than from the named companies, the Government was under the affirmative obligation (if it wished its own view to prevail) to clarify the meaning of the contract in definitive fashion before the plaintiff was bound. It did make such an attempt, and it did reveal its own view. But when the plaintiff demurred the Government did not adequately indicate that it stood steadfast by its announced opinion. There was a fatal insufficiency in the defendant's effort to communicate to plaintiff that the contract was to be interpreted as the Government understood it. Largely because of this lapse, the plaintiff was left with the mistaken impression that the defendant, rather than insisting, would accept plaintiff's rendering of the contract. The Government, in a word, was very lax in seeing the matter through. Since the burden of clarification was the defendant's, it must bear the risk of an insufficient attempt, even though the plaintiff's obtuseness likewise contributed to the continuance of the misunderstanding. If there had been no communication by defendant to plaintiff between the receipt of the bids and the making of the award, the defendant would have had to suffer the consequences of its poorly drafted specifications. The ineffective attempt to put things right does not place the defendant in a better position. Only an adequate effort to reach the plaintiff's mind could have that result.

Two objections may be made to our taking this ground. The inconclusive discussions between the parties show, it may be said, that there was no "meeting of the minds" on the issue which concerns us, and therefore no valid contract. There was no subjective coming together, it is true, but an enforceable agreement came into being nevertheless. The design of the contract can be picked from the terms and words of the invitation, objectively read with the aid of rules of contract construction (which are distillates of the common experience and the common sense of justice). It is a normal characteristic of the class of cases in which the courts have held ambiguities against the drafter that the parties' minds have failed to meet on the specific point in dispute. That gap has not been permitted to swallow the whole contract except perhaps where the gulf is far closer to the bounds of the entire consensual perimeter than here. For a contract to exist there does not have to be, and rarely is, a subjective "meeting of the minds" all along the line....

The other objection is that the plaintiff is bound by the opposing view of the contract because it twice extended the defendant's time to make the award (on February 8 and 18, 1957) after the Air Force's representatives had told plaintiff of their attitude. This contention must be rejected for the reason given above. Although it had the burden, the defendant simply did not make it clear enough that it stood by its position despite the plaintiff's disagreement. When the latter extended the time for the award it did not comprehend that the Government was insisting on its own construction. This state of affairs was attributable, in substantial measure, to defects in the defendant's course of communication to plaintiff on the subject of the source of the five components. Plaintiff was also at fault, but the risk of a failure to clarify lay largely upon the Government and could have been averted only by a more sufficient effort than was made.

We hold, therefore, that the defendant was wrong in demanding that only products of (or authorized by) the named manufacturers could be used for the five components. The contract did not so require. The issue of the amount of damages or recovery has not been tried and we are not called upon to pass upon any aspects of that question. We leave all such problems to the trial under Rule 38(c), including the issue of which party has the burden of showing that the components plaintiff planned to use would or would not have been available, and would or would not have qualified under this contract.

The plaintiff is entitled to recover and judgment is entered to that effect. The amount of recovery will be determined under Rule 38(c).

NOTES AND QUESTIONS

1. *Limits on the rule of thumb:* The Court of Claims has been unwilling to resolve all ambiguities in favor of the contractor.[34] In *National By-Products, Inc. v. United States*,[35] the Court refused to apply the rule of the *WPC* case, even though the parties had "two contrary understandings of the 'deal' [which] were both objectively reasonable

---

34. In Beacon Constr. Co. v. United States, 314 F.2d 501, 504 (Ct. Cl. 1963), a contractor bidding on a government construction job noticed an ambiguity in the bid documents, but did not inquire of the government contracting officer — choosing instead to bid on the basis of the Maine trade practice. A dispute subsequently arose, and the Court of Claims ruled against the contractor, noting that a "prime purpose of these contractual provisions relating to ambiguities and discrepancies is to enable potential contractors (as well as the Government) to clarify the contract's meaning before the die is cast." When a contractor "is presented with an obvious omission, inconsistency, or discrepancy of significance, he must consult the Government's representatives if he intends to bridge the crevasse in his own favor."

35. 405 F.2d 1256, 1272 (Ct. Cl. 1969).

in the totality of the circumstances." The court noted: "Here, there was no root fault on the part of the Government from which the later misunderstanding flowered." Would the test be different in a case involving a supplier and a private non-governmental buyer? *See* Restatement (Second) of Contracts §§ 20, 201.

   2. Of latent and patent ambiguity: In *States Roofing Corp. v. Winter*,[36] a recent case following *WPC*, the Federal Circuit divided over whether there was a latent or a patent ambiguity. The court referred to *WPC* as setting a still-applicable "rule of *contra proferentum*," literally meaning "against the one bringing forth" and commonly used to refer to interpretation against the drafter of standard terms. The *States Roofing* majority found a latent ambiguity that made it reasonable for the contractor to understand the contract as requiring only waterproof paint on the roofing of a naval facility, rather than three-ply felt flashing. Applying the test that a "patent ambiguity" is one that is "obvious, gross, glaring, so that plaintiff contractor had a duty to inquire about it at the start," the court concluded that the ambiguity in the case was only latent. A dissenter conceded that the contract had omitted a specification for a three-layer waterproofing membrane — which would have clarified that flashing was expected — and instead used only the word "layers," but said this was a "glaring" ambiguity and that a reasonable contractor would have inquired what the term meant. What type of ambiguity was involved in *Raffles*? What type of ambiguity was involved in *WPC*? What makes an ambiguity glaring and therefore patent, requiring inquiry, as opposed to an ambiguity that is latent?

3. When Is It Too Late to Discover a Mistake and Avoid the Contract?

a. Introducing the Problem of the Mistaken Bid

   People often make offers based on mistakes. When should we let them back out of contracts formed when the other party accepted the mistaken offer? Professor Lon Fuller, in his classic article exploring the reliance and expectation interests,[37] justified holding people to contracts and protecting their expectation interests because of the difficulty of proving reliance. For example, when I think I have a deal with you, I am likely to stop looking for other suppliers of the same item. At the least, your failure to perform costs me the chance to find other bargains. This explanation for holding people to promises suggests several problems. On one hand, buyer may rely on seller's promise even before they make a legally binding contract. Seller, however, wants to withdraw because it made a mistake. Should buyer's reliance be protected? On the other hand, the injury actually or likely caused by buyer's reliance after the parties made a legally binding contract may be very small, as compared to the burden on seller if it is held to its mistaken promise. Should this matter?

---

   36. 587 F.3d 1364, 1372 (Fed. Cir. 2009).
   37. Lon Fuller & William R. Perdue Jr., *The Reliance Interest in Contract Damages: Pt. 1*, 46 Yale L.J. 52 (1936).

Legal formalism would ignore both situations. Under this theory, a bargainer is free to back out of any transaction before the magic moment of closing the deal took place. Conversely, once a deal is closed, absent fraud or a *mutual* mistake going to the essence of the transaction, a bargainer has to live with any mistakes. However, the solutions offered by legal formalism fail to track with much of business life. Many transactions involve an incremental process of give-and-take. It is hard to find any magic moment of commitment that matters to the parties. After parties work together, either may suffer losses if the other backs out. Expectations of fairness and good faith grow as the transaction progresses.

Should the law recognize these business practices, or should judges demand that parties go through formalities that mark when the parties make a contract? Alternatively, how much weight should courts give to contract formalities? Suppose seller submits an offer that buyer accepts. This creates a legally binding contract. Shortly afterward, seller discovers he made a substantial mistake in calculating the price he quoted. Buyer has done little in reliance. Should the law offer relief from the mistake?

We must keep several questions distinct. First, we might ask as a matter of ethics whether a person who has made a promise based on a mistake should stand behind it. Would the good person back out if her lawyer told her that no legally binding agreement had been made under the rules of contract law? Second, we might ask whether the ethical person would hold another to a contract once she discovers their agreement was based on the other's mistake. Third, we can ask whether legal rules should reflect whatever moral decisions we reach. We might conclude that most people will offer to stand behind their promises based on mistakes. Most who might benefit from such errors may refuse to accept the benefits of these promises. Most people are ethical, or they are subject to private sanction systems that offer all the regulation that is needed.

We will look at several situations in which one party makes a promise based on a mistake. In each situation, the other party has no reason to know that a mistake has been made. In some cases courts enforce the agreement, while in other cases enforcement is denied. In some cases relief is given to a party even though the formalities of a contract were not met. Can we formulate a principled and coherent explanation of these cases?

Buyers of goods or services often use competitive bidding. Statutes may require governmental units to operate this way to save money and minimize favoritism and kickbacks. Plans and specifications are drawn by architects, and engineers and owners make them available to interested general contractors. General contractors then ask subcontractors and suppliers to make bids. A bid is a statement that the firm making it will do some part of the project for a certain amount. Typically subcontractors give general contractors bids shortly before the general must submit a prime bid to the corporation or governmental unit having the work done. Though some bids may be submitted in writing, more typically the bidder telephones them to the general contractor just before the deadline or emails them the night before. The process can be hectic and chaotic.

Each general contractor then takes the best bids, adds its own estimates for work its crew will do, and then includes a sum to cover the expense of coordinating the work and taking the risks involved. A general must both keep the amount of the bid as low as possible to get the job and keep it high enough to make money on the project. The owner makes a contract with the lucky general contractor. Then the general usually makes contracts with selected subcontractors and material suppliers of goods and services at guaranteed prices.

Clearly, there is a great deal of room for error in this process. Some building contractors, subcontractors, and material suppliers are highly professional and use the most advanced methods of preparing bids, including the use of software that checks for errors. Others operate in a more seat-of-the pants fashion, scorning paperwork. A general or a subcontractor may misread plans and specifications. These documents may be ambiguous or conflict with one another. A contractor may assume that it can make something in a customary way, but an owner's architect may have demanded a special and more costly procedure in a clause buried in lengthy and poorly organized specifications. A contractor may make an error in data entry or in computation. A component (sometimes a room, or a whole floor) can be inadvertently omitted during the last-minute calculations.

Mistakes can hurt everyone involved. If a subcontractor must perform a mistaken bid, it may go broke. But a general contractor may have relied on that bid in computing its offer to the owner, and if the subcontractor backs out, the general contractor must cope with the loss. If the owner calls for new bids because of the mistakes, this may increase the price of the building. Ideally, bidders would avoid making mistakes; however, this is easier said than done.

We will explore the range of choices open to courts in these cases, and the advantages and disadvantages of each. The cases expose the eternal tension between a desire for orderly, clear, certain rules and the urge to provide relief when those clear rules seem to work a hardship. We begin with the war horses of traditional contract courses—the mailbox rule and the firm offer—and then move to other rules that implicate the same policies. Throughout, we will ask whether courts are protecting free choice, holding people to the consequences of their negligence, or making decisions based on ideas of social engineering or sympathy. Keeping in mind Professor Horwitz's arguments, we will ask whether developments in these areas systematically favor the powerful.

b. The Mailbox Rule

Under the classic common law "mailbox rule," an acceptance creates a legally binding contract when it is mailed.[38] Nothing happening between the time of mailing

---

38. There are a number of wonderful subproblems. The offeree must have addressed the letter of acceptance properly. It must have adequate postage. The person relying on the existence of a contract must prove both that he mailed the acceptance and when he did this. While there are presumptions that help, sometimes it is not easy to prove you mailed a letter. We can worry whether the rule applies to modern methods of communication such as computer systems linked by telephone lines. At least

and the time of receipt affects the formation of the contract. (All *other* communications—offers, rejections, and revocations—take effect only when they are received.)

Suppose, for example, that a buyer sends a purchase order by mail to a manufacturer. The order is designated as an offer to be accepted by the manufacturer, which proceeds to deposit its acceptance in the mail. Before receiving the acceptance, buyer discovers that its purchase order made a mistake as to quantity, and its representative telephones manufacturer, attempting to withdraw the offer.

The common law is clear.[39] The offeror's attempt to revoke the offer is too late because the acceptance has already been mailed. The rule has been rationalized in terms of protecting an offeree's likely reliance. Once it mails a letter of acceptance, an offeree must take that contract into account in its planning. It may not seek other contracts and may prepare to perform the one it just accepted. The mailbox rule means that the offeree need not wait for the offeror to learn of the acceptance before the offeree can begin to rely on the contract's existence. The offeror knows that it is in an uncertain situation once it makes an outstanding offer; an offeror who wishes to be free from this uncertainty could specify, in the offer, that an acceptance will be effective only when received by the offeror.

An offeree's possible reliance after acceptance by mail is a standard part of making contracts by correspondence, if the mailbox rule is applicable. Notice that the rule applies and there is a contract although the offeree cannot show that it suffered any reliance loss. As you might expect, in many situations offerees will not assert their contract rights. Offerees often allow offerors to back out when they believe that the reason for the attempted revocation of an offer is a mistake, rather than that the offeror found another deal at a better price.

Notwithstanding the venerability and widespread acceptance of the mailbox rule, in 1949 the Court of Claims announced an acceptance-when-received rule. *Dick v. United States*[40] involved the following sequence of communications:

(1) After an extended exchange of telegrams, a manufacturer sent the Coast Guard a bid to supply propellers for an ice-breaking vessel.

(2) The Coast Guard mailed its purchase order to the manufacturer, offering to buy the propellers.

(3) The manufacturer mailed its acceptance of the order to the Coast Guard.

(4) While the letter of acceptance was in transit, the manufacturer discovered that the order was for two *sets* of two propellers and not one set of two propellers as it had assumed. (That is, the Coast Guard ordered four propellers while the manufac-

---

judged by appellate reports, the rule is not a pressing modern problem. Perhaps this makes it good material for bar examinations.

39. The United Nations Convention on the Sale of Goods rejects the common law rule. Article 15 § 1 provides that an acceptance is effective when it reaches the offeree. Even the putatively irrevocable offer can be so revoked.

40. 82 F. Supp. 326 (Ct. Cl. 1949).

turer's representatives thought they were agreeing to supply only two for the price they quoted.) The manufacturer telegraphed the Coast Guard, informing it of the mistake and saying that the price quoted should be doubled. This telegram arrived *before* the Coast Guard received the letter of acceptance.

(5) The Coast Guard's contracting officer told the manufacturer that they would make a new contract. Relying on this, the manufacturer supplied the four propellers (two sets) the Coast Guard wanted. However, the Comptroller General ruled that the contracting officer had no authority to give away the government's rights. A contract was formed when the manufacturer placed a letter of acceptance in the mail. As a result, the government paid the manufacturer only the price set forth in its purchase order, which the manufacturer mistakenly thought was for only one set of propellers instead of the two sets ordered.

On these facts, the United States Court of Claims changed its rule to acceptance-when-received. It found that the government should pay the manufacturer for both sets of propellers supplied. We are almost certain there was no reliance by the offeror on the letter of acceptance. Note that in the case, it was the offeree who made a mistake, and the offeree overtook its mailed communication with a telegraph. The first thing the Coast Guard received in response to its offer was a communication telling it to disregard the earlier mailed but not-yet-received acceptance because of a mistake. Thus, the *Dick* case reached the right result in terms of protecting expectations and reliance, but violated the mailbox rule.

Six years later, the Court of Claims decided *Rhode Island Tool Co. v. United States*.[41] It applied its acceptance-when-received rule and found no contract. An offeror tried to revoke its offer after the offeree had mailed a letter of acceptance but before the offeror had received it. The court assumed there could be but one rule covering both the *Dick* and *Rhode Island Tool* situations. It had to adopt an acceptance-when-mailed or an acceptance-when-received rule for all situations.

Several writers have suggested that we need different rules for different situations. To oversimplify, in the *Dick* situation the rule should be acceptance-when-received. In the *Rhode Island Tool* situation, however, it should be acceptance-when-mailed. This makes sense if the primary goal is to protect likely reliance. In the *Dick* situation, the Coast Guard's officials did not know that the manufacturer had mailed an acceptance before they learned it had made a mistake. An offeror cannot rely on an acceptance before learning of its existence. In the *Rhode Island Tool* case, however, an

---

41. 128 F. Supp. 417 (Ct. Cl. 1955). The United States Court of Claims has continued to follow its acceptance-when-received rule. *See, e.g.*, Romala Corp. v. United States, 20 Cl. Ct. 435 (1990). However, other courts have continued to apply the common law acceptance-when-mailed rule and rejected the Court of Claims position. *See, e.g.*, Soldau v. Organon, Inc., 860 F.2d 355 (9th Cir. 1988); Morrison v. Thoelke, 155 So. 2d 889 (Fla. App. 1963). Under the Court of Claims acceptance-when-received rule, an offeree could post a letter of acceptance, estimate when it would arrive, and make the final decision as to whether to accept at the last minute before the letter was delivered. In this way, the offeree could watch market fluctuations that much longer before making a final commitment. Is this a reason for rejecting the Court of Claims rule?

offeree had deposited a letter of acceptance in the mail and should have been entitled to start relying from that point on. Other writers worry about binding one party to a contract when the other party is not bound. However, they concede that perhaps courts should give relief in the *Dick* situation on the ground of mistake. Consider the mistake possibility after we have studied traditional and modern views about such relief.

Would the mailbox rule apply to an acceptance sent by email or by fax?[42] The short answer is that we don't know. Courts have not faced cases involving this problem. Both forms of communication usually are fast, and so parties do not generally face the delays involved in letters being mailed, carried to another city, and delivered. It is this delay that makes it possible for the offeree to put a letter of acceptance in the mail, and the offeror to attempt to revoke after the mailing but before the letter is received. Some contracts are made when customers go to a website such as those run by catalog merchants like Lands' End or Eddie Bauer. These merchants typically give customers the right to return goods within a reasonable time. This policy avoids many of the problems of the mailbox rule. Of course, to trigger the mailbox rule, the communication must be properly addressed. The Uniform Electronic Transactions Act (UETA) § 15 defines what constitutes sending and receipt of electronic records, providing, for example, that if an email is misaddressed, it has not been "sent," but it has nothing to say about what constitutes acceptance of a contract, other than that it can be done by electronic means. See UETA § 7(b).[43] By 2010, UETA had been adopted in 47 states. Furthermore, the federal Electronic Signatures in Global and National Commerce Act (E-SIGN) makes electronic communications effective to form contracts in any state.[44]

The Uniform Computer Information Transactions Act (UCITA), which only Maryland and Virginia have enacted and which only applies to software and certain digital content contracts, provides a "receipt" rule for formation by an electronic acceptance. See UCITA § 203(4)(A). "Receipt" is elaborately defined in UCITA in terms of either "being delivered to and available at a location or system designated by agreement" or in the absence of agreement, in the case of an electronic communication, "coming into existence in an information processing system or at an address in that system in

---

42. *Compare* Amelia Rawls, *Contract Formation in an Internet Age*, 10 COLUM. SCI. & TECH. L. REV. 200 (2009) (arguing that the mailbox rule is outdated) *with* Valerie Watnick, *The Electronic Formation of Contracts and the Common Law "Mailbox Rule,"* 56 BAYLOR L. REV. 175 (2004) (advocating for the continued relevance of the mailbox rule).

43. *See* Watnick, *supra* note 42, at 197–98 (noting that UETA does not set a rule for when acceptance occurs in electronic contract formation, but arguing that problems of proof may be reduced by a dispatch rule, rather than a receipt rule, for effectiveness of an emailed acceptance because e-mail is not necessarily nearly instantaneous).

44. 15 U.S.C. §§ 7001 *et seq.* The federal legislation, which was enacted because of impatience on the part of national enterprises with waiting for completion of the uniform law's drafting and enactment process, also adds some consumer protections not present in UETA.

a form capable of being processed by or perceived from a system of that type by a recipient, if the recipient uses, or otherwise has designated or holds out, that place or system for receipt of notices of the kind to be given and the sender does not know that the notice cannot be accessed from that place." UCITA § 101(53). This definition gives a flavor of the tortuous drafting style of UCITA, one of the reasons it failed to gain wide enactment. Another was its perceived bias toward producers of software and other digital products and against their customers.[45]

Reported contract cases involving the mailbox rule, whether involving electronic or postal mail, are few and far between. Why do you think this is so?

c. The Firm Offer

Another change in traditional contract rules affects who has responsibility for mistaken bids and offers. Since the 1960s courts and legislatures have created more liability, even though parties have not followed settled procedures for forming contracts. Again we must understand the consequences and ask who benefits and who suffers from the changes.

Suppose Seller offers to sell goods to Buyer at a specified price. Buyer neither accepts nor rejects the offer. Seller, eager to make a sale, says, "Take your time and think about this deal. You'll find it is a good price for goods of this quality." Seller leaves. Buyer then gets another offer for the same type of goods from Competitor, but the price is higher. Buyer rejects Competitor's offer, planning to accept Seller's proposal. However, before Buyer can communicate, Seller revokes its offer. (Seller may have found another customer for the goods it has, or may have discovered an error in the calculations upon which it quoted that price, or may simply have changed its mind.) Buyer has lost its possible deal with Competitor. May Buyer recover from Seller? The traditional common law rule was clear: offers are revocable until they are accepted. Buyer had no right to rely on an unaccepted offer. It should have known it did not have a contract. Thus, Buyer could not recover.[46]

Suppose Seller was very eager to make a sale. She says, "Take your time and think about this deal. You'll find it is a good price for goods of this quality. I promise not to revoke this offer for one week." Under the common law rules, the case for Buyer

---

45. *See also* Jean Braucher, *New Basics: 12 Principles for Fair Commerce in Mass-Market Software and Other Digital Products*, Consumer Protection in the Age of the "Information Economy" 177 (Jane K. Winn ed., 2006) (discussing the opposition to UCITA from myriad perspectives, particularly that of both business and consumer customers of digital products).

46. Some writers would explain this result in terms of mutuality of obligation. Buyer is free to reject seller's offer or ignore it. If buyer has this freedom, seller should have it too. Equal treatment is an important value in our legal system. However, there is no requirement that our law treat people who have done different things equally. Thus, the question remains whether seller's actions warrant courts treating seller differently than they treat buyer. Seller has made an offer. Buyer has done nothing. Does this difference in their behavior call for different treatment by the courts? Mutuality does not answer the question.

is no stronger. Seller's promise not to revoke lacks consideration. It would not be en-forceable, and Seller could revoke without liability to Buyer. Buyer could make a promise not to revoke enforceable by paying for an "option."[47]

There have been changes in these rules. Section 2-205 of the Uniform Commercial Code offers a very limited change in the rules. It provides:

> An offer by a merchant to buy or sell goods in a signed writing which by its terms gives assurance that it will be held open is not revocable, for lack of consideration, during the time stated or if no time is stated for a reasonable time, but in no event may such period of irrevocability exceed three months; but any such term of assurance on a form supplied by the offeree must be separately signed by the offeror.

Notice that the rule applies only to merchants. The promise to hold open an offer must be in a signed writing. The statute limits the duration of the option. Moreover, the Code imposes a special rule for a form contract supplied by the offeree.

This cautious relaxation of the consideration doctrine stands in contrast to the court-fashioned rule applicable to subcontractor bids in building construction. Think about bidding in building construction. Typically, an owner invites bids on the plans and specifications for a project. Several general contractors plan to bid on the job. They calculate their bids from their own estimates of the costs of that part of the work they plan to carry out with their own crew, as well as sub-bids from subcontractors and suppliers of machinery and materials. Sub-bids may be written, but in the past they were often transmitted at the last minute by telephone. Today, as more and more processes move online, emailed subcontractor bids have become common.

The owner usually awards a contract to construct the building to the low-bidding general contractor. Suppose one subcontractor refuses to stand behind its bid and enter a contract. Assume the subcontractor revokes its offer (its bid) before the general contractor accepts it to form a contract. The common law rule allowed subcontractors to back out if they did so before their bids were accepted.

The general contractor relied on the subcontractor's bid. The general used this sub-bid in calculating its bid on the contract. Moreover, this reliance is foreseeable and reasonable. Can general contractors find a theory of liability to hold subcontrac-tors or suppliers? Soon after the first Restatement of Contracts was published, a lawyer for a general contractor sued a supplier of materials that had submitted a bid based on mistaken calculations. The lawyer tried to use § 90, providing that "[a] promise which the promisor should reasonably expect to induce action or forbearance of a

---

47. In some jurisdictions, seller's promise would be enforceable if it were stated in a sealed in-strument. In the United States, few people, other than those advised by lawyers, are likely to use this method of making binding promises.

definite and substantial character on the part of the promisee, and which does induce such action or forbearance, is binding if injustice can be avoided only by enforcement of the promise." It was not clear whether this provision applied to reliance on bids.

Judge Learned Hand of the United States Court of Appeals for the Second Circuit was a member of the American Law Institute. He helped draft the Restatement of Contracts. He wrote the opinion in this first attempt to use § 90 in a bidding case. He refused to apply it to block withdrawal of a bid. "[A]n offer for an exchange is not meant to become a promise until a consideration has been received.... In the case at bar the defendant offered to deliver the linoleum in exchange for the plaintiff's acceptance, not for its bid, which was a matter of indifference to it.... There is no room in such a situation for the doctrine of 'promissory estoppel.'"[48]

There were many cases suggesting disagreement with Judge Hand's position. However, the major breakthrough came in an opinion of Justice Roger Traynor of the Supreme Court of California in 1958. His opinion in *Drennan v. Star Paving Co.*[49] is cited often, and represents the prevailing view. In the *Drennan* case, a paving subcontractor telephoned an oral bid to a general contractor. The subcontractor's representative did not promise to keep the bid open. There was no finding that this was the custom among subs and generals in that area. The subcontractor refused to enter a contract based on its bid to the general. Justice Traynor found an implied secondary promise in the bid that the subcontractor would keep its offer open for a reasonable time. This implied promise became irrevocable by the sub under § 90 once the general relied on it by using the sub-bid in its prime bid.[50]

Was Justice Traynor's decision based on choice, or fault, or another theory of liability? While some suppliers have more bargaining power than the general contractors with whom they deal, in the usual situation a large general contractor is seeking to hold a smaller subcontractor to its bid. Subcontractors as a group have a stake in the bidding process. Most will stand behind their bids and eat their losses when they make mistakes. Generals may not ask subcontractors who refuse to honor their bids to submit them in future transactions. However, there is no guarantee that the general who receives the prime contract will award a contract to the subcontractor with the

---

48. *See* James Baird Co. v. Gimbel Bros., 64 F.2d 344, 346 (2d Cir. 1933).

49. 51 Cal. 2d 409, 333 P.2d 757 (1958). For a discussion of the Hand and Traynor positions, see Alfred S. Konefsky, *Freedom and Interdependence in Twentieth-Century Contract Law: Traynor and Hand and Promissory Estoppel*, 65 U. Cin. L. Rev. 1169 (1997) ("In *Baird*, Learned Hand viewed the commercial transaction at issue through the lens of individualism and formalism. Traynor, however, impatient with the traditional application of individualism to contract law, sought to transform that law by sanctioning the increasingly interdependent activities of marketplace actors.").

50. Applying *Drennan*, the Nevada Supreme Court held that "the district court may award expectation, reliance, or restitutionary damages for promissory estoppel claims." The Court shied away from an all-inclusive rule, instead reminding us of the "general requirements that damages be foreseeable and reasonably certain." Dynalectric Co. of Nev., Inc. v. Clark & Sullivan Constructors, Inc., 255 P.3d 286, 289 (Nev. 2011).

lowest bid. Even if a general does offer the contract to the low-bidding subcontractor, the general may seek to bargain for an even lower price. In other words, the general may shop for a better deal or may try to negotiate with the sub, practices called "bid shopping" and "bid chopping."

Is the firm-offer rule just another example of the law being twisted in the interests of the powerful behind apolitical-seeming abstractions? None of the judges writing opinions applying Restatement § 90 to subcontractor bids explains why "injustice can be avoided only by enforcement of the promise." Scholars and politicians tell us that judges should not make major political choices but should leave them to the legislature. Why don't they leave this choice to legislation? Organized lobbying groups represent many general contractors, subcontractors, and materials suppliers. Isn't their failure to seek legislation significant? If courts can hold subcontractors to their bids under § 90, they must then consider whether to offer relief for mistake under other provisions. Wouldn't it be easier just to continue the common law position? Are subcontractors who back out and refuse to honor bids likely to hurt general contractors often? How do we know that reputational sanctions are not enough?

How should jurists answer questions such as these? Most of these questions are normative, but they rest on assumptions about the likely consequences of various rules courts could adopt. Facts alone cannot answer normative questions. Nonetheless, data can sharpen normative issues when they let us see how various proposals might operate. The study discussed below fills in some of the blanks, though it cannot establish once and for all "the facts" relevant to subcontractor bids.[51] It does offer far more information than legal decision-makers usually have about a problem. Begin by assessing the quality of this information. Flawed data can mislead, or it can be suggestive and thus of value. Once you have some confidence about the facts, you still have to decide what approaches they call for.

The *Virginia Law Review* Study of Construction Bidding

A study of generals and subs doing business in Virginia, conducted and published by the editors of the *Virginia Law Review*, provides a snapshot of bidding practices as of the mid-1960s.[52] Of 94 subs surveyed, 53 responded. Sixty-seven of 100 generals sent back questionnaires. What follows is a summary and paraphrase of the study.

Most of the subs said that they submitted their bids within one to four hours of the general's deadline for submitting a bid. This had the effect of exerting time pressure on the general to minimize pre-submission bid-shopping.

---

51. At best, this study is a snapshot of the situation in Virginia in the mid-1960s. We cannot be sure the information would hold for other states today. Moreover, the respondents are not an ideal random sample of the relevant population. As is true whenever respondents are asked questions, we cannot be sure that all of them understood the questions or told the exact truth.

52. Note, *Another Look at Construction Bidding and Contracts Formation*, 53 Va. L. Rev. 1720 (1967).

Although some bids were submitted in writing with a statement that they would not be withdrawn for a certain period of time, most were oral, indicating that § 2-205 of the code did not cover many bids made to generals.

A clear majority of subs said they had difficulties with generals who bid-shop before awarding a subcontract. They also believed that it was unethical for a general contractor to bid-shop either before or after the award of the prime contract. Generals did not specifically say they engaged in bid-shopping, but only about half indicated that they always used the low bid from among those submitted by the subs. Many generals qualified their answer by stating that they used the low bid unless the low bidder had a poor reputation, had performed unsatisfactorily on previous jobs, or was in financial trouble. Eleven of 65 generals responded that they typically used a sub's bid to estimate what that portion of the job should cost, and they retained the option of doing the work themselves or finding someone who could beat that price.

Generals were also asked if it was customary to conduct further negotiations with subs before concluding an agreement. Of the generals who responded, 25 said they usually negotiated further. Of these 25, 20 stated that the purpose of the negotiations was only to clarify terms other than price. Only two indicated that they did bargain about price (the practice referred to as bid chopping).

Most subs responded that they felt the need to counter a general's efforts to bid-shop. Thirty-one of 45 subs indicated that they would not in the future submit bids to a bid-shopping general, but not one of the subs mentioned he would take the general to court.

Subs were unanimous in saying they would feel bound to go ahead and perform the work at their original bid price if it was discovered that the sub made a mistake in the bid but that the general had used the bid in its own bid. The majority of generals considered both parties bound to each other as of the time that the general used the bid. Neither generals nor subs ascribed much importance to whether a bid was "firm." One sub said a bid's status as "firm" was irrelevant: "Our word is our bond and our reputation paramount." Most subs stated that they felt compelled to do the job once the general had relied because they felt morally or legally bound.

When a general decided to use a sub's bid in his own bid to the awarding authority, rarely was the sub notified that the general was using it prior to the general's bid. More frequently, a sub was notified immediately after the general used a sub's bid in his own bid or after the general was awarded the prime contract. However, about half of the subs indicated that they were notified at some later time.

Finally, generals and subs were both asked what objection, if any, they would have if a court found that a contract was formed so that the parties were bound to perform as of the time the sub's bid was used by the general in his own bid. This contract would only take effect if the general received the prime contract. This question was most important to subs, but surprisingly their reactions were not unanimous. Forty-eight subs expressed their approval. Many elaborated, saying such things as "Wonderful!" or "I think this is the way it should be." Of the five subs who were skeptical of finding a contract at this point in the dealing, none had strong reservations. Two believed a general should not be required to deal with a sub he found unacceptable after bid opening.

Of generals, 28 objected to a court's finding of a contract while 35 did not. The fact that a majority of generals did not object is surprising in light of the fact that the legal change posited by the question would bind the general earlier than under existing law. Many generals, both some who objected and some who did not, noted that a sub's reliability was paramount. One solution suggested by them was to treat differently solicited subs or bids from subs the general knew, which the law could do by recognizing a trade usage that use of such bids creates a contract.

Both generals and subs raised an objection about the difficulty of proving whose bid was used. This practical point does not concern the wisdom of finding a contract but rather raises an administrative hurdle with solutions possible. As in certain public contract bidding, generals could protect themselves by posting their subs' names with their bids. At least one trade association recommended this approach.

A weightier concern was the sloppiness of some sub-bids, often caused by time pressures. As one general stated:

> None of them get their final bids to us until shortly before bid time—when the estimators must, within about three hours, take (over the phone) the sub's bid, get from him what he has covered—and evaluate all sub-bids, which entails adding to or deducting from a sub-bid, whatever he can find is the right price, for the work not included in some, and the extra work included by others. In a job in which there may be 35 sub-bid items the estimators may have 150 to 200 sub-bids to evaluate, choose one in each category, transfer the unit prices (which are part of so many bids) onto our sheets, then if there are alternates, add those bids up, add the alternates up, put them in our bid, say a prayer, and submit our bid.

The extent of this type of challenge for generals was not known.

The main concern of most objecting generals was the possibility of having to deal with an "unknown" bidder. Generals wanted to investigate such subs before awarding the subcontract. Furthermore, some subs might not be registered and therefore not qualified to do the work, or some might not have a sufficient labor force to do the job. Generals viewed all these circumstances as grounds for objection to subs.

———

Before—and, at an accelerating pace, after—the turn of the twenty-first century, bidding practices moved online. The following article describes the transition, focusing on highway contracting in Iowa and Wisconsin in regular "lettings" of contracts by each state's Department of Transportation. Before the Internet age, "lettings" required contractors to set up operations in a hotel in the state capital for assembly of bids, but online bidding changed this and many other practices.

Technology Applications: Internet Bidding

Gov't Eng'g 34–36 (Jan.–Feb. 2005)[53]

Iowa DOT Phases in Internet Bidding

For contractors, bidding on highway construction projects for the Iowa Department of Transportation (Iowa DOT) used to involve a great deal of logistics. Contractors would bring a small army to the letting hotel, along with various support equipment like fax machines, computers, and printers. There they would set up camp for a few days and prepare their bids.

"Over the years, this monthly pilgrimage was getting more difficult," said Roger Bierbaum, Iowa DOT Contracts Engineer. "Then one time a blizzard hit the day before a letting. Many of Iowa's larger contractors, especially those from the far corners of the state, began to push Iowa to allow Internet bid submission."

Since 1994, Iowa's contractors had been able to use the American Association of State Highway and Transportation Officials' (AASHTO, www.aashto.org) Trns•port Expedite® software to submit their bids. This is referred to as one-way bidding, since contractors download bidding files from Bid Express® (Bidx.com™, an Info Tech, Inc. Company, www.infotechfl.com), an online information service, and then submit their bids either on paper or on a disk. Iowa DOT started testing two-way electronic bidding with Bid Express in January 2000....

Digitally signed Internet bids were first accepted during the April 2001 letting. [According to Bierbaum,] "At the first letting, ten contractors submitted a total of 52 bids over the Internet. By October 2001, about 40 percent of the bids in the letting were submitted over the Internet. Through our February 2002 letting, 793 bids were submitted over the Internet for bids that totaled over $1.1 billion. For each subsequent letting, we were getting more contractors submitting bids over the Internet for the first time."

In calendar year 2003, the Iowa DOT received 2,501 bids over the Internet (81 percent of the bids submitted) for a value over $2.5 billion. These days, the only non-Internet bids they receive are for the small, non-highway projects, or unique projects that attract new contractors.

Most agencies that implement electronic bidding see benefits quickly in terms of error reduction and an easier, more streamlined letting process. Bierbaum can point to an instance where Internet bidding literally saved the state millions of dollars. "We had a situation where a bidder at the letting hotel determined he would be the only bidder on a project. He submitted a bid, which he thought to be close enough to the state's estimate so a contract would be awarded. An unexpected bidder stayed at home and submitted a bid over the Internet for $8 million less and 'stole' the contract."

Internet bidding can also speed up the [way] ... projects can be set up and bid. "We had several times where we needed to take bids under 'emergency' conditions.

---

53. Available at https://bidx.com/site/goveng_0105.pdf.

We receive information from our field offices and send a fax to the contractors that we think are qualified, informing them of the special letting. We tell them when the letting documents will be posted and when the letting will be. Using Bid Express, we have been able to compress the time from submittal of scope, to the contractor beginning work, to less than a week."

Bierbaum reports that there are more advantages for the agency. "We have seen greater competition. Some contractors are bidding on more projects than they did in the past because they have more resources bidding from their home office than they did bidding from a hotel room. We've also heard that contractors can more easily include last-minute quotes in their bids, which results in lower bid prices for the DOT."

The process of implementing Internet bidding included some "lessons learned" for Bierbaum and his staff—advice that he would gladly share. "We learned you don't forget the agency's private key needed to open the bids. We won't change the time of the letting by addendum again. We needed a backup Internet provider, in case the DOT's primary Internet system goes down. We needed something faster than an inkjet printer so the hundreds of bids submitted over the Internet can be printed and so we can quickly post the 'as-read' bids."

All of these minor lessons learned aside, Bierbaum points out that the process was smooth and the support and implementation services provided by the software supplier have always been on target.

Wisconsin Reaps Benefits of Internet Bidding

Wisconsin Department of Transportation (WisDOT) first became aware of Bid Express in 1997 when [it was] implementing the AASHTO pre-construction software modules offered by Info Tech. WisDOT had an existing service that it was using to communicate bidding information to contractors.

"During our evaluation assessment we determined that we had three options: create new interfaces from the newly implemented modules to the existing bidding service, develop a new bidding service to interface, or use the Bid Express service that already interfaced," said David Castleberg, Construction Engineering Technology Supervisor with WisDOT.

The software was fairly new at the time and was offered to WisDOT as a way to provide current services to its contractors and expand on those services in the future using the Internet. "We decided to take the plunge and be the first state to offer bidding information on Bid Express."

Once the decision was made, it was time to convince the contractors that this was a good idea. "The biggest challenge facing the contractors in the initial or one-way bidding process was working on the Internet to get their information," Castleberg said.

It was also a change for them to go from an all-paper process to a partially electronic process. As a result, WisDOT phased in the use of the software. "When we first implemented, paper was still the main form for bid entry and considered the 'controlling' document. Preparing the bid using Expedite was still optional and the completed Expedite file was submitted on a diskette. They still submitted a signed paper printout with this method. After a year we went to mandatory use of Expedite and submission of bids on diskette with paper printout backup. Paper still controlled."

Contractors immediately felt the impact of the implementation, but quickly saw the benefits, too. "The time savings for the contractor was the 24/7 access to Bid Express to download their bid files, and in preparing and editing the bids using Expedite," he said. With Bid Express, the contractors also had access to planholders and eligible bidders lists that were helpful to those subcontractors who needed to know to whom they should potentially submit quotes.

There were immediate benefits on the agency side, too. WisDOT received fewer support calls from contractors looking for bidding information and implemented simple procedures for creating the bid files and posting information to Bid Express, which saved time over the old way of doing business.

However, the biggest impact for the department was clearly on the post-letting processing side. With the bid files on diskette, it was a simple process to load the data for further processing. "We no longer had to hand-key all the bid data from paper forms submitted by the contractor. Previously, we had hired six temporary employees each month to key the data from the paper forms. This processing took four to six hours once all the edit checking was done. With one-way bidding, we dropped down to three temps working for two to four hours."

Castleberg and his team felt that the next step was to go with two-way electronic bidding. With this method, bidding information is not only downloaded from the Bid Express website, but also completed bids are submitted back via the Internet. He knew that the contractors might not be eager to get on board. But given the success of one-way bidding, they forged ahead.

"The contractors were reluctant when we first proposed the idea of two-way bidding to them. They were hesitant to remove themselves from physically handing off their bid proposal. They had questions about creating digital IDs, error checking, verification of receipt of bids, and Internet connection failures. However, I believe that we did a good job of advanced planning with the contractors, so that we were able to answer their questions and rest their fears. Once they realized that it would not be a difficult process for them to manage and they realized the benefits to them, they were ready. We worked with a group of 10 to 15 contractors, trained them, and conducted two pilot lettings before our final roll-out of two-way bidding."

This group of pilot contractors sold the idea to the rest of the industry. Wisconsin's first two-way letting was a success. There were 21 proposals to let and 99 bids were submitted. Of those, 46 were submitted over the Internet. The contractors did not report any problems. Castleberg attributes this to good planning and training. With two-way bidding, the agency eliminated the remaining three temporary employees.

Castleberg says that two-way bidding quickly became the norm simply because the contractors like it. "This was evident in the number of contractors submitting bids electronically—even though it wasn't mandatory. They could still submit bids on diskette, but this soon became a small percentage of the bids submitted. Because they were submitting bids from their offices they no longer had to travel to Madison every month for the letting. This saved them hundreds of dollars each month in travel and hotel costs. The department still held a public reading of the results, but since they were being posted on Bid Express, the contractors could also view the results at their office."

Use of Bid Express has also changed the process for getting subcontractor quotes. "Previously, most of the quoting was done in person at the hotel, the evening before the letting. Now quotes are done in advance by fax and email; therefore contractors are preparing their bids in a more timely fashion. Plus, with Bid Express, contractors who bid in Wisconsin, as well as neighboring states like Iowa, Michigan, and Minnesota can use the same Bid Express service for preparing those bids."

Castleberg advises agencies interested in implementing Bid Express to start with good planning and to get the contractors involved early. "The more they feel involved, and perceive they are part of the process, the better buy-in you will have from them." He also feels that the training and pilot lettings were vital to the process...."Our biggest benefit, in addition to reducing the number of staff needed, is in the savings of processing time. A typical letting contains 45 proposals with 175 bids submitted. Prior to one-way bidding, we were still processing and analyzing as late as 5 P.M. to 7 P.M. on the day of the letting. With one-way bidding, we are done by 3 P.M. to 4 P.M., and with two-way bidding we are done by 1 P.M."

Castleberg and his team do less error checking because the Expedite application does extensive error checking prior to submittal. Do errors sometimes appear? "Our only errors are from the handful of diskette proposals with paper corrections and a possible 'paper only' submittal."

In Wisconsin, diskettes are mandatory if not submitting two-way, and a paper-only submittal costs the contractor $75 for processing. "We have averaged 92 percent of bids being submitted via the Internet since we implemented two-way bidding. As a result, the department discontinued holding the public reading at a local hotel that had been used for over 25 years and moved it to a conference room in our own building. Where there used to be over 200 persons in attendance at the letting, we are now lucky if one or two contractors stop in for the reading."

In February 2010, the Wisconsin Department of Transportation announced that it was making electronic submission of bids mandatory in the absence of waiver of the requirement for certain small bids or on a case-by-case basis.[54] Other states have followed suit.[55] For example, the Kansas Department of Transportation no longer ac-

---

54. *See* http://wisconsindot.gov/Pages/doing-bus/contractors/hcci/default.aspx.

55. As of 2011, 37 state transportation agencies had moved to online processes. Ward Zerbe, *Internet Bidding Adoption in Large Transportation Agencies—From Innovation to the Norm*, presented at the 2011 Annual Conference of the Transportation Association of Canada. http://conf.tac-atc.ca/english/annualconference/tac2011/docs/m2/zerbe.pdf.

cepts handwritten or typewritten bids; all contractors submit their bids online.[56] How do the electronic bidding procedures described in the article likely affect the legal issues that arise? Note that electronic bidding led to earlier submission of sub-bids, typically by either email or fax. General contractors could also set up websites for submission of sub-bids to them.

Consider the following decision in light of the Virginia study and the more recent transition to electronic bidding. How does the court know that the Wisconsin courts would hold that a subcontractor cannot withdraw a mistaken bid once the general contract has used that bid in computing its bid on the prime contract? Would you expect the issues to change with electronic bidding?

JANKE CONSTRUCTION CO. v. VULCAN MATERIALS CO.

United States District Court, Western District of Wisconsin
386 F. Supp. 687 (1974), *aff'd*, 527 F.2d 772 (1976)

ROSENSTEIN, J.

In this action, plaintiff, a general contractor, alleges that defendant, a producer of construction materials, including reinforced concrete pipe, agreed to provide plaintiff with pipe and fittings at a per unit cost, for a marine construction project at the University of Wisconsin at Milwaukee, Wisconsin; that defendant expressly warranted and represented to plaintiff that defendant's products would meet the specifications required for that project; that plaintiff, in reliance thereon, used defendant's prices in bidding on the marine project and was awarded the contract; that following the award, defendant proposed to provide plaintiff with pipe and fittings which did not meet the specifications and which were rejected by the project engineers; and that plaintiff was thereby compelled to purchase the specified materials from another supplier at a higher cost, sustaining damages of $40,442.40.

Jurisdiction is based on diversity of citizenship and the parties do not contest that Wisconsin law applies. The case was tried to this Court without a jury, briefs were submitted, and the matter is now ripe for disposition.

Plaintiff, a Wisconsin corporation with its principal offices near Wausau, Wisconsin, has been engaged in various types of construction work, including highway, sewer, airport, and marine projects. Defendant, a New Jersey corporation, operates quarries and has sand, gravel, aggregate, and redi-mix concrete plants in several states. In 1970, it also operated a concrete pipe plant located in Illinois which produced only AWWA (American Water Works Association) Specification C302 pipe.

In February 1970, the State Bureau of Engineering, on behalf of the Regents of the University of Wisconsin, publicly invited submission of sealed bids for the construction of condenser water transmission lines, lake piping, and a pumping station for the University of Wisconsin-Milwaukee campus. The project was intended to pro-

---

56. *See* http://www.ksdot.org/burconsmain/ppreq/downloadebs.asp.

vide the University with its own cooling system. The bids were to be opened at 2:00 P.M., on March 10, 1970, in Madison, Wisconsin.

The general construction, land, marine, and electrical work portions of the project were to be bid on separately, each portion requiring a separate lump-sum bid. The marine portion of the work included the furnishing and installation of water intake and return lines into Lake Michigan. The materials required for marine piping included concrete subaqueous pipe in full compliance with either AWWA Specification C300 or AWWA Specification C301. The main contract also contained an "or equal" clause, permitting use of nonspecified materials of equal quality to those specified if they were considered equally acceptable to and approved by the project engineers.

Plaintiff, intending to bid on the marine work, obtained price quotations from suppliers of the various materials required for that portion of the project. On March 5, 1970, Jerry Janke, then vice-president of plaintiff, received by telephone from a Vulcan representative price quotations for the various concrete pipe items to be used in the marine work. Janke made a memorandum of the prices quoted, but did not inquire during this conversation whether defendant proposed to supply C300 or C301 pipe, nor did the caller specify the quality or type of pipe Vulcan intended to furnish.[57] Defendant's prices were $40,000 below that quoted by Interpace, another subaqueous concrete pipe supplier.

On the evening of March 9, 1970, Jerry Janke and his brother, James Janke, owner of plaintiff, checked in at a Madison hotel for the purpose of submitting their bid the next day. Around midnight they were visited in their hotel room by Alex Barry, then general manager of Vulcan's Wisconsin operation, and Peter W. Fox, a salesman for defendant's sand, gravel, crushed limestone, and redi-mix concrete.

While it is not clear whether the visit was only social or included some discussion of Vulcan's ability to furnish the pipe for the project, all parties present at that visit agree that there was no reference to the particular specifications or type of pipe that Vulcan proposed to supply. The next day, shortly prior to submitting his bid, James Janke met Barry in the hallway of the State Office Building. Janke was concerned because of the disparity in the prices quoted by Vulcan and Interpace. He requested and received assurance from Barry that Vulcan could furnish the pipe for the project. During that meeting Barry also placed a telephone call to someone at Vulcan who confirmed his statement.

According to Barry, Janke merely inquired at this meeting whether Vulcan could reduce its quoted prices on the pipe, and his telephone call to Vulcan's vice-president was made only to confirm his statement that prices would not be reduced.

Janke, who had relied upon Vulcan's quoted pipe prices in calculating his prime bid, thereupon submitted it and was subsequently awarded the contract.

---

57. [1] Janke stated: "Pipe suppliers or any supplier giving quotations on projects normally don't bother to call you with a price or quotation unless they know they are going to be able to furnish the material, so I normally don't ask. If they call up and say I have some prices for you on this job, we want to sell it, I take the prices."

Within the week after the bid opening plaintiff received a written quotation from Vulcan setting forth the same prices that were quoted to Jerry Janke over the telephone on March 5, but stating that the quotation was for AWWA C302 pipe. The writing is dated March 6, but it is not known when it was mailed.

The record does not indicate the date when plaintiff discovered that defendant was offering to supply C302 pipe and not the pipe listed in the specifications. However, between March 10 and March 23, James Janke met three times in Milwaukee and in Madison with the engineers for the State of Wisconsin, a representative from the University, Alex Barry, and Art Littva of Vulcan's engineering department in an effort to persuade the State to accept the C302 pipe. Littva then sent Janke specifications and shop drawings showing use of the C302 pipe on the marine project, and requested Janke to submit them under the "or equal clause." The plans were submitted as requested, and were rejected by the State's consulting engineers as not approved.

In response to James Janke's inquiry as to why the pipe did not meet specifications the engineers stated that the pipe was not AWWA C300 or C301 as specified; was not steel cylinder type; was not designed for an internal pressure of 5 psi; and did not have a beam strength equal to the pipe specified.

The engineers subsequently requested Janke to submit shop drawings using design conditions and materials as specified, stating that time was critical to the completion of the project. Plaintiff was then forced to buy the specified pipe from Interpace at a cost of $197,093.50, which was $39,992.40 over the $157,101.10 it would have paid for Vulcan's pipe in accordance with the latter's quotation. James Janke considered $150 to $200 per day to be the reasonable and fair value of his time spent in attending the meetings at Madison and Milwaukee with the state engineers on Vulcan's pipe....

Plaintiff has had previous dealings with defendant, having purchased C302 pipe from it for a project in Racine, Wisconsin.

Evidence was adduced at the trial as to the normal bidding practices in the construction industry in the area. The contemplated project is generally listed or advertised in trade magazines and in the "Dodge Reports," a daily construction news service which lists proposed construction activity for various areas of the country. A subscriber to the Dodge Reports for a particular area may inspect the plans for a project in any Dodge plan room located in that area. The University of Wisconsin-Milwaukee project plans were available in Dodge plan rooms located in Milwaukee, Madison, Green Bay, and Eau Claire, Wisconsin.

An interested materials supplier checks the plans and specifications to determine if he can supply any of the required materials. He then submits a quotation by telephone, mail, or both to the contractors interested in bidding on the project. It is in this manner that contractors usually obtain quotations from the competing suppliers and subcontractors. These quotations are used by the contractors to estimate their own costs in preparing their bids. Normally, the 24-hour period preceding the prime bid deadline is one of great activity, with the subcontractors and suppliers making the rounds of the contractors who are still preparing their bids. By this time the first quotations have generally become known and the prices are often revised downward at the last minute, with the prime contractors revising their bids accordingly.

The contractor usually purchases the materials from the supplier whose prices he relied upon in preparing his bid. However, the contract is not entered into until after the contractor has been awarded the contract and the project engineers have approved the material, if such approval is needed. The supplier then prepares the shop drawings for the project after the successful bidder signs a letter of intent to purchase the material.

The Janke brothers testified that the supplier normally submits a price on material that will meet the specifications. However, Jerry Janke stated, if the supplier were offering non-specified material under the "or equal" clause he would, in the normal course of trade, alert the contractor to that fact so that the latter, if he relies upon this quotation, would note on his [the general's] bid that he proposed to supply alternate material under the "or equal" clause and that his bid is based on the substitute material.

In this manner the contractor would protect himself from having to perform on the bid, if it were accepted, in the event that the project engineers rejected the non-specified material as unsuitable.

Jerry Lapish, a marine contractor appearing for defendant, testified that when a quotation is received it is customarily the contractor's responsibility to check the specifications listed for the material on the quotation with the material specifications listed in the project contract to determine for himself whether the supplier is offering non-specified material.

Plaintiff views this action as one grounded in contract and governed by the Uniform Commercial Code, which was adopted by Wisconsin (Wis. Stat. chs. 401–409.) It contends that (1) defendant breached an alleged contract to furnish suitable and acceptable materials for the project, and (2) knowing that plaintiff relied upon its skill and judgment in furnishing the materials for the project, defendant had impliedly warranted their fitness for that particular purpose.

I agree with defendant that no binding contractual obligation existed under the Code. The mere use of Vulcan's bid was not an acceptance in law which gave rise to a contract with plaintiff. *N. Litterio & Company v. Glassman Construction Company*, 319 F.2d 736, 115 U.S. App. D.C. 335 (1963); *Drennan v. Star Paving Company*, 51 Cal. 2d 409, 333 P.2d 757 (1958)....

Defendant had not offered to make its bid irrevocable, nor was there an option supported by consideration. Thus its bid does not meet the "firm offer" requirement of Wis. Stat. §402.205, which states:

> An offer by a merchant to buy or sell goods in a signed writing which by its terms gives assurance that it will be held open is not revocable, for lack of consideration, during the time stated or if no time is stated for a reasonable time....

However, the absence of a contractual basis to plaintiff's claim is not fatal to its action. The facts which plaintiff has pleaded and relied upon to support its claim and to which defendant has responded in entering its defense give rise to the application of the doctrine of promissory estoppel. This doctrine is expressed in the Restatement of the Law of Contracts § 90 as follows:

> A promise which the promisor should reasonably expect to induce action or forbearance of a definite and substantial character on the part of the promisee and which does induce such action or forbearance is binding if injustice can be avoided only by enforcement of the promise.

In *Hoffman v. Red Owl Stores, Inc.*, 26 Wis. 2d 683, 696, 133 N.W.2d 267, 274 (1965), the Supreme Court of Wisconsin, in a significant and what may prove to be a far-reaching opinion, expressly adopted the doctrine of promissory estoppel, stating:

> Because we deem the doctrine of promissory estoppel, as stated in § 90 of Restatement, 1 Contracts, is one which supplies a needed tool which courts may employ in a proper case to prevent injustice, we endorse and adopt it.

In *Hoffman*, the court found that defendants had promised to establish plaintiffs as franchise operators of one of their stores in a certain town if they would invest a specific amount of capital and fulfill other conditions. During a two-year period of negotiations, plaintiffs, relying upon defendants' promise, and in fulfillment of the conditions, sold their bakery and grocery businesses and a building, moved to another town, incurred moving expenses, made a down payment on a lot, and paid one month's rent on a home in the town where they had been led to believe that a franchised store would be available. Negotiations finally broke off after defendants demanded a larger capital investment than originally requested. The Court found that the factual elements of promissory estoppel were present and concluded that injustice would result if plaintiffs were not granted some relief because of defendants' failure to keep their promises which induced plaintiffs to act to their detriment.

The opinion is significant in that the Court clearly distinguished between an action on a promise based on promissory estoppel and one based on breach of contract.[58] The Court further held that a promise actionable under § 90 need not have all the elements of an offer that would result in a binding contract between the parties if the promisee were to accept the same....

Having gained a firm foothold in Wisconsin, the doctrine has been extended there to third persons and held applicable as a basis for relief in actions by employees to receive pension benefits. *Scheuer v. Central States Pension Fund*, 358 F. Supp. 1332 (E.D. Wis. 1973).

Although the Wisconsin authorities have not had occasion to consider the applicability of promissory estoppel to construction bidding cases, the doctrine has found

---

58. [4] As the Court observed in *N. Litterio & Company v. Glassman Construction Company, supra*, 319 F.2d at 738, the authorities do not "always keep clear the distinction between traditional rules of contract law and the principles of promissory estoppel." For a more extensive treatment of this subject, *see* Stanley D. Henderson, *Promissory Estoppel and Traditional Contract Doctrine*, 78 YALE L.J. 343 (1969).

increasing acceptance in other jurisdictions as a basis for a cause of action in litigation involving construction bids....

[T]here is no logical reason, particularly in light of the language used in *Hoffman*, why § 90 of the Restatement should not apply to the situation herein. "It is only right and just that a promise a promisor knows will induce action of a substantial character be enforced if it is in fact relied on." *E. A. Coronis Associates v. M. Gordon Construction Co.*, 216 A.2d 246, 251 (1966).

The rationale for application of promissory estoppel to construction bidding cases is perhaps best expressed in *Drennan v. Red Star Paving Company, supra*. That case involved an oral bid by a subcontractor for certain work at a school project on which plaintiff, the general contractor, was about to bid. As defendant's bid was the lowest, plaintiff computed his own bid on the basis of defendant's bid price. Plaintiff was the successful bidder but was informed the next day by defendant that it would not do the work at its quoted price. The California Supreme Court, applying the promissory estoppel rule to prevent defendant's revocation of its bid stated (333 P.2d at 760):

> The very purpose of § 90 is to make a promise binding even though there was no consideration "in the sense of something that is bargained for and given in exchange." (See 1 Corbin, Contracts, 634 *et seq.*) Reasonable reliance serves to hold the offeror in lieu of the consideration ordinarily required to make the offer binding.

> When plaintiff used defendant's offer in computing his own bid, he bound himself to perform in reliance on defendant's terms. Though defendant did not bargain for this use of its bid neither did defendant make it idly, indifferent to whether it would be used or not. On the contrary it is reasonable to suppose that defendant submitted its bid to obtain the subcontract. It was bound to realize the substantial possibility that its bid would be the lowest, and that it would be included by plaintiff in his bid. It was to its own interest that the contractor be awarded the general contract; the lower the subcontract bid, the lower the general contractor's bid was likely to be and the greater its chance of acceptance and hence the greater defendant's chance of getting the paying subcontract. Defendant had reason not only to expect plaintiff to rely on its bid but to want him to. Clearly defendant had a stake in plaintiff's reliance on its bid. Given this interest and the fact that plaintiff is bound by his own bid, it is only fair that plaintiff should have at least an opportunity to accept defendant's bid after the general contract has been awarded to him.

> It bears noting that a general contractor is not free to delay acceptance after he has been awarded the general contract in the hope of getting a better price. Nor can he reopen bargaining with the subcontractor and at the same time claim a continuing right to accept the original offer.

> ...

Under the guidelines set down in *Hoffman*, if plaintiff is to prevail in an action under § 90 of the Restatement, it must establish that a definite promise was made by defendant with the reasonable expectation that it would induce action of a definite and substantial character on plaintiff's part; that plaintiff had acted in justifiable reliance upon the promise to its detriment; and that injustice can be avoided only by enforcement of the promise.

I find substantial evidence to support each of the afore-described elements of promissory estoppel.

Jerry Janke received a definite offer by telephone on March 5, 1970, from Vulcan to supply the concrete subaqueous pipe required for the University of Wisconsin-Milwaukee project at the quoted prices. At no time prior to the awarding of the contract was plaintiff informed that defendant was proposing to furnish anything other than the pipe specified in the project plans. Furthermore, I find that throughout its course of dealing with the Janke brothers on this particular bid, defendant intentionally, and successfully, represented to plaintiff through its agents that it "would supply the pipe for the job" (R. 34), that is, the pipe specified in the plans.

The Janke brothers, not unreasonably, had relied upon the representations of Vulcan's Wisconsin representative, Alex Barry, whom they knew from previous business dealings, and who continued to assure them up to the bid deadline that Vulcan could and would supply the required pipe.[59] Accordingly, the Jankes, men of limited formal education and with no engineering or technical experience in concrete subaqueous piping, were never alerted to the fact that they were relying upon a bid which was based on non-specified material. If they had known that defendant was offering pipe under the "or equal" clause, they would have conditioned their bid in like manner if they still wanted to use Vulcan's pipe.

I find that plaintiff acted with reasonable care and prudence in relying upon Vulcan's offer, and that this offer included, as represented to plaintiff, a proposal to furnish the specified concrete subaqueous pipe.

Plaintiff suffered substantial detriment by acting in reliance upon defendant's bid. It was compelled to go forward on the contract and supply the specified pipe when defendant's products were rejected as unsuitable. Upon defendant's refusal or inability to furnish the required material, plaintiff had to purchase it from Interpace, the other pipe supplier, at a price which was $39,992.40 over defendant's bid. Injustice can be avoided only by enforcement of the promise; accordingly, plaintiff is entitled to reliance damages.

[The court found that Barry had both real and apparent authority to make representations on behalf of Vulcan. It is worth noting that the "apparent authority" rule in agency law seems to embody an objective theory of contract formation.]

One question remains. Can the statute of frauds, raised by defendant as a defense in the context of plaintiff's contractual claim, be raised as a defense to a claim for

59. [5] Barry's recollection that his last-minute meeting with James Janke on March 10 and his confirming phone call to Vulcan's vice president concerned an attempt by Janke to get a lower price on the pipe seems scarcely credible in view of the fact that Vulcan's price was $40,000 below the quote Janke had received from Interpace.

damages based on the theory of promissory estoppel? The issue has not been raised in the Wisconsin courts and there is a split of opinion in other jurisdictions where this question has been considered.

[The court noted that some courts, like New York, have declined to use promissory estoppel to defeat a statute of frauds defense. Other states, like Hawaii, in *McIntosh v. Murphy*,[60] have no such reservations. The District of Columbia, in the *Litterio* case, *supra*, held that promissory estoppel could be used in cases of oral promises.]

I agree with the statement in *Litterio* as to the inapplicability of the statute. The statute of frauds relates to the enforceability of *contracts*; promissory estoppel relates to *promises* which have no contractual basis and are enforced only when necessary to avoid injustice. The Wisconsin Supreme Court clearly stated in *Hoffman* that a promise which could not meet the requirements of an offer that would ripen into a contract if accepted by the promisee is nonetheless enforceable to avoid injustice if the other elements of promissory estoppel are present. To allow defendant to raise the statute of frauds herein as a defense to prevent enforcement of a promise that is actionable under § 90 of the Restatement would defeat the spirit and intent of *Hoffman*. Accordingly, I find the statute is not applicable in an action based on promissory estoppel.

Turning now to plaintiff's claimed damages, the rule in Wisconsin is that "where damages are awarded in promissory estoppel instead of specifically enforcing the promisor's promise, they should be only such as in the opinion of the court are necessary to prevent injustice." *Hoffman, supra*, 26 Wis. 2d at 701, 133 N.W. 2d at 276. I find that the sum of $39,942.40 [*sic*; should be $39,992.40], which represents the difference between what would have been paid for the pipe under defendant's bid and the actual cost to plaintiff in purchasing it from Interpace, is a proper item of damages. However, the damages claimed for the time James Janke spent in attending meetings with the state engineers after the contract was awarded and with the knowledge that defendant would not supply the required pipe are not recoverable under the promissory estoppel doctrine. These actions were not taken in reliance upon defendant's promise but were part of an effort to get the State to accept defendant's nonspecified pipe. In other words, they were not induced by defendant's bid.

It is hereby ordered that judgment be entered in favor of plaintiff in the amount of $39,942.40 [*sic*, $39,992.40] plus costs.

NOTES AND QUESTIONS

1. *The Restatement (Second) of Contracts solution:* At this point, you should consult § 87 of the Restatement (Second) of Contracts. Those drafting the Restatement (Second) of Contracts were aware of cases such as *James Baird Co. v. Gimbel Bros.*[61] and *Drennan v. Star Paving Co.*[62] Rather than adopting a stringent rule that *no* firm offers, or *all*

60. 52 Haw. 29, 469 P.2d 177 (1970).
61. 64 F.2d 344 (2d Cir. 1933).
62. 51 Cal. 2d 409, 333 P.2d 757 (1958).

firm offers, were enforceable against a bidder, they fashioned an intermediate position, embodied in § 87. Consider the adequacy of the Restatement's solution in light of the Virginia survey and the later adoption of electronic bidding for some contracts.

2. *The legislative decision:* Suppose you were a legislator considering a bill to deal with the legal enforceability of bids by subcontractors submitted to general contractors. Thus, you are free to decide how to vote entirely on the merits of the proposal. In light of the Virginia survey, would you have adopted the solution of the court in the *Janke Construction* case, the Restatement (Second) of Contracts,[63] or something else?

3. *Electronic records and signatures:* The article above about electronic bidding for Department of Transportation contracts in Iowa and Wisconsin indicates that subs now often submit their sub-bids by email. UETA, discussed above in connection with the description of the mailbox rule, provides in § 8(a) that a requirement for a writing can be met with an electronic record. Is an email "signed"? UETA § 2(8) defines an electronic signature as "an electronic sound, symbol, or process attached to or logically associated with a record and executed or adopted by a person with the intent to sign the record." *See also* UCC § 1-201(b)(37) and its comment 37.

4. *Equality and the subcontractor's rights:* Suppose a general contractor uses a subcontractor's bid, and under cases such as *Janke Construction Co., Inc. v. Vulcan Materials Co., Inc.*, the subcontractor cannot withdraw it. The general contractor then receives the award from the state agency or owner. Now can the subcontractor successfully sue the general contractor if it does not award the subcontractor the contract? The Minnesota Supreme Court, which had followed *Drennan v. Star Paving Co.*, decided that symmetry did not require that the subcontractor gain rights. In *Holman Erection Co. v. Orville E. Madsen & Sons, Inc.*,[64] a general contractor declined to award a contract to a subcontractor whose bid it had used (and had listed on its own winning bid). In a suit brought by the disappointed sub, the court directly addressed the apparent unfairness of allowing the general to choose another sub, while at the same time refusing to allow subs to refuse to accept contracts at the general's option. The court reasoned that the general has, and must, rely on the subcontractors, while the subs have no reciprocal need to rely on getting a contract. In addition:

> The bidding process puts the subcontractor and the general in very different positions as to the content of the subcontract. The subcontractors have the luxury of preparing their bids on their own timetable, subject only to the

---

63. For an attack on the approach of the Restatement, *see* Margaret Kniffin, *Innovation or Aberration: Recovery for Reliance on a Contract Offer, as Permitted by the New Restatement (Second) of Contracts*, 62 U. Det. L. Rev. 23, 39 (1984). She says: "[B]efore the general is bound or has bound the sub, the general cannot reasonably expect to be protected from risk." Kniffin also suggests that while the sub can better predict the probability that a loss will occur, the general has better ability to insure against losses caused by subs withdrawing their bids. Generals will increase the amount they bid to cover such risks. Furthermore, under the Restatement rule, offerors (subcontractors) will be uncertain whether they are bound to contracts for some time after they submit their bids. Do you find her arguments persuasive?

64. 330 N.W.2d 693 (Minn. 1983).

deadline for submitting their bids to the general contractors. The same bid goes to all the general contractors and covers the same work. The generals, on the other hand, are dealing with all the various construction aspects of the project and with numerous potential subcontractors. They compile their bids, as the various subcontractor bids are received, within a few hours of the deadline for submission of the prime bid. Specifics are necessarily given less than thorough consideration and are left for future negotiations....

Although supplying some certainty and symmetry to the construction industry, ... a decision [in favor of subcontractors whose bids have been used by generals] would also impose a rigidity on the process and result in greater cost to awarding authorities and potential detriment to general contractors. If such a change is to take place, it is one properly brought before the legislature.[65]

5. *Representing the bidder who wants out:* Suppose you are retained to represent a bidder who does not want to perform under the terms and conditions of the bid it made. First, you establish that the general contractor seems willing to sue your client. In other words, the damages claimed are substantial, and your client has sufficient assets to make it worth seeking a judgment. Second, the other-than-legal sanctions are not strong enough to prompt your client to perform and swallow its losses. Third, your client probably made a mistake in preparing its bid so that it is far too low.

What can you do to defend your client? Of course, you would like to win a total victory, but remember that if you can fashion a plausible theory, you might be able to settle the case for far less than the general's total damages. The following strategies are worth considering:

(a) *Attack the firm-offer rule:* You might try to persuade the court in your state to reject the firm-offer rule reflected in Restatement (Second) of Contracts § 87. This would be playing a long shot. Court after court has adopted the rule. Many of these decisions fail to offer convincing arguments to justify holding bidders once generals have used their bids. Nonetheless, you would have to be very persuasive to convince a court that Justice Traynor's *Drennan v. Star Paving* opinion, the Restatement (Second) of Contracts, almost all writers in the law reviews, and the great weight of authority were wrong.

(b) *Construe the bid:* Lawyers, seeking a way out for clients caught in contracts that have turned out unfavorably, know that they may find legal ammunition if they read written documents or carefully consider testimony about the deal. If the case can be made, it is always nice to say that your client is ready, willing, and able to perform its side of the bargain. However, it never promised to do A, B, and C, as the plaintiff contends. Rather, it only promised to do A, B, and D. (This tactic is feasible only if your client is willing to perform A, B, and D.) Plans and specifications for building construction are often ambiguous if not contradictory.

---

65. *Id.* at 698–99.

A few cases have said that the bidder can reserve a right to withdraw the bid after a general has used it. However, if you want to use such language, you face all the fine print problems. For example, in *Lyon Metal Products, Inc. v. Hagerman Construction Corp.*,[66] a general contractor sued a manufacturer of athletic lockers that had made a mistaken bid. The manufacturer's bid was submitted on its quotation form. On the reverse side a clause printed in very small type stated: "This quotation may be withdrawn and is subject to change without notice after 15 days from date of quotation."[67] The general relied on the supplier's bid, but it did not make a contract with the manufacturer before 15 days had passed. The manufacturer attempted to withdraw its quotation, arguing that it was entitled to withdraw the bid unless it was accepted within 15 days. Nonetheless, the court found the general's reliance reasonable and held the manufacturer to the bid. It noted that the bid was in small print on the back of the quote, was not brought to the attention of the general, and was arguably inconsistent with terms in the specifications.

(c) *Use the rules of mistake and Restatement § 90:* To trigger Restatement (Second) § 90, reliance must be reasonable. If a general knew or should have known that a bid was based on a mistake, then it cannot reasonably rely on it. For example, in *Maurice Electrical Supply Co., Inc. v. Anderson Safeway Guard Rail Corp.*,[68] the court found that "plaintiff's reliance was not reasonable because of the great difference in price quotes received from defendant and the other two potential suppliers.... While the price quotes obtained from the other two suppliers were quite similar to each other, they were anywhere from 50 to almost 100 percent higher than the price quotes given by defendant. In such circumstances, plaintiff's reliance was not justifiable."[69] The court noted: "While a party may reasonably rely on an unusually low price quote if it reconfirms the price quote prior to reliance, here the Court found plaintiff did not reconfirm the price quote prior to bidding on the resale contract."[70]

To similar effect, the Supreme Court of Utah, in *Tolboe Construction Co. v. Staker Paving & Construction Co.*,[71] found that a general contractor's reliance was not reasonable, although its estimator telephoned the subcontractor and asked it to review its bid. Defendant's bid was 290 percent below that of the next lowest bid and 350 percent below the other bid submitted. Experts testified that they had never seen a disparity in bids for asphalt paving as large as the one in this case. Another general contractor who bid on the project received the same erroneous bid from defendant and rejected it, assuming that it must be mistaken. The telephone call did not alert defendant to the problem.[72]

---

66. 391 N.E.2d 1152 (Ind. Ct. App. 1979).

67. *Id.* at 1153.

68. 632 F. Supp. 1082 (D.D.C. 1986).

69. *Id.* at 1090.

70. *Id.* at 1091, n.14.

71. 682 P.2d 843 (1984).

72. The court said: "According to plaintiff's own version of the request, defendant's estimator was merely informed, as would be any bidder whose bid was 10 to 15 percent below the next lowest bid, that his bid was substantially low, and further was asked to reconfirm it. Nothing was mentioned by

In an earlier decision, *Union Tank Car Co. v. Wheat Bros.*,[73] the Utah Supreme Court described the firm-offer rule as one involving a balancing of the equities. Wheat Brothers bid $22,500 to paint four steel tanks, based on the erroneous assumption that they could use ordinary paint that cost $6/gallon. Their bid was $6,000 lower than any others because in fact the specifications required "phenoline" paint, which cost $26/gallon. Union Tank's representative had called John Wheat to invite a bid and Wheat had phoned in a bid later in the day. A document subsequently sent to Wheat described the job, listed the Wheat Brothers' price, and noted that the job was to be done "as per attached specifications"; the specifications referred to "phenoline" paint, but there was no indication that the paint was extraordinarily expensive. Wheat Brothers signed the document. They then discovered the cost of the paint and sought to withdraw the offer. However, Union Tank had used the Wheat Brothers bid, and had been awarded the contract.

The Utah court found that the balance of equities favored Wheat Brothers. Union Tank was in control of the situation. It could have warned Wheat Brothers about the high cost of phenoline paint; it was obvious that Wheat Brothers' bid was based on the price of ordinary paint. Union Tank called twice to verify the bid, but did nothing to alert Wheat Brothers to the high cost of phenoline paint.

(d) *Try to prove bid shopping and chopping:* Most of the states that have adopted the position of Justice Traynor's *Drennan* decision have followed his suggestion that a general contractor loses the right to hold a sub to its bid if the general engages in bid shopping or bid chopping. That is, the general cannot negotiate with other subcontractors for a cheaper offer after it gets the award and still hold the sub whose bid the general used. Nor can the general negotiate with the sub whose bid the general used and still hold the sub to the original bid.[74]

(e) *Assert the Statute of Frauds:* Often bids of subcontractors and material suppliers are made orally by telephone at the last minute before a general must submit its bid. Contracts for the sale of services need not be in writing unless they cannot be performed within one year. Contracts for the sale of goods for a price of $500 or more, however, come under § 2-201 of the UCC. Furthermore, § 2-205 provides that merchants can make firm offers "in a signed writing which by its terms give assurance that it will be held open."

Remember that the *Janke Construction Co.* case finds that the Statute of Frauds applies to enforcing contracts but not to claims based on promissory estoppel. Thus, Restatement (Second) of Contracts § 90 makes an oral bid of a supplier of goods irrevocable once a general has used it. The court notes in a footnote that the Restatement

---

plaintiff with respect to the large disparity between defendant's bid and the others, or of any other apparent error. Thus we conclude that plaintiff's request for verification did not validate the erroneous bid nor justify plaintiff's reliance." *Id.* at 848.

73. 15 Utah 2d 101, 387 P.2d 1000 (1964).

74. *See, e.g.,* N. Litterio & Co., Inc. v. Glassman Constr. Co., Inc., 319 F.2d 736 (D.C. Cir. 1963); Haselden-Langley Constructors, Inc. v. D.E. Farr & Assocs., Inc., 676 P.2d 709 (Colo. App. 1983).

(Second) of Contracts, in what became § 139,[75] provides that a court can enforce a promise because of reliance to avoid injustice, despite the Statute of Frauds. This provision calls for a case-by-case balancing of factors.

But the court in *C.R. Fedrick, Inc. v. Borg-Warner Corp.*,[76] came to a different result. The federal court predicted that the Supreme Court of California would not apply promissory estoppel in a case involving a bid to supply goods for a price of $500 or more. While California had recognized that equitable estoppel might be used to overcome the provisions of the Statute of Frauds, the court declined to apply the doctrine in this case. It decided that equitable estoppel required either a promise not to assert the Statute of Frauds or a representation that a writing was not required; mere reliance on the alleged oral contract was not enough. The Court of Appeals further decided that equitable estoppel to assert the Statute of Frauds requires a greater degree of detrimental reliance than does promissory estoppel. Finally, the Court of Appeals found that the California legislature had resolved the policy questions by passing § 2-201 of the UCC. Section 2-201(3) itself offers limited exceptions to the writing requirements of subsections (1) and (2), and it was not proper for the court to create new exceptions.

While firm offers and consideration may have been the issue of the 1950s and 1960s, oral firm offers and the Statute of Frauds provoked more dispute in subsequent decades. Consider what you have learned about electronic bidding. When subs submit their sub-bids to generals by email, is there a Statute of Frauds defense? See Note 3 above.

6. *Mistakes, bids, and government contracts:* Governmental agencies cannot give away the taxpayer's money. Contracting officers are seldom authorized to be sympathetic, or to compromise to preserve a relationship. If contracting officers are given too much discretion, some might sell it for bribes. Hard and fast rules may also help ward off political influence. These reasons suggest governments could justifiably have the benefit of different rules than commercial enterprises. However, bidding mistakes are a recurrent problem and seem to call for some relief. Cases and statutes have attempted to deal with it by creating standards for relief. How should the balance be struck? The following cases show two approaches.

MARANA UNIFIED SCHOOL DIST. NO. 6 v. AETNA CASUALTY AND SURETY CO.

Arizona Court of Appeals
144 Ariz. 159, 696 P.2d 711 (1985)

BIRDSALL, C.J.

This appeal arises from a complaint filed by the appellee, Marana Unified School District, seeking judgment on a bid bond given by appellants, L.G. Lefler, Inc., doing

---

75. The court cited § 217A in a tentative draft version, and this became § 139 in the published version of the Restatement.

76. 552 F.2d 852 (9th Cir. 1977).

business as Defco Construction Company, principal, and the Aetna Casualty and Surety Company, surety. The bond was provided pursuant to A.R.S. § 34-201(A)(3) because Defco submitted a bid proposal to construct a junior high school building for the appellee. The statute provides:

> 3. That every proposal shall be accompanied by a certified check, cashier's check or a surety bond for five percent of the amount of the bid included in the proposal as a guarantee that the contractor will enter into a contract to perform the proposal in accordance with the plans and specifications, or as liquidated damages in event of failure or refusal of the contractor to enter into the contract. The certified check, cashier's check, or surety bond shall be returned to the contractors whose proposals are not accepted, and to the successful contractor upon the execution of a satisfactory bond and contract as provided in this article.

Although Defco was the low bidder, it refused to enter into a contract with the appellee because it had made a mathematical mistake in its proposal.

The trial court entered summary judgment in favor of the Marana District.... The appellants' cross-motion for summary judgment was denied.

The facts considered in the light most favorable to the appellants may be summarized as follows. The appellee gave notice of its intent to receive sealed bids for the construction of the school pursuant to A.R.S. § 34-201. The bids were required to be submitted by 4 P.M., February 2, 1982, at which time they were opened. The appellant's bid was for $4,890,000 together with alternates, all of which totalled $5,936,500. The bid bond attached to the proposal was "in the sum of five percent of contract bid." No actual figures were set forth on the bond but the proposal referred to the required bid bond amount as five percent of the "base bid," which would have been $244,500. Nine other contractors submitted bids. Defco's was the lowest base bid. The next lowest base bid was $5,447,000. The architect's estimated cost for the construction without alternates was $4,900,000. Defco's bid was within two-tenths of one percent of that estimate.

After all bids were opened, the architect and school district officials reviewed them and a written recommendation was made that day to accept Defco's base bid together with two alternates totalling $5,253,080.

At about the same time, Defco personnel were rechecking their figures since it appeared that a mistake may have been made. The employee who had tabulated Defco's bid sheet then discovered that she had used $42,000 as the bid for the structural steel when the correct figure was $412,000, a mistake of $370,000.

According to the employee's affidavit attached to the appellants' cross-motion for summary judgment, she was still receiving telephone bids from subcontractors and suppliers and working on Defco's bid up until 3:30 on February 2; she found a mistake in her first tabulation of some 170 items on the bid sheet and did a second tabulation, then added the figures six times. Since this brought her so close to the time the bid had to be submitted, there was no time to have another employee check her figures.

Defco advised appellee by telephone within one and one-half hours of the bid opening of the mistake, which came to $398,752 with the addition of other items based on percentages of the $370,000 error. A letter containing the same information was delivered to the school within three hours after the bid was opened at 4 P.M. In the letter Defco asked to meet with the school officials to show them the calculator tapes and bid sheet that revealed how the error had occurred.

[After two school board meetings, and confirmation that Defco was unwilling to perform if awarded the contract, the architect was instructed to re-bid the job.]

The important issue presented by this appeal is whether a low bidder for a public contract may refuse to enter into a contract because of a mistake in the bid without forfeiting the bid bond. Although this question has never been decided in Arizona, it has been the subject of numerous opinions in our sister states and federal courts....

It is the appellee's position that the statute permits no escape from forfeiture. There is authority to support such a result. These decisions are cited by the appellees: *Board of Edn. v. Sever-Williams Co.*, 22 Ohio St. 2d 107, 258 N.E.2d 605, *cert. denied*, 400 U.S. 916, 91 S. Ct. 175 (1970), and *A.J. Colella, Inc. v. County of Allegheny*, 391 Pa. 103, 137 A.2d 265 (1958).... The reasoning in these decisions is generally the same, that this is the purpose of the statute and to permit exceptions would materially weaken the purpose of the bidding procedure for public contracts and make the bid bond requirement meaningless. In *Colella* the court opines that plea of a clerical mistake would make the system of sealed bids a mockery. *Sever-Williams* speaks of possible abuse of the bidding procedure, *i.e.*, favoritism or fraud....

We do not agree with the reasoning or result in those cases. Nor do we believe that the Arizona legislature intended that there be no relief from forfeiture of the bid security for equitable reasons. We agree with the appellants that unless the legislature clearly indicates an intention to do so, its enactments shall not be construed so as to change established common law. *Terry v. Linscott Hotel Corp.*, 126 Ariz. 548, 617 P.2d 56 (1980); ... The doctrine of rescission for unilateral clerical mistake was set forth by the United States Supreme Court as early as 1900. *See Moffett, Hodgkins, & Clarke Co. v. City of Rochester*, 178 U.S. 373, 20 S. Ct. 957 (1900).

We believe the trial court erred in granting summary judgment in favor of the appellee. We follow those decisions which hold that when relief from the forfeiture is legally justifiable, statutes like Arizona's do not mandate the forfeiture. The cases upon which we rely all arise under a statute or bid solicitation which, on its face, prohibits a withdrawal of bids.... In these cases the bidder notified the public authority of the mistake prior to acceptance of the bid. Clearly this notice was promptly given by Defco before the appellee had accepted the bid. [The Arizona statute also prohibited bidders from withdrawing their bids for 45 days.]

A starting point is the decision in *Moffett, Hodgkins, & Clarke Co. v. City of Rochester, supra*. The mistake in *Moffett* resulted from mathematical errors committed by an extremely nearsighted engineer working in great haste with a voluminous number of specifications. Affirming a decree in favor of the contractor, the Supreme Court said that the contractor was not endeavoring to withdraw or cancel a bid or bond in contravention of the city charter, since the contractor was proceeding upon the theory that the bid read at the meeting of the board was one which it had never intended to make, and that the minds of the parties had never met. The Court added that if the city was correct in its contention that the charter provision barred any remedy, then there would be no redress for a bidder on a public work, no matter how aggravated or palpable his blunder. A material mistake of fact in a bid justifies a conclusion that there has been no meeting of the minds because the bidder did not intend to make the erroneous bid....

What appear to be the majority decisions rely upon the equitable remedy of rescission. In these decisions the courts have held or recognized that the bidder who had notified the public authority of the mistake prior to acceptance of the bid was entitled to a decree rescinding the bid, or to similar equitable relief, despite a statute similar to A.R.S. § 34-201(A)(3)....

These cases generally set forth certain criteria to be satisfied before a forfeiture can be avoided. The criteria are summarized in yet another especially comprehensive decision, *City of Baltimore v. De Luca-Davis Construction Co.*, 210 Md. 518, 524, 124 A.2d 557, 562 (1956).

> 1, the mistake must be of such grave consequences that to enforce the contract as made or offered would be unconscionable; 2, the mistake must relate to a material feature of the contract; 3, the mistake must not have come about because of the violation of a positive legal duty or from culpable negligence; 4, the other party must be put in status quo to the extent that he suffers no serious prejudice except the loss of his bargain....

Other cases have added as an additional reason for permitting rescission that the public body knew or had reason to know that a mistake had been made.... We do not understand that to be a requirement for rescission. It is indeed difficult to envisage a fact situation where the public body would know that a sealed bid contained a mistake prior to its opening unless the bidder discovered and gave notice of the mistake. After that, unless the bid is accepted and a contract made, it seems immaterial whether upon opening the bid the public body knew or should have known. At least in the instant case, where the appellant notified the appellee within three hours and before any attempted acceptance of the bid, it does not appear to be material.

Other courts admonish that a bidder should not be able to withdraw a bid under circumstances profitable to the bidder or which would permit any collusion or connivance among bidders to the detriment of the public.... Nothing suggests any such problems in the record before us.

Turning to the four conditions required by *De Luca* and other decisions, we believe they are all satisfied by the undisputed evidence before the trial court. We consider them in order.

First, was the mistake of such consequence as to make enforcement of the contract unconscionable? From our analysis of the reported decisions this refers not to the bid bond, since it contains no mistake, but to the mistake in the bid. That mistake was in the amount of almost $400,000. This was approximately 8 per cent of the base bid of $4,890,000. Although we believe this to be unconscionable on its face, we compare it to the amounts involved in other reported cases. Thus we find: [The court then cited 10 cases finding mistakes of unconscionable size. Rounding off the amounts, they can be summarized as follows: Mistake of $34,000 on bid of $464,000; mistake of $20,000 on bid of $141,000; mistake of $150,000 on bid of $883,000; mistake of $590,000 on bid of $1,769,000; mistake of $100,000 on bid of $1,367,000; mistake of $301,800 on bid of $780,000; mistake of $35,000 on bid of $173,000; mistake of $50,000 on bid of $145,000; mistake of $145,000 on bid of $1,242,000 and mistake of $182,000 on bid of $3,547,000.]

Although some of these are proportionately greater than the mistake of Defco, some are smaller in proportion to the bid, and we believe the amount of the mistake was of such grave consequence that it would be unconscionable to enforce it.

The appellee argues, however, that forfeiture of the 5 percent bid bond is not unconscionable because it is the very bid contract that was bargained for and made by the parties. This argument does not go to the issue of unconscionability but rather to the principal issue, *i.e.*, must the bid bond be forfeited despite the presence of legal justification for the refusal to enter into the contract. In all of the cases cited above, the discussion of unconscionability concerns the amount of the mistake in the bid and not the bid security. In each case it appears that the bid security sought to be forfeited was required by statute or by the bidding documents. Thus if unconscionability was to be determined by reference to the fact that the parties knew the amount of the penalty to be exacted, we believe that would have been decisive in many of those cases. We find no such holding. Assuming, *arguendo*, that we should look to the forfeiture of the bid bond rather than the amount of the mistake, one quarter of a million dollars is still, in the vernacular, a lot of money, and we believe it would be unconscionable to require even this forfeiture in the instant case.

The second condition, that the mistake must relate to a material feature of the contract, cannot be disputed. The amount to be paid for the construction is clearly a material feature of the contract.

The third condition concerns the question of whether the mistake constituted culpable negligence or the violation of a positive legal duty. If either, then this third requirement is unsatisfied. Since there is no contention that the appellant violated any legal duty, we must determine only whether there was "culpable negligence." Generally a mechanical, clerical, or mathematical error satisfies this condition whereas an error in judgment does not. In fact this distinction highlights the inequitable result of the trial court's decision in this case. The mistake was not one of judgment, as for example, underestimating the cost of labor or materials. It was not intended. We believe this distinction also serves to show the real purpose for the statute requiring forfeiture of the security. The bidder who makes an error in judgment should be penalized if he then refuses to execute the contract. On the other hand, the bidder who submits a bid which is different than that which he intended to make is entitled to relief.... The type of mistake satisfying this condition has been variously referred to as resulting from some reasonable excuse, ... based upon an erroneous omission and not involving gross negligence, ... and honest and not gross negligence, ...

At least one jurisdiction, Illinois, requires that the party seeking rescission prove that the mistake occurred notwithstanding the exercise of reasonable care. Thus in the present case the appellee argues there was lack of reasonable care. Deposition testimony revealed that the normal procedure would have been to have a second person total the figures on the bid spreadsheet and run a tape on those prices as a check on the work of the original clerk. This procedure was not followed. Likewise, the original clerk notified one of the estimators working on the project just prior to the bid deadline that her work had not been double-checked. *See also John J. Calnan Co. v. Talsma Builders, Inc.*, 67 Ill. 2d 213, 367 N.E.2d 695 (1977), where the court considered the failure of a subcontractor to utilize its own bid procedures. Despite finding this to be less than the exercise of reasonable care, the case is distinguishable since the mistake was not discovered until performance under the contract had begun and it was impossible to return the general contractor to status quo.

We reject the reasonable care standard since it appears to be nothing more than a test for negligence. We agree with the rationale appearing in the comment to § 157 of the Restatement, Second, Contracts. Section 157 concerns the effect of the fault of the party seeking relief from a mistake and provides:

> A mistaken party's fault in failing to know or discover the facts before making the contract does not bar him from avoidance or reformation under the rules stated in this Chapter, unless his fault amounts to a failure to act in good faith and in accordance with reasonable standards of fair dealing.

The comment to the section states:

> The mere fact that a mistaken party could have avoided the mistake by the exercise of reasonable care does not preclude either avoidance or reformation. Indeed, since a party can often avoid a mistake by the exercise of such care, the availability of relief would be severely circumscribed if he were to be barred by his negligence. Nevertheless, in extreme cases the mistaken party's fault is a proper ground for denying him relief for a mistake that he otherwise could have avoided. Although the critical degree of fault is sometimes described as "gross" negligence, that term is not well defined and is avoided in this Section as it is in the Restatement, Second, of Torts. Instead, the rule is stated in terms of good faith and fair dealing.

Defco's burden of showing good faith and fair dealing is satisfied and not in dispute. No facts are suggested by affidavit, deposition, or otherwise from which it could be inferred that there was a lack of good faith or fair dealing.

Another method of testing the mistake to determine if it could be "culpable negligence" is comparing it to the other mistakes for which the courts have granted relief.

Such a comparison shows several factual situations which are strikingly similar to the instant case....

Thus we are left with the question of whether the appellee has been placed in status quo so that it suffers no serious prejudice except loss of bargain.

The minutes of the Marana school board meeting of February 4 show that the board rejected all bids and instructed the architect to prepare to rebid the construction contract. All of the rejected bids, including the bid the appellant intended to make, exceeded the architect's estimate by over $350,000. Obviously the board decided to try again. These facts were before the court for its consideration on the cross-motions for summary judgment. The appellants contend that they established that the school had been put in status quo. The appellee offered nothing to refute this conclusion. No evidence shows that the appellee contends that it suffered serious prejudice, or, in fact, any prejudice except the loss of a bargain that was never intended by the appellants.

We reverse the judgment and direct the trial court to enter judgment in favor of the appellants. HATHAWAY, J., and WILLIAM N. SHERRILL, Superior Court Judge, concur.

———————

Many states have statutes dealing with mistakes in bidding on public construction. You must always check to see if such a statute controls if you are faced with this type of case. The following case deals with a statute and also suggests some methods that could be used in private bidding as well.

GLASGOW, INC. v.
PENNSYLVANIA DEPARTMENT OF TRANSPORTATION

Pennsylvania Commonwealth Court
851 A.2d 1014 (2004)

Opinion by JUDGE PELEGRINI.

Glasgow, Inc. (Glasgow) petitions this Court to review a final determination of the Secretary of Transportation denying Glasgow's bid protest, challenging the rejection by the Department of Transportation (Department) of Glasgow's apparent low bid to perform a road reconstruction project in Montgomery County (the Project).

Glasgow submitted a bid to the Department to perform the Project in the amount of $10,335,645.80. The bid was submitted in accordance with the Department's bid requirements via the Department's new internet bidding system, known as the Electronics Contract Management System (ECMS). The Department's bid specification for the Project included a special provision called "Designated Special Provision 7" (DSP7) entitled "Disadvantaged Business Enterprise Requirements." It provides:

> **Responsive.** When the goal established by the Department is met or exceeded, the apparent low bidder is required to electronically submit evidence of such solicitation and commitments, by accessing the Department's ECMS web page by selecting and submitting DBE Participation for Federal Projects by

3:00 o'clock P.M. prevailing local time within seven (7) calendar days after the bid opening. When the seventh calendar day after the bid opening falls on a day the PENNDOT offices are closed, submit the DBE Participation for Federal Projects by 3:00 o'clock P.M. prevailing local time on the next business day. (Reproduced Record at 5b.)

The bid specifications also provided what would occur if the apparent low bidder did not timely submit the Disadvantaged Business Enterprise (DBE) information. In Paragraph IV of DSP7, the Department notified and informed all bidders of the following:

> *When the above required documentation is not provided by the apparent low bidder within the time specified, the bid will be rejected* and the apparent next lowest bid will be notified by telephone to electronically submit evidence of such solicitations and commitments, by accessing the Department's ECMS web page by selecting DBE Participation for Federal Projects by 3:00 o'clock P.M. prevailing local time within seven (7) calendar days notification. (Reproduced Record at 5b.) (Emphasis added.)

On July 17, 2003, Glasgow received an e-mail from the Department advising it that it was the apparent low bidder for the Project. The e-mail further advised Glasgow to submit its DBE participation information for the Project by 3:00 P.M. July 24, 2003. This information was to be submitted via the ECMS and placed on the Department's website.

On July 23, 2003, Glasgow placed all relevant DBE information on the Department's website; the information indicated that the DBE participation in Glasgow's bid was 7.1 percent, exceeding the 7 percent goal required by the Department for the Project, and the DBE subcontractors named by Glasgow on the website electronically "acknowledged" receipt of their selection via the Department's website. Glasgow's estimator, however, neglected to take the next step, which was to press the "submit" button. Taking the failure to hit the submit button as a failure to submit the information, the Department rejected Glasgow's bid because the information had not been "submitted" by the required time. It awarded the contract to the next lowest bidder, whose bid was $432,626 higher than Glasgow's.[77]

Glasgow filed a bid protest with the Department. Without holding a hearing, the Secretary of Transportation (Secretary) denied the protest by letter dated August 18, 2003. The Secretary accepted Glasgow's contention that its estimator simply forgot to press the submit button. The Secretary, however, noted that the bidding instructions expressly stated that when the required DBE documentation is not provided by the apparent low bidder within the time specified, the bid will be rejected.

---

77. [1] The bidding instructions pertaining to the submission of DBE information provide that the low bidder's failure to "submit" such information by the date and time provided *will* result in the award of the contract to the next lowest bidder, provided that the next lowest bidder timely submits its DBE information.

The Secretary stated two reasons for the rejection of Glasgow's contention that the submission requirement should be waived because the DBE information was available on the Department's website. First, he stated that such information was "not readably [sic] accessible." (Secretary's Letter Decision at 2.) Second, he stated that until a contractor submits the required information, it "has a great deal of flexibility regarding the use of particular subcontractors." *Id.* The Secretary also noted the Department's longstanding practice, prior to the implementation of the ECMS, of rejecting bids when a bidder innocently forgets to fax or attach "Attachment A" setting forth the bidder's information regarding DBE participation. The Secretary determined that a bidder's failure to hit the submit button is no different than a bidder's failure, under prior procedure, to timely mail or fax "Attachment A." This appeal followed.[78]

Glasgow contends that the Department abused its discretion by failing to waive what Glasgow denominates as insubstantial and immaterial irregularity in the bidding process; *i.e.*, by treating Glasgow's bid as not "submitted" when it failed to click on the submit button to submit the required information.

While a governmental body has the discretion to waive non-material bid defects where the non-compliance (1) does not deprive the agency of the assurance that the contract will be entered into and performed and (2) does not confer a competitive advantage on the bidder, ... the failure to submit the information in this case is not a waivable defect. Where specifications set forth in a bidding document are mandatory, they must be strictly followed for the bid to be valid, and a violation of those mandatory bidding instructions constitutes a legally disqualifying error for which a public agent may reject a bid.... While a bidding entity may waive a bid defect, it may not do so if it involves the waiver of a mandatory requirement that the bid instructions treat as non-waivable.... While the Department could have provided otherwise, it removed any discretion it had to waive the time to submit the information when it provided in the bid instructions that the bid would be rejected if the information was not provided within the time specified.

Even if the failure to submit the information was a waivable defect, the Department did not abuse its discretion in rejecting Glasgow's bid, even though the Department had received all the DBE information on its website. The Department found that until Glasgow hit the submit button no information had been provided; there were just "screens" that were filled, and Glasgow did not have a commitment and had no responsibility to commit to the DBE subcontractors it listed until it actually clicked on the submit button. In other words, Glasgow would be able to delete their inclusion absent the formal step of hitting the submit button. We find that where governmental entities are at the beginning stages of implementing electronic bidding, determining

---

78. [2] This Court's scope of review of an agency decision is limited to determining whether constitutional rights were violated, an error of law was committed, or necessary findings of fact are supported by substantial evidence.... Further, judicial review of discretionary acts of governmental bodies requires an "affordance of deference" towards such acts....

the requisites for a proper bid should be left to the discretion of the agency, especially at this early stage....

Moreover, if we were to adopt Glasgow's position that they are not required to click the submit button, that would make clicking the button superfluous when it is not. All of us, when using a debit or credit card, are used to "swiping" the card, then receiving a message of "is this amount okay?" and then having to push a button indicating assent. Until we push the button, even though the bank has all the information, it is not okay for the bank to charge the account. Similarly, when one goes on the internet to buy a book or book a trip, one submits all the information to the vendor's site, and after it has the information and has recapsulized the transaction, the site requires one to click on a submit button. Only when that occurs is the party bound to the terms of the transaction and only then is your credit card charged. What occurred here is no different than what occurs in normal, everyday commercial transactions; until the submit button was clicked, Glasgow, as the Department found, was not bound by any of its representations.

Accordingly, because the Department did not abuse its discretion in rejecting Glasgow's bid, its decision is affirmed.

Dissenting opinion by PRESIDENT JUDGE COLINS.

I respectfully dissent to the majority's thoughtful analysis of this novel issue. I believe that the Department's decision constitutes a hyper-technical interpretation of its bidding requirements, exulting form over substance, and resulting in an unnecessary additional burden on taxpayers in the amount of $432,626.

At the outset, I question whether Glasgow's submission was deficient. I disagree with the majority's conclusion that Glasgow failed to "submit" the necessary DBE information on time, and I question the majority's acceptance of the Department's factual and legal characterizations of Glasgow's submission.

The Department recognized Glasgow as the apparent lowest qualified bidder following the completion and submission of bids by Glasgow and its competitors. All that remained was for Glasgow to submit information concerning its proposed DBE subcontractors by the deadline in the manner required by the bidding instructions. Glasgow placed the information on the Department's website. Thus, the Department had the DBE information available for viewing by the submission dates and time. This information exceeded the Department's requirements. The DBE subcontractors acknowledged their selection via the website. The only missing element was the scrolling down of the web page and the clicking on the submit button found there. Both parties acknowledge that Glasgow's failure to do so was simply an oversight.

Further, it is well established that the submission of a bid constitutes an "offer" and becomes a binding contract when the bid is accepted by the agency. *Muncy Area School District v. Gardner*, 91 Pa. Cmwlth. 406, 497 A.2d 683 (1985). Glasgow, therefore, would have no grounds to assert that its DBE subcontractor information was not binding upon it had the Department gone forward with the contract. Moreover, the Department has the right to monitor, with appropriate enforcement mechanisms, the construction project to ensure that its DBE requirements are being met. Therefore, the "practical" implications of Glasgow failing to hit the submit button, as described by the Department, are a non-issue.

Even if Glasgow's submission was defective, I would reverse the Secretary's decision. Our Supreme Court has held that a governmental body may waive bid defects where the noncompliance (1) does not deprive the agency of the assurance that the contract will be entered into and performed and (2) does not confer a competitive advantage on the bidder. *Gaeta v. Ridley School District*, 567 Pa. 500, 508–9, 788 A.2d 363, 368 (2002). As discussed above, the Department had definite assurance of Glasgow's performance. Further, the competitive bidding process had already run its course by the time Glasgow was requested to set forth its DBE subcontractor information, because the Department had named Glasgow lowest responsible bidder. Thus, the failure to hit the submit button in no way conferred upon Glasgow a competitive advantage necessitating the rejection of its bid.... JUDGE SMITH-RIBNER and JUDGE FRIEDMAN join in this dissent.

NOTES AND QUESTIONS

1. *Mistaken bids on public projects:* As the *Marana Unified School District* case indicates, some courts require that the bond be forfeited despite clerical errors. *See, e.g., J.D. Graham Const., Inc. v. Pryor Public Schools*,[79] where the court distinguished the *Marana* decision because of the differences in the text of the Arizona and Oklahoma statutes dealing with public bidding. Other courts offer relief under a number of theories with many qualifications. *See, e.g., Powder Horn Constructors, Inc. v. City of Florence*,[80] where the court, by a four-to-three vote, followed the approach of the *Marana* case. The majority and dissenting opinions review the law review writing and the Restatement (Second) of Contracts position. The Arizona and Colorado courts refuse to require that the public body knew or should have known of the mistake. This means considering whether there should be a remedy for a unilateral mistake by the bidder when officials of the public body had no reason to recognize that a mistake had been made. The *Glasgow* majority, by contrast, takes a very strict approach to compliance with statutory procedures.

2. *What if the* Marana *case had involved electronic bidding?* Recall what you have learned about the impact of electronic bidding in Wisconsin and Iowa. Would the use of electronic bidding likely have caught the error that occurred in *Marana*? What sorts of errors do you think such bidding catches and misses?

3. *Private construction and mistaken bids:* Suppose the owner seeking bids for construction is not a unit of government but a business corporation. Would the doctrine of *Marana Unified School District v. Aetna* offer relief for bidding mistakes in such a case? If not, are there any avenues open to a bidder who has made a serious error? Many cases say that I cannot snap up your offer, knowing it to be mistaken. The dif-

_____

79. 854 P.2d 917 (Okla. Civ. App. 1993).
80. 754 P.2d 356 (Colo. 1988).

ficulty, of course, comes in deciding that I knew or should have known of your error. It is not necessarily enough that your bid is the lowest one I received. It is not necessarily enough that it is entirely out of the range of the other bids. Your very low bid might rest on a mistake, but it might also rest on efficiency or competitive conditions. Assuming that you cannot show that I knew or should have known your bid rested on a mistake, can you recover for your mistake that I did not share?

4. *Protecting subs:* The Pennsylvania statute at issue in Glasgow protects certain subs that qualify as "disadvantaged business enterprises" (DBEs). DBEs are subs owned by women and minorities, and the concept is taken from federal highway funding regulations of the U.S. Department of Transportation. The Pennsylvania statute requires that information on commitments to DBEs has to be provided in a timely manner to the state DOT. This has the effect of limiting the time during which generals can try to shop and chop sub-bids. Could a similar process be used to protect subs who bid on private contracts? Who might implement such a system?

d. Unilateral Mistakes in Communicating: I Meant "X" but Said "Y"

Courts have always been reluctant to grant relief to a bargainer who makes a mistake in entering a contract. In part, this reflects the prevailing view that a deal is a deal. A court will not relieve a life insurance company of liability because it did not expect the insured to die so soon. A trader on a commodities exchange cannot claim an excuse because he thought the market would go up but it went down. A consumer may want a red car instead of the black one he bought, but has no right to insist the seller exchange automobiles. You have a right to rely on the deal, even if I made a mistake. Furthermore, taking responsibility for my errors should give me reason to be careful and avoid them.

Nonetheless, many writers have advocated more relief for bargainers' mistakes — at least when relief would not hurt the other party. In recent years courts have moved in this direction. However, most of the cases where they have been willing to grant relief involve different kinds of mistakes than the ones we've mentioned.

Section 503 of the first Restatement of Contracts reflects the common law core rule. It says a "mistake of only one party that forms the basis on which he enters into a transaction does not of itself render the transaction voidable...." The Comment says: "There is a contract formed by the acceptance of an offer even though the offer is made under a mistake or fails to express what the offeror intends. The objective appearance of his acts is controlling...." Under this classic view, my mistake would be the basis for relief only if my error was caused by your fault or where you know or have reason to know of my error.[81]

---

81. Section 504 of the original Restatement provides "where *both parties* have an identical intention as to the terms to be embodied in a proposed written conveyance, assignment, contract or discharge, and a writing executed by them is materially at variance with that intention, either party can get a

The first Restatement reflects an objective theory of contracts. I am bound by my actions and not my intentions. You have a right to rely on what a reasonable person would think I meant. My errors in judgment and communication are no excuse unless you caused or should have known of them. If, however, we share a mistake, then there is a chance for relief.

This core position is much less forgiving than the results of the cases. Few would state the law this way today without a long list of exceptions. While we still think a deal is a deal, we want to be sure what the deal really was. People make mistakes calculating and communicating constantly. We are more willing to ask whether there is good reason to give one party the benefit of another's error. We can see some of the problems with unilateral mistake by tracing the struggles of the Supreme Court of Wisconsin with the issue.

In *Miller v. Stanich*,[82] the Supreme Court of Wisconsin found a unilateral mistake warranted reworking a lease. In 1922, Michael Stanich leased a butcher shop for $75 a month. The term of the lease was five years and there was an option to renew the lease at the same rent for an additional five years. In 1926, S. Miller bought the property from Stanich's lessor, subject of course to the lease to Stanich.

As the first five-year term was coming to an end, Stanich went to his lawyer to talk about negotiating an extended renewal of his lease. Stanich wanted to renew the lease at $75 a month for five years, from 1927 to 1932, and wanted another option to renew at the same rent for a third five-year term (from 1932 to 1937). Stanich's lawyer drafted a lease reflecting his client's wishes, sending two copies of this lease to Miller's building manager. The manager telephoned Stanich's lawyer and told him, "I don't think that Mr. Miller will sign those leases." Stanich's lawyer responded that to save time, he would also send Miller two copies of a lease which ran from 1927 to 1932 but which had no option to renew for the third term. Stanich's lawyer drafted such a lease. The two leases were the same except one contained 23 additional words granting an option to renew from 1932 to 1937. Both sets of leases (two copies of each version) were sent to Miller, at his home in Marshfield, Wisconsin.

Although Miller was the president of a wholesale fruit and cold storage business, he could neither read nor write English. His son read the leases to him. They discovered that one set contained an additional five-year renewal option while the other did not. Miller did not want to renew Stanich's lease at all because he thought that the $75 a month rent was far too low, and he clearly did not want to give Stanich an option to renew for an additional five years at that rent.

Miller drove to Wisconsin Rapids to see his lawyer, R.B. Graves. Miller asked if he had to renew the lease. Graves told him that Stanich had a right to renew the lease from 1927 to 1932. There was no discussion about granting Stanich a right to renew

decree that the writing shall be reformed so that it shall express the intention of the parties, if innocent third persons will not be unfairly affected thereby."

82. 202 Wis. 539, 230 N.W. 47 (1930). Much of our description of the case is taken from the briefs and record on appeal.

again from 1932 to 1937. Apparently, Graves read only one copy of the lease—one that did not have the additional 23 words granting Stanich an option to renew from 1932 to 1937. Apparently, he assumed there were four copies of the same lease. Graves dated two copies of the lease and gave them to Miller. Miller took all four copies back to Marshfield. He signed the two copies Graves had dated and sent them to his building manager, who passed them along to Stanich. Graves, of course, had dated the wrong set. As a result, Miller had mistakenly signed the copies that gave Stanich an option to renew for the third five-year term.

In late June 1927, Miller had a chance to sell the building. To make the sale, he had to buy out Stanich's lease. Miller and Stanich met in Milwaukee. Stanich asked $9000 to surrender his rights under the lease. Miller said that this was too much for only a five-year term. Stanich said, "No, it is not five. It is ten." Miller and Graves then tried to persuade Stanich that a mistake had been made. However, Stanich insisted that he had a lease for five years with an option to renew at the same rent for another five.

Miller then sued to have a court reform the lease and cancel the option to renew for an additional five years from 1932 to 1937. The trial court reformed the lease, striking out the option to renew. It found "at no time was there a meeting of the minds ... to execute a lease for five years with the privilege to renew the same for another period of five years."

On appeal, the Supreme Court of Wisconsin *first* issued an opinion by Justice Fritz, joined by four other justices. Justice Fritz stated:

> Although plaintiff may have made a mistake in signing and sending to defendant the copies of the lease which contained the provision giving defendant an option for a further renewal, nothing had occurred because of which the defendant had reason to believe that plaintiff did not intend to agree to that provision, or that plaintiff had made a mistake. Defendant, in good faith, had submitted two forms. Without being misled by any trick or artifice on the part of any one, plaintiff signed and sent the two copies, containing the clause for another option, to defendant for his signature. When defendant also signed those copies, he was entitled to assume that the minds of the parties had met as to all terms embodied in the signed instruments, and that the plaintiff, by signing, had evidenced his intention to agree to all of those terms. Nothing had been done by plaintiff, on which defendant had knowledge, that indicated an intention on plaintiff's part not to consent to the option for the additional extension. Nothing had occurred which can be said to evidence a meeting of the minds of the parties to another contract, which plaintiff is now entitled by reformation to have expressed in the lease which he voluntarily signed. There was no mutual mistake. At best, it was merely a unilateral mistake, without any fraud on the part of the defendant. Under the circumstances there was no ground for reformation.[83]

---

83. 202 Wis. at 542, 230 N.W. at 48.

Justice Fowler, joined by Justice Stevens, dissented:

> The case is so simple that to my mind the mere statement of it proves the decision of the court wrong.... [P]laintiff promptly, and before defendant had taken any steps whatever in reliance upon the provision for a five-year extension, comes into a court of equity and asks relief on the ground of mistake.... There was ... no meeting of the minds of the parties in respect to the extension.... Mere inadvertence in signing the wrong lease is not such negligence as should bar plaintiff from relief.... Where no one is injured by a mistake except the party making it, and no one has changed his position in consequence of it, relief may be granted, although a high degree of care was not exercised....
>
> It is true ... that equity does not reform instruments for mistake unless the mistake is mutual, and the mistake here involved is not mutual, but unilateral. But equity rescinds written instruments for unilateral mistakes.... The complaint in terms erroneously asks for reformation of the lease by striking out the clause for extension. The plaintiff, strictly speaking, is not entitled to the particular form of relief he asks for, because the defendant did not by signing the lease returned to him agree to a lease without the extension. But the fact is proved and found by the court that entitles plaintiff to rescission of the lease signed by him. Striking from that lease the provision for extension, and letting the lease stand as so changed, affords the plaintiff precisely the same relief that he would have were the lease declared canceled and the defendant adjudged to have the right to hold the premises for the extended term provided for by the original lease. Strictly speaking, that is the relief that should have been adjudged. But the error of decreeing reformation instead of rescission did not affect the substantial rights of the defendant....[84]

The Supreme Court of Wisconsin granted a motion for rehearing, and the case was reargued.[85] This time Justice Fowler wrote an opinion for the new majority, and Justice Fritz dissented. The court changed its decision. The majority opinion stated:

> Equitable relief from a mutual mistake is frequently given by a reformation of the contract. But a contract will not be reformed for an unilateral mistake. Equitable relief may, however, be given from an unilateral mistake by a rescission of the contract. Essential conditions to such relief are: (1) The mistake must be of so grave a consequence that to enforce the contract as actually made would be unconscionable. (2) The matter as to which the mistake was made must relate to a material feature of the contract. (3) Generally the mistake must have occurred notwithstanding the exercise of ordinary diligence by the party making the mistake. (4) It must be possible to give relief by way of rescission without serious prejudice to the other party except the loss of his bargain. In other words, it must be possible to put him *in statu quo*.

84. *Id.* at 544–46, 230 N.W. at 49–50.
85. 202 Wis. 548, 233 N.W. 753, 753 (1930).

The Supreme Court of Wisconsin ordered a judgment canceling the lease if plaintiff executed and filed with the clerk of the court a lease with the terms he had intended to sign and deliver.

Miller v. Stanich could have marked a real retreat by the Wisconsin court from an objective theory of contract or the beginning of a general relief-of-hardship doctrine. However, in retrospect, it seems just an odd instance in Wisconsin jurisprudence — since one could argue that it has been overruled implicitly or at least limited to a very narrow exception. On the other hand, it is a resource available in the event a future court chooses to use it.

The Supreme Court of Wisconsin first cited its *Miller v. Stanich* decision eight years later in *Willett v. Stewart.*[86] The facts of the *Willett* case are complicated because of the tangled relationships among the parties. In June of 1929, Mr. and Mrs. Willett, both of whom were then in their seventies, owned property mortgaged to Mr. Garland. About 10 acres of this land were referred to as the Bristol Tile Works, consisting of a factory, machinery, and land from which workers took clay as a raw material. The Willetts' home occupied another acre or more and was part of the same tract of land. The description in the Willetts' deed covered both the Bristol Tile Works and their home.

The Willetts wanted to convey the portion of their land which contained the Bristol Tile Works to John and Zelba Runge. Zelba was the Willetts' daughter and John was her husband. William Runge, John's brother, practiced law in the same office as Calvin Stewart; Stewart was the municipal judge for Kenosha County. An associate in their law office drafted the conveyance from the Willetts to John and Zelba. He mistakenly used the same description of the property he found on the original deed. The Willetts signed the conveyance, which they were not aware conveyed *both* the Bristol Tile Works *and their home* to their daughter and son-in-law.

Judge Stewart had some money to invest. William Runge suggested that Stewart loan John and Zelba about $7,000, secured by a mortgage on the Bristol Tile Works. Judge Stewart agreed. The same associate drafted the mortgage securing Judge Stewart's loan to John and Zelba and used the same mistaken description of the property he had used in the original conveyance. This subjected the Willetts' home to Judge Stewart's mortgage.

John and Zelba Runge failed to make payments and failed to keep the Bristol Tile Works insured. In 1936, Judge Stewart began foreclosure procedures. The Willetts sued for reformation so that the mortgage would not apply to their home.

The trial court reformed the mortgage to exclude the Willetts' home. It relied on Judge Stewart's testimony:

> William Runge did not tell me there were any buildings on the property used for residential purposes. I was not told that anyone lived in any of the buildings on the land that was mortgaged to me. At the time I loaned the

---

86. 227 Wis. 303, 277 N.W. 665 (1938). Again, we have taken much of the information about the case that follows from the briefs and record on appeal.

money, … I didn't have the Willett home in my mind. The first time I knew the Willett home was included in the description was after we started to foreclose. Prior to that time I never thought anything about whether or not the Willett home was included in my mortgage.

Stewart did not see the premises before making the loan. The trial court said: "[I]f the defendant Calvin Stewart was in any way misinformed as to the extent or value of the property on which he was to be given a mortgage to secure the loan he was making to the defendants, John and Zelba Runge, it was because of statements made to him by William Runge, a brother of John Runge, an attorney sharing an office with Mr. Stewart at the time." While some of the proceeds of the loan had gone to pay off the Garland mortgage on the home, Mr. and Mrs. Willett were not responsible for anything said by William Runge.

The case was appealed to the Supreme Court of Wisconsin. Neither side mentioned *Miller v. Stanich* in its briefs. Both sides offered rather weak legal analyses. Both attorneys tried to convince the court that the equities favored their clients. Judge Stewart's lawyer pointed out that if the Willetts gained reformation of the mortgage, they would own their home free and clear of security interests while Judge Stewart would have loaned over $7,000 on the property now valued at no more than $2,500. His brief spoke of a conspiracy between William Runge, Judge Stewart's former associate in practice, and Runge's relatives. The Willetts' lawyer responded that the low value of the Bristol Tile Works was caused by the Depression and not by any fault of the Willetts. Moreover, he objected to the expression of personal anger "against a young lawyer who had the moral courage to testify against his former office associate, who at the time happened to be a judge before whom the lawyer would have occasion to appear from time to time."

The Supreme Court of Wisconsin reversed the decree reforming the mortgage. It said, "no doubt, there was a mutual mistake as between the Willetts and the Runges." However, Judge Stewart loaned money on the representation that it would be secured by a mortgage on about 11? acres of land. Without the Willetts' homestead, there would be less than 11 acres included. The court quoted language from *Jentzsch v. Roenfanz*:[87] "If the mistake has not been mutual but has been made inadvertently on one side and yet in good faith by the other, if any amendment or reformation of the contract can, under any circumstances, be made, it cannot be made so as to make the agreement conform merely to the views of the party seeking reformation, but only to the original views of both parties."[88] The court then cited *Miller v. Stanich* as supporting this proposition, but it did not discuss the case. Finally, the court concluded "there was no mutual mistake such as is necessary for reformation on the part of the Stewarts."[89]

---

87. 185 Wis. 189, 201 N.W. 504 (1924).

88. 277 N.W. at 668.

89. *Id.* We can notice another odd fact about the case. Judge Stewart benefits from a mistake made by a lawyer working in Stewart's law office. Today we might consider fiduciary duty and agency theories if we were representing the Willetts. Indeed, Judge Stewart's firm seems to have represented both sides

How does the *Willett* case differ from *Miller v. Stanich*? Both involve drafting mistakes made by lawyers concerning documents related to real estate.[90] It is likely that neither Stanich nor Judge Stewart relied on a literal reading of the rights granted to them by the documents in a way related to their economic interests. Stanich thought he had a five-year renewal plus an option to renew for five more years at a very favorable rent. Judge Stewart thought he had a mortgage on 11? acres of land, but he did not think he had a mortgage on any residential property. Stanich lost only his expected gain as a result of the decision in his case.[91] Judge Stewart would have found himself with security worth only $2,500 to cover a $7,000 debt if the Willetts had won.

Does the distinction between the *Miller* and the *Willett* cases turn on the remedy? In *Miller* the court could rescind and rely on the option to renew contained in the original lease to put the parties where they should have been. In *Willett*, rescission would have ended Judge Stewart's security interest in the Bristol Tile Works as well as the Willett home. Reformation to exclude the home was needed. However, why can't judges rewrite legal documents to arrive at what they see as appropriate results? In the *Willett* case, would reformation of the mortgage be anything more than making the paper deal conform to the real deal? Or to the deal Judge Stewart would have made had he known the facts in 1929?

In 1983, the Supreme Court of Wisconsin cited the *Miller* case as allowing rescission for unilateral mistake only where there was "the exercise of ordinary diligence by the party making the mistake."[92] An administrative agency had found that the party who wrote a contract containing such a mistake had "failed to act with due care in preparing the original agreement." Similarly, in *Carney-Rutter Agency, Inc. v. Central Office Buildings, Inc.*,[93] the court noted that "the negligence of respondent's officers in not reading the lease, which reading would have disclosed the existence of the termination clause, bars them from having reformation."

---

to the transaction. Lawyers may not benefit from such a conflict of interest. None of this was raised at trial or on appeal.

90. In the 21st century, we can consider malpractice actions as solutions to the problems presented by the cases. In the 1930s, it is unlikely that any of the lawyers involved carried insurance or had enough money to pay judgments that anyone might gain from malpractice actions.

91. However, consider Fuller and Perdue's comment in light of Stanich's position:

The difficulties in proving reliance and subjecting it to pecuniary measurement are such that the business man knowing, or sensing, that these obstacles stood in the way of judicial relief would hesitate to rely on a promise in any case where the legal sanction was of significance to him. To encourage reliance we must therefore dispense with its proof. For this reason it has been found wise to make recovery on a promise independent of reliance, both in the sense that in some cases the promise is enforced though not relied on (as in the bilateral business agreement) and in the sense that recovery is not limited to the detriment incurred in reliance.

Lon Fuller & William S. Perdue Jr., *The Reliance Interest in Contract Damages: Pt. 1*, 46 YALE L.J. 52, 62 (1936).

92. Dep't of Transp. v. Transp. Comm'n, 111 Wis. 2d 80, 330 N.W.2d 159 (1982).

93. 263 Wis. 244, 57 N.W.2d 348 (1953).

Wisconsin intermediate appellate courts had cited *Miller v. Stanich* in only seven other decisions concerning mistake as of 2016. In a 1994 opinion,[94] a court of appeals dismissed the appellant's contention that Wisconsin had adopted the Restatement (Second) of Contracts' view of unilateral mistake, finding no evidence of this. It commented on appellant's citation to the *Miller* case by observing in a footnote: "The [appellant] offers only a 1930 case, *Miller v. Stanich*, in which the court stated that a party might be entitled to rescission based on unilateral mistake if he or she can establish 'fraud' on the part of the other party, or that the other party knew that the first party 'was laboring under a mistake.'" Perhaps remarkably, this statement occurs in Justice Fritz's first opinion, which was overturned on rehearing. We can hope that it is an unusual misreading of a precedent. In *Town of Kronenwetter v. City of Mosinee*,[95] the court cited the *Miller* decision for the proposition that you can get recovery for mutual mistake.

Wisconsin courts of appeal did consider the unilateral mistake doctrine seriously in two decisions. In *Redevelopment Authority for the City of Kenosha v. Passarelli*,[96] the Redevelopment Authority for the City of Kenosha made an offer of $127,000 for a parcel of land on which the Passarellis owned a tavern. The Authority's lawyer had intended to make an offer for the tavern parcel as well as five other parcels of land belonging to the Passarellis. An appraisal had valued the tavern property as worth about $65,000. A secretary had prepared the offer based on legal descriptions given to her. She had given it to an assistant city attorney for review. Five legal descriptions had been omitted from the offer that was to go to the Passarellis. This was not noticed by the supervising attorney. The court relied on the *Miller* case's requirements and affirmed the trial court's grant of rescission of the contract because of unilateral mistake. It said that "the trial court was entitled to conclude that a generally reliable procedure was used, and that the mistake therefore occurred despite the exercise of ordinary diligence."

In 2007, a court of appeals affirmed a decision that an employee of the Milwaukee police department did not have a right to rescind her resignation because her case did not satisfy the requirements of *Miller v. Stanich*. In *Kamermayer v. City of Milwaukee*,[97] the appellate court criticized the argument of the plaintiff's lawyer. The lawyer did not establish that the mistake went to a material feature of the contract. The plaintiff's former attorney had gone over the details of the proposed settlement of the dispute concerning discharging the plaintiff. The lawyer did not establish how it was possible to give relief without serious prejudice to the City of Milwaukee. And the plaintiff's lawyer argued that "she is not required to offer proof that enforcement of the contract as made would be unconscionable ..." The appellate court emphasized the test of the *Miller* case in affirming the trial court's decision.

---

94. Erickson by Wightman v. Gundersen, 515 N.W.2d 293 (Wis. Ct. App. 1994) (The case name is correct; it involved a suit brought on behalf of Erickson.).

95. 1995 Wisc. App. LEXIS 1318.

96. 155 Wis. 2d 466, 458 N.W.2d 532 (1990).

97. 307 Wis. 2d 443, 745 N.W.2d 88 (2007).

What does this exercise in Shepardizing *Miller v. Stanich* suggest about how likely courts in other states are to adopt the Restatement (Second) of Contracts' position on unilateral mistake?

Why has *Miller v. Stanich* had such a limited application? If we read the decision narrowly, it may be that it applies only to a situation very unlikely to occur. One can get relief for a unilateral mistake that a court views as innocent only when a court can be almost certain there has been no reliance. In addition, perhaps it must be a situation in which a court can bring about a proper result by rescission rather than reformation. If a court calls off the mistaken transaction, some other transaction must exist that defends the rights of both parties.

In the *Miller* case, an illiterate person could not protect himself by reading the lease, and he relied on his lawyer. The lawyer made an error that anyone might make. (Indeed, Stanich's lawyer has some responsibility for creating a situation in which it was easy to make a mistake. He drafted two detailed and complex commercial leases that differed only by 23 words, which were easy to overlook.) Stanich could not argue that he had relied in any substantial way on a lease to begin five years in the future. Stanich clearly wanted to renew for five years, whether or not he got an option to renew for an additional five beyond that. Finally, since the original lease stood, all a court had to do was rescind the mistaken renewal.

In the *Willett* case, however, the Supreme Court of Wisconsin could not be sure that Judge Stewart had not relied on representations about the total number of acres of land that would be security for his loan. Moreover, rescission of the mortgage would have left Judge Stewart without any security. Reformation was needed, but the court was unwilling to write a contract for the parties that they ought to have written for themselves.

Is there reason to have an expansive unilateral mistake doctrine that would allow the reworking of contracts and other legal documents to achieve good ends? Consider the following, and ask how Sharp, Kessler and Fine, and the authors of the Restatement would have dealt with *Miller* and *Willett*. As you read the selections, ask yourself how easy the criteria they suggest would be to apply.

Malcolm Pitman Sharp, *Promissory Liability II*

7 U. Chi. L. Rev. 250, 267 (1939)

The extreme and simple case of unilateral mistake is indeed the case where one signs the wrong paper and sends it off to his correspondent by way of the acceptance of an offer already made; discovering the mistake at once, and notifying the correspondent before the communication has in any way affected his conduct. Here it appears persuasively that the same reasons which require relief in cases of mutual error may also require relief in any case of unilateral mistake.

The objective theory of contracts is not really threatened by such a suggestion, for relief from the consequences of the transaction will be allowed subject only to equitable limitations. Thus it is commonly said that change of position on the part of the person relying on the transaction will defeat relief for mistake. The mistaken person has perhaps merely by making a promise assumed some risk. He seems, however, in no worse a position than one who negligently misstates a fact. Apart from odd decisions about the measure of damages for deceit, a consistent treatment of liability would, it seems, require the mistaken party at most to make good the loss of the other party from the transaction as a whole, as a condition of relief against other consequences of the transaction. The mistaken party would thus of course make restitution and compensate the other party normally for expenses incurred in reliance on the promise as made; but the mistaken person would be relieved from liability for expectation damages.

Culpa in Contrahendo?

What follows is *our summary* of the arguments of Friedrich Kessler and Edith Fine, advanced in an important article entitled *Culpa in Contrahendo, Bargaining in Good Faith, and Freedom of Contract: A Comparative Study.*[98] We offer the summary in lieu of their more extended comments.

The German doctrine of *culpa in contrahendo* provides that parties to a prospective contract have a legal duty to negotiate the contract in good faith. If a party fails to negotiate in good faith and this prevents the parties from reaching their ultimate contractual objective, the blameworthy party can be legally required to compensate the injured party for expenses incurred in relying on the prospective contract. Though American contract law has not [at least at the writing of the Kessler and Fine article] adopted a doctrine equivalent to *culpa in contrahendo*, good faith and fair dealing are expressed in the laws pertaining to preliminary agreements, firm offers, mistake, and misrepresentation. Further, doctrines such as negligence, estoppel, and implied contract have served many of the same functions of *culpa in contrahendo*.

Culpa in contrahendo developed, in large part, as an attempt to deal with the problem of unilateral mistake. Civil law countries, such as Germany, had previously followed the subjective theory of contract because it was widely believed that the objective theory provided too much protection for the promisee and resulted in waste. The subjective theory of contract formation, however, which might imply a broad right of avoidance in the case of unilateral mistake, also seemed to be problematic. Neither the objective nor the subjective theory seemed to strike the right balance in allocating the burden of unilateral mistake. Therefore, *culpa in contrahendo* emerged in German law as a middle ground between accepting either theory. *Culpa in contrahendo* created an incentive to avoid careless promises, and at the same time, it gave some protection to those who might rely on the promises.

Under German law, a unilateral mistake entitles the mistaken party to void a legal exchange only when certain requirements are met. First, it must be the case that the

---

98. 77 HARV. L. REV. 401 (1964).

mistaken party would not have agreed to the contract terms if the party had known the true facts and thus appreciated the significance of assent. Second, the mistake must fall within one of three enumerated (but hard to capture in a summary) categories. The errors must generally be either errors in "purport" or intention, or mistakes as to the characteristics of persons or subject matter that are characterizable as essential. Errors in calculation have been considered to be errors in purport, and so operative and excusing—so long as the negotiations brought home to the other party that the mistaken price, for example, was intended to be the result of accurate calculations. Under these circumstances, the mistaken party is allowed to rescind the contract. However, the mistaken party is still liable for the amounts expended by the non-mistaken party in relying on the contract unless the non-mistaken party either knew or should have known of the mistake.

Some American writers have been critical of the German law treatment of unilateral mistake. First, they criticize the German law for not providing a remedy for intangible injuries suffered by a promisee who relies on a promise. The fact that non-economic injuries are difficult to calculate was the driving force behind common law rulings allowing recovery for the full expectation interest. Second, American commentators contend that adhering to the objective theory of contracts and allowing a promisee to recover the full expectation interest (rather than merely the reliance interest) is a strong incentive for parties to avoid careless manifestations of assent.

The first Restatement of Contracts, which can be taken to represent the conventional view of the matter in the United States, states that the mistake of one party does not automatically render a transaction voidable even when the mistake formed the basis for the mistaken party to enter into the contract. But there is a growing body of case law that offers relief for mistake, and which emphasizes some of the same factors that are important under the doctrine of *culpa in contrahendo*. Exceptions in the American law have been carved out for fraud and misrepresentation. Courts are also increasingly considering notions of good faith and fair dealing, even at the expense of creating unpredictability in the marketplace. This has led to exceptions being made for unconscionability and for mistakes of which the other party should have been aware. Relief is also available for material mistakes as to essential terms. Usually when relief is denied, the unilateral nature of the mistake is only one of a number of factors considered. Often courts, in denying relief, stress the immateriality of the mistake, the fact that parties could not be restored to their prior positions, and negligence on the part of the mistaken party. Also, while miscalculations of price, or errors as to quantity, are generally sufficient, several decisions denying relief in such cases have emphasized the fact that the goods had already changed hands or that the parties had materially altered their positions. As Kessler and Fine put it:

> To sum up, in attempting to find acceptable solutions mediating between the legitimate interests of both promisor and promisee, traditional doctrine in this country has been redefined by a body of case law too large to be ig-

nored. In this process of refinement of our law of contract, *culpa in con-trahendo* and notions of unjust enrichment have played a significant role. While in the civil law countries *culpa in contrahendo* has been used in large measure to mitigate the will theory, the common law starting from the other end has employed it as one of its weapons to soften the rigor of the objective theory of contracts. In this country the process of mitigation has found further manifestation in the notion that a mistaken party should be protected against oppressive burdens when rescission would impose no substantial hardship on the party seeking enforcement of the contract. Thus a link has been established between operative mistake and unjust enrichment. Here is an instance where the common law will look into adequacy of consideration. This variance from the general rule is not surprising, since the ordinary interest in protecting a price mutually arrived at is not present here.[99]

The Restatement's Synthesis of Common Law Rules

The Restatement (Second) of Contracts contains a number of rules dealing with unilateral mistakes. Those who drafted it were influenced by cases such as *Miller v. Stanich* and the Kessler and Fine article. As a way to give some content to the Restatement's abstractions, ask yourself how a court adopting the Restatement (Second) of Contracts would decide the *Miller* and *Willett* cases. You should also ask what the likely impact of the Restatement might be on bargaining to settle cases. At this point you should consult Restatement (Second) §§ 153–55, 157–58, and 204. The Restatement's approach to unilateral mistake has been well received in the courts.[100] The following case does not cite the Restatement's provisions on unilateral mistake. Nonetheless, does it take the approach advocated by the Second Restatement?

S.T.S. TRANSPORT SERVICE, INC. v. VOLVO WHITE TRUCK CORP.

United States Court of Appeals, Seventh Circuit
766 F.2d 1089 (1985)

CUDAHY, J.

Plaintiff appeals from a finding of unilateral mistake and rescission of a contract of sale. We affirm the judgment of the district court....

---

99. *Id.* at 436.

100. *See* Gregory E. Maggs, *Ipse Dixit: The Restatement (Second) of Contracts and the Modern Development of Contract Law*, 66 GEO. WASH. L. REV. 508, 526 (1998) (in a study of adoption of new approaches to contract law issues taken in the Second Restatement, finding 89 cases that cited § 153, none of them rejecting it but three finding its elements unsatisfied without deciding whether to adopt the section, one of these being the *Erickson* case, *supra* note 94, and another misunderstanding the section). A 2015 LEXIS search reveals 174 cases in which § 153 is cited.

Plaintiff-appellant S.T.S. Transport Service, Inc. ("S.T.S.") is an Illinois corporation whose principal place of business is located in Alsip, Illinois. Since its incorporation in 1978, S.T.S. has leased tractor trucks and trailers to other companies and has also hauled freight for customers. Volvo White Truck Corporation ("Volvo White") is a Virginia corporation with its principal place of business in Greensboro, North Carolina. There is a branch dealership of Volvo White in Alsip, Illinois. In 1979 and 1980 S.T.S. bought trucks and heavy equipment from White Motor Company ("White Motor"), a truck manufacturer whose assets were purchased in 1981 by Volvo White.

Early in 1981 S.T.S. expressed an interest in purchasing eight new tractor trucks from White Motor in Alsip. In order to avoid a down payment, S.T.S. wanted to trade in trucks it already owned and use its equity in those trucks as a down payment. After appraising the trucks S.T.S. intended to trade in, and after some negotiations concerning the appraised value, White Motor offered to sell S.T.S. eight 1981 Road Commander trucks on the following terms:

(a) The 1981 Road Commander trucks would be sold to S.T.S. for a price of $58,749 each;

(b) S.T.S. would trade White Motor one used truck for each new truck purchased;

(c) S.T.S. would continue to make payments (to financing companies) on the used trucks through July 1981;

(d) White Motor would value six of the used trucks at the same amount that S.T.S. would owe on them in July 1981: $26,560 each;

(e) White Motor would give S.T.S. a credit of $25,000 on another of the trucks;

(f) White Motor would arrange financing for S.T.S.

Provision (d) meant that S.T.S. would receive no credit for any equity in six of the trucks it owned, but that White Motor would simply pay off the amount still owed by S.T.S. on those trucks. The list price of the Road Commander trucks was $80,784. The offer price of $58,749 was reached by adding a profit of $2,200 to the Alsip branch's base cost of $56,549 for the trucks. These terms were confirmed in a March 10, 1981, letter from White Motor to S.T.S. Apparently they were not satisfactory to S.T.S., and negotiations were suspended.

In August, 1981, while White Motor [remember—the assets of White Motor were later bought by Volvo-White] was the subject of bankruptcy proceedings, S.T.S. solicited a new offer from them. White Motor recalculated its costs and sent a letter, dated August 17, 1981, which set out the specifications of the eight Road Commander Trucks, and which concluded with the following paragraphs:

Net delivered price F.O.B. Alsip, including preparation, but excluding state/local taxes is ... $273,176.00.

We will pay off balance due to White Motor Credit Corporation on the (6) 1979 Western Stars. We assume you will make your payment to White

Motor Credit Corporation on December 14, 1981, and then begin a new note with White Motor Credit Corporation effective January 30, 1982, as your first payment on the new equipment. There will be no prepayment return to you; that figure ($9,035) is included in the above figures.

We will also pay off the "estimated" money owed to I.T.T. of $31,755 once your trades are turned in. This is the estimated balance after your November 30, 1981, payment to I.T.T. We will receive the 1978 Freight-liner and 1977 Peterbilt as trades and we will also receive the 1979 Western Stars.

Hope this isn't confusing. I just net'd everything out and gave you the bottom line. It's a good deal for you for two reasons: there is a $3,500.00 U.T.A. on this deal, and we expect 6 percent 1982 increase by September 1, 1981. You are actually purchasing 1982 units at 1981 prices with $3,500 off on top.

What do you think!!!!!!!

A moment's calculations makes clear how widely the price suggested in the August 12 letter diverges from the earlier price. Eight trucks at the March 10 price of $58,749 would total $469,992; there was to be no credit for the equity of any of the trucks traded in, except for one, and the credit for that one was to be $25,000. Subtracting that credit from the total for the eight trucks would result in a net price of something just under $445,000. The new net price named in the August letter is some $170,000 — over $20,000 a truck — less.

Appellee Volvo White claims that the August figure was the result of a miscalculation. Intending to offer the eight new trucks for the lower price of $56,530 each, for a total of $452,240, White Motor subtracted from that figure not only $42,000 in credit that it was now willing to allow on the trade-in of two trucks, but the $137,064 in assessed value on six other trucks, an amount which equalled the outstanding debt on the trucks. Since S.T.S. was to be credited with no equity on those six used trucks, the assessed value should not have been subtracted from the price of the new trucks. White Motor merely intended to wipe out S.T.S.'s remaining debt on those trucks. By subtracting the amount they did from the price of the new trucks, White Motor in effect offered to credit S.T.S. with an amount equal to the amount of the debt remaining on each truck.

In response to further inquiries by S.T.S, White Motor sent out a second letter on September 2, 1981. This letter was in all respects identical to the August 17 letter, except that in place of the last line of the August letter the September 2 letter contained the following paragraph regarding interest rate charges:

If prime rate increases from todays [sic] rate of 20.5%, your rate to be charged will be 2.5% below the existing prime on date of delivery. If prime decreases, your rate will be the then existing add-on rate charged by White Motor Credit Corporation.

Both letters were sent out by Joseph LaSpina, manager of the Alsip branch. LaSpina admitted at trial that he did not review the August 17 letter before it went out, and that he did not review or sign the September 2nd letter; his name was signed on the first page by his secretary.

S.T.S. accepted the offer. In December 1981, S.T.S. turned over to Volvo White all of the trade-in vehicles. S.T.S. also entered into a new lease agreement with Suburban Truck & Trailer, under the terms of which Suburban would lease five of the new trucks from S.T.S. for three years. S.T.S. expected the lease to produce gross income before expenses of $37,876.49 per truck per year.

In January 1982, [before the eight new trucks were delivered to S.T.S.] the parties became aware of the problem. Volvo White informed S.T.S. that the net purchase price for the new trucks was $452,000, and S.T.S. insisted that under the contract the purchase price was $273,176. On January 15, 1982, Volvo White sent a letter admitting that it had made a clerical error in the contract. It offered to go ahead at the $452,000 price or to call off the transaction, and it confirmed that the eight trade-ins, now in Volvo White's lot, would remain the property of S.T.S. until the deal was closed. Maintaining that it could not use the trade-in vehicles in its new leasing contract with Suburban, and maintaining that under the terms of the contract Volvo White should have taken over payments of the used trucks, S.T.S. neither reclaimed the trucks nor kept up payments on them. They were repossessed and sold later in the year for approximately $20,000 per truck. [The eight new trucks were never delivered to S.T.S.]

S.T.S. claims that it lost an equity of $70,900 that it had built up in those trade-in units. It also claims that it lost a profit of $372,352 that it would have earned under its lease with Suburban.

S.T.S. had apparently been experiencing some financial difficulty in the latter half of 1981. In January and February 1982, it sold its remaining tractor trucks. This lawsuit was commenced on June 11, 1982. A trial in the Northern District of Illinois was held during the week of June 13, 1983. S.T.S. sought as damages its lost profits under the Suburban lease. Volvo White counterclaimed for an unpaid balance on parts and materials Volvo White had provided to S.T.S.

The district court found first that S.T.S. had a duty to mitigate its damages. It found that S.T.S. should have gone ahead with the purchase at the higher price, so that it might fulfill its own commitment to provide trucks for Suburban, reserving the right to sue Volvo White for the difference under the UCC. It found that since the plaintiff did not mitigate in that way, it could not realize any of the damages it claimed.

But the district judge also found that the contract contained a mistake with respect to the price term, a mistake that would not have been discovered by merely proofreading the document. Since she found a mistake, she also found that the mistake could be excused and the contract rescinded if the plaintiff could be returned to the *status quo ante*. She found that the costs of the parts and labor that were the subject of Volvo White's counterclaim were incurred in the process of getting the trucks ready for the trade-in, so that the *status quo* could be restored with respect to those obligations by excusing them. On the other hand, she was persuaded by the testimony of witnesses that S.T.S. intended to go out of business at the end of 1981, and that "there is nothing really to restore it to in that regard." Accordingly, she entered judgment for the plaintiff on the counterclaim [denying Volvo-White's claim for parts and materials] but against the plaintiff on its principal claim [the S.T.S. claim for lost profits and equity on trade-in trucks].

On the question of equity, the district judge found that the used trucks probably could have been sold by S.T.S. for more than they were sold for after repossession, but that since S.T.S. had not taken advantage of the opportunity to reclaim the trucks, it was stuck with the price the trucks had actually been sold for. At that price, there was no equity, since the trucks were sold for less than the amount owed on them.

If the contract is void because of a mistake, then there is no question of mitigation, since the duty to mitigate (if there is such a duty) arises out of the breach of a valid contract. Where the court applies the doctrine of mistake, the parties are excused from the contract and consequently there is no breach. Thus, if the district court properly found a mistake concerning the price term and properly voided the contract, we need not reach the issue of mitigation.

The parties have stipulated that Illinois law governs. The sale of the trucks would be governed by the Uniform Commercial Code, chapter 26 of the Illinois Revised Code; but under § 1-103 of the Code [Eds.: § 1-103(b) as revised in 2001], mistake and certain other questions are governed by the common law. 26 Ill. Rev. Stat. § 1-103.

Although the traditional case in which a contract is found to contain a mistake is one in which the parties understand a key term differently (hence, a case in which the mistake is mutual), the cases have also voided contracts—though more reluctantly—where only one party is mistaken as to the facts. In the typical case of this sort, a seller or contractor will miscalculate in adding up a list of items. Under the appropriate circumstances courts will now recognize a right to avoidance of this sort of mistake....

[The court excludes errors of judgment from the kinds of errors which may permit avoidance of the contract.]

As the law now stands, three conditions must be fulfilled before a contract can be rescinded: (1) the mistake must relate to a material feature of the contract; (2) it must have occurred despite the exercise of reasonable care; and (3) the other party must be placed in the position it was in before the contract was made....

The mistake in this case relates to the price, which must be conceded to be material. The mistake must also have occurred in spite of the exercise of reasonable care. Although reasonable care is as difficult to be precise about in this sort of case as it is elsewhere, there are some fairly clear groupings of mistake cases that can serve as guideposts. Most helpful is the knowledge that Illinois courts will generally grant relief for errors "which are clerical or mathematical." *Cummings v. Dusenbury*, 129 Ill. App. 3d 338, 84 Ill. Dec. 615, 619, 472 N.E.2d 575, 579 (1984). The reason for the special treatment for such errors, of course, is that they are difficult to prevent, and that no useful social purpose is served by enforcing the mistaken term. No incentives exist to make such mistakes; all the existing incentives work, in fact, in the opposite direction. There is every reason for a contractor to use ordinary care, and, if errors of this sort—

clerical or mathematical—slip through anyway, the courts will generally find it more useful to allow the contract to be changed or rescinded than to enforce it as it is. Naturally there are cases of extreme negligence to which this presumption should not apply; and there is an exception of sorts where the contract has been relied upon. We will have something to say about this last at a later point.

Although it would be wrong to suppose that "merely" mathematical or clerical errors are easily distinguished from other errors such as those of judgment—a miscalculation about the economic climate, say—the distinction is clear enough for ordinary purposes. A merely mathematical or clerical error occurs when some term is either one-tenth or ten times as large as it should be; when a term is added in the wrong column; when it is added rather than subtracted; when it is overlooked.

The error involved here is of that sort, but if anything more difficult to detect. The Alsip manager, LaSpina, made the crucial calculations. The assessed value of the used trucks was subtracted from the price of the new trucks. Such a procedure is perfectly appropriate, ordinarily; whoever buys a new car expects to have the price reduced by the value of the trade-in. Here, however, the assessed value was set so as to match the outstanding debt on the trucks. Even so, had the offer been for S.T.S. to pay off the remaining debt on the trucks before they were traded in, the calculation would have been correct. But that was not the offer; Volvo White offered to take over the remaining debt on the trade-ins, so that there was nothing in the way of trade-in value to be subtracted from the purchase price. The assessed value was completely offset by the outstanding debt.

However foolish this mistake, once made it would not easily have been detected. S.T.S. points out that Volvo White conceded in testimony that neither of the two letters containing the term in question were reviewed by LaSpina before going out. But such an omission ought to bar rescission only if it would have resulted in the error's being detected. Here, the mistaken calculations were made by LaSpina, and there is little reason to suppose that he would have detected the error had he proofread the letters before they went out. The error involved, therefore, was not one that would have been detected by the exercise of ordinary care, and we do not think that the trial judge erred in rejecting the defense of negligence.

The question of reliance is no different from the question whether the parties can be put into the position they were in at the time the contract was signed. Here, S.T.S. claims that it lost the equity it had in the trucks traded in. If it did in fact lose those trucks because of reliance on the contract; and if in fact there was equity in the trucks—that is, if the market value of the trucks exceeded the remaining debt—then S.T.S. is entitled to claim that equity as the price of putting it back into the position it would have been in had it not relied on the contract.

The district court found that S.T.S. could have reclaimed its trucks at any time. At the time it became apparent that Volvo White was not going to honor the contract as written, sometime in January 1982, S.T.S. could have arranged to sell the trucks on its own. A party to a contract cannot be allowed to create damages by continuing to rely on a contract which has either been breached, or been void from the start. As of January 1982, S.T.S. was on notice that one of those two situations applied....

Instead, S.T.S. refused to make further payments, and the trucks were repossessed and sold for amounts less than the amounts still owed on each. S.T.S. might have complained of the reasonableness of these sales, but it did not; in any case the sales do not appear to have been unreasonable.[101] The district court therefore correctly found that any loss of equity—if there was equity to begin with—was due to conduct of S.T.S., and that restoring S.T.S. to the status quo did not require payment for lost equity.

S.T.S. also incurred certain obligations in preparing the trucks for the trade-in; Volvo White has counterclaimed for repayment of approximately $9500 for parts and services priced during this period. The district judge found that these obligations were legitimately incurred in reliance on the contract and that before the contract can be rescinded those obligations must be excused. She therefore dismissed the counterclaim and rescinded the contract. Volvo White does not reassert its counterclaim on appeal.

Since the district court properly rescinded the contract, the question of mitigation does not arise. The judgment of the district court is affirmed.

NOTES AND QUESTIONS

1. *Mistaken calculations:* The Volvo White dealer's initial offer was calculated as follows:

Price for 8 at $58,749 each:	$469,992
Less credit for 1 used truck:	*$25,000*
Total to be paid by S.T.S.:	$444,992

[6 *trucks traded in and dealer pays off amounts due*]

The second mistaken offer was calculated as follows:

Price for 8 at $56,530 each:	$452,240
Less credit for 2 used trucks:	*$42,000*
Subtotal:	$410,240 [Correct amt.]
Less assessed value of 6 trucks:	*$137,064* [Mistake]
Mistaken total:	$273,176

2. *The buyer's interest:* Why does the buyer lose the benefit of the bargain? Should it have seen the mistaken calculation? At the time the second offer was made, the court tells us White Motor was the subject of bankruptcy proceedings. Could the buyer rea-

---

101. [1] The trucks were sold for $20,000 each. Volvo White had appraised the trucks at $22,000–23,000; testimony for S.T.S. would have set the value at $30,000. Considering the conditions under which the trucks were sold, the selling price does not appear unreasonable, whichever estimate of market value we choose.

sonably assume that it was getting a great deal as part of clearing out the inventory of an almost bankrupt manufacturer? However, the next-to-last sentence of the second offer says: "You are actually purchasing 1982 units at 1981 prices with $3,500 off on top." Was this enough to alert the buyer that the calculations were mistaken?

3. *The authority of the S.T.S. case:* In *Chicago Litho Plate Graining Co., Ltd. v. Allstate Can Company*,[102] the court read the *S.T.S.* decision as an example of rescission for unilateral mistake "in the limited circumstances as suggested by the Restatement (Second) of Contracts, § 153(a)." *S.T.S.* purported to be an application of Illinois law in a diversity of citizenship case. The case was recognized as a proper reading of Illinois law in *Estate of Blakely v. Federal Kemper Life Assur. Co.*[103] In the *Blakely* decision, an insurance company had charged too large a premium for the deceased's life insurance because it made the wrong calculation. The policy had lapsed before the insured's death. The executor argued that the overpayments extended the duration of the policy so that it would have been in effect when the insured died. Summary judgment for the estate was affirmed. This was not an appropriate case to grant either reformation or restitution for the insurance company's unilateral mistake. Giving the estate back the premiums paid would not give the estate the insurance that the insured thought that he had bought. *See also Prudential Ins. Co. of America v. S.S. American Lancer*,[104] which cites the *S.T.S.* decision with approval in a case involving a clerical error.

Professor Melvin Eisenberg classifies the type of mistake involved in the case as "mechanical error" and highlights that the court justified its approach in terms of incentives for optimal precaution, which in particular avoids incentives for too much precaution (triple- and quadruple-checking).[105]

An Illinois intermediate appellate court, considering *In re Marriage of Mary Anne Doran*,[106] cited both the *S.T.S.* and *Estate of Blakely* decisions as examples of a doctrine that allowed reformation of a written contract for a "scrivener's error." This is a clerical error that is the result of a minor mistake, or inadvertence in drafting a document so that it fails to reflect the agreement of the parties. The court must be able to determine from the language of the contract that a term is "manifestly incongruous" with the rest of the written agreement. Does the *Doran* case accurately reflect either the *S.T.S.* decision or the Restatement (Second)'s unilateral mistake doctrine?

C. UNENFORCEABLE CONTRACTS, RESTITUTION, AND RELIANCE

People can make mistakes about whether they made a contract or if they did, what its terms are. If the mistake is discovered soon enough, all that is lost is the chance

102. 838 F.2d 927, 931 (7th Cir. 1988).
103. 267 Ill. App. 3d 100, 640 N.E.2d 961 (1994).
104. 870 F.2d 867 (2d Cir. 1989).
105. Melvin A. Eisenberg, *Mistake in Contract Law*, 91 Cal. L. Rev. 1573, 1585 (2003).
106. 2012 Ill. App. Unpub. LEXIS 2229 (Ill. App. Ct. 2d Dist. 2012).

that they might have made as good, or better, a bargain elsewhere. However, in some situations reliance losses may be much greater. You will not be surprised when we tell you that restitution serves to clean up the mess in some cases. Suppose that buyer and auto dealer think they have made a contract, but are mistaken. Dealer delivers the car to buyer before discovering that there was no contract. When the mistake is discovered, buyer won't go through with the deal. Buyer has been unjustly enriched, and seller can recover the car in a restitution action. Things are less clear when there has been a reliance loss that does not create an economic benefit for the other party. Furthermore, even where there is a benefit, there are problems when the buyer reasonably thought she was buying something else or that the deal had not yet been closed. Seller has suffered a loss, but it may not be clear that buyer should pay for it.

We have placed this material here for teaching reasons. It relates both backward and forward. That is, we considered situations where people have been mistaken about whether they made contracts or what the terms were. The material in this section suggests that the question is more than the choice between "contract" or "no contract." Up to this point, we did not want to raise restitution and reliance questions because we thought you had enough on your plate, but now it is time to add these issues. Those who accept realist jurisprudence insist that judges and lawyers do not decide (1) is there a contract or can it be rescinded for mistake?, and then (2) if there is no contract, can some or all of the reliance losses be recovered? Rather, anyone considering a close question as to whether a contract was formed may be influenced by the consequences of deciding one way or the other and by possibilities for remedial alternatives to expectation damages, such as reliance damages, reformation, restitution for benefits conferred, or some combination of these forms of relief.

VICKERY v. RITCHIE

Massachusetts Supreme Judicial Court
202 Mass. 247, 88 N.E. 835 (1909)

Knowlton, C.J.

This is an action to recover a balance of $10,467.16, alleged to be due the plaintiff as a contractor, for the construction of a Turkish bath house on land of the defendant. The parties signed duplicate contracts in writing, covering the work. At the time when the plaintiff signed both copies of the contract, the defendant's signature was attached, and the contract price therein named was $33,721. When the defendant signed them the contract price stated in each was $23,200. Until the building was completed, the plaintiff held a contract under which he was to receive the larger sum, while the defendant held a contract for the same work, under which he was to pay only the smaller sum. This resulted from the fraud of the architect who drew the contracts, and did all the business and made all the payments for the defendant. The contracts were on typewritten sheets, and it is supposed that the architect accomplished the fraud by changing the sheets on which the price was written, before the signing by the plaintiff, and before the delivery to the defendant. The parties did not discover the discrepancy between the two writings until after the building was substantially completed. Each of them acted honestly and in good faith, trusting the statements of the architect. The architect was indicted, but he left the commonwealth and escaped punishment.

The auditor found that the market value of the labor and materials furnished by the plaintiff, not including the customary charge for the supervision of the work, was $33,499.30, and that their total cost to the plaintiff was $32,950.96. He found that the land and building have cost the defendant much more than their market value. The findings indicate that it was bad judgment on the part of the defendant to build such a structure upon the lot, and that the increase in the market value of the real estate, by reason of that which the plaintiff put upon it, is only $22,000. The failure of the parties to discover the difference between their copies of the contract was caused by the frequently repeated fraudulent representations of the architect to each of them.

The plaintiff and defendant were mistaken in supposing that they had made a binding contract for the construction of this building. Their minds never met in any agreement about the price. The labor and materials were furnished at the defendant's request and for the defendant's benefit. From this alone the law would imply a contract on the part of the defendant to pay for them. The fact that the parties supposed the price was fixed by a contract, when in fact there was no contract, does not prevent this implication, but leaves it as a natural result of their relations. Both parties understood and agreed that the work should be paid for, and both parties thought that they had agreed upon the price. Their mutual mistake in this particular left them with no express contract by which their rights and liabilities could be determined. The law implies an obligation to pay for what has been done and furnished under such circumstances, and the defendant, upon whose property the work was done, has no right to say that it is not to be paid for. The doctrine is not applicable to work upon real estate alone. The rule would be the same if the work and materials were used in the repair of a carriage, or of any other article of personal property, under a supposed contract with the owner, if, through a mutual mistake as to the supposed agreement upon the price, the contract became unenforceable....

The principle has often been applied when the ground for an implication of an agreement to pay was much less strong than in the present case. In *Butterfield v. Byron*, 153 Mass. 517, ... where the owner was to do a part of the work in the erection of a building, and a contractor was to do the rest, under an express contract for an agreed price, it was held that, when the building was destroyed by lightning, so that the contract became impossible of performance, the contractor might recover, on a *quantum meruit*, the fair value of the labor and materials that he had furnished. This was on the ground that, when the contract came to an end without the fault of either party, there was an implication that what was furnished was to be paid for, and if it could not be paid for under the contract it should be paid for on a *quantum meruit*....

If the law implies an agreement to pay, how much is to be paid? There is but one answer. The fair value of that which was furnished. No other rule can be applied. Under certain conditions the price fixed by the contract might control in such cases. In this case there was no price fixed.

The defendant contends that because the erection of a Turkish bath house on Carver street was not a profitable investment, and therefore, through a seeming error of judgment on the part of the defendant, the building did not add to the value of the land so much by a large sum as it cost, the plaintiff must suffer the consequences of the defendant's mistake and be precluded from recovery....

[N]owhere, so far as we have been able to discover, does the law, as applied to such cases in other jurisdictions, make the right of the contractor depend in any degree upon the profit or loss to the owner, arising from his wisdom or folly, or good fortune or bad fortune, in erecting the building upon his land....

In this case there was no express contract. The plaintiff's right is to recover upon an implied contract of an owner to pay for labor and materials used upon his [owner's] property at his [owner's] request.... [I]n cases of the class to which the present one belongs the right does not depend upon the ultimate benefit received by the owner....

In all cases to which this general principle has been applied, the recovery has been upon a *quantum meruit* for that which was furnished, subject to diminution of the amount by the price named in the contract, if that was very low. The right of recovery depends upon the plaintiff's having furnished property or labor, under circumstances which entitle him to be paid for it, not upon the ultimate benefit to the property of the owner at whose request it was furnished....

It follows that the plaintiff is entitled to recover the fair value of his labor and materials.

Exceptions sustained.

NOTES AND QUESTIONS

1. *The AIA treatment of the problem:* Architects, builders, and owners make many building contracts today using standard forms drafted by the American Institute of Architects (AIA). In almost all building contracts, the owner and not the builder selects the architect, who serves as agent for the owner. Principals are usually liable for contracts made by their agents acting within the scope of their actual or apparent authority. They are also liable for their agents' torts committed in the scope of employment. In light of agency law, should the owner who selected the architect be responsible for the architect's fraud and mistakes?

2. *Calculating the amount of restitution:* If liability is based on restitution, how much should the builder in *Vickery v. Ritchie* be able to recover? Consider the possibilities, rounding off the sums:

(a) Increased value of owner's land	$22,000
(b) Owner's contract price	$23,000
(c) Half the difference between construction cost and the added value to the land, or ($32,750 − 22,000 = 10,750; ½ x 10,750 = 5,375 + 22,000)	$27,375
(d) Cost of construction	$32,750

(e) Market value of labor & material, but not including
    supervision $33,500

(f) Builder's contract price $33,721

Does your answer turn on choice, fault, benefit, loss-sharing, or some form of social engineering?

3. *The Restatement of Restitution's solution:* Section 10 of the Restatement (Third) of Restitution (2010) offers still another solution to the *Vickery v. Ritchie* problem:

> A person who improves the real or personal property of another, acting by mistake, has a claim in restitution as necessary to prevent unjust enrichment. A remedy for mistaken improvement that subjects the owner to a forced exchange will be qualified or limited to avoid undue prejudice to the owner.

Comment h to § 10 states that the analysis of § 155 of the first Restatement is being carried forward. Section 10's Illustration 27, based on the facts of *Vickery*, indicates that the owner should pay the price it agreed to pay because that reveals the "subjective valuation" the owner put on the improvement.

4. *Recovering for reliance expenses and calling it restitution:* The *Vickery* case deals with the situation in which the work done by the builder, in the mistaken belief that there was a contract, was clearly received by the landowner. The *Vickery* case is interesting because the cost incurred by the builder so substantially exceeded the increase in the value of the land—which we might expect to be an unusual occurrence. (Do you see why?) Nevertheless, it is undeniable that plaintiff's work had really enriched the defendant; the question was by *how much*, and whether to focus on increases in asset value or the imputed value of work done at one's request. This undeniable fact of enrichment apparently provides the justification for a recovery on a restitution theory. But the court seems candid in admitting that the benefit recovered by the defendant, though the ground for the claim, is not the measure of the recovery. In contrast, the Restatement of Restitution suggests that the award cannot exceed its "value in advancing the purposes of the recipient." The measure of recovery seems more clearly constrained by the substantive rationale for the claim, which is said to be the avoidance of unjust enrichment.

But what happens when a person, mistakenly believing herself to be party to an enforceable contract, incurs expenses which seem not to benefit the other party to the *un*enforceable contract at all? Remember the next-to-last paragraph in *S.T.S. Transport, Inc. v. Volvo White Truck Corp.*? It appears that in preparing the used trucks to be traded in, S.T.S. repaired them, buying parts and services from Volvo White on credit. Volvo White had asked to be paid for these parts and services. The trial court had dismissed Volvo White's claim (for reasons that are either ill-considered or unclear), and Volvo White had not pressed the claim on appeal. But what if Volvo White *had* insisted that the court address its counterclaim?

First, it is not clear that the delivery of parts and services to S.T.S. should even have been regarded as part of the ill-fated transaction involving the sale of the eight new trucks. Second, even if S.T.S. was obliged to repair the trucks, and to buy services and parts from Volvo White, S.T.S. may have received the benefit of those parts and services when the used trucks were subsequently resold after being repossessed. The repairs and parts may have increased the liquidation value of the trucks. *But let's assume* that, perhaps because the trucks sat unused on the Volvo White lot for several months, the parts and services were never of any measurable economic benefit to S.T.S. Should Volvo White receive nothing? Or should it be paid something because it provided goods and services to another upon the request of that other? Is this like *Vickery*?

The 1928 Connecticut case of *Kearns v. Andree*[107] allowed recovery of reliance expenses. In *Kearns* the seller incurred expenses in remodeling a house to suit the tastes of a buyer who then refused to complete the transaction. The buyer was held to be entitled to refuse, since the court held the contract to be insufficiently definite. The court concluded, however, that the disappointed seller was entitled to recover expenses it had incurred "in good faith and in the honest belief that the agreement was sufficiently definite to be enforced,"[108] subject to a deduction to the extent that any of those expenses were of any benefit to the seller. The court said, "He has performed those services at the request of the other party to the contract, and in the expectation, known to the other, that he would be compensated therefor. Here is a sufficient basis for an implication in law that reasonable compensation would be made."[109] The court disallowed a claim for additional remodeling to meet the needs of a second buyer, on the ground that to allow such recovery would be to permit recovery upon an unenforceable contract. *Kearns v. Andree* was distinguished in 1941 in *R.F. Baker & Co. v. P. Ballentine & Sons*.[110] Finally, in *Automobile Insurance Co. v. Model Family Laundries*,[111] the Connecticut court asserted that the true ground for recovery in cases like *Kearns v. Andree* was quasi-contract for unjust enrichment, and that quasi-contract required that defendant receive a benefit.

In *Ramsey v. Ellis*,[112] the Supreme Court of Wisconsin attempted to clear up the confusion. The court said: "*Quantum meruit* is a distinct cause of action from an action for unjust enrichment, with distinct elements and a distinct measure of damages." *Quantum meruit* is based on an implied contract to pay reasonable compensation for services rendered at the defendant's request. Unjust enrichment is based on a benefit conferred on the defendant. If the defendant has asked for the services in a situation where she knows they are not a gift, the plaintiff can recover in *quantum meruit* whether or not providing the requested services has resulted in a tangible economic gain to the defendant. The defendant has made a choice to request the services.[113]

---

107. 107 Conn. 181, 139 A. 695 (1928).

108. 139 A. at 698.

109. *Id.*

110. 127 Conn. 680, 20 A.2d 82 (1941).

111. 133 Conn. 433, 52 A.2d 137 (1947).

112. 168 Wis. 2d 779, 484 N.W.2d 331, 333 (1992). *See* Midcoast Aviation, Inc. v. Gen. Elec. Credit Corp., 907 F.2d 732 (7th Cir. 1990).

113. *See also* Candace Kovacic, *A Proposal to Simplify Quantum Meruit Litigation*, 35 Am. U. L. Rev. 547 (1986).

Courts, however, often confuse restitution and *quantum merit* and deny any remedy when there is no tangible economic benefit, even if the defendant has requested the services.[114] The hard cases are, of course, those where the defendant requested the services as part of what the parties thought was a contract, but where the contract is not enforceable. Defendant made a choice to gain plaintiff's services under the terms of the unenforceable contract, but she might not have made that choice had she known that she would have to pay the reasonable price of those services.

The paradox was addressed head-on in the California case of *Earhart v. William Low Company*.[115] Earhart Construction Company made a contract with William Low Company to construct the Pana Rama Mobile Home Park. The contract was subject to the conditions that William Low obtain the needed financing and that Earhart Construction secure a performance bond. Neither condition was ever fulfilled. The park was to be built on land owned by William Low and an adjoining tract owned by Ervie Pillow. There was a special use permit altering the zoning regulations to allow a mobile home park to be built on Pillow's land. However, it would expire on May 27th, without possibility of renewal unless work on the property was "diligently underway" by that date. William Low Company made a contract to buy the Pillow tract subject to financing. On May 25th, William Low's representative telephoned Fayette L. Earhart and said it had obtained the necessary financing. It urged Earhart to move the necessary equipment onto the property and begin work immediately to save the special use permit. Earhart's crew began work at once. It worked for a week, often in the presence of William Low. On June 1st, Earhart Construction submitted a request for a progress payment. Fayette Earhart then learned that William Low had not obtained the needed financing. William Low refused the bill, and it later signed a contract with another construction company to build the park.

The trial court awarded Earhart Construction the reasonable value of the work done on William Low's tract but refused to award anything for the work done on the land owned by Ervie Pillow. It explained; "All he pays for is the value of what he got, notwithstanding how much it cost the plaintiff to produce it."[116] In other words, work done on the Pillow land at the request of the William Low Company was not a benefit to it. The trial court followed several California decisions, which held that there must be a direct benefit to justify restitution and that the satisfaction of obtaining compliance with a request was not enough.

The Supreme Court of California reversed. Justice Tobriner relied on a dissenting opinion by former Chief Justice Roger Traynor, which "urged that we abandon the unconscionable requirement of 'benefit' to the defendant and allow recovery in *quantum meruit* whenever a party acts to his detriment in reliance on another's represen-

---

114. *See* Peter Linzer, *Rough Justice: A Theory of Restitution and Reliance, Contracts and Torts*, 2001 Wis. L. Rev. 665, 764–72 (discussing the unreported opinion in Shore v. Motorola, 210 F.3d 376 (7th Cir. 2000)).

115. 158 Cal. Rptr. 887, 600 P.2d 1344 (1979).

116. *Id.* at 890, 600 P.2d at 1347.

tation that he will give compensation for the detriment suffered."[117] Traynor argued that benefit conferred was a pure fiction. Allowing recovery would place the loss where it belongs—on the party whose requests induced performance in justifiable reliance on the belief that the requested performance would be paid for. It was enough that plaintiff performed the work on the Pillow property at the urgent request of defendant. Plaintiff reasonably relied, believing that defendant would pay for the work.

Justice Clark dissented on this point. He said: "Absent promise of payment, a person who does no more than request an attorney to consult with a potential client does not incur an obligation to pay the attorney for the consultation."[118] Justice Clark said that William Low Company might have benefited from saving the special use permit. This increased the time William Low had to obtain financing. However, "[b]y commencing work to maintain the permit, thereby increasing the time to obtain financing, plaintiff also increased the likelihood that his contract would be effective. Because the benefits to plaintiff are substantially similar to those to defendant company, there is no unjust enrichment, and no basis for finding an implied in fact promise to pay."[119]

5. *Same result—different theory:* Is there another way in which one could provide relief to those who rely on unenforceable contracts? If there is, it might be possible to apply it, and avoid the potentially unfortunate effects of stretching the concept of benefit in restitution cases (if not, as some might assert, eliminating it altogether). What about using Restatement § 90? The Wisconsin Supreme Court held in *Hoffman v. Red Owl*[120] that Hoffman was entitled to recover the losses he had reasonably incurred in relying on Red Owl's promise, even though that promise was not definite enough to support a contract. Should cases of indefiniteness be treated differently than cases of unilateral mistake? Would the utilization of § 90 as a theory allow courts to get to just outcomes without doing violence to existing restitutionary doctrines? Or doesn't it matter? What difference does it make so long as the courts are able to arrive at results which square with our sense of justice?

6. *No recovery for a monstrosity:* In *Dunnebacke v. Pittman,*[121] the Supreme Court of Wisconsin rejected a builder's claim to compensation based on unjust enrichment. Pittman had done various small jobs for the Gilligans on their property on Lake Michigan in Kenosha County. He and Mrs. Gilligan several times discussed the need for a breakwater to protect the property from erosion, but they never agreed on specifications or a price and Mrs. Gilligan never gave a go-ahead for the project. While the Gilligans were away for two weeks, Pittman built a massive V-shaped wall that made it impossible to go from one side of the property to the other along the beach

---

117. *Id.* at 892–93, 600 P.2d at 1359–60 (citing Citizens Eng'g Co. v. North Am. Aviation, Inc., 65 Cal. 2d 396, 410, 420 P.2d 713, 723 (1966)).

118. *Id.* at 897, 600 P.2d at 1354.

119. *Id.* at 897, 600 P.2d at 1355.

120. 26 Wis. 2d 683, 133 N.W.2d 267 (1965).

121. 216 Wis. 305, 257 N.W. 30 (1934).

without stepping into the water. When she saw the new breakwater on her return, Mrs. Gilligan told Pittman it was a monstrosity and she wanted it removed. The court found that no contract had been made and that there was no unjust retention of a benefit to justify restitution recovery.

How is *Dunnebacke* different from *Vickery v. Richie*? How is it different from *Kearns v. Andree* (discussed in Note 4, *supra*)? Can you rationalize the no-recovery result in *Dunnebacke* with the recoveries in the other two cases? If not, which one reaches the better result?

While the case appears to be a suit between the builder of the wall and the property owners, the record indicates that the supplier of the cement used in the wall was never paid. It was attempting to assert the builder's rights. Pittman, the builder of the wall, did not have sufficient assets to pay for the cement. He was a small handyman builder, and the case took place in the middle of the Great Depression. The supplier was seeking to assert Pittman's claim, if any, against the property owner. We can wonder whether the case might have been decided differently had Pittman himself been the real party in interest. As between a supplier of materials and an owner who received little tangible benefit, who should take the loss of the value of the cement?

Those who work on the property of others or supply materials are often protected by statutes giving them liens on property that has been improved. However, these statutes require the mechanic or materialman to follow certain procedures. For example, Wis. Stat. § 779.41(1) provides: "Every mechanic and every keeper of a garage or shop, and every employer of a mechanic who transports, makes, alters, repairs or does any work on personal property *at the request of the owner or legal possessor of the personal property*, has a lien thereon for his just and reasonable charges therefor, ... and may retain possession of the personal property until the charges are paid." They also protect those who have a recorded security interest. Several cases involve attempts by those who otherwise would have been protected by these statutes but who failed to follow procedures to assert a right to recover for unjust enrichment. The Supreme Court of Wisconsin has been unsympathetic to attempts to get around the statutory requirements for liens. The restitutionary end-run has not worked.[122]

---

122. *See, e.g.*, Gebhardt Bros., Inc. v. Brimmel, 31 Wis. 2d 581, 143 N.W.2d 479 (1966); Indus. Credit Co. v. Inland G.M. Diesel, Inc., 51 Wis. 2d 520, 187 N.W.2d 157 (1971).

Chapter 2

INCOMPLETE PLANNING, FLEXIBILITY, AND ENFORCEABILITY

A. SPECIFYING ENDS BUT NOT MEANS: "WE CAN WORK IT OUT!"

1. Building Construction and Ordinary People

KLIMEK v. PERISICH

Oregon Supreme Court
231 Or. 71, 371 P.2d 956 (1962)

PERRY, J.

This is an action brought by the plaintiff to recover damages from the defendant for breach of contract to remodel an old dwelling house into a rooming house.

The jury returned a verdict for the plaintiff which was set aside and judgment entered notwithstanding the verdict for the defendant. The plaintiff has appealed.

[Much of the court's opinion consists of extracts from the trial court testimony. We offer a summary of it here. At the beginning of the opinion, the court observed that "both plaintiff and defendant were born in Yugoslavia, and while they now speak and understand English, the record discloses limitations in this regard." It seems that Mrs. Klimek, the plaintiff, had purchased an old building with hopes of turning it into a boarding house. She had conversations with Mr. Perisich, a builder, about the remodeling. Apparently, Mr. Perisich told Mrs. Klimek that he was not sure how many rooms she could get out of the house but that the cost of refurbishing would run $8,000, $9,000, or at the most $10,000.

Blueprints for the remodeling were obtained but no specifications covering materials to be used were ever drafted. The parties did not enter into a formal contract; Mr. Perisich simply began remodeling the building. Although Mr. Perisich was supervising the job, he was paid the same as the other carpenters. Mr. Perisich received no compensation for helping Mrs. Klimek obtain plans and building permits. Mrs. Klimek herself testified that no arrangements were made between the parties as to who would do the required plumbing, heating, or electrical wiring, but as these items became necessary both she and Mr. Perisich would search for the most reasonable price. Mrs. Klimek took care of paying bills for materials, services, and the workmen's wages. Mrs. Klimek ran out of money before the work was done, was unable to get financing, and sued Mr. Perisich to recover damages.]

We have set forth only the evidence of the plaintiff, as this is an action at law, and if there is substantial evidence of the formation of a contract, as sued upon, the finding of the jury must be sustained....

To constitute a contract such as here present, there must be an offer and an acceptance....

An offer must be certain so that upon an unqualified acceptance the nature and extent of the obligations of each party are fixed and may be determined with reasonable certainty....

As to an acceptance of an offer: "It is well settled that when a contract is to be founded on offer and acceptance, it must be shown that the latter coincides precisely with the former. Unless this appears, there is no agreement." ... *Northwestern Agencies v. Flynn*, 138 Or. 101, 106, 5 P.2d 530.

In other words, there must be a meeting of the minds as to the obligations each assumes under the contract before it can be said that a contract exists.

In the matter before us the plaintiff agreed to pay money and the defendant agreed to render services; therefore both the amount to be paid and the services to be rendered must be reasonably certain.

As stated by ... CORBIN ON CONTRACTS, § 100, p. 315:

> It is not always the price in money that is left uncertain in an agreement; sometimes it is that for which the price is to be paid. If no method is agreed upon for rendering this subject matter sufficiently definite for enforcement, the agreement must nearly always fail of legal effect; it is not customary for courts to fill the gap by finding that a "reasonable" amount of goods or land or labor has been agreed upon as the exchange for the money....

The trial court, in granting judgment for the defendant, notwithstanding the verdict of the jury, based its opinion upon the indefiniteness of the subject matter of the offer. The plaintiff contends that the subject matter of the offer is sufficiently definite in that the parties agreed upon a maximum amount to be paid by the plaintiff for the remodeling of a certain building; that the extent and requirements for remodeling were certain, although no specifications were agreed upon; that the minimum requirements of the building code of the city of Portland required certain materials to be used, and this supplied the lack of specifications as to the work to be done and the material to be used by the defendant. Defendant contends that no agreement existed other than to perform labor at an hourly rate and there was no agreement as to the extent of remodeling or the materials to be used, and therefore no contract existed between the parties.

The difficulty with plaintiff's contentions that the minimal requirements of the city building code are sufficiently definite as a substitute for specifications is that there is no evidence that the parties agreed that compliance with the minimal requirements of the building code would constitute a satisfactory execution of the purported contract, and also there is no evidence that the building code specifies the extent of the remodeling, or the kinds or types of materials that could be satisfactorily used in the remodeling of this particular. Also there is no evidence of what the parties agreed was necessary to constitute a remodeling of the structure.

The building code of the city of Portland was not introduced into evidence, and therefore the jury could not determine whether the building code covered these requirements....

The plaintiff cites and relies upon a number of cases, such as *Helm v. Speith*, 298 Ky. 225, 182 S.W.2d 635. [There] the parties agreed that the building should be contracted to comply with the minimal requirements of the Federal Housing Administration, and the Federal Housing Administration requirements were introduced into evidence.... [Here] as previously stated, there is no evidence that the parties agreed that the minimal requirements of the Portland building code were agreed upon as a basis of their negotiations, nor was it introduced into evidence.

The trial court correctly held that there was no contract.

There is additional reason why the judgment of the trial court should be affirmed. An examination of the evidence of the plaintiff, in our opinion, is such that reasonable minds could reach only the conclusion that at all times the plaintiff knew that the statements made by the defendant with relation to the cost of remodeling of the structure were only estimates and that the plaintiff knew this to be such, therefore the words and actions of the defendant could only be construed as not an offer to remodel the building to the satisfaction of the plaintiff at a fixed maximum amount, nor as an acceptance of such an offer.

The judgment of the trial court is affirmed.

NOTES AND QUESTIONS

1. *An additional argument from defendant's brief:* In his brief, defendant argued that a promise to guarantee the cost of a construction project is enforceable only if there is consideration for it. In this case, the defendant received only a carpenter's wages for the work that he did. There was no mechanism by which defendant could share in any cost savings on component parts of the project:

> There is no question but what a contractor can guarantee a maximum cost of construction, but before that is done there must be an allegation and proof that the agreed figure that is the ceiling price must be a guaranteed maximum cost. In the case at bar, it is clear that the parties merely agreed that this "would be the cost." There is no allegation or proof that the defendant guaranteed this to be the maximum cost and there is no allegation or proof that

defendant agreed to be liable for any costs in excess of $10,000. Nor is there any consideration for the alleged guarantee.

2. *The building code as a gap filler:* Should the Supreme Court of Oregon have found that the contract was too indefinite to be enforced, in view of the jury's verdict for the plaintiff? Plaintiff argued in her brief that the parties implicitly agreed that the building code provided minimum specifications. Apparently, the jury was not charged that it needed to decide this issue. If we assume that plaintiff had raised this question at trial and in her request for jury instructions, should the appellate court have remanded the case for a new trial on this question? Would this depend on the degree to which the Portland building code specifies what is required in a rooming house?

3. *How formal must a building contract be?* In *Lichty v. Merzenich,*[1] Dr. Merzenich hired Mr. Lichty to build a residence. Under the original contract, Lichty was paid by the hour for his services, plus $0.25 for each hour of additional labor employed on the job. A year later, the project was proving to be slower and more costly than expected. Dr. Merzenich prepared a list of things he thought necessary to finish the job. He asked Lichty what it would cost to complete them. Lichty argued that Dr. Merzenich asked for an estimate. Dr. Merzenich contended that he asked for a bid.

A few days later they met at the building site and discussed matters. Lichty suggested that they each write a figure on pieces of paper and turn them over simultaneously. They did. Dr. Merzenich's figure was $5,000; Lichty's was $6,500. Merzenich testified:

> [W]e agreed that he would do it. He agreed to do it for [$]6500 with a provision that we allow plus or minus 10 percent, not to exceed $6800 total.

> In other words, if it came in under [$]6200, I was to receive the benefit of the doubt on the 10 percent. If it came in over, I would pay him over.[2]

Dr. Merzenich also testified that Lichty would not sign the slip because he did not have a contractor's license, but they shook hands on it.

The trial court found there was a contract for a specific sum. The Supreme Court of Oregon affirmed. Justice Linde said: "[T]he manner of arriving at the remaining costs by turning over slips on which each party had proposed a sum would seem an odd way for a builder and a dentist to arrive at an estimate of labor and materials; it appears more consistent with an attempt to negotiate an agreed price."[3] The court continued:

> Plaintiff also contends that the terms of the parties' discussion of the work to be completed, while adequate as an estimate, were too indefinite to form the essential elements of a contract, citing *Klimek v. Perisich.*... The decision [in the Klimek case] illustrates the relevant principles but also the limited usefulness of matching facts among individually unique, nonformalized per-

---

1. 278 Or. 209, 563 P.2d 690 (1977).
2. *Id.* at 211, 563 P.2d at 692.
3. *Id.* at 213, 563 P.2d at 692.

sonal transactions.... Dr. Merzenich's list of work to be completed, which in another setting might have left a contractor's commitment too undefined, here drew meaning from the parties' collaboration on the project for a full year.[4]

While Justice Linde may be able to avoid contrasting these cases because he is a judge, the rest of us cannot put aside the point so easily. Is there a difference between the *Klimek* and *Lichty* cases? Does the difference turn on the definiteness and completeness of the agreement, or on something else?

4. *Promissory estoppel as an alternative when there is reliance?* In an officially unreported decision, the U.S. District Court in Oregon relied on *Klimek* in another case involving an indefinite promise, *Kraft v. Arden*.[5] Kraft, a provider of piano tuning and repair services, sued a piano supply manufacturer and its principal owner, Arden, for breach of an alleged contract for an exclusive distributorship of the manufacturer's piano supplies. After discussions with Arden, Kraft believed they had an agreement on "fundamentals," but he admitted that many details had not been settled, including the amount of a minimum monthly order requirement, what sort of infrastructure and how much capacity Kraft would be expected to develop, the timetable for doing so, and how much Kraft would pay for customer lists. The court cited *Klimek* for the principle that "the subject matter of the agreement must be sufficiently definite to determine the nature and extent of the obligations of each party." The court went on to consider a promissory estoppel (reliance on a promise) cause of action and found that the promise, if any, was so indefinite that there was no reasonable basis for Arden and his company to foresee Kraft's reliance, which involved acquiring warehouse space, office space, and computer systems. It said an indefinite promise can sometimes justify reliance when there is a basis for the promisor to reasonably expect reliance, such as an employment relationship or a request that the promisee rely. Finding no such basis, the court granted summary judgment to the defendants.

Would reliance on a promise have been a better theory than standard contract formation in *Klimek*? Was there a basis for the promisor to expect reliance? If so, what should be the remedy?

5. *The limits of the law for ordinary people:* In the *Klimek* case, it is likely that neither party came away from the Oregon courts thinking justice was done. Of course, in theory Mrs. Klimek could have gone to an architect and a large construction company. They would have given her a firm price and a form contract that would have protected their interests and few of hers. Mr. Perisich could have hired a lawyer to draft an agreement limiting his liability so he would never have been sued. However, Mrs. Klimek and Mr. Perisich lacked the education, experience, wealth, and social status to make detailed legal planning realistic. Could the court have done any better to compensate for these problems?

---

4. *Id.* at 213, 563 P.2d at 692–93.
5. 2008 U.S. Dist. LEXIS 91001.

2. The UCC and Indefiniteness:
Transactions in Goods between Major Corporations

BETHLEHEM STEEL CORP. v. LITTON INDUSTRIES, INC.

Pennsylvania Superior Court
321 Pa. Super. 357, 468 A.2d 748 (1983)

WICKERSHAM, J.

The central issue in this case is whether a certain written option agreement is a contract. [The trial judge, sitting without a jury, had ruled that the plaintiff-appellant had failed to meet its burden to show the parties intended to be contractually bound.]

Basically the complaint alleged that on or about April 25, 1968, Litton entered into an agreement with Bethlehem whereby Litton would construct and deliver and Bethlehem would purchase a one-thousand-foot self-unloading ore vessel. The vessel constructed under the agreement was delivered, accepted, and the price paid therefor.

The complaint further alleged that Litton extended to Bethlehem by letter dated April 25, 1968 "a written offer good until December 31, 1968, for the entry into an option agreement for five vessels." Furthermore, it was alleged that on or about December 31, 1968, Bethlehem accepted Litton's offer to enter into an option agreement under which Bethlehem was granted the right for a period of five years after the execution of the option agreement to obtain from Litton from one to five vessels for prices varying between $22,400,000 and $18,400,000 each. Further, the complaint alleged that Bethlehem, pursuant to the option agreement, by letter dated November 16, 1973, exercised its option for two vessels and thereby ordered the first and second vessels in accordance with the option agreement. On December 26, 1973, Bethlehem, pursuant to the option agreement, exercised its option for an additional (third) vessel.

Finally, the complaint alleged that Litton expressly and unequivocally refused to perform in accordance with its obligations under the option agreement; that Litton demanded the payment of a price for each vessel many millions of dollars in excess of the price provided for in the option agreement and indicated delivery dates substantially later than the delivery provided in the option agreement. Damages were sought in a sum in excess of $95,000,000.00 together with interest and costs....

In its defense, Litton responded, *inter alia*: (1) PX-1 (the letter of December 31, 1968) was never intended to be and was not a contract; (2) no contract was formed in any event because the vital terms left for later negotiation could not be filled by the court on a reasonably certain basis; (3) any purported "option agreement" had been rejected prior to exercise by Bethlehem's assertions that it would "never" order another vessel from Litton; (4) since an "option" unsupported by consideration is revocable at will, any purported "option agreement" had been revoked prior to exercise by Litton's notice to Bethlehem that the Erie shipyard was to be closed; (5) any purported "option" had never been properly exercised; and (6) Litton had never breached or repudiated any "agreement" which might have existed.

On June 28, 1978, a non-jury trial began and Judge Louik filed his adjudication on June 6, 1979. It provided, in part, as follows:

[Beginning of an extended excerpt from the trial court opinion.]

After a protracted trial of approximately nine months with over 12,000 pages of testimony and some 500 exhibits, this matter is now before the Court for determination. The claim in excess of 95 million dollars, together with a counterclaim, is based on a two-page letter between two giant corporations....

For background purposes, it should be noted that on April 25, 1968, at a formal signing ceremony, the plaintiff and defendant entered into a ship-construction contract for a newly designed 1,000-foot self-unloading ore vessel. This vessel, known as Hull 101, was commissioned "The *Cort.*" ...

In addition, there is in evidence as PX-4 a document which was executed on that very same day, April 25, 1968, together with a document dated December 31, 1968, in evidence as PX-1. These are the documents in issue in the instant case.

The primary and fundamental question now before the Court is whether or not there has been an option contract. The plaintiff's claim is based upon the following two-page letter:

Erie Marine, Inc.
Erie, Pennsylvania
April 25, 1968

Bethlehem Steel Corporation
Bethlehem, Pennsylvania
Attn: Ralph K. Smith

Gentlemen:

Reference is made to the ship construction contract signed by our companies this date for the construction by us of a 1,000-foot self-unloading ore vessel for you. Reference is also made to my letter to you of this date extending to you an option to purchase either one or two additional vessels upon the terms therein set forth.

We hereby extend to you an offer to enter into an option agreement to have us construct for you from one to five additional vessels in accordance with "Specifications covering the Construction of a Self-Unloading Bulk Carrier for Bethlehem Steel Corporation" (Number Y 917) dated March 1968, addendum number 1 thereto dated March 28, 1968, and addendum number 2 thereto dated April 17, 1968. This offer to enter into an option agreement shall be firm and irrevocable until December 31, 1968, at 5:00 P.M. E.S.T.

The terms of the option agreement are to be as follows:

(a) The specifications for the vessels shall be the specifications referred to above, except for mutually agreeable reduced test schedules of the vessels, if the testing of the vessel to be delivered under the contract executed this date proves successful.

(b) Bethlehem to have the right at any time within five years after the effective date of the option agreement to order from one to not more than a total of five vessels, for delivery within 24 months from the date of the order for the first vessel ordered and for delivery within 24 months plus four months for each additional vessel ordered within any one calendar year; provided however no vessel shall be scheduled for delivery between November 31 and March 31.

(c) The price of the vessel shall be as follows:

1st vessel ordered	$22,400,000.00
2nd " "	$21,400,000.00
3rd " "	$20,400,000.00
4th " "	$19,400,000.00
5th " "	$18,400,000.00

(d) The vessel prices are subject to escalation for both labor and material for a base price of $20,400,000.00 for each vessel and based upon Fourth Quarter 1968 mutually agreed upon index such as:

Material—"Material index for Bureau of Ships steel vessel contracts" furnished to the Naval Ship Systems Command by the Bureau of Labor Statistics of the U.S. Department of Labor.

Labor—"Index of changes in straight-time average hourly earnings for selected shipyards" (June 1962 = 100) for steel ship construction, furnished to the Naval Ship Systems Command by the Bureau of Labor Statistics of the U.S. Department of Labor.

At the time of exercise of the option for any vessel, the escalation shall be computed to the date of contract execution, and an appropriate contract clause will be included therein providing for quarterly escalation thereafter. We will furnish you the labor and material percentages subject to escalation by May 15, 1968.

(e) The terms and conditions of the ship construction contracts to be in accordance with the attached terms and conditions and any other mutually agreed to terms and conditions and shall contain a clause giving to Bethlehem the right to cancel at any time upon the payment of all of our costs incurred to date of cancellation, including similar vendor and subcontractor cancellation charges, plus 15 percent of such costs.

Very truly yours,
George K. Geiger

In response to this letter, a letter dated December 31, 1968, was sent by Bethlehem to Erie which stated in part: "We hereby accept your offer of an option to have you construct for us from one to five additional vessels." In all other respects, the letter of December 31, 1968, is merely identical repetition of the language in the letter of April 25, 1968....

On November 16, 1973, plaintiff sent a letter to defendant stating that it exercises its option to order two vessels and then on December 26, 1973, plaintiff sent another letter to defendant stating that it exercises its option to order a third vessel....

Defendant did not enter into any ship construction contract with plaintiff and did not construct any vessels under the letters of November 16, 1973, and December 26, 1973....

Conclusion of Law

1. Bethlehem has not sustained its burden of proof, either in law or in fact, of imposing liability on Litton-Erie, and a finding accordingly will be entered in favor of Litton-Erie on Bethlehem's claim....

[End of excerpt from trial court opinion.]

Scope of Review

It is quite clear that the scope of appellate review of a finding on contractual intent is limited — indeed narrowly circumscribed.

The "intent to contract" is a question of fact for the trier-of-fact.... It is axiomatic that a trial judge's findings of fact, sustained by the Court *en banc*, have the weight of a jury verdict and cannot be disturbed on appeal if supported by competent evidence in the record....

We have reviewed the entire trial record and viewing the evidence in the light most favorable to the victorious party below, a fair distillation of the evidence would indicate the following scenario.

This controversy arose out of ship construction on the Great Lakes. Litton, a newcomer to the Lakes, tried unsuccessfully through its subsidiary, Erie, to develop a market for a unique and revolutionary supertanker-type ore vessel, 1,000 feet long with novel self-unloading features. In seven years of effort (from 1967 to 1973), however, Litton sold only one ore vessel ("Hull 101" [the *Cort*]) — to Bethlehem.

In 1968, Litton and Bethlehem exchanged two incomplete letters, one dated April 25, 1968 (PX-4), and the other dated December 31, 1968 (PX-1), concerning an offer to negotiate a long-term option agreement for construction of up to five novel multimillion-dollar vessels at Litton's new shipyard. In the words of Judge Louik: "If anything, there is one matter that is absolutely clear, and that is that the writing provides that further agreements between the parties are necessary." During the ensuing years, Litton repeatedly attempted to interest Bethlehem in commencing the negotiations contemplated. These efforts were in vain, however, and from late 1972 through early 1973 Litton repeatedly informed Bethlehem of its intention to close the Erie shipyard unless ship construction orders were immediately forthcoming. When Bethlehem disclaimed interest in purchasing any additional ships and no other contracts were obtained, Litton began closing its Erie yard and disbanding its workforce.

Thereafter, however, Bethlehem notified Litton that it wished to negotiate a ship construction contract pursuant to PX-1. When the parties were unable to agree on contractual terms, Bethlehem commenced this action, contending that despite the parties' failure to agree upon the myriad terms explicitly left for future negotiations, the mere exchange of the letters in 1968 bound the parties to a "contract" for the construction of novel ships worth millions of dollars.

The April 25, 1968 Letter (PX-4)

After four months of careful negotiation and drafting and redrafting of contract terms, representatives of Litton and Bethlehem met on April 25, 1968, for the ceremonial exchange of a contract for the immediate construction of Hull 101, the only 1000-foot vessel actually sold by Litton, for the firm fixed price of $17,994,138.00 ("Hull 101 Contract"). Bethlehem's Board of Directors had insisted upon "great precision" in every aspect of the sale, especially price. The Hull 101 Contract was fully performed and is not at issue here.

During the two to three hours that the parties were together on April 25, 1968, primarily for the exchange of the Hull 101 contract, they jointly drafted a two-page letter (PX-4), extending a last-minute sales promotional offer to negotiate a long-term option agreement for up to five additional Hull 101 type vessels. The parties clearly understood that PX-4 was not part of the consideration for the Hull 101 Contract. With one exception, none of the representatives at the April 25 meeting even was aware before that meeting that such an offer was to be made or drafted that day. On its face, PX-4 clearly was not an option agreement; rather, it expressly provided for future negotiations which, if successfully completed, would have resulted in an option agreement which, in turn, if properly exercised, would have resulted in formal execution of a formal written ship construction contract.

In hurriedly drafting PX-4 during a part of their short meeting on April 25, the parties explicitly agreed that price escalation would be included in any long-term option agreement and ship construction contract upon which they might subsequently agree. The parties further expressly acknowledged, however, that because escalation was so critical and so complex, they would postpone the negotiations necessary for agreement upon that vital subject.

PX-4 thus was jointly drafted during the less than three-hour meeting on April 25 in the form of a two-step offer to enter into a future option agreement in order to provide until the end of the year for the parties to investigate and develop the terms of an appropriate escalation clause and the other important matter intentionally left for future negotiation and agreement.

Having taken more than four months to negotiate a contract for a single vessel (Hull 101), on which construction was to begin immediately for a fixed price with no escalation, the parties recognized that negotiation of a long-term option agreement for up to five novel multimillion-dollar vessels providing for price escalation would be infinitely more complex and time consuming.

On several occasions from May through November of 1968, Litton sought to negotiate the terms of an option agreement. On each occasion, Bethlehem replied that it was not yet willing to spend the time and effort required for such negotiations, since it would not even consider additional 1000-foot ore vessels until the revolutionary Hull 101 had been successfully operated for at least one season.

By December of 1968, aware that the PX-4 offer was about to lapse, but still unwilling to devote the time necessary to negotiate the terms essential for a definitive option agreement and ship construction contract, Bethlehem sought to preserve the status quo.

Between April 25 and December 31, 1968, there were no discussions, negotiations, or agreements between the parties with respect to any of the terms, including escalation, expressly left for future negotiation and mutual agreement under PX-4.

In short, whatever the parties had intended by drafting PX-4 was unchanged by PX-1. In PX-4 the parties had explicitly contemplated negotiations and agreements necessary to create a binding option contract. PX-1 did not resolve any of the substantive terms left open for negotiation in PX-4; as the record clearly reveals, it was adopted as an accommodation to Bethlehem's request for a "holding pattern."

From 1968 through 1973, Litton attracted no other customers to its Erie shipyard. Indeed, by early 1973, Litton officials warned Bethlehem that the Erie yard would be closed unless Bethlehem ordered additional ships. Bethlehem officials had previously stated, however, that they were "disgusted" by the "slow" construction of Hull 101, and by 1973, rather than express any objection to the closing of the Erie yard, repeatedly insisted that they would never order any additional ships from Litton. Thus, without any hope of future business from Bethlehem, Litton "mothballed" its Erie yard.

Thereafter, in full knowledge of the fact that the Erie Shipyard had dismissed most of its labor force for lack of business, Bethlehem notified Litton by letter that it was planning to "exercise its options" for ore vessels. Significantly, however, Bethlehem expressly acknowledged that the terms of an option agreement had to be negotiated before Bethlehem could exercise any option.

At subsequent meetings, Litton advised Bethlehem that although it had closed down its shipyard in reliance upon Bethlehem's representations, it was willing to build vessels if the parties could reach agreement on a ship construction contract, which Litton was at all times willing to negotiate. The parties, however, never agreed on any of the material terms left open in PX-4 and PX-1, including escalation — found by the trial judge to be "one of the most critical provisions of a ship construction contract". Nor would Bethlehem accept any of Litton's alternative proposals.

Judge Louik carefully considered all the relevant factors under the common law and under the Uniform Commercial Code — the letters themselves, the discussions at the time of the exchange of the letters, the surrounding circumstances, subsequent conduct, the nature of the contemplated construction contract, and the parties' prior dealings—and found that the parties did not intend to enter a binding agreement until they mutually agreed on the critical terms intentionally deferred, including the terms of a price escalation clause, and reduced those terms to a formal ship construction contract. The Court alternatively found that under § 2-204(3) of the UCC, no contract had been formed—because the Court simply could not, on "a reasonably certain basis," fill in the price escalation terms and other missing contract provisions in order to provide for "an appropriate remedy." ...

Returning now to relevant portions of the adjudication of Judge Louik dated June 6, 1979, our review of the record supports the correctness of the court's conclusions, as follows:

[The court again quotes from the trial court opinion.]

Discussion

While a great many legal issues have been presented by both parties in this trial, their determination and even their relevance depend upon the resolution of one elementary factual dispute: Did both Bethlehem and Litton intend a legally binding option to arise from the two-page letter of April 25, 1968? ...

Uniform Commercial Code

One of the contentions of Bethlehem is that these agreements come within the Uniform Commercial Code and, therefore, gaps, (if any appear in the documents), may be filled in by the Court....

Even if the Uniform Commercial Code is applicable, the Court must first find that there was intent to enter into a contract by the two letters (PX-4 and PX-1). The same criteria has to be used in this regard as is used in determining whether or not there is a contract at common law. Even if the Court had found that there was such an intent, there then arises the matter of ability of the Court to fill in the gaps because, if anything is clear in PX-4 and PX-1, it is that gaps exist which must be filled in.

If a contract did exist, there are three general areas in which gaps appear which would require the Court's intervention to fill.

The first term obviously left open was the original escalation index which would be used to calculate the increase in cost per vessel over the time between PX-1 to the date of contract execution.

The only aspect of this stage of escalation that the documents provided is that an index method of escalation shall be used for this portion of escalation, and that the index shall be mutually agreed upon, as evidenced by the language "mutually agreed upon index such as." Because the parties established the method of arriving at the index as mutual agreement, and because of the complexity of negotiations of escalation clauses in the shipbuilding industry, the Court cannot fill in such a gap in light of Code § 2-305 (4).

The second gap relates to "second-stage escalation," which PX-4 and PX-1 establishes as the escalation from the execution of the construction contract to the end of the escalation period: "An appropriate contract clause will be included therein providing for quarterly escalation thereafter."

An escalation clause is a complex, detailed contractual provision negotiated between parties to provide a means necessary to calculate and pay escalation. It is an equitable concept that escalation clauses must be such as not to give the builder a windfall nor to have the builder suffer losses due to inflation. Because of inflation since the middle 1960s, the escalation clauses became one of the most critical provisions of a ship construction contract. There are many essential elements to be negotiated in an escalation clause, some of which are very critical, such as the indexes to be used, the escalatable amount, the amount escalatable each computation period, the duration of escalation, payment, and the method of computation. These elements can have numerous possible variations resulting from negotiations between the parties. One of the most critical elements and perhaps the heart of an escalation clause is the amount escalatable each computation period. This is called the "apportionment," which can have an infinite number of possible variations and will vary from ship to ship depending upon the time of construction, the place of construction, needs and desires of the parties.

The third gap which the Court would have to fill if it found a contract otherwise existed, arises from the language indicated that the terms and conditions were to be in accordance with the sample contract and "any other mutually agreed-upon terms and conditions." In view of the fact that the sample form of contract was for a fixed-price contract, there must of necessity be changes required since the writings clearly indicate that the parties contemplated an escalation contract. Such a contract would require additional terms and conditions from those that appear in the sample form.

In addition, there are numerous other terms which might be expected to be in a ship construction contract of this magnitude. Evidence of this can be found in the contract (DX-12) proposed by the plaintiffs at the September 24, 1973, meeting with defendants. This proposed contract varied substantially from the sample contract in at least 12 separate items (See Finding 28). These altered or added terms strongly suggest that, at least in the mind of Bethlehem, there were many items left out of the sample contract, or left to be negotiated at a later time.

The breadth of these gaps can only be appreciated in light of the nature of the vessel. According to David Klinges, Bethlehem's Senior Maritime Attorney:

> As you can appreciate this was to be a new departure for maritime transportation for Great Lakes. It contemplated a new revolutionary way of building ships and a new revolutionary way of transporting and discharging.

The apportionment in quarterly escalation, if nothing else, must be one to be negotiated between the parties. Apportionment does not depend upon the actual use of labor or material in a particular quarter, but is an item negotiated between the parties depending upon what the parties are aiming at, either for the purpose of securing payments earlier during the construction period or for a later payment, but higher escalation. The extent of the escalation period can also vary, the payment of escalation amounts can vary, and a host of factors can move the parties to a variety of allocation of apportionment. This is also recognized by plaintiff in its Request for Findings, Point 30.59, where they ask the Court to find:

> In the shipbuilding industry, a party entering a contract would, in negotiating an escalation clause, submit to the other party the form of escalation clause desired, and if the owner submitted a proposal that the builder did not like, the builder would make his feelings known to the buyer. Point 30.59.

All of the expert testimony indicated that such clauses could not be materialized from the air by the Court. Because of the nature of negotiations in shipbuilding and the extreme complexity of the undertaking, such a clause would require careful negotiations between the parties and would need to be custom-tailored to fit the project. There is nothing in the record upon which the Court could extract such a clause.

Because of the nature of the gaps as has been discussed in this Option, it would appear that only the parties are the exclusive entities capable of filling in the gaps. Because these gaps are so wide, the Court cannot make a new contract for the parties.

When we consider all of the above elements and the fact that the parties involved here are two of the largest corporations in this country, and PX-4 is only a two-page letter, the language of Mr. Justice Cohen in the case of *Essner v. Shoemaker*, 393 Pa. 422, [143 A.2d 364 (1958)] is most appropriate:

> It is difficult to believe that the principals, experienced in real estate dealings as they were, would intend to ... [assent unequivocally] to an oral agreement in a transaction involving more than a quarter of a million dollars, [and] complicated by assignments, mortgages, and taxes.

[End of second extended extract from trial court opinion.]

... In summary, we agree with the finding of the lower court that there was no enforceable contract between the parties.... Order affirmed.

[JUDGE HESTER's dissent follows. ROWLEY and WIEAND, JJ., joined in it.]

... For the reasons that follow, I would reverse and remand to the lower court for further proceedings consistent with this Opinion....

The threshold issue to be resolved in the instant appeal concerns the contractual intent of the parties. Unlike the majority, which views this issue as a question of fact, I believe the issue of contractual intent is a question of law or ultimate fact. Undeniably, the basic findings of fact of the lower court should not be disturbed if these findings are based upon competent evidence, unless the lower court committed an abuse of discretion or error of law in admitting the evidence from which the findings of fact were derived. However, the contractual intent of the parties as an ultimate fact or conclusion of law is subject to independent appellate scrutiny....

[I]t is clear that the Code applies to the instant case. The issue, as refined by the language of the Code, thus becomes: "Did the parties intend to enter into a contract for sale, whereby Bethlehem would have the right to exercise its option to order specially-manufactured future goods from Litton, resulting in a contract to sell future goods?" ...

The Code states [under the heading "Options and cooperation respecting performance"]:

> (a) Specifying particulars of performance—An agreement for sale which is otherwise sufficiently definite (§ 2204(c)) to be a contract is not made invalid by the fact that it leaves particulars of performance to be specified by one of the parties. Any such specification must be made in good faith and within limits set by commercial reasonableness." 13 Pa. C.S.A. § 2311(a).

In the instant case, the time of performance, and whether performance would be required at all, was specifically left to Bethlehem as an option. The time within which Bethlehem was required to exercise its option was specified, so there is no issue concerning "commercial reasonableness." ...

The lower court did not specifically decide whether the Code applies. Rather, the trial court improperly relied upon numerous pre-Code decisions and other authority not involving a contract for the sale of goods.

For instance, the lower court repeatedly cited *Upsal Street Realty Company v. Rubin*, 326 Pa. 327, 192 A. 481 (1937), involving an application for a lease, which along with location, term, and rental amount, provided, "Selection of colors will be made after lease is signed." Citing a comment to § 26 of the Restatement of the Law of Contracts, the Court in *Upsal* found that this language was evidence that the parties intended no binding agreement by stating:

> [I]f the preliminary agreement is incomplete, it being apparent that the determination of certain details is deferred until the writing is made out; or if an intention is manifested in any way that legal obligations between the parties shall be deferred until the writing is made, the preliminary negotiations and agreements do not constitute a contract.

Id. at 330, 192 A. at 483. Referring to the above-quoted section of *Upsal*, the lower court reasoned:

> In light of the formality of the signing of the first fixed-price contract for Hull 101 [the *Cort*], this language dictates that a final writing be signed before the parties intended to be legally bound.... Another aspect of this language indicates a conclusion that [the letter of April 25, 1968] was merely an expression of preliminary accord.

As will be further discussed *infra*, the lower court's reliance on *Upsal* is misplaced, since the principles stated therein were specifically displaced by particular provisions of the Code. 13 Pa. C.S.A. § 1103....

From § 2204 of the Code, it is clear that the existence of a contract is initially dependent upon the intent of the parties. If the parties have intended to contractually obligate and benefit each other, their contract is enforceable even if certain terms are left open or are left to be agreed upon in the future. In other words, the Code specifically contemplates that the parties may "agree to agree" with respect to certain terms. The comment to § 2204 acknowledges that, depending upon how many terms are uncertain, an agreement may be defeated due to "indefiniteness" if there is no reasonably certain basis for granting an appropriate remedy. However, the Code specifically provides "gap-filling" so as to avoid defeating a contract which the parties otherwise intended....

Under the Code, parties can expressly agree to be contractually bound, even though certain terms are left open to be negotiated or agreed upon at a future time. It does not matter whether the original agreement is "a preliminary accord," "an agreement to agree," or "an agreement to negotiate." The crucial inquiry is whether the parties intended to enter into an agreement; and, if the parties left certain terms to be negotiated at a future time, then those parties contemplate that those terms will be filled in, on a reasonable basis, through the mutual good-faith negotiations of the parties....

The Code also states: "Every contract or duty within this title imposes an obligation of good faith in its performance or enforcement." 13 Pa. C.S.A. § 1203. Therefore, if parties agree to agree concerning certain open contractual terms, then both parties must attempt to negotiate those terms, on a reasonable basis and in good faith.

As evinced by the letter of April 25 and December 31, 1968, as well as other discussions, negotiations, communications, and "course of dealing" between the parties, it is clear that the parties intended to enter into an agreement that would give Bethlehem the right to exercise its option to order as many as five 1000-foot, self-unloading ore vessels from Litton at any time during a five-year period.

The letter of April 25, 1968, from Litton to Bethlehem states, *inter alia*:

> We hereby extend to you an offer to enter into an option agreement to have us construct for you from one to five additional vessels ... this offer to enter into an option agreement shall be firm and irrevocable until December 31, 1968, at 5 p.m. E.S.T.

This correspondence expressly represents itself to be "an offer to enter into an option agreement," which is "firm and irrevocable." See 13 Pa. C.S.A. § 2205.

The letter of December 31, 1968, from Bethlehem to Litton states: "We hereby accept your offer of an option to have you construct for us from one to five additional vessels." Said letter of December 31, 1968, was executed by George K. Geiger on behalf of Litton and Erie under a heading "AGREED TO."

These two letters are "sufficient to show agreement" for the purposes of 13 Pa. C.S.A. § 2204(a). The letter of December 31, 1968, operated as an acceptance of Litton's offer to enter into an option agreement, for the purposes of 13 Pa. C.S.A. § 2206(a).

Furthermore, the conduct of the parties manifests that they both recognized the existence of such a contract. [Judge Hester then enumerated several letters in which representatives of Litton and Bethlehem seemed to acknowledge that a binding agreement was in force.]

In determining that the parties had not intended to create a legally binding option agreement, the lower court heavily relied on "the fact that the parties involved here are two of the largest corporations in this country, and [the letter of April 25, 1968] is only a two-page letter," citing *Essner v. Shoemaker*, 393 Pa. 422, 143 A.2d 364 (1958).

I cannot agree with the majority that this reasoning is supported by the evidence. The letters of April 25 and December 31, 1968, incorporate by reference the detailed specifications concerning the construction of the self-unloading ore carrier for Bethlehem Steel Corporation, which were used by the parties in connection with the construction of the *Cort*. These specifications serve the purposes of identifying the specially manufactured vessels, as contemplated by the parties at the inception of their agreement.

Furthermore, both letters incorporated by reference the *pro forma* Ship Construction Contract which consists of 26 pages and 21 articles and which was also used as the basis of the agreement between the parties for the construction of the *Cort*. This *pro forma* contract sets forth in detail many contractual terms including specifications, approval and inspection, delivery schedule and manner of delivery, terms of payment, manner of inspection, trial runs, schedule of trial runs, place of delivery and acceptance, allocation of risk of loss, allocation of insurance proceeds, events of default, remedies in the event of default, manner of modification of the agreement, responsibility to defend alleged patent infringements, confidential information, passing of title, schedule of payments, selection of vendors and subcontractors, choice of materials and manufacturers, manner of assignment, governing law, settlement of disputes by arbitration, indemnification against third-party personal injury claims, manner of notice, a "no oral modification" clause, and an integration or "zipper" clause.

As stated in the letters of April 25 and December 31, 1968, "the terms and conditions of the ship construction to be in accordance with the attached terms and conditions and any other mutually agreed to terms and conditions." Thus, the parties specifically agreed that any ship construction contract concerning any vessel ordered by Bethlehem pursuant to its option would be based upon the detailed *pro forma* contract as drafted by Mr. Davis, an attorney for Litton.

[Judge Hester then catalogued certain additional terms which supplemented the *pro forma* agreement.]

The use of the *pro forma* contract by the parties as the basis of the Ship Construction Contract of April 25, 1968, sharply brings into focus the relevancy of the "course of dealing" between the parties. 13 Pa. C.S.A. § 1205. It is apparent from the documentation of the transaction between the parties which occurred on April 25, 1968, that Litton's offer to Bethlehem to enter into an option agreement was part of this overall transaction, perhaps a contract "sweetener." The course of dealing between the parties with respect to the construction of the *Cort* amplifies the intentions of the parties to be legally bound to each other on the basis of the option agreement. Litton obviously desired to enter the shipbuilding industry as evinced by its construction of a ship for Bethlehem. Clearly Litton was hopeful that it would be able to build additional vessels for Bethlehem in the future and granted options to Bethlehem accordingly. As part of the ship construction contract for the *Cort*, Litton specifically gave Bethlehem a right of first refusal to purchase any of the ships described in its quarterly shipbuilding schedule.

By letter of July 10, 1968, Litton gave notice to Bethlehem of its projected shipbuilding schedule, offered Bethlehem the right of first refusal on projected Hull 102, and submitted to Bethlehem a proposed form of contract which was identical to the *pro forma* contract referenced in the letters of April 25, 1968, and December 31, 1968. The suitability of these basic contractual terms was therefore repeatedly recognized by Litton. The fact that the letters of April 25 and December 31, 1968, specified that the ship construction contract might also contain "any other mutually agreed to terms and conditions" does not indicate that the parties did not intend to be legally bound *unless* such additional terms were agreed upon. The parties were obviously able to agree to terms concerning the construction of the *Cort* and consented to similarly negotiate in good faith at some future time regarding any additional terms.

This "course of dealing" between the parties was not considered by the court below. However, Litton itself recognized the relevancy of this course of dealing and interrelationship between the construction of the *Cort* and the option agreement. The letter of April 25, 1968, which was drafted by Litton, began as follows:

> Reference is made to the ship construction contract signed by our companies this date for the construction by us of a 1000-foot self-unloading ore vessel for you. Reference is also made to my letter to you of this date extending to you an option to purchase either one or two additional vessels upon the terms therein set forth.

Thus did Litton make references to the "course of dealing" between the parties. This evidence cannot be ignored, for under the Code, "course of dealing" is always relevant....

As author of the letter of April 25, 1968, Litton was in control of the terms of the offer. Litton also offered and controlled the attached *pro forma* contract. I cannot understand how Litton, as a large corporation, could conceivably have delivered the letter of April 25, 1968, to Bethlehem without intending to be legally bound by the terms stated herein. The letter of April 25, 1968, created a power of acceptance by Bethlehem, which was exercised by the jointly executed letter of December 31, 1968, was prepared by both the parties and was intended to be a final expression of the terms included therein. "The official commentary to [13 Pa. C.S.A. § 2203] recognizes that the parties may condition their assent on formalities, but must do so expressly. Official commentary to § 203, 1 Uniform Laws Annotated, Uniform Commercial Code 107 (West, 1968)." ...

In addition to the previously mentioned course of dealing between the parties, the following conduct by both parties additionally supports the existence of a contract, for the purposes of 13 Pa. C.S.A. §2204(a):

[Judge Hester then catalogued 16 instances in which, in letters or corporate documents, either Litton or Bethlehem or both seemed to acknowledge the existence of a contract. This list includes, for example:]

6. In February, 1973, before Bethlehem notified Litton of the exercise of its option, Litton internally listed "Bethlehem Steel Corporation's option to purchase five additional vessels" as one of its "Contractual Obligations."

9. In its financial plan of July 1973, Litton acknowledged the outstanding option as follows: "It should be noted that Bethlehem has an option for construction of up to five (5) new vessels. That option will not expire until December 31, 1973. The terms of the option, if exercised by Bethlehem, would result in substantial losses by Litton." ...

Finally, and perhaps most importantly, my review of the record does not indicate a single instance whereby Litton denied Bethlehem's right to exercise its option, nor did Litton ever deny that the letter of December 31, 1968, was intended to be a legally binding agreement, prior to the expiration of the option period on December 31, 1973....

Having concluded that the parties intended to make a contract, the next question to be addressed is whether "there is a reasonably certain basis for giving an appropriate remedy." 13 Pa. C.S.A. §2204(c).

In addition to the previously mentioned contractual terms contained in the specifications and *pro forma* contract, the letters of April 25 and December 31, 1968, contain definite terms relating to the period of the option, time of delivery of the vessels, base prices for the vessels, a base index of "Fourth Quarter 1968," "quarterly escalation" of price during construction, specific labor and material percentages (supplied by Litton's letter of May 8, 1968), and a clause providing for Bethlehem's right to cancel subject to liquidated damages.

The terms which were left open by the parties are as follows:

(1) The index by which the material and labor cost escalation would be computed;

(2) "an appropriate contract clause ... providing for quarterly escalation thereafter";

(3) "any other mutually agreed to terms and conditions," in addition to the terms and conditions of the *pro forma* ship construction contract.

Concerning "any other mutually agreed to terms and conditions," the word "any" implies that the failure of the parties to agree to any such additional terms would not affect their intention to be legally bound pursuant to the option agreement. Litton repeatedly recognized the suitability of the *pro forma* contract for the construction and purchase of the vessels in question....

At the meeting on September 24, 1973, Bethlehem submitted to Litton a proposed contract containing additional terms and conditions that were not included in the *pro forma* contract. However, many of these proposed additional terms and conditions were previously included by the parties in the ship construction contract relating to the *Cort*. Therefore, it would appear that Bethlehem did attempt to negotiate in good faith concerning any additional terms and conditions, based upon the course of dealing between the parties relating to the construction of the *Cort*.

The other open terms directly relate to the ultimate price for the construction of the vessels. The Code [at 13 Pa. C.S.A. §2305] specifically addresses this issue as follows:

Open Price Term

(a) General rule—the parties if they so intend can conclude a contract for sale even though the price is not settled. In such a case the price is a reasonable price at the time for delivery if:

(2) the price is left to be agreed by the parties and they fail to agree;

(d) Intent not to be bound without established price.—Where, however, the parties intend not to be bound unless the price be fixed or agreed and it is not fixed or agreed there is no contract.

The parties intended to be bound by the option agreement of December 31, 1968. Therefore, the ultimate price of the vessels was "left to be agreed by the parties and they fail[ed] to agree." 13 Pa. C.S.A. §2305(a)(2).

Under the circumstances, the price for the vessels "is a reasonable price at the time for delivery." However, the parties did specifically agree to stated base prices for the vessels. Therefore, the "reasonableness" of the ultimate price term must be related to the stated base prices, as escalated by a "reasonable" index (using a base of "Fourth Quarter 1968").

The lower court bifurcated this case and received only evidence relating to the issue of liability. Since the lower court improperly held that the parties had not intended a binding agreement, and since the lower court did not address the various sections of the Code cited herein, this case should be remanded for additional findings of fact, conclusions of law, and on the development of an appropriate record on matters not already in the record. I would reverse.

NOTES AND QUESTIONS

1. *The end of the appellate story:* Bethlehem Steel Corporation appealed to the Supreme Court of Pennsylvania. Three justices of that court did not participate in the case. The remaining four justices were evenly divided, and so the order of the Superior Court was affirmed.[6] Eleven appellate judges considered the case. Six found

---

6. Bethlehem Steel Corp. v. Litton Indus., Inc., 507 Pa. 88, 488 A.2d 581 (1985).

enough evidence in the record to support the trial court's conclusion that no contract was formed, while five would have reversed. We can only speculate about what might have happened if some or all of the three Pennsylvania Supreme Court justices who did not consider the case had participated in the decision. How would you have voted?

2. *Relationship to the* Klimek *case:* Instead of a woman seeking to run a rooming house and a builder, the *Bethlehem Steel* case involves two of the largest corporations in the world. The parties in each case intended some commitment to one another. Did the Pennsylvania courts serve the interests of Bethlehem Steel and Litton Industries any better than the Oregon courts served Klimek and Perisich?

3. *Contract formation through email:* At the time *Bethlehem Steel Corp. v. Litton Industries, Inc.* was decided, parties communicated through letters. Commerce now moves more quickly. Firms tend to notify one another of opportunities through email. In *Republic Bank, Inc. v. West Penn Allegheny Health System, Inc.*,[7] the 10th Circuit found that emails can add up to a contract. Republic Bank's agent initially contacted the defendant by phone, leaving a voicemail inquiring into its interest in purchasing several pieces of medical equipment. The defendant responded by email, stating: "We are interested in [the equipment]. Our offer is as follows ..." The email included the amount the defendant was willing to pay. About a week later, Republic's agent responded, telling the defendant that "your offer" had been conveyed to Republic's president and promising to get back with an answer shortly. After a week, Republic's agent sent an email to the defendant that stated: "I met with the bank president this morning and he gave me approval to sell [the equipment] for the total amount offered [in the defendant's original email]." He noted that how one of the items would be shipped remained unclear, but said: "We can discuss that issue." The defendant acknowledged receipt of this email. Soon afterwards, Republic's agent sent a draft contract to the defendant. About two months later, the defendant notified Republic that it no longer wanted to purchase the equipment.

In the wake of the defendant's repudiation, Republic auctioned the equipment. It later sued the defendant for the difference between the auction proceeds and the amount the defendant agreed to pay in its email. The defendant took the position that the email exchange was nothing more than an "agreement to agree." It further argued that Republic's response was not an acceptance. Republic disagreed, arguing that a binding contract had been created via email. Relying on the language of § 2-204, the 10th Circuit agreed, finding that the email exchange formed a contract, and that the defendant could be held liable for the breach of that contract.

4. *A different court, a different contract, a different result:* *Oglebay Norton Co. v. Armco, Inc.*,[8] concerned a 1957 contract for shipping iron ore on the Great Lakes.

---

7. 2012 U.S. App. LEXIS 7383 (10th Cir. 2012).

8. 52 Ohio St. 3d 232, 556 N.E.2d 515 (1990). For a more recent case following *Oglebay Norton, see* Westlake Vinyls, Inc. v. Goodrich Corp., 518 F. Supp. 2d 955 (W.D. Ky. 2007), noting that the two-step analysis of the Ohio Supreme Court involved first determining whether there was an intent to be bound despite an open price and then filling in a reasonable price; also reasoning that either a trade usage or course of dealing could fill the gap.

Oglebay was to provide ore boats if and when Armco wished to transport ore from Lake Superior to the lower Great Lakes. Armco was to pay "the regular net contract rates for the season in which the ore is transported, as recognized by the leading iron ore shippers in such season for the transportation of iron ore."[9] If there was no recognized regular net contract rate, "the parties shall mutually agree upon a rate for such transportation, taking into consideration the contract rate being charged for similar transportation by the leading independent vessel operators engaged in transportation of iron ore from The Lake Superior District."[10] The contract was modified four times during the period from 1957 to 1980. In 1980 the contract was amended so that Oglebay Norton was required to provide vessels with self-unloading capability. Armco was to pay an extra 25 cents per ton shipped in self-unloading ore boats. Oglebay Norton began a $95 million capital improvement program to meet this provision of the amended contract.

The parties had a complex long-term continuing relationship. Armco held a seat on Oglebay Norton's Board of Directors and owned Oglebay Norton stock. They were partners, owning and developing the Eveleth iron ore mine in Minnesota.

From 1957 to 1983 the parties established shipping rates by referring to those indicated in *Skillings Mining Review*. After 1983, such information was no longer available from this source. The parties failed to negotiate mutually acceptable rates in 1984 and 1985. Oglebay Norton billed at one rate but Armco paid at a much lower rate, which Oglebay Norton was forced to accept. In 1986, Oglebay Norton filed a declaratory judgment action, asking the court to declare the rate demanded in its 1985 invoices as the contract or to declare a reasonable rate for its services. The trial court found that the parties intended to be bound to a contract even if they could not agree on a price for Oglebay Norton's services. It then set a reasonable rate based on expert testimony, Oglebay Norton's past charges for carrying Armco's iron ore, and evidence of what others were charging for those services. Finally, the trial court ordered that "if the parties were unable to agree upon a rate for the upcoming seasons, then the parties must notify the court immediately. Upon such notification, the court, through its equitable jurisdiction, would appoint a mediator and require the parties' chief executive officers ... to meet for the purpose of mediating and determining the rate for such season, i.e., that they mutually agree upon a rate."[11]

The Ohio Supreme Court affirmed the judgment. It relied on Restatement (Second) of Contracts § 33. Section 33 provides that if the parties intend to conclude a contract and the pricing mechanism fails, the contract will be enforced and the price will be a reasonable price. (This section, in substance, applies UCC § 2-305 to contracts that are not transactions in goods.) The Ohio court rejected old cases that found agreements to agree to be unenforceable. It said that there was sufficient evidence to support the trial court's findings of fact about the intent to be bound and the reasonable price.

---

9. 52 Ohio St. 3d at 232, 556 N.E. 2d at 516.

10. *Id.*

11. *Id.* at 234, 556 N.E.2d at 518.

How did Oglebay Norton establish a reasonable price? It was not a thing existing in the world. The trial court, sitting as trier of fact, had to create it by exercising judgment. In 1996, a magazine story[12] pointed out that there was not much competition among shipping companies on the Great Lakes because the steel companies owned their own fleets or were closely associated with particular operators of ore boats. The story noted: "Rates in the later trade are difficult to get hold of. Published rates are nothing more than a starting point, and with such an incestuous relationship between shippers and carriers, no one talks about what they actually pay." Oglebay Norton tried to subpoena information about rates from independent vessel operators and captive fleets, but the trial court quashed these subpoenas before the trial because Oglebay Norton had no right to this proprietary information. The appellate court noted that the trial court could have allowed Oglebay Norton to gain the information but imposed a protective order so that those rates would not be disclosed to others.

The dispute between Oglebay Norton and Armco came at a time when the American steel industry was in decline. The contract called for Oglebay Norton to supply Armco's requirements of carrying iron ore on the Great Lakes. Despite the order to mediate price, Armco could decrease its needs for such iron ore. At one point in the 1990s, Armco bought much of its iron ore from Brazil. It was shipped by barge up the Mississippi and then the Ohio River to Armco's plants. Obviously, this supply of iron ore was not covered by the contract with Oglebay Norton.

The court said that the trial court's order for mediation "neither added to nor detracted from the parties' significant obligations under the contract." Its order "would merely facilitate in the most practical manner the parties' own ability to interact under the contract." A trial court "may exercise its equitable jurisdiction and order specific performance if the parties intend to be bound by a contract where determination of long-term damages would be too speculative." The court stressed the "unique and long-lasting business relationship between the parties."[13]

Suppose you agree with the dissenting judges in *Bethlehem Steel Corp. v. Litton Industries, Inc.*, and conclude that the parties in that case intended to be bound whether or not they agreed on an escalator clause. Would the mediation approach taken by the Ohio trial court have solved the problem of fashioning an appropriate escalator clause? Suppose the mediator fails to lead the parties to an agreement on a reasonable price or reasonable escalator clause. Then what happens?

5. The UCC and indefiniteness: The fact that the parties did not agree to a term that most of us think essential to a deal is some evidence they had yet to make a commitment. However, the UCC says that is all it is—some evidence. The two-page signed letter may have been drafted at the last minute, but which party is responsible for that? The long-term continuing relationship between the two firms was not last-minute and casual. Why wasn't Bethlehem's reliance on the option reasonable and foreseeable? The UCC tells courts to work things out if there is enough so that a court can fashion

12. Paul F. Conley, *A Long Season Ends for Great Lakes Fleet*, J. Com., Feb. 29, 1996, at 18.
13. *Id.* at 238, 556 N.E.2d at 521.

a remedy. The standard is no more than that the courts should fashion reasonable terms. How should they do this? Must the remedy reflect risk assumption and choice, or can judges engage in rate-making when the parties have failed to do it?

Professor Edwin W. Patterson studied Article 2 of the Uniform Commercial Code for the New York Law Revision Commission. In reviewing § 2-305, he wrote:

> The last sentence of subsection (4) provides for restitution in case the "agreement" fails to be a contract. It is well to have this sentence to show that an alleged buyer and seller may *think* they have a contract and *act* as if they had one, and yet not have one. The "buyer" is, in such a case, required to make *specific* restitution if able to do so. Perhaps this is the simplest solution; yet the *remedy* of specific restitution is limited in other cases to *unique* chattels. While this sentence does not cover all the problems of restitution, it will serve as a guidepost to the case law on that subject.

Does or should the adequacy of available restitutionary remedies have any bearing on a court's determination as to whether the parties have made a contract enforceable under UCC § 2-305?

6. *Indefiniteness in the courts and the puzzle of deliberately indefinite contracts:* You have seen that some courts are more willing to fill gaps in contracts than others. Professor Robert Scott gathered reported decisions applying indefiniteness doctrine over a five-year period, 1998 to 2002, and found that, of 137 randomly selected cases from a larger pool, 48 percent found no intent to be bound or otherwise did not reach the question of supplying a reasonable term, 55 denied enforcement despite a finding that an agreement had been concluded, and only 34 supplied a gap-filling term.[14] He further noted that "[a]ll contracts are incomplete"[15] because possible future states of affairs cannot all be anticipated and dealt with, so that a more useful category to think about is deliberately incomplete contracts in which parties fail to agree on readily available, verifiable terms. This is the type of case that the courts are least likely to enforce.

To explain why parties enter into deliberately indefinite contracts despite considerable doubt that they will be enforced, Scott offers the theory that they are "self-enforcing" because of reputational sanctions for breach and also because of the benefits of repeated interactions between the parties.[16] He further argues that courts should not enforce such contracts because legal enforcement may "crowd out" behavior based on reciprocal fairness, the object of self-enforcing contracts.[17] He offers this theory as a justification for the traditional common law approach of refusing to enforce con-

---

14. Robert E. Scott, *A Theory of Self-Enforcing Indefinite Agreements*, 103 Colum. L. Rev. 1641, 1652–53 (2003).

15. *Id.* at 1650.

16. *Id.* at 1660.

17. *Id.* at 1689–90.

tracts where important terms have been left unresolved and as a reason for courts to abstain from intervention where reciprocity fails.

While agreeing that self-enforcement is strong in relational contracts, Professor William Whitford questions Scott's theory as applied to such contracts because it could create incentives for opportunistic behavior when one party has invested more in performance than the other, so that the latter can drive a very hard bargain.[18] Whitford says that facilitating opportunism was unlikely to have been the parties' intent at the time of contract formation, meaning respect for the parties' autonomy supports enforcement despite indefiniteness when a relational contract breaks down. Are parties who have had a long relationship more likely to cooperate if no resort to judicial enforcement is possible, or might the possibility of judicial enforcement reinforce cooperative adjustment?

7. *The effect of reliance on indefiniteness:* In *Dawson v. General Motors*,[19] a Cadillac dealer wanted to invest in expanding the service facilities on the Chicago premises that it subleased from General Motors. General Motors leased the building from the owner of the property. The dealer did not want to invest its money unless it could be assured that it would receive renewals of its lease. In response to Dawson's letter, an official of Cadillac wrote: "It is ... Cadillac Motor Car Division's plan to exercise the remaining five-year options extending through 2011.... While Cadillac cannot guarantee the annual lease rate will not increase, it is anticipated the percent of increase will be a maximum of three percent for each five-year option which is to be exercised." Dawson went ahead with the remodeling and informed Cadillac about the investments that it was making. Cadillac discovered that Dawson was selling cars made by manufacturers other than General Motors at the dealership. It then raised the rent beyond the amount specified in the letter. The trial court granted Cadillac's motion to dismiss the dealer's complaint because Cadillac's letter was too vague to constitute an offer that could be turned into a contract. The United States Court of Appeals for the Seventh Circuit reversed. It said: "The Illinois courts have not been shy about enforcing promises made in the context of ongoing negotiations and often involving preliminary or 'incomplete' agreements.... It is particularly noteworthy in this regard that one party's acquiescence in the other's reliance on the preliminary agreement is a factor that supports enforcement." To what extent, if at all, does the *Dawson* opinion help distinguish the *Bethlehem Steel* case from *Oglebay Norton v. Armco*?

8. *Judicial enforcement of agreements to agree:* Classic doctrine dismisses agreements to agree as illusory and unenforceable. What about an obligation to bargain in good faith? In *Thompson v. Liquichimica of America, Inc.*,[20] the parties stated: "[I]t is understood that all parties will exercise their best efforts to reach an agreement on or

---

18. William C. Whitford, *Relational Contracts and The New Formalism*, 2004 Wis. L. Rev. 631, 640–41.

19. 977 F.2d 369, 371, 374 (7th Cir. 1992).

20. 481 F. Supp. 361 (S.D.N.Y. 1979).

before May 15, 1979."[21] The court found an obligation to negotiate in good faith. "Such an agreement does not require that the agreement sought be achieved, but does require that the parties work to achieve it actively and in good faith." Compare *Reprosystem, B.V. v. SCM Corp.*[22] The Second Circuit found that since no contract was formed, there was no obligation to act in good faith. If the United States District Court's analyses were accepted as the law, how, if at all, would it affect the result in the *Bethlehem Steel* case? On the one hand, Bethlehem attempted to exercise its option after it knew that Litton had taken significant steps to close its shipyard. Moreover, Litton had told Bethlehem that the shipyard would close unless it got more orders for the self-unloading ore carriers. On the other hand, Litton's construction of the first ore carrier was long delayed, and Bethlehem's officials doubted Litton's ability to produce these ore carriers efficiently.

B. FLEXIBLE PRICE AND QUANTITY: "I'LL BUY WHAT I WANT AT A FAIR PRICE"

A classic issue in the law of contracts involves what businesspeople call flexibility. Buyer and seller make what they see as a contract. However, their agreement gives buyer discretion as to how much it will order. Seller, in turn, has discretion as to the price it will charge. Many judges and legal scholars during the mid-20th century saw such bargains as offending contract theory because the parties had not made specific commitments to buy a specified amount for a stated price. Nonetheless, despite questions about legal enforceability, businesspeople continued to make these arrangements. Since almost every state has adopted Article 2 of the UCC, the classic problems about flexibility have been transformed. Some of the old struggles remain, but we must discuss them with a new vocabulary. However, since the UCC's provisions are a response to older law, we must consider a little history to understand the statutory scheme.

While much legal thought assumes discrete transactions between strangers, many important economic transactions involve long-term continuing relationships, almost bordering on joint ventures or partnerships. For example, Sellerco is Buyerco's supplier; Buyerco is Sellerco's account. There may be no document establishing and regulating their relationship. When Buyerco needs to restock its inventory, it simply orders from Sellerco. Both parties often assume some obligation to each other. In times of shortage, Sellerco will take care of Buyerco as best it can. Buyerco may cancel orders for goods it cannot use. However, its officials feel some obligation to place additional orders later or to be reasonable when Sellerco is late on deliveries of future

---

21. *Id.* at 362.
22. 522 F. Supp. 1257 (S.D.N.Y. 1981), *rev'd*, 727 F.2d 257 (2d Cir. 1984).

orders. There are advantages to dealing this way. Buyers can cut the costs of finding reliable high-quality performance at an acceptable price by dealing with a small group of suppliers whose reputation cements the relationship. The loss of the status of regular supplier would be costly, and so the threat of turning elsewhere serves as a sanction pressing for good performance.

As long as parties leave matters to customary patterns, it is unlikely that they will create a legally binding contract until the buyer orders goods and the seller accepts the order. While parties may feel ethical obligations to continue to place and fill orders, most lawyers would think the parties are legally free to walk away at any time. They do not make definite commitments for the future. They assume tacitly that their relationship will continue.

Instead of leaving matters to custom or practice, parties may draft what they call contracts covering their long-term relationship. However, the world of business involves fluctuating demand and rising prices. Businesspeople are likely to seek flexibility. Buyers cannot be sure how many parts #123 they will use in the coming quarter or year. Sellers, in turn, hesitate to promise to fill all orders for part #123 at 50 cents each for several months or more. If the price of the special type of steel needed to make part #123 jumps 20 percent during the course of the year, a fixed-price contract could be disastrous.

There are several techniques for dealing with these risks. A seller may make a continuing offer subject to a series of acceptances by the buyer. For example, suppose the seller promises to supply all the #123s that buyer orders at 50 cents each.[23] Each time the buyer orders, this would close a contract for the amount ordered at that price. If the seller made a promise in writing to hold such an offer open for a specific term, it might be enforceable under UCC § 2-205. However, absent such a firm offer, seller could withdraw the offer as to future deliveries. Sellers may also promise to fill all orders at a specified price, but reserve the right to withdraw their offer at any time. Buyers may order their projected needs for, say, the first quarter of the year, but reserve the right to cancel their order for convenience — perhaps agreeing to pay a specified cancellation charge. Sellers also may promise to supply part #123 for six months as ordered by the buyer but at "seller's price in effect at the time and place of shipment" or at "market price." The parties may use elaborate price escalation clauses so that the contract price tracks some index of prices in the trade. Buyers may

---

23. You must be careful to distinguish the situation in the text, where the seller promises to fill orders at a quoted price, from one where the seller merely announces that its price is 50 cents a unit. Typically, an advertisement or a catalogue is not an offer committing a seller to supply goods at the quoted price. Sellers seldom take the risk of promising to supply anyone with all of the #123s they care to order. Sometimes it is difficult to decide whether a seller's communication is a promise or only information. In addition, advertisements that state a price that is not available may be a "bait and switch" that constitutes an unfair trade practice, so that saying that "an ad is not an offer" may be very misleading if that statement suggests no liability. *See* Jay M. Feinman & Stephen R. Brill, *Is an Advertisement an Offer? Why It Is, and Why It Matters*, 58 Hastings L.J. 61 (2006).

agree to buy all or part of their requirements from seller. They can draft this clause to limit the obligation—for example, a buyer may promise to take "33 percent of the requirements of its Austin, Texas, plant, but no less than 1000 units and no more than 10,000 units." We will consider these and other techniques to gain flexibility in the materials that follow.

Flexible quantity and price terms created problems for courts applying the common law of contracts. For example, some judges asked whether a seller who had the power to change the price had really promised to do anything. Seller might want to back out of the deal to serve another preferred customer. Seller could then set a price at $1 million per item, forcing buyer to back out. On the other hand, many courts found requirements contracts to lack mutuality of obligation. It was not certain that a buyer would have any requirements, and the amount of requirements was largely within the control of the buyer. Some courts adopted a middle position: they would enforce contracts calling for a seller to supply the requirements of an existing business, but they would not enforce new business requirements contracts since the needs of a new business offered no standard by which to measure a commitment.

The "jobber," or distributor requirements contract, was particularly troublesome. Suppose a producer agrees to supply all of a distributor's requirements of the producer's product. The distributor makes no promise to have any requirements of that product. If the distributor's customers want the product, then the distributor will order some from the producer. If a producer had to fill orders but a distributor did not have to place any, the arrangement seemed to lack mutuality.

Suppose Ace Beer Co. agreed to supply Acme Distributors with all of its requirements of Ace beer. Acme also distributed King, Queen, and Jack beers, which were made by Ace's competitors. On the one hand, if Ace beer were not very popular, Acme's salespeople would spend their time promoting King, Queen, and Jack beers. They would do little more than take any orders for Ace that tavern and liquor store owners wanted to place. Indeed, Acme might not order any Ace beer under this contract. On the other hand, if Ace beer suddenly became the rage with drinkers, Acme could make almost unlimited demands on the brewer to supply the needed product. To make matters worse, suppose that Ace had agreed to supply Acme with beer at $1.00 per case. Because of unanticipated increases in prices of raw materials, the cost to all brewers to produce a case of beer jumped to at least $1.25 a case. Acme Distributors had no requirements contracts with the other breweries, and they all increased their prices to cover the increase in their costs. Acme then might offer Ace beer to taverns and liquor stores at an extremely favorable price. Now they would promote it with great efforts. The demand could grow for a product on which the brewer lost at least 25 cents a case. Courts in many states refused to enforce these distributor requirements contracts, saying they lacked mutuality.

Many writers, notably Yale's Professor Arthur Corbin, attacked the refusal of courts to keep up with modern business practices. These writers noted that sellers could not name just any price they pleased—"seller's price in effect at time and place of shipment" meant the price the seller was quoting to the trade. This was at least influenced, if not controlled, by the market. Moreover, the mutuality requirement was an unnecessary addition to the requirement of consideration. A promise to buy one's requirements satisfied the consideration doctrine, whatever the likelihood there would be any requirements. The buyer gave up its freedom to buy elsewhere, whatever the likelihood that it would buy anything. Courts said they were interested in the existence and not the adequacy of consideration. If a seller thought a promise to buy requirements had value, why should courts refuse to enforce the contract when the buyer was a new business? The seller's business judgment may have been poor, but courts seldom recognize this as a reason for relief. Moreover, courts could push jobber or distributor requirements contracts into the consideration mold simply by implying a promise to use reasonable efforts to promote and sell the product.

The UCC changed the common law response to flexibility in long-term contracts. Its drafters were aware of the academic criticism of the case law and modern business practices. Rather than asking whether a contract was formed when the parties left issues of quantity and price open, the Code usually finds a binding contract and then directs courts to interpret the obligation assumed in light of standards such as commercial reasonableness or good faith. First, we will look at flexible pricing and then we will consider flexible quantity. However, we must recognize that often both go together. A seller may agree to supply the buyer's requirements only if there is a clause in the contract protecting the seller against rising costs of production.

1. Flexible Pricing

We can consider arrangements under which the price fluctuates from the perspective of the policymaker considering a legal response or that of a lawyer drafting an escalator clause. First, to what extent, if at all, are flexible pricing clauses socially desirable? Should the likely or possible consequences of these clauses affect courts' judgments about whether a particular clause is legally enforceable?

Escalator clauses may increase prices beyond actual increases in costs. For example, some sellers may be able to set high base prices that reflect estimates of increasing costs. Then on top of this amount, they provide for an increased price if certain costs increase. Thus, they may be able to justify increasing prices beyond an amount that reflects their actual costs. Other sellers have substantial control over their costs of labor and materials. An escalator clause may weaken their resistance to cost increases that they can pass along directly to their customers without renegotiation. Sellers' escalator clauses may have an "upward bias" as well. A drafter must weigh components of cost in the formula used. How does she deal with items drawn from old inventories purchased at lower prices or from fixed costs that do not increase? How does the clause deal with changes in methods of production that may, at least in part, offset increased raw materials costs? How does the clause deal with an industry-wide index of costs that fits a particular seller's costs poorly?

Of course, sellers may have little freedom to draft escalator clauses or to put into effect the prices called for by such clauses in their contracts. In a highly competitive market, buyers may be able to negotiate for fixed prices based on the threat to take their business elsewhere. Or buyers may refuse to honor contracts if sellers exercise the option to raise prices. Of course, a seller could always sue, but this threat is often a paper tiger. Suing a customer jeopardizes future sales. Such litigation is costly and uncertain.

Professor Daniel Farber argues that there are high costs when businesses rely on flexible long-term continuing relationships.[24] He says:

> [T]hese informal incentives are costly; to the extent that inadequate legal incentives cause excessive use of informal incentives, economic efficiency suffers.... Customers will tend to deal with sellers with whom they have dealt before and will tend not to engage in a widespread search for sellers. As a result, their willingness to shop for better prices can decrease. Furthermore, entry by new sellers becomes more difficult, because a reputation for reliability cannot be immediately established. Although these effects on behavior are difficult to quantify, they nevertheless represent real costs, because they impede the market's movement toward equilibrium.

> Farber is obviously right when he suggests that not all markets are highly competitive, but do the costs of flexible long-term relationships outweigh the benefits? Dr. Arthur Okun, an economist who was the chairperson of President Lyndon Johnson's Council of Economic Advisors and a scholar at the Brookings Institution, suggested that long-term continuing relationships are a major part of why we can have falling demand and rising prices at the same time.[25] Structures fashioned by lawyers — such as flexible pricing clauses and requirements contracts — can foster these relationships.

Okun points out that in "auction markets," supply and demand affect prices directly. Stocks and bonds, agricultural commodities, some primary metals, and things such as cotton and lumber are sold this way. However, most product transactions take place in *customer markets* rather than *auction markets*. Okun explains: "As long as there are costs associated with shopping and limited information about the location of the lowest price in the marketplace, buyers do not find it worthwhile to incur all the costs required to find the seller offering the lowest price."[26] While the Internet now often facilitates price research, in what circumstances might a buyer consider price information alone insufficient?

Whether or not flexible price terms are socially desirable, lawyers are frequently asked by clients to draft them. It is difficult to write a long-term contract when the

---

24. Daniel A. Farber, *Reassessing the Economic Efficiency of Compensatory Damages for Breach of Contract*, 66 VA. L. REV. 1443, 1465–66 (1980).

25. ARTHUR OKUN, PRICES & QUANTITIES: A MACROECONOMIC ANALYSIS (The Brookings Institution 1981).

26. *Id.*

drafter anticipates price volatility, but the following case deals with one solution as well as its potential for abuse.

SHELL OIL CO. v. HRN, INC.
Texas Supreme Court
144 S.W.3d 429 (2004)

PHILLIPS, C.J.

In this case, we must decide whether the price fixed by a refiner for the sale of its gasoline under an open-price-term contract with its dealers was in good faith as required by § 2.305(b) of the Texas Business and Commerce Code. The dealers claim that the refiner's pricing practices are forcing them out of business and therefore are not in good faith. The trial court concluded that the refiner had established its good faith as a matter of law, but the court of appeals reversed the summary judgment, concluding that circumstantial evidence raised a fact issue about the refiner's good faith. Although the refiner's price was commercially reasonable when compared to the prices of other refiners in the relevant market, the court found some evidence in the record to suggest that the refiner's price might have been influenced by improper subjective motives such as the desire to force some of its dealers out of business. Because we conclude that the refiner established as a matter of law that its price was fixed in good faith as defined in the Code, we reverse the judgment of the court of appeals and render judgment that plaintiffs take nothing.

I

Plaintiffs are several hundred lessee dealers in 17 different states who lease service stations and buy gasoline from Shell, operating those stations as independent businesses. Each dealer and Shell enter into two agreements: a Lease and a Dealer Agreement. Shell's relationship with its lessee dealers is also governed by the federal Petroleum Marketing Practices Act ("PMPA"), which regulates the grounds for termination and nonrenewal of petroleum franchise relationships. 15 U.S.C. §§ 2801–2806.

In the Dealer Agreement, each dealer agrees to buy Shell-branded gasoline from Shell at the "dealer prices ... in effect" at the time of purchase. Shell's price to its dealers is referred to as the DTW ("dealer tank wagon") price because it includes delivery to the dealer's station by a Shell tanker truck. The DTW pricing provision is an "open price term" governed by § 2.305(b) of the Texas Business and Commerce Code (which corresponds to § 2-305 (2) of the Uniform Commercial Code). Open-price-term contracts are commonly used in the gasoline refining and marketing industry due to price volatility.

Shell markets gasoline to the public through a retail network that includes not only lessee dealers, but open dealers and company-operated stations as well. First, Shell acts as a franchisor, leasing service stations to franchisees such as the dealers here that sell Shell-branded gasoline. Second, Shell sells Shell-branded gasoline directly to the public through company-operated stations. Finally, Shell sells branded and unbranded gasoline to jobbers. Some jobbers are wholesale distributors, selling Shell-branded and unbranded gasoline to stations operated by independent business owners. Other jobbers are also independent retail dealers, selling Shell-branded and unbranded gasoline directly to the public.

Jobbers operate fleets of trucks to pick up gasoline at refiners' terminals and distribute it to their own stations or to independent ones. Jobbers may have distribution agreements with several refiners simultaneously. Jobbers pay a "rack" price that is available for gasoline bought and picked up at Shell's terminals. The DTW price is typically higher than the rack price, although Shell does not set either price in relation to the other.

Shell's agreements with the dealers prohibit them from selling any gasoline except Shell-branded gasoline. Although the contracts with the dealers do not require them to buy Shell gasoline exclusively from Shell itself, agreements between Shell and its jobbers effectively eliminate the only major alternative source for Shell-branded gasoline. When a jobber sells gasoline to a dealer, the jobber is retroactively charged the DTW price for that product, not the lower rack price it otherwise would pay.

The dealers claim that Shell's pricing practices are forcing them out of business. Although Shell has the right under the Dealer Agreement to fix the DTW price at which the dealers must buy its gasoline, all parties agree that it must exercise this right in good faith. *See* Tex. Bus. & Com. Code § 2.305(b). Dealers claim that Shell's DTW prices cannot be set in good faith because they are so high that they put dealers at a competitive disadvantage. Dealers further assert that Shell's DTW pricing is part of a plan to replace them with company-operated outlets which are more profitable for Shell.

Shell moved for summary judgment on dealers' good-faith pricing claims, contending that it was entitled to judgment as a matter of law because it charged a posted price applied uniformly to all dealers and was a commercially reasonable price as well. Rather than contest the commercial reasonableness of Shell's DTW prices, Dealers argued that fact issues existed as to whether Shell had acted in bad faith by setting its DTW price with the subjectively improper motive of running dealers out of business.

The trial court granted Shell's motion for summary judgment. The court of appeals reversed and remanded the case for trial, concluding that the dealers had raised fact issues about Shell's subjective good faith when setting its DTW price.

II

Most contracts for the sale of goods specify a price, but some do not because either the parties fail to consider the issue directly or purposefully leave it for later determination. When a contract for the sale of goods does not specify a price, § 2.305 of the Uniform Commercial Code[27] supplies default rules for determining whether a

---

27. [2] That section of the UCC, dealing with open-price-term contracts, is codified as § 2.305 of Texas Business and Commerce Code and provides:

(a) The parties if they so intend can conclude a contract for sale even though the price is not settled. In such a case the price is a reasonable price at the time for delivery if
  (1) nothing is said as to price; or
  (2) the price is left to be agreed by the parties and they fail to agree; or

contract exists and what the price should be. This section is one of a series of provisions in Article 2 of the Code that fill common "gaps" in commercial contracts.

In this instance, the Code imposes on Shell the obligation of good faith when fixing its DTW price under the Dealer Agreement, providing that "[a] price to be fixed by the seller or by the buyer means a price for him to fix in good faith." Tex. Bus. & Com. Code § 2.305(b). Good faith is defined elsewhere in the Code to mean "honesty in fact and the observance of reasonable commercial standards of fair dealing." *Id.* § 1.201(b)(20). Official Comment 3 to § 2.305(b) further elaborates on the good faith requirement, creating a presumption in the normal case that a seller's posted price or price in effect is also a good faith price:

> 3. Subsection [b], dealing with the situation where the price is to be fixed by one party, rejects the uncommercial idea that an agreement that the seller may fix the price means that he may fix any price he may wish by the express qualification that the price so fixed must be fixed in good faith. Good faith includes observance of reasonable commercial standards of fair dealing in the trade if the party is a merchant. (§ 2-103). *But in the normal case a "posted price" or a future seller's or buyer's "given price," "price in effect," "market price," or the like satisfies the good faith requirement.*

Tex. Bus. & Com. Code § 2.305(b), cmt. 3 (emphasis added). Despite this definition and comment, or perhaps because of them, Shell and the dealers urge conflicting ideas about what good faith should mean in this case.

Shell argues that a good faith price, as § 2.305(b) requires, is one that is commercially reasonable and non-discriminatory. Because its DTW price fell within the range of DTW prices charged by other refiners in the relevant geographic markets (was commercially reasonable) and was applied uniformly among similarly situated dealers (was non-discriminatory), Shell submits that summary judgment was appropriate. According to Shell, the chief concern of the drafters in adopting § 2.305(b) was to prevent suppliers from charging two buyers with identical pricing provisions different prices for arbitrary or discriminatory reasons. The drafters, however, also wished to minimize judicial intrusion into the setting of prices under open-price-term contracts. To balance these concerns, the drafters created a presumption under Official Comment 3 that a "posted price" or "price in effect" is a good faith price that may be rebutted only by evidence of discrimination. Shell asserts that because the dealers brought

---

(3) the price is to be fixed in terms of some agreed market or other standard as set or recorded by a third person or agency and it is not so set or recorded.

(b) A price to be fixed by the seller or the buyer means a price for him to fix in good faith.

(c) When a price left to be fixed otherwise than by agreement of the parties fails to be fixed through fault of one party the other may at his option treat the contract as cancelled or himself fix a reasonable price.

(d) Where, however, the parties intend not to be bound unless the price be fixed or agreed and it is not fixed or agreed there is no contract. In such a case the buyer must return any goods already received or if unable so to do must pay their reasonable value at the time of delivery and the seller must return any portion of the price paid on account.

forth no such evidence here, this is a normal case where the posted price or a price in effect is a good faith price under § 2.305.

The dealers respond that Shell's concept of good faith and the "normal case" under § 2.305 is too narrow. They reject the notion that discriminatory pricing is the only way to rebut Comment 3's posted price presumption. Instead, the dealers submit that the definition of good faith incorporates two elements: a subjective element, "honesty in fact," and an objective element, "the observance of reasonable commercial standards of fair dealing." *See* Tex. Bus. & Com. Code § 1.201(b)(20). They conclude that both elements must be satisfied before a case is considered normal and before the posted price presumption can apply.

III

The dealers rely extensively on the Fifth Circuit Court of Appeals' recent decision in *Mathis v. Exxon* Corp., 302 F.3d 448 (5th Cir. 2002), which also involved open-price contracts between an oil refiner and its dealer/franchisees. Those dealers similarly complained that the refiner had breached its duty of good faith by purposefully setting its dealer price for gasoline at uncompetitively high levels to run them out of business. The *Mathis* court identified the central issue to be whether good faith required observance of both subjective and objective good faith in light of the apparent "safe harbor" described in Official Comment 3. *Id.* at 454–55. The refiner contended that a price fixed according to an established price schedule was within the safe harbor described in Comment 3. The court reasoned, however, that this safe harbor was not absolute because it applied only to "normal cases," or those cases in which an open price term was set with subjective good faith. Thus, the court placed the following limitation on Comment 3's safe harbor:

> [Comment 3] avoids challenges to prices set according to an open price term unless that challenge is outside the normal type of case. Although price discrimination was the type of aberrant case on the minds of the drafters, price discrimination is merely a subset of what constitutes such an aberrant case. Any lack of subjective, honesty-in-fact good faith is abnormal; price discrimination is only the most obvious way a price-setter acts in bad faith—by treating similarly situated buyers differently. *Id.* at 457.

In support of its interpretation, the court cited *Nanakuli Paving & Rock Co. v. Shell Oil Co.*, 664 F.2d 772, 806 (9th Cir. 1981), and *Allapattah Servs. v. Exxon Corp.*, 61 F. Supp. 2d 1308, 1322 (S.D. Fla. 1999), *aff'd*, 333 F.3d 1248 (11th Cir. 2003).

The court of appeals in this case adopted the reasoning in *Mathis*, concluding that good faith under § 2.305 encompasses both subjective and objective elements. Although a commercially reasonable price might establish the oil company's objective good faith, it would not alone be sufficient if there were also evidence that the company's price might have been influenced by its desire to replace franchisees with more profitable company-owned stores (a lack of subjective good faith). Because the court concluded that the dealers had presented sufficient circumstantial evidence on Shell's subjective intent to drive them out of business, it reversed the summary judgment.

IV

Most courts have rejected the approach of the Fifth Circuit and the court below in interpreting the good faith requirement of § 2.305. Instead, the majority of decisions suggest that a commercially reasonable DTW price, that is, one within the range of DTW prices charged by other refiners in the market, is a good faith price under § 2.305 absent some evidence that the refiner used pricing to discriminate among its purchasers. *See, e.g.,* ... *Wayman v. Amoco Oil Co.,* 923 F. Supp. 1322, 1332 (D. Kan. 1996) *aff'd mem.,* 145 F.3d 1347 (10th Cir. 1998) ... As the court in *Wayman* observed, "it is abundantly clear ... that the chief concern of the UCC Drafting Committee in adopting § 2-305 (2) was to prevent discriminatory pricing—i.e., to prevent suppliers from charging two buyers with identical pricing provisions in their respective contracts different prices for arbitrary or discriminatory reasons." *Wayman,* 923 F. Supp. at 1346–47.

The dealers themselves concede that Shell is not obligated to price its gasoline with their interests in mind or to protect them from competition. They further explain that their theory in this case does not turn on the DTW price set by Shell but rather on the reason why Shell chose to charge that price. Likewise, the court of appeals concludes that this is not the normal case because the price, although commercially in line with that charged by other refiners to their lessee dealers, may have been motivated by an improper underlying purpose to eliminate some dealerships.

It is not apparent, however, why the intent behind a commercially reasonable, non-discriminatory price should matter for purposes of a breach of contract claim under § 2.305(b). Dealers do not contend that they are entitled to any particular price and do not disagree that Shell's DTW price is within the range charged by other refiners to their dealers. Thus, if these dealers were charged the same DTW price by another refiner who did not have a similar plan to thin their ranks, presumably the price would pass muster under the dealers' view of § 2.305. Premising a breach of contract claim solely on assumed subjective motives injects uncertainty into the law of contracts and undermines one of the UCC's primary goals—to "promote certainty and predictability in commercial transactions." *Am. Airlines Employees Fed. Credit Union v. Martin,* 29 S.W.3d 86, 92, 43 Tex. Sup. Ct. J. 1196 (Tex. 2000).

Beyond prohibiting discriminatory pricing, the drafters wished to minimize judicial intrusion into the setting of prices under open-price-term contracts. They understood that requiring sellers in open-price industries, such as the oil and gas industry, to justify the reasonableness of their prices in order to satisfy § 2.305 would "mean[] that in every case the seller is going to be in a lawsuit" and that every sales contract would become "a public utility rate case." Walter D. Malcolm, *The Proposed Commercial Code: A Report on Developments from May 1950 through February 1951,* 6 BUS. LAW. 113, 186 (1951). The drafters reasonably foresaw that almost any price could be attacked unless it benefited from a strong presumption. Thus, they adopted a safe harbor, Comment 3's posted price presumption, to preserve the practice of using "sellers' standard prices" while seeking "to avoid discriminatory prices." *Id.; see also* Tex. Bus. & Com. Code § 2.305, cmt. 3.

The reasoning in *Mathis* and the court of appeals in this case negates the effect of Comment 3's "safe harbor" by concluding that circumstantial evidence of "any lack of subjective, honesty-in-fact good faith" is sufficient to create an "abnormal" case in which the posted-price presumption no longer applies. *See Mathis*, 302 F.3d at 457. The effect is to allow a jury to determine in every § 2.305(b) case whether there was any "improper motive animating the price-setter," even if the prices ultimately charged were undisputedly within the range of those charged throughout the industry. *Id.* at 454. This result appears to conflict with the drafters' desire to eliminate litigation over prices that are nondiscriminatory and set in accordance with industry standards. Although the subjective element of good faith may have a place elsewhere in the Code, *see, e.g., La Sara Grain Co. v. First Nat'l Bank*, 673 S.W.2d 558, 562–63, 27 Tex. Sup. Ct. J. 382 (Tex. 1984) (applying subjective good faith to a negotiable instrument), we do not believe this subjective element was intended to stand alone as a basis for a claim of bad faith under § 2.305. Rather we conclude that allegations of dishonesty under this section must also have some basis in objective fact which at a minimum requires some connection to the commercial realities of the case. *See* 2 JAMES J. WHITE & ROBERT S. SUMMERS, UNIFORM COMMERCIAL CODE § 17.6 at 167 (4th ed. 1995) (noting that "the subjective rule never prevailed in Article 2 with respect to merchants" and that in "various other articles of the Code there has been a movement from subjective to objective definitions of good faith").

The two cases relied on by *Mathis* appear to make a similar connection. In *Nanakuli*, a buyer of asphalt under an open-price-term contract asserted that the seller had breached its § 2.305 duty of good faith by failing to follow industry custom when changing its price. 664 F.2d at 778. The buyer established that by trade custom and usage the sellers of asphalt on the island of Oahu, Hawaii, price-protected their buyers by providing notice of price increases and an opportunity for the buyer to complete projects bid under the old price. The seller, however, abandoned this practice, raising the price without notice. The buyer complained that the price increase was not in good faith because the seller had not observed "reasonable commercial standards of fair dealing in the trade." *Nanakuli*, 664 F.2d at 805. Disregarding the posted-price presumption, the court concluded that this was not a normal case because the dispute was "not over the amount of the increase — that is, the price that the seller fixed — but over the manner in which that increase was put into effect." *Id.* The price increase failed to conform to commercially reasonable standards both in "the timing of the announcement and [the seller's] refusal to protect work already bid at the old price." *Id.* at 806.

In *Allapattah*, another case involving a refiner and its dealer network, the dispute concerned the calculation of a discount that was to be applied to the refiner's posted price. *Allapattah*, 61 F. Supp. at 1312–13. The refiner implemented a discount for cash program to offset the costs of credit card processing, which the dealers alleged resulted in their being charged twice for the cost of credit. The court concluded that these allegations were not the normal case contemplated under § 2.305 if there was evidence that the refiner double-charged to recover its costs of credit while representing to its buyers that its price was net of credit costs. *Id.* at 1322. The posted-price presumption did not apply, according to the court, because the dispute was not about price but rather the "manner in which the wholesale price was calculated without considering the doubled charge for credit card processing." *Id.*

Both of these cases recognize that a price, commercially reasonable on its face, may nevertheless be applied in a dishonest fashion. But in both of these cases, the allegation of bad faith resulted in a commercial injury distinct from the price increase itself. Here the dealers' claim of bad faith appears to be inextricably tied to the amount of the price set by Shell. We agree with those decisions that have upheld the posted price presumption against similar attacks. Applying that presumption, these courts have generally rendered judgment as a matter of law on similar claims under § 2-305 where the refiner used a posted price which it fairly applied to similarly situated purchasers.

V

The dealers maintain, however, that even though Shell used a posted price it nevertheless violated its duty of good faith by setting its DTW price too high with the conscious intention of driving some of its franchisees out of business. And the court of appeals agreed that there was enough circumstantial evidence to raise a fact issue about Shell's subjective motives and therefore its good faith. According to the court, this evidence generally included: (1) the DTW price itself, which was on the high end of the wholesale pricing spectrum, (2) the "captive" nature of the relationship between Shell and its franchisees, and (3) the general decline in the business fortunes of Shell franchisees.

Shell argues that these circumstantial factors are either irrelevant, unrelated to Shell's pricing, or unsupported by the record. Shell submits that there is no evidence that its DTW price caused any particular dealer to fail or be uncompetitive in the market. And even if there were evidence of this, Shell submits it would not raise a fact issue about its good faith because § 2.305 does not require a competitive price or the lowest price available. Moreover, Shell argues that the fact that some franchisees have experienced declining sales, lost money, or gone out of business does not raise a fact issue about whether Shell had a bad-faith plan to price them out of business. Instead, Shell suggests that market forces beyond its control are at the root of these problems. Shell points out that the dealers' own expert agreed that the lessee dealer is "a class of trade whose economic viability is dying" due to broader market forces, including the entry of mass merchandisers into gasoline retailing.

We agree with Shell that the court of appeals' list of circumstantial factors are not evidence that Shell lacked good faith when fixing its DTW price. The DTW price, the captive nature of the franchisee relationship, and the business losses suffered by the dealers are variations of the same theme: Shell's DTW price is too high for the dealers to compete with other gasoline retailers. But good faith under § 2.305(b) does not mandate a competitive price for each individual dealer, nor could it. The competitive circumstances of each dealer in the same pricing zone may vary from station to station, and yet Shell must treat them all the same.

The court of appeals, however, suggests that because the dealers paid more than most of the other gasoline retailers in Houston, the DTW price itself is some evidence of Shell's subjective bad faith. ("73–80 percent of [the dealers'] Houston competition paid rack price—or lower—for gas."). We cannot agree that a relatively high, yet commercially reasonable, price is evidence of bad faith. A good-faith price under §2.305 is not synonymous with a fair market price or the lowest price available....

Each dealer contractually agreed to buy gasoline at the DTW price applicable only to Shell-branded lessee-dealers. The court of appeals' wholesale cost analysis indiscriminately compares Shell's DTW price to prices available to other classes of trade, with different contractual buying arrangements. Included in the comparison are branded and unbranded jobbers who pick up their gasoline at terminals, open dealers who own their own premises, and company-owned stores operated by other refiners. Evidence that different prices are available to different classes of trade is not evidence of bad faith under §2.305.

Moreover, the court's description of the dealers as "captive buyers required to purchase Shell-branded gas at Shell's price" is not evidence of bad faith or an abnormal case within the meaning of Comment 3. Dealers are only "captive" as a result of their own choice to become Shell-branded lessee dealers, which involved their agreement to buy gasoline from Shell at the DTW price, rather than at rack or some other price. That is the nature of a long-term franchise. Such "captivity" is therefore the "normal" case.

Because the summary judgment evidence establishes that Shell's posted price was both commercially reasonable and fairly applied to the dealers, we reverse the judgment of the court of appeals and render judgment that the plaintiffs take nothing.

NOTES AND QUESTIONS

1. *The merchant definition of good faith:* The merchant definition of good faith in Article 2 has long included both reasonable commercial standards of fair dealing and honesty in fact, while the Article 1 definition, otherwise applicable throughout the UCC, was just "honesty in fact." UCC Uniform Text (2000), §§1-201(19) and 2-103(1)(b). In the 2001 revision of Article 1, the UCC's sponsors amended the uniform text definition of good faith to also include both elements rather than just honesty in fact (except as otherwise provided in Article 5 on Letters of Credit). See UCC Uniform Text (2003), §1-201(b)(20). Despite the change in the uniform text, some states have retained the "subjective good faith only" definition in Article 1, while also retaining the combined objective and subjective tests for merchants in Article 2. One of the major backers of the "good faith only" standard, leading to resistance to changing the Article 1 definition, was the American Bankers Association, which was concerned about an objective standard being applicable under Articles 3 and 4, dealing with checks and notes, and Article 9, dealing with secured transactions (loans backed by collateral).

Clearly, Shell Oil Co. is a merchant and thus subject to the two-part test under Article 2. Which of the two tests was in issue in the Shell case? What were the arguments of the parties about the meaning of that standard? Ordinarily, subjective honesty is a lower standard and easier to establish than objectively reasonable fair dealing. Was that true in this case? Why or why not?

2. *The reasons for the volatility of oil prices:* Oil prices are highly volatile, ranging from a high of $140 per barrel in early 2008 to a low of $37 in early 2016. The reasons include expanding world demand, with price inelasticity in the short term, and a rigid supply that is subject to uncertainties, making oil prices extremely sensitive to small shocks and news.[28] This is the backdrop against which Shell used dealer agreements with an open price term that empowered it to set the price, subject to the good-faith constraint at issue in the case. Does the analysis of the case constrain Shell's power over its dealers sufficiently?

3. *Dealing with price volatility:* Contract drafters can attempt to address price volatility in various ways. UCC § 2-305 seeks to make open price terms more acceptable, but it only directly applies to sales of goods. Furthermore, an open price term does not necessarily address the parties' goals, as explained by Professor Thomas R. Hurst:

> Despite the increasing acceptance of the open-price contract evidenced by Uniform Commercial Code § 2-305 and, to a lesser extent, by the courts at common law, its usefulness is mitigated by the following considerations. First, the open-price contract may be unsatisfactory to the buyer if his main purpose in entering into the contract is to protect himself against future increases in price or to the seller if he wishes to lock into a sale at the prevailing market price to protect himself against future price declines. Thus, to the extent that a contract provides for *future* determination of the price, it fails to accomplish these objectives. If, however, the major purpose for entering into a contract for future delivery is to assure the buyer a supply of an essential product or the seller a market for his output and the parties are content that the contract price be determined at the time of delivery, then the open-price contract should be satisfactory.
>
> Second, the open-price contract is of limited utility when it is difficult to find a formula by which the price will be determined. For this reason, open-price contracts are most commonly used in agreements for the sale of homogeneous commodities or for services that are regularly bought and sold in an active market. Conversely, a contract for a manufactured product involving a variety of materials and substantial labor costs in its production will not normally be suitable for an open-price contract.
>
> Third, in using an open-price contract, considerable care should be exercised in specifying the manner in which the price is to be determined. For example, if the contract specifies that the price is to be the "market price,"

---

28. Clifford Krauss, *Oil Prices: What's Behind the Drop? Simple Economics*, N.Y. TIMES, Mar. 30, 2016.

there is often considerable room for argument as to just what is the market price. Disputes that may arise include what price is meant when trading is inactive, whether customary discounts from listed market prices should be taken into account, and whether the prices of one or two sellers who habitually undercut the majority of sellers in a given market should be taken into account.

Finally, in some situations a contract calling for payment of the current "market price" or a "reasonable price" at the time of delivery might be subject to challenge if the market is severely distorted by shortages, strikes, or price-wars. Hence, if the parties decide that the use of the open-price contract is desirable, they should specify as precisely as possible the manner in which the price is to be determined and the circumstances, if any, that would render the formula inapplicable.[29]

Hurst pointed out that doctrines of frustration of purpose, impossibility, or impracticability of performance, codified in UCC § 2-615, sometimes relieve a party of obligation. He also noted two other ways of dealing with price volatility, cost-plus contracts and indexing. Cost-plus contracts, however, do not give sellers incentives to minimize costs of production, and furthermore there can be controversy about what counts as a "cost." Indexing is well accepted by the judiciary, but a suitable index may not be available and even if available, is sometimes discontinued, a point that should be addressed in the contract.

4. *Specific examples of flexible pricing:* Consider the following examples of flexible pricing clauses. As to each, ask first whether the clause is legally enforceable under the UCC.[30] Ask also whether the clause creates a workable governance structure so that the parties can perform under the contract.

— Acknowledgment of order form of a major American producer of steel:

Our base prices, together with related lists of Extras and Deductions, are subject to changes without notice, and all orders and contracts are accepted subject to price in effect at time of shipment.

— Requirements contract between a major American producer of aluminum and a major American automobile manufacturer:

The price for primary aluminum pig, ingot, and billet sold by [the aluminum company] and purchased by Buyer [the automobile company] hereunder shall be [the aluminum company's] current published price (including transportation allowance, if any) in effect at the date of delivery for the

---

29. Thomas R. Hurst, *Contract Drafting in an Inflationary Era*, 28 U. FLA. L. REV. 879 (1976). Reprinted with permission.

30. Consider UCC §§ 2-204, 2-305, and 2-311. Do not overlook § 2-204(3) and the first official comment to § 2-305.

products involved, unless the price as quoted in "American Metal Market"[31] (or, in the event that "American Metal Market" quotations shall be unavailable or inapplicable, as quoted in some other recognized trade publication) is lower, in which case the price quoted in the "American Metal Market" shall apply.

If Buyer receives a legitimate offer from some other domestic United States supplier source to sell to Buyer aluminum of the same quality as sold by [the aluminum company], Buyer may communicate to [the aluminum company] the quantity, price, and terms so offered to Buyer and if [the aluminum company] is unable or unwilling to meet such price and terms for such quantity, Buyer may, without such action constituting a breach of this agreement, purchase from such other source such quantity at the price and terms so quoted.

—Long-term contract for sale of paper used by one of the largest American manufacturers of this product:

3. The price(s) to apply to shipments made on this contract during each calendar quarter ... shall be specified by the Seller not less than fifteen (15) days in advance of the first day of the calendar quarter for which such price(s) is/are specified. In the event that the Seller shall not have thus specified such price(s), the price(s) for the preceding calendar quarter shall continue in effect for the calendar quarter as to which no price(s) shall have been so specified.

4. In case the Seller shall, as to any such calendar quarter, specify a revision in price(s) and the price(s) so specified for such calendar quarter is/are higher than the price(s) at which Buyer can secure an equivalent grade and quality of paper to be delivered by a responsible person during such calendar quarter, the price(s) shall be subject to a satisfactory adjustment by mutual agreement.

—Purchase order of a manufacturer of automobile components such as brakes and transmissions:

Buyer may at any time make changes in writing relating to this order including changes in the drawings or specifications, method of shipment, quantities, packing, or time, or place of delivery. If such changes result in an increase or decrease in cost of, or time required for, the performance of this contract, an equitable adjustment shall be made in the contract price, delivery schedule or both.

Consider the following comments, made in the course of an interview with a partner in a large law firm with a business practice:

Many courts are hostile to clauses calling for negotiation or settlement on a fair basis. Yet this is just what the parties want at the time they draft the contract, and a lawyer often cannot get them to be more specific. They are un-

---

31. This is a trade publication that reports market prices of metals.

willing to work out standards for settlement since there are too many facts that are uncertain and too much remains that cannot be foreseen. Businessmen do not like to deal with hypothetical cases.

What is a lawyer to do in a situation in which the client wants more flexibility than the rules seem to permit?

2. Flexible Quantity

a. Blanket Orders

Major American automobile manufacturers and some other firms with a great deal of bargaining power use blanket order purchasing. The arrangement allows a buyer to separate two functions of contract: an elaborate document drafted by a team of lawyers helps parties plan their transaction, but the buyer makes the minimum commitment possible to purchase anything from the seller. The following article describes practices as of the early 1970s. As automobile manufacturers in the 1980s attempted to follow Japanese methods of management, they often dealt with far fewer suppliers and gave them real commitments so they could invest in new technology.[32] Also, this way they were able to hold much smaller inventories and counted on suppliers delivering just enough to keep the assembly lines moving. Nonetheless, blanket order purchasing continues to be used widely.

Stewart Macaulay, *The Standardized Contracts of United States Automobile Manufacturers*

7 INT'L ENCYCLOPEDIA COMP. L. Ch. 3, sec. 3-21 to 3-30, 3-51 (1973)[33]

... 21. The automobile industry in the United States is large, very complex, and has great economic power. The major manufacturers are run as bureaucratic structures designed to operate efficiently at all levels. Those people and organizations that deal with the manufacturers have patterned their conduct to accommodate this model of economic efficiency. However, new models of automobiles must be designed several years before they are offered to the public and the demand for new automobiles fluctuates significantly. Bureaucratic operation in the service of economic efficiency, time-span and fluctuating demand are all critical factors that are reflected in many different kinds of exchange transactions found in this industry. In this paper we will

---

32. *See* NEW YORK TIMES, Aug. 8, 1985, at 25; *see also* General Motors, *Selling to General Motors* (July 14, 2010), *available at* http://www.gmsupplypower.com/apps/r4psanon/portal/content/news/supplypower/2010-07-14%20Selling%20to%20General%20Motors.pdf (reporting that GM acquires $130 billion worth of goods and services annually and relies on "lean manufacturing" and "just-in-time" procedures, including in the handling of raw materials, components, and finished products).

33. Copyright © koninklijke BRILL NV. Reprinted with permission.

consider some of the exchange relationships between the manufacturers and their suppliers, their dealers, and their customers in order to generalize about contract as it is found in this kind of large-scale industry.

A. Contracts to Build and Sell Cars

i. *The Manufacturers and Their Suppliers*

a. Description of the Relationship ...

22. Although the manufacturers can and do make in their own plants some of almost all of the parts that go into an assembled automobile, they also buy many of these parts from suppliers. There are a number of reasons why they purchase from outside suppliers. First, the manufacturer gets a product without investing additional capital in buildings, machines, and a trained work force. Second, the manufacturer gets a yardstick which can be used to measure the efficiency of its own division making the same item. If a division making grease seals can produce them at 2 cents each, but an outside supplier can make them for 1? cents each, the manufacturer knows he must re-examine the efficiency of his internal operation. Third, the manufacturer increases the chance that he may benefit from technological innovation. The supplier's designers and engineers may be able to suggest a different design or an improved manufacturing process. On the other side, most businesses, but not all, that can produce parts for automobiles want to sell their output to the automobile manufacturers because of the possibilities for extremely high-volume production which, in an efficiently managed firm, can be highly profitable.

There are three additional factors influencing the course a manufacturer-supplier relationship takes: First, the mass production techniques of American automobile manufacturing require that the assembly line not be stopped. When, for example, a particular Ford sedan arrives at a certain point on the assembly line four hubcaps must be there ready to be installed. It would be extremely costly to the manufacturer if the line had to be stopped because the supplier's machines that stamp out hubcaps broke down, because a supplier's inventory was not great enough to meet the demand, or because the parts were lost in shipment. However, demand for automobiles and even for particular types of automobiles fluctuates. To a great extent, this second factor offsets the first. The easiest way to avoid stopping assembly lines would be to produce large quantities of parts far in advance of need. Yet this approach increases costs because of the possibility of waste and the loss of the use of funds thus devoted to inventories. If, for example, the demand for station wagons declines during the year, exhaust pipes that fit only station wagons that will never be produced are mere scrap metal. Third, component parts can be defective, the defect can cause injury to property or person, and in United States law the injured party in such cases has increasingly been gaining rights against manufacturers. Not surprisingly, one finds that manufacturers wish to hold suppliers responsible for such claims, and the suppliers must defend themselves against the costly results of seemingly minor defects in the parts they make.

b. The Blanket Order System

aa. The System Described

23. The *manufacturers* have accommodated all of these economic and legal factors in an imaginative piece of transaction architecture that is usually called a "blanket order."[34] Coupled with the suppliers' great desire to do business with the automobile manufacturers, the blanket order system almost always ensures that parts will arrive at the assembly plants at the right time, that the suppliers will take the risk of scrapped parts caused by fluctuations in demand, and that the suppliers will be responsible for claims caused by defects. Moreover, the system gives the manufacturers great leverage to ward off price increases caused by the suppliers' increased costs.

This is how it works: Some time before the beginning of the model year, the manufacturer will issue a blanket order to a supplier of, for example, tailpipes designed specifically for one of the manufacturer's station wagons. The blanket order states a number of "agreements." One of the most important is the price per unit. This price is computed on the basis of an estimated number of units to be ordered, and it will not be increased if fewer are actually ordered. Thus, the manufacturer has made the supplier run the risk that he will not even recover his cost of producing the items actually shipped to the manufacturer in the event that the manufacturer uses substantially fewer than the estimated number. And the blanket order does not oblige the manufacturer to take and pay for *any* of the parts described in it. That obligation comes only when the manufacturer sends the supplier documents called "releases." The idea seems to be that the blanket order creates a force which is held back until released little by little.

Each month, sometimes more often, the manufacturer sends the supplier a release, ordering him to manufacture and ship a specified number of the parts each week. On the release form, the manufacturer also will estimate the number of parts he will require for the next two or three months, but this estimate, to quote one manufacturer's form, "is for planning purposes only and does not constitute a commitment." Typically, manufacturers do not send releases calling for more parts than they will need in a month since their monthly estimates of sales are fairly accurate. However, sometimes they do order too few or too many parts. If there is an increase in public demand for a particular model, the blanket order allows the manufacturer to send another release form to the supplier calling for increased deliveries. Such sudden increases may be a great strain on the supplier if he does not have unused capacity for production. Moreover, a supplier must always guard against a breakdown of his machinery, which temporarily destroys his ability to meet the manufacturer's demands.

---

34. [78] Many divisions of the General Motors Corporation use what are called requirements contracts rather than blanket orders. However, because of the way General Motors' requirements contracts are written and administered, the two systems are essentially the same in operation. The General Motors standard agreement form for production requirements calls for it to "purchase … approximately the percentage shown on the attached exhibit (of) the Buyer's requirements." Legally, the key word would be "approximately" since it might be interpreted to undercut any commitment to buy.

As a result, the supplier usually makes more than the number of parts ordered by the manufacturer so that the supplier will have an inventory to cover anticipated future demands. He builds this inventory at his own risk since the blanket order clearly provides that "Seller shall not fabricate any articles covered by this order, or procure materials required therefor, or ship any articles to Purchaser, except to the extent authorized by ... written releases ... Purchaser will make no payments for finished work, work in process, or raw material fabricated or produced by Seller in excess of Purchaser's written releases."

If a manufacturer has "released" too many parts in light of a sudden decrease in demand, the blanket order gives it the right to cancel the amount ordered in whole or in part. It then is obligated to pay the contract price for each part finished and "the cost to Seller (excluding profit or losses) of work in process and raw material, based on any audit Purchaser may conduct and generally accepted accounting principles."[35]

bb. Blanket Orders and American Contract Law

(1) Legal Enforceability

24. American contract law would likely support the manufacturer's plan for the transaction so that, when the law is combined with the market situation, the manufacturer's interests would be favored. Under the law there must be an exchange of promises or of performances to create a legally enforceable contract. In a blanket order the manufacturer makes no promise until it sends a "release," and so until then there has been no exchange and contract rights have not been created. In effect, at the manufacturer's request, the supplier makes an offer — a promise to supply certain goods if they are ordered — which the manufacturer accepts every time it sends a release. The continuing offer and the many acceptances create a series of contracts. It is possible that two developing doctrines in the common law of the United States might be applied in the future to offer remedies despite the absence of a contract. Reliance by the manufacturer on the supplier's promise to fill all orders might receive legal protection, in the unlikely event it were needed, by the growing "firm offer" doctrine. Reliance by the supplier on any assurances (most likely implied ones) of the manufacturer that it would order a reasonable quantity might be protected by the development of rules requiring fairness in negotiations.

25. One can only speculate about the legal situation in light of general principles of contract law and the Uniform Commercial Code, since litigation-testing these conclusions is unlikely.[36] The large automobile manufacturers try to avoid placing total

---

35. [79] General Motors' requirements contract reserves no such right. Interviews, however, indicate that General Motors occasionally does cancel these contracts and pays what it deems reasonable cancellation charges. These charges would be no more than those stated in the text.

36. Eds. note: As of 1973, when this article was written, there was only one case involving a manufacturer-supplier dispute. This case arose shortly after General Motors started using the blanket order system, and the supplier claimed he was misled. The court was very critical of the General Motors blanket order system. *See* Streich v. Gen. Motors Corp., 5 Ill. App. 2d 485, 126 N.E.2d 389 (1955). Another case arose in the 1980s, and led, after five years of litigation with GM, to a three-paragraph opinion by the Sixth Circuit. The opinion represented a victory for General Motors' assertion

reliance on any one supplier, and other suppliers usually can increase production so that a manufacturer's assembly line is not stopped for lack of an item. Thus manufacturers tend to avoid injury rather than litigate for compensation. On the other hand, no automobile parts supplier is likely to bring a case against a manufacturer; the loss on any one order is very unlikely to be large enough to justify jeopardizing future business. Of course, the trustee of a bankrupt supplier would be free of this constraint. However, in light of the uncertainty of the supplier's legal position, many trustees would think it unwise to risk the cost of legal action against a manufacturer.

26. What are the consequences of the legal situation? If we assume that the developing reliance and fairness doctrines would not apply, the parties get legal rights only after the manufacturer has issued a release and only as to the goods ordered in that release. This means that there can be a great deal of reliance by the supplier that is unprotected by contract rights. On the other hand, legally the supplier would be free to refuse to continue the relationship by revoking his outstanding offer to supply the parts as ordered by the release forms. As we have said previously, few suppliers who were not going out of business could afford to exercise such a right; very few situations short of bankruptcy would justify losing the good will of General Motors, Ford, Chrysler, or American Motors. Most importantly for the manufacturer, it does get legal rights once a release is issued. As a result, it manages to avoid any question that the supplier will bear liability for injuries caused by defective parts which it ships. Once the parts are ordered by a release there is a contract that the manufacturer has written, and the disclaimers and limitations of remedy so typically found in documents drafted by sellers are thus avoided. As between Chrysler and its suppliers, the responsibility for compliance with federal safety and air pollution regulations is also clearly placed on the supplier.

(2) Remedies

27. The standard blanket order documents drastically limit the remedies to which a supplier would otherwise be entitled under American contract law once a legally binding contract is created by the issuance of a release. Typically, the manufacturer reserves a right to cancel the goods ordered by its release, either in whole or in part. Under American contract law such a cancellation would be a breach if not authorized by the agreement, and, absent a contract provision to the contrary, the seller would be entitled to recover what he had spent in performance before the buyer's notice of cancellation plus the profit he would have made had he been allowed to complete his performance. Most blanket order cancellation clauses, however, exclude a right to profit except as to those parts which have been completed before cancellation. Thus even when a contract is formed by a release, the supplier's rights in most situations will be minimal. The manufacturer gains a practical commitment from the supplier

---

that its blanket order did not obligate it to order any specific number of parts from a supplier. Pro-Par Indus., Inc. v. Gen. Motors Corp. 884 F.2d 580 (6th Cir. 1989) (unpublished opinion). The major point still seems valid. Pro-Par was an inexperienced supplier. At the time of the litigation it was in bankruptcy, and so had no continuing relationship to protect. And it lost.

to meet the demands of its assembly line. It retains maximum flexibility by making no commitment to buy any parts until a release is given and making only a very limited payment if it wishes to cancel after one is sent.

c. The Absence of a Reform Movement

28. There are no statutes attempting to regulate this relationship, and no movement seeking such legislation has been discovered. Insofar as statutes in the United States are the result of pluralistic struggle and compromise, one essential element of pluralism seems lacking. It would be hard to form a group of suppliers to seek legislation. Supplying the manufacturers is very profitable for a firm that can accept all of the risks allocated to it by the blanket order system. Such successful firms would hesitate to jeopardize their standing with the manufacturers by supporting an organization taking a stand antagonistic to the manufacturers's interests. Without the most successful firms, such a group would lack political power. Firms that do not wish to assume the risks of the blanket order system can easily seek other customers since their facilities are not limited to producing original-equipment automobile parts. "Exit" is a relatively cheap remedy for dissatisfaction in this case.[37] The facilities devoted to producing original-equipment parts can be converted readily to producing parts for repairing automobiles—the so-called "after market"—or to supplying related industries such as truck or industrial engine manufacturers which, generally, do not have the bargaining power to use the blanket order system. "Voice"—using private or legal power to change the allocation of risks—would entail high costs and the chances of success would not be great in light of the many resources of the manufacturers.

Moreover, insofar as statutes flow from the efforts of those with access to the communications media attempting to enhance their status and power by acting as champions of the deserving underprivileged, this seems an unpromising area. The auto parts suppliers typically are not small businessmen but only smaller organizations than the giant auto manufacturers. The image of the suppliers is that of junior partners who are well-paid for taking large but acceptable risks: it would be hard for an ambitious United States senator to champion them as the exploited victims of the corporate system.

Finally, insofar as one explains United States legislation as an instrument of the powerful to further their interests, no statutory action is needed in this area. The common law of contracts serves to legitimate and support the manufacturers' procedures by minimizing or denying rights to the suppliers.

29. In summary, the manufacturers have tailored a relationship whereby they get most of the advantages of producing parts in a division of their own firms while preserving most of the advantages of dealing with an outside organization. The suppliers

---

37. [87] *See* the analysis in Albert O. Hirschman, Exit, Voice and Loyalty (Cambridge, Mass. 1970).

are offered a chance to make high profits in exchange for assuming great risks. Most suppliers are eager for the chance to play the blanket order game.[38] The public may get better automobiles at a lower price as a result of the system, but one cannot be sure. There are important parallels to the contract system used by the United States government to procure military equipment such as tanks and aircraft. Since experience may change the need for a weapon or call for a modification in its design, the government retains great power to change or terminate its orders to private industry while paying less than the damages specified in general contract law.... It is thought that the risks in dealing with the United States government are reflected in higher prices paid to the weapons industry on government contracts. The automobile manufacturers may also pay for the flexibility in the blanket order system. However, unlike the United States government, the manufacturers make some of their own needs of each type of part. They can turn to their own divisions if prices are too high, and they can negotiate about prices with suppliers in the light of detailed knowledge about what it costs to make the item. Moreover, unlike the government's, the manufacturers' decisions and negotiations are not directly subject to a political process.

ii. *Evaluation: Benefits at What Price?*

a. The Balance of Gains and Costs

51. Undoubtedly, this kind of rationalized planning has advantages. It is not an insignificant part of a system that has produced great wealth for executives of auto-

---

38. [88] The blanket order system may not be very different from the pattern of expectations that would exist if the manufacturers made contracts for fixed quantities of parts with their suppliers. Study of the contract documents typically used in other industries and interviews with businessmen and their lawyers disclose that in many situations purchasers assume they may "cancel" their orders when a change in demand causes them to no longer need the items ordered; suppliers usually accept this as one of the risks of business, particularly if the item in question is not being made specially for the buyer but is what the seller offers in the normal course of his business. At times the contract documents contain cancellation clauses, but even where they do not, the right to cancel is widely but not always assumed to exist. After cancellation, the key question is what the buyer must pay to the seller to use this privilege. The obligation is not always clear. Many purchasers think that the supplier is not entitled to his full anticipated profit on the transaction. Many would limit cancellation charges to payment at the contract rate for items completed before cancellation and payment for the raw materials that cannot be salvaged in partially completed items. Thus, the conventional measure of contract damages in the United States contract law awards an aggrieved party more than many businessmen think appropriate. Of course, the possibility of a breach of contract action with its damage measure defined as the net profit on the entire transaction had it been performed plus expenditures in part performance, may serve indirectly as one factor in inducing industrial buyers to cancel only when suppliers would accept as legitimate the reasons for not wanting the goods. It may be that it is legitimate to cancel an order for steel when there is no demand for the product that the buyer planned to manufacture with the steel; it would not be legitimate to cancel because another supplier of steel offered a lower price. Another way of viewing the matter is that businessmen recognize far broader impossibility and commercial frustration excuses for nonperformance than does the law. In summary, the pattern of risk allocation found in the blanket order system may deviate far more from the contract lawyer's model of business than from the actual expectations of those managing the relationships between large business corporations. *See* Stewart Macaulay, *Non-Contractual Relations in Business. A Preliminary Study*, 28 Am. Soc. Rev. 55 (1963).

mobile manufacturers, stockholders in these companies, automobile dealers, parts suppliers, and even, to some extent, for workers employed by this industry and its satellites. The high demand for automobiles produces opportunities for profit and jobs in many related industries and has a major impact on the total American economy. The system may have produced less expensive automobiles than could be made by any other, since one can assume that if the manufacturers had had to assume all of the risks they avoid by these contracts, they would have passed on these costs to buyers in the form of higher prices for new cars.

NOTES AND QUESTIONS

1. *Understanding the arrangement's functions:* Creating a blanket order system costs major buyers something. Why don't they avoid these costs by buying their needs on the market? Why are suppliers interested in blanket orders? Why don't they sell on the market to those who want to buy, rather than accept arrangements under which buyers make so little commitment to them? Does the blanket order system help minimize costs of production, or does it increase those costs and contribute to inflation when they are passed along to consumers?

A 2008 industry newsletter reported that several cases had been initiated that challenged "the very notion of blanket purchase orders," but that no supplier was willing "to take the risk of letting this go to a decision." Instead, problems were ultimately solved through negotiation. "The reality is that the procurement industry has too much vested in blanket purchase orders. It may not be in anyone's interest to see that get ruled illegal."

2. *Blanket orders when a seller has superior bargaining power:* Sellers with superior bargaining power will use a different structure for blanket orders than those of the automobile manufacturers described by Macaulay. For example, in *Franklin v. Demico, Inc.*,[39] Demico contracted to supply electronic circuit boards to Python Corporation under the "Demico Blanket Order Policy." Python agreed to purchase large quantities of circuit boards. However, it could give 90 days notice and increase or decrease the amounts called for. If it decreased the amounts called for, there would be a "bill-back" to reflect a higher price per unit. This arrangement, of course, reflects the usual practice of charging less per unit when goods are ordered in large quantities. Under the Demico policy, Python bills a buyer on the assumption that it will order enough units in the future to qualify for a quantity discount. If it does not, it owes additional amounts for those units it has received and paid for. The Georgia court upheld this arrangement. It found that the supplier had proved its damages with reasonable certainty under the bill-back system.

b. Requirements and Output Contracts

Requirements and output contracts are one of the places where classic contracts scholarship touches modern business practices. A requirements contract is one under

---

39. 347 S.E.2d 718 (Ga. Ct. App. 1986).

which a seller agrees to supply all the part #123 that buyer requires, and buyer agrees to buy all its requirements of that part from seller.[40] An output contract is one under which a seller agrees to deliver to buyer all the output of a particular factory or farm. These contracts raise a number of practical and legal questions. Most were recognized in a classic article written in the 1930s, in which Harold C. Havighurst and Sidney M. Berman[41] dealt with the problems of mutuality and enforceability found in the common law cases. The Uniform Commercial Code solves or transforms most of these problems. We will survey the transformation of the requirements and output contract problem from mutuality to UCC interpretation.

Havighurst and Berman also pointed out that lawyers and judges had to interpret the risks taken by each side as a result of promises to supply all the buyer's requirements. The seller risks that the buyer will have either no requirements or too many requirements. In a falling market for seller's goods, buyer can get them elsewhere cheaper. Thus, buyer has an incentive to look for ways out of the requirements contract. First, buyer may change the design of the product in which it used what seller was to supply so that buyer no longer has any requirements for seller's goods. Suppose buyer had a contract to buy its requirements of fuel oil from seller. Can buyer switch to natural gas to heat and power its factory? Second, mergers and consolidations can affect requirements contracts. Suppose a contract calls for buyer to purchase "all requirements for the Seattle plant" from seller. Buyer then is merged into a multinational corporation that closes the Seattle plant. However, multinational makes the same product at its Houston plant, free of labor unions and state regulation. Has seller any rights against multinational? Third, suppose buyer goes bankrupt and ceases doing business. Has seller a claim in the bankruptcy proceedings on the theory of an implied promise to have requirements?

Suppose, on the other hand, the requirements contract calls for a fixed price and the market price for the goods in question increases rapidly. Now the buyer may demand too many goods from the seller. Suppose buyer ordered the goods for use in buyer's own manufacturing process. Once the market takes off, may buyer order additional items and resell them at a higher price? Suppose buyer is merged into a multinational corporation that uses its marketing skills and capital to double the demand for buyer's product. Must seller supply these additional requirements at the lower contract price?

Those who drafted Article 2 of the UCC were well aware of Havighurst and Berman's article. Sections 2-306, 1-201, 2-103 (1)(b) and the Official Comments to these sections tell us something about how the Code proposes to solve these problems. (Of course, those drafting requirements and output contracts can and do deal with these problems explicitly. Indeed, we raise them, in part, so that you will see them if you are ever called on to draft such documents.)[42] However, what are the require-

---

40. A buyer may also agree to buy a specified percentage of its requirements, the requirements of a particular plant, or the units needed to produce a particular product.

41. *Requirement and Output Contracts*, 27 ILL. L. REV. 1 (1932).

42. *See* Note, *Requirements Contracts: Problems of Drafting and Construction*, 78 HARV. L. REV. 1212 (1965).

ments and output contracts problems that are likely to extend into the future?[43] We will look at a case considering the Code's resolution of one of the problems raised by Havighurst and Berman. Then we will study two of the most common problems involving requirements contracts today—whether a distributorship is a requirements contract governed by the UCC, and the impact of UCC § 2-201(1) on provisions for flexible quantity. That section, you may recall, says that a "writing is not insufficient because it omits or incorrectly states a term agreed upon but the contract is not enforceable under this paragraph beyond the quantity of goods shown in such writing." How does UCC § 2-306 track with this apparent demand that parties show the quantity in writing?

EMPIRE GAS CORP. v. AMERICAN BAKERIES CO.

United States Court of Appeals, Seventh Circuit
840 F.2d 1333 (1988)

POSNER, C.J.

This appeal in a diversity contract case presents a fundamental question—surprisingly little discussed by either courts or commentators—in the law of requirements contracts. Is such a contract essentially a buyer's option, entitling him to purchase all he needs of the good in question on the terms set forth in the contract, but leaving him free to purchase none if he wishes provided that he does not purchase the good from anyone else and is not acting out of ill will toward the seller?

Empire Gas Corporation is a retail distributor of liquefied petroleum gas, better known as "propane." It also sells converters that enable gasoline-powered motor vehicles to operate on propane. The sharp rise in gasoline prices in 1979 and 1980 made American Bakeries Company, which operated a fleet of more than 3,000 motor vehicles to serve its processing plants and bakeries, interested in the possibility of converting its fleet to propane, which was now one-third to one-half less expensive than gasoline. Discussions between the companies resulted in an agreement in principle. Empire Gas sent American Bakeries a draft of its standard "Guaranteed Fuel Supply Contract," which would have required American Bakeries to install a minimum number of conversion units each month and to buy all the propane for the converted vehicles from Empire Gas for eight years. American Bakeries rejected the contract and Empire Gas prepared a new one, which was executed on April 17, 1980, and which was "for approximately three thousand (3,000) [conversion] units, more or less depending upon requirements of Buyer, consisting of Fuel Tank, Fuel Lock Off Switch, Converter & appropriate Carburetor & Small Parts Kit," at a price of $750 per unit. American Bakeries agreed "to purchase propane motor fuel solely from EMPIRE GAS CORPORATION at all locations where EMPIRE GAS has supplied carburetion and dispensing equipment as long as EMPIRE GAS CORPORATION remains in a reasonably competitive price posture with other major suppliers." The contract was to last for four years.

---

43. *See* Caroline N. Bruckel [now Brown], *Consideration in Exclusive and Nonexclusive Open Quantity Contracts Under the UCC: a Proposal for a New System of Validation*, 68 MINN. L. REV. 117 (1983).

American Bakeries never ordered any equipment or propane from Empire Gas. Apparently within days after the signing of the contract American Bakeries decided not to convert its fleet to propane. No reason has been given for the decision.

Empire Gas brought suit against American Bakeries for breach of contract and won a jury verdict for $3,254,963, representing lost profits on 2,242 conversion units (the jury's estimate of American Bakeries' requirements) and on the propane fuel that the converted vehicles would have consumed during the contract period....

The heart of this case is the instruction concerning American Bakeries' obligation under the contract. If there were no legal category of "requirements" contracts and no provision of the Uniform Commercial Code governing such contracts, a strong argument could be made that American Bakeries agreed to buy 3,000 conversion units or *slightly* more or *slightly* less, depending on its actual needs, and hence that it broke the contract by taking none. This is not only a semantically permissible reading of the contract but one supported by the discussions that the parties had before the contract was signed (and these discussions are admissible to explain though not to change the parties' undertakings), in which American Bakeries assured Empire Gas that it was planning to convert its entire fleet. American Bakeries insisted on adding the phrase "more or less depending upon requirements of Buyer" just in case its estimate of 3,000 was off, and this is quite different from supposing that the phrase was added so that American Bakeries would have no obligation to buy any units at all.

The parties agree, however, that despite the negotiating history and the inclusion in the contract of a specific estimate of quantity, the quoted phrase sorted the contract into the legal bin labeled "requirements contract" and thereby brought it under the governance of § 2-306 (1) of the Uniform Commercial Code ... Over American Bakeries' objection the judge decided to read the statute to the jury verbatim and without amplification ... [However,] the law is [not] what a jury might make out of statutory language. The law is the statute as interpreted. The duty of interpretation is the judge's. Having interpreted the statute he must then convey the statute's meaning, as interpreted, in words the jury can understand. If § 2-306 means something different from what it seems to say, the instruction was erroneous.

The interpretive question involves the proviso [in § 2-306 (1)] dealing with "quantity unreasonably disproportionate to any stated estimate." This limitation is fairly easy to understand when the disproportion takes the form of the buyer's demanding more than the amount estimated. If there were no ceiling, and if the price happened to be advantageous to the buyer, he might increase his "requirements" so that he could resell the good at a profit.... This would place him in competition with the seller—a result the parties would not have wanted when they signed the contract. So the "unreasonably disproportionate" proviso carries out the likely intent of the parties. The only problem is that the same result could easily be reached by interpretation of the words "good faith" in the preceding clause of § 2-306 (1), thus making the proviso redundant. But redundancies designed to clarify or emphasize are common in legal drafting, and anyway the Uniform Commercial Code has its share of ambiguities ... *see Wisconsin Knife Works v. National Metal Crafters*, 781 F.2d 1280, 1288 (7th Cir. 1986).

The proviso does not distinguish between the buyer who demands more than the stated estimate and the buyer who demands less, and therefore if read literally it would forbid a buyer to take (much) less than the stated estimate. Since the judge did not attempt to interpret the statute, the jury may have read it literally, and if so the judge in effect directed a verdict for Empire Gas. The stated estimate was for 3,000 units; American Bakeries took none; if this was not unreasonably disproportionate to the stated estimate, what buyer shortfall could be?

So we must decide whether the proviso should be read literally when the buyer is demanding less rather than more than the stated estimate. There are no cases on the question in Illinois, and authority elsewhere is sparse, considering how often (one might think) the question must have arisen. But the clearly dominant approach is not to construe the proviso literally, but instead to treat the overdemanding and underdemanding cases differently.... We think this is right....

Granted, there is language in the Official Comments (not official in Illinois, be it noted) which points to symmetrical treatment of the overdemanding and underdemanding cases: "the agreed estimate is to be regarded as a center around which the parties intend the variation to occur." UCC § 2-306, comment 3. But there is no elaboration; and the statement is in tension with the statement in comment 2 that "good faith variations from prior requirements are permitted even when the variation may be such as to result in discontinuance," for if that principle is sound in general, why should it cease to be sound just because the parties included an estimate of the buyer's requirements? A tiny verbal point against the symmetrical interpretation is the last word of the proviso—"demanded." The statement that "no quantity unreasonably disproportionate to any stated estimate ... may be ... demanded" is more naturally read as applying to the case where the buyer is demanding more than when he is reducing his demand below the usual or estimated level.

More important than this verbal skirmishing is the fact that the entire proviso is in a sense redundant given the words "good faith" in the main clause of the statute. The proviso thus seems to have been designed to explicate the term "good faith" rather than to establish an independent legal standard. And the aspect of good faith that required explication had only to do with disproportionately *large* demands. If the buyer saw an opportunity to increase his profits by reselling the seller's goods because the market price had risen above the contract price, the exploitation of that opportunity might not *clearly* spell bad faith; the proviso was added to close off the opportunity. There is no indication that the draftsmen were equally, if at all, concerned about the case where the buyer takes less than his estimated requirements, provided, of course, that he does not buy from anyone else. We conclude that the Illinois courts would allow a buyer to reduce his requirements to zero if he was acting in good faith, even though the contract contained an estimate of those requirements.

This conclusion would be greatly strengthened—too much so, as we shall see— if the only purpose of a requirements contract were to give the seller a reasonably assured market for his product *by forbidding the buyer to satisfy any of his needs by buying from another supplier....* The buyer's undertaking to deal exclusively with a particular seller gives the seller some, although far from complete, assurance of having a market for his goods; and of course he must compensate the buyer for giving up the opportunity to shop around for a better deal from competing sellers.

There was no breach of *this* obligation.... If the obligation were not just to refrain from buying a competitor's goods but to buy approximately the stated estimate (or, in the absence of any estimate, the buyer's "normal" requirements), the contract would be altogether more burdensome to the buyer. Instead of just committing himself not to buy from a competitor even if the competitor offered a better product or terms of sale, he would be committing himself to go through with whatever project generated the estimate of required quantity, no matter what happened over the life of the project save those exceptional events that would excuse performance under the related excuses of *force majeure*, impossibility, impracticability, or frustration. This would be a big commitment to infer from the inclusion in the contract of an estimated quantity, at least once the parties concede as they do here that their contract really is a requirements contract and not a contract for the estimate itself—not, in other words, a fixed-quantity contract.

Both extreme interpretations—that the buyer need only refrain from dealing with a competitor of the seller, and that the buyer cannot go significantly beneath the estimated quantity except in dire circumstances—must be rejected, as we shall see. Nevertheless the judge should not have read the "unreasonably disproportionate" proviso in §2-306 (1) to the jury. The proviso does not apply, though the requirement of good faith does, where the buyer takes less rather than more of the stated estimate in a requirements contract.

This error in instructions requires reversal and a new trial on liability unless it is clear either that American Bakeries acted in good faith or that it acted in bad faith, since the statute requires the buyer to take his "good faith" requirements from the seller, irrespective of proportionality. The Uniform Commercial Code does not contain a definition of "good faith" that seems applicable to the buyer under a requirements contract. Compare §2-104 (1) with §2-103 (1)(b). Nor has the term a settled meaning in law generally; it is a chameleon.... Clearly, American Bakeries was acting in bad faith if during the contract period it bought propane conversion units from anyone other than Empire Gas, or made its own units, or reduced its purchases because it wanted to hurt Empire Gas (for example because they were competitors in some other market). Equally clearly, it was not acting in bad faith if it had a business reason for deciding not to convert that was independent of the terms of the contract or any other aspect of its relationship with Empire Gas, such as a drop in the demand for its bakery products that led it to reduce or abandon its fleet of delivery trucks. A harder question is whether it was acting in bad faith if it changed its mind about conversion for no (disclosed) reason. There is no evidence in the record on why it changed its mind beyond vague references to "budget problems" that, so far as appears, may have been nothing more than a euphemism for a decision by American Bakeries not to allocate funds for conversion to propane.

If no reason at all need be given for scaling back one's requirements even to zero, then a requirements contract is from the buyer's standpoint just an option to purchase up to (or slightly beyond, i.e., within the limits of reasonable proportionality) the stated estimate on the terms specified in the contract, except that the buyer cannot refuse to exercise the option because someone offers him better terms. This is not an unreasonable position, but it is not the law. Among the less important reasons for this conclusion are that option contracts are dealt with elsewhere in the Code, see § 2-311, and that the Official Comments to § 2-306 state that "a shut-down by a requirements buyer for lack of orders might be permissible where a shut-down *merely to curtail losses* would not." UCC § 2-306, comment 2 (emphasis added). More compelling is the Illinois Code Comment to § 2-306 which states that "this section ... is but a codification of prior Illinois decisional law," which had made clear that a requirements contract was more than a buyer's option. "By the original agreement, appellant was entitled to order all the coal which was required or needed in its business for the season named; by the modified contract, appellant was restricted to the privilege of ordering twelve thousand tons. It was not the intention here to contract for the mere option or privilege of buying coal at a future time, but simply to limit the quantity to be bought.... It was not intended to be an option contract." *Minnesota Lumber Co. v. Whitebreast Coal Co.*, 160 Ill. 85, 96–97, 43 N.E. 774 (1896). "Requirements" are more than purely subjective "needs," which would be the equivalent of "wants." [citations omitted].

These cases are old, but nothing has happened to sap their strength ... The statement of an estimate invites the seller to begin making preparations to satisfy the contract, and although no reliance expense was incurred by the seller in this case, a seller is entitled to expect that the buyer will buy something like the estimated requirements unless it has a valid business reason for buying less. More important than the estimate (which was not a factor in the Illinois cases just cited) is the fact that ordinarily a requirements contract is terminated after performance has begun, rather than before as in the present case. Whether or not the seller can prove reliance damages, the sudden termination of the contract midway through performance is bound to disrupt his operations somewhat. The Illinois courts interpret a requirements contract as a sharing of risk between seller and buyer. The seller assumes the risk of a change in the buyer's business that makes continuation of the contract unduly costly, but the buyer assumes the risk of a less urgent change in his circumstances, perhaps illustrated by the facts of this case where so far as one can tell the buyer's change of mind reflected no more than a reassessment of the balance of advantages and disadvantages under the contract. American Bakeries did not agree to buy conversion units and propane for trucks that it got rid of, but neither did Empire Gas agree to forgo sales merely because new management at American Bakeries decided that its capital would be better employed in some other investment than conversion to propane.

The general distinction that we are trying to make is well illustrated by *Southwest Natural Gas Co. v. Oklahoma Portland Cement Co.*, 102 F.2d 630 (10th Cir. 1939), which to the drafters of the Uniform Commercial Code exemplified "reasonable variation of an extreme sort" (at least in the absence of an estimate, but that is irrelevant, for reasons we have explained). UCC § 2-306, comment 2. A cement company agreed to buy all of its requirements of gas from the seller for 15 years. Seven years later, the cement company replaced its boiler, which had worn out, with more modern equipment; as a result its need for gas fell by 80 percent. The court deemed this a bona fide change in the cement company's requirements. It would have been unreasonable to make the company replace its worn-out plant with an obsolete facility.

It is a nice question how exigent the buyer's change of circumstances must be to allow him to scale down his requirements from either the estimated level or, in the absence of estimate, the "normal" level. Obviously it need not be so great as to give him a defense under the doctrines of impossibility, impracticability, or frustration, or under a *force majeure* clause. Yet, although more than whim is required … how much more is unclear. There is remarkably little authority on the question. This is a good sign; it suggests that, while we might think it unsatisfactory for the law to be unclear on so fundamental a question, the people affected by the law are able to live with the lack of certainty. The reason may be that parties linked in an ongoing relationship—the usual situation under a requirements contract—have a strong incentive to work out disagreements amicably rather than see the relationship destroyed by litigation.

The essential ingredient of good faith in the case of the buyer's reducing his estimated requirements is that he not merely have had second thoughts about the terms of the contract and want to get out of it.… Whether the buyer has any greater obligation is unclear … but need not be decided here. Once it is decided (as we have) that a buyer cannot arbitrarily declare his requirements to be zero, this becomes an easy case, because American Bakeries has never given any reason for its change of heart. It might seem that once the district judge decided to instruct the jury in the language of the statute, American Bakeries was foreclosed from arguing that it had scaled down its requirements in good faith; a reduction to zero could never be proportionate if, as the instruction implied, the proviso on disproportion applies to reductions as well as increases in the buyer's takings. But the judge did not make this decision until the instructions conference. Until then American Bakeries had every opportunity and incentive to introduce evidence of why it decided not to convert its fleet to propane. It introduced none, and even at the argument in this court its counsel could give no reason for the change of heart beyond a hint that it was due to a change in management, which would not be enough by itself to justify a change in the buyer's requirements.

Even though Empire Gas had the burden of proving breach of contract and therefore (we may assume) of proving that American Bakeries acted in bad faith in reducing its requirements from 3,000 conversion units to zero … no reasonable jury could have failed to find bad faith, and therefore the error in instructing the jury on proportionality was harmless. Empire Gas put in evidence, uncontested and incontestable, showing that American Bakeries had not got rid of its fleet of trucks and did have the financial wherewithal to go through with the conversion process. After this evidence came in, American Bakeries could avoid a directed verdict only by introducing some evidence concerning its reasons for reducing its requirements. It not only introduced no evidence, but as is plain from counsel's remarks at argument it has no evidence that it would care to put before the jury—no reasons that it would care to share with either the district court or this court. It disagrees with the standard of good faith, believing that so long as it did not buy conversion units elsewhere or want to hurt Empire Gas it was free to reduce its requirements as much as it pleased. It does not suggest that it has a case under the standard we have adopted, which requires at a minimum that the reduction of requirements not have been motivated solely by a reassessment of the balance of advantages and disadvantages under the contract to the buyer....

The jury's finding of liability must stand; but was there error in the assessment of damages? American Bakeries objects violently to the assumption made by Empire Gas's expert witness that the vehicles converted by American Bakeries, had it honored what Empire Gas contends were its obligations under the contract, would have run 100 percent on propane. The conversion units would have been dual units, which permit the driver by a flick of a switch in the engine to run his vehicle on either gasoline or propane. But since the parties agree that the price of propane was lower than that of gasoline throughout the entire contract period, a driver would have switched his conversion unit to gasoline only when he was low on propane and too far away from a propane station to reach it before he ran out. This factor was not big enough to upset the expert witness's calculations significantly. The calculation of damages is estimation rather than measurement, and it is foolish to prolong a lawsuit in quest of delusive precision.

The other complaints about the damage assessment are equally inconsequential, and do not require discussion. A great weakness of American Bakeries' case was its failure to present its own estimate of damages, in the absence of which the jury could have no idea of what adjustments to make in order to take account of American Bakeries' arguments. American Bakeries may have feared that if it put in its own estimate of damages the jury would be irresistibly attracted to that figure as a compromise. But if so, American Bakeries gambled double or nothing, as it were; and we will not relieve it of the consequences of its risky strategy....

The judgment is affirmed.

[JUDGE KANNE's dissent is omitted.]

NOTES AND QUESTIONS

1. *A different view:* Relying on a "plain meaning" approach to statutory interpretation, the Alabama Supreme Court rejected Judge Posner's analysis.[44] The Alabama court held that § 2-306's "unreasonably disproportionate" language does apply when a buyer orders an amount less that an agreed-upon estimate. The court said that a buyer of coal breached its contract by purchasing only 41 percent of the amount of

---

44. Simcala, Inc. v. Am. Coal Trade, Inc., 821 So. 2d 197 (Ala. 2001).

coal it had estimated it needed in the contract because that amount was unreasonably disproportionate to the estimate. Two justices dissented and said the majority's decision was inconsistent with the purpose of the statute. If the Alabama Supreme Court had wanted to justify its decision in terms of purpose in addition to relying on the statutory language, how might it have done so? What is the best analysis of the purpose of the "unreasonably disproportionate" clause of § 2-306 (1)?

2. *Practical problems:* A seller faces some real difficulty in determining just when requirements have become "unreasonably disproportionate." Parties face similar practical problems in asserting that demands are not made in good faith. Cheryl R. Guttenberg[45] asserts:

> The distinction between good and bad faith reductions in requirements that the Seventh Circuit adopted in *Empire Gas* is of no ... practical use.... The court stated that seller assumes the risk of changes in buyer's circumstances that make continuation of the contract unduly costly, but does not assume the risk of less urgent changes. It is unclear when a change in circumstances makes performance of the contract unduly costly and when a change is less urgent. The court offered no guidelines other than that something more than whim is required.... [T]his distinction leaves an expansive middle ground where a court's application of the distinction would be wholly unpredictable.[46]

She advocates a business reason rule: "It would define good faith as buyer providing seller with a business reason for a reduction. 'Business reason' means an economic reason, such as business losses or a more profitable alternative investment."[47] She asserts this rule "would provide contracting parties with definite guidelines."[48] This would be efficient because the parties will not have to expend resources bargaining for a more explicit allocation of risk.

Contrast Judge Posner's explanation of why there are few cases construing § 2-306 (1):

> There is remarkably little authority on the question. This is a good sign; it suggests that, while we might think it unsatisfactory for the law to be unclear on so fundamental a question, the people affected by the law are able to live with the lack of certainty. The reason may be that parties linked in an ongoing relationship—the usual situation under a requirements contract—have a strong incentive to work out disagreements amicably rather than see the relationship destroyed by litigation.[49]

---

45. *And Then There Were None: Requirements Contracts and the Buyer Who Does Not Buy*, 64 WASH. L. REV. 871 (1989).
46. *Id.* at 882.
47. *Id.* at 880, 882.
48. *Id.* at 883.
49. Empire Gas Corp., 840 F.2d at 1334.

3. *Two examples applying the "good faith" test:* Consider these two examples of the application of this concept:[50]

> (i) [T]he controversy in *Orange & Rockland Utilities, Inc. v. Amerada Hess Corp.*[51] concerned the alleged breach of a fixed-price contract for the oil requirements of a utility. Both parties expected the oil to be used as a supplement to the utility's primary fuel, natural gas, but a rapid rise in fuel prices made it more profitable for the utility to sell its natural gas reserves and substitute for the gas the cheap oil it could obtain under the fixed-price Amerada Hess contract. Additionally, the company's access to cheap oil enabled it to increase dramatically its sales of electricity to other utilities, thereby further increasing its own needs for oil. Under these circumstances, the trial court found that all of the utility's increased requirements were incurred in bad faith. By selling greater amounts of electricity to other utilities, Orange & Rockland was forcing the oil company to supply indirectly the needs of those other utilities at low prices; by selling its reserves of gas and substituting oil, it was seizing an opportunity to reap substantial profits at the expense of the oil company.
>
> (ii) In contrast, in *Eastern Air Lines, Inc. v. Gulf Oil Corp.*,[52] a supplier's assertion of the buyer's bad faith was rejected. Eastern had been "fuel freighting"—obtaining fuel in excess of its known requirements at low-priced refueling stations [run by other companies] and thereby obviating the need to obtain fuel at higher-priced stations [run by Gulf]. Gulf attacked fuel freighting as a bad-faith practice,[53] but because fuel freighting was an established practice in the industry, the court found that it had probably been taken into consideration during contract negotiations, and held that Eastern had not breached its obligation of good faith.

If increases under a contract that contains no estimate develop slowly and steadily over a long period, they are arguably allowable on the theory that the parties to a long-term contract should anticipate such increases. A slow and steady increase also means that each year's requirements are not unreasonably disproportionate to the prior year's orders. The pre-Code case of *Ehrenworth v. George F. Stuhmer & Co.*[54] upheld the buyer's 8,000 percent increase in orders over a seven-year period under a requirements contract.

4. *Supplying the buyer's requirements of . . . what?* Lawyers and engineers put effort into defining which of the buyer's needs the seller will have a right to supply. This

---

50. Note, *Requirements Contracts, "More or Less," Under the Uniform Commercial Code*, 33 RUTGERS L. REV. 105 (1980).
51. 59 A.D.2d 110, 397 N.Y.S.2d 814 (1977).
52. 415 F. Supp. 429 (S.D. Fla. 1975).
53. Gulf contended that slight changes in its prices vis-a-vis those of companies operating refueling stations in other cities led to drastic alterations in Eastern's refueling patterns.
54. 229 N.Y. 210, 128 N.E. 108 (1920).

becomes more difficult when the businesses are large and complex, as is illustrated by *Whitesell Corp. v. Whirlpool Corp.*[55] In 1995, the two firms entered a long-term "Strategic Alliance Agreement." Whitesell was to be Whirlpool's supplier of its requirements of cold-headed/threaded fasteners. The agreement listed the parts currently being supplied; parts that might be supplied in the future if Whitesell were the low bidder for them; parts that would not be covered by the agreement; and the Whirlpool manufacturing divisions that were subject to the agreement.

The relationship "became strained," and in 2004 Whitesell brought suit against Whirlpool for breach of contract. It contended that Whirlpool had ordered fasteners from other suppliers that should have been purchased from Whitesell. The jury found for Whitesell on a number of its claims and awarded damages of more than $25 million. The appellate court affirmed the award. This involved finding that there was sufficient evidence to support the jury's interpretation of the contract. There were many issues. For example, did the requirements contract cover fasteners that Whirlpool bought from others as "safety stock," in order to have an inventory to cover delays by Whitesell? Did it cover fasteners used by other suppliers when Whirlpool ordered component parts of Whirlpool products from them? Did it cover the requirements of the Benton Harbor plant, which was not listed as a manufacturing division in the Strategic Alliance Agreement? That is, was Whirlpool's obligation to buy from Whitesell limited to the requirements of its manufacturing divisions?

It is likely that the drafters of the Strategic Alliance Agreement did not foresee all of these questions as raising issues to be defined by a court. As we have noted in Volume 1 of these materials, master supply agreements involve a long process that is likely to build knowledge and trust. Here, Whitesell obtained a promise from Whirlpool that Whirlpool would buy its requirements from Whitesell. Such a commitment may have been needed to justify the investment in being ready to supply large numbers of fasteners. Whirlpool, we can note, might have been willing to make such a commitment in light of the remedy limitation that the Strategic Alliance Agreement contained. It said: "In no event shall Buyer be liable to Seller for damages arising from any performance or breach." The court found that this violated § 2-719 of the Uniform Commercial Code. The clause did not allow for minimum adequate remedies. The court quoted the official comment to that section of the Code: "It is of the very essence of a sales contract that at least minimum adequate remedies be available."

What is the lesson of the *Whitesell* case for transaction-planning lawyers? They could invest more time in defining the precise requirements covered by the contract; this would probably require a great deal of foresight and technical knowledge. Another route might be not to agree to purchase the buyer's entire requirements from the seller. Of course, the buyer would have to convince the seller to enter the deal without such a commitment. This is common practice in the U.S. automobile industry, which deals under "blanket orders."

55. 496 Fed. Appx. 551, 554–55 (6th Cir. 2012).

c. Distributorships — Is a Distribution Contract a Requirements Contract?

A very common commercial arrangement involves a manufacturer who contracts with a distributor to promote and deliver the manufacturer's goods within a defined territory. The distributors often provide warehousing and delivery services, as well as acting as a sales force. A distributor may carry several "lines" from several different manufacturers. A distributor generally prefers to be the exclusive source for a manufacturer's product in the region. Only if the distributor "has an exclusive" can the distributor be sure of capturing all of the value of its promotional efforts and developing long-term loyal customers. The distributor acts as a conduit for the goods. The contracts between manufacturers and distributors involve duties that make the distributors look, for some purposes, as if they were the part-time employees or agents for the manufacturer, but for other purposes as if they were buyers of goods for resale. What difference does the characterization of the agreement make? One important difference is that if the transaction between a manufacturer and a distributor is characterized as a sale of goods, the UCC applies. And the application of the UCC may yield different results from the application of common law.

An example of such a question arose in the case of *Famous Brands, Inc. v. David Sherman Corp.*[56] In the course of Famous Brands' purchase of a liquor wholesaler (Midland), Famous sought reassurance that Sherman would continue to supply it with Everclear and other liquor brands. Sherman's representative replied, "If [the proposed sale] happens, I want you to know that we will be more than happy to have you distribute Everclear alcohol and any other brands that Midland will be selling for us." Later, Sherman said that Famous could "count on" Sherman. Shortly thereafter, Sherman terminated the distributorship, apparently because Famous refused to carry a full line of Sherman's products. Famous sued to enforce the distributorship agreement. The trial court granted Sherman's motion for summary judgment on the grounds that (1) the terms of the contract were too indefinite, and (2) there was no mutuality of obligation.

The Eighth Circuit reversed, finding that since the parties had operated under the agreement for over a year, there was a jury issue as to whether an implied contract had arisen. In addition, the court found that the "no mutuality" objection was not well-founded. First, the arrangement could be regarded as a "requirements" contract, recognized as valid in South Dakota's adoption of § 2-306 of the UCC. In addition, the plaintiff had a plausible promissory estoppel argument, based on reliance by Famous on Sherman's reassurance that it could continue as a distributor.

Section 2-306 (2) of the UCC says that a "lawful agreement by either the seller or the buyer for exclusive dealing in the kind of goods concerned imposes unless otherwise agreed an obligation by the seller to use best efforts to supply the goods and by the buyer to use best efforts to promote their sale." But how much effort is "best"

---

56. 814 F.2d 517, 519 (8th Cir. 1987).

efforts? If either the buyer or the seller does nothing, this would seem to violate the obligation. However, if either of them takes some action, it will be difficult to judge if they should have done more.[57] How much must a seller invest to see that goods get to its distributor quickly? How much must a distributor spend on advertising and promotion? We would not be surprised to see litigation about this issue turn into a battle of experts. The seller's expert would find the buyer's judgments less than best efforts, while the buyer's expert would find them more than enough. What is a court to do then? The burden of proof would help in some cases, but we should expect real difficulty in others.

The next case discusses in an extended fashion the implications of the characterization of a distributorship. In *Famous Brands*, characterizing the contract as governed by the UCC imposes an obligation of good faith, and since the UCC validates requirements contracts, this arguably avoids some common law challenges that are based on the higher standard of definiteness that may apply if the common law rule applies.

The UCC, however, is a two-edged sword. In the next case, the distributor seeks to avoid application of the Code, since the Code may require a signed writing in cases where the common law would not.

LORENZ SUPPLY CO. v. AMERICAN STANDARD, INC.

Michigan Supreme Court
419 Mich. 610, 358 N.W.2d 845 (1984)

Levin, J.

The principal question presented is whether the distributorship agreement[58] between Lorenz and American Standard is a "contract for the sale of goods" within the meaning

---

57. In *Bloor v. Falstaff*, 601 F.2d 609 (2d Cir. 1979), the contract required Falstaff to use best efforts to promote and maintain a high volume of sales of Ballantine beer. The court decided that Falstaff did not use best efforts. However, Victor Goldberg, in *Great Contracts Cases: In Search of Best Efforts: Reinterpreting* Bloor v. Falstaff, 44 St. Louis U. L.J. 1465 (2000), argues that the court was mistaken in light of the nature of the deal and the purposes of the clause. Goldberg concedes that the lawyers did not frame the issue for the court properly, and they did not create a record that would have helped the court see the purposes of the clause. His article reinforces the idea that "best efforts" is an extremely difficult concept to apply.

58. [1] Plaintiff Lorenz Supply Company and defendant American Standard, Inc., entered into an agreement whereunder Lorenz agreed to purchase $420,000 worth of plumbing inventory from American Standard. The jury found that, at the same time, the parties agreed that Lorenz was to become a distributor of American Standard products in the Detroit area. The terms of the inventory sale agreement, but *not* the distributorship agreement, were set forth in writing. Subsequently, a dispute arose concerning the performance of the inventory sale agreement. Lorenz withheld payments totaling $65,100 for goods received because it believed that it was owed over $70,000 for alleged errors pertaining to the inventory sale. American Standard then refused to supply additional products under the distributorship agreement unless Lorenz paid cash in advance. Lorenz filed the instant action claiming breach of both the written inventory sale agreement and the oral distributorship agreement. The complaint sought $2,000,000 in damages. American Standard counterclaimed for approximately $72,000 for products delivered under the inventory sale agreement.

of § 2-201 of the Uniform Commercial Code.[59] We hold that it is not and affirm the decision of the Court of Appeals affirming the judgment entered by the circuit court on the jury's verdict in favor of Lorenz.

I. Lorenz pleaded and the jury found that Lorenz entered into a distributorship agreement with American Standard. The only written evidence of this agreement was a letter from American Standard to Lorenz that "welcome[d]" Lorenz "to the numbers of American Standard distributors across the country."

Section 2-201 does not require that the terms of a contract for the sale of goods, other than the quantity term, be expressed in writing.[60] The requirements of § 2-201 are satisfied if the writing indicates that "a contract of sale has been made between the parties" and "specif [ies] a quantity." 2 ANDERSON, UNIFORM COMMERCIAL CODE (3d ed.), § 2-201:97, p. 61.[61]

The concurring opinion recognizes that the quantity term of a distributorship agreement is generally uncertain, and to require that it be stated with certainty would put most distributorship agreements out of compliance with § 2-201 and, hence, if a distributorship agreement is a "contract for the sale of goods," make them unenforceable. The concurring opinion seeks to avoid this dilemma by inferring a quantity term. The quantity term must, however, under § 2-201, be specifically stated.[62]

A requirements or output term of a contract, although general in language, nonetheless is, *if stated in the writing*, specific as to quantity, and in compliance with § 2-201.[63] However, not all distributorship agreements are requirements or output contracts. The jury was not asked to decide whether the instant distributorship agreement contained a requirements or output term, and this Court would exceed its role if it were to imply a provision akin to a requirements term.[64] Under the construction

---

59. [2] M.C.L. § 440.2201; M.S.A. § 19.2201.

60. [3] The Official Comment to § 2-201 provides, in part:

The required writing need not contain all the material terms of the contract and such material terms as are stated need not be precisely stated. All that is required is that the writing afford a basis for believing that the offered oral evidence rests on a real transaction.... *The only term which must appear is the quantity term* which need not be accurately stated but recovery is limited to the amount stated. The price, time and place of payment or delivery, the general quality of the goods, or any particular warranties may all be omitted. (Emphasis added.)

61. [4] It appears that most, if not all, commentators agree with Anderson's observation that § 2-201 requires that a writing must specify a quantity. *See, e.g.,* CALAMARI & PERILLO, THE LAW OF CONTRACTS, § 313, p. 486; WHITE & SUMMERS, UNIFORM COMMERCIAL CODE (2d ed.), § 2–4, pp. 59–60; 3 DUESENBERG & KING, UNIFORM COMMERCIAL CODE SERVICE (Bender), § 2.04[2][a], pp. 2–59.

62. [5] ... [Official Comment to UCC 2-201] and Doral Hosiery Corp. v. Sav-A-Stop, Inc., 377 F. Supp. 387, 389 (E.D. Pa. 1974)....

63. [6] *See* Cox Caulking & Insulating Co. v. Brockett Distributing Co., 150 Ga. App. 424, 426, 258 S.E.2d 51 (1979); 3 DUESENBERG & KING, UNIFORM COMMERCIAL CODE SERVICE (Bender), § 2.04[2][a], pp. 2–59; 2 ANDERSON, UNIFORM COMMERCIAL CODE (3d ed.), §§ 2-201:113, 2-201:114, p. 70.

64. [7] Other courts have refused to hold that a distributorship agreement contains an implied term that the seller will supply the buyer with its requirements. *See, e.g.,* Eastern Dental Corp. v. Isaac

advanced in the concurring opinion, American Standard could maintain an action against Lorenz for failure to purchase its requirements whether the parties agreed thereto or not.

Because many distributorship agreements are not requirements or output contracts and in such cases the quantity term is generally uncertain, we conclude that the drafters of the Uniform Commercial Code did not intend that all distributorship agreements be regarded as "contract[s] for the sale of goods."[65]

II. A writing that satisfies § 2-201 does not prove the terms of a contract; such a writing merely removes the statutory bar to the enforcement of the contract whether its terms—other than the quantity term which alone must be specified in writing—be written, oral, or partly written and partly oral. In the instant case, the letter from American Standard to Lorenz welcoming him as a distributor indicates that a contract was made between the parties. If one concludes, as would the author of the concurring opinion, that the letter satisfies the requirements of § 2-201, then the terms of the instant agreement, whatever those terms might be, are enforceable. Because the terms of a contract for the sale of goods, other than the quantity term, need not be stated in writing, the declaration in the concurring opinion that § 2-201 applies to distributorship agreements does not bear on the disputed terms of the instant distributorship agreement.... *Affirmed.*

BRICKLEY, J. (concurring).

This case presents for the first time in this state the question whether the Uniform Commercial Code, MCL § 440.1101 *et seq.*; MSA § 19.1101 *et seq.*, and its Statute of Frauds, MCL § 440.2201; MSA § 19.2201, are applicable to a distributorship agreement, and whether the Statute of Frauds' quantity requirement can be satisfied by a writing stating that one party is a distributor of another's products. I would answer yes to both questions.

I. In July of 1972, plaintiff Lorenz Supply Company was engaged in a family-owned and operated business selling "in the wall" plumbing items, such as pipes and valves, in the Detroit area. Defendant American Standard, Inc., a major manufacturer of diversified products, was planning to close out a heating and plumbing distribution outlet in Troy, run by its Amstan supply division.

Plaintiff's president, Robert Lorenz, desirous of expanding his plumbing line to "out of the wall" fixtures, such as sinks and faucets, entered into negotiations with defendant's local management. These negotiations resulted in an agreement whereby Lorenz would purchase $420,000 worth of inventory from defendant's Troy warehouse and take responsibility for its outstanding delivery orders. As part of the inducement

---

Masel Co., Inc., 502 F. Supp. 1354, 1364 (E.D. Pa. 1980); Cavalier Mobile Homes, Inc. v. Liberty Homes, Inc., 53 Md. App. 379, 395, 454 A.2d 367 (1983).

65. [8] We express no opinion on the question whether a distributorship agreement may fall within the broader category of "transactions in goods" within the meaning of § 2-102 of the UCC, MCL § 440.2102; MSA § 19.2102. See FARNSWORTH, CONTRACTS, § 8.16, p. 612; 3A CORBIN, CONTRACTS, § 700, p. 309.

for the inventory sale, Lorenz was to be made a "preferred" distributor of defendant's products. Plaintiff's president testified at trial that defendant promised to use its best efforts to supply items on a regular basis as they were needed and that plaintiff could distribute defendant's products for as long as it desired.

The arrangement for the inventory sale was reduced to a specific writing that set forth the details for transfer of the goods. The goods were to be transferred from the defendant's warehouse in August 1972. When Mr. Lorenz inquired as to the distributorship part of the arrangement, he was advised that it was the policy of defendant not to have written distributorship agreements. However, in the following month plaintiff received a confirmation letter from an official of defendant corporation. It expressed "happiness with the way our whole negotiations turned out with regard to your purchase of the Amstan inventory and, more importantly, to welcome you to the numbers of American Standard distributors across the country." Lorenz immediately began to enlarge his facilities and augment his staff in preparation for the distributorship and its expected enhancement of his business.

Unfortunately, happiness did not become a hallmark of the relationship. Lorenz first became concerned that defendant was not honoring the terms of their agreement at the time of the inventory transfer in August of 1972, when he received reports that some of the fastest-selling inventory from the Troy warehouse was seen departing for destinations other than plaintiff's business. Lorenz would later testify that some of the fastest-selling items from the inventory were sold to other distributors. Lorenz also testified that defendant overcharged him for some of the items he received from the sale, and charged for some items not received at all. Lorenz further testified at trial that, when he complained to defendant about these various errors, he was told on several occasions that restitution would be made for the missing inventory, and that he should keep track of the billing errors so that the total amount could be offset against his account at a later date.

The dispute between the parties and efforts to resolve it continued through the remainder of 1972 and into 1973. Finally, in December 1973, plaintiff, claiming that it was owed $72,000 by defendant as a result of the alleged errors, refused to pay approximately $65,000 otherwise owing to defendant.[66] Defendant, disputing these assertions, advised plaintiff that it would be cut off from further products if it did not pay on its account. When the payment was not received by January 1974, defendant placed plaintiff on "credit hold," meaning that plaintiff could receive additional products only by paying cash in advance.

Meanwhile, plaintiff filed suit for breach of contract. Defendant denied a breach and counterclaimed for the monies due according to defendant's accounting. Robert

---

66. [1] Plaintiff was to pay defendant $420,000, in six $70,000 monthly installments, for the inventory in defendant's Troy warehouse. Plaintiff was also purchasing additional materials from the defendant under the distributorship arrangement. The record is not clear as to precisely how much of the disputed credits or debits between the parties was attributable to the inventory sale as opposed to ongoing purchases of non-inventory merchandise. It is likely the accounts were combined.

Lorenz testified at trial that he secured additional financing, at great personal cost, in order to continue to buy essential items from defendant in cash. This in turn compounded his financial problems. Finally, in June 1974, defendant advised plaintiff that because of "restrictions placed on your orders by the credit department ... we are cancelling all open orders as of June 15, 1974." Plaintiff filed for bankruptcy in March 1975, and at the time of trial was a defunct corporation.

Plaintiff offered evidence at trial that it was saddled with a quarter-million dollar "dead" inventory because it was denied essential related products by defendant, both because it did not receive promised material from the Troy warehouse and because of the refusal of the defendant to continue to furnish products under the distributorship agreement. Lorenz further testified that, in spite of contracting for $420,000 worth of inventory from the Troy warehouse, he received only $260,000 worth of products.

The trial judge instructed the jury that there were "two separate issues that are at issue in this case; one, an issue with respect to the sale of the inventory at the Troy warehouse of American Standard, and the second issue being permitting Lorenz Supply Company to distribute American Standard's products in the Detroit area."

[The jury found a breach of the inventory sale, and damages to plaintiff of $45,000. The jury also found plaintiff had been the victim of a breach of the distributorship agreement with damages of $255,000. After the trial judge ordered a new trial on defendant's counterclaim, the parties stipulated to plaintiff's liability of $69,873.40 and avoided a retrial on that issue.]

Defendant argued before the Court of Appeals, as it does here, that the distributorship agreement was a "transaction in goods" under Article 2 (Sales) of the Uniform Commercial Code and, therefore, was subject to the Statute of Frauds of that article, thus making it unenforceable since the letter welcoming the plaintiff as a distributor did not satisfy the "writing" requirement. Defendant also contested the admission of certain evidence relating to lost profits and argued that the jury's erroneous verdict on the counterclaim invalidated the entire verdict and should have entitled them to a new trial on all issues. Finally, defendant argues that even if it is enforceable, the distributorship agreement was terminable at will, thus precluding any damage award for lost profits.

The letter from defendant to plaintiff, which is the only written evidence of the distributorship aspect of the arrangement between the parties, reads as follows:

> Dear Bob:
>
> Now that you have officially joined the family of American Standard distributors, I want to record with you my extreme happiness with the way our whole negotiations turned out with regard to your purchase of the Amstan inventory and, more importantly, to welcome you to the numbers of American Standard distributors across the country.
>
> Ed and I are most enthusiastic about your ability to help us participate in larger measure in the Detroit market and I hope the opportunity will soon

present itself when I can express my sincerest welcome to those other Lorenz personnel who I have not yet met but on whom we are counting for the strongest possible support in a very difficult market.

It is a pleasure to have you with us and I trust that our association will be mutually beneficial for many years to come.

Sincerely yours,

Bren O'Connell

The Court of Appeals, 100 Mich. App. 600, 608, 300 N.W.2d 335 (1980), found that the distributorship agreement did not come within the purview of the UCC since the "agreement did not require Lorenz to buy a certain quantity of goods or, indeed, to buy *any* goods from the defendant in the future." Rather, they said, "This agreement envisioned an ongoing economic relationship." The Court did allow that "Lorenz was granted the status of a 'preferred distributor' who would be entitled to purchase plumbing fixtures manufactured by the defendant in the future." Based on that relationship—that plaintiff need not buy but defendant must sell—the Court found the distributorship agreement to be outside of the Uniform Commercial Code and its Statute of Frauds and therefore enforceable.

The Court of Appeals further said that even if it had found the UCC to be applicable, the letter from the defendant to the plaintiff was a "sufficient written memorandum of the previous oral agreement to satisfy the requirements" of the Statute of Frauds. The Court further stated that "Lorenz never undertook to buy any of defendant's products, so the $500 statutory amount was never triggered." Finally, it said, "Although the quantity term is omitted, in the context of a distributorship agreement such an indefiniteness is inherent to the relationship and would not defeat the validity of the contract where the parties agreed. *See* MCL 440.2204(3); MSA 19.2204(3); MCL 440.2306(1); MSA 19.2306(1)." The Court did not deal with the counterclaim verdict question.

I disagree with both the analysis and conclusion of the Court of Appeals.

Dealing first with the Court of Appeals dictum that the $500 limit of the Statute of Frauds was not triggered, I see nothing in the record or arguments of the parties that would indicate that there was to be a $500 limit on what was to be covered by the distributorship agreement. To the contrary, the record reflects that thousands of dollars' worth of products were sold by defendant to plaintiff. The other two points of the Court's holding, that the UCC was not applicable to this type of distributorship agreement and the question of the satisfaction of the quantity term, are important issues, largely novel to our jurisprudence.

II. On the applicability of the UCC, the Court of Appeals did not distinguish between the "transaction in goods" criteria for the general application of Article 2 and the more specific finding of a "contract for the sale of goods," critical for the applicability of the Statute of Frauds. Instead, the Court of Appeals opined that the distributorship agreement did not fit the Statute of Frauds "contract for the sale of goods" definition and therefore held that the UCC, seemingly in its entirety, does not apply.

Appellants argue forcefully that such an interpretation would leave a major and fast-growing type of commercial activity outside the code. I agree.

Section 2-102 of the UCC, MCL § 440.2102 *et seq.*; MSA § 19.2102 *et seq.*, provides: "Unless the context otherwise requires, this article applies to *transactions in goods*" (emphasis added), whereas the Statute of Frauds of the UCC, MCL § 440.2201, MSA § 19.2201 provides:

> [A] *contract for the sale of goods* for the price of $500 or more is not enforceable by way of action or defense unless there is some writing sufficient to indicate that a contract for sale has been made.... A writing is not insufficient because it omits or incorrectly states a term agreed upon but the contract is not enforceable under this paragraph beyond the quantity of goods shown in such writing. (Emphasis added.)

MCL § 440.2106; MSA § 19.2106 defines "contract for sale" as both a "present sale of goods and a contract to sell goods at a future time."

"Transaction in goods" is a broad term and on its face would seem to cover an agreement that has as its purpose the ongoing transfer of title to goods between the parties. The UCC is to be "liberally construed," MCL § 440.1102; MSA § 19.1102, and is designed to "provide its own machinery for expansion of commercial practices. It is intended to make it possible for the law embodied in this act to be developed by the courts in the light of unforeseen and new circumstances and practices." UCC § 1-102, Official Comment 1. [Eds.: § 1-103 (a) and Official Comment 1, as revised in 2001.]

The predominant holdings among those states which have considered this issue are to the effect that a distributorship agreement is subject to the UCC, although there is anything but a consistent rationale for the holdings. Because cases involving distributorship agreements have involved different sections of Article 2, the courts have variously focused on the words "transaction in goods," "contract for the sale," or "goods." We have found nowhere a case which is precisely on point with the facts of this case, nor has our research disclosed a case with the exact legal analysis that we think is required to properly resolve the issue before us.

Our conviction that Article 2 itself contemplates a distributorship agreement is buttressed by our observation that sections of Article 2 other than the Statute of Frauds quite clearly include distributorship agreements within their scope. Section 2-306, MCL § 440.2306; MSA § 19.2306, which validates contract terms that measure quantity by the output of the seller or the requirements of the buyer, clearly encompasses agreements that contemplate ongoing commercial arrangements such as are involved in a normal distributorship. Indeed, Official Comment No. 1 to this section states that "[i]t applies to such contracts of nonproducing establishments such as dealers or distributors as well as to manufacturing concerns." Similarly, § 2-309, MCL § 440.2309; MSA § 19.2309, which deals with a "contract ... for successive performances [that] is indefinite in duration," clearly lends itself to a distributorship arrangement.

Cases from other jurisdictions support this conclusion....

The more difficult and separate question is the applicability of the Statute of Frauds, MCL § 440.2201; MSA § 19.2201, to the distributorship agreement. I see it as a separate question because the term "contract for the sale of goods" is clearly more restrictive than the term "transaction in goods."

The prevailing authority clearly favors holding a distributorship agreement to be a "contract for the sale of goods." . . .

My observation of the conflicting views represented in the . . . cases is that the majority of holdings implicitly say that a distributorship agreement is subject to the Statute of Frauds because it is a contract *dealing* with the sale of goods (or, stated differently, a contract for the sale of goods once removed). The minority view, adopted by our Court of Appeals in this case, says that, because the distributorship does not itself bind the parties to a specific transfer of specific goods, it is not a "contract for the sale of goods"; rather, as defendant characterizes it, it is "akin to an umbrella underneath which there were a series of commercial transactions between merchants."[67]

I think it wise when interpreting a uniform act, to join what is developing as a clear majority on this question, especially because of our previously mentioned conviction that it furthers the overall intent and scope of the UCC, and to consider the arrangement a contract for the sale of goods.

III. This does not end the inquiry, however. The key factual question in this case is whether the letter from defendant's agent to plaintiff's president satisfied the quantity requirement necessary for a contract to be enforceable under the Statute of Frauds.

In *Cavalier, supra,* the majority view of the Statute of Frauds is applied for the first time in combination with the "quantity" requirement of the Statute of Frauds with the result that unless a distributorship agreement writing specifies a quantity it is unenforceable.

I cannot, as did the Court of Appeals, completely dismiss the quantity requirement even though I agree that "in the context of a distributorship agreement such an indefiniteness is inherent in the relationship." 100 Mich. App. 600, 300 N.W.2d 335.

---

67. [4] We are not troubled by the relatively indefinite nature of most distributorship agreements; we believe that both the requisite consideration and mutuality can be found to exist despite the inherently imprecise terms. The UCC, with its provisions for successive performances, MCL § 440.2309; MSA § 19.2309, and indefinite quantity terms, MCL § 440.2306; MSA § 19.2306, envisions very loose arrangements that are reinforced by the code with its requirement of "good faith." MCL § 440.1203; MSA § 19.1203. *See* J.W. Knapp Co. v. Sinas, 19 Mich. App. 427, 172 N.W.2d 867 (1969). Furthermore, in the typical distributorship arrangement, an agreement by one party to sell without a corresponding agreement by the other to buy, as the Court of Appeals suggests exists in the instant case, is usually accompanied by other forms of consideration, such as exclusive territories, best efforts by the distributor to market the manufacturer's products, and the like. As such, these arrangements are distinguishable from those agreements whose quantity term is totally unascertainable. The Michigan court does not enforce contracts calling for the purchase or sale of such goods as may be "desired," "ordered," or "wished." Such contracts are distinguishable from the usual output or requirements contracts because the promisor is not bound to deliver or accept any sufficiently definite quantity. MCLA § 440.2306 practice commentary, p. 247.

Indeed, if the quantity term was construed to require a numerically specific quantity of goods, the net result would be that most distributorships by their nature could never comply with the Statute of Frauds. It would indeed be an anomalous result to hold such contracts subject to the UCC and its Statute of Frauds and then proceed to hold them all unenforceable for lack of a sufficiently definite quantity term.

The code obviates such an interpretation in § 2-306, which provides:

> (1) A term which measures the quantity by the output of the seller or the requirements of the buyer means such actual output or requirements as may occur in good faith, except that no quantity unreasonably disproportionate to any stated estimate or in the absence of a stated estimate to any normal or otherwise comparable prior output or requirements may be tendered or demanded.

While this provision does not specifically refer to § 2-201, it would be difficult to argue that it does not impliedly define quantity as it is used in § 2-201. As previously noted, the official comment to § 2-306 states specifically that it applies to "contracts of nonproducing establishments such as dealers or distributors as well as to manufacturing concerns."

In *Kubik v. J & R Foods of Oregon, Inc.*, 282 Or. 179, 187–188, 577 P.2d 518 (1978), the Oregon Supreme Court, in interpreting an exclusive dealing contract, stated:

> As noted, ORS 72.3060 [the counterpart of § 2-306] is a statute designed, among other things, to define 'quantity' — as that item is required by the UCC's own Statute of Frauds — in those situations in which, because of the nature of the contract, a particular quantity cannot be identified in advance with certainty.

I may not go so far as to suggest that § 2-306 is intended to define quantity in § 2-201, but I think it indicates at least that Article 2 of the UCC does not contemplate any rigid definition of the term *quantity* as it is used anywhere in Article 2, including § 2-201. If it did not refer to the word *quantity* in § 2-201, then § 2-306 would be without purpose.

Traditional restrictions on requirements contracts and the need to have the quantity term ascertainable have been based on the need to supply consideration in such contracts. The UCC, particularly § 2-306, makes it clear that the code intends contracts to be upheld even where the terms are indefinite by reading into such contracts "good faith" requirements, thus allowing a quantity term as imprecise as an agreement to furnish the distributor with his needs.

The obvious purpose of the Statute of Frauds is to require the understanding of the parties regarding the quantity of goods involved to be spelled out in the writing. Even if the quantity is as imprecise as an agreement to furnish the goods that the plaintiff needs to serve his customers, it is important to have that understanding in writing. As the Maryland court stated in *Cavalier Mobile Homes, Inc. v. Liberty Homes, Inc.*, 53 Md. App. 379, 395, 454 A.2d 367 (1983):

The Statute of Frauds requires that even where the quantity term is not numerically stated, there must be some writing which indicates that the quantity to be delivered under the contract is a party's requirements.

The letter in question was signed by the party "against whom enforcement is sought" — an agent of the defendant. The only question remaining is whether the language of the letter shows that the parties intended that defendant was obliged to supply plaintiff with its requirements, indefinite though it was.

The letter from defendant to plaintiff stated: "Now that you have officially joined the family of American Standard distributors," and "more importantly, to welcome you to the numbers of American Standard distributors across the country," and "Ed and I are most enthusiastic about your ability to help us participate in larger measure in the Detroit market."

It is perfectly clear from this writing that plaintiff was to be a distributor for defendant, who would supply plaintiff with products to sell "in the Detroit market"; it is equally obvious that in a distributorship the manufacturer must furnish the distributor with sufficient goods to be a successful distributor. The specific quantity of goods to be delivered under the distributorship agreement could have been determined only by the demand generated, and could not have been calculated in advance. Rather, the quantity term was as specific as necessary under these circumstances. The only thing left unsaid in the letter are the words "we will supply those goods necessary for you to represent us in your area." It would have been redundant to do so because the words of welcome to the "family of American Standard distributors" told it all. The word *distributorship* means the practice of a manufacturer furnishing its distributor with the products it needs to fill its orders. The parties have never, throughout the course of this litigation, disputed the fact that the defendant was required to furnish those goods ordered by the plaintiff, subject to certain conditions. The disagreement is over whether the defendant was justified in cutting off the plaintiff from further deliveries because plaintiff refused to pay its bill.

I conclude that the agreement between the parties was a contract for the sale of goods under the UCC and its Statute of Frauds and that there was a writing satisfying the quantity requirement of that statute. The distributorship agreement should be enforceable.

NOTES AND QUESTIONS

1. *Requirements contracts versus distributorships and franchises:* The *Lorenz Supply* case suggests some of the problems courts have faced when those who hold distributorships and franchises try to bring their relationships within the Uniform Commercial Code. Many modern cases raise this issue. Remember that many states have passed statutes regulating distributorships and franchises. Should the courts add to this regulation the obligations imposed by UCC § 2-306? What should courts do in states that have no distributorship or franchise statute? Consider the implications of the text of UCC § 2-306 (2) on this question. In 2008, the U.S. District Court for the Eastern District of Michigan said that *Lorenz* was still good law in Michigan, but it

took a minority position in saying that the UCC is not applicable to agreements for distribution of goods; furthermore, it said that the doctrine of promissory estoppel might make it unnecessary to meet the Statute of Frauds even if the transaction were subject to Article 2.[68]

2. *Requirements contracts and the Statute of Frauds:* The *Lorenz Supply* case also suggests some of the difficulties courts have faced in reconciling §§ 2-306 and 2-201 of the UCC. In *Cox Caulking & Insulating Co. v. Brockett Distributing Co.,*[69] Cox Caulking & Insulating Co. was the insulation subcontractor on a construction project. It made an oral agreement to buy the needed insulating material from Brockett Distribution Co. A Brockett official wrote a letter saying that it had "submitted a price of $2.62 a bag for the above project." The letter earlier defined the project as the "Cardinal and Hunt Joint Venture in Hinesville, Georgia." The Court of Appeals of Georgia acknowledged "the quantity need not be designated numerically where the memorandum evidences a requirements or output contract." However, it said, "[W]e reject appellant's contention that the phrase 'for the above project' was sufficient as a term of quantity. We conclude, instead, that the phrase merely designated the project that was the subject of the letter and that the letter contained no such 'term which measure[d] the quantity by the output of the seller or the requirements of the buyer.' Code § 109A-2-306 (1)."[70] As a result, the court affirmed summary judgment in favor of Brockett.

Professor Caroline N. Brown[71] writes that the *Cox Caulking & Insulating Co.* case "is perhaps the most notorious example of § 2-201's potential for thwarting the effects of the Code sections that approve open quantity contracts." She continues: "[T]he difficulty was the omission of such a magic word as 'all' or 'requirements' which would allow a *certain* quantitative determination by reference to the project." She notes that UCC § 2-306 does not require these magic words. Professor Brown says:

> The cornerstone of the difficulty concerning quantity lies in the initial determination that the statute requires quantity to "appear." This rule is almost universally accepted, despite the absence of any clear statutory direction to that effect. As construed in cases like *Cox Caulking*, the test imposed for quantity is stricter than the test recognized for the writing's sufficiency to show that the asserted transaction is genuine.[72] The sufficiency requirement, which is clearly *central* to the purpose and language of the statute, may be satisfied by merely an "indication." Quantity, on the other hand, must "appear," according to the language of the official comment to § 2-201. The court in *Cox Caulking* apparently took this language to mandate that the quantity

---

68. KP Bldg. Prods., Inc. v. Ciraulo Bros. Bldg. Co., 2008 U.S. Dist. LEXIS 104916 (E.D. Mich., Dec. 30, 2008) (unpublished opinion).

69. 150 Ga. App. 424, 258 S.E. 51 (1979).

70. *Id.* at 426, 258 S.E. at 52.

71. Caroline N. Bruckel [now Brown], *The Weed and the Web: Section 2-201's Corruption of the UCC's Substantive Provisions—The Quantity Problem*, 1983 U. Ill. L. Rev. 811, 819, 820, 822, 856–57. Copyright © 1984 by the Board of Trustees of the University of Illinois. Reprinted by permission.

72. Eds. note: See the first sentence of § 2-201(1).

term be mechanically ascertainable solely from the face of the writing (together with any reference indicated as necessary to quantify it). In accordance with many courts, the *Cox Caulking* court effectively ruled that if *any* inferences must be drawn from circumstances outside the writing to establish quantity, the memorandum is insufficient.

This standard is highly inappropriate, for it subordinates the central issue of sufficiency to the peripheral one. It can, and does, result in a refusal of recovery to a plaintiff who clearly establishes a legitimate agreement. This plaintiff will lose even after producing a written memorandum sufficient to "indicate" quantity as well as the agreement's legitimacy, if the written term requires even an obvious inference to give it substance....

The official comment to § 2-201 ... begins by echoing the drafters' primary concern to reverse the prior rule requiring all essential terms to be stated; it then notes that the only goal of the writing requirement is to establish a credible evidentiary basis for a real transaction. Two sentences later, however, the comment falls into confusion, seeming to recognize a requirement that quantity be stated....

[T]he *single* statutory standard to determine the sufficiency of a memorandum should be its indication of a real transaction. No quantity term need be shown or even indicated in the writing; thus, the only standards affecting quantity are the Code's substantive standards. Consequently, the quantity term may be established by an unsigned writing or by oral allegations sufficient to satisfy the trier of fact, or supplied by implication from usage or conduct, or by law under § 2-306.

When the writing *does* contain a quantity term, § 2-201(1) directs that it serve as a ceiling on enforceability. Even this limitation, however, should give way to avoid manifest injustice when no statutory purpose is served by maintaining it. In cases where granting the plaintiff relief seems especially compelling, the statutory guideline properly yields to the overriding purpose of avoidance of fraud. Safety for the defendant *must* be weighed against injustice to the plaintiff before any coherent place for § 2-201 may be discovered in the Code.

Can you defend the courts against Professor Brown's attack? Can you answer her arguments? As she notes, there are many cases involving the relationship between UCC §§ 2-306 and 2-201, and most courts have insisted that the quantity term must be stated in writing. In answering Professor Brown, assume that it is not enough to argue that her position does not follow the majority view.

This is not the only time we will consider a substantive doctrine alongside the Statute of Frauds. Compare, for example, *Janke Construction Co. v. Vulcan Materials Co., supra* Chapter 1. Might judges comfortable with classic contract law seek to reach the old results by using the Statute of Frauds to offset legal realist innovations such as the firm offer and the enforceability of requirements contracts? Professor Stanley

D. Henderson, for example, in his article on promissory estoppel, discussed those decisions that denied "any basis whatsoever for operation of the doctrine [of promissory estoppel] in opposition to the Statute of Frauds." He said: "These decisions surely reflect some lingering doubts about the general legitimacy of the reliance ground of enforcement of promises."[73] Could the same thing be said about the judicial reaction to oral flexible quantity terms?

C. BUSINESS DOCUMENTS AND FORMING CONTRACTS

Businesspeople often sign written agreements. Sometimes a business contract is signed with a formal ceremony. The signatures of high officials representing both sides are symbolic acts of commitment, marking a sharp line between being free to back out and being bound. However, on other occasions a deal is closed by a handshake or phone call. Papers are signed to keep accountants and lawyers happy. The parties may be in the midst of performing before anyone thinks about a formal ceremony.

Even where written documents are used, the situation may be unclear. For example, a letter may convey information with no intention of commitment. "I wouldn't think of selling for less than $500,000, and I might get more if I put the property on the market. Furthermore, unless you are thinking of buying for cash, I would need adequate security for your obligation." Contrast this with a letter saying, "I am willing to sell the Jones Farm to you for $500,000, payable in cash now." On the other hand, we may have a single commitment but too many documents. Seller may send its proposal and Buyer may respond with its purchase order. However, the two forms contain terms that do not match. Often the parties do not notice the inconsistency and start to perform. Is there a legally enforceable contract? If so, what are its terms?

Business patterns do not always neatly fit the categories of contract law. Judges and legislators could demand that businesspeople change their ways, and sometimes they do. However, generally judges, lawyers, and law professors see contract law as facilitative and supportive of the market. When business reality does not fit into legal categories, many think that the legal categories should be changed. As we have noted before in these materials, Professor Duncan Kennedy points out that older teachers of common law subjects explained many problems in terms of the core and a periphery of exceptions to deal with hard cases. In the core situations, many lawyers will assume that the theories work, but there will always be a few peripheral situations that cause difficulty. Kennedy, however, asserts that the periphery tends to swallow the core in area after area. We are about to consider an area in which we can ask about the status of "core" and "periphery." Once again we encounter our familiar questions: Is liability based on choice, responsibility for careless use of language, social planning to serve the market, or something else? Furthermore, do the rules favor larger, more bureau-

---

73. Stanley D. Henderson, *Promissory Estoppel and Traditional Contract Doctrine*, 78 YALE L.J. 343, 381–82 (1969).

cratically organized businesses; the underdog consumer or small business; or are the impacts random?

Should the law insist on a signed written document that functions as a kind of magical symbol, dividing obligation from freedom? Or should it try to give effect to the understandings of the parties? Two provisions of the Uniform Commercial Code indicate conflicting views. UCC § 2-204(1) says a "contract for sale of goods may be made in any manner sufficient to show agreement, including conduct by both parties which recognizes the existence of such a contract." Subsection (2) says "an agreement sufficient to constitute a contract for sale may be found even though the moment of its making is undetermined." Nonetheless, if the price of the goods is $500 or more, UCC § 2-201 requires "some writing sufficient to indicate that a contract for sale has been made between the parties and signed by the party against whom enforcement is sought." While these provisions can be reconciled, they point in different directions. How do businesspeople regard the practice of documenting transactions?

— Interview with the Purchasing Agent of a large manufacturer of small electric appliances:

> Mr. X does make orders at times by telephone, but he always confirms them later by a written purchase order. For example, recently he was buying a complete new appliance to be marketed under his firm's brand name and to be manufactured by one of the large well-known appliance manufacturers. So far only an order to buy the tooling necessary to make the appliance has been issued. In order to have the manufacturer ready to go, Mr. X has called and told it to begin buying materials. He has given them the number of the purchase order that will be sent to the manufacturer, over the telephone. The formal purchase order for the materials is now in the process of being written and approved. Mr. X is sure that the manufacturer has gone ahead and started buying materials at this point because once it has a purchase order number it is safe.

— Interview with the general counsel of an automobile parts manufacturer:

> Mr. Y remarked that, unless something is unusual about a transaction, the house counsel is seldom called in until after a contract has been made and problems develop in performance. People in this corporation often write "letters of intent" in purchasing situations without going through either the purchasing department or the house counsel. In his view these letters of intent often go far towards creating binding offers or contracts. In one case, Mr. Y found that nothing was in the file indicating any commitment on the part of a manufacturer as to how a $50,000 machine would perform, and his company's engineers seemed to have made a binding contract through a fairly vague letter of intent. The engineers said they had intended to refer the matter to the purchasing department to have a formal contract drafted but had overlooked the matter as they were anxious to get started.

— Interview with the general counsel of a manufacturer of a well-known small consumer item:

Most people would rather not put things in writing. It is amazing how in casual conversations people will agree to one thing after another and will reach almost complete agreement. Then one asks for a signature on a document embodying that agreement. That seems to be a very disruptive act. At this point, many people back out and say, "No, I'd better think about that before I sign," even though they have orally agreed to everything in the written contract.

—From *How a Great Corporation Got Out of Control—The Story of General Dynamics*:[74]

Convair's [the Convair Division of the General Dynamics Corporation] first target was United, which it had listed as a prospect for 30 aircraft. For a time things seemed to be going Convair's way in its pursuit of this critical $120 million sale. Boeing, Douglas, and Convair were all in competition for the United contract, but Convair had the edge with its 880, for it was then the only true medium-to-long-range jet aircraft being offered. All Boeing could offer was essentially the long-range 707, too big and, for its seating capacity, 50,000 pounds too heavy to suit United. The size could be reduced, of course, and some of the weight chopped out, but not 50,000 pounds unless Pratt & Whitney could substantially lighten the engines, the JT3C-6's used on the 707 aircraft. With Pratt & Whitney unwilling to make this effort, United's board decided in favor of the 880 on September 27, 1957, subject to a final going-over by United engineers.

Soon thereafter, United's President William Patterson called G.D.'s Executive Vice President Earl Johnson ... out of a board meeting to tell him Convair was "in." But perhaps the most consequential call was one Pratt & Whitney's Chairman H. Mansfield "Jack" Horner then made on Patterson himself. Spurred on by Boeing, Horner had been galvanized into action, and now he wanted to know whether something couldn't be done about getting Boeing back into the competition, if Pratt & Whitney could come up with a lighter engine. Patterson referred him to United's engineers, who made very encouraging noises. They themselves had been pushing Pratt & Whitney for just that. Both Boeing and Pratt & Whitney then went into a crash program, the former to scale down the 707, the latter to develop a lighter engine than the JT3C-6.

On or about October 10, 1957, Convair's Sales Vice President Jack Zevely and United's Financial Vice President Curtis Barkes had happily worked out 18 articles of a 19-article contract and in 15 minutes more would have finished the 19th, merely a statement of where the notices were to be sent, when a call came through for Barkes. As Zevely recalled this fall: "He came back, shaken, and said, 'Sorry, Boeing's back in the competition.'"

---

74. From Fortune Magazine, Feb. 1962, © Time, Inc. Used under license. Part II, at 120, 121–22.

It was indeed. Pratt & Whitney engineers had managed to get 750 pounds out of the JT3C-6 engine.... Boeing engineers had shortened the fuselage of the 707, reduced the weight of such heavy items as the landing gear, and improved its cost per mile. Within a few weeks Boeing had come up with a new medium-range aircraft — the 720 — 45,000 pounds lighter than the 707. United then invited Boeing and Convair to cut their prices and both did.... In November, United's chief engineer John Herlihy compared Convair's 880 and Boeing's 720 and then strongly recommended the latter.... [T]he 720 with its lower operating costs per passenger-mile was a better buy than the 880 with a $200,000 cheaper price tag. On November 28, 1957, United's board approved purchase of 11 Boeing 720s, with options for 18 more.

— Interview with the vice president in charge of merchandising of a firm in the textile industry:

Things can be worked out informally, you decide to close and do, and then something comes up and you change your mind. You look for something that has been omitted, argue that things really hadn't been closed but there was another point remaining for negotiation, and then you back out. You just simply refuse to go through with things. It is more just to end things at this point, if you change your mind, than to string the other guy along or to maneuver in your performance of the contract to minimize what he gets out of it. At times it is better to break off. It is nice to find a subject of negotiation that has not been completed to save a little face when you do this. Of course, it is not absolutely necessary.

1. Formation Doctrine and "Letters of Intent"

Businesspeople, particularly in international trade, often deal on the basis of letters of intent. According to Marvin Leon: "Litigation over letters of intent fills libraries."[75] Ralph Lake says:

In general, letters of intent can be classified into four types: letters designed to provide information; framework agreements intended to govern only the negotiation process; memorializations of partial agreements during a negotiation process; and documents erroneously entitled letters of intent that are, in actuality, legally enforceable contracts.[76]

Why write a letter of intent? Lake, writing as the Europe and Middle East legal counsel of Holiday Inns, Inc., noted that modern business transactions are increasingly complex. Contracts contain hundreds or thousands of pages.

---

75. Marvin Leon, *Lessening the Risk of Letters of Intent*, Los Angeles Lawyer, Nov. 2001, at 20, 24 (finding 106 reported federal appellate decisions in seven years, from 1994 through 1999).

76. Ralph Lake, *Letters of Intent: A Comparative Examination Under English, U.S., French, and West German Law*, 18 Geo. Wash. J. Int'l L. & Econ. 331, 331–32 (1984). Reprinted by permission.

The negotiation of such contracts can be a lengthy process and often requires the resolution of numerous details. Participation of financial institutions, government agencies, subcontractors, consultants, and other professionals is essential. Therefore, precontractual agreements that have moral, if not legal effect, are useful in bringing order to the complexity.[77]

Also, letters of intent serve to exclude lawyers from the negotiation process until the final stages. Writers of letters of intent sometimes believe they will incur no obligations and will obtain a commitment from the other party. Lake tells us:

> [G]enerally, English law does not recognize precontractual liability. United States courts have the doctrine of promissory estoppel at their disposal and increasingly impose an obligation to negotiate in good faith. French law imposes liability in tort for actions prior to contractual execution. West German law uses the doctrine of *culpa in contrahendo* to impose precontractual liability.[78]

The following case involves a dispute over a real estate transaction. The parties' letter of intent made it explicit that there was no contract of sale yet, but controversy still ensued on the basis of some procedural promises.

LOGAN v. SIVERS CO.

Oregon Supreme Court
343 Or. 339, 169 P.3d 1255 (2007)

GILLETTE, J.

This case arises out of a property owner's promise to a prospective buyer to refrain from soliciting or accepting offers from other potential buyers for a specified period of time, during which time the parties anticipated that they would be able to negotiate a binding agreement for the sale and purchase of the property in question. At issue is the enforceability of such a promise, when it is made in the context of a "letter of intent" that elsewhere expressly provides that only a fully executed purchase and sale agreement will create binding obligations between the parties. Also at issue is the proper measure of damages for a breach of a "nonsolicitation" provision in that context, should the breach be actionable. The Court of Appeals held that the owner's promise was enforceable and that a jury permissibly could conclude that the appropriate measure of damages was plaintiff's increased tax liability resulting from her inability to buy the property in question. *Logan v. D. W. Sivers Co.*, 207 Or. App. 231, 141 P.3d 589 (2006). For the reasons that follow, we affirm in part and reverse in part the decision of the Court of Appeals. In so doing, we agree with the Court of Appeals that nonsolicitation promises like the one involved here may be enforceable. However, we also are of the view that in this case, the letter of intent contained no promise by defendant, the breach of which would serve as the basis for an award of the kind of damages that plaintiff seeks here.

---

77. *Id.* at 332.
78. *Id.*

The relevant facts are as follows. In January 2003, plaintiff realized a substantial profit — $3.9 million — on the sale of a piece of productive land that had belonged to her family for a number of years. [Plaintiff planned to buy other property with the proceeds to take advantage of a federal tax "exchange" provision, 26 USC § 1031 of the federal tax code, which required her to designate up to three replacement properties and purchase one of them within statutory deadlines.] ... If she failed to meet those deadlines, she would have to treat some or all of the $3.9 million that she had earned on the sale of the original property as a capital gain, increasing her overall tax liability by an amount potentially exceeding $900,000.

In early March, plaintiff already had designated two potential replacement properties and had obtained signed letters of intent from the owners of those properties. She told her real estate agent at that time that she also was interested in purchasing a nearby shopping mall that was not then on the market. Her real estate broker contacted defendant, the owner of the shopping mall, about a possible purchase of the mall. The broker told defendant's president that plaintiff was a "motivated 1031 buyer." Defendant's president understood that to mean that the buyer had to acquire replacement property within a relatively short period of time in order to secure the tax advantages provided by § 1031.

After some preliminary negotiations, plaintiff and defendant entered into a letter of intent that set out a framework for defendant's sale of the shopping mall to plaintiff, including a purchase price ($5.28 million) and a closing date (June 30, 2003). The letter of intent contained several provisions that are relevant to the present controversy. First, it listed several "conditions of purchase," including "[a] fully executed Purchase and Sale Agreement [to be finalized and signed] within approximately fifteen (15) days of signature by both parties of this Letter of Intent; Purchaser shall provide the initial draft of the Purchase and Sale Agreement."

In addition, the agreement contained a nonsolicitation clause: "Seller and/or its representatives agree that it will not seek nor enter into a letter of intent or purchase agreement for sale of the Property with any third party for a period of sixty (60) days from the date this Letter of Intent is signed by both parties and becomes effective."

Finally, the letter of intent stated, at considerable length, the extent to which it was not intended to constitute a binding agreement for the sale and purchase of the property. However, that statement contained an important qualification: "Seller and Purchaser acknowledge that this Letter of Intent proposal is not a binding agreement and that it is intended solely to establish the principal terms of the purchase and as a basis for the preparation of a binding Purchase and Sale Agreement. The Purchase and Sale Agreement shall be subject to Seller's and Purchaser's approvals and approval by their respective counsel, and only a fully executed Purchase and Sale Agreement shall constitute a binding transaction and binding obligation between the parties; *provided, however, that in consideration of Purchaser's good faith efforts to review the due diligence material provided by Seller, Seller agrees to be bound to provide the required due diligence documents to Purchaser within the time required and to comply with the Non-Solicitation provision set forth above.*" (Emphasis added.)

As soon as defendant executed the letter of intent, plaintiff designated the shopping mall as her third § 1031 replacement property—just in time to meet the 45-day identification deadline on March 17, 2003.

Over the next few weeks, plaintiff's broker called defendant's officers on a number of occasions to ask for due diligence materials and to tell them that a draft purchase and sale agreement soon would be complete. On April 4, 2003, the 21st day after the letter of intent was signed, plaintiff's broker learned that defendant had accepted another party's offer to purchase the property. Plaintiff's broker attempted to salvage the deal between plaintiff and defendant, and plaintiff's lawyer immediately sent a draft purchase and sale agreement to defendant by e-mail. However, defendant already had committed to the other offer and refused to negotiate any further with plaintiff or her agents.

By that time, plaintiff had decided that one of her other designated replacement properties was too problematic to purchase. Although plaintiff did purchase the third designated property, that purchase absorbed only a small part of plaintiff's gain on the sale of the original property. Plaintiff was required to pay over $900,000 in taxes on the remaining gain, a result that she would have avoided if she had succeeded in purchasing defendant's shopping mall.

Plaintiff then brought the present action against defendant, alleging that defendant had breached its promise to refrain from seeking offers on the property or from entering into any agreement to sell the property to others for 60 days. Among other things, plaintiff sought over $900,000 in consequential damages, based on the tax effects of her failure to make a timely § 1031 exchange.

The case went to trial and defendant eventually moved for a directed verdict on a number of alternative grounds, three of which are at issue here. Defendant argued, first, that the letter of intent was a mere "agreement to agree" and, as such, was unenforceable in its entirety; second, defendant argued that any failure by defendant to adhere to its promise to refrain from accepting other offers was excused by a failure of a condition precedent, viz., execution of a final purchase and sale agreement within "approximately 15 days"; and, third, defendant argued that, in any event, plaintiff was not entitled to recover damages measured by the tax loss consequences of her failure to make the hoped-for § 1031 exchange. The trial court initially indicated that it would grant defendant's motion for a directed verdict on two of the grounds but, upon plaintiff's request ... it allowed the case to go to the jury. The jury returned a verdict for plaintiff, awarding her an amount in damages that was equivalent to her tax losses. Upon defendant's motion, however, the trial court then reinstated its previous order granting a directed verdict and entered judgment for defendant.

Plaintiff appealed to the Court of Appeals, arguing that the trial court had erred in overriding the jury's verdict. The Court of Appeals agreed with all of plaintiff's arguments, holding that (1) the letter of intent contained terms that were enforceable; (2) evidence in the record supported the jury's implicit determination that plaintiff had satisfied her obligations under a provision calling for execution of a purchase and sale agreement within "approximately 15 days"; (3) evidence in the record also supported the jury's implicit conclusion that defendant's breach of its obligations under the letter of intent had caused plaintiff's tax losses and that the tax loss was a foreseeable result of the breach. *Logan*, 207 Or. App. at 242–48. Consistent with those holdings, the Court of Appeals reversed and remanded with instructions to the trial court to reinstate the jury's verdict for plaintiff. *Id.* at 249. We allowed defendant's petition for review of that decision.

Defendant first objects to the Court of Appeals' holding that the letter of intent contained at least some terms that were enforceable, including defendant's promise not to solicit or accept other offers on the property for a 60-day period. Defendant contends that the letter of intent was merely a framework for future negotiations, expressing nothing more than the parties' hope that agreement could be reached. Such agreements, defendant argues, are not enforceable.

That argument has the wrong focus. Although a provision of the letter of intent *does* expressly provide that the parties intend only to set out a framework for a future purchase and sale agreement and that the letter, as a whole, is nonbinding and "subject to approval," the last part of that provision identifies three specific terms as exceptions to that general nonbinding intent: "provided, *however*, that *in consideration* of Purchaser's good faith efforts to review the due diligence material provided by Seller, *Seller agrees to be bound* to provide the required due diligence documents to Purchaser within the time required *and* to comply with the Non-Solicitation provision set forth above." (Emphasis added.) Those words clearly convey that the parties intended that the three specified promises—defendant's promises to provide due diligence materials and to abide by the nonsolicitation agreement, and plaintiff's return promise to review the due diligence material in good faith—be binding. Thus, unless those terms are so indefinite that a court cannot determine what the parties intended, they form a contract that *is* binding....

Defendant responds that the terms *are* too indefinite. It contends that the letter of intent is, at best, an "agreement to negotiate" and that such agreements categorically are too indefinite to be enforced. That is so, defendant argues, because agreements to negotiate leave all terms unresolved, still subject to negotiation. In so arguing, however, defendant is focusing on the label, rather than the substance, of the parties' promises. The enforceability of a contract or agreement does not depend on whether it properly may be categorized as "preliminary," or an "agreement to agree," or and "agreement to negotiate." Rather, it is the contents of the agreement and what the parties intended that is important. And, with respect to those contents and that intent, we can state categorically that this agreement, although narrowly drawn, does contain an exchange of promises that the parties intended to be binding and that are sufficiently definite to allow a jury or court to determine what is required of each party. Thus, those promises *are* binding; with respect to each of the three promises, the parties' obligations are clearly identified and ascertainable, and it simply is a matter of determining whether, how, and when one or more of them was breached. (As noted, the jury found a breach and the evidence supports such a finding.)

Defendant argues, however, that, even if the letter of intent contains terms that otherwise are binding, they were *only* binding as long as the parties chose to continue negotiations. And, defendant notes, the parties were under no obligation to continue the negotiation in this case. It therefore insists that, in the absence of any such obligation, either party could have walked away at any point and thereby ended any and all obligations under the letter of intent—including the obligations under the nonsolicitation agreement.

In that regard, defendant likens the present case to *Feldman v. Allegheny Inter., Inc.*, 850 F.2d 1217 (7th Cir. 1988), a case that also involved a seller's breach of an exclusive dealings provision that appeared in the context of an otherwise nonbinding letter of intent. Defendant notes that, in *Feldman*, the court held that the seller's obligation under the exclusive dealings provision to refrain from negotiating with other parties continued only so long as both parties elected to pursue the transaction. As the *Feldman* court put it, although the parties were bound by the exclusive dealings provision: "Both parties were free to end the arrangement and move on if they felt that discussions were progressing too slowly or they had reached a stalemate and believed they had better prospects elsewhere." *Id.* at 1223.

The foregoing quotation demonstrates why *Feldman* is not on point. By its own clear terms, the exclusive dealings provision in that case only was operative "while the proposed acquisition is being pursued." *Id.* at 1219. In the present case, however, the nonsolicitation provision is *not* couched in terms of the parties' continued commitment to negotiations but, instead, speaks in terms of a specific period of time—60 days—during which it shall be operative. Assuming that defendant is correct that the letter of intent imposes no obligation on the parties to continue negotiating until an agreement is reached, that fact has no bearing on defendant's obligations under the 60-day nonsolicitation provision, and clearly does not render that provision unenforceable. Defendant might choose to walk away from its negotiations with plaintiff, but the prohibition on selling the property to, or soliciting, other parties for a period of 60 days would remain in force and would make such a choice by defendant less likely—the very reason plaintiff would seek defendant's promise on that point in the letter of intent.

We conclude that, although the letter of intent was not, as a whole, a binding agreement for the sale and purchase of the property in question, it did contain certain promises that were binding, one of which was defendant's promise to neither solicit nor accept other offers on the property for a period of 60 days. The Court of Appeals thus was correct in holding that the trial court erred in granting a directed verdict to defendant on that ground.

We turn to defendant's second argument for reversing the Court of Appeals—that defendant was excused from its obligations under the agreement because plaintiff failed to perform a condition precedent. Defendant contends, in particular, that plaintiff failed to satisfy a "condition of purchase" that required her to produce the first draft of a purchase and sale agreement with sufficient speed that a final agreement could be "fully executed" within "approximately 15 days." The record shows that plaintiff did not deliver a draft purchase and sale agreement to defendant until 21 days after the letter of intent was executed.

The Court of Appeals concluded that the trial court had correctly rejected that argument. After stating that the question of whether plaintiff had failed to satisfy her obligations under the "approximately 15 day" condition was for the jury to decide, and that the jury had found that the longer period was permissible, the Court of Appeals held that there was "ample evidence" supporting the jury's implicit finding that plaintiff had timely performed: "First, there was evidence that the parties intended that the term 'approximately' be flexible, and from that the jury could infer that the parties were not in a great hurry to execute the draft agreement. Second, there was evidence that defendant acquiesced in plaintiff's delay in delivering the agreement by never objecting to the delay. Third, there was evidence that the closing date contemplated by the letter of intent could be maintained so long as the parties executed the purchase and sale agreement within 45 days of signing the letter of intent. The jury could have inferred that, under those circumstances, 21 days was a reasonable period of time within which to deliver the draft agreement because that left ample time for the parties to execute the agreement and close on the date originally contemplated." *Logan*, 207 Or. App. at 248.

… There is no question that the words "approximately 15 days" are ambiguous in this context and that, as such, it is for the trier of fact to ascertain what the parties intended by those words. *See Pacific First Bank v. New Morgan Park Corp.*, 319 Or. 342, 347–48, 876 P.2d 761 (1994) (if contract is ambiguous, the trier of fact must ascertain the intent of the parties and construe the contract consistently with that intent). Here, as the Court of Appeals correctly described it, the trier of fact (the jury) implicitly found that plaintiff had fully satisfied her obligation to provide a draft agreement with sufficient speed that the condition of a fully executed agreement within "approximately 15 days" could be met. We need only determine whether a reasonable jury could so find, based on the evidence that was before it.

As to that issue, we agree with the Court of Appeals that there was at least some evidence in the record that would allow a jury to conclude that the parties intended the term "approximately 15 days" to be flexible. When asked at trial about what she thought the term meant, plaintiff declined to name any particular time limit and would say only that there was "no date certain that the deal was dead." Another witness who was called by the plaintiff as an expert in commercial real estate transactions confirmed the idea that the term might be entirely flexible. He testified that, in most commercial real estate transactions, "if there's not a time-is-of-the-essence clause, dates specified in the agreement are treated as flexible and are not drop-dead dates."

Defendant does not point to anything in the record that would preclude a reasonable jury from finding that, consistent with the foregoing testimony, the parties intended to describe a flexible deadline when they referred to a time period of "approximately 15 days." It is true that the letter of intent involved multiple steps and cascading deadlines—evidence that the jury might have accepted, had it wished to do so—but the deadlines involved were not so inescapably tight and the steps were not so interdependent that a delay of six days or even longer in producing a draft purchase and sale agreement would make it impossible as a matter of law to close the deal as the parties had envisioned—by June 30, 2003. We conclude that the defendant was not entitled to a directed verdict on the ground that, in waiting 21 days before submitting a draft purchase and sale agreement to defendant, plaintiff had failed to perform a condition precedent to defendant's obligations. The Court of Appeals did not err in so holding.

We turn to the question of damages. Defendant argues that the damages that the jury awarded and that the Court of Appeals reinstated, which were based on the taxes that plaintiff would have been able to avoid if she had been able to purchase the property at issue and effect a § 1031 exchange, were not available to plaintiff as a matter of law. Defendant contends that any such damage award ultimately and necessarily rests on the idea that plaintiff had an enforceable contractual right to purchase the property, an idea that is contrary to the express terms of the contract.

In reinstating that damage award, the Court of Appeals posited a fairly involved string of inferences that would have allowed the jury to conclude, from the evidence in the record, that plaintiff's tax losses were a direct consequence of defendant's breach of the nonsolicitation provision. One step in that string of inferences is particularly notable, i.e., an inference that "although defendant retained the right to back out of the negotiations, the jury could infer that defendant would not have done so had it not entertained a better offer from another party, and that the parties would have entered into a binding purchase and sale agreement." *Logan*, 207 Or. App. at 244. Also significant is the Court of Appeals' holding that the jury reasonably could find, based on the evidence in the record, that tax losses arising out of plaintiff's inability to timely purchase a replacement property were a foreseeable and natural result of defendant's breach of the nonsolicitation provision—in spite of the absence of any actual obligation on defendant's part to sell the property to plaintiff. *Logan*, 207 Or. App. at 245–46.

The difficulty with the foregoing analysis is that it fails to give proper consideration to the specific wording of the contract at issue and, particularly, to the parties' express and thorough disclaimer of any intent to bind themselves to a purchase and sale. We return to the operative words of the parties' agreement to illustrate the point. In doing so, we emphasize again that the agreement contained only three binding promises: (1) plaintiff's promise to conduct a good faith review of "due diligence" documents provided by defendant; (2) defendant's promise to provide the due diligence documents within a certain time; and (3) defendant's promise to comply with the nonsolicitation provision. What is absent is any binding obligation to bargain in good faith to achieve the contemplated sale—each party remained free to sit on its hands and do nothing. Each party also might hope that the other would not behave in that way, but such a party had nothing beyond that—hope—on which to risk its financial circumstances. As the parties' agreement put it: "Only a fully executed Purchase and Sale Agreement shall constitute a binding transaction and binding obligation between the parties." The parties clearly intended, and clearly had the right to expect, that

that disclaimer would shield them from any liability for failing to carry through with the sale that then was being contemplated. In the face of such a disclaimer, it is irrelevant that a reasonable person in the same position as defendant might have foreseen that plaintiff would suffer tax losses down the road if defendant declined to go through with the contemplated sale, either by selling to another party in breach of the non-solicitation provision or otherwise. It also is irrelevant whether defendant would have sold the property to plaintiff if it had not been diverted by another party's offer. The parties expressly declined, in the letter of intent, to assume the risks of injury inherent in a completed contract of purchase and sale. Defendant cannot now be saddled with those very same liabilities on the theory that, because defendant likely would have sold the property to plaintiff except for its breach of its lesser promise not to sell the property to someone else for 60 days, those liabilities are the natural and foreseeable consequences of defendant's breach. We repeat the important distinction here: Defendant's obligation not to solicit or sell to others for 60 days did *not* include any promise to negotiate in good faith — or at all — during that 60-day period.

In arguing otherwise, plaintiff relies on *Senior Estates v. Bauman Homes*, 272 Or. 577, 583–84, 539 P.2d 142 (1975), a case that recognizes and explains Oregon's long-established rule that, in an appropriate case, the victim of a breach of contract may recover not only her loss of bargain damages, but also consequential damages. The Oregon rule, as stated in that case, is straightforward: "*The plaintiff may recover such damages, including gains prevented as well as losses sustained, as may reasonably be supposed to have been within the contemplation of both parties at the time of the making of the contract as the proximate and natural consequence of a breach by defendant.*" *Id.* at 585 (quoting *Blagen v. Thompson*, 23 Or. 239, 248, 31 P.647 (1892); emphasis in original).

We have no quibble with that rule when the circumstances support its application. On the facts of the present case, however, they do not. We note again that the parties were at pains in their letter of intent to identify what they were *not* agreeing to do: Defendant was not agreeing to sell, or even to negotiate in good faith toward selling, and plaintiff was not agreeing to buy, or even to negotiate in good faith toward buying, the property in question. The document in this case contains the opposite understanding: "Seller and Purchaser acknowledge that *this Letter of Intent proposal is not a binding agreement* and that it is intended solely to establish the principal terms of the purchase and as a basis for the preparation of a binding Purchase and Sales Agreement.... [O]nly a fully executed Purchase and Sale Agreement shall constitute a binding transaction and binding obligation between the parties." (Emphasis added.) The foregoing pledge *not* to be bound to buy or sell is entitled to enforcement. *See, e.g., Senior Estates*, 272 Or. at 590 (although vendor of real estate was entitled to certain consequential damages from defaulting purchasers, award could not include amount for title insurance costs because, "by the terms of the contract itself, [plaintiff] was to assume [that] expense").

Put differently, defendant's nonsolicitation promise was directed to the *manner* of the negotiations and not to their *outcome*, and the damages that may be deemed to have arisen from defendant's breach of that promise are similarly limited. Under the narrow and specific bargain struck by the parties here, plaintiff may be able to charge defendant with any expenses that she incurred (and wasted) in attempting to negotiate a final agreement with defendant for the purchase and sale of defendant's property. But, because defendant never agreed to sell or even to negotiate in good faith toward the sale of the property to plaintiff (and, in fact, explicitly disclaimed any such agreement when it signed the letter of intent), plaintiff cannot, under this contract, charge defendant with losses that flowed from her inability to finally purchase it. The trial court properly set aside the jury's award of damages of that kind (*i.e.*, damages that were based on taxes that plaintiff could have avoided had she succeeded in timely purchasing defendant's property), and the Court of Appeals erred when it ordered the trial court to reinstate the jury's verdict. That part of the Court of Appeals decision must be reversed.

The decision of the Court of Appeals is affirmed in part and reversed in part. The judgment of the circuit court is affirmed in part and reversed in part, and the case is remanded to the circuit court for further proceedings.

KISTLER, J. (concurring in part and dissenting in part).

This case arises out of an increasingly common practice in real estate sales. The parties signed a letter of intent setting out the principal terms of a proposed sale of real property. The letter of intent made clear that it did not impose a binding obligation on either party to go through with the sale. It did, however, impose a binding obligation on defendant, for a period of 60 days, not to solicit or enter into a sale agreement with anyone other than plaintiff. Although defendant breached that promise, the majority holds that plaintiff cannot recover expectation damages for defendant's breach. That is so even though the jury implicitly found (and there is evidence to support its finding) that defendant would have gone through with the sale to plaintiff at the agreed-upon price if defendant had honored the 60-day, nonsolicitation provision. The majority cites no authority in support of its holding, and both the case law and the commentary lead to precisely the opposite conclusion. I respectfully dissent from the decision denying plaintiff her expectation damages.[79]

The relevant facts are straightforward.... [D]efendant "agree[d] that it will not seek nor enter into a letter of intent or purchase agreement for sale of the Property with any third party for a period of sixty (60) days" from the date that the parties signed the letter of intent.

Defendant breached that promise when it entered into an agreement, within 21 days of signing the letter of intent, to sell the property to someone other than plaintiff. For the purposes of determining the damages resulting from that breach, it is important to recognize that not only was there evidence from which the jury could have

---

79. [6] The majority correctly holds that defendant's promise not to solicit or enter into a sale agreement for 60 days with a third party was a binding contractual obligation. It also correctly holds that plaintiff's failure to comply strictly with a condition precedent did not bar her from seeking to enforce the nonsolicitation provision. I concur in those parts of the majority's decision.

found that plaintiff would have gone forward with the proposed sale if defendant had dealt only with her, but there was also evidence from which the jury could have found that, if defendant had honored the 60-day nonsolicitation provision, it would have sold the property to plaintiff in accordance with the terms set out in the letter of intent. Specifically, defendant's president, Dennis Sivers, testified that defendant had wanted to sell the property quickly so that defendant could complete a "1031 exchange" of its own—a deal that had to be closed soon after the end of the 60-day nonsolicitation period. According to Sivers, defendant was so eager to close its own 1031 exchange that it would have gone through with the sale of the property to plaintiff for $5.28 million—the price on which the parties had tentatively agreed in the letter of intent.

In light of that testimony, as well as the other evidence introduced at trial, the jury reasonably could have found three critical facts. *See Northwest Natural Gas Co. v. Chase Gardens, Inc.*, 333 Or. 304, 310, 39 P.3d 846 (2002) (explaining that appellate courts must uphold jury verdicts unless there is "no evidence" to support the elements of a claim). First, although defendant had no legal obligation to go through with its proposed sale to plaintiff, defendant in fact would have gone through with the sale to plaintiff if it had complied with its promise to deal only with plaintiff during the 60-day period. Second, the parties would have agreed on all the material elements of the sale, as stated in the letter of intent. *See Povey v. Clow*, 146 Or. App. 760, 764, 934 P.2d 528 (1997) (listing material elements of land sale contracts). Finally, defendant was on notice that, if plaintiff did not purchase defendant's property, she would suffer a substantial tax loss because of her inability to defer recognizing the gain from her earlier sale. In short, there was evidence to support the jury's finding that, if defendant had honored the nonsolicitation provision, it would have sold its property to plaintiff, and she would not have suffered over $900,000 in tax losses. Put differently, there was evidence to support the jury's award of over $900,000 in expectation damages to plaintiff.

Despite that evidence, the majority holds as a matter of law that plaintiff may not recover the expectation damages that defendant's breach caused. The majority's holding appears to rest solely on the following proposition: Because defendant "declined ... to assume the risks of injury inherent in a completed contract of purchase and sale," it "cannot now be saddled with those very same liabilities." Slip op at 16. The majority effectively transforms the parties' lack of final agreement on the sale of the property into a disclaimer of liability for breaching a provision on which they did agree.

The primary problem with the majority's reasoning is that the letter of intent does not contain a disclaimer of liability. No provision in that letter purports either to define or limit the measure of plaintiff's damages for a breach of the nonsolicitation provision. More specifically, no provision in the letter states that defendant will not be liable for plaintiff's expectation damages should defendant breach the nonsolicitation provision. The provision stating that the letter of intent is not a binding agreement to sell land is just that: It limits the scope of the parties' agreement; it does not limit the scope of their remedies for a breach of a provision on which they did agree. The majority errs in reading into the unambiguous terms of the letter of intent a limitation on liability that the parties did not include.... *See Yogman v. Parrott*, 325 Or. 358, 361, 937 P.2d 1019 (1997) (in construing a contract, courts may not insert what the parties have omitted).

Fairly read, the terms of the letter of intent provide no support for the majority's decision. Beyond that, the majority's decision is at odds with the weight of authority, which would not preclude plaintiff, as a matter of law, from recovering her expectation damages. One of the leading decisions on the issue is *Venture Associates v. Zenith Data Systems.*, 96 F.3d 275 (7th Cir. 1996). In that case, the plaintiff had proposed to buy a subsidiary of the defendant corporation. *Id.* at 276–77. The parties signed a letter of intent that stated, as the letter of intent does here, that it did not create a binding obligation to go through with the sale. *Id.* at 277. The letter of intent did, however, impose a binding obligation on the parties to negotiate in good faith toward a final agreement.[80] *Id.* As negotiations wore on, the defendant became concerned about the plaintiff's solvency and eventually abandoned the negotiations on that basis, selling the subsidiary to a third party. *Id.* at 278–79. The plaintiff sued, arguing that the defendant had breached its duty to negotiate in good faith and seeking expectation damages based on the terms in the letter of intent. *Id.* at 278.

Faced with the question whether the plaintiff could recover expectation damages at all, given the parties' lack of a final agreement, Judge Posner, writing for the majority, held that it could. He reasoned: "Damages for breach of an agreement to negotiate may be, although they are unlikely to be, the same as the damages for breach of the final contract that the parties would have signed had it not been for the defendant's bad faith. If, quite apart from any bad faith, the negotiations would have broken down, the party led on by the other party's bad faith to persist in futile negotiations can recover only his reliance damages — the expenses he incurred by being misled, in violation of the parties' agreement to negotiate in good faith, into continuing to negotiate futilely. *But if the plaintiff can prove that had it not been for the defendant's bad faith the parties would have made a final contract, then the loss of the benefit of the contract is a consequence of the defendant's bad faith, and, provided that it is a foreseeable consequence, the defendant is liable for that loss — liable, that is, for the plaintiff's consequential damages.*" *Id.* at 278 (emphasis added). Judge Posner explained that "[t]he difficulty, which may well be insuperable, is that since by hypothesis the parties had not agreed on *any* of the terms of their contract, it may be impossible to determine what those terms would have been and hence what profit the victim of bad faith

---

80. [8] The majority suggests that, if the letter of intent in this case had included a requirement that the parties bargain in good faith rather than a nonsolicitation provision, the result might be different. Given the majority's holding, however, it is difficult to see a principled basis for that distinction. Under the majority's reasoning, the provision stating that the letter of intent does not create a binding obligation to go through with the sale would create a disclaimer of liability that would operate equally in both situations.

would have had. But this goes to the practicality of the remedy, not the principle of it." *Id.* at 278–79 (citation omitted; emphasis in original).

In his treatise on contracts, Farnsworth agrees with Judge Posner that, in principle, an injured party is entitled to expectation damages even if, as a practical matter, there may be difficulties of proof in such cases. E. ALLAN FARNSWORTH, 1 FARNSWORTH ON CONTRACTS, § 3.26b at 397 (3d ed. 2004). Farnsworth observes, however, that the concern that plaintiffs can never prove damages in this type of case may be overstated. As he notes, the difficulty of proving expectation damages in this type of case "may not be insuperable, because parties do not usually make agreements to negotiate until the negotiations are well advanced, so that what remains to be negotiated may be no more extensive than if the parties had made an agreement with open terms. In a growing number of decisions courts have indicated a willingness to consider awarding damages based on expectation." *Id.*[81]

Burton and Andersen reach the same conclusion, reasoning that "when the parties have worked out many of the principal economic terms of their final contract in detail, there is no obstacle to allowing expectation damages based on the bargain tentatively agreed to, but never consummated." STEVEN J. BURTON & ERIC G. ANDERSEN, CONTRACTUAL GOOD FAITH: FORMATION, PERFORMANCE, BREACH, ENFORCEMENT, § 8.4.2.3 at 365 (1995). *See also* Melvin Aron Eisenberg, *The Emergence of Dynamic Contract Law*, 88 CAL. L. REV. 1743, 1809 (2000) (arguing that, if a breaching party wants to avoid paying expectation damages, it should offer evidence that the deal would have broken down even absent the breach); Charles L. Knapp, *Enforcing the Contract to Bargain*, 44 N.Y.U. L. REV. 673, 723 (1969) ("In some cases ... the main terms of performance ... may have been so agreed upon ... that an expectation remedy can be computed with as much certainty as is usually required.").

Thus, in *Evans, Inc. v. Tiffany & Co.*, 416 F. Supp. 224, 240 (N.D. Ill. 1976), the court awarded the plaintiff expectation damages after finding that those damages were sufficiently certain and that the parties would have reached a final agreement had the defendant not breached its duty to negotiate in good faith. Similarly, in *Milex Products v. Alra Laboratories*, 237 Ill. App. 3d 177, 177 Ill. Dec. 852, 603 N.E.2d 1226, 1235–37 (1992), the court awarded the plaintiff expectation damages, including lost profits, for the defendant's breach of its duty to negotiate in good faith, finding that those profits were within the parties' contemplation and not too speculative.... Following the majority of courts and commentators, I would hold that a jury may award expectation damages on a proper evidentiary showing. I also would hold that, given our limited standard of review, plaintiff's evidentiary showing in this case sufficed; that is, we cannot say that there was "no evidence" from which the jury could have found that plaintiff had proved her right to recover expectation damages. *See Northwest*

---

81. [10] Interestingly, Farnsworth's views evolved from his early categorical rejection of expectation damages in cases such as this: *See* E. Allan Farnsworth, *Precontractual Liability and Preliminary Agreements: Fair Dealing and Failed Negotiations*, 87 COLUM. L. REV. 217, 267 (1987) (arguing against expectation damages but in favor of reliance damages and damages for lost opportunities).

Natural Gas Co., 333 Or. at 310 (stating that standard of review).[82] The Court of Appeals correctly held that, on this record, plaintiff was entitled to recover her expectation damages for defendant's breach.

It may be that, in many cases, a jury will find as a matter of fact that, even if the parties had honored a nonsolicitation agreement, they still would not have entered into an agreement to sell the property. Alternatively, even if there were evidence that the parties would have reached some agreement, the terms of that agreement may be too speculative to permit a jury to calculate expectation damages with reasonable certainty. In this case, however, the evidence permitted the jury to find that defendant would have entered into an agreement to sell the land to plaintiff if it had honored the nonsolicitation provision. Moreover, the evidence of the terms that the parties would have reached was sufficiently certain to uphold the jury's award. There is no basis in principle or in law to deny plaintiff the full extent of the damages that the jury awarded her. I respectfully dissent from the majority's contrary holding.

DURHAM and WALTERS, JJ., join in this opinion.

NOTES AND QUESTIONS

1. *What remedy under the majority decision?* The *Logan* majority remanded the case for further proceedings. What should the measure of a remedy be on remand? Would any substantial amount be recoverable? If not, does this mean that in essence the defendant can get away with making a contract with a third party in violation of the nonsolicitation term?

2. *Variation on a theme:* The dissent argues that the majority is wrong to suggest that the result in the case might have been otherwise if the contract had contained a term stating an obligation to negotiate in good faith. On the issue of whether expectation damages are recoverable, should such a clause matter?

3. *"How crazy is your client?"* *Logan* suggests that parties can avoid liability on the basis of letters of intent by explicitly providing that there is no contract and no liability as of yet, particularly if procedural promises are also avoided. So why might an attorney choose to use a letter that is ambiguous as to whether there is liability? Consider this type of negotiation: Letters of intent are often used in bringing together directors, actors, scripts and financing to make motion pictures. *See, e.g., Roth v. Garcia Marquez.*[83] A prominent entertainment lawyer offered a continuing legal education program about "the negotiation game." He said that sometimes a lawyer for an actor or producer will want enforceability, but often such a lawyer will not; or he or she will want it against the other party but not against the lawyer's client. Sometimes the

---

82. [12] The majority does not rest its contrary holding on the ground that the consequential damages that the jury awarded were either too speculative or not foreseeable. Rather, it holds that, no matter what the proof, plaintiff could not recover expectation damages.

83. 942 F.2d 617 (9th Cir. 1991).

lawyer will *want* uncertainty about whether a contract has been formed. The entertainment lawyer said that some of the factors to consider are:

(1) How committed is your client to making the picture?

(2) How crazy is your client (that is, does he change his mind frequently and does he irritate people)?

(3) Why might your client like to back out (the nature of the script, the person named as director, changes in the cast, other opportunities)?

(4) Is the producer of the picture good for the money?

(5) Why would the producer back out (better talent becomes available, money falls through, creative differences)?

(6) How replaceable is your client?

(7) What is the exposure if your client walks away from a binding agreement?

The lawyer listed 15 steps on a continuum between written evidence that essential points have been clearly left open and, on the other end, a fully signed written agreement. Steps in the middle leave matters in more or less doubt.

2. Business Documents and Commercial Practices

People can make contracts in many ways, but those who repeatedly make agreements often follow patterns. Lawyers for larger firms attempt to structure these patterns so that they fit into the models favored by the legal system. Some businesspeople, however, pay little attention to lawyers' advice. Usually, business agreements are carried out well enough so that commercial life goes on. Now and again, however, deals collapse. Businesspeople and their lawyers may then look in their files to determine their legal position—assuming enough is involved to make an inquiry, or a struggle, worthwhile. Sometimes business practices offset what the lawyers who drafted the documents tried to achieve.

People can draft detailed blueprints of their transactions. While we might wish that parties would do this in all situations, human behavior is flexible and sloppy. Businesspeople write letters that cover some, but usually not all, of the terms of their deal. The provisions in my letter may not match those in your letter. We may not notice this, or we may ignore it. Businesses may use printed form documents designed for routine transactions to memorialize complex and unusual bargains. Lawyers may attempt to create careful procedures, which businesspeople then find cumbersome and ignore. We will review some of the forms frequently used and then turn to the legal problems created by business behavior and business forms.

Business forms: The documents for exchanges serve both business and legal functions. When these functions conflict, we should not be surprised that the commercial function usually wins out. First, let's look at *documents used by sellers.* Price lists and catalogues usually give information to potential customers about standard items (often called "shelf goods"). A firm's sales department usually has a *proposal/quotation form.* Sellers use this form to state that they will supply some item at an indicated price. Proposals tend to be made for sales of specially made items or large orders of standard items. A proposal form serves as a checklist so that a seller will not fail to cover important matters as a result of oversight; it usually must be signed so that someone in the seller's organization will take responsibility for the transaction.

A sales department may also use an *acknowledgment of order form*. Buyers place orders after they have looked at a seller's price list or catalogue, talked with a sales-person, or asked for a formal proposal. Most sellers routinely acknowledge these orders for a number of reasons. The form functions as a means of controlling the sale within the seller's organization. Some copies go to the seller's production or shipping department. Some go to the financial department so that the buyer will be billed. The *acknowledgment of order* copy goes to the customer. It serves to tell the buyer that the order was received, what the seller thinks should be shipped, and how much the seller will charge.

A sales department may also use a sales representative's *order form*. Salespeople visit potential customers and talk with them. If they get an order, they fill in the blanks on this form. This serves as a checklist. The sales representative must determine such things as the necessary sizes, speeds, where the product will be shipped, and how the customer will pay for it.

Buyers, if their organizations are big enough, also have form documents. Purchasing departments may have a *request for quotation form*, which is sent to sellers asking for bids. If sellers fill out the form, the buyer gains information needed to choose between competitors. Obviously, the functions of this form and sellers' forms overlap. Both buyer and seller may prefer their own forms. A buyer's form, for example, is likely to demand more precise specifications of delivery dates than will be given on a seller's form.

A company big enough to have a purchasing department is likely to have a printed *purchase order*. This form commits the company to buy and gives the transaction an internal control number. It tells the financial department that the company will be billed by the seller, and tells the buyer's receiving department to accept the shipment when it arrives. Some buyers send with their purchase orders their own *acknowledgment of order form*, asking sellers to sign and return it. Obviously, the functions of this form and sellers' acknowledgments overlap.

Selling and buying patterns: If any of several patterns of behavior are followed, there will be little question about when or whether the parties have agreed to sell and buy and what is to be supplied at what price. For example:

(A) The engineers and purchasing agents of the buyer may negotiate with the seller's engineers and sales representatives for a machine made for the buyer's pur-poses—for example, the buyer wants a machine that automatically cleans, fills, and seals glass jars at a given rate per hour. Preliminary ideas are exchanged. The seller drafts a proposal, either in a letter or on a proposal form, which contains detailed specifications, prices for alternatives, a delivery date, and two lines for signatures.

Authorized representatives of both seller and buyer sign the form. While engineers, corporate officers, and even lawyers might have to interpret the terms, it is likely that the parties have a deal and that they can determine what it is.

(B) The purchasing agent of a corporation seeking to buy glass jars wants to discover which manufacturer will furnish the corporation with the best delivery date at the best price. The purchasing agent sends a request for quotation form to several man- ufacturers. The form states: "THIS IS NOT AN ORDER." Each manufacturer fills in the blanks that ask for a description of the product, prices, delivery schedules and the like, and signs it. The purchasing agent selects a lucky supplier. The purchasing department prepares a purchase order and sends it to that seller. Again, the parties have a deal, and they probably can determine what it is.

(C) A purchasing agent seeking to buy glass jars may study products and prices from catalogues. She selects a supplier and sends a purchase order that has an acknowledgment-of-order copy. The supplier's authorized agent signs the acknowledgment-of-order copy and returns it. There is a deal.

(D) A sales representative calls on a purchasing agent and they discuss the price of glass jars. The salesperson fills out an order form and the purchasing agent signs it. Typically, this form states: "This order is subject to acceptance at Seller's home of- fice." Sellers may want to check a buyer's credit, inventory, or production capacity. Sales representatives are seldom given the power to make these decisions. The home office approves the order. The seller may send the buyer an acknowledgment-of-order form, or it may just ship the goods. Again, there is a deal.

(E) The preceding patterns do not contemplate the role of the Internet. Websites have now largely supplanted printed catalogues. A purchasing agent may locate a much-needed part for a new line of manufacturing on the website of a previously unfamiliar company. Having had no personal interactions with this company, but after verifying the company's bona fides, the agent orders the desired number of parts through the online order form—which typically does not allow for negotiated terms.

Businesspeople often follow these patterns. If the buyer is a large corporation, its suppliers may be smaller organizations. Large corporations, which have many em- ployees with the power to make contracts, may insist that their employees follow standardized procedures. The small suppliers often go along with a large buyer's pro- cedures, since a good customer is always right!

Life does not always run smoothly. Anyone who has worked for a major corporation knows that there is always some give in the rules. Moreover, while those at the lower levels may follow routines, those higher in the organization often assert their own independence and discretion. For example, lawyers and others may plan and draft careful procedures which both serve business functions and limit liability for breach of warranty. Sales representatives use the proper forms and get buyers' signatures. Then, a vice president writes a letter to one of the buyer's officials. The vice president explains the meaning of the deal, or says that his firm would never use its rights against a customer such as the buyer. Even when the order is placed online and the terms are stated to be non-negotiable, a vice president may be willing to haggle if the customer is sufficiently important. This may give rise to a series of emails or other communications that ostensibly establish a different price or change the manner of delivery.

Suppose seller sends buyer a quotation form, stating a price for a particular product. The buyer immediately sends a purchase order back to the seller. Does this create a legally enforceable contract? The answer turns in large part on whether a court would classify the quotation as an offer, or only as a preliminary negotiation. Catalogues and advertisements directed to the world at large usually are not offers. Buyers are held to understand that sellers do not guarantee to have sufficient inventory or productive capacity to supply the world at the listed price. Additionally, typos and other errors are inevitable in any printed work. Catalogues and advertisements are useful ways to convey information, but some of this usefulness would be lost if sellers had to proofread them with great care to avoid being held to mistaken prices. Finally, a seller may be willing to supply the item, but only subject to a credit check.

Some price quotations are similar to advertisements. A quotation, however, that is directed to a particular buyer and is for a specified quantity is another matter. If the quotation is sent in response to a buyer's inquiry, the seller can foresee that the buyer is likely to rely on it. Clearly, the surrounding circumstances and the words used in the quotation will be important. Many proposal forms attempt to answer the question by their express terms. For example, the proposal form used by one major corporation states in large print: "This proposal will become a binding contract when signed by the purchaser and thereafter accepted by an officer of the [seller corporation] at its home office in Boston, Massachusetts, U.S.A."

a. The Battle of the Forms: Magic through Contract Drafting

The "Battle of the Forms" has been a pet of contracts scholars for many years. Casebook authors dwell on it, and scholars write articles about it. You should ask whether it is a sufficiently large problem for businesspeople to justify all the attention. Online order forms may now provide a way for a seller to "win" the battle of the forms by reducing the number of forms to one, the seller's. Indeed, in this context, the fighting issue is whether the seller can delay revealing terms until after order and payment online, either by putting them in the shipping box or embedding them in a digital product.[84] The Uniform Commercial Code has an elaborate section designed to solve problems involving multiple and delayed forms; you should ask whether it does so. Our focus here will not be on one-form transactions but rather on the "battle of the forms." This battle can still take place when the Internet is used for formation, for example, when forms are exchanged as attachments to emails, or when a buyer

---

84. These issues are addressed in Hill v. Gateway 2000, Inc. 105 F.3d 1147 (7th Cir. 1997), and Pro-CD v. Zeidenberg, 86 F.3d 1447 (7th Cir. 1996), cases included in Volume I of these materials. *See also infra* Note 2 after the *Steiner* case.

follows up an order on the seller's website by sending its own terms by email to a seller's agent prior to the time the seller ships.

The business model versus the legal model of contract: Many business transactions follow patterns that involve the exchange of inconsistent business forms. In some instances a lawyer will have to determine whether any contract has been made or what its provisions are. An all-too-common type of transaction would proceed as follows:

(1) Buyer has a seller's catalogue, or a seller's web address, which gives access to what amounts to an online catalogue. Buried in the catalogue (whether electronic or paper), along with technical details about products and other handy bits of information, are the seller's terms of sale.[85] They are written in legal language and presented in small type. Buyer's purchasing agent has dozens, if not hundreds, of catalogues, or web addresses, provided by her suppliers. She has never read the terms and conditions in seller's particular catalogue, although she has a general idea of what most sellers put on their forms. She finds the item she wants in the catalogue, notes its price, and telephones or emails seller's office to ask if the item is available at the catalogue price. Seller's agent says "Yes."

(2) The purchasing agent tells an office assistant to fill in a pre-drafted purchase order form. The agent checks it and may or may not sign it. There are many terms and conditions on the copy that is sent to the seller. The purchasing agent has read these terms and conditions in the past, but she now has only a general idea of what they say and mean. Buyer's purchase order protects its interests; its terms almost certainly add to or conflict with any seller's conditions of sale. For example, buyer may demand a broad warranty while sellers will offer a narrow warranty. The second copy of the purchase order is an acknowledgment form. Sellers are asked to sign and return it, thus "agreeing" to all of buyer's terms and conditions.

(3) The purchase order and acknowledgment copy are sent to seller.

(4) An assistant sales manager receives the purchase order and acknowledgment copy from buyer. He reads only part of the document, ignoring the fine print buried at the bottom or on the back as is customary. He decides to fill the order. (Of course, his decision is based on seller's capacity to manufacture the items, its inventory, its backlog of orders, and, importantly, buyer's credit rating.)

(5) The assistant sales manager tells an office assistant to write up the order. She fills in a description of the item ordered, the price, an estimated delivery date, and any other necessary information on a set of business forms. Several copies from this set will go to the accounting or billing department for use as an invoice and for financial records. Several will go to production or shipping to get the item ordered, made, and shipped.

---

85. Sometimes the terms are not on the website but are delivered with the product; we then have a case of delayed terms, not addressed here. *See* Jean Braucher, *Delayed Disclosure in Consumer E-Commerce as an Unfair and Deceptive Practice*, 46 Wayne L. Rev. 1805, 1860–62 (2000) (in a survey of the top 100 personal computer (PC) software companies by revenue in 1999, finding that 64 companies provided for online orders and of those only eight, 12.5 percent, disclosed terms prior to the time that a customer had to provide a credit card number and enter an order).

One copy of this set is marked "Customer's Acknowledgment." On the reverse side of this document or at the bottom in small print all of the seller's terms and conditions of sale are restated—which are not necessarily the same as those stated in seller's catalogue! The document reads: "We accept your order subject to the terms and conditions stated in this acknowledgment." Of course, the sales manager has not read his firm's terms and conditions for a number of years, but he has a general idea of what is covered.

(6) Seller sends the acknowledgment copy of the seller's set of business forms to buyer. Buyer's acknowledgment of order form is not signed and returned. It is filed by seller with buyer's purchase order. (Or, to really complicate matters, seller sends *both* its acknowledgment form and buyer's acknowledgment form back to buyer, even though they are inconsistent.)

(7) When buyer receives seller's acknowledgment, the major terms such as price and quantity are checked against the purchase order to see that the order has been interpreted correctly. No one at the buyer's office reads the fine print on the seller's form.

(8) The purchase order and the seller's acknowledgment are filed away by buyer.

(9) One of two things happens:

(a) Most commonly, the goods are delivered on time, seller is paid in full, and the goods work perfectly (or well enough that buyer is satisfied);

OR

(b) The goods are not delivered at all or arrive late, buyer does not pay seller, or the goods prove to be defective.

In most instances, the inconsistent or additional terms and conditions on buyer's and seller's forms will not matter to anyone. The seller may not deliver the goods at all or they may arrive late, the goods may be defective, or the buyer may not pay on time. Nonetheless, buyer and seller will negotiate a settlement without reading what is said on the faces or backs of business forms. They will not involve their lawyers. However, in those few instances where there is a major problem that cannot be resolved easily, someone may begin to read purchase order clause 1(a)(ii)(cc)(5) and wonder whether it is part of a binding contract.

The traditional common law answer seemed easy; it is often called the "mirror image" rule. As was said in *Clark v. Burr*,[86] "The acceptance of an offer upon terms varying from those of the offer, however slight,[87] is a rejection of the offer."[88]

---

86. 85 Wis. 649, 55 N.W. 401 (1893).

87. There are dicta suggesting that a purported acceptance with a "slight," "insubstantial," or "immaterial" variation would not defeat the formation of a contract and make the purported acceptance a counteroffer. However, the point is not considered in any of these cases. *See, e.g.,* Hess v. Holt Lumber Co., 175 Wis. 451, 185 N.W. 522 (1921); Russell v. The Falls Mfg. Co., 106 Wis. 329, 82 N.W. 134 (1900). In light of UCC § 2-207, a lawyer seeking to overcome or limit the common law rule in non-Code situations might draw on these dicta as the basis for arguing that the Code only restates and clarifies the common law rule in Wisconsin. The lawyer would have to overcome the phrase "however slight" in the *Clark* case and some of the discussion in Leuchtenberg v. Hoeschler, 271 Wis. 151, 72 N.W.2d 758 (1955).

88. 85 Wis. at 655, 55 N.W. at 403. *See also* Morris F. Fox & Co. v. Lisman, 208 Wis. 1, 237 N.W. 267, 240 N.W. 809, 242 N.W. 679 (1932).

The Wisconsin court further explained that "[a]n attempted acceptance of an offer, if coupled with any condition that varies or adds to the offer, is not an acceptance, but a counter-proposition or counter-offer.... [T]here must be an acceptance of the counter-offer in order to complete the contract.... [A]cceptance of a counter-offer can be inferred from any conduct on the offeree's part indicative thereof, but ... mere silence bears no such significance."

These common law rules are substantially modified by § 2-207 of the Uniform Commercial Code. However, Article 2 of the Code applies only to "transactions in goods." The common law rules may still apply to all other kinds of transactions, such as sales of real estate and services. These kinds of transactions are less likely to be conducted by the exchange of forms with inconsistent terms, but the problem can arise here as well as in sales of goods. For example, in *Leuchtenberg v. Hoeschler*,[89] the buyer offered to buy a lot with a depth of "about 150 feet." The owner tried to accept the offer but drew a line through the number 150 and substituted "120." The purported acceptance was a counteroffer, and no contract was formed.

The common law solution to the battle of the forms meant that even after an exchange of documents that both buyer and seller assumed formed a contract, either might be able to back out without legal liability. Thus, there was a chance that the law would leave reliance unprotected, which contracts scholars assumed was a significant problem. If we assume that the opinions expressed by businesspeople and their lawyers in the excerpts that follow are typical, is there a problem? Does the UCC solve it? After you have studied § 2-207 of the UCC, consider whether the problems with that section are worse than those that businesspeople faced under the common law.

—Interview with the purchasing agent of a manufacturer of heavy industrial and construction equipment:

> The company is willing to rely on a supplier's acknowledgment form. The purchasing department is concerned primarily about whether the vendor received the order and entered it properly. Moreover, the purchasing department wants the vendor's number for the transaction to help the company in expediting matters in case of delay. Perhaps we are a bit lax in not following up and insisting that vendors send us our own acknowledgment forms, but the legal department has never made an issue of the matter. The purchasing department's job is to get material here on time; not to arrange for improbable lawsuits. The company never has trouble on terms and conditions, and so it doesn't spend any time on the matter.

—Interview with the purchasing agent of a manufacturer of nationally advertised electrical appliances:

> The purchasing department is too busy getting the items needed to spend its time reading and checking terms and conditions. The company does not

---

89. 271 Wis. 151, 72 N.W.2d 758 (1955).

need legal sanctions since in every case it gets what it wants. We have never referred to the back of a buying or selling form to get performance from a supplier. A telephone call stressing the agreed schedule for delivery and the specifications is far more effective. All of the company's vendors have been doing business with the firm for years.

—Interview with the purchasing agent of a large manufacturer of industrial and residential electrical equipment:

The purchasing department will review all of a vendor's terms of acceptance, and if it finds any disagreement with the company's way of doing business, it will take the matter up with the vendor. It does not mind if the vendor simply adds items as long as they are not contrary to the usual way of doing business. This is true although additional items might prevent the formation of a legally binding contract. It is interested in a legally binding contract only in the case of building construction or large capital items such as automation machinery. In normal business one does not pay any attention to the problem of legal enforceability.

—Interview with the owner of a small manufacturer of sporting goods:

We buy a great deal of metal from a large supplier. The supplier has many terms and conditions on its acknowledgment form, but this company is a good one to do business with and would never refer to all this fine print to weasel out. If they did refer to terms and conditions and surprised us with some gimmick, they would lose our account. Moreover, I would comment about this when I went to business meetings. One behaves decently in business and doesn't run to lawyers or contract clauses.

—Interview with the sales and production managers of a manufacturer of packaging machinery:

The company has recently redrafted its standard contract for selling its machines. It now insists that its contract be signed or any modifications be carefully approved. Before these forms were drafted and this procedure was installed, the company was often on the edge of trouble. It is easy to fail to deliver on time when you are manufacturing machinery engineered for the customer's product and his factory. It takes five months or more to design and build this machinery. You cannot always predict how long it will take to solve some special problem. Yet customers' purchase orders tend to demand firm delivery dates. At present, a competitor is being sued for $600,000 for missing a delivery date on a packaging machine. The customer had arranged a TV presentation to promote a packaging idea that was to be produced on the machine. He had committed his production to the machine and had torn his plant down to install it. Our competitor did not get the machine there on time. The customer had to put his factory back together again and use the old machinery. The customer claims it suffered a loss of reputation when it could not supply its distributors with the item it had advertised. This suit has caused a lot of rethinking in this industry.

—Interview with the purchasing agent of a manufacturer of machine tools:

Terms and conditions might have significance in 1 or 2 percent of all cases. We do not read them. I have been purchasing agent for 11 years and with the company for 16. During that time we've had only three or four disputes on terms and conditions, and we've never lost much money. Our experience shows that elaborate procedures to check the 8,000 to 15,000 purchase orders and acknowledgments that pass through here each year would not be justified.

—Interview with the general counsel of a manufacturer of machinery that puts products into containers. He supplied letters written by him to be sent out by his firm's sales manager to indicate how the company takes exception to a customer's conditions of purchase:

The sales manager first acknowledges "your most valued purchase order." Then he states: "We have followed the practice for years of selling our machinery under a uniform type of contract under which our liabilities are limited. For those liabilities for which we are responsible under the contract, we purchase insurance so that our annual cost can be anticipated and our selling prices adjusted accordingly." He goes on to discuss the warranties demanded by the customer. Next he states: "We are certain that we can arrange an acceptable contract that will protect you. Our insurance companies, however, have asked us to obtain additional information so that they can advise us whether our present coverage is sufficient and what costs would be involved in acquiring additional protection." Then he states: "In making such comments we want you to know that we are desirous of meeting every reasonable request and that our only objection will be to situations where insurance protection is not reasonably available or the cost thereof was not anticipated in the selling price of the equipment, or where the condition is contrary to a long-established and desirable policy of the company." He next makes a show of accepting as many of the customer's conditions as he can. He objects to conditions dealing with warranty, excuses for failure to perform, and inspections. He makes, in the course of his argument, several references to the fact that his terms and conditions have been accepted by the customer's major competitors. He ends his letter by saying: "We regret the length of this discussion and hope that we have not in any manner indicated an intention to avoid reasonable responsibility to provide and install a first-class unit of equipment. However, it becomes impossible for us to operate under a different contract in the plant of each customer and we have, therefore, established our selling prices on the basis of our uniform contract provisions."

In another letter, the sales manager argues that if the extensive guarantees demanded by the customer are given, it will only be a bonanza for the insurance companies and an additional cost for the seller and its customers. "This kind of protection is not necessary when dealing with a company of our standing. We fear that making an exception in a few cases will lead to a general breakdown of our rule."

—Interview with the general counsel of a manufacturer of machinery that puts products in containers:

> Typically, our purchasing agent's authority to buy is limited to signing for 5 to 10,000 dollars on any one purchase order. The extent of exposure on any order is trivial. There are so many purchase orders that we have many small risks spread over many transactions. If we are buying a more expensive item, the transaction must be approved by an official of the company. He will, as a matter of regular procedure, route the matter to the legal department for approval. Then we can see that the company is protected.

—Interview with the general counsel of a manufacturer of heating and cooling equipment:

> You must ask how much time is justified in checking the terms and conditions on customers' forms and seeing that a contract is negotiated in every case. You could get agreement in every case, but this is not practical. Until I came to the company six months ago, someone, but not a lawyer, checked every order. I have set a check point so that only the more important transactions are subject to a careful reading and negotiation for agreement with the customer. The breakdown is designed to catch messy situations and to take a chance on the rest. First, all orders involving more than $25,000 are checked. Second, orders under this amount are not checked unless: (1) they involve government contracts; (2) they involve a retainage provision which allows the customer to retain, say, 10 percent of the price until the transaction is completed (with many customers you can never get that 10 percent no matter how well you perform); or, finally, (3) they involve aircraft products, which always involve special problems of products liability. Of course, if you have trouble with a particular account, you deal on a tailor-made contract with the best security you can get, if you deal at all. This is an insurance-like approach. You must balance the risk and degree of difficulty against the cost of avoiding all possible liability. You should not spend $100 to save $50.

—Interview with a partner in a law firm in a large city with a corporate practice:

> I can think of many disputes where it was wonderful to find that the back of the documents protected my client and not the other party although perhaps there was no enforceable contract. You need arguments for negotiating a settlement. What are you going to say on the telephone?

—Interview with the general counsel of a large manufacturer of paper and paper products:

The important thing about a contract is not its legal enforceability but its meaning when read by the other side. There is a moral sanction. You can look at the man on the other side of the table and say, "You have agreed to this. Are you going to back out and not honor your word?" But this is a business where buyers and sellers know each other very well.

Before the Uniform Commercial Code was passed, many lawyers relied on "the last shot principle" in planning for their firm in its role as seller. Normally, the last document sent in a "battle of the forms" situation is a seller's acknowledgment of a buyer's order. Under pre-Code law, if a seller sent an acknowledgment with additional or different terms from those on the buyer's purchase order, it would be a counteroffer rather than an acceptance. No contract would be formed at this point. However, if the seller shipped goods and the buyer accepted them, the buyer's action also accepted the counteroffer and formed a contract on the seller's terms. Of course, the buyer might get the last shot. Suppose a seller offered goods on a proposal form, the buyer sent a purchase order with inconsistent terms and conditions, and the seller responded by shipping the goods. Now the act of shipment would probably constitute acceptance of buyer's counteroffer.

Lawyers drafting forms for buyers and sellers tried to cope with the common law's last shot approach. For example, the selling forms of the Anaconda American Brass Company provided that "seller's failure to object to provisions contained in any communications from buyer will not be deemed as an acceptance of such provisions or as a waiver of the provisions hereof." On the other hand, the purchase order of the Pabst Brewing Company provided that "you accept all the terms and conditions on the front and reverse sides of this order ... by failing to make prompt written objection to these terms and conditions, even if you fail to sign or return the acknowledgment copy to us." Several major corporations used clauses on their purchase orders that read: "Buyer recognizes that seller may for operating convenience desire to utilize its own form of acknowledgment, contract, or other document in connection with this transaction. Therefore, it is agreed that any provisions in the form of acceptance used, which modify, conflict with, or contradict any provision of this contract or order, shall be deemed waived." Of course, the legal effect of these clauses is debatable, but they give lawyers something to argue about as part of negotiations in the event of a dispute.

b. Section 2-207 of the Uniform Commercial Code

Section 2-207 of the UCC purports to wipe out the common law approach to the battle of the forms and start over. Some scholars have argued that the rise of the Internet and "shrink-wrap" or "click-wrap" contracts have made § 2-207 largely irrelevant. Although the number of cases that hinge on § 2-207 has decreased, they have not disappeared. A solid grasp of this section is essential for any business lawyer.

We begin by looking at the text of the statute. As always, one must consider the structure of the legislation and touch all the bases rather than rip a phrase or paragraph out of context. Then we'll turn to some appellate opinions to highlight problems.

Subsections (1) and (2) of § 2-207 go together. If a case does not fit within them, then you must go on to subsection (3). Subsection (1) deals with whether a contract has been formed. If a contract has been formed under subsection (1), then we look to subsection (2) to determine its terms. If a contract has not been formed under subsection (1), then we turn to subsection (3) and not the common law or the last shot doctrine.

Section 2-207(1) asks whether there is a contract. It says that a "definite and seasonable expression of acceptance" closes a deal and creates a contract. Notice that we must have a communication that a court will classify as an acceptance. Reading the statute literally, a preliminary negotiation, an offer, or a counteroffer does not come under UCC § 2-207(1). However, if we have an acceptance, it creates a contract even if it states "terms additional to or different from those offered or agreed upon." Clearly, this overturns much of the common law rule. Under the common law, a purported acceptance that states "terms additional to or different from those offered or agreed upon" is only a counteroffer. Under the UCC, it can close a contract. However, it does not have this effect if "acceptance is expressly made conditional on assent to the additional or different terms." Courts have had great difficulty interpreting this last clause.

What are the terms of a contract created under subsection (1)? Additional terms are proposals for additions to the contract. In effect, the Code says that we treat the communication as if it said, "I accept your offer and we have a deal now. However, I propose we also add term XYZ to our contract." Between merchants, these proposals become part of the contract unless any of the three qualifications in subsection (2) apply:

(a) the offer expressly limits acceptance to the terms of the offer;

(b) the terms materially alter the offer; or

(c) notification of objection to the terms has already been given or is given within a reasonable time after notice of them is received.

Notice that the "materially alter" provision goes to the *terms* of a deal formed under subsection (1), and not to whether there is a contract formed under subsection (1).

Suppose instead of additional terms, the acceptance contains different terms that do not alter the contract materially and to which there is no objection. Do added terms become part of the deal while different terms drop out? Courts and writers have struggled with this question.

Assume the buyer's and seller's forms do not create a contract under subsection (1). Now we turn to subsection (3). "Conduct by both parties which recognizes the existence of a contract is sufficient to establish a contract for sale although the writings of the parties do not otherwise establish a contract." Suppose the seller offered goods on its proposal form. The buyer accepted the offer by sending a purchase order to seller, but the terms printed on the purchase order expressly made acceptance conditional on assent to the additional or different terms found there. Thus, under UCC § 2-207(1), the writings of the parties would not create a contract. However, seller then ships the goods ordered, and buyer accepts and pays for them. This seems to be conduct by both of them which "recognizes the existence of a contract." If a court finds this to be true, a contract is established.

What are its terms? Subsection (3) says that they are those on which the writings of the parties agree, "together with any supplementary terms incorporated under any other provisions of this Act." The proposal and purchase order are likely to agree on the description of the goods and their price. Often the seller's form disclaims warranties and limits remedies, while the buyer's form claims these rights. The warranty and remedy provisions found in these documents would drop out of the deal. The UCC provisions on warranties and remedies would fill the gap. Notice that this is not the last shot principle, in which the party that last submitted a document gets its terms and conditions as the contract.

MCCARTY v. VERSON ALLSTEEL PRESS CO.

Illinois Appellate Court, First District
89 Ill. App. 3d 498, 411 N.E.2d 936 (1980)

ROMITI, J.

[A Nash Bros. employee was injured using a machine manufactured by Verson. The employee sued Verson, who settled. Verson then sued Nash Bros. for indemnification under a clause in the form that accompanied its price quotation.] The trial court, after a bench trial, found that the clause was part of the contract and entered judgment for [Verson] in the amount of $322,745.44. We disagree and reverse.

In early 1971, Nash Bros. Co. (hereinafter called buyer), and Verson Allsteel Press Company (hereinafter called seller), entered into oral negotiations regarding the sale of a punch press from the seller, Verson, as a manufacturer, to Nash, the buyer. These negotiations centered almost completely around the technical specifications of the subject punch press. At no time during this period of oral negotiation were any discussions had regarding the indemnification of seller by buyer for injuries caused by defects in seller's presses.

On May 19, 1971, seller sent buyer a document entitled Proposal No. 5575-1-RB. It stated: "In accordance with your request, we are pleased to offer the following press brake equipment for your consideration...." A detailed list of "General Specifications" and "Items Included" followed. The proposal concluded:

> Point of operation guards are not included with this equipment. It is the employer's responsibility to provide guards, devices, tools, or other means to effectively protect all personnel from serious injury which may otherwise occur as a result of any particular machine use or activity. Thank you for this opportunity to offer our equipment. Should you require any additional information, please let us know.

This offer was subject to 30 days' acceptance.

At the foot of the first page of the proposal was the legend: "All quotations, orders and contracts are subject to acceptance of home office."

Enclosed with the May 19th proposal was a copy of seller's form "Conditions of Sale—Machinery." In pertinent part, these provided:

... 7. WARRANTY—WARRANTY LIMITATIONS—INDEMNITY ...

(c) Customer assumes and shall bear all responsibility for providing adequate and sufficient safeguards, work handling tools and safety devices to protect fully the operator and any other users of the goods at all times, in accordance with the prevailing federal, state, and local codes and industry-accepted standards. Verson shall bear no liability whatsoever for the failure of customer to order, install, or use such safeguards, work handling tools or safety devices.

Customer shall establish and use, and require all persons operating the equipment to use, all proper and safe operating procedures, including but not limited to procedures set forth in any manuals or instruction sheets relating to the equipment. Customer shall not remove or modify any devices, warning sign, or manual furnished with, or installed upon or attached to the goods.

NOTWITHSTANDING ANY PROVISION OF THESE TERMS AND CONDITIONS, THE WARRANTY CONTAINED IN THIS PARAGRAPH, AS LIMITED HEREIN, IS THE ONLY WARRANTY EXTENDED BY VERSON IN CONNECTION WITH ANY SALE BY IT AND IS IN LIEU OF ALL OTHER WARRANTIES, EXPRESS OR IMPLIED, INCLUDING WARRANTIES OF MERCHANTABILITY AND FITNESS FOR PURPOSE.

8. INDEMNITY. Customer hereby (1) waives, releases, and discharges any and all claims of any and every kind (including but not limited to injury to or death of any person or damage to property), which it may have at any time against Verson, its agents or employees, by reason of or arising out of any claimed improper design, specifications, or manufacture of the goods sold hereunder, or of devices; and (2) covenants to indemnify and hold harmless Verson, its agents and employees of, from and against any and all loss, damage, expense, claims, suits or liability which Verson or any of its employees may sustain or incur at any time for or by reason of any injury to or death of any person or persons or damage to any property, arising out of any claimed improper design or manufacture of the goods sold hereunder, or of any claimed inadequate or insufficient safeguards or safety devices....

14. ACCEPTANCE-WHOLE AGREEMENT,

ALL ORDERS ARE VALID AND BINDING UPON VERSON ONLY UPON ACKNOWLEDGMENT BY A DULY AUTHORIZED OFFICER OR DEPARTMENT MANAGER OF VERSON, BY ANY ACKNOWLEDGMENT OR ACCEPTANCE BY CUSTOMER IN ANY MANNER OF VERSON'S PROPOSAL, OR BY THE SUBMISSION OR ISSUANCE OF CUSTOMER'S OWN PURCHASE ORDER BASED ON SUCH PROPOSAL, CUSTOMER UNCONDITIONALLY ACCEPTS AND AGREES TO BE BOUND BY THE TERMS AND CONDITIONS HEREIN, SUCH TERMS AND CONDITIONS

SHALL CONSTITUTE THE COMPLETE AGREEMENT BETWEEN CUS-
TOMER AND VERSON AND SHALL NOT BE SUPERSEDED BY ANY
CONDITIONS OR PROVISIONS IN CUSTOMER'S ORDER WHICH MAY
CONFLICT WITH, BE CONTRARY TO OR OTHERWISE VARY FROM
THOSE HEREIN CONTAINED. ALL PREVIOUS COMMUNICATION BE-
TWEEN THE PARTIES HERETO, WHETHER VERBAL OR WRITTEN,
WITH REFERENCE TO THE SUBJECT MATTER HEREOF, IS HEREBY
ABROGATED, IT BEING UNDERSTOOD THAT THERE ARE NO OTHER
AGREEMENTS, UNDERSTANDINGS, GUARANTEES OR WARRANTIES
WHATEVER, EXPRESS OR IMPLIED, EXCEPT AS CONTAINED IN VER-
SON'S PROPOSAL, AND THESE CONDITIONS.

Verson Allsteel Press Co.

On or about May 28, 1971, seller sent buyer its Proposal No. 5575-1-RB Revised.
This document contained language almost identical to the May 19, 1971, proposal
in its opening and conclusion. It also provided that the prices were subject to thirty
days' acceptance and that all quotations, orders and contracts were subject to the acceptance of the home office. The enclosures included another copy of seller's "Conditions of Sale — Machinery." Various changes were made, however, in the "General
Specifications" and "Included Items."

On June 8, 1971, seller sent buyer a letter, on its own stationery, reducing the price
of the press that was the subject of its proposals. On the face of this letter was printed:

All quotations, orders and contracts are subject to acceptance of home office
and are contingent upon strikes, fires or other causes beyond our control.

Seller's "Conditions of Sale" were not included with this document and did not appear
therein.

On June 16, 1971, buyer sent seller its form "PURCHASE ORDER." On its face
was typed:

IN ACCORDANCE WITH YOUR QUOTATION PROPOSAL NO. 5575-1-
RB REVISED AND LETTER DATED 6-8-71, WE WISH TO PURCHASE
THE FOLLOWING:

A detailed list of "General Specifications" and "Included Items" was then typed on
each of seven pages. On the front of each page was printed the following:

This Purchase Order Is Subject To The Terms and Conditions Below and On
The Reverse Side.

PLEASE ACKNOWLEDGE THIS ORDER AT ONCE UPON ATTACHED
COPY. This order is not binding until accepted. This order shall become a
binding contract when Vendor executes and returns the attached Acknowledgment copy or ships any of the items, or renders any of the services, ordered
herein. When accepted, the terms and conditions on the face and reverse
sides of this order will constitute the complete agreement between Purchaser
and Vendor. No additional or different terms that may be contained in Ven-

dor's forms or otherwise proposed by Vendor will be binding upon Purchaser unless accepted in writing signed by Purchaser.

On the back of each page were buyer's "Terms and Conditions." In pertinent part these provided:

PURCHASE ORDER

Terms and Conditions

1. ACCEPTANCE OF ORDER. This order is an offer to purchase upon the conditions and terms below and on the reverse side hereof and at the prices stated herein and may be withdrawn at any time prior to the actual receipt by Purchaser of Vendor's unconditional, written acceptance hereof. No modifications of, or exceptions to, any of the terms, conditions, or provisions of this order by Vendor shall be of any effect unless and until accepted in writing by Purchaser. Any delivery (complete or partial) by Vendor pursuant hereto prior to actual receipt of Vendor's unconditional, written acceptance hereof, shall constitute Vendor's acceptance of this order in accordance with all terms, conditions, and provisions thereof....

On June 25, 1971, seller responded to the buyer's Purchase Order by returning a copy of the buyer's Acknowledgment form, signed by Walter C. Johnson, Vice-President of Verson, as follows:

ACCEPTED:

Verson Allsteel Press Company (Vendor) _____

Date _____

/s/ Walter C. Johnson

Walter C. Johnson

Vice President, Marketing Industrial Products

The cover letter accompanying the Acknowledgment provided:

Gentlemen:

We acknowledge and express our sincere gratitude for your subject order, covering a # B-1110-250 and a # B-3010 Verson Major Series Press Brakes. The order has been entered in our production schedule for shipment of the B-1110-250 during the month of October, 1971, and the B-3010 during the month of November, 1971.

Based upon the previous correspondence, our formal proposal and your purchase order, the enclosed acknowledgment copies of our production orders give our terms, specifications, and pricing.

Point of operation guards are not included with these equipments. It is the employer's responsibility to provide guards, devices, tools, or other means to effectively protect all personnel from serious injury which may otherwise occur as a result of any particular machine use or activity. Again, please accept our thanks for your purchase order.

The maintenance manual delivered with the machine also stated that "Providing safe working conditions and safety devices are the sole responsibility of the user."

In 1974 an employee of the buyer was injured while operating the press, allegedly because of defects in the sufficiency of safety guards and warning devices on the press. He collected workmen's compensation benefits from the buyer and then sued the seller, which settled for $300,000. Seller in turn sued buyer on the alleged indemnification agreement.[90]

At trial Johnson, seller's vice-president, testified the price of the machinery did not vary with the inclusion or exclusion of the indemnification agreement. He also volunteered the statement that they would not sell the machine without such an agreement. Buyer's contracting officer testified that he was familiar with the purchase of this type of machine and that when some other press manufacturer had wanted a similar indemnification agreement, they refused. He could recall no other occasion in his eight and one-half years of employment at buyer's where a manufacturer had required an indemnification agreement as a condition of sale.

The trial court held that the buyer was bound by the indemnification agreement.

I. The rights of the parties are governed by § 2-207 of the Uniform Commercial Code....

The seller, relying on *Alan Wood Steel Co. v. Capital Equipment Enterprises, Inc.* (1976), 39 Ill. App. 3d 48, 349 N.E.2d 627, contends that the price quotation was an offer, although any contract was subject to approval by the home office; that since the price quotation was an offer the order must have been an acceptance of the offer; and that, therefore, the terms in the price quotation are binding.

We are not convinced, however, that *Alan Wood* is controlling. It is true that that case stated that the price quotation, which, like the price quotation in the present case, provided that no order was binding until acceptance by the seller, was an offer. However it does not appear from the case that this question had been litigated by the parties. Furthermore, the court in *Alan Wood* stated that the buyer orally accepted the offer by telephone before mailing the purchase order. Obviously, therefore, both parties in that case were treating the price quotation, not the purchase order, as the offer.

A price quotation, if sufficiently detailed as was the price quotation in the present case, may constitute an offer.... It does not follow, however, that a price quotation which is not binding when accepted by a buyer but only becomes binding if and when accepted by the seller, who is under absolutely no obligation to accept it, can by itself be treated as an offer.... It follows that where the so-called offer is not intended to give the so-called offeree the power to make a contract there is no offer....

---

90. [1] Prior to 1977 Illinois did not permit a manufacturer held liable for a products liability injury to a buyer's employee to seek common law indemnification from the employer of the employee for its negligence in maintaining or altering the machine. This rule was overturned in 1977 by the Illinois Supreme Court in Stevens v. Silver Manufacturing Co. (1977), 70 Ill. 2d 41, 374 N.E.2d 455, which held, however, that its ruling was prospective only. Accordingly, since the injury occurred in 1974, the seller cannot recover from the buyer unless it can prove a contractual right to indemnification.

In *West Penn Power Co. v. Bethlehem Steel Corp.* (1975), 236 Pa. Super. 413, 348 A.2d 144, *allocatur refused*, the court refused to treat a proposal requiring acceptance by its home office as an offer since the clause was clearly intended to prevent formation of a contract by the unilateral action of the other party, saying at 236 Pa. Super. 426, 427, 348 A.2d 152:

> The first legal issue involved in this conclusion concerns the validity of the "Acceptance" clause. There can be no doubt about appellee's right to include this clause in its proposal to appellants, nor about the effect of the clause. The clause kept the proposal in effect for seven days but precluded the formation of a contract except upon approval by appellee's home office. Such a clause is valid in Pennsylvania under the common law of contracts. If the seller does not authorize the contract or accept the order within a reasonable time, the buyer may revoke its order, but there is no contract until the terms of the clause are met. *McCrea v. Automatic Heat, Inc.*, 161 Pa. Super. 545, 55 A.2d 564 (1947). "The purpose of [the inclusion of such a standard acceptance clause] is that the negotiating agent shall have no power to bind his principal, and that expressions of agreement on the paper shall therefore be no more than an offer to be accepted or rejected by the principal at his pleasure." 1 CORBIN CONTRACTS, § 33, at 128–29 (1963).

II. Even if we were to treat the seller's price quotation as an offer and the buyer's purchase order as an acceptance ... it does not follow under the facts in the present case that the provisions in the seller's proposal would control. The seller unconditionally signed the buyer's acknowledgment form sent with the purchase order. The purchase order retained by the seller provided on its face above the purchaser's signature, in fairly large sized print, that when the order was accepted, the terms and conditions on the face and reverse sides of this order would constitute the complete agreement between the purchaser and vendor and that no additional or different terms contained in the vendor's forms would be binding on the purchaser. Where the seller signs the buyer's acknowledgment without expressly conditioning that signature, the seller accepts the conditions in the buyer's forms ... even though the price quotation contained a provision that the buyer by ordering any of the listed merchandise agreed to the enumerated conditions of sale.... The seller could, of course, have avoided this result by not signing the acknowledgment at all or by expressly conditioning the signature as did the seller in *Lincoln Pulp & Paper Co. v. Dravo Corp.* (D. Me. 1977), 445 F. Supp. 507, where the seller said on the acknowledgment that it was accepted in accordance with the accompanying letter, and the letter said conditions on back of form were not acceptable.

III. Furthermore, even if we were to treat the price quotation as an offer, it does not follow that the purchase order was necessarily an acceptance of that offer, despite the provision in the seller's condition of sale which, apparently, attempts to make any purchase order, regardless of its terms, an acceptance of all of the seller's terms. (Absent proper punctuation, it is impossible to decipher the precise meaning of paragraph 14.) While it is true that the offeror has total control over its own offer and may condition *acceptance* to the terms of the offer (Ill. Rev. Stat. 1969, ch. 26, par. 2-207(2)(a)), as apparently the seller did here, nevertheless it is not true that the first party to a sales transaction will always get his own terms. In most commercial transactions which party processes its terms first is purely fortuitous ... and "it must be recognized that the offeree should not be compelled to accept the terms of the offer if he does not want them, and he ought also to be free to respond with a counteroffer." 3 R. DUESENBERG & L. KING, UNIFORM COMMERCIAL CODE SERVICE (MB) § 3.06[3] (1977).

Under § 2-207(1) of the Uniform Commercial Code ... any definite and seasonable expression of acceptance operates as an acceptance even though it is not a mirror image of the offer unless the acceptance is expressly made conditional on assent to the additional or different terms. However that section still requires a definite expression of acceptance and does not change the basic common-law requirement that there must be an objective manifestation of mutual assent.... No contract can be found where the offeror could not reasonably treat the response of the offeree as an acceptance (*Air Products and Chemicals, Inc. v. Fairbanks Morse, Inc.*, 58 Wis. 2d 193, 206 N.W.2d 414 (1973)), and parties may initially exchange printed forms which differ so radically that the second cannot be treated as an acceptance of the first. *Koehring Co. v. Glowacki*, 77 Wis. 2d 497, 253 N.W.2d 64 (1977). Here the purchase order clearly, expressly, and repeatedly stated that it was an offer to be accepted by the seller and that no contract existed until it was accepted by the seller. We cannot distort this definite expression of an offer into a "definite and seasonable expression of acceptance."

IV. Seller's signing of the purchase order acknowledgment acted as an acceptance of the order. Indeed, the seller admitted this in its request to admit that "Verson Allsteel Press Company by Walter C. Johnson, Vice-President, accepted the purchase order and signed it on Page 1." Nor did seller dispute this point in its brief, although it was raised by the buyer. The mere fact that the seller enclosed its "Conditions of Sale" with the accompanying letter merely stating that enclosed copies gave its terms, specifications and pricing was not sufficient to make the acceptance a counteroffer instead of an acceptance, since to prevent such an assent from being an acceptance under § 2-207(1) it must be *expressly* made conditional on assent to the additional or different terms. This provision is construed narrowly to apply only to an acceptance that clearly reveals that the offeree is unwilling to proceed without agreement to the additional terms.... [See] *Dorton v. Collins & Aikman Corp.*, 453 F.2d 1161 (6th Cir. 1972), which held that even a statement that acceptance subject to all the terms and conditions on reverse side was not "expressly made conditional on assent to the additional or different terms."

Under § 2-207(2) of the Commercial Code the terms enclosed with the letter were merely to be construed as proposals for additions to the contract. They did not, however, become part of the contract since, as the seller admits, they materially altered it....

V. If we were to assume, contrary to the cases, that seller's acceptance was expressly made conditional on assent to the conditions set forth in its "Conditions of Sale," the result would still be the same. In that case, under § 2-207(1) of the Commercial Code the acknowledgment would act as a counteroffer, not an acceptance.... Following this reasoning, since the only contract formed would be that formed by the parties' conduct, their rights would be controlled by § 2-207(3) of the Code.... This section provides that the terms of the particular contract consist of those on which the *writings* of the parties agree and the code provisions. It is well established that under this provision terms contained only in one of the party's forms are not part of the contract....

VI. The seller argues, however, that the court's finding was proper because the parties intended to make the indemnity clause part of the contract, pointing to the testimony of seller's marketing vice-president that seller would never have sold the press without the indemnity provision. There is absolutely no evidence in the record that this intent was communicated to the buyer. To the contrary, the only evidence in the record is that there was no discussion between the parties regarding the indemnification of the seller....

Seller, however, contends that the terms of the "Conditions of Sale" were incorporated into the buyer's order by the language "in accordance with your quotation Proposal No. 5575-1-RB Revised and letter dated 6-8-71," relying on the well-established axiom that typewritten provisions prevail over printed ones. This rule is applicable only where there is a conflict between typed and printed portions of a document.... A contract must be read as a whole ... and neither the printed portion nor the typewritten portion should be disregarded unless there is a conflict between the two. Rather, a typewritten provision of a contract should prevail over inconsistent printed stipulations only as far as it is apparent that the parties intended to modify or disregard such printed stipulations, and where the antagonism is merely apparent, the difference should be reconciled, if possible, by any reasonable interpretation.... Reading the purchase order as a whole it is clear the general phrase "in accordance with" was intended only to identify the pertinent price quotations and not to incorporate the "Conditions of Sale" attached to only one of those quotations in direct conflict with the many provisions of the purchase order specifically stating that the seller's conditions were not binding.

The seller also contends that the buyer is bound by the indemnity provision because it failed to object to it. The indemnity provision only appeared in the "Conditions of Sale" which, as we have already determined, did not become part of the contract. The other notices sent to the buyer repeatedly informed the buyer that the responsibility for installing safety devices was on the buyer but did not contain an indemnification clause. Such unobjected-to notice might be construed as modifying the contract so as to remove any warranties relating to the safety of the machine, but obviously could not be considered to change the contract to add an indemnification clause never referred to in such notice. To the contrary, an indication that the seller was not relying on any indemnification clause is the fact that while the notices reaffirmed the buyer's duty to install safety devices, a duty first mentioned in the "Conditions of Sale," they failed to make any reference to the indemnification clause also in the same conditions. Since the accident occurred before the decision in *Stevens v. Silver Manufacturing Co.*, 70 Ill. 2d 41, 374 N.E.2d 455 (1977), the claim does not and cannot arise out of the buyer's failure to install effective devices. It can arise only if the buyer did in fact agree "to indemnify ... Verson ... against any and all loss, damage, expense, claims, suits or liability which Verson ... may sustain or incur at any time for or by reason of any injury to or death of any person or persons or damage to any property, arising out of any claimed improper design or manufacture of the goods sold hereunder, or any claimed, inadequate or insufficient safeguards or safety devices."

Since we believe it is clear as a matter of law that the indemnification clause cannot be found to be part of the contract agreed upon by the parties, the judgment of the trial court is *Reversed*.

NOTES AND QUESTIONS

1. *Section 2-207 and substantive policy concerning the clauses in question:* The seller tried to convince the court that the safety obligation was that of the buyer who was to use the machine in a particular setting for a particular purpose. It said that the buyer's "safety device obligation was not an overlooked item in a 'battle of forms,' but a prime point expressly reiterated at least 10 different times in the documents exchanged between the parties."

2. *The buyer's views about indemnity:* The buyer responded that the case "remains one in which Verson, as seller, is attempting to foist a hold-harmless clause (which is contrary to the policies embodied in the UCC) on its buyer, Nash, after the fact of sale, and without procuring any agreement, written or otherwise, from Nash with respect to the clause."

The buyer pointed out that the parties had never discussed the clause during negotiations. It continued:

> This court is asked to decide whether the manufacturer of an unreasonably dangerous machine can attempt to enforce a hold-harmless clause in the "contract" of sale of the machine, and, thereby, escape liability for its failure to equip the machine with safety devices. It is submitted that to allow such a practice would be to effectively remove a manufacturer's obligation to create its products safely. Certainly, if one realizes that he will be reimbursed for any damages he may be required to pay on account of his responsibility for another's injuries, he will no longer be as inclined to take precautions which will prevent the injury. It is the prevention of this injury with which the law of products liability is concerned....

> Verson has marketed a product which is unreasonably dangerous due to its lack of safety devices, and has, simultaneously, attempted to transfer its liability for injuries caused thereby to Nash. A minute clause on the back of Verson's printed form is the means by which Verson seeks to effectuate this transfer. Verson's attempted transfer of the financial responsibility for its violation of a duty which it could not delegate cannot, and should not, be tolerated if the policies embodied in the doctrine of strict tort liability are to be preserved.

3. *Sneaking provisions into deals:* Professor John E. Murray asserts: "If a party would not reasonably understand that certain terms were included in the contract *ab initio*, they will not be included, because their inclusion would unfairly surprise and oppress the party against whom they would have operated. Section 2-207, therefore, may be viewed as addressing incipient unconscionability—its philosophy is identical to 2-302's."[91] Suppose the seller's representative had called the attention of buyer's officials to the hold-harmless clause and to the problem of installing safety devices on the machine. Is it likely that this would have made a difference in the negotiations or other behavior of the parties?

STEINER v. MOBIL OIL CORP.

California Supreme Court
20 Cal. 3d 90, 569 P.2d 751 (1977)[92]

Tobriner, J.

In this case, over one year after apparently accepting plaintiff's offer, the Mobil Oil Corporation sought to impose upon plaintiff the very contractual terms which plaintiff expressly rejected in his offer. As justification for its conduct, Mobil asserted that the crucial provision of plaintiff's offer was lost in the labyrinth of the Mobil bureaucracy, and thus that Mobil decisionmakers had no opportunity to pass on plaintiff's offer as such. As we shall see, however, the trial court correctly concluded that § 2207 of the California Uniform Commercial Code bars Mobil from in this way converting its own error into plaintiff's misfortune.

Section 2207, subdivision (1), provides that parties may form an agreement, even if the terms of offer and acceptance do not entirely converge, if the offeree gives a definite expression of acceptance, and if the terms of acceptance do not explicitly condition agreement upon the offeror's consent to the offeree's new proposed terms. In this case, as the trial court found, defendant Mobil did not condition its acceptance of plaintiff's offer upon plaintiff's agreement to Mobil's alteration of plaintiff's offer and thus a contract was formed. Section 2207, subdivision (2), provides in turn that, if the terms of the offer and acceptance differ, the terms of the offer become part of

---

91. John E. Murray, *The Chaos of the "Battle of the Forms": Solutions*, 39 Vand. L. Rev. 1307, 1322 (1986).

92. Eds. note: It is interesting to note that Mobil Oil was represented by McCutchen, Black, Verleger & Shea, a firm that had an office on Wilshire Boulevard and had 25 partners and 33 associates. Steiner was represented by Mr. Lazaroni and Mr. Sapiro, who were solo practitioners. Mr. Lazaroni had been in practice for more than 50 years at the time of this case; Mr. Sapiro had been in practice for more than 30 years. Marc Galanter, *Contract in Court; Or Almost Everything You May or May Not Want to Know About Contract Litigation*, 2001 Wis. L. Rev. 577, 621, distinguishes what he calls uphill litigation from downhill litigation. An individual suing a corporation is an example of uphill litigation; a corporation suing an individual is downhill. He finds that uphill litigation does not succeed as often as downhill. He also points out that contracts casebooks tend to feature an atypical selection of uphill cases where the plaintiff wins. He comments: "The casebooks reflect the uphill struggle and magnify its success—perhaps both encouraging those eager to engage in that struggle but also offering reassurance that the law embodies a benign balance, so that it doesn't really matter which side one is on."

a contract between merchants if the offer expressly limits acceptance to its own terms, or if the varying terms of the acceptance materially alter the terms of the offer. As the trial court found, under either of these clauses, the terms of Steiner's offer must prevail, because Steiner's offer was expressly conditional upon Mobil's agreement to provide a guaranteed discount, and Mobil's substitution of a discount terminable at its discretion materially affected Steiner's interests.

Accordingly, the trial court did not err in granting judgment for plaintiff, and we shall thus affirm its judgment.

1. *The facts in this case*

… Joseph R. Steiner is an independent service station operator … [leasing his station from a third party and buying gasoline from Mobil].

In 1971, the third party who leased the service station property to Steiner informed him that the property was for sale. Steiner contacted Mobil sales representative Tony Montemarano. Montemarano informed Steiner that Mobil would not purchase the property, but that Mobil was interested in assisting Steiner in making the purchase.

Thereafter, Steiner entered into extended negotiations with J.S. Chenen, Mobil's area manager and Montemarano's superior. Steiner and Chenen agreed that Mobil would supply the down payment on the property, amounting to $30,000. In return, Steiner would enter into a 10-year contract with Mobil. The contract would treat the cash advance as a prepaid competitive allowance, to be amortized over the 10-year period through Steiner's purchase of 5.8 million gallons of gasoline.

The negotiations did not terminate with the agreement concerning the down payment. Steiner had concluded that he would not be able to do business successfully if he were compelled to purchase gasoline from Mobil at the standard tank wagon price. As the trial court found, Steiner told Chenen that he, Steiner, "needed a firm competitive allowance for the length of his distributor's agreement to make his cash flow adequate to meet the payments on the property." Steiner and Chenen agreed that a satisfactory arrangement with Mobil would include not only the $30,000 prepaid competitive allowance, but also a further competitive allowance reducing Mobil's tank wagon price by 1.4 cents per gallon. Mobil would also supply Steiner with $3,000 worth of improvements.

As Chenen made clear to Steiner, neither Chenen nor his immediate supervisor, district manager D.L. Dalbec, possessed the authority to accept the negotiated terms on Mobil's behalf. The negotiations therefore did not culminate in an agreement as such but rather in a proposal to be submitted to R.D. Pfaff, the division general manager, who did possess authority to agree to the proposal on Mobil's behalf.

Moreover, the proposal did not take the form of a documented single contract. Chenen and Steiner utilized a series of standard Mobil forms in putting together the proposal, modifying the forms where necessary. Steiner signed those of the forms, such as the basic retail dealer contract, which required his signature. The package of documents which comprised the proposal, therefore, needed only Pfaff's approval to become effective.

Near the close of the process of negotiating and assembling the proposal, Steiner obtained a copy of the standard Mobil form that would embody the 1.4 cents per gallon competitive allowance. This form, which did not require Steiner's signature, stated: "This allowance may be changed or discontinued by us at any time upon notice to you in writing...." Upon receipt of the form Steiner immediately contacted Chenen by telephone, told Chenen that he would not go ahead with the deal if Mobil could revoke the competitive allowance at any time, and demanded assurances that no such revocation would occur.

In order to placate Steiner, Chenen, after consultation and authorization from Dalbec, sent Steiner a letter, dated December 2, 1971, which declared "[¶] The ten-year Retail Dealer Contract dated December 15, 1971, effective January 1, 1972, is signed by you on the basis that Mobil grant a $30,000 Prepaid Competitive Allowance, and a *$.014 Competitive Allowance at time of delivery.* [¶] If Mobil management does not accept in full the above conditions outlined in your competitive offer, the above mentioned contract will be void." (Italics added.)

[The trial court found that Chenen was authorized to write Steiner and that Chenen and Dalbec's knowledge of Steiner's firm insistence on a competitive allowance was attributable to Mobil. Chenen and Dalbec, under the circumstances, "were obligated in the exercise of good faith and ordinary care and diligence" to inform Pfaff of the terms of Steiner's offer.]

In fact, however, Chenen and Dalbec did *not* transmit to Pfaff the letter which Chenen had sent to Steiner; Mobil's copy of that letter remained in the district office files. In preparing the proposal for submission to Pfaff, Chenen and Dalbec assembled a package that included the various documents that Steiner had executed, the standard form providing the revocable 1.4 cents per gallon competitive allowance, and various memoranda explaining the advantages of the deal for Mobil. Early in 1972, several months after Chenen and Dalbec had transmitted the proposal to him, Pfaff approved it as submitted.

Chenen informed Steiner of Pfaff's approval by telephone. Steiner had called Chenen to find out what was happening with the proposal that they had negotiated. Chenen told Steiner that Mobil had a check for him, and that the next thing for Steiner to do was to *open an escrow account* and *proceed with the purchase of the property.*

Subsequently, Montemarano delivered to Steiner at his service station a manila folder containing the documents approved by Pfaff. These documents, the trial court found, were "numerous and complex in nature." Nonetheless, there was no cover letter describing the contents of the folder. Although the folder included Mobil's standard competitive allowance form, with its clause providing for revocation at will, Montemarano did not call this fact to Steiner's attention.

Thus, as the trial court found, at no time after Chenen sent Steiner the December 2 letter "did Mobil advise [Steiner] that a non-cancellable allowance would not be part of the agreement." Moreover, Steiner "did not at any time reread all of the documents delivered to him by Mobil, particularly the form letter ... setting forth the provision regarding the 1.4 cents per gallon competitive allowance being cancellable." Mobil did not "specifically bring" to Steiner's attention "the statements made in the form letter ... concerning the cancellable condition of the competitive allowance."

By April 1972, Steiner had completed the process of acquiring the service station property. Beginning in March, Mobil afforded Steiner the benefit of the 1.4 cents per gallon competitive allowance in billing him for gasoline and continued to do so until the summer of 1973. On July 16, 1973, Chenen informed Steiner by letter that, in accordance with the provisions of Mobil's notice of competitive allowance, Mobil would reduce Steiner's discount to 0.5 cents per gallon as of August 1, 1973.

Steiner brought this suit in the Los Angeles County Superior Court, seeking declaratory and monetary relief. The trial court, sitting without a jury, found that Mobil "had reason to know" that Steiner would not enter into an agreement unless Mobil agreed that he "was to have a non-cancellable ... competitive allowance ... to run as long as the distributor agreement was in force." Moreover, the trial court found, in returning the package of documents to Steiner, "Mobil intended to make a contract, not to make a counter-offer." The trial court concluded that "in the exercise of good faith and reasonable care and diligence Mobil was required to specifically bring to the attention of plaintiff the statements made in the form letter sent by Dalbec concerning the cancellable condition of the competitive allowance."

The trial court ruled that, under California Uniform Commercial Code § 2207, Mobil had entered into a contract with Steiner that guaranteed Steiner a 1.4 cents per gallon discount for 10 years. "Mobil made a definite and seasonable expression of acceptance of plaintiff's offer, although its reply contained a material term different from that offer." Moreover, "[i]n accepting plaintiff's offer Mobil did not either orally or in writing expressly condition its acceptance upon plaintiff's assent to the different terms as to the competitive allowance in Mobil's acceptance." The trial court granted Steiner a declaratory judgment to that effect, and awarded Steiner damages of $4,953.63. Mobil appeals the trial court's judgment.

2. *Under California Uniform Commercial Code § 2207, Steiner's contract with Mobil grants Steiner a 1.4 cents per gallon discount for the duration of the contract.*

[The California UCC applies to this dispute, and § 2-207 (§ 2207 in the Cal. code) is the critical section.]

Under traditional common law, no contract was reached if the terms of the offer and the acceptance varied.... This "mirror image" rule of offer and acceptance was plainly both unfair and unrealistic in the commercial context ... [since it ignored the parties' mutual and reasonable understandings that there was a deal].

Section 2207 rejects the "mirror image" rule. *See, e.g., Roto-Lith, Ltd. v. F.P. Bartlett & Co.* 297 F.2d 497, 500 (1st Cir. 1962). "This section of the Code recognizes that in current commercial transactions, the terms of the offer and those of the acceptance will seldom be identical." *Dorton v. Collins & Aikman Corp.* 453 F.2d 1161, 1166 (6th Cir. 1972).

Under § 2207, for example, the parties may conclude a contract despite the fact that, after reaching accord, they exchanged forms that purport to memorialize the agreement, but which differ because each party has drafted his form "to give him advantage." WHITE & SUMMERS, UNIFORM COMMERCIAL CODE, p. 23 (1972); *see, e.g., Rite Fabrics, Inc. v. Stafford-Higgins Co., Inc.* 366 F. Supp. 1 (S.D.N.Y. 1973). Similarly, the parties may form a contract even if the terms of offer and acceptance differ because one or the other party, in stating its initial position, relies upon "forms drafted to cover the majority of [its] transactions in a uniform, standard manner" (DUESENBERG & KING, SALES AND BULK TRANSFERS UNDER THE UNIFORM COMMERCIAL CODE § 3.02, p. 3–9 [1976]), and subsequently fails to amend its form to reflect the deal which the other party claims was actually negotiated. *See, e.g., Ebasco Services Inc. v. Pennsylvania Power & L. Co.*, 402 F. Supp. 421, 434–35 (E.D. Pa. 1975).

In place of the "mirror image" rule, § 2207 inquires as to whether the parties intended to complete an agreement.... If the parties intend to contract, but the terms of their offer and acceptance differ, § 2207 authorizes a court to determine which terms are part of the contract, either by reference to the parties' own dealings (*see* § 2207, subds. (1), (2)), or by reference to other provisions of the code. *See* § 2207, subd. (3).

Section 2207 is thus of a piece with other recent developments in contract law. Instead of fastening upon abstract doctrinal concepts like offer and acceptance, § 2207 looks to the actual dealings of the parties and gives legal effect to that conduct. Much as adhesion contract analysis teaches us not to enforce contracts until we look behind the facade of the formalistic standardized agreement in order to determine whether any inequality of bargaining power between the parties renders contractual terms unconscionable, or causes the contract to be interpreted against the more powerful party, § 2207 instructs us not to *refuse* to enforce contracts until we look below the surface of the parties' disagreement as to contract terms and determine whether the parties undertook to close their deal. Section 2207 requires courts to put aside the formal and academic stereotypes of traditional doctrine of offer and acceptance and to analyze instead what really happens. In this spirit, we turn to the application of § 2207 in this case.

Section 2207, subdivision (1), provides: "A definite and seasonable expression of acceptance or a written confirmation which is sent within a reasonable time operates as an acceptance even though it states terms additional or different from those offered or agreed upon, unless acceptance is expressly made conditional on assent to the additional or different terms."

In this case, as the trial court found, Mobil provided "[a] definite and seasonable expression of acceptance." Steiner offered to enter into a 10-year dealer contract with Mobil only if Mobil, among other things, agreed to advance Steiner $30,000, and to give Steiner a 1.4 cents per gallon competitive discount on the price of Mobil gasoline for the duration of the contract. When Steiner telephoned Chenen, Mobil's employee, to inquire as to the fate of Steiner's offer, *Chenen told Steiner that Mobil had a check for him, that he should open an escrow account, and that he should go ahead with the purchase of the service station property*—in context a clear statement that Mobil had approved the deal.

Moreover, through Montemarano, another Mobil employee, Mobil returned to Steiner various executed documents in an envelope unaccompanied by any cover. The documents provided written confirmation of the deal. The fact that Mobil returned the documents without in any way calling Steiner's attention to them is further evidence that Mobil regarded the process of negotiation as over and the deal as complete.

As the trial court also found, Mobil did not in any way make its acceptance "expressly ... conditional" on Steiner's "assent to the additional or different terms." Chenen, in telling Steiner to go ahead with the purchase, did not suggest that Mobil had conditioned its acceptance. In returning the executed documents, Mobil enclosed no cover letter; again, it did not use the occasion in any way to condition expressly its acceptance.

Thus, neither of the restrictions which limit § 2207, subdivision (1)'s application are relevant in this case. Despite the fact that the terms of Mobil's acceptance departed partially from the terms of Steiner's offer, Mobil and Steiner did form a contract. To determine the terms of this contract, we turn to § 2207, subdivision (2).

Section 2207, subdivision (2), provides: "... additional terms are to be construed as proposals for addition to the contract. Between merchants such terms become part of the contract unless:

(a) The offer expressly limits acceptance to the terms of the offer;

(b) They materially alter it; or

(c) Notification of objection to them has already been given or is given within a reasonable time after notice of them is received."

Under § 2207, subdivision (2), Mobil's revocable discount provision does *not* become part of the agreement between Steiner and Mobil. In order to become part of the agreement, Mobil's provision must not fall within *any* of the categories defined by § 2207, subdivision (2), subsections (a), (b), and (c). Mobil's term, however, clearly comes within subsections (a) and (b).

Subsection (a) provides that no additional term can become part of the agreement if Steiner's offer "expressly limit[ed] acceptance to the terms of the offer." § 2207, subd. (2)(a). Mobil concedes that Steiner's offer provided that the competitive allowance of 1.4 cents per gallon would run for the full length of the 10-year dealer contract. Chenen's December 2 letter to Steiner explicitly acknowledges Mobil's awareness that "[i]f Mobil management does not accept in full the above conditions outlined in your competitive offer, the above mentioned contract is void."

Moreover, Mobil's acceptance falls within subsection (b) since without question the acceptance "materially alter[ed]" the terms of Steiner's offer. *See* § 2207, subd. (2)(b). The Uniform Commercial Code comment notes that a variation is material if it would "result in surprise or hardship if incorporated without express awareness by the other party...." §2-207, Uniform Commercial Code, com. 4. Here, Steiner clearly indicated to Mobil in the course of the negotiations that, without the 1.4 cents per gallon discount, he could not economically operate the service station. Mobil's alteration, therefore, amended the terms of the offer to Steiner's significant detriment; accordingly, the alteration was necessarily "material."

To reiterate, subsections (a), (b), and (c) of §2207, subdivision (2), operate in the alternative. If any one of the three subsections applies, the variant terms of an acceptance do not become part of an agreement. Here, as we have seen, the provisions of both subsections (a) and (b) are met. Mobil's declaration that the 1.4 cents per gallon discount was terminable at Mobil's discretion did not become part of the contract. Instead, Steiner and Mobil formed a contract incorporating the terms of Steiner's offer: Under this contract, Steiner was guaranteed a 1.4 cents per gallon discount throughout the 10-year period of the dealer contract.[93]

Thus, on their face, subdivisions (1) and (2) of §2207 confirm the trial court's conclusion that Mobil breached its agreement with Steiner. We now turn to Mobil's

---

93. [5] The parties do not challenge the finding of the trial court that both Steiner and Mobil are "merchants" within the meaning of §2104, subdivision (1), and thus within the meaning of §2207, subdivision (2), as well. Moreover, the parties do not argue that the applicability of §2207, subdivision (2), subsections (a), (b), and (c) turns upon whether the terms of Mobil's acceptance were additional to, or instead different from, Steiner's offer. Despite the parties' agreement in this case, however, the question of the relevance of the distinction between "additional" and "different" terms has become a matter of some controversy among courts and commentators. Section 2207, subdivision (1), refers to acceptances in which terms are either "additional to or different from" the terms of an offer. Section 2207, subdivision (2), however, expressly concerns itself with only "additional terms." Noting this difference, several courts and commentators have concluded that §2207, subdivision (2), applies if an acceptance *adds* terms to an offer, but does not apply if an acceptance *alters* the term of an offer. *See, e.g.,* American Parts Co., Inc. v. American Arbitration Ass'n, 8 Mich. App. 156, 154 N.W.2d 5, 11 (1967); Duesenberg & King, *supra,* §3.03 (1), pp. 3-33 to 3-38. Other courts and commentators, however, suggest that §2207, subdivision (2), applies without regard to whether the varying terms of an acceptance differ from or add to an offer. *See, e.g.,* Ebasco Services Inc. v. Penn. Power & L. Co., *supra,* 402 F. Supp. 421, 440 & fn. 27; Comment, *Section 2-207 of the Uniform Commercial Code—New Rules for the "Battle of the Forms,"* 32 U. Pitt. L. Rev. 209, 211 (1971). We conclude that the applicability of §2207, subdivision (2), should not turn upon a characterization of the varying terms of an acceptance as "additional" or "different." First, Uniform Commercial Code comment 3 specifically states that "[w]hether or not additional *or different* terms will become part of the agreement depends upon the provisions of subsection (2)." (Italics added; see also UCC com. 2.) Second, the distinction between "additional" and "different" terms is ambiguous. Since an offer's silence with respect to a particular issue may indicate an intent to adopt the code's gap-filling provisions, even an acceptance term which at first glance appears to be plainly "additional" is at least arguably "different." *See* Air Products & Chem., Inc. v. Fairbanks Morse, Inc., 58 Wis. 2d 193, 206 N.W.2d 414, 424 (1973). Third, the distinction between additional and different terms serves no clear purpose. If additional and different terms are treated alike for purposes of §2207, subdivision (2), an offeror does not, as some contend, lose "the ability to retain control over the terms of his offer." Duesenberg & King, *supra,* at p. 3-37. Under §2207, subdivision (2), if the offeror wishes to retain such control, he may do so by framing his offer so that it "expressly limits acceptance to the terms of the offer...." §2207, subd. (2)(a).

opposing argument that we should adopt an interpretation of §2207 that conflicts with the trial court's conclusion.

3. *Contrary to Mobil's argument, California Uniform Commercial Code §§2204 and 2207 do not incorporate the traditional rule that parties to a contract must mutually assent to all essential terms.*

We set forth Mobil's contentions, which, although elaborately developed, can be simply stated. Section 2207 does not apply if the general contract formation rules of §2204 are not met. Section 2204 does not change the traditional rule that, in order to create an enforceable contract, the parties must mutually assent to all essential terms of the supposed agreement. In order to square §2207 with §2204, Mobil argues, we must construe §2207, subdivision (1), to provide that there is no "definite" acceptance unless the parties agree to all essential terms. Moreover, Mobil contends, we must also hold that, under the same section, an acceptance that alters an essential term of an offer is an acceptance "expressly made conditional on assent" to the variant term. Finally, Mobil concludes that, since its acceptance, in changing the duration of the discount, modified an essential term of Steiner's offer, i.e., price, we must find that Steiner cannot claim a continued discount.

As we shall explain, Mobil's arguments do not survive scrutiny. The official comments accompanying §2204, other provisions of the code, and the case law interpreting §2204 all support the conclusion that §2204 does not require mutual assent to all essential terms. Mobil's interpretations of the definite agreement and conditional acceptance provisions of §2207, subdivision (1), likewise conflict with other subdivisions of §2207.

a. *California Uniform Commercial Code §2204 does not incorporate the traditional requirement of mutual assent to all essential terms.*

Section 2204 incorporates three subdivisions. The third of these subdivisions directly refutes Mobil's claims. "Even though one or more terms are left open a contract for sale does not fail for indefiniteness if the parties have intended to make a contract and there is a reasonably certain basis for giving an appropriate remedy." §2204, subd. (3).

Section 2204, subdivision (3), does not, by its terms, require parties to a contract to assent to *all* essential terms. Instead, this provision states that a court, if it is to enforce a contract, must first make two findings. Initially, the court must find some basis for concluding that the parties engaged in a process of offer and acceptance, rather than inconclusive negotiations. Second, the court must find that it possesses sufficient information about the parties' incomplete transaction to apply the provisions of the California Uniform Commercial Code that fill in the gaps in parties' contracts.[94] As we have already seen, both of these minimal requirements are met in this case:

---

94. [7] These provisions, of course, include §2207; they also include, for example, §2305, which deals with open price terms, §2307, which fixes otherwise open delivery provisions, and §2309, which sets a duration for otherwise indefinite contracts.

the parties did not engage in inconclusive negotiations, and § 2207 readily fills in the terms of their contract.

To overcome the literal language of § 2204, subdivision (2), Mobil argues that the traditional requirement of "a meeting of the minds upon the essential features of the agreement" (*Ellis v. Klaff*, 96 Cal. App. 2d 471, 478, 216 P.2d 15 [1950]); ... is so fundamental that the code could not conceivably have rejected it. The California code comment, however, explicitly states: " '[A] meeting of the minds on the essential features of the agreement' is not required." § 2204, com. 2.

Other code provisions sustain the comment's view. As we have already pointed out, § 2207, subdivision (2)(b), expressly acknowledges the possibility that parties may reach a contract without agreeing to all "material" terms. Mobil does not attempt to distinguish "material" from "essential" terms; in any event, we do not think that it could successfully do so. Section 2305, subdivision (1), provides an even more dramatic refutation of Mobil's argument. As we have noted, Mobil treats price as an "essential" term. Nonetheless, this section states: "The parties if they so intend can conclude a contract for sale even though the price is not settled." § 2305, subd. (1).

The case law interpreting § 2204 reinforces the interpretation offered by the code comment and the implication of other code provisions: the rules of contract formation under the California Uniform Commercial Code do not include the principle that the parties must agree to all essential terms in order to form a contract. Courts have held that, under § 2204, subdivision (3), parties may form a contract even though they do not agree as to the terms of payment..., the time or place for performance..., or the quantity of the goods sold ... —all terms that might appear to be "essential" to an agreement.

More significantly, in view of Mobil's emphasis on the essential character of price terms, a number of courts have held that, under § 2204, subdivision (3), the parties may frame a contract without fully agreeing as to price.... Concededly, one court has suggested in dictum that § 2204, subdivision (3), incorporates the requirement of assent to essential terms. *See Blackhawk Heat. & P. Co., Inc. v. Data Lease Fin. Corp.*, 302 So. 2d 404, 408 (Fla. 1974). We think, however, that the Delaware Supreme Court stated the prevailing view: "[T]he omission of even an important term does not prevent the finding under [section 2204, subdivision (3)] that the parties intended to make a contract." *Pennsylvania Co. v. Wilmington Trust Co.*, 39 Del. Ch. 453, 463, 166 A.2d 726 (1960).[95]

---

95. [8] In the instant case, Steiner and Mobil, at Mobil's instigation, arranged their dealings in a way that clearly distinguished preliminary bargaining from the process of offer and acceptance as such. As we have seen, Steiner and Chenen initially negotiated the terms of Steiner's offer. Chenen and Dalbec then submitted the offer to Pfaff, who accepted it on Mobil's behalf. Other Mobil employees treated Pfaff's decision as terminating negotiations: Chenen told Steiner to go ahead with the service station purchase; Montemarano delivered the contract documents to Steiner without comment or cover letter. Thus, because of the hierarchical structure Mobil imposed on the bargaining, the trial court could conclude, as it did, that Mobil intended to accept Steiner's offer and not merely to continue negotiations. In this case, thus, the serious nature of the contract provision in dispute does not

b. *California Uniform Commercial Code § 2207, subdivision (1), should not be narrowly read to conform to the principle of mutual assent to all essential terms.*

As we have seen, § 2204 quite clearly does *not* incorporate the rule that parties must mutually assent to all essential terms. Mobil has thus failed to establish the premise that it would postulate as justifying a narrow reading of § 2207, subdivision (1). We shall, however, briefly consider Mobil's other and further arguments concerning the construction of § 2207, and show that these arguments, taken in isolation, are consistent neither with the language of § 2207, subdivision (1), nor with the logic of § 2207 as a whole.

Initially, Mobil focuses on § 2207, subdivision (1)'s requirement of a "definite ... expression of acceptance." Mobil would define "definite" by reference to the extent of the difference between offer and acceptance: the more significant the divergence, the less definitely a response is an acceptance. This construction suffers from two flaws. First, in § 2207, subdivision (1), "definite" modifies "expression" and not "acceptance," and thus refers to the *process* of offer and acceptance and not to the *terms* of the acceptance itself. Second, in any event, § 2207 as a whole bars any interpretation of "definite" which, as Mobil urges, would exclude from the ranks of acceptances all but collateral variations on the terms of offers. Section 2207, subdivision (2)(b)'s concern with material variations necessarily implies that acceptances incorporating such variations can satisfy the requirements of subdivision (1).

Mobil would also construe the final clause of § 2207, subdivision (1), which provides that, if acceptance "is expressly made conditional on assent to ... additional or different terms," the "acceptance" does not operate as an acceptance but as a counteroffer. Specifically Mobil argues that we should read this provision broadly, by adopting the interpretation advanced in *Roto-Lith, Ltd. v. F. P. Bartlett & Co., supra,* 297 F.2d at page 500: "a response which states a condition materially altering the obligation solely to the disadvantage of the offeror is an 'acceptance ... expressly ... conditional on assent to the additional ... terms.'"

Again, however, Mobil's construction does not accord with the language of the section. Such an interpretation of the conditional acceptance clause would transform acceptances into counteroffers without regard to whether the acceptance is in fact, as § 2207, subdivision (1), requires, "expressly made conditional on assent to ... additional or different terms." Moreover, under Mobil's reading, the conditional acceptance clause of § 2207, subdivision (1), would largely duplicate the function of the material variation clause of § 2207, subdivision (2)(b).

As Mobil concedes, courts and commentators alike have repeatedly criticized the *Roto-Lith* interpretation of § 2207, subdivision (1).... Most courts have rejected *Roto-Lith*, and have instead interpreted the conditional acceptance clause literally, as we

---

preclude a finding that they intended to conclude a contract; the parties' negotiating procedure itself reveals their intent. In other cases, in which negotiations are not so well organized, the importance of a term which the parties leave open may very well be a decisive measure of whether the parties intended to enter into a contract....

did earlier.... Recognizing the superiority of the majority view, we reject Mobil's attempt to advance the *Roto-Lith* interpretation of § 2207, subdivision (1).

4. *Conclusion.*

In this case, as we have seen, the trial court correctly concluded that under § 2207 the guaranteed discount included in the terms of Steiner's offer, and not Mobil's standard revocable discount provision, became part of the agreement between Mobil and Steiner. Mobil cannot assert as a defense the failure of its own bureaucracy to respond to, or even fully recognize, Steiner's efforts to modify the standard Mobil dealer contract.

The judgment is affirmed.

[BIRD, C.J., MOSK, J., CLARK, J., RICHARDSON, J., MANUEL, J., and JEFFERSON, J., concurred.]

NOTES AND QUESTIONS

1. *Of offers and acceptances:* Suppose the court had found that the package of forms created by Chenen and Steiner and submitted to Pfaff was a proposal and not an offer. Then assume the court found that the manila folder containing the documents approved by Pfaff was an offer. Finally, assume that Steiner's actions in acquiring the service station property and running the business under the competitive allowance were deemed an acceptance. Would a court decide the case for Mobil?

Remember that UCC § 2-207(1) applies only to a "definite and seasonable expression of acceptance." However, does anything of substance turn on whether a court classifies Mobil's documents in the manila folder as the offer, or as an acceptance of Steiner's offer? Justice Tobriner wrote: "Instead of fastening upon abstract doctrinal concepts like offer and acceptance, § 2207 looks to the actual dealings of the parties and gives legal effect to that conduct.... Section 2207 requires courts to put aside the formal and academic stereotypes of traditional doctrinal offer and acceptance and to analyze instead what really happens." Can a court put aside the "formal and academic stereotype" of an acceptance when § 2-207(1) says it applies to an acceptance? Should the section be amended to avoid this problem?

In light of the fact that Steiner had objected in the strongest possible way to giving Mobil the right to change the competitive allowance, could we make an argument for him based on UCC §§ 2-204 and 1-201(b)(3)?

2. *Section 2-207 and "a written confirmation":* As we have discussed, § 2-207 applies to the exchange of two or more forms. However, it also applies to a different situation. Suppose the buyer and seller make an oral contract in a telephone conversation. Then the seller sends the buyer a printed form confirming that order. There are terms on the confirmation form additional to or different from the oral order. We could read the *Steiner* case as involving a variation of this situation. Steiner and the lower-ranking Mobil officials put together an offer. Then Chenen, Mobil's area manager, told Steiner that the deal had been approved and that Steiner should buy the property. The folder with all the Mobil standard terms was a written confirmation of that telephone call.

(Of course, this reading requires us to assume that under the law of agency Chenen had apparent authority to pass along a commitment by Mobil.) If we read the forms in the folder as a written confirmation, would the result in the case change?

Suppose a buyer telephones a seller and orders a computer or computer software. The seller's employee takes the order. Nothing is said about warranties, remedy limitations, arbitration, or any other terms beyond a description of the goods and the price. The goods are shipped to the buyer along with a seller's document (an invoice or a page in the instruction manual) that contains a disclaimer of warranties, a remedy limitation, and an arbitration clause. Does § 2-207 apply? In *ProCD, Inc. v. Zeidenberg*,[96] Judge Easterbrook said "Our case has only one form; UCC 2-207 is irrelevant." In *Step-Saver Data Systems, Inc. v. Wyse Technology*, Judge Wisdom applied § 2-207 to a situation somewhat like our hypothetical; he did not think that you must have two documents for this section to apply.[97] Which United States Circuit Judge reads statutes the best? *See also* Comment 1 to § 2-207.

3. *Why did the middle managers create the mess?* Unfortunately, the briefs cast no light at all on the most interesting question raised by the case: Why did the middle managers of Mobil create the problem by not telling their supervisor about the competitive allowance provision? Compare the role of the architect in *Vickery v. Ritchie*, *supra* Chapter 1.

4. *The interpretation of § 2-207(2) — "additional vs. different" terms:* In one of the long footnotes in *Steiner* the court addresses an argument that arises in the course of interpreting § 2-207(2). The question is whether there is an important distinction between "different" and "additional" terms. The question arises because § 2-207(1) refers to acceptances in which terms are either "additional to or different from" the offered terms, whereas § 2-207(2) seems to concern itself only with "additional" terms. The court mentions, in that footnote, the case of *Air Products & Chemicals, Inc. v. Fairbanks Morse, Inc.*,[98] the facts of which may serve not only to illuminate that issue, but as a useful review and drill concerning the difficulties of applying § 2-207.

It seems that Air Products wanted to buy some large electric motors from Fairbanks Morse. After discussions about the specifications of the motors, Air Products verbally agreed to buy several. Air Products then submitted a purchase order. Fairbanks Morse returned an executed copy of the purchase order together with Fairbanks Morse's acknowledgment of order form. Air Products asserted that the motors failed to perform properly, and brought suit against Fairbanks Morse. (The complaint alleged 43 causes of action; they must have been really mad!) Fairbanks Morse interposed as a defense a limitation of liability term contained on its acknowledgment of order form. The front of the Fairbanks form contained the following language, which the Wisconsin Supreme Court described as being printed "in reasonably bold face type at the bottom."

96. 86 F.3d 1447, 1452 (7th Cir. 1996).
97. 939 F.2d 91 (3d Cir. 1991).
98. 58 Wis. 2d 193, 206 N.W.2d 414 (1973).

You might note that § 2-207 contains no explicit requirement of conspicuousness. Does this mean the appearance of the clause is irrelevant?

> WE THANK YOU FOR YOUR ORDER AS COPIED HEREON, WHICH WILL RECEIVE PROMPT ATTENTION AND SHALL BE GOVERNED BY THE PROVISIONS ON THE REVERSE SIDE HEREOF UNLESS YOU NOTIFY US TO THE CONTRARY WITHIN 10 DAYS OR BEFORE SHIPMENT WHICHEVER IS EARLIER.
>
> BEFORE ACCEPTING GOODS FROM TRANSPORTATION COMPANY SEE THAT EACH ARTICLE IS IN GOOD CONDITION. IF SHORTAGE OR DAMAGE IS APPARENT REFUSE SHIPMENT UNLESS AGENT NOTES DEFECT ON TRANSPORTATION BILL. ACCEPTANCE OF SHIPMENT WITHOUT COMPLYING WITH SUCH CONDITIONS IS AT YOUR OWN RISK.
>
> THIS IS NOT AN INVOICE. AN INVOICE FOR THIS MATERIAL WILL BE SENT YOU WITHIN A FEW DAYS.

The reverse side of the "acknowledgment of order" contained six printed provisions that were immediately preceded by the following statement:

> The following provisions form part of the order acknowledged and accepted on the face hereof, as express agreements between Fairbanks, Morse & Co. ("Company") and the Buyer governing the terms and conditions of the sale, subject to modification only in writing signed by the local manager or an executive officer of the Company:

Provision 6, which became the subject of the dispute between the parties, provided:

> 6. — The Company nowise assumes any responsibility or liability with respect to use, purpose, or suitability, and shall not be liable for damages of any character, whether direct or consequential, for defect, delay, or otherwise, its sole liability and obligation being confined to the replacement in the manner aforesaid of defectively manufactured guaranteed parts failing within the time stated.

Fairbanks Morse asserted that Paragraph 6 became part of the contract, and effectively limited its liability. Air Products asserted that Paragraph 6 did *not* become part of the contract and therefore, that Air Products was entitled to rely on the Code's provisions governing the implied warranties of merchantability, fitness for a particular purpose, and providing for recovery of consequential damages. The trial court had concluded, apparently without thoroughly considering UCC § 2-207(2)(b), that since the terms limiting damages were completely new and additional proposed terms, and since the parties were merchants, the terms became part of the contract.

Air Products advanced two arguments to seek to avoid Paragraph 6. They first argued that § 2-207(2) only applies to "additional" terms; that is, only terms that can be characterized as "additional" can become part of the contract by reason of the application of § 2-207(2). Air Products then, of necessity, argued that Paragraph 6 was a "different," as opposed to an "additional," term, and so was not included *via* §2-207(2). They argued that terms are "additional" if they concern a subject matter not addressed in the offer, and that they are "different" if they concern a subject matter which was covered but dealt with in a variant way. Air Products then argued that their offer must be regarded as including the terms expressly included *and* the terms implied by law—such as the implied warranty and damages claims. *Voila!* By this logic, the Fairbanks Morse confirmation contains a "different" term because it is at variance with the terms of the offer, which included the implied terms concerning warranty and liability.

Fairbanks Morse sought to parry the thrust of this argument by asserting that recovery of consequential damages is not included in every contract by implication, since they are only recoverable "in a proper case" (§2-714 (3)). As a result, even if you accept the first steps of the Air Products argument, Paragraph 6 is okay because recovery of consequential damages is not among the terms that could fairly be implied in a contract otherwise silent on the topic.

The court expressed doubt about the basic premise of the entire debate, suggesting that the Code should not be interpreted as creating an important distinction between "different" and "additional" terms. But in addition to suggesting that the argument was perhaps irrelevant, the court rejected Fairbanks Morse's counterargument by carrying it one step further. The court noted that the Comment to §2-715 observes that sellers are liable to buyers for consequential damages in cases in which the seller "had reason to know of the buyer's general or particular requirements at the time of contracting." In this case Fairbanks Morse was aware of the needs of Air Products, making it a "proper case" for recovery of consequential losses—and so a recovery of consequential loss was implicit in the contract.

Air Products' second argument was more direct, since it was not based on the argument that "additional" terms and "different" terms should be treated differently—an argument that has been widely criticized. Air Products argued that the disclaimer in the Fairbanks Morse acknowledgment was a material alteration of the agreement and could become a part of the contract only if expressly agreed to. To quote from the court's decision:

> Hartford and Air Products contend that the eradication of a multimillion-dollar damage exposure is *per se* material. Fairbanks bases its argument on the ground that consequential damages may not be recovered except in "special circumstances" or in a "proper case." (§§2-714 (2) and (3)). As already stated, these "special circumstances" would seem by comment 3 to §2-715 to be referring to situations that concern instances where the seller [had] reason to know of buyer's general or particular requirements at the time of contracting. "Consequential damages resulting from the seller's breach include (a) any loss resulting from general or particular requirements and needs of which the seller at the time of contracting had reason to know and which could not reasonably be prevented by cover or otherwise; …" UCC §2-715 (2)(a).

While the comment 4 clearly indicates that a disclaimer of an implied warranty of merchantability is material, there is no good reason to hold that a disclaimer that has the effect of eliminating millions of dollars in damages should become a part of a contract by operation of law.

We conclude that the disclaimer for consequential loss was sufficiently material to require express conversation between the parties over its inclusion or exclusion in the contract.[99]

5. *An additional argument in* Air Products v. Fairbanks Morse: The lawyers for Fairbanks Morse made an argument in their brief that seems not to have been confronted in the court's opinion. The argument, essentially, was that the Code, in §2-719(3), provides that limitations on consequential damages are valid unless unconscionable. This goes to whether a limitation on consequential damages should be regarded as a material alteration of the offer. In the commercial world in which Air Products and Fairbanks Morse were resident, such limitations were, allegedly, quite common, and in the words of the Fairbanks Morse brief, they "effectuate the very purpose of §2-719[,] which is to encourage and facilitate the allocation of risks associated with the sale of goods, particularly those occurring in a commercial setting."

Suppose Fairbanks Morse's lawyers commissioned a survey of machinery manufacturers and purchasers, and this survey showed that in, say, 92.66 percent of all contracts for the sale of machinery, consequential damages were ruled out. Would, or should, this information change the court's decision? Suppose the clause was found in 60 percent of all contracts? In 40 percent? Would an attitude survey be better? Suppose businesspeople were asked whether they expected to be able to recover consequential damages, and 85 percent said that they would not in the ordinary case. Would this be relevant to the application of §2-207 to the Fairbanks Morse situation? How does the Supreme Court of Wisconsin get its data on whether the remedy limitation materially alters the contract created by Fairbanks Morse's acceptance? Or is it a question of data?

6. *Once bitten, twice shy:* You might be interested to learn that as a result of the litigation with Fairbanks Morse, Air Products adopted the following language in its purchase order form. This is the 15th clause printed in small type on the back of the form:

This Order shall be binding upon the parties either upon receipt of Seller's acknowledgment of its acceptance hereof or commencement of its performance of the work contemplated by this Order. No terms or conditions in Seller's order acknowledgment form or in any other form of acceptance of this Order, shall bind Buyer or modify Seller's obligations hereunder, unless accepted in writing by Buyer.

7. *Additional or different terms and the "knock-out" rule:* UCC §2-207(1) finds a contract created by an acceptance "even though it states terms additional to or different from those offered...." Subsection (2), however, talks about "additional terms" but says nothing about "different" ones. The courts in both the *Steiner* and *Air Products* cases

---

99. *Id.* at 213–14, 206 N.W.2d at 424–25.

seem to think that the distinction between additional and different terms should not matter. Not all courts follow that approach, and some adopt a "knock-out rule" for different terms. In a diversity case applying Pennsylvania law,[100] the 10th circuit reasoned:

> Section 2-207(2) is silent on the treatment of terms stated in the acceptance that are *different*, rather than merely additional, from those stated in the offer. It is unclear whether "different" terms in the acceptance are intended to be included under the aegis of "additional" terms in § 2-207(2) and, therefore, fail to become part of the agreement if they materially alter the contract. Comment 3 suggests just such an inclusion.[101] However, Comment 6 suggests that different terms in exchanged writings must be assumed to constitute mutual objections by each party to the other's conflicting terms and result in a mutual "knock-out" of both parties' conflicting terms; the missing terms to be supplied by the UCC's "gap-filler" provisions.[102] At least one commentator, in support of this view, has suggested that the drafting history of the provision indicates that the word "different" was intentionally deleted from the final draft of § 2-207(2) to preclude its treatment under that subsection.[103] The plain language, comments, and drafting history of the provision, therefore, provide little helpful guidance in resolving the disagreement over the treatment of different terms pursuant to § 2-207.

> Despite all this, the cases and commentators have suggested three possible approaches. The first of these is to treat "different" terms as included under the aegis of "additional" terms in § 2-207(2). Consequently, different terms in the acceptance would never become part of the contract, because, by definition, they would materially alter the contract (i.e., the offeror's terms). Several courts have adopted this approach. *E.g., Mead Corporation v. McNally-Pittsburg Manufacturing Corporation*, 654 F.2d 1197 (6th Cir. 1981) (applying Ohio law); *Steiner v. Mobil Oil Corporation*, 20 Cal. 3d 90, 141 Cal. Rptr. 157, 569 P.2d 751 (1977); *Lockheed Electronics Company, Inc. v. Keronix, Inc.*, 114 Cal. App. 3d 304, 170 Cal. Rptr. 591 (1981).

> The second approach, which leads to the same result as the first, is that the offeror's terms control because the offeree's different terms merely fall

---

100. Daitom, Inc. v. Pennwalt Corp., 741 F.2d 1569, 1578–79 (10th Cir. 1984).

101. [7] Comment 3 states (emphasis added):
Whether or not *additional or different* terms will become part of the agreement depends upon the provision of subsection (2).
It must be remembered that even official comments to enacted statutory text do not have the force of law and are only guidance in the interpretation of that text....

102. [8] Comment 6 states, in part:
Where clauses on confirming forms sent by both parties conflict each party must be assumed to object to a clause of the other conflicting with one on the confirmation sent by himself....
The contract then consists of the terms expressly agreed to, terms on which the confirmations agree, and terms supplied by the Act, including subsection (2).

103. [9] *See* D.G. Baird & R. Weisberg, *Rules, Standards, and the Battle of the Forms: A Reassessment of § 2-207*, 68 VA. L. REV. 1217, 1240, n.61 (1982).

out; § 2-207(2) cannot rescue the different terms since that subsection applies only to *additional* terms. Under this approach, Comment 6 (apparently supporting a mutual rather than a single-term knock-out) is not applicable because it refers only to conflicting terms in confirmation forms following *oral* agreement, not conflicting terms in the *writings* that form the agreement. This approach is supported by Professor Summers. J. J. WHITE & R. S. SUMMERS, UNIFORM COMMERCIAL CODE, § 1–2, at 29 (2d ed. 1980).

The third, and preferable approach, which is commonly called the "knock-out" rule, is that the conflicting terms cancel one another. Under this view the offeree's form is treated only as an acceptance of the terms in the offeror's form that did not conflict. The ultimate contract, then, includes those non-conflicting terms and any other terms supplied by the UCC, including terms incorporated by course of performance (§ 2-208), course of dealing (§ 1-205), usage of trade (§ 1-205) [Eds. note: § 1-303, as revised in 2001], and other "gap fillers" or "off-the-rack" terms (e.g., implied warranty of fitness for particular purpose, § 2-315). As stated previously, this approach finds some support in Comment 6. Professor White supports this approach as the most fair and consistent with the purposes of § 2-207. WHITE & SUMMERS, *supra*, at 29. Further, several courts have adopted or recognized the approach. *E.g., Idaho Power Company v. Westinghouse Electric Corporation*, 596 F.2d 924 (9th Cir. 1979) (applying Idaho law, although incorrectly, applying § 2-207(3) after finding a contract under § 2-207(1).

… We are of the opinion that this is the more reasonable approach…. Thus, we are of the conclusion that if faced with this issue the Pennsylvania Supreme Court would adopt the "knock-out" rule.

How would this analysis work as applied to *Steiner*?

8. *One more example:* Given the complexity of § 2-207, it should not be a surprise that courts adopt different ways of applying it on multiple issues. One more example is *Northern States Power Co. v. International Telephone and Telegraph Corp.*[104] Northern States Power Company (NSP) contracted with International Telephone and Telegraph Corporation (ITT) for anchors used in erecting power line towers. Each anchor consisted of a 10-foot-long section capable of being augured into the ground. Guy wires were attached from the anchors to points near the top of the tower. Welds on some anchors were defective, and towers fell. NSP had to replace all of the anchors. NSP sued for damages of over $2,400,000. ITT moved for summary judgment, arguing that NSP's claim was barred by ITT's remedy limitation.

The court denied the motion. The trier of fact could find that the remedy limitation was part of the contract. NSP had sent a request for quotation to ITT. ITT responded with a proposal containing a detailed remedy limitation. During the negotiations, the parties did not discuss limitation of liability. NSP issued a purchase order that

---

104. 550 F. Supp. 108 (D. Minn. 1982).

did not specifically mention the remedy limitations in ITT's proposal. It did say: "Confirming Verbal Order of 8-11-78 Per Your Proposal #780049 of 7-16-78."[105] ITT then issued a sales acknowledgment, which again included the remedy limitation. NSP did not respond, and the parties proceeded to perform the contract.

While the court cited § 2-207, it did not discuss the terms of the statute. It said only:

> The purchase order (offer) makes no express reference to the limitation of liability clause. The sales acknowledgment (acceptance) does contain the clause, but this reference to the clause does not necessarily mean the acknowledgment varies from the terms of the purchase order. Prior to the purchase order Meyer [a division of ITT] had submitted a proposal that included a special reference to the limitation of liability clause, and NSP had placed a verbal order during discussions between the parties. The subsequent purchase order could be merely a written verification of the verbal order; it made express reference to Meyer's proposal.... On this record the trier of fact could find the limitation of liability clause part of the contract between the parties.[106]

The court also decided that the trier of fact could find that ITT's remedy limitation "failed of its essential purpose" and was ineffective under § 2-719. Is the result consistent with *Steiner* and *Air Products*?

SCIENTIFIC COMPONENTS CORP. v. ISIS SURFACE MOUNTING, INC.

United States District Court, Eastern District of New York
539 F. Supp. 2d 653 (2008)

IRIZARRY, DISTRICT JUDGE.

Plaintiff Scientific Components Corporation, d/b/a Mini-Circuits Laboratory ("Mini-Circuits" or "Plaintiff") brings this breach of contract action against defendant ISIS Surface Mounting, Inc. ("ISIS" or "Defendant"), alleging that Defendant repudiated the contract between the parties by cancelling orders it had placed with Plaintiff. Plaintiff now moves for summary judgment finding Defendant liable for breach of contract and awarding Plaintiff damages, as a lost-volume seller, in the amount of $382,773.31, plus interest and attorneys' fees. Defendant claims that no contract existed between the parties and that, in any event, Plaintiff is not a lost-volume seller and is not entitled to any damages. Defendant cross-moves for summary judgment dismissing this action.

The court finds that a contract existed between the parties and that Defendant breached the contract. However, as described below, Plaintiff does not qualify as a lost-volume seller. Accordingly, Plaintiff's motion for summary judgment is granted with respect to the issue of breach of contract liability but not with respect to Plaintiff's

105. *Id.* at 110.
106. *Id.* at 112.

damages claim. Defendant's motion is denied. The calculation of damages is referred to United States Magistrate Judge Cheryl L. Pollak....

Mini-Circuits is a New York corporation that manufactures and sells electronic components primarily used in the wireless communications industry.... ISIS is a California corporation in the business of manufacturing electronic equipment....

The following facts are undisputed unless otherwise indicated. Sometime during or prior to January 1999, Western Multiplex engaged ISIS to manufacture component parts for electronic equipment. Subsequently, Western Multiplex contacted Mini-Circuits and requested that Mini-Circuits sell electronic components to ISIS and extend any established pricing agreements and volume discounts to ISIS. Starting 1999 until December 2000 or later, ISIS placed numerous orders for the purchase of electronic components from Mini-Circuits.

To place an order, ISIS submitted to Mini-Circuits purchase order forms listing the items ordered, the quantity, the price, and the anticipated delivery date. In addition, each purchase order form contained the following language displayed in all-capital letters: "ISIS RESERVES THE RIGHT TO CHANGE THIS P.O. IN ITS ENTIRETY OR IN PART, WITHIN 30 CALENDER [*sic*] DAYS [*sic*] NOTICE WITH NO LIABILITY TO ISIS."

In response to ISIS's orders, Mini-Circuits sent acknowledgment forms listing the items ordered, the quantity, the price, the shipment method, and the delivery date. Each acknowledgment form also stated in all-capital letters: "ACCEPTANCE OF YOUR COMPANY'S ORDER IS EXPRESSLY MADE CONDITIONAL ON YOUR COMPANY'S ASSENT TO THE TERMS AND CONDITIONS ON THE FACE AND REVERSE SIDE OF THIS ACKNOWLEDGMENT; THESE TERMS AND CONDITIONS ARE ALSO CONTAINED ON THE REVERSE SIDE OF MINI-CIRCUITS' INVOICE." The relevant disputed term contained on the reverse side of the acknowledgment form stated: "Notwithstanding the rights of Company contained herein, Purchaser shall not have the right to accelerate, postpone, cancel (other than as provided in Paragraph 7) or otherwise modify delivery dates specified on the face hereof. If Purchaser attempts to do so, it will be deemed to have repudiated this contract." Paragraph seven of Mini-Circuits' terms and conditions permitted the purchaser to cancel only in the event of excessive delay. ISIS never expressly assented to the terms and conditions set forth in Mini-Circuits' acknowledgment forms.

On March 28, 2001, ISIS cancelled all of its open orders with Mini-Circuits, stating that "Western Multiplex has cancelled with us so we have no requirements." Plaintiff alleges that the agreed-upon price of the items Defendant cancelled (the "cancelled items") was $817,101.16. The components ISIS cancelled were standard catalogue items. The items manufactured for ISIS bore identifying "run numbers but were not segregated from other similar parts."

Starting March 28, 2001, Mini-Circuits re-sold some portion of the cancelled components to Pemstar and SMTC, subcontractors engaged by Western Multiplex for the same project for which ISIS had previously been engaged. ISIS also claims that, after its March 28 cancellation, it rescheduled delivery of $162,43.16 of the cancelled items. In addition, Mini-Circuits purportedly re-sold a portion of the cancelled components directly to Western Multiplex and other third parties. However, Mini-Circuits claims that, despite reasonable efforts, it was unable to re-sell some of the cancelled items. Mini-Circuits did not credit any re-sales or rescheduled deliveries against the amount it claimed ISIS owed.

Dispute over cancellation charges ensued. On January 21, 2002, Lesley Barretta of ISIS sent an electronic mail ("e-mail") to "Kevin" of Mini-Circuits, with a carbon copy to others, objecting to Mini-Circuits' most recent calculation of the cancellation charges. She wrote:

> As we have stated since the beginning of this ordeal, ISIS POs clearly state that we can revise or cancel our orders outside of standard lead time with NO liability to ISIS. In addition all of the parts we canceled are standard catalog items, therefore not NC NR. When we originally received your cancellation charges they were approximately $313k, now you have added almost $500k.?? This is not acceptable. We gave you a spreadsheet indicating the corrections that needed to be made to the original charges, bringing the total to $221,134.08. As requested by ISIS and Western Multiplex, the orders received from Pemstar and SMTC were to be deducted from the orders we canceled. This did not happen. We are working on resolving the remaining issues with Western, but we need realistic numbers from our suppliers. Please review your information and send me a number we can work with.

On October 8, 2002, Mini-Circuits filed the instant action. Mini-Circuits now moves for summary judgment, and ISIS cross-moves for summary judgment....

The first issue is whether a contract existed between ISIS and Mini-Circuits. ISIS claims that no contract existed, pursuant to §2-207(1) of the Uniform Commercial Code ("UCC §2-207"), and Mini-Circuits, unsurprisingly, argues the contrary, contending that a contract existed based on the parties' conduct.

The court holds that an enforceable contract existed between ISIS and Mini-Circuits. UCC §2-207(1) states that:

> A definite and seasonable expression of acceptance or a written confirmation which is sent within a reasonable time operates as an acceptance even though it states terms additional to or different from those offered or agreed upon, unless acceptance is expressly made conditional on assent to the additional or different terms.

In this case, Mini-Circuits' acknowledgment forms set forth additional and/or different terms and, furthermore, clearly stated that "ACCEPTANCE OF YOUR COMPANY'S ORDER IS EXPRESSLY MADE CONDITIONAL ON YOUR COMPANY'S ASSENT TO THE TERMS AND CONDITIONS ON THE FACE AND REVERSE SIDE OF THIS ACKNOWLEDGMENT." Accordingly, under UCC §2-207, Mini-Circuits' forms did not serve as acceptances establishing contractual obligations but, instead, operated as counteroffers. *See Stemcor USA, Inc. v. Trident Steel Corp.*, 471 F. Supp. 2d 362,

367 (S.D.N.Y. 2006) ("If ... the seller's response is 'expressly made conditional on assent' to the divergent terms, then the proviso in paragraph (1) [of UCC § 2-207] provides that no contract is formed, and instead the seller's response constitutes a counteroffer."); *C. Itoh & Co. v. Jordan Int'l Co.*, 552 F.2d 1228, 1235–36 (7th Cir. 1977) (applying New York law, holding the same).

Although ISIS did not explicitly accept Mini-Circuits' counteroffers, pursuant to UCC § 2-207(3), "[c]onduct by both parties which recognizes the existence of a contract is sufficient to establish a contract for sale although the writings of the parties do not otherwise establish a contract." Here, both ISIS's prior and subsequent conduct reflects its understanding that a contract was created between the parties in the instant conflict. Mini-Circuits and ISIS had conducted business apparently without any problems from 1999 to March 2001. Starting in 1999, ISIS sent Mini-Circuits purchase order forms, and Mini-Circuits, in turn, sent ISIS acknowledgment forms containing the aforementioned conditional acceptance language. Through this exchange of forms, the parties agreed upon the material terms concerning price and quantity. In addition, the parties engaged in negotiations over shipping dates. Although ISIS never expressly assented to Mini-Circuits' acknowledgment forms, neither did ISIS object to the forms or engage in any behavior suggesting it did not intend to enter into a contractual relationship. Instead, ISIS continued to submit additional purchase order forms. This conduct serves as some evidence of its intent to enter into contractual obligations with Mini-Circuits.

In addition, subsequent to ISIS's March 28, 2001, cancellation e-mail, Mini-Circuits apparently sent ISIS a bill for cancellation charges amounting to "almost $500k." Although ISIS objected to the imposition of the cancellation charges in general, ISIS nonetheless asserted that Mini-Circuits' calculation should be corrected to $221,134.08, and sent Mini-Circuits a spreadsheet it had prepared setting forth its calculation of the cancellation charges. Moreover, ISIS asked Mini-Circuits to "review your information and send me a number we can work with." It is clear to the court, based on the foregoing evidence concerning ISIS's prior and subsequent conduct, that ISIS intended to enter into a contract and, further, that ISIS understood that it had entered into a valid and enforceable contract when it cancelled its order. Therefore, an enforceable contract existed between ISIS and Mini-Circuits.

Both Mini-Circuits and ISIS expend a considerable amount of effort in their submissions debating the issue of whose, if either's, cancellation provision controls. However, regardless of whose cancellation provision applies, if either's, ISIS breached the contract and is liable for its breach.

Mini-Circuits argues that its cancellation clause, which does not permit ISIS to cancel orders for convenience, became a part of the contract. ISIS argues, however, that Mini-Circuits' provision concerning cancellation rights was "knocked out" by its own conflicting cancellation clause listed on its purchase order forms, which provided that ISIS was able to change its order for any reason within 30 calendar days of the order. ISIS provides no dispute to Mini-Circuits' assertion that ISIS failed to cancel within its own 30-day cancellation period.

Mini-Circuits' cancellation clause does not control here. When a contract is not established by the parties' writings but rather by the parties' conduct, under UCC § 2-207(3), "the terms of the particular contract consist of those terms on which the writings of the parties agree, together with any supplementary terms incorporated under any other provisions of this Act." ISIS's cancellation provision stated that "ISIS RESERVES THE RIGHT TO CHANGE THIS PO IN ITS ENTIRETY OR IN PART, WITHIN 30 CALENDER [sic] DAYS [sic] NOTICE WITH NO LIABILITY TO ISIS." Mini-Circuits' cancellation clause stated, in pertinent part, that "Purchaser is entitled to cancel only that portion of any order which is excessively delayed" and thus did not permit ISIS to cancel within 30 days, as provided in ISIS's cancellation clause. The parties' writings do not agree on what ISIS's cancellation rights were under the contract; thus, pursuant to UCC § 2-207(3), neither clause became a part of the agreement, and the UCC supplies any missing terms. *See Stemcor USA, Inc.*, 471 F. Supp. 2d at 367 (stating that, when the parties' conduct recognizes the existence of a contract, "paragraph (3) of § 2-207 defines the terms of the agreement as those upon which the parties agree together with any supplemental default terms provided elsewhere in the UCC.").

Although the UCC does not provide terms concerning cancellation rights that would be appropriate here, the instant legal problem requires only an application of basic contract principles. ISIS appears to argue that, if Mini-Circuits' cancellation provision does not apply, ISIS escapes any liability at all. This argument is entirely untenable. As to the first 30 days after ISIS submitted a purchase order, it is unclear whether ISIS had the ability to alter or cancel the order, as discussed above. As to the ensuing period, however, the parties' writings do not provide any dispute that both parties were under a contractual obligation to perform. Moreover, neither the UCC nor contract law permits a party to a contract to cancel its obligations without liability. It is thus clear that ISIS's cancellation constituted an anticipatory repudiation of its contractual obligations, for which it is liable.

[The Court went on to conclude that plaintiff was not a lost-volume seller and to assign the question of appropriate damages to a U.S. magistrate.]

NOTES AND QUESTIONS

1. *Anticipatory repudiation:* The U.S. District Court in *Scientific Components* could have cited UCC § 2-610, recognizing the concept of anticipatory repudiation, also a feature of the common law of contracts. It means saying or otherwise indicating that one is going to breach before the time for performance. We discuss anticipatory repudiation and § 2-610 in Chapter 5 of these materials.

2. *Who, buyer or seller, is likely to be happy with subsection 2-207(3) more of the time?* Note who included the "expressly made conditional" language in its form in *Scientific Components*. Is that likely to be the usual pattern? Consider that when subsection 2-207(3) comes into play to supply terms because the contract was formed by conduct, this means including the implied warranty of merchantability under § 2-314 and consequential damages under the buyer's remedy provisions of §§ 2-712

through 2-715. Winning the battle of the forms is difficult indeed, especially for sellers, a point considered further in the next section.

c. Lawyers Cope with § 2-207:
Business Procedures and Drafting Practices

Lawyers have struggled with the problems posed by the need to anticipate the application of § 2-207. For every controversy that has ripened into a lawsuit, requiring lawyers to figure out how to apply § 2-207 after a transactional breakdown, there are many more instances in which lawyers have struggled to draft forms to avoid problems, or to give their clients an edge if a problem arises.

Frederick D. Lipman, *On Winning the Battle of the Forms: An Analysis of Section 2-207 of the Uniform Commercial Code*
24 Bus. Law. 802–805 (1969)[107]

The victorious attorney in the battle of forms must direct his strategy toward making the first offer. The Code favors the party who makes the first offer by giving him the best opportunity to have his terms of sale become part of any subsequent contract. The offeror need only wait and hope that the offeree will do any one of the following things:

(1) expressly accept the offer or do so by actions that are a reasonable mode of acceptance (e.g. commencing work);

(2) send an Expression of Acceptance document that does not make the acceptance expressly conditional on assent to the additional or different terms; or

(3) send a Confirmation document that does not make the acceptance expressly conditional on assent to the additional or different terms.

In either of the three events, the first offeror has obtained a contract with his opponent, without negotiation, containing his own terms of sale and, at worst, only the non-material additions of the offeree's form. The Code's favoritism of the first offeror is reminiscent of the favoritism shown by the common law "last shot doctrine" to the last offeree.

If the seller is to make the first offer, the seller must have a quotation form in his arsenal of weapons and be prepared to "fire it off" to the buyer before the buyer can make the first offer. If the buyer is to make the first offer, the buyer must be prepared to send the seller either a request for quotation form or a purchase order form before the seller can "fire off" his quotation form. It is difficult, but not impossible, to make an offer out of the buyer's request for quotation form, since the buyer will generally use the request for quotation form merely to request an offer from the seller with respect to certain goods described in the buyer's form. Therefore, the buyer must rely

---

107. Reprinted by permission.

heavily on the purchase order form. In the natural sequence of events, if a quotation form is issued by the seller, it will be issued before the buyer's purchase order is issued, and thus the buyer generally has a built-in disadvantage in this regard. Of course, the buyer was also disadvantaged under the common law "last shot doctrine," whereby the buyer was usually deemed to have accepted the seller's last offer when the buyer accepted or used the goods.

If your client is not the first offeror, but in fact the offeree, do not despair; all is not lost, provided certain defensive strategy is employed. Your client must scrupulously avoid engaging in any of the three actions previously set forth and immediately "fire off" a rejection and counteroffer. Of course, your client would not want to call the document "a rejection and counteroffer" since these terms are too harsh and legalistic in tone and might arouse the suspicions of the offeror. Rather the document must have that effect without really saying it.

If your client is the seller who has just received the buyer's purchase order, you can advise him to "fire off" his sales acknowledgment. If your client is the buyer who has just received the seller's quotation form, you can advise him to "fire off" a purchase order. In both cases, however, the form must contain either and preferably both of the following clauses to constitute a rejection and counteroffer:

(1) a clause negating the fact that it is an Expression of Acceptance or Confirmation document.

(2) a clause expressly making any acceptance contained in the form conditional on the offer's assent to your additional or different terms.

All defensive moves in a battle have certain inherent risks. The risk of making a rejection and counteroffer is that no contract is thereby formed and, if nothing more is done, either party can with legal immunity walk away from the transaction. The advantage is that by sending the counteroffer, the offeree avoids being bound by all the terms of sale of the offeror. In addition, although there is a risk that a contract will never be formed, the likelihood is that the parties will commence performance and will be deemed to have formed a contract under paragraph (3) of §2-207. Such a contract will be deemed to contain only those terms on which the forms of the two parties agree, plus such other terms as are read in by the Code. On balance, the risk of not having a contract ultimately formed is very small in the normal transaction and the defensive move previously described is generally well worth the risk.

The Arsenal

Since the prime purpose of engaging in the battle of forms is to save the time and expense of negotiating terms, the attorney had best prepare his arsenal of forms by contemplating all eventualities in the battle. Thus, in preparing the sales acknowledgment form, the seller's attorney must anticipate the possibility that a contract has already been formed between the parties by virtue of the exchange of the quotation form and purchase order form. On the other hand, the buyer's attorney must realize that the purchase order may in any given transaction be either the first offer or the Expression of Acceptance or Confirmation document sent in response to the seller's quotation form. The following are a few thoughts in drafting documents in the arsenal of forms:

(a) Buyer's request for quotation form—Print the buyer's terms of purchase on this form. Insert a clause stating that any quotation sent in response to the request for quotation is deemed subject to the buyer's terms of purchase, unless seller specifically states the contrary in the typewritten portion of seller's quotation form.

(b) Seller's quotation form—Insert the clauses contemplated by clauses (a) and (c) of §2-207(2). State that the dispatch of buyer's purchase order is an acceptance of the quotation if the purchase order agrees with the quotation with respect to certain basic terms, e.g., description of goods, quantity, price and delivery schedule.

(c) Buyer's purchase order form—Insert the clauses contemplated by clauses (a) and (c) of paragraph (2) of §2-207 and add the following clause: "Any acceptance contained herein is expressly made conditional on seller's assent to the additional or different terms contained herein." State that the seller's commencement of work or shipment is a mode of acceptance of the purchase order if the sales acknowledgment agrees with the purchase order with respect to certain basic terms, e.g., description of goods, quantity, price, and delivery schedule.

(d) Seller's sales acknowledgment form—State that the form is to be disregarded if a contract has already been formed on seller's terms of sale and insert the following clause: "Any acceptance contained herein is expressly made conditional on buyer's assent to the additional or different terms contained herein."

Training the Manpower

The victor in the battle of the forms will not satisfy himself merely with a well-stocked forms arsenal. The manpower who will use the forms, i.e., the purchasing and selling agents, must also be trained in their use and misuse. Purchasing agents must be trained to avoid making verbal agreements with respect to goods they wish to purchase. Such verbal agreements could convert the purchase order subsequently sent from an offer into a confirmation document. In such situations, the terms of the verbal agreement of the purchasing agent and, at best, the non-material alterations made to that verbal agreement by the purchase order form would constitute the terms of the contract. If it is absolutely necessary for the purchasing agent to make a verbal agreement, the purchasing agent should be trained to make the terms of the purchase order form part of the verbal agreement, where feasible. Of course, purchasing agents must also be advised to never verbally accept the seller's quotation form. Likewise, selling agents must be cautioned against making verbal agreements or verbally accepting purchase orders.

Certain limits must also be placed upon the extent to which the purchasing and selling agents can automatically use their respective forms without consulting an attorney. Very large orders or contracts containing unusual terms must, by standard operating procedure, be reviewed by an attorney.

The degree of sophistication of the manpower using the forms may well determine the ultimate victor in the battle of the forms.

NOTES AND QUESTIONS

1. *Drafting drawbacks:* Is the drafting suggested by Lipman always a good idea? In *Salt River Project Agricultural Improvement & Power District v. Westinghouse Electric Corp.*,[108] such drafting caused problems for a buyer.

In the early 1970s, Westinghouse sold power plant equipment to the Salt River Project (SRP). In May 1976, there was an explosion causing $1.9 million in damage to the SRP power plant. SRP alleged that the damage was caused by a malfunction of a $15,000 control device it had purchased from Westinghouse in 1973. It sued Westinghouse, alleging causes of action in strict products liability; breaches of express and implied warranties; and negligence in design, manufacture, and installation of the control device. Westinghouse moved for summary judgment on the strict products liability and breach of warranty theories and partial summary judgment on the negligence theory, which would limit SRP's recovery to $15,000, the price of the control device. The court of appeals affirmed the grant of summary judgment to Westinghouse.

The transaction under which the control unit was purchased involved a battle of the forms. SRP's purchase order stated:

> This Purchase Order becomes a binding contract, subject to the terms and conditions hereof, upon receipt by Buyer at its Purchasing Department of the acknowledgment copy hereof, signed by Seller, or upon commencement of performance by Seller, whichever occurs first. Acceptance of this Purchase Order must be made on its exact terms and if additional or different terms are proposed by Seller such response will constitute a counteroffer, and no contract shall come into existence without Buyer's written assent to the counteroffer. Buyer's acceptance of or payment for material shipped shall constitute acceptance of such material subject to the provisions herein, only, and shall not constitute acceptance of any counteroffer by Seller not assented to in writing.[109]

Westinghouse returned an acknowledgment form. On its face it said "SEE REVERSE SIDE FOR TERMS AND CONDITIONS." There, Westinghouse gave a warranty that the goods would be as described in the acknowledgment and would be free of defects in workmanship and materials. All other warranties were disclaimed in a provision printed in capital letters. It also limited its liability, stating that it would not be liable for consequential damages nor for more than the price of the product sold in this transaction.

The Court of Appeals found "as a matter of law that the exclusions of warranty and limitation of liability set forth in Westinghouse's Acknowledgment form are enforceable against SRP." It explained:

---

108. 143 Ariz. 437, 694 P.2d 267 (Ct. App. 1983), *modified en banc*, 143 Ariz. 368, 694 P.2d 198 (1984).

109. *Id.* at 440, 694 P.2d at 270.

Paragraph I of the "Terms and Conditions of [SRP's] Purchase Order" dictated how the SRP order could or could not ripen into a binding contract by expressly providing: (1) that it could only be accepted on its "exact terms"; (2) that any contrary document would constitute only a "counteroffer," and (3) that no contract would result from such an exchange unless SRP assented to the counteroffer in writing.

The Westinghouse Acknowledgment did not accept SRP's Purchase Order on its "exact terms." The Acknowledgment's warranty exclusions and limitation of liability clauses are substantially different from those contained in the SRP Purchase Order; therefore, the Acknowledgment became a "counteroffer" as was contemplated by the express terms of SRP's Purchase Order. The pivotal question before us then is whether SRP accepted the Westinghouse counteroffer.

The record reveals that SRP failed to object to the changed terms contained in the Acknowledgment. SRP took delivery of the LMC [Local Maintenance Controller], paid for it and made extended use of it.... A contract for the sale of goods may be made in any manner sufficient to show agreement, including *conduct* by both parties that recognizes the existence of a contract.... UCC § 2-204(1). Furthermore, an offer to make a contract shall be construed as inviting acceptance in any manner and by any medium reasonable in the circumstances.... UCC § 2-206(1). The "counteroffer" embodied in the Westinghouse Acknowledgment was accepted by SRP's conduct manifested through SRP's acceptance, payment for, and use of the LMC. This was true even in the absence of SRP's express assent. Where, as here, an offeree uses a seller's goods for his own purposes, that action will be deemed to constitute an acceptance of the terms of the counteroffer or offer.... While SRP's Purchase Order specifically states that any counteroffer can only be accepted by SRP when that acceptance is in writing, the SRP Purchase Order terms concerning the acceptance of the counteroffer do not control. Because SRP's original offer was rejected, the rejected offer could not govern how the new Westinghouse "counteroffer" could or would be accepted. Absent any limiting language in the counteroffer that would restrict the manner of acceptance, the acceptance of the counteroffer would be governed by the general provisions of the UCC....

We find no support for SRP's argument that ... UCC § 2-207, the so-called "battle of the forms" provision, applies in this case because SRP's own Purchase Order rejected in advance its possible application. The SRP order distinctly stated that a responsive document containing any different or additional terms would operate as a counteroffer and could not be an acceptance of the SRP offer.... [Section 2-207] comes into play when there has in fact been a "definite and seasonable expression of acceptance." The Westinghouse Acknowledgment was not such an "expression of acceptance" because the SRP Purchase Order would not permit it to be one. Thus, the exchange of documents that occurred in this case is wholly outside the scope of … [§ 2-207].[110]

Professor John E. Murray comments:

> The first reaction to this bizarre situation may be to regard the buyer's draftsman as a classic illustration of one who, in Llewellyn's words, tried to "draft to the edge of the possible" and was hoisted on his own excessively drafted petard. Further reflection, however, reveals a more troubling analysis.… In *Salt River* the seller's form is not a counteroffer by its own language. Instead, it becomes a counteroffer by *unread* language in the buyer's purchase order. Section 2-207 has no application. *Salt River* thus provides the most recent example of the "last shot" principle.… [T]his kind of analysis may appear at any time because of chaotic judicial interpretations in this area.[111]

Would a careful application of § 2-207(3) produce a different result in the *Salt River* case? See Official Comment 7 to that section. Moreover, could we say that in this case a remedy limited to the amount of the purchase price "failed of its essential purpose" under § 2-719(2), because it "operates to deprive … [the buyer] of the substantial value of the bargain"?

2. *Arguing the* Salt River *case as a matter of policy:* Assuming a good technical argument could be made for liability under §§ 2-207(3) and 2-719(2), did the court, nonetheless, reach the right result? Consider the policies sought by the courts in *McCarty v. Verson Allsteel Press Co.*, *Steiner v. Mobil Oil Corp.*, and *Air Products & Chemicals, Inc. v. Fairbanks Morse, Inc.* Would they favor Westinghouse in this case? Make a case that they would … and then make a case that they would not. Remember the policies justifying the *Hadley v. Baxendale* rule in carrying out this exercise.

3. *What do you tell the client?* Should lawyers drafting form contracts be able to fashion forms that they know will protect their clients, whatever the actual negotiations between representatives of the parties? In seeking the actual expectations of the parties, does UCC § 2-207 undercut a lawyer's ability to structure transactions?

4. *Evaluations of § 2-207:* Professor Alexander M. Meiklejohn[112] points out that § 2-207 is based on Karl Llewellyn's idea that businesspeople give blanket assent to all of the terms and conditions that they do not read, except those that are unreasonable or unconscionable. As an empirical matter, Meiklejohn doubts that this is true. As a result, § 2-207 produces results different from what were likely the real expectations of the parties. Instead of the complexities of § 2-207, courts should look

---

110. *Id.* at 444–45, 694 P.2d at 267.

111. John E. Murray, *The Chaos of the "Battle of the Forms": Solutions*, 39 Vand. L. Rev. 1307, 1354 (1986).

112. Alexander M. Meiklejohn, *Castles in the Air: Blanket Assent and the Revision of Article 2*, 51 Wash. & Lee L. Rev. 599 (1994).

to the agreement of the parties. It is likely that they assume that the usages of their business will control unless they really negotiate for something different.

Professor Victor Goldberg[113] would also abandon § 2-207. He advocates a rule calling for courts faced with conflicting forms to enforce all the terms found on one form, based on which one was the most fair expression of the deal. This would give drafters an incentive to take account of the interests of the other side.

Do you see any problems with either of these approaches? If neither satisfies you, could we defend the common law "last shot" rule on the basis that it is close to a random flipping-a-coin solution to the problem? If no means-ends solution works well, what is wrong with leaving the matter to chance?

5. *Amended § 2-207:* We hesitate to mention that the sponsors of the UCC attempted to "fix" § 2-207 as part of a set of amendments they approved in 2003, but which have not been enacted anywhere. The proposed amended section is superficially cleaner in its drafting, but it is also broader and vaguer: it seems to cover all contracts under Article 2 and provides for most of the issues to be resolved by its subsection (b), under which the terms are those "to which both parties agree." Here is the full amended version:

> Subject to Section 2-202 [dealing with parol evidence], if (i) conduct by both parties recognizes the existence of a contract although their records do not otherwise establish a contract, (ii) a contract is formed by an offer and acceptance, or (iii) a contract formed in any manner is confirmed by a record that contains terms additional to or different from those in the contract being confirmed, the terms of the contract are:
>
> (a) terms that appear in the records of both parties;
>
> (b) terms, whether in a record or not, to which both parties agree; and
>
> (c) terms supplied or incorporated under any provision of this Act.

This provision was not well received by commercial interests, who anticipated that it would take decades of litigation to achieve the degree of certainty there is under the existing § 2-207.

d. Remember the UN Convention on Contracts for the International Sale of Goods

You should, at this point, have a fair appreciation for the difficulties both with the perceived problems the UCC sought to "solve" in the original version of § 2-207, and the problems with the solution. A certain measure of consternation would not be an unusual reaction upon a first reading of the previous pages. Unfortunately, the picture

---

113. Victor Goldberg, *The "Battle of the Forms": Fairness, Efficiency, and the Best-Shot Rule,* 76 Or. L. Rev. 155 (1997).

is just slightly more confusing still. Though you might face a dispute concerning your domestic client's purchase or sale of goods, requiring an analysis of incomplete or contradictory paperwork, the answer might not be in the Uniform Commercial Code. Another body of law might apply.

The development of trade across state boundaries led to the need for a code of commercial law that would be more or less uniform from one state to another; this was the impetus for the Uniform Sales Act and later the UCC. Similarly, the growth of international trade led to the need for a code that would govern international sales of goods: hence the Convention on Contracts for the International Sale of Goods (CISG). The Convention was approved by a diplomatic conference in Vienna in 1980, and the process of adoption by individual countries began immediately. As of 2016, 84 nations — including the United States, Australia, China, France, Germany, Mexico, Canada, and Sweden — had subscribed to the Convention. Contracts for the international sale of goods entered into by parties in countries that have ratified the Convention are subject to CISG unless the contract for sale explicitly designates another law (such as the UCC) as governing. Many of the rules of the Convention are the same as those of the U.S. common law or the UCC, but there are important differences.

The Convention excludes a number of contracts that would be covered under the UCC. First, the Convention is not applicable to consumer sales. Second, the Convention does not apply when a government is a party to the contract. Further, the Convention excludes transactions pertaining to securities or the sale of ships, aircraft, and electricity. In addition, claims for personal injury or death caused by goods are not covered. Finally, parties to an international contract are free to exclude the application of the Convention or vary the effects of its provisions, even more freely than parties to contracts governed by the UCC and its sections 1-301 and 1-302.

We will, on occasion, call your attention to the Convention when we think it would be useful or interesting to do so; we do not intend, however, to provide an exhaustive summary of the Convention's rules. It is important that you know that the Convention provides the default standards for international sales of goods involving participating nations, and that the rules may be different from those you might otherwise expect to apply.

We are calling your attention to the Convention at this point because the manner in which the CISG deals with the battle of the forms is different from the UCC solution. Article 19(1) of the Convention is analogous to the common law "mirror image" rule. It provides that "a reply to an offer which purports to be an acceptance but contains additions, limitations or other modifications is a rejection of the offer and constitutes a counteroffer." But paragraph (2) states that unless the offeror objects, a reply is an acceptance if the additional or different terms do not materially alter the terms of the offer. The terms of a contract thus formed would incorporate the modifications included in the acceptance of the offer. Paragraph (3) goes on to furnish a non-exclusive list of terms that are considered material. These relate to price, quality, and quantity of goods, place and time of delivery, means of settling disputes, and the extent of a party's liability. The impact of Article 19 is likely to be that fewer enforceable contracts will result under the Convention than under the UCC, so long as the parties have not performed. If there is performance, Article 18 provides that the "conduct of the offeree indicating assent to an offer is an acceptance." Therefore, when one party has met its contractual obligation, the "last shot" doctrine would indicate what the terms of the contract are.

D. CLOSING THE DEAL BUT LEAVING A WAY OUT

Bargainers often want to close a deal but, at the same time, leave a way out. I want you to be committed, but I want to be able to call things off. I may not be sure whether it is a good deal, and I may want some time to think about it. I may want to control my salespeople who dealt with you. I may want to investigate your credit or my ability to perform. I may want time to seek financing to pay for my purchase, but I may not be sure I can find a lender willing to put up the money on acceptable terms.

If the parties are willing to put their cards on the table and have received good legal advice, legally enforceable contracts can be created that achieve these purposes. An *option* is perhaps the easiest way to preserve a business opportunity while buying time. For example, a TV producer thinks she may want to fashion a television show or series based on a novel. She can buy an option from the novelist or the publisher. In exchange for money, the novelist or publisher agrees not to sell the rights to anyone else for a specified time. On the other hand, a bargainer can make its performance *subject to a condition*. We can agree we have a contract, provided that I am awarded a different government contract.

As always, things can be more complicated. A common problem is created by a practice sellers have long used to limit the authority of their salespeople to close contracts.[114] The salesperson calls on a customer and writes an order on the seller's standard form. The customer and the salesperson sign, and the customer is likely to think that the deal is closed. However, the form states: "Any quotation by Seller on the face hereof or on any attachment hereto is merely an invitation for an offer from potential customer(s). All resulting customer offers (orders) are thus subject to acceptance at Seller's offices at the address shown on the face here, before any contract is formed." The customer, thinking there is a deal, is not likely to back out, but the seller can decide whether or not to accept the order. We can view this as a condition, but it is a condition that goes to creating a contract. Furthermore, it is a condition left in the hands of the seller. The seller has said no more than that it will perform if it wants to.

Such clauses usually work as their drafters intend. There are many cases saying that if an order is subject to acceptance at the home office, no contract is formed

---

114. *See* Cole-McIntyre-Norfleet Co. v. Holloway, 141 Tenn. 679, 214 S.W. 817 (1919).

until such acceptance is given.[115] However, these clauses raise all the problems of fine print, duty to read, and even the battle of the forms. Can the buyer reasonably rely on such a transaction when seller has not accepted buyer's order? In some situations, sellers try to have it both ways. They want buyers to think they (the buyers) are bound, but sellers want the power to back out if it suits their purposes. Do sellers have a duty to approve or reject orders within a reasonable time? Can the seller's conduct create an obligation, even when it has not accepted the order?

In the case that follows, Judge Posner reviews many of the issues about flexibility and indefiniteness we have considered so far, and also notes that reserving a right of home office approval can work to keep a solicitation from being an offer. Why didn't that technique succeed for the defendant?

ARCHITECTURAL METAL SYSTEMS, INC. v. CONSOLIDATED SYSTEMS, INC.

United States Court of Appeals, Seventh Circuit
58 F.3d 1227 (1995)

POSNER, C.J.

The district judge granted summary judgment for the defendant in a suit for breach of contract (a diversity suit, governed by Illinois law), and we must decide whether he did so prematurely. The facts, construed, in light of the procedural setting, as favorably to the plaintiff as the record permits, are (slightly simplified) as follows:

On January 20, 1992, Mellon Stuart, the general contractor on a project to rehabilitate a train station, solicited bids for a subcontract to provide the metal decking required by the project. AMS, the plaintiff in this suit, was interested in the subcontract. AMS is a middleman, not a fabricator, so it asked for price quotations from fabricators, including CSI, the defendant. CSI's Memphis office submitted a price quotation which stated however that any actual order must be approved by CSI's headquarters in South Carolina. Armed with CSI's price quotation (which CSI sent to Mellon Stuart as well as to AMS), AMS on February 12 submitted a $1.9 million bid to Mellon Stuart. Mellon Stuart accepted AMS's bid two days later, on February 14. But shortly afterward, Mellon Stuart altered its specifications (as it had reserved the right to do) with regard to the painting of the metal decking, and invited AMS to submit a revised bid. AMS sent the altered specs to CSI and to another fabricator, Bowman, for revised price quotations. Both Bowman and on March 24, CSI, submitted revised price quotations to AMS. CSI's new price was $769,033, less than half of Bowman's price. AMS submitted a revised bid to Mellon Stuart on April 6 after informing CSI that it would be submitting CSI's price quotation to Mellon Stuart and that it wanted to be sure that the quotation was correct (and it was so assured),

---

115. *See, e.g.,* Foremost Pro Color, Inc. v. Eastman Kodak Co., 703 F.2d 534 (9th Cir. 1983); Meekins-Bamman Prestress, Inc. v. Better Construction, Inc., 408 So. 2d 1071 (Fla. App. 1982).

and after extracting CSI's agreement to post a performance bond if CSI got the order. CSI's price quotation did not contain the clause in the previous one requiring approval by headquarters.

Mellon Stuart thought AMS's new price too high. Negotiations ensued, and AMS lowered the price slightly, to $1,884,195. On April 14 Mellon Stuart formally accepted AMS's new bid. AMS informed CSI of this, and there was some further discussion of specifications, leading CSI to submit a new bid to AMS on April 24 but with prices identical to those in the March 24 bid for items included in both bids. The clause requiring approval by headquarters was again omitted. The parties then discussed escalation terms and, according to notes taken by AMS's negotiator, reached agreement on them. On April 28, CSI's salesman in Memphis (Allen), with whom AMS had been dealing, faxed AMS that "we look forward to working with you on the transit project." On the same day, AMS prepared and mailed a purchase order to CSI, but at the same time it told Allen that the order was a mere formality; they had a deal.

CSI, however, responded to AMS's purchase order on May 1 with a revised bid in which it raised its price by 73 percent, claiming that it had made a mistake in calculating the price in its previous bids. AMS rejected the bid, insisting that CSI honor the deal previously struck. When CSI refused, AMS turned to another supplier—to whom it had to pay $260,967 more than the price in CSI's bid of April 24. This suit, to recover that addition, followed. AMS argues both conventional breach of contract and promissory estoppel. The parties agree that the issues are governed by the Uniform Commercial Code as interpreted by the courts of Illinois.

Regarding the contract claim as distinct from the claim of promissory estoppel, the district court held that CSI's price quotations were not offers and anyway were not accepted. They were not offers first because they lacked detail and second because they were conditioned on approval by CSI's headquarters. The record does not support either conclusion. The test for an offer is whether it induces a reasonable belief in the recipient that he can, by accepting, bind the sender. *McCarty v. Verson Allsteel Press Co.*, 89 Ill. App. 3d 498, 44 Ill. Dec. 570, 411 N.E.2d 936, 943 (Ill. App. 1980); RESTATEMENT (SECOND) OF CONTRACTS § 24 (1981). A lack of essential detail would negate such a belief, since the sender could not reasonably be expected to empower the recipient to bind him to a contract of unknown terms. "I would like to buy your hamster" is not intended to empower the recipient of that solicitation to reply: "My price is $1 million. We have a contract." Granted, the degree to which the reasonable recipient will think a vague offer intended to empower him to create by acceptance a legally enforceable contract depends on the courts' attitudes toward vague offers. The more willing the courts are to interpolate missing terms, the more difficult it is for the recipient of a vague offer to interpret the intentions behind the offer. In Michigan during the heyday of the Toussaint decision (*Toussaint v. Blue Cross & Blue Shield*, 408 Mich. 579, 292 N.W.2d 880, 885 [Mich. 1980]) from which the Supreme Court of Michigan has recently backed off, *Rowe v. Montgomery Ward & Co.*, 437 Mich. 627, 473 N.W.2d 268, 273–75 (Mich. 1991), no promise was too vague to support an enforceable contract (at least of employment), so no inference that a vague offer was not really an offer could be drawn from its vagueness. Illinois has never gone that far; contracts in Illinois really can fail for indefiniteness, *see, e.g., Academy Chicago Publishers v. Cheever*, 144 Ill. 2d 24, 161 Ill. Dec. 335, 578 N.E.2d 981 (Ill. 1991), and, since this is so, the recipient of a hopelessly vague offer should know that it was not intended to be an offer that could be made legally enforceable by being accepted.

CSI's April 24 price quotation was not hopelessly vague. It specified the items to be sold, the quantity and price of each item, and the delivery terms. These are the essential terms of a contract for the sale of goods. As long as the remaining terms, covering warranty, excuses, remedies, and so forth, can be pieced out from trade usage, an unexplored issue in this case, the contract will not fail for indefiniteness, *Wait v. First Midwest Bank/Danville*, 142 Ill. App. 3d 703, 96 Ill. Dec. 516, 491 N.E.2d 795, 801 (Ill. App. 1986), or—what amounts to the same thing—the "offer" be deemed the mere solicitation of an offer, as in *McCarty v. Verson Allsteel Press Co.*, *supra*, 411 N.E.2d at 943. The parties had ironed out their differences over escalation terms and the bond, and having done so thought they had a deal—a contract. That is, they thought they had resolved the only potential deal-busting disagreements. At any rate there was enough evidence of this to preclude summary judgment for the defendant.

The Uniform Commercial Code, its draftsmen mindful of the haste and sloppiness, and disregard for lawyerly niceties, that characterize commercial dealing, tolerates a good deal of incompleteness and even contradiction in offer and acceptance. This is clearest in its rejection of the common law" "mirror image" rule. Under the UCC, the fact that the acceptance contains different terms from the offer does not convert the acceptance into an offer or otherwise make it ineffective as an acceptance. UCC § 2-207; *Northrop Corp. v. Litronic Industries*, 29 F.3d 1173 (7th Cir. 1994). The parties have a contract despite the discrepancies. The course of dealing here is typical of the commercial practices that under the UCC result in the formation of enforceable contracts.

A person can prevent his submission from being treated as an offer by suitable language conditioning the formation of a contract on some further step, UCC § 2-207(2)(a); *La Salle National Bank v. Vega*, 167 Ill. App. 3d 154, 117 Ill. Dec. 778, 520 N.E.2d 1129, 1133 (Ill. App. 1988); *Northrop Corp. v. Litronic Industries, supra*, 29 F.3d at 1179, such as approval by corporate headquarters. The district judge thought that the inclusion of such a clause in previous price quotations by CLS put AMS on notice that such approval would be required even for price quotations not containing the clause. That is a *non sequitur*. For all AMS knew, the clause had been left out because the Memphis office had obtained the requisite approval from the home office in South Carolina. What is more, in an affidavit submitted by AMS to which the district judge unaccountably failed to refer, a former officer of CLS stated that home-office approval was not in fact required. We suppose it could be argued that even if the clause was not intended seriously, unless AMS knew this it would not think the price quotation an offer and therefore would not intend to accept it and so create a binding contract. Whether this tortuous reasoning has any basis in law is irrelevant, however, because AMS treated the price quotations as offers and because the last two quotations, those of March 24 and April 24, omitted the clause. CSI argues that the omission was inadvertent and known by AMS to be such, but these obviously are issues for trial rather than for summary judgment.

Equally premature is the judge's conclusion that if the price quotations were offers, AMS did not accept them because its acceptance, which the judge deemed to be the purchase order of April 28, contained discrepant terms. We have already pointed out that a discrepancy between offer and acceptance does not prevent the formation of a contract. CSI's brief contains an imposing list of discrepancies, which it describes as "radical," but admits that there is not a shred of evidence that they were potential deal-busters. An example of one of these "radical" discrepancies is that CSI's March 24 and April 24 price quotations specify "G-90" steel while the purchase order specifies "G-60" steel. We have no idea what this difference signifies. For all we know it is (to persons knowledgeable in the trade) an obvious typographical error, inverting "9" and thus turning it into "6." The Uniform Commercial Code, moreover, does not make even "radical" differences between offer and acceptance a ground for concluding that there is no contract. If there is an offer and an acceptance, then, however discrepant (within reason) their terms are, there is a contract, and the question is merely *what* the terms are. *Northrop Corp. v. Litronic Industries, supra*, 29 F.3d at 1175, 1179. (The possibilities are the terms in the offer, the terms in the acceptance, or "default" terms interpolated by the court.) Nor is it even clear that the purchase order here, with its discrepant terms, *was* the acceptance. The acceptance may have been oral.

Which brings us to the question whether the contract, if there was one, was made unenforceable by the Statute of Frauds. We think not. Between the price quotations and the purchase order (whether or not it was the formal acceptance of CSI's offer), there was enough indication of the terms of the parties' contract to satisfy the UCC's not very demanding Statute of Frauds. UCC §2-201; *Monetti, S.P.A. v. Anchor Hocking Corp.*, 931 F.2d 1178, 1182–83 (7th Cir. 1991).

Since the case must go back to the district court for a trial, we should consider whether AMS's alternative theory of liability, that based on promissory estoppel, is also viable. The theory is simply that AMS, in deciding what price to bid for the contract with Mellon Stuart, reasonably relied, to its detriment, on CSI's expressed willingness to sell metal decking at the low price in the March 24 and April 24 price quotations. We adhere to the view tentatively adopted in *Goldstick v. ICM Realty*, 788 F.2d 456, 464–66 (7th Cir. 1986), and since confirmed (as a prediction of Illinois law) by two decisions of the Illinois Appellate Court, *First National Bank v. McBride*, 267 Ill. App. 3d 367, 204 Ill. Dec. 676, 642 N.E.2d 138, 142 (Ill. App. 1994); *Dickens v. Quincy College Corp.*, 245 Ill. App. 3d 1055, 185 Ill. Dec. 822, 615 N.E.2d 381, 386 (Ill. App. 1993), that the Statute of Frauds is applicable to a promise claimed to be enforceable by virtue of the doctrine of promissory estoppel. That is not a problem here; the alleged promise is the price quotations, which are written, not oral.

The judge, while intimating that the statute of frauds might bar AMS's claim of promissory estoppel, rejected the claim on different grounds. The first was that AMS had not relied on CSI's price quotations, since it had entered into a binding contract with Mellon Stuart on February 14, before it had received final bids from CSI. This ignores the fact that Mellon Stuart reopened the bidding after altering its specifications, which required AMS to submit a new bid. AMS submitted its new bid on April 6, after and in reliance on CSI's price quotations of March 24 (which essentially were repeated on April 24), and became bound on April 14, when Mellon Stuart accepted the new bid. So far as we can determine from the record, AMS was under no contractual obligation to Mellon Stuart to submit a revised bid, let alone at a particular price. Had it known how much CSI would charge, it might have submitted a higher bid, or no bid; either way, it would not have been in breach of the contract previously made with Mellon Stuart on the basis of AMS's February bid. The contract based on that bid, the contract that took effect on February 14 when Mellon Stuart accepted AMS's bid of two days earlier, became defunct when Mellon Stuart altered the specs and invited a new bid.

Second, the judge thought that AMS's reliance on CSI's price quotations could not be reasonable, given the disparity between CSI's price and Bowman's. The judge ruled that AMS should have known, or at least suspected, that CSI's price had been computed erroneously. At the argument of the appeal, CSI's lawyer rather recklessly argued that whenever one bid is at least 50 percent lower than the next lowest, acceptance of the low bid does not create a binding contract; the buyer is on notice of the existence of a mistake. There is no such rule of law. *Community Consolidated School District No. 169 v. Meneley Construction Co.*, 86 Ill. App. 3d 1101, 42 Ill. Dec. 571, 409 N.E.2d 66, 68 (Ill. App. 1980); *Chicago City Bank & Trust Co. v. Wilson*, 86 Ill. App. 3d 452, 41 Ill. Dec. 466, 407 N.E.2d 964, 968 (Ill. App. 1980). It would lead to absurdities. If a person hailed a cab, asked what the price would be to his destination, was told $10, said it was too high, hailed another cab, was quoted by that cabbie a price of $5, and agreed, the second cabbie would be able to demand a higher price, on the ground that the passenger should have known by reason of the discrepancy in prices that the $5 price had been computed erroneously.

There are circumstances in which a mistake can be inferred from the price in the offer. *See, e.g., Vincent DiVito, Inc. v. Vollmar Clay Products Co.*, 179 Ill. App. 3d 325, 128 Ill. Dec. 393, 534 N.E.2d 575, 577 (Ill. App. 1989); *S.N. Nielsen Co. v. National Heat & Power Co.*, 32 Ill. App. 3d 941, 337 N.E.2d 387, 389–90 (Ill. App. 1975); 2 E. Allan Farnsworth, Farnsworth on Contracts §9.4 (1990). Suppose that CSI's bid had been not $769,033, but $7,690.33. AMS could not cry "Gotcha!" It would know that a mistake had been made. Perhaps it should have drawn that inference here. But that would depend on the circumstances. Bowman's bid could have been mistaken on the high side. There is no evidence of that but there is evidence that there were special reasons why Bowman's price was much higher than CSI's that had nothing to do with mistake by anyone. The judge's comment on that evidence was: "We are not persuaded that these factors justify reasonable reliance." This is not the language of summary judgment. The weighing of evidence is the task for trial. The function of summary judgment is to determine whether there are contestable issues. Whether a 56 percent discrepancy between two bids to supply metal decking for the rehabilitation of a train station should make a bulb light up in the brain of the person to whom the bids have been submitted remains profoundly uncertain on this record. We note that CSI does not as one of its defenses to the breach of contract claim seek reformation of the contract on the ground of mistake. We express no view on whether that course remains open to it in the further proceedings that must be conducted in the district court. Reversed and remanded.

NOTES AND QUESTIONS

1. *Posner's hamster hypothetical — one for the ages?* Judge Posner is a master at opinion writing,[116] and in the decision you have just read he also displays his talent for coming up with memorable hypotheticals, one involving a hamster sale and the other involving a contract for taxi services. The hamster hypothetical involves this exchange: "I would like to buy your hamster," with the response, "My price is $1 million. We have a contract." What is good and bad about this hypothetical to demonstrate the point that Judge Posner is trying to make with it? How might it be varied to make other points?

2. *What constitutes an "acceptance at the home office"?* In *Nordyne, Inc. v. International Controls & Measurements Corp.*,[117] the seller sent a price quotation for an improved version of a control panel that buyer had been purchasing for a number of years. The quotation provided that any action brought under this agreement would be tried in Onondaga, New York. The document also stated: "All orders are subject to acceptance by the Seller at its home office in Cicero, New York." Buyer asked to see samples of the new control panel. Seller supplied them on September 12, 1997, along with a letter that said "Full-blown manufacturing of this device is awaiting your sign-off of these check samples as approved for production. Please review the samples and 'sign off' this document and send it back by return fax so that we may fulfill your production requirements in a timely manner." The buyer signed the seller's production approval form, and then two days later it issued a purchase order for 20,000 units at the quoted price. This purchase order said nothing about the place of trying any lawsuit. Buyer alleged that the control panels were defective and sued in a federal court in Missouri. The trial court dismissed the complaint for improper venue because the forum selection clause in the seller's proposal governed. Buyer argued that there had been no approval. The appellate court affirmed. It said: "The fact that ICM's home office issued the letter of September 12, 1997, asking for Nordyne's production approval, *i.e.*, Nordyne's acceptance of ICM's offer, undermines Nordyne's argument that the quotation was not an offer because it required ICM's home office approval.

---

116. *See* Kate O'Neill, *Rhetoric Counts: What We Should Teach When We Teach Posner*, 39 SETON HALL L. REV. 507 (2009) ("Judge Posner's rhetoric is a good chunk of his message, not just the means by which he conveys it. When the author is as skilled as Judge Posner, law professors' inattention to rhetoric allows students, and perhaps faculty as well, to receive more information than they may consciously perceive as being communicated.").

117. 262 F.3d 843 (8th Cir. 2001).

This approval in fact occurred, and thereafter Nordyne approved the beginning of production." Do you see any problem with the court's analysis? Was the buyer's request for manufactured samples of the new control panel an offer? Wouldn't the buyer be free to look over the samples and decide not to buy? When the buyer signed the production approval form and faxed it back to the seller, was this an offer? Would seller be reasonable in thinking that buyer had made a commitment before buyer issued a purchase order?

3. *Silence as acceptance:* "Subject to approval at the home office" clauses raise the classic problem of "silence" as acceptance of an offer. The older black-letter rule was that silence could not be taken as an acceptance. This position seems to have been an over-generalization of the idea that I cannot force you to act to ward off a contract. Suppose I park my ten-year-old Ford Taurus in your driveway and send you the keys with a letter saying that unless you reject my offer within three days, I will deem you to have agreed to buy the car for $1,000. Individualistic contract law refuses to allow me to force you to act; your inaction would not be taken by courts to be an agreement to buy the car.

However, courts were never easy with a rule saying that "silence" could never be an acceptance. On the one hand, a person receiving such an offer could rely on it and get hurt. On the other hand, a person receiving such an offer could try to play it both ways. If she or he desired to enforce the contract, inaction could be called an acceptance. If she or he desired not to be bound, inaction could be called a rejection. The cases cannot be explained in terms of whether silence was a manifestation of acceptance — one must turn to other factors.

For example, in *Kukuska v. Home Mutual Hail-Tornado Ins. Co.*,[118] a farmer filed an application for insurance on July 3; the insurance company gave notice of rejection of the application at 11:00 A.M. on August 1; and the crops were destroyed by a storm later that afternoon. The court found the insurance company liable. It said that three theories support such a conclusion: silence as acceptance; an implied contract to act promptly; and a duty arising from the franchise created by being licensed as an insurance company in the state. The court observed: "If the insurer is under such a duty and fails to perform the duty within a reasonable time and, as a consequence, the applicant sustains damage, it is not vastly important that the legal relationship be placed in a particular category."[119]

Later, in *Sell v. G.E. Supply Corp.*,[120] the same court found that inaction had not created liability. The plaintiff applied to become a distributor for Hotpoint refrigerators and ordered five. The order, written on a G.E. Supply Corporation form, was "subject to approval" by G.E. Supply. Seventeen days later, General Electric Contracts Corporation notified plaintiff that it would purchase his customers' installment payment contracts. However, 19 days later plaintiff received a telegram saying that the appli-

---

118. 204 Wis. 166, 235 N.W. 403 (1931).
119. *Id.* at 405.
120. 227 Wis. 242, 278 N.W. 442 (1938).

cation to become a distributor had been disapproved. It explained that there was a shortage of refrigerators, and it had decided to allocate production to the existing distributors rather than add new ones. The Supreme Court of Wisconsin, finding no liability, pointed out that there was a good reason for rejecting the application, the decision was relatively prompt, and plaintiff's reliance was not particularly great.

The "silence cannot be acceptance" rule was further shaken in *Morris F. Fox & Co. v. Lisman.*[121] Here, plaintiff made an offer on a form drafted by defendant that stated a contract was "subject to approval at home office." Defendant considered the deal and plaintiff's credit and made a note on plaintiff's offer indicating that defendant had accepted the contract. However, this letter was filed away, and no notice of acceptance was ever given to plaintiff. While other things were communicated by defendant to plaintiff, the court stressed that the letter showed defendant's intention to accept and found that a contract had been made. Compare *International Filter Co. v. Conroe Gin, Ice and Lt. Co.,*[122] reaching a similar result.

All in all, cases such as *Hills v. Wm. B. Kessler, Inc.*[123] and the three Wisconsin decisions just discussed suggest that some courts have been willing to regulate the reservation of a right of approval after the business adopting the practice creates a situation where an applicant can be hurt by reliance. Regulation appears particularly likely when the one reserving the right does not use it for legitimate business purposes or, as in the *Morris F. Fox & Co.* case, where the legitimate business purposes of the procedure have been served. Compare Restatement (Second) of Contracts § 69.

4. *Estoppel and good faith in bargaining:* In *Iacono v. Toll Brothers,*[124] the plaintiffs sued for specific performance of a contract to purchase real property. Defendants were developers. They listed units in Colts Neck Estates with a real estate broker. The broker sold buyers a house to be built by the developers on a contract form provided by the developers. This form provided:

> This Agreement has been obtained by Seller's salesman or agent who has no authority to bind Seller to this Agreement. This Agreement shall not be binding upon Seller unless signed by Seller within thirty (30) calendar days from the date below. Otherwise, the deposit money will be returned to the Buyer without interest....[125]

Buyers conceded that they were aware of the clause and understood it. They paid a deposit, but defendants never signed the form. Almost two months after buyers signed the contract, defendants notified them there was no deal. The trial court found that a binding contract had been formed. The appellate court reversed this judgment. However, it remanded the case for findings necessary to determine whether the defendants were equitably estopped. The defendants had not returned the deposit, and

---

121. 208 Wis. 1, 237 N.W. 267, 240 N.W. 809, 242 N.W. 679 (1932).
122. 277 S.W. 631 (Tex. Civ. App. 1925).
123. 41 Wn. 2d 42, 246 P.2d 1099 (1952).
124. 217 N.J. Super. 475, 526 A.2d 256 (1987).
125. *Id.* at 477, 526 A.2d at 257.

they had waited almost two months before writing plaintiffs, rejecting the agreement of sale. Plaintiffs requested several modifications in the design of the house defendants were to build, and defendants agreed to these changes. Plaintiffs tendered checks in partial payment for construction charges, which defendants accepted and deposited. The defendants' construction superintendent referred to the house as "your home" or "your new home." Plaintiffs were not in the real estate market looking for another house at a time of sharply rising real estate values.

The court said there were a number of unresolved issues:[126]

> [W]hether Toll Brothers' [the defendants] silence or conduct or both following April 13, 1985 [30 days after the agreement was signed by the buyer], induced reliance by plaintiffs that Toll Brothers had accepted the agreement of sale; whether such reliance, if found factually, was reasonable and in good faith in the light of plaintiffs' concessions that they knew of and understood the import of the home office acceptance clause in the agreement of sale; whether plaintiffs, relying upon Toll Brothers' silence or conduct or both, changed their position to their detriment by staying out of the rising real estate market as purchasers for a significant time interval after April 13, 1985.

> Plaintiffs would be entitled to judgment on remand only if the determination of all the foregoing fact questions is in the affirmative. If so, there should be a further factual determination as to whether the Statute of Frauds was met.

Notice that while the buyers and the developers may not have entered a binding contract, they did enter a continuing relationship. Can we explain the court's decision in terms of a duty of good faith in negotiations? That is, the developers would have several acceptable reasons for not wanting real estate brokers to have the power to bind them to contracts. For example, if the developers had only a certain number of lots, and various brokers might sell more than the total available. Developers might want to investigate the credit of buyers or institutions providing financing for buyers. However, developers might also want to be able to reject buyers in order to discriminate on the grounds of race or religion. In the *Iacono* case, the buyers argued that the developers tried to back out so they could benefit from a rapidly rising housing market. Can we view these cases finding at least a possible liability despite "subject to approval" clauses as American versions of *culpa in contrahendo*? *See* Kessler & Fine, *supra* Chapter 1.

5. *"Subject to financing" clauses:* Buyers of real estate and other expensive items often insist that contracts be drafted with a "subject to financing" clause. Buyers must shop for the property they want to purchase and shop for a loan on terms they find acceptable. This way of closing a deal while leaving a way out provokes several problems for courts. Does the buyer have any obligation to look seriously for financing? Must the buyer accept a reasonable offer of credit from a lending institution, or is the offer's acceptability left to the buyer's discretion?

---

126. *Id.* at 480–81, 526 A.2d at 259.

Some courts solve such problems by refusing to consider them. They refuse to enforce contracts subject to financing, or they refuse to enforce them unless the parties
have agreed to the amount, terms, and conditions of the loan that the buyer will
seek.[127] They explain that such clauses leave buyers too much discretion. Furthermore,
courts would be burdened by trying to judge the reasonableness of financing buyers
could have obtained. On the one hand, financing could be reasonable in the sense
that the loan was what most lenders were offering. On the other hand, such a loan
could burden a particular borrower greatly in light of his or her personal situation.
Courts would have to decide whether a reasonable person in the buyer's position
would have made the sacrifices of lifestyle needed to produce enough money to make
the monthly payments. For example, perhaps a buyer would be reasonable in rejecting
a loan that would make him unable to pay for his child's college education. Would
he be reasonable in rejecting one that would require him to sell his sports car?

Finally, this position may serve to protect inexperienced buyers, who must first
shop for a house and then shop for financing. They may overestimate their ability to
make loan payments out of a modest income. Classic mistake doctrine would offer
them little relief. However, if their lawyer can attack their contract with the seller, a
court can overturn the deal without being forced to craft a new mistake rule. For example, in *Perkins v. Gosewehr*,[128] a contract for the sale of a house for $65,000 provided:
"This offer is contingent upon buyer obtaining a first mortgage loan commitment
for $52,000." The appellate court found that "the statement of the amount of the loan
does not fill the evidentiary void, and does not establish that the parties reached a
meeting of the minds concerning the primary objective of the 'subject to financing'
clause, i.e., what financing would be affordable or desirable to the buyers and acceptable to the sellers. In the absence of such evidence, the contract is void for indefiniteness."[129] The trial court had concluded that the buyers "were in over their heads"
and could not afford the monthly payments needed to buy the house.

Courts do, however, usually uphold such conditions.[130] Compare the outcome in

---

127. *See, e.g.*, Gerruth Realty Co. v. Pire, 17 Wis. 2d 89, 95, 115 N.W.2d 557, 560 (1962).
128. 98 Wis. 2d 158, 295 N.W.2d 789 (1980).
129. *Id.* at 164–65, 295 N.W.2d at 792.
130. Professor Farnsworth noted:

    A surprisingly wide variety of matters can be left to the satisfaction of one of the parties
without making the agreement unenforceable. Courts have, for example, allowed the buyer
of real estate to condition its obligation on its satisfaction with governmental action on
zoning and development plans and engineers' and architects' feasibility studies. They have
even allowed the parties to leave the precise nature of the financing obtained by the buyer
to its own satisfaction. While it scarcely can be sound practical advice to say merely "subject
to financing," such language has passed muster. Courts have been equally tolerant with
similar conditions commonly found in commitments to lend that leave matters to the
lender's discretion. Thus it has been held that the commitment of a lender that had agreed
to finance a shopping center was not illusory although it was conditioned on leases in the
shopping center not being "unsatisfactory or otherwise unacceptable" to the lender.

    Courts, however, have been less tolerant of terms that condition the agreement on ap-

Perkins with that in *Wiggins v. Shewmake*.[131] In that case, the buyers agreed to purchase a house provided they were able to obtain a "13 percent conventional loan." The buyers were denied a loan by one lender. The seller got a commitment from a bank for such a loan to the buyers, but they refused to accept it. They obtained a loan on another home, which they purchased shortly thereafter. Seller sued, and the trial court found that the buyers had failed to use due diligence in carrying out their good faith duty to obtain financing. Seller was awarded consequential damages. The South Dakota Supreme Court affirmed, saying:

> [T]he circumstances surrounding the contract can make the clause sufficiently certain enough to grant specific performance.... Enforcement by specific performance of a residential real estate purchase contract does not require an expansive recitation of mortgage financing details.
>
> Excessive detail may be counterproductive to enforcement of the contract by unwarrantedly narrowing the contingency clause to an extent that makes its fulfillment improbable. It also ignores the fiscal realities that the total effect of the financing terms is often more important than the variation in individual details, which often offset each other. For the latter reason, financing clause terms are better stated in essentials so that inconsequential variances resulting from current financial market conditions do not preclude consummation of the transaction....
>
> [T]he trial court found that "conventional loan," as used in the agreement, is a loan directly through a local lending agency not guaranteed by a governmental agency. Several local banking officials testified that this was the common understanding of the term....
>
> [A] purchaser, such as the Shewmakes, is under an implied promise to use his best efforts to bring about the happening of the condition.... The Shewmakes did indeed fail to exercise their best efforts when they refused to accept offered financing that comported with the exact language of the purchase agreement.[132]

---

proval by a party's lawyer, a kind of term that often appears if there is a division of responsibilities between managers and lawyers. The key is the extent of responsibility given to the lawyer under the term. Sometimes the agreement is conditioned on the lawyer's approval of the agreement itself. Such a provision invites the inference that the lawyer's responsibility includes a review of the advisability of the deal, and courts have held that this makes the party's obligation illusory. Sometimes, however, the agreement is conditioned on the lawyer's approval of documents such as guarantees or closing papers. Here, even though the lawyer's discretion may be said to extend to "substance" or "content" as well as form, it is easier for a court to reject the argument that the lawyer's responsibility includes a review of the advisability of the deal.

E. Allan Farnsworth, *Precontractual Liability and Preliminary Agreements: Fair Dealing and Failed Negotiations*, 87 Colum. L. Rev. 217, 247–48 (1987).

    131. 374 N.W.2d 111 (S.D. 1985).

    132. *Id.* at 115–16.

Does this result better protect the expectations of the parties than those found in the Wisconsin cases? Does it reflect another instance of an American approach to *culpa in contrahendo*? *See* Kessler & Fine, *supra* Chapter 1. Do you see any problems with the approach of the South Dakota court?

Chapter 3

THE DEAL IS CLOSED —
BUT WHAT IS IT?

A. INTRODUCTION

Two leading contract scholars recently began a law review article about contract interpretation by stating:

> Interpretation issues are hard; the doctrine is difficult and the issues are complex.... This is unfortunate because contract interpretation remains the largest single source of contract litigation between business firms.[1]

Interpretation and drafting are obviously related activities. To draft contracts well, a lawyer must first know something about how courts give meaning to those contracts that come before them. To become an expert contract drafter takes years of practice, ideally with a lot of feedback from more experienced lawyers. Some law schools offer upper-level courses in contract drafting or include drafting exercises in first-year legal writing courses.[2]

Lawyers sometimes make deliberate choices not to draft as well as they might, or they may be under time deadlines that prevent them from doing their best possible work. Professor Claire Hill has written about why complex business contracts so often contain obvious drafting shortcomings.[3] There has long been an idea that parties and their lawyers bargain in the shadow of the law. If they have a dispute, they take into account what a court might decide and adjust their relationship accordingly, without actually litigating. Hill adds the idea of bargaining "in the shadow of the lawsuit," that is, the parties know when they bargain that they may end up in a dispute that

---

1. Allan Schwartz & Robert E. Scott, *Contract Interpretation Redux*, 119 Yale L.J. 926, 926 (2010). More recently, Professor Scott, along with Professors Gilson and Sable, affirmed this view: "Contract interpretation remains the most important source of commercial litigation and the least settled, most contentious area of contemporary contract doctrine and scholarship." *See* Ronald J. Gilson, Charles F. Sabel, Robert E. Scott, *Text and Context: Contract Interpretation as Contract Design*, 100 Cornell L. Rev. 23, 25 (2014) (footnote omitted).

2. There are now some published teaching materials available that are designed to teach about contract drafting. *E.g.*, Scott Burnham, Drafting and Analyzing Contracts (LexisNexis, 3d ed. 2003).

3. Claire Hill, *Bargaining in the Shadow of the Lawsuit: A Social Norms Theory of Incomplete Contracts*, 34 Del. J. Corp. L. 191, 192–195 (2009). Reprinted by permission.

neither party anticipated. Furthermore, the parties may prefer flexibility to work something out then as opposed to trying to spell out many contingencies in advance.

How do parties bargain in the shadow of the lawsuit? First, they do less than they might to "complete" their contracts. All immediate issues are addressed, as are parties' (or their lawyers') "hot button" issues and other issues that become salient to one or both parties. But the form documents used for the transaction are not kept up-to-date, nor is the final product in a particular transaction cleaned up to eliminate confusing cross-references and possible ambiguities before the parties bind themselves to it (or afterwards, for that matter). While parties do ask themselves throughout the contracting process what they might have missed, the inquiry is not nearly as systematic as it might be....

In my account, in contracting, parties are not principally trying to set forth an agreement for a court to enforce. The contracting process, and the contract that results, importantly serves to create the parties' relationship and to set the stage for dispute resolution consistent with preserving the relationship, as well as to keep available the backstop of enforcement if needed.... [C]reating the relationship involves defining what the relationship is; parties bargain to determine what they want and write it down in a document they can bind themselves to and later bring to court.... If parties seek to capture the last, costliest attempt at precision, they probably will not commensurately reduce their endgame costs. Indeed, they may increase such costs. Bargaining more than the community norm may shrink the reputational penumbra otherwise created by the contract, encouraging an ethos in which whatever is not prohibited is permitted. Accommodation that might help relationship preservation may thereby be crowded out, replaced by a more literalistic and opportunistic mindset on the part of both parties....

In other work, I have made the (perhaps uncontroversial) claim that contracts are unnecessarily long and complicated, and not infrequently have "ambiguities that too readily allow for multiple interpretations."[4] Contracts are redundant, with cumbersome, inartful, and imprecise drafting. What I have called "band-aid" fixes are often used: "anything in the foregoing to the contrary notwithstanding," or "for purposes solely of this Section Z, word A shall mean and include ..."[5] Matters would be bad enough if parties "started fresh" in every transaction with a real fill-in-the-blanks form, but they do not. They start with what they call a form, but what is actually an already heavily cluttered document used in a previous deal and not "cleaned up." Add in the force of cumulation, not only for negotiated terms but also for so-called "boil-

---

4. [3] *See* Claire A. Hill, *Why Contracts are Written in "Legalese,"* 77 CHI.-KENT L. REV. 59, 75 (2001).
5. [4] Considering the circumstances in which the contracts are drafted—late at night, by people who have had very little sleep—that band-aid solutions, rather than more global solutions, are used is not surprising. But why does contracting proceed in this way? ... I have also discussed the contracting process in more depth in Claire A. Hill, *A Comment on Language and Norms in Complex Business Contracting*, 77 CHI.-KENT L. REV. 29 (2001) (arguing that when parties bind themselves to a contract, they are binding themselves as much or more to a relationship as they are to each of the specific terms of the contract)....

erplate," and the result is a contract that is not nearly as clear as it could be, and that offers manifold opportunities for disputes after the fact. Some (indeed, probably many) of these opportunities could be addressed at the time of contracting. Parties could "clean up" contracts before signing them-but they do not.... The stereotype of bleary-eyed corporate lawyers negotiating late into the night is indeed true. Lawyers do not take a dispassionate day or two after the dust clears to afford their more rested selves a chance to review and correct, if necessary, what their very tired selves wrote.

Turning to the question of how courts interpret often poorly drafted contracts, an initial question is who decides, judge or jury. In our system, that issue turns on whether interpretation is considered to raise legal or factual issues. When a contract is oral, there are obvious questions about who said what to whom, and these issues are obviously factual. If one of the parties so requests, and there is credible conflicting evidence, the jury will get to decide what was said, as well as what those words meant. But the law has long taken the position that the interpretation of a writing raises a question for the judge rather than the jury.[6] As we will see, there are numerous exceptions to this proposition. Often matters that need to be weighed when considering the interpretation of a written contract, such as scope of a trade usage or existence of a course of dealing, can introduce conflicting evidence concerning facts that, when a party so requests, are resolved by a jury. In those circumstances the interpretation issue can usually be assigned to the jury as well. But the initial question we address is why the interpretation of a written contract might ever be considered a legal question. Many have suggested that this proposition is basically an unprincipled rule reflecting skepticism of the wisdom of juries.[7] Professor William Whitford has critiqued this interpretation rule in the following way:[8]

A. The Fact/Law Distinction in General

The most important standard for distinguishing questions of fact from questions of law is the general/particular distinction. If the significance of a determination is limited to a particular case, we call it a fact issue, even though by no means would it be considered a "fact" as that term is used in ordinary language. Consider for example an issue that often arises in determining expectation damages for breach—in what situation would the plaintiff be if the contract had not been broken (*e.g.*, how much profit would she make). A layman would term such a determination an informed guess at

---

6. There is conflict in the authorities whether the reason for this rule is that textual interpretation is a question of law, or a fact question that is reserved for the judge. The authorities are reviewed thoroughly in Judge Newman's concurrence in Antilles Steamship, Ltd. v. Members of the Am. Hull Ins., 733 F.2d 195, 202 (2d Cir. 1984). Judge Newman concludes that textual interpretation of a written contract raises a legal issue.

7. Most famously, Charles T. McCormick, *The Parol Evidence Rule as a Procedural Device For Control of the Jury*, 41 YALE L.J. 365 (1932).

8. William C. Whitford, *The Role of the Jury in Contract Interpretation*, 2001 WIS. L. REV. 931, 932–36. Copyright © 2010 by The Board of Regents of the University of Wisconsin System. Reprinted by permission of the Wisconsin Law Review.

best, but because its significance is limited to the case, we consider it a fact rather than a law question....

The general/particular distinction has its gray areas, as all dichotomies do. The indistinctness is most prominent in issues of law application, sometimes called mixed questions of fact and law. Many law application issues involve the specification of a general legal standard to particular facts. A common example is the determination of negligence in a tort case. Sometimes we use the occasion of a law application to further specify a general standard, in a way that will help determine the outcome of future cases through the doctrine of precedent. In such circumstances, the general/particular distinction suggests that law application should be considered a question of law. In other circumstances we regard each law application as *sui generis* (as is typically the case when applying the negligence standard), and in those circumstances law application is likely to be considered a question of fact, even though a good deal of discretion is exercised in applying a general standard to particular facts.

A consideration distinct from the general/particular dichotomy for distinguishing between fact and law questions is the type of reasoning process used to resolve the issue. Inductive reasoning processes are used in determining both fact and law questions. However, if a deductive reasoning process is used to reach a decision, the determination is always made by a court, even if the determination is only relevant to the particular case. Sometimes we say that the determination is a factual one, because it is particular, but for the court, because there is only one reasonable conclusion to be drawn (the deductively correct one), it amounts to the same thing as considering the determination a legal one.

B. Contract Interpretation Principles

... The most commonly used principle in contract interpretation is that words and acts are to be interpreted from the perspective of the listener, not the speaker or actor. This is called the objective approach to interpretation. And normally the objective approach is applied by asking not what the listener understood, but what a reasonable person in the position of the listener would have understood, or perhaps more precisely believed the speaker to have intended....

Application of this objective interpretation principle should not be understood as requiring a finding of historical or pure fact. There is no existential reality to the reasonable person; nor is ascertaining her understanding or belief a matter of taking a statistical average. Rather, applying the objective interpretive principle is better understood as an instance of law application, the specification of a standard similar to application of the negligence principle in tort law. In accordance with the usual approach to law application questions, when contract interpretation is particular to a single contract, the issue of interpretation of even a written contract should be deemed a question of fact, appropriate for jury decision when there are competing plausible interpretations. One might justify an exception for standard form contracts (SFKs), especially insurance contracts, because these contracts are frequently the subject of multiple cases, and for contract language that appears in many contracts (*e.g.*, "time is of the essence"). In each circumstance the interpretation of contract language in one case could influence the outcome of a subsequent case, and so interpretation could be considered general. But in the great number of contract cases in which the language to be interpreted is idiosyncratic to the contract at issue, at the level of principle the interpretation question should be considered one of fact. The generally stated rule with respect to written contracts is to the contrary, however....

The final principle of interpretation to be discussed here is the so-called plain meaning rule. If words are deemed to have a natural meaning, then interpretation of a writing may be viewed as raising a legal issue because the reasoning process is deductive. There is only one right answer, even assuming the words being interpreted are idiosyncratic and no precedent is being set....

C. Conclusion

The often stated rule is that the interpretation of a written contract is a question of law. There are many exceptions to this statement, as will be detailed (later).... In this section, however, I have evaluated the general proposition from the point of view of what I call "principle." Unless one adopts a plain or natural meaning approach to interpretation, making the reasoning process deductive, the better arguments from principle are that the textual interpretation of a writing raises a fact question whenever the conclusion is particular to the individual case and contract....

B. TEXTUAL OR CONTEXTUAL INTERPRETATION OF CONTRACTUAL LANGUAGE?

We begin this section with long passages from one of the classic works reviewing the legal principles governing the interpretation of written contracts. A basic issue is always whether the person(s) (judge or jury) doing the interpretation are limited to the written contractual language or can consider other matters that may bear on what one or both parties understood that language to mean.

Edwin W. Patterson, *The Interpretation and Construction of Contracts*
64 COLUM. L. REV. 833 (1964)[9]

I. Interpretation, Construction, and Inference Distinguished

A. *Interpretation.* What is interpretation? It is the process of endeavoring to ascertain the meaning or meanings of symbolic expressions used by the parties to a contract, or of their expressions in the formative stage of arriving at the creation of one or more legally obligatory promises. Since most contracts are temporary in their effects, the process of interpretation often consists merely of the direct application of the symbols used to the factual situation that gives rise to controversy. For example, if *S*, a farmer, has agreed for a stated price to sell and deliver to *B*, a grocer, four dozen eggplants, and on the appointed day *S* tenders as his performance to *B* four dozen eggs, an objective observer could, without formulating any *general* conception of the genus and species of "eggplant," give a *particular* interpretation that the tender was not within the terms of the contract; and this interpretation might well support a *particular* legal evaluation that *B* was under no duty to accept the eggs in performance, and possibly that *S* has breached his contractual duty....

B. *Construction.* Construction, which may, in this writer's opinion, be usefully distinguished from interpretation, is a process by which legal consequences are made to follow from the terms of the contract and its more or less immediate context, and from a legal policy or policies that are applicable to the situation. Construction may be applicable along with interpretation, or it may take over when interpretation wholly or partly fails. Take three possible cases:

1. An action has been brought upon an alleged contract which has vague and meaningless expressions of what would normally be important terms; *e.g.*, the quality and quantity of goods are vague, and so is the price. In such a case the symbolic conduct will ordinarily be adjudged to be too indefinite to be enforced. "The court cannot make a contract for the parties," is the basic policy. Yet if goods have been delivered and accepted, the context may show that no gift was intended, as the recipient knew, and the court will construe (imply) a duty to pay the reasonable value of the goods. The policy seems to be to prevent unjust enrichment, yet the duty construed is contractual, not quasi-contractual.

2. An action has been brought by *P* upon a written contract, partly printed and partly typed, the terms of which are chosen and drafted by *D*, defendant. On interpretation of the terms it appears that a crucial term, such as a condition precedent of *D*'s promise, is ambiguous, that is, has two possible meanings, one of which is more favorable in its effect to *D*, and the other of which is more favorable to *P*. If the latter interpretation will signify that *P* has fulfilled the condition, then the court will usually construe the crucial term *contra proferentem*, that is, unfavorably to the party drafting the contract, *D*, and favorably to the other party, *P*. This construction may be based upon the inference that *D* in drafting the instrument intended only the meaning favorable to *P*, otherwise it would have excluded that meaning by more explicit drafting; or it may be based upon a policy of equalizing the inequality of the one-sided bargain. This principle of construction is frequently applied to insurance contracts (where sometimes, it seems, the court conjures up the ambiguity) and to other "contracts of adhesion."

Reserved. This article originally appeared at 64 COLUM. L. REV. 833 (1964) (*passim*). Reprinted by permission.

3. An action is brought by *P* upon a contract that contains an unconscionable condition of *D*'s contractual duty or an unconscionable limitation or extension of the measure of damages for a breach by *D*. In such a case the court may, under exceptional circumstances, and in direct denial of the meaning that interpretation properly would give, construe the unconscionable term to be unenforceable in this action and in this sense "void." Here construction overrides interpretation. Such uses of construction are exceptional....

D. *Court and Jury.* Even in a case in which a jury is the trier of issues of fact, the interpretation and construction of a written contract is within the exclusive province of the judge. While the judge may be called upon, in this process, to determine several issues of "fact," such as those inferences referred to above, the relevant dictionaries, and relevant circumstances, yet the meaning of a written instrument is often called "a question of law." This characterization of the rule is a surviving fiction (or semifiction). The continuance of the rule is justified by the judge's superior equipment— his education and legal experience—to interpret written instruments and to give them reliability. As a determination of law, the trial judge's interpretation of the meaning of a written contract is not as conclusive upon an appellate court as his "findings of fact" would be and hence may be set aside as an "error of law."

Where the contract is partly oral and partly written, the judge may instruct the jury as to the meaning of the written part and, with other instructions, leave the remaining issues of interpretation to be determined by the jury. If the jury is directed to bring in a general verdict (*i.e.*, for the plaintiff or for the defendant), it may in so doing exercise its views of jury equity and thus impair the reliability of written instruments. This possibility may account for the reluctance of courts to admit parol evidence and other extrinsic aids to interpretation, and for their adherence to the "plain meaning" of the contract....

II. "Plain Meaning" and the Several Dictionaries

The ideal result that legal draftsmen seek to attain and that judicial interpreters commonly seek to find in a written contract is that a judge should be able, by reading the contract without lifting his eyes from the page, to determine its one and only "true" meaning in relation to the issues being litigated. Once this "true" meaning has been ascertained, no other evidence should be permitted to fritter away the meaning and thus make written contracts unreliable. What I have called the "true" meaning is transformed into "plain meaning" in the standard set of maxims of interpretation. In accordance with this ideal, if the court finds a "plain meaning" of the relevant terms of the writing, it will exclude various kinds of proof, discussed in this and the next two sections, that would contradict or qualify the plain meaning. If, however, the written contract on its face contains an ambiguity, then evidence extrinsic to the contract will be admitted....

How seriously ... should one take the "plain meaning" rule that is stated in many judicial opinions? ... [T]o quote the words of a brilliant judge (Learned Hand), "there is a critical breaking point ... beyond which no language can be forced...." This breaking point is the limit of "plain meaning." It serves to fulfill one or more of the basic purposes of the law of contracts.

Yet the plain meaning rule must be taken with reservations. The first one is that it does not apply in case of an "ambiguity," which may be cleared up by extrinsic aids; only the courts can say when there is an ambiguity. A second one, less important, is that a "plain meaning" provision may be deemed unconscionable and thus unenforceable. A third one is more important than either of these: the term of a contract that at first sight seems to have only one "plain" meaning may have two to a dozen meanings in a standard or universal dictionary of the vernacular. From among these the court, if it looks at the universal dictionary, has to *select* the one meaning that is "plainly" *appropriate* in this case. Usually, however, the crucial interpretation is not dependent on a single word but is dependent upon a phrase or a sentence that is not listed in a dictionary and to which the court gives its own interpretation.

A fourth reservation to the "plain meaning" rule is that a local, trade, or other special usage may give to a term a meaning very different from that given to it by the common or universal dictionary, and when one reads the contract terms with the proof of the usage, of which both parties knew or should have known, the appropriate meaning is no longer merely the "plain" one. A striking example is the old English case involving a suit by a lessee of a rabbit warren against his lessor, who by the terms of the written lease agreed to pay the lessee, at the expiration of the lease, "£60 per thousand" of rabbits left in the warren, and the lessor proved that by local usage, of which the lessee had reason to know, the term "thousand" meant "1,200," so that for 19,200 rabbits, the lessee was entitled to recover just 16 times £60. It is not easy to match this case with one in which the contract term, unaided by a special usage, had as "plain" a meaning as "thousand," and the special usage had a "plain" and plainly contradictory meaning. Does the admission of the usage for such a purpose contradict the late Judge Learned Hand's statement that there is a "breaking point" beyond which no language can be forced? And what of the famous dictum of Judge Oliver Wendell Holmes, Jr.? "It would open too great risks if evidence were admissible to show that when they [the parties] said 'five hundred feet' they agreed that it should mean 'one hundred inches,' or that 'Bunker Hill monument' should signify the 'Old South Church.'"

The late Professor John H. Wigmore, who first developed the notion that there are several "dictionaries," besides the ordinary lexicon, in which symbols may have meaning (*e.g.*, trade or technical usages), apparently thought there was a contradiction. Yet Learned Hand certainly, and Holmes probably, was referring to the latitude of discretionary interpretation of words taken in their "ordinary dictionary" sense. This restrictive view would, it is believed, be appropriate if, as in the case of a recorded deed to land, third persons had innocently relied upon the ordinary meaning. If a trade or local usage can be proved and if it was known to both parties at the time when the written instrument was signed, then a different case is presented and the special usage should control.... [For example] a promise by *R*, a seller of books by subscription, was to pay his salesman, *E*, a commission on "every order," yet *R* was allowed to prove that "every order" meant, in the subscription book business, "every order where five volumes were taken and paid for by the subscriber." In such cases there is a substantial variance between the contract term in its ordinary sense and the usage meaning; yet the contract term does not manifest an intention not to be "bound" by the usage. On the other hand, an extreme case, such as the "1,000 rabbits" case, might be taken to express such an intention, and the court should require stricter than usual proof that there was such a linguistic usage, that the objector may fairly be charged with knowledge of it, and that the contract term was not intended to exclude it.

If the interpretation of the contract requires ascertainment of the meaning of a scientific or technical term that the court cannot find in any standard dictionary, the scientific or technical linguistic usage as to the meaning of the term may be proved by the testimony of expert witnesses who are familiar with it. For instance, a contract in litigation contained a promise to purchase dyes, "Amacid Blue Black KN," and expert testimony was admissible to prove the meaning of the quoted term. Here the term had no "plain meaning" to the court, and not even ambiguous meanings — it was meaningless. Hence the "plain meaning" rule was not applicable. Cases of this type give no difficulty.

Despite numerous dicta that a "plain meaning" cannot be explained by a special usage, it is believed that the law as laid down in judicial precedents is otherwise. A contract to sell 125,000 "chickens, 2½–3 lbs." was, by the aid of expert testimony and of terminology derived from the U.S. Department of Agriculture, interpreted by the court to include "stewing chickens," as the seller interpreted it, and not limited to "broilers or fryers," as the buyer argued it should be. The Restatement, which does not recognize the "plain meaning" rule, states as the standard of interpretation of a contract contained in a single written instrument ("integrated") "the meaning that would be attached to the ... [instrument] by a reasonably intelligent person acquainted with all operative usages...."

... The "plain meaning" rule serves as a last resort, to guide a court that has found no aids to interpretation nor signs of intention in the transactional context and no basis for an "equitable construction," and thus falls back upon the literal wording of the contract for which the court does not see any rational basis. Either poor drafting of the contract or supervening unforeseen circumstances have made the contract scarcely intelligible, and the court refuses, under the guise of "equitable interpretation," to make a new contract for the parties.

III. Extrinsic Aids: Relevant Circumstances

An extrinsic aid is anything outside of the written instrument in which the terms of a contract are embodied ("integrated") and which may be used in ascertaining the meaning of these terms. The ideal process of interpretation outlined in Part II can rarely, if ever, be realized: the contra-document usually does not "speak for itself." In suggesting that such a document *may* carry its own meaning I refer only to the *interpretation* of the contract, not to its validity or to the proof of its performance.

In case of dispute as to the genuineness of the signatures, the authority of agents to sign on behalf of their principals, or the identity of agents and principals, extrinsic proof may be used. So, if a claim is made that the contract was induced by fraud or duress and is therefore voidable, proof of conduct of the parties and other facts outside the contract are admissible. The same is true when a dispute arises as to the facts of performance of the contract. A written contract *may* be so carefully drawn with explicit provisions, definitions of terms, and recitals of fact, that, as to some disputes that *do* arise (but not as to all disputes that *might* arise) its meaning is clear in relation to the particular dispute without the aid of extrinsic proof.

Yet proof of many of the circumstances of the transaction that would tend to show how the contract came to be made, the motivation or purposes of the parties in making it, the particular characteristics of the subject matter, and the like, are admissible to show its meaning....

A. *Course of Performance.* The conduct of both parties to a contract in the course of its performance is, if it indicates that they gave a particular meaning to its terms, provable as evidence of that meaning. This kind of proof is frequently called the "practical construction" of the parties. The basis of inference in such cases is often an admission by one party, by his conduct, that the contract has a certain meaning. For instance, the fact that *P*, a trucking company, did not in its monthly billings to the other party, a freight forwarder, make any claim for certain alleged "receiving charges" referred to in the contract, was deemed sufficient evidence of the meaning of the provision concerning "receiving charges" to justify a denial of a later claim for such charges....

One party's performance in accordance with his interpretation, favorable to his own interests, may, if the other party consents to or acquiesces in this interpretation, create a practical construction unfavorable to the latter. If the latter gives an *express* assent to the former, who afterward acts in reliance on it, an estoppel may be created. Hence practical construction may entrap a party who is not alert to detect and repudiate practical interpretations with which he disagrees. "Self-serving" interpretations by one party are not often given effect. At least they should be limited to cases of knowledge and acquiescence by the other party.

For contracts to sell goods the Uniform Commercial Code gives a clearer and more restrictive meaning of course of performance than can be found in judicial opinions [§ 2-208(1)]:

> Course of Performance or Practical Construction.... Where the contract for sale involves repeated occasions for performance by either party with knowledge of the nature of the performance and opportunity for objection to it by the other, any course of performance accepted or acquiesced in without objection shall be relevant to determine the meaning of the agreement.

This language avoids the pitfalls of the doctrine.

B. *Prior Utterances and Thoughts.* [We have omitted Patterson's brief summary of the parol evidence rule, since we take up that topic somewhat later, in more detail.]

C. *Recitals.* Recitals are statements of a factual character inserted in written contracts for the purpose of explaining and clarifying their terms. They are frequently worded as "whereas" clauses, and are useful aids to interpretation.

IV. Extrinsic Aids: Course of Dealing and Trade Usages

"Custom conquers all" is a maxim that had somewhat greater reliability in previous centuries than in this one. Still, it may serve to remind us that the transactions with which lawyers and judges have to deal take place in an ordered and established society for the most part, and that the social matrix envelops every word that the parties may utter, or every sentence that they may sign. What is this social matrix? It includes, above all, the common or universal language of the community, for which no dictionary is ordinarily needed by parties, lawyers, judge, or jury. It includes the vocabulary of lawyers when relevant. It includes a previous course of dealing (if any) between these same parties to this contract. It includes the linguistic usages discussed in Part III above that give meaning to special terms in the contract, and also those *additive* usages that may add terms to the contract where the contract itself is silent and does not exclude such usages.

A. *Course of Dealing.* A prior course of dealing between the parties to a contract has long been recognized by courts as relevant to the interpretation of their contract. A contract by *D* to supply *P* with chemicals at "ruling market rates" was followed by deliveries, monthly rendition of accounts by *D* to *P*, and payment by *P*. Then *P* discovered he had been paying jobber's rates, rather than the lower exporter's rates, and sued for the difference. Prior dealings between *P* and *D* (and also their prior conversations) were relied on by the court to show that *P* had not been overcharged. A course of dealing may, it seems, consist of a repeated practice of one party that was known to the other, which the jury might find helpful in determining their rights— here a buyer's belated claim for breach of warranty. Yet one party's practice, unknown to the other, can not establish a course of dealing. The regular accounts rendered by one party to another and acquiesced in by failure to object within a reasonable time may be held effective against the latter on the basis of two older doctrines, estoppel or account stated. Course of dealing, sometimes confused with "custom" or "usage," has seldom been relied upon in reported case law.

The Uniform Commercial Code defines the term [§ 1-205(1)]:

> A course of dealing is a sequence of previous conduct between the parties to
> a particular transaction which is fairly to be regarded as establishing a common
> basis of understanding for interpreting their expressions and other conduct.

This definition, far superior to any previous judicial attempts, gives some objectivity ("sequence of conduct establishing") to the term, yet the requirement of knowledge of the sequence, "between the parties," is left to "fairly" and "common basis of understanding." The trier of fact will, it seems, have considerable discretion; yet it is somewhat limited by the hierarchy of persuasiveness discussed below.

B. *Additive and Linguistic Usages.*

… Although a trade or class usage resembles a custom, such usages are not required to have existed "from time immemorial," as are English local customs. The original of a trade usage need not be veiled in mystery. It may be embodied in regulations adopted by a trade association, of which one party is a member, if the regulations are known to the other party. However, if the nonmember was not aware of the trade rule when the contract was made, he is not bound by it. American courts have been less careful than English courts in requiring proof from which it might be inferred that one party knew, or had reason to know, of a usage relied on by the other. Under a contract by a seller to deliver potatoes f.o.b. railroad cars in Virginia, a jury found that the seller was aware of a usage by which payment by the New York buyer was to be deferred until after the potatoes arrived in New York and were inspected by him. On the other hand, a court in Arkansas held that a remote nonresident, dealing with a New York buyer, was not charged with knowledge of a New York usage, and a New York court held a usage of fruit buyers in New York was not so long and well-established as to be imputed to a fruit grower shipping fruit from Oregon to the New York market. Ordinarily the "insider" tries to impute knowledge of his group's usage to the "outsider." However, on the principle of reciprocity, the "outsider" should not be allowed to claim the benefit of the "insider's" usage if the "outsider" was not aware of it when the contract was made, and in Virginia it was so held. With respect to *knowledge* by a party of a trade usage so as to make it binding upon him the Uniform Commercial Code seems to provide three categories: (1) parties engaged in the vocation or trade, (2) parties who are aware, and (3) parties who should be aware are deemed to have knowledge.…

C. *"Unreasonable" Usages and the Hierarchy of Authority.* While usage may often be used to smooth the channels of commercial transactions, yet parties to contracts sometimes seek to prove usages with which their lawyers may mislead juries. There has thus grown up the judicial doctrine that a court will not permit proof of an "unreasonable" or an unlawful usage. [For example, a] Missouri court held that a usage of used-car dealers to turn back the speedometer mileage on used cars, after making "improvements" on them, was deceptive and contrary to the public good. On the whole, judicial supervision of usages has been salutary.

The Commercial Code seeks to express the requirement of reasonableness along with a statement as to which source of interpretation prevails when they are in conflict with each other: "The express terms of an agreement and an applicable course of dealing or usage of trade shall be construed wherever reasonable as consistent with each other; but when such construction is unreasonable express terms control both course of dealing and usage of trade and course of dealing controls usage of trade." [UCC § 1-205(4).] An alleged usage that contradicts express terms of the contract is to be rejected. A course of dealing between these two parties is more likely to express their expectations than a conflicting usage that may be the practice of other persons.

D. *Notice of Intention to Prove Usage.* As another safeguard against the false usage as an escape hatch for delinquents the Uniform Commercial Code provides that one party's evidence of a usage shall not be admissible "unless and until he has given the other party such a notice as the court finds sufficient to prevent unfair surprise to the latter." ...

V. Secondary Maxims of Interpretation and Construction

In addition to or in conjunction with the principles of interpretation and construction of contracts set forth above, courts rely upon and purport to use a number of maxims of interpretation, some of which are very broad but most of which are applicable only to special situations. There is some doubt whether they have reliable guidance value for judges, or are merely justifications for decisions arrived at on other grounds, which may or may not be revealed in the opinion. This rather cynical view is supported by two observations. One is that for any given maxim that would persuade a judge to a certain conclusion, a contrary maxim may be found that would persuade him to the opposite (or contradictory) conclusion. For instance, the courts often quote the maxim "the court cannot make a contract for the parties," and, somewhat less frequently, they make statements such as: "The law does not favor, but leans against, the destruction of contracts because of uncertainty; and it will, if feasible, so construe agreements as to carry into effect the reasonable intentions of the parties if that [*sic*] can be ascertained."

[The author then provides other possibly contradictory maxims.]

The second reason, referred to above, for believing that the maxims of interpretation are ceremonial rather than persuasive is that in many instances the court will set forth in its opinion the whole battery of maxims and then proceed to decide the case on the basis of an analysis of the terms of the contract and the facts of the dispute, without indicating which maxim or maxims, if any, were applied or invoked in reaching that decision. In a system of law based on judicial precedents, a clear statement of the operative facts and the legal reasons is a part of judicial responsibility. However, the court's awareness of the quoted maxims is a part of the context of its reasoning. Moreover, the lawyers on each side of a controversy would do well to quote to the court the relevant maxims for their positions....

In this brief treatment we can only quote a list of standard maxims, which may not be complete. The ones most often phrased in Latin are given first:

1. *Noscitur a sociis.* The meaning of a word in a series is affected by others in the same series; or, a word may be affected by its immediate context. The example for the next maxim may be taken to illustrate this one.

2. *Ejusdem generis.* A general term joined with a specific one will be deemed to include only things that are like (of the same genus as) the specific one. This one if applied usually leads to a restrictive interpretation. *E.g., S* contracts to sell *B* his farm together with the "cattle, hogs, and other animals." This would probably not include *S*'s favorite house-dog, but might include a few sheep that *S* was raising for the market.

3. *Expressio unius exclusio alterius.* If one or more specific items are listed, without any more general or inclusive terms, other items although similar in kind are excluded. *E.g.,* S contracts to sell B his farm together with "the cattle and hogs on the farm." This language would be interpreted to exclude the sheep and S's favorite house-dog.

4. *Ut magis valeat quam pereat.* By this maxim an interpretation that makes the contract valid is preferred to one that makes it invalid.

5. *Omnia praesumuntur contra proferentem.* This maxim states that if a written contract contains a word or phrase that is capable of two reasonable meanings, one of which favors one party and the other of which favors the other, that interpretation will be preferred which is less favorable to the one by whom the contract was drafted. This maxim favors the party of lesser bargaining power, who has little or no opportunity to choose the terms of the contract, and perforce accepts one drawn by the stronger party. Such "contracts of adhesion" are discussed below. However, the maxim is commonly invoked in cases that do not reveal any disparity of bargaining power between the parties.

6. *Interpret contract as a whole.* A writing or writings that form part of the same transaction should be interpreted together as a whole, that is, every term should be interpreted as a part of the whole and not as if isolated from it. The maxim expresses the contextual theory of meaning, which is, perhaps, a truism.

7. *"Purpose of the parties."* "The principal apparent purpose of the parties is given great weight in determining the meaning to be given to manifestations of intention or to any part thereof." This maxim must be used with caution. In fact, the two parties to a (bargain) contract necessarily have different purposes....

8. *Specific provision is exception to a general one.* If two provisions of a contract are inconsistent with each other and if one is "general" enough to include the specific situation to which the other is confined, the specific provision will be deemed to qualify the more general one, that is, to state an exception to it. A lease of a truck-trailer provided that the lessee should be absolutely liable for loss or damage to the vehicle, yet another clause stated that no party's liability should be increased by this contract. It was held that the former was more specific and therefore controlled the general provision, hence the lessee was liable. A careful draftsman would have stated the former as an exception to the latter, and the court in effect does it for him.

9. *Handwritten or typed provisions control printed provisions.* Where a written contract contains both printed provisions and handwritten or typed provisions, and the two are inconsistent, the handwritten or typed provisions are preferred. This maxim is based on the inference that the language inserted by handwriting or by typewriter for this particular contract is a more recent and more reliable expression of their intentions than is the language of a printed form. While this maxim is used in interpreting insurance contracts and other contracts of adhesion, it is also applicable to all contracts drawn up on a printed form.

10. *Public interest preferred.* If a public interest is affected by a contract, that interpretation or construction is preferred that favors the public interest. The proper

scope of application of this rule seems doubtful. It may have some appropriate uses in construing contracts between private parties. However, as applied to government contracts it would, if applied, be used to save the taxpayers' money as against those contracting with the government. But this is not, it is believed, a standard of interpretation or construction uniformly applied to government contracts.

This battery of maxims is never fired all together. The judge or other interpreter-construer of a contract may, by making prudent choices, possibly obtain some useful guides for his reasoning and justifications for his conclusion.

VI. Contracts of Adhesion and Compulsory Contracts

[We have omitted Patterson's treatment of this topic. Briefly, Patterson notes that if the drafter of a contract was in a stronger bargaining position than the other signer, a court under the influence of twentieth-century views might favor the weaker party whenever possible. This is consistent with the general rule of interpretation favoring construction against the drafter, but is an extension of it. The origins of the idea that there are some contracts — contracts of adhesion — that are in some respects "pretended contracts" seemed to originate in France. A French scholar suggested that those contracts expressing the intentions of only one party (the drafter) should be treated, in a sense, as private legislative enactments. There may be sound reasons, grounded in efficiency concerns, to enforce such contracts, but they threaten assumptions about contract as the expression of two or more parties sharing some common intention. Whether the adhesion contract is subject to different interpretive rules is a question that neither courts nor scholars have answered with any clarity.]

NOTES AND QUESTIONS

1. *Times change?* Professor Edwin Patterson was writing in the 1960s, a time when the view was popular, in law as well as other fields, that language had no natural meaning and always had to be understood in context. He states that the "plain meaning" rule "serves as a last resort," available only when context does not provide another interpretation. As we will see later in this chapter, the idea that language has a natural, or "plain" meaning, which should not be varied by consideration of context, has experienced a revival. While there are still many supporters of the contextual approach to interpretation advocated by Professor Edwin Patterson, there are also numerous supporters of a "plain meaning" approach, also called textualism, to interpretation that would favor resort to evidence about context only "as a last resort" — *i.e.*, when the words used are ambiguous and yield no "plain" meaning.

2. *Llewellyn and the primacy of express terms:* Though Professor Edwin Patterson would clearly be considered in the contextualist school of interpretation today, he ultimately endorses the primacy of express terms (often written terms) in interpretation, as can most clearly be seen in Section IV(C) of his article, where he says that "An alleged usage that contradicts express terms of the contract is to be rejected," citing UCC § 1-205(4). Professor Dennis Patterson has persuasively argued that this interpretation of the UCC is not consistent with the intent or philosophy of Code

architect Karl Llewellyn.[10] Llewellyn believed that contractual obligations should be based on what a reasonable person in the position of the contracting party would understand, and that in ascertaining that understanding, context, especially usages of trade and courses of dealing, were as important as express terms, even written ones. All the evidence needed to be considered in coming to conclusions about the meaning of a contract.

There are many provisions in the Code and its comments that reflect Professor Dennis Patterson's understanding of Llewellyn's intent. Section 1-201(b)(3) defines "Agreement" as "the bargain of the parties *in fact*, as found in their language or by implication from other circumstances including course of performance, course of dealing, or usage of trade" (emphasis supplied).[11] Comment 3 to this section provides "the word [agreement] is intended to include full recognition of usage of trade, course of dealing, course of performance ... and the ... circumstances as effective parts thereof...." The first part of § 1-303(e) reads similarly:[12]

> [T]he express terms of an agreement and any applicable course of performance, course of dealing, or usage of trade must be construed whenever reasonable as consistent with each other. If such a construction is unreasonable: (1) express terms prevail over course of performance, course of dealing, and usage of trade; (2) course of performance prevails over course of dealing and usage of trade; and (3) course of dealing prevails over usage of trade.

Professor Edwin Patterson, in supporting the ultimate primacy of the written word, relies on the ideas in the second sentence. This ordering of the constitutive elements of interpretation, privileging express terms and to a lesser extent course of dealing, is called a "totem pole approach in the analysis of the meaning of agreement" by Professor Dennis Patterson.[13] The totem pole approach to interpretation is arguably supported by the second sentence in § 1-303(e) (as well as by the language of § 2-208(2), which reads similarly), but Professor Dennis Patterson would argue that it conflicts fundamentally with the importance of the Code's definition of "agreement," quoted above.

As you read the next two cases, addressing usages of trade in contract interpretation, consider whether the courts are adopting a "totem pole" approach, giving primacy to express (and here written) terms. Note that these cases cite to the original Article 1 provisions rather than the 2001 revision.

---

10. Dennis Patterson, *Good Faith, Lender Liability, and Discretionary Acceleration: Of Llewellyn, Wittgenstein, and the Uniform Commercial Code*, 68 TEX. L. REV. 169 (1989).

11. We quote here the text of Revised UCC § 1-201(b)(3) (2001). The original Article 1, in § 1-201(3), defined agreement similarly but in slightly different words. Revised Article 1, with some nonuniform variations, had been enacted by about 40 states as of 2010.

12. The counterpart provision in original Article 1, with similar substance but slightly different words, was § 1-205(4).

13. Dennis Patterson, *supra* note 10, at 193.

FEDERAL EXPRESS CORP. v.
PAN AMERICAN WORLD AIRWAYS, INC.

United States Court of Appeals, Eighth Circuit
623 F.2d 1297 (1980)

McMILLIAN, J.

Appellant Federal Express Corporation, which operates an air express cargo service, appeals from a judgment of the district court dismissing its claim of damages for breach of contract in a diversity action against appellee Pan American World Airways, Inc. For the reasons stated below, we affirm.

This case involves contracts for the sale of a particular kind of jet aircraft called the Falcon 20 Jet, manufactured by Avions Marcell Dassault and marketed at the time of the contracts in the United States by the Business Jets division of appellee. The controversy is over a provision in the sales contracts calling for appellee to provide to appellant (the buyer) "initial training" for flight personnel on a "flight simulator," a machine designed to recreate conditions that might be encountered in flight and to test the responses of the trainee. While we do not attempt to detail the facts of the case, which are admirably set forth in the district court's opinion, some background is required for an understanding of the parties' dispute.

Appellant Federal Express came into existence after Frederick W. Smith, a young but experienced pilot and aircraft industry businessman, sought to set up a new kind of air express delivery service. He planned to use Falcon 20 Jets for this purpose, an inventive idea that created a new function for what had been primarily a "corporate jet," normally used by large enterprises for transportation of personnel. Smith took his plan to Mr. C.C. Flemming, an executive officer of the Business Jets division of appellee, who was supportive, and the parties arranged in 1971 for a sale of a total of twenty-five jets, two at once and the other twenty-three for future delivery. After some delays while appellant obtained financing and while regulatory changes were made that enabled appellant to go into business, the twenty-three aircraft were delivered between October 1972, and May 1973.

The contracts called for delivery of the aircraft in a "green" condition, that is, without modifications for appellant's particular needs and without finished instruments or interiors. Appellant subsequently modified the aircraft as they were delivered, with the modifications on the last aircraft completed by December 1974.

The contracts also called for appellee to provide certain training for appellant's personnel, including the "initial training" for aircraft crews on the flight simulator which is at issue in this case. In regard to this training, the schedule provided by appellee with the first two aircraft purchased in 1971 varied from that provided under the contract for the twenty-three aircraft delivered in 1972–73. The training schedule covering the first two aircraft provided:

> Seller shall arrange to provide, at its expense, initial training of flight and maintenance personnel of buyer as follows: … Flight Simulator Training.… Up to 30 hours per crew.…

A similar printed training schedule was appended to the subsequent contract for the twenty-three with a typed alteration in the first sentence to read:

> Seller shall arrange to provide, at its expense, for each Aircraft, initial training of flight and maintenance personnel.…

A modification of this provision occurred in September 1972, when appellant had encountered delays in obtaining financing that postponed the delivery dates envisioned under the contract, and the parties negotiated a letter agreement under which appellant agreed to waive all rights to training under the original contract except the simulator time.

The only flight simulator for the Falcon 20 aircraft in existence at the time of the contract was owned by a firm called Flight Safety, Inc., which had purchased the simulator from appellee. Under terms of the simulator sale, Flight Safety agreed upon notice of appellee to supply to customers of the Business Jets division who purchased Falcon 20 aircraft "initial training" of flight personnel, "including use of the Simulator as necessary," without charge to Business Jets or the customer. Business Jets, however, apparently did not notify Flight Safety, Inc., of the sale to appellant.

Nor did appellant request training until July 1975. In the meantime, appellant made certain other arrangements for training. It set up a Veterans Administration-approved school for veterans who could make use of federal training funds and trained about 400 Falcon Jet pilots, about 200 of whom appellant employed. In 1973, it ordered its own Falcon simulator, a $1.25 million machine, but its financial sources balked and appellant transferred the simulator to Flight Safety, Inc., where it was installed in early 1975. On July 3, 1975, having sold its flight school, appellant contracted with Flight Safety, Inc., to provide simulator training for flight personnel on a continuing basis, allowing appellant 1,000 hours of training a year and covering Falcon Jets as well as other aircraft.

A week later, on July 10, 1975, appellant requested from appellee the "30 hours per crew, per aircraft, for initial flight simulator training" appellant considered itself entitled to under the sales contracts. Appellee refused, and this lawsuit ensued.

The result below hinged upon the meaning of "initial training" of flight personnel in the sales contracts. Appellant urged that the meaning of "initial training" must be taken from the Federal Aviation Administration regulations covering training of flight crew members, which defines "initial training" as that "required for crew members" in order to qualify them for service on a type of aircraft. 14 C.F.R. § 121.400(c)(1) (1979). Under appellant's interpretation, therefore, the phrase "initial training" refers to the status of the crew to be trained, and the "initial training" for pilots provided under the contracts would be available to appellant to train two crew members per aircraft at appellee's expense at any reasonable time upon appellant's demand. The district court found that, under the contracts for the first two aircraft, this interpretation would be proper.

The court also found, however, that the phrase, "for each aircraft, initial training," which appeared in the contract for the additional twenty-three aircraft, was on its face susceptible of a second interpretation, which appellee advanced: whatever training of crew the buyer needed at the time of the purchase to put the aircraft into its initial operation. Under appellee's interpretation, therefore, "initial training" refers to the status of the aircraft, and under the contract training would be available for two crew members per aircraft only as required at the time of purchase to provide an initial crew for appellant to operate the aircraft.

The court concluded that the phrase "initial training" was ambiguous. Applying the law of New York, which has adopted the Uniform Commercial Code, New York Uniform Commercial Code Annotated (McKinney 1964) (hereinafter NYUCC), the court resolved the ambiguity by interpreting the writing in light of trade usage. NYUCC §§ 1-205(4), 2-208(2). Finding that the trade usage was for the seller of this kind of aircraft to provide only initial training for an original crew to put a particular aircraft into service for a buyer, the court interpreted the writing as consistent with this usage....

Appellant argues that the district court erred on three points, each of which requires reversal: (1) appellant contends that the contract was not ambiguous and clearly referred to initial training in the sense of the training required to qualify any crew member; (2) appellant contends that trade usage for sale of a single aircraft as a "corporate jet" does not apply to this sale of a fleet of aircraft intended to be used as cargo vehicles; ... [We omit discussion of appellant's third point.]

As a preliminary matter, we note that the parties agree that New York law controls, and we note also that because the contract was primarily for the sale of goods, NYUCC § 2-105(1), the Uniform Commercial Code applies to it.... We note that the district court decided the case under the Code and neither party challenges the applicability of the Code to this transaction.

Turning to the ambiguity issue, appellant's own argument suggests that the contract was ambiguous. Although appellant contends that the regulation of the Federal Aviation Administration controls the meaning of the parties' written agreement, there is a facial difference between the regulation that defines "initial training" of flight crew and *dispatchers*, 14 C.F.R. § 121.400(c)(1) (1979), and the written sale agreement, which calls for "initial training" of flight crew and *mechanics*. On this basis alone, we would consider some doubt justified that the contract phrase referred to the same thing the FAA regulations referred to. Furthermore, we think it would do violence to the plain sense of the words to read the phrase "for each aircraft, initial training" without understanding the phrase to refer at least ambiguously to the training required for initial use of the aircraft. We therefore fully agree with the district court's conclusion that the contract was ambiguous....

Next, appellant asserts that usage of trade in sales of "corporate jets" was inapplicable to this case, because sale of a whole fleet of aircraft for cargo service is unique and fundamentally different than other sales of single aircraft for personnel transport purposes.[14] In particular, appellant urges that when used as a "corporate jet" the Falcon would only require one flight crew for relatively infrequent use, while the use of Falcons in a cargo business required five or six different flight crews for each aircraft because of much more frequent use. Therefore different training provisions would be anticipated under this sale.

Whatever the validity of this distinction, it does not avail appellant. The critical point is that this transaction involved the same aircraft and virtually the same written agreement as the "corporate jet" sales. The usage in those cases therefore had some relevance to this transaction, and the trial court clearly was correct in considering it. NYUCC § 1-205.... The existence and scope of trade usage is a matter of fact. NYUCC § 1-205(2); 1 R. Anderson, Uniform Commercial Code § 1-205-6. "In case a dominant pattern has been fairly evidenced, the party relying on the usage is entitled to go to the trier of fact on the question of whether such dominant pattern has been incorporated into the agreement." Draftsmen's Comment 9, NYUCC § 1-205. The dominant pattern in this case was the pattern that buyers of Falcon aircraft had a contract right to certain training for the first crew to fly the aircraft. We find no error in the conclusion of the trial court that usage of trade shown by other sales of Falcon Jets was applicable to this contract to explain the meaning of the indefinite term "initial training," and we certainly see no reason to find this conclusion clearly erroneous. Fed. R. Civ. P. 52(a).

Appellant argues that in any event New York law requires construction of ambiguities in a writing against the drafting party. It is true that New York courts have shown some tendency to do so where the party who drafted the agreement takes a position that has little support outside some verbal ambiguity....

But the Uniform Commercial Code specifically requires the written language of the parties' agreement to be construed consistently with applicable trade usage, and this statutory rule of construction must prevail. NYUCC § 1-205....

Accordingly, the judgment of the district court is affirmed.

NOTES AND QUESTIONS

1. *Ambiguity:* Judge McMillian assumes that terms in a contract must be ambiguous before a court can consider evidence such as usage of trade. Is this holding consistent

---

14. [4] Appellant suggests that it was misled at trial by the district court, which indicated at one part of the trial in passing that custom of trade would not be determinative. Appellant asserts that thereafter it considered the case to depend entirely upon the "clear language of the contract." If so, appellant should have looked more closely at the Uniform Commercial Code, which rejects the law of *custom of trade* as a guide to contract meaning, and instead adopts the approach that the language is to be read in light of *trade usage*, a very different approach according to the comments of the code draftsmen. *See* NYUCC § 1-205 and Draftsmen's Comments 4 and 5 to § 1-205. *See generally* [Joseph H.] Levie, *Trade Usage and Custom Under the Common Law and the Uniform Commercial Code*, 40 N.Y.U. L. Rev. 1101 (1965); R. Nordstrom, Handbook of The Law of Sales 157 (1970). Consideration of trade usage was not only consistent with, but also required for, determination under the Code of the meaning of the contract language. NYUCC §§ 1-205, 2-208.

with Llewellyn's view on the proper way to ascertain the meaning of a contract or with the views of Professor Edwin Patterson? In your view, was the written contract ambiguous? Did the term "initial training" have a plain meaning?

2. *Why are usages of trade relevant?* Is trade usage relevant to the interpretation of contracts because a contractual party is so likely to know of the trade usages that the usages are evidence of actual intentions? Or is it because if courts hold people to the usages of their trades, this lowers the cost of transacting business because the outcome of litigation is more predictable, and it also saves valuable court time? Are the reasons consistent? Could it be both reasons? Are there other reasons for believing trade usage relevant?

3. *Which trade usage?* The court resorts to trade usages for the sale of corporate jets. Why did appellant claim that this trade usage was not applicable? Should it matter that the written contract was virtually the same contract that appellee used for the sale of Falcon 20s as corporate jets? The court seems to imply that this fact matters, but do you agree?

During the trial, Frederick W. Smith, the CEO of Federal Express, was asked whether airline crews flew only particular aircraft. He responded:

> No. In that regard, it would probably be the most dramatic difference between corporate and airline-type flying, and *I am very familiar with both of those fields.* In the case of corporate aviation, with a few notable exceptions of some major companies ... generally the business jet operation has a specific crew for a specific aircraft, and as long as these people are employed, they fly the aircraft.... In the airline business, on the other hand, because of the considerably higher utilization of the aircraft ... the crews are never married to the aircraft. They rotate among all of the given aircraft of a given type in the airline's fleet. So the unusual nature of this contract [between Federal Express and Pan American] ... was the fact that the Falcon aircraft for the first time was going to be put into the regime of airline operations.

Does the italicized sentence support the court's resort to trade usages for corporate jet sales?

4. *Construction against the drafter:* Judge McMillian refused to construe the contract against Pan American, the firm that drafted it. He said: "But the Uniform Commercial Code specifically requires the written language of the parties' agreement to be construed consistently with applicable trade usage, and this statutory rule of construction must prevail." Do you agree with this conclusion? Obviously Pan American could have drafted the contract to make more specific that the promised training applied only once per aircraft sold. Does Official Comment 6 to § 1-205 indicate that the maxim of construction about interpreting ambiguities against the drafter should no longer be applied but that tests of good faith and unconscionability must be used instead? Does it make any difference which approach is taken?

5. *Contra Proferentem:* As noted above, this is idea of "construing" an ambiguity "against" the drafter is sometimes referred to by the Latin term "*contra proferentem.*"

In a recent paper,[15] Professors Leib and Thel explore this doctrine. Although usually assumed to be a doctrine meant to protect unsophisticated consumers from contract terms ambiguously drafted by a more sophisticated and/or powerful commercial counterpart (*e.g.*, an insurance company), Leib and Thel find that it can play an important role in disputes among commercial actors, even if equally powerful or sophisticated. "[T]he core focus of a court's decision about the application of *contra proferentem*," they explain—

> turns on whether there was negotiation between the parties and/or joint drafting. Although some courts wonder aloud whether it makes sense to give sophisticated parties the benefit of the rule at all (implicitly assuming the rule serves the interests of nondrafters, not those of drafters), most acknowledge that the weight of authority does not limit the rule's application except in cases of joint negotiation and joint drafting.

> Some courts also focus on whether parties were represented by counsel. But just having a sophisticated nondrafting party isn't enough to form a general exception to the rule. The crux seems to be actual negotiation, deliberation, and dickering over terms.

Do you think there is any role for the *contra proferentem* doctrine—construction against the drafter—when two parties have negotiated the terms of a contract? How is a judge or jury supposed to know which party "drafted" which provision? If it was truly negotiated, would not both parties have contributed to the final language? Contracts sometimes contain clauses that say, in substance, "the parties agree that if there is an ambiguity, this contract will not be construed against either party," attempting to contract out of *contra proferentem*. Could those provisions be found to be ambiguous? If so, what then? Might such questions lead us to think that usage of trade and course of dealing are more efficient interpretive strategies?

6. *An academic challenge to the UCC:* In a series of articles, Professor Lisa Bernstein launched a sophisticated attack on the UCC strategy of encouraging consideration of usage of trade and course of dealing in interpreting contracts (which she calls the "incorporation strategy").[16] Bernstein's first point is that usages of trade are often imprecise. Drawing on impressive empirical studies of several different industries, she notes, as an example, that in the hay industry the term "bale" means different things in different parts of the country, and even in particular localities it may not have a precise definition.[17]

---

15. Ethan J. Leib & Steve Thel, *Contra Proferentem and the Role of the Jury in Contract Interpretation*, 87 Temp. L. Rev. 773, 781–82 (2015).

16. The leading articles are Lisa Bernstein, *Private Commercial Law in the Cotton Industry: Creating Cooperation Through Rules, Norms and Institutions*, 99 Mich. L. Rev. 1724 (2001); Lisa Bernstein, *The Questionable Empirical Basis of Article 2's Incorporation Strategy: A Preliminary Basis*, 66 U. Chi. L. Rev. 710 (1999); and Lisa Bernstein, *Merchant Law in a Merchant Court: Rethinking the Code's Search for Immanent Business Norms*, 144 U. Pa. L. Rev. 1765 (1996).

17. 66 U. Chi. L. Rev. 710, 720–725.

It is widely conceded that Bernstein is correct to point to the vagueness of trade usages in many circumstances. Yet some precise usages clearly exist. Professor Macaulay, in commenting on Professor Bernstein's work, wrote:

> If you go to a lumber yard and ask for a "two by four," the board tendered will not measure two inches by four inches. It will be approximately one and one-half inches by three and one-half inches. I bought a bird feeder that the instructions said was designed to be mounted on a two by four. The mounting bracket is too small to fit a board two inches by four inches, but it fits nicely on a board one and one-half by three and one-half. This suggests that those who made the bird feeder were well aware of the usage of trade.[18]

Bernstein concedes that there are usages of trade, some of them precise, and that some courses of dealing have developed. But she argues that the parties to most contracts would not want these "implicit" rules applied in adjudication, or what she calls "end game situations." There are at least two concerns that she expresses. The first is having to prove the existence of a consistent usage or trade or course of dealing can increase the cost of litigation. Realizing this, in order to simplify litigation, parties may prefer that courts apply a "plain," or at least most evident, meaning of the written contractual language. The second concern is if an established course of dealing can be used to aid in the interpretation of the written language of the contract, in performing contracts one or both parties may be reluctant to grant informal concessions from strict contractual entitlements, for fear that he/she/it will be foreclosed in the future from insisting upon strict compliance with the written language.

We will have occasion to revisit Professor Bernstein's concerns after we read the next case, and then again later in this chapter and in the next chapter.

7. *The jury once again:* Presumably a jury was not impaneled at trial in the *Federal Express* case. If there had been a jury, whose job—judge or jury—would it have been to ascertain the relevant usage of trade? If contractual meaning is to be determined solely from the written language of the contract—as Professor Bernstein might advocate—then the jury would be excluded, since interpretations of writings are considered to raise solely legal issues. It might even be possible to foreclose a trial altogether, deciding the case on summary judgment. No doubt such litigation would be less expensive, but would the result be more just?

8. *Are the common law and the UCC consistent?* We have examined the UCC's approach to interpretation and its endorsement of a broad contextualist approach. The Restatement (Second) of Contracts endorses this approach to interpretation. Consider the following Restatement sections.

§ 220. Usage Relevant to Interpretation

(1) An agreement is interpreted in accordance with a relevant usage if each party knew or had reason to know of the usage and neither party knew or

---

18. Stewart Macaulay, *Relational Contracts Floating on a Sea of Custom? Thoughts about the Ideas of Ian Macneil and Lisa Bernstein*, 94 Nw. U. L. Rev. 775, 787 (2000).

had reason to know that the meaning attached by the other was inconsistent with the usage.

§ 221. Usage Supplementing an Agreement

An agreement is supplemented or qualified by a reasonable usage with respect to agreements of the same type if each party knows or has reason to know of the usage and neither party knows or has reason to know that the other party has an intention inconsistent with the usage.

Despite these Restatement provisions, some commentators assert that the majority common law approach to interpretation takes a textualist approach that privileges the plain or most evident reading of a written contract, avoiding resort to evidence about usages of trade or courses of dealing in most cases.[19] We will return to this issue about the correct characterization of the common law when we consider the parol evidence rule in the next section of this chapter.

NANAKULI PAVING AND ROCK CO. v. SHELL OIL CO.

United States Court of Appeals, Ninth Circuit
664 F.2d 772 (1981)

HOFFMAN, J.

Appellant Nanakuli Paving and Rock Company (Nanakuli) initially filed this breach of contract action against appellee Shell Oil Company (Shell) in Hawaiian State Court in February 1976. Nanakuli, the second largest asphaltic paving contractor in Hawaii, had bought all its asphalt requirements from 1963 to 1974 from Shell under two long-term supply contracts; its suit charged Shell with breach of the later 1969 contract. The jury returned a verdict of $220,800 for Nanakuli on its first claim, which is that Shell breached the 1969 contract in January 1974, by failing to price-protect Nanakuli on 7200 tons of asphalt at the time Shell raised the price for asphalt from $44 to $76. Nanakuli's theory is that price protection, as a usage of the asphaltic paving trade in Hawaii, was incorporated into the 1969 agreement between the parties, as demonstrated by the routine use of price protection by suppliers to that trade, and reinforced by the way in which Shell actually performed the 1969 contract up until 1974. Price protection, appellant claims, required that Shell hold the price on the tonnage Nanakuli had already committed because Nanakuli had incorporated that price into bids put out to or contracts awarded by general contractors and government agencies. The District Judge set aside the verdict and granted Shell's motion for judgment n.o.v., which decision we vacate. We reinstate the jury verdict because we find that, viewing the evidence as a whole, there was substantial evidence to support a finding by reasonable jurors that Shell breached its contract by failing to provide protection for Nanakuli in 1974.... We do not believe the evidence in this case was such that, giving

---

19. *E.g.*, Robert E. Scott, *The Uniformity Norm in Commercial Law: A Comparative Analysis of the Common Law, in* THE JURISPRUDENCE OF CORPORATE AND COMMERCIAL LAW 149 (Jody S. Kraus & Steven D. Walt eds., 2000).

Nanakuli the benefit of all inferences fairly supported by the evidence and without weighing the credibility of the witnesses, only one reasonable conclusion could have been reached by the jury....

Nanakuli offers two theories for why Shell's failure to offer price protection in 1974 was a breach of the 1969 contract. First, it argues, all material suppliers to the asphaltic paving trade in Hawaii followed the trade usage of price protection and thus it should be assumed, under the UCC, that the parties intended to incorporate price protection into their 1969 agreement. This is so, Nanakuli continues, even though the written contract provided for price to be "Shell's Posted Price at time of delivery," F.O.B. Honolulu. Its proof of a usage that was incorporated into the contract is reinforced by evidence of the commercial context, which under the UCC should form the background for viewing a particular contract. The full agreement must be examined in light of the close, almost symbiotic relations between Shell and Nanakuli on the island of Oahu, whereby the expansion of Shell on the island was intimately connected to the business growth of Nanakuli. The UCC looks to the actual performance of a contract as the best indication of what the parties intended those terms to mean. Nanakuli points out that Shell had price-protected it on the two occasions of price increases under the 1969 contract other than the 1974 increase. In 1970 and 1971 Shell extended the old price for four and three months, respectively, after an announced increase. This was done, in the words of Shell's agent in Hawaii, in order to permit Nanakuli to "chew up" tonnage already committed at Shell's old price.[20]

Nanakuli's second theory for price protection is that Shell was obliged to price-protect Nanakuli, even if price protection was not incorporated into their contract, because price protection was the commercially reasonable standard for fair dealing in the asphaltic paving trade in Hawaii in 1974. Observance of those standards is part of the good-faith requirement that the Code imposes on merchants in performing a sales contract. Shell was obliged to price protect Nanakuli in order to act in good faith, Nanakuli argues, because such a practice was universal in that trade in that locality.

Shell presents three arguments for upholding the judgment n.o.v. or, on cross-appeal, urging that the District Judge erred in admitting certain evidence. First, it says, the District Court should not have denied Shell's motion *in limine* to define trade, for purposes of trade usage evidence, as the sale and purchase of asphalt in Hawaii, rather than expanding the definition of trade to include other suppliers of materials to the asphaltic paving trade. Asphalt, its argument runs, was the subject matter of the disputed contract and the only product Shell supplied to the asphaltic paving trade.[21] Shell protests that the judge, by expanding the definition of trade to

---

20. [4] Price protection was practiced in the asphaltic paving trade by either extending the old price for a period of time after a new one went into effect or charging the old price for a specified tonnage, which represented work committed at the old price. In addition, several months' advance notice was given of price increases.

21. [5] Shell's argument would, in effect, eliminate all trade usage evidence. First, it argues that its own acts were irrelevant as mere waivers, not acts in the course of the performance of the contract. Second, it contends that all acts of price protection by the only other asphalt supplier in Hawaii,

include the other major suppliers to the asphaltic paving trade, allowed the admission of highly prejudicial evidence of routine price protection by all suppliers of aggregate. Asphaltic concrete paving is formed by mixing paving asphalt with crushed rock, or aggregate, in a "hot-mix" plant and then pouring the mixture onto the surface to be paved. Shell's second complaint is that the two prior occasions on which it price-protected Nanakuli, although representing the only other instances of price increases under the 1969 contract, constituted mere waivers of the contract's price term, not a course of performance of the contract. A course of performance of the contract, in contrast to a waiver, demonstrates how the parties understand the terms of their agreement. Shell cites two UCC Comments in support of that argument: (1) that, when the meaning of acts is ambiguous, the preference is for the waiver interpretation, and (2) that one act alone does not constitute a relevant course of performance. Shell's final argument is that, even assuming its prior price protection constituted a course of performance and that the broad trade definition was correct and evidence of trade usages by aggregate suppliers was admissible, price protection could not be construed as reasonably consistent with the express price term in the contract, in which case the Code provides that the express term controls.

We hold that the judge did not abuse his discretion in defining the applicable trade, for purposes of trade usages, as the asphaltic paving trade in Hawaii, rather than the purchase and sale of asphalt alone, given the unusual, not to say unique, circumstances.... Additionally, we hold that, under the facts of this case, a jury could reasonably have found that Shell's acts on two occasions to price-protect Nanakuli were not ambiguous and therefore indicated Shell's understanding of the terms of the agreement with Nanakuli, rather than being a waiver by Shell of those terms.

Lastly we hold that, although the express price terms of Shell's posted price of delivery may seem, at first glance, inconsistent with a trade usage of price protection at time of increases in price, a closer reading shows that the jury could have reasonably construed price protection as consistent with the express term.... Our decision is reinforced by the overwhelming nature of the evidence that price protection was routinely practiced by all suppliers in the small Oahu market of the asphaltic paving trade and therefore was known to Shell; that it was a realistic necessity to operate in that market and thus vital to Nanakuli's ability to get large government contracts and to Shell's continued business growth on Oahu; and that it therefore constituted an intended part of the agreement, as that term is broadly defined by the Code, between Shell and Nanakuli.

I. History Of Nanakuli-Shell Relations Before 1973

Nanakuli, a division of Grace Brothers, Ltd., a Hawaiian corporation, is the smaller of the two major paving contractors on the island of Oahu, the larger of the two

Chevron, the marketing division of Standard Oil Company, were irrelevant to prove trade usage because Chevron at one time owned all or part of the paving company it supplied and routinely price-protected Hawaiian Bitumuls (H.B.). The court correctly refused to bar that evidence since the one-time relationship between the two went to the weight, not the admissibility, of the evidence. Nanakuli was given permission to offer evidence in rebuttal that Chevron price-protected other customers in California with whom it had no such relationship in the event Shell tried to impeach that evidence.

being Hawaiian Bitumuls (H.B.). Nanakuli first entered the paving business on Oahu in 1948, but it only began to move into the largest Oahu market, Honolulu, in the mid-1950s. Until 1964 or so, Nanakuli only got small paving jobs, such as service stations, driveways, and small subdivision streets; it was not in a position to compete with H.B. for government contracts for major roads, airports, and other large jobs. In the early sixties Nanakuli owner Walter Grace began to negotiate a mutually advantageous arrangement with Shell whereby Shell, which had a small market percentage and no asphalt terminals in Hawaii, would sign a long-term supply contract with Nanakuli that would commit Nanakuli to buy its asphalt requirements from Shell. On the other hand, Nanakuli would be helped to expand its paving business on Oahu through a guaranteed supply and a discount on its asphalt prices. Nanakuli's growth would expand the market for Shell's asphalt on the island, which would justify Shell's capital investment of half a million dollars on Oahu, to which asphalt would be brought in heated tankers from Shell's refinery in Martinez, California.

Shell signed two five-year contracts in 1963: a supply contract with Nanakuli itself and a distributorship with Grace, which provided for a $2 commission on all Nanakuli's sales. In fact, almost all Nanakuli's sales were to itself and thus the commission operated, according to Shell's Hawaiian representative, Bohner, primarily as a discount mechanism. Lennox, who succeeded Grace as president in 1965 at Grace's death,[22] testified that its purpose was "to make us competitive in our paving operation with our competitor [H.B.] who is much larger than ourselves because they were a distributor for the Standard Oil Company's asphalt operation." Lennox and Smith, who joined Nanakuli as vice-president in 1965 and eventually succeeded Lennox, both saw Nanakuli's and Shell's relationship as that of partners. That characterization was not denied by Bohner, Shell's Hawaiian representative from 1964 to 1978, who, in fact, essentially corroborated their description of the close relations between the two companies. As a symbol of that relationship, Nanakuli painted its trucks "Shell white," placed Shell's logo on those trucks, chose the same orange as used by Shell for its own logo, and put the Shell logo on its stationery.

In 1966 Pacific Cement and Aggregates (P.C. & A.), Nanakuli's landlord at its rented rock quarry at Halawa, was bought by Lone Star Cement Corporation, which later became Lone Star Industries. Lone Star requested that Nanakuli upgrade its plant facilities at the quarry, which Nanakuli estimated would cost between $250,000 to $300,000. Nanakuli, knowing Shell was eager to build up its paving business on Oahu, approached Shell for direct financing of the plant, an idea to which Shell was initially receptive. Lennox testified that Shell "had a sizeable installation at Iwilei and they didn't think we were selling enough of their product and they wanted us to sell more and that's why we enlarged our plant." Shell management philosophy later changed and it was decided not to finance the plant directly but rather to offer Nanakuli an additional $2 volume discount on all sales over five thousand tons to

---

22. [11] After Grace died, new supply and distributorship contracts were signed, the latter substituting Nanakuli for Grace as Oahu distributor for Shell.

help finance the plant, according to Bohner. Lennox testified that Shell authorized Nanakuli to tell Lone Star that Shell, with a million-dollar investment in Hawaii, fully supported Nanakuli's plant expansion plans. In 1968 two top Shell asphalt officials came from the mainland to discuss Nanakuli's expansion: Blee from San Francisco and Lewis from New York.[23] Together with Bohner and Nanakuli's Lennox and Smith, they met with officials of Nanakuli's bank to discuss the loan and repayment schedule. The three contracts were finally signed after long negotiations on April 1, 1969. They were to parallel the amortization schedule of the bank loan for the plant: a supply contract, a distributorship contract, and volume discount letter, all three to last until December 31, 1975, at which point each would have the option to cancel on six months' notice, with a minimum duration of over seven years, April 1, 1969, to July 1, 1976. Such long-term contracts were certainly unusual for Shell and this one was probably unique among Shell's customers, at least by 1974.

Lennox's testimony, which was partially stricken by the court as inadmissible, was that Shell's agreement with Nanakuli in 1969 included a commitment by Shell never to charge Nanakuli more than Chevron charged H.B., in order to carry out the underlying purpose of the agreement to make Nanakuli competitive with H.B. and thus expand its and Shell's respective businesses on Oahu. This testimony was ruled inadmissible as parol evidence.[24] ... Nanakuli's offer of proof by Lennox was that Shell agreed "to sustain that price during those contracts in the same way in which Standard Oil Company [Chevron] sustained its price to the principal paving contractor on the island, Hawaiian Bitumuls, if there was any price increase" and to "not exceed Standard Oil's [Chevron's] posted price for asphalt sold to Hawaiian Bitumuls." It was agreed that Nanakuli would have to submit bids on a fixed-price basis and be price-protected to compete with H.B. "We understood that Shell gave us the same protection in our bidding and our purchase of asphalt from them to incorporate in our work," Lennox did testify, adding that by that means Nanakuli could compete with H.B. and Shell would thereby benefit. He said Nanakuli understood the price term to mean that Shell would not increase prices without advance notice and would hold the price on work bid for enough time to allow Nanakuli to use up the tonnage bid at the old price. Smith's testimony backed up that of Lennox: the price was to be "posted price as bid as was understood between the parties," further explaining that it was to be Shell's price at time and place of delivery, except for price increases, at which point the price was time and place of bid for a period of time or a specified tonnage....[25]

_____

23. [12] The hierarchical structure was that Bohner reported to Blee, who reported to Lewis.

24. Eds. note: We will cover the parol evidence rule later in this chapter. The discussion of it in this opinion is omitted. One effect of the application of the parol evidence rule by the trial court was to exclude consideration of course of dealing evidence. That is why the opinion excerpted here discusses just trade usage evidence.

25. [16] The principal reason the judge initially refused to allow any such testimony and one major reason for his inclination to grant the defendant's motion for a directed verdict, was his belief that there was no ambiguity in the express price term of "posted price at time of delivery." He was reluctantly persuaded to allow the evidence because of Shell's answer to interrogatory 11, asking its understanding of the contract term, that it had never had a posted price although it did have a list price.

II. Trade Usage Before And After 1969

The key to price protection being so prevalent in 1969 that both parties would intend to incorporate it into their contract is found in one reality of the Oahu asphaltic paving market: the largest paving contracts were let by government agencies and none of the three levels of government—local, state, or federal—allowed escalation clauses for paving materials. If a paver bid at one price and another went into effect before the award was made, the paving company would lose a great deal of money, since it could not pass on increases to any government agency or to most general contractors. Extensive evidence was presented that, as a consequence, aggregate suppliers routinely price-protected paving contractors in the 1960s and 1970s, as did the largest asphaltic supplier in Oahu, Chevron. Nanakuli presented documentary evidence of routine price protection by aggregate suppliers.... The smallness of the Oahu market led to complete trust among suppliers and pavers.... None of the aggregate companies had a contract with Nanakuli expressly stating price protection would be given; Nanakuli's contract with P.C. & A. merely set out that P.C. & A. would not charge Nanakuli more than it charged its other customers....

[The court summarized evidence that Chevron had given price protection to H.B., and that there was no mention of price protection in the written contract between H.B. and Chevron.]

In addition to evidence of trade usages existing in 1969 when the contract at issue was signed, the District Judge let in evidence of the continuation of that trade usage after 1969, over Shell's protest. He stated that, giving a liberal reading to § 1-205, he felt that later evidence was relevant to show that the expectation of the parties that a given usage would be observed was justified. The basis for incorporating a trade usage into a contract under the UCC is the justifiable expectation of the parties that it will be observed. That later evidence consisted here of more price protection by the aggregate companies on Oahu, as well as continued asphalt price protection. Chevron after 1969 continued price-protecting H.B. on Oahu and, on raising prices in 1979, price-protected Nanakuli on the island of Molokai, where Nanakuli purchased its asphalt from Chevron. Additionally, Shell price-protected Nanakuli in 1977 and 1978 on Oahu.[26]

The court stated its doubts about Nanakuli's case at the time it denied Shell's directed verdict motion: lack of ambiguity in the express term and inconsistency between the trade usage of that term. When first requested to allow evidence of prior dealings the judge asked, "Can you point out what terms [in the written contract] are supposed to be ambiguous?" However, the Code lets in evidence of prior dealings, usage, and performance under § 2-202(a) even if the contract terms are clear: "This section definitely rejects: ... (c) The requirement that a condition precedent to the admissibility of the type of evidence specified in paragraph (a) is an original determination by the court that the language used is ambiguous." Haw. Rev. Stat. § 490:2-202, Comment 1.

26. [17] We do not need to decide whether usage evidence after a contract was signed is admissible to show that a party's reliance on a given usage was justifiable, given its continuation, because part of that evidence dealing with asphalt prices was admissible to show the reasonably commercial standards of fair dealing prevalent in the trade in 1974, and the part dealing with the continuation of price protection by aggregate suppliers after 1969 was not so extensive as to be prejudicial to Shell.

III. Shell's Course Of Performance of the 1969 Contract

The Code considers actual performance of a contract as the most relevant evidence of how the parties interpreted the terms of that contract. In 1970 and 1971, the only points at which Shell raised prices between 1969 and 1974, it price-protected Nanakuli by holding its old price for four and three months, respectively, after announcing a price increase. In the late summer of 1970, Shell had announced a price increase from $35 to $40 a ton effective September 1, 1970. When Nanakuli protested to Bohner that it should be price-protected on work already committed, Blee wrote Bohner an in-house memo that, if Bohner could not "convince" Nanakuli to go along with the price increase on September 1, he should try to "bargain" to get Nanakuli to accept the price raise by at least the first of the year, which was what was finally agreed upon. During that four-month period, Nanakuli bought 3,300 tons. Shell announced a second increase in October 1970, from $40 to $42 effective December 31st. Before that increase went into effect, on November 25 Shell increased the raise to $4, making the price $44 as of the first of the year.[27] Shell again agreed to price-protect Nanakuli by holding the price at $40, which had been the official price since September 1, for three months from January to March, 1971. Shell did not actually raise prices again until January 1974, but at several points it believed that increases would be necessary and gave several months' advance notice of those possible increases. Those actions were in accord with Shell's own policy, as professed by Bohner, and that of other asphalt and aggregate suppliers: to give at least several months' advance notice of price increases. On January 14, 1971, Shell wrote its asphalt customers that the maximum 1971 increase would be to $46. On July 9, 1971, another letter promised the price would not go over $50 in 1972. In addition, Bohner volunteered on direct the information that Shell price-protected Nanakuli on the only two occasions of price increases after 1974 by giving six months' advance notice in 1977 and three or four months' advance notice in 1978, a practice he described as "in effect carry-over pricing," his term for price protection. By its actions, Bohner testified, Shell allowed Nanakuli time to make arrangements to buy up tonnage committed at the old price, that is, to "chew up" tonnage bid or contracted.

IV. Shell-Nanakuli Relations, 1973–74

Two important factors form the backdrop for the 1974 failure by Shell to price-protect Nanakuli: the Arab oil embargo and a complete change of command and policy in Shell's asphalt management. The jury was read a page or so from the World Book about the events and effect of the partial oil embargo, which shortened supplies and increased the price of petroleum, of which asphalt is a byproduct. The federal government imposed direct price controls on petroleum, but not on asphalt. Despite the international importance of those events, the jury may have viewed the second factor as of more direct significance to this case. The structural changes at Shell offered a possible explanation for why Shell in 1974 acted out of step with, not only the trade

---

27. [18] That November letter also announced a "new pricing policy" of Shell, setting out a requirement that firm contractual commitments be made with Shell within 15 days of accepting a bid.

usage and commercially reasonable practices of all suppliers to the asphaltic paving trade on Oahu, but also with its previous agreement with, or at least treatment of, Nanakuli.

Bohner testified to a big organizational change at Shell in 1973 when asphalt sales were moved from the construction sales to the commercial sales department. In addition, by 1973 the top echelon of Shell's asphalt sales had retired. Lewis and Blee, who had negotiated the 1969 contract with Nanakuli, were both gone.[28] Their duties were taken over by three men: Fuller in San Mateo, California, District Manager for Shell Sales, Lawson, and Chippendale, who was Shell's regional asphalt manager in Houston. When the philosophy toward asphalt pricing changed, apparently no one was left who was knowledgeable about the peculiarities of the Hawaiian market or about Shell's long-time relations with Nanakuli or its 1969 agreement, beyond the printed contract.

Shell had begun rethinking its asphalt pricing policies several years before. Swanson, who succeeded Lewis in New York in 1970, wrote an internal memorandum on April 21, 1970, in which he discussed frankly the advantages and disadvantages of price protection of its asphalt buyers. Such a practice assured Shell of captive-volume sales, he wrote. The practice of granting carry-over pricing at times of price increases, however, had the unfortunate side effect of depressing prices in the asphalt market everywhere else, the memorandum concluded. This rethinking apparently led to a November 25, 1970, letter setting out "Shell's New Pricing Policy" at its Honolulu and Hilo terminals. The letter explained the elimination of price protection: "In other words, we will no longer guarantee asphalt prices for the duration of any particular construction projects or for the specific lengths of time. We will, of course, honor any existing prices which have been committed for specific projects for which we have firm contractual commitments." The letter requested a supply contract be signed with Shell within 15 days of the receipt of an award by a customer.

The District Judge based his grant of judgment n.o.v. largely on his belief that, had Nanakuli desired price protection, it should have complied with Shell's request in that 1970 letter, by which we assume he meant Nanakuli should have made a firm contractual commitment with Shell for each project on which its bid was successful within 15 days of award. That conclusion, however, ignores several facts. First, compliance by Nanakuli with the letter's demand that a contract be signed within 15 days of an award would have offered Nanakuli little, if any, protection. Nanakuli still would have been stuck with only charging the government the price incorporated into its bid if Shell raised its price between bid and award. The purpose of price protection was to guarantee the price in effect when a paver made a bid because of the often lengthy time span between bid and award. Second, if price protection was a part of Nanakuli's 1969 agreement with Shell, Shell had no right to terminate unilaterally that protection. Third, the letter was addressed to "Gentlemen" with Nanakuli's name

28. [19] Lewis had left earlier, his position in New York having been taken over by Swanson. Later a Houston office took charge of asphalt sales for Nanakuli's region.

typed in at the top; it was apparently addressed to all Shell's Hawaiian customers. Fourth, Nanakuli officials testified that they did not believe the letter was applicable to its unusual situation of already having a long-term contract with Shell. Smith and Lennox both testified that they did not view the letter as applicable to that supply contract but only to sales it might make to third parties under the distributorship contract. Shell characterized that argument as disingenuous, given Nanakuli's infrequent, if not nonexistent, sales to third parties. Nevertheless, the letter does assume that a Shell customer would need to sign a contract or purchase order setting forth the terms of sale as well as the price for any asphalt they would need to buy after an award. Nanakuli, on the other hand, already had a supply contract with all the terms of sales set forth, a point its two officials made repeatedly at trial. For example, Smith testified he saw no need to notify Shell because Bohner knew of each project and because the supply contract was a firm contractual commitment with Shell.[29] Shell had added in the 1970 letter: "All previous contractual commitments made prior to the date of this letter will, of course, be honored." Smith's reading of this was that Nanakuli's supply contract with Shell *was* a firm contractual commitment by Shell and that no further contract was needed. "We felt that this letter was unapplicable [*sic*] to our supply contract, that we already had a contractual commitment with Shell Oil Company which was not to end before 1975." Smith said he did not discuss with Bohner that part of the letter that also announced the increase in asphalt prices to $44 on January 1, because "[t]here was no need to. The price had been protected before. He knew it. We knew it…." Given Nanakuli's particular agreement, as it understood the agreement to be, the jury could have believed that Nanakuli officials reacted reasonably in believing that parts of the letter dealing with the need to notify Shell of awards won did not apply to Nanakuli.

Nanakuli's strongest argument as to its failure to comply with the letter was that there was no need to notify Shell, as Bohner already knew of each project as it was bid and each award as it was made. Lennox testified: "The Shell Oil representative was in our office frequently and knew what jobs we had successfully bid." At another point Lennox said: "The Shell representative was in the office and was fully aware of what we were doing and what jobs we had gotten. He was familiar and was more or less a partner in this thing; he even attended the bid openings at times. He was fully aware and congratulated us every time we got a nice big job because it was more for Shell." Bohner kept his principals informed of Nanakuli's projects, Lennox said. He added, "[W]e had always been protected and our understanding was that we were protected and it wasn't necessary to keep making notices." Smith in his deposition said that Bohner only told him that he lacked the authority to grant price protection "after the fact." Since he knew nothing about how Shell arrived at its pricing, Smith assumed Bohner could carry out Shell's agreement to price-protect Nanakuli each time it was needed without consulting the mainland.

---

29. [22] "We already had a supply contract. Why would we need another supply contract?" Smith asked. "There was no need to write. We had our supply contract. We didn't need to enter a new contract with the Shell Oil Company with every successful project."

After Shell's December 31, 1973, letter arrived on January 4, 1974 [raising the price from $44 to $76], Smith called Bohner, as he had done before at times of price increases, to ask for price protection, this time on 7200 tons. Bohner told Smith that he would have to get in touch with the mainland, but he expected that the response would be negative. Smith wrote several letters in January and February asking for price protection. After getting no satisfaction, he finally flew to California to meet with Lawson, Fuller, and Chippendale. Chippendale, from the Houston office, was acknowledged by the other two to be the only person with authority to grant price protection. All three Shell officials lacked any understanding of Nanakuli and Shell's long, unique relationship or of the asphaltic trade in Oahu. They had never even seen Shell's contracts with Nanakuli before the meeting. When apprised of the three and their seven-year duration, Fuller remarked on the unusual nature of Nanakuli's relations with Shell, at least within his district. Chippendale felt it was probably unique for Shell anywhere. Smith testified that Fuller admitted to knowing nothing, beyond the printed page of Nanakuli's agreement with Shell, of the background negotiation or Shell's past pricing policies toward Nanakuli. Chippendale could not understand why Nanakuli even had a distributorship contract giving it a $2 commission on sales; he thought Nanakuli had been paid "illegally." No one had ever heard about Shell giving price protection to Nanakuli before. Instead of asking Bohner directly, Chippendale told Fuller to search the files for something on paper. Fuller testified that Shell would not act without *written* proof of Shell's past price protection of Nanakuli. He admitted he was unable to find anything in the files before 1972 because the departments had been reorganized in that year, about which he informed Chippendale. Chippendale accordingly decided to deny Nanakuli any price protection and wrote a draft of a letter for Fuller to send Nanakuli. He wrote a note to Fuller that he should adopt the "least said" approach with Nanakuli and check any letters with the legal department. When asked at trial if he had ever simply asked Bohner about Shell's past pricing practices toward Nanakuli, Fuller answered, "No, I didn't know we had it, other than the standard policy if we had one which we didn't."[30] Chippendale told Smith in the California meeting that, although 7200 tons represented an infinitesimal amount for Shell, it would set a bad precedent for Shell, since price protection was not Shell's "*current* policy" (emphasis supplied). Shell people told him, Smith testified from contemporaneously made notes, that "any past practice was inapplicable at the present time."[31] Smith testified from those same notes that he had left the meeting under the impression that Shell was going out of business in Hawaii.

---

30. [24] Fuller only found out the background to the Shell-Nanakuli 1969 agreement and Shell's past price protection of Nanakuli in an August 11, 1974, in-house memo from Bohner. Bohner explained in that memo that Shell only built its two terminals in Hawaii in 1963 because of long-time firm commitments from Nanakuli on Oahu and James W. Glover, Ltd., at Hilo....

31. [25] ... Smith testified that Chippendale told him to try to pass on the asphalt price increases, which Nanakuli unsuccessfully tried to do. Smith wrote Chippendale on February 14, "Our attempts ... have met with utmost resistance and threats of litigation." By December 1973, Nanakuli, in reaction to Shell's November letter, had already begun inserting escalation clauses in its contract bids, which

We conclude that the decision to deny Nanakuli price protection was made by new Houston management without a full understanding of Shell's 1969 agreement with Nanakuli or any knowledge of its past pricing practices toward Nanakuli. If Shell did commit itself in 1969 to price-protect Nanakuli, the Shell officials who made the decisions affecting Nanakuli in 1974 knew nothing about that commitment. Nor did they make any effective effort to find out. They acted instead solely in reliance on the 1969 contract's express price term, devoid of the commercial context that the Code says is necessary to an understanding of the meaning of the written word. Whatever the legal enforceability of Nanakuli's right, Nanakuli officials seem to have acted in good faith reliance on its right, as they understood it, to price protection and rightfully felt betrayed by Shell's failure to act with any understanding of its past practices toward Nanakuli.

V. Scope Of Trade Usage

The validity of the jury verdict in this case depends on four legal questions. First, how broad was the trade to whose usages Shell was bound under its 1969 agreement with Nanakuli: did it extend to the Hawaiian asphaltic paving trade or was it limited merely to the purchase and sale of asphalt, which would only include evidence of practices by Shell and Chevron? Second, were the two instances of price protection of Nanakuli by Shell in 1970 and 1971 waivers of the 1969 contract as a matter of law or was the jury entitled to find that they constituted a course of performance of the contract? Third, could the jury have construed an express contract term of Shell's posted price at delivery as reasonably consistent with a trade usage and Shell's course of performance of the 1969 contract of price protection, which consisted of charging the old price at times of price increases, either for a period of time or for specific tonnage committed at a fixed price in non-escalating contracts? Fourth, could the jury have found that good faith obliged Shell to at least give advance notice of a $32 increase in 1974, that is, could they have found that the commercially reasonable standards of fair dealing in the trade in Hawaii in 1974 were to give some form of price protection?

We approach the first issue in this case mindful that an underlying purpose of the UCC as enacted in Hawaii is to allow for liberal interpretation of commercial usages. The Code provides: "This chapter shall be liberally construed and applied to promote its underlying purposes and policies." Haw. Rev. Stat. §490:1-102(1). Only three purposes are listed, one of which is "[t]o permit the continued expansion of commercial practices through custom, usage and agreement of the parties; ..." Id. §490:1-102(2)(b).

The Code defines usage of trade as "any practice or method of dealing having such regularity of observance in a *place, vocation, or trade* as to justify an expectation that it will be observed with respect to the transaction in question." Id. §490:1-205(2) (emphasis supplied). We understand the use of the word "or" to mean that parties can be bound by a usage common to the *place* they are in business, even if it is not the usage of their particular vocation or trade.... This language indicates that Shell would be bound not only by usages of sellers of asphalt but by more general usages

---

were mostly rejected. By March 1974, local and state governments allowed such clauses for paving materials, although the federal government still does not allow escalation clauses for asphalt.

on Oahu, as long as those usages were so regular in their observance that Shell should have been aware of them. This reading of the Code, in our opinion, achieves an equitable result. A party is always held to conduct generally observed by members of his chosen trade because the other party is justified in so assuming unless he indicates otherwise. He is held to more general business practices to the extent of his actual knowledge of those practices or to the degree his ignorance of those practices is not excusable: they were so generally practiced he should have been aware of them.

... [E]ven if Shell did not "regularly deal" with aggregate supplies, it did deal constantly and almost exclusively on Oahu with one asphalt paver. It therefore should have been aware of the usage of Nanakuli and other asphaltic pavers to bid at fixed prices and therefore receive price protection from their materials suppliers due to the refusal by government agencies to accept escalation clauses. Therefore, we do not find the lower court abused its discretion or misread the Code as applied to the peculiar facts of this case in ruling that the applicable trade was the asphaltic paving trade in Hawaii. An asphalt seller should be held to the usages of trade in general as well as those of asphalt sellers and common usages of those to whom they sell. Certainly, under the unusual facts of this case it was not unreasonable for the judge to extend trade usages to include practices of other material suppliers toward Shell's primary and perhaps only customer on Oahu. He did exclude, on Shell's motion *in limine*, evidence of cement suppliers. He only held Shell to routine practices in Hawaii by the suppliers of the two major ingredients of asphaltic paving, that is, asphalt and aggregate. Those usages were only practiced towards two major pavers. It was not unreasonable to expect Shell to be knowledgeable about so small a market. In so ruling, the judge undoubtedly took into account Shell's half-million dollar investment in Oahu strictly because of a long-term commitment to Nanakuli, its actions as partner in promoting Nanakuli's expansion on Oahu, and the fact that its sales on Oahu were almost exclusively to Nanakuli for use in asphaltic paving. The wisdom of the pre-trial ruling was demonstrated by evidence at trial that Shell's agent in Hawaii stayed in close contact with Nanakuli and was knowledgeable about both the asphaltic paving market in general and Nanakuli's bidding procedures and economics in particular.

Shell argued not only that the definition of trade was too broad, but also that the practice itself was not sufficiently regular to reach the level of a usage and that Nanakuli failed to show with enough precision how the usage was carried out in order for a jury to calculate damages. The extent of a usage is ultimately a jury question. The Code provides: "The existence and scope of such a usage are to be proved as facts." Haw. Rev. Stat. § 490:1-205(2).[32] The practice must have "such regularity of observance ... as to justify an expectation that it will be observed...." *Id.* The Comment explains:

> Therefore, it is not required that a usage of trade be "ancient or immemorial," "universal," or the like.... [F]ull recognition is thus available for new usages and for usages currently observed by the great majority of decent dealers, even though dissidents ready to cut corners do not agree. *Id.*, Comment 5.

---

32. [27] Written trade codes, however, are left to the court to interpret. *Id.*

The Comment's demand that "not universality but only the described 'regularity of observance'" is required reinforces the provision only giving "effect to usages of which the parties 'are or should be aware.' ..." *Id.*, Comment 7. A "regularly observed" practice of protection, of which Shell "should have been aware," was enough to constitute a usage that Nanakuli had reason to believe was incorporated into the agreement.[33]

Nanakuli went beyond proof of a regular observance. It proved ... that price protection was probably universal practice by suppliers to the asphaltic paving trade in 1969.[34] It had been practiced by H.C. & D. since at least 1962, by P.C. & A. since well before 1960, and by Chevron routinely for years, with the last specific instance before the contract being March 1969, as shown by documentary evidence. The only usage evidence missing was the behavior by Shell, the only other asphalt supplier in Hawaii, prior to 1969. That was because its only major customer was Nanakuli and the judge ruled prior course of dealings between Shell and Nanakuli inadmissible. Shell did not point in rebuttal to one instance of failure to price-protect by any supplier to an asphalt paver in Hawaii before its own 1974 refusal to price-protect Nanakuli. Thus, there clearly was enough proof for a jury to find that the practice of price protection in the asphaltic paving trade existed in Hawaii in 1969 and was regular enough in its observance to rise to the level of a usage that would be binding on Nanakuli and Shell.

Shell next argues that, even if such a usage existed, its outlines were not precise enough to determine whether Shell would have extended the old price for Nanakuli for several months or would have charged the old price on the volume of tonnage committed at that price. The jury awarded Nanakuli damages based on the specific tonnage committed before the price increase of 1974. [The court considers Code Sections and Comments that eliminate the need to prove usages and related damages with "mathematical accuracy."] The manner in which the usage of price protection was carried out was presented with sufficient precision to allow the jury to calculate damages at $220,800.

VI. Waiver or Course of Performance

Course of performance under the Code is the action of the parties in carrying out the contract at issue, whereas course of dealing consists of relations between the parties *prior* to signing that contract. Evidence of the latter was excluded by the District Judge; evidence of the former consisted of Shell's price protection of Nanakuli in 1970 and 1971. Shell protested that the jury could not have found that those two instances of price protection amounted to a course of performance of its 1969 contract, relying on two Code comments. First, one instance does not constitute a course of

---

33. [28] White and Summers write that Code requirements for proving a usage are "far less stringent" than the old ones for custom. "A usage of trade need not be *well known*, let alone 'universal.'" It only needs to be regular enough that the parties expect it to be observed. White & Summers, *supra* §3-3 at 87 (emphasis supplied). "Note particularly [in §§ 1-205(1) & (2)] that it is not necessary for both parties to be consciously aware of the trade usage. It is enough if the trade usage is such as to 'justify an expectation' of its observance." *Id.* at 84.

34. [30] All evidence was that trade usage continued to be universally practiced after 1969, even by Shell.

performance. "A single occasion of conduct does not fall within the language of this section...." Haw. Rev. Stat. §490:2-208, Comment 4. Although the Comment rules out one instance, it does not further delineate how many acts are needed to form a course of performance. The prior occasions here were only two, but they constituted the only occasions before 1974 that would call for such conduct. [The court discusses another occasion Shell seemed in discussions to have recognized Nanakuli's right to price protection.]

Shell's second defense is that the Comment expresses a preference for an interpretation of waiver.

> 3. Where it is difficult to determine whether a particular act merely sheds light on the meaning of the agreement or represents a waiver of a term of the agreement, the preference is in favor of "waiver" whenever such construction, plus the application of the provisions on the reinstatement of rights waived.... is needed to preserve the flexible character of commercial contracts and to prevent surprise or other hardship. *Id.*, Comment 3.

The preference for waiver only applies, however, where acts are ambiguous. It was within the province of the jury to determine whether those acts were ambiguous, and if not, whether they constituted waivers or a course of performance of the contract. The jury's interpretation of those acts as a course of performance was bolstered by evidence offered by Shell that it again price-protected Nanakuli on the only two occasions of post-1974 price increases, in 1977 and 1978.

VII. Express Terms as Reasonably Consistent With Usage on Course of Performance

Perhaps one of the most fundamental departures of the Code from prior contract law is found in ... the definition of an agreement between two parties. Under the UCC, an agreement goes beyond the written words on a piece of paper. "'Agreement' means the bargain of the parties in fact as found in their language or by implication from other circumstances including course of dealing or usage of trade or course of performance as provided in this chapter (§§ 490:1-205 and 490:2-208)." *Id.* § 490:1-201(3). Express terms, then, do not constitute the entire agreement, which must be sought also in evidence of usages, dealings, and performance of the contract itself. The purpose of evidence of usages, which are defined in the previous section, is to help to understand the entire agreement.

> [Usages are] a factor in reaching the commercial meaning of the agreement which the parties have made. The language used is to be interpreted as meaning what it may fairly be expected to mean to parties involved in the particular commercial transaction in a given locality or in a given vocation or trade.... Part of the agreement of the parties ... is to be sought for in the usages of trade which furnish the background and give particular meaning to the language used, and are the framework of common understanding controlling any general rules of law which hold only when there is no such understanding. *Id.* § 490:1-205, Comment 4.

Course of dealings is more important than usages of the trade, being specific usages between the two parties to the contract. "[C]ourse of dealing controls usage of trade." *Id.* § 490:1-205(4). It "is a sequence of previous conduct between the parties to a particular transaction which is fairly to be regarded as establishing a common basis of understanding for interpreting their expressions and other conduct." *Id.* § 490:1-205(1). Much of the evidence of prior dealings between Shell and Nanakuli in negotiating the 1963 contract and in carrying out similar earlier contracts was excluded by the court.

A commercial agreement, then, is broader than the written paper and its meaning is to be determined not just by the language used by them in the written contract but "by their action, read and interpreted in the light of commercial practices and other surrounding circumstances. The measure and background for interpretation are set by the commercial context, which may explain and supplement even the language of a formal or final writing." *Id.*, Comment 1. Performance, usages, and prior dealings are important enough to be admitted always, even for a final and complete agreement; only if they cannot be reasonably reconciled with the express terms of the contract are they not binding on the parties. "The express terms of an agreement and an applicable course of dealing or usage of trade shall be construed wherever reasonable as consistent with each other; but when such construction is unreasonable express terms control both course of dealing and usage of trade and course of dealing controls usage of trade." *Id.* § 490:1-205(4)....

Our study of the Code provisions and Comments, then, form the first basis of our holding that a trade usage to price-protect pavers at times of price increases for work committed on nonescalating contracts could reasonably be construed as consistent with an express term of seller's posted price at delivery. Since the agreement of the parties is broader than the express terms and includes usages, which may even add terms to the agreement, and since the commercial background provided by those usages is vital to an understanding of the agreement, we follow the Code's mandate to proceed on the assumption that the parties have included those usages unless they cannot reasonably be construed as consistent with the express terms....

Some guidelines can be offered as to how usage evidence can be allowed to modify a contract. First, the court must allow a check on usage evidence by demanding that it be sufficiently definite and widespread to prevent unilateral *post hoc* revision of contract terms by one party.... Although the Code abandoned the traditional common law test of nonconsensual custom and views usage as a way of determining the parties' probable intent ... thus abolishing the requirement that common law custom be universally practiced, trade usages still must be well settled....

Evidence of a trade usage does not need to be protected against perjury because, as one commentator has written: "[A]n outside standard does exist to help judge the truth of the assertion that the parties intended the usage to control the particular dispute: the existence and scope of the usage can be determined from other members of the trade." Roger W. Kirst, *Usage of Trade and Course of Dealing: Subversion of the UCC Theory*, 1977 U. ILL. L.F. 811, 839 (1977)....

Here the evidence was overwhelming that all suppliers to the asphaltic paving trade price-protected customers under the same types of circumstances. Chevron's contract with H.B. was a similar long-term supply contract between a buyer and seller with very close relations, on a form supplied by the seller, covering sales of asphalt, and setting the price at seller's posted price, with no mention of price protection. The same commentator offers a second guideline:

> Because the stock printed forms cannot always reflect the changing methods of business, members of the trade may do business with a standard clause in the forms that they ignore in practice. If the trade consistently ignores obsolete clauses at variance with actual trade practices, a litigant can maintain that it is reasonable that the courts also ignore the clauses. Similarly, members of a trade may handle a particular subset of commercial transactions in a manner consistent with written terms because the writing cannot provide for all variations or contingencies. Thus, if the trade regards an express term and a trade usage as consistent because the usage is not a complete contradiction but only an occasional but definite exception to a written term, the courts should interpret the contract according to the usage. Kirst, *supra*, at 824....

Here, the express price term was "Shell's Posted Price at time of delivery." A total negation of that term would be that the buyer was to set the price. It is a less than complete negation of the term that an unstated exception exists at times of price increases, at which times the old price is to be charged, for a certain period or for a specified tonnage, on work already committed at the lower price on nonescalating contracts. Such a usage forms a broad and important exception to the express term, but does not swallow it entirely. Therefore, we hold that, under these particular facts, a reasonable jury could have found that price protection was incorporated into the 1969 agreement between Nanakuli and Shell and that price protection was reasonably consistent with the express term of seller's posted price at delivery.

VIII. Good Faith in Setting Price

Nanakuli offers an alternative theory why Shell should have offered price protection at the time of the price increases of 1974. Even if price protection was not a term of the agreement, Shell could not have exercised good faith in carrying out its 1969 contract with Nanakuli when it raised its price by $32 effective January 1 in a letter written December 31st and only received on January 4, given the universal practice of advance notice of such an increase in the asphaltic paving trade. The Code provides: "A price to be fixed by the seller or by the buyer means a price for him to fix in good faith." Haw. Rev. Stat. § 490:2-305(2). For a merchant good faith means "the observance of reasonable commercial standards of fair dealing in the trade." *Id.* 490:2-103(1)(b). The comment to § 2-305 explains, "[I]n the normal case a 'posted price'... satisfies the good faith requirement." *Id.,* Comment 3. However, the words "in the normal case" mean that, although a posted price will usually be satisfactory, it will not be so under all circumstances. In addition, the dispute here was not over the amount of the increase — that is, the price that the seller fixed — but over the manner in which that increase was put into effect. It is true that Shell, in order to observe the good faith standards of the trade in 1974, was not bound by the practices of aggregate companies, which did not labor under the same disabilities as did asphalt suppliers in 1974. However, Nanakuli presented evidence that Chevron, in raising its price to $76, gave at least six weeks' advance notice, in accord with the long-time usage of the asphaltic paving trade. Shell, on the other hand, gave absolutely no notice, from which the jury could have concluded that Shell's manner of carrying out the price increase of 1974 did not conform to commercially reasonable standards. In both the timing of the announcement and its refusal to protect work already bid at the old price, Shell could be found to have breached the obligation of good faith imposed by the Code on all merchants. "Every contract or duty within this chapter imposes an obligation of good faith in its performance or enforcement," *id.* § 490:1-203, which for merchants entails the observance of commercially reasonable standards of fair dealing in the trade. The Comment to § 1-203 reads:

> This section sets forth a basic principle running throughout this Act. The principle involved is that in commercial transactions good faith is required in the performance and enforcement of all agreements or duties. Particular applications of this general principle appear in specific provisions of the Act.... It is further implemented by § 1-205 on course of dealing and usage of trade.

… Chevron's conduct in 1974 offered enough relevant evidence of commercially reasonable standards of fair dealing in the asphalt trade in Hawaii in 1974 for the jury to find that Shell's failure to give sufficient advance notice and price-protect Nanakuli after the imposition of the new price did not conform to good faith dealings in Hawaii at that time.

Because the jury could have found for Nanakuli on its price protection claim under either theory, we reverse the judgment of the District Court and reinstate the jury verdict for Nanakuli in the amount of $220,800, plus interest according to law.

Reversed and remanded with directions to enter final judgment.

[Special concurrence by JUDGE KENNEDY omitted.]

NOTES AND QUESTIONS

1. *The parol evidence rule:* Part of this decision concerns proposed testimony (by Lennox and Smith) about conversations between the parties at the time the contract was signed. This testimony was excluded by the trial court because of the parol evidence rule, which we will next consider. Does the Court of Appeals base its ruling for Nanakuli on those conversations?

2. *Price protection in the asphalt trade:* The *Nanakuli* case is not the only dispute arising out of the custom of price-protecting distributors of asphalt. When OPEC caused petroleum prices to rise drastically in the early 1970s, the United States government regulated prices charged by major oil companies. Asphalt, however, was largely unregulated. Thus, the oil companies could make up some of what they lost

on asphalt pricing under the regulations controlling other petroleum products. When the major oil companies withdrew price protection, their distributors suffered losses on bids outstanding, which they had calculated at the old prices. Some distributors other than Nanakuli also sued.[35]

3. *Expectations vs. bureaucratic control:* The person in the field made a deal with a customer. As is often true, their deal was inconsistent with the "legislation" of the organization, as announced in its printed form contracts. The people in Shell's home office knew little about what was going on in Hawaii. Shell's managers in corporate headquarters wanted the ability to exert control at their discretion. Their lawyers fashioned lengthy documents protecting Shell's interest, warding off liability, and claiming maximum flexibility.

At the same time, Shell's agents in the field dealt with their own problems. They worked in specific business contexts influenced by the competitive situation. They did not go by the book. They created expectations inconsistent with the literal language of Shell's standard form contracts. And headquarters ignored all this until there was a very substantial price increase, which they wanted to pass on to Nanakuli.

One can speculate about the ultimate motives of Shell headquarters in this case. One of the unusual aspects of this case is, as the opinion reveals, the parties continued to do business all during this litigation, and Shell even granted Nanakuli price protection at a later date. Perhaps there was a management decision to pass along the huge price increase in 1974 to distributors in all circumstances, and headquarters felt they could not make an exception for Nanakuli without running into trouble with other distributors. But of course Nanakuli was in a unique situation among distributors because they had a long-term supply contract, as the opinion makes clear.

Should courts honor the "real deal" or the "paper deal"? The court's approach in the *Nanakuli* case places real burdens on the home office. They cannot know for sure what their agents have said and done. Nonetheless, Nanakuli's people were likely to be less cautious about reading and understanding written documents than people in more distant relationships. Nanakuli and Shell were not in an arms-length relationship. They were quasi-partners, and officials of Nanakuli and Shell's local representative worked together for their mutual benefit for a long time. In short, we are suggesting that the case reflects far more than a technical construction of the provisions of the

---

35. In at least two cases the distributors lost. In W.H. Barber Co. v. McNamara-Vivant Contracting Co., Inc., 293 N.W.2d 351 (Minn. 1979), a jury found that the supplier's representatives had promised price protection. The Supreme Court of Minnesota affirmed the judgment for the supplier, ruling that there was no writing adequate to show the quantities of asphalt to be supplied, and the contractor did not establish that the supplier was estopped to assert the Statute of Frauds. In Lige Dickson Co. v. Union Oil Co. of Cal., 96 Wash. 2d 291, 635 P.2d 103 (1981), the Supreme Court of Washington made a similar ruling. Although a Union Oil official had conceded that "there was an unwritten custom in the liquid asphalt business in the Tacoma area, well known and acted upon by suppliers and users, that any increase in price of liquid asphalt would not be applicable to manufacturers' then-existing contracts," nonetheless, the court said that "we cannot help but foresee increased litigation and confusion as being the necessary result of the eroding of the UCC" if promissory estoppel is held to override § 2-201.

Uniform Commercial Code. The court looked to the relationship in addition to the abstractions of formal contract law.

4. *Does* Nanakuli *discourage informal concessions in contract performance?* Recall Professor Bernstein's criticisms, summarized in Note 5 following the preceding case. Does the holding in *Nanakuli* discourage large companies from making concessions to contracting parties in the performance of long-term contracts, for fear that they will be held to them in the future under a course-of-dealing theory? In other words, do you think that after *Nanakuli* Shell prohibited its agents from encouraging Shell's suppliers to bid on government contracts by implicitly or explicitly promising them price protection?

5. *Did the price-protection usage extend to big price increases?* Recall that Professor Bernstein has argued that many trade usages are quite vague. Note that all the instances of price protection relied on by the court to establish a usage of trade and a course of dealing concerned situations in which the underlying price increase was relatively modest. The price increase that gave rise to this litigation was enormous, perhaps the highest in this industry's history. Was it appropriate for the court to rely on a practice developed in connection with smaller price increases to interpret the contract as providing for price protection in connection with very large price increases as well?

6. *Other possible doctrines for deciding this case:* Though the court does not consider them, two other doctrines the court might have used to reach a decision in favor of Nanakuli are promissory estoppel (reliance on a promise) and waiver. You are probably somewhat familiar with these doctrines, which will be considered in greater detail later in this chapter (promissory estoppel) and in Chapter 4 (waiver). Consider whether you believe a decision could have been reached for Nanakuli on either of these doctrines. If it could have, would such a decision have been a superior doctrinal basis for the result? You should consider these questions again after you study these doctrines.

7. *Is the jury a fair decision-maker?* As we have emphasized repeatedly in these materials, one possible reason for taking a textualist approach to the interpretation of written contracts is to avoid the necessity of a jury decision. In *Nanakuli* there was a jury trial, and the jury returned a verdict for the plaintiff. The trial took place in Honolulu. Do you suspect that Shell Oil Co. felt that it could not get a fair hearing before a Honolulu jury in a case brought by a local company? Is that a sufficient reason to reject reliance on trade usages and courses of dealing in interpreting written contracts?

C. THE PAROL EVIDENCE RULE

The parol evidence rule is not easy to understand. A famous treatise states: "Few things are darker than [the parol evidence rule], or fuller of subtle difficulties."[36]

---

36. James B. Thayer, A Preliminary Treatise on Evidence at the Common Law 390 (1898).

This short note and the following excerpt from a famous law review article should help sort the cases that follow. While the rule may be difficult for judges, lawyers, and law students, it is clear that it is an important doctrine in modern contract law.

Perhaps the place to start is distinguishing these materials on the parol evidence rule from the preceding materials on the interpretation of written documents. Under the UCC, nothing about the parol evidence rule prevents consideration of usages of trade and courses of dealing in interpreting a written document. This is made clear in the Code's section adopting and specifying the common law parol evidence rule, § 2-202(1). The parol evidence rule deals with consideration of communications between the parties concerning the current contract other than the signed writing itself. A few examples will further amplify the scope of the parol evidence rule.

Let's begin with the easiest case. Seller and Buyer are negotiating a complicated contract. They have been exchanging oral and written communications for weeks. As a result, both have file folders filled with formal drafts of provisions, scraps of paper with handwritten proposals, notes, and letters. They have tried to consider matters one by one. However, the bargaining about point five has reopened their tentative agreement about point three. Of course, there also have been oral concessions and proposals. Some of these are reflected in the notes in the files and some remain only imperfectly in the memories of the parties.

Finally, Seller confesses that she is uncertain where the parties stand. Despite Seller believing they have agreed on everything and have a contract, it is not written down anywhere from beginning to end. Seller proposes that she draft a clean text from which they can work. Buyer thinks this is a good idea. Two days later, Seller and Buyer meet again. Seller presents Buyer with a detailed written contract. She says, "I think this is our deal. Look it over. If I've left out anything, tell me. If I've got something wrong, we can change it. If there's more to negotiate, at least we'll know where to start." A day later Buyer returns and says, "You've done a remarkable job in capturing just what we have agreed. I have one small problem in clause 2, but if we can solve that, we have a contract." Together they work out the problem in clause 2. Seller then says to Buyer, "Now, are you sure that this writing expresses your understanding of our deal? We haven't left anything out? I don't want any misunderstandings or mistakes." Buyer responds, assuring Seller that the writing reflects perfectly his understanding of their agreement. He says, "My lawyer and I have been through all of the earlier material. Of course, you made some changes to harmonize the entire deal, but I can live with them in order to close a contract. The document is our deal." They change the document to reflect the few corrections to clause 2, and subsequently sign it.

A year later, Buyer sues Seller for breach of contract. Buyer offers as evidence the text of a preliminary draft of clause 23, which both Buyer and Seller had initialed. This draft is dated a week before Buyer and Seller signed the writing to close their deal. Clause 23 in the preliminary draft declares that if X occurs, then

Buyer shall have right Y. Clause 23 in the writing they signed to create a contract declares, on the other hand, if X occurs, then Buyer shall not have right Y but only right Z.

The parol evidence rule would bar admission of the preliminary draft of clause 23 as evidence. Here, it is just a matter of free contract. Buyer and Seller agreed that their entire agreement was expressed in the writing they signed to create a contract. Implicitly, they also agreed that the final writing superseded and overturned all prior inconsistent agreements—after all, this was the point of starting with a clean draft. If parties agree that a particular document states their entire agreement and amends or repeals all prior bargains, then courts will give effect to their choice.

However, our story, while understandable, is atypical. People seldom expressly agree that a writing they sign is the final crystallization of their contract.[37] They just sign written documents called contracts. We could presume that everyone understands, or should understand, any writing he or she signs. We know, however, this is not the case in many instances. If clause 23 in a prior letter and clause 23 in the written contract conflict, it is likely the product of mistake. Courts could approach the situation much as the British judges did in *Raffles v. Wichelhaus* and find no agreement, at least if neither of the parties has yet performed. On the other hand, perhaps it is easier for courts to presume later formal writings supersede whatever is said in earlier correspondence and conversations. And it may help bureaucratically run organizations to ignore choice and hold people to whatever they signed.

Typical cases present even more difficulty. For example: Buyer offers into evidence a letter from Seller, written before their final contract was signed. In it, Seller agrees to something that is not covered in the final document. Should courts view the omission of this provision as an implied agreement that there should be no such clause in the contract? Should courts recognize that people may put some but not all of their bargain in a final writing? Should courts seek the actual intentions of the parties or create presumptions to protect writings?

Suppose Buyer offers a preliminary draft of clause 23 in evidence. Buyer does not seek to have it enforced as part of the contract. Rather, Buyer argues that the preliminary draft is relevant to interpreting the meaning of clause 23 in the final agreement. The written document says that if X occurs, Buyer shall have right Z. However, what are the boundaries of right Z? Buyer argues that it should be interpreted in light of the definition of right Y in the preliminary draft—that the decision to reject Y

---

37. Lawyers drafting form contracts commonly insert a clause, called a "merger" clause, saying the writing is intended to be the final and complete expression of the parties' agreement, with the precise purpose in mind of invoking the parol evidence rule in any subsequent litigation. We will consider later what effect merger clauses in form contracts should or do have. Is insertion of a merger clause that the other party is not expected to read or understand a type of fraud? Should you feel a personal sense of guilt if you use guile, and legal knowledge, to take advantage of the trusting or unwary?

implies something about Z. Should courts consider this evidence? Must they first determine that the scope of right Z is ambiguous?

Suppose, on the other hand, Buyer wants to show that clause 23 was never supposed to be effective. Rather, it was written into the contract to comply with requirements of the Mexican government. Buyer and Seller agreed in a prior letter that the clause would have no effect. Should this evidence be admitted? Suppose, instead, Buyer wants to show that Buyer and Seller agreed in a side agreement that clause 23 would be effective only if the Mexican government could not be persuaded to waive its regulation in the case of this transaction. Should this evidence be admitted?

Finally, suppose Buyer wants to have the court *reform* the final written contract to change the term "right Z" to "right Y." Buyer wants to offer evidence of prior agreements to show that Seller's computer software was mistakenly programmed, producing the wrong clause when a typist entered "ALT 25." "ALT 25" should have produced language giving Buyer "right Y." Instead, it produced language giving the Buyer "right Z." Neither Buyer nor Seller discovered the error before they signed the document. Can Buyer contradict the writing in a reformation action? Is the claim really different from the original case, where Buyer wanted to contradict a final writing with a preliminary draft?

Obviously, a great deal turns on whether courts seek to carry out real choices. They may seek other goals without announcing them openly. We can now turn to consider what courts have done with such cases.

John D. Calamari & Joseph M. Perillo, *A Plea for a Uniform Parol Evidence Rule and Principles of Contract Interpretation*
42 IND. L.J. 333 (1967)[38]

Any reader of advance sheet[39] is well aware that most of the contract decisions reported do not involve offer and acceptance or other subjects usually explored in depth in a course in contracts but rather involve the parol evidence rule and questions of interpretation, topics given scant attention in most courses in contracts. Although a number of articles have appeared recently on these subjects, for the most part they tend to express the individual view of the writer as to what the law should be. While the authors of this paper will state their views, their principal purpose is to set forth the basic problems involved and to offer a guide for comprehending the reasons for the many contradictory decisions in these areas. Much of the fog and mystery surrounding these subjects stems from the fact that there is basic disagreement as to the meaning and effect of the parol evidence rule and as to the appropriate goals to be achieved by the process of contractual interpretation. The cases and treatises of the

---

38. Reprinted with permission.

39. Eds note: An "advance sheet" was an early report of a recent case, issued prior to inclusion in the full volume of an official case reporter. Today, most consumers of judicial opinions obtain them electronically, and so are unlikely to use "advance sheets" to remain current.

contract giants tend to conceal this conflict. While frequently masking disagreement by using the same terminology, Professors Williston and Corbin are often poles apart in the meaning they attach to the same term. Often starting from what superficially appear to be the same premises, they frequently advocate different results in similar fact situations. The polarity of their views reflects conflicting value judgments as to policy issues that are as old as our legal system and that are likely to continue as long as courts of law exist. Although many writers and courts have expressed their views on the subject and have made major contributions to it, concentration on the analyses of Professors Williston and Corbin will point up the fundamental bases upon which the conflicting cases and views rest.

I. The Parol Evidence Rule

The Area of Substantial Agreement

There is a rule of substantive law that states that whenever contractual intent is sought to be ascertained from among several expressions of the parties, an earlier tentative expression will be rejected in favor of a later expression that is final. More simply stated, the contract made by the parties supersedes tentative promises made in earlier negotiations. Consequently, in determining the content of the contract, the earlier tentative promises are irrelevant.

The parol evidence rule comes into play only when the last expression is in writing. Professor Corbin states the rule as follows: "When two parties have made a contract and have expressed it in a writing to which they have both assented as the complete and accurate integration of that contract, evidence, whether parol or otherwise, of antecedent understandings and negotiations will not be admitted for the purpose of varying or contradicting the writing." Professor Williston's formulation is not to the contrary: "Briefly stated," he writes, "this rule requires, in the absence of fraud, duress, mutual mistake, or something of the kind, the exclusion of extrinsic evidence, oral or written, where the parties have reduced their agreement to an integrated writing." Both agree that this, too, is a rule of substantive law that also operates as an exclusionary rule of evidence merely because prior understandings are irrelevant to the process of determining the content of the final contract. The similarity between the parol evidence rule and the rule stated in the preceding paragraph is obvious. The main and important difference is that where the last expression is not in writing the jury determines whether the parties intended the second expression to supersede the first. This is to say that this question of intention is determined as is any other question of intention stemming from oral transactions. Where the later expression is in writing, however, this question is usually determined by the trial judge. At an early date it was felt (and the feeling strongly remains) that writings require the special protection that is afforded by removing this issue from the province of unsophisticated jurors.[40]

---

40. [10] It is often assumed that the parol evidence rule protects the "haves" against the "have nots," since it is the former who ordinarily draft written contracts and the latter who receive the sympathy of the jury. *See* McCormick, *The Parol Evidence Rule as a Procedural Device for Control of the Jury*, 41 YALE L.J. 365, 427–28 (1932). Surprisingly, however, a substantial number of the reported

While it is unanimously agreed that the parol evidence rule applies to *prior* expressions, and has no application to an agreement made *subsequent* to the writing, there is no unanimity as to expressions *contemporaneous* with the writing. Williston and the Restatement take the position that contemporaneous expressions should be treated the same as prior expressions except that contemporaneous writings should be deemed to be a part of the integration. Corbin appears to argue that expressions are either prior or subsequent to the writing and that therefore the word "contemporaneous" merely clouds the issue. Everyone agrees that the parol evidence rule does not apply to a separate agreement; that is, an agreement that has a separate consideration.

A distinction is drawn between a total and a partial integration. Where the writing is intended to be *final* and *complete*, it is characterized as a total integration and may be neither contradicted nor supplemented by evidence of prior agreements or expressions. But where the writing is intended to be *final* but *incomplete*, it is said to be a partial integration; although such a writing may not be *contradicted* by evidence of prior agreements or expressions, it may be *supplemented* by evidence of consistent additional terms. Thus, in approaching a writing, two questions must be asked: (1) Is it intended as a final expression? (2) Is it intended to be a complete expression?

Is the writing intended as a final expression? Writings that evidence a contract are not necessarily "final" embodiments of the contract. Exchanges of letters or memoranda that show the conclusion of a contract may have been intended to be read in the light of more far-ranging conversations and documents. Or, the parties may have intended their writing to be tentative and preliminary to a final draft. In these cases, the parol evidence rule does not bar enforcement of the entire agreement as proved by the writing read in the context of prior and contemporaneous expressions. It is agreed that any relevant evidence is admissible to show that the writing was not intended to be final. Although the question of finality is frequently characterized as one of law in order to remove it from the province of unsophisticated jurors, it is actually a question of fact—one of intention—which the trial judge determines. To be considered final the writing need not be in any particular form and need not be signed. The crucial requirement is that the parties have regarded the writing as the final embodiment of their agreement....

Is the writing a complete or partial integration? Once it is determined that the writing is intended to be final and therefore an integration, it becomes necessary to ascertain whether the integration is complete (so that it cannot be contradicted or supplemented) or only partial (so that it cannot be contradicted but may be supplemented by evidence of consistent additional terms). It seems to be generally agreed that this is a question of law in the sense that it is determined by the trial judge.

The Parol Evidence Rule: The Major Area of Conflict

Apparent agreement by Professors Williston and Corbin, except as noted, on the rules stated above conceals real conflict. The battleground upon which they express

---

cases dealing with the rule involve sizable transactions between persons with apparently strong bargaining power.

disagreement is a major one: the concept of total integration. This, of course, is the area in which most of the cases arise. Both assert that the existence of a total integration depends on the intention of the parties. Williston does so primarily in a section entitled "Integration Depends Upon Intent." Corbin's emphasis on intent runs throughout his entire discussion of the rule. It appears, however, that in this context they use the term "intent" in ways that are remarkably dissimilar. A typical fact situation will illustrate this. *A* agrees to sell and *B* agrees to purchase Blackacre for $10,000. The contract is in writing and in all respects appears complete on its face. Prior to the signing of the contract *A*, in order to induce *B*'s assent, orally promises him in the presence of a number of reputable witnesses that if *B* will sign the contract, *A* will remove an unsightly shack on *A*'s land across the road from Blackacre. May this promise be proved and enforced? This depends upon whether the writing is a total integration.

Williston argues that if the intention to have a total integration were to be determined by the ordinary process of determining intention, the parol evidence rule would be emasculated. He points out that the mere existence of the collateral oral agreement would conclusively indicate that the parties intended only a partial integration and that the only question that would be presented is whether the alleged prior or contemporaneous agreement was actually made. This would be a question of fact for the jury, thus eliminating the special protection that the trial judge should afford the writing.

Williston, therefore, suggests that the issue of partial or total integration should be determined according to the following rules.

(1) If the writing expressly declares that it contains the entire agreement of the parties (what is sometimes referred to as a merger clause), the declaration conclusively establishes that the integration is total unless the document is obviously incomplete or the merger clause was included as a result of fraud or mistake or any other reason exists that is sufficient to set aside a contract. As previously indicated, even a merger clause does not prevent enforcement of a separate agreement supported by a distinct consideration.

(2) In the absence of a merger clause, the determination is made by looking to the writing. Consistent additional terms may be proved if the writing is obviously incomplete on its face or if it is apparently complete but, as in the case of deeds, bonds, bills, and notes, expresses the undertaking of only one of the parties.

(3) Where the writing appears to be a complete instrument expressing the rights and obligations of both parties, it is deemed a total integration unless the alleged additional terms were such as might naturally be made as a separate agreement by parties situated as were the parties to the written contract.

Thus in the hypothetical case given, Williston's view is that the collateral promise to remove the unsightly shack could not be enforced. The writing was apparently complete on its face and contracting parties would ordinarily and naturally have included such a promise in the writing. Many might agree with this result, but can it be seriously argued that this result is based on the parties' intent that the agreement be integrated? How can a rule based on the intention of the parties be emasculated by seeking to determine their actual expressed intent? It is quite clear that the expressed intent shown by overwhelming evidence is at variance with an intent to have the writing serve as their complete agreement.

Professor Corbin takes a contrary view as to the proper result in our hypothetical case: "It can never be determined by mere interpretation of the words of a writing whether it is an 'integration' of anything, whether it is 'the final and complete expression of the agreement' or is a mere partial expression of the agreement." Elsewhere, he states: "Since the very existence of an 'integration'... is dependent on what the parties thereto say and do (necessarily extrinsic to the paper instrument), at the time they draw that instrument 'in usual form,' are we to continue like a flock of sheep to beg the question at issue, even when its result is to 'make a contract for the parties,' one that is vitally different from the one they made themselves?" When Professor Corbin speaks of the intent of the parties he emphatically means their actual expressed intent.

Thus, two schools of thought are on the scene, one determined to seek out the intent of the parties, the other speaking of intent but refusing to consider evidence of what the intent actually was....

Fictions have been enormously important in the development of our law. In an era when the law was deemed unchangeable and eternal, they provided almost the only mechanism for avoiding the impact of rules deemed unwise. Their use today serves only to obfuscate what should be clear. Shorn of language indicating a fictitious search for intent, the courts and writers who adopt a Willistonian approach are saying this: *When parties adopt a written form that gives every appearance of being complete and final, they are required to incorporate in that form their entire agreement. If they fail to do so, unincorporated agreements relating to the same subject matter are void....*

Professor Corbin has an easy task in demolishing the Willistonian approach. In treating the matter of integration as a question of intent, as Professor Williston purports to do, he shows the absurdity of excluding all relevant evidence of intent except the writing itself. But, as we have seen, Williston ... [is] unconcerned about the true intention of the parties. Rather, shorn of rote language of fiction indicating a search for intention ... [he is] advocating and applying a rule of form. Since (and even before) the common law had its genesis, there has been a deeply felt belief that transactions will be more secure, litigation will be reduced, and the temptation to perjury will be removed, if everyone will only use proper forms for his transactions. The Statute of Wills and the Statute of Frauds are but examples of this belief. Professor Corbin, by attacking the apparent arguments of Williston's position, has not expressly come to grips with the substance of his position. This is not to suggest that either he or Professor Williston have been unaware of the true nature of their disagreement. Rather, they seem for the most part to have been content not to make explicit the basis of their differing views. The purpose of the above discussion is to bring their differences into bold relief so that the debate on this matter can break away from the bland assumption that everyone agrees as to the statement of the parol evidence rule and that there is merely some confusion as to its application.

The debate involves the question: is the public better served by giving effect to the parties' entire agreement written and oral, even at the risk of injustice caused by the possibility of perjury and the possibility that superseded documents will be treated as operative, or does the security of transactions require that, despite occasional injustices, persons adopting a formal writing be required, on the penalty of voidness of their oral and written side agreements, to put their entire agreement in the formal writing[?]

The conflict is an old one. Rules excluding evidence on the ground that it is likely to be false are not strangers to the law. Formerly, parties and interested third persons were incompetent to testify on the ground that their testimony would be unworthy of belief. The Statute of Frauds and Statute of Wills embody similar considerations. The authors believe, however, that the possibility of perjury is an insufficient ground for interfering with freedom of contract by refusing to effectuate the parties' entire agreement.

The whole thrust of our law for over a century has been directed to the eradication of exclusionary rules of evidence in civil cases. Thus parties may now testify, their interest in the outcome affecting only the weight and not the admissibility of the evidence. Dissatisfaction with rigid application of the parol evidence rule has resulted in the strained insertion of fact situations into the categories where the parol evidence rule is inapplicable. Thus, to circumvent the rule fraud has been found and reformation has been granted in situations where these concepts are not ordinarily deemed applicable. Moreover, whole categories of exceptions have been carved out; for example, a deed absolute may be shown to be a mortgage. Professor Thayer's summation of the parol evidence problem warrants repetition: "Few things are darker than this, or fuller of subtle difficulties." When any rule of law is riddled through with exceptions and applications difficult to reconcile, it is believed that litigation is stimulated rather than reduced. If the policy of the parol evidence rule is to reduce the possibility of judgments predicated upon perjured testimony and superseded documents, it may be effectuated to a large extent by continuing to leave control over determining the question of intent to integrate in the hands of the trial judge. Finally, the trend of modern decisions, as Williston suggests, "is toward increasing the liberality in the admission of parol agreements." This tendency of the courts is in no small measure due to the influence of Professor Corbin's treatise.

It is of little moment whether the views of the authors of this article as to what the law should be are convincing. The essential point being made here is that there is no uniform parol evidence rule. Rather, there are at least two rather dissimilar rules which, for convenience, may be denominated the Corbin Rule and the Williston Rule. In view of the confusion engendered by having two contradictory rules expressed in the same terminology, it is remarkable that a few states have shown a degree of consistency. New York, despite some inconsistent cases, generally maintains a rigorously Willistonian approach.... Some states, such as Connecticut, reach results consistent with Corbin's test, while utilizing the most varied reasoning. Perhaps most states are consistently erratic. Such is the confusion that in any state a decision may be reached that is ludicrous in result and analysis or sensible in result but strained in analysis.

It is hoped that once the source of confusion is comprehended, courts will achieve a greater degree of consistency by consciously choosing one of the competing rules. The widespread adoption of the Uniform Commercial Code may give impetus to a consistent and enlightened approach if it is applied to cases not specifically under its coverage. An official comment to § 2-202 states:

> [C]onsistent additional terms, not reduced to writing, may be proved unless the court finds that the writing was intended by both parties as a complete and exclusive statement of all terms. If the additional terms are such that, if agreed upon, they would *certainly* have been included in the document in the view of the court, then evidence of their alleged making must be kept from the trier of fact. (Emphasis added.)

Thus, the Code requires the court to ascertain the intention of the parties, and it can be assumed that the codifiers meant a true expressed intention and not a fictitious intention. The trial judge has an important function in making this determination. If he finds that it is certain the parties would have incorporated the additional term into the writing if they had agreed upon it, he excludes evidence of the alleged term from the jury's consideration. If it is merely improbable that the parties would have agreed to the term without incorporating it into the writing, the jury must determine whether the additional term was agreed upon....

III. The Relationship Between the Parol Evidence Rule and Rules and Standards of Interpretation

Before the parol evidence rule may be invoked, the judge must determine that the parties intended the writing to be final. The question of intent is determined according to the standards and rules of interpretation discussed above. Conversely, the parol evidence rule should have no effect on the question of interpretation—the *meaning* of language. Stated otherwise, before the parol evidence rule can be invoked to exclude evidence, the *meaning* of the writing must be ascertained since one may not determine whether a writing is being contradicted or supplemented until one knows what the writing means.

This should mean that evidence of prior and contemporaneous expressions is always admissible to aid in determining the meaning of the integration, and Corbin so states. Williston is cautiously in accord. Such evidence may be introduced, he grants, but not to prove that the intention of the parties is at variance with the appropriate local meaning of the words. The evidence may be considered only on the question of whether the parties contracted with reference to a local or trade usage or, if this local or trade meaning is ambiguous, on the question of what meaning the parties attached to the words. Even accepting his premise that the true intention of the parties is usually irrelevant, there are two difficulties with Williston's position on the admissibility of this evidence. First, it assumes that the court can successfully ignore the parties' real intention when it is shown by the evidence. Second, it involves a great deal of tension with the exclusionary aspects of his version of the parol evidence rule. If evidence of prior and contemporaneous expressions is not admissible to prove terms supplementary to or at variance with a total integration, but is admissible to show the meaning of the integration, the astute trial lawyer will characterize his evidence on what are really supplementary or contradictory terms as evidence on the true meaning of the contract. Although the function of this evidence is to demonstrate the "meaning of the writing," once it is admitted the court may find it difficult (and unjust) to disregard what may be clear and convincing proof that the writing is not the complete agreement of the parties. Williston's grand structure meticulously separating the parol evidence rule, standards of interpretation, and primary and secondary rules of interpretation seems to collapse into this procedural pitfall.

It is little wonder, then, that many courts that share Williston's concern for the "security of transactions" have retreated even further from the intention of the parties to the …"plain meaning rule," holding that if a writing appears clear and unambiguous on its face, its meaning must be determined from the four corners of the instrument without resort to extrinsic evidence of any nature. This approach excludes evidence of trade usage and prior dealings between the parties as well as evidence of surrounding circumstances and prior and contemporaneous expressions. The latest legislative ruling on the matter, the Uniform Commercial Code, explicitly condemns the plain meaning rule and explicitly allows use of evidence of a course of dealing or course of performance to explain the agreement "unless carefully negated."

1. Search for Truth or Defense of Form?

BINKS MANUFACTURING CO. v. NATIONAL PRESTO INDUSTRIES, INC.

United States Court of Appeals, Seventh Circuit
709 F.2d 1109 (1983)

COFFEY, J.

This appeal involves a contractual dispute concerning the manufacture and sale of an "industrial spray finishing and baking system." Binks Manufacturing Company, the System's manufacturer, brought an action in federal district court to collect the purchase price of the System. Presto Manufacturing Company counterclaimed alleging damages resulting from defective design and manufacture of the System as well as late delivery. The jury returned verdicts in favor of Binks on its purchase price claim and against Presto on its counterclaims. We affirm.

I.

Presto is engaged in the manufacture and sale of electrical appliances, including hamburger cookers. Binks Manufacturing Company is a leading manufacturer of industrial spray finishing equipment. In 1975, Presto management decided to increase its production capacity of electric hamburger cookers and as part of its expansion plan, determined to purchase an automatic system designed to coat aluminum castings (the principal components of hamburger cookers) with a non-stick "teflon-like" coating for installation at its Alamogordo, New Mexico plant. Presto entered into negotiations with Binks Manufacturing Company for the design and manufacture of the system.

The negotiations between Binks and Presto continued from October 1975 through March 1976, resulting in a contract with Binks agreeing to manufacture "a custom designed, custom built automatic spray application and oven curing system intended to apply coatings to various Presto products" (hereinafter the "System"). The System was to consist of one continuous conveyor 858 feet long, designed to carry an aluminum casting through a six-step manufacturing process: (1) a booth in which the castings would be sprayed with a primer; (2) an oven where the primer would be baked on to the aluminum castings; (3) a cooling area; (4) a booth where the castings would be sprayed with a non-stick coating; (5) three progressively hotter ovens in which the non-stick coating would be baked on to the aluminum castings over the primer; and (6) a final cooling area....

[The contract provided for delivery of the system not later than June 2, 1976; the contract contained a clause providing that "time is of the essence." In fact, due to unforeseeable and apparently unavoidable problems encountered by a Binks subcontractor (Radiant Products), delivery was not accomplished until July 19, 1976.]

Binks offered to supervise installation of the System, but Presto chose not to accept the offer and hired their own local independent contractors to install the System. According to Binks, Presto's independent contractors committed installation errors of major proportions, including a failure to properly align and anchor the conveyor equipment. Binks further contends that Presto insisted upon initially operating the System at maximum capacity, thereby ignoring Binks's advice that the System be brought up to full capacity only gradually.

After installation of the System had been completed, Presto personnel made several unsuccessful attempts to operate the System's conveyor. In the ensuing weeks representatives of Presto, Binks, and Radiant [the oven subcontractor] made other attempts to operate the System, but experienced a myriad of problems. Binks contends that Presto's independent contractors failed to properly synchronize the electric motors used to run the conveyor, causing the conveyor to run sporadically and jam. These problems in conveyor synchronization continued for some two months, causing the System to operate at less than half capacity.

Binks and Presto disagree as to the underlying cause of the System's faulty performance. Presto alleges that the System was defectively manufactured in that the conveyor, contrary to the contract specifications, was totally enclosed in the System's ovens, causing the conveyor components to overheat, contributing to the twisting, bending, and eventually breakage of the conveyor chain.

Binks, on the other hand, contends Presto: (1) improperly installed the System; (2) inadequately lubricated the conveyor; (3) operated the System's oven at excessive temperatures; (4) ignored Binks's advice in initially operating the System at maximum capacity; and (5) ran defective castings through the System, resulting in pieces breaking off the castings and jamming the conveyor.

Binks also asserts that Presto abused the System by "double loading" the castings used to make upper components of the hamburger cookers, thereby exceeding the System's maximum capacity set forth in the contract. According to Binks, "double loading" the System resulted in twice as many upper burger castings being loaded into the System per hour as specified in the contract (2,250 "upper double burger" castings per hour instead of the 1,125 castings per hour outlined in the contract and 4,500 "upper square burger" castings per hour rather than the 2,250 castings per hour set forth in the contract)....

... Binks and Presto made several unsuccessful attempts to reach a negotiated settlement and failing to achieve this, on November 4, 1977, Binks filed a complaint seeking recovery under the contract for the balance of the purchase price. Presto answered by filing a $9.5 million counterclaim against Binks alleging late delivery of the System, breach of contractual warranties, breach of implied warranties, negligence and misrepresentation in connection with the design, manufacture, and sale of the spraying and baking system....

The case came to trial on March 1, 1982, and after the four-week jury trial, judgment was entered in favor of Binks on its claim for the balance of the purchase price and [against Presto's counterclaims].

On appeal, Presto contends that the district court erred:

1. In granting Binks's pre-trial motion in limine, precluding Presto from introducing parol and extrinsic evidence to attempt to show that the parties intended to define the maximum capacity of the System in terms of pounds of castings per hour, rather than the number of castings per hour....

II. The Motion in Limine Concerning the Issue of Maximum Capacity

Presto's counterclaim against Binks alleged that the System designed and manufactured by Binks was defective, resulting in repeated breakdowns and loss of production. Binks answered that the System's breakdowns were not a result of defective design or manufacture, but rather were caused by Presto's abuse of the System, particularly Presto's practice of "double loading" the System.

Therefore, to establish this "double loading" theory at trial, it became necessary to determine the System's "maximum capacity" as defined in the parties' contract. The parties agree that the following provision of the contract sets forth the System's maximum capacity:

One Item of Equipment designed to coat any one of the following parts on one and/or both sides in quantities, as listed at the conveyor rate of 25 fpm with either 16 or 18 inch spindle spacing:

#60-001* Upper Double Burger at (13 oz.)   1,125 pcs./hr.
#60-002* Lower Double Burger at (24 oz.)   1,125 pcs./hr.

#60-003* Upper Square Burger (9.5 oz.)	2,250 pcs./hr.
#60-004* Lower Square Burger (12 oz.)	2,250 pcs./hr.
#60-121* Upper Round Burger (7 oz.)	2,250 pcs./hr.
#60-120 Lower Round Burger (5 oz.)	2,250 pcs./hr.

#28-006 Fry Pan at 3.8#—Quantities as later established.

> * Asterisk to indicate item coated on both sides. Hinges on 60-001 and 60-003 coated both sides.

The maximum capacity of the system is limited to the above parts or parts of similar size and cross section with a maximum loading of 4,500 pounds per hour and 4,500 #/hr. of work holders, which would pass through each oven.

Based on the foregoing contractual language, Binks takes the position that the "maximum capacity" of the System for the castings specified in the contract is defined in terms of the *number* of castings that the System can handle per hour consistent with the design of the machine. Presto, however, contends that extrinsic evidence concerning negotiation and performance of the contract demonstrates that the parties intended the maximum capacity of the System to be defined in terms of *pounds* of castings run through the System per hour; *i.e.*, 4,500 pounds of castings per hour. Presto further argues, and Binks concedes, that Presto never loaded the System with more than 4,500 pounds of castings per hour.

Presto, in support of its contention that the parties intended the System's maximum capacity to be defined in *pounds* per hour, sought to introduce extrinsic evidence pertaining to the negotiation and performance of the contract.[41] On February 25, 1976, four days before trial, Binks presented a motion *in limine* seeking an order precluding Presto from presenting extrinsic evidence to show that the parties intended to define the maximum capacity of the System in terms of pounds per hour rather than number of castings per hour. After hearing arguments, the court ruled in favor of Binks on the motion *in limine* and stated:

> I conclude that so far as the six identified parts are concerned, the specified maximums of the system are those numbers appearing opposite each of the items [in the contract provision quoted above] and not the number of items which would aggregate 4,500 pounds.

Presto contends the court committed reversible error in ruling that Presto could not introduce extrinsic evidence to show that the parties intended to define the System's maximum capacity in pounds per hour.

In evaluating Presto's challenge to the district court's ruling, we must bear in mind that our role as an appellate court is not to consider a case *de novo*. Rather, our role

---

41. [6] This extrinsic evidence included, *inter alia*: (1) a quotation submitted by Binks several days prior to formation of the contract stating "approximately 4,500 pounds of aluminum work pieces ... will pass through each oven per hour"; (2) a March 9, 1976, letter from Binks's project engineer to Presto reciting: "The System capacity increased from 1500 to 4500 #/Hr."; and (3) that Binks participated in designing the work holders in which castings were placed, and allowed for "double loading" of castings.

in reviewing the district court's ruling on the motion *in limine* is limited as "decisions regarding the admission and exclusion of evidence are peculiarly within the competence of the district court and will not be reversed on appeal unless they constitute a clear abuse of discretion." *Ellis v. City of Chicago*, 667 F.2d 606, 611 (7th Cir. 1981)....

Guided by these principles, we turn to the issue of whether the court abused its discretion by precluding Presto from introducing extrinsic evidence to establish that the parties intended the System's maximum capacity for "Upper Double Burger" and "Upper Square Burger" castings to be defined in pounds per hour, rather than number of castings per hour. The admissibility of extrinsic evidence to interpret the contract in this case is governed by Ill. Rev. Stat. ch. 26, § 2-202 [Uniform Commercial Code § 2-202]....

Thus, it is evident that under UCC § 2-202, evidence of a prior agreement or a contemporaneous oral agreement must be excluded if (1) the writing (here the contract between the parties) was intended as the final expression of the parties' agreement with respect to the maximum capacity term; *and* (2) the proffered evidence *contradicts* or is *inconsistent* with the terms of the written contract.... It is evident from the record that both Binks and Presto agree that their written contract was intended to be the final expression of their agreement; therefore, the crucial question is whether the interpretation urged by Presto (*i.e.*, that the parties intended the System's maximum capacity for "Upper Square Burger" and "Upper Double Burger" castings to be a function of pounds of castings per hour) contradicts or is inconsistent with the terms of the written contract.

Although the Uniform Commercial Code itself fails to delineate or set forth when extrinsic evidence contradicts or is inconsistent with written terms of a contract, this court recently defined "inconsistency" for the purpose of UCC § 2-202 as "the absence of reasonable harmony in terms of the language and respective obligations of the parties." *Luria Bros. & Co. v. Pielet Bros. Scrap Iron*, 600 F.2d 103, 111 (7th Cir. 1979). Applying this definition of "inconsistency" to this case, it is clear that if the court were to allow the admission of extrinsic evidence tending to show that the maximum capacity of the System for "Upper Square Burger" and "Upper Double Burger" castings was defined in terms of pounds per hour it would necessarily lead to an "absence of reasonable harmony" between the terms of the written contract and the proffered extrinsic evidence of the parties' purported intent. Presto's theory that the System's maximum capacity for the upper burger castings was defined as 4,500 pounds of such castings per hour would render almost meaningless the express language of the written contract which, after reciting a specified number of each particular casting, states "the maximum capacity of the System is limited to the above parts...." On the other hand, the district court's well-reasoned interpretation of the written contract gave meaning to each and every provision of the contract; for each of the six castings listed, the maximum capacity of the System was defined in number of parts per hour, while for other unspecified castings which Presto might decide to run through the System in the future, the maximum capacity was defined in pounds of castings per hour. Thus, the court's decision to exclude the extrinsic evidence of the parties' intent is amply supported by the basic principles of contract interpretation that a written contract should be given a construction that "harmonizes all the various parts" of the contract so that no provision is "conflicting with, or repugnant to, or neutralizing of any other." *Zannis v. Lake Shore Radiologists, Ltd.*, 73 Ill. App. 3d 901, 29 Ill. Dec. 569, 392 N.E.2d 126, 129 (1979).

Furthermore, the district court's decision to preclude Presto from introducing extrinsic evidence regarding the maximum capacity issue pays credence to the policy underlying the parol evidence rule as set forth in UCC § 2-202. This court in *Luria Bros.*, 600 F.2d at 110 n.5, stated:

> The parol evidence rule ... is a rule of substantive law. Evidence is excluded not because it is not credible or not relevant but because of a policy favoring the reliability of written representations of the terms of a contract.

This policy of upholding the integrity of written contracts and favoring written terms over extrinsic evidence is particularly relevant in cases of this nature involving a written contract between two large corporations presumably represented by competent counsel. Such parties should be held to the terms of their written contract whenever it is reasonable to do so, as it is incumbent upon courts to uphold the dignity of a contract whenever possible by preventing parol evidence from being used to negate the terms of written contracts. The First Circuit's words in *Intern. Business Machines v. Catamore Enterprises*, 548 F.2d 1065, 1073 (1st Cir. 1976), *cert. denied*, 431 U.S. 960, 97 S. Ct. 2687, 53 L. Ed. 2d 278 (1977) are particularly apt in this case:

> The morass of business dealings between two companies described on this record, their promises oral and written, the disparity of their understandings, the frustration of expectations, the inevitable recriminations and conflicting memories—all this is not unique, new, or infrequently encountered. The law in its effort to facilitate just resolutions of such controversies has, over the centuries, developed certain aids or guides to decision.... The first is the substantive principle that when, in the course of business transactions between people or corporations, free and uncoerced understandings purporting to be comprehensive are solemnized by documents which both parties sign and concede to be their agreement, such documents are not easily bypassed or given restrictive interpretations.

Additionally, as this lawsuit involved a lengthy and complicated fact situation, admitting extrinsic evidence would have increased the possibility of unnecessarily confusing the jury, a possibility § 2-202 is designed to avoid:

> But the way [§ 2-202] is worded, the trial is certainly not to be a free-wheeling affair in which the parties may introduce before the jury all evidence of terms, including the writing, with the jury then to decide on terms. Rather, it is plain from the rule and from prior history of similar rules that some of the evidence is to be heard initially only by the judge and that he may invoke the rule to keep this evidence from the jury. WHITE & SUMMERS, THE LAW UNDER THE UNIFORM COMMERCIAL CODE 77 (2d ed. 1980). *See also* Charles T. Mc-

Cormick, *The Parol Evidence Rule as a Procedural Device for Control of the Jury*, 41 Yale L.J. 365 (1932).

In summary, we conclude that the district court's order barring Presto from introducing extrinsic evidence regarding the intended maximum capacity of the System was not an abuse of discretion as it properly held the parties to the written terms of their contract, accorded with the basic principle of law favoring the dignity of a written contract, and avoided unnecessarily confusing the jury....

Conclusion

We agree with the rulings of the trial court and hold that: (1) the district court did not err in precluding Presto from introducing extrinsic evidence to attempt to prove that the parties intended the maximum capacity of the System to be defined solely in terms of pounds of castings per hour....

NOTES AND QUESTIONS

1. *Interpretation as a surrogate for the real dispute:*[42] Presto's small hamburger cookers were very successful, and a large Christmas market was anticipated in 1976. Seller's delivery was six weeks late. Presto was in a tough spot once Binks announced it would be late. The minutes of a November 15, 1976, meeting of the seller's officials said that "Presto has made commitments on their products and they cannot make their commitments. Presto is desperate. Their frying pans are a commitment to Sears for the Christmas rush." Seller's brief states:

> Binks and its suppliers recommended that Presto break in the System gradually after installation. Presto started up the system "full bore" and thereby increased the chance that the conveyor later would drag and the ovens would not seal properly. When the K was made, the parties assumed the ovens would run 8 hours a day 5 days a week, but Presto decided to operate it 24 hours per day 6 days a week. Presto had no program of preventive maintenance until 6 months after installation.

The trial court ruled that the seller was excused from liability for late delivery by the delay of an oven subcontractor caused by a supplier's strike and an injury to a key employee. The trial court also suggested that Presto had waived any damages arising from late delivery by accepting delivery, not terminating the contract, and not making a written claim at that time.[43] Presto could still sue for damages ($9.5 million was claimed) for delivery of a defective product, however. Note that this dispute about whether the goods were defective is partly a surrogate for the responsibility for the delay and the efforts made to overcome the lost time.

---

42. Much of the information contained in this and subsequent notes come from an interview by one of the authors with an attorney for Presto and from a review of the appellate briefs and the trial record in this case.

43. We will return to the issue of what victims of breach can do when we look at waiver and the required notices of an intention to hold a seller liable for damages under the Uniform Commercial Code in Chapters 4 and 5 of these materials.

2. *The excluded parol evidence:* The key items of parol evidence excluded by the trial court are described in a footnote to the opinion. In its brief, Binks offered this justification for describing the machine's capacity not just in terms of weight per hour:

> There was an important reason for expressing the maximum capacity of the System in terms of specific hourly quantities for the identified parts. The ovens in the System baked Presto's coatings by "impinged high velocity hot air" — jets of hot air directed at the parts as they progressed through the ovens. An increase in the number of parts passing back and forth through the ovens would obstruct the impinged air and, therefore, decrease the efficiency of the ovens. On the other hand, the "maximum loading" provision in the contract established the weight above which the loading of the parts (4500 pounds) and the work holders (4500 pounds) would exceed the weight-bearing tolerances of the entire System, including the conveyor and conveyor drives....

> Binks has never contended that it was improper to load 2 parts per work-holder, so long as the applicable pieces-per-hour limitation was not exceeded. These overall limits could have been observed even when work holders were being doubleloaded simply by doubling the distance between work holders.

3. *Ambiguities and the parol evidence rule:* Courts often address parol evidence rule issues by asking whether the writing was ambiguous and looking at parol and other evidence to resolve the issue. Presto argued that the trial court should have looked at the course of performance to indicate the proper construction of the contract. The work holder was designed to allow two parts per holder and thus a load more than what the trial court found to be the contractual maximum for number of pieces per hour. The system was operated with Binks's knowledge, and Presto double-loaded the system at the 24-hour test run, and Binks's officials did not object. Would you find this evidence persuasive?

Apparently Binks's engineers drafted the language in the proposal form that became the contract between the parties. Should the court have construed the language most strongly against Binks, the party that drafted it?

4. *The purpose of the parol evidence rule:* According to the court, what is the purpose of the parol evidence rule? Does the court limit interpretation to consideration of the language of the written contract because it thinks the written language better describes the parties' intent? Or is there some other reason? If there is another reason, would you describe this decision as contrary to the principle of freedom of contract?

5. *The jury once again:* We have noted before that one possible reason for privileging the language in a written contract over other evidence of the parties' intentions is to exclude a possibly unreliable jury from making determinations of fact. In this case, however, it was not possible to exclude the jury entirely, because there was conflicting evidence about why the machine did not perform properly (an issue clearly appropriate for jury consideration, should either party demand it). Do you think that the parol evidence rule should be waived in any case where a jury is going to hear the case regardless? Certainly the advantages of a more efficient dispute resolution process, by avoiding a jury trial, are not then achievable.

In this case a large national concern (Presto) was seeking $9.5 million in damages against a considerably smaller machinery company (Binks). Do you think considerations of that nature ever influence a jury?

6. CISG and parol evidence: A court applying the Convention on Contracts for the International Sale of Goods (CISG) has the authority to consider extrinsic evidence that contradicts the "paper deal;" the Convention contains no parol evidence rule. In Article 8(3) the Convention states that "[i]n determining the intent of a party … due consideration is to be given to all relevant circumstances of the case including the negotiations, any practices which the parties have established between themselves, usages and any subsequent conduct of the parties." If the contract had been governed by the CISG, would the result in *Binks v. Presto* have been different?

2. Of Partial Integrations and Side Agreements

MITCHILL v. LATH

New York Court of Appeals
247 N.Y. 377, 160 N.E. 646 (1928)

Appeal, by permission, from a judgment of the Appellate Division of the Supreme Court in the second judicial department, entered May 27, 1927, unanimously affirming a judgment in favor of plaintiff entered upon a decision of the court on trial at Special Term in an action to compel specific performance of an alleged contract to remove an ice house....

ANDREWS, J.

In the fall of 1923 the Laths owned a farm. This they wished to sell. Across the road, on land belonging to Lieutenant-Governor Lunn, they had an ice house which they might remove. Mrs. Mitchill looked over the land with a view to its purchase. She found the ice house objectionable. Thereupon "the defendants orally promised and agreed, for and in consideration of the purchase of their farm by the plaintiff, to remove the said ice house in the spring of 1924." Relying upon this promise, she made a written contract to buy the property for $8,400, for cash and a mortgage and containing various provisions usual in such papers. Later receiving a deed, she entered into possession and has spent considerable sums in improving the property for use as a summer residence. The defendants have not fulfilled their promise as to the ice house and do not intend to do so. We are not dealing, however, with their moral delinquencies. The question before us is whether their oral agreement may be enforced in a court of equity.

This requires a discussion of the parol evidence rule — a rule of law that defines the limits of the contract to be construed. *Glackin v. Bennett*, 226 Mass. 316. It is more than a rule of evidence and oral testimony even if admitted will not control the written contract, *O'Malley v. Grady*, 222 Mass. 202, unless admitted without objection. *Brady v. Nally*, 151 N.Y. 258. It applies, however, to attempts to modify such a contract by parol. It does not affect a parol collateral contract distinct from and independent of the written agreement. It is, at times, troublesome to draw the line. Williston, in his work on Contracts (§ 637) points out the difficulty. "Two entirely distinct contracts," he says, "each for a separate consideration may be made at the same time and will be distinct legally. Where, however, one agreement is entered into wholly or partly in consideration of the simultaneous agreement to enter into another, the transactions are necessarily bound together.... Then if one of the agreements is oral and the other is written, the problem arises whether the bond is sufficiently close to prevent proof of the oral agreement." That is the situation here. It is claimed that the defendants are called upon to do more than is required by their written contract in connection with the sale as to which it deals.

The principle may be clear, but it can be given effect by no mechanical rule. As so often happens, it is a matter of degree, for as Professor Williston also says, where a contract contains several promises on each side it is not difficult to put any one of them in the form of a collateral agreement. If this were enough written contracts might always be modified by parol. Not form, but substance is the test.

In applying this test the policy of our courts is to be considered. We have believed that the purpose behind the rule was a wise one not easily to be abandoned. Notwithstanding injustice here and there, on the whole it works for good. Old precedents and principles are not to be lightly cast aside unless it is certain that they are an obstruction under present conditions. New York has been less open to arguments that would modify this particular rule, than some jurisdictions elsewhere. Thus in *Eighmie v. Taylor*, 98 N.Y. 288, it was held that a parol warranty might not be shown although no warranties were contained in the writing.

Under our decisions before such an oral agreement as the present is received to vary the written contract, at least three conditions must exist, (1) the agreement must in form be a collateral one; (2) it must not contradict express or implied provisions of the written contract; (3) it must be one that parties would not ordinarily be expected to embody in the writing; or put in another way, an inspection of the written contract, read in the light of surrounding circumstances, must not indicate that the writing appears "to contain the engagements of the parties, and to define the object and measure the extent of such engagement." Or again, it must not be so clearly connected with the principal transaction as to be part and parcel of it.

The respondent does not satisfy the third of these requirements. It may be, not the second. We have a written contract for the purchase and sale of land. The buyer is to pay $8,400 in the way described. She is also to pay her portion of any rents, interest on mortgages, insurance premiums, and water meter charges. She may have a survey made of the premises. On their part the sellers are to give a full covenant deed of the premises as described, or as they may be described by the surveyor if the survey is had, executed and acknowledged at their own expense; they sell the personal property on the farm and represent they own it; they agree that all amounts paid them on the contract and the expense of examining the title shall be a lien on the property;

they assume the risk of loss or damage by fire until the deed is delivered; and they agree to pay the broker his commissions. Are they to do more? Or is such a claim inconsistent with these precise provisions? It could not be shown that the plaintiff was to pay $500 additional. Is it also implied that the defendants are not to do anything unexpressed in the writing?

That we need not decide. At least, however, an inspection of this contract shows a full and complete agreement, setting forth in detail the obligations of each party. On reading it one would conclude that the reciprocal obligations of the parties were fully detailed. Nor would his opinion alter if he knew the surrounding circumstances. The presence of the ice house, even the knowledge that Mrs. Mitchill thought it objectionable, would not lead to the belief that a separate agreement existed with regard to it. Were such an agreement made it would seem most natural that the inquirer should find it in the contract. Collateral in form it is found to be, but it is closely related to the subject dealt with in the written agreement—so closely that we hold it may not be proved.

Where the line between the competent and the incompetent is narrow the citation of authorities is of slight use. Each represents the judgment of the court on the precise facts before it. How closely bound to the contract is the supposed collateral agreement is the decisive factor in each case.... Attention should be called also to *Taylor v. Hopper*, 62 N.Y. 649, where it is assumed that evidence of a parol agreement to remove a barn, which was an inducement to the sale of lots, was improper.

We do not ignore the fact that authorities may be found that would seem to support the contention of the appellant.... But the fixed form of a deed makes it inappropriate to insert collateral agreements, however closely connected with the sale. This may be cause for an exception. Here we deal with the contract on the basis of which the deed to Mrs. Mitchill was given subsequently, and we confine ourselves to the question whether its terms may be modified....

Our conclusion is that the judgment of the Appellate Division and that of the Special Term should be reversed and the complaint dismissed, with costs in all courts.

LEHMAN, J. (dissenting).

I accept the general rule as formulated by Judge Andrews. I differ with him only as to its application to the facts shown in the record. The plaintiff contracted to purchase land from the defendants for an agreed price. A formal written agreement was made between the sellers and the plaintiff's husband. It is on its face a complete contract for the conveyance of the land. It describes the property to be conveyed. It sets forth the purchase price to be paid. All the conditions and terms of the conveyance to be made are clearly stated. I concede at the outset that parol evidence to show additional conditions and terms of the conveyance would be inadmissible. There is a conclusive presumption that the parties intended to integrate in that written contract every agreement relating to the nature or extent of the property to be conveyed, the contents of the deed to be delivered, the consideration to be paid as a condition precedent to the delivery of the deeds, and indeed all the rights of the parties in connection with the land. The conveyance of that land was the subject matter of the written contract and the contract completely covers that subject.

The parol agreement which the court below found the parties had made was collateral to, yet connected with, the agreement of purchase and sale. It has been found that the defendants induced the plaintiff to agree to purchase the land by a promise to remove an ice house from land not covered by the agreement of purchase and sale. No independent consideration passed to the defendants for the parol promise. To that extent the written contract and the alleged oral contract are bound together. The same bond usually exists wherever attempt is made to prove a parol agreement that is collateral to a written agreement. Hence "the problem arises whether the bond is sufficiently close to prevent proof of the oral agreement." *See* Judge Andrews's citation from WILLISTON ON CONTRACTS, § 637.

Judge Andrews has formulated a standard to measure the closeness of the bond. Three conditions, at least, must exist before an oral agreement may be proven to increase the obligation imposed by the written agreement. I think we agree that the first condition that the agreement "must in form be a collateral one" is met by the evidence. I concede that this condition is met in most cases where the courts have nevertheless excluded evidence of the collateral oral agreement. The difficulty here, as in most cases, arises in connection with the two other conditions.

The second condition is that the "parol agreement must not contradict express or implied provisions of the written contract." Judge Andrews voices doubt whether this condition is satisfied. The written contract has been carried out. The purchase price has been paid; conveyance has been made; title has passed in accordance with the terms of the written contract. The mutual obligations expressed in the written contract are left unchanged by the alleged oral contract. When performance was required of the written contract, the obligations of the parties were measured solely by its terms. By the oral agreement the plaintiff seeks to hold the defendants to other obligations to be performed by them thereafter upon land which was not conveyed to the plaintiff. The assertion of such further obligation is not inconsistent with the written contract unless the written contract contains a provision, express or implied, that the defendants are not to do anything not expressed in the writing. Concededly there is no such express provision in the contract, and such a provision may be implied, if at all, only if the asserted additional obligation is "so clearly connected with the principal transaction as to be part and parcel of it," and is not "one that the parties would not ordinarily be expected to embody in the writing." The hypothesis so formulated for a conclusion that the asserted additional obligation is inconsistent with an implied term of the contract is that the alleged oral agreement does not comply with the third condition as formulated by Judge Andrews. In this case, therefore, the problem reduces itself to the one question whether or not the oral agreement meets the third condition.

I have conceded that upon inspection the contract is complete. "It appears to contain the engagements of the parties, and to define the object and measure the extent of such engagement"; it constitutes the contract between them and is presumed to contain the whole of that contract. *Eighmie v. Taylor*, 98 N.Y. 288. That engagement was on the one side to convey land; on the other to pay the price. The plaintiff asserts further agreement based on the same consideration to be performed by the defendants after the conveyance was complete, and directly affecting only other land. It is true, as Judge Andrews points out, that "the presence of the ice house, even the knowledge that Mrs. Mitchill thought it objectionable, would not lead to the belief that a separate agreement existed with regard to it"; but the question we must decide is whether or not, *assuming* an agreement was made for the removal of an unsightly ice house from one parcel of land as an inducement for the purchase of another parcel, the parties would ordinarily or naturally be expected to embody the agreement for the removal of the ice house from one parcel in the written agreement to convey the other parcel. Exclusion of proof of the oral agreement on the ground that it varies the contract embodied in the writing may be based only upon a finding or presumption that the written contract was intended to cover the oral negotiations for the removal of the ice house which led up to the contract of purchase and sale. To determine what the writing was intended to cover, "the document alone will not suffice. What it was intended to cover cannot be known till we know what there was to cover. The question being whether certain subjects of negotiation were intended to be covered, we must compare the writing and the negotiations before we can determine whether they were in fact covered." WIGMORE ON EVIDENCE (2d ed.) § 2430.

The subject matter of the written contract was the conveyance of land. The contract was so complete on its face that the conclusion is inevitable that the parties intended to embody in the writing all the negotiations covering at least the conveyance. The promise by the defendants to remove the ice house from other land was not connected with their obligation to convey, except that one agreement would not have been made unless the other was also made. The plaintiff's assertion of a parol agreement by the defendants to remove the ice house was completely established by the great weight of evidence. It must prevail unless that agreement was part of the agreement to convey and the entire agreement was embodied in the writing.

The fact that in this case the parol agreement is established by the overwhelming weight of evidence is, of course, not a factor which may be considered in determining the competency or legal effect of the evidence. Hardship in the particular case would not justify the court in disregarding or emasculating the general rule. It merely accentuates the outlines of our problem. The assumption that the parol agreement was made is no longer obscured by any doubts. The problem then is clearly whether the parties are presumed to have intended to render that parol agreement legally ineffective and non-existent by failure to embody it in the writing. Though we are driven to say that nothing in the written contract which fixed the terms and conditions of the stipulated conveyance suggests the existence of any further parol agreement, an inspection of the contract, though it is complete on its face in regard to the subject of the conveyance, does not, I think, show that it was intended to embody negotiations or agreements, if any, in regard to a matter so loosely bound to the conveyance as the removal of an ice house from land not conveyed.

The rule of integration undoubtedly frequently prevents the assertion of fraudulent claims. Parties who take the precaution of embodying their oral agreements in a writing should be protected against the assertion that other terms of the same agreement were not integrated in the writing. The limits of the integration are determined by the writing, read in the light of the surrounding circumstances. A written contract, however complete, yet covers only a limited field. I do not think that in the written contract for the conveyance of land here under consideration we can find an intention to cover a field so broad as to include prior agreements, if any such were made, to do other acts on other property after the stipulated conveyance was made.

In each case where such a problem is presented, varying factors enter into its solution. Citation of authority in this or other jurisdictions is useless, at least without minute analysis of the facts. The analysis I have made of the decisions in this State leads me to the view that the decision of the courts below is in accordance with our own authorities and should be affirmed.

CARDOZO, C.J., POUND, KELLOGG, and O'BRIEN, JJ., concur with ANDREWS, J.; LEHMAN, J., dissents in opinion in which CRANE, J., concurs.

Judgment accordingly.

NOTES AND QUESTIONS

1. *Background from the briefs and record:* The buyers sued for specific performance. On December 20, 1926, the trial court issued a decree ordering the seller to remove the ice house by December 25th or to pay the buyers $8,000. The court found that the sellers orally promised to remove the ice house by the spring of 1924. Relying on this promise, the buyers bought the farm for $8,400. The deed was delivered on December 19, 1923. The buyers made extensive repairs and improvements, spending over $23,000, "during the course of some of which the defendants were employed." The presence of the ice house and the operation of the ice business decreased the value of the property by $8,000.[44]

2. *The likely impact of the decision:* What lessons might the decision teach the rest of us? Are future buyers in Mrs. Mitchill's position likely to learn that they cannot trust sellers but must get these promises in writing? Can we count on real estate brokers and lawyers to tell her? What is likely to happen in cases where parties deal without brokers or lawyers? To what extent is a demand to put promises such as this one in writing an attack on the integrity of the other party?

3. *1928 sexism?* Can we explain the Court of Appeals' decision as sexist? Did the court, a group of older male middle- or upper-class lawyers, assume that concern with aesthetics is feminine and thus frivolous and unimportant? Property values are conventionally tangible and part of the male sphere. Legal institutions

---

44. The Inflation Calculator, *available at* http://www.westegg.com/inflation, tells us that what cost $8,400 in 1923 would cost $104,698.56 in 2009; what cost $23,000 in 1923 would cost $286,674.63 in 2009.

respond only to this male world of deeds and dollars. Recall that the formal written contract was made between Mrs. Mitchill's husband and the sellers. The men took care of business, and only then was she able to assert her concerns. She gained a promise that prompted her to agree to the deal, but it was treated as of little consequence—as a woman's whim. To the extent that women trust others more than men and assume cooperation rather than conflict, the Court of Appeals penalizes this desirable tendency. Is the foregoing a plausible, likely, or fair analysis of the case? Or is this note sexist insofar as it assumes that Mrs. Mitchill was not the business brains of the family and perfectly capable of taking care of herself in the world of business?

4. *Social class and the* Mitchill *case:* Suppose we speculated on the relationship between Catherine Mitchill and Charles Lath and their families. The Mitchills were able to spend $23,000 in 1923 for improvements on a farmhouse on a lake that was to be a summer residence. Apparently, the Laths were farmers who ran an ice business. (On the other hand, they could afford to fight a case to the Court of Appeals.) The Mitchills hired the Laths to remodel what was once their house. They went from owners to workers subject to the commands of others. It is easy to imagine that the Laths could have harbored resentments about the circumstances that caused them to sell the property, or to the way in which they were treated by the Mitchills. Should there be an inquiry into such questions? If not, can justice be done?

Justice Andrews said: "We are not dealing ... with their [the Laths'] moral delinquencies." How might Charles Lath justify failing to remove the ice house to himself and his friends? Remember that Mrs. Mitchill found a plain and practical building where work was done offensive. The Laths were able to win by asserting their legal rights. Is such an assertion a form of moral delinquency?

5. *Is the* Mitchill *standard good law under the UCC?* Judge Andrews's opinion spoke of additional terms "that parties would not ordinarily be expected to embody in the writing." Official Comment 3 to UCC § 2-202 talks of "additional terms ... such that, if agreed upon ... would certainly have been included in the document...." Is the difference between these two formulations of the standard significant? In what setting? To whom?[45]

---

45. A lower New York court suggested in George v. Davoli, 91 Misc. 2d 296, 299, 397 N.Y.S.2d 895, 897 (City Ct. Geneva 1977), that the *Mitchill* case "does not apply herein as its application to the instant case [a transaction in goods covered by Article 2 of the UCC] has been changed by legislative enactment (Uniform Commercial Code § 2-202, sub (b)) that took effect in 1964." In the case of Braten v. Bankers Trust Co., 60 N.Y.2d 155, 162, 456 N.E.2d 802 (1983), the court of appeals indicated that the *Mitchill* case was alive and well, at least outside the area covered by Article 2 of the UCC, finding in that case that evidence of an oral promise to delay enforcing foreclosure rights contradicted the document since it did not appear in the writing and "such a fundamental condition would hardly have been omitted."

MASTERSON v. SINE

California Supreme Court
68 Cal. 2d 222, 436 P.2d 561 (1968)

Action for declaratory relief to establish plaintiff's right to enforce an option to repurchase certain real property. Judgment declaring plaintiff's right to exercise the option reversed.

TRAYNOR, C.J.—

Dallas Masterson and his wife Rebecca owned a ranch as tenants-in-common. On February 25, 1958, they conveyed it to Medora and Lu Sine by a grant deed "Reserving unto the Grantors herein an option to purchase the above described property on or before February 25, 1968" for the "same consideration as being paid heretofore plus their depreciation value of any improvements Grantees may add to the property from and after two and a half years from this date." Medora is Dallas's sister and Lu's wife. Since the conveyance Dallas has been adjudged bankrupt. His trustee in bankruptcy and Rebecca brought this declaratory relief action to establish their right to enforce the option.

The case was tried without a jury. Over defendants' objection the trial court admitted extrinsic evidence that by "the same consideration as being paid heretofore" both the grantors and the grantees meant the sum of $50,000 and by "depreciation value of any improvements" they meant the depreciation value of improvements to be computed by deducting from the total amount of any capital expenditures made by defendant grantees the amount of depreciation allowable to them under United States income tax regulations as of the time of the exercise of the option.

The court also determined that the parol evidence rule precluded admission of extrinsic evidence offered by defendants to show that the parties wanted the property kept in the Masterson family and that the option was therefore personal to the grantors and could not be exercised by the trustee in bankruptcy.

The court entered judgment for plaintiffs, declaring their right to exercise the option, specifying in some detail how it could be exercised, and reserving jurisdiction to supervise the manner of its exercise and to determine the amount that plaintiffs will be required to pay defendants for their capital expenditures if plaintiffs decide to exercise the option.

Defendants appeal. They contend that the option provision is too uncertain to be enforced and that extrinsic evidence as to its meaning should not have been admitted. The trial court properly refused to frustrate the obviously declared intention of the grantors to reserve an option to repurchase by an overly meticulous insistence on completeness and clarity of written expression.... It properly admitted extrinsic evidence to explain the language of the deed ... to the end that the consideration for the option would appear with sufficient certainty to permit specific enforcement.... The trial court erred, however, in excluding the extrinsic evidence that the option was personal to the grantors and therefore nonassignable.

When the parties to a written contract have agreed to it as an "integration"—a complete and final embodiment of the terms of an agreement—parol evidence cannot be used to add to or vary its terms.... When only part of the agreement is integrated, the same rule applies to that part, but parol evidence may be used to prove elements of the agreement not reduced to writing....

The crucial issue in determining whether there has been an integration is whether the parties intended their writing to serve as the exclusive embodiment of their agreement. The instrument itself may help to resolve that issue. It may state, for example, that "there are no previous understandings or agreements not contained in the writing," and thus express the parties' "intention to nullify antecedent understandings or agreements." *See* 3 CORBIN, CONTRACTS (1960) § 578, p. 411. Any such collateral agreement itself must be examined, however, to determine whether the parties intended the subjects of negotiation it deals with to be included in, excluded from, or otherwise affected by the writing. Circumstances at the time of the writing may also aid in the determination of such integration....

California cases have stated that whether there was an integration is to be determined solely from the face of the instrument ... and that the question for the court is whether it "appears to be a complete ... agreement." ... Neither of these strict formulations of the rule, however, has been consistently applied. The requirement that the writing must appear incomplete on its face has been repudiated in many cases where parol evidence was admitted "to prove the existence of a separate oral agreement as to any matter on which the document is silent and which is not inconsistent with its terms"—even though the instrument appeared to state a complete agreement.... Even under the rule that the writing alone is to be consulted, it was found necessary to examine the alleged collateral agreement before concluding that proof of it was precluded by the writing alone. *See* 3 CORBIN, CONTRACTS (1960) § 582, pp. 444–446. It is therefore evident that "[t]he conception of a writing as wholly and intrinsically self-determinative of the parties' intent to make it a sole memorial of one or seven or twenty-seven subjects of negotiation is an impossible one." 9 WIGMORE, EVIDENCE (3d ed. 1940) § 2431, p. 103. For example, a promissory note given by a debtor to his creditor may integrate all their present contractual rights and obligations, or it may be only a minor part of an underlying executory contract that would never be discovered by examining the face of the note.

In formulating the rule governing parol evidence, several policies must be accommodated. One policy is based on the assumption that written evidence is more accurate than human memory.... This policy, however, can be adequately served by excluding parol evidence of agreements that directly contradict the writing. Another policy is based on the fear that fraud or unintentional invention by witnesses interested in the outcome of the litigation will mislead the finder of facts.... McCormick has suggested that the party urging the spoken as against the written word is most often the economic underdog, threatened by severe hardship if the writing is enforced. In his view the parol evidence rule arose to allow the court to control the tendency of the jury to find through sympathy and without a dispassionate assessment of the probability of fraud or faulty memory that the parties made an oral agreement collateral to the written contract, or that preliminary tentative agreements were not abandoned when omitted from the writing. *See* McCormick, Evidence (1954) § 210. He recognizes, however, that if this theory were adopted in disregard of all other considerations, it would lead to the exclusion of testimony concerning oral agreements whenever there is a writing and thereby often defeat the true intent of the parties. *See* McCormick, *op. cit. supra*, § 216, p. 441.

Evidence of oral collateral agreements should be excluded only when the fact finder is likely to be misled. The rule must therefore be based on the credibility of the evidence. One such standard, adopted by § 240(1)(b) of the Restatement of Contracts, permits proof of a collateral agreement if it "is such an agreement as might *naturally* be made as a separate agreement by parties situated as were the parties to the written contract." (Italics added; *see* McCormick, Evidence (1954) § 216, p. 441; *see also* 3 Corbin, Contracts (1960) § 583, p. 475, § 594, pp. 568–569; 4 Williston, Contracts (3d ed. 1961) § 638, pp. 1039–1045.) The draftsmen of the Uniform Commercial Code would exclude the evidence in still fewer instances: "If the additional terms are such that, if agreed upon, they would *certainly* have been included in the document in the view of the court, then evidence of their alleged making must be kept from the trier of fact." (Cmt. 3, § 2-202, italics added.)[46]

The option clause in the deed in the present case does not explicitly provide that it contains the complete agreement, and the deed is silent on the question of assignability. Moreover, the difficulty of accommodating the formalized structure of a deed to the insertion of collateral agreements makes it less likely that all the terms of such an agreement were included.[47] *See* 3 Corbin, Contracts (1960) § 587; 4 Williston, Contracts (3d ed. 1961) § 645; 70 A.L.R. 752, 759 (1931); 68 A.L.R. 245 (1930). The statement of the reservation of the option might well have been placed in the recorded deed solely to preserve the grantors' rights against any possible future purchasers, and this function could well be served without any mention of the parties' agreement that the option was personal. There is nothing in the record to indicate that the parties to this family transaction, through experience in land transactions or otherwise, had any warning of the disadvantages of failing to put the whole agree-

---

46. [1] Corbin suggests that, even in situations where the court concludes that it would not have been natural for the parties to make the alleged collateral oral agreement, parol evidence of such an agreement should nevertheless be permitted if the court is convinced that the unnatural actually happened in the case being adjudicated. 3 Corbin, Contracts, § 485, pp. 478, 480; *cf.* Murray, *The Parol Evidence Rule: A Clarification*, 4 Duquesne L. Rev. 337, 341–342 (1966). This suggestion may be based on a belief that judges are not likely to be misled by their sympathies. If the court believes that the parties intended a collateral agreement to be effective, there is no reason to keep the evidence from the jury.

47. [2] *See Goble v. Dotson*, 203 Cal. App. 2d 272, 21 Cal. Rptr. 769 (1962), where the deed given by a real estate developer to the plaintiffs contained a condition that grantees would not build a pier or boathouse. Despite this reference in the deed to the subject of berthing for boats, the court allowed plaintiffs to prove by parol evidence that the condition was agreed to in return for the developer's oral promise that plaintiffs were to have the use of two boat spaces nearby.

ment in the deed. This case is one, therefore, in which it can be said that a collateral agreement such as that alleged "might naturally be made as a separate agreement." *A fortiori*, the case is not one in which the parties "would certainly" have included the collateral agreement in the deed.

It is contended, however, that an option agreement is ordinarily presumed to be assignable if it contains no provisions forbidding its transfer or indicating that its performance involves elements personal to the parties.... The fact that there is a written memorandum, however, does not necessarily preclude parol evidence rebutting a term that the law would otherwise presume. In *American Industrial Sales Corp. v. Airscope, Inc.*, 44 Cal. 2d 393, 397–398 (1955), we held it proper to admit parol evidence of a contemporaneous collateral agreement as to the place of payment of a note, even though it contradicted the presumption that a note, silent as to the place of payment, is payable where the creditor resides.... Moreover, even when there is no explicit agreement—written or oral—that contractual duties shall be personal, courts will effectuate presumed intent to that effect if the circumstances indicate that performance by substituted person would be different from that contracted for....

In the present case defendants offered evidence that the parties agreed that the option was not assignable in order to keep the property in the Masterson family. The trial court erred in excluding that evidence.

The judgment is reversed....

BURKE, J.—

I dissent. The majority opinion:

(1) Undermines the parol evidence rule as we have known it in this state since at least 1872 by declaring that parol evidence should have been admitted by the trial court to show that a written option, absolute and unrestricted in form, was intended to be limited and nonassignable;

(2) Renders suspect instruments of conveyance absolute on their face;

(3) Materially lessens the reliance that may be placed upon written instruments affecting the title to real estate; and

(4) Opens the door, albeit unintentionally, to a new technique for the defrauding of creditors.

The opinion permits defendants to establish by parol testimony that their grant to their brother (and brother-in-law) of a written option, absolute in terms, was nevertheless agreed to be nonassignable by the grantee (now a bankrupt), and that therefore the right to exercise it did not pass, by operation of the bankruptcy laws, to the trustee for the benefit of the grantee's creditors.

And how was this to be shown? By the proffered testimony of the bankrupt optionee himself! Thereby one of his assets (the option to purchase defendants' California ranch) would be withheld from the trustee in bankruptcy and from the bankrupt's creditors. Understandably the trial court, as required by the parol evidence rule, did not allow the bankrupt by parol to so contradict the unqualified language of the written option.

The court properly admitted parol evidence to explain the intended meaning of the "same consideration" and "depreciation value" phrases of the written option to purchase defendants' land, as the intended meaning of those phrases was not clear. However, there was nothing ambiguous about the granting language of the option and not the slightest suggestion in the document that the option was to be nonassignable. Thus, to permit such words of limitation to be added by parol is to *contradict* the absolute nature of the grant, and to directly violate the parol evidence rule.

Just as it is unnecessary to state in a deed to "lot X" that the house located thereon goes with the land, it is likewise unnecessary to add to "I grant an option to Jones" the words "*and his assigns*" for the option to be assignable. As hereinafter emphasized in more detail, California statutes expressly declare that it *is* assignable, and only if I add language in writing showing my intent to withhold or restrict the right of assignment may the grant be so limited. Thus, to seek to restrict the grant by parol is to *contradict* the written document in violation of the parol evidence rule.

The majority opinion arrives at its holding via a series of false premises which are not supported either in the record of this case or in such California authorities as are offered....

At the outset the majority in the present case reiterate that the rule against contradicting or varying the terms of a writing remains applicable when only part of the agreement is contained in the writing, and parol evidence is used to prove elements of the agreement not reduced to writing. But having restated this established rule, the majority opinion inexplicably proceeds to subvert it.

Each of the ... cases cited by the majority ... holds that although parol evidence is admissible to prove the parts of the contract not put in writing, it is *not admissible* to vary or *contradict* the writing or *prove* collateral *agreements* which are *inconsistent* therewith. The meaning of this rule (and the application of it found in the cases) is that if the asserted unwritten elements of the agreement would contradict, add to, detract from, vary, or be inconsistent with the written agreement, then such elements *may not* be shown by *parol* evidence.

The contract of sale and purchase of the ranch property here involved was carried out through a title company upon written escrow instructions executed by the respective parties after various preliminary negotiations. The deed to defendant grantees, in which the grantors expressly reserved an option to repurchase the property within a ten-year period and upon a specified consideration, was issued and delivered in consummation of the contract. In neither the written escrow instructions nor the deed containing the option is there any language even suggesting that the option was agreed or intended by the parties to be personal to the grantors, and so nonassignable....

Options are property, and are widely used in the sale and purchase of real and personal property. One of the basic incidents of property ownership is the right of the owner to sell or transfer it....

The right of an optionee to transfer his option to purchase property is accordingly one of the basic rights that accompanies the option unless limited under the language of the option itself. To allow an optioner to resort to parol evidence to support his assertion that the written option is not transferable is to authorize him to limit the option by attempting to restrict and reclaim rights with which he has already parted. A clearer violation of two substantive and basic rules of law—the parol evidence rule and the right of free transferability of property—would be difficult to conceive....

[The dissent quarreled with the majority's assertion that its decision was consistent with previous cases. The dissent concluded this section by characterizing the example of a promissory note as "obviously specious."] Rarely, if ever, does a promissory note given by a debtor to his creditor integrate *all* their agreements (that is not the purpose it serves); it may or it may not integrate *all* their present contractual rights and obligations; but relevant to the parol evidence rule, at least until the advent of the majority opinion in this case, alleged collateral agreements which would vary or contradict the terms and conditions of a promissory note may not be shown by parol....

Upon this structure of incorrect premises and unfounded assertions the majority opinion arrives at its climax: The pronouncement of "several policies [to] be accommodated ... *[in] formulating the rule governing parol evidence.*" (Italics added.)[48] Two of the "policies" as declared by the majority are: written evidence is more accurate than human memory;[49] fraud or unintentional invention by interested witnesses may well occur.

I submit that these purported "policies" are in reality two of the basic and obvious reasons for adoption by the Legislature of the parol evidence rule as the policy in this state. Thus the speculation of the majority concerning the views of various writers on the subject and the advisability of following them in this state is not only superfluous but flies flatly in the face of established California law and policy. It serves only to introduce uncertainty and confusion in a field of substantive law that was codified and made certain in this state a century ago.

However, despite the law which until the advent of the present majority opinion has been firmly and clearly established in California and relied upon by attorneys and courts alike, that parol evidence may *not* be employed to vary or contradict the terms of a written instrument, the majority now announce that such evidence "should be excluded only when the fact finder is *likely to be misled,*" and that "[t]he rule must therefore be based on the *credibility of the evidence.*" (Italics added.) But was it not, *inter alia*, to avoid misleading the fact finder, and to further the introduction of only the evidence that is most likely to *be* credible (the written document), that the Legislature adopted the parol evidence rule as a part of the substantive law of this state?

---

48. [7] It is the *Legislature* of this state that *did the formulating* of the rule governing parol evidence nearly a century ago when in 1872, as previously noted, §§ 1625 of the Civil Code and 1856 of the Code of Civil Procedure were adopted. And as already shown herein, the rule has since been consistently applied by the courts of this state. The parol evidence rule as thus laid down by the Legislature and applied by the courts *is the policy* of this state.

49. [8] Although the majority declare that this first "policy" may be served by excluding parol evidence of agreements that directly contradict the writing, such contradiction is *precisely* the *effect* of the agreement sought to be shown by parol in this case.

Next, in an effort to implement this newly promulgated "credibility" test, the majority opinion offers a choice of two "standards": one, a "certainty" standard, quoted from the Uniform Commercial Code,[50] and the other a "natural" standard found in the Restatement of Contracts,[51] and concludes that at least for purposes of the present case the "natural" viewpoint should prevail.

This new rule, not hitherto recognized in California, provides that proof of a claimed collateral oral agreement is admissible if it is such an agreement as might *naturally* have been made a separate agreement by the parties under the particular circumstances. I submit that this approach opens the door to uncertainty and confusion. Who can know what its limits are? Certainly I do not. For example, in its application to this case, who could be expected to divine as "natural" a separate oral agreement between the parties that the assignment, absolute and unrestricted on its face, was intended by the parties to be limited to the Masterson family?

Or, assume that one gives to his relative a promissory note and that the payee of the note goes bankrupt. By operation of law the note becomes an asset of the bankruptcy. The trustee attempts to enforce it. Would the relatives be permitted to testify that by a separate oral agreement made at the time of the execution of the note it was understood that should the payee fail in his business the maker would be excused from payment of the note, or that, as here, it was intended that the benefits of the note would be *personal* to the payee? I doubt that trial judges should be burdened with the task of conjuring whether it would have been "natural" under those circumstances for such a separate agreement to have been made by the parties. Yet, under the application of the proposed rule, this is the task the trial judge would have, and in essence the situation presented in the instant case is no different....

Comment hardly seems necessary on the convenience to a bankrupt of such a device to defeat his creditors. He need only produce parol testimony that any options (or other property, for that matter) that he holds are subject to an oral "collateral agreement" with family members (or with friends) that the property is nontransferable "in order to keep the property in the family" or in the friendly group. In the present case the value of the ranch which the bankrupt and his wife held an option to purchase has doubtless increased substantially during the years since they acquired the option. The initiation of this litigation by the trustee in bankruptcy to establish his right to enforce the option indicates his belief that there is substantial value to be gained for the creditors from this asset of the bankrupt. Yet the majority opinion permits defeat of the trustee and of the creditors through the device of an asserted collateral oral

---

50. [9] "If the additional terms are such that, if agreed upon, they would *certainly* have been included in the document in the view of the court, then evidence of their alleged making must be kept from the trier of fact." (Cmt. 3, § 2-202; italics added.).

51. [10] *Viz.*, proof of a collateral agreement should be permitted if it "is such an agreement as might *naturally* be made as a separate agreement by parties situated as were the parties to the written contract." (Restatement of Contracts, § 240, subd. (1)(b); italics added.).

agreement that the option was "personal" to the bankrupt and nonassignable "in order to keep the property in the family"![52] ...

I would hold that the trial court ruled correctly on the proffered parol evidence, and I would affirm the judgment.

[McComb, J., concurred.]

NOTES AND QUESTIONS

1. *Justice Traynor:* Roger Traynor was a member of the University of California—Berkeley law faculty when he was appointed to the Supreme Court of California in 1940. He served on that court until his retirement in 1970. Henry Friendly, a much respected judge, wrote a tribute on the occasion of Justice Traynor's death. He said, "Roger Traynor was the ablest judge of his generation in the United States. I say this without hesitation, qualification, limitation, or fear of successful contradiction."[53]

Walter Schaefer, another famous appellate judge, wrote:[54]

> "Roger Traynor is a law professor's judge," said the late Professor Harry Kalven, pointing out that his own casebook on torts used eight Traynor cases and that "we would have been well advised to have used more." ...
>
> That Roger Traynor was also a judge's judge is obvious from the frequent citation of his opinions. A Traynor opinion is always sound currency, always to be reckoned with. His influence on judges was enhanced by his warm personal relationships with so many of them. Over a span of just short of ten years, he served on the faculty of the Appellate Judges Seminar at New York University Law School. There he met for two weeks each year with twenty to twenty-five judges of top state courts and federal courts of appeals. The atmosphere was informal; common problems were discussed frankly and lasting friendships resulted....

Although Justice Traynor's opinions in many cases have had great influence on courts in other states, *Masterson v. Sine* has not had great influence outside of California. Why not?[55]

2. *The interests of others:* One of the plaintiffs in this case was Dallas Masterson's trustee-in-bankruptcy. A trustee acts on behalf of the creditors of the bankrupt debtor. As Justice Burke observes in his dissent, the value of the real estate transferred to the Sines had no doubt appreciated to the point where it exceeded, perhaps by a considerable amount, the price that Dallas and Rebecca Masterson would be required to

---

52. [14] As noted at the outset of this dissent, it was by means of the bankrupt's own testimony that defendants (the bankrupt's sister and her husband) sought to show that the option was personal to the bankrupt and thus not transferable to the trustee in bankruptcy.

53. Henry Friendly, *Ablest Judge of His Generation*, 71 CAL. L. REV. 1039, 1039 (1983).

54. Schaefer, *A Judge's Judge*, 71 CAL. L. REV. 1050, 1051 (1983).

55. For a discussion of Justice Traynor's opinions, *see* Stewart Macaulay, *Mr. Justice Traynor and the Law of Contracts*, 13 STAN. L. REV. 812 (1961).

pay under their option to purchase. If the trustee could have exercised the option held by Dallas to half the property (the option to the other half being held by Dallas's wife, who had not filed bankruptcy), the trustee could have resold the property for more than he or she had paid for it. The profits on the resale would have gone to repay Dallas's creditors, if any profits remained after deductions for the trustee's costs and fees.

At the time this case was litigated, the Bankruptcy Act vested in the trustee-in-bankruptcy all "transferable or leviable" property owned by the debtor at the time of the filing of bankruptcy. That is why the Sines were able to defeat the trustee's suit to exercise the option by showing that Dallas's option was personal and not transferable. The trustee did not own the option. Such a showing did not destroy Dallas's option, however. If Dallas later received a discharge of unsecured debts in bankruptcy (most debtors do), he could exercise the option afterwards, resell the real estate, and pocket the profits, probably leaving his unpaid creditors without any ability to obtain repayment from the asset. That is why Justice Burke refers to the parol testimony about the nontransferability of the option as "a device to defeat ... creditors." (This analysis assumes that the original transfer of the real estate from the Mastersons to the Sines could not be shown to have been done with the intent of defeating the Mastersons' creditors, in which case it could have been set aside under the Uniform Fraudulent Conveyances Act. This topic is beyond the scope of this note.)

In 1978, the Bankruptcy Act, which is federal legislation applicable in all states, was extensively revised. Since then, the Bankruptcy Code has provided that the trustee-in-bankruptcy becomes vested with all property interests of the debtor even if a "provision in an agreement ... restricts or conditions transfer of such interest by the debtor."[56] Consequently, if *Masterson v. Sine* were to recur today, the bankruptcy trustee's action to enforce the option against the Sines would not be defeated by a showing that Dallas's option was nontransferable.

3. *Justice Traynor on construction of documents:* *Masterson v. Sine* is but one of several decisions written by Justice Traynor concerning interpreting and construing written documents. Roughly, he adopts Professor Corbin's approach. For example, in *Pacific Gas & Elec. Co. v. G.W. Thomas Drayage & Rigging Co.*,[57] there was a contract for repairs on a steam turbine. It provided that G.W. Thomas was to indemnify PG & E "against all loss ... resulting from ... injury to property ... in any way connected with the performance of this contract." PG & E sued to recover damages for an injury to the turbine itself. G.W. Thomas offered evidence that the parties intended the indemnity clause to cover only injury to the property of third parties. The trial court refused to consider this evidence because the contract had a "plain and clear" meaning. The Supreme Court of California reversed. The question was the credibility of this evidence and not its admissibility.

56. 11 U.S.C. §541(c)(1).
57. 69 Cal. 2d 33, 442 P.2d 641, 643 (1968).

Justice Traynor reinforced (and perhaps even extended) this view in *Delta Dynamics, Inc. v. Arioto*.[58] In *Delta*, the court heard a case where the trial court refused to hear evidence that the parties intended cancellation of the contract as the exclusive remedy for a failure by a distributor to sell a specified number of safety devices. The Supreme Court of California reversed. Justice Traynor wrote: "The test of admissibility of extrinsic evidence to explain the meaning of a written instrument is not whether it appears to the court to be plain and unambiguous on its face, but whether the offered evidence is relevant to prove a meaning to which the language of the instrument is reasonably susceptible."[59] However, Justice Traynor also suggests that credible evidence does not necessarily mean evidence conforming to an objective standard. That implies that all credible evidence should be admitted provisionally to prove the intentions of the parties. Indeed, he even suggests that the evidence may be credible and establish a meaning to which the language of the document is not reasonably (objectively) susceptible. If this is the case, then it could be argued that courts must look at all the offered evidence to see if this interpretation is believable.[60]

Contrast Justice Traynor's approach with that of the Seventh Circuit's approach in *Binks Manufacturing Co. v. National Presto Industries, Inc.* What are the advantages and disadvantages of each approach?

4. *Later developments:* For 10 to 15 years after *Masterson v. Sine* and Justice Traynor's other decisions on interpretation of contracts, the California appellate courts generally followed his approach. However, Professor Ralph James Mooney asserted in 1995:

> California judges have largely abandoned Justice Traynor's admonitions that words have no fixed meanings and that courts should interpret contracts in ways that would have made sense to both parties considering the language at the transaction's outset. As always, the principal beneficiaries of the newer, more absolutist interpretations are the economically dominant parties who drafted the language.[61]

One of the most colorful attacks occurred in *Trident Center v. Connecticut Gen. Life Ins. Co.*[62] In that case, a partnership consisting of an insurance company and two of Los Angeles's largest and most prestigious law firms brought an action in federal court for a declaratory judgment. California law governed the transaction. The partnership asserted that it had the right to prepay a loan of more than $56 million. The 12.25 percent rate that had seemed reasonable in 1983 compared unfavorably with 1987 market rates and Trident (the partnership plaintiff) started looking for ways of refinancing the loan to take advantage of the lower rates. The defendant lender brought a motion to dismiss, claiming that the loan documents clearly and unambiguously

---

58. 69 Cal. 2d 525, 446 P.2d 785 (1968).

59. *Id.* at 528, 446 P.2d at 787 (*quoting* Pacific Gas & Elec. Co. v. G.W. Thomas Drayage & Rigging Co., 69 Cal. 2d 33, 37, 442 P.2d 641, 644 (1968)).

60. For a discussion, see W. Richard West Jr., *Chief Justice Traynor and the Parol Evidence Rule*, 22 Stan. L. Rev. 547 (1970).

61. Ralph James Mooney, *The New Conceptualism in Contract Law*, 74 Or. L. Rev. 1131, 1165 (1995).

62. 847 F.2d 564 (9th Cir. 1988).

precluded prepayment during the first 12 years of the loan. The trial court granted the motion and dismissed the plaintiff's complaint. Moreover, the trial court also sanctioned the plaintiff for filing a frivolous lawsuit.

The United States Court of Appeals for the Ninth Circuit reversed. Judge Kozinski said:

> The contract documents are lengthy and detailed; they squarely address the precise issue that is the subject of this dispute; to all who read English, they appear to resolve the issue fully and conclusively.
>
> Plaintiff nevertheless argues here, as it did below, that it is entitled to introduce extrinsic evidence that the contract means something other than what it says. This case therefore presents the question whether parties in California can ever draft a contract that is proof to parol evidence. Somewhat surprisingly, the answer is no.[63]

Judge Kozinski analyzed Justice Traynor's opinion in the *Pacific Gas & Electric Co.* case. He was highly critical:[64]

> We question whether this [Justice Traynor's] approach is more likely to divulge the original intention of the parties than reliance on the seemingly clear words they agreed upon at the time....
>
> *Pacific Gas* casts a long shadow of uncertainty over all transactions negotiated and executed under the law of California. As this case illustrates, even when the transaction is very sizeable, even if it involves only sophisticated parties, even if it was negotiated with the aid of counsel, even if it results in contract language that is devoid of ambiguity, costly and protracted litigation cannot be avoided if one party has a strong enough motive for challenging the contract. While this rule creates much business for lawyers and an occasional windfall to some clients, it leads only to frustration and delay for most litigants and clogs already overburdened courts.
>
> It also chips away at the foundation of our legal system. By giving credence to the idea that words are inadequate to express concepts, *Pacific Gas* undermines the basic principle that language provides a meaningful constraint on public and private conduct. If we are unwilling to say that parties, dealing face to face, can come up with language that binds them, how can we send anyone to jail for violating statutes consisting of mere words lacking "absolute and constant referents"? How can courts ever enforce decrees, not written in language understandable to all, but encoded in a dialect reflecting only the "linguistic background of the judge"? Can lower courts ever be faulted for failing to carry out the mandate of higher courts when "perfect verbal expression" is impossible? Are all attempts to develop the law in a reasoned and principled fashion doomed to failure as "remnant[s] of a primitive faith in the inherent potency and inherent meaning of words"? ...

---

63. *Id.* at 565.
64. *Id.* at 569, 570.

By holding that language has no objective meaning, and that contracts mean only what courts ultimately say they do, *Pacific Gas* invites precisely this type of lawsuit. With the benefit of 20 years of hindsight, the California Supreme Court may wish to revisit the issue. If it does so, we commend to it the facts of this case as a paradigmatic example of why the traditional rule, based on centuries of experience, reflects the far wiser approach.

Judge Kozinski noted that the defendant could move for summary judgment after completion of discovery. He said that the motion would succeed "unless Trident [the plaintiff] were to come forward with extrinsic evidence sufficient to render the contract reasonably susceptible to Trident's alternative interpretation, thereby creating a genuine issue of fact resolvable only at trial."

Did Judge Kozinski read Justice Traynor's opinions correctly or plausibly? Two months after the *Trident* decision was announced, another panel of judges on the United States Court of Appeals for the Ninth Circuit raised this question very politely. In *A. Kemp Fisheries, Inc. v. Castle & Cooke, Inc.*,[65] the court said:

> The broad language in *Trident* suggests that under California law courts must always admit extrinsic evidence to determine the meaning of disputed contract language. *Trident* held only that courts may not dismiss on the pleadings when one party claims that extrinsic evidence renders the contract ambiguous. The case must proceed beyond the pleadings so that the court may consider the evidence. If, after considering the evidence, the court determines that the contract is not reasonably susceptible to the interpretation advanced, the parol evidence rule operates to exclude the evidence. The court may then decide the case on a motion for summary judgment.

5. *The costs of a contextualist approach:* If a court can dismiss a case on the pleadings when it thinks documents are unambiguous, rather than allowing the parties to develop evidence by discovery and otherwise before considering a motion for summary judgment, obviously it can save litigation costs. Of course, it may increase what we might call "error costs"—the costs of having a court adopt an interpretation varying from what the parties intended. In the vast academic literature on interpretation, the question whether admitting evidence about context will increase or decrease error costs is hotly contested. It seems self-evident that by allowing contextualist evidence, such as the Mastersons' testimony about what was intended, the courts increase the risk that they will be misled about the parties' intent by self-serving, and perhaps even perjured, testimony. But by relying solely on a "plain meaning" approach to the interpretation of written language, the court risks adopting the meaning implied by an inartfully drafted contract. Recall, in this context, Professor Hill's comments in the introductory pages to this chapter on how written business contracts are drafted. Is it not likely that in some cases a court is more likely to reach a result consistent with the parties' intentions by taking a contextualist approach to interpretation?

---

65. 852 F.2d 493, n.2 (9th Cir. 1988).

Another kind of cost that needs to be considered is the effect of interpretation rules on the drafting of contracts. If courts taking a contextualist approach to interpretation are good at ascertaining what the parties intended, perhaps parties can then expend less effort and expense in the drafting of contracts, leaving it to the courts to fill in details and correct errors. Concern has been expressed by some commentators, however, about the possibility that erroneous interpretations by contextualist courts can cause contractual parties to expend greater resources in the drafting of contracts. The argument is that they may be driven to be very specific in their written contract to reduce the risk that courts will adopt an erroneous interpretation after hearing evidence about context. All this assumes that when drafting contracts, parties consider the rules governing interpretation and draft their contracts with those rules in mind. How likely is that? Consider again Professor Hill's comments in the introductory pages to this chapter.

6. *What do contractual parties prefer?* After considering all the evidence, some leading commentators have argued that we should adopt the interpretative approach that parties prefer. And these commentators argue that the evidence suggests that large, sophisticated parties prefer a textualist approach. The evidence is based on an empirical study of the choice of law clauses in over 2,800 contracts attached to Form 8-K filings[66] during the first half of 2002, finding that, overall, choice of law is nearly six times as likely to favor New York over California.[67] The sample of contracts in the study consisted of "a reasonably rich variety of relations" and included contracts related to security purchase agreements, credit, mergers, and settlements (among others). Though the type of contract varied, each was sufficiently important to the filing party's operations that it would have been the result of careful negotiation and drafting. When the contracts are divided by type, New York law is preferred in 10 out of 13 categories.

The authors of the study attribute New York's dominance to the state's commercial history and its longstanding efforts to attract commercial contracts. Other commentators, however, argue that this correlation suggests that the parties prefer the rule of *Mitchill v. Lath, supra*, to the rule of *Masterson v. Sine, supra*, because the interpretative approach of the former carries fewer total costs than the approach of the latter.[68] Can you think of other reasons why sophisticated parties, or their lawyers, might prefer in these kinds of contracts the contract law of New York to that of California? The study did not include any contracts for the sale of goods under Article

---

66. Form 8-K is promulgated by the U.S. Securities and Exchange Commission and used by publicly-traded companies to report certain material corporate events and keep investors informed. For a list of events that require disclosure *see* Form 8-K, https://www.sec.gov/answers/form8k.htm. For background on Form 8-K, *see* Jennifer B. Lawrence & Jackson W. Prentice, *The SEC Form 8-K: Full Disclosure or Fully Diluted? The Quest for Improved Financial Market Transparency*, 41 Wake Forest L. Rev. 913 (2006).

67. Theodore Eisenberg & Geoffrey P. Miller, *The Flight to New York: An Empirical Study of Choice of Law and Choice of Forum Clauses in Publicly-Held Companies' Contracts*, 30 Cardozo L. Rev. 1475 (2009).

68. *E.g.*, Alan Schwartz & Robert E. Scott, *Contract Interpretation Redux*, 119 Yale L.J. 926, 955–57 (2010).

2 of the UCC or any ordinary construction contracts. Would the reasons that sophisticated parties prefer New York law in the contracts studied necessarily apply to other types of contracts?

3. A More Recent California Decision

DORE v. ARNOLD WORLDWIDE, INC.

California Supreme Court
39 Cal. 4th 384, 46 Cal. Rptr. 3d 668, 139 P.3d 56 (2006)

WERDEGAR, J.

Plaintiff alleges against his former employer various causes of action in connection with his termination. The trial court granted the employer summary judgment, but the Court of Appeal reversed. We agree with the trial court and, accordingly, reverse the judgment of the Court of Appeal.

Background

Plaintiff Brook Dore was employed with an advertising agency in Colorado as a regional account director specializing in automobile accounts. In late 1998, Dore discussed with his employer the possibility of relocating to the employer's Los Angeles office.

In 1999, Dore learned that a management supervisor position was available in the Los Angeles office of defendant Arnold Worldwide, Inc., formerly known as Arnold Communications, Inc., (hereafter AWI). Dore interviewed with several AWI officers and employees. According to Dore, he was never told during the interview process that his employment would be terminable without cause or "at will." Dore alleges he was told that AWI had landed a new automobile account and needed someone to handle it on a long-term basis. He also was told that, if hired, he would "play a critical role in growing the agency," that AWI was looking for "a long-term fix, not a Band-Aid," and that AWI employees were treated like family. Dore alleges he learned that the two people previously holding the position for which he was being considered had been terminated for cause—one for committing financial indiscretions, the other because his work had not satisfied a client. Dore states that AWI offered him the management supervisor position by telephone in April 1999, and he orally accepted.

Later that same month, Dore received a three-page letter from Sharon McCabe, senior vice-president of AWI, dated April 6, 1999 (AWI's letter), purporting to "confirm our offer to join us as Management Supervisor in our Los Angeles office" and to state "[t]he terms of this offer." AWI's letter then listed, in bullet-pointed sections, a commencement date, compensation details, and various benefits (including reimbursement of relocation expenses, parking at the AWI offices, various types of insurance, expense reimbursement, and vacation).

AWI's letter also stated: "You will have a 90-day assessment with your supervisor at which time you will receive initial performance feedback. This assessment will also be the time that you will work with your supervisor to set objectives against which you will be evaluated at the time of your annual review. After your assessment is complete, you and your supervisor will have the opportunity to discuss consideration for being named an officer of Arnold Communications."

In a separate paragraph central to the present dispute, AWI's letter stated: "Brook, please know that as with all of our company employees, your employment with Arnold Communications, Inc., is at will. This simply means that Arnold Communications has the right to terminate your employment at any time just as you have the right to terminate your employment with Arnold Communications, Inc., at any time."

AWI's letter requested that Dore sign and return the letter signifying his acceptance of these employment terms. Dore read and signed the letter.

AWI terminated Dore's employment in August 2001. Thereafter, Dore sued AWI ... alleging (1) breach of contract, (2) breach of the implied covenant of good faith and fair dealing, (3) intentional infliction of emotional distress, (4) fraud, and (5) negligent misrepresentation. AWI ... filed a motion for summary judgment.

The trial court granted AWI's motion on the ground that Dore could not establish the existence of either an express or an implied-in-fact agreement that his employment was terminable only for cause.... Dore appealed.

The Court of Appeal affirmed in part and reversed in part. The court ... reversed the judgment in favor of AWI. The court remanded the matter to the trial court with directions to vacate its order granting summary judgment to AWI and enter a new order granting summary adjudication to AWI only on Dore's negligent misrepresentation cause of action. We granted AWI's petition for review.

Discussion

Dore alleges that AWI, by various oral representations, conduct, and documents, led him reasonably to understand there existed between AWI and himself an implied-in-fact contract that provided he would not be discharged from his employment except for cause. AWI contends that its oral representations, conduct, and documents could not reasonably have raised any such understanding in Dore.

We take the facts from the record that was before the trial court when it ruled on AWI's motion for summary judgment. We review the trial court's decision *de novo*, considering all the evidence set forth in the moving and opposing papers except that to which objections were made and sustained. We liberally construe the evidence in support of the party opposing summary judgment and resolve doubts concerning the evidence in favor of that party....

Dore acknowledges that a clear and unambiguous at-will provision in a written employment contract, signed by the employee, cannot be overcome by evidence of a prior or contemporaneous implied-in-fact contract requiring good cause for termination. (*See* cases cited in *Guz v. Bechtel National, Inc.*, 24 Cal. 4th 317, 340, 100 Cal. Rptr. 2d 352, 8 P.3d 1089 [2000]). But he contends this rule cannot govern here because AWI's letter neither constitutes nor contains a clear and unambiguous agreement that his employment would be terminable without cause.

A. Dore's Contract Claims

1. "At any time"

The Court of Appeal below agreed with Dore that AWI's letter, signed by Dore, was not clear and unambiguous with respect to cause for termination. Notwithstanding the letter's statement that "your employment with Arnold Communications, Inc., is at will," the court reasoned, by going on to define the term "at will" to mean that AWI had the right to terminate Dore's employment "at any time," AWI impliedly relinquished the right to terminate Dore without cause. We disagree.

The Courts of Appeal are in conflict over whether a provision in an employment contract providing for termination "at any time" or upon specified notice is, without more, reasonably susceptible to an interpretation allowing for the existence of an implied-in-fact agreement that termination will occur only for cause. The Court of Appeal in *Bionghi v. Metropolitan Water Dist. of So. California*, 70 Cal. App. 4th 1358, 83 Cal. Rptr. 2d 388 (1999), held such a provision is not thus susceptible; those in *Seubert v. McKesson Corp.*, 223 Cal. App. 3d 1514, 273 Cal. Rptr. 296 (1990), *Wallis v. Farmers Group*, 220 Cal. App. 3d 718, 269 Cal. Rptr. 299 (1990), and *Bert G. Gianelli Distributing Co. v. Beck & Co.*, 172 Cal. App. 3d 1020, 219 Cal. Rptr. 203 (1985) held it is. . . .

Seubert concerned a wrongful termination action brought by a regional sales manager of a computer systems company against his employer for breach of contract, misrepresentation, and breach of the implied covenant of good faith and fair dealing. Notwithstanding the plaintiff had signed an employment application stating that "if hired, my employment is for no definite period and may, regardless of the date of payment of my wages and salary, be terminated at any time without any prior notice." . . . [T]he Court of Appeal, looking to other factors indicating the application "was not intended to be the entire employment agreement between the parties," ruled that extrinsic evidence supported the existence of an implied contract requiring cause for termination. . . .

In *Wallis*, an insurance agent entered into an agreement with the insurer she represented that provided her agency could be "terminated by either the Agent or [the insurance company] on three (3) months written notice. . . ." After she was terminated, the agent brought an action alleging the parties had both an express oral and an implied-in-fact agreement that she would be terminated only for cause. The Court of Appeal found that, notwithstanding the contract was integrated on the subject of termination, because its termination provision was silent as to whether good cause was required, the language was reasonably susceptible of meaning either that no cause was required or that a separate agreement requiring good cause existed. Therefore, the court held, extrinsic evidence was admissible to determine the meaning of the written agreement. . . .

In *Gianelli*, independent local beer wholesalers and distributors brought an action against a brewer of an imported brand of beer, alleging the brewer's termination of their distribution contracts without good cause breached those contracts. Each complaining party had signed a distribution agreement providing it would "continue in effect unless and until terminated at any time after January 1, 1973, by thirty days' written notice by either party to the other...." The Court of Appeal held the agreements could reasonably be interpreted as consistent with an implied requirement of good cause for termination....

The termination clause at issue in *Bionghi* provided that the agreement "may be terminated by [the employer] hereto 30 days after notice in writing...." The Court of Appeal held that the plain language of the clause was not reasonably susceptible to an interpretation requiring the employer to have good cause for termination...."In our view," the court stated, "a contract that provides that it may be terminated on specified notice cannot reasonably be interpreted to require good cause as well as notice for termination, unless extrinsic evidence establishes that the parties used the words in some *special sense*. Instead, such a contract allows termination with or without good cause ..." (italics added).

We disagree with Dore that the verbal formulation "at any time" in the termination clause of an employment contract is *per se* ambiguous merely because it does not expressly speak to whether cause is required. As a matter of simple logic, rather, such a formulation ordinarily entails the notion of "with or without cause."

2. AWI's letter

That the phrase "at any time" is not in itself ambiguous with respect to cause for termination does not preclude the possibility that AWI's letter, when considered as a whole, contains ambiguity on the topic. As California courts previously have observed, the "meaning of language is to be found in its applications. An indeterminacy in the application of language signals its vagueness or ambiguity. An ambiguity arises when language is reasonably susceptible of more than one application to material facts. There cannot be an ambiguity *per se*, *i.e.*, an ambiguity unrelated to an application...." (Citations omitted.)

Accordingly, "[e]ven if a contract appears unambiguous on its face, a latent ambiguity may be exposed by extrinsic evidence that reveals more than one possible meaning to which the language of the contract is yet reasonably susceptible." *Morey v. Vannucci*, 64 Cal. App. 4th 904, 912, 75 Cal. Rptr. 2d 573 (1998). "The test of admissibility of extrinsic evidence to explain the meaning of a written instrument is not whether it appears to the court to be plain and unambiguous on its face, but whether the offered evidence is relevant to prove a meaning to which the language of the instrument is reasonably susceptible." *Pacific Gas & E. Co. v. G.W. Thomas Drayage etc. Co.*, 69 Cal. 2d 33, 37, 69 Cal. Rptr. 561, 442 P.2d 641 (1968), citing numerous authorities.

In this case, the trial court recognized that the presumption of at-will employment codified in § 2922 of the Labor Code can be overcome by an express or implied agreement to the contrary. *See Guz v. Bechtel National, Inc., supra....* Nevertheless, the court ruled that because the express written contract—i.e., AWI's letter—controls, it need not consider whether Dore's proffered extrinsic evidence establishes the existence of an earlier implied agreement to terminate only for cause.

The Court of Appeal, in reaching the contrary conclusion, relied primarily on the fact that AWI's letter, after stating that Dore's employment is "at will," defines "at will" in a manner that refers expressly only to the duration of the contract (*i.e.*, as meaning "that Arnold Communications has the right to terminate your employment at any time") and does not state explicitly whether cause is required. The Court of Appeal also relied on evidence extrinsic to the letter, in particular, that AWI required Dore to sign a postemployment noncompetition and nondisclosure agreement.

The trial court's ruling was correct. The language of the parties' written agreement is unambiguous. AWI's letter plainly states that Dore's employment with AWI was at will. Indeed, as the trial court observed, Dore admitted as much and further admitted that he "read, signed, understood, and did not disagree with the terms of the letter." Even the Court of Appeal acknowledged that the term "at will" when used in an employment contract normally conveys an intent [that] employment may be ended by either party "at any time without cause." Although AWI's letter also states that AWI would provide Dore a "90-day assessment" and "annual review," these provisions, in describing AWI's employee evaluation schedule, neither expressly nor impliedly conferred on Dore the right to be terminated only for cause.

That AWI's letter went on to define at-will employment as employment that may be terminated at any time did not introduce ambiguity rendering the letter susceptible of being interpreted as allowing for an implied agreement that Dore could be terminated only for cause. In defining at-will employment, AWI used language similar to the language the Legislature used in our statutory provision. Labor Code § 2922 says that an "employment, *having no specified term,* may be terminated at the will of either party on notice to the other." (Italics added.)

"An at-will employment may be ended by either party 'at any time without cause,' for any or no reason, and subject to no procedure except the statutory requirement of notice." *Guz v. Bechtel National, Inc., supra....* For the parties to specify—indeed to emphasize—that Dore's employment was at will (explaining that it could be terminated at any time) would make no sense if their true meaning was that his employment could be terminated only for cause. Thus, even though AWI's letter defined "at will" as meaning "at any time," without specifying it also meant without cause or for any or no reason, the letter's meaning was clear.

Nor did Dore's proffered extrinsic evidence render AWI's letter ambiguous concerning whether he could be terminated only for cause. As noted, Dore declared that he was told his role would be "critical" because AWI "needed a long-term fix" of certain problems and wanted Dore to "build a relationship" with an important new client. He also testified that he learned in interviews that some people at AWI had been employed there for long periods and he was assured the company had a family atmosphere. Even if credited, such evidence would not support an inference that Dore reasonably understood AWI's letter as consistent with a promise not to terminate him without cause. "When a dispute arises over the meaning of contract language, the first question to be decided is whether the language is 'reasonably susceptible' to the interpretation urged by the party. If it is not, the case is over." (Citation omitted.)

We conclude, in sum, that AWI's letter contained no ambiguity, patent or latent, in its termination provisions. Accordingly, we agree with the trial court that no triable issues of fact exist with respect to Dore's causes of action for breach of contract and breach of the implied covenant of good faith and fair dealing.

B. Dore's Fraud Claim

Dore alleges that AWI induced him to leave his longstanding, secure employment with an advertising agency in Denver and relocate to Los Angeles by promising him that his employment with AWI would continue indefinitely so long as he performed in a proper and competent manner, that he would not be demoted or discharged except for good cause, and that he would be given notice and a meaningful opportunity to respond to any unfavorable evaluations of his performance. Dore alleges these promises were false in that AWI had no intention of performing them at the time they were made and that he justifiably relied on AWI's promises and suffered damages when AWI failed to perform them....

AWI contends it was entitled to summary judgment on Dore's promissory fraud cause of action because Dore produced insufficient evidence of misrepresentation, intent not to perform, and reliance. As we agree with AWI on the reliance point, we need not address the others.

Dore conceded in his deposition that no one at AWI specifically told him he would be employed there so long as his work was satisfactory or that he could be fired only for good cause. Dore admits, moreover, that he read, signed, and understood AWI's letter stating "the terms" of his employment. As demonstrated above, the letter did not contain promises of long-term employment or that termination would be only for cause; AWI expressly and unambiguously stated that Dore's employment was at will. For all these reasons, we agree with the trial court that Dore's admission he signed AWI's letter stating his employment was at will and terminable at any time as a matter of law defeats any contention that he reasonably understood AWI to have promised him long-term employment.

In accordance with the foregoing, we agree with the trial court that there exists no triable issue of fact with respect to Dore's cause of action for fraud.

Disposition

For the foregoing reasons, the judgment of the Court of Appeal is reversed.[69]

WE CONCUR: George, C.J., Kennard, Chin, and Moreno, JJ.

Concurring Opinion by Baxter, J.

I agree with the result reached by the majority and with the bulk of their reasoning. Dore signed, and admitted he read, understood, and did not disagree with, Arnold Worldwide's (AWI) letter stating the terms of his employment. This letter could hardly

_____

69. [2] *Seubert v. McKesson Corp., supra; Wallis v. Farmers Group, supra;* and *Bert G. Gianelli Distributing Co. v. Beck & Co., supra,* are disapproved to the extent they are inconsistent with this opinion.

have made it clearer that the employment was "at will." ... No rational person could believe this language meant both parties were obliged to continue the employment relationship except upon "good cause." The words "at will" and "at any time," as used in the letter, would make no sense if the parties really meant the opposite—that good cause was required for termination.

It follows beyond doubt that the letter expressed the parties' mutual understanding the relationship could be terminated by either party as desired, for any or no reason. I therefore concur in the majority's conclusion that the letter contained no ambiguity, patent or latent, and that the extrinsic evidence proffered by Dore could not contradict the letter's plain meaning.

However, I cannot join the majority's general endorsement of *Pacific Gas & E. Co. v. G.W. Thomas Drayage etc. Co....* (*Pacific Gas*). *Pacific Gas* essentially abrogated the traditional rule that parol evidence is not admissible to contradict the plain meaning of an integrated agreement by concluding that, even if the agreement "appears to the court to be plain and unambiguous on its face," extrinsic evidence is admissible to expose a *latent* ambiguity, *i.e.*, the possibility that the parties actually intended the language to mean something different....

Read in its broadest sense, *Pacific Gas* thus stretched the unremarkable principle that extrinsic evidence is admissible to resolve a contractual ambiguity into a rule that parol evidence is always admissible to demonstrate ambiguity despite facial clarity. The effect is that, despite their best efforts to produce a clear written agreement, parties can never confidently conduct their affairs on the basis of the language they have drafted.

Predictably, the *Pacific Gas* decision has drawn strong criticisms.... Judge Kozinski succinctly expressed them in *Trident Center v. Connecticut General Life Ins. Co....* : "Under *Pacific Gas*, it matters not how clearly a contract is written, nor how completely it is integrated, nor how carefully it is negotiated, nor how squarely it addresses the issue before the court; the contract cannot be rendered impervious to attack by parol evidence. If one side is willing to claim that the parties intended one thing but the agreement provides for another, the court must consider extrinsic evidence of possible ambiguity. If that evidence raises the specter of ambiguity where there was none before, the contract language is displaced and the intention of the parties must be divined from self-serving testimony offered by partisan witnesses whose recollection is hazy from passage of time and colored by their conflicting interests." (Citation omitted.)

To their credit, it appears the majority here have declined to apply *Pacific Gas* quite so broadly. On the one hand, they repeat mischievous statements from *Pacific Gas* and its progeny that extrinsic evidence of intent may be admissible even when the contract's language appears "unambiguous on its face." ... On the other hand, however, they assert that "[a]n ambiguity arises [only] when language is reasonably susceptible *of more than one application to material facts.*" (Italics added.)

If I understand the majority's premise, a "latent" ambiguity is simply one that becomes manifest when one attempts to apply the contract's language to the specific facts that gave rise to the parties' legal dispute. Even then, extrinsic evidence is admissible only to prove a meaning the contract's language will reasonably accommodate. Thus here, the majority are able to say, in effect, that the language of AWI's letter is not ambiguous as applied to the particular facts (*i.e.*, Dore's termination) that gave rise to the dispute between AWI and Dore.

I entirely agree that *Pacific Gas* should be limited at least to the extent the majority imply. I hope the majority's limiting "gloss" will be noted by the bench and bar, and will signal that written agreements whose language appears clear in the context of the parties' dispute are not open to claims of "latent" ambiguity.

Still, it may be time for a fuller reconsideration of the meaning and scope of *Pacific Gas*. I am open to undertaking such a comprehensive reexamination in an appropriate case. With that caveat, I concur in the majority's reasoning and result.

I CONCUR: Corrigan, J.

Concurring Opinion by Moreno, J.

I concur in the majority opinion, but write separately to emphasize one point.

The majority opinion devotes substantial attention to employment agreements that authorize termination "upon notice," or after a specified notice period.... But the written agreement before us did not use the words "upon notice," or any equivalent phrasing. Instead, the agreement allowed for termination "at any time." Our analysis is properly directed at this "at any time" language. The majority opinion has no occasion to express, and does not express, any view as to whether providing for termination "upon notice" also connotes a mutual intention to create an at-will employment arrangement.

In my view, a provision that allows for termination "upon notice" does not, by itself, shed light on whether the parties intended an at-will employment contract, or a relationship terminable only for cause. I concur in the majority opinion with the understanding that it takes no position on this issue.

NOTES AND QUESTIONS

1. *Logic or cultural understanding?* The court says that as a "matter of simple logic," "at any time" ordinarily "entails ... with or without cause." Do you agree? Is it nonsensical to have an agreement providing for dismissal only for cause but without the need for a warning or a notice period before pay ceases? Could this be a plausible interpretation of the letter sent to Dore? Is it a likely interpretation by anyone familiar with employment practices in America?

2. *Is* Masterson *implicitly overruled?* Do you think that the California Supreme Court as constituted in 2006 would have reached the same decision as that court did when *Masterson v. Sine* was decided in 1968? Would the 2006 court have concluded that a real estate option was absolute and assignable "as a matter of simple logic" even though the writing was silent on the issue of assignability?

D. SUBVERSIVE DOCTRINES: EXCEPTIONS TO THE PAROL EVIDENCE RULE

1. Reformation

To what extent, if at all, can a party seeking to contradict a written contract *reform* the document and avoid the parol evidence rule? Historically, reformation has been considered a remedy available only in equity, which means that a party seeking reformation is not entitled to a jury trial. Reformation has been granted only rarely, with the exception of real estate contracts, in which it is a more common remedy. The following cases are illustrative.

BELK v. MARTIN

Idaho Supreme Court
136 Idaho 652, 39 P.3d 592 (2001)

WALTERS, J.

This is an appeal following a trial without a jury where the district court determined a farm lease contained a unilateral mistake regarding the rental amount. As a result, the district court reformed the lease to provide that the dollar amount of the lease should be $14,768.00 rather than $1,476.80. We affirm.

Factual and Procedural Background

Howard and Lois Belk owned farmland located in Canyon County, Idaho. The farm consisted of seven fields totaling 113.6 acres, which had been rented to various tenants for many years. In October of 1995, William Ekberg, brother of Lois Belk, advertised the land for rent in the newspaper. Defendants Allen and Meliah Martin ("Martin") responded to the advertisement. A meeting to discuss the leasing of the farmland was attended by Mr. Martin, Mr. Ekberg, Plaintiffs Gary Belk and Carole Cannon ("Plaintiffs" or "Respondents"), who were the son and daughter of the Belks, and Carole's husband, Warren Cannon.

At the meeting, the parties agreed upon the fields that were to be leased; that the lease was a cash lease; that the payment of rent would be due after harvest; that the payment of rent would be secured by a crop lien; and that the lessors would pay real property and water assessments on the property. Martin took possession of the land immediately thereafter and began preparation work for the upcoming farm season.

A written lease was prepared by Ms. Cannon's attorney in December 1995 but not signed until the parties met again in late February or March of 1996. In between the negotiation of the lease and the signing, both Howard and Lois Belk passed away; Ms. Cannon was appointed personal representative of their estates and signed the lease in that capacity. At no time prior to the signing of the lease did the Plaintiffs review the lease. Before signing the lease, Martin requested that the date of termination be changed from August 15, 1996 to November 15, 1996. Both Mr. Martin and Ms. Cannon initialed the change. No other changes were made to the lease. The lease, as written, provided for rent in the amount of $1,476.80. A farm products financing statement for security of the payment of rent was also signed and subsequently filed.

On November 15, 1996, Martin did not pay the rent but retained possession of the farmland; two fields of unharvested corn remained. By letter dated November 27, 1996, Plaintiffs demanded payment of the rent, an accounting, and requested that Martin not re-enter the property without permission. A second demand letter was sent to Martin's attorney on December 2, 1996. On December 4, 1996, the parties entered into an interim agreement allowing the harvesting of the corn to be completed. The agreement stated that the amount of rent was disputed and provided that the proceeds from the sale of the crops on the farmland would be placed in an interest-bearing trust account up to the disputed amount. For a variety of reasons, including weather and mechanical breakdowns, by December 19, 1996, Martin had not yet completed the harvest of the corn. Respondents engaged Sam Hall to combine one of the corn fields. On January 8, 1997, Martin engaged Sam Hall to combine the second field. The Cannons paid Sam Hall $1,191.30 for combining the two corn fields.

A complaint was filed April 17, 1997, whereby Plaintiffs sought reformation of the lease, payment of rent, reimbursement for the corn-harvesting expenses, recovery of interest, and for attorney fees and costs. Martin filed an amended answer and counterclaim requesting specific performance of the lease and recovery of his attorney fees and costs. The case was tried without a jury on July 15 and 16, 1998. On the first day of trial, the district court heard and denied Martin's motion *in limine* seeking to prevent extrinsic evidence from being presented.

Following the trial, the district court issued its Memorandum Decision and Order finding that a valid lease, with a termination date of November 15, 1996, existed. The trial court also determined that the parties had agreed to a rental fee of $130 per acre for 113.6 acres, thereby totaling $14,768.00 rather than the $1,476.80 stated in the rental provision of the lease. The basis for the district court's conclusion was that the lease contained a unilateral mistake made by the Plaintiffs of which Martin had knowledge. The court therefore reformed the rental provision of the lease to $14,768.00. Further, the district court awarded the corn-harvesting expenses paid by the Cannons.... The Martins then pursued this appeal....

Discussion

Appellant Martin asserts that the district court erred by finding the lease contained a unilateral mistake made by the Respondents. Martin argues specifically that the district court (1) erred by allowing extrinsic evidence to vary the terms of an integrated and complete contract and by denying Martin's motion *in limine*, which sought to prevent extrinsic evidence; [and] (2) erred by reforming the lease....

A. Extrinsic Evidence

Martin argues the district court erred by allowing extrinsic evidence to be presented at trial because the farm lease was a complete, integrated, and unambiguous contract. Further, Martin asserts that extrinsic evidence is only admissible when a mutual mistake is alleged rather than when the mistake was unilateral. Respondents counterargue that extrinsic evidence is allowed to determine the intentions of the parties when the written instrument does not memorialize the true intent of the parties.

The parol evidence rule provides:

> If the written agreement is complete upon its face and unambiguous, no fraud or mistake being alleged, extrinsic evidence of prior or contemporaneous negotiations or conversations is not admissible to contradict, vary, alter, add to, or detract from the terms of the contract.

... Parol evidence, however, is allowed to clarify that a term of the contract was a mistake. *Beard v. George*, 135 Idaho 685, 689, 23 P.3d 147, 151 (2001).... Parol evidence is also admissible to prove that by reason of mutual mistake the written agreement does not express the parties' true intent. *Bailey v. Ewing*, 105 Idaho 636, 641, 671 P.2d 1099, 1104 (Ct. App. 1983)....

Extrinsic evidence should be allowed where there has been a unilateral mistake made by a party and the other party has knowledge of the mistake. This type of unilateral mistake is a ground for reformation where extrinsic evidence may be admissible to show the intent of the parties....

In this case, mistake, albeit a unilateral mistake, was alleged by Respondents. Since Respondents' mistake in the rental provision was known by Martin, the parties' negotiations and prior discussions as well as other relevant parol evidence was permissible to show the lease contained an error and did not reflect the true intentions of the parties. This Court holds the district court did not err when it allowed extrinsic evidence to be presented by Respondents to show that the lease did not reflect the intent of the parties as to the rental and duration provisions.

1. *Untimely Filing of Motion* in Limine

Martin argues the trial court abused its discretion when it denied his motion *in limine* for being untimely. The motion sought to exclude presentation of any extrinsic evidence pertaining to the unambiguous lease.

The evidence which Martin sought to exclude was properly held by the district court to be admissible. Accordingly, we conclude that the district court did not err in denying Martin's motion *in limine*.

B. Reformation

Martin argues that the district court erred by reforming the lease because a unilateral mistake cannot serve as a basis for reformation. Martin testified that he realized that the rental provision in the lease was different than the parties had agreed upon. Martin asserted that he thought the Respondents had changed their minds as to the rental amount. Respondents, however, did not know that the amount stated in the contract was different than agreed upon because they did not read the contract prior to signing it. Respondents argue that their unilateral mistake may be reformed since Martin had knowledge of the mistake.

"Reformation of an agreement can be awarded if one party has knowledge that the other party suffers from a unilateral mistake." *Graber v. Comstock Bank*, 111 Nev.

1421, 905 P.2d 1112, 1116 (1995). Reformation is proper when the evidence shows that the instrument does not reflect the true intentions of the parties.... "By reforming an instrument, the court gives effect to the contract which the parties did in fact make, but which by reason of mistake was not expressed in the writing executed by them." *Uptick Corp. v. Ahlin*, 103 Idaho 364, 372, 647 P.2d 1236, 1244 (1982).

The district court found that the parties had entered into a valid lease and that Martin knew the rental provision was incorrect. The district court properly recognized that a failure to read a contract does not excuse a party's performance.... Although Ms. Cannon failed to read the lease prior to signing, the district court found that since Martin knew of the error and failed to alert the Respondents to it, this was sufficient to excuse performance to the extent of the error.... The district court further found that because the mistake was unilateral and known by Martin, the equitable remedy of reformation was available even though the mistake was a product of negligence. *Aitken v. Gill*, 108 Idaho 900, 902, 702 P.2d 1360, 1362 (Ct. App. 1985).

The district court also determined that the testimony of the Respondents and Mr. Ekberg, as well as the notes in the attorney's file, corroborated the parties' agreement that the rent would be $130 per acre for 113.6 acres. The district court found the testimony of the witnesses familiar with the farmland supported the fact that $130 per acre was a fair rental value for the farmland, despite Martin's complaints about the conditions of the farmland. "It is the province of the district judge acting as trier of fact to weigh conflicting evidence and testimony and to judge the credibility of the witnesses."... We will not substitute our view of the facts for the view of the district court....

The district court thoroughly analyzed and weighed all of the evidence presented at trial and found a valid crop-year lease between the parties, which contained a unilateral mistake made by the Respondents and a termination date of November 15, 1996. Upon a showing of knowledge of the mistake in the rental provision by Martin, the district court reformed the lease to state the correct rental amount of $14,768.00 for the term of the lease. This Court holds that the district court did not err by reforming the lease that contained a unilateral mistake of which Martin had knowledge. Although there is conflicting testimony, the factual findings of the district court are supported by substantial and competent evidence. The district court's findings are not clearly erroneous and therefore are affirmed....

Conclusion

This Court affirms the trial court's finding that the lease contained a unilateral mistake to which Martin had knowledge. The district court properly reformed the lease to reflect the parties' intent....

CHIEF JUSTICE TROUT and JUSTICES SCHROEDER, KIDWELL, and EISMANN concur.

NOTES AND QUESTIONS

1. *Mistake:* Mistake, mutual or in some cases (as in this case) unilateral, is the most common ground for reformation. The mistake normally concerns the terms of

the written contract, not the underlying subject matter of the contract. In the principal case, for example, if the parties had intended an amount of rent as stated in the contract, but the plaintiffs could show that at the time of contract they labored under a mistaken estimate of the fair rental value of the property, there may not have been a remedy available. Courts do, however, sometimes grant relief when the mistake concerns the underlying subject matter of the contract, not just the terms of the writing. There is some discussion of this kind of mistake in Chapter 6, *infra*.

2. *Why this exception to the parol evidence rule?* It is self-evident that the result in this case is inconsistent with the usual statement of the parol evidence rule. There was nothing ambiguous about the price stated in the written contract. Do you think admitting extrinsic evidence to show that there was a mistake undermines the policy concerns that support a strict (or "hard") parol evidence rule? Certainly it lengthens the litigation; no longer is it possible to resolve the case on summary judgment. Does the fact that reformation is an equitable remedy, so that there is no jury trial, sufficiently justify the reformation exception to the parol evidence rule?

3. *Would reformation have worked in* Mitchill v. Lath? The plaintiff in *Mitchill v. Lath* sought specific performance of a side agreement to remove an ice house. Suppose plaintiff had sought to reform the principal real estate sale contract to include, as a term of the contract, that the seller would remove the ice house from a neighboring parcel of land, and then sought specific performance of the reformed contract. Would plaintiff have succeeded? What would plaintiff have had to prove to win in Idaho? Do you think a New York court should allow an exception to its rather strict parol evidence rule if the plaintiff seeks reformation?[70]

4. *Does it matter that this case concerned "small" people?* The contract in *Belk v. Martin* was between individuals. Suppose the contract had been between large corporations—as in *Federal Express v. Pan American World Airways*, *supra*, or *Binks Manufacturing v. National Presto Industries*, *supra*—and there was an argument that the price term was mistakenly misstated. Should the court be more reluctant to admit evidence normally barred by the parol evidence rule than it was in *Belk v. Martin*?

JOHNSON v. GREEN BAY PACKERS

Wisconsin Supreme Court
272 Wis. 149, 74 N.W.2d 784 (1956)

Action by the plaintiff Clyde Johnson against defendant the Green Bay Packers, Inc., for reformation of contract and to recover damages for breach of contract.

Plaintiff's complaint contained two causes of action stated in the alternative, the first of which prayed for reformation of the contract entered into between the parties on June 30, 1948, and for the recovery of damages by plaintiff for breach of the con-

---

70. Note that since the plaintiff in *Mitchill v. Lath* sought the remedy of specific performance, the case was already in equity and there was no possibility of a jury trial. By requesting reformation as a remedy, the plaintiff would not have compromised an otherwise available right to a jury.

tract as so reformed; while the second cause of action prayed for recovery of damages by the plaintiff for breach of the contract as originally written without first being re-formed. The answer interposed by the defendant ... contained denials of most of the material allegations of plaintiff's complaint. The action was tried to the court without a jury.... A summary of the testimony and evidence adduced at the trial follows.

Johnson, a professional football player, had a contract with the Los Angeles Rams for the 1947 season. This was a "season" contract under which Johnson could not be released during the season at the option of the Rams. The contract also provided that the Rams had the right to renew the contract for the 1948 season. At the end of the 1947 season the Rams informed Johnson that they would employ him for the 1948 season, but not on the basis of a season contract. This was not satisfactory to Johnson and the parties failed to agree on terms. The Rams then traded Johnson to the de-fendant Packers.

About June 1st, Lambeau, in behalf of the defendant Packers, contacted Johnson by phone and arranged an appointment.... At the first meeting between Mr. and Mrs. Johnson and Lambeau at the latter's home contract terms were discussed for the employment of Johnson by the Packers. Johnson testified that he insisted on a "season" contract like he had had with the Rams and that Lambeau agreed thereto. This Lambeau denied.

Later, Lambeau and Johnson met at the Hotel Roosevelt in Hollywood on or about June 30, 1948. Lambeau produced a printed form of contract in blank which was in triplicate (one for the player, one for the Packers, and one for the commissioner of the National Football League). Lambeau wrote in longhand the figure "$7,000" on the face of the contract. Johnson then brought up the fact that a "season" contract had been agreed on, whereupon Lambeau turned over the contract and wrote in longhand on the back:

> *$7,000 season 1948*   *Season contracts*
>
> *Minimum $7,000 1949*   *E. L. L.*

Both Johnson and Lambeau signed the contract in triplicate and Lambeau retained all copies for the purpose of sending them in to the Packers to be typed and made to conform to the verbal understanding of the parties, after which one of the three would be returned to Johnson.

Johnson testified that at the time of these negotiations at the Hotel Roosevelt he asked Lambeau to strike out paragraph 6 on the printed forms of the contract, covering the power of the Packers to release the player, to which Lambeau replied that he would send the contracts in and have them "fixed" as agreed.

Several weeks later Johnson received his copy of the contract, which bore the afore-mentioned notations in ink on the back made by Lambeau, but he noted that para-graph 6 had not been stricken. Such paragraph 6 reads as follows:

> The player represents and warrants that he is and will continue to be suffi-ciently highly skilled in all types of football team play to play professional football of the caliber required by the league and by the club, that he is and

will continue to be in excellent physical condition, and agrees to perform his services hereunder to the complete satisfaction of the club and its head coach. (If in the opinion of the head coach the player does not maintain himself in excellent physical condition or fails at any time during the football seasons included in the term of this contract to demonstrate sufficient skill and capacity to play professional football of the caliber required by the league and by the club, or if in the opinion of the head coach the player's work or conduct in the performance of this contract is unsatisfactory as compared with the work and conduct of other members of the club's squad of players, the club shall have the right to terminate this contract upon written notice to the player of such termination.)

As soon as Johnson received his copy, he called Lambeau and protested that the printed portion of the contract that gave the Packers the right to release Johnson during the season (paragraph 6) had not been stricken as agreed. Lambeau replied that Johnson should not worry, that the commissioner did not like the contracts to be cut up or have portions crossed out, that his (Lambeau's) word was as good as gold, and that Johnson had a two-year "season" contract. Johnson accepted this explanation by Lambeau, Johnson's testimony on this point being as follows:

> Well, as closely as I can remember, I took him at his word, plus the notation on the back of the contract that it was a two-year seasonal.

Johnson later came to Green Bay, went into training, and played two exhibition games. On or about September 16, 1948, the defendant Packers then terminated Johnson's employment by written notice sent by mail, reading as follows:

Notice of Termination

Attention of Clyde Johnson

Dear Sir: Date: September 16, 1948

You are hereby notified that the Green Bay Packers, Inc., a member of the National Football League, pursuant to paragraph 6 of its contract with you dated June 30, 1948, hereby terminates said contract, effective immediately, for the reason[s] checked below:

☐ In the opinion of the head coach, you are not and have not maintained yourself in excellent physical condition.

☒ In the opinion of the head coach, you are failing and have failed to demonstrate sufficient skill and capacity to play professional football of the caliber required by the league and by the club.

☒ In the opinion of the head coach, your work and conduct in the performance of your contract is unsatisfactory as compared with the work and conduct of other members of the club's squad of players.

Remarks:

Club

By /s/ E. L. Lambeau

The only compensation Johnson received from the Packers was $100 travel money for the trip to Green Bay. Johnson played the remainder of the 1948 season with the Los Angeles Dons and his earnings from such source were $6,000. Early in the spring of 1949 Johnson wrote to the Packers and informed them that he was ready, willing, and able to play for them in 1949, but received no answer. The total amount of his earnings and income for the period of August through December, 1949, was $1,007.25. The answer of the defendant raises no issue that Johnson should have attempted to earn more during such period, or to take other action to mitigate damages.

Following the trial, the trial court made and filed a memorandum decision in which he determined that the plaintiff Johnson was entitled to have his contract of employment with the defendant for the football seasons of 1948 and 1949 reformed by striking out paragraph 6 thereof, and that Johnson should recover from the defendant the agreed compensation for said two seasons less his earnings from other sources....

Judgment was ... rendered ... in favor of plaintiff and against the defendant. From such judgment the defendant has appealed.

CURRIE, J.

The following issues are raised on this appeal:

(1) Whether reformation may be decreed to delete a provision in a contract, where such provision was left in the contract with the consent of the aggrieved party, even though such consent was obtained in reliance upon a contemporaneous oral promise that was not kept;

(2) Whether the judgment in behalf of Johnson can be affirmed on the ground set forth in plaintiff's second cause of action, i.e., that the trial court should have enforced the contract as written giving effect to the written portion over the conflicting printed paragraph 6; ...

[Issues 3 & 4 deleted.]

Without dispute, it appears from the facts found by the trial court that, when Johnson in the summer of 1948 received back his copy of the contract of employment, he at once discovered that paragraph 6 thereof had not been deleted as agreed between the parties, and that he immediately called the matter to Lambeau's attention. Lambeau then explained to Johnson that paragraph 6 had not been deleted because the league commissioner did not like contracts with parts crossed out, but assured Johnson that the original agreement for a "season" contract for the years 1948 and 1949 would be lived up to. Upon such verbal assurance from Lambeau, Johnson did not renew his request that paragraph 6 be deleted but entered into employment with such paragraph still in the contract.

In *Touchett v. E Z Paintr Corp.*, 263 Wis. 626, 630, 58 N.W.2d 448, 59 N.W.2d 433 (1953), this court had before it a cause of action for reformation of contract, and in its opinion stated:

> There is a further rule of law that the court will not insert a provision in a contract which was omitted with the consent of the parties asking for refor-

mation, although such consent was given in reliance on an oral promise of
the other party that the omission would not make any difference.

We consider the above-quoted principle to be equally applicable to the facts in the
instant case. The fact that here we are concerned with the failure to delete a clause
necessary to conform the written contract to the prior verbal understanding of the
parties, while in the *Touchett* case the written contract failed to include a paragraph
covering a matter previously agreed upon by the parties in parol, we deem to be of
no significance. In both situations the aggrieved party accepted the contract as written
and entered into performance thereof upon the oral promise of the other party that
the failure of the contract to read as agreed would not make any difference. We, therefore, conclude that it was error for the trial court to have decreed reformation of the
contract by ordering the deletion of paragraph 6.

Counsel for Johnson urge that, even if the contract be not reformed so as to delete
paragraph 6 thereof, the written provisions indorsed on the back of plaintiff's copy
of the contract by Lambeau, being in direct conflict with the printed provisions of
paragraph 6, must prevail over such printed provisions. In other words, it is urged
that the trial court should have reached the same result by a proper interpretation of
the contract as written....

We deem that the point under consideration is ruled in plaintiff's favor by the case
of *Tollefson v. Green Bay Packers, Inc.*, 256 Wis. 318, 41 N.W.2d 201 (1950). Such case
involved an action to recover damages for breach of contract of employment by Tollefson, a professional football player, against the same defendant as in the instant case.
Most of the provisions of the contract were in printed form, as in the instant case,
and Lambeau, manager of the Packers, wrote in longhand in paragraph 1, which
covered the matter of Tollefson's compensation, "minimum $3,600 for season." Para-
graph 7, one of the printed clauses of the agreement, provided that the contract
might be terminated any time by the Packers giving notice in writing within 48 hours
after the date of the last game in which Tollefson had participated. This court interpreted such words to mean that, unless discharged for cause, Tollefson was entitled
to the full sum of $3,600 whether he participated in the games played by the Packers
or not. In its opinion, this court stated (p. 322):

> *Where written provisions are inconsistent with printed provisions* [of a contract],
> *an interpretation is preferred which gives effect to the written provisions.* Re-
> statement, 1 Contracts, p. 328, §236(e).... (Emphasis supplied.)

Lambeau in the instant case testified on his adverse examination that if the provision
contained in paragraph 6 of the printed form of the contract were deleted then the
contract would have constituted that which is known "in the trade" as a "season contract." This corroborates Johnson's testimony that it was verbally agreed between him
and Lambeau that he was to have a "season" contract for both years 1948 and 1949
under which the Packers would have no right to terminate the same except for cause,
and that the notation placed on the back of Johnson's copy of the contract in longhand
by Lambeau, and initialed by him, were in order to comply with Johnson's request

that he have a "season" contract for such two years. As we view it, the only material difference in the facts of the *Tollefson* case and the one at bar is that the governing provision written in longhand in the former was written on the face of Tollefson's contract, while in the instant case it was written on the back of the contract. However, inasmuch as the parties intended the provision in the instant case with respect to a "season" contract to be part of the contract, its location, whether on the face or back, is wholly immaterial....

Inasmuch as the provisions of paragraph 6 directly conflict with the provision in Lambeau's handwriting for "season" contracts for each of the years 1948 and 1949, the latter provision must govern....

NOTES AND QUESTIONS

1. *Background from briefs and record:* The record contains coach Lambeau's testimony about the contract with Johnson. He said:

> Johnson did not insist on a seasonal contract. He mentioned a seasonal contract, and I said, I don't sign players for season contracts, no players, because anyone that doesn't have enough confidence in their ability shouldn't be playing this game of football. I said that we needed big tackles, and you are a big boy [Johnson was 6 feet 6 inches tall and weighed 265 pounds], and all you have to do is your best and you have nothing to worry about.

> I remember that he was quite concerned. We agreed to terms and he was quite concerned about being cut. At that time, as you know, there were players—mostly in the All-America Conference—that were being signed for tremendous salaries and then asked to take a cut; and Mr. Johnson was quite concerned about the talk around about players being cut, which is true. When I say "cut," I mean and have reference to a reduction in salary, and not being eliminated from the squad. I told him that I was willing to sign anything, that if he played with our ball club that his salary would not be cut for two years. I never made a statement to the effect that at that time or any other time that if he signed with me I would either play him, pay him, or trade him. I don't make statements like that.... I did not discuss with him at that time, or at any other time before the contract was signed, that any contract he signed with me would not be subject to his release.... The notation "7000 season 1948, minimum 7000 1949," and a bracket and then "season contracts, E.L.L."... is in my handwriting.... I don't remember anything like Mr. Johnson calling me and complaining after he got his copy [of the contract] from the Commissioner. I don't remember him complaining that his contract was not a season contract.... A seasonal contract does not necessarily mean that a player cannot be dismissed.... When the portion of the contract that gives the club the right to release them is deleted from the printed portion, that would be a season contract, of course.

2. *"No cut contracts" today:* Today athletes participating in professional sports are usually represented by skilled agents and are often unionized as well. We might expect

the problem presented in this case to belong to the past. But the problem can still arise.[71] A hornbook on sports law notes:

> Players are always after the "no-cut" contract. We have seen that the term "no-cut" is really inappropriate.... What is really sought is a guaranteed salary, whether the player stays on the team or not. But what is meant by a guarantee? That term is only slightly less ambiguous. Is the salary guaranteed even if the player defaults and refuses to play? Obviously, no club would agree to such one-sidedness. Thus, there is a need to specify under what circumstances the salary will be paid, and under what conditions it will not. The National Basketball Association has set forth different approaches in its Allowable Amendments to the Uniform Player Contract.... These guides should be consulted when contemplating the various possibilities. But even those provisions may not anticipate all grounds for dispute.[72]

3. *Another case:* With the important exception of real estate contracts, reformation of a written contract is rarely granted in contract law, as the opinion indicates. But there are a few cases where the theory succeeds. In *Bollinger v. Central Pennsylvania Quarry Stripping and Construction Co.*[73] the contract allowed the defendant to deposit construction waste from a highway construction project on plaintiff's farmland. Plaintiff claimed that the parties had agreed orally that defendant would first remove topsoil and later deposit the removed topsoil on top of the construction waste. At the beginning of the construction project defendant acted in that way, but later stopped, saying the written contract said nothing about removing and later restoring the topsoil. Plaintiffs testified that they had signed the written contract without reading it, just assuming that the contract, drafted by defendant, contained all that had been agreed upon. The Pennsylvania Supreme Court affirmed a trial court decision to reform the written contract to reflect the plaintiff's view of the deal, stating:

> Once a person enters into a written agreement he builds around himself a stone wall, from which he cannot escape by merely asserting he had not understood what he was signing. However, equity would completely fail in its objectives if it refused to break a hole through the wall when it finds, after proper evidence, that here was a mistake between the parties, that it was real and not feigned....

Note that *Bollinger* is not a real estate sale or lease case, but the contract did affect real estate. Perhaps that helps explain why the court was amenable to a reformation argument. As in all reformation cases, there is no claim that a term of the written contract is ambiguous and hence that it is appropriate to admit extrinsic evidence to determine the parties' intent. What might account for courts' occasional proclivity

---

71. For another case, *see* Chuy v. Philadelphia Eagles Football Club, 595 F.2d 1265 (3d Cir. 1979).

72. Robert C. Berry & Glenn M. Wong, Law and Business of the Sports Industries, Vol. 1 at 260–61 (1986).

73. 229 A.2d 741 (Pa. 1967).

to seemingly ignore the parol evidence rule in reforming written contracts? Is it important the reformation is considered an equitable remedy?

4. *Why didn't the parol evidence rule bar recovery in the principal case?* In the *Johnson* case, the court was unwilling to reform the written contract, yet Johnson was still able to recover notwithstanding paragraph 6. Why? Did the court act contrary to the parol evidence rule? If Curly Lambeau had not added handwritten words on the back of the printed contract, would the result have been different?

2. Promissory Estoppel

In any case where a party tries to rely on oral promises when there is a written contract, our old friend, promissory estoppel (reliance on a promise), might provide another avenue for escaping the consequences of the parol evidence rule. There are obvious pitfalls in such a theory. An important idea underlying the parol evidence rule is that the written contract is a better indication of what the parties "really" intended. If there is evidence of oral promises contradicting the written contract, it may be that the parties did not intend the oral statements to be legally binding, or that they changed their minds before the written contract was signed. Nonetheless, as with reformation, an occasional promissory estoppel claim based on an oral promise is successful. And in these circumstances the remedy sought is not equitable, so the case can get to the jury.

EHRET CO. v. EATON, YALE & TOWNE, INC.
United States Court of Appeals, Seventh Circuit
523 F.2d 280 (1975)

Fairchild, C.J.

This appeal raises questions concerning the interpretation of an exclusive sales contract and the application of the parol evidence rule and promissory estoppel. It also raises the question whether the trial judge abused his discretion by offering a remittitur and granting a new trial. Jurisdiction is founded on diversity. All parties to this appeal have accepted Illinois law as controlling.

The plaintiff, Ehret Company, acted as a manufacturer's sales representative for the defendant, Eaton Company, in the Milwaukee and Chicago territories until the termination of their 1966 contract. This termination was effected by notice in compliance with the "Duration of Agency" clause and took effect on September 30, 1968.

There was evidence that the defendant's products, worm gears and lubricating systems, required the plaintiff to engage in "Development Work" of up to 10 years prior to the consummation of a sale. It was necessary, during this pre-sale development, for the plaintiff to engineer, design, and adapt the defendant's products into either the customers' finished product or into the customers' own manufacturing equipment. Before signing the 1965 contract, Mr. Ehret objected to the "Duration of Agency" clause, which reads:

12. Duration of Agency

This Sales Agreement may be altered by our mutual consent and may be terminated by either of us upon thirty (30) days' notice in writing. In the event of cancellation of this Agreement or abridgment of the territory herein covered, no commission will be paid on any orders which have not been properly received, in writing, and accepted by us in writing before the termination of the Agreement or abridgment of the territory, or on orders which purchasers will not accept delivery of and pay for within three (3) months from the date of cancellation of the Agreement or abridgment of the territory.

His objections were raised in an April 28, 1965 letter to the General Sales Manager of Eaton Company, Mr. Witzenburg. Mr. Ehret showed concern for the possibility that Eaton Company could cancel the contract after Ehret Company had expended considerable time and money in procuring a sale, but before an order was placed, and also that orders placed prior to termination may not be shipped within 90 days.

On April 29, 1965, Eaton Company responded, with a letter from Mr. Witzenburg declining to change the contract, stating:

It is true in the event of cancellation by either party, our company would not be obligated to pay a commission on orders that were received before the date of final cancellation but were not released for shipment three months after cancellation. However, in those few cases where the contract has been cancelled by us we have always been much more liberal than provided for in the contract.

The normal procedure is to allow full credit for all orders received within 30 days after final cancellation date, provided that they resulted from quotations made prior to the date of cancellation and if released for shipment within five months of the date of cancellation. In fact, in two cases, we have extended that protection to orders received under the same circumstances but shipped within a period of one year after cancellation.

Neither you nor we expect that the new contracts will be cancelled by either one of us, so that this discussion is probably academic only. However, we cannot alter the terms of the contract. The same contract must exist with you as with all of our other representatives and in the very unlikely event of cancellation, you will have to rely on receiving extremely fair treatment.

After receiving Mr. Witzenburg's letter, Ehret Company entered into the Commission Sales Agreement containing the "Duration of Agency" clause on April 30, 1965.

On March 31, 1966, Eaton, Yale and Towne, Inc., formerly Eaton Company, sent a letter to the Ehret Company requesting that a new contract be signed reflecting the defendant's name change. This new contract, signed and dated June 2, 1966, contained the same "Duration of Agency" clause as the 1965 contract. In addition, the new contract contained an integration clause which stated that "[u]pon its receipt, it will constitute an entire Agreement between us as of the date set forth above (January 1,

1966). This Agreement cancels all prior Sales Agreements between us, including the latest one dated May 1, 1965."

On August 28, 1968, Eaton, Yale and Towne, Inc. sent a letter to Ehret Company terminating their 1966 agreement as to both the Chicago and Milwaukee territories, effective September 30, 1968. In this letter the defendant expressed its intent to construe literally the "Duration of Agency" clause stating, "In effecting this cancellation, full credit will be given your office for all acceptable orders dated September 30, 1968, and before, provided they are shipped prior to December 31, 1968." Later, and after negotiation, Eaton, Yale and Towne, Inc. agreed to pay Ehret Company on all orders received prior to termination regardless of when shipped. Eaton tendered this amount, $51,000.00, to Ehret Company, of which $44,000.00 was accepted.

The plaintiff contends that it is entitled to better treatment than described in the "Duration of Agency" clause, (and better than Eaton actually extended) relying on Mr. Witzenburg's April 29, 1965 letter, which stated that "you (Ehret Company) will have to rely on receiving extremely fair treatment."

The defendant's motion for summary judgment was denied. The plaintiff's motion for partial summary judgment was granted, determining that defendant was estopped from asserting the "Duration of Agency" clause of the contracts to limit commissions. At trial, the defendant's motion for directed verdict was denied and the jury's verdict awarded plaintiff $546,000.00. The defendant's motion for judgment N.O.V. was denied and the defendant's motion for a new trial was granted after the plaintiff refused a remittitur of $408,119.25. The jury's verdict awarded $120,000.00 to the plaintiff in the second trial.

The plaintiff appeals challenging the order setting aside the first jury verdict and the granting of a new trial. On its appeal the defendant contends that the 1966 contract on its face is a complete representation of the agreement between the parties, and that in any event the plaintiff failed to prove damages based on the meaning of the "extremely fair treatment" letter.

The trial judge correctly held, as a matter of law, that the defendant was estopped from asserting the "Duration of Agency" clause of the 1965 and 1966 contracts. As stated in *Dill v. Widman*, 413 Ill. 448, 109 N.E.2d 765, 769 (1952):

> The general rule is that where a party by his statements or conduct leads another to do something he would not have done but for the statements or conduct of the other, the one guilty of the expressions or conduct will not be allowed to deny his utterances or acts to the loss or damage of the other party. The party claiming the estoppel must have relied upon the acts or representations of the other and have had no knowledge or convenient means of knowing the true facts. Fraud is a necessary element but it is not essential that there be a fraudulent intent. It is sufficient if a fraudulent effect would follow upon allowing a party to set up a claim inconsistent with his former declarations.

All of the elements necessary to form an estoppel are present in this case. The plaintiff was induced to sign the 1965 and 1966 contracts only in reliance on the defendant's representation that it would not enforce the "Duration of Agency" clause, but would give "extremely fair treatment" in the unlikely event of termination. The plaintiff also relied on a letter, which preceded the 1966 contract, from Eaton Company stating that a new contract must be signed to reflect Eaton Company's name change. If the defendant were allowed to disclaim its representations after receiving the benefits therefrom, this would have the fraudulent effect that an estoppel was designed to prevent. Usually the question of estoppel is for the jury except where, as in this case, the facts presented leave but one inference; then it becomes a question of law. *Bituminous Casualty Corp. v. City of Harrisburg*, 315 Ill. App. 243, 42 N.E.2d 971 (1942).

The Milwaukee territory was not mentioned in the written contracts, but evidence was adduced that the parties understood it to be covered by the same terms and conditions as the written Chicago agreement. The question was submitted to the jury, which found that the "extremely fair treatment" letter was also applicable to the Milwaukee contract and territory. This finding was not contested on appeal; therefore both territories are treated similarly for the purpose of this order.

The question of damages was submitted to the jury on the theory of a possible breach of a contract to give the plaintiff extremely fair treatment. Support for the treatment as an enforcible promise of the promise which, as a result of plaintiff's reliance, creates an estoppel is supported by Restatement, Contracts, § 90 and Restatement 2d, Contracts, § 90 (Tent. Draft No. 2, 1965). Following this view, admission of the "extremely fair treatment" letter is not in conflict with the parol evidence rule as the defendant contends. An estoppel is an equitable remedy that has its own independent force.

We now turn to the interpretation of the contract, specifically the "Duration of Agency" clause, as modified by the "extremely fair treatment" letter. The meaning of the term "extremely fair treatment" is neither plain nor clear, but is susceptible to numerous interpretations. Parol evidence is always permitted to assist in determining the meaning and effect of a contract term from the intent of the parties. *Ortman v. Stanray Corp.*, 437 F.2d 231 (7th Cir. 1971).[74] This is especially true where the words used, by their very nature, are ambiguous. The trial court properly allowed the introduction of the extrinsic evidence, not to vary or contradict the written contract, but to explain a term that became part of the agreement by means of an estoppel.

---

74. Eds. note: The 7th Circuit later overruled the preceding sentence in this opinion, holding that under Illinois law the court must first find that a written contract is ambiguous before allowing a jury to hear extrinsic evidence about the parties' conversations and written exchanges before concluding a written contract. The court held, however, that a judge could consider the extrinsic evidence before deciding whether the written contract was ambiguous. Sunstream Jet Express v. Int'l Air Serv., 734 F.2d 1258 (7th Cir. 1984). Nothing in the *Sunstream* decision questions the resort to promissory estoppel in the principal case.

The quantum of damages was dependent on the jury's determining the meaning of the phrase "extremely fair treatment," whether the plaintiff received "extremely fair treatment," and if not, what would compensate the plaintiff for commissions or allowances it would have received if it had been given "extremely fair treatment." The defendant contends that there was no evidence presented to support the jury's verdict. We disagree. There was sufficient evidence to establish that it took up to 10 years for the plaintiff to develop a customer prior to an order being placed. It was this concern of the plaintiff that prompted the defendant's promise of "extremely fair treatment" and it was on this basis that the jury awarded damages.

The defendant's contention that the 1966 contract superseded its representation of "extremely fair treatment" we find to be without merit under the circumstances because of defendant's representation of the limited purpose of the 1966 contract.

We recognize that there is authority in jurisdictions other than Illinois for the proposition that the promise which becomes the basis for the estoppel is not to be enforced as a promise, and that damages, if awarded, "should be only such as in the opinion of the court are necessary to prevent injustice." *Hoffman v. Red Owl Stores, Inc.*, 26 Wis. 2d 683, 701, 133 N.W.2d 267, 276 (1964).... We think, however, that in the circumstances of this case, this latter theory produces the same result as determining damages under the contract. Giving the estoppel only the effect of depriving defendant of its right to limit commissions due after termination to those computed according to the 1966 contract, and seeking only an amount of damage needed to produce an equitable result, plaintiff would be entitled to compensation, reasonably determined, for the time and effort it expended as the defendant's sales agent without being afforded sufficient opportunity to recoup from the venture....

The plaintiff's computation of damages is based on Eaton's sales figures for the five years after termination. Of this amount Ehret contends that it is entitled to the "development credit" portion of the commissions from customers that it had serviced while acting as Eaton's representative. The plaintiff borrowed the term "development credit" from the defendant's agreement, which provided for the allocation of commission where one representative worked on a project for which an order was placed outside his territory. The representative who performed the "development work," described above, was entitled to 80 percent of the sales commission for the gear products and 60 percent of the sales commission for the lubrication products. For the five-year period the portion of commissions equivalent to the development credit is equal to $910,000.00. The jury's verdict in the first trial was three-fifths of this amount, or $546,000.00. The trial judge held that a three-year development credit was excessive and offered a remittitur that would bring the figure to less than one year over the commission already paid. Plaintiff elected not to remit. The basis for the jury award at the second trial is not readily apparent. It was less than the amount offered by the court.

Under the circumstances, we find no fault in using the Eaton Company's sales figures and the "development credit" concept for the years subsequent to the termination, to determine damages for the breach of defendant's promise to give "extremely fair treatment," or alternatively, an allowance of an amount necessary to prevent injustice.

The plaintiff's contention on its appeal is that the trial judge abused his discretion by offering a remittitur and granting a new trial. There is no doubt that the federal district court has the power to offer a remittitur and, if refused, grant a new trial. *Dimick v. Schiedt*, 293 U.S. 474, 55 S. Ct. 296, 79 L. Ed. 603 (1935). The standard for appellate review of a trial judge's order granting a new trial for an excessive verdict has been explained in *Taylor v. Washington Terminal Co.*, 409 F.2d 145, 149, 133 U.S. App. D.C. 110 (1969), *cert. denied*, 396 U.S. 835, 90 S. Ct. 93, 24 L. Ed. 2d 85:

> The trial judge's view that a verdict is outside the proper range deserves considerable deference. His exercise of discretion in granting the motion is reviewable only for abuse. Thus we will reverse the grant of a new trial for excessive verdict only where the quantum of damages found by the jury was *clearly* within "the maximum limit of a reasonable range." (Emphasis in original.)

Since the damage issue in this case is dependent upon the interpretation of a vague term, or, in the alternative the determination of an amount or equitable grounds, we cannot say that the first jury verdict was clearly within this "reasonable range." On appeal, the trial judge's opportunity to view the "living courtroom" must be given great weight, especially when assessing the intent of the parties. We can find no abuse of discretion and accordingly affirm the judgment of the district court.

The Clerk of this court is directed to enter judgment affirming the judgment appealed from.

SWYGERT, C.J. (dissenting).

I cannot agree with the majority's conclusion that it was proper to give the jury free reign to decide what constitutes "extremely fair treatment." I concur in the portion of the opinion upholding the finding of equitable estoppel based on the letter of April 29, 1975. But I do not understand why the majority concludes that the perimeters of this estoppel are to be based only on a single phrase of that letter, viewed out of context.

Equitable estoppel has been invoked in this case to override the written contract between these parties because it would be unfair to allow the defendant to rely on that contract in light of the April 29 letter. Yet, it seems to me, it is just as unfair to ignore the very instrument that necessitates the use of the equitable estoppel doctrine. I believe this is what the majority has done. We are concerned with a dispute arising in a commercial context. Certainly, Eaton, Yale & Towne never agreed that in case of cancellation plaintiff would receive whatever a jury thought to be "extremely fair treatment." In the same letter in which this now-seized-upon phrase was used, the "normal procedure" was specifically spelled out: full credit for all orders received within 30 days after final cancellation date and shipped, at most, within one year after cancellation. I think that the phrase "extremely fair treatment" must be read to refer to this statement of the normal procedure. The phrase must be given contours if we are to reach an equitable result and the contours are those contained in the same letter. It is interesting to note that to a considerable extent plaintiff, at one time, agreed with my view of what is "equitable" since a letter was written on October 22, 1968, requesting this "fair treatment" which "would involve full payments for all orders booked before October 1, 1968, regardless of when shipped."

The majority approves the "legal" conclusion that equitable estoppel must apply, but then relies on the "jury question" rubric in regard to the issue of what should fill the void created by disregarding the contract. I do not think that we can interfere with a contract in the name of equity and then ignore the question of the "equitable-ness" of the outcome of that interference. I would hold that Ehret is entitled to no more than that which would be received under the most liberal interpretation of Eaton's "normal procedure" as defined in the letter of April 29.

NOTES AND QUESTIONS

1. *Is* Ehret *still good law?* No Illinois court, or other federal court applying Illinois law, has relied on the *Ehret* decision to avoid the parol evidence rule using promissory estoppel. The statement in the *Ehret* opinion that "[p]arol evidence is always permitted to assist in determining the meaning and effect of a contract term from the intent of the parties," citing *Ortman v. Stanray Corp.*, has been explicitly overruled as an incorrect statement of Illinois law by *Sunstream Jet Express v. Intl. Air Serv. Co.*, 734 F.2d 1258 (7th Cir. 1984).[75] But that decision does not explicitly address the promissory estoppel argument, and the 7th Circuit has not explicitly overruled *Ehret* in that respect.[76] As of this writing the Illinois Supreme Court has not addressed the point, but several intermediate appellate courts in Illinois or federal district courts applying Illinois law have held that the parol evidence rule bars a promissory estoppel claim based on pre-contract communications where the contract is fully integrated.[77]

In other jurisdictions there are few, if any, decisions upholding promissory estoppel as a way around the parol evidence rule. Several decisions have suggested that if the parol evidence rule would foreclose consideration of evidence about prior agreements or negotiations, then it was not possible to base a promissory estoppel claim on those earlier agreements and negotiations.[78] Such decisions are inconsistent with the opinion in *Ehret*.

In light of these later precedents, it would seem unlikely a court would rely on *Ehret* to uphold a promissory estoppel claim. Might it be wrong for a court to do so as a matter of law?

---

75. We will look more closely at the Illinois parol evidence rule and when extrinsic evidence can be admitted when we study AM Int'l v. Graphic Mgmt. Assocs., *infra* (part E of this chapter).

76. In Coldwell Banker v. Karlock, 686 F. 2d 596 (7th Cir. 1989), the court questioned whether *Ehret* is still good law on the promissory estoppel point, but stopped short of explicitly disapproving the case on that point.

77. Prentice v. UDC Advisory Services, 648 N.E.2d 146, 153 n.4 (Ill. App. 1995) (stating, erroneously we believe, that *Sunstream Jet Express* overrules the *Ehret* case on the promissory estoppel theory as well); Snellman v. A.B. Dick Co., 1987 U.S. Dist. LEXIS 2306 (N.D. Ill., Mar. 20, 1987).

78. *E.g.*, IBM v. Medlantic Healthcare Group, 708 F. Supp. 417 (D.C. 1989).

2. *The potential of promissory estoppel:* Professor Michael Metzger has argued that courts should use the promissory estoppel doctrine to avoid the parol evidence rule.[79] He argues:

> Estoppel could enhance the effectuation of the parties' true intent in a written contract, an objective shared by modern formulations of the parol evidence rule, and could minimize the injustice associated with mechanical applications of the rule. Estoppel also could provide a better doctrinal explanation for the results courts reach in many parol evidence cases than the traditional parol evidence rubric that courts currently employ affords. Such doctrinal clarity would result in the focusing of judicial attention in parol evidence cases on the real issues that ultimately will determine whether a court will give legal effect to an extrinsic promise, a consequence likely to provide a much needed measure of clarity and predictability in the administration of the parol evidence rule. Finally, promissory estoppel's application in parol evidence cases would be consonant with the tendency of twentieth-century contract law to elevate substance over form in the pursuit of just results, a tendency of which the reliance principle is merely one manifestation.

Do you agree that resort to promissory estoppel would bring needed clarity to the parol evidence rule? Would resort to promissory estoppel become a vehicle for judicial repeal of the historic parol evidence rule? Is that appropriate in a democracy? The parol evidence rule is itself a judicially created rule, but it has been around for a long time and the state legislatures have not chosen to alter it. Is that a relevant consideration?

3. Mitchill v. Lath *once again:* If the case had arisen in Illinois, could the plaintiff in *Mitchill v. Lath, supra,* have used promissory estoppel as a theory for obtaining a remedy for removal of the ice house? Could the remedy be specific performance (*i.e.,* removal of the ice house)? If the remedy would be limited to damages, what would be the measure of damages?

4. *Expectations versus bureaucratic control, revisited:* The *Ehret* case is an example of a common type of fact situation. The parties are quite different in size, and have both signed a standard form contract drafted by the dominant party. In discussions or letters, however, they have discussed other terms. *Nanakuli v. Shell, supra,* is another fact situation of this nature. The bureaucratic policies of the larger organization often make it impractical for that organization to alter the language of its standard form contract. If the parol evidence rule is applied strictly in such circumstances, the effect is to reinforce the terms of the standard form contract. If an agent of the larger organization participated in discussions or letter exchanges with the smaller party that led the latter to have different expectations, is that right? Is it sufficient to say that the smaller party should have read the standard form contract before signing it and have insisted on some written revision of the standard form contract (as the plaintiff did in *Johnson v. Green Bay Packers, supra*)?

---

79. *See* Michael Metzger, *The Parol Evidence Rule: Promissory Estoppel's Next Conquest?*, 36 Vand. L. Rev. 1383, 1466 (1983).

A brief look at some of the litigation involving Burroughs Corp. may serve to make the abstract problem described in the foregoing paragraph more concrete. In the 1960s and '70s Burroughs was a profitable company selling, among other things, computers and installed software to small commercial users.[80] Many of its customers became dissatisfied, and they filed at least 190 cases against Burroughs. Although Burroughs emphasized that this represented only a small fraction of its installed base of users, and that other computer equipment companies had suffered similar problems leading to litigation, no other company faced as many cases as Burroughs did. Burroughs blamed the customers for inexperience in using computers, for neglecting to send operators to Burroughs's training sessions, and for having unrealistic expectations. The customers charged that Burroughs oversold its computers, put products on the market before they were developed properly, and either encouraged or allowed its sales force to misrepresent what the machines could do. Though there is no doubt a fair amount of truth in both sides of the story, a computer consultant said, "Burroughs has a long and colorful history of announcing machines before they are fully developed, shipping them without software, and having hardware breakdowns in the user's shop." Some Burroughs salespeople testified for plaintiffs and suggested that they only said what they were instructed to say in the sales meetings.

Some of the other computer suppliers adopted a strategy of settling disputes with customers. Burroughs was more litigious. The chief weapon in its defensive strategy was the standard form contract, which it required its customers to sign. The terms of the contract were described in *Badger Bearing Co. v. Burroughs Corp.*[81] A provision on the front page of the contract provided that there was a three-month warranty, governed by the terms on the reverse side of the form. On the reverse side were two clauses; the first was a limitation of remedy clause, and the second a merger clause:

> Seller ... shall not be held responsible ... in any event under this agreement for more than a refund of the purchase price, less reasonable rental for past use, upon return of the equipment to Seller with Seller's prior written consent. (Purchaser hereby expressly waives all incidental and consequential damages.)

> There are no understandings, agreements, representations, or warranties, express or implied (including any regarding merchantability or fitness for a particular purpose), not specified herein, respecting this contract or equipment hereunder. This contract states the entire obligation of seller in connection with this transaction.[82]

The express warranty offered by Burroughs was relatively narrow. In addition, the terms were in many cases accompanied by a provision that cut the time for filing claims from the four or six years provided by most state statutes to just two years. Burroughs sometimes brought cross-actions against its customers, and some lawyers

---

80. In 1986, Burroughs merged with Sperry to form Unisys Corporation.
81. 444 F. Supp. 919 (E.D. Wis. 1977), *aff'd without opinion*, 588 F.2d 838 (7th Cir. 1978).
82. *Id.* at 920–21.

accused Burroughs of delaying the progress of litigation by extensive (and allegedly unnecessary) use of pre-trial procedures.

Burroughs won some and lost some. In the *Badger Bearing* case, in which the customer had experienced 76 service calls in two and a half years on a $62,590 computer, Judge Gordon, the trial judge, found that any warranties that might have been breached had been successfully disclaimed and that Badger had not established that any material misrepresentations had been made. Although the outcome represented a victory for Burroughs, Judge Gordon did find that the sales agreement was not intended as a final expression of the contract and allowed Badger to try to prove the existence of terms that contradicted the sales form. Unfortunately for Badger, the judge then concluded that the plaintiff had failed to prove that the disclaimer language had been "negotiated out" of the contract. As a result, the disclaimers stood. Judge Gordon also ruled that the contractual disclaimers could not be used to prevent Badger from proceeding on the tort theories of negligent misrepresentation or strict responsibility for misrepresentation.[83] But Badger failed to prove those claims. And so, in *Badger Bearing*, the effort to use the parol evidence clause or merger clause proved ineffective, as it did for similar reasons in *Sierra Diesel Injection Service, Inc. v. Burroughs Corp.*[84] An Arizona court, however, found that "since the contract specifically negated the alleged misrepresentations, [plaintiff's] claims for negligent misrepresentation, fraud, and consumer fraud, based upon statements made prior to the signing of the contract, were not actionable because of the parol evidence rule."[85] The Fifth Circuit seemed to follow the same approach in *Earman Oil Co. v. Burroughs Corp.*[86] Other cases, which turned on other factors and other UCC sections, met with similarly mixed success for Burroughs.

The Burroughs cases could be described in at least two different ways. Some might suggest that they represent a situation in which a major company attempted to use its superior market power to abuse its customers, who were not in a position to evaluate the company's promises. The fact that the provisions were available to customers does not mean that the customers assented to them in any meaningful way, especially since they were inconsistent with all of the other signals being sent by the seller. If that is your view, you would probably be disappointed in those courts that seemed to permit Burroughs to use its forms and the parol evidence rule to escape justice.

On the other hand, some would paint a more benign picture. They would argue that if one wants companies like Burroughs to bring new and innovative products to market, they must be able to free themselves from the burden of claims for consequential damages based on misrepresentations by their salespeople. In the long and even medium term, they would assert we can rely on the desire to protect commercial reputation to prompt most companies to fix defective machines or give refunds. Com-

---

83. A potential fraud exception to the parol evidence rule is considered in the next subsection of these materials.

84. 874 F.2d 653 (9th Cir. 1989).

85. Kalil Bottling Co. v. Burroughs Corp., 127 Ariz. 278, 619 P.2d 1055 (Ariz. Ct. App. 1980).

86. 625 F.2d 1292 (5th Cir. 1980).

panies that don't do this will wither and disappear. Furthermore, most customers should know better than to rely on the statements of salespeople who are known to be working on commission. In a sense, the relationship between Burroughs and its customers could be seen as a kind of partnership. By trial and error both producer and customer attempt to get a new product to operate properly, sharing the rewards and risks. If we impose liability, we can expect to increase the cost to everyone of spreading the benefits of computers. Much of any damages award will be siphoned off to pay lawyers' fees and litigation costs. In the long run, this argument concludes, enforcing merger clauses and disclaimers is in the best interest of most people in society, even though in the short run firms like Badger Bearing must pay a price.

Do you find either argument convincing? Can you offer others or strike the balance?

3. Fraud

When the parol evidence rule is applied to bar evidence supporting a claim, it is often because the evidence conflicts with language in a written contract. But what if the contract itself is invalid for some reason? Suppose, for example, that a party claims it was a victim of duress when it signed a contract, and the contract contained a clause stating that both parties signed the contract free of any coercion. Would the parol evidence rule bar evidence of the claimed duress? That has been too extreme a position for the courts. And essentially for the same reason, fraud has long been considered an exception to the parol evidence rule, as is illustrated by the following case. But as the notes after the case explain, in many ways the fraud exception has been narrowed in recent decades.

ANDERSON v. TRI-STATE HOME IMPROVEMENT CO.

Wisconsin Supreme Court
268 Wis. 455, 67 N.W.2d 853 (1955)

[Plaintiffs, the Andersons, were husband and wife. He was a machinist with 30 years' experience. She had no business experience. Spector, the president of Tri-State, called on the Andersons. He persuaded them to sign a contract calling for the installation of Perma-loy siding on their home. The jury found that Spector told the Andersons that Tri-State guaranteed the siding against chipping, cracking, rusting, or peeling for at least 30 years. He said that the siding had been tested under all climatic conditions in their area, and the paint on the siding was not affected by snow, ice, or salt water. These statements were false, which Spector did not know but should have known. He made the statements recklessly, having no knowledge about testing. The written contract did not mention a 30-year guarantee nor did it contain statements about testing and the impact of snow, ice, or salt water. The writing did contain a "no representations" clause.]

CURRIE, J.

The contract entered into between plaintiffs and defendant company under date of April 6, 1950, contained the following clause:

> The company prohibits the making of any promises, or representations, unless it is inserted in writing in this agreement before signing....

The first question that faces us on this appeal is whether such clause is effective to bar plaintiffs' cause of action grounded upon the alleged false representations of defendant's president and agent, which induced the plaintiffs to enter into the contract.... [W]e conclude that it is not.

An excellent statement of the policy reasons that have caused courts to refuse to construe so-called "integration" clauses, and contract clauses attempting to bar liability for false representations, as being effective to bar causes of action based upon fraudulent representations inducing a contract, is set forth in *Bates v. Southgate*, 308 Mass. 170, 182, 31 N.E.2d 551, 558 (1941), as follows:

> As a matter of principle it is necessary to weigh the advantages of certainty in contractual relations against the harm and injustice that result from fraud. In obedience to the demands of a larger public policy the law long ago abandoned the position that a contract must be held sacred regardless of the fraud of one of the parties in procuring it. No one advocates a return to outworn conceptions. The same public policy that in general sanctions the avoidance of a promise obtained by deceit strikes down all attempts to circumvent that policy by means of contractual devices. In the realm of fact it is entirely possible for a party knowingly to agree that no representations have been made to him, while at the same time believing and relying upon representations which in fact have been made and in fact are false but for which he would not have made the agreement. To deny this possibility is to ignore the frequent instances in everyday experience where parties accept, often without critical examination, and act upon agreements containing somewhere within their four corners exculpatory clauses in one form or another, but where they do so, nevertheless, in reliance upon the honesty of supposed friends, the plausible and disarming statements of salesmen, or the customary course of business. To refuse relief would result in opening the door to a multitude of frauds and in thwarting the general policy of the law.

1 Restatement, Agency, p. 579, § 260, states in effect that a principal, by inserting in a contract that he is not liable for the representations of his agent, may relieve himself from liability in an action for deceit to recover damages for the agent's fraudulent representations inducing the execution of the contract, but cannot by such a clause bar the other party's cause of action for rescission. However, 3 WILLISTON, CONTRACTS (rev. ed.), p. 2283, § 811A, points out that such rule, insofar as it relates to the barring of an action of damages for deceit, is not applicable where the fraud is attributable to the principal. In the case at bar, the defendant did not contend that Spector, its president, was not authorized to make the false representations claimed by the plaintiffs, but denied that any such representations were made by him. It seems to us that, where a corporation clothes its president with authority to execute a contract on its behalf, it is in no position to contend that such president was without authority to make representations of fact for the purpose of inducing the execution of the contract.

It appears that the authorities are divided on the question of whether an action to recover damages for deceit can be maintained against a principal for fraudulent representations of an agent, which induced the entering into of the contract, where the contract contains a clause negativing the existence of any representations not incorporated in the contract. Anno. 127 A.L.R. 132, 143 *et seq.* In a recent case the Iowa Supreme Court held that such an action could be maintained against the principal. *Hall v. Crow*, 240 Iowa 81, 34 N.W.2d 195 (1948). We, however, find it unnecessary here to pass upon the issue of whether an honest principal by proper contract provision cannot protect himself from liability to respond in damages in an action at law for fraud grounded upon the unauthorized fraudulent representations of his agent.

[After a brief discussion of whether the jury's finding was supported by adequate evidence, the court turned to the question of whether a false promise can stand as the premise for a fraud claim.]

[D]efendant contends that the [false representation] constitutes merely an unfulfilled promise as to future events and, therefore, no liability can be grounded thereon....

The principal contention made here by the plaintiff is that he has sustained damages in reliance upon the promissory misrepresentations made by the defendants. It is a well-established rule of law that fraud must relate to a present or pre-existing fact, and it cannot ordinarily be predicated on unfulfilled promises or statements made as to future events.... *Beers v. Atlas Assurance Co.*, 215 Wis. 165, 171, 253 N.W. 584, 687 (1934).

. . .

[T]his court in *Alropa Corp. v. Flatley*, 226 Wis. 561, 565, 277 N.W. 108, 110 (1938), adopted the position contended for by Mr. Justice Fairchild ... [in a concurring opinion in *Beers*] recognizing ... an exception to the general rule, that an unfulfilled promise to perform a future act cannot be the basis of an action for deceit, and declared:

> To amount to a fraud upon the purchaser the representations must relate to present or pre-existing facts, and it cannot ordinarily be predicated on unfulfilled promises or statements made as to future events. *Beers v. Atlas Assurance.*... One of the exceptions to this rule is that *when promises are made upon which the purchaser has a right to rely, and at the time of making them the promisor has a present intent not to perform them, the promises may amount to fraudulent representations and liability result.* (Emphasis supplied.)

. . .

Furthermore, we believe a reasonable construction of the representation, that Spector and his company (the defendant) "*guaranteed the siding against chipping, cracking, rusting, or peeling for at least 30 years,*" to be that the defendant had a policy of so guaranteeing all Perma-loy siding installed on buildings of its customers for 30 years. In other words, the representation had reference to the existence of a general business policy of defendant rather than to a promise that was restricted to the siding to be installed on plaintiffs' home....

We conclude that, whether construed as an unfulfilled promise, which when made defendant had no intention of performing, or as a statement of an existing general business policy, the representation as to the guaranty is sufficient upon which to ground plaintiffs' cause of action for fraud and deceit....

NOTES AND QUESTIONS

1. *The economic loss doctrine:* Since the decision in *Anderson*, courts have developed an "economic loss" doctrine that limits suits in tort for misrepresentation in the course of negotiating a contract, where the damage is economic loss. Wisconsin has been among the most aggressive states in extending the economic loss doctrine. Although in many jurisdictions the doctrine applies only where both parties to the contract are commercial entities, Wisconsin now applies the doctrine where the buyer is a consumer as well.[87] As a result the plaintiff in the *Anderson* case could no longer recover for fraud or other misrepresentation in Wisconsin. And since the contract contained a merger clause—negating the making of any promises, etc., not included in the written contract—recovery for breach of warranty would also have been foreclosed.

In an article, Professor Jean Braucher explored the history of economic recovery for fraud by a contract party, finding the idea that an economic loss rule bars a fraud action when there is a contract to be a recent development led by federal rather than state judges, and questioned by Judge Richard Posner:[88]

As late as the mid-1980s, no authority on torts seems to have thought that an "economic loss rule" applied to the law of intentional misrepresentation or fraud. This tort is not centrally targeted at dangerous behavior or products that cause personal injury and accidental loss to property. Fraud is a pecuniary loss tort, not typically associated with physical harm.[89] In the core fraud case, the defendant knowingly lies to the plaintiff, who justifiably relies and suffers economic loss. More often than not, the form of the reliance is entering into a transaction....

Clearly, the common law did not cut off fraud liability if there was a contract; initially, a contract was an essential element to a deceit action, and the late development was allowing recovery without a contract. The common law also did not cut off fraud liability when the loss was only pecuniary or

---

87. Below v. Norton, 310 Wis. 2d 713, 751 N.W.2d 351 (2008). Wisconsin has also extended the doctrine to include not just economic loss but also most loss to property. *See* Ralph C. Anzivino, *The Disappointed Expectations Test and the Economic Loss Doctrine*, 92 MARQ. L. REV. 749 (2009). Where there is personal injury, misrepresentation causes of action still are available in Wisconsin, and the parol evidence rule does not bar evidence of the making of any misrepresentation respecting the product sold.

88. Jean Braucher, *Deception, Economic Loss and Mass-Market Customers: Consumer Protection Statutes as Persuasive Authority in the Common Law of Fraud*, © 2006 by Arizona Board of Regents and Jean Braucher. Reprinted with permission of the author and publisher. This article originally appeared in 48 ARIZ. L. REV. 829, 836–38, 844–45 (2006).

89. [44] *See* W. Page Keeton et al., PROSSER AND KEETON ON THE LAW OF TORTS 726–27 (5th ed. 1984).

financial. The final edition of Prosser and Keeton on the Law of Torts, published in 1984, also identified tort theories of misrepresentation and nondisclosure (originally called the common law action of deceit) as "confined in practice very largely to the invasion of interests of a financial or commercial character, in the course of business dealings."[90]

More recently, Professor Dobbs has explored the idea of an economic loss rule in misrepresentation cases under headings dealing with negligent and innocent misrepresentation, but not in his discussion of intentional misrepresentation.[91] Even where the misrepresentation is only negligent, Dobbs raises doubt that an economic loss rule makes sense in some transactional contexts:

When the facts are peculiarly within the knowledge of the defendant and inaccessible to the plaintiff, commercial dealings between the parties must come to a halt unless the plaintiff can put confidence in reasonable accuracy of the defendant's statements. So courts sometimes impose a duty of care when the defendant had peculiar knowledge or expertise.[92]

He also describes the core case of misrepresentation, involving intentional fraud, as one that concerns liability for "commercial harm" in "the bargaining context."[93]

In a case decided in 1999, Judge Posner suggested that the origin of some courts' discovery of an "economic loss rule" barring common law fraud recovery is in reading dicta out of context, treating broad language as if it were a statute not limited by the facts of the case.[94] ... As an aside, Judge Posner noted that even if there is an economic loss rule cutting off fraud liability, it is important to distinguish commercial contracting parties from "consumers and other individuals not engaged in business."[95] This is certainly right and related to another dubious argument for a contract-only approach to fraud: the parties "could easily have protected themselves from the misrepresentation of which they now complain."[96] Posner recognized that this is a particularly unrealistic idea for consumers, but he sets forth the arguments that a commercial buyer should insist that oral representations be written down:

To allow him to use tort law in effect to enforce an oral warranty would unsettle contracts by exposing sellers to the risk of being held liable by a jury on the basis of self-interested oral testimony and perhaps made to pay punitive as well as compensatory damages. This menace is averted by channeling disputes into warranty (contract) law, where oral warranties can be expressly

90. [47] *Id.* at 726 (explaining the reason for this in terms of other torts typically being used when, for example, personal injury resulted, although fraud could also have been used).
91. [48] *See* DAN B. DOBBS, THE LAW OF TORTS (2000) at 1353, 1356.
92. [49] *Id.* at 1351.
93. [50] *Id.* at 1343.
94. [51] All-Tech Telecom, Inc. v. Amway Corp., 174 F.3d 862, 866–67 (7th Cir. 1999).
95. [101] *Id.* at 866.
96. [102] *See id.*

disclaimed, or extinguished by operation of the parol evidence rule.... It is true that, in principle, the cheapest way to prevent fraud is to punish the fraudfeasor; but in practice, owing to the ever-present possibility of legal error, the really cheapest way in some cases may be to place a burden of taking precautions on the potential victim.

Having stated this position as a vigorous advocate might, Judge Posner immediately questioned it, even in the business-to-business context, noting that eliminating the commercial fraud tort would add transaction costs in "every commercial contract, not just the tiny fraction that end up in litigation," as parties resorted to longer contracts and longer negotiations to spell out all representations. He also noted that the law has "safeguards against false [fraud] claims, such as pleading with particularity" or in some jurisdictions a heightened burden of proof. He ended by finding the balance of considerations close and declining to decide the issue.

Do you agree with Judge Posner that at least consumers should be able to recover in fraud for economic loss? Of course, consumers may be able to use state consumer protection statutes in such circumstances, unless the "economic loss rule" is extended to bar use of these statutes too, as a few courts have held. Of the competing considerations Judge Posner identifies, which is the greater risk for commercial fraud, exaggerated stories about oral fraud or adding to transaction costs as commercial parties feel compelled to get every representation in writing? Or is there some other consideration greater than either of these?

Braucher also noted that UCC Article 2 made a change in the remedial law of fraud in some jurisdictions by extending expectation-based remedies under Article 2 to cases involving fraud, recognizing the overlapping nature of breach of contract and fraud. Section 2-721 states, "Remedies for material misrepresentation or fraud include all remedies available under this Article for non-fraudulent breach." Braucher comments, "If a fraud cause of action would not lie in cases where there is a breach of contract, there would be no need to extend the expectancy measure of damages to fraud actions. In sum, the UCC in Article 2 emphatically does not contemplate a separation of the realms of tort and contract and is quite comfortable blending them to produce commercial law."[97]

2. *Merger clauses, fraud, and the parol evidence rule:* As the court indicates, there is a clash in authority among the states about whether a merger clause bars introduction of evidence of the making of a misrepresentation, when the merger clause denies the making of representations like the very one alleged. As one might expect, states adopting a conservative or strict parol evidence rule (like New York) tend to bar fraud claims where there is a merger clause. But an exception is created for what is characterized as "fraud in the inducement." This kind of fraud concerns misrepresentations about some extraneous matter that may have induced one party to enter the contract. For example, in *Wall v. CSX Transportation*, 471 F.3d 410 (2d Cir. 2006),

---

97. 48 ARIZ. L. REV. at 842–43.

the plaintiff, a former employee of the defendant, claimed it entered into a contract settling various claims arising from his termination because of the defendant's representation that it would provide plaintiff with a "neutral" job reference. Nothing was stated in the job agreement about job references. Plaintiff alleged the defendant had not and had never intended to abide by that representation. The complaint was held to state a valid cause of action for fraud under New York law.[98]

3. Mitchill v. Lath *again:* One element of any fraud claim is that the party making the misrepresentation knew that the statement was untrue and intended to mislead by making it. Could the plaintiff in *Mitchill v. Lath, supra,* have won her case if she alleged the promise to remove the unsightly ice house was fraudulent? What would she have had to prove to establish fraud? Would a New York court have considered the alleged false statement to be "fraud in the inducement" or ordinary fraud? See the discussion of the *Wall* case in the previous note.

4. *Merger clauses and legal ethics:* A merger clause states that the parties agree that the written document is the final and complete expression of their agreement. If, in fact, the parties agreed that a written document should have this effect, the clause makes their choice clear, and insertion of the clause may serve to protect one, or the other, or both parties. Problems arise when a merger clause does not express the parties' bargain in fact but reflects the drafting skill, craft, or even trickery of the lawyer for the more sophisticated party. Do even fairly experienced businesspeople realize that these clauses purport to cancel the legal effect of all a salesperson's representations and promises (if those promises are not also stated in the written contract, itself)? Or is it the case that lawyers who insert such clauses in sales contracts to be used in transactions with unsophisticated consumers are structuring fraud? Is it ethically permissible for a lawyer to use his or her training to trick the unsuspecting? Or are lawyers entitled to assume that their clients are ethical people and will use the rights granted by form contracts only to ward off unjustified claims by those who want something for nothing? It could be argued that clients who use clauses hidden in form contracts to injure their customers will be disciplined by the market. Moreover, some would assert that lawyers are hired to implement their clients' not-unlawful wishes, and not to pass moral judgment on them. Lawyers, under this view, are expected to protect their clients by drafting such clauses, not to protect the interests of non-clients. What do you think? How would you respond if asked to draft a merger clause for a form contract, where you were reasonably sure that parties (other than your client) signing the contract would neither notice nor understand the legal effect of the clause?

5. *Constructive fraud:* In *Adams v. Adams,* 89 P.3d 743 (Alaska 2004), a commercial lease contained a clause granting the lessee an option to purchase. The clause, however,

---

98. A Seventh Circuit decision, applying Illinois law, held that a "no reliance" clause in a written contract barred even a "fraud in the inducement" claim, where both parties were commercial entities, or as the court colorfully put it, "big boys." The "no reliance" clause stated: "The parties are not relying on representations or statements made by the other party or by any persons representing them except for the representations and warranties expressed in this Release." Extra Equipamentos e Exprotacao Ltd. v. Case Corp., 541 F.3d 719 (7th Cir. 2008).

was headed "Right of first refusal." In earlier drafts of the agreement the clause had given the buyer only a right of first refusal — essentially a right to match any offers to buy should the owner/lessor decide to sell. In preparing the final draft, the lessee had changed the substance of the clause without changing the heading. Nobody called the owner/lessor's attention to the change and he signed the lease without noticing it. The Alaska Supreme Court held that this constituted "constructive fraud," entitling the owner/lessor to introduce parol evidence showing his real intent, even though his testimony about intending to grant lessee only a right of first refusal clearly conflicted with the contractual language granting the lessee an option to purchase. By labeling the fraud "constructive" the Court exempted the owner/lessor from any need to show that the lessee intended to mislead the owner. The lessee had testified that he had assumed that owner would reread the lease and notice the change before signing it.

E. CONCLUSIONS ABOUT THE PAROL EVIDENCE RULE

AM INTERNATIONAL, INC. v. GRAPHIC MANAGEMENT ASSOCIATES, INC.

United States Court of Appeals, Seventh Circuit
44 F.3d 572 (1995)

Posner, C.J.

This diversity breach of contract suit, governed by Illinois law, was brought by AM International ("AM" for short) against Graphic Management Associates (GMA). The district judge entered judgment on the pleadings for GMA. Fed. R. Civ. P. 12(c). The appeal raises surprisingly fundamental questions of contract law.

Both parties are manufacturers of printing machines used in the newspaper business. One of these machines is called a "newspaper inserting machine," and it comes equipped with what is called a Missed Insert Repair System (MIRS). These are complicated and expensive machines, which must be customized to the purchaser's specifications. AM brought a suit against GMA, charging that GMA's newspaper inserting machines with MIRS infringed a patent of AM's. The case was settled on December 27, 1988. The settlement included a license agreement, effective the same day, which entitled AM to a royalty of $200,000 on each MIRS-equipped newspaper inserting machine made by GMA and "shipped after ... [Dec. 27, 1988] and before the expiration of" the patent, which was to expire on July 23, 1991. But there was an exception: "[B]eginning on January 1, 1991 and continuing to July 23, 1991 [the date of the expiration of the patent], royalty shall accrue on the receipt by GMA of a bona fide purchase order for a product, provided that product is shipped prior to December 31, 1991."

In January 1990, the owner of the *Philadelphia Inquirer* ordered nine MIRS-equipped machines from GMA. Four were not shipped until after December 31,

1991, and AM concedes that no royalty is due on any of those machines. The other five machines were shipped between September and November of 1991, and thus before December 31, and as to those AM contends that royalty is due. The district judge disagreed, thinking the contract too clear against AM's contention to allow the taking of parol evidence to determine the parties' true intentions. The judge did, however, mention some of that evidence, which had been obtained in discovery before GMA moved for judgment on the pleadings, en route to his conclusion that the evidence was inadmissible to alter the apparent meaning of the contract.

When judges say that a contract is "clear on its face," they mean simply that an ordinary reader of English, reading the contract, would think its application to the dispute at hand certain. That describes this case to a T. AM is entitled to royalties on machines shipped by GMA before July 23, 1991, unless the purchase order was received between January 1 and July 23, in which event AM is entitled to royalties on machines shipped by GMA until December 31. The purchase order for the five machines in issue was received before January 1, so the exception did not come into play, and therefore AM would have been entitled to royalties on the machines only if they had been shipped before July 23, which they were not.

The text contains no clue that the contract might mean something different from what it says. GMA says that that is the end of the case; and there is plenty of judicial language, from Illinois cases as from cases from other states, that if the language of a contract appears to admit of only one interpretation, the case is indeed over.... This is the "four corners" rule. AM ripostes that the doctrine of "extrinsic ambiguity" entitled it to present evidence that although the contract appears to be clear, anyone who understood the real-world context would know that it does not mean what it seems to mean. And there are many cases that say this, too.... Can these lines of cases be reconciled? If so, how? If not, how are we to decide this case?

Rules of law are rarely as clean and strict as statements of them make them seem. So varied and unpredictable are the circumstances in which they are applied that more often than not the summary statement of a rule—the terse formula that judges employ as a necessary shorthand to prevent judicial opinions from turning into treatises—is better regarded as a generalization than as the premise of a syllogism. Take the rule that if a contract is clear on its face, the court will not permit the taking of evidence to contradict that "clear" meaning. The famous contract in *Raffles v. Wichelhaus*, 2 H. & C. 906, 159 Eng. Rep. 375 (Ex. 1864) ... was clear on its face. It called for the shipment of a specified amount of cotton from one port to another on the ship Peerless. Clear as a bell. Only there were two (if not more) ships Peerless, and it was impossible to tell which one the contract referred to. The contract was unclear because clarity in a contract is a property of the correspondence between the contract and the things or activities that it regulates, and not just of the semantic surface.

Take another example. Suppose the parties to the contract in *Raffles* had been members of a trade in which the term "cotton" was used to refer to guncotton rather than to the cotton used in textiles. The ordinary reader of English would not know about this special trade usage, and so would suppose the contract unambiguous.

Again, the ambiguity is in the reference, that is, the connection between the word and the object that it denotes.

There has to be a means by which the law allows these surfaces to be penetrated, but without depriving contracting parties of the protection from the vagaries of judges and juries that they sought by reducing their contract to writing. A review of the doctrines that allow this penetration of semantic surfaces suggests that the key is the distinction between what might be called "objective" and "subjective" evidence of ambiguity. We use these terms informally, rather than with any approach to philosophical precision. By "objective" evidence we mean evidence of ambiguity that can be supplied by disinterested third parties: evidence that there was more than one ship called Peerless, or that a particular trade uses "cotton" in a nonstandard sense. The ability of one of the contracting parties to "fake" such evidence, and fool a judge or jury, is limited. By "subjective" evidence we mean the testimony of the parties themselves as to what they believe the contract means. Such testimony is invariably self-serving, being made by a party to the lawsuit, and is inherently difficult to verify. "Objective" evidence is admissible to demonstrate that apparently clear contract language means something different from what it seems to mean; "subjective" evidence is inadmissible for this purpose. AM relies on our decision in *FDIC v. W.R. Grace & Co.*, 877 F.2d 614 (7th Cir. 1989), the principal case in this court dealing with extrinsic ambiguity and a case in which we were, as here, interpreting Illinois law, but overlooks our observation that "the nature of the offer of proof to show an [extrinsic] ambiguity is … critical." *Id.* at 622. We said that "a self-serving statement … that a party did not understand the contract to mean what it says (or appears to say) will not suffice"; only "an offer to show that anyone who understood the context of the contract would realize it couldn't mean what an untutored reader would suppose it meant will [suffice]." *Id.* at 622.

There is a further screen to protect the parties from the uncertainties of trial. Objective evidence claimed to show that an apparently clear contract is in fact ambiguous must be presented first to the judge, and only if he concludes that it establishes a genuine ambiguity is the question of interpretation handed to the jury.…

There are exceptions to the rule that only objective evidence can be used to alter the meaning of a clear contract, but they are consistent with the underlying principle. If the parties agree to an idiosyncratic meaning, the court will honor their agreement. *Skycom Corp. v. Telstar Corp.*, 813 F.2d 810, 814–16 (7th Cir. 1987).… Or if one party charges fraud, the court will go behind the face of the contract—but it will require the party to prove fraud by clear and convincing evidence, … thus imposing a heightened standard of proof, a device analogous to requiring objective evidence.…

So far, so good; but when one speaks in a diversity case of rules of contract law such as the parol evidence or "four corners" rules that erect procedural obstacles to a party's efforts to avoid being bound by the words of his contract, questions can arise concerning the seam between the doctrine of *Erie R.R. v. Tompkins*, 304 U.S. 64, 58 S. Ct. 817, 82 L. Ed. 1188 (1938), and the dictates of the Seventh Amendment. Are these "substantive" rules because of their effect on the behavior of contracting parties outside the courtroom—on their decision how to structure their relations (whether even to have contractual relations), what forms of words to use in their written contracts (whether even to have a written contract), and so on? Or are they "procedural" rules because they involve the relation between judge and jury, governed in federal courts by the Seventh Amendment? If they were treated as procedural rules, a substantial wedge would be driven between state contract cases and federal diversity contract cases. So it comes as no great surprise that rules of contract interpretation, such as the parol evidence and four corners rules, are deemed substantive, because of their effect on the conduct of contracting parties outside the courtroom, even though the rules operate through limiting the kinds of evidence that are admissible.... No doubt suspicion of juries plays a role in the doctrines that limit the admissibility of evidence by which a party seeks to avoid the consequences of his written words; but the rules do not differentiate between judge and jury; they bind the former as much as the latter.

The rule that a claim of extrinsic ambiguity is to be "screened" by the judge before being submitted to the jury ... is different. That is a rule about the division of functions between judge and jury, and in federal court that division is governed by the Seventh Amendment rather than by state law.... But these cases did not involve a state procedural rule limited to a particular field of law, such as contract law, and arguably motivated by substantive rather than procedural concerns, as in this case.... The rule that the judge must be satisfied that extrinsic evidence creates a legitimate ambiguity before he can submit the dispute over the contract's meaning to the jury is a sensible rule, and if not bound to follow it under Erie we can still adopt it as a rule of federal common law to guide procedure in diversity breach of contract suits. We need not consider the extent to which it is already implicit in Rule 56 of the Federal Rules of Civil Procedure (summary judgment). There is a sense in which a motion for summary judgment requires the judge to "screen" the evidence in advance of trial to make sure it creates a genuine issue of material fact.

The principle that allows the court in some but not all cases to search beneath the semantic surface for clues to meaning is not limited to contract cases. Even the strongest devotees of the "plain meaning" rule of statutory interpretation, a rule that resembles the "four corners" rule of contract law, allow it to bend when necessary to avoid absurd results.... An absurdity in the application of the plain meaning rule usually results from a comparison of the apparently plain meaning to the real-world setting in which the contract or statute is to be applied. It is the same point that a clear document can be rendered unclear—even have its apparent meaning reversed—by the way in which it connects, or fails to connect, with the activities that it regulates. Discrepancy between the word and the world is a common source of interpretive problems everywhere.

With this understanding of the law, we can wrap up our discussion of this case in short order. AM presented no objective evidence that the contract means something different from what it seems to mean. No relevant custom or usage of the trade was tendered for the judge's consideration. There is no indication of the sort of "latent" ambiguity, resulting from uncertain reference or correspondence, that was present in the *Raffles* case. AM points out that the contract does not expressly discuss purchase orders received before January 1, 1991, and not filled till after July 23. But if a contract says "X after January 1," we hardly expect it to say "and not-X until January 1," since that is plainly implied.

AM argues that it is arbitrary — absurd — to distinguish between purchase orders received before or after January 1, 1991, when it is obvious that the parties intended AM to receive royalties on all allegedly infringing machines, and therefore on all machines made before the expiration of the patent. But that is not at all obvious, and in fact is obviously incorrect. AM concedes that no royalty was due on the four machines ordered by the owner of the *Philadelphia Inquirer* that were shipped after December 31, 1991, even if those machines happened to have been made before July 23, 1991, and therefore infringed the patent, since a valid patent excludes others from manufacturing, as well as selling, the patented device. 35 U.S.C. § 154. So not all infringing machines trigger a royalty obligation; and why should the five shipped after the expiration of the patent but before December 31 do so? If the parties ... being competitors can be assumed to be knowledgeable about the subject matter of the contract, had wanted AM to obtain royalties on all machines shipped before December 31, whenever ordered — which is AM's position — they could have said so in just those words. They did not; and there is no objective evidence that their failure to do so must be overlooked if the contact is to be enforced in conformity with the parties' intentions when they signed it. Although the January 1, 1991, cut-off date for GMA's obligation to pay royalties on infringing machines is arbitrary, as all such temporal lines are, it is not absurd that there should have been a cut-off date. The obvious reason for extending the royalty expiration date from the patent expiration date to some months later was to discourage GMA from delaying shipment in order to escape having to pay the royalty, which was sizable. The danger of strategic delay would be less acute for orders that GMA received long in advance of the expiration of AM's patent — orders received, for example, before January 1, 1991. Customers will not wait indefinitely for the delivery of the goods that they order, and GMA would be unlikely, therefore, to delay shipment on orders received before 1991 until after the expiration of the patent in late July. The more acute danger was manipulation of the shipment date of last-minute orders, so a cut-off date was chosen that in effect extended the final royalty expiration date for last-minute orders only.

This interpretation of the reason for the January 1, 1991, cut-off date is conjecture. But it shows that interpreting the contract in accordance with its actual language does not produce absurd results. It thus underscores AM's failure to present objective evidence that the apparent clarity of the contract is an illusion. Without such evidence, the interpretation of the contract presents a question of law, for the judge to decide (not ignoring context, *Florida East Coast Ry. v. CSX Transportation*, Inc., 42 F.3d 1125, 1129 (7th Cir. 1994), but ignoring disputed evidence), and judgment on the pleadings is therefore appropriate.

So when GMA, after discovery was completed, moved for judgment on the pleadings on the ground that the contract was unambiguous, AM was required to demonstrate the existence of objective evidence that the contract was not so clear as it seemed to be. In its brief in opposition to GMA's motion for judgment on the pleadings, AM argued that there was evidence demonstrating an extrinsic ambiguity, tendered that evidence in the form of affidavits, and asked the district judge to convert GMA's motion into a motion for summary judgment and deny the recharacterized motion on the ground that there was a genuine issue of material fact concerning the meaning of the contract, precluding summary judgment. Fed. R. Civ. P. 12(c). This was a proper procedure for AM to follow.... But its affidavits do not create a factual issue concerning the existence of an extrinsic ambiguity. The strongest of them is the affidavit of a patent expert who opined that "[i]n my 30 years of patent practice, I have never seen, handled, or heard of a patent license in which there was a royalty exclusion window [of the kind suggested by GMA]." What does that prove? That such a provision is unusual? That AM was fooled? It is not evidence that the parties were employing a special vocabulary, so that the meaning of the contract is opposite to what an outsider would think. It is not the sort of evidence that would authorize a jury to ignore the language of the contract. So the judge was right to grant GMA's motion, though he should have said that he was ruling on a motion for summary judgment, because the propriety of granting the motion depended on a determination that AM's affidavits did not create a genuine issue of material fact.

AFFIRMED.

NOTES AND QUESTIONS

1. *Is the Posner parol evidence rule the law?* Professor Posner's decision strikes a compromise between historically competing positions, admitting "objective," but not "subjective," extrinsic evidence without the need first to show an ambiguity in the writing. Posner's rule has not fared well in the Illinois state courts, however. The Illinois Supreme Court has addressed the parol evidence rule at length only once since the decision in *AM International*, and it applied a "four corners" rule, excluding all kinds of extrinsic evidence unless the writing was deemed ambiguous on its face.[99] Judge Posner's decision in *AM International* was not discussed. Intermediate Illinois appellate courts continue to apply the Illinois Supreme Court position.[100]

In the meantime, federal courts rely on *AM International* as a controlling authority on Illinois law. In *Cole Taylor Bank v. Truck Ins. Exchange*,[101] Judge Posner suggested that distinguishing objective from subjective testimony, as a way of showing that a seemingly clear contract really is ambiguous, explains the debate between Justice Traynor in cases such as *Masterson v. Sine* and Judge Kozinski in *Trident Center*. Judge Posner notes: "[T]he risk of erroneous interpretations would be very great if parties

---

99. Air Safety v. Teachers Realty Corp., 706 N.E.2d 882 (Ill. 1999).
100. *E.g.*, Lease Mgmt. Equip. Corp. v. DFO P'ship, 910 N.E.2d 709 (Ill. App. 2009).
101. 51 F.3d 736 (7th Cir. 1995).

could not present even unimpeachable evidence that the clarity of the written contract was illusory."[102]

2. *Another attempt to synthesize the decisions:* Judge Posner's decision can be understood as an attempt to create a uniform parol evidence rule (as called for by Professors Calamari and Perillo, *supra*). Some commentators have applauded the effort on the merits, finding Posner's rule a reasonable compromise of conflicting positions.[103]

Long before Posner's decision, Professors Robert Childres and Steven J. Spitz[104] advocated a different way to synthesize the precedents and come up with a uniform parol evidence rule. They studied the 149 cases relevant to the parol evidence rule cited in volumes 10 through 15 of West's General Digest, Fourth Series.[105] They found they could order the apparent chaos of the parol evidence rule by classifying the cases in terms of the status of the parties to the contracts in question.

They divided the cases into categories they labeled as (a) formal contracts, (b) informal contracts, and (c) contracts involving an abuse of the bargaining process. Formal contracts are transactions between parties with some expertise and business sophistication. The parties can be regarded as professionals, and the agreements are negotiated fairly and in detail. Informal contracts are agreements between people who lack sophistication in business. Abuse of bargaining power cases include contracts of adhesion and unconscionable contracts as well as other contracts objectionable on public policy grounds.

Courts protect written documents in formal contract situations. They do not allow oral evidence to replace contract language with an alleged prior understanding. They will allow parties to show that the writing was not a complete statement of the contract. For example, parties may not have defined all their obligations because they deal under the assumption that usages of trade will govern. Businesspeople can prove side agreements. However, courts frequently ignored the parol evidence rule in informal contracts. About 27 percent of the cases in the sample involved these situations. Courts refused to hear extrinsic evidence in only three reported cases involving informal contracts. The approach here was obviously inconsistent with both that in the formal situation and the language of the rule itself. Often courts strained to find terms in the written document to be ambiguous so parol evidence could be admitted. In those cases where courts upheld the written document, the courts frequently in-

---

102. *Id.* at 737. More recent federal decisions relying on *AM International* for Illinois law include Joy v. Hay Group, Inc., 403 F.3d 875 (7th Cir. 2005) and Evergreen Invs. v. FCL Graphics, 334 F.3d 750 (8th Cir. 2003).

103. *E.g.*, William C. Whitford, *The Role of the Jury (and the Fact/Law Distinction) in the Interpretation of Written Contracts*, 2001 Wis. L. Rev. 931, 959–62. Without explicitly citing Judge Posner's opinion, Professor Steven Burton has written a whole book essentially arguing for the distinction that Posner draws between objective and subjective extrinsic evidence. Steven J. Burton, Elements of Contract Interpretation (Oxford University Press 2009).

104. Robert Childres & Steven J. Spitz, *Status in the Law of Contract*, 47 N.Y.U. L. Rev. 1 (1972).

105. Roughly, these volumes reported cases decided during the decade of the 1960s.

dicated that they did not believe the alleged oral agreement had been made. Finally, any person who alleged inferior bargaining position or an abuse of bargaining power usually got his evidence to the trier of fact. A third of the cases in the sample involved an abuse of bargaining power, and the courts in all but seven of them allowed the evidence to be considered.

Childres and Spitz conclude: "Once it is made explicit that no single rule can be expected to operate across all status lines, we can get about the business of trying to create new categories and rules." The authors concede that their categories may be crude and imprecise. Their study tells us only about reported appellate cases. Furthermore, some might suspect that the reactions of courts in the 1960s might differ substantially from reactions today. Interestingly, in 1991 Michael Lawrence[106] sought to replicate the Childres and Spitz analysis, using Wisconsin cases. He concluded that the outcomes in the cases supported the Childres and Spitz hypothesis with "striking frequency."

Professor William Whitford[107] labels the Childres and Spitz approach "denial." They find consistency in the application of the parol evidence rule by inventing new categories, but Whitford is skeptical that the consistency is really there.

> My primary quarrel is with the vagueness of their categories. The distinctions between "formal" and "informal," and between "substitution" and "variation," are not precise. The result is a great risk of coder bias, with cases applying a hard [parol evidence rule] pushed into the "formal" contract and "substitution" categories and cases admitting extrinsic evidence pushed into the other categories, in order to validate the preconceived hypotheses. Another weakness is that the study cannot show that the same pattern will prevail over time. The hypothesis is that judges bend the black letter rules to achieve what they perceive as the proper result in the cases, and that there is consistency across judges in what is perceived as the just result. Today there is a greater willingness to recognize differences in judges' basic sensibilities than there once was. Some judges will be much more devoted to efficiency in contract performance as a policy goal, others to autonomy values, still others to redistribution values. And judges will differ in what is the best strategy to achieve autonomy values. So even if Childres and Spitz correctly found a consistency in result in the 1960s, there is no guarantee that the consistency would continue over time, nor would I expect it to.

3. *Professor Robert Scott's approach:* Professor Robert Scott does not think there is some unrecognized consistency in previous decisions, but, like many others, he longs for a uniform parol evidence rule. Scott's solution to the uniformity problem is a return to a plain-meaning approach to interpretation and a strict parol evidence rule.

---

106. Comment, *The Parol Evidence Rule in Wisconsin: "Status in the Law of Contracts" Revisited,* 1991 WIS. L. REV. 1071.

107. William C. Whitford, *The Role of the Jury (and the Fact/Law Distinction) in the Interpretation of Written Contracts,* 2001 WIS. L. REV. 931, 959.

Often, this will defend writings at the cost of defeating actual expectations. Professor Scott seems ready to trade having courts enforce the understandings of the parties for something approaching certainty or predictability in court decisions. He says:

> [T]he efficient regulation of contract does not require that every relational norm be judicialized or that the legal mechanism operates efficiently viewed on its own terms, but rather that it operates efficiently in concert with social norms of trust, reciprocity, and conditional cooperation that also regulate relational contracts. Under the formalist approach, these norms would not be legally enforceable contract terms ... but they nevertheless would be enforced by social sanctions that would effectively constrain the parties' incentives to exploit changed circumstances strategically.[108]

4. *Professor Justin Sweet's approach:* Like Professor Scott, Professor Justin Sweet would prefer a uniform parol evidence rule, but with a preferred approach of barring extrinsic evidence in interpreting written contracts only in rare cases. Professor Sweet argues:[109]

> [T]rue integration should be the only basis for any rule that limits provability of prior oral agreements. The desirable objectives now sought through the parol evidence rule can be accomplished more directly through other accepted legal doctrines. To make the integration concept work, however, there is a need for workable and realistic methods of recognizing the objective trappings of a true integration. A model of a truly integrated contract should be created and criteria developed for identification of truly integrated writings....
>
> The hallmark of a truly integrated contract is that it is put together carefully and methodically. In this sense it resembles the creation of a statute or a treaty. A good deal has occurred before the act of integration. The person preparing the integration, usually the attorney, gathers all the evidence of what has transpired in order to prepare a draft. He will look at letters, wires, memoranda, agreements, contracts, and any other data relevant to the final document.... Drafts are exchanged and revised. Provisions are traded, eliminated, or modified. Each party uses its persuasiveness to support inclusion or deletion of specific clauses. Language is reviewed carefully with a view toward achieving phraseology satisfactory to both parties. Usually, a clause stating that the writing covers the entire transaction is included. Attorneys look over the final draft and confer with the top negotiators in order to iron out final details. The final draft is prepared and the date set for execution. Top executives of the contracting parties and other interested persons gather to sign or to witness the execution of the agreement....

---

108. Robert E. Scott, *The Case for Formalism in Relational Contract*, 94 Nw. U. L. Rev. 847, 861 (2000). *See also* Robert E. Scott, *Is Article 2 the Best We Can Do?*, 52 Hastings L.J. 677 (2001).

109. Justin Sweet, *Contract Making and Parol Evidence: Diagnosis and Treatment of a Sick Rule*, 53 Cornell L. Rev. 1036 (1968). Copyright © 1968 by Cornell University. All Rights Reserved.

Obviously, the percentage of contracts made in this manner is small. It can be argued that if we protect only true integrations of this sort, we are in effect abolishing the parol evidence rule. But these are the only types of written agreements which can confidently be assumed to integrate the entire transaction in one repository....

Even a contract put together in a manner suggested by the above model would not invariably integrate everything relating to the transaction. Contracts which appear to be integrated contracts *may* not contain everything. Oral agreements may be made simultaneously with the execution of a complete and final-looking written agreement, and may nevertheless be enforceable.

Sweet then lists nine factors a court should consider in deciding whether a written document truly was intended as a final and complete expression of the parties' contract. Two important factors, he lists, are the "bargaining situation" and the "degree of standardization of the writing." He says: "The greater the one-sidedness of the bargaining situation, the less likely it is that the bargain was concluded by an integrated writing." Furthermore, "[t]he greater the standardization of the writing, the less likely that the transaction was concluded by an integrated writing."

5. *Professor Whitford and the best of all possible worlds:* Professor Whitford, the skeptic who questions whether Professors Childres and Spitz have discovered a true synthesis of the decisions, concludes his article by saying:[110]

The prophecy of continued confusion and conflict may be a source of despair for many. But we have lived with this conflict for decades. And maybe life isn't so bad. Undoubtedly things could be better, and it is possible that the unsettled law of contract interpretation is holding us back. It is also possible that it just doesn't make much difference whether we have a coherent and consistent law of interpretation or continued confusion and conflict. If it doesn't make much difference, then the promoters of efficiency in contract performance as an important value will need to reevaluate their position. Their position is premised on the idea that predictability in how a lawsuit will be decided is very important to the efficient performance of transactions. That is the essential rationale for keeping interpretation away from juries, assumed to be unpredictable. That we have persevered for so long with such unpredictability in how courts will decide contract interpretation cases weakens this rationale, and strengthens the case for tilting the balance more toward the pursuit of autonomy values [*i.e.*, trying to enforce actual expectations].... That probably means, in light of our traditions for drawing the fact/law distinction, giving juries a more consistent role in contract interpretation.

---

110. Whitford, *supra* note 107, at 964.

Chapter 4

PROBLEMS CONCERNING THE ADJUSTMENT OR MODIFICATION OF PERFORMANCE TERMS

It is hard to make a contract to be performed over time that will continue to satisfy everyone concerned as it is performed. People often expect to make adjustments and changes during the course of performance. Often contracts are written with provisions designed to track with changing conditions. We have already seen flexible quantity and price arrangements. Frequently, however, people write what appear to be absolute contracts with no provision for changes, yet as both parties anticipated, they make adjustments as circumstances change. The practice of making adjustments, without providing for doing so in advance, is common but has presented a series of challenges for the legal system.

One problem, already covered to some extent in these materials,[1] is the doctrine of consideration. Suppose a contract modification is one-sided: it changes only one party's right or obligation under the contract. For example: a creditor might agree to accept $600 in full satisfaction of a $1,000 debt. At one time, this kind of contractual modification caused the legal system a great deal of difficulty. It was said that there was no consideration for the creditor's agreement to release the debtor of liability upon payment of $600, as the debtor already had a pre-existing legal duty to pay this amount (and more). Over the years, courts have found ways to enforce a one-sided contractual modification in most cases notwithstanding the consideration doctrine. Section 2-209(1) of the Uniform Commercial Code has now established an explicit exception to the consideration doctrine for contractual modifications in contracts for the sale of goods. In other types of contracts, courts have found alternative ways to reach a similar result. Sometimes they hold that the parties to a modification have implicitly agreed first to rescind the earlier contract and then to create a new contract with different terms (sometimes called a novation), with both the rescission agreement and the new contract supported by consideration on quite tra-

---

1. *See* Chapter 3, Volume I, of these materials, where the consideration doctrine and the pre-existing duty rule are first discussed.

ditional grounds. Other times courts have held that an agreement to modify the original contract in a one-sided way (in the sense of changing only one side's obligation) is enforceable by relying on principles that we now recognize as promissory estoppel. But the estoppel theory (reliance on a promise) usually requires that the party seeking enforcement of the modification show reliance on the promised modification. The following case illustrates waiver, still another doctrine used to enforce contract changes lacking consideration.

A. WAIVING CONDITIONS CONTRASTED WITH MODIFYING CONTRACTS

CLARK v. WEST

New York Court of Appeals
193 N.Y. 349, 86 N.E. 1 (1908)

[Plaintiff, an author, sued defendant, a publisher, for breach of contract. The trial court overruled defendant's demurrer to the complaint. The Appellate Division reversed this decision and sustained the demurrer. But the Court of Appeals reversed the Appellate Division, ruling that the complaint stated a cause of action.

Clark, the plaintiff, alleged that he had entered a contract with the West Publishing Company to write and prepare for publication a series of law books. Manuscripts were to be satisfactory to West. Clark promised "to totally abstain from the use of intoxicating liquors during the continuance of this contract, and the payment to him in accordance with the terms of this contract of any money in excess of $2 per page is dependent on the faithful performance of this as well as the other conditions of this contract." Clark was to be paid $2 a page for each manuscript accepted by West. The contract also stated that if Clark "abstains from the use of intoxicating liquor and otherwise fulfills his agreements ... he shall be paid an additional $4 per page."

Clark's complaint alleged that West published Clark's three-volume work on corporations. The book was successful, and West received large net receipts. The work contained 3,469 pages. West paid Clark at a rate of $2 per page ($6,938). It refused to pay Clark the additional $4 a page. Clark fully performed the contract, except he "did not totally abstain from the use of intoxicating liquor during the continuance of said contract, but such use by the plaintiff was not excessive and did not prevent or interfere with the due and full performance by the plaintiff of all the other stipulations in said contract."

The complaint stated that the intoxicating liquor condition had been waived. Long prior to the completion of the book, West had full knowledge that Clark drank intoxicating liquor. It did not then terminate the contract. Its agents failed to object. They continued to "exact and require of the plaintiff performance of all the other stipulations and conditions." West continued to receive installments of manuscript and continued to make advance payments. It published the book. At no time did

West's agents "notify or intimate to the plaintiff that defendant would insist upon strict compliance, or that defendant intended to take advantage of plaintiff's said breach." "[W]ith full knowledge of plaintiff's said use of intoxicating liquors, defendant repeatedly avowed and represented to the plaintiff that he was entitled to and would receive said royalty payment [the full $6 a page], and plaintiff believed and relied on said representation, and in reliance thereon continued in the performance of said contract."]

WERNER, J.

. . . .

Briefly stated, the defendant's position is that the stipulation as to plaintiff's total abstinence is the consideration for the payment of the difference between $2 and $6 per page, and therefore could not be waived except by a new agreement to that effect based upon a good consideration; that the so-called waiver alleged by the plaintiff is not a waiver, but a modification of the contract in respect of its consideration. The plaintiff, on the other hand, argues that the stipulation for his total abstinence was merely a condition precedent, intended to work a forfeiture of the additional compensation in case of a breach, and that it could be waived without any formal agreement to that effect based upon a new consideration.

The subject matter of the contract was the writing of books by the plaintiff for the defendant. The duration of the contract was the time necessary to complete them all. The work was to be done to the satisfaction of the defendant, and the plaintiff was not to write any other books except those covered by the contract unless requested to do so by the defendant, in which latter event he was to be paid for that particular work by the year. The compensation for the work specified in the contract was to be $6 per page, unless the plaintiff failed to totally abstain from the use of intoxicating liquors during the continuance of the contract, in which event he was to receive only $2 per page. That is the obvious import of the contract construed in the light of the purpose for which it was made, and in accordance with the ordinary meaning of plain language. It is not a contract to write books in order that the plaintiff shall keep sober, but a contract containing a stipulation that he shall keep sober so that he may write satisfactory books. When we view the contract from this standpoint, it will readily be perceived that the particular stipulation is not the consideration for the contract, but simply one of its conditions, which fits in with those relating to time and method of delivery of manuscript, revision of proof, citation of cases, assignment of copyrights, keeping track of new cases and citations for new editions, and other details that might be waived by the defendant, if he saw fit to do so. This is made clear, it seems to us, by the provision that, "in consideration of the above promises," the defendant agrees to pay the plaintiff $2 per page on each book prepared by him, and if he "abstains from the use of intoxicating liquor and otherwise fulfills his agreements as hereinbefore set forth, he shall be paid an additional $4 per page in manner hereinbefore stated." The compensation of $2 per page, not to exceed $250 per month, was an advance or partial payment of the whole price of $6 per page, and the payment of the two-thirds, which was to be withheld pending the performance of the contract, was simply made contingent upon the plaintiff's total abstention from the use of intoxicants during the life of the contract....

It is obvious that the parties thought that the plaintiff's normal work was worth $6 per page. That was the sum to be paid for the work done by the plaintiff, and not for total abstinence. If the plaintiff did not keep to the condition as to total abstinence, he was to lose part of that sum.... This, we think is the fair interpretation of the contract, and it follows that the stipulation as to the plaintiff's total abstinence was nothing more nor less than a condition precedent. If that conclusion is well-founded, there can be no escape from the corollary that this condition could be waived; and, if it was waived, the defendant is clearly not in a position to insist upon the forfeiture that his waiver was intended to annihilate. The forfeiture must stand or fall with the condition. If the latter was waived, the former is no longer a part of the contract. Defendant still has the right to counterclaim for any damages that he may have sustained in consequence of the plaintiff's breach, but he cannot insist upon strict performance....

The theory upon which the defendant's attitude seems to be based is that, even if he has represented to the plaintiff that he would not insist upon the condition that the latter should observe total abstinence from intoxicants, he can still refuse to pay the full contract price for his work. The inequity of this position becomes apparent when we consider that this contract was to run for a period of years, during a large portion of which the plaintiff was to be entitled only to the advance payment of $2 per page; the balance being contingent, among other things, upon publication of the books and returns from sales. Upon this theory the defendant might have waived the condition while the first book was in process of production, and yet, when the whole work was completed, he would still be in a position to insist upon the forfeiture because there had not been strict performance. Such a situation is possible in a case where the subject of the waiver is the very consideration of a contract ... but not where the waiver relates to something that can be waived. In the case at bar, as we have seen, the waiver is not of the consideration or subject matter, but of an incident to the method of performance. The consideration remains the same. The defendant has had the work he bargained for, and it is alleged that he has waived one of the conditions as to the manner in which it was to have been done. He might have insisted upon literal performance, and then he could have stood upon the letter of his contract. If, however, he has waived that incidental condition, he has created a situation to which the doctrine of waiver very precisely applies.

The cases that present the most familiar phases of the doctrine of waiver are those that have arisen out of litigation over insurance policies where the defendants have claimed a forfeiture because of the breach of some condition in the contract ... but it is a doctrine of general application that is confined to no particular class of cases. A "waiver" has been defined to be the intentional relinquishment of a known right. It is voluntary and implies an election to dispense with something of value, or forego some advantage which the party waiving it might at its option have demanded or insisted upon.... In the recent case of *Draper v. Oswego Co. Fire R. Ass'n*, 190 N.Y. 12,

16, 82 N.E. 755, Chief Judge Cullen, in speaking for the court upon this subject, said: "While that doctrine and the doctrine of equitable estoppel are often confused in insurance litigation, there is a clear distinction between the two. A 'waiver' is the voluntary abandonment or relinquishment by a party of some right or advantage.... The doctrine of equitable estoppel, or estoppel *in pais*, is that a party may be precluded by his acts and conduct from asserting a right to the detriment of another party who, entitled to rely on such conduct, has acted upon it.... As already said, the doctrine of waiver is to relieve against forfeiture; it requires no consideration for a waiver, nor any prejudice or injury to the other party."....

In the ... complaint, the plaintiff alleges facts and circumstances that we think, if established, would prove defendant's waiver of plaintiff's performance of [the] contract stipulation [calling for total abstinence]....

NOTES AND QUESTIONS

1. *Conditions, penalties and forfeitures:* This case discusses what are called "conditions" on promises, a topic we consider extensively in Chapter 5 *infra*. Broadly speaking, conditions are provisions in a contract providing that a party's performance is conditional upon the happening of some event, commonly a performance by the other party. The effect of conditions, if enforced, is to entitle one party not to perform some part, perhaps all, of a contract, irrespective of the actual harm caused by the non-occurrence of the condition. In this case, of course, West sought to avoid its promise to pay an extra $4 per page.

As we discussed extensively in Chapter 2 of Volume 1 of these materials, the law has long placed limitations on contract provisions explicitly providing for penalties for breach. The penalty principle is a clear limitation on freedom of contract, but one that contract law has long embraced. Despite the similarity in policy concerns, however, the penalty principle is not explicitly extended to bar enforcement of conditions that look like a penalty. The law nonetheless has responded to similar policy concerns by invoking other doctrines, of which waiver is a prime example.

2. *The benefits and limitations of waiver as a doctrine:* As the court indicates, waiver does not require the proof of reliance by the party seeking its benefit. In that respect, waiver is a more useful doctrine than estoppel. But waiver does require some action by the other party that can be understood as at least an implied promise not to enforce the condition. In *Clark v. West*, the complaint alleged that "with full knowledge of plaintiff's [continued] use of intoxicating liquors, defendant repeatedly avowed and represented to the plaintiff that he ... would receive [the full] royalty payment." The allegation is interpreted as an implied promise to waive the explicit contractual condition on payment of more than $2 per page (*i.e.*, abstention from alcohol). Courts in other circumstances have been quite ingenious in finding implied waivers to avoid forfeitures.

To enforce a waiver, a party must show an implied or express promise but not consideration or reliance thereon. However, it is widely recognized that the party making the waiver can revoke it at any time before there is reliance. This ability to revoke a waiver is recognized by both the Restatement (Second) of Contracts, § 84(2) and the Uniform Commercial Code, § 2-209(5).

3. *Waiver in context—some history:* The opinion in *Clark v. West* tells us that much of the development of waiver came from judicial opinions dealing with insurance contracts. Spencer Kimball studied insurance regulation in Wisconsin from 1835 to 1959.[2] He found that courts regulated the administration of insurance claims. They attempted to balance two policies: they tried to give effect to the reasonable expectations of the parties while at the same time preserving the integrity of the insurance fund by preventing unwarranted raids on it by persons not entitled to share. Major fires destroyed large cities throughout the second half of the 19th century, and the insurance companies were faced with the threat of serious losses.

> [I]t became industry policy to tighten up loss settlement practices. Suspicion of arson seldom resulted in a defense frankly based on an allegation of criminal incendiarism; instead the companies used whatever technical defenses came to hand. Moreover, to protect the companies against fraudulent and exorbitant claims, and to give time for adequate investigation, it was industry policy to delay settlement as long as possible under the contract. Though insurance men were presumably actuated only by creditable motives, no device can be imagined more calculated to harm the industry's public relations than a set policy of arbitrary delay of loss settlement for the maximum period permitted by law.[3]

Loss settlement usually involved two steps, each of which the policy made a condition to recovery. First, the insured had to give notice of loss within a certain time. Second, it had to submit proofs of the amount of loss within another specified time after the notice of loss. Insured persons and entities often missed the deadlines. Kimball says: "[T]he judges were not willing to forfeit the insured's protection by reason of his failure to perform these technical conditions, so long as they could possibly rationalize a contrary result without overtly discarding the canon that freedom of contract was a basic value."[4] This provoked a game between the courts and insurance company lawyers.

> The industry men saw it as a game, the object of which for them was finding and using language so explicit that the court could find in it no latent ambiguity. Though in fact the courts were less hostile than company men supposed, industry committees frequently made drafting suggestions for making the contracts so airtight that even a judge with a strong bias against insurance companies could not misunderstand.... Occasionally someone expressed a more pessimistic view—that the courts were creating liability arbitrarily outside the contract. If that were true, more careful drafting would help little.[5]

---

2. SPENCER KIMBALL, INSURANCE AND PUBLIC POLICY (Wisconsin Press 1960).
3. *Id.* at 215.
4. *Id.* at 213.
5. *Id.* at 211–12.

Lawrence Friedman[6] developed these ideas further. He argued first that classic contract law was grounded in abstraction; it assumed a system of doctrine that appears to be constructed by the deduction of rules from principles. The principles are universal. That is, they are applicable whether the parties are rich or poor, without regard to the subject matter of the transaction, and are unchanging over time. But, Friedman argued next, it is not feasible for a rapidly developing economy to cope with such abstract law, which gives no regard to context and change. How was the idea of abstract contract law applied to serve the needs of a developing economy? Two of the tools that Friedman suggests the courts used to bridge this gap were waiver and estoppel. He noted:

> It might offend a purist to talk in one breath about estoppel, waiver, ratification, election of remedies, laches, and accord and satisfaction. These were all different concepts, with different histories and uses. They had in common, however, that they all related to particular acts of particular parties, subsequent to the formation of a contract but affecting the contract rights of the actors. And they were all ideas that could be used to bend rules of higher generality. Though they themselves could be expressed in terms of rules, they constituted statements of reasons (derived from the facts of particular cases) why some more general rule should not be applied.

> ... A concept like estoppel is in essence antithetical to pure contract abstraction. A party is "estopped" for reasons that are peculiar to his or her opponent's situation. Abstraction, however, abhors the special and the particular. [Friedman then notes that the use of these concepts was common throughout the period he was studying (1836 to 1958) but was perhaps more common at the end of the 19th century. The use of the doctrines to give relief in individual cases avoided the "bother or embarrassment" of making radical changes in the formal doctrine.]

> Waiver and estoppel were not used only on a case-by-case basis. If the court had a consistent bias of values in a given area of transactions, it sometimes applied one or more of these concepts consistently in handling such transactions. This warping and sliding process was characteristic of the way the common law developed. After a generation or two in which a court consistently found that not the general rule but the "exception" applied to whatever case was at hand, the original general rule turned into a mummified corpse. Historically the insurance companies were on the losing end of such a process, which, by the use of "estoppel" and "waiver," created what amounted to a set of rules for construing insurance policies so as to aid the insured. This process of attrition took place frequently in the law; and in the 20th century "legal realism" gave dead rules decent burial in many instances simply by pointing out that the old rules were no longer used even when legal literature still paid them lip service.

---

6. LAWRENCE FRIEDMAN, CONTRACT LAW IN AMERICA: A SOCIAL AND ECONOMIC CASE STUDY (Wisconsin Press 1965). Reprinted by permission of The University of Wisconsin Press.

4. *Getting performance from a delinquent:* Suppose the West Publishing Co. editor in charge of Clark's book wants to get the best book written on time or as close to on time as possible. The editor knows Clark has a problem with alcohol. The editor becomes aware of Clark's drinking. What does the opinion in *Clark v. West* suggest that the editor should do to preserve West's rights to pay only $2 a page for the manuscript? Could the editor do anything less than give Clark formal notice that the publisher would not pay the added $4 a page? What might a reasonable editor fear would be the consequence of such a notice?

Furthermore, the court seems to see the case as one involving forfeiture. West has the book, but now it won't pay the contract price for it. Is the quality of the book necessarily the same as West had hoped for? Is it possible that Clark's book produced while drinking is acceptable but that he could have written an excellent one had he not taken a single drink? The court says West could sue for its damages caused by Clark's drinking. How would you compute them?

5. *Modifications, duress and good faith:* Contractual modifications are entirely normal, and common, in many contractual situations. The modern tendency to enforce modifications can therefore be seen as consistent with freedom of contract values. In recognizing and enforcing a modification, the court is enforcing the deal that a reasonable businessperson observing the parties' behavior would assume the parties intended as the enforceable deal.

Sometimes, however, contractual modifications are the product of pressures that one party brings on another that may not be entirely appropriate. A British casebook noted:[7]

> An agreement running over a period of time may give a party the scope for "opportunism," by taking advantage of the other's circumstances to threaten a breach of contract unless the deal is renegotiated in his favor. Frequently the opportunity for such extortion arises from the operation of the contract itself. Even if the parties met on an equal footing originally, when the time for performance draws near one party may be heavily dependent on the other; he may face serious losses if he does not get the other's performance and has nowhere that he can readily obtain a substitute.

Contract law has occasionally relied on the doctrine of duress to invalidate modifications resulting from such bargaining behavior. But the requirements for satisfying the duress doctrine are often hard to determine and satisfy, resulting in instances where the court has found it convenient to just say that there is no consideration for the contractual modification. A much discussed example is *Alaska Packers' Assn. v. Domenico.*[8] In this case, the owner of a fishing boat hired a crew to work on the boat for the duration of the relatively short season in the Alaskan waters. When the boat was in remote waters, and where it was not possible to hire

---

7. H.G. Beale, W.D. Bishop & Michael Furmston, Contract: Cases and Materials 491 (Butterworths 1985).

8. 117 Fed. 99 (9th Cir. 1902).

other workers given the short season, the crew mutinied and refused to work further unless they were promised higher wages. The captain promised the higher pay, but when the ship returned to shore he reneged. The court held that the promise for the wage increase was not supported by consideration. The decision is often applauded today in its result, but argued that duress would have been a more satisfactory rationale.[9]

As mentioned above, the Uniform Commercial Code has created an explicit exception to the consideration doctrine for contractual modifications. UCC § 2-209(1). Official Comment 2 attempts to account for modifications resulting from inappropriate bargaining, stating:

> [M]odifications ... must meet the test of good faith imposed by this Act. The effective use of bad faith to escape performance on the original contract terms is barred, and the extortion of a "modification" without legitimate commercial reason is ineffective as a violation of the duty of good faith. Nor can a mere technical consideration support a modification made in bad faith.

The Official Comment adds a good deal of substantive law to the text of the statute. Professor Robert Hillman[10] concluded that courts read the text of § 2-209(1) and ignore the Official Comment, enforcing modifications without considering the issue of good faith. He proposed an amendment to § 2-209(1) adding two sentences to it: "An agreement modifying a contract made as a result of economic or other duress is not enforceable. The burden of establishing that a modification involving a material net loss to the party opposing its enforcement was not a product of duress is on the party seeking to enforce the modification." Why haven't courts taken something such as this approach, following the invitation in the UCC comment?

6. *Elections contrasted with waivers:* An "election of remedies" may be seen as different from a "waiver" of right. For example, one of the most important remedies granted buyers by the UCC is the right to reject or return defective goods and have no obligation to pay for them. However, under UCC § 2-606(1)(a), a buyer "accepts" goods when "after a reasonable opportunity to inspect the goods," he signifies to the seller "that he will take or retain them in spite of their nonconformity." If the defect could have been detected by a reasonable inspection and the buyer has no "reasonable assumption that ... [the] ... nonconformity would be cured," then the buyer cannot return them. He has given up this remedy and *elected* to do nothing or seek damages. The seller need offer no new performance nor prove that he relied on the statement. Does this kind of election of remedies significantly differ from a waiver of rights? The buyer's choice may be less than ideally free when confronted by a delivery of defective but usable goods. She may no longer have time to find

---

9. The case, and the analysis of it in this paragraph, is discussed in Judge Richard Posner's decision in *Selmer v. Blakeslee-Midwest*, 704 F.2d 924 (1983). The *Selmer* case is included as a principal case in Volume I of these materials. If you have access to this volume, see also Note 4 following the *Selmer* case.

10. Robert Hillman, *Policing Contract Modifications under the UCC: Good Faith and the Doctrine of Economic Duress*, 64 Iowa L. Rev. 849 (1979).

substitutes. Of course, she can accept the goods and sue for damages, but often this will not provide an adequate remedy. Yet under the language of the Code, this does not seem to matter.

B. "WRITTEN MODIFICATIONS ONLY" CLAUSES

Part A showed that both at common law and under the Code, modern courts are generally willing to enforce contractual modifications, notwithstanding the older common law. But this decisional trend has raised a number of practical problems for contract parties. First, a large organization will have many employees dealing with the other party, and they may want to make sure that any modifications are approved by an appropriate company official. Second, a party may be concerned about the possibility of claims that there was agreement to a modification when no such agreement was intended. Courts can find implied agreements to modify a contract, even when there was not an explicit modification. A claim that there was an implied modification agreement can become more credible if evidence is introduced about oral discussions at the time of contracting, notwithstanding the parol evidence rule. For example, in *Clark v. West*, if Clark had introduced testimony that at the time of contract an official from West stated that it did not intend to enforce the condition respecting use of intoxicating beverages so long as Clark met deadlines and his work was of good quality, it would be easier for a court to interpret West's subsequent behavior in accepting the manuscript and not protesting about the drinking as a waiver of the condition. Yet reliance on pre-contract discussions is what the parol evidence rule is supposed to prevent, especially in a state like New York, which follows a more formalist version of that rule.[11]

Concerned about problems such as these, a party will sometimes insert into a written contract a provision that neither an agreement to modify the contract nor a waiver of any of its provisions will be effective unless put in a writing signed by a specified official of each party. As the following cases illustrate, such provisions have not always been successful in avoiding oral or implied modifications and waivers.

UNIVERSAL BUILDERS, INC. v.
MOON MOTOR LODGE, INC.

Pennsylvania Supreme Court
430 Pa. 550, 244 A.2d 10 (1968)

EAGEN, J.

[This was an appeal from a final equitable decree ordering the defendant to pay the plaintiff the balance due on a construction contract, plus extras. Plaintiff sought money damages for work done under both the basic and a supplemental agreement. The defendant denied it owed plaintiff any money for work done, claiming both a

---

11. *See* Mitchill v. Lath in Chapter 3 of these materials.

set-off for uncompleted work and damages for delay. The trial court entered a decree for the balance due and denied all counterclaims.]

Briefly, the background facts of this case are as follows. On August 16, 1961, the plaintiff, Universal Builders, Inc. (hereinafter Universal), entered into a written contract with the defendant, Moon Motor Lodge, Inc. (hereinafter Moon), for the construction of a motel and restaurant in Allegheny County. The contract provides, *inter alia*, that all change orders must be in writing and signed by Moon and/or the Architect and that all requests for extension of time must be made in writing to the Architect. The contract specifications also required that a certain proportion of a reinforcing substance be used in the building walls. The masonry subcontractor failed to use the specified proportion. When this defect was discovered, Moon magnified its importance, withheld from Universal a progress payment to which Universal was entitled, threatened to expel Universal from the job, and thereby induced Universal to enter into the supplemental agreement. The supplemental agreement, dated March 27, 1962, provides, *inter alia*, that Universal will pay Moon $5000 as damages for the absence of the reinforcing material, that Universal will perform certain additional work at no additional cost to Moon, [and] that the date for completion of the project is extended from April 1, 1962, to July 1, 1962....

Universal substantially completed performance on September 1, 1962, and left the construction site on October 1, 1962. After filing this suit, Universal went into bankruptcy. The trustee prosecuted this action and won a final decree in the lower court....

Moon urges that the lower court erred in several respects.

First, Moon submits that the chancellor erred in not enforcing the contract provision that extras would not be paid for unless done pursuant to a written, signed change order.

Unless a contract is for the sale of goods, see the Uniform Commercial Code — Sales, the Act of April 6, 1953, P.L. 3, § 2-209(2), as amended, 12 A P.S. § 2-209(2), it appears undisputed that the contract can be modified orally although it provides that it can be modified only in writing.... Construction contracts typically provide that the builder will not be paid for extra work unless it is done pursuant to a written change order, yet courts frequently hold that owners must pay for extra work done at their oral direction.... This liability can be based on several theories. For example, the extra work may be said to have been done under an oral agreement separate from the written contract and not containing the requirement of a written authorization.... The requirement of a written authorization may also be considered a condition which has been waived....

On either of the above theories, the chancellor correctly held Moon liable to pay for the extras in spite of the lack of written change orders. The evidence indicates that William Berger, the agent of Moon, requested many changes, was informed that they would involve extra cost, and promised to pay for them. In addition, Berger frequently was on the construction site and saw at least some of the extra work in progress. The record demonstrates that he was a keen observer with an extraordinary knowledge of the project in general and the contract requirements in particular. Thus it is not unreasonable to infer that he was aware that extra work was being done without proper authorization, yet he stood by without protesting while the extras were incorporated into the project. Under these circumstances there also was an implied promise to pay for the extras.

C.I.T. Corp. v. Jonnet, 419 Pa. 435, 214 A.2d 620 (1965), does suggest that such non-written modifications are ineffective unless the contract provision requiring modifications to be in writing was first waived. That case, however, is misleading. Although it involved a contract for the sale of movable bar and restaurant equipment, which is a contract for the sale of "goods" controlled by the Uniform Commercial Code—Sales, *supra*, §2-101 *et seq.*, as amended, 12 A P.S. §2-101 *et seq.*, it overlooks that legislation, in particular §2-209....

From subsection (5) it can be inferred that a provision in a contract for the sale of goods that the contract can be modified only in writing is waived, just as such a provision in a construction contract is waived, under the circumstances described by Restatement, Contracts, §224 (1932), which provides: "The performance of a condition qualifying a promise in a contract within the Statute [of Frauds or in a contract containing a provision requiring modifications to be in writing (§407)] may be excused by an oral agreement or permission of the promisor that the condition need not be performed, if the agreement or permission is given while the performance of the condition is possible, and in reliance on the agreement or permission, while it is unrevoked, the promisee materially changes his position." Obviously a condition is considered waived when its enforcement would result in something approaching fraud.... Thus the effectiveness of a non-written modification in spite of a contract condition that modifications must be written depends upon whether enforcement of the condition is or is not barred by equitable considerations, not upon the technicality of whether the condition was or was not expressly and separately waived before the non-written modification.

In view of these equitable considerations underlying waiver, it should be obvious that when an owner requests a builder to do extra work, promises to pay for it and watches it performed knowing that it is not authorized in writing, he cannot refuse to pay on the ground that there was no written change order.... When Moon directed Universal to "go ahead" and promised to pay for the extras, performance of the condition requiring change orders to be in writing was excused by implication. It would be manifestly unjust to allow Moon, which misled Universal into doing extra work without a written authorization, to benefit from non-performance of that condition.

Next, Moon submits that the lower court erroneously dismissed its counterclaim for delay damages. The lower court denied Moon any recovery for the delay because it resulted from Moon's own acts in ordering many changes. There is authority for this position.... In this case, however, the contract expressly conditions the allowance of any time extension on the submission of a written request to the Architect. This condition specifically applies to delays caused by the owner's, *i.e.*, Moon's, own acts. Article 18 of the General Conditions provides: "If the contractor be delayed at any time in the progress of the work by any act or neglect of the Owner or the Architect, or of any employee of either, or by any separate contractor employed by the Owner, or by changes ordered in the work ... then the time of completion shall be extended for such reasonable time as the Architect may decide. No such extension shall be made for delay occurring more than seven days before claim therefor is made in writing to the Architect...."

Consequently, the case authority on which the lower court based its decision is not controlling.

The evidence that Universal conformed with the procedure required by Article 18 is slight; what evidence there is has been largely discredited. However a condition precedent such as the one contained in Article 18 can of course be waived ... and there is evidence to support at least a partial waiver.

By executing the Supplemental Agreement (which extends the time of substantial completion from April 1, 1962, to July 1, 1962) without reference to the procedure established by Article 18, Moon certainly waived Article 18 with reference to that extension. It is not apparent, however, that this waiver applies to subsequent delays. Apart from the execution of the supplemental agreement, there is no evidence that Moon expressly or impliedly promised that the condition precedent contained in Article 18 would not apply to subsequent delays. We think it does so apply....

Finally, we have carefully considered the record and we agree with the lower court that there was sufficient evidence to establish the amount of Universal's claim for extras and that there was not sufficient evidence to establish Moon's set-off claim for uncompleted work.

The decree of the lower court therefore was correct, except insofar as it failed to allow Moon's counterclaim for delay damages, as before indicated, for the period from July 1, 1962, to September 1, 1962.

Decree vacated and record remanded for entry of a decree consonant with this opinion. Each party to bear own costs.

Dissenting Opinion by MUSMANNO, J.:

I believe an injustice is being done the defendant in this case. The lower court awarded the plaintiff $42,283.29, for extras, but the record shows that only $900 of such extras was earned on two signed change orders agreed to in writing. Yet the agreement specifically provides that, except in an emergency endangering life or property, no claim for an addition to the contract price was to be valid unless the work was done pursuant to the owner's written, signed order, and after written notice given by the contractor before proceeding with the work. I am disturbed that the Majority could have reached its conclusion when the record shows that *there was no such writing....*

Even the plaintiff did not contend that the requirement in writing was waived by agreement of the parties.... The most that the plaintiff has shown are oral modifications of the work called for under the contract, which is exactly what is prohibited by the solemn agreement entered into between the parties. The oral modification certainly cannot be used as evidence of a waiver, for otherwise, a requirement of writing would become meaningless. This Court clearly pointed out this fundamental proposition of law in *C.I.T. Corp. v. Jonnet*, 419 Pa. 435, 438 (1965), where this writer, speaking for the Court, said: "Nowhere, however, do the defendants allege cancellation by the plaintiff of the express term of the original conditional sale contract that 'no waiver or change in this contract or related note, shall bind such assignee (in this case, the plaintiff) unless in writing signed by one of its officers.'"

"This specific condition stands as a stone wall in the path of the defendants' contention. However, they believe they have found a way around this formidable barrier by citing the case of *Kirk v. Brentwood M.H., Inc.*, 191 Pa. Superior Ct. 488, 492 (1960) where the Superior Court said that '[e]ven where the written contract prohibits a non-written modification, it may be modified by subsequent oral agreement.' This is true but there must first be a waiver of the requirement that has been spelled out in the contract. Otherwise, written documents would have no more permanence than writings penned in disappearing ink. If this, the defendants' argument, were to prevail, contractual obligations would become phantoms, solemn obligations would run like pressed quicksilver, and the whole edifice of business would rest on sand dunes supporting pillars of rubber and floors of turf. Chaos would envelop the commercial world." ...

It was the plaintiff's duty to support its claim for extras with competent evidence, which in my opinion it wholly failed to produce. I cannot, therefore, go along with the Majority's conclusions as to recoveries to be permitted....

BELL, C.J., joins in this dissenting opinion.

NOTES AND QUESTIONS

1. *Modifications and freedom of contract:* In an earlier Pennsylvania case, *Wagner v. Graziano Construction Co.*,[12] the court said: "The most iron-clad written contract can always be cut into by the acetylene torch of parol modification.... The hand that pens a writing may not gag the mouths of the assenting parties." This colorful statement is consistent with the historic common law position. The parol evidence rule itself does not apply to parol modifications made *after* a writing is executed. On one hand, we can agree that our written document cancels all prior agreements, and courts will apply the principles of free contract to enforce our choice. On the other hand, if we can agree that our written contract cannot be modified or cannot be modified except by a specified procedure, nonetheless we remain free to change our minds and agree to make changes apart from this procedure.

Do you understand the dissenting opinion by Justice Musmanno to be disagreeing with this proposition? If not, what did he want to happen before the parties would be allowed to make an enforceable oral change order?

2. *Modifications and the Statute of Frauds:* Even if the statute of frauds requires the original contract to be in writing to be enforceable, the courts will enforce an

---

12. 390 Pa. 445, 448, 136 A.2d 82 (1957).

oral modification that has been relied upon. The court cites a section (§224) of the original Restatement of Contracts to that effect. Restatement (Second) of Contracts, §150, is to similar effect. This oral modification rule is broadly consistent with the part the performance exception to the statute of frauds, and more precisely consistent with promissory estoppel exception to the statute (if one exists). Note that there must be reliance on the oral modification agreement for it to be enforceable when the statute of frauds otherwise applies.

The Uniform Commercial Code, Article 2, contains a somewhat different rule than the common law. Section 2-209(3) applies the statute of frauds, where applicable, to modifications. However, an oral modification unenforceable as a modification can nonetheless operate as an enforceable waiver. §2-209(4). These provisions are examined in greater depth in the next case.

3. *Written modification clauses in modern building contracts:* Building construction projects traditionally involve making detailed plans and specifications, getting bids from contractors, and finally executing a contract to build according to the plans and specifications. Building contracts often require all changes to be approved by the architect in writing.

Professor Emanuel Halper comments:[13]

> [T]he goal of limiting changes in the scope of the work to those memorialized in formal change orders is a laudatory but usually unattainable ideal. Developers and their field personnel often request changes on the spur of the moment, and they often find it impractical to wait until the architect can actually prepare formal drawings and specifications to describe the change. Thus, the contractor has a dilemma. Should he ignore a change order request until the architect gets around to preparing the formal documentation, or should he take a chance and immediately perform the work? A decision to wait may be wasteful because he may be proceeding with work that he will have to demolish or alter later in order to conform to the change order. Furthermore, delay might irritate the developer. On the other hand, a decision to go ahead might result in the developer's refusal to pay for the changed work.

Under modern "design-build/fast track" construction methods, those involved in building complicated structures merge the design and performance steps to minimize delays and cut costs. For example, a builder may make a contract before the plans and specifications are final. Often these contracts contain the standard provisions calling for written change orders signed by the architect. Nonetheless, all involved understand that changes and adjustments to the preliminary plans and specifications will be made as work progresses, difficulties are encountered, and practical solutions found. There often will be a high volume of change orders, and frequently owners, project managers, architects, and builders will shortcut procedures for changes set

---

13. Emanuel B. Halper, *Negotiating Construction Contracts III*, 18 REAL ESTATE REV. 45 (Summer 1988).

forth in contract documents and handle modifications informally to avoid delays and paperwork.

In these circumstances, can an owner assert the formal provisions calling for written modifications to be approved by the owner, the architect, or both, to resist paying for extras? While there always is a risk that courts and arbitrators will find that there has not been a waiver of the formal procedure, courts and arbitrators have enforced "the real deal" rather than the "paper deal" in a number of cases.

For example, in *Southern Maryland Hospital Center v. Edward M. Crough, Inc.*,[14] Crough and the hospital entered a construction management contract. Crough was to provide design consultation and direct construction of a major structure. The agreement included the American Institute of Architect forms, calling for written change orders to be signed by both the owner and the architect in order to modify the design, the date for completion, or the amounts to be paid. Even before the owner signed the construction management agreement, the owner knew that the structural engineer was having a problem with soil borings. The plan called for "spread footings," but Crough and the structural engineer decided that the building needed a mat foundation. This modification of the plan required many other changes in the design as well. Crough, however, never prepared nor requested anyone else to prepare a change order reflecting the mat foundation and the other extras. Both the architect and the owner knew of the changes.

In arbitration under the procedures established by the AIA form contracts used by the parties, the arbitrators awarded compensation for all extras despite the failure to follow the formal change order procedure. The trial court granted enforcement of the award, and the appellate court affirmed. It noted that the owner was aware of all the changes in the scope of the work and had been advised by Crough of the estimates of the increased costs caused by the changes. There was no suggestion that the changes were not required, not performed in a workmanlike manner, nor that the prices charged were unfair and unreasonable. Finally, the appellate court pointed out that courts would refuse to enforce an arbitration award only when it was based on "a completely irrational interpretation of the contract." The arbitrators could find that the owner knowingly permitted noncompliance with the strict terms of the agreement and thus waived its rights.

CENTRAL ILLINOIS PUBLIC SERVICE CO. v. ATLAS MINERALS, INC.

United States District Court, District of Illinois
965 F. Supp. 1162 (1997)

Mills, J.

A contract between a coal company and a public utility to supply coal [sic]. During the term of the contract, things did not go well for the coal company. Now that the

---

14. 48 Md. App. 401, 427 A.2d 1051 (1981).

term of the contract has expired, the parties disagree whether each side held up its end of the bargain. To resolve this case, the Court must untangle the parties' extensive dealings and must unravel and apply two provisions of the Uniform Commercial Code.

I. Background

A. Parties and Characters

Defendants Atlas Minerals, Inc. (Atlas) and Indiana Coal Company (Indiana Coal) are both Indiana corporations. Indiana Coal is the successor to two merged companies: Buck Creek Coal, Incorporated, and Buck Creek Mining, Incorporated. Atlas was the marketing representative for the Buck Creek companies (for simplicity's sake, the Court will call Defendants collectively: Atlas).

Atlas Minerals, Inc. was wholly owned by Walter Pieper. Pieper was also a principal in Buck Creek. From 1986 to 1994, Richard Bartholomew acted as the Vice President of Marketing for Atlas. Charles Schulties became an investor in Buck Creek in 1992, and assumed an active management role in mid-1994 when Pieper became ill.

Central Illinois Public Service Company (CIPS) is an Illinois public utility supplying electricity to central and southern Illinois. CIPS operates several coal-burning power plants in Illinois. CIPS buys coal to burn in its power plants by entering long-term purchase contracts (like the one at issue in this case) and by making "spot" purchases (open-market purchases with durations of less than one year).

In 1988–89, CIPS's Fuel Procurement Section handled the utility's purchases of coal. Mark Cochran, an engineer and attorney, headed the Fuel Procurement Section. The Fuel Procurement Section fell within CIPS's Purchasing and Stores Department, headed by James Birkett. John Prief and Bruce Garner worked for Cochran in the Fuel Procurement Section. In 1990, Dennis Kirchner took over Cochran's post when Cochran was promoted.

B. The Contract

On June 22, 1989, Atlas and Indiana Coal entered into a Coal Sale and Purchase Agreement (the contract) with CIPS. Through the contract, Atlas agreed to sell coal from the Buck Creek mine near Sullivan, Indiana, to CIPS to burn at its Newton, Illinois, Generating Station Unit Number 2. Due to a geologic anomaly, the Buck Creek mine produces both high- and low-sulphur coal. The contract was for the purchase of "compliance coal," coal that produces less than 1.2 pounds of sulphur dioxide per 1,000 BTUs of energy released when the coal is burned. At the Buck Creek mine, compliance coal came from the north section and high-sulphur coal from the south section of the mine.

The parties' 16-page contract specifies delivery schedules and prices for the coal, and describes in detail the properties of the coal to be supplied. It also specifies its term: "This Agreement shall commence on June 22, 1989, and continue through December 12, 1995. No suspension of an obligation under this Agreement by reason of Force Majeure (as hereinafter defined) shall extend the term of this Agreement, except upon mutual consent of the SELLER and BUYER." The parties agreed that Illinois law would govern the contract. For purposes of this litigation one of the most important contract provisions is this: "This Agreement contains the entire agreement between the parties hereto, and no alteration or modification thereof shall be binding unless in writing and signed by the BUYER and SELLER."

The contract specified that from June 1, 1990, to December 31, 1990, Atlas would sell and tender a minimum of 100,000 tons of coal, less any tonnage excused by reason of a force majeure. From January 1, 1991, to December 31, 1995, Defendants were required to sell at least 235,000 tons per year and not more than 250,000 tons per year (the contract allowed CIPS to elect to receive any quantity between 235,000 and 250,000 tons per year). The contract set prices for the coal that started at $22.27 per ton for the first 50,000 tons of coal delivered during the June 1, 1990, to December 31, 1990, period. The final price, for the January 1, 1995, through December 31, 1995, period was either $27.37 per ton or $27.85 per ton, depending on the method of shipment. At the time the parties entered the contract, the prices were below the market price for purchases of coal on the "spot" market. The contract did not contemplate delivery of any coal beyond the specified annual allocations, unless the parties amended the contract.

The contract defined the term "force majeure" as:

> [A]ny causes beyond the reasonable control of the party affected thereby, such as acts of God; acts of the public enemy; insurrections; riots; strikes; labor disputes; fires; explosions; floods; breakdown or damage to plants, equipment, or facilities; accidents of navigation; interruptions to transportation; river freeze-ups; embargoes; orders or acts of military or civil authority (executive, judicial, or legislative), including but not limited to, any regulation, direction, order, or request (whether valid or invalid) made by any governmental authority or person acting therefor, which is complied with in good faith; or other such causes of a similar or dissimilar nature which wholly or partly prevent the mining, delivering, and/or loading of coal by SELLER, or the receiving, transporting and/or delivering of coal by the carrier of the coal, or the accepting, utilizing and/or unloading of the coal by BUYER. The doctrine of *ejusdem generis* shall not be applied to exclude any event dissimilar to the enumerated events, but which is beyond the reasonable control of a party.

The effect of a force majeure under the contract was to allow the party suffering the force majeure to cease performance upon notice to the other party. Thus, if one party suffered a force majeure event and gave notice to the other party, the notifying party was excused from performing its obligations under the contract from the beginning of the force majeure until the condition ceased. The contract specified, however, that "[a]ny deficiencies in deliveries of coals hereunder, which are excused by Force Majeure, shall not be made up except by mutual consent of the parties."

C. The Course of Performance

The relationship between CIPS and Atlas was troubled, primarily because the Buck Creek mine did not live up to expectations. The mine's disappointing performance has led to bankruptcy for Indiana Coal and, predictably, to this lawsuit.

Problems began early and continued through the life of the contract. In 1990, Buck Creek experienced severe mining difficulties and wrote to CIPS to claim a force majeure. In a November 30, 1990, letter to CIPS, Rick Bartholomew stated that Indiana Coal had encountered mining difficulties and wished to excuse a production shortfall of 69,629 tons.

On December 4, 1990, representatives of CIPS, Atlas, and Indiana Coal met to discuss the 1990 shortfall. On December 21, 1990, Dennis Kirchner of CIPS wrote back to Indiana Coal:

> ... At this time, [CIPS] does not believe it is appropriate to Force Majeure this tonnage. Our Agreement guarantees CIPS 100,000 tons of coal (less applicable Force Majeure) in 1990 and 250,000 annual tons of coal (less applicable Force Majeure) for the period of January 1, 1991, through December 31, 1995. Accordingly, CIPS would like to further discuss this issue with Atlas [] and Buck Creek [].

> Because of the poor mining conditions experienced by Atlas during the start-up and your discussions regarding the effect it has had on cash flow of the mine, CIPS would be willing to discuss (1) the delivery of the subject tonnage at such time when production levels of compliance coal have stabilized (including delivery after December 31, 1995); and (2) a price or pricing mechanism for the subject coal that is agreeable to both parties.

Representatives of the parties again met on January 25, 1991. At the meeting, Atlas proposed making up the 1990 shortfall in two installments of 15,000 tons each in 1994 and 1995, followed by a third installment of 39,629 tons in 1996. On February 7, 1991, John Prief [of CIPS] wrote to Rick Bartholomew of Atlas and stated:

> During our meeting of January 25, 1991, in Springfield, Illinois, you proposed the following possibilities for making up the shortfall of the 1990 shipments (69,629 tons):

> (1) For each of the years 1994 and 1995, deliveries would be accelerated by approximately 15,000 tons. CIPS would pay the applicable price for each year, as stated in our Agreement.

> (2) For the year 1996, deliveries would be accelerated by approximately 39,629 tons. CIPS would pay the 1995 price, plus any escalation that would be based on an indicator agreed to by both parties.

> As stated in our letter of December 21, 1990, CIPS is agreeable to making up the tonnage at an agreed-to price that differs from the contract price. We would, however, prefer to have the tonnage made up as soon as production levels permit. This would afford both parties the possibility of making up tonnage in any future adverse mining conditions.

On February 18, 1991, Rick Bartholomew responded to Prief's letter:

> In response to your letter of February 7, 1991, I have listed below for your review our thoughts regarding the 1990 shortfall tonnage—69,629 tons.

(1) 1994 — 15,000 tons delivered in addition to the 1994 base contract tonnage. This tonnage would be priced at the 1994 contract price.

(2) 1995 — 15,000 tons delivered in addition to the 1995 base contract tonnage. This tonnage would be priced at the 1995 contract price.

(3) 1996 — 39,629 tons delivered in addition to the contract tonnage elected by [CIPS] — 1996. The 1996 shortfall tonnage would be priced at the 1995 contract price, adjusted (+) by an escalator of 6 percent. The base contract tonnage for 1996 would follow the pricing guidelines of our agreement.

(4) Tonnage considered as surplus to (1) our operations and (2) our required base contract tonnage, during 1991, 1992, and 1993, will be shipped to satisfy our shortfall tonnage requirement. This coal will be delivered following negotiation of, and approval by, [CIPS]. Pricing would be governed by the contract price in effect at the time of delivery.

John, if the above conditions are satisfactory to [CIPS], we are prepared to execute a Memorandum or Letter of Agreement, following these guidelines.

In a February 22, 1991, telephone call, CIPS indicated to Bartholomew that Atlas could ship its excess production to make up the 1990 shortfall. Then, on March 6, 1991, J.L. Lisenbee, CIPS's Vice President for Corporate Services,[15] responded to Bartholomew's February 18, 1991, letter. He wrote:

After reviewing your letter of February 18, 1991, regarding the 1990 delivery shortfall of 69,629 tons, [CIPS] would like to propose the following:

1. During each of the contract years 1994 and 1995, CIPS shall receive, in addition to the contractual tonnage stated in Article III, 15,000 tons at the applicable price for each year as stated in Article X;

2. During 1996, CIPS shall have the option to receive 39,629 tons. The price for this tonnage shall be determined by a mutually agreed-to method of adjusting the 1995 contract price as stated in Article X of the subject Agreement;

3. In the event surplus tonnage of the quality specified in the Agreement is mined prior to 1994, CIPS shall have the right of first refusal to such tonnage. The price per ton shall be at the price stated in Article X for the year in which it was delivered; and

4. The terms and conditions of this Letter Agreement shall not be considered precedential.

If you are in agreement with the above stated, please have the appropriate person sign below and return one executed original of the letter to my attention.

Atlas never executed the proposed agreement.

---

15. [1] Lisenbee was the CIPS corporate official authorized to enter into a written amendment of the contract.

Also on March 6, 1991, CIPS declared a force majeure with respect to 3,972 tons of coal due to a condenser leak at the Newton power plant. The parties met in March 1991 to discuss CIPS's force majeure claim. In a memorandum of the meeting, Bartholomew indicates that he told CIPS's representatives that he thought their force majeure claim was trivial and made Atlas reconsider its position regarding the 69,629 tons it had proposed to force majeure. The memorandum also indicates that Atlas considered the possibility of selling excess coal produced in 1991 on the open market instead of using it to make up the 1990 shortfall on the CIPS contract. On March 21, 1991, Bartholomew wrote to Walter Pieper to suggest a written response to CIPS's March 6, 1991, proposal. The proposed response was actually sent to CIPS. It stated:

> In reference to the proposed letter of agreement dated March 6, 1991 and executed by Mr. J.L. Lisenbee, regarding the 1990 shortfall/force majeure [sic] tonnage, Atlas Minerals-Buckcreek would like to propose the following. The format suggested follows that indicated in my letter to you dated February 18, 1991, and deviates slightly from the method suggested in Mr. Lisenbee's letter.
>
> (1) During each of the contract years 1994 and 1995, CIPS shall receive, in addition to the contractual tonnage stated in Article III, 15000 [sic] tons at the applicable price for each year as stated in Article X;
>
> (2) During 1996, CIPS shall have the option to receive 39,629 tons. The price for this tonnage shall be determined by a mutually agreed-to method of adjusting the 1995 contract price as stated in Article X of the subject agreement;
>
> (3) Any tonnage considered as surplus to (1) Atlas-Buckcreek operations and (b) our required base contract tonnage, during 1991, 1992, 1993 can be shipped *at the sole discretion* of Atlas-Buckcreek to satisfy our 1990 shortfall/force majeure [sic] tonnage. Pricing would be governed by the applicable contract price in effect at the time of shipments.
>
> Acknowledging all of our previous correspondence and discussion regarding this tonnage, we propose the format indicated above, to resolve this issue. Please consider that we have not altered our position regarding the legitimacy of our original force majeure [sic] claim, however, we wish to resolve the problem in a manner satisfactory to CIPS....
>
> John, if Sections I, II, and II above represent a satisfactory method of addressing our 1990 force majeure/shortfall [sic] tonnage, please incorporate the language in a letter of agreement, and we will execute the letter to resolve this issue.

These letters did not culminate in a written agreement to dispose of the Force Majeure claims or to make up the 1990 delivery shortfall.[16]

---

16. Eds. note: Recall that under the contract deficiencies in deliveries because of a force majeure event were not to be made up except by mutual consent of the parties.

By the end of 1991, Atlas had delivered 274,304 tons of coal. CIPS paid for the first 69,629 tons at the 1990 contract price. CIPS paid the 1991 price for the remaining 204,675 tons, leaving a shortfall for 1991 of 45,325 tons. On October 1, 1991, CIPS informed Atlas in writing that it wished to receive 250,000 tons of coal in 1992.[17] In a December 12, 1991, meeting, the parties discussed shipment schedules for 1992. The parties concurred that any coal delivered in 1991 above the 250,000 tons required by the contract would be applied to the 1990 shortfall.

In January 1992, Atlas sought additional financing for its operations from Old National Bank of Evansville, Indiana. In its loan proposal, Atlas repeatedly indicated that its contract with CIPS expired in 1995. Atlas stated: "The bulk of the low-sulfur coal is sold under contract with [CIPS] and Pfizer through 1995." Atlas also listed its current contracts and their termination dates. The CIPS contract was listed as expiring on December 31, 1995, "with CIPS having the option to extend for a three-year period...."

In early 1992 Atlas must have been optimistic about the coming year, because on March 19, 1992, Bartholomew wrote CIPS and proposed a delivery schedule for the remainder of 1992 that would not only make up all existing deficits, but would also leave a 41,000-ton surplus at year's end. On his file copy of the letter, Bartholomew wrote a note to Pieper in which he expressed doubt that CIPS would agree to accept 41,000 tons of surplus coal in 1992. Bartholomew indicated that if CIPS refused, Atlas would insist on selling that surplus to another buyer and crediting it against its obligation to CIPS.

CIPS initiated the only written amendment to the contract when, on September 4, 1992, it wrote to Atlas to complain about the coal's moisture content and Gross Calorific Value. The parties resolved CIPS's complaints in a written amendment signed by J.L. Lisenbee and Bartholomew. The amendment provided that "[e]xcept as hereby amended, the Agreement and each and every provision and condition thereof, is and shall remain in full force and effect."

On September 29, 1992, CIPS informed Atlas that it wished to receive 250,000 tons of coal during 1993. During the negotiations about coal quality, Bartholomew wrote CIPS a letter regarding coal shipments for the remainder of 1992. He stated that Atlas had encountered mining problems and anticipated ending 1992 with a "carry-over of 1992 'tonnage due'. Per our discussion, we will deliver any 1992 carry-over tonnage at 1992 contract pricing." On October 28, 1992, Bartholomew wrote CIPS with a proposed delivery schedule for 1993. He estimated that Atlas would deliver between 280,000 to 290,000 tons of coal and said that Atlas would like to ship any excess coal to make up contract deficits.

---

17. Eds. note: Recall that under the contract CIPS was obligated to take 235,000 tons in 1992 and had the option to take an additional 15,000 tons (totaling 250,000 tons).

The parties again met to discuss 1993 shipments on November 9, 1992. At the meeting, CIPS indicated that it wanted to receive 300,000 tons of coal during 1993. In a follow-up letter, CIPS stated:

> With respect to 1990 through 1992 shipments from the Buck Creek Mine to CIPS, it is projected that the cumulative shortfall will equal approximately 134,000 tons (see attached information). It is CIPS's position that this initial 134,000 tons, or whatever the cumulative shortfall might be as of December 31, 1992, shipped during 1993, will be billed at the 1992 price.... All remaining tonnage shipped during 1993, up to 250,000 tons, will be billed at the 1993 price....

Atlas delivered 167,387 tons of coal in 1992. CIPS paid for the first 45,325 tons at the 1991 price, and the remaining 122,062 tons at the 1992 price.

1993 was not a good year for Atlas. In April, the United Mine Workers of America, who had just been chosen to represent miners at the Buck Creek mine, began a strike. During all of 1993, Atlas only delivered 83,605 tons of coal, all of which CIPS bought at the 1992 price.

1994 was little better. That year, Atlas shipped 129,756 tons of coal. CIPS paid for the first 44,333 tons at the 1992 price, and the balance (85,423 tons) at the 1993 price. In December 1994, Atlas lost its other major contract for coal. Atlas had previously supplied high-sulfur coal from the south section of its mine to Hoosier Energy's Merom generating plant. The contract expired in December 1994 and was not renewed. Upon receiving the bad news, Atlas shut down its entire mine.

The loss of the Merom contract and the subsequent shutdown of the mine triggered a series of events in late 1994 and early 1995. First, Atlas's bank exercised its right under security agreements with Atlas to direct CIPS to forward all payments directly to the bank. When CIPS learned of this development, it sent Atlas two letters on January 13, 1995. The first letter was a notice that CIPS was terminating the contract effective July 13, 1995. The termination was pursuant to a provision in the contract that allowed either party to terminate the agreement if the other failed to deliver or purchase 50 percent of the tonnage required during a six-month period. The second letter demanded adequate assurances of performance pursuant to § 2-609 of the Illinois Commercial Code.

The parties met on January 16, 1995. Charles Schulties (who had stepped in as the manager of the mine) indicated that Old National Bank had been on the verge of providing additional financing, but had backed down when it learned of CIPS's position. In order to obtain financing necessary to reopen the Buck Creek mine, Atlas requested "assurances relative to the marketing of [its] coal" from CIPS. Atlas stated that financing was contingent on such assurances. In a letter sent on January 17, 1995, Schulties proposed to resume deliveries in February 1995 and continue them at a rate of 15,000 to 20,000 tons per month until December 1995 and then at a rate of 19,000 to 30,000 tons per month in 1996. On January 27, 1995, CIPS faxed a letter to Atlas at 11:06 A.M. The letter stated that CIPS would accept deliveries during 1995 on a probationary basis, but would not accept any coal past the December 31, 1995, termination date in the contract. The letter also spelled out various other terms and conditions for CIPS to continue buying coal from Atlas. One hour and fifteen minutes after CIPS faxed the letter to Atlas, Bartholomew left a voice mail message for Kirchner. The message stated that Atlas would resume shipments to Newton the following Monday morning.

Atlas resumed shipments to Newton on January 30, 1995. Then, in July 1995, Atlas approached CIPS about the possibility of continuing to contract past December 31, 1995. CIPS refused to do so. In a meeting on October 2, 1995, Schulties told CIPS that he believed that Atlas was entitled to ship all of the coal contracted for under the contract, even if that meant CIPS would have to accept delivery in 1996 and beyond. CIPS disputed that claim. Atlas delivered 250,048 tons of coal in 1995. CIPS paid the 1993 price for the first 164,577 tons and the 1994 price for the remaining 85,471 tons.

D. The Proceedings Before this Court

CIPS filed its Complaint for Declaratory Judgment on December 1, 1995. In its Complaint for Declaratory Judgment, CIPS sought a declaration that: (1) the contract between CIPS and Atlas terminated on December 31, 1995; (2) CIPS has no further obligations under that contract after December 31, 1995; and (3) CIPS complied with its obligations under the contract. Defendants answered on January 8, 1996. Defendants also raised as an affirmative defense the claim that the contract was extended by agreement, course of dealing, and waiver. Finally, Defendants asserted a counterclaim for breach of contract. CIPS answered the Counterclaim on January 29, 1996. In February 1996, the Court allowed CIPS to amend its Complaint to include a claim for damages based on Atlas's alleged failure to timely deliver the agreed-upon quantities of coal.

On January 19, 1996, creditors of Indiana Coal Company filed an involuntary bankruptcy petition under Chapter 7 of the Bankruptcy Code. On Indiana Coal's motion, the bankruptcy court converted the case to one under Chapter 11. The bankruptcy court also modified the automatic stay to allow this case to proceed.

On March 19, 1996, after informing the Court that they had filed for bankruptcy under Chapter 11, Defendants filed an Amended Answer and Counterclaim. CIPS answered the Amended Counterclaim on March 27, 1996, and raised three affirmative defenses. CIPS added a fourth affirmative defense later....

II. Analysis

The Court will only reach the first two motions for summary judgment and will dispose of this case entirely based on those motions. Specifically, the Court finds that CIPS never waived the December 31, 1995, termination date, so the contract must be enforced as written, at least with respect to the termination date. The Court, however, rejects CIPS's damages claim because CIPS waived its right to enforce the contract's delivery schedule by acquiescing in Atlas's course of performance. Finally, the Court concludes that CIPS was not required to accept more than 250,000 tons of coal during 1995, as Atlas contends. Thus, CIPS is entitled to a declaratory judgment stating that CIPS has done all that the contract required and Atlas is entitled to judgment in its favor on Count II of the Amended Complaint.

A. The Law

The contract in this case was one for the sale of goods, namely coal. Accordingly, it is governed by Article 2 of the Illinois Commercial Code....

To resolve the dispute in this case, the Court must reconcile and then apply three parts of the UCC. The *first* is the UCC provision that allows contracting parties to agree that their written contracts may not be modified except by a signed writing. The *second* is the UCC provision that allows "attempts at modification" to waive terms in a written contract, despite a clause in the contract allowing only written and signed modifications. The *third* provision is the UCC's rule on course of performance, which states that although course of performance is generally an interpretive tool, it may also be relevant to show a waiver of any terms inconsistent with the course of performance.

Unlike the common law, which takes a skeptical view of contract provisions requiring modifications to be in writing, *see Williams v. Jader Fuel Co.*, 944 F.2d 1388, 1394 (7th Cir. 1991) (reciting the common law principle that parties may orally modify a contract even after they include a contract provision requiring modifications to be in writing), the UCC strictly enforces such provisions.... In § 2-209(2), the UCC states: "A signed agreement which excludes modification or rescission except by a signed writing cannot otherwise be modified or rescinded, but except as between merchants such a requirement on a form supplied by the merchant must be separately signed by the other party."

Not unlike the common law, however, the UCC provides some relief to parties who have agreed in writing that their agreement may not be changed except in writing and who have then performed or orally agreed to perform in a manner different from that specified by the written contract. In § 2-209(4), the Code provides that "[al]though an attempt at modification or rescission does not satisfy the requirements of [§ 2-209(2)] it can operate as a waiver." The leading case on §§ 2-209(2) and (4) is *Wisconsin Knife Works v. National Metal Crafters*, 781 F.2d 1280 (7th Cir. 1986). In that case, the United States Court of Appeals for the Seventh Circuit, applying Wisconsin's Uniform Commercial Code, rejected a claim that delivery dates in a contract had been modified because the party asserting modification had not identified a written modification. *Id.* at 1284–85. The court then examined whether the parties had waived the delivery dates by virtue of an attempted modification. The court concluded that to prove that an attempt at modification led to a waiver, the party asserting waiver must prove not only the existence of an oral modification (or other modification that does not comply with the contract's terms) but must also prove that it relied on the alleged waiver. *Id.* at 1287–88....

To add another layer of complexity, UCC § 2-208 also speaks to the issue....

By its terms, § 2-208 is primarily an interpretive tool. *See* § 2-208(1) (course of performance "shall be relevant to determine the meaning of the agreement"); § 2-208, cmt. 1 ("This section ... rounds out the set of factors which determine the meaning of the 'agreement.'").... Section 2-208 also permits course of performance to "show a waiver or modification of any term inconsistent with" the contracting parties' course of performance. § 2-208(3). Section 2-208(3), however, states that course of performance can only show waiver or modification of inconsistent terms "[s]ubject to the provisions of" § 2-209. This qualification seems intended to achieve a limited purpose: subjecting waivers by course of performance to § 2-209(5), which allows retraction of a waiver. § 2-208, cmt. 3 ("Where it is difficult to determine whether a particular act merely sheds light on the meaning of a term of the agreement, the preference is in favor of 'waiver' whenever such construction, plus the application of the provisions on reinstatement of rights waived ... is needed to preserve the flexible character of commercial contracts and to prevent surprise or other hardship.").[18]

Waiver is not defined in the UCC, but its meaning is well established. Generally, "waiver in contract law is the intentional relinquishment of a known right." *Sethness-Greenleaf, Inc. v. Green River Corp.*, 65 F.3d 64, 67 (7th Cir. 1995)....

The burden is on Atlas to prove that CIPS waived any provisions of the written contract. *See Wisconsin Knife Works*, 781 F.2d at 1285. Waiver seems like a factual issue. However, when the relevant facts of the case are undisputed and only one possible inference may arise from those facts, waiver is a legal question.... Thus, to win on its waiver claims, Atlas must show, by reference to undisputed facts, that CIPS intentionally relinquished its right under the contract.

B. The Termination Date

1. The Contract

In contract law, the place to start is with the written contract, if there is one. In this case, the parties — both sophisticated participants in the coal market — signed a detailed written contract. The contract ended by its terms on December 31, 1995, and it stated that the parties could not modify it unless they did so in a writing signed by both parties. UCC § 2-209(2) provides an easy answer; initially Atlas admits that no written modification exists that alters the December 31, 1995, termination date. Thus, under the terms of the contract (which are fully enforceable under § 2-209(2)) the termination date remained December 31, 1995.

2. Attempt at Modification?

The Court, then, must pass to the next question under UCC § 2-209: did the parties attempt to modify the contract's termination date, and if so, does their attempt

---

18. [3] In this case, the only question is whether the parties waived any of the contract's provisions. The contract precluded all modifications except those written and signed by both parties. Section 2-209(4) only allows attempts at modification to constitute waivers. Section 2-208(3) allows course of performance to show either a waiver or a modification of a term inconsistent with the course of performance. But since that section is expressly subject to § 2-209's provisions on modification, it appears that the question here is limited to whether any terms of the contract were waived by course of performance. Waiver and modification are distinct concepts. "[I]f the court asks whether the conduct of the parties amounted to a 'modification,' it will determine whether there was assent by applying the usual rules for the formation of contracts; if the court asks whether the conduct amounted to a 'waiver,' it may give effect to more dubious manifestations of assent." 2 E. ALLAN FARNSWORTH, FARNSWORTH ON CONTRACTS § 8.5, p. 375 (1990).

support Atlas's claim that CIPS waived the termination date? From the facts the Court has already recited, it is obvious that the parties did not attempt to modify the termination date of the contract. Additionally, nothing in CIPS's conduct suggests that CIPS intentionally relinquished its right to cease performance on December 31, 1995.

The contract provided for coal deliveries in the years 1990–95. Problems with deliveries began in 1990. At that time, Atlas sought to declare a force majeure with respect to 69,629 tons of coal to be delivered in 1990. CIPS's December 12, 1990, letter shows that CIPS did not want to excuse delivery of that coal under the contract's force majeure clause and instead wanted to work out an alternate schedule for delivery of the 1990 shortfall. Initially, CIPS proposed taking deliveries of coal in 1996. Indeed, the initial proposal was for Atlas to make up the 1990 shortfall by delivering 15,000 tons of coal in both 1994 and 1995 and 39,629 tons in 1996. On February 18, 1991, Atlas wrote to CIPS with a revised proposal for making up the shortfall. In that letter, Atlas suggested the same deliveries for 1994 and 1995 but proposed that CIPS could take 39,629 tons in addition to "contract tonnage elected by [CIPS] — 1996." By the time CIPS sent its proposed formal letter agreement to Atlas on March 6, 1991, the proposal was for CIPS to have an option to purchase 39,629 tons of coal in 1996. Atlas's March 21, 1991, response to that proposal stated: "During 1996, CIPS shall have the option to receive 39,629 tons."

Atlas claims that the contract was amended in early 1991 to bar the parties from filing further force majeure claims and to allow Atlas to deliver all 1,350,000 tons of coal contemplated by the agreement, regardless of the year of delivery. The parties' correspondence does not support either claim. Even if the correspondence and discussion of the parties can be considered "an attempt at modification" under UCC § 2-209(4), the attempted modification dealt only with the 1990 tonnage shortfall. Additionally, the best evidence of the extent of the purported attempted modification are the letters of March 6, 1991, and March 21, 1991, and neither letter discusses modifying the contract's termination date or barring the parties from filing force majeure claims. At best, the letters show that the parties agreed to make up the 1990 tonnage shortfall as quickly as possible with CIPS having an *option* to buy coal in 1996.

The overall course of events further limits the impact of the March 1991 letters. By the end of 1991, Atlas had delivered 274,034 tons of coal. CIPS paid the 1990 contract price for the first 69,629 tons. Neither side protested this; therefore, the issue of the 1990 tonnage shortfall was resolved. The discussions regarding the 1990 tonnage shortfall were the last time until early 1995 that the parties expressly discussed the contract's termination date.

Of course, delivery problems did not end with the 1990 tonnage shortfall. As just noted, Atlas came up 45,325 tons short by the end of 1991. To remedy this situation, Atlas proposed a delivery schedule for 1992 that would have made up that deficit and ended 1992 with a delivery *surplus*. By the end of 1992, however, Atlas still lagged behind in deliveries and proposed to deliver any "1992 carry-over tonnage at 1992 contract pricing." This routine continued, with Atlas falling farther and farther behind on deliveries, until December 1994. Despite the fact that it was becoming increasingly difficult to do so, it appears from all of the evidence that the parties intended to make up all of the tonnage shortfalls by the end of 1995. And nothing in the record indicates that the parties discussed going beyond that year.

The parties' agreement for 1995 deliveries, the agreement that allowed the Buck Creek mine to stay open, expressly barred deliveries in 1996. When the Atlas mine shut down in December 1994, it reopened only after assurances by CIPS that it would continue to accept coal in 1995. In response to CIPS's notice of termination and demands for adequate assurances, Atlas proposed a delivery schedule that would have spanned 1995 and 1996. In a counteroffer, CIPS said it would accept coal on a probationary basis in 1995 only. Atlas's representative accepted this proposal by leaving a telephone message for CIPS stating that Atlas would resume shipments within the next few days. Again, to the extent the January 1995 negotiations can be considered "an attempt at modification," the modification consisted of reinstating the contract (which would have terminated in July 1995 if CIPS had not agreed to accept deliveries for all of 1995) for the purpose of delivering coal in 1995 only.

The preceding summary demonstrates that the parties never attempted to modify the termination date. At the very least, the evidence shows that modifying the termination date was initially placed on the bargaining table, but subsequently withdrawn....

Even if the facts could support a claim that the parties attempted to modify the contract's termination date, the facts do not permit a finding that that provision was waived. To prove a waiver, Atlas would have to show that CIPS intentionally relinquished its right to cease performance on December 31, 1995. *See Sethness-Greenleaf, Inc.*, 65 F.3d at 67 (stating that a waiver requires intentional relinquishment of a known right). The evidence reveals no conduct which could possibly show that. Finally, Atlas makes a great deal out of the fact that CIPS never explicitly withdrew its proposal to accept deliveries in 1996. Atlas apparently means to rely on UCC § 2-209(5), but that provision is inapplicable because CIPS never waived the termination date.

3. Course of Performance

The final step under the UCC is to determine whether course of performance might play a role in deciding whether the contract terminated on December 31, 1995. Course of performance is primarily an interpretive tool. UCC § 2-208(1) (stating that course of performance "shall be relevant to determine the meaning of the agreement"); *Sethness-Greenleaf, Inc.*, 65 F.3d at 67 ("'[C]ourse of performance' can be used to flesh out an ambiguous or incomplete agreement."). As far as the termination date is concerned, the contract was neither ambiguous nor incomplete. Thus, course of performance is only relevant to the extent it is evidence of a waiver. § 2-208(3).

The course of performance under the contract was that until 1995, whenever Atlas was unable to deliver a year's tonnage, CIPS allowed Atlas to deliver that tonnage in following years, but at the price stated in the contract for the year Atlas should have delivered the coal. That course of performance has implications for the contract's internal delivery schedule, but not for the termination date. There is no course of performance that might shed light on the validity or meaning of the termination date provision. And even if CIPS had taken coal after December 31, 1995, a single instance of conduct does not amount to course of performance. *See* §2-208, cmt. 4 ("A single occasion of conduct does not fall within the language of this section....").

Furthermore, to the extent that performance within the contract's term is relevant to interpreting or applying the termination date, the Court must first decide if that course of performance may be reasonably construed consistently with the termination date. §2-208(2) ("The express terms of the agreement and any such course of performance, as well as any course of dealing and usage of trade, shall be construed whenever reasonable as consistent with each other; but when such construction is unreasonable, the express terms shall control course of performance...."). The parties abandoned the internal delivery and price schedules to allow Atlas to make up shortfalls—that much is evident in their conduct and communications. It is not inconsistent with that course of performance to conclude that performance should cease on the contract's termination date. Indeed, the parties' correspondence and conduct demonstrates that they abandoned the internal delivery and price schedules in order to make up shortfalls before the end of the contract. Thus, the Court can construe the termination date and the course of performance (*i.e.* abandoning the internal delivery and price schedules) consistently with each other, so the Court need not disregard the express term (the termination date). In any event, when the terms of a contract conflict with the course of performance, §2-208(2) provides that the express terms govern. Accordingly, even if the course of performance and the termination date cannot be construed consistently with each other, the termination date would control.

In summary, the Court finds as follows: (1) the parties did not modify the contract's termination date in writing, as the contract required; (2) the parties did not attempt to modify the contract's termination date so that term could not have been waived; and (3) there is no course of performance relevant to interpreting or applying the contract's termination date. Accordingly, the parties' contractual obligations ceased on December 31, 1995....

III. Conclusion

The parties in this case entered into a five-year contract for the sale and purchase of coal. The contract had both a fixed end date and fixed delivery and price schedules. Because the coal mine could not produce according to the contract, the parties abandoned the delivery and price schedules in the hope that the mine would catch up before the contract terminated. At the beginning of the contract's final year, the mine shut down and reopened only after CIPS agreed to buy only as much coal that year as it had originally promised....

In this lawsuit, Atlas has claimed that the parties modified the contract in various ways. Atlas cannot prove most of those claims. The only alteration the Court finds was of the internal delivery and price schedules, which the parties waived. Accordingly, the Court will enforce the contract's termination date, but will not permit CIPS to recover damages for late deliveries that occurred during the contract's term.

In short, the Court finds that both parties to this contract may simply walk away from the contract. CIPS was not obliged to accept any more coal than it did. Atlas and Indiana Coal performed as required under the contract, as modified by course of performance. Neither side owes the other any damages. This result is no doubt of little comfort to Indiana Coal, which is now in bankruptcy. But in light of the mine's miserable performance during the term of its contract with the utility, the Court cannot justly place blame anywhere but with the mine....

NOTES AND QUESTIONS

1. *Force majeure clauses:* Contract clauses excusing performance on the occurrence of various events are extremely common and are called "force majeure" clauses. We will study them in Chapter 6 *infra.*

2. *Comparing the Code and the common law:* Would this case have been decided differently if it had not been governed by Article 2?

3. *Course of performance:* In this case, course of performance is relied upon to establish an agreement by CIPS to accept a later shipment of coal when the force majeure clause was invoked to excuse delivery shortfalls in 1990 and later years. Without such an agreement, CIPS would have been under no obligation to accept the delivery shortfalls in later years. We can consider these agreements as a kind of modification of the original contract. Because the modifications dealt with delivery shortfalls excused by force majeure, the contract provision requiring that contract modifications be in writing apparently did not apply. Therefore, the court did not need to rely on § 2-209(4).

Review the discussion of course of performance in *Nanakuli Paving and Rock Co. v. Shell Oil Co.* in Chapter 3. There the court relied on course of performance to help it interpret the meaning of the original contract, not to establish a post-contract modification. Would the result in *Nanakuli* have been different if the court had utilized course of performance evidence in the way the court did in *CIPS v. Atlas*? You may assume that the contract between Nanakuli and Shell contained a clause requiring modifications to be in writing.

4. *CISG and modification-in-writing clauses:* The Convention on International Sale of Goods provides in Article 29 that "[a] contract may be modified or terminated by the mere agreement of the parties." At the same time, the Article gives effect to contract clauses that require modifications to be in writing. However (and we might have expected the however), the Article goes on to provide that "a party may be precluded by his conduct from asserting such a provision to the extent that the other party has relied on that conduct." How different is the approach taken by the CISG from the UCC or from the common law?

Chapter 5

PERFORMANCE AND BREACH OF CONTRACT

A. THE MAIN THEMES — PROMISES, CONDITIONS, AND THE ROLE OF COURTS

1. The Logic of "Conditions"

Suppose S and B make a legally enforceable contract under which S contracts to sell an antique car to B for $40,000. They agree in their written contract that S is to rebuild the engine before delivery of the car. After S and B close the deal, many things must happen before the transaction is completed. What happens to B's obligations if S does not perform some or all of his? Does it matter that S comes close to performing all his obligations but does not quite make it? Not surprisingly in a society that gives a high place to individual choice, courts and lawyers attempting to answer these questions give great weight to the parties' agreement. However, often the parties have said little about the details involved in carrying out their contract. In many instances, having just made a deal, they do not want to think about what will happen if one or both parties fail to perform. Many clients do not want their lawyers to raise too many "what-ifs."[1] Courts are often called on to fill in gaps in planning.

Students may have difficulty with questions of performance and breach of contracts. Some have even told us that they consider the material in this chapter to be boring and frustrating because it is so uncertain. Part of the difficulty comes from turning to complex issues before a number of simple matters are understood. Thus, it may help to consider some relatively easy examples in order to establish a vocabulary and see the logic of orthodox conditions analysis.

---

1. *See* George W. Dent, Jr., *Business Lawyers as Enterprise Architects*, 64 Bus. Law. 279, 310 (2009) ("Because the parties often duck known sore points and are unaware of lurking problems, lawyers play a crucial role in ferreting out difficulties and finding solutions. This task is rendered trickier because spotting problems may cause a deal to collapse, whereupon the lawyers may be blamed for 'queering' the deal. In many cases, this accusation is not warranted, but in some it is. . . ."); *see also* Claire A. Hill, *Bargaining in the Shadow of the Lawsuit: A Social Norms Theory of Incomplete Contracts*, 34 Del. J. Corp. L. 191, 215 (2009) ("[S]eeking additional increments of precision may signal one's propensity to litigate, which may in turn signal that one is a less desirable transacting partner.").

Assume seller promises in a written contract to deliver a specific car to buyer on April 7th if buyer is then ready, willing, and able to pay $40,000 to seller. Buyer, in turn, promises to pay $40,000 on April 7th if seller is then ready, willing, and able to deliver the specific car. Assume further that on April 7th, seller fails to deliver the goods and she does not have a legally adequate excuse. Buyer, who was ready, willing, and able to pay on April 7th, did not pay because seller failed to make delivery.

Suppose now an unlikely event: seller sues buyer for failing to pay $40,000. *Seller would lose because buyer did not breach his promise.* Buyer did not make an unqualified promise to pay $40,000. He promised to pay *only if* seller was ready, willing, and able to deliver the goods. Seller was not. Putting the matter in the vocabulary of contracts, a *condition precedent* to buyer's duty to perform was not fulfilled, and this failure serves to shield him from liability. Conditions precedent are usually in the form of "if" or "when" clauses qualifying promises to perform. If the qualifications are not met, then my promise literally does not bind me to do anything. I cannot be held liable for failing to do what I never promised to do.

Now assume the same contract and facts but add that buyer came to seller's place of business on April 7th with $40,000, asked for delivery of the goods, and indicated clearly that he had the money and was ready to pay if seller was ready to deliver. As before, seller refused to deliver. Buyer could sue seller and win a judgment for damages because seller has failed to perform her promise—the conditions on that promise were fulfilled and so there was an obligation to perform.[2]

Notice that in the example, the *conditions* to buyer's promise and to seller's *promise* are almost the same. Buyer promises to pay *if and when seller delivers*. Seller promises to deliver *if and when buyer pays*. Paying is both a condition and a promise; delivering, also, is both condition and promise. But paying is a condition to the promise to deliver and delivering is a condition to the promise to pay.

Keep one thing clear: *a party always sues for breach of promise and not breach of condition.* Although it is not uncommon, the phrase *breach of condition* is misleading insofar as it connotes that someone did something she was not supposed to do — "failure of condition" is probably a more descriptive term. A failure of condition is a *defense* and often ends the obligation to perform a qualified promise.

Notice, as well, that an aggrieved party often gets rights based on both a breach of promise and a failure of a condition flowing from the same actions by the defaulting party. The buyer refuses to pay because seller refuses to deliver. The buyer can both sue the seller for breach and defend any suit brought by the seller claiming damages because buyer failed to pay the purchase price. When the promise on one side is the same as the condition on the other, lawyers often speak of *concurrent conditions*.

---

2. Put aside for the moment the question of whether buyer could do anything less than engage in the elaborate ceremony we sketched and still meet the conditions of seller's promise. We will get to this later.

While this may be a useful shorthand, it does not describe the situation very well. Paying the money is both promise and condition, as is delivering the goods.

Let's change the facts slightly to illustrate another possibility. Assume that seller promises to deliver the car on April 7th, (a) if buyer is then ready, willing, and able to pay $40,000, *and* (b) if the components needed to rebuild the engine arrive from England on or before March 27th. Buyer promises to pay $40,000 on April 7th if seller is ready, willing, and able to deliver at that time. The components fail to arrive from England on or before March 27th. Buyer is at seller's place of business on April 7th ready, willing, and able to pay. Seller, of course, fails to deliver. Buyer sues seller for breach of contract. Buyer would lose his suit because seller did not breach his promise, which was to deliver *only if* the components arrived on time. They did not arrive on time, and so there was no breach. Seller did not promise that they would arrive on time, but he negotiated the contract so that he would not assume this risk. Here we have an express condition precedent to seller's duty to deliver, *which is not also a promise.* Of course, seller could not sue buyer for failure to pay $40,000, since that promise to pay was still qualified by a condition that seller deliver the car.[3] In this case, the conditions would give each party a defense to a suit by the other.

Finally, let's illustrate a more complicated situation. Suppose buyer wants to purchase a car from a seller who first needs to borrow $30,000 to finance the acquisition of the car and repair parts. X Bank agrees to provide the needed money. X Bank conditions its loan to seller on seller entering into a contract with buyer in which buyer expressly promises to pay $30,000 to X Bank on May 1st *whether or not seller has delivered the car on April 7th.*[4] Seller does enter into such a contract with buyer. As a result of this contract, X Bank on March 5th pays $30,000 to seller, less its charges for financing the deal. Seller, however, fails to deliver on April 7th, with no legally sufficient excuse. Buyer refuses to pay X Bank on May 1st, asserting seller's non-delivery as a defense.

X Bank would win in a suit against the buyer. Buyer's promise to pay was not conditioned on delivery of the car by seller. The bank was not taking the risk of problems in the seller-buyer transaction. It advanced money to seller and bargained for a right to be repaid by buyer even if seller failed to perform. Buyer's remedy would be to sue seller for failure to deliver the goods. Seller, in turn, might have a cause of action against buyer for any damages caused by buyer's failure to pay X

---

3. Sometimes courts or lawyers talk of a "failure of consideration" in situations such as this one. Notice that this is not the same thing as an "absence" of consideration. Formation and performance of contracts are different things. Buyer and seller made a legally enforceable contract, supported by the consideration of their promises to pay and deliver. However, since seller failed to deliver goods, he cannot sue buyer. "Failure of consideration" is too easy to confuse with "absence of consideration," and so the term is not favored by contracts teachers.

4. X Bank is also likely to keep a security interest in the goods until it is paid, so that it can sell them to recover some or all of its money if buyer fails to pay.

Bank. X Bank likely would have reserved a right to hold seller responsible if Buyer failed to pay. In this kind of case, lawyers often speak of *independent promises*— that is, promises that are unqualified by reference to performance by other parties. They are rare in two-party situations, but they can serve a function when the deal involves more than two people.

Planning the transaction to minimize risks: So far we've stated the obvious: courts usually enforce promises as made, and if a person puts a qualification on a promise, then she hasn't promised to act unless or until something happens. But there is more to the matter than this. Conditions reflect assumptions of risk by the parties. On one hand, they can be geared to allocate risks of events external to the particular deal. For example, our seller promised to perform provided that component parts arrived from England by a certain date. Seller also might provide that it would perform only if its shop were not damaged by some natural disaster before it could do the work. Of course, if buyer had sufficient bargaining power, it might demand that seller *promise* to deliver goods whether or not component parts arrived from England. Under such a contract, seller would have to get parts from England, find substitutes elsewhere, or be liable to pay damages to buyer for non-delivery of the goods.

Furthermore, conditions reflect a structuring of a relationship so that one person has sanctions to induce the other to perform. For example, it is often advantageous to arrange things so that the other person performs first before you must act. (That is, the other person's promise is unconditional and must be performed on a certain date. Your promise, however, is to be performed later and is conditioned on receiving the other's full performance.) If you have the bargaining power and skill to negotiate such a contract, you take no risk of losing your performance if the other person breaches the contract, as you would if you had to pay in advance before he was to perform.

Of course, if the contract requires that you pay in advance but the other person fails to perform, you are likely to have a cause of action for breach of contract or restitution. However, you may have to hire a lawyer to evaluate your case, draft documents, gain personal jurisdiction over the other party, win a verdict, and defend it on appeal. And *then* you must find some non-exempt assets owned by the other party to satisfy your judgment, and hope the other party isn't bankrupt. You avoid all this if you can make her go first and perform before you have to pay.

If the other person must perform before you act, you may have another tactical advantage. If you think that the other person's performance is defective, you can deduct an allowance from your performance and offer it to her in full settlement.[5] Since she has performed, she must accept the offer or take legal action against you to recover the balance. She must make this difficult choice. Moreover, since the other person wants to be sure that you perform after she does, she has some incentive to perform

---

5. *See* UCC § 2-717.

well and on time. Her interest in keeping you happy may grow as she invests more and more effort in her performance and seeks to guard that investment by making you a satisfied customer who feels some obligation to pay for the fine performance.

We do not find too many contracts where all the risks in performance rest solely on one side.[6] Rather, leverage is used to provide incentives for both sides to perform.

For example, frequently an owner who wishes a building constructed agrees to pay a down payment and then installments at specified times as the building is erected. In this way, the owner helps the builder finance construction. The builder does not have to provide or borrow all the money needed to purchase labor and materials during the course of performance. The builder also minimizes the risk that she will not be paid for the work that she has done by limiting the amount put into the building before the owner pays. If one or more payments are missed or late, the builder may have the right to suspend working on the job until she is paid for what is due. On the other hand, an owner is likely to negotiate for the right to hold back, say, 10 percent of the value of the work done at each installment; this "hold-back" will be paid to the builder only upon full completion of the job. Thus, the builder is given an incentive to finish the work and do it well. All of this can be expressed in the language of conditional promises—the builder *promises* to perform *provided* that the down payment and installments are paid on time; the owner *promises* to pay the installments *provided* the builder is performing, and *promises* to pay the amount held back *provided* the builder completes the structure on time and according to plans and specifications.

People planning a transaction can rely on forms of leverage that only awkwardly conform to a conditions analysis. On one hand, if the transaction is part of a long-term continuing mutually advantageous business relationship, the other's continued satisfaction is a powerful incentive to perform. If she becomes dissatisfied, there is a risk that she will end the relationship and turn to a competitor. On the other hand, where continuing relationships or the right to withhold one's own performance do not seem to offer enough leverage, there may be other things that can be done. One can insist that the other person buy a bond to guarantee his performance. One can insist that money be paid to a neutral third party who will hold it until the return performance is completed—an "escrow" arrangement. A party selling goods can retain a security interest in them, thereby retaining some right to reclaim the goods if payment is not made as agreed. (While the threat of losing the machine, the TV, or the car may induce performance, a seller who repossesses may be hard-pressed to

---

6. Employment contracts once tended to be out of balance. Today statutes, with some exceptions, require wages to be paid frequently rather than withheld for long periods of time. Still, employees usually work first and then get paid. Compare performances of motion pictures, plays, rock concerts, and the like. Typically, a member of the audience pays first and then sees the performance. Why is this order of performance customary? Imagine the consequences of a custom in which the audience saw the show and then paid on the way out. However, restaurants manage to collect in all but a few situations when they present the bill after their customers have eaten the food.

gain much from a resale of used goods.) Bonds, escrow arrangements, and conditional sales provisions can be expressed in terms of conditions, but they are sufficiently different from the questions of the timing of performance and the right to withhold performance to warrant special mention.

2. Interpretation and Construction

Courts must interpret or construe contracts to determine whether the promises they contain are subject to a condition or conditions, and, if so, what that condition is, and whether a condition is also a promise.

Even when the parties spell things out, they are likely to leave a few questions unanswered by the express words of their agreement. In the examples we've considered, the parties expressly said that the seller would be ready, willing, and able to deliver on April 7th if the buyer was ready, willing, and able to pay $40,000 then. As a result, we know that if the buyer cannot pay, the seller need not deliver and cannot be sued for failing to do so.

But even in this simple case, questions remain. Suppose buyer refuses to come to seller's place of business with the money but insists that seller bring the car to buyer's place of business and pick up the money there. The contract is silent about where money and goods are to be exchanged. UCC § 2-308, following common law tradition, fills the gap in the contract and tells us that in most instances a buyer must go to a seller's place of business unless they agree otherwise.

Suppose buyer offers seller a personal check calling for a bank to pay seller $40,000. Has buyer met the condition on seller's promise to deliver so that the buyer is entitled to the goods? Or must a buyer tender cash? UCC § 2-511(2) fills this gap and tells us that "tender of payment is sufficient when made by any means or in any manner current in the ordinary course of business unless the seller demands payment in legal tender and gives any extension of time reasonably necessary to procure it."

Contracts frequently, if not typically, are less explicit than our example. People often neglect to spell out who is to do what and when, in the event that certain contingencies occur. A seller may offer to sell goods for a specified sum, and the buyer may sign a letter saying little more than "I accept your offer." Nothing is said about whether the buyer must pay in advance, whether the seller must deliver before the buyer pays, or whether they must pay and deliver at the same time. And whatever order of performance we select, *when* are these things to take place?

There is a common law rule, implicit in the UCC, that pushes one party to go first. If a contract calls for one performance that by its nature takes time and another that can be done instantly, the one that takes time must be done first. For example, I promise to work for you for a month. You promise to pay me $1,000 for my services. Under this rule of construction, I must do the work before you must pay me. Why is there such a rule? Does it reflect custom? Does it protect wealth and power at the expense of the dominated? Does it prompt efficient behavior?

Courts must often supply "constructive conditions" to fill such gaps in contracts, and the process very much resembles instances in which courts "imply" promises. At this point, review the passage from Professor Patterson in Chapter 3[B], *supra*. And consider the following case, in which the court must decide whether an express condition is also an implied promise.

JACOBS ASSOCIATES v. ARGONAUT INSURANCE CO.

Oregon Supreme Court
580 P.2d 529 (1978)

DENECKE, C.J.

Plaintiff is an engineering firm that provided services used in construction of the Portland General Electric (PGE) Company headquarters building in Portland. The services were provided for Target Dredging and Pile Driving Company. Target has since been adjudicated bankrupt without paying plaintiff $10,891.94 due under its subcontract. In accordance with its contract with PGE, Target secured a bond through defendant. After Target was adjudicated bankrupt, plaintiff instituted this action asserting that it was a third-party beneficiary on the bond executed by defendant. Defendant demurred to plaintiff's complaint on the ground that it failed to state facts constituting a cause of action. The demurrer was sustained. Plaintiff refused to plead further. Judgment was entered for defendant and plaintiff appealed.

The bond at issue in this case is of standard form. After reciting that Target as principal and defendant as surety are bound to PGE in the sum of $820,771, the bond lists the "conditions" that will void the obligations. The bond recites:

NOW, THEREFORE, THE CONDITION OF THIS OBLIGATION IS SUCH that if the Contractor [Target] shall

(a) Pay all persons, firms, and corporations who perform labor or furnish equipment, supplies, and materials for use in the work under the Contract;
...

(d) Fully complete the work as provided in the Contract, free from all liens and claims of any kind whatsoever, and in all other particulars shall faithfully and fully perform the Contract on its part according to all the terms, covenants, and conditions thereof, and within the time specified therein;

(e) Fully indemnify and save harmless the Owner [PGE] against and from all cost and damage which it may suffer by reason of a default in the performance of any of the foregoing provisions, and fully reimburse and repay the Owner all outlay and expense which the Owner may incur in making good any such default; then this obligation shall be void; otherwise the same shall remain in full force and effect.

1. It is clear that the conditions have not all been satisfied and that the bond remains in effect. The question, however, is whether plaintiff is [a] party that may maintain an action on the bond.

Plaintiff candidly admits that the question was squarely answered in the negative by this court in *Tait & Co. v. D. Diamond Corp.*, 228 Or. 602, 365 P.2d 883 (1961). In *Tait* we recognized that our decision followed the minority rule and that our approach had been strongly criticized, but we felt that our prior decisions dictated the result. *Parker v. Jeffery*, 26 Or. 186, 37 P. 712 (1894), and *Pankey v. National Surety Co.*, 115 Or. 648, 239 P. 808 (1925).

In *Parker* and *Pankey* we held we would not imply a promise to pay the third-party plaintiff. We did not interpret the language of the bond to constitute a promise, only a condition.

This is the principal ground for the dissent; that is, that the surety did not promise to pay laborers and the words of condition are irrelevant on the issue of to whom the surety owes the obligation to pay.

The difficulty is caused by the archaic form that continues to be used in surety bonds. Most courts have not interpreted the archaic form literally but consider the words of condition to be words of promise. To do otherwise would be erroneous in instances even more obvious than in this case.

Corbin states:

> Words of "condition" are not words of "promise" in form; but in this class of cases it is sound policy to interpret the words liberally in favor of the third parties. In a majority of states, it is already done; and without question the surety's rate of compensation for carrying the risk is sufficiently adjusted to the law. The compensated surety has become an institution that is well suited to carry the risk of the principal contractor's default, whereas individual laborers and materialmen are frequently very ill-prepared to carry the risk. The legislatures have recognized this fact, and in the case of public contracts have required surety bonds to protect the third parties. While this has not been done in the case of private construction, and while the courts should not on their own motion put such a provision into a private surety bond, they may well interpret a bond that is expressly conditioned on the payment of laborers and materialmen as being a promise to pay them and made for their benefit. The words reasonably permit it, and social policy approves it...." [4 CORBIN, CONTRACTS §800, 177–178 (1951)].

Some sureties have discarded the ancient form and inserted language expressly providing that unpaid laborers shall have a direct action against the bond. In our opinion this was not intended to change the surety's obligation from that stated in the archaic form but to express that same obligation in understandable language.

If the dissent is correct, that language in the bond in this case, "Pay all persons ... who perform work ..." does not amount to a promise to pay persons such as plaintiff, the quoted condition is completely superfluous. PGE does not need this condition for protection; it is fully protected by other conditions in the bond. Condition (d), before quoted, includes a requirement that the work shall be completed, free of all liens and claims. Condition (e) provides that the contractor shall fully indemnify

PGE against damage suffered by reason of any default in contractor's performance. Because the above-quoted condition is unnecessary to protect PGE, the inference necessarily arises that it is a promise to pay an unpaid laborer or materialman....

We conclude, therefore, that our decisions in *Parker* and *Pankey* were incorrectly decided.

2. When an express promise to pay a third party has been found, the subjective intent of the promisee, in this case PGE, is immaterial; the third party can maintain an action against the promisor surety. The general principle that is the basis for that proposition has always been the law in Oregon. "On the second point, the authorities with us are quite decisive that when A., for a valuable consideration, agrees with B. to pay his debt to C., the latter can enforce the contract against A." *Baker & Smith v. Eglin*, 11 Or. 333, 334, 8 P. 280 (1883).

This same principle applies to contracts of surety:

> And thirdly, the third party has an enforceable right if the surety promises in the bond, either in express words or by reasonable implication, to pay money to him. If there is such a promissory expression as this, there need be no discussion of "intention to benefit." We need not speculate for whose benefit the contract was made, or wonder whether the promisee was buying the promise for his own selfish interest or for philanthropic purposes. It is a much simpler question: Did the surety promise to pay money to the plaintiff?" 4 CORBIN, CONTRACTS, *supra*, at 163–164.

3. In addition to the lack of persuasive precedents supporting *Tait*, it should be overruled because it failed to follow a recognized rule of the construction of contracts. The defendant in this case is a compensated surety; its business is writing surety bonds for a fee. The universal rule is that a compensated surety is regarded as an insurer and the contract it draws will be construed most strongly against it....

In *Tait* we chose not to repudiate our former decisions because we stated: "[A]n untold number of surety contracts have been entered into in reliance upon the unequivocal holdings of this court," and we could not "judge the repercussions that could occur within the construction industry by an abrupt reversal of the rule." 228 Or. at 604–605.

We are now of the opinion that in *Tait* we were unrealistic in our concern over the possible magnitude of the effect of repudiating our former decisions, and since *Tait* the effect of repudiating our former decisions has been lessened by changes in the mechanic's lien laws. The only persons who are vitally interested in bringing an action on the payment provision of a bond are those who have no lien rights in the owner's property or who failed to perfect their lien rights. At the time of *Tait* most persons performing services for or furnishing material to a construction project had statutory mechanic's lien rights. ORS 87.010. Since *Tait* the legislature provided for lien rights for more classes of persons, including engineers such as plaintiff. (Plaintiff did not have lien rights at the time it performed the work for Target.) For these reasons the number of persons affected by a change would be small.

In addition, the defendant and other sureties can change the form of their bonds and clearly provide that unpaid engineers, laborers, and materialmen have no right of action. This will not affect outstanding bonds; however, as we observed, this will not be of concern to many sureties or claimants.

If this were a "custom" contract, "tailor-made" for these parties for this project, it is very unlikely that we would repudiate the interpretation reiterated in *Tait*. In that situation it would be likely that the parties relied upon our holding in *Tait* and wrote the clause accordingly. But that is not the situation in this case. This is a standard clause in bonds. It is not part of a contract of adhesion but it is not a clause that is normally negotiated. Under these circumstances there is no reason we should not overrule our past decisions interpreting the clause to the contrary if we conclude the past decisions are clearly erroneous....

We hold that the plaintiff has a right of action against the surety. *Tait & Co. v. D. Diamond Corp.*, *supra*, is overruled. Therefore, the demurrer should be overruled.

Reversed and remanded for setting aside the judgment for defendant and for further proceedings.

[LINDE concurred, noting that the majority found the bond to contain a promise, while the dissent found the absence of such a promise to be clear. To decide this case on the pleadings would be to suggest that "the parties clearly understood something, but we disagree on what they clearly understood." The demurrer was improper, since there were factual issues that might have given plaintiff a victory if resolved in favor of plaintiff. LENT, J., joined in Linde's concurrence.]

HOLMAN, J., dissenting. [BRYSON joined in the dissent.]

The majority takes a condition of a bond and makes it a promise. The surety made no promise to pay parties other than the owner, Portland General Electric Company (PGE). The words of the contract provide that "... *if the Contractor* shall (a) Pay all persons, firms, and corporations who perform labor or furnish equipment, supplies, and materials for use in the work," there will be no obligation of the surety under the bond. (Emphasis added.) Thus, the language from the contract quoted by the majority provides no obligation upon the surety to pay but provides only that *if the contractor* pays, no obligation can exist under the bond. It is a provision for the benefit of the surety. The words are not words of promise on the part of the surety but are words that specify a condition which, if fulfilled, nullifies the surety's obligation. *They say nothing about to whom the surety owes the obligation.*

The words that indicate in whose favor the obligation runs are as follows:

> ... TARGET DREDGING & PILE DRIVING CO ... and ARGONAUT IN-SURANCE COMPANY, ... are jointly and severally held and *firmly bound unto* PORTLAND GENERAL ELECTRIC COMPANY, ... in the sum of ... $820,771.00 ... *for the payment whereof to the Owner* the Contractor binds itself, its successors and assigns, and *the Surety binds itself*, its successors and assigns firmly by these presents.

… In view of the quoted language from the agreement, I do not understand how the majority comes to the conclusion that the contracting parties intended that the bond should also run in favor of someone else. A contract is a matter of the intention of the parties, and there is no evidence here that this contract was intended to benefit anyone other than PGE. The contract, although drawn in an archaic form, is clear and unambiguous....

The purpose of a bond of this kind is to save an owner harmless from the expense of clearing liens which might be filed upon the premises being constructed. A bond of this kind is given because those in the position of PGE require it for their protection. The premium on the bond is a cost of doing business and is reflected in the contractor's bid. Neither the contractor nor the owner is interested in enhancing the premium, and thus the amount of the bids on the property being constructed, by securing coverage for anyone other than the owner. Unless the milk of human kindness runs thicker in the veins of public utilities and contractors than is generally apparent, there is no real basis for believing there was an intention to benefit anyone other than PGE....

If there is an ambiguity, because of the archaic form of the bond, as to what the parties intended, it would be proper to submit proof showing what the parties did intend. Whether the parties intended those in the position of plaintiff to be beneficiaries would then be a question of fact. However, even if the contract is treated as being ambiguous, plaintiff is in no position to recover in the face of the literal wording of the bond and in the absence of evidence that the parties intended otherwise. The majority not only construes the wording contrary to its literal meaning but it does so *as a matter of law* without the necessity of evidence that the words of condition were intended as words of promise. I have no quarrel with the law of third-party beneficiary contracts as stated by the majority nor with its application to plaintiff if such was the intent of the parties, but that intent cannot be conjured out of the language of the contract.

The majority contends it was not necessary that the condition, which it construes as a promise, be in the contract unless it was intended as a promise. I would counter by contending that if the parties intended to benefit anyone other than PGE, they would have said so instead of using words of condition. In addition, we know that sureties state everything at least three different ways because courts construe contracts against them if such contracts do not completely cover every possible contingency. We now hold that any duplication arising out of any statements made by sureties will be construed against them.

[The dissenting judge notes the majority's reliance on Corbin. He quotes Corbin, and then observes:] A reading of the text preceding and following the quoted material makes it apparent that his reason for such a statement is that he believes a better social result would follow if sureties were made responsible to all claimants—not because he believes the parties to such a contract usually intend to so agree.

The majority's result is appealing because the bonding company can distribute the risk through premiums and because it is a way of assuring the payment of all workmen and materialmen. Whether one wants to twist the words to reach what is considered a good social result depends upon how important one considers the right of the parties to make their own contract. This is the kind of public policy that is usually handled by legislatures, and the law has been settled in this state for 95 years without any legislative action.

NOTES AND QUESTIONS

1. *An argument from Jacobs Associates' brief:* Jacobs Associates argued that the *Tait* decision ought to be overruled. Much of Jacobs Associates' argument turned on Oregon decisions after 1961, and also on stressing that the *Tait* decision was contrary to the great weight of authority in the United States. However, it also said in its brief:

> Unfortunately, because this case was not allowed to proceed beyond the demurrer stage, plaintiff did not have the opportunity to engage in any discovery. Plaintiff therefore admittedly does not have actual data to buttress the argument it is about to make but since the Court in the *Tait* case was making certain assumptions 16 years ago, plaintiff believes it would be proper to suggest some alternative assumptions for application in 1977. In fact, plaintiff will be so bold as to contend that, given the present state of the law on this subject in the country today, plaintiff has great faith that the facts would support the following contentions:
>
> > 1. The great majority of jurisdictions in this country would allow plaintiff a right of action against defendant as a third-party beneficiary of the type of bond involved in this case.
> >
> > 2. The bond set forth in Exhibit "A" is probably a standard form of bond employed by defendant in most areas of the country where it does business.
> >
> > 3. Defendant's actuaries have determined a premium rate for such bonds and have probably based such a premium on an analysis of the risks being covered; and being prudent actuaries have built into their premium structure the risk of the right of recovery by third-party subcontractors which such third parties have under the laws of most jurisdictions.
> >
> > 4. The defendant probably does not discount its standard premium to reflect its reduced exposure in Oregon when it writes Oregon bonds.

2. *A digression on third party beneficiaries:* Once the court in the *Jacobs Associates* case found that Argonaut had *promised* the owner to pay all those who had worked on the Portland headquarters building, it then allowed *Jacobs Associates* to sue to enforce that promise as a "third-party beneficiary."

Nineteenth and early twentieth-century courts struggled with the idea of allowing a person who was not a party to a contract to sue to enforce it. Today it is clear that beneficiaries of some contracts between others can sue in almost all states. Moreover, in some circumstances, the parties to the contract may not be able to rescind it without the consent of the beneficiaries.

As you might expect, there is both a core of clear cases and a periphery of uncertain ones. The first Restatement of Contracts divided all beneficiaries of other people's contracts into three kinds: creditor, donee, and incidental. Incidental beneficiaries could not sue. For example, owner and builder make a contract to construct a beautiful house on a vacant lot. If the house were built, it would increase the value of neighbor's adjoining property. Builder breaches the contract with owner, and the house is not built. Neighbor would be an "incidental beneficiary" and could not sue the builder.

Creditor and donee beneficiaries could sue. For example, A sells his painting to B for $1,000. Instead of paying the money to A, B is to pay it to C. This will satisfy a debt that A owes C. B fails to pay. C may sue B as a "creditor beneficiary." Or B buys A's painting for $1,000. A is to deliver it to C, who is B's mother. It is a birthday gift. A fails to deliver the painting. C can sue A. She is a "donee beneficiary."

Restatement (Second) of Contracts § 302 abandons the creditor, donee, and incidental beneficiary scheme. It keeps the idea that incidental beneficiaries cannot sue. However, those who can sue are called "intended beneficiaries." To be one, a person must show that "recognition of a right to performance in the beneficiary is appropriate to effectuate the intention of the parties." In addition, one must show either:

a) the performance of the promise will satisfy an obligation of the promisee to pay money to the beneficiary; or

b) the circumstances indicate that the promisee intends to give the beneficiary the benefit of the promised performance.

Restatement (Second) of Contracts § 311 states a general rule and some exceptions concerning the power of the original parties to change or end a beneficiary's rights. Generally, the parties who made the contract can modify it without the consent of the beneficiary. They do not have this power if their contract provides that the third-party beneficiary's rights cannot be changed. Also, if a beneficiary "materially changes his position in justifiable reliance on the promise or brings suit on it or manifests assent to it at the request of the promisor or promisee," the beneficiary's rights cannot be changed.

Martinez v. Socoma Companies, Inc.[7] is an example of third-party beneficiary doctrine in American history. As part of President Lyndon Johnson's "War on Poverty," Socoma and two other corporations made contracts with the Secretary of Labor. However, they entered these contracts just three days before President Johnson's term ended and President Richard Nixon would take office. The companies agreed to lease space in a public building and adapt the space so items could be manufactured there. They also promised to train and employ in the facilities for at least 12 months, at minimum-wage rates, a specified number of East Los Angeles residents certified as disadvantaged by the government. They further agreed to provide these employees with opportunities for promotion to available supervisory-managerial positions and with options to purchase stock in the corporation that employed them. The corporations failed to perform, and officials of the Nixon administration did not assert the government's rights against the corporations.

---

7. 11 Cal. 3d 394, 521 P.2d 841 (1974).

A legal services program, representing disadvantaged unemployed persons, brought a class action claiming that they were third-party beneficiaries of the contract between the United States government and the three corporations. Demurrers to the complaint were sustained, and the Supreme Court of California affirmed by a 4–3 vote. This meant that the disadvantaged unemployed persons could not sue the corporations that had failed to perform their promises.

The majority found that the "benefits to be derived from defendants' performance were clearly intended not as gifts from the government to such persons but as a means of executing the public purposes stated in the contracts and in the underlying legislation. Accordingly, plaintiffs were only incidental beneficiaries and as such have no right of recovery."[8] The majority relied greatly on the first Restatement of Contracts in its opinion.

What is involved in a case such as this? Do classifications such as "incidental," "donee," or "intended" beneficiaries raise the relevant issues? If the corporations had breached their promises, the United States could sue for contract remedies, settle the case, or abandon its rights. Why might government officials decide to allow the corporations to abandon their commitment without being subject to a suit? Should this decision be left in the hands of those appointed by elected officials or should those speaking for the unemployed of East Los Angeles be able to make the decision? Neither the majority nor the dissent in the *Martinez* case discussed the situation in these terms.

3. Conditions and Forfeitures: Free Contract, Material Breach, and Fairness

A major problem faced by the courts in the area of performance and breach of contracts is that of fairness and the prevention of forfeitures. The parties, for example, may have provided in their contract that if one fails to perform, the other has no obligation to carry out his or her promise. The default in performance may be relatively minor. Calling off the contract may cause either extreme reliance losses or a great forfeiture which benefits the party who is not in default — or, in some cases, both reliance losses and forfeiture.

Consider several examples:

(1) Suppose a college student contracted to cut the grass of a homeowner. The student agreed to start at 10:00 A.M. on June 1. The homeowner agreed to provide the mower and fuel, and to pay $100 when the job was done. The student arrived just before 10:00. The homeowner discovered that he had forgotten to buy fuel, but asked the student to wait for 15 minutes while he went to a nearby gas station to get some. The student refused to wait and left, declaring that the homeowner had breached the contract. Could the student recover damages, although he did not perform, by arguing that his non-performance was excused by failure of a condition? Could the home-

---

8. *Id.* at 397, 521 P.2d at 843.

owner recover damages from the student if he was unable to hire another person to mow the lawn for less than $150?

(2) Suppose a famous pop singer agrees to perform at a nightclub. She promises to perform there on the night of April 7th, singing in shows lasting no less than 30 minutes and no more than one hour, to begin at 9:00 and 11:00 P.M. She is to be paid $10,000 for the performances. Suppose the singer performs for 45 minutes at the 9:00 show and the audience is enthusiastic. However, the singer cuts the 11:00 show short and sings for only 20 minutes because the audience fails to respond to her act. Assume that the owner of the club is in no way responsible for the reaction of the audience at the 11:00 show. The owner asserts that since the singer did not perform for at least 30 minutes at the 11:00 show, she did not perform her part of the contract, and, as a result, the owner owes the singer nothing. Are the singer's lawyers likely to collect the $10,000? Anything? Could they assert with any real chance of success that since she performed the 9:00 show, she should be paid $5,000 for it? Since she also performed 20/30ths of the 11:00 show, should she be paid two-thirds of $5,000 (or $3,333), making a total of $8,333 earned for the night of April 7th? Of course, this would be subject to a set-off of any damages the club owner could prove had been caused by the singer's failure to perform for 10 minutes.

(3) Suppose a contract calls for a seller to manufacture and install a machine by April 7th that will do certain specified things. The buyer promises to pay $100,000 if the machine is installed by April 7th. The machine cannot be resold to anyone else since it is tailored to the buyer's specific needs. The seller spends $85,000 to make and install the machine, and it is in place on April 7th. However, it will not quite do the things specified, although it comes close. On April 8th, seller could make adjustments which would cost $1,000, and they would make the machine perform as specified in the contract. While the buyer would lose the use of the machine for a day, it would be valuable to him on the 8th and thereafter. May the buyer refuse to allow these adjustments on the 8th and be free of any obligation under the contract, since the condition to his promise was not met precisely?

On one hand, these examples could be seen as raising a question of interpretation of the contract. We might doubt in example (3) whether the seller had in fact assumed the risk without a clear showing from the facts that he was aware he was entering into an $85,000 gamble. We might wonder whether the buyer's conduct was in good faith or was merely a pretext to bail out of what now seems to be a poor deal. On the other hand, suppose it is clear that the buyer has drafted the contract to put the risk of timely performance on the seller. Will courts accept this allocation of risk, or will they impose some standard of fairness and consider whether to enforce the contract as written?

Suppose a court accepts the contractual allocation of risk and finds that the condition to one party's obligation to perform has not been met. Does this mean that the other party gets no recovery, even for benefits conferred on the first party? For example, in example (2) above, should the club owner have to pay the singer something, even if the court finds that full performance by the singer was a condition precedent to recovery of the contract price? The singer would likely still have a claim in restitution for benefits conferred by partial performance, here likely measured by the *quantum meruit* standard. However, the singer may not regard this as a fair solution. She may have secured a highly favorable contract, so that the contract price would be considerably higher than the *quantum meruit* rate. Moreover, in some states, courts say that a party in default (or perhaps one in "willful" default) cannot recover restitution and that could prevent recovery.

The drafters of written contracts attempted to structure the transactions to gain advantages for their clients. Consider the role of courts in these cases, and consider the lessons for those planning commercial transactions.

DAVIS v. ALLSTATE INSURANCE CO.

Wisconsin Supreme Court
101 Wis. 2d 1, 303 N.W.2d 596 (1981)

DAY, J.

… The principal question on review is: Did the court of appeals err in overturning the trial court's finding that the Allstate Insurance Company (Allstate) exercised bad faith in the course of handling Ronald D. Davis's (insured's) claim under a contract of fire insurance?

The insured is an attorney who graduated from law school in 1974 and immediately entered the private practice of law in Milwaukee.

In 1975, insured obtained a standard "deluxe" business owner's fire and extended coverage insurance policy from Allstate in the amount of $8,000. The policy coverage was based on Allstate's inspection of the insured's business personal property, which resulted in a written report placing an approximate value of $7,500 on the property in plaintiff's office. A second Allstate inspection in February 1976 estimated the value of plaintiff's business property at $11,100. Based on this second estimate, the policy limit was increased to $15,000 on Allstate's recommendation. In October 1976, Allstate conducted another inspection and recommended that the policy limits be raised to $25,000; however, the policy was not amended.

On February 22, 1977, a fire destroyed all of the contents of insured's law office, including invoices and receipts for purchases of the contents of the office. Allstate was notified of the loss on the day following the fire.

Bruce Piette, an Allstate claims adjuster, was assigned to the claim. He investigated the fire between February 24 and May 15, 1977, and recommended to Allstate a "cash-out" settlement of $14,860.04, which was approved by Mr. Piette's supervisor, Larry Peterson, a commercial claims supervisor.

On May 15, 1977, the insured filed a sworn proof-of-loss statement detailing the property destroyed in the fire and the value of each item, claiming losses in excess of the policy limit of $15,000. Internal Allstate memoranda stated that both Piette and Peterson believed the proof of loss to be substantially completed in proper form.

In a separate internal memorandum, Mr. Piette stated he would offer the plaintiff a lower amount initially, and go up to $14,860 if necessary.

Jerome Mondl, Piette and Peterson's supervisor, rejected their recommendations. He advised Peterson to reject insured's proof-of-loss for lack of documentation of purchase of the individual items of property claimed. Mr. Mondl did authorize settlement of $4,148.53, which Piette offered the insured to satisfy the claim. This offer was rejected.

The insured then brought this action seeking damages for the fire loss and compensatory and punitive damages for bad faith. The case was tried before a jury. The jury returned a special verdict finding that the insured substantially performed the conditions required by the policy to recover his claim and found damages for losses to his personal property of $14,860.04. The jury also found that Allstate exercised bad faith in the course of its handling of the claim and awarded compensatory damages resulting from the defendant's bad faith of $12,103 and punitive damages of $30,000.

Allstate's motions after verdict were denied and the trial court affirmed the jury's verdict and judgment was entered in the amount of the jury's verdict plus costs and disbursements for a total of $57,306.54.

The defendant filed a notice of appeal from the entire judgment.

The court of appeals affirmed the jury's finding that the insured substantially performed his obligations under the insurance contract to recover his claim. The court rejected Allstate's contention that an insured must supply certified invoices or receipts establishing the cost of each item of lost property as a precondition to recover, characterizing that theory as "nonsense." The court of appeals found that an insured need only substantially comply with the proof-of-loss requirements in the insurance contract, which he had done. Accordingly, the jury's verdict finding $14,860.04 as the amount of damage to the insured's personal property was affirmed.

Turning to the bad faith issue, the court of appeals found insured's claim to be "fairly debatable," thus shielding Allstate from charges of "bad faith." Relying on this court's decision in *Anderson v. Continental Ins. Co.*, 85 Wis. 2d 675, 691, 271 N.W.2d 368 (1978), the court held the trial court erred in presenting the bad faith issue to the jury and reversed the jury's findings on that issue.

This court granted the insured's petition for review.

The first question on review is: Did the insured satisfy the conditions of the standard fire insurance policy concerning proof of ownership and valuation of property lost in the fire?

The insurance policy was the standard form required by § 203.06, Stats. 1973.[9]

---

9. [1] The Standard Policy incorporated by reference to § 203.01 provides in lines 90–122:
   Requirements In Case Loss Occurs. The insured shall give immediate written notice to this Company of any loss, protect the property from further damage, forthwith separate the

It is clear that insured failed to comply with that part of the insurance contract providing that:

> The insured ... shall produce for examination all books of account, bills, invoices, and other vouchers, or certified copies thereof if originals be lost....

He did, however, provide the company with a sworn proof of loss setting out in detail the items lost and the value of each.

The record shows that Allstate's employees did not demand certified copies of the invoices that were lost in the fire until June 10, 1977, nearly four months after the insured's loss occurred. In fact, the record amply supports the insured's contention that until that date, Allstate agreed to verify ownership and valuation by checking with the vendors of the lost property and later by referring to the insured's tax records. The record also shows that insured cooperated with the defendant in determining ownership and valuation of the property.

Substantial performance with the terms of the contract is necessary for insured to recover under the policy. Where a party has met the essential purpose of the contract, he has substantially performed under the contract....

We conclude that, on this record, the jury correctly found that the insured substantially performed his obligations under the contract. Allstate on this review does not challenge the affirmance by the Court of Appeals of the award of $14,860.04 to the insured for damage to his property.

The second question is: Did Allstate exercise bad faith in the handling of the insured's claim?

The controlling case on the law of bad faith is *Anderson v. Continental Ins. Co.*, 85 Wis. 2d 675, 271 N.W.2d 368 (1978). Bad faith is an intentional tort "which results

---

damaged and undamaged personal property, put it in the best possible order, furnish a complete inventory of the destroyed, damaged, and undamaged property, showing in detail quantities, costs, actual cash value, and amount of loss claimed; and within sixty days after the loss, unless such time is extended in writing by this Company, the insured shall render to this Company a proof of loss, signed and sworn to by the insured, stating the knowledge and belief of the insured as to the following: the time and origin of the loss, the interest of the insured and of all others in the property, the actual cash value of each item thereof, and the amount of loss thereto, all encumbrances thereon, all other contracts of insurance, whether valid or not, covering any of said property, any changes in the title, use, occupation, location, possession, or exposures of said property since the issuing of this policy, by whom and for what purpose any building herein described and the several parts thereof were occupied at the time of loss and whether or not it then stood on leased ground, and shall furnish a copy of all the descriptions and schedules in all policies and, if required, verified plans and specifications of any building, fixtures, or machinery destroyed or damaged. The insured, as often as may be reasonably required, shall exhibit to any person designated by this Company all that remains of any property herein described, and submit to examinations under oath by any person named by this Company, and subscribe the same; and, as often as may be reasonably required, shall produce for examination all books of account, bills, invoices, and other vouchers, or certified copies thereof if originals be lost, at such reasonable time and place as may be designated by this Company or its representative, and shall permit extracts and copies thereof to be made.

from a breach of duty imposed as a consequence of the relationship established by contract." *Anderson, supra,* 85 Wis. 2d at 688. The duty imposed on an insurance company has been characterized as being analogous to that of a fiduciary. *Anderson, supra,* 85 Wis. 2d at 688. "Bad faith" is defined as deceit, duplicity, or insincerity. *Anderson, supra,* 85 Wis. 2d at 692.

In order to show a claim for bad faith, this court has held that:

> ... a plaintiff must show the absence of a reasonable basis for denying benefits of the policy and the defendant's knowledge or reckless disregard of the lack of a reasonable basis for denying the claim. *Anderson, supra,* 85 Wis. 2d at 691.

The insurer is, however, entitled to challenge the claim on the basis of debatable law or facts....

Allstate contends that no bad faith issue was presented because the failure of the insured to supply certified invoices or receipts showing the cost of each claimed item of property provided a reasonable basis for denying the claim.

The court of appeals found the issue of valuation to be fairly debatable as a matter of law. We disagree.

The insured submitted upon request a sworn proof-of-loss statement to Allstate, claiming damage to his property under the policy of $15,000. The proof-of-loss statement placed a value on each of nearly four hundred items destroyed by the fire. The testimony of two of defendant's claims personnel considered the statement to be substantially complete. The same Allstate employees recommended a cash payment to plaintiff of nearly $15,000. Allstate investigators had recommended an increase in coverage on plaintiff's property to $25,000 only four months before the fire. Allstate's claims adjuster confirmed the insured's purchase of many of the major items shown on the proof-of-loss statement. After recommending a cash settlement of nearly $15,000, Allstate's claims adjuster noted in his records that:

> When I get authorization I will attempt to cash out insured for a complete loss. I will start at a low price and work my way up. I'm not going to offer the full amount at first. There is no harm in offering a lower amount at first. I can always go up.

The insured testified that he spoke with Allstate's Commercial Claims supervisor after the claims adjuster offered only $4,000 to settle the claim. He testified that the supervisor told him:

> We know we owe the money but if you don't take the $4,000, we are not going to offer you anything else and if you don't take the settlement we'll just turn it over to our lawyers and we'll tie you up for the next two or three years in a [sic] litigation and you won't see a dime.

The claims adjuster also wrote to his supervisor stating that:

> I don't feel we should drag this out to [sic] much longer. Insured is more than willing to supply us with tax records [which had been requested by Allstate to verify ownership].

Allstate introduced evidence at trial showing that the insured had represented the value of his office property at $350 to $3,500 and in one case claimed the property was merely rented by him. These representations were not made to Allstate but in divorce and bankruptcy proceedings and on personal property tax returns.

But whatever the insured's motives were in those proceedings, it is apparent from its interoffice memos that Allstate was not misled as to the property's ownership or value, even if others may have been.

We conclude that the evidence before the trial court was sufficient to submit the bad faith question to the jury and find no error in submitting the question.

The jury was obviously persuaded that the property was worth what insured had claimed. That figure was almost identical to the amount recommended by Allstate's representatives to their superiors to settle the claim and $10,000 less than the coverage limits recommended by Allstate's underwriters four months before the fire. Accordingly, the jury determined that Allstate had no reasonable basis for denying the claim.

Because there is ample evidence to support that conclusion, we reverse that part of the court of appeals' decision overturning the award of damages for bad faith, and reinstate the award for bad faith of $12,103 in compensatory damages and $30,000 in punitive damages found by the jury and approved by the trial court. Accordingly, we uphold the entire judgment of the trial court for $57,306.54....

NOTES AND QUESTIONS

1. *The behavior of insurance companies:* Given the amount involved, a great deal of legal work was devoted to Davis's claim. If courts insisted on literal rather than substantial compliance with the conditions in the insurance policy, we would get easy and quick answers. Why are courts and lawyers willing to spend so much effort on cases such as that of Mr. Davis?

In thinking about exact and substantial performance, consider the third paragraph of Justice Day's opinion carefully. Is it likely that the salespeople from Allstate explained to Mr. Davis the record-keeping requirement and the risk that records would be destroyed in the very fire being insured against? What if they had done so? Moreover, consider Allstate's sales tactics in the transaction. What expectations did it create as it sold Davis more and more insurance?

What is the lesson of the Allstate loss for insurance companies? Would you expect Allstate to change its practices? In what way? Should Allstate be able to use technical defenses when they suspect that a policy holder is making a questionable claim?

In a 2010 book,[10] Professor Jay Feinman argues that, beginning in the 1990s, insurance companies increasingly sought to improve their profitability through strategies of delaying payment on claims, denying valid claims, and litigating cases that would previously have been settled. These strategies represented a repudiation of the pre-

---

10. Jay M. Feinman, Delay, Deny, Defend: Why Insurance Companies Don't Pay Claims and What You Can Do About It (Portfolio, Penguin Group 2010).

viously prevailing ethic, within the insurance industry, of honoring the terms of insurance policies. Some companies reduced premiums to attract customers, who legitimately expected to be paid promptly when they presented valid claims, but then the companies systematically reduced or delayed payment on those claims.

Assuming Feinman is correct that insurance industry practices have changed, how likely is the legal system to react to those changes? Could a court consider evidence like that presented by Feinman, in the context of litigating a particular claim? Should it?

2. Regulation of insurance settlements: Many courts recognize a tort of bad faith performance of an insurance contract. Why isn't an insurance company privileged to bargain to settle claims? What was wrong with taking advantage of Mr. Davis's need for money to continue his law practice? Suppose Mr. Piette had made an opening offer of $8,000 (twice the offer he did make). Would the situation have been different? Recall the discussions of waiver and estoppel in insurance cases by Kimball and Friedman in Chapter 4, §A, Note 3.

The California courts were the first to find insurers liable when they denied or delayed legitimate claims. However, California law now recognizes that when there is a genuine dispute about coverage, courts may conclude as a matter of law that the denial of coverage or delay in payment did not constitute bad faith and may grant summary judgment for the insurance company.

In *Wilson v. 21st Century Ins. Co.*,[11] the Supreme Court of California said:

> In this first-party insurance bad faith action, the question on review is whether summary judgment was properly granted for the insurer. Eight months after plaintiff Reagan Wilson was injured in an automobile accident by a drunk driver, her insurer, defendant 21st Century Insurance Company (21st Century), rejected her demand for payment of the $100,000 policy limit on her underinsured motorist coverage. Although Wilson's treating physician had opined that the 21-year-old woman had "degenerative disc changes as a result of occult disc injury at the levels in her neck from her high-speed motor vehicle accident," and that these spinal changes were atypical for her age and "almost certainly" caused by the automobile accident, 21st Century rejected the claim on the asserted ground that she had suffered only soft-tissue injuries in the collision and had "pre-existing" degenerative disc disease. Because, based on the undisputed facts in the summary judgment record, a jury could reasonably find 21st Century reached this medical conclusion without a good-faith investigation of the claim and without a reasonable basis for genuine dispute, … summary judgment on plaintiff's bad faith cause of action was improper.[12]

In dissent, Justice Chin argued:

---

11. 42 Cal. 4th 713, 171 P.3d 1082 (2007).
12. *Id.* at 716.

The majority's holding can only drive up the cost of underinsured motorist insurance—contrary to the clear public policy of keeping the costs of such insurance low.... By allowing plaintiff to proceed with her lawsuit for bad faith even though a genuine dispute existed over the extent of her injuries until 21st Century paid the policy limits, the majority encourages unwarranted and costly lawsuits, the unnecessary hiring of doctors and lawyers, and the resulting increase in our automobile insurance premiums. 21st Century's reasonable and cautious behavior in light of the facts here should be encouraged on behalf of all consumers, not punished.[13]

3. *Substantial performance:* The substantial performance standard that the court applied in *Davis v. Allstate*, notwithstanding the contract language, is the same standard that is generally applied at common law to determine if failure of a condition excuses a party's future performance. Sometimes the phrase *material breach* is used instead of *substantial performance*. Consider Restatement Second of Contracts, § 237:

> [I]t is a condition of each party's remaining duties to render performances to be exchanged under an exchange of promises that there be no uncured *material* failure by the other party to render any such performance due at an earlier time (emphasis added).

See also Restatement Second of Contracts, §§ 236 and 243. The Restatement provides guidelines for determining whether a failure of performance is "material"; *see* §§ 241 and 242.

The late Professor Malcolm Sharp wrote that the "best statement of these ordinary tests [for materiality], and perhaps the best portion of the work, is § 241 in the Second Restatement."[14] Professor Eric G. Andersen challenges the Restatement's approach to material breach.[15] He says that "the relevant Restatement provisions seem enigmatic at best." They "resemble a list of ingredients rather than a recipe; no real guidance is provided on the order or proportions in which to combine the provisions." They "fail to identify an underlying, unifying principle more specific than 'fairness' or 'justice.' ..."

Professor Andersen offers his solution. We should not look at the burden on the defaulting party. Rather, he advocates an expanded view of restitution for a party in default, to protect any interest of the defaulting party from excessive forfeiture.[16] In

---

13. *Id.* at 728–29.

14. Malcolm Sharp, *Promissory Liability II*, 7 U. Chi. L. Rev. 250, 272 (1939).

15. Eric G. Andersen, *A New Look at Material Breach in the Law of Contracts*, 21 U.C. Davis L. Rev. 1073 (1988). *Cf.* Jean Braucher, *E. Allan Farnsworth and the Restatement (Second) of Contracts*, 105 Colum. L. Rev. 1420, 1424–25 (2005) (describing how self-conscious the decisions were to create flexible, open-ended provisions in the Restatement in general, following the approach of Karl Llewellyn in the Uniform Commercial Code, to avoid dogmatism about policy and leave discretion to courts).

16. As discussed earlier, in the second paragraph preceding the *Davis v. Allstate Insurance* case, the party who has materially breached a condition—but nonetheless has already extended benefits to the other party—can recover in restitution for the value of the benefits conferred. The measure of recovery in restitution is often less—perhaps much less—than the recovery available if the breach of condition is deemed immaterial. In advocating a more expansive recovery in restitution where

this way, we can be sure that the victim will have the right to cancel when she must turn elsewhere in order to protect her expectation interest. Andersen asserts: "Cancellation should be invoked only when a breach so impairs the interest in future performance that the victim has reasonable cause to bring the contract to an end, so that the bargained-for security [of performance], or its economic equivalent, may be acquired elsewhere."

Consider Professor Andersen's criticism of the Restatement's balancing test. Does Andersen's approach significantly limit the amount of judgment and discretion necessary when a court considers whether to allow one party to cancel? To what extent, if at all, does it make a court's task easier? If it does, and if the goal is to get a fair result based on all of the facts of the particular case, don't we have to give the courts scope to make intuitive judgments based on the likely impact of the court's decision on both parties to the deal?

4. *Substantial performance in building contracts:* Courts often use substantial performance in contracts to erect or repair buildings. For example, suppose owner promises to pay when builder constructs the building according to plans and specifications. Courts generally read the builder's *promise* as one to build to plans and specifications. However, they read the *constructive condition* on the owner's promise to pay as requiring only substantial performance of the contract in good faith.

Where substantial performance occurs, the owner must pay the full contract sum although he or she did not get exactly what was bargained for. Of course, the owner has a cause of action for damages for the builder's failure to perform the promise to meet plans and specifications. This might seem to approximate compensation for loss. However, at least in some cases, the owner's damages are measured as the difference between the value of the house as it stands and as it would be had the contract been performed exactly. Often this produces only a token sum, leaving the owner's interest in having good craftsmanship unprotected insofar as it is not reflected in market values.

Where there is no substantial performance, the owner is excused from making further payments. However, since the owner owns the imperfectly constructed building and retains possession and use of it, in almost all jurisdictions he must still compensate the builder in restitution. Restitution is likely to be measured by the *quantum meruit* standard, less payments already received. What is the practical difference in the measure of buyer's compensation, depending on whether substantial performance is deemed to have occurred?

5. *Experts' certificates in building contracts and substantial performance:* Under many construction contracts, owners are to pay only when the builder obtains an *architect's or engineer's certificate* that the work has been done. Why might owners insert such a provision? Why might builders? Suppose the architect or engineer refuses to grant the certificate. May the builder claim the contract price, less a set-off for the

---

benefits have been conferred, Anderson is advocating that we minimize the differences between a material and immaterial breach of condition.

owner's damages, on the ground that the builder has substantially performed? We can contrast two views:

In *Coorsen v. Ziehl*,[17] the Wisconsin court found that the satisfaction of the architect "is a condition precedent to the right to sue for the contract price, unless the refusal to certify should be disregarded on the grounds of fraud or bad faith, or clear evidence of mistake, on the part of the architect."

However, in the classic case of *Jacob & Youngs, Inc. v. Kent*,[18] Justice Cardozo found that a builder could recover despite his failure to obtain the required architect's certificate when the builder had substantially performed and where "the defect was insignificant in its relation to the project" and denial of recovery would result in a great forfeiture. One of the specifications for plumbing work provided that "all wrought iron pipe must be well galvanized, lap welded pipe of the grade known as 'standard pipe' of Reading manufacture." About nine months after occupying the country residence, the owner discovered that some of the pipe "instead of being made in Reading, was the product of other factories." The owner had not yet paid $3,483 of the price. The builder was directed by the architect to do the work anew. Carrying out the order would have meant the demolition at great expense of substantial parts of the completed structure. The omission of Reading pipe "was neither fraudulent or willful. It was the result of the oversight and inattention of the plaintiff's subcontractor." The builder sued for the unpaid balance.

The trial court excluded evidence that the pipe installed was of the same quality, appearance, and market value as Reading pipe, and it directed a verdict for the defendant owner. The Court of Appeal reversed and directed a judgment for Jacob & Youngs by a 4–3 vote. In an opinion by Judge Cardozo, the Court said:

> The courts never say that one who makes a contract fills the measure of his duty by less than full performance. They do say, however, that an omission, both trivial and innocent, will sometimes be atoned for by allowance of the resulting damage, and will not always be the breach of a condition followed by a forfeiture.... Considerations partly of justice and partly of presumable intention are to tell us whether this or that promise shall be placed in one class or another.... This is not to say that the parties are not free by apt and certain words to effectuate a purpose that performance of every term shall be a condition of recovery ... This is merely to say that the law will be slow to impute the purpose ... where the significance of the default is grievously out of proportion to oppression of the forfeiture.

The dissent said that Kent "had a right to contract for what he wanted." "It may have been a mere whim on his part, but even so, he had a right to this kind of pipe, regardless of whether some other kind, according to the opinion of the contractor

---

17. 103 Wis. 381, 79 N.W. 562 (1899).
18. 230 N.Y. 239, 129 N.E. 889 (1921).

or experts, would have been 'just as good, better, or done just as well.' He agreed to pay only upon condition that the pipe installed were made by that company and he ought not be compelled to pay unless that condition be performed."

Richard Danzig[19] studied the background of the *Jacob & Youngs* case. The contract was lengthy and detailed. It created a system whereby the builder was to be paid when it obtained architect's certificates, but it did not expressly state the circumstances under which certificates should be granted or denied. All that was said was that the builder was entitled to a certificate when "in the Architect's judgment the work called for ... has been satisfactorily executed...." Paragraph 22 of the General Conditions stated: "Where any particular brand of manufactured article is specified, it is to be considered as a standard. Contractors desiring to use another shall first make application in writing to the Architect, stating the difference in cost, and obtain their written approval of the change." Jacob & Youngs, of course, had made no such written application nor received written approval of a substitution of brands of pipe.

Kent was a successful New York lawyer, and there is no evidence that he had any connection with the Reading Pipe Company. There were four major brands of wrought-iron pipe on the market, and an informant said that they were of the same quality and price. Wrought-iron pipe cost 30 percent more than steel pipe, and was used in quality construction before World War I, but it is almost never used today. It was normal trade practice to ensure the quality of wrought-iron pipe by naming a manufacturer known not to use iron containing steel scrap. The specifications themselves were imprecise. Apparently, it was impossible to make lap-welded wrought iron in all of the sizes necessary for the house, as called for by the specifications.

Why did Kent object to the pipe? Danzig reports he was told: "The old man would go all over town to save a buck." However, he may have used the substitution as an expression of his frustration with Jacob & Youngs's performance of the contract. Completion of the job was long delayed. Jacob & Youngs did additional work that added to Kent's bill.

Suppose Kent drafted the contract and specified Reading pipe as an easy way to avoid questions about the quality of the pipe installed in the house. Instead of having to argue about how good or bad other kinds of pipe were, Kent wanted to plan the transaction so that there was but a simple yes/no distinction. He had to pay for Reading pipe; he didn't have to pay for anything else. Doesn't Judge Cardozo take away this clarity from those who are planning transactions? Indeed, if the builder must tear down the house and install the specified brand, wouldn't this make people in the construction industry more careful students of the specifications?[20]

---

19. RICHARD DANZIG, THE CAPABILITY PROBLEM IN CONTRACT LAW 108–28 (Foundation Press 1978).

20. *See* Jody S. Kraus & Robert E. Scott, *Contract Design and the Structure of Contractual Intent*, 84 N.Y.U. L. Rev. 1023 (2009). They say that the owner "might have intentionally conditioned his payment obligations on the installation of Reading *brand* pipe, rather than Reading *quality* pipe, in order to lower the expected costs of enforcing that requirement."

VAN IDERSTINE CO. v. BARNET LEATHER CO.

New York Court of Appeals

242 N.Y. 425, 152 N.E. 250 (1926)

LEHMAN, J.

... On September 10th, 1920, the parties entered into another contract for the sale of 6,000 vealskins, delivery to be made in September, "to be received by Jules Star & Co. subject to their approval." ...

... Jules Star & Co. rejected the entire quantity of 6,000 skins which the plaintiff tendered in attempted performance of its contract of September 10th, 1920, and defendant refused to accept them.

The plaintiff has brought this action to recover damages suffered because of the defendant's refusal to accept the skins which plaintiff offered to deliver....

... In the second cause of action as amended at the trial the plaintiff alleged that any condition for approval by a representative of Jules Star & Co. of the skins to be delivered under the contract of September 10th was waived and excused because the approval was unreasonably withheld, and because defendant prevented Jules Star & Co. from giving such approval and "because defendant and said Jules Star & Co. wrongfully and knowingly colluded to withhold that approval, with intent to avoid defendant's having to accept the said skins." The issues raised by the denial to these allegations were submitted to the jury and decided in favor of the plaintiff....

We have pointed out that under both contracts sued upon, the seller agreed to make delivery subject to the approval of Jules Star & Co. The parties chose to stipulate that such approval must be given. It constitutes a condition which, unless waived or excused, must be fulfilled before the buyer can be compelled to accept skins that are tendered. Concededly approval of Jules Star & Co. has not been given....

... [T]he condition was waived also in regard to the contract which forms the basis of the second cause of action if refusal of approval by Jules Star & Co. was the result of bad faith on the part of Jules Star & Co. in which the defendant had some share. If by its own interference and wrong the defendant prevented the plaintiff from obtaining the stipulated approval, then the plaintiff may recover without it. We have pointed out that in the second cause of action the plaintiff has pleaded that the condition was waived and excused not only because of wrongful act on the part of the defendant but because approval was "unreasonably withheld," and the serious question raised upon this appeal is whether the plaintiff may recover under its contract upon proof that it offered to deliver skins which in quality complied with the contract requirements, and that the representative of Jules Star & Co. unreasonably withheld its approval of these skins.

The trial judge charged that if "approval was unreasonably withheld, whether Barnet had anything to do with it or not, the plaintiff could recover. Star must have acted honestly. If he showed an honest judgment the defendant is entitled to a verdict." Though the parties have stipulated that the approval of Jules Star & Co. must be obtained for any skins delivered under the contract, under the rule laid down in the charge, the plaintiff may become liable for damages if he insists upon this stipulation being carried out. It places upon the buyer the risk of determining whether Jules Star & Co. have acted reasonably; it makes the buyer determine whether approval should reasonably have been given, though not he but Jules Star & Co. were to approve of the quality of the skins. In effect it makes the buyer a guarantor of both the honesty and the good judgment of Jules Star & Co.

It is said that authority for the rule laid down in the charge may be found in many cases in this and other jurisdictions where the courts have considered the effect of unreasonable or dishonest refusal of architect or engineer to approve of work done or materials furnished, under building contracts when such approval was made a condition precedent to payment.... In those cases it must be remembered that by the nature of the contracts, if failure to obtain approval deprived the contractor of right to recover the agreed compensation the result would be that the benefit of work actually performed and materials actually furnished could be appropriated by the owner without payment, though in other respects the contractor had fully complied with his contract. It would cause forfeiture of agreed price for agreed service without any fault on the contractor's part. In the same manner as the courts have evolved the rule that under contracts of that nature there may be recovery for substantial performance, they have evolved a rule that permits recovery without stipulated certificate of approval where the certificate has been wrongfully or unreasonably refused....

So, too, in some cases where the contract shows that the person whose approval is required under the contract is merely an agent of a buyer, selected by the buyer to pass upon the goods in the buyer's place, wrong on the part of the agent is imputed to the principal....

Here the contract is of different nature. The parties agree that a designated broker acting as expert and not simply as the buyer's agent must pass upon the goods and delivery must be made subject to the expert's approval. Refusal to approve by the expert does not enable the buyer to obtain property from the seller without payment. According to the terms of the contract it merely permits him to refuse to accept the goods because he stipulated not merely for goods of a certain quality but for goods of that quality approved by a particular expert. To compel him to accept and pay for the goods without such approval is to impose liability upon him that he had not agreed to assume, and gives compensation to the seller for goods not delivered in full compliance with contract. The theoretical soundness of the rule applied to building contracts has not escaped criticism. It rests upon the basis that enforcement of the contract according to its strict terms would cause forfeiture of compensation for work done or materials furnished. The rule should not be extended by analogy where the reason for the rule fails.... Unless the certificate has been withheld dishonestly and in bad faith, and the defendant is a party to that bad faith through control of the expert or collusion with him, there may be no recovery under the second cause of action.

There are cases where parties stipulate for the approval or certificate of a third person, not as part of the contractual obligation of either party to the contract but rather as machinery for avoiding dispute between the parties as to whether these obligations have been properly performed. Question may then arise as to whether the stipulated approval or certificate constitutes in full sense a condition precedent to recovery, or whether there may be recovery based on substantial performance, upon proof that in other respects the contract has been fully complied with. Such question we do not now decide. Doubtless there are cases where such hardship would be imposed upon a party who performs work or manufactures goods at the special instance of another if payment were withheld merely because approval is wrongfully refused, that argument may well be made that such result was not intended by the parties. Here we have no such circumstances. The plaintiff's obligation is only to deliver certain goods, and by express stipulation there may be no delivery without approval of a third party. It has done nothing for which it might legally or equitably expect compensation until delivery is made. If approval is withheld the plaintiff cannot perform; it loses the profit which it might have otherwise made by delivery of goods at a contract price higher than the then prevailing market price. It assumed this risk. It still retains the goods and may sell them at market price. The defendant should not be required to pay the contract price unless the plaintiff performs according to contract "subject to the approval" of the third party....

The judgments should be reversed and a new trial granted, with costs to abide the event.

CARDOZO, POUND, and ANDREWS, JJ., concur; HISCOCK, C.J., McLAUGHLIN, and CRANE, JJ., dissent.

NOTES AND QUESTIONS

1. *Material from the briefs and record — the buyer's story:* The briefs and record in the case disclose that the jury was presented with two conflicting stories about the transaction. It was agreed that calfskins from farmers and butchers outside of New York City were likely to be of lower quality than New York City skins. Those slaughtering calves in New York City exercised care so that the skins would not be marked, and it was customary in New York City to use a special salt that did not discolor in the tanning process. The Barnet Leather Company, the buyer, offered evidence that before the contract involved in the case was signed, representatives of the seller had tried to sell calfskins to Barnet. Barnet refused because Van Iderstine "does not handle skins that are satisfactory to us, on account of buying outside skins, and our experience has been such that we have refrained from buying from you since last year."

Jules Star & Co. was a broker handling calfskins. It offered seller's skins to buyer on the standard form contract in the industry. The contract provided that the skins were "to be received by Jules Star & Co.'s representative subject to their approval." Star told his employees to bend over backwards to find the skins acceptable if possible, but they found that the skins were not of acceptable quality. Van Iderstine's representatives asked that Jules Star himself look at the skins. He did, and he testified:

I could not approve of that kind of skins, that is not what the contracts call for.... I found that the condition of the skins was very bad, they were ... in the worst shape I have ever been presented with New York City skins by anybody. I did not trust my eyes when I really saw this lot of poor stuff laying there coming out of that pack, and satisfying myself from all over that they were poor all the way through.... [The] custom of the trade is to reject a lot of skins if a proportion of these country and resalted and old outside city skins is mixed in with a supposedly first-class New York City first salted skin.

Van Iderstine's representatives then contacted Mr. Barnet, the buyer, and complained about the rejection. Barnet testified:

So I told both of them that Mr. Star was our representative and the skins had been sold subject to his approval and that was final, as it had been final in every other transaction we had ever made through Star with them, or with anybody else, and that we would not have inserted in our contract that they were subject to the approval of Jules Star if it did not mean something. They were not satisfied, nevertheless, with Star's rejection and they begged me to come over. I decided that I would go over in all fairness to determine whether these skins were as Star reported to us or not, but without any obligation of any kind on our part.... [It] was a shame to call that [material offered] a first salted New York City skin and try to force him [Star] to take that kind of stuff.

Finally, the buyer offered the testimony of a former Van Iderstine Company employee. He said that Van Iderstine collected many skins from farmers and others outside New York City, including people known in the business to offer lower-quality goods. Then Van Iderstine would mix the best of the outside skins in with New York City skins, offering all of them at New York City prices.

2. *Material from the briefs and record — the seller's story:* Van Iderstine, the seller, offered evidence that told a very different story. The salesman who handled the deal testified that in fact the skins offered were clean, fresh New York City calfskins. After Barnet claimed that the skins were badly scored, dirty, and not clean and bright as New York City's should be, the salesman said he responded: "The reason you do not want these skins, Mr. Barnet, is not because they are not New York City's, but due to the fact that the market has dropped badly."

3. *The trial judge's view of the evidence:* The jury found for Van Iderstine, the plaintiff seller, based on the evidence and instructions quoted. The buyer moved for a new trial in part because it was against the weight of the evidence, but its motion was denied. The trial judge said "the court would not have disturbed the verdict whichever way it went, although its impressions upon the trial were distinctly in favor of the merit of the plaintiff's [seller's] claim, and the impression has not been changed by the further consideration of the testimony."

4. *Can you distinguish* Jacob & Youngs v. Kent? The famous case of *Jacob & Youngs v. Kent*, described in the note immediately preceding the *Van Iderstine* case, was decided by the same court only five years earlier. Judge Cardozo, who concurred with the majority in *Van Iderstine*, wrote the majority opinion in *Jacob & Youngs*. Can the cases be distinguished? In one case the expert's lack of certification is upheld in the face of a claim of substantial performance, and in the other the expert's action is overridden.

5. Van Iderstine *under the UCC:* Would the *Van Iderstine* case be decided differently today now that such a transaction in goods is governed by the UCC? Section 2-513 deals with a buyer's right to inspect goods, but it does not mention inspections by experts. Would a sale of calfskins "to be received by Jules Star & Co.'s representative subject to their approval" be governed by §2-515(b)? It provides:

> In furtherance of the adjustment of any claim or dispute ... the parties may agree to a third party inspection or survey to determine the conformity or condition of the goods and may agree that the findings shall be binding upon them in any subsequent litigation or adjustment.

Does this section cover only claims or disputes that have already arisen, or would it apply to potential claims or disputes that might arise as well? Does the first phrase mean adjusting any existing claim or dispute, or would it also include adjusting any potential claim or dispute?

4. Conditions of Satisfaction

HELPRIN v. HARCOURT

277 F. Supp. 2d 327 (S.D.N.Y. 2003)

MARRERO, DISTRICT JUDGE.

Plaintiff Mark Helprin filed a complaint against defendants Harcourt Brace Jovanovich, Inc., and Harcourt, Inc., alleging that Harcourt committed fraud by making certain misstatements and concealing its failure to fulfill certain obligations pursuant to a publishing agreement between Helprin and Harcourt (the "Agreement") ... and breached the Agreement by ... failing to publish Helprin's second work produced pursuant to the Agreement ... Harcourt in turn filed a motion pursuant to Rule 12(b)(6) of the Federal Rules of Civil Procedure to dismiss the complaint in its entirety.... For the reasons discussed below, the Motion is [denied].

I. FACTS

At its heart, the instant case is more than a dispute between two parties over the interpretation of a contract. It is "a dispute over creativity and the respective responsibilities of an author and his publisher." *Doubleday & Co., Inc. v. Curtis*, 599 F.Supp. 779, 780 (S.D.N.Y. 1984). Yet, despite the disagreement that brings the parties before the Court, certain facts are undisputed.

Both parties acknowledge that Helprin is a world-famous, talented author whose previous works have earned both commercial and critical acclaim. In addition, both parties agree that in 1989, Helprin and Harcourt entered into the Agreement, which obligated Helprin to produce five works over an indefinite time period in exchange for, among other things, a $2,000,000 advance and royalties from sales of the works.... In conjunction with the signing of the agreement, Harcourt purchased a $2,000,000 insurance policy on Helprin's life to protect Harcourt in the event that Helprin died before he was able to fulfill his obligations under the agreement. Finally, both parties concur that in 1995, Harcourt published the first work by Helprin under the Agreement, entitled *Memoir from Antproof Case* (the "First Work"), and Helprin did not submit a draft of his next work (the "Contested Work") until October 24, 2002. Past those points of agreement lie the contested issues of the instant litigation.

In the complaint, Helprin alleges he received no response to his submission of the Contested Work until December 17, 2002, when Dan Farley, president of Harcourt, informed Helprin via letter that Harcourt was rejecting the Contested Work for publication because it was "unacceptable as defined in paragraph 16 of the Agreement." ... In the Agreement, the standard for determining what constitutes an "acceptable" Work is described as follows:

> A Work shall be "acceptable" under this Agreement if such Work meets a standard comparable to the literary merit of [Helprin's] previous works.

The Agreement further stated that in the event Harcourt did reject a Work because it was not acceptable, Helprin would regain all rights with respect to such Work upon notice of the rejection. Helprin then would be obligated to use his best efforts to sell the Work to another publisher, and some of the payments he received from such a deal would first go to Harcourt to reimburse it for certain portions of the Advance that went unrecouped because of the rejection.

Helprin alleges that Harcourt's rejection of the Contested Work was a breach of contract motivated by Harcourt's belief that the Contested Work would not be commercially successful and by Harcourt's desire to avoid spending money on advertising and promoting the Contested Work....

II. DISCUSSION

A. Standard of Review

Dismissal of a complaint for failure to state a claim pursuant to Fed. R. Civ. P. 12(b)(6) is proper only where it appears beyond doubt that the plaintiff can prove no set of facts in support of his claim that would entitle him to relief.... On a motion to dismiss pursuant to Fed. R. Civ. P. 12(b)(6), a court accepts all well-pleaded factual assertions in the complaint as true and draws all reasonable inferences in favor of the plaintiff.... ...

B. Breach of Contract Claim Based on Rejection of the Contested Work

Helprin's first claim for relief alleges that Harcourt breached the Agreement when it rejected the Contested Work. Harcourt responds that paragraph 8 of the Agreement prevents Helprin from instigating a lawsuit because it provides that:

> [I]f a Work is not published within the time provided in Paragraph 6 ...
> [Helprin] may thereafter request [Harcourt] by written notice ... to publish

such Work within six months after [Harcourt's] receipt of [Helprin's] request. If, after receipt of such notice, [Harcourt] fails to publish such Work within such period, this Agreement will terminate with respect to such Work immediately and automatically at the end of such period, all rights to such Work will revert to [Helprin] on the effective date of termination without further obligation or liability on the part of [Harcourt], and [Helprin] will have the right to retain any advances previously paid, *but will be entitled to no other compensation, remedy, or damages,* and [Helprin] will retain the right to sell such Work to another publisher and retain the proceeds. [Harcourt's] failure to publish a Work that it has accepted according to the provisions of paragraphs 16 and 17 hereof will not alter the conditions under which [Helprin] is deemed to have satisfied his obligation in regard to such Work. (Emphasis added by the Court.) Paragraph 6 requires that "within eighteen months after delivery and acceptance of the final revised manuscript of a Work hereunder, [Harcourt] will publish such Work at its own expense," and Harcourt contends that the Contested Work is an acceptable Work for purposes of paragraphs 6 and 8—despite Harcourt's rejection of it—because "Helprin has pleaded [in the Complaint] that [the Contested Work] met the standards of paragraph 16(a) and therefore under that paragraph's express terms it is deemed to be accepted by Harcourt."

1. *What Constitutes an "Acceptable" Work?*

Harcourt's argument raises the crucial question at the heart of Helprin's claim: what constitutes an "acceptable" work under the Agreement? To answer that question, the Court first looks at paragraph 16(a) of the Agreement, which states as follows:

[Harcourt] recognizes its obligation to give editorial assistance to [Helprin] in order to assist [him] in making the manuscript of each Work hereunder acceptable for publication by [Harcourt]. However, [Harcourt] reserves the right to determine the amount and usefulness of its editorial assistance and whether or not its editorial intervention will result in an acceptable manuscript that merits publication by [Harcourt]. A Work shall be "acceptable" under this Agreement if such Work meets a standard comparable to the literary merit of [Helprin's] previous works. When the manuscript of a Work meets the foregoing standard, [Harcourt] shall notify [Helprin] of its acceptance thereof in accordance with paragraph 17 hereof. [Helprin] recognizes [his] obligation to deliver manuscripts that are complete and acceptable in accordance herewith and to participate in the editorial process for that purpose.[21]

Helprin contends that this paragraph was drafted in a way that "substantially alter[ed Harcourt's] discretion in accepting or rejecting a manuscript." However, in

---

21. [2] A handwritten footnote to paragraph 16(a)—which appears to be initialed by both signatories to the Agreement, Helprin and Peter Jovanovich, and which neither party contests as being inaccurate—provides that "the final shape of the manuscript will be determined according to the author's sole discretion."

reviewing other cases before this Court involving similar contractual obligations, the Court reaches a different conclusion.

In prior cases with analogous fact patterns, the publishing agreements at issue have allowed the publisher to terminate the contract if, in the publisher's sole discretion, it deemed the submitted manuscript to be unsatisfactory. *See Doubleday & Co. v. Curtis,* 763 F.2d 495, 497 (2d Cir.1985) (contract could be terminated if delivered manuscript was not "satisfactory to Publisher in content and form."); *Random House, Inc. v. Gold,* 464 F.Supp. 1306, 1307 (S.D.N.Y.), *aff'd,* 607 F.2d 998 (2d Cir.1979) (same); *Nance v. Random House, Inc.,* 212 F. Supp. 2d 268, 272 (S.D N.Y. 2002) (author's "manuscripts had to be 'complete and satisfactory to [the] Publisher,' and … publishers could reject a manuscript if they found it 'unacceptable for any reason.' ") (citations omitted); *Random House, Inc. v. Curry,* 747 F.Supp. 191, 193 (S.D.N.Y. 1990) (contract could be terminated "if any manuscript that is delivered is not, in the Publisher's judgment, satisfactory …"); *Dell Publishing Co., Inc. v. Whedon,* 577 F.Supp. 1459, 1460 (S.D.N.Y. 1984) (author had to return advances if delivered work was not satisfactory to publisher "in form, style and content"); *Harcourt Brace Jovanovich, Inc. v. Goldwater,* 532 F.Supp. 619, 620 (S.D.N.Y. 1982) (author required to deliver to publisher a work "satisfactory to the publisher in form and content."); *see also Chodos v. West Publishing Co., Inc.,* 292 F.3d 992, 997 (9th Cir. 2002) (publisher could terminate agreement if publisher deemed work or portion thereof unacceptable and author did not cure such identified problems within thirty days of notice of such problems).

Despite Helprin's contention, the Court finds the portion of paragraph 16(a) set forth above to endow the publisher in this action with the same type of discretion as that conferred by similar contract language employed in the previously cited cases. In a contractual relationship such as this one, it would be illogical for the acceptability of the Work for publication to be ultimately judged by the author. If that were the case, Helprin could submit any writing to Harcourt, regardless of its coherence, artistic merit, or state of completion, and unilaterally declare it to be an acceptable work comparable to the literary merit of his previous works. Since the Agreement does not provide for an outside individual or panel to judge the quality of the submitted Work, the decision as to whether the Work is an "acceptable manuscript that merits publication by Harcourt" must logically fall in the final analysis to the only other party to the Agreement, namely the publisher, Harcourt....

Such a conclusion is bolstered by a closer reading of paragraph 16(a) as a whole. The first sentence notes that Harcourt is obligated to provide editorial assistance to Helprin in order to help make the Work "acceptable for publication *by [Harcourt]*." … (Emphasis added by the Court.) Through this clause, Harcourt acknowledged that it would need to participate in the revision process to ensure that the Work would satisfy its own standard of acceptability for publication.

Later in the paragraph, in the sentence immediately following the definition of "acceptable," Harcourt makes it a condition precedent that the submitted Work satisfy the standard of acceptability before Harcourt will notify Helprin that Harcourt accepts the submitted Work for publication. (*See* Agreement, *supra,* at ¶ 16(a)) ("When the manuscript of a Work meets the foregoing standard, [Harcourt] shall notify [Helprin] of its acceptance thereof in accordance with paragraph 17 hereof.") This same sentence makes reference to paragraph 17 in defining how notification should be made. Paragraph 17, entitled Notice of Acceptance or Termination, reads:

> Termination of this Agreement and *acceptance by [Harcourt] of a finally revised manuscript* shall be made only by a specific written notice signed by an Officer of [Harcourt]. Editorial comments concerning the intent or execution of a Work, approvals of parts of the manuscript, acknowledgment of the physical receipt of a manuscript, requests for changes, and other matters in communications to [Helprin] will not constitute acceptance or conditional acceptance by [Harcourt].[22] (Emphasis added by the Court.)

Thus, as the [italicized] terms unequivocally provide, the ultimate acceptance of a "finally" edited work is to be given "by Harcourt." In order for Harcourt to accept a submitted Work, it has to execute a written notice signed by an officer of the company explicitly stating *Harcourt's* acceptance of the Work. The second sentence's clarification that certain preliminary editorial comments and other communications to Helprin that do not explicitly express Harcourt's acceptance "do not constitute acceptance" demonstrates the intent of the parties to make clear that, as a condition precedent, Harcourt had to determine to unequivocally accept the Work in order for the acceptance to qualify under the Agreement's definition.

Another manifestation of this intent is contained in paragraph 16(c), discussed below, governing the procedure to be followed in the event Harcourt does determine that a manuscript of the Work "*is not acceptable to Harcourt.*" (Emphasis added by the Court.) As a result, for Harcourt now to contend in its response to Helprin's allegations that paragraph 8 is relevant because Helprin has pleaded that the Contested Work is acceptable invokes a form of circular reasoning that the Court rejects. A contract provision cannot be read to have been fulfilled simply because, in a pleading and without more, one party says so. The claim at issue does not involve Helprin's view of the quality of the Contested Work—which would most likely be favorably biased—but rather Harcourt's assertion in its letter dated December 17, 2002, that the Contested Work was not acceptable. Consequently, paragraphs 6 and 8 are inapplicable to the factual situation as Helprin has pleaded it.

2. Harcourt's Good Faith

Having rejected both Helprin's contention that the acceptability clause is distinct from other such clauses in the publishing industry and Harcourt's assertion that paragraphs 6 and 8 should govern the situation presented here, ... the Court turns to paragraph 16(c), which contemplates a prospect identical to the factual situation at hand:

---

22. [4] Because the paragraph is titled "Notice of Acceptance *or* Termination," the Court assumes that the first sentence should have read, or at least be interpreted as saying: "Termination of this Agreement *or* acceptance by Harcourt...."

> In the event that Harcourt determines in accordance with this Agreement that the manuscript of a Work is not acceptable to it, it shall so notify Helprin and upon such notice all rights with respect to such Work granted or transferred to Harcourt under this Agreement will automatically revert to Helprin.

The paragraph continues by stating that upon such rejection, Helprin is obligated to use his best efforts to sell the Work to another publisher and, if successful, return some of the profits from that sale to Harcourt so Harcourt could recoup the portion of the advance that applied to the Contested Work. In light of paragraph 16(c), Harcourt might be inclined to argue that it is under no obligation to publish a submission that it finds unacceptable. Harcourt does not make such an argument, perhaps in part because of the existence of a significant body of precedent in this Court that directly addresses when a publisher is permitted to reject a submitted work from an author who is under contract with that publisher.

In at least six cases in recent years with similar fact patterns to the instant case, the Court has interpreted comparable "acceptability" clauses as granting publishers wide discretion to terminate publishing contracts if the submitted draft is not acceptable, "provided that the termination is made in good faith, and that the failure of the author to submit a satisfactory manuscript was not caused by the publisher's bad faith." *Curtis,* 763 F.2d at 501; *see also Gold,* 464 F.Supp. at 1308; *Nance,* 212 F.Supp.2d at 272; *Curry,* 747 F.Supp. at 193; *Whedon,* 577 F.Supp. at 1462; *Goldwater,* 532 F.Supp. at 624. The Court reached these holdings based in part on analogous breach of contract cases considered by New York courts where the satisfactory performance of one party was to be judged by another party. In such cases, the New York courts required the party terminating the contract to act in good faith.

In *Curtis,* for example, the Court observed that:

> This principle — that a contract containing a "satisfaction clause" may be terminated only as a result of honest dissatisfaction — would seem especially appropriate in construing publishing agreements. To shield from scrutiny the already chimerical process of evaluating literary value would render the "satisfaction" clause an illusory promise, and place authors at the unbridled mercy of their editors.

763 F.2d at 500; *see also Goldwater,* 532 F. Supp. at 624 ("It cannot be, however, that the publisher has absolutely unfettered license to act or not to act in any way it wishes and to accept or reject a book for any reason whatever. If this were the case, the publisher could simply make a contract and arbitrarily change its mind and that would be an illusory contract.").

Furthermore, testimony at some of the Court's cases established that publishing industry practice has always involved "significant editorial changes, and that it is 'inconceivable'... that a publisher would reject a completed manuscript written under contract, without first offering or providing some editorial assistance to revise it." *Whedon,* 577 F. Supp. at 1463 n. 4; *see also Goldwater,* 532 F. Supp. at 624 (observing that both parties' witnesses testified that the "custom of the trade" establishes an implied good faith obligation on the part of a publisher to engage in appropriate editorial work with the author).

Thus, in determining whether the publisher in each of the foregoing cases acted in good faith, the Court focused primarily on the amount of editorial assistance the publisher provided. A publisher that provided a "detailed and lengthy editorial analysis of the shortcomings in the plot, characters and pacing of the submitted draft" demonstrated its good faith in offering sufficient editorial assistance. *Nance,* 212 F. Supp. 2d at 273; *see also Curtis,* 763 F.2d at 498, 501 (finding that publisher's thorough review and offers of subsequent help demonstrated good faith); *Gold,* 464 F. Supp. at 1307–10 (finding that publisher's editorial comments and assistance demonstrated good faith). A publisher that did "nothing approaching any [kind of] sensible editorial activity" and failed to provide any "comments of a detailed nature designed to give the author an opportunity to remedy defects" failed the test and could be considered in possible breach of its agreement. *Goldwater,* 532 F. Supp. at 624; *Whedon,* 577 F. Supp. at 1462–63 (concluding that publisher did not act in good faith when calling manuscript unsatisfactory because it did not offer "detailed explication of the problems it saw in the manuscript, and an opportunity to revise [the manuscript] along the lines its editors suggested.").

Based on the Complaint, the Court finds that Helprin has pled sufficient facts to state a sufficient claim at this point in the litigation that Harcourt did not act in good faith when judging the Contested Work unacceptable. Helprin alleges that he sent the Contested Work to Harcourt, and less than two months later received a letter back saying only that the Contested Work was being rejected because it was unacceptable as defined in paragraph 16 of the Agreement. There is no indication at this stage from either party that Harcourt offered any further editorial comments or assistance, nor has it been alleged by either party that Harcourt allowed Helprin an opportunity to cure whatever defects Harcourt found in the Contested Work. As a result, the Court finds that Helprin has met his burden to state a claim with regard to breach of contract based on rejection of the Contested Work....

E. Helprin's Requested Forms of Relief

In addition to Harcourt's opposition to Helprin's claims, Harcourt contends that some forms of relief requested by Helprin in the Complaint are improper. Specifically, among various remedies, Helprin seeks: (1) rescission of the Agreement, causing the rights to all Works written by Helprin under the Agreement to revert to him, leaving Helprin with no further obligations to Harcourt, and providing Harcourt with no further rights under the Agreement, [and] (2) punitive damages of $10 million....

1. *Rescission*

Helprin seeks rescission of the Agreement on the ground that a material breach has occurred. "Under New York law, 'rescission is an extraordinary remedy, appropriate only where the breach is found to be material and willful, or, if not willful, so substantial and fundamental as to strongly tend to defeat the object of the parties in making the contract.'" (citations omitted) ... "Courts generally permit rescission of a contract only when it appears reasonably feasible to return the parties to their respective positions prior to the contract." (citations omitted)

Harcourt contests Helprin's request, asserting that the alleged breach is not material, willful, substantial or fundamental, that Helprin has not offered to restore the status quo, and that he has an adequate remedy at law. The Court is not persuaded that the alleged breach is not significant enough to qualify for rescission. The test for determining the materiality of a breach for purposes of rescission is whether the alleged breach is "of such nature and such importance that the contract would not have been made without it." Richard A. Lord, *Williston on Contracts* § 68:2, at 42 (4th ed. 2003). Assuming that Helprin's allegation that Harcourt rejected the Contested Work in bad faith is correct, it is fair to conclude that such a rejection could serve to undermine the entire purpose of the Agreement, which was to produce the Works for Harcourt to publish.

Harcourt's other arguments fail as well. Harcourt asserts that the right of rescission cannot be exercised without a return or an offer to return such benefits.... [T]he New York Court of Appeals has stated that it is sufficient for the offer to return the benefits to be stated in the complaint. While Helprin did not make such an offer in the complaint, and in fact requested that Harcourt be declared unable to recoup any of the advance, Helprin has also indicated his willingness to follow the Court's orders if the Court demands that he return a portion of the advance in order to be entitled to rescission. (*See* Memorandum of Mark Helprin in Opposition to Defendants' Motion to Dismiss Pursuant to Fed. R. Civ. P. 12(b)(6), undated, at 10.) Because the restoration of benefits to Harcourt consists simply of returning the unrecouped portion of the advance, and therefore is easily identifiable and performable by Helprin, the Court is not inclined to dismiss Helprin's request for rescission at this time solely based on his initial failure to offer to return the unrecouped portion of the advance.

Finally, Harcourt asserts that Helprin's claim for breach of contract based on the rejection of the Contested Work can be adequately remedied by money damages reflecting lost royalties. This argument ignores Helprin's concerns regarding his ability to publish future Works under the Agreement and the possible lost trust between him and Harcourt that could make it difficult for a working relationship to continue in the future. If the trier of fact eventually finds these concerns have merit, money damages may not be sufficient as a remedy. Thus, at this stage of the proceeding, the Court is satisfied that Helprin's allegations on these issues demonstrate that a request for rescission should be maintained as a possible remedy should the instant case be resolved in favor of Helprin.

2. Punitive Damages

Helprin also seeks $10 million in punitive damages against Harcourt. Under New York law, punitive damages are not available in the ordinary breach of contract case.... However, such damages are available if the plaintiff demonstrates, at a minimum, that the defendant's conduct was (1) actionable as an independent tort; (2) egregious in nature; and (3) directed towards plaintiff.... The Court is not persuaded that Helprin has alleged sufficient facts to sustain a claim of egregious tortuous conduct that is independent from Harcourt's alleged bad faith rejection of the Contested Work. *See Continental Info. Sys. Corp. v. Federal Ins. Co.*, No. 02 Civ. 4168, 2003 WL 145561, at *3 (S.D.N.Y. Jan. 17, 2003) (finding that in order to obtain punitive damages, plaintiff must allege tortuous conduct "independent of plaintiff's claim of bad faith denial of insurance coverage"). As a result, Harcourt's motion to strike Helprin's request for punitive damages is granted....

III. ORDER

For the reasons described above, it is hereby

ORDERED that Harcourt's motion to dismiss with regard to the first claim in the Complaint is DENIED; and it is further

ORDERED that the claim for punitive damages in the first claim in the Complaint is stricken....

NOTES AND QUESTIONS

1. *What remedy did each party want?* The plaintiff, Mark Helprin, sought rescission of the Agreement, which the court holds would require plaintiff to return the "un-recouped" part of the advance. Suppose plaintiff did not seek rescission. What were plaintiff's rights under the contract once Harcourt rejected the second manuscript? See the description of the contract terms in the opinion's fact section. With respect to the second manuscript, is there a difference between the two remedies? Of course, rescission would leave plaintiff free to submit future manuscripts to publishers other than Harcourt.

2. *Another publishing case:* Joan Collins, an actress who played a scheming businesswoman on the television series *Dynasty*, made a contract to write two books for Random House. Her agent, Irving (Swifty) Lazar,[23] negotiated a clause providing that all she had to submit was a "complete manuscript." In other words, he had sufficient bargaining power to negotiate the standard "satisfactory to the publisher" clause out of the contract. Ms. Collins submitted two manuscripts, but Random House argued that it was not liable to pay her for them because they were unreadable and unpublishable. She sued, and the issue tried to a jury was whether what she had submitted

---

23. Irving Lazar's obituary tells us that Lazar went to Fordham University and then Brooklyn Law School, where one of his professors — recognizing Lazar's well-honed persuasive talents — hired him to solicit students for a bar preparation class. Lazar graduated in 1930, worked briefly in a Manhattan law office representing show business clients, and became an agent at the Music Corporation of America. The reason, he said, was simple: he preferred an agent's 10 percent commission to an attorney's 1 percent. Dubbed Swifty after he accepted a dare and made five movie deals in one day for his friend Humphrey Bogart, Lazar had since the 1940s commanded record-setting fees for hundreds of writers, producers, directors, choreographers, composers, and lyricists around the world. "I am a literary agent. A national literary agent.... You can't be a Hollywood agent and handle Moss Hart, Teddy White, Arthur Schlesinger, Roald Dahl, Noel Coward, Francoise Sagan, Georges Clouzot," Lazar once told *New York* magazine. Amy Wallace, *Agent Swifty Lazar, Pioneer Deal-Packages, Dies at 86*, L.A. Times, Dec. 31, 1993, at A1. Lazar often negotiated very high fees from publishers for books written (or said to be written) by his celebrity clients.

was a "complete manuscript." A Random House lawyer summarized one of her plot lines: "Stephanie has a miscarriage and tells a doctor or nurse not to tell anyone, while she goes about trying to adopt a baby. In the meantime, she pretends for eight months to be pregnant. When the husband of her best friend sees her without her pregnancy disguise, she murders him. Then she runs to the forest to give birth to her imaginary child."[24] The jury found for Ms. Collins on the first manuscript but for Random House on the second. One juror said: "A good editor can virtually take the phone book and turn it into something reasonable."[25]

The then-Director of Legal Services for the Authors' Guild said:

> As Collins discovered with her repeated humiliation in and out of court, the price for standing up for your contractual rights can be dear. Most writers cannot afford litigation and, faced with wrongful rejection of their manuscripts, can only write off the time, work, and enormous personal and financial cost of writing a book nobody wants anymore....
>
> Whether Collins submitted two manuscripts as the parties honestly envisioned them was a question for the jury. But, even though the jury found Collins had lived up to her side of the bargain on one book, the verdict does not represent a victory for writers. Random House and other publishers will simply do what they've always done when a court has held their own contract language against them: They'll adjust their contracts and practices to maintain their current level of control over their authors.[26]

3. *How else might publishers exert control?* Publishers have another way to reject books for which they contracted that they later decide they do not want to publish. Typically, publishing contracts set a date by which the author is to submit a manuscript. Authors often fail to meet these submission dates. The publisher can cancel the deal because of the delay. However, authors with strong reputations usually get an advance payment from the publisher when they sign the contract. While the publisher would have a cause of action to recover the advance in most cases, in practical terms, few authors would be able to repay it. The *New York Times* reported:

> Often by the time a book is canceled, a good bit of ... [the] advance has been paid to the writer, and the disenchanted publisher wants the money back. Usually, the only practical way to get it is for another publisher to buy the book and give the writer an advance large enough to live on and at the same time pay back at least some of the advance to the first publisher. Since any other method of recovery is largely wishful thinking, trashing the product doesn't help.[27]

---

24. N.Y. Times, Feb. 13, 1996, at A13.
25. N.Y. Times, Feb. 14, 1996, at A1.
26. Kay Murray, *Collins Verdict: Beware, Book Authors*, Newsday, Feb. 21, 1996, at A29.
27. Martin Arnold, *Making Books; The Many Ways of Saying "No,"* N.Y. Times, Apr. 30, 1998, at E3.

4. ***Personal approval in house-building contracts:*** In *Haymore v. Levinson*,[28] owners and builder entered a contract for the construction of a house. $3,000 of the purchase price was placed in escrow until the "satisfactory completion of the work." The owners gave the builder a list of things to be done, and after these items were finished, they refused to release the money because they still were not satisfied. The builder recovered $2,739,[29] and the owners appealed, asserting that there had been no "satisfactory completion" of the contract. They argued that the phrase should be given a subjective meaning: "unless they are satisfied and so declare, the money is not payable."

The Supreme Court of Utah affirmed. It said that if the work were reasonable under the circumstances, the builder was entitled to recover. The court said that where the purpose of the contract is "pleasing taste, fancy, or sensibility of another," then a subjective standard will be applied. Where, however, the purpose is operative fitness, mechanical utility, or structural completion, an objective standard will be applied: "that is, the party favored by such a provision has no arbitrary privilege of declining to acknowledge satisfaction and he cannot withhold approval unless there is apparent some reasonable justification for doing so."

The owners argued that free contract required a subjective standard. "If parties are not legally bound by their contracts, there could be no order or progress in the business world." Moreover, "a house should rank high among those aesthetic things which are dependent upon personal satisfaction and taste." The owners spent a substantial sum to buy a home. "There they would live their lives, and there they would entertain their friends, relatives, and social visitors. It would be difficult to say that the finishing and decorating of a house does not contribute to one's personal fancy, taste, and judgment."

The court rejected this argument. Why? Building contractors often complain that the last installment is difficult to collect. They say that homeowners often cannot visualize what will be built from a set of drawings, and they often have unrealistic expectations about cost, time, progress, and quality. Homeowners complain that it is very difficult to get builders to finish a job. In the *Haymore* case, the owners complained of such matters as: the dishwasher protruded two inches beyond the rest of the cabinet because it was the wrong size, acoustical tile had started to fall off the basement ceiling, there was a hole in one of the basement bedroom walls, the doors in the house were warped, and cement walls and slabs had cracked. The builder offered experts who said that the defects were minor and not structural, and the builder testified that it tried to make repairs until the owners ordered its workers off the premises.

Do courts seem appropriate places to resolve disputes of this sort?

---

28. 8 Utah 2d 66, 328 P.2d 307 (1958).

29. The Inflation Calculator, *available at* http://www.westegg.com/inflation, tells us that what cost $2,700 in 1958 would cost $22,355.59 in 2015.

B. CONDITIONS AND THE UNIFORM COMMERCIAL CODE

1. The General Pattern

To what extent does the UCC follow the approach of the Restatement (Second) of Contracts for cases coming within Article 2? Standing alone, § 2-601 appears to state what has been called the "perfect tender" rule. With some important qualifications, it says that "if the goods ... fail *in any respect* to conform to the contract, the buyer may ... reject the whole...." [Emphasis added.] For example, in a pre-UCC case, *Frankel v. Foreman & Clark*,[30] the court permitted rejection of an entire shipment of coats although the jury found that there was a trivial or inconsequential failure to comply with the contract, involving only 1 or 2 percent of the coats. Would a court be likely to reach this result under the UCC? White and Summers[31] think not, saying:

> [T]he code ... erodes the [perfect tender] rule. First of all, § 2-601 renders the perfect tender rule inapplicable to installment contracts, and 2-612 permits rejection in such contracts only if "the nonconformity substantially impairs the value of that installment...." The seller's right to cure a defective tender, in 2-508 ... is a further restriction upon the buyer's apparent right to reject for insubstantial defects under 2-601. Additional restrictions upon the perfect tender rule in 2-601 may be found in 2-504 (an improper shipment contract that causes a late delivery is grounds for rejection only if "material delay or loss ensues")[32] and in the Code's general invitations to use trade usage, course of dealing, and course of performance in interpretation.... The courts may also deny rejection for what they regard as insubstantial defects by manipulating the procedural requirements for rejection. That is, if the court concludes that a buyer ought to be denied his right to reject because he has suffered no or only minor damage, the court might arrive at that conclusion by finding that the buyer failed to make an effective rejection (for example, because his notice was not timely).

> We conclude, and the cases decided to date suggest, that the foregoing changes have so eroded the perfect tender rule that the law would be little changed if 2-601 gave the right to reject only upon "substantial" nonconformity.

---

30. 33 F.2d 83 (2d Cir. 1929).

31. Uniform Commercial Code at 415–16 (6th ed., 2010).

32. Eds. note: *See* Monte Carlo Shirt, Inc. v. Daewoo Int'l (America) Corp., 707 F.2d 1054 (9th Cir. 1983).

Acceptance, Rejection, Cure, Revocation under Article II:

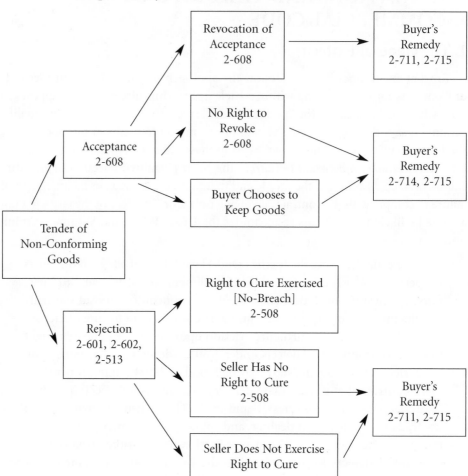

The above chart should help you see the pattern of the UCC's sections related to tender, acceptance, rejection, cure, revocation of acceptance, notices, and remedies.[33] We will be exploring these issues in greater detail in the pages that follow.

2. Inspection and Acceptance of the Goods

The following opinion illustrates the UCC's basic approach to a buyer's right to reject or return a defective performance.[34] Remember, however, that a seller may have a right to cure a defective performance under § 2-508. Furthermore, under § 2-612 installment contracts are treated differently. We will consider these variations later.

---

33. The chart is not complete. We have tried to diagram the basic pattern to help you understand it. You should ask yourself what you would add to the chart as you master all of the nuances of Article 2's sections dealing with performance of contracts.

34. However, if a defect is a seller's late delivery to a carrier, UCC § 2-504 controls.

ARDEX COSMETICS OF AMERICA v. LOGOTECH, INC.

United States District Court, Northern District of New York
2002 U.S. Dist. LEXIS 1545, 2002 WL 169393 (2002)

TREECE, J.

This is a civil action for breach of contract involving the sale of adhesive labels by defendant Logotech, Inc. ("Logotech") to plaintiff Ardex Cosmetics of America, Inc. ("Ardex")....

Finding of Facts

Ardex is a New York corporation involved in, *inter alia*, the manufacturing of perfumes and oils, which are then packaged and sold in labeled bottles to retailers.... In 1997, Ardex created a new line of oils called Ancient Oils. These oils would be contained in an amber color, cylinder-type bottle approximately two inches in height. On or about April 8, 1997, Ardex received substantial orders for the Ancient Oils line from Family Dollar of Charlotte, North Carolina. The orders were to be tentatively delivered on July 21 and August 18, 1997. To complete the order, Moses Sukljian [an Ardex manager] entered into negotiations with Logotech, a New Jersey printing company that specializes in the production of adhesive labels for many types of packages, including bottles.

There were various stages to these negotiations, such as selecting artwork, selecting colors, and determining the size of the labels. Ardex sent Logotech several samples of the Ancient Oils bottle in order to determine the specifications for the labels. Logotech was aware of the urgency of this production due to the Family Dollar order. Logotech quoted the labels at a cost of $11.42 per thousand, plus several production costs. On June 27, 1997, Ardex ordered two million labels, but contested the production costs. In July 1997, Logotech shipped the test labels to Ardex. After receiving the first shipment, Ardex began placing the labels on the Ancient Oils bottles with a label machine.... Lorretta Sukljian was in charge of this aspect of production and immediately noticed that the labels did not properly adhere to the bottles.

On or about July 12, 1997, Moses Sukljian advised Logotech's salesperson, Randy Fiorey ("Fiorey"), that the labels were peeling away from the bottles and suggested that Logotech use another type of adhesive for the remaining labels. Logotech informed Ardex that it experienced a similar problem with the sample bottles. Logotech suggested washing and then placing the labels on the bottles, a process Logotech found successful with the sample bottles. Ardex attempted this course of action after attempting to heat the labels and/or heat the bottles and then put the labels on, with the hope of activating the adhesion on the labels, which was to no avail.... Indeed, washing the bottles proved to be the soundest solution....

Logotech began delivering the two million labels on or about August 5, 1997, continuing into November 1997. Logotech then billed Ardex $30,982.42, which included the production charges that Moses Sukljian challenged. Ardex continued to experience some problems with the labels, notwithstanding the washing of the bottles prior to applying the labels. From the receipt of the initial delivery in July of the test sample labels and continuing for months thereafter, the parties discussed the problem. Nonetheless, Ardex was concerned about meeting the Family Dollar order and continued the production of their product line. The then-president of Logotech, Tuvia Leibovitz, ... [said] that the only successful remedy was to wash the bottles.

Moses Sukljian accepted Leibovitz's assertion that it was the bottles that were causing the labels to peel off. Thus, Ardex went through the arduous task of removing the first run of 255,000 labels from the bottles as well as washing and drying 550,000 bottles and then putting on labels. As mentioned earlier, this process worked best, but the labels still did not adhere properly. Ardex continued to complain. Within a week after the August 5, 1997 delivery, Logotech representative Bombardier arrived at Ardex with the hope of resolving the dilemma. Indeed, there were other occasions when Bombardier and/or Fiorey visited Ardex either to determine how things were going or to collect moneys toward the account. The last meeting occurred in February 1998.

Despite the problems, Ardex used approximately 810,000 labels on the Ancient Oils bottles, of which approximately 660,000 bottles were sent to Family Dollar. On November 5, 1997, ... Sukljian sent a check to Logotech ... in the amount of $25,322.42 ($30,982 minus the challenged production costs), with the notation "payment full" [sic]. A second check was given to Bombardier and Fiorey at the February 1998 meeting in the amount to $1,200 with the same notation. No further negotiations occurred between the parties after February 1998. Replacement of the labels was never offered by Logotech nor any other remedy provided.

Sometime in 1998, Bombardier left Logotech and began working for a competitor, Mid-Atlantic Labels, Inc. ("Mid-Atlantic").... Very interested in gaining Ardex's business, it appears that he approached Moses Sukljian on two accounts: purchase of machinery and purchase of labels for the Ancient Oils line of products....

Eventually Mid-Atlantic secured an order from Ardex for one million labels at a price substantially lower than the contract price for the same labels with Logotech. These labels were used immediately upon their delivery on or about December 17, 1998. The Mid-Atlantic labels adhered to the bottles without the bottles being washed, although approximately 100,000 Mid-Atlantic labels were placed on bottles that had been pre-washed by Ardex. The successful implementation of these Mid-Atlantic labels dispelled the notion for Moses Sukljian that a "film" or "residue" was the caused for the Logotech labels not sticking to the bottles. Rather, this was a "red flag" for him that Logotech's product was defective and the sole cause for this label debacle.

In January 1999, Logotech sent a bill for the balance it believed still due. In the same month, Ardex sent a letter to Logotech advising that "we never accepted these labels as useable merchandise," reiterated the problem with the labels, informed them that they had more than one million "defective" labels remaining, and sought a refund for the "unusable" labels. The unused labels were not returned to Logotech because Ardex felt they were unusable for anyone and thus worthless.

Ardex commenced this breach of contract action on or about December 13, 1999.

Conclusions of Law

This matter concerns the sale of goods (labels) in New York; therefore, the parties' rights and obligations are governed by Article 2 of the New York Uniform Commercial Code (N.Y. UCC).... Under N.Y. UCC §2-601, upon delivery of goods, the buyer has the right to accept or reject, in whole or in part, such goods that fail to conform to the contract. "Acceptance of the goods occurs when the buyer after a reasonable opportunity to inspect the goods signifies to the seller that the goods are conforming or that he will take or retain them in spite of their nonconformity" N.Y. UCC §2-606(1)(a).

When a buyer accepts nonconforming goods, he may revoke his acceptance of the goods pursuant to N.Y. UCC §2-608 ...

Here, Ardex noticed that the test labels did not properly adhere to the bottles and suggested that Logotech use a different adhesive on the remaining two million labels. When the first shipment arrived on or about August 15, 1997, the labels again failed to properly adhere to the bottles and again Ardex immediately informed Logotech of the problem. The parties then began negotiating a solution. While the best solution was washing the bottles prior to applying the labels, Ardex never expressed its satisfaction with the labels, but neither did Ardex unequivocally express its dissatisfaction. Despite these problems, on November 5, 1997, Ardex paid Logotech $25,322.42 for the labels. This payment constitutes acceptance of the nonconforming goods. However, Ardex's continued complaints to Logotech demonstrates that it accepted the nonconforming labels under the reasonable assumption that the adhesion problem would be seasonably cured. Thus, the issues are: whether the nonconformity was a "substantial impairment"; and whether Logotech seasonably cured the nonconformity and, if not, whether Ardex revoked its acceptance within a reasonable time.

"Substantially Impaired"

There is no dispute that the labels did not properly adhere to the bottles, regardless of whether the bottles were pre-washed. This defect clearly substantially impaired the value of the labels to Ardex. Logotech, however, contends that Ardex failed to prove that the labels did not stick because of a defect in the labels. Rather, Logotech contends that a residue or film on the bottles may have caused the problem. Ardex, however, sent sample bottles to Logotech for it to determine what adhesive needed to be used on the labels so they would properly adhere to the bottles. Logotech sent the labels to Ardex without indicating that it experienced any problems affixing the labels to the bottles. Therefore, Logotech sent nonconforming goods.

"Seasonably Cured"

The next issue is whether the solution of washing the bottles "seasonably cured" the nonconformity. Washing the sample bottles worked for Logotech and appeared to work relatively well for Ardex. Indeed, more than 600,000 Ancient Oils bottles were sent out to Family Dollar. Nonetheless, Ardex continued to lodge complaints with Logotech and the parties continued to discuss the issue until February 1998. Since Ardex never accepted Logotech's "cure" of pre-washing the bottles, and Logotech did not provide any other acceptable alternative, Logotech failed to "seasonably cure" the nonconforming labels.

Timely Revocation

The final issue is whether Ardex's revocation of acceptance in January 1999 was both timely and reasonable. "Reasonable time is not an inflexible term. It depends commonly on the circumstances of each case." ...

Here, Ardex continued to discuss the problems with the labels through February 1998. These negotiations were sufficient to extend Ardex's time to revoke its acceptance of the goods. *See* N.Y. UCC § 2-607(2) and (3).... The parties' mutual attempts to cure the nonconformity, however, ended in February 1998. Since no other cure was proffered by Logotech after February 1998, it should have been readily apparent to Ardex that it had to either retain the nonconforming goods or revoke its acceptance. *See* N.Y. UCC § 2-608(2).

Ardex contends that it did not become aware of the nonconformity until it secured new labels from Mid-Atlantic in December 1998. However, Ardex did not formally notify Logotech of its revocation until it received a bill from Logotech for the balance due on the account. It is this Court's opinion that it was this bill, and not the Mid-Atlantic labels, that raised the ire of Ardex. Thus, Ardex's contention is unpersuasive and it should have known it had an obligation to provide timely revocation of acceptance in February 1998.... Ardex did not send its unequivocal notice of revocation until January 1999. Waiting approximately one year to revoke is unreasonable under these circumstances. This untimely notice precludes Ardex from recovering the contract price....

Damages

Ardex's failure to reject or revoke the acceptance of the labels, however, does not impair any other remedy provided by Article 2 of the N.Y. UCC for nonconformity. *See* N.Y. UCC § 2-607(2).... Moreover, repeated complaints made within a reasonable time upon the receipt of the first shipment of labels is sufficient to recover damages. Since Ardex almost immediately informed Logotech that the labels were not properly adhering to the bottles, Ardex may recover damages pursuant to N.Y. U.C.C. § 2-714, which states in pertinent part:

> (1) Where the buyer has accepted goods and given notification (subsection (3) of § 2-607) he may recover as damages for any nonconformity of tender the loss resulting in the ordinary course of events from the seller's breach as determined in any manner which is reasonable....

The only issue is whether Ardex has proven damages.... Ardex has failed to provide such proof to this Court. Ardex withdrew its claim for lost profits prior to trial. Instead, Ardex seeks recovery for labor costs incurred when its employees spent time removing approximately 250,000 labels and washing approximately 910,000 bottles before securing new labels to them. The only evidence provided to the Court is a pile of payroll records and vague testimony by current and former employees that they spent hours a day for approximately one year peeling labels and washing bottles. This evidence is both qualitatively and quantitatively deficient. [The court found that Ardex's evidence failed to establish the cost of removing the labels and washing the bottles.]

It is hereby ordered that judgment be entered for defendant Logotech, Inc.

NOTES AND QUESTIONS

1. *The burden on the aggrieved party:* The court finds that Logotech, the seller, supplied defective labels. Nonetheless, it wins the lawsuit. Ardex certainly complained to Logotech, and Logotech misdiagnosed why the labels would not stick. What did Ardex do that cost it its rights? From a businessperson's standpoint, did it do anything that was unreasonable? Is the lesson of the case that a business needs legal advice when it faces a breach of contract?

2. *Section 2-601 and acceptance of the goods:* Consider UCC §§ 2-606 and 2-602. What did Ardex, the buyer, do that constituted an acceptance of the defective labels? Does a buyer have to know that goods are defective in order to accept them and thus lose its rights to reject them for any defect under § 2-601?

3. *Did the court apply the wrong section of Article 2?* After you study the *Midwest Mobile Diagnostic Imaging* case later in the course, ask yourself why the *Logotech* decision did not apply § 2-612 of the UCC. *See* § 2-612(1). Also consider whether applying the installment contract rules would have taken the court to a different result after you study *Midwest Mobile Diagnostic Imaging.*

3. Cooperation and Good Faith

ADMIRAL PLASTICS CORP. v. TRUEBLOOD, INC.
United States Court of Appeals, Sixth Circuit
436 F.2d 1335 (1971)

WEICK, J.

This appeal arose out of an action for damages filed in the District Court by Admiral Plastics Corporation (Admiral) of New York against Trueblood, Inc. (Trueblood) of Dayton, Ohio, for breach of contract in which Trueblood agreed to design and manufacture for Admiral three injection blow mold machines, at a cost of $39,750.00 per machine. Jurisdiction was based on diversity of citizenship. The case was governed by Ohio law.

The District Court, sitting without a jury, found that both parties failed to act in good faith and failed to cooperate in the performance of the contract, thus rendering the contract void. The District Court entered judgment in favor of Admiral for $29,812.50, which was the amount of its down payment to Trueblood, and dismissed Trueblood's counterclaim. Both parties appeal. We affirm.

In 1965, Admiral was a leading manufacturer and supplier of plastic containers, which were extensively used in the food, beverage, and pharmaceutical industries. Admiral could not meet the ever-increasing demand for its product, and as a result, began investigating machine manufacturing companies to determine which company could best supply Admiral with the injection blow mold machines it needed to increase production. Paul Marcus, the chief engineer for Admiral, contacted Trueblood, a manufacturer of injection mold machines, and was informed that Trueblood had never built a blow mold machine, but would consider doing so if Admiral provided the specifications.

Marcus made several trips to Trueblood's plant, the last preliminary meeting being on May 17, 1966. At this meeting Marcus described the features of the machine required by Admiral and stated that it would want Trueblood to build only the rear portion of the machine, in order to protect Admiral's trade secrets. On May 24, 1966, Marcus called Trueblood and asked for a firm quotation on the price of the machine. Trueblood quoted $39,750.00 per machine, and Marcus ordered three machines to be manufactured by Trueblood. Marcus stated that the written purchase order, the specifications, and a check for 25 percent of the total purchase price would be forthcoming.

By June 22, 1966, Trueblood had not received the purchase order, specification letter, or check from Admiral. Trueblood advised Marcus of this fact, and on June 28, Marcus informed Trueblood that the purchase order had been written, but would not be sent until the middle of July, at the end of Admiral's fiscal year. Thereafter, on July 20, 1966, Trueblood received from Admiral a check for $29,812.50, a six-page specification letter dated May 24, 1966, and the purchase order.

The specification letter stated that Trueblood would redesign (where necessary), manufacture, assemble, and test three injection blow molding machines and furnish all engineering drawings of the machine and that the delivery dates for the machines were November 1, November 15, and December 1, 1966. On July 21, 1966, Trueblood informed Admiral that there were discrepancies between the specification letter and the previous discussions with Marcus. After being assured that the specifications would be revised, Trueblood deposited Admiral's check of $29,812.50, but did not sign the purchase order.

On August 25, 1966, Marcus visited Trueblood's plant and expressed concern over the lack of progress in the construction of the machines, and the fact that Trueblood had not forwarded the design drawings. Marcus was informed that the component parts had been ordered, and also that Trueblood had not received the revised specifications. Marcus revised the specifications upon his return to New York, and Trueblood received them on September 9, 1966. These revised specifications satisfied Trueblood, except for the terms of payment, and the fact that Trueblood considered the data on the machine's automatic sequence of operation to be inadequate.

On October 19, 1966, an engineer of Admiral visited Trueblood's plant and discovered that little work had been done on the manufacture of the machines. Only one of the three machines ordered was in any stage of construction, and only to the extent of the basic weldment.

On October 26, 1966, Marcus informed Trueblood that one of the component parts ordered by Trueblood, the Egan reciproscrew, was the wrong size, and that a larger one was required. Trueblood told Marcus that to reorder the part would entail added expense. Marcus instructed Trueblood to order the larger reciproscrew and that Admiral would bear the added expense.

No design drawings of the machines were furnished to Admiral as of November 1966. On November 11, 1966, a Trueblood official visited Admiral's plant to observe Admiral's machines in operation, in order to aid Trueblood in the making of the design drawings. However, no drawings were ever furnished to Admiral.

On December 1, 1966, the Admiral engineer again visited Trueblood's plant, and again observed little progress on the construction of the machines. He was informed that the earliest possible delivery date would be March 1, 1967. Thereafter, on December 8, 1966, Admiral's attorney contacted Trueblood, asserting that Trueblood was in default, and threatened legal action unless Trueblood signed the purchase order. At this same time, Trueblood ceased work on the drawings and on the machines. No machine was ever delivered to Admiral, and Trueblood did not return the $29,812.50 down payment.[35] Both parties claimed substantial damages as the result of the other's alleged lack of performance and breach of contract.

The District Court held that Admiral and Trueblood entered into a valid contract under UCC 2-204.... With this there can be no dispute. The District Court recognized that the contract was one for the manufacture and sale of unique machines, in the designing of which neither company had any experience. It was understandable, therefore, that certain terms were left unspecified and that difficulty was encountered in designing and producing the machines. This in no way detracts from the validity of the contract.

The nature of the contract made it imperative that both parties cooperate to the fullest extent in order for the machines to be successfully designed and built. The UCC recognizes such situations where good faith and cooperation are necessary to the successful fulfillment of a contract. UCC 1-203 and 2-311. The District Court determined that both parties failed to act in good faith and failed to cooperate in the performance of the contract, thus terminating their respective obligations and rendering the contract void.

Each party has urged that whatever its shortcomings were, they were caused by the other party's initial failure to cooperate and subsequent breach of contract. The District Court found that lack of progress on the machines could not be attributed to the conduct of any one party to the contract, and we agree. There was evidence that Admiral was delinquent in furnishing the specifications, as was Trueblood in failing to furnish the machine design drawings.

The evidence is not clear as to who was at fault for ordering the wrong size Egan reciproscrew, but a resolution of this is not necessary, as both parties were sufficiently

---

35. [1] The difficulty of performing this contract for the custom-made machines is exemplified by the fact that Admiral hired, on November 7, 1966, one Ephraim Natkins as chief engineer, and on January 21, 1967, one Eli Jaffe as engineer. Both men worked almost exclusively on designing the injection blow mold machines that were finally manufactured and delivered by a Connecticut company, between September 1967 and January 1968.

at fault in other instances which justify the finding of mutual breaching of the contract. In our opinion, the findings of fact adopted by the District Court are supported by substantial evidence and are not clearly erroneous. The District Court was correct in dismissing Trueblood's counterclaim for damages against Admiral, and in not awarding to Admiral any money damages other than the return of its down payment.

The only question remaining is whether the District Court was correct in ordering the refund of Admiral's down payment of $29,812.50. We think it was.

The UCC does not provide a remedy for the specific situation of a mutual breaching of a contract.[36] We must therefore turn to other state principles of law and equity. UCC 1-103.

The rule in Ohio is: "Mutual delinquency gives rise to the presumption of mutual assent to a rescission."

We construe the parties' actions in this case, illustrated by their failure to cooperate and failure to perform tasks called for by the contract within a reasonable time, as evidence of a mutual rescission.... In *Brown v. Johnston*, 95 Ohio App. 136, 108 N.E.2d 298 (1952), a contract was mutually rescinded, and the purchaser was allowed to recover the money that he had paid on the purchase price, in excess of the benefits conferred upon him while the contract was in existence. Since Admiral received no benefits from Trueblood during the existence of the contract, it is entitled to the return of its down payment.

The judgment is affirmed in each appeal. Costs will be assessed against each appellant.

NOTES AND QUESTIONS

1. *Information from the record about the transaction:* Admiral manufactured clear plastic bottles that looked like glass but were much stronger and lighter. It wanted Trueblood to build machines to which it would attach parts that it had developed. Ray Trueblood testified that Admiral's general manager came to the Trueblood plant at the beginning of the negotiations. "We ... started to discuss his special machine and he wouldn't tell me too much because he said it was a secret, what produced over the front end was a secret and he wanted us to produce the main part of the machine in the rear." The specifications were written by Admiral's general manager, who had a degree in mechanical and industrial engineering, and they were sent to Trueblood in a seven-page letter drafted in outline form. After four pages of specifications, the following appears: "All other details may be worked out between the authorized personnel of Admiral and Trueblood." Trueblood was to design the hydraulic and electrical systems, but Trueblood's engineers were never certain about the sequence of operation. One of Admiral's engineers conceded that Trueblood's

---

36. [2] In our opinion UCC § 2-718 is not applicable to this case. The section bears some resemblance, in that it pertains to a buyer's right to restitution of his payments on the contract. However, the section specifically applies when "the seller justifiably withholds delivery of goods because of the buyer's breach." That is not the case here.

engineers would not have been able to prepare the hydraulic and electrical circuitry if they did not understand the sequence of operation. Neither Trueblood nor Admiral ever took steps to clear up the difficulty and get the project underway. Each seemed to assume that the other party was responsible for working out these matters. After the dispute arose, Admiral bought machines from another manufacturer. This time, Admiral's engineers designed exactly what they wanted in great detail. Even so, once the machines were delivered it took some effort to adjust them and make modifications so that they would work.

2. *Formation and performance:* The opinion of the trial court in the *Admiral Plastics* case suggests some of the relationships between classical notions of contract formation and a more relational contract approach based on the UCC:

> This is another one of those disturbing cases caused by the failure of both parties to have the benefit of counsel. This agreement does not pertain to the ordinary purchase of known or advertised machinery but pertains exclusively to a new type, a custom-type piece of machinery requiring the intense cooperation of each side in order to manufacture an injection blow mold machine....

> Before the enactment of the Uniform Commercial Code [*See* UCC §2-204] the evidence presented would be conclusive that no contract ever existed between these parties because there had never been a meeting of the minds regarding the obligations of each party to this transaction. Equity in such a case would restore the parties to the same position that they were on the date plaintiff claims, May 24, 1966.

> Applying the provisions of the Uniform Commercial Code, a consideration of all the evidence shows a contract between plaintiff and defendant that was breached by failure of both parties to cooperate in the performance of the contract. In law and in equity this Court concludes that each party should bear its own losses.

Does it matter whether a court follows the approach of the appellate or the trial court?

3. *Loss sharing?* Should each party bear its own losses? Trueblood, the manufacturer, expended time and effort designing and beginning production of the machine. Moreover, the Admiral order was placed on the production line in its plant, and this affected its ability to accept other orders and the scheduling of those it did accept. Admiral, however, invested time and effort negotiating the contract and trying to help Trueblood perform. In its complaint it claimed:

> [Admiral had] been damaged and will continue to be damaged in that it will be obliged to expend other and additional monies for the purchase of such machines from other suppliers at prices more expensive than those provided for by the agreement; it has lost and will continue to lose profits on the sale of plastic containers from the dates on which said machines were to have been delivered and in production to and including the dates on which substitute machines may be delivered and be in production; it has lost the value

of drawings, materials, and parts prepared at its expense specifically for use in said machines and has suffered other and further losses and damages in the aggregate amount of $324,962.50.

Should the court leave parties where it finds them when it deems both parties to be in breach? Should the court attempt to adjust the losses so that each party bears the same amount? Or, should it adjust so that the party more at fault, if possible to determine, bears a higher loss? Whatever the goal, is there any justification for allowing buyer to recover its down payment?

4. Good faith, long-term continuing relations, and the UCC—quasi-fiduciary obligations? In *Conoco, Inc. v. Inman Oil Co., Inc.*,[37] Conoco was found to have breached its implied obligation of good faith to one of its distributors. From 1967 to 1972, Inman Oil Co. obtained most of the products it sold from Sinclair Oil Co. and Shell Oil Co. St. Joe Minerals Corp., a lead mining company, was one of its major customers. Conoco had been unable to sell products to St. Joe Minerals. Conoco and Inman held a series of meetings in 1972. Their officials agreed to cooperate in Conoco's attempt to persuade St. Joe to switch from Sinclair products to Conoco products to be supplied by Inman as a distributor. The effort was successful, and there were no problems until 1980.

Conoco operated through two divisions. Conoco Wholesale and Commercial Operations (WCO) sold petroleum products directly to large commercial and industrial users. Conoco Branded Division sold to distributors such as Inman. In 1981, WCO decided to bid directly on the St. Joe Minerals account and bypass Inman Oil. It was successful. The loss of the lucrative, long-time St. Joe account was a significant factor in Inman Oil going out of business in 1982.

The Court of Appeals reversed the finding that Conoco had acted in good faith. It found that the relationship was governed by the UCC. It said:

> Conoco had earlier obtained St. Joe as an indirect Branded Division customer through the efforts and good will of Inman Oil. On the basis of its longstanding relationship with and confidence in Inman Oil, St. Joe had agreed to transfer much of its business from Sinclair to Conoco. However, Conoco evidently felt no obligation to repay this substantial favor by continuing to channel its St. Joe business through Inman Oil. Moreover, having acquired St. Joe as a direct customer [by submitting bids below its jobber price quotations], Conoco then refused to permit Inman Oil to serve as the delivery agent....

The Court of Appeals remanded the case, directing a federal magistrate to find Inman Oil's damages as a result of Conoco's direct bids on the St. Joe account.[38]

---

37. 774 F.2d 895 (8th Cir.1985).

38. *Cf.* Bloor v. Falstaff Brewing Corp., 601 F.2d 609 (2d Cir. 1979); *see also* E. Allan Farnsworth, *On Trying to Keep One's Promises: The Duty of Best Efforts in Contract Law*, 46 U. PITT. L. REV. 1 (1984).

4. Notice: § 2-607(3)(a) — And a Note on § 2-608(2)

EASTERN AIR LINES, INC. v. MCDONNELL DOUGLAS CORP.

United States Court of Appeals, Fifth Circuit
532 F.2d 957 (1976)

AINSWORTH, J.

This important Florida diversity case involves an appeal from a judgment for damages for breach of contract in favor of Eastern Air Lines against McDonnell Douglas Aircraft, Inc., based on a jury verdict in Eastern's favor for the sum of $24,552,659.11 plus costs of $241,149.02 — one of the largest jury verdicts ever reviewed by this Court. Involved is a series of contracts covering the years 1965–1968 by which Douglas Aircraft, Inc.,[39] agreed to manufacture and sell to Eastern Air Lines nearly 100 jet planes for approximately a half-billion dollars. Suit was filed by Eastern against Douglas on July 31, 1970, based on allegations that 90 of these planes were delivered a total of 7,426 days late. It was not until July 12, 1973, after almost three years of pretrial motions and discovery and four and one-half months of trial, that the jury's verdict was rendered in the District Court.

Our review of the case convinces us that the District Court made a diligent effort to resolve the many difficult matters before it. Nevertheless, we conclude that the trial judge committed substantial and prejudicial errors in a number of his rulings and instructions to the jury, which require reversal of the judgment and a new trial. Accordingly, we reverse and remand.

I. Background

Eastern Air Lines decided in 1964 to replace what remained of its outmoded propeller-driven fleet in an effort to reverse a serious five-year financial decline. Ever since the advent of the commercial jet age in 1959, Eastern had lagged behind its competitors in the purchase of jet-powered planes. Consequently, the company's decision to order 100 new planes made it the last major trunk carrier to purchase a large number of jet aircraft.

Although Eastern is one of the largest passenger carriers in the world, its route system has historically been composed of relatively short segments. In 1964, only Boeing and Douglas could offer a small, twin-engine, short-range jet suited to Eastern's needs. Eastern's decision to purchase the Douglas DC-9 rather than Boeing's 737 was based in part on Douglas's offer to lease it a number of DC-9-14s as an interim plane

---

39. [1] As will be noted below, Douglas merged with the McDonnell Aircraft Company on April 28, 1967 to become the McDonnell Douglas Corporation. Although we will occasionally refer to "Douglas" in discussing acts that antedated the merger, the company will generally be denominated "McDonnell" or "McDonnell Douglas" during the course of this opinion.

until the larger "stretched" DC-9-31's were available.[40] Boeing had been unable to provide Eastern with an equivalent aircraft as a substitute for its short-haul, twin-engine 737 which was not due to be delivered until a year after Douglas was to begin producing the DC-9-31. For its longer-range flights, Eastern also ordered a number of DC-8-61 jets, which are Douglas' equivalent of the Boeing 707.[41]

Letters of intent providing for Eastern's lease or purchase of DC-9-14s and for its purchase of the "stretched" DC-9-31 and the DC-8 planes were signed in February 1965. The following July, Douglas and Eastern entered into the first three of what was to be a series of eight contracts providing for the delivery of a total of 99 planes. Five of the eight contracts were amended, some a number of times, between 1965 and 1968.

Although varying in details, all the agreements are basically similar; each required Douglas to manufacture a number of planes at a stipulated price per aircraft to be paid upon the delivery of each plane at Douglas's California plant. Each jet was designated for delivery during a particular calendar month. In addition, every contract contained two provisions that are of special importance to these appeals. One clause is a choice of law provision that requires that the contracts' construction and performance be determined under California law. The other provision is an "excusable delay" clause that exempts Douglas from liability for delays beyond its control and not its fault.

Problems developed in the Douglas-Eastern relationship before even the first plane was scheduled to be delivered. In January 1966, it became evident to both parties that Douglas would be unable to complete its DC-9-14 jets in time to meet the contract delivery dates. In an early exchange of letters on the subject, Douglas attributed the delivery delays to "our nation's rapidly increasing commitments in Southeast Asia," and Eastern replied by expressing concern and noting that "[i]t appears to us that some of this slippage really should have been avoidable."

Subsequently it appeared that the delays could not be confined to the DC-9-14 deliveries. During 1966 and 1967, Douglas repeatedly revised its scheduled delivery of DC-8s and DC-9-31s. These further delays were viewed with "great concern" by Eastern executives, who informed Douglas that the late deliveries were imposing a "substantial burden" on the airline.

Throughout this period, Douglas was confronted with a mounting financial crisis which, to some extent, was the result of the DC-8 and DC-9 delivery delays. In the summer of 1966, Douglas forecast a loss of almost $30 million in its operations for the year. By November, Douglas's cash shortage reached such catastrophic proportions

---

40. [2] The DC-9 is a "second generation" commercial jet with two engines mounted on its tail and is designed for short to medium-haul service. The DC-9-14 is capable of carrying approximately 65 passengers, while the "stretched" model DC-9-31 can carry 100 passengers.

41. [3] The DC-8-61 planes ordered by Eastern are large (200 passenger), medium-range (2,000 miles), four-engine jets. The Model 61 is a larger and more advanced version of the DC-8 introduced in 1959.

that the company's creditors insisted that a solvent merger partner be found. The natural choice was the McDonnell Aircraft Company, whose military and space activities effectively complemented Douglas's strength in the commercial aircraft field. After McDonnell infused into Douglas over $68 million in new funds, a merger was consummated on April 28, 1967. The new McDonnell Douglas Corporation assumed all the obligations and liabilities of the former Douglas Aircraft Company.

Delivery delays continued after the merger until the last of the planes was delivered in January 1969. On the average, each of the 90 late planes was delivered 80 days after the month specified in the contract date. Several months after performance had been completed under the last of the eight contracts, Eastern wrote McDonnell on May 29, 1969, presenting a claim for damages resulting from the late deliveries over the previous three years. The airline alleged that these delays could not be deemed excusable under the applicable clause in the agreements. McDonnell rejected the claim and suit was filed in the District Court for the Southern District of Florida.

On the order of the District Judge, the trial was bifurcated with the liability phase to be tried first; to be followed, if necessary, by a trial on damages before the same jury. The greater part of the three-month liability trial was devoted to McDonnell's efforts to prove that the delivery delays were the product of events covered by the excusable delay clause in each contract. Although McDonnell produced evidence that some of the deliveries were late because of strikes and labor shortages, the heart of its defense was that most of the delays were caused by the rapid military buildup occasioned by the war in Vietnam. During the 1966–1968 escalation of the war, the Government asked the aviation industry to accord specific military projects priority over civilian production. Although military priority, in some cases, was gained through written directives and ratings issued pursuant to the Defense Production Act of 1950 ("D.P.A."), the Government often effectively achieved the same result by more informal and less direct means. McDonnell endeavored to show that, because its subcontractors cooperated with this "jawboning" policy of the Government, there were serious delays in the delivery of parts vital to DC-8 and DC-9 production. Throughout the course of this phase of the trial, however, the District Judge took the position that the only excusable delays were those resulting from written government orders issued in strict compliance with procurement regulations. As a result, the trial judge refused to allow the jury to consider evidence of less formal efforts by the Government to expedite military production.

McDonnell Douglas also contended that Eastern had failed to give timely and reasonable notice of the breaches, that one of the contracts was no longer enforceable, and that Eastern should be estopped from pursuing any of its claims. The District Court, however, ruled against McDonnell on all these issues.

At the close of the liability trial, the jury was instructed that McDonnell bore the burden of proving that the delays were caused by events that were excused under the contracts. Furthermore, according to the court's instructions, no event could be an excuse unless it was not reasonably foreseeable at the time the particular contract was entered into. On May 16, 1973, the jury's verdict, in the form of answers to special interrogatories, found that none of the 7,426 days of delay was excusable.

During the six-week damages phase of the trial, each side presented testimony concerning the effect of the delivery delays on Eastern's operations during the 1966–1968 period. Eastern's expert estimated the airline's lost profits to be $23,400,000 while McDonnell's expert witness was of the opinion that no such damages resulted from the delays. The airline presented evidence to support its claims for damages resulting from surplus pilot time expense, wasted pilot training, and wasted schedule expense. In addition to these claims, the District Judge permitted the jury to consider Eastern's contention that, under Florida law, it was entitled to prejudgment interest from the time of the breach. On July 12, 1973, the jury returned a special verdict awarding Eastern a total of $22,219,601 in compensatory damages and $9,650,715 in pre-judgment interest....

In its appeal, McDonnell Douglas's most fundamental contentions concern the District Court's rulings on excusable delay, Eastern's obligation to give reasonable and timely notice of breach, and the enforceability of one of the contracts....

III. Notice of Breach Under the Uniform Commercial Code

During the trial and in final instructions to the jury, the District Court held that Eastern need not prove, as a predicate for recovery in this suit, that it had given McDonnell Douglas reasonable and timely notice of the delivery delays. McDonnell strongly contests the trial judge's rulings for Eastern on this issue and argues either that the airline should, as a matter of law, be barred from any recovery or, alternatively, that the issue of timely notice should have been submitted to the jury.

The statute governing this question is § 2-607(3)(a) of the Uniform Commercial Code, which provides in part as follows:

(3) Where a tender has been accepted

(a) the buyer must within a reasonable time after he discovers or should have discovered any breach notify the seller of breach or be barred from any remedy; ...

McDonnell contends that the trial judge denied it the benefits of this provision, both by ruling that § 2-607 does not apply to late deliveries and by holding in the alternative that Eastern gave adequate notice. Because we are unable to agree with the District Court's ruling on either ground, we hold that the question of timely notice under § 2-607 should have been submitted to the jury.[42]

A. Applicability of UCC § 2-607(3)(a)

Even though § 2-607, by its very terms, governs "any breach," the trial court found the notice requirement to be inapplicable to delivery delays because a seller necessarily has knowledge of this sort of contract violation. Relying on the case of *Jay V. Zim-*

---

42. [31] Notification under § 2-607 is an integral part of a buyer's cause of action and is not an affirmative defense of the seller. Therefore, the buyer must both plead and prove that the notice requirement has been complied with.

merman Company v. General Mills, Inc., E.D. Mo., 1971, 327 F. Supp. 1198, 1204, the District Judge concluded that notice is useless where a breach is apparent to both parties.[43] The trial court apparently was of the view that the sole function of §2-607 is to inform the seller of hidden defects in his performance. Under this approach, the only purpose of notice is to provide the seller with an opportunity to remedy an otherwise unknown nonconforming tender....

Section 2-607's origins, however, reveal that it has a much broader function. The Code's notice requirement was derived from decisional law in California and several other states that sought to ameliorate the harsh common law rule that acceptance of goods by the buyer waived any and all of his remedies.... This approach was codified under §49 of the Uniform Sales Act, which was adopted in California as Civ. Code §1769.

As Professor Williston, the author of the Sales Act, has noted, §49 continued the common law rule treating a seller's tender of goods as an offer of them in full satisfaction. 3 S. WILLISTON, CONTRACTS §714 (rev. ed. 1961). The buyer, though, was permitted to accept the offer without waiving any claims if he gave the seller prompt notice to this effect.... This approach reconciled the desire to give finality to transactions in which goods were accepted with the need to accommodate a buyer who, for business reasons, had to accept the tendered goods despite unsatisfactory performance by the seller.... Pre-UCC decisions in California and elsewhere, therefore, recognized that the primary purpose of notice is to inform the seller that, even though his tender has been accepted by the buyer, his performance is nonetheless considered a breach of contract.

Under §49 it was irrelevant whether a seller had actual knowledge of a nonconforming tender. Instead, the critical question was whether the seller had been informed that the buyer considered him to be in breach. Consequently, in Professor Williston's words, "the section is applicable not only to defects in quality but to breach of any promise or warranty, as, for instance, *delay in time*." 5 S. WILLISTON, CONTRACTS

---

43. [32] In relevant part, the *Zimmerman* opinion reads as follows:

   In the present, as in any case involving late delivery, both the seller and the buyer are necessarily fully aware *prior* to tender that the seller's contract obligation to timely deliver has not been complied with. It would be an unreasonable, if not absurd, construction of the statute to require a renewed notice of breach *after* acceptance of the goods under the facts here involved. A party has notice of a fact when he has actual knowledge of it. Section ... 1-201 (25) of the Uniform Commercial Code. The purpose of a notice in the context of this section ... is to *inform* the seller of matters that would not normally come to the buyer's attention until *after* the goods came into his possession. The legislative intent was to make provision with respect to the effect of acceptance of allegedly defective or inferior goods or those allegedly not meeting warranted standards of quality. In that situation it is reasonable to require the buyer to inform the seller of the existence of a possible factual dispute relating to matters of which the buyer presumably was not aware prior to his acceptance of a tender of the goods.

Jay V. Zimmerman Company v. General Mills, Inc., E.D. Mo., 1971, 327 F. Supp. 1198, 1204 (emphasis in original).

§ 714 at 409 (3d ed. 1961) (emphasis supplied). Pre-UCC decisions, therefore, applied the notice requirement in delivery delay cases....

As the drafters of Article 2 acknowledge, § 2-607 continues the basic policies underlying § 49 of the Uniform Sales Act. Indeed, the notice requirement developed in pre-UCC cases is entirely consistent with the Article 2 goals of encouraging compromise and promoting good faith in commercial relations. As Comment 4 to § 2-607 indicates, the purpose of notice is not merely to inform the seller that his tender is nonconforming, but to open the way for settlement through negotiation between the parties. In the words of the California Supreme Court, "the sound commercial rule" codified in § 2-607 also requires that a seller be reasonably protected against stale claims arising out of transactions that a buyer has led him to believe were closed. *Pollard v. Saxe & Yolles Development Company*, 12 Cal. 3d 374, 115 Cal. Rptr. 648, 525 P.2d 88 (1974).... Early warning permits the seller to investigate the claim while the facts are fresh, avoid the defect in the future, minimize his damages, or perhaps assert a timely claim of his own against third parties....

Given these undeniable purposes, it is not enough under § 2-607 that a seller has knowledge of the facts constituting a nonconforming tender; he must also be informed that the buyer considers him to be in breach of the contract. The Code's notice requirement, then, is applicable to delivery delays as well as other breaches.... Accordingly, we decline to follow the reasoning of the *Zimmerman* decision, and we find that the trial court erred in not applying § 2-607 to the delivery delays at issue in this case.

B. Adequate Notice Under § 2-607(3)(a)

Turning next to the lower court's alternative rationale for ruling against McDonnell on the issue, we must determine whether the notice given by Eastern was both sufficient and timely as a matter of law. Finding the facts "essentially uncontradicted," the trial court concluded that Eastern adequately informed McDonnell that it considered the delivery delays to be an actionable breach:

> Eastern's management repeatedly protested the delays and requested negotiation of the dispute, but they were always put off by McDonnell Douglas with the assurance that the matter would be taken up once the assembly line was back on schedule. When production was again on-line many months later it became obvious to Eastern that no good-faith settlement negotiations would take place.

Because the court's ruling was, in effect, a directed verdict, it can be sustained only if there is no conflict in substantial evidence and the inferences from these facts "point so strongly and overwhelmingly" in favor of Eastern that reasonable men could not have arrived at a contrary verdict.... As will be demonstrated below, the adequacy and timeliness of notice under § 2-607 typically depend upon the reasonableness of the buyer's efforts to communicate his dissatisfaction.... Therefore, whether the notice requirement has been complied with is a question that is particularly within the province of the jury.... Applying this standard of review to the facts, we find that there was at least one substantial factual dispute before the court and that the trial judge's interpretation of the facts in the case was not the only reasonable inference that could be drawn from them. We, therefore, reverse on this issue as well. We do not agree, however, with McDonnell's contention that, as a matter of law, Eastern's notice was inadequate and untimely.

As we have seen, the contractual relationship between Douglas and Eastern stretched over a number of years and was governed by a series of separate agreements, several of which were amended a number of times. The complexity of these agreements and the large number of planes involved required the parties to be in constant communication with each other. Indeed, throughout this period, Eastern was informed of all significant developments by one of its own engineers who was in residence at the Douglas plant. Eastern, therefore, often knew of anticipated delivery delays before being formally informed of them by Douglas.

By early January of 1966, both parties were aware that production under Contract 65-41-L, the agreement with the earliest delivery dates, was behind schedule. Douglas did not officially notify Eastern of the impending delays until February, when it sent several letters ascribing the DC-9-14 production difficulties to delays by subcontractors and a shortage of skilled labor. In Douglas's view, all of these problems were due to "our nation's rapidly increasing commitments in Southeast Asia." Douglas also indicated that it was making every effort to mitigate the impact of its subcontractors' difficulties.

Eastern replied on March 15, stating that it was "most disappointed with the delivery status" of the DC-9-14s. The airline noted that it had repeatedly expressed concern over the lack of early notification by Douglas. Without contesting Douglas's assertions concerning the Vietnam War, Eastern stated that:

> It appears to us that some of this slippage really should have been avoidable if corrections had been rigorously pursued when it first became apparent. In light of this, we believe the Douglas Company has a responsibility to assist Eastern wherever possible in the reduction of our own pre-inauguration activities. Some of the areas that assistance would be beneficial [sic] are training (flight crews, cabin attendants, mechanics, and inspectors) and additional introductory service support.
>
> While it may be too early to evaluate completely, we assume your corrective actions will preserve the presently planned deliveries for the DC-9-31 and the DC-8-61 currently on order by Eastern.

On May 4, Douglas wrote Eastern expressing its willingness to discuss ways of "minimizing the difficulties these delays are causing you." Douglas, however, asked the airline to defer such conversations until production was back on schedule. There was no further correspondence concerning Contract 65-41-L, and ... the agreement itself was terminated on July 14, 1966.

By fall of 1966, however, it became apparent that there also would be delays in the delivery of the DC-9-31 and DC-8-61 planes. Between October 1966 and September

1967, Douglas wrote Eastern at least four times informing the airline of further delays in the production of these two types of aircraft. In a September 28, 1967 letter, written after the April merger, McDonnell Douglas again attributed the delays to "the worker shortage and continuing material and equipment shortages."

Eastern's first formal response to this series of announcements came on October 6, 1967. This letter informed McDonnell that "the delays in aircraft delivery have been very expensive to Eastern Airlines and we must view continuing slippage with great concern." Eastern went on to state:

> [T]he delivery delays have cost Eastern so heavily that it would now appear that we made a mistake in going the DC-9 and DC-8-61 routes. Terms that were offered to us by another manufacturer would have been far less costly and although all aircraft manufacturers have suffered to some degree from common problems, it is apparent that the delivery schedules offered to us by your competitors have been more realistic than those attained by Douglas....
>
> The delivery record of your current series of aircraft must necessarily be taken into account as we evaluate the purchase of the next series of airplanes. Unless there is concrete evidence that we can expect the DC-10 to be delivered in accordance with schedules offered by Douglas, it will be very difficult for us to decide in favor of your product as compared with that of another manufacturer.

On November 7, 1968, Eastern's Chief Financial Officer, Mr. Simons, wrote McDonnell Douglas asking that every effort be made to deliver several planes on schedule because a delay during the peak holiday season would place "a substantial burden on Eastern which is more severe than that imposed on your other customers."

There were no further significant written communications from Eastern until May 29, 1969, when McDonnell was formally presented with a claim for damages, in a letter from Eastern reading, in part, as follows:

> Eastern has made a full study of such delays and their economic impact and has concluded that Eastern has sustained very substantial damages as a result of delays that cannot be deemed "excusable" within the meaning of the definition in the applicable Purchase Agreements. At its meeting on May 27, 1969, our Board of Directors instructed management to present and process a claim for such damages.

In addition to this undisputed documentary evidence, the District Court had before it testimony concerning Eastern's attitude toward the delivery delays. Eastern's Chairman, Floyd Hall, testified that he "talked with almost every one of the top officials [of Douglas and then of McDonnell Douglas] at one time or another.... [E]very time I met them I reminded them of the late delivery of their aircraft." ...

Eastern contends that these facts are more than sufficient to constitute adequate notice as a matter of law. The Code, in Eastern's view, does not require the buyer to inform the seller that he is presenting a claim under the contract. This contention is based on Comment No. 4 to § 2-607, which states, in part, that "[t]he content of the notification need merely be sufficient to let the seller know that the transaction is still troublesome and must be watched." Eighth Circuit decisions[44] and at least one commentary[45] have relied on this sentence from Comment No. 4 for the proposition that almost any indication of dissatisfaction on the buyer's part meets the requirements of § 2-607. Under this standard, there would be little doubt that Eastern's letters concerning the delays constituted sufficient notice under the UCC.

It appears that Comment No. 4 was aimed at remedying a rule adopted under § 49 of the Uniform Sales Act by some courts that a mere complaint of a breach was not adequate notice. In California and a number of other states, for example, a buyer was required to indicate that he intended to look to the seller for damages. Several jurisdictions, moreover, required the buyer to specify in detail the basis for his claim that the contract was breached....

These technical requirements were dispensed with because they frequently served to deny an uninformed consumer of what was otherwise a valid claim. As is noted in the draftsmen's comments, "[T]he rule of requiring notification is designed to defeat commercial bad faith, not to deprive a good faith consumer of his remedy."[46] Eastern is therefore correct in asserting that notice under § 2-607 need not be a specific claim for damages or an assertion of legal rights....

However, the fact that the Code has eliminated the technical rigors of the notice requirement under the Uniform Sales Act does not require the conclusion that any expression of discontent by a buyer always satisfies § 2-607. As Comment 4 indicates, a buyer's conduct under § 2-607 must satisfy the Code's standard of commercial good faith. Thus, while the buyer must inform the seller that the transaction is "still troublesome," Comment 4 also requires that the notification "be such as informs the seller that the transaction is claimed to involve a breach, and thus opens the way for normal settlement through negotiation."

---

44. [43] Bonebrake v. Cox, 499 F.2d 951, 956–67 (8th Cir. 1974) (letter informing seller that equipment not installed within meaning of contract was sufficient notice as a matter of law); Lewis v. Mobil Oil Corporation, 438 F.2d 500, 509 (8th Cir. 1971) (constant communications from buyer concerning his suspicion that improper oil was being supplied were sufficient to support jury verdict of adequate notice); Boeing Airplane Company v. O'Malley, 329 F.2d 585, 593–96 (8th Cir. 1964) (failure to perform properly in front of seller's expert and resulting shutdown of buyer's operations was sufficient evidence for jury's finding on notice).

45. [44] J. White & R. Summers, Handbook of the Law under the Uniform Commercial Code 347–48 (1st ed., 1972). The authors of this treatise conclude that

Quite clearly the drafters intended a loose test; a scribbled note on a bit of toilet paper will do.... Under [Comment No. 4], it is difficult to conceive of words which, if put in writing, would not satisfy the notice requirement of 2-607. Indeed a letter containing anything but the most exaggerated encomiums would seem to tell the seller that the transaction "is still troublesome and must be watched."

46. [49] Uniform Commercial Code § 2-607, Comment 4.

In arguing that these requirements have been complied with, Eastern cannot rely on the same minimal standards of notice developed for ordinary consumers. The measure of good faith required under the Code varies with a buyer's commercial status. Unlike an ordinary purchaser, a merchant's good faith is measured by "reasonable commercial standards of fair dealing in the trade."[47] Therefore, as the Comments to § 2-607 indicate, what constitutes adequate notice from an inexperienced consumer may not be sufficient in a transaction between professionals.[48] While an ordinary purchaser is generally ignorant of his obligation to give timely notice, a merchant buyer should be well aware that some form of notice is a requirement of his trade. We find merit, then, in those decisions which have indicated that, under § 2-607, merchants will be held to a higher standard than ordinary buyers....

We note, moreover, that the trial judge's rationale for ruling against McDonnell on the notice issue appears to have been based on a single letter written by Douglas in response to Eastern's March 15, 1966, request for aid in reducing its "pre-inauguration activities." In his post-trial memorandum, the District Judge appeared to infer a waiver of Douglas's right to notification concerning any future breaches from its request that this aid be postponed. In our view, though, the March 15 letter from Eastern does not constitute adequate notice as a matter of law. Indeed, a close reading of the communication reveals that Eastern's primary concern was the lack of early notification of impending delivery delays rather than the validity of Douglas's contention that these delays were the product of the Vietnam War. Although Eastern expressed the view that some of the delays should have been avoided, it requested merely that Douglas help to mitigate the delays' impact upon Eastern's operations. A jury, therefore, might reasonably infer from this correspondence that Eastern was not claiming a breach of the particular contract involved.[49]

More importantly, the District Court's reliance on these two particular letters evidences a failure to recognize that the buyer's good faith is the governing criterion under § 2-607. As we have seen, the Code's draftsmen disposed of rigid technical requirements which would frustrate the notice requirement's design of defeating commercial bad faith.[50] Therefore, the fact that dissatisfaction may once have been communicated to the seller should not preclude an inquiry into the buyer's good

---

47. [51] Section 2-103(1)(b)....

48. [52] Although the following statement concerns the time in which notification must be given, we consider it equally applicable to the issue of the content of adequate notice under § 2-607:

> The time of notification is to be determined by applying commercial standards to a merchant buyer. "A reasonable time" for notification from a retail consumer is to be judged by different standards.... Uniform Commercial Code § 2-607, Comment 4.

49. [54] The exchange of letters relied on by the trial judge was concerned exclusively with delays arising under Contract 65-41-L which ... cannot be the subject of an action by Eastern.

50. [55] Indeed, the Code focuses so heavily on the buyer's conduct that notice is deemed given merely if the notifying party has taken reasonable steps to give the requisite notice to his counterpart. Uniform Commercial Code § 1-201(26) [Cal. Comm. Code § 1201(26)]. Thus, if a reasonable effort has been made by the buyer, it is not necessary that the seller actually learn of the breach for a buyer's rights to be preserved under § 2-607....

faith as evidenced by his entire course of conduct.... Even though adequate notice may have been given at one point in the transaction, subsequent actions by the buyer may have dissipated its effect. The buyer's conduct, then, taken as a whole, must constitute timely notification that the transaction is claimed to involve a breach.[51]

It is particularly important in continuing contractual relationships—such as the one that bound Eastern and McDonnell Douglas together for almost four years—that all of a buyer's dealings with a seller be evaluated under the good faith standard. An overly mechanical application of the notice requirement to complex or ongoing agreements would frequently frustrate the § 2-607 design of defeating commercial bad faith.

Reviewing Eastern's entire course of conduct during the years 1965–1969, and recognizing that Eastern must be held to a higher standard of good faith than an ordinary consumer, we conclude that a jury could reasonably find, as one of its options, that adequate notice was not given. In analyzing the record before us ... we give McDonnell the benefit of every reasonable inference.

We note first that even Eastern's most strongly worded communications can reasonably be construed as an effort to prod McDonnell Douglas into minimizing the Vietnam War's impact upon production rather than as a claim for breach. As we have seen, Eastern's March 15, 1966 letter to Douglas—perhaps its single most forceful expression of dissatisfaction—can be viewed as a request for aid in minimizing the impact of the delays rather than an assertion that Douglas had violated the contract.

Eastern, moreover, did not dispute McDonnell Douglas's contention that the delays were caused by the Vietnam War until the airline presented its formal claim for damages in 1969. Indeed, throughout the life of all the contracts, Eastern was advising its shareholders,[52] the public,[53] and, in sworn testimony, the Federal Government,[54] that war-related defense priorities were causing the delivery delays. Inasmuch as the "excusable delay" clause found in all the contracts provides that the "[s]eller shall not be ... deemed to be in default" on account of delays caused by "governmental priorities," Eastern may well have led McDonnell to believe that it was not in breach of the agreements.

We disagree with Eastern's contention that it "had no choice but to accept what Douglas was saying as the truth." Eastern was in constant communication with its

---

51. [56] We emphasize that even though a buyer's notification under this test may be adequate in terms of content, it may nonetheless be untimely. See Uniform Commercial Code § 2-607, cmt. 4. The jury could have found, for example, that Eastern had given timely notice with regard to only some of the delivery delays.

52. [57] Eastern's 1966 Annual Report, for example, stated that the aircraft deliveries were being delayed because of "the war demands on the aerospace industry and its suppliers."

53. [58] On March 2, 1966, an Eastern press release stated that its "ability to increase available seat miles ... is being restricted by the slow rate of the new aircraft deliveries by both Boeing and Douglas caused by the military requirements in Viet Nam."

54. [59] Before the Civil Aeronautics Board, on December 8, 1967, Eastern stated that "Eastern, like other purchasers, has experienced substantial delays in delivery of DC-9-31 aircraft, largely because of military requirements for the Vietnam conflict."

own engineer who was in residence at the Douglas plant throughout this period.[55] Furthermore, Eastern and, indeed, the entire aviation industry were aware that Douglas's catastrophic financial crisis was, to some degree, precipitated by internal management difficulties. As early as the summer of 1966, therefore, Eastern had ample opportunity to assert then, as it does now, that the delivery delays were caused by internal problems rather than the Vietnam War. It failed to do so.

Eastern's commercial good faith is subject to further challenge because it continued to negotiate new contracts and amend old ones throughout the period in which the delays occurred. Two of the agreements, in fact, were executed in October of 1967 after 44 of the planes were already late. At no time during the negotiation and execution of any of these contracts did Eastern seek a settlement of its claims or even dispute McDonnell's Vietnam excuse. This may very well have led McDonnell to believe that, even though Eastern was unhappy about the delays, it did not consider them to be a breach of the contract.[56] ...

The evidence reflected in the record, however, is ... insufficient to support a directed verdict in favor of McDonnell Douglas on the issue of notice. There was no evidence at trial concerning the "reasonable standards of fair dealing" in the commercial aviation industry. We, therefore, cannot determine whether Eastern's conduct failed to satisfy contemporary standards of commercial good faith.... In conclusion, therefore, the issue of notice under UCC § 2-607 should have been submitted to the jury with instructions that it determine whether Eastern's conduct throughout the life of the contracts constituted adequate and timely notice to McDonnell that it was considered to be in breach of the contracts.

NOTES AND QUESTIONS

1. *The Fifth Circuit elaborates on* Eastern Air Lines: The United States Court of Appeals for the Fifth Circuit explained its *Eastern Air Lines* decision in *T.J. Stevenson & Co. v. 81,193 Bags of Flour.*[57] In a dispute concerning whether or not the nation of Bolivia had given an adequate § 2-607(3)(a) notice of its objection to insect-infested wheat flour it was buying, the Fifth Circuit re-affirmed and explained its decision in *Eastern.* Applying Illinois law,[58] the court observed:

---

55. [60] At oral argument, in fact, Eastern's counsel stated that the airline's representative at the Douglas plant "had a better estimate of when the planes were coming out than Douglas did."

56. [62] We recognize, of course, that once an airline begins to build a fleet with a particular make of airplane it cannot easily switch to a competing manufacturer. Eastern, therefore, is correct in pointing out that as of 1965, it was effectively "married" to Douglas. The conjugal nature of its relationship with Douglas, however, did not relieve Eastern of its obligation of commercial good faith. As we have seen, the notice requirement reconciles the seller's right to early warning of claims for breach with the need to accommodate the buyer who, for reasons of necessity, has to accept a tender that is not in full compliance with the contract. In a continuing contractual relationship, therefore, the buyer must decide whether the benefits of claiming a breach of contract outweigh the need for a close rapport with the seller.

57. 629 F.2d 338 (5th Cir. Ala. 1980).

58. The contract between the seller and Bolivia specified that Illinois law applied. The seller was based in the Midwest region of the United States.

(i) Notice Under §2-607(3)(a)

In Illinois it is well-established that §2-607(3)(a)'s requirement of notification of breach of warranty need not be in any particular words and is ordinarily a question of fact, looking to all the circumstances of the case. Notice need not be written. It may be given in a single communication or derived from several. It is also well-established that "notice under §2-607 need not be a specific claim for damages or an assertion of legal rights." *Eastern Air Lines, Inc. v. McDonnell Douglas Corp.*, 532 F.2d 957, 976 (5th Cir. 1976)....

Beyond these principles, however, Courts have disagreed in their interpretations of §2-607(3)(a)'s notification requirement. A few decisions, largely from the Eighth Circuit and from Oregon, have held that the seller need only be informed that "the transaction is still troublesome and must be watched." And if the troublesome nature of the transaction is moreover apparent or already known to the seller, no notice at all is required. In *Eastern Air Lines, Inc. v. McDonnell Douglas Corp.*, *supra*, however, this Court decided that for merchant buyers §2-607(3)(a) requires something more than the minimal notification endorsed by those Courts. 532 F.2d at 970–80. We held that the dual policies of "encouraging compromise" and "promoting good faith in commercial relations," *id.* at 972, underlie the notice requirement of §2-607(3)(a). Notice consequently must fulfill those policies; merely indicating that the transaction is troublesome is not enough. One way in which the policies are fulfilled is by notice informing the seller that the buyer regards the contract as breached by the seller, though specific legal rights need not be invoked. *Id.* at 973, 976.

The *Eastern Air Lines* interpretation of §2-607(3)(a) has been adopted by the vast majority of Courts that subsequently have considered the issue. It is also significant that the Eighth Circuit, which decided three cases which we declined to follow in *Eastern Air Lines*, recently decided a case under Illinois law and adopted the *Eastern Air Lines* view of notification. *Southern Illinois Stone Co. v. Universal Engineering Corp.*, 592 F.2d 446, 452 (8th Cir. 1979). Because we regard the Eighth Circuit as very knowledgeable concerning Illinois law and considering the wide acceptance of *Eastern Air Lines*' view of notification, we hold that Illinois law requires application of the *Eastern Air Lines* principles to this case....

Our *Eastern Air Lines* decision grew out of McDonnell Douglas's late delivery over a period from 1965 to 1969 of aircraft ordered by Eastern. The contract required a high degree of cooperation and communication between the parties. Beginning even before the expected time of the first aircraft's delivery, Eastern continuously expressed dissatisfaction with the delivery schedule. Finally, Eastern sued for damages. The District Judge found that that evidence of Eastern's communications with McDonnell Douglas was sufficient to permit a directed verdict that §2-607(3)(a) notice had been given. A jury then considered other issues and returned a verdict in Eastern's favor. We reversed, ruling that examination of the "entire course of conduct during the years 1965–1969" revealed enough doubt concerning notification to preclude a directed verdict for either party and to require evaluation by the jury as fact-finder. 532 F.2d at 978. We emphasized that Eastern's expressions of dissatisfaction were less than unequivocal in view of the parties' cooperative arrangement and Eastern's failure to cancel future aircraft deliveries. It was not clear to a reasonable certainty that Eastern's alleged notice was sufficient to encourage compromise by McDonnell Douglas. Furthermore, there was evidence that created a jury question concerning the second policy of notification, the encouragement of commercial good faith. For example, Eastern at times praised McDonnell Douglas's performance and made public statements that might "well have led McDonnell to believe that it was not in breach of the agreement." *Id.* at 978. During the 1965–1969 period encompassing the alleged breaches of contract, Eastern negotiated several new contracts with McDonnell Douglas without attempting to raise or settle its claims under the original contract. Added to this were the assurances by Eastern during 1968 that it would not seek delay damages from McDonnell Douglas. All of this, we held, created a question of the adequacy of Eastern's notification, which was a fact question calling for resolution by the fact-finder.

Eastern Air Lines ... teaches two concepts. First, the factfinder's determination of the mixed law-fact issue of notice, if based on a correct understanding of the law, is to be given great weight. Second, § 2-607(3)(a) notice must be evaluated from the perspective of the policies it seeks to encourage: compromise by the parties, and conduct within the bounds of commercial good faith.

Applying these concepts to the instant case we first observe that while the District Judge did not make elaborate findings concerning notice, he did treat it as a fact question and recognized that *Eastern Air Lines* requires more than minimal notice:

> "A purpose of § 2-607 notice requirement is to inform the seller that his tender is nonconforming, *but also to open the way for settlement* through negotiations between the parties." *T.J. Stevenson & Co. v. 81,193 Bags of Flour*, 449 F. Supp. 84, 129 (S.D. Ala. 1976) (emphasis supplied).

Because of this appreciation for the appropriate legal standard, we give great weight to the District Judge's conclusion that "the facts are sufficient to find that Bolivia gave adequate notice under § 2-607(3)(a) to ADM."[59] *Id.*

Second, the record reveals a number of specific communications, as well as additional inferable ones, between Bolivia and ADM, that must be evaluated for adequacy under the § 2-607(3)(a) policies.[60]

---

59. Eds. note: ADM was the seller.
60. T.J. Stevenson & Co. v. 81,193 Bags of Flour, 629 F.2d 338, 359–62 (5th Cir. Ala. 1980).

The court then proceeded to consider a number of communications between Bolivia and ADM Milling Co., the seller. The wheat flour itself had been shipped from Mobile, Alabama, to Arica, Chile. Bolivia initially refused to allow the flour to be unloaded in Chile, but eventually allowed the unloading of the flour; it was eventually sold in Chile at reduced prices. The court concluded its discussion of the notice issue:

> We find four aspects of the record that indicate that Bolivia gave proper notice *after* accepting the flour in Arica: (i) the fact that, as stated above, communications concerning the flour problems were ongoing; (ii) prior communications, including the September 25 telex, indicated Bolivia's staunch position with respect to live infestation; (iii) Bolivia's action in refusing to allow the flour to be discharged in Arica, an action consistent with a position that the contract had been breached; and (iv) Bolivia's October 24, 1974, telex stopping further letter of credit payments and asserting that the flour was contaminated when it left ADM's hands. From these facts and inferences, the District Judge was entitled to conclude that *Eastern Air Lines'* first policy of encouraging compromise was fulfilled, since ADM had full knowledge that the flour was infested and that Bolivia regarded live infestation as a breach of contract.
>
> Similarly, the second policy of encouraging commercial good faith is fulfilled under the facts and permissible inferences of this case. Bolivia acted in good faith. There was nothing about its conduct that was unreasonable with respect to ADM.... For example, Bolivia complained to ADM in Mobile and again after the flour reached South America and was found "reinfested." Unlike the buyer in *Eastern Air Lines*, Bolivia did not try to continue its relationship with ADM; to the contrary, it rejected the ... flour and stopped payments under the letter of credit. Bolivia never gave ADM any assurances that ADM would not be liable....
>
> We therefore have a situation converse to that in *Eastern Air Lines*. In the instant case, there is a fact-finding, not a directed verdict, of adequate notice based on all the evidence. The notice encouraged compromise, notwithstanding ADM's adamant refusal to even consider doing so. And the buyer acted in commercial good faith in contrast to the seller's questionable conduct—as compared to the reverse situation in *Eastern Air Lines*. We cannot say that the District Judge was wrong in finding that Bolivia gave adequate notice of breach to ADM under § 2-607(3)(a). Bolivia's claim for damages ... is therefore not barred under the UCC's notice requirement.[61]

The court went on to find that ADM was not entitled to raise Bolivia's failure to comply with a notice procedure outlined in the ADM contract, since ADM had effectively waived that condition in the course of dealing with Bolivia after the infestation was discovered.

---

61. *Id.* at 364.

2. Proof of good or bad faith: As the Fifth Circuit notes, the question of good faith was never submitted to the jury in the *Eastern Air Lines* case. For teaching purposes, we can sketch the situation based on reports in business publications as well as opinions in the case, but of course, a jury might find some of our "facts" not to have been proven. Given this qualification, let's first look at Eastern Air Lines. It was not a healthy corporation. Eastern lost money in seven of the ten years from 1960 to 1970. It competed with Delta on many of its routes, and Delta was well managed. As the court notes, "Ever since the advent of the commercial jet age in 1959, Eastern had lagged behind its competitors in the purchase of jet-powered planes." It was the "last major trunk carrier to purchase a large number of jet aircraft." On many of its routes it flew the Lockheed Electra, a prop-jet that was both slower than a pure jet and unpopular with passengers because of a number of serious crashes when the plane was introduced. In the early 1960s, Eastern had alienated business passengers and had a reputation for trying to save money by providing poor service. Employee morale was very low. There was an organization of those who had to fly Eastern regularly that had a newsletter called "WHEALs"—the letters stood for "We Hate Eastern Air Lines."

A new management tried to remedy the situation. It ordered 60 Boeing 727s, and it had received about half of them by 1965. It was heavily in debt for these purchases, but the 727 was not well suited for many of Eastern's routes. Thus, it entered eight contracts for Douglas DC-8 and DC-9 jets between July 1965 and October 1967. A major factor in selecting Douglas rather than Boeing planes was Douglas's willingness to lend Eastern the money to buy the DC-8s and DC-9s at favorable rates. When Douglas fell behind on deliveries in mid-1966, it disappointed all of the airlines that had bought planes from it. However, airlines such as TWA, United, Delta, and Continental did not have to cancel flights on existing schedules. Eastern had to cancel about 5 percent of its June service because it had no pilots to fly additional piston aircraft, since it had been concentrating on jet pilot training.

Eastern had a profit of $24.1 million in 1967, but it reported a loss of $11.9 million in 1968, and it had a sharp drop in earnings in the first half of 1969. In May 1969, Eastern's board of directors instructed management to bring suit against McDonnell Douglas for the losses caused by the delays in performing the contracts to deliver the DC-8 and DC-9 aircraft. During the course of the litigation in the 1970s, Eastern's fortunes continued up and down. It had unsuccessful merger discussions with Pan American. As a result of its dispute with McDonnell Douglas, Eastern ordered the Lockheed L-1011 rather than the McDonnell Douglas DC-10. However, Lockheed experienced great delivery delays when Rolls-Royce defaulted on the contract to produce the engines for the L-1011. Then one of Eastern's L-1011s crashed in the Everglades under circumstances that generated negative publicity for both the plane and Eastern's pilots.

The Douglas Aircraft Corporation was the most successful producer of passenger aircraft in the world from the 1930s to the 1950s. However, it lost its position when it decided to produce the DC-7, the last piston engine transport sold in great numbers, rather than manufacturing a jet aircraft. The Boeing Corporation developed a plane that could refuel jet bombers in flight so they could continue on patrol for longer periods, and when the United States Air Force bought the tanker, it paid to create the necessary manufacturing facilities. The tanker was converted by Boeing into the 707, the first successful passenger jet aircraft. Douglas found itself two to three years behind Boeing before it could offer the DC-8, and it lost its position as the major producer of commercial aircraft. Douglas saw a market for a plane smaller than either the 707 or the DC-8, and it developed the twin-engined DC-9. Technically, it was a fine aircraft. Douglas worked hard to sell it to the airlines, battling Boeing's 737. In order to make sales, Douglas was willing to tailor the DC-9 to the wishes of its customers, and so production could not be completely standardized.

The *Wall Street Journal*,[62] *Business Week*,[63] and *Fortune*[64] all reported that Douglas was a victim of its own success because it sold more DC-9 aircraft than it could deliver on time. This point was the subject of great controversy in the *Eastern Air Lines* trial. The business journals all reported that Douglas had underestimated the market and accepted orders exceeding its production capacity. It had to hire many new workers whose lack of experience delayed production. Douglas managers were reported to be better aircraft engineers and salespeople than experts in production.

Douglas, however, pointed to the expansion of the Vietnam War as the major cause of its problems. Commercial jet aviation was in competition with military production, and war production came first. Douglas, and Boeing as well, experienced delays caused by Pratt and Whitney's inability to supply all the ordered engines; Douglas was also delayed by its suppliers of landing gear and galleys. There was a debate about what part of the problem was caused by Douglas's mismanagement and what part by the unexpected demands of the war escalation.

Douglas was in great financial trouble, and its major lenders pushed for a merger with a profitable corporation to salvage the situation. The McDonnell Aircraft Corporation was primarily a producer of military aircraft, and it had the cash needed to keep Douglas in production. The two firms merged on April 28, 1967. It was clear that McDonnell was the dominant partner in the new firm; its people took over operation of Douglas. They set revised production schedules, and deliveries of DC-8 and DC-9s caught up to the new schedules in late 1967.

Suppose that during 1966 to 1969, Eastern had been advised by lawyers who interpreted § 2-607(3)(a) exactly as the Fifth Circuit read it in the *Eastern Air Lines* and *T.J. Stevenson* decisions. What would they have told Eastern's management to do? If Eastern had given a § 2-607(3)(a) notice that would have passed the court's test, what would have been the likely result? Would Eastern have received more planes sooner, or fewer planes later? Suppose Eastern had given proper § 2-607(3)(a) notices and Douglas, in response, said that Eastern would have to give up its claims to damages

62. Jan. 26, 1967, at 28.
63. Oct. 22, 1966, at 175–80.
64. Dec. 1966, at 167–71.

or receive no special favors in the delivery of DC-9 aircraft. Would this be the exercise of economic duress, or just the negotiations that the court says § 2-607(3)(a) is designed to bring about? Given Eastern's great need for the planes and Douglas's great difficulties (which business publications attributed in part to bad management), what — if anything — was wrong with trying to get Douglas to perform and then suing for the damages caused by the delays?

3. *McDonnell Douglas's case for bad faith:* McDonnell Douglas's brief is not a dispassionate document. A few excerpts will show its response to the idea that Eastern could "string along" Douglas:

> The acquisition of Douglas by McDonnell … occurred only after McDonnell had been assured by Douglas that no claims had been asserted against it as the result of late deliveries of aircraft. True, letters from Eastern and other airlines had expressed concern over the status of future deliveries … Eastern, like most of the other airlines, was vitally interested in witnessing the marriage of Douglas to a solvent bridegroom, so as to insure the delivery of the many planes still on order. Hence, Eastern refrained from asserting any claims which might have frightened the groom and cancelled the wedding.… Eastern had a change of heart as its financial picture deteriorated. When Charles Simon arrived on the scene [as Eastern's vice president in charge of financial affairs], he reversed the decisions previously made and persuaded Eastern to pursue the "fat-cat" McDonnell in order to brighten its financial outlook.…

> Besides being morally suspect and inherently prejudicial, Eastern's conduct is precisely the type prohibited by § 2-607 of the UCC.… Eastern's string-along tactics deprived defendant of an opportunity to enter into meaningful settlement negotiations during the critical period when its entire production program was being disrupted and delayed; to take what steps it could to minimize its own potential damages, by preserving claims against subcontractors or suppliers or otherwise; or to prepare a proper defense to this action. Additionally, defendant's willingness to enter into further contractual arrangements with plaintiff would doubtless have been influenced had it been aware of Eastern's litigious designs.…

> Although … Eastern stoutly professes that it gave a series of notifications to McDonnell throughout the 1966–69 period, Eastern's true attitude and the philosophy underlying the "string-along" theory is strikingly conceded … [in] its brief, where it acknowledges that by making claims against defendant while some of the planes were still undelivered, it would be "in the awkward position of having to sue the seller to whom [it] must continue to look for further deliveries." Eastern therefore admits, in effect, that it gambled under § 2-607 … and did not alert defendant to its designs for fear of jeopardizing the future deliveries which first Douglas and then McDonnell were working so hard to expedite. It is now time for Eastern to pay the price for that gamble.…

4. *The settlement:* Professor Stewart Macaulay[65] reports what happened after the Fifth Circuit's reversal and remand for a new trial:

> The delays ... were an important factor in Eastern's decision to buy Lockheed L-1011 wide-body jets rather than the McDonnell Douglas DC-10. This was a serious loss to McDonnell Douglas.... The suit was filed in 1970, and the Fifth Circuit's opinion reversing the district court judgment was handed down almost six years later. Rather than retry the case, McDonnell Douglas and Eastern reached a complicated settlement. Eastern returned nine older-model DC-9 jets and leased nine newer-model DC-9s at a price lower than usual....
>
> The settlement reached gave Eastern much-needed newer planes that were larger, quieter, and burned less fuel; importantly, it did not require Eastern to try to borrow money in order to do this. McDonnell Douglas apparently sought the resumption of close business relations after the earlier divorce.

The Fifth Circuit stressed that promoting compromise was an important objective of § 2-607(3)(a). All in all, the entire process did promote a compromise. However, it took two years of pretrial proceedings, about five months of trial, and almost two years in which the case was on appeal. Suppose Eastern had given a proper § 2-607(3)(a) notice when Douglas fell behind on the delivery schedule for the DC-8s and DC-9s. What kind of settlement could have been reached then?

Eastern Air Lines, which was founded in 1926, went out of business in January 1991. Some people said that it was a victim of airline deregulation. It could not compete with the low-price carriers that had entered the market. McDonnell Douglas merged with Boeing Aircraft Corporation in 1997.

Both Eastern and Douglas were famous corporations with long histories in aviation. Neither was able to cope successfully with major changes in the businesses of designing and building passenger aircraft and flying them in competition with other airlines.

PAULSON v. OLSON IMPLEMENT CO., INC.

Wisconsin Supreme Court
107 Wis. 2d 510, 319 N.W.2d 855 (1982)

CALLOW, J.

This is an appeal from judgments ... dismissing this breach of warranty action against defendants Olson Implement Company, Inc., and Super Steel Products Corporation....

The facts generating this litigation may be summarized as follows: The plaintiff corporation, Breezy Prairie Farms, Inc., had two stockholders, Ronald Paulson and Kenneth Wachholz, who are neighboring dairy and grain farmers.... In the fall of

---

65. Stewart Macaulay, *Elegant Models, Empirical Pictures, and the Complexities of Contract*, 11 LAW & SOC'Y REV. 507, 517–18 (1977).

1975 the plaintiffs contacted Lawrence Olson, of Olson Implement Company, Inc., to inquire about a grain drying and handling facility for their corn harvest. In January of 1976 Olson, accompanied by David Miller of Super Steel Products Corporation, went to the Paulson home to discuss such a facility with both Paulson and Wachholz. Paulson testified they informed Olson and Miller that they "definitely wanted something to keep up with [their] daily harvesting schedule, and that [they] were harvesting approximately 5000 bushels a day and [they] wanted a dryer that would dry what [they] harvested in one day, or 5000 bushels." After they had looked over Super Steel's literature on drying bins, they testified Miller informed them that Super Steel was experimenting with a new stirating device, a "seven-screw, seven-auger stirator," and that it would more than double the capacity of the 30-foot drying bin advertised in the brochure (which had three auger stirators and dried 2,400 bushels of corn in 24 hours). Paulson testified that Olson and Miller then left the farm to "figure out a facility and come back and give us a price on it."

On March 11, 1976, Olson and Miller returned to the Paulson farm with a written proposal, on a Super Steel form, setting forth the specifications and cost of a seven-auger stirator drying bin and a storage bin. No contract was signed or agreement reached on the purchase of the facility, and Olson and Miller left the farm to enable the plaintiffs to discuss the proposal and the financing arrangements. On March 17, 1976, the plaintiffs gave Olson a check for $2,000 as a down payment to hold the price on the bin....

Throughout the summer of 1976 Paulson and Wachholz had contact with Olson regarding whether they would purchase the bin if they obtained additional acreage and whether their crop was coming along well enough to warrant purchasing the bin. On or about September 20, 1976, Paulson and Wachholz went to Olson's office and signed an agreement to purchase the drying facility. According to the plaintiffs' testimony, at the time of the signing of the purchase agreement, Olson affirmed Miller's earlier representations that the drying equipment would dry 5,000 bushels of corn in a 24-hour period.

After receiving their drying bin, Paulson and Wachholz dried three or four bins containing 5,000 bushels of corn and discovered that instead of 24 hours it took approximately 40 to 50 hours to dry. Paulson phoned Olson to complain about this, and both Miller and Olson stopped by the farm on several occasions in 1976 to discuss any problems with the facility. On one of these occasions, the defendants recommended increasing the drying temperature to alleviate the problem. This was done, but it provided no improvement in the drying time. Olson then replaced a drying fan with a new one from his shop. Paulson testified this "made no difference."

Paulson testified at trial that in 1977 Miller put a new drying floor in the facility because "[h]e felt the floor was restricting the air flow." Plaintiffs continued to have problems drying corn in 1977 and continued to complain to Olson. Wachholz and Paulson stated nothing was done about their complaints and that it took them 40 to 50 hours to dry 5,000 bushels of corn. Plaintiffs' harvest time was delayed, and they were forced to leave 325 acres of corn standing in the field until the spring of 1978.

The failure of the facility to dry 5,000 bushels in 24 hours continued into 1978, requiring Paulson and Wachholz to secure storage space for the corn they could not put in the dryer. This involved considerable expense in hauling and securing off-farm storage. On October 5, 1978, Paulson and Wachholz commenced suit against Olson Implement Company, Inc., Super Steel Products Corporation, and Specialized Products, Inc., alleging breach of warranty as the grain drying unit never dried 5,000 bushels of corn in 24 hours.

The jury returned a special verdict on August 1, 1980, finding that both Olson Implement Company, Inc., and Super Steel Products Corporation warranted that the drying equipment sold to the plaintiffs had a drying capacity of 4,800 to 5,000 bushels of corn in a 24-hour period; that the plaintiffs relied upon this warranty in purchasing the equipment; and that they were damaged as a result of their reliance on the warranty. The trial court, in a decision and order following the verdict, responding to motions by the defendants, dismissed the action against defendants for the following reasons....

[The action was dismissed against Olson Implement because the plaintiffs' pleading did not allege having given notice within Wis. Stat. § 402.607, and because the trial court determined "as a matter of law a two-year delay in giving notice would be unreasonable."]

Section 402.607(3)(a), Stats., requires that a buyer notify a seller of a breach of contract within a reasonable time or be barred from any remedy. In the instant case, the issue of notice was not presented to the jury. The trial court concluded as a matter of law that the requisite notice had not been provided, and this conclusion we may independently review. The trial court noted that, although the grain drying equipment was installed and used in 1976, the lawsuit was not commenced until October 5, 1978.

Examining the trial court's first proposition that plaintiffs' complaint was defective as it failed to assert notice, we note that, while the plaintiffs' complaint and amended complaint may not have been artfully drafted, under our liberal pleading rules we believe the issue of notice was apparent. At paragraph 11 of plaintiffs' amended complaint the following appears, in part: "That defendants told plaintiff's [sic] agents [Paulson and Wachholz] the reason the bin was not performing properly was caused by poor floor construction and a new floor was constructed by defendants in the summer of 1977." ... Obviously, a new floor would not have been installed without the plaintiffs having informed the defendants of dissatisfaction with the drying equipment. Super Steel alleged as an affirmative defense that plaintiffs had failed to provide notice within a reasonable time of the alleged defect in the grain drying bin....

The defendants and the trial court cite several pre-Code cases for the proposition that notice must apprise the seller that the buyer looks to seller for damages for such breach.

We note that with the adoption of the Uniform Commercial Code, this is no longer intended to be a requirement of notice.... The official comments to UCC § 206-7 reveal the following:

The content of the notification need merely be sufficient to let the seller know that the transaction *is still troublesome and must be watched.* There is no reason to require that the notification which saves the buyer's rights under this section must include a clear statement of all the objections that will be relied on by the buyer.... *Nor is there reason for requiring the notification to be a claim for damages or of any threatened litigation or other resort to a remedy.* Comment 4, UCC § 2-607 (emphasis added).

While this comment is not law, we find it persuasive authority which we adopt in order to protect purchasers.

In the instant case, the plaintiffs, after they had attempted to dry three or four bins of corn, provided notice within approximately two months following installation of the facility that the grain drying equipment was not performing as expected. This was not unreasonable....

The principal reason for requiring notice "is to enable the seller to make adjustments or replacements or to suggest opportunities for cure to the end of minimizing the buyer's loss and reducing the seller's own liability to the buyer." WHITE & SUMMERS, HANDBOOK OF THE LAW UNDER THE UNIFORM COMMERCIAL CODE, 421 (Hornbook Series, 2d ed. 1980). Other obvious policies inherent in the notice requirement are to permit the seller to assist the buyer in minimizing the buyer's losses and to expedite the return of the goods to the seller before they have substantially depreciated.

In the instant case the record contains numerous instances where Olson and Super Steel went to the Paulson and Wachholz farm and attempted to alleviate the grain drying problems about which plaintiffs repeatedly complained. The defendants inspected the equipment; recommended increasing the drying temperature; Olson replaced a drying fan; and Super Steel's representative, Miller, installed a new drying floor facility. It appears to us that the purpose of the notice provision, enabling the seller to cure the defect, has been effected. Only after the seller proved unable to remedy the situation did the plaintiffs commence the instant action. There is nothing in the record to indicate that the plaintiffs were not the good faith purchasers that the Uniform Commercial Code seeks to protect through liberal notice requirements. As we view the record, the defendants acknowledged the warranty and their responsibilities under it by attempting to repair the defects of which Paulson and Wachholz complained.... Thus we hold that Paulson and Wachholz provided the requisite notice to the defendants in this action....

By the Court. —The judgments of the trial court dismissing the defendants from this action are reversed, and the jury verdict against the defendants is reinstated.

NOTES AND QUESTIONS

1. *Distinctions:* Could the *Paulson* and the *Eastern Air Lines* decisions both exist in the same jurisdiction, assuming its courts were concerned about consistency? Suppose one were to argue that in the *Eastern* opinion the court distinguished consumer from merchant buyers, holding the latter to a much higher burden of giving notice

in order to comply with §2-607(3)(a). However, *Paulson* could be taken to suggest that more refined categories are needed. Consumers may constitute one group and large bureaucratically organized corporations well-served by legal staff, such as Eastern Air Lines, may constitute another. However, Breezy Prairie Farms, Inc., is still a different kind of entity. Much like consumers, such smaller businesses do not get day-to-day legal advice and are likely to deal less formally. Unlike an Eastern Air Lines, the Breezy Prairie Farms of the world cannot be expected to comply with unknown and hard-to-discover procedures.

Do you see any problems with such an analysis? For example, what does the consumer/business distinction have to do with the Fifth Circuit's position on promoting settlements? Do you see any statutory basis for a distinction based on the type of buyer seeking to assert rights?

2. The functions of §2-607 notice—settlement—a variety of views: In *Shooshanian v. Wagner*,[66] the Supreme Court of Alaska found that a retail consumer gave adequate notice under §2-607 by filing a complaint to initiate a lawsuit. It noted:

> The majority of courts do not allow the filing of a complaint to serve as notice. We disagree, and are of the opinion that a complaint filed by a retail consumer within a reasonable period after goods are accepted satisfies the statutory notice requirement. The filing of a complaint is certainly not a bar to the negotiation and settlement of claims. To the contrary, the prospect of going to trial is often a powerful incentive to a defendant to investigate the claims against it and arrive at a reasonable agreement. A defendant may more easily and effectively prepare for either settlement or trial when it may compel discovery and so determine for itself the basis for a plaintiff's claims of liability. Allowing a consumer's complaint to serve as notice will not prevent a defendant manufacturer from raising the issue of timeliness if it has been prejudiced by an unreasonable delay....
>
> In some cases, a consumer may not even know who produced an allegedly defective product until he files a complaint and begins discovery. A rule requiring notice prior to suit could effectively prevent an injured consumer from joining a manufacturer as a party defendant in a suit already begun.

Three years earlier, in *Armco Steel Corp. v. Isaacson Structural Steel Co.*,[67] the Supreme Court of Alaska, by a three-to-two vote, found that filing a complaint was not adequate notice in a business transaction. Should the Alaska court's argument in the *Shooshanian* case be limited to consumer plaintiffs?

Professor John C. Reitz[68] says: "The promotion-of-settlement justification for the notice rule depends on the questionable premise that the sooner the parties begin negotiations after breach, the greater the chances of settlement." He continues: "A

---

66. 672 P.2d 455, 462–63 (Alaska 1983).
67. 611 P.2d 507 (Alaska 1980).
68. John C. Reitz, *Against Notice: A Proposal to Restrict the Notice of Claims Rule* in UCC §2-607(3)(a), 73 CORNELL L. REV. 534, 536 (1988).

closely related premise, namely that settlement negotiations started before litigation are more likely to result in settlement than those started after the initiation of litigation, has apparently led some courts to hold that pleadings cannot constitute notice and that notice with or after the pleadings comes too late to satisfy the rule." Reitz thinks both assertions are overgeneralizations. Moreover, suppose a buyer who has accepted goods gives a proper § 2-607(3)(a) notice. Does this necessarily mean that either seller or buyer will negotiate in good faith for a settlement?

The Mississippi Court of Appeals justified a strict § 2-607(3)(a) notice rule in *Peavey Electronics Corp. v. Baan USA, Inc.*,[69] which involved a merchant buyer of software. The court argued that a seller needs protection against stale claims arising out of transactions that a buyer has led him to believe were closed. "Early warning permits the seller to investigate the claim while the facts are fresh, avoid the defect in the future, minimize his damages, or perhaps assert a timely claim of his own against third parties." It is not enough that the seller knows of the failure to perform the contract. The seller is entitled to know that he must meet a claim for damages. This helps avoid situations where the buyer has not paid for goods and then fashions hard-to-dispute claims about their poor quality as a device to avoid payment.

3. Sections 2-607(3) and 2-608(2) notices distinguished: Most of us know very little about Gertrude Stein, other than the fact that she authored that immortal line "Rose is a rose is a rose is a rose." Is it true that "A notice is a notice is a notice?" It seems not. Different words may, for some purposes and in some situations, mean the same thing. It is equally true, although sometimes confusing and a bit inconvenient, that the same word may mean different things. UCC § 2-607(3) requires that the buyer notify the seller of the breach "or be barred from any remedy." The very next section of the Code deals with revocation of acceptances, and provides in § 2-608(2) that "[revocation] … is not effective until the buyer notifies the seller of it." We have just seen that what constitutes a notice can prove to be a subject of great (and critical) controversy. Can we carry over to § 2-608 notices the jurisprudence of the meaning of notice under § 2-607? It *is* the same statute, the same Article, the same Part, and the words are only inches apart in the statutes. But, asking the question as we have should suggest that the answer may be no.

The court in *Solar Kinetics Corp. v. Joseph T. Ryerson & Son, Inc.*,[70] discussed the requirements for a notice of revocation. Solar Kinetics, the buyer, had been awarded damages for breach. Seller counterclaimed for the price of unused goods remaining in buyer's possession. As a defense to that claim, Solar Kinetics sought to show that it had revoked its acceptance.

> Since revocation "is not effective until the buyer notifies the seller of it," Conn. Gen. Stat. Ann. § 42a-2-608(2), the third condition is met only if the buyer gives the seller effective notice of revocation within a reasonable time after the buyer knew or should have known of the seller's breach. Plaintiff

69. 10 So. 3d 945, 958 (Miss. Ct. App. 2009).
70. 488 F. Supp. 1237, 1244–50 (D. Conn. 1980).

insists that the jury has already decided this question and seeks to support this claim by reference to the following interrogatory:

Do you find the plaintiff has shown by a fair preponderance of the evidence that it gave Ryerson notice of any of its claims within a reasonable time after it knew or should have known of any breach of the contract by Ryerson?

While the jury did answer this question in the affirmative, its finding does not, contrary to plaintiff's assertion, amount to a finding of notice of revocation. In order to have found that Ryerson was liable to Solar Kinetics for breach of warranty, the jury was only required to find that a notice of breach was given to the seller pursuant to §42a-2-607(3). The content of the limited notice necessary to preserve a claim for damages need only "be sufficient to let the seller know that the transaction is troublesome and must be watched." UCC §2-607, comment 4. The official comments to the section on revocation, however, make it clear that the *content* of notice required under §2-608 is generally more than "the mere notification of breach" required under §2-607.... Consequently, when the jury concluded that adequate §2-607 notice had been given, it had no occasion to consider and rule on the question of whether or not Solar Kinetics had given the more extensive §2-608 notice necessary for revocation.

Nor does the language of the question itself suggest that the jury was being asked to make more extensive findings than were necessary to resolve the breach-of-warranty claim. All the question asks is whether notice of "any claim" was given. When the question is considered in light of the oral instructions given to the jury, it is clear that the jury was asked only to find whether Ryerson was given the limited notice required by §42a-2-607. Thus, it is clear that the jury's affirmative answer to the question concerning adequate notice of breach of contract does not estop this court from reaching a different conclusion with respect to the notice required for revocation....

While the various authorities who have considered the question have uniformly insisted that a notice of revocation must contain more than a mere notice of breach, they differ widely over how much more. Some have suggested that as little as conduct manifesting a buyer's desire to get his money back will suffice.... An intermediate position requires the buyer to notify the seller that he considers the seller to be in breach and that he desires to revoke his acceptance as to particular goods. The strictest test was recently set forth in the case of *Lynx, Inc. v. Ordnance Products*, 273 Md. 1, 327 A.2d 502 (1974), where the court held that notice of revocation "should inform the seller that the buyer has revoked, identify the particular goods as to which he has revoked, and set forth the nature of the nonconformity...." 273 Md. at 16, 327 A.2d at 513.... However, consideration of the cases reveals two significant trends. First, those cases that have found an effective notice of revocation based on minimal communications with the seller are generally cases where the dissatisfied buyer is the ultimate consumer. The notice required for revocation is generally more content-specific in a transaction between merchants....

Second, courts have been reluctant to allow a buyer in litigation to justify his earlier attempted revocation by reference to defects in the goods that he only discovered after the supposed revocation.... Both of these trends are in accord with the policy expressed in the UCC official comment 5 to § 2-608, which provides:

The content of the notice under subsection (2) is to be determined in this case as in others by considerations of good faith, prevention of surprise, and reasonable adjustment. More will generally be necessary than the mere notification of breach required under the preceding section. On the other hand, the requirements of the section on waiver of buyer's objections do not apply here. The fact that quick notification of trouble is desirable affords good ground for being slow to bind a buyer by his first statement. Following the general policy of this Article, the requirements of the content of notification are less stringent in the case of a non-merchant buyer.

The first line of cases is in accord with the Code's stricter treatment of interactions between merchants. The second line of cases adopts a rule designed to prevent surprise and to allow the seller to have an opportunity to make a reasonable adjustment with the buyer. Where the seller does not know the grounds for revocation it may be substantially prejudiced in its efforts to respond reasonably and in good faith to a supposed revocation. Thus, both of the rules adopted by other courts serve to highlight aspects of the official comment.... [The court discussed the communications between Solar Kinetics and the seller, finding in each instance that though there was a notice of a defect, there was no notice of revocation.]

Effective notice is an absolute prerequisite to the revocation of acceptance. Since Solar Kinetics failed to set forth the particular nonconformity on which it was relying to revoke, its attempted revocation was ineffective.

Consider UCC § 2-608, Comment 5, and § 2-607, Comment 4, second paragraph. What functions should the notices required under these sections serve? Why should more notice be given in a case where buyer wants to return the goods than where buyer wants to sue for breach of warranty after accepting the goods? What does the interplay between the two notice provisions, as explained in the comments, suggest about the decision in the *Eastern Air Lines* case?

4. *Written notices:* In *Prompt Electrical Supply Co., Inc. v. Allen-Bradley Co.,*[71] a former distributor sued Allen-Bradley. Allen-Bradley counterclaimed for payment for electrical equipment shipped to plaintiff. Plaintiff said that the goods were defective; Allen-Bradley would not accept their return. In granting summary judgment for Allen-Bradley, the court noted that while plaintiff gave Allen-Bradley *oral notice* of

71. 492 F. Supp. 344 (E.D.N.Y. 1980).

the alleged defects, Allen-Bradley's terms and conditions of sale required that notice of an alleged defect must be given Allen-Bradley *in writing* promptly upon discovery. Do you see a problem with upholding a written notice requirement that appears in the terms and conditions of a seller's printed form? *See* § 1-302, relied upon by the court. The section permits the parties to vary provisions of the Code by "agreement." Section 1-201(3) defines "agreement" as "the bargain of the parties in fact."

5. *Section 2-605 demands specification of defects:* Suppose a seller has supplied goods that are defective in several respects. Buyer and seller negotiate about the problem. Seller demands in writing "a full and final written statement of all defects on which the buyer proposes to rely." Buyer makes such a statement. Later buyer discovers still another serious defect. Suppose seller could not prove that it had changed its position materially in reliance on the statement of defects. Why should buyer lose the right to seek a remedy for the unlisted serious defect in the goods?

6. *How quickly must the aggrieved party notify the other party?* We've considered the content of the notices called for by §§ 2-607 and 2-608. There is another often-litigated question—when must the notice be given? Section 2-607(3)(a) says that "the buyer must within a reasonable time after he discovers or should have discovered any breach, notify the seller …" to avoid being barred from any remedy. Section 2-608(2) has a similar provision also requiring notice within a reasonable time. How fast must the buyer act? Official Comment 4 to § 2-607 tells us that courts should treat merchant and consumer buyers differently. A court should turn to "commercial standards" to judge a merchant buyer. The notice should not "deprive a good faith consumer of his remedy."

On one hand, in *Wilson v. Tuxen*,[72] the Wilsons purchased 50 adult dairy cows from Tuxen in August 2001. Some of the cows began exhibiting health problems within several months of the sale. In June 2002, two of the cows tested positive for Johne's disease,[73] and several more tested positive after that. The Wilsons gave Tuxen notice of breach in April 2003. The court decided that the notice was not given within a reasonable time:

> [T]he Wilsons allege the diseased herd caused them serious collateral con-
> sequences, including loss of their farm. As a result, their claimed damages
> are almost ten times the purchase price of the herd. Timely notice would
> have given Tuxen the opportunity to replace the diseased animals or take
> other steps intended to limit those collateral consequences. Whether Tuxen

---

72. 312 Wis. 2d 705, 732–73, 754 N.W.2d 220, 233 (Ct. App. 2008).

73. The University of Wisconsin School of Veterinary Medicine's website tells us: Johne's (pronounced "Yoh-nees") disease and paratuberculosis are two names for the same animal disease. Named after a German veterinarian, this fatal gastrointestinal disease was first clearly described in a dairy cow in 1895. A bacterium named Mycobacterium avium ss. paratuberculosis causes Johne's disease. *See* http://www.johnes.org/general/faqs.html#1. The disease kills some cows and decreases milk production in others. As with other mycobacterial infections (for instance, human tuberculosis), multiple antibiotics must be injected or given orally daily for months. For most animals, this is cost-prohibitive as well as infeasible.

would have availed himself of that opportunity—or whether a solution would actually have been reached—is beside the point. Wisconsin Stat. § 402.607 required a notice of breach when a business solution to this problem was most likely to still be available.[74]

On the other hand, in *Marvin Lumber and Cedar Co. v. PPG Industries*,[75] Marvin manufactured wooden doors and windows. It used PPG's wood treatment on the doors and windows from 1985 to 1988. The wood treatment failed to prevent premature rot and decay in these wood products. PPG claimed that Marvin should have discovered any breach no later than 1990. Marvin gave notice in April 1993. The trial court ruled as a matter of law that Marvin had given notice within a reasonable time. The Court of Appeals affirmed the trial court's decision that the notice was timely. The Eighth Circuit said:

> The undisputed testimony ... was that numerous factors could have contributed to the rot problems. And it was not until a committee of Marvin employees studied the problem in 1992 and 1993 that a determination was made that PILT [the PPG product] was the common denominator in the products about which Marvin was receiving complaints.... Shortly after Marvin realized that the pattern of rot complaints it was receiving had only PILT in common, in spite of the promises of superior performance it had received from PPG regarding the wood treatment, it notified PPG—well within a "reasonable" time.

5. Section 2-508: The Seller's Right to Cure

T.W. OIL, INC. v.
CONSOLIDATED EDISON CO. OF NEW YORK, INC.

New York Court of Appeals
57 N.Y.2d 574, 443 N.E.2d 932 (1982)

Fuchsberg, J.

In the first case to wend its way through our appellate courts on this question, we are asked, in the main, to decide whether a seller who, acting in good faith and without knowledge of any defect, tenders nonconforming goods to a buyer who properly rejects them, may avail itself of the cure provision of subdivision (2) of § 2-508 of the Uniform Commercial Code. We hold that, if seasonable notice be given, such

---

74. *Compare* Fitl v. Strek, 269 Neb. 51, 690 N.W.2d 605 (2005). Fitl bought a Mickey Mantle Topps baseball card from Strek for $17,750 in September of 1995. Fitl put the card in a safe-deposit box. In May of 1997, Fitl sent the card to Professional Sports Authenticators. It found the card valueless because it had been touched up and trimmed. The Supreme Court of Nebraska affirmed the trial court's judgment ordering Strek to pay Fitl $17,750 plus costs. The court said that timely notice had been given: "[T]here is no evidence that Strek could have made any adjustment or taken any action that would have minimized his liability. In its altered condition, the baseball card was worthless."

75. 401 F.3d 901, 908–09 (8th Cir. 2005).

a seller may offer to cure the defect within a reasonable period beyond the time when the contract was to be performed so long as it has acted in good faith and with a reasonable expectation that the original goods would be acceptable to the buyer.

The factual background against which we decide this appeal is based on either undisputed proof or express findings at Trial Term. In January 1974, amidst the fuel shortage produced by the oil embargo, the plaintiff (then known as Joc Oil USA, Inc.) purchased a cargo of fuel oil whose sulfur content was represented to it as no greater than 1 percent. While the oil was still at sea en route to the United States in the tanker *M T Khamsin*, plaintiff received a certificate from the foreign refinery at which it had been processed informing it that the sulfur content in fact was 0.52%. Thereafter, on January 24, the plaintiff entered into a written contract with the defendant (Con Ed) for the sale of this oil. The agreement was for delivery to take place between January 24 and January 30, payment being subject to a named independent testing agency's confirmation of quality and quantity. The contract, following a trade custom to round off specifications of sulfur content at, for instance, 1 percent, 0.5%, or 0.3%, described that of the *Khamsin* oil as 0.5%.[76] In the course of the negotiations, the plaintiff learned that Con Ed was then authorized to buy and burn oil with a sulfur content of up to 1 percent and would even mix oils containing more and less to maintain that figure.

When the vessel arrived, on January 25, its cargo was discharged into Con Ed storage tanks in Bayonne, New Jersey.[77] In due course, the independent testing people reported a sulfur content of 0.92%. On this basis, acting within a time frame whose reasonableness is not in question, on February 14 Con Ed rejected the shipment. Prompt negotiations to adjust the price failed; by February 20, plaintiff had offered a price reduction roughly responsive to the difference in sulfur reading, but Con Ed, though it could use the oil, rejected this proposition out of hand. It was insistent on paying no more than the latest prevailing price, which, in the volatile market that then existed, was some 25 percent below the level that prevailed when it agreed to buy the oil.

The very next day, February 21, plaintiff offered to cure the defect with a substitute shipment of conforming oil scheduled to arrive on the *S.S. Appollonian Victory* on February 28. Nevertheless, on February 22, the very day after the cure was proffered, Con Ed, adamant in its intention to avail itself of the intervening drop in prices, summarily rejected this proposal too. The two cargos were subsequently sold to third parties at the best price obtainable, first that of the *Appollonian* and, sometime later, after extraction from the tanks had been accomplished, that of the *Khamsin*.

There ensued this action for breach of contract,[78] which, after a somewhat unconventional trial course, resulted in a nonjury decision for the plaintiff in the sum of

---

76. [1] Confirmatorily, Con Ed's brief describes 0.92% oil as "nominally" 1% oil.

77. [2] The tanks already contained some other oil, but Con Ed appears to have had no concern over the admixture of the differing sulfur contents. In any event, the efficacy of the independent testing required by the contract was not impaired by the commingling.

78. [4] The plaintiff originally also sought an affirmative injunction to compel Con Ed to accept the *Khamsin* shipment or, alternatively, the *Appollonian* substitute. However, when a preliminary in-

$1,385,512.83, essentially the difference between the original contract price of $3,360,667.14 and the amount received by the plaintiff by way of resale of the *Khamsin* oil at what the court found as a matter of fact was a negotiated price which, under all the circumstances,[79] was reasonably procured in the open market. To arrive at this result, the Trial Judge, while ruling against other liability theories advanced by the plaintiff, which, in particular, included one charging the defendant with having failed to act in good faith in the negotiations for a price adjustment on the *Khamsin* oil (Uniform Commercial Code, § 1-203), decided as a matter of law that subdivision (2) of § 2-508 of the Uniform Commercial Code was available to the plaintiff even if it had no prior knowledge of the nonconformity. Finding that in fact plaintiff had no such belief at the time of the delivery, that what turned out to be a 0.92% sulfur content was "within the range of contemplation of reasonable acceptability" to Con Ed, and that seasonable notice of an intention to cure was given, the court went on to hold that plaintiff's "reasonable and timely offer to cure" was improperly rejected (*sub nom. Joc Oil USA v. Consolidated Edison Co. of N.Y.*, 107 Misc. 2d 376, 390, 434 N.Y.S.2d 623 ...)

II.

We turn then to the central issue on this appeal: Fairly interpreted, did subdivision (2) of § 2-508 of the Uniform Commercial Code require Con Ed to accept the substitute shipment plaintiff tendered? In approaching this question, we, of course, must remember that a seller's right to cure a defective tender, as allowed by both subdivisions of § 2-508, was intended to act as a meaningful limitation on the absolutism of the old perfect tender rule, under which, no leeway being allowed for any imperfections, there was, as one court put it, just "no room ... for the doctrine of substantial performance" of commercial obligations (*Mitsubishi Goshi Kaisha v. Aron & Co.*, 16 F.2d 185, 186 (1926) [LEARNED HAND, J.]....

In contrast, to meet the realities of the more impersonal business world of our day, the Code, to avoid sharp dealing, expressly provides for the liberal construction of its remedial provisions (§ 1-102) so that "good faith" and the "observance of reasonable commercial standards of fair dealing" be the rule rather than the exception in trade (*see* § 2-103, subd. [1], par. [b]), "good faith" being defined as "honesty in fact in the conduct or transaction concerned" (Uniform Commercial Code, § 1-201, subd. [19]). As to § 2-508 in particular, the Code's Official Comment advises that its mission is to safeguard the seller "against surprise as a result of sudden technicality on the buyer's part." (Uniform Commercial Code, § 2-106, Comment 2)....

[There are two parts to § 2-508. The first, which had its counterpart before the enactment of the Code, provides for a cure when the time for performance has not

---

junction was denied on the ground that the plaintiff had an adequate remedy at law, it amended its complaint to pursue the latter remedy alone.

79. [5] These circumstances included the fact that the preliminary injunction was not denied until April so that, by the time the *Khamsin* oil was sold in May, almost three months had gone by since its rejection.

yet expired. The second part, new with the Code, provides an opportunity for cure in some cases even though the time for performance has passed.]

Since we here confront circumstances in which the conforming tender came after the time of performance, we focus on subdivision (2). On its face, taking its conditions in the order in which they appear, for the statute to apply (1) a buyer must have rejected a nonconforming tender, (2) the seller must have had reasonable grounds to believe this tender would be acceptable (with or without money allowance), and (3) the seller must have "seasonably" notified the buyer of the intention to substitute a conforming tender within a reasonable time.

In the present case, none of these presented a problem. The first one was easily met, for it is unquestioned that, at 0.92%, the sulfur content of the *Khamsin* oil did not conform to the 0.5% specified in the contract and that it was rejected by Con Ed. The second, the reasonableness of the seller's belief that the original tender would be acceptable, was supported not only by unimpeached proof that the contract's 0.5% and the refinery certificate's 0.52% were trade equivalents, but by testimony that, by the time the contract was made, the plaintiff knew Con Ed burned fuel with a content of up to 1 percent, so that, with appropriate price adjustment, the *Khamsin* oil would have suited its needs even if, at delivery, it was, to the plaintiff's surprise, to test out at 0.92%. Further, the matter seems to have been put beyond dispute by the defendant's readiness to take the oil at the reduced market price on February 20. Surely, on such a record, the trial court cannot be faulted for having found as a fact that the second condition too had been established.

As to the third, the conforming state of the *Appollonian* oil is undisputed, the offer to tender it took place on February 21, only a day after Con Ed finally had rejected the *Khamsin* delivery and the *Appollonian* substitute then already was en route to the United States, where it was expected in a week and did arrive on March 4, only four days later than expected. Especially since Con Ed pleaded no prejudice (unless the drop in prices could be so regarded), it is almost impossible, given the flexibility of the Uniform Commercial Code definitions of "seasonable" and "reasonable," to quarrel with the finding that the remaining requirements of the statute also had been met.

Thus lacking the support of the statute's literal language, the defendant nonetheless would have us limit its application to cases in which a seller *knowingly* makes a nonconforming tender that it has reason to believe the buyer will accept. For this proposition, it relies almost entirely on a critique in Nordstrom, Law of Sales (§ 105), which rationalizes that, since a seller who believes its tender is conforming would have no reason to think in terms of a reduction in the price of the goods, to allow such a seller to cure after the time for performance had passed would make the statutory reference to a money allowance redundant.[80] Nordstrom, interestingly enough,

---

80. [8] The premise for such an argument, which ignores the policy of the Code to prevent buyers from using insubstantial remediable or price adjustable defects to free themselves from unprofitable bargains (Hawkland, Sales and Bulk Sales Under the Uniform Commercial Code, pp. 120–22), is that the words "with or without money allowance" apply only to sellers who believe their goods will

finds it useful to buttress this position by the somewhat dire prediction, though backed by no empirical or other confirmation, that, unless the right to cure is confined to those whose nonconforming tenders are knowing ones, the incentive of sellers to timely deliver will be undermined. To this it also adds the somewhat moralistic note that a seller who is mistaken as to the quality of its goods does not merit additional time (Nordstrom, *loc. cit.*). Curiously, recognizing that the few decisions extant on this subject have adopted a position opposed to the one for which it contends, Con Ed seeks to treat these as exceptions rather than exemplars of the rule....

That the principle for which these cases stand goes far beyond their particular facts cannot be gainsaid. These holdings demonstrate that, in dealing with the application of subdivision (2) of § 2-508, courts have been concerned with the reasonableness of the seller's belief that the goods would be acceptable rather than with the seller's pretended knowledge or lack of knowledge of the defect....

It also is no surprise then that the aforementioned decisional history is a reflection of the mainstream of scholarly commentary on the subject.... [Citations omitted.]

White and Summers, for instance, put it well, and bluntly. Stressing that the Code intended cure to be "a remedy which should be carefully cultivated and developed by the courts" ... the authors conclude, as do we, that a seller should have recourse to the relief afforded by subdivision (2) of § 2-508 of the Uniform Commercial Code as long as it can establish that it had reasonable grounds, tested objectively, for its belief that the goods would be accepted.[81] It goes without saying that the test of reasonableness, in this context, must encompass the concepts of "good faith" and "commercial standards of fair dealing" that permeate the Code (Uniform Commercial Code, § 1-201 (20); §§ 1-304, 2-103(1)(b)).

As to the damages issue raised by the defendant, we affirm without reaching the merits. At no stage of the proceedings before the trial court did the defendant object to the plaintiff's proposed method for their calculation, and this though the plaintiff gave ample notice of that proposal by means of a preliminary statement and pretrial memorandum filed with the court.... And, even after the decision at *nisi prius* revealed that the Judge had acted on such an assumption, so far as the record shows, no motion was ever made to correct it....

For all these reasons, the order of the Appellate Division should be affirmed, with costs.

---

be acceptable with such an allowance and not to sellers who believe their goods will be acceptable without such an allowance. But, since the words are part of a phrase that speaks of an otherwise unqualified belief that the goods will be acceptable, unless one strains for an opposite interpretation, we find insufficient reason to doubt that it intends to include both those who find a need to offer an allowance and those who do not.

81. Eds. note: The court was quoting and referencing the second edition of WHITE & SUMMERS, UNIFORM COMMERCIAL CODE (1980). This reference work is now in its sixth edition. The relevant discussion, to similar effect, is at page 440.

NOTES AND QUESTIONS

1. *Arguments by plaintiff and defendant:* Not surprisingly, Con Edison and Joc Oil emphasized different aspects of the dispute in their arguments to the trial court. Mr. Goldstein, lawyer for Con Edison, attempted to describe as unreasonable Joc Oil's conduct upon discovering that the oil had a higher sulphur content than the contract provided. After noting that oil prices had fallen $4.50 per barrel since the contract was formed, Goldstein urged:

> What did Joc Oil offer to give us off on the oil that was defective? They offered to give us off at most 80 cents a barrel....

> Well, 80 cents a barrel as a reduction is nowhere near the prevailing market price for that oil, 1 percent oil, on February 14th or February 15th or February 20th or February 21st, any of those dates, because on those dates the oil was selling for $13 a barrel, so they wanted to take a price of $17.875 a barrel, which we had agreed to pay for 0.5% maximum sulfur oil and reduce that to not more than $17.075 a barrel, and ask us to pay that price for oil that was selling for $13 a barrel at the time they asked us to accept it....

> Joc Oil is the party that put us in the position of having to figure out what to do with the defective product. We didn't ask for 0.92% oil. We asked for 0.5% maximum sulfur oil. They delivered to us a defective product and then they asked us to do something that would make them get paid for it. They asked us to accept the oil at far more than we would have paid for that oil if we went out to buy it on the day that they asked us to buy it.

> I don't want to belabor the point, but I think it goes without saying that their position was unreasonable. If they would have come down ... to the then-prevailing price we would have bought it, because we stipulated to that.

> They wanted us to swallow a huge chunk of money because of their error....

> ... [W]hen you talk about a substitute shipment, you have to consider what is doing with this substitute shipment. It is very nice to say, o.k., we learned that the oil is defective that we delivered to you; we've got another barge and here it is; that is a reasonable way, perhaps, of offering a substitute shipment, because there is no delay there. But Joc Oil didn't do that; it said, we got a ship coming in, this is on February 21st, we have a ship coming in, it is due to arrive February 28th, we will give you that shipment at the old contract price.

> And we said we don't want that ship, we ordered a shipload of oil that was supposed to arrive between January 24 and January 30, and although it arrived it didn't meet specifications. Don't tell us you are going to give us a shipload of something that will meet specifications five weeks or six weeks later. We are not going to buy it at the old contract price because the market price is way down....

The argument of Mr. Maloof, counsel for plaintiff, emphasized the cure.

[W]e were in the position to make Con Ed one hundred percent whole according to the contract. They should not have the advantage of a drop in the market that occurred from extraordinary military pressures in the Middle East; why should Con Ed get the benefit of that drop in the market and Joc Oil suffer so badly.... Mr. Elias ... offered 80 cents and Mr. Doyle responded with an arbitrary offer of market value.... The market value, according to the papers and the guides, was $13 a barrel. This meant that Joc would have taken a bath of 188,000 barrels times more than $4 a barrel, which is over $700,000, and this is what Con Ed wanted them to do because they were innocently surprised when the oil arrived at 0.92%, and Mr. Goldstein admitted, admitted that we didn't know that it was 0.92, so we are innocent parties....

Now did we offer the conforming shipment on the *Appollonian Victory* seasonably? Well, on February 20th we had this meeting with Mr. Doyle, it broke up. On the next day we offered the conforming shipment. Seasonably means reasonably. I think that is pretty close. Nobody is going to talk about doing these things in a couple of hours. We were quite fortunate to find it, find that we owned it, and offered it on February 21st to be delivered on February 28th. I don't think there is a big question [about] that and I do hope that you will agree.

2. ***Can a money allowance constitute cure?*** Joc Oil was careful to offer, as a cure, a conforming shipment (the *Appollonian* oil). Suppose it had simply offered to lower the price to reflect the difference in the market price of 0.5% and 1.0% maximum sulfur oil at the time of contract, before the fall in oil prices? Most courts would hold that was not a sufficient offer of cure. However, White and Summers[82] say: "Despite the modest violence it does to the language of §2-508(2), we believe that the buyer who complains of some insubstantial nonconformity which can be recompensed by a reduction in the price should be made to accept such a reduction as cure even if there is no usage in the trade to accept such reductions." In a footnote to this passage in the first edition that is not included in later editions, they go on to say: "One must remember that there are many defects which cannot be cured by a money allowance.... [A] price reduction does not ... cure a quality defect which makes the goods unusable or unsalable."

HEAD v. PHILLIPS CAMPER SALES & RENTAL, INC.

Michigan Court of Appeals
234 Mich. App. 94, 593 N.W.2d 595 (1999)

CORRIGAN, C.J.

In this dispute over a pop-up camper, plaintiff Mary Head appeals ... the judgment of no cause of action on her claim for revocation of acceptance.... This case presents an issue of first impression regarding the effect of a seller's previous attempts to repair

---

82. Uniform Commercial Code 443 (6th ed., West 2010).

defective goods where the buyer revokes acceptance under [UCC § 2-608(1)(b)]. We hold that, while a seller has no right to cure after the buyer revokes, the seller's efforts to repair are relevant to the determinations whether the defect substantially impaired the value of the goods and whether the buyer revoked acceptance within a reasonable time after discovering the defect. In this case, the trial court erroneously instructed the jury that defendant Phillips's attempts to repair the camper could support a defense to plaintiff's claim. We therefore affirm in part, vacate the judgment in part, and remand for further proceedings consistent with this opinion.

I. Factual Background and Procedural Posture

Plaintiff purchased a pop-up camper from defendant Phillips in July 1992.... Plaintiff took delivery of the camper a few days later. Plaintiff soon discovered that the roof "leaned" toward the door and that the door would not lock. She returned the camper to Phillips six days after taking delivery. Phillips replaced the lock and advised plaintiff that the leaning condition was normal for a pop-up camper.

Plaintiff first took the camper on a trip in late July 1992. According to plaintiff, she had difficulty latching the door and assembling the awning. The sides and roof of the camper were unstable and swayed. The refrigerator did not work properly. Plaintiff notified Phillips of these problems on her return home. She experienced the same difficulties during another trip in early August, and cut that trip short when the refrigerator stopped working. Further, in preparing to leave the campsite, plaintiff had considerable difficulty hitching the camper to her van. Plaintiff notified Phillips of these additional problems after she returned home. She then delivered the camper to Phillips on August 31, 1992, for repairs.

Defendant Phillips returned the camper to plaintiff in late September 1992. According to plaintiff, she needed her husband's assistance to assemble the camper and the camper continued to "sway." Moreover, plaintiff could not close the camper. She called Phillips for assistance. A Phillips employee then came to her home and successfully closed the camper. Soon thereafter, plaintiff returned the camper to Phillips. Plaintiff initially requested the return of the purchase price, but ultimately agreed to further repairs. Phillips transported the camper to the manufacturer for the repairs.

In late November 1992, defendant Phillips notified plaintiff that the repairs were complete and she could pick up the camper. Plaintiff inspected the camper at Phillips's place of business and discovered that it continued to lean. She refused to take possession and told Phillips that she no longer wanted the camper. Phillips declined to refund her money and requested another opportunity to repair the camper. Plaintiff agreed. Phillips attempted to repair the camper during December 1992 and January 1993. When plaintiff requested a refund in January, Phillips refused.

In February 1993, defendant Phillips notified plaintiff that she could pick up the camper. Plaintiff's stepdaughter retrieved the camper from Phillips and transported it to plaintiff's home. Plaintiff, however, could not open the camper. Further, plaintiff, noting apparent changes in the camper, believed that it was not the one that she had purchased. She compared the vehicle identification number (VIN) on the certificate of origin, title, and registration with that on the camper and discovered that they differed by one number.[83] Plaintiff demanded a refund in a letter dated March 19, 1993. Defendant Phillips refused her request.

Plaintiff commenced this action in August 1993, asserting ... claims against defendants for revocation of acceptance.... The jury found for defendant Phillips on plaintiff's claim for revocation....

Plaintiff subsequently moved for judgment notwithstanding the verdict (JNOV) on her claim for revocation on the ground that defendant Phillips's failure to convey marketable title to her substantially impaired the value of the camper.... The trial court denied plaintiff's motions for JNOV....

II. Revocation of Acceptance

Plaintiff first contends that the trial court erroneously instructed the jury that defendant Phillips's efforts to repair the camper could support a defense to her claim for revocation of acceptance....

UCC §2-608(1)(b)

This case presents a question of first impression regarding the effect of a seller's attempts to repair where the buyer revokes acceptance under §2-608 of the Uniform Commercial Code (UCC).... The statute provides: [The Court quotes §2-608 in full.] This case does not fall within subsection 1(a) because the record does not reflect that plaintiff knew of the defect when she accepted the camper. Further, although the parties to a sales agreement may limit remedies and damages for a breach, UCC §2-719, the parties' agreement in this case contained no such limitation.[84] Therefore, plaintiff did not have to prove that a limited remedy failed in its purpose or operated to deprive her of the value of the bargain to pursue other UCC remedies, including revocation. Consequently, we must determine whether a seller has a right to cure when a buyer revokes his acceptance on the basis of a defect that was not known at the time of acceptance, UCC §2-608(1)(b), and, if not, the effect of a seller's previous attempts to repair on the buyer's right to revoke.

This issue involves a question of statutory interpretation, which we review *de novo*.... Judicial construction is not permitted where the plain and ordinary meaning of the statutory language is clear.

A majority of courts considering this question have concluded that a seller has no right to cure after a buyer revokes his acceptance under §2-608(1)(b) of the UCC.

---

83. [1] The sticker attached to the camper states that the VIN is 1RKTC2600M1000135, whereas the certificate of origin, title, and temporary registration list the VIN as 1RKTC3600M1000135.
84. [2] The contract provided:
> It is expressly agreed that there are no warranties, express or implied, made by the selling dealer or the manufacturer on the motor vehicle, chassis or parts furnished hereunder except, in the case of a new motor vehicle the warranty expressly given to the purchaser upon the delivery of such motor vehicle or chassis.

The manufacturer's warranty limited the remedy to repair and replacement. The sales agreement did not similarly limit plaintiff's remedies against defendant Phillips.

E.g., American Honda Motor Co. v. Boyd, 475 So. 2d 835, 840 (Ala. 1985); *U.S. Roofing, Inc. v. Credit Alliance Corp.*, 228 Cal. App. 3d 1431, 1443–44, 279 Cal. Rptr. 533 (1991); ... *Gappelberg v. Landrum*, 666 S.W.2d 88, 89–91 (Tex. 1984).... A minority of courts have reached the opposite result on the basis of either policy considerations, *Fitzner Pontiac-Buick-Cadillac, Inc. v. Smith*, 523 So. 2d 324, 327–28 (Miss. 1988), or the determination that § 2-608(3) incorporates a seller's right to cure under § 2-508. *Ayanru v. General Motors Acceptance Corp.*, 130 Misc. 2d 440, 445, 495 N.Y.S.2d 1018 (1985); *Oberg v. Phillips*, 615 P.2d 1022, 1026 (Okla. App. 1980).

We adopt the majority approach to the construction of § 2-608(1)(b). Under the plain language of UCC § 2-608(1)(b), a seller has no right to cure a defect that was not discoverable when the buyer accepted the goods. The Legislature explicitly granted the seller a right to cure in UCC § 2-508, and implicitly granted a similar right in UCC § 2-608(1)(a) (acceptance with knowledge of a nonconformity that the seller will seasonably cure). The Legislature granted no such right in UCC § 2-608(1)(b). We will not read a right to cure into § 2-608(1)(b) where the Legislature granted that very right in other sections, but did not do so here.

We further conclude that UCC § 2-608(3) does not incorporate the seller's right to cure under § 2-508. Section 2-608(3) grants a buyer who revokes his acceptance "the same rights and duties with regard to the goods involved as if he had rejected them." Those rights and duties are set forth in provisions such as § 2-602(2)(b) and (c), § 2-603, and § 2-604 ...; see *Colonial Dodge, Inc. v. Miller*, 420 Mich. 452, 460, 362 N.W.2d 704 (1984). Section 2-608(3) does not similarly extend the seller's rights and duties. Further, to incorporate a right to cure into § 2-608 would ignore the policies that underlie the distinction between rejection and acceptance within the UCC. Under UCC § 2-601, the buyer may reject a tender if the goods "fail in any respect to conform to the contract." If a buyer rejects a nonconforming tender, the seller may have a right to cure the defect. UCC § 2-508. The seller can also recover damages if the buyer wrongfully rejects. UCC § 2-703. Once the buyer accepts the tender, however, he loses the ability to reject the goods. The buyer must pay for the goods at the contract rate, UCC § 2-607(1), and may only revoke his acceptance if the defect substantially impairs its value to him. UCC § 2-608(1). If the defect does not rise to this level of severity, the buyer is limited to those remedies available for a breach of contract. The seller, in turn, loses the right to cure, but gains the benefit of the higher substantial impairment standard for revocation. Further, if the buyer wrongfully revokes, the seller may recover damages. UCC § 2-703.

We certainly recognize that policy reasons do exist for extending a seller's right to cure to the revocation context. These reasons include the minimization of economic waste, the improvement of uniformity, and the reduction in the costs of bargaining over the existence and scope of the right to cure. See generally Foss, *The seller's right to cure when the buyer revokes acceptance: Erase the line in the sand*, 16 S. ILL. U.L.J. 1, 1–17 (1991); Sebert, *Rejection, revocation, and cure under Article 2 of the Uniform Commercial Code: Some modest proposals*, 84 Nw. U. L. R. 375, 392–98, 425–28 (1990). We will not, however, debate the public policy interests at stake in § 2-

608(1)(b). In our view, that debate is for the Legislature, not this Court.... Accordingly, under the plain language of the statute, a seller has no right to cure when a buyer revokes acceptance under UCC § 2-608(1)(b).

A seller's attempts to repair are not, however, irrelevant to a determination whether a buyer rightfully revoked acceptance under § 2-608(1)(b). The uncertainty inherent in the substantial impairment standard encourages the buyer to allow the seller to repair rather than risk paying damages for wrongful revocation. See UCC § 2-608, Official Comment 4. The seller's attempts to repair are likewise a factor in determining whether the buyer notified the seller of revocation within a "reasonable time" after discovering the defect. *Id.* Moreover, the ease of repair may be relevant to the question whether the defect substantially impairs the value of the goods to the buyer. See *Haverlah v. Memphis Aviation, Inc.*, 674 S.W.2d 297 (Tenn. App. 1984). We next consider whether the trial court adequately instructed the jury regarding these principles.

B. Jury Instructions

In this case, the trial court instructed the jury that defendant Phillips's efforts to repair the camper could provide it with a defense to plaintiff's claim for revocation:

> [T]his case involves a claim by the buyer for breach of a contract for the sale of goods. A contract for the sale [of] goods is an agreement between a buyer and a seller who, by their words and conduct, show that they intended to make a contract. The buyer has the burden of proving that a contract exists at the time of the purchase, that the seller breached the contract, and that the buyer was damaged by the breach of contract. *Now, the seller has the burden of proving the defense of the buyer failed to revoke the contract within a reasonable period of time; and two, that the seller has made all reasonable and necessary efforts to repair any alleged defects.*
>
> *Now, also keep in mind that the seller's good-faith efforts do not excuse its failure to have the item repaired and returned to the plaintiff within a reasonable period of time. So where a — a dealer has limited its obligation under the agreement to repair a particular item, they do not have an unlimited time to make the repairs, but rather must repair within a reasonable time.*
>
> All right, now that had to do with revocation. Let me go over it again. The buyer has the burden of proving that the contract exists at the time of purchase, the seller breached the contract, the buyer was damaged by the breach of contract. *The seller has the burden of proving the defense that the buyer failed to revoke the contract within a reasonable period of time, and that the seller has made all reasonable and necessary efforts to repair any alleged defects. But again that has to be done within a reasonable period of time.*
>
> All right, now the buyer's revocation of acceptance. A buyer must accept goods from the seller if the goods and the manner, time, and place of their delivery conform to the contract. In this case, the buyer accepted the goods and then revoked the acceptance. The buyer is entitled to revoke acceptance of the goods only if those goods do not conform to the contract and the non-

conformity substantially impairs the value of those goods to the buyer and if the buyer notified the seller of the revocation within a reasonable time after the buyer discovered, or should have discovered, the nonconformity and the buyer accepted the goods on the reasonable assumption that the nonconformity would be cured and it was not cured within the time agreed, or the buyer did not discover the nonconformity and the buyer's acceptance was reasonably induced, either by difficulty of discovery before acceptance or by the seller's assurances.

Now, the buyer has the burden of proving that he or she gave the seller the required notification. In this case the defendants admit that they received the required notification. If you determine that the buyer rightfully revoked the acceptance, then the seller has breached the contract. If you determine that the buyer has wrongfully revoked the contract—or excuse me, the acceptance, then the buyer has breached the contract. [Emphasis added by the Court of Appeals.]

We conclude that the trial court erroneously instructed the jury on the applicable law and theories of the parties. Because defendant Phillips conceded that plaintiff's acceptance of the camper was induced by the difficulty of discovery of the nonconformity and that plaintiff gave the required notification, two issues remained for determination by the jury: (1) whether plaintiff revoked her acceptance within a reasonable time, and (2) whether the nonconformity substantially impaired the value of the camper to plaintiff. Plaintiff bore the burden of proof regarding both these issues. UCC §§ 2-607(4), 1-201(8). The trial court, however, erroneously instructed the jury that defendant Phillips's "reasonable and necessary efforts to repair" could provide a defense to plaintiff's claim for revocation. The trial court also improperly instructed [the jury] regarding a seller's limitation of remedies to repair when the sales agreement contained no such limitation. These errors were not harmless because the trial court's confusing instructions pertained to the critical issues at trial. We vacate the judgment for defendant Phillips on plaintiff's claim for revocation of acceptance and remand for a new trial....

VI. Remaining Issues

Plaintiff asserts that the trial court erred in denying her motion for judgment notwithstanding the verdict on the ground that the defects in the camper and the discrepancy in VIN substantially impaired its value to her. We disagree. In reviewing the trial court's decision on a motion for JNOV, we view the evidence in a light most favorable to the nonmoving party to determine whether reasonable jurors could reach different conclusions. *Zander v. Ogihara Corp.*, 213 Mich. App. 438, 441; 540 N.W.2d 702 (1995). "If reasonable jurors could honestly have reached different conclusions, neither the trial court nor this Court may substitute its judgment for that of the jury." *Id.*

We conclude that the trial court properly denied plaintiff's motion. Because plaintiff premised her motion below solely on the VIN issue, we will not consider her additional grounds for JNOV first raised on appeal. Regarding her VIN argument, plaintiff has provided no legal support for her contention that the discrepancy in the VIN either rendered the conveyance void or substantially impaired the value of the camper to her as a matter of law. This Court will not search for authority to sustain or reject a party's position. Plaintiff has effectively abandoned this issue by failing to cite any supporting legal authority.

Affirmed in part, vacated in part, and remanded.

NOTES AND QUESTIONS

1. *Applying the minority view:* The court notes that there is a division of authority respecting the right to cure after a proper revocation of acceptance. White and Summers make a strong policy argument for the minority view, as do the law review articles cited by the court.

> Certainly a case can be made for [the minority] approach. The Code itself says that it is to "be construed liberally" in order "to promote its underlying purposes and policies." A stated policy of the Code is to incorporate commercial practices and custom. A reading of the cases indicates that most buyers allow, or even desire, an opportunity to cure by the seller before the buyer resorts to the more drastic action of revocation. Two policies not stated in the Code, but clearly evident in its provisions, are to facilitate the settlement of disputes by the parties themselves, and to minimize economic waste. Allowing the seller the chance to cure might go further toward these goals than permitting the buyer unilaterally to revoke and sending the parties to court to see if the revocation was justified.[85]

If the Michigan Court of Appeals had followed this advice, what more would plaintiff have had to prove to justify recovery of her purchase price? Note that plaintiff allowed defendant several opportunities to repair.

2. *Limiting remedies:* As the second footnote in the opinion makes clear, the defendant, the dealer, had not inserted a provision limiting remedies to repair or replacement, at the seller's option. Such a provision was in the manufacturer's warranty. "Limitation of remedy" clauses such as this one are pervasive, and they are enforced unless they "fail of their essential purpose" or are unconscionable. *See* UCC § 2-719(2) and (3). What arguments could you have made for plaintiff if the dealer's contract had contained the traditional limitation-of-remedy clause?

3. *How much burden can a seller put on the buyer in attempting to cure?* In *Travelers Indemnity Co. v. Maho Machine Tool Corp.*,[86] a complex machine tool had been shipped to Singapore, but it had been damaged by rust. The machine had to be returned to Germany for reconditioning. The seller proposed that the buyer do the following: (1) file a claim with its insurance carrier; (2) return the damaged machine to Germany,

---

85. WHITE & SUMMERS, UNIFORM COMMERCIAL CODE 437 (6th ed. 2010).
86. 952 F.2d 26 (2d Cir. 1991).

where it would be reconditioned and resold; (3) accept a replacement machine that would arrive within a month; and (4) use a smaller but similar machine that the seller would loan the buyer for the period of time between returning the machine and the arrival of its replacement. The buyer had expected to finance the purchase of the machine by a loan from a Singapore bank that would have been secured by the machine itself. Without the machine, the bank would not loan the money. Buyer did not have sufficient funds available to pack and ship the defective machine from Singapore to Germany. The trial court found that the seller had complied with UCC §2-508(2). The Second Circuit reversed. It said: "The law of sales does not impose upon the buyer any obligation to assume the expenses of the seller in effecting a cure for the delivery of nonconforming goods." Could the plaintiff in the *Head* case have used this holding to her advantage?

6. CISG and Imperfect Performance

We have offered, in the preceding chapters, notes that offer a glimpse of the manner in which the Convention on Contracts for the International Sale of Goods (CISG) deals with the topics covered in this course. In most cases, the CISG either adopts a rule that tracks the UCC, or it chooses a variation that reflects the common law approach — or perhaps an approach that is widespread in other parts of the world. When it comes to the issue of the treatment of breach, notice, cure, and remedy, we have concluded that it is appropriate to merely call your attention, in the broadest terms possible, to the CISG approach. To do more would require more time and space than we believe appropriate here. The changes are too significant.

Professor Curtis Reitz[87] suggests that "[t]he most important ... [differences between CISG and the UCC] deal with the performance stage of sales contracts, particularly when a performance is late or is qualitatively or quantitatively deficient." The CISG creates, to some extent, a different structure than the Code; it rejects the perfect tender rule as a starting point for defining a buyer's rights, makes distinctions between late performance and the tender of nonconforming goods, provides for a remedy in which a buyer can insist on repair, adopts a concept it calls "fundamental breach" as the critical point in establishing a right to "avoid" a contract, and generally "seeks to keep troubled contracts going forward despite failings to a greater extent than the rules of the Commercial Code."[88] If you have a transaction governed by the CISG, you should realize that the CISG provides a different structure of rights and remedies. Our brief warning should also stand as more evidence that the rules we have been discussing represent one set of choices from among competing possibilities, and not the inevitable result of the application of "legal science" to the problem.

---

87. Curtis R. Reitz, *The Uniform Commercial Code and the Convention on Contracts for the International Sale of Goods, in* Negotiating and Structuring International Commercial Transactions (American Bar Association 1991).

88. *Id.*

7. Two Classic, But Troublesome, Problems

a. Installment Contracts and the Failure to
Perform Part of the Deal

Installment contracts often present several problems to lawyers and courts. Suppose supplier is to perform steps A, B, C, and D while buyer is to pay $100,000. UCC § 2-307 states the common law rule: "Unless otherwise agreed all goods called for by a contract for sale must be tendered in a single delivery and payment is due only on such tender...." The same idea is contained in the rule that when one performance takes time while the other can be done all at once, then the performance that takes time must be performed first. In other words, unless they agree otherwise, sellers of goods and services must complete the job before the buyer must pay for it.

Suppose, however, that supplier and buyer's contract looks like this:

Supplier does:	Buyer pays:
Step A	$25,000
Step B	$15,000
Step C	$35,000
Step D	$25,000
Total:	$100,000

Then assume that supplier completes Step A, but has not yet begun the other steps. Must buyer pay supplier $25,000 then? UCC § 2-307 continues, providing: "[B]ut where circumstances give either party the right to make or demand delivery in lots the price if it can be apportioned may be demanded for each lot."

Building contracts often provoke difficult problems. For example, suppose a builder has promised to do steps A, B, C, and D. The owner has promised in turn to make the four payments indicated as each step is completed. Often the owner is not buying step A for $25,000. Step A may be worth much more or much less than $25,000. Rather, the parties have agreed on a payment schedule, which serves several purposes. With such a payment schedule, the builder does not have to finance the entire job until completion. Rather than borrowing money to pay for needed materials, wages, and subcontractors, the builder can settle its debts with the money the seller pays at designated times. Furthermore, the builder lessens its credit risk. It does not want to take the chance that it will build an entire structure and then discover that the owner cannot raise enough money to pay for it. In a pay-as-you-go contract, the builder only risks losing its investment of time and materials made between payments. Owners may also benefit from installment contracts. They can appraise the quality of performance at each step before they pay, rather than waiting to the end—when at least some defects will be harder to cure.

But what happens when one party fails to perform as called for by the contract? Suppose that builder completes step A and owner pays $25,000. Builder then completes step B, but owner fails to pay the $15,000 that is due. Must builder continue and finish steps C and D? Can it exercise "self-help" remedies? May builder suspend performance until owner pays the $15,000 that is due? May builder call off the entire contract and move its workers to another job? Suppose owner is eager to have builder complete the job and says that he will pay builder just as soon as he can. Should this matter?

First, we'll look at installment contract problems in the setting of building contracts, and then we'll turn to transactions in goods and one of the Uniform Commercial Code's less satisfactory sections.

PALMER v. WATSON CONSTRUCTION CO.

Minnesota Supreme Court
265 Minn. 195, 121 N.W.2d 62 (1963)

SHERAN, J.

The appeal is from an order of the district court denying defendants' motion for judgment notwithstanding the verdict or, in the alternative, a new trial.

The action was instituted by plaintiff to recover progress payments, retained percentages, and damages for breach of contracts for excavation and backfilling, one being dated August 26, and the other September 20, 1960. In response defendant Watson Construction Company asserted default by plaintiff and counterclaimed for damages occasioned by his failure to perform.

The subject matter of the contracts was excavation, backfilling, sodding, and seeding to be performed in connection with the construction of four buildings and connecting tunnels being built at the state hospital at Brainerd pursuant to a prime contract between defendant and the State of Minnesota.

Relevant contract provisions fixing the obligations of these parties included the following:

The Contractor agrees— ...

(h) To pay the Subcontractor on demand for his work or materials as far as executed and fixed in place, less the retained percentage....

The subcontractor's obligations are described as follows:

Section 3. The Subcontractor agrees to complete the several portions and the whole of the work herein sublet by the time or times following: As required by the progress of the job. Subcontractor agrees to provide sufficient equipment to complete the excavation of the four buildings this fall and, further agrees that if he does not provide proper equipment to complete his contract, the contractor has the right to bring in additional equipment and charge the cost of same against his contract.

The contracts involved do not contain provisions governing resolution of disputes between the parties as to quantities of work performed for purpose of progress payments where, as here, there was no certification by the architect.

On October 6, 1960, plaintiff submitted to defendant a statement for work completed as of September 20, 1960, which included a claim for $7,760 for excavation of 19,400 cubic yards of earth at 40 cents per cubic yard. Upon receipt, defendant disputed the quantity of excavation for which it had been billed and sent plaintiff a check that included the sum of $5,400, less retained percentage, representing payment for excavation of 13,500 cubic yards of material. Protracted negotiations then ensued, during the course of which plaintiff insisted that he was entitled to payment based upon his figures, which represented the quantity of material that he claimed he had in fact removed. Defendant persisted in its refusal to accept these figures on the theory that if the quantity of material claimed by plaintiff had in fact been removed, plaintiff had "overexcavated," *i.e.*, excavated from the foundation grade to the level of the ground at an angle in excess of that prescribed by defendant and by proper and customary standards of workmanship....

Although plaintiff submitted statements for and received payment on account of additional excavation performed during the month of November, the disagreement with respect to the quantity for which he was entitled to payment in connection with the digging done by him and included in the October 6 billing was never resolved. Apparently construction work on the project was resumed in February 1961, but plaintiff declined to perform further under his subcontracts unless he was paid in conformity with his calculations....

Correspondence between defendant and plaintiff and plaintiff's attorney during February, March, and April reveals that the parties had reached an impasse. By letter dated March 2, 1961, which reviews the February correspondence and reflects the persistence of the disagreement, defendant wrote, "Further, we are requesting at this time a definite statement from Mr. Palmer as to whether he intends to complete his contract." By letter dated March 6, 1961, defendant advised plaintiff that it was correcting the grade level in one of the basements and completing the backfilling on this building and would backcharge the expense to plaintiff. On March 16, 1961, defendant wrote to plaintiff, "If we do not hear from you by return mail that you intend to complete your contract on this project, it will be necessary for us to hire another contractor to complete your contract on a time and material basis. Any costs over and above your total contract price will necessarily have to be assumed by your firm." On March 20, 1961, plaintiff's attorney wrote to defendant as follows: "Mr. Palmer has always been willing to complete his contract but he is not going to complete the contract unless you fulfill your obligation to make payment as set forth above." In addition, this letter contains a statement that plaintiff was unable to pay another subcontractor and that defendant was placing plaintiff "in a position where he cannot proceed with the contract by reason of this inability to pay."

The jury was instructed that if refusal by plaintiff to continue performance under the contract was justified, he was entitled to recover not only for the excavation and other contract services actually performed, but also for such profits as he would have realized had performance been completed and payment made according to the agreement. The jury was informed that if plaintiff's refusal to proceed was not justified, defendant was entitled to recover damages on its counterclaim. No instructions were given or requested that plaintiff would be entitled to recover in *quantum meruit* for the services in fact performed by him up to the point when the disagreement brought work to a halt....

... [I]t is our opinion that the evidence does not sustain the verdict in so far as it includes damages for loss of the profit anticipated in the event of full performance. A party to a contract who is entitled to progress payments may treat the failure to make such payments when due as a breach of the contract, which will justify him in refusing to perform further and which will give legal basis for a claim for the reasonable value of the services performed or material supplied pursuant to the contract.... His alternative course is to continue with performance and recover the contract price in full upon completion.... It is true that a party ready, willing, and able to perform may recover damages for breach of contract, as distinguished from the reasonable value of the services rendered or material supplied, if he is prevented from performance by an act or omission of the other contracting party.... We are committed in this state, however, to the rule that nonpayment of installment obligations is not in and of itself such prevention of performance as will make possible suit for loss of profits even though the party entitled to payment may lack working capital....

Although the letter written by plaintiff's attorney on March 20 stated that nonpayment was interfering with the discharge of Palmer's obligation to his subcontractor and thus preventing completion, there is nothing in the testimony of the subcontractor, who was called as a witness in behalf of plaintiff, to support this argument adequately. While the parties to a construction contract could make nonpayment of progress payments such an event as would empower the party entitled to the money to discontinue performance and sue for that which he would have earned had the contract been completed, we find no such provision in the agreements here involved. It is conceivable that refusal to make progress payments without justification and under circumstances where the refusal is intended to make performance by the contractor impossible could be considered such prevention of performance as would justify recovery of profits for breach of an indivisible contract. For the present, it is sufficient to say that this is not such a case.

Reversed and remanded for a new trial.

NOTES AND QUESTIONS

1. The general contractor argued that even if the grading contractor had performed properly, there was a breach only of the progress payment provisions and not the whole contract. It quoted *New York Life Ins. Co. v. Viglas*[89] as stating that to justify treating a contract as completely broken, a repudiation "must at least amount to an unqualified refusal or declaration of inability substantially to perform according to the terms of its obligation." The brief continued, saying that "[t]he trial judge in his memorandum attempts to distinguish ... case law ... on the basis that [the grading

---

89. 297 U.S. 672 (1936).

contractor's] financial resources were insufficient to let him finish the job.... [T]his contention has been repeatedly raised, examined on the merits in trial, and has been held as a matter of law inapplicable." The general contractor quoted a passage from *Beatty v. Howe Lumber Co.*:[90]

> It could make no difference with the legal liability of the defendant whether the plaintiffs were rich or poor. If they had been rich, or had ample means, it is evident, from the record, that they would or could have continued to perform the services.... [One may recover when another prevents perform-ance]..., but ... this right does not rest in the mere default in payment of an installment when it becomes due, especially when ... there was no denial of the legal right of the plaintiffs to proceed in the performance of the contract unaffected by the conduct or default of the defendant.

As with many legal questions, there is another view of the question of whether late payments constitute cause for a contractor's refusal to proceed. In *Cork Plumbing Co., Inc. v. Martin Bloom Associates, Inc.*,[91] the court stated:

> Because of the nature of construction contracts and the contractor's need for funds to meet expenses and proceed with construction, courts have dis-tinguished construction contracts from other installment contracts with re-spect to the subcontractors' right to terminate for non-payment of installments. This judicial sentiment is expressed in *Brady Brick & Supply Co. v. Lotito*, 43 Ill. App. 3d 69, 1 Ill. Dec. 844, 848, 356 N.E.2d 1126, 1130 (1976):
>
>> The failure to pay an installment of the contract price as provided in a building or construction contract is a substantial breach of contract and gives the contractor the right to consider the contract at an end, to cease work, and to recover the value of the work already performed....[92]
>
> We recognize that the facts in every construction contract might not warrant a termination upon failure to pay an installment, but the present facts, par-ticularly the repeated failure to keep payments current coupled with [defen-dant's] statements about future payments, permit such a resolution. We must consider the effect of delays on the builder's finances, and "[s]ince the builder's risks depend largely upon the financial resources of the debtor, ... a non-payment by an obligor who is of doubtful solvency ... *or who accompanies his non-payment by words of near repudiation is almost certain to be held a vital breach.*" (Emphasis added.) 3A Corbin on Contracts, § 692.

2. *The measure of damages:* The jury determined that the general contractor wrong-fully failed to make a full progress payment. The court determined that the subcon-tractor was entitled to stop work on the job and sue for damages as well. What should be the measure of recovery? The court determined that plaintiff could recover the

<hr>

90. 77 Minn. 272, 79 N.W. 1013, 1015 (1899).
91. 573 S.W.2d 947 (Mo. Ct. App. 1978).
92. Eds. note: The measure of damages in a case such as this is covered in the next note.

reasonable value of services and materials provided, but that it could not recover lost profits for the part of the contract not yet performed.

Courts often distinguish between "partial" and "total" breaches of contract in discussing such questions. Under a *partial breach*, the contract continues despite the default. Nonetheless, the aggrieved party can recover a judgment for the payment that has been missed. Under a *total breach*, the contract is at an end. Now damages are not measured by the installment payments in the contract but are to be calculated in terms of the expectation, reliance, or restitution interests. How do we know whether a breach is "partial" or "total"? Courts often ask whether the breach was substantial or material. If not, the aggrieved party is often required to continue to perform in the face of the other's less-than-substantial breach. In this case, however, the Minnesota court appeared to uphold the jury's denial of defendant's counterclaim, while still denying the plaintiff's claim for lost profits. The court implicitly created a middle ground in which the partial failure to make a progress payment entitled the plaintiff to cease performance without committing a breach, yet the failure was still not a total breach that would entitle plaintiff to recover lost future profits.

Damages issues are particularly difficult when builders "front-load" the contract. Contracts sometimes provide that owners pay far more than the builders have invested in the job in the early progress payments. This minimizes the builder's risks as owners are paying in advance of the builders' performance, and it allows the builder to fund the next stage of construction without having to borrow funds to buy materials and pay laborers. But suppose an owner refuses to make the first progress payment, and builder ceases to continue work on the project. If cessation of performance is deemed rightful, should the builder recover the full progress payment owed under the contract? How might you measure a different recovery? Courts reach different results on this issue.[93]

3. *Legislation by a private government — the American Institute of Architects forms:* The American Institute of Architects (AIA) has drafted form contracts covering most of the building process. It has done this for many years. Professor Justin Sweet traces the process back to 1888.[94] The documents have been revised from seven to 15 years apart, but more recently the AIA has issued revisions about every 10 years. There are rival collections of contract forms available to those entering into building construction contracts, but the AIA's standard contracts still command most of the market.

AIA's Form A101 is signed by the parties to a construction contract. It addresses such terms as the parties, the price for the job, the payment process, dispute resolution, insurance, and bonds. Form A201 states the complex general conditions. A101 contains eight pages; A201 runs to 39 pages. In the realm of building transactions, these general conditions serve as something roughly analogous to the Uniform Commercial

---

93. For a case discussing these issues, see Fuller v. United Electric Co., 70 Nev. 448, 273 P.2d 136 (1964).

94. Justin Sweet, *The American Institute of Architects: Dominant Actor in the Construction Documents Market*, 1991 Wis. L. Rev. 317, 323; *see also* Thomas J. Stipanowich, *Reconstructing Construction Law: Reality and Reform in a Transactional System*, 1998 Wis. L. Rev. 463.

Code. Instead of being passed by legislatures, they are fashioned by private associations playing a public function. The process does serve to give us a more or less uniform national "law" of building construction contracts without all of the problems of getting 50 state legislatures to enact a statute. We might wonder how well a private association such as the AIA or the Associated General Contractors of America (AGC) takes into account all of the interests at stake in construction. Indeed, Professor Sweet has noted that state legislatures have increasingly passed statutes that deal with specific aspects of building contracts. Indeed, a lawyer faced with a construction contract must check the relevant state statutes to be sure that the only norms applicable are those found in the standard form contract used by the parties.

The provisions in these form contracts come before the courts only occasionally. In part, this is because those in the construction industry are familiar with the substance of the provisions; in part, it is because reputation and trust are very important.[95] There is some tendency among building construction professionals to dislike legal approaches to solving problems in their world. These professionals resist contract provisions that might offend those involved in the process. They ask for a more friendly style of contract language.[96] Professor Stipanowich notes:

> Increasingly, sophisticated owners sponsoring major commercial projects write their own contract documents, often using the AIA standard documents or other prototypes as a starting point. In the case of repeat players, such administrative costs can be amortized over a series of projects. For other owners, however, there is no choice but to make use of some existing model.[97]

4. *The AIA contract provisions on progress payments:* To what extent, if at all, would the following provisions in the current AIA forms affect the resolution of the dispute in *Palmer v. Watson*?

AIA Document A401, Contractor-Subcontractor Agreement,[98] provides:

> § 4.7 If the Contractor does not pay the Subcontractor through no fault of the Subcontractor, within seven days from the time payment should be made as provided in this Agreement, the Subcontractor may, without prejudice to other available remedies, upon seven additional days' written notice to the Contractor, stop the Work of this Subcontract until payment of the amount owing has been received. The Subcontract Sum shall, by appropriate Modification, be increased by the amount of the Subcontractor's reasonable costs of demobilization, delay, and remobilization.

95. *See* William A. Klein & Mitu Gulati, *Economic Organization in the Construction Industry: A Case Study of Collaborative Production under High Uncertainty*, 1 Berkeley Bus. L.J. 137 (2004) ("[I]n construction, though the identity of the participants will generally change from project to project, the industry persists and the participants are in for the long haul, which, of course, affects how people behave on any particular project.").

96. These paragraphs draw heavily from Justin Sweet, *Standard Construction Contracts in the USA*, unpublished paper (2010).

97. Stipanowich, *supra* note 94, at 487.

98. The 2007 contract is the most recent one published by the AIA.

§ 7.1. The Subcontractor may terminate the Subcontract ... for nonpayment of amounts due under this Subcontract for 60 days or longer. In the event of such termination by the Subcontractor for any reason which is not the fault of the Subcontractor, Sub-subcontractors or their agents or employees or other persons performing portions of the Work under contract with the Subcontractor, the Subcontractor shall be entitled to recover from the Contractor payment for Work executed and for proven loss with respect to materials, equipment, tools, and construction equipment and machinery, including reasonable overhead, profit, and damages.

b. Installment Contracts and the UCC

MIDWEST MOBILE DIAGNOSTIC IMAGING, L.L.C. v. DYNAMICS CORP. OF AMERICA

United States District Court, Western District of Michigan
965 F. Supp. 1003 (1997)

ENSLEN, C.J.

I. Introduction

Plaintiff Midwest Mobile Diagnostic Imaging, L.L.C. [hereinafter "MMDI"] brings this diversity action against defendant Ellis & Watts, d/b/a Dynamics Corporation of America [hereinafter "E&W"], seeking damages for (1) breach of a sales contract for the purchase of four mobile MRI units[99] and (2) misrepresentation. Defendant, the seller, counterclaims for damages, alleging that the buyer is in breach. Having considered the evidence submitted and the legal arguments of the parties made during a three-day bench trial, and having reviewed the exhibits submitted, the Court enters the following Findings of Fact and Conclusions of Law pursuant to Federal Rule of Civil Procedure 52(a). To the extent that any findings of fact also constitute conclusions of law or vice versa, they are so adopted. . . .

III. Contentions of the Parties

MMDI contends that, after its rightful rejection of a nonconforming trailer tendered by E&W on December 13, 1995, E&W repudiated the contract in its entirety. E&W's repudiation, whether anticipatory or not, destroyed whatever right to cure E&W may have had and gave MMDI the right to cancel the contract, which it then did. MMDI argues it is entitled to damages.

E&W counters that its tender on December 13, 1995, was both timely and in conformity with contract specifications. Consequently, MMDI's rejection was wrongful.

---

99. [1] A mobile MRI unit is, in effect, a mobile MRI clinic. It is a semi tractor trailer that contains an MRI scanner and the computer equipment necessary to operate such a machine. It is designed to function as a temporary extension of the hospital that it is serving, with an interior which generally matches the hospital environment.

E&W continues that, even if the trailer were not conforming, E&W had a right to cure pursuant to Uniform Commercial Code [hereinafter "UCC"] § 2-508, and MMDI could not cancel the contract without first requesting adequate assurances from E&W in writing pursuant to UCC § 2-609. Since plaintiff did not satisfy § 2-609 and a reasonable time for performance had not expired, MMDI's cancellation of the contract on December 18, 1995, constituted anticipatory repudiation.

IV. Facts

Plaintiff Midwest Mobile Diagnostic Imaging, L.L.C ("MMDI") is a Delaware limited liability company, with offices in Kalamazoo, Michigan, engaged in the business of furnishing equipment and personnel for magnetic resonance imaging (MRI) scans to hospitals in southwestern Michigan. In 1995, MMDI had three mobile MRI units servicing area facilities.

Defendant Ellis & Watts ("E&W") is a New York corporation whose principal place of business is in Cincinnati, Ohio, which engineers, designs, and manufactures trailers for mobile medical uses, including mobile MRI systems.

Under Michigan regulations, the number of mobile MRI scanners that may be licensed is strictly limited. Consequently, companies wishing to provide this service must seek a Certificate of Need from the State. In 1995, the demand for these mobile MRI units exceeded that which MMDI could supply. MMDI, therefore, sought and received a Certificate of Need to begin operating a fourth mobile MRI unit.

In April 1995, plaintiff commenced negotiations with defendant to purchase four mobile MRI trailers, each designed to house a state-of-the-art, ACS NT 1.5T MRI scanner system, which plaintiff would purchase separately from Philips. During these initial negotiations, E&W became aware that MMDI had an immediate need for the first trailer because of the growing demand for its services.

As a consequence, the parties agreed that delivery of the first trailer would occur in September 1995 with the rest to follow in monthly installments. However, during final negotiations in Kalamazoo on August 10, 1995, the parties agreed to delete a clause in the written contract requiring that all four trailers be delivered in 1995. While no specific delivery dates were ultimately included in the written contract, E&W understood that early delivery of the first trailer was of great importance to MMDI. At the time of signing, the parties expected delivery of the trailers to occur in October, November, and December 1995 and January, 1996. The delivery dates were, however, contingent upon coordination with Philips and agreement of the parties.

In addition to the timing of the project, during negotiations the parties also made representations concerning the design of the trailer. On April 17, 1995, Robert Freudenberger of E&W faxed a signed purchase agreement to Jerry Turowski of MMDI. Attached to the form contract were two drawings. One of the drawings depicted a three-dimensional illustration of the interior of a mobile MRI system trailer upon which was written: "Spacious, efficient layout with clean, aesthetically pleasing interior." (Exh. 2.) In addition, these drawings, and all others reviewed by MMDI both before and after contract signing, did not depict a bracing structure surrounding the scanner magnet.

On August 10, 1995, Mr. Turowski and Mr. Freudenberger executed a purchase agreement for four E&W trailers. (Exh. 9.) With the signing of the contract, MMDI paid E&W a deposit in the amount of $63,000. On August 11, 1995, Mr. Andrew Pike, President of E&W, countersigned the purchase agreement in Cincinnati, Ohio. Under the parties' agreement, E&W was to construct the four trailers in accordance with Philips's specifications. Once certified by Philips, the trailers could be delivered. (Exh. 9, ¶ 3.)

On September 7, 1995, plaintiff and defendant met in Kalamazoo to discuss the delivery schedule. On September 21, 1995, MMDI sent a letter indicating that, as a result of that meeting, MMDI expected delivery of the first trailer on November 6, 1995. The letter also noted the parties' understanding that the trailer would be "show" ready for MMDI's open house in Kalamazoo, Michigan, on November 3, 1995. E&W did not respond to this letter. During the course of construction, the parties discussed several alterations to the trailer and consequently, again renegotiated the delivery date for the first trailer. Ultimately, the parties agreed upon a December 1, 1995 delivery date. Under the expectation that the trailer would be delivered on that date, MMDI scheduled patients assuming the trailer would be ready for use beginning December 4, 1995.

On November 3, 1995, indicating that the trailer was cosmetically complete, E&W presented the trailer to MMDI to show at its open house in Kalamazoo, during which representatives of MMDI and many of its customers inspected the trailer. At that time, the scanner magnet was free from any metal, bracing structures. The trailer was then returned to E&W for final adjustments and testing.

As of mid-November 1995, the first E&W trailer was fully fabricated and substantially all equipment was installed and ready for testing by Philips. In anticipation of the December 1 delivery date, E&W invoiced MMDI on November 10, 1995 for the full purchase price of the first trailer. (Exh. 20.) On November 16, 1995, E&W sent a follow-up letter requesting payment prior to shipment of the trailer on November 30 in accordance with the purchase agreement. (Exh. 9, 22.) MMDI paid $321,500 to E&W on November 17, 1995. (Exh. 20.)

On November 28, 1995, the first trailer failed to meet contract specifications in a test conducted by Philips. The test indicated that the trailer did not comply with Philips's specifications for magnetic shielding in the side walls of the trailer. This failure occurred despite the fact that, throughout the construction of the trailer, Philips had repeatedly noted the importance of the proper fabrication of this feature in its correspondence with E&W. (Exhs.13, 17, 19.)

When the parties discovered that the trailer had failed the test, they met to discuss potential solutions to the situation. At that time, E&W stated unequivocally that: (1) the trailer was defective; (2) the defect was entirely its fault and responsibility; and (3) it would cure the problem. E&W also indicated a willingness to reimburse MMDI for at least part of the expenses it might incur in renting another trailer to substitute for the one that E&W had not completed. As a result of the need for a cure, E&W failed to tender a conforming trailer on the December 1 delivery date and MMDI was forced to cancel appointments that had been scheduled with patients for December 4, 1995.

During the following two weeks, E&W designed a reinforcement structure to contend with the wall-flexing problem. The solution consisted of multiple large steel beams placed around the scanner magnet in a cage-like structure, which prevented removal of the magnet's outer covers and dramatically changed its appearance. Such a bracing structure had never been used with a mobile MRI scanner by any manufacturer. During this period, E&W exchanged multiple letters and sketches with Philips in which Philips's representatives indicated several concerns with the bracing structure. E&W made adjustments to address some of these concerns. Ultimately, Philips approved the design as a temporary solution to the wall-flexing problem.

On December 7, 1995, E&W sent MMDI a schedule indicating that the decision whether to proceed with this design would be made on December 12, 1995. The letter indicated: "if no go at this point, alternate plans established." Although MMDI had reviewed drawings of the interior during the course of construction, E&W did not include a sketch of the reinforcement design in this correspondence.

On December 12, 1995, Philips's representatives retested the trailer with the bracing structure in place and found that the flexing problem had been remedied. Thus, the trailer was approved for use on a temporary basis. However, because the structure impaired service of the scanner magnet, Philips would not certify the trailer for permanent use with the structure in place.

On December 13, 1995, Mr. Turowski of MMDI arrived at E&W to inspect the new design for the first time. After viewing the trailer and speaking with Philips's representatives, Mr. Turowski concluded that the bracing structure was unacceptable for several reasons. Mr. Turowski and Mr. Andrew Pike of E&W then placed a telephone conference call to Dr. Azzam Kanaan and Dr. Ilydio Polachini at MMDI. At that time, Mr. Turowski indicated that, with the bracing structure, the trailer did not conform to the contract obligations because: (1) service of the scanner magnet would be impeded and, in cases, would be more dangerous; (2) its appearance was objectionable; and (3) the resale value of the trailer would be diminished.

Mr. Pike countered that the structure in place conformed to the parties' agreement, that this was the design that met the Philips specification, that it had been approved by Philips, and told MMDI to accept it the way it was. Further, Mr. Pike stated that the materials had already been purchased to install this design in the second trailer, that this was the best design that one could come up with, and that he did not know if it could be done any differently. Finally, Mr. Pike refused to pay rent for a replacement unit or to refund MMDI's previous payment.

The following day, December 14, 1995, Mr. Pike sent a letter to Dr. Kanaan at MMDI (Exh. 29.), indicating that E&W was working with "this design" to see if it could be made more aesthetically pleasing. The letter made no reference to the servicing problems, safety concerns, or concerns about a potential diminution in resale value resulting from the use of the bracing structure. Mr. Pike again asserted the validity of the contract and refused to refund MMDI's payment for the trailer.

On December 18, 1995, acting in good faith, MMDI advised E&W in writing that the Purchase Agreement was canceled. On December 19, 1995, MMDI rented a mobile MRI unit to replace the one it had expected to receive from E&W. On December 21, 1995, MMDI executed a contract with a third party for the manufacture and construction of two trailers to house two of the Philips 1.5T MRI scanner systems.

On December 22, 1995, Mr. Freudenberger sent a letter to Mr. Turowski, reiterating that the first trailer was ready for shipment and requesting instructions on how to ship it. In addition, the letter indicated that E&W was finalizing the design for an alternative bracing structure that would neither impede the servicing of the magnet components nor negatively impact the aesthetics of the trailer interior. Mr. Freudenberger also suggested that, after final testing and seeking MMDI's input regarding the aesthetics of the design, the design "would be considered the permanent solution" for the trailer. The design would then be incorporated into the second trailer, at which time the first trailer would be returned to E&W and retrofitted with the new design at no cost to MMDI. E&W, however, maintained that the purchase agreement was still effective and continued to refuse to refund MMDI's payment. Soon after this correspondence, the parties ceased communication. Ultimately, E&W did remove the offending reinforcement structure and replaced it with an alternative design, which was approved for permanent use by Philips. In the time since this replacement solution was fabricated and installed, E&W has sold two of the trailers to a third party.

On January 9, 1996, MMDI filed the instant suit for damages resulting from breach of contract and misrepresentation. E&W retained payments made by MMDI in the amount of $384,500. Further, MMDI incurred expenses in the amount of $185,250 for the lease of a mobile MRI scanner and trailer between December 19, 1995, and April 20, 1996.

V. Analysis

A. Breach of Contract

The primary issue for resolution by the Court is whether MMDI rightfully rejected E&W's tender of the first trailer and then subsequently canceled the contract, or if its actions in mid-December constituted anticipatory repudiation of the contract. Having previously determined that Michigan law controls in the instant case, the Court simply notes that the Michigan version of the Uniform Commercial Code [hereinafter the "UCC"] applies to this sales contract....

1. Installment Contract

Before turning to the specific questions of rejection and cancellation, the Court must first resolve a threshold issue. Under the UCC, the parties' rights to reject, cure, and cancel under an installment contract differ substantially from those defined under a single delivery contract. Consequently, resolution of whether the contract is an installment contract is of primary concern. Section 2-612(1) defines an "installment contract" as "one which requires or authorizes the delivery of goods in separate lots to be separately accepted...." The commentary following this section emphasizes that the "definition of an installment contract is phrased more broadly in this Article [than in its previous incarnation as the Uniform Sales Act] so as to cover installment deliveries tacitly authorized by the circumstances or by the option of either party." § 2-612, comment 1.

Plaintiff argues that the contract between itself and E&W does not constitute an installment contract because it authorizes delivery in commercial units, and not lots, as required by subsection (1). However, upon review of the Code section defining those terms, it becomes clear that those terms are not mutually exclusive. Section 2-105 defines a "lot" as a "parcel or single article which is the subject matter of a separate sale or delivery, whether or not it is sufficient to perform the contract." The same section defines a commercial unit as "such a unit of goods as by commercial usage is a single whole for purposes of sale and division of which materially impairs its character or value on the market or in use. A commercial unit may be a single article (as a machine) or a set of articles (as a suite of furniture or an assortment of sizes) or a quantity (as a bale, gross, or carload) or any other unit treated in use or in the relevant market as a single whole." Thus, a lot, which is the measure of goods that the contract states will be delivered together in one installment, can be a single commercial unit. Consequently, § 2-612 applies wherever a contract for multiple items authorizes the delivery of the items in separate groups at different times, whether or not the installment constitutes a commercial unit.

The contract between MMDI and E&W for the sale of four trailers authorizes the delivery of each trailer separately. While the written contract does not explicitly state this delivery schedule, it does authorize separate delivery. Paragraph 2 of the contract assumes separate delivery dates by setting out a payment schedule wherein the balance for each unit is due at the time of shipment. Furthermore, based on the parties' testimony it is clear that both parties understood the trailers would be delivered in separate installments. Indeed, neither party disputes that they agreed to have the trailers delivered at four separate times. Therefore, the Court finds that the contract in dispute is an installment contract.

2. Right of Rejection

Section 2-612, therefore, is the starting point for the Court's analysis of MMDI's actions on December 13, 1995.... Under § 2-612, the buyer's right to reject is far more limited than the corresponding right to reject under a single delivery contract defined under § 2-601. Under § 2-601, a buyer has the right to reject, "if the goods or tender of delivery fail in any respect to conform to the contract...." Known as the "perfect tender" rule, this standard requires a very high level of conformity. Under this rule, the buyer may reject a seller's tender for any trivial defect, whether it be in the quality of the goods, the timing of performance, or the manner of delivery. To avoid injustice, the Code limits the buyer's correlative right to cancel the contract upon such rejection by providing a right to cure under § 2-508. § 2-508, comment

2. Under § 2-508, the seller has a right to cure if s/he seasonably notifies the buyer of the intent to do so, and either (1) the time for performance has not yet passed, or (2) the seller had reason to believe that the goods were in conformity with the contract. Thus, § 2-508's right to cure serves to temper the buyer's expansive right to reject under a single delivery contract....

Section 2-612 creates an exception to the perfect tender rule.... Under subsection (2), a buyer may not reject nonconforming tender unless the defect substantially impairs the value of the installment. In addition, "if the nonconformity is curable and the seller gives adequate assurances of cure," the buyer must accept the installment. § 2-612, comment 5. But even if rejection is proper under subsection 2, cancellation of the contract is not appropriate unless the defect substantially impairs the value of the whole contract. § 2-612(3), comment 6. Because this section significantly restricts the buyer's right to cancel under an installment contract, there is no corresponding necessity for reference to § 2-508; the seller's right to cure is implicitly defined by § 2-612.[100]

a. Delivery Date

Before proceeding with the analysis of MMDI's December 13 rejection, the Court initially notes that E&W's tender on December 13 constituted a cure attempt for the wall-flexing defect which delayed the delivery of the first trailer beyond the agreed-upon delivery date. Although under § 2-612 the delivery date does not cut off the seller's right to cure, it does have an effect on the rights of the parties....

In the instant case, the original, written contract included no definite delivery date. Instead, the contract left the delivery term to be agreed upon at a later date. At the time of execution, the parties both expected delivery of the first trailer to take place in October. During the months after the execution of the contract, however, the parties modified the deadline for the first installment of the contract on several occasions. As noted above, upon review of the testimony and documentary evidence, the Court finds that, whatever delivery date the parties had agreed upon prior to November 1995, by early November they had renegotiated their agreement to establish a December 1, 1995 delivery date. See § 2-209 (sales contract may be modified by oral or written agreement without consideration, so long as agreement does not state otherwise).

Defendant argues, however, that, even if the parties had at one point agreed upon a December 1, 1995 deadline, when the first trailer failed the Philips road test on No-

---

100. [6] Courts of other jurisdictions have reached differing conclusions with regard to the interaction between §§ 2-612 and 2-508. *See, e.g.*, Arkla Energy Resources v. Roye Realty & Dev., Inc., 9 F.3d 855 (10th Cir. 1993); Bodine Sewer, Inc. v. Eastern Illinois Precast, Inc., 97 Ill. Dec. 898, 906, 493 N.E.2d 705, 713; Bevel-Fold, Inc. v. Bose Corp., 9 Mass. App. Ct. 576, 402 N.E.2d 1104, 1108 (1980); Continental Forest Prods., Inc., v. White Lumber Sales Inc., 256 Or. 466, 474 P.2d 1, 4 (1970). This Court does not find the arguments of these other courts persuasive, however, and notes that their decisions are not binding on this Court. Nevertheless, the Court also notes that, since the time for delivery of the first installment had already passed on December 1, 1995 (*see infra* § 2(a)) and defendant could not have reasonably believed and, in fact, did not believe that the trailer was in conformity with the contract on that date, defendant had no right to cure under § 2-508.

vember 28, 1995, the parties renegotiated the delivery term to allow E&W a reasonable time to cure the defect. While E&W is correct that, as of December 1, it had a reasonable time in which to cure the wall-flexing problem, the Court disagrees that MMDI's willingness to wait for a cure constitutes an agreement to extend the delivery deadline. Because the parties believed that the defect was curable and E&W, without solicitation, unequivocally promised to cure it, under § 2-612, MMDI had no choice but to accept an offer of cure. To reject the installment on November 28 would have constituted a violation of § 2-612. The Court, therefore, finds that any negotiations the parties engaged in regarding delivery after discovery of the wall-flexing problem, did not constitute a modification of the delivery date for the first installment, but rather involved negotiation regarding cure. Since no specific date for delivery of a cure was agreed upon during those negotiations, under § 2-309(1), E&W had a reasonable time to effectuate a cure. Although there is some question as to whether further delay would have been reasonable, the Court finds that, as of December 13, 1995, a reasonable time had not yet passed. Therefore, defendant's tender of a cure was timely.[101]

b. Substantial Impairment of the Installment

The Court's conclusion that E&W's December 13 tender was an attempt to cure the November 28 breach raises another question: which standard of conformity applies to cure under an installment contract, perfect tender or substantial impairment? Looking to the rationale behind § 2-612, the Court notes that the very purpose of allowing the seller time to cure under this section is to permit it additional time to meet the obligations of the contract. The assumption is that, because the parties have an ongoing relationship, the seller should be given an opportunity to make up the deficiency. This section was not designed to allow the seller to have a never-ending series of chances to bring the item into conformity with the contract. Nor was it enacted to force the buyer to accept a nonconforming product as satisfaction of the contract. Consequently, it is logical that a tender of cure should be required to meet the higher "perfect tender" standard. On its face, however, § 2-612, which generally defines a buyer's right to reject goods under an installment contract, requires only substantial impairment in this context as well. Thus, there is some question as to which is the appropriate standard. The answer is not crucial, however, since the trailer in this case fails under both standards. Because a decision on this point will not affect the ultimate outcome in this case, the Court declines to address the issue. Instead, the Court proceeds with the substantial impairment analysis provided by § 2-612.

---

101. [7] Defendant contends that because under ¶ 3 of the purchase agreement (Exh. 9), delivery was conditioned upon certification by Philips and the condition was not yet satisfied, defendant's duty to perform had not yet arisen on December 13. The argument is unavailing, however, given that it was defendant's deficient performance that prevented certification of the trailer both in late November and mid-December 1995. *See* Kentucky Skilled Craft Guild v. General Electric Co., 431 F.2d 62, 68 (6th Cir. 1970) (*quoting* Gulf Oil Corp. v. American Louisiana Pipe Line Co., 282 F.2d 401 [6th Cir. 1960]). ("'Where liability under a contract depends upon a condition precedent one cannot avoid his liability by making the performance of the condition precedent impossible, or by preventing it.'").

To establish substantial impairment of the value of an installment, the buyer "'must present objective evidence that with respect to its own needs, the value of the goods was substantially impaired.'" ... See also § 2-612, comment 4. The existence of such nonconformity depends on the facts and circumstances of each case, and "can turn not only on the quality of the goods but also on such factors as time..., and the like." § 2-612, comment 4.... Finally, whether nonconformity rises to the level of substantial impairment may be judged by reference to the concept of material breach under traditional contract law....

In the instant case, plaintiff alleges several aspects in which defendant's December 13 tender failed to conform to contract obligations. Plaintiff contends that the trailer tendered on December 13 with the bracing structure did not conform to the parties' agreement because: (1) it was not and could not be certified by Philips without conditions for use with the 1.5T scanner and (2) its interior design did not conform with the parties' agreements. Because of these defects, MMDI argues that the value of the trailer was reduced substantially. Defendant, on the other hand, contends that the contract required only that the trailer meet the technical specifications provided by Philips, and that, therefore, the December 13 trailer was in complete compliance with its terms.

The written contract signed by the parties in this case is relatively skeletal and thus, requires interpretation. The Court's fundamental purpose in interpreting the terms of the contract is to give effect to the intent of the parties as it existed at the time the agreement was made...."The meaning of the agreement of the parties is to be determined by the language used by them and by their action, read, and interpreted in the light of commercial practices and other surrounding circumstances.'" 1 Williston on Sales § 10-2, 431 (quoting 1 Corbin on Contracts § 2.9 (rev. ed.)). See also § 1-203 [Eds.: § 1-304 as revised in 2001] (setting out the requirement of good faith and requiring the Court to interpret "contracts within the commercial context in which they are created, performed, and enforced"). Furthermore, the Code explicitly authorizes courts to look to the parties' course of dealings and performance and to the usage of terms in trade in interpreting the terms of the contract. §§ 1-205 [Eds.: § 1-303 as revised in 2001], 2-202, and 2-208.

As instructed by the commentary to § 2-612, the Court begins the substantial impairment analysis by looking to the "normal and specifically known purposes of the contract." § 2-612, comment 4. Reviewing the evidence presented, the Court finds that the primary purpose of the contract was to provide the plaintiff with four trailers for use with the Philips 1.5T scanner. With that in mind, the parties agreed that the trailers would be constructed in accordance with the specifications provided by Philips and that the trailer would be not be ready for delivery until Philips's certification had been received.[102] Philips did not, however, ever certify the trailer for unconditional

---

102. [8] Although the contract does not explicitly state that the trailers must be constructed in accordance with Philips's specifications, the parties have stipulated that the contract so required and the Court, therefore, begins its analysis from this premise. In addition, it is undisputed, indeed the defendant asserted repeatedly in its trial brief, that, under the contract, delivery of the trailer was conditioned upon certification of the unit by Philips.

use with the bracing structure. Because the bracing structure prevented normal service of the scanner magnet, it was only approved as a temporary fix.[103]

The general rule in cases where third-party approval is required as a condition of performance is one of strict compliance.... Such conditions will only be excused where the third party acts in bad faith or dishonestly. In the instant case, there was no credible evidence presented that Philips acted in bad faith by withholding approval. On the contrary, there was extensive evidence presented detailing the inherent problems with the long-term use of such a bracing solution, which demonstrated the reasonableness of Philips's refusal to certify the trailer. The bracing structure's shape and orientation prevented removal of the outer panels from the scanner magnet and made some repairs to the magnet more difficult and more dangerous. Furthermore, in order to perform certain repairs, the steel brace would have to be unbolted and removed. Once removed, the scanner magnet would have to be recalibrated and retested. Consequently, Philips's decision to refuse certification was entirely justified. Having found no evidence of bad faith or dishonesty on the part of Philips, the Court finds that defendant's failure to meet this condition constituted a breach of the parties' agreement.... Given that the central purpose of the trailer was to house a Philips 1.5T scanner, the failure to meet the standard for Philips's certification substantially impaired the value of the trailer. The Court, therefore, finds that this failure to conform to the parties' agreement, in and of itself, constituted a material breach.

In addition to violating the requirement that the trailer receive certification from Philips, plaintiff correctly asserts that defendant breached yet another term of the contract. The Court notes that the bracing structure also violated the parties' implied agreement regarding the design of the interior of the trailer. During the course of the parties' dealings both before and after the contract signing, MMDI reviewed numerous representations of the trailer's interior layout and design. Many of these drawings showed the location of the scanner and detailed the location of every structure in the trailer. None of them, however, depicted a cage-like brace made up of multiple large steel beams surrounding the scanner magnet. These drawings, when coupled with E&W's own statement that the trailer was cosmetically complete without the brace when it was presented at the open house, convince the Court that there was an implied agreement that the trailer would not have such a structure.

Furthermore, it is clear that, when the contract was executed, the parties both understood that the trailer's interior was meant to be aesthetically pleasing. It is the very nature of a mobile MRI trailer to function as an extension of the hospital it services. Since E&W was in the business of constructing trailers for mobile medical uses, it no doubt understood that the appearance of the trailer's interior could impact the comfort of MMDI's patients. Indeed, it is apparent that E&W realized such aesthetics

---

103. [9] Defendant argues that Philips did approve the trailer with the structure and that the testimony and documentary evidence reveal this to be so. However, review of the evidence convinces the Court that, in fact, while Philips may have approved the brace as a temporary solution to bring the wall-flexing problem within specification, it never approved the steel brace for permanent use with the Philips scanner.

were important to the value of the trailer, since, in its initial negotiations with MMDI, E&W included a cut-away drawing of the interior of a mobile unit which read: "Spacious, efficient layout with clean, aesthetically pleasing interior." The Court, therefore, finds that the agreement between the parties required that the interior of the trailer be aesthetically pleasing.

Such a condition of satisfaction by one of the parties to the contract will only be excused if approval is withheld unreasonably.... In the instant case, upon review of photographs of the bracing structure and testimony of those experienced in this industry, and in light of the fact that the interior of the trailer should match that of a hospital and not a construction site, the Court finds that plaintiff's refusal to approve the aesthetics of the design was commercially reasonable. Given that an integral aspect of the trailer's function is to serve as a clinic for patients undergoing medical procedures, and given MMDI's clients' expectations after having viewed the trailer at the open house, such a defect in the trailer's interior also reduced the value of the trailer substantially.

Upon review of the evidence, the Court finds that the bracing structure substantially impaired the value of the first trailer. Although the trailer met the express technical Philips specifications for wall-flexing, it was never certified by the manufacturer. The failure of this condition does not relieve defendant of liability because it was defendant's failure to properly construct the trailer that prevented certification. In light of the specific facts and circumstances of this case, the Court finds that this deficiency substantially impaired the value of the installment. When coupled with the trailer's failure to conform with the aesthetic requirements of the contract and the delay caused by the cure attempt, the Court holds that the cure attempt clearly constitutes a substantial breach within the meaning of § 2-612(2).

Substantial impairment, however, does not in itself justify rejection of the installment. As noted above, the buyer must still accept tender if the defect can be cured and the seller gives adequate assurances. Under § 2-612, as opposed to § 2-609, it is incumbent upon the seller to assure the buyer that cure would be forthcoming.... Defendant has failed in this regard. The Court notes that neither E&W's statements during the December 13 conference call nor the letter sent the following day constituted adequate assurances. On the contrary, during the December 13 conference call, Andrew Pike, the President of E&W, denied the existence of a defect, disclaimed any continuing obligation to cure under the contract, and stated that he did not believe a better design could be made that would remedy the wall-flexing problem. Furthermore, on December 14, Mr. Pike again ignored the servicing problems that the bracing structure had caused, ignored the fact that the bracing structure had not been approved for permanent use by Philips, and reiterated his doubt that the design could be constructed in a more aesthetically pleasing manner. Under these circumstances, the Court finds that MMDI's rejection of E&W's cure on December 13 constituted a rightful rejection under § 2-612(2).[104]

---

104. [10] Defendant argues that, as of December 13, it still had a right to cure under § 2-508 and that it was not required to give assurances unless plaintiff requested them in writing under § 2-609.

3. Cancellation

a. Substantial Impairment of Contract as a Whole

The fact that rejection of one installment is proper does not necessarily justify cancellation of the entire contract. Under § 2-612(3) the right to cancel does not arise unless the nonconforming goods substantially impair the value of the entire contract. Indeed, as noted above, the very purpose of the substantial impairment requirement of § 2-612(3) is to preclude parties from canceling an installment contract for trivial defects....

Whether a breach constitutes "substantial impairment" of the entire contract is a question of fact. *Bill's Coal Co. v. Board of Public Utilities*, 887 F.2d 242, 247 (10th Cir. 1989). To make such a determination, the Court should consider "the cumulative effect of [the breaching party's] performance under the contract, based on the totality of the circumstances...." Ultimately, "[w]hether the nonconformity in any given installment justifies cancellation as to the future depends, not on whether such nonconformity indicates an intent or likelihood that future deliveries will also be defective, but whether the nonconformity substantially impairs the value of the whole contract." § 2-612, comment 6. Thus, the question is one of present breach which focuses on the importance of the nonconforming installment relative to the contract as a whole. If the nonconformity only impairs the aggrieved party's security with regard to future installments, s/he "has the right to demand adequate assurances but not an immediate right to cancel the entire contract." § 2-612, comment 6. The right to cancel will be triggered only if "material inconvenience or injustice will result if the aggrieved party is forced to wait and receive an ultimate tender minus the part or aspect repudiated." § 2-610, comment 3 (noting the test for anticipatory repudiation under § 2-610 is the same as the test for cancellation under § 2-612(3)).

In the instant case, there is substantial evidence that one of the primary purposes of this contract was to provide MMDI with a fourth mobile MRI trailer so that it could meet the growing demand for its services. Thus, impairment of one of the four installments would have a substantial negative impact on MMDI. Moreover, an early delivery time was of primary importance to MMDI, as E&W was well aware. By failing to cure the November 28 breach on the first installment, E&W substantially delayed completion of the remainder of the contract, which delayed MMDI's ability to begin use of the 1.5T MRI trailer it had promised to its customers at the open

---

The Court reiterates that, under § 2-508, defendant's right to cure was cut off on December 1. Furthermore, § 2-612, unlike § 2-609, does not require the aggrieved party to request assurances. In an installment contract, where the seller's right to cure is more expansive, it stands to reason that the burden would fall on the seller to show that it had the present ability and the intent to cure any remaining defect. Allied Semi-Conductors Int'l Ltd. v. Pulsar Components Int'l, Inc., 907 F. Supp. 618 (E.D.N.Y. 1995). In the instant case, defendant gave no indication that it either had the capability to satisfy the contract or the will to do so. On the contrary, E&W's President gave MMDI the impression that cure was not possible and indicated clearly that he was not required to do anything more under the contract. Under such circumstances, MMDI's rejection was rightful.

house on November 3. Having found that substantial injustice would be done to plaintiff if it were required to accept the remaining three trailers after substantial delay as satisfaction of the contract, the Court finds that plaintiff rightfully canceled the contract on December 18, 1995....

4. Damages

Having found that plaintiff rightfully rejected defendant's tender of cure on December 13, 1995, and subsequently properly canceled the contract, the Court finds that plaintiff is entitled to damages. Plaintiff has requested reimbursement of the amount it already paid for the nonconforming installment in the amount of $384,500 as well as damages in the amount of $185,250 incurred for the lease of a rental mobile MRI trailer between December 19, 1995, and April 20, 1996, to replace the trailer E&W failed to produce. Under §2-711, a buyer who has rightfully canceled a contract may recover, among other things: (1) the amount that has already been paid, (2) damages for "cover" as defined in §2-712, and (3) any damages of nondelivery, including consequential and incidental damages, as defined by §2-715. Under §2-715, incidental damages include "any reasonable expense incident to the delay or other breach." Thus, plaintiff is clearly entitled to return of the amount already paid for the item it never received. Plaintiff is also entitled to recover the amount paid for a replacement rental unit. Though this amount does not constitute cover it is allowable as incidental to the delay produced by E&W's breach. Had E&W made conforming tender on December 13, 1995, plaintiff would not have been forced to contract with another company for the trailers and to wait until spring for the first one. The Court, therefore, finds plaintiff is entitled to both expectation and consequential damages under the Code and awards plaintiff a sum total of $569,250 for the breach of contract claim....

VI. Conclusion

For the foregoing reasons, plaintiff is awarded expectation and incidental damages in the amount of $569,250. Plaintiff's claim of misrepresentation is deemed waived and dismissed. Defendant's counterclaim for damages is denied and its motion for judgment on partial findings pursuant to Federal Rule of Civil Procedure 52(c) is deemed moot.

NOTES AND QUESTIONS

1. *Cure under §2-612:* The court decides that we need look only to §2-612 to deal with cure in an installment contract. If we confine ourselves to the language of this section, what do we learn about "cure"? For example, could the seller argue that, under subsection (2), a buyer does not have the right to reject an installment even if its nonconformity substantially impairs the value of that installment, in cases where the nonconformity can be cured? The text says only: "and cannot be cured." Literally, the statute seems to say that there is no right to reject if a nonconformity can be cured, *whether or not the seller cures it*. Section 2-612 leaves much unsaid about the subject of cure in installment contracts. However, look at Official Comment 5. Here we find a small essay about cure. It goes far beyond the text of §2-612. To what extent

is Official Comment 5 the law? Did it seem to influence the court's decision in *Midwest Mobile Diagnostic Imaging*?

The court says that we do not need to look at § 2-508, which deals with cure. However, it finds that the seller would not win if § 2-508 were applied. Suppose § 2-508 were applied to installment contracts. Would it make any substantial difference?

2. *Needy buyers and defective installments:* Suppose MMDI needed these units immediately. The seller delivered the first one in the same condition as in the case. MMDI, however, took the first unit and put it into service to avoid breaching its contracts with the various local hospitals that were going to make use of the machine. MMDI also communicated with the seller and stressed its need for the rest of the units, although it said they must comply with the contract specifications. Notice § 2-612(3)'s last sentence: "But the aggrieved party reinstates the contract if he accepts a nonconforming installment without seasonably notifying of cancellation or if he brings an action with respect only to past installments or demands performance as to future installments." Official Comment 7 is another essay that expands a great deal on the text of the statute. However, if you were serving as MMDI's lawyer, what would you tell its officials to do when the seller tendered the first defective unit when MMDI needed it to avoid breaching its own contracts with the hospitals? How much help does the text plus Official Comment 7 give you?

3. *The gaps in the drafting of § 2-612:* Ellen Peters's article *Remedies for Breach of Contracts Relating to the Sale of Goods Under the Uniform Commercial Code: A Roadmap for Article Two*[105] is still an often-quoted and important analysis of this part of the Code. Professor (and later Justice) Peters says that § 2-612 "is reasonably clear at the extremes":

> [A] If the breach is trivial and curable, the buyer must accept the installment and cannot categorically refuse further installments. He may, however, be able to reduce or postpone payments otherwise due upon delivery.... [She cites §§ 2-609 and 2-717 for this idea.]

> [B] On the other hand, incurable breaches so substantial as to impair the value of the contract as a whole will privilege total rejection of installment and contract....

> [C] It is the middle ground which remains unnecessarily uncertain. Consider the following cases:

>> (1) the defect is trivial and incurable;

>> (2) the defect is trivial, curable, but not cured;

>> (3) the defect is substantial as to the installment only and not curable;

>> (4) the defect is substantial as to the installment only, curable, but not cured;

>> (5) the defect is substantial as to the installment, and as to the contract, and seller actually tenders adequate cure....

---

105. 73 Yale L.J. 199, 225–27 (1963). Reprinted by permission.

The present language of 2-612 is a law professor's delight. Introduced at the proper moment, when the class in commercial law needs to be shaken up, it guarantees at least two class hours of wandering through a maze of inconsistent statutory standards and elliptical cross-references....

Would the *Midwest Mobile Diagnostic Imaging* case be an example of the third, the fourth, or another of Peters's categories?

4. *An almost real problem to test your understanding of § 2-612:* You should consider your understanding of § 2-612 and the *Midwest Mobile Diagnostic* case by considering the following problem. Suppose a contract calls for several goods to be delivered at different times. Assume that it is subject to Article 2 of the UCC.[106] This problem is based on an actual dispute between the University of Wisconsin-Madison (UW) and Globe Ticket and Label Company. The contract provisions are the actual ones used by the UW. However, some of the details have been changed to pose issues relevant to our purposes here, and so the parties have been given other names. Nonetheless, the question is very close to the problem faced by lawyers representing UW-Madison and Globe Ticket.

The University of Southern Michigan's Fighting Wasps emerged in the 1990s as a football power. Its men's and women's basketball and men's ice hockey teams, the other three of the four so-called "income sports," have also had great success. The University of Southern Michigan ("the University," or "USM") depends on what it earns from these programs to fund all its other athletic programs, as well as the maintenance, modernization, and construction of stadiums, rinks, and courts. It sells season tickets to all of these income sports. A season ticket holder buys a ticket to a particular seat (or seats) for all games played by the team for a particular season. The buyer pays in advance, and usually a few weeks to a month before the first game, s/he is sent tickets for each home game the team will play for that particular season. Sales of season tickets in all four sports are critical to the University's ability to plan and count on receiving certain sums of money, and season tickets cut the risks associated with having any team having a very bad year because the seats are sold no matter what the record of the particular team.

USM had purchased the sets of season tickets from WWL Ticket Corporation for many years. In 2000, USM made a contract to buy all of its season tickets from a new supplier, Ball Ticket and Label Company. Ball bid $200,000, which was $50,000 less than WWL Ticket Corporation. Ball was well known in the industry and regularly produced tickets for professional and university football, basketball, and hockey teams.

The contract between USM and Ball was made on forms drafted by the University's Purchasing Services department. Ball was to send season tickets "directly to the indicated ticket holder by the US Postal Service via Priority Mail."

There were to be 60,000 general public, 15,000 student, and 1,000 limited view *football* season tickets printed and distributed. "All season tickets will be delivered di-

---

106. *See* UCC §§ 2-307 and 2-612.

rectly to individual ticket holders by Priority Mail. The tickets must be mailed on or before August 10, 2001." Ball indicated a specified price for printing the football tickets and the cost of distributing them.

There were to be 17,500 general public and 2,500 student men's *basketball* season tickets printed and distributed. "All season tickets will be delivered directly to individual ticket holders by Priority Mail. The tickets must be mailed on or before October 30, 2001." Ball indicated a specified price for printing the men's basketball tickets and the cost of distributing them.

There were to be 9,500 general public and 2,500 student *women's basketball* season tickets printed and distributed. "All season tickets will be delivered directly to individual ticket holders by Priority Mail. The tickets must be mailed on or before October 30, 2001." Ball indicated a specified price for printing the women's basketball tickets and the cost of distributing them.

There were to be 14,000 general public series 1, and 14,000 general public series 2, *men's ice hockey* season tickets printed and distributed. Generally, series 1 tickets were for games played on Fridays and series 2 tickets were for games played on Saturdays. "All season tickets will be delivered directly to individual ticket holders by Priority Mail. The tickets must be mailed on or before September 15, 2001." Ball indicated a specified price for printing each series of hockey tickets and the cost of distributing them.

The dates for mailing had been established so that season tickets would arrive well before the first game. For example, hockey season tickets were to be mailed on or before September 15th, but the first game was not until October 19th.

The University's Special Conditions of Bid were incorporated into the contract via the bidding process. For purposes of this problem, you may assume that the Special Conditions contained no provision relevant to this problem (though in fact there were several, not fully consistent with one another).

Ball Ticket mailed the 60,000 general public football season tickets in four mailings of 15,000. The first was put in the mail on Friday, August 10, 2001; the second on Saturday, August 11th; the third on Monday, August 13th; and the fourth on Thursday, August 16th. The USM Fighting Wasps were to play their first football game against the University of Virginia on Saturday, August 25, 2001. All of the season tickets arrived at the mailing addresses of the general public season ticket holders before the August 25th game. However, many season ticket holders were concerned when their tickets had not arrived as the date for the game approached and called the Athletic Ticket Department. On Wednesday, August 22nd, Ball Ticket's National Sales Manager issued a statement that was reported in the press and on television. He said that a combination of peak season and staffing problems at Ball Ticket's soon-to-be-closed printing and distribution center in Tacoma, Washington, caused the problems. He explained that some disgruntled employees quit when it was announced that the Tacoma plant was to be closed. This left a thin workforce that was less than diligent about getting work out on time.

Ball Ticket's representatives traveled to the campus to meet with USM Athletic Department officials on August 22, 2001. Ball Ticket's representatives verbally assured USM that there would be no more problems because the account was now being handled at Ball Ticket's new processing headquarters in Pennsylvania. Ball Ticket was to mail all of the two series of general public hockey season tickets before September 15, 2001. Twenty-eight thousand season tickets were to be sent to season ticket holders. Twenty thousand were mailed on or before September 15th; 8,000 were mailed over the next four weeks. The first hockey game was on Friday, October 19th. About 2,500 season tickets had not been received by the night of the first game, and the USM athletic ticket office had to issue duplicate tickets for these season ticket holders so that they could get into the October 19th game. These ticket holders had to stand in line at will-call to receive their tickets. The problem was reported and discussed in both local newspapers. All of the delayed 2,500 season tickets arrived in either Saturday's or Monday's mail; that is, all tickets had arrived by Monday, October 22nd.

On Monday, October 22, 2001, the USM athletic ticket department canceled its order with Ball Ticket for men's and women's basketball season tickets. USM sent Ball Ticket a written contract termination notice, and it informed Ball that it could expect breach of contract proceedings under the contract.

Ball Ticket responded in writing on the 23rd. It objected that it had not breached its contract and asserted that it was entitled to print the basketball tickets. It explained that Ball Ticket had its headquarters and a large plant in Franklin, Pennsylvania. The Pennsylvania plant was running near capacity in August and early September of 2001 because this is a peak time when work must be done for the many universities that are Ball Ticket's customers for tickets. Despite paying its workers to work overtime, the Pennsylvania plant was not able to finish distributing all of the USM hockey tickets on time. It argued that its delay was trivial and showed nothing about its ability to deliver the basketball tickets. Late September and October is always a slow time because all of the work for football will have been completed well before then. The Pennsylvania plant would have had adequate capacity and workers to print and distribute USM basketball season tickets by about October 30th.

The University of Southern Michigan placed an emergency order for these tickets with WWL, the firm that had produced season tickets for the University for a number of years before being replaced by Ball Ticket. It had to pay $27,396.03 more for WWL to print and distribute these tickets than it would have paid Ball Ticket for the same work.

You work for USM's legal department. The University's general counsel asks you to write a detailed memorandum discussing the University's legal position as a result of the problems with the football and hockey tickets and the University's response to these problems. She tells you that she has heard that Ball Ticket is considering suing the University and asserting that the University, rather than Ball Ticket, breached the contract. She wants to know all the legal theories that Ball Ticket is likely to raise, whether USM has any response to them, and whether USM can recover the extra costs of obtaining the tickets from WWL. The state of Southern Michigan has no special contract law that governs all state contracts, and none of the various specific provisions of its laws applicable to state contracts are relevant to this case. The case will be governed by the general contract law of Southern Michigan. That state has passed the Uniform Commercial Code.

c. The Long Wait: Delay and Calling Off the Deal after One Has Given Extensions

FAIRCHILD STRATOS CORP. v. LEAR SIEGLER, INC.

United States Court of Appeals, Fourth Circuit
337 F.2d 785 (1964)

Bell, J.

[The Hufford Corporation Division of Lear Siegler, Inc. (hereafter Hufford), appealed from a judgment awarding Fairchild Stratos Corporation (hereafter Fairchild), damages upon a finding that Hufford breached a special warranties contract. The court affirms the finding of a breach but not the amount of damages.]

The background facts of this case are rather complex; the legal issues are reasonably simple. Generated by Fairchild's invitation to bid, Hufford on January 4, 1960, submitted proposals to design, fabricate, and install a stretch wrap forming press in Fairchild's Hagerstown, Maryland plant. The press, according to the district court, was to be "a sophisticated piece of machinery, the purpose of which was, with a high degree of automation, to pull and stretch a sheet of aluminum to conform to dies for half sections of boat hulls so as to cause the formation of aluminum half-boat hulls which could be thereafter welded together to make a complete hull for certain aluminum pleasure boats that [Fairchild] desired to manufacture and sell." In its proposals, Hufford made certain affirmations of fact that are germane to the present controversy.

Hufford stated that "the equipment will be designed and built so that *no hand work* will be required in the formation of parts." (Emphasis in original.) Hufford further stated that "the stretch forming equipment will be capable of producing formed boat hull halves at a rate of ten (10) parts per hour or six (6) minutes per part on existing dies constructed by Fairchild...." This statement was qualified in two respects: first, by the statement that it could not be expected that the press would, immediately after installation, be capable of producing parts at the guaranteed rate until operators had been trained and the machine's functions refined, and second, as a consequence, Hufford was "to provide a qualified operating crew for a period of three (3) months to bring this facility to a full-scale production capacity, simultaneously training [Fairchild's] personnel in operational procedures, maintenance, tooling, etc." The cost of providing the crew was to be borne by Fairchild.

Hufford agreed to manufacture and ship components in the order required for installation, so that installation could proceed concurrently with the latter stages of machine manufacture. Shipments were to start approximately four months from the date of receipt of the proposals and were to be completed two months thereafter. The purchase price was to be paid in six installments, five during the time that Hufford was shipping parts to Fairchild and installing them at Fairchild's plant and the sixth upon the completion of shipment, installation, and acceptance of the parts by Fairchild.

Fairchild issued a purchase order on January 21, 1960, accepting Hufford's proposals. Fairchild, in the purchase order, suggested that the cost of the operating crew be prorated, so that if less than three months was required, Fairchild's obligation would be accordingly reduced. Fairchild also suggested that shipments begin within four months from January 15, 1960 (the date of Fairchild's acceptance of the proposals by telephone), and be completed two months thereafter. Hufford agreed to these suggestions on February 2, 1960, and as of that date the terms and conditions of the contract were made explicit.

By the terms of the contract, Hufford was obligated to begin shipment of the components of the press on May 15, 1960, and to complete deliveries by July 15, 1960. This schedule was not met. Hufford's first shipment, that of rails for the press, was not made until July 12, 1960; the final shipment was not made until September 8, 1960; and not until November 21, 1960, did the press become operable. Thus, Hufford from the beginning was late in deliveries and acknowledged this fact in intercompany correspondence. For instance, a July 1, 1960, memorandum from Hufford's president stated:

> We are badly behind schedule on this machine. Our customer is in serious need for production from the machine to introduce their new line of boats in time to meet the marketing season.

The operating crew which was to be provided for a three-month period arrived at Fairchild's plant and began work on the press on October 31, 1960. Initial attempts to stretch matching half hulls failed. Some measure of success was achieved on December 22, 1960, when a matching pair of half hulls was stretched; but it was found that when the half hulls were trimmed and put on the assembly jig, the tumble home area[107] lacked any formation at all. It was this area that was to present the major difficulties in the press's operation right up until Hufford's breach. After the December experience, Hufford undertook to redesign the machine assembly used in forming the tumble home area.[108] Discussions were held within the period between January 6, 1961, and February 10, 1961, between representatives of the two companies to discuss problems in connection with the press and to try to work out an agreement as to what would constitute an acceptable half hull. Fairchild requested a completion date for the press's qualification, and Hufford's representative stated that Hufford ex-

---

107. [3] Described by the district court as the area in the stern of the boat "where the sides bend inward to join. It may be likened to the base of an isosceles triangle."

108. [4] Formation of the tumble home area was to be achieved by imposing localized pressure on the aluminum sheets by the use of heavy pressure rubber rollers.

pected the press to be ready for acceptance by April 7, 1961. Fairchild, waiving any claim it may have had to hold Hufford in breach at a prior date, orally advised Hufford that June 1, 1961, was the deadline for qualification.

Hufford, purporting to confirm the oral agreements between the parties, submitted a written memorandum in which it agreed to redesign and modify the machine element to provide configuration in the tumble home area and proposed a set of standards to determine whether the half hulls were in conformity with the die and with each other. Fairchild replied in writing, suggesting specific tolerances of stand off from the die in both the tumble home and forward areas of the boat and gave formal notice of the June 1, 1961, deadline. Hufford wrote and declined to accept specific tolerances as dimensional limitations, but it reiterated its memorandum position that the stand off in the tumble home area would be no more than that which could be pushed into position against the die by hand pressure. Hufford again acknowledged, without guaranteeing, its target date of April 7, 1961. On April 5, 1961, Hufford stretched two half hulls on the press. Although there was marked improvement in conformation on the second half hull, the stern area stood approximately two feet from the die, and it was impossible to force it into position by hand. Under these circumstances, Fairchild refused to give written confirmation that the machine was functioning properly.

Additional corrective work was done on the press by Hufford representatives and on April 15, 1961, they began stretching half hulls with Fairchild personnel as onlookers or helpers in loading and unloading the press. On April 24, 1961, Hufford representatives stretched three half hulls, and the third, as the most satisfactory, was left on the die for Fairchild's inspection. The following day, April 25, 1961, Hufford's representative advised Fairchild that he was ready for the qualification test. That same day, upon Fairchild's inquiry, Hufford's representatives prepared a test procedure and delivered it to Fairchild. It was agreed by the parties that the qualification run would consist of six half hulls of each hand rather than the ten upon which they had previously agreed.

The qualification run was never undertaken. Instead, Fairchild and Hufford reached an impasse. Hufford insisted that Fairchild accept the standards for forming sequence and procedures as set forth in Hufford's memorandum of April 25, 1961, and further insisted that if these standards were met by the qualification test, Fairchild must accept the press without regard to whether or not it could produce acceptable boat hulls. Fairchild adamantly refused, advising Hufford that it might undertake the qualifying test at any time but that Fairchild would accept or reject the press only on the basis of its operating characteristics and that there was no substitute for actual demonstration. This impasse came to a head on May 26, 1961, when Fairchild sent a telegram to Hufford stating that:

> Fairchild awaits proof of press by actual operation by Hufford. June 1st nearly here. If Hufford fails to heed our warning regarding this firm deadline litigation will undoubtedly follow shortly.

Although duly warned, Hufford failed to meet the June 1, 1961, deadline, and on May 31, 1961, stated its willingness to "start acceptance test on June 5." Fairchild on

June 2, 1961, notified Hufford not to send test personnel and on June 23, 1961, formally rescinded the contract. Thereafter, Fairchild brought this declaratory judgment action.

I. Breach of Contract

In its memorandum opinion the district court exhaustively delineated the pre-contract negotiations between the parties, the causes for delay in shipment of the component parts, and the problems attending the installation and functioning of the press. We need not cover the same ground. Suffice it to say that the district court had ample support in the record to conclude that whatever delay in the final performance of the contract could be attributable to Fairchild, it "was considerably less than the extension of the date for performance granted by Fairchild" and that failure to meet the June 1, 1961, deadline was the fault of Hufford alone. Applying the law of Maryland, conceded by the parties to govern, the district court found the ultimate facts and conclusions of law to be as follows:

> 1. Hufford agreed to build and install a stretch press *and to complete shipment thereof* by July 15, 1960, and especially warranted the press to be capable of producing within three months from that date "... boat hull halves at a rate of ten (10) parts per hour or six (6) minutes per part on existing dies constructed by Fairchild," and that the stretch press would be "... designed and built so that *no hand work* will be required in the formation of the parts."
>
> 2. Hufford failed to perform the contract or to fulfill its special warranty by June 1, 1961, notwithstanding that Fairchild waived performance by Hufford prior to that date, and had agreed to a less rigorous test to determine the acceptability of the stretch press.
>
> 3. Fairchild's refusal to extend Hufford's date of performance beyond June 1, 1961, was fair and reasonable under all of the circumstances.
>
> 4. Whether the boat press is capable of performance in accordance with the special warranty is unknown, but, in view of the repeated failure of the stretch press to perform, the conclusion is inescapable that it is extremely unlikely that the boat press possesses this capability, absent an actual demonstration that it possesses this capability.
>
> 5. Hufford had an obligation to demonstrate the production capability of the stretch press on or before June 1, 1961, and its refusal to meet that obligation was arbitrary, unreasonable, and without legal justification, so that Hufford's refusal constituted a material legal breach of the contract.
>
> 6. Fairchild had a legal right to refuse to accept the stretch press and to rescind the contract. Fairchild *refused further performance of* the contract on *and after* June 2, 1961, *and formally rescinded it by notice dated June 23, 1961*, because of Hufford's breach of warranty and Hufford's unjustified refusal to perform.

7. Fairchild is entitled to judgment on Hufford's counterclaim and to damages and supplementary declaratory relief, as hereafter discussed. (Italics represent modifications in initial findings by the district court.)

On appeal, Hufford makes three basic contentions with respect to the above ultimate findings: (1) that Hufford had no contractual obligation to demonstrate the press's capabilities by June 1, 1961; (2) that Hufford's failure to demonstrate by June 1, 1961, was not such a material breach of the contract as to warrant Fairchild's rescission; and (3) that Fairchild's failure to perform its own contractual obligation prevented rescission. We discuss these contentions *seriatim*.

(1) *Hufford's Contractual Obligations.* Hufford strenuously contends that it had no contractual obligation to demonstrate the press's warranted capabilities by performing an acceptance test. While it is true that the contract did not provide by express language that Hufford must conduct such a test, the contract did provide that Hufford guaranteed a press that would produce ten parts an hour of such conformation to existing dies that no hand work would be required in their formation. These warranties, clearly spelled out in the contract, of necessity required Hufford to demonstrate their fulfillment. These warranties constituted the contractual standard that Hufford was required to meet by an acceptance test. Fairchild properly rebuffed Hufford's attempts to superimpose additional parts standards that were neither expressly provided for nor implicit in the terms of the contract. Fairchild was concerned with a satisfactory finished product; the method by which Hufford was to establish the press's capabilities was not Fairchild's concern. Fairchild had a right to expect a press of a guaranteed production rate producing parts of such quality as to require no hand work in their formation. Under the contract Fairchild could not insist upon more, but conversely, it had a right to demand no less.

(2) *The Materiality of Hufford's Breach.* The district court, after finding that Hufford's failure to demonstrate the press's warranted capabilities by June 1, 1961, constituted a breach of the contract, further found that the breach was material and justified Fairchild's rescission. Hufford contends, however, that even if it be assumed that Hufford's failure to demonstrate the press's warranted capabilities amounted to a breach of the contract, such breach may not be deemed so material as to defeat the parties' just expectations. Hufford points to its willingness to tender performance on June 5, 1961, and argues that its purported breach resulted in only two lost working days—by no reasonable standard a material breach.

Hufford's argument carries some force. Generally "in the contracts of merchants, time is of the essence," *Norrington v. Wright*, 115 U.S. 188, 203, 6 S. Ct. 12, 29 L. Ed. 366 (1885), and the failure of the seller to meet a promised day of performance permits the buyer to rescind. We think, however, that the present contract may not be viewed as an ordinary mercantile contract. It is more akin to the contract discussed in *Beck & Pauli Lithographing Co. v. Colorado Milling & Elevator Co.*, 52 F. 700 (8th Cir. 1892). There, in considering a seller's action for the purchase price of custom-made stationery, the Eighth Circuit reversed a directed verdict for the buyer. The court declined to accept the buyer's contention that the seller's delay of one day in delivery constituted a material breach of the contract, for as the court stated:

> [I]n contracts for work or skill, and the materials upon which it is to be bestowed, a statement fixing the time of performance of the contract is not ordinarily of its essence, and a failure to perform within the time stipulated, followed by substantial performance after a short delay, will not justify the aggrieved party in repudiating the entire contract, but will simply give him his action for damages for the breach of the stipulation. *Tayloe v. Sandiford*, 5 L.Ed. 384, 7 Wheat. 13, 17]; *Hambly v. [Delaware, M. & V.] Railroad Co.*, 21 Feb. Rep. 541, 544, 554, 557. 52 F. at 703.

We think that this was, as in the *Beck* case, a contract for "work or skill" and "time [was] not ... of its essence." Thus, Hufford's delay of two working days in demonstrating that the press performed in accordance with its warranted capabilities, nothing else appearing, would not have justified Fairchild's rescission. But ours is a different case. It will be recalled that the contract contemplated that shipment of component parts of the press was to begin May 15, 1960, and was to be completed by July 15, 1960, at which time Hufford was given three months to bring the press up to its warranted capabilities. By October 15, 1960, Hufford was to have completed its contractual obligations and was to receive the final installment payment, and Fairchild was to begin mass production and distribution of aluminum pleasure boats. This schedule was not met, and in view of the sophistication of the press, the first of its kind, it seems improbable that the parties expected the schedule to be met to the day. Significantly, Fairchild waived a demonstration of the press's warranted capabilities until June 1, 1961. This date seemed an eminently reasonable deadline in view of Hufford's assurance, repeated in correspondence, that it would have the press ready by April 7, 1961. Thus, we are not faced here with the situation where a seller in a contract for "work or skill" fails to meet a specified day for performance. Rather we are faced with a seller who failed to meet a contract performance date, failed to meet a subsequent date set by himself, and then failed to meet an even later date set by the buyer. Even in out-of-the-ordinary mercantile contracts, there must come a day when a long-suffering buyer may demand performance or opt rescission. In our case that day came on June 1, 1961....

We conclude that the district court correctly held that Hufford's failure to demonstrate the warranted capabilities of the press by June 1, 1961, constituted a material breach of the contract and entitled Fairchild to rescind....

NOTES AND QUESTIONS

1. *The reasons for Fairchild's actions:* Why did Fairchild let matters drag on for so long? Why did it then insist on calling off the deal? Lear Siegler contended that in July 1960 Fairchild was under pressure from its bankers to eliminate money-losing projects. Its brief tells the story this way:

> In January 1960, plaintiff was negotiating to become the sole source of supply for aluminum boats for Sears, Roebuck & Company and was interested

in launching a program of boats of its own design. Plaintiff was also building F27 airplanes and radar antennas. For use in these projects, plaintiff requested and received from defendant a quotation on the desired stretch press, and on January 25, 1960, issued to defendant a purchase order for it. On February 3, 1960, the plaintiff's Directors voted ... to approve the purchase of the press. The basis of this approval was that a contract to assemble 1,300 boats for the 1960 Sears season had been received; and although the press was not involved in the Sears program for 1960, it would be required for the production for 1961 and subsequent years, as well as for plaintiff's own line of boats [and] its airplane and radar programs. The Sears program for 1961 contemplated a minimum of 10,800 and a maximum of 13,800 boats.

On February 23, 1960, the plaintiff entered into a contract with Miracle Marine, Inc., Theodore Cromp, President, under which Miracle Marine, Inc., was to participate in design, development, advertising, sales promotion, and the establishing of dealerships for a line of marine products to be manufactured by plaintiff....

Commencing in February, 1960, while the stretch press was being manufactured, plaintiff undertook the manufacturing of boats for Sears and Miracle Marine using boat hull halves from a Sears inventory and those purchased from Allied Products Incorporated. This effort was pursued vigorously until a Sears request for stop work was received on June 17, 1960, because of structural failure of plaintiff's boats in tests at the Sears Test Center, Fort Myers, Florida. Manufacturing for inventory was allowed to continue until July 19, 1960, on the assumption that structural fixes would resolve the problem. Subsequent testing of the structural fixes showed that the problem was not resolved, therefore, a management decision was made on July 19, 1960, to stop work on the boat program....

On September 14, 1960, the Directors were told that the cooperative attitude of Sears would reduce by approximately one-half the indicated loss on the boat program and that expenses on the boat program had been written off as incurred. An attempt was then made to sell the boat program, including the press, but the prospective purchaser, Miracle Marine, could not finance the purchase. Finally, on November 28, 1960, Fairchild advised all distributors that a decision had been reached not to renew their agreements at their expiration and immediate termination was invited....

[Thus, when Fairchild canceled the contract on June 1, 1961, its] boat program had terminated much earlier.... No practical or production use was to be made of the parts [produced at the demonstration of the machine] and they were nothing more than test pieces to be run for demonstration purposes.

As we might expect, Fairchild's brief tells the story differently:

The 1960 Sears boat program had absolutely no connection with or relevance to the pending lawsuit.

Difficulties with the Sears boats did not mean abandonment by Fairchild of its own boat program, based on mass production from the Hufford press. Fairchild's own program was only abandoned after June 1, 1961, when the Hufford press failed to prove out. The Hufford [Lear Siegler] brief fails to differentiate between the Sears boat program and the Fairchild boat program, which was geared to the boat press.

The trial judge responded to Lear Siegler's argument by saying that "Fairchild's activities can only be characterized as those of prudence and caution, because it was obvious to Fairchild throughout the period that it was communicating with its distributors and seeking to sell the stretch press that Hufford was badly in default under the contract. That Fairchild sought to minimize its damages does not mean that it caused a breach of the contract. At most, Fairchild had a motive in failing to waive all of Hufford's defaults under the contract, but if, as is hereafter concluded, Hufford breached the contract, Fairchild's motive in asserting the breach is immaterial."

2. *The* **Fairchild** *case under the UCC:* The *Fairchild* case was decided before the Uniform Commercial Code went into effect in most states. How would the *Fairchild* case be decided under the UCC? Under § 2-601, Fairchild would have had a right to reject the defective delivery. Under § 2-606 (1)(b), Fairchild may have accepted the goods by failing to make an effective rejection. However, it is questionable whether Hufford ever made a delivery or tender to start the reasonable time for inspection running.[109] Under § 2-503(1), "[t]ender of delivery requires that the seller put and hold *conforming goods* at the buyer's disposition...." This was not done.

Perhaps under § 2-208(3), the course of performance showed a waiver of the original delivery date. See also § 1-303, as revised in 2001. Section 2-209(5) allows a retraction of a waiver "by reasonable notification ... that strict performance will be required of any term waived...." Yet Fairchild probably cannot demand that Lear Siegler meet the original contract date after Fairchild waived it. Section 2-209(5) blocks retractions of waivers when they would be "unjust in view of a material change of position in reliance on the waiver."

Could Fairchild, after such a waiver and reliance, then set a reasonable deadline for completion of the machine and declare the contract at an end if Lear Siegler failed to meet it? Section 2-309(1) provides that the "time for shipment or delivery or any other action under a contract if not provided in this Article or agreed upon shall be a reasonable time." We might think that after a waiver that has been relied upon, the time has not been "agreed upon." Then Lear Siegler would have a reasonable time in which to perform. Official Comment 1 tells us: "It thus depends upon what constitutes acceptable commercial conduct in view of the nature, purpose and circumstances of the action to be taken." However, this comment continues, saying: "Agreement as to a definite time, however, ... may be found in a term implied from the contractual circumstances, usage of trade or course of dealing or performance as well as in an express term. Such cases fall outside of this subsection since in them the time for action is

---

109. *See* UCC § 2-602(1).

'agreed' by usage." Fairchild's action in setting a new time and Lear Siegler's acceptance of it could be viewed as an agreement by course of dealing or performance.

The Code seems written to deal with contracts for delivery of "shelf goods." It does not seem too helpful in situations where a seller and a buyer enter a "quasi-partnership" to assemble a large custom-made machine in the buyer's plant, and to work out difficulties as part of an ongoing process. We can always fall back on notions of agreement and the reasonable expectations of the parties. However, once the buyer allows the seller to miss deadlines for completion and gives the seller second and third chances in this kind of relationship, it is often hard to determine the reasonable expectations of the parties.

The following decision involves specially made goods, but something less than the long-term continuing relationship we found in the *Fairchild* case. The opinion was written by Professor (later Justice) Ellen Peters, an expert on the Uniform Commercial Code. (Be sure to notice her comments about the lawyers' "total disregard" of Article 2 of the UCC; this degree of unfamiliarity with the UCC is probably less common today, since the UCC has been in force in most states — and taught in law schools — for more than 40 years.) We can ask whether Justice Peters reaches a sensible result, and whether she finds adequate authority and help in the text of Article 2 to deal with a long-delayed performance.

BEAD CHAIN MANUFACTURING CO. v. SAXTON PRODUCTS, INC.

Connecticut Supreme Court
183 Conn. 266, 439 A.2d 314 (1981)

PETERS, J.

This is an action for the breach of a contract for the purchase of specially manufactured electronic parts. The plaintiff, the Bead Chain Manufacturing Company, the seller, sued the defendant, Saxton Products, Inc., the buyer, for failure to accept delivery of goods tendered pursuant to the contract of sale, and for failure to pay related costs and damages. The defendant denied the plaintiff's allegations and entered both special defenses and a counterclaim. After a trial to the court, judgment was rendered for the plaintiff on the complaint and on the counterclaim, and this appeal followed.

The underlying facts are not, on this appeal, in dispute. After more than a year of discussion, negotiation, and examination of handmade samples, the defendant Saxton in January, 1973, sent to the plaintiff Bead a purchase order for five million electrical components known as female contacts. The contract called for the production of special new tooling for these newly designed parts. The purchase order described the material out of which the goods were to be made and specified that they were to conform to "Sketch S-1318." A month later, a superseding design drawing was prepared by Bead and approved by Benjamin Jarmolow, Saxton's chief engineer and vice president. The idea for and the design of the female contacts was initially provided by Jarmolow, who made some changes in it subsequent to the original submission. After receipt of the initialed drawing from Jarmolow in February, 1973, Bead began to prepare for production, by manufacturing the necessary tooling and producing preproduction samples in conformity with the initialed drawing.

Although the contract called for the first installment of 250,000 contacts to be delivered by the middle of June, 1973, Bead first sent 100 preproduction samples to Saxton for its approval in August of that year. These samples were lost. When this loss came to light upon inquiry by Bead, further preproduction samples were delivered in October, 1973, and February, 1974. Small installments, 1000 each, of finished contacts were delivered in April and May of 1974. Until July, 1974, Saxton neither rejected any of these tenders nor made any complaint about their conformity with Jarmolow's design or about their timeliness. In July, confronted with a bill for the costs of tooling, Saxton for the first time stated that the contacts were defective because they lacked "memory" characteristics, *i.e.*, the ability to return to their original shape after having been deformed. "Memory" characteristics were, according to Saxton, essential to the incorporation of this component in the electrical products that Saxton intended to market and to sell. Saxton never suggested what specific design modifications would be required to make the contacts acceptable. Further discussions proved fruitless, and this lawsuit ensued.

The trial court, after extensive proceedings, found all of the issues for the plaintiff, the seller Bead. It concluded that the contract required Bead to provide electrical contacts in accordance with the specifications in the initialed design drawing, rather than requiring Bead to design the contacts subject to the buyer Saxton's approval. Essentially, the court concluded that the basic responsibility for design rested with Jarmolow, Saxton's engineer, while Bead's responsibility was to manufacture goods in conformity with that design.... Finally the court determined that Saxton could not rely on contract provisions making time of the essence with regard to Bead's performance, when Saxton, by its conduct, had waived compliance with the delivery dates specified in the purchase order. Having thus concluded that Saxton was in breach in refusing to accept the tendered female contacts and in refusing to pay the tooling charges stipulated in the purchase order, the court awarded the plaintiff Bead damages in the amount of $8411 plus interest and costs. The defendant Saxton's appeal challenges each of these conclusions, in whole or in part.

Before we address the merits of the defendant's claims of error, we must observe that this case has been presented with virtually total disregard of the relevant provisions of our statutes, in particular Article 2 of the Uniform Commercial Code, General Statutes § 42a-2-101 *et seq.* While it is true that the Code incorporates, by reference, supplementary general principles of contract law and of the law merchant, § 42a-1-103, such supplemental bodies of law cannot displace those provisions of the Code that are directly applicable. Article 2 applies to all contracts for the sale of goods, whether those goods be existing at the time of sale or whether, as in this case, they are to be specially manufactured. *See, e.g.,* §§ 42a-2-106(1); 42a-2-201(3)(a); 42a-2-704(2).

The defendant's first claim of error challenges the court's conclusion that the defendant waived contract provisions concerning the time for delivery. The defendant's purchase order made time of the essence, providing: "The dates of delivery in quantities herein specified are of the essence of this order, and delivery must be effected within the time specified. If deliveries are not made on time and in the quantities specified, Buyer reserves the right to cancel and to purchase elsewhere and hold Seller accountable therefor." At the trial, the defendant relied on this provision both as a defense to the plaintiff's claim for damages and as the basis of its counterclaim. We agree with the trial court that this clause, in the circumstances of this case, neither excused the defendant's nonperformance nor supported its own cause of action "because the defendant did not exercise its right to cancel in a timely fashion."

Under the Uniform Commercial Code, "[r]ejection of goods must be within a reasonable time after their delivery or tender. It is ineffective unless the buyer seasonably notifies the seller." General Statutes § 42a-2-602(1). Although a buyer must be afforded a reasonable opportunity to inspect goods to determine whether they should be rejected, §§ 42a-2-606(1)(b), 42a-2-513(1), he must exercise his right to inspect in a timely fashion. Section 42a-2-602 establishes a policy that requires the buyer to act with reasonable speed in determining whether to reject and requires prompt implementation of rejection by notification to the seller. *See* White & Summers, Uniform Commercial Code (2d ed.) § 8-3, p. 309. The parties, in their contract, may establish guidelines to determine whether any action required by the Code has been taken within a reasonable time, but their agreement may only fix a time period "which is not manifestly unreasonable." § 42a-1-204(1). [Eds.: § 1-302(b), as revised in 2001.]

Applying these statutory provisions to the case before us, we conclude that Saxton's protracted delay in rejecting the contacts tendered by Bead, coupled with its delay in notifying Bead of their alleged nonconformity, obligated Saxton to accept those deliveries. It would be manifestly unreasonable, in the circumstances of this case, to permit a printed time-of-the-essence clause in Saxton's contract form to extend for six months or more its opportunity to inspect and to reject.

... [O]ne of the relevant factors in determining timeliness is the course of performance between the parties after the sale but before the formal rejection. This course-of-conduct factor in effect incorporates the common law principles of waiver which the trial court found persuasive in this case....

Contrary to the defendant's assertion, Saxton's silence in the face of Bead's deliveries now precludes it from complaining about defects, such as delay in delivery, that were readily apparent at the time of tender....[110]

The defendant's third claim of error is that the trial court could not reasonably have concluded that the defendant's conduct constituted a breach of the contract. The court found the defendant in breach for refusing to accept the parts shipped to it in 1974 and for refusing to pay the tooling charges. We have already noted that

---

110. [1] The defendant also adverts to a printed contract provision reserving to the buyer "the right to reject any material which does not fulfill the specifications of the order or time of delivery." This clause is as vulnerable as is the time-of-the-essence clause to the implications of §§ 42a-2-602 and 42a-1-204. [Eds.: § 1-302(b), as revised in 2001.]

Saxton failed effectively to reject the goods tendered to it. Saxton's rejection was wrongful[111] because, as the trial court found, the contacts that were tendered conformed to the design drawing initialed by Saxton's engineer, Jarmolow. Saxton might have bargained for a sale on approval; the trial court found that it had not done so.[112] A manufacturer of parts does not impliedly warrant that his goods will meet a buyer's special requirements unless, "at the time of contracting, the seller has reason to know any particular purpose for which the goods are required and that the buyer is relying on the seller's skill or judgment to select or furnish suitable goods." § 42a-2-315. No such implied warranty was alleged or proven in this case. Absent a statutory warranty or definitive contract language, the determination of what the parties intended to encompass in their contractual commitments is a question of the intention of the parties, unless the trial court could not reasonably have arrived at the conclusion that it reached....

[The Court's discussion of damages is omitted. The Court concluded that plaintiff was entitled to its costs, including reasonable overhead, plus lost profits.]

NOTES AND QUESTIONS

1. *The background as disclosed by the briefs:* Saxton issued a purchase order for one million female contacts to be delivered in four installments. The first was to be delivered on June 18, 1973, the second on September 17, 1973. The contacts were to be part of a solderless connector which had been designed by B. Jarmolow, who was the Chief Engineer of Saxton. Bead Chain Manufacturing Company did not assume any responsibility for the electrical or mechanical properties of the connector, since Jarmolow did not disclose how it was to be used by Saxton. Jarmolow left Saxton before the pre-production samples were delivered in August 1973. It is likely that no one at Saxton saw the solderless connector project as of great importance once Jarmolow left the firm.

Bead Chain received no response to the August delivery of pre-production samples and inquired about the matter. It was told they had been lost. It then sent samples

---

111. [2] The Uniform Commercial Code makes a distinction between a rejection that is ineffective and a rejection that is wrongful. An ineffective rejection is a rejection that is procedurally defective, the buyer having improperly delayed in rejecting the goods or, more typically, in notifying the seller. § 42a-2-602(1). The consequence of an ineffective rejection is that the buyer is held to have accepted the goods, § 42a-2-606(1)(b), and thereafter becomes liable for their purchase price. § 42a-2-607(1). A wrongful rejection is a rejection that is substantively incorrect, the buyer having improperly asserted that a tender is nonconforming when in fact the tender meets the specifications of the contract of sale. The consequence of a wrongful rejection is that the buyer is in breach and the seller is entitled to invoke any of the remedies available to a seller aggrieved by a buyer's breach. § 42a-2-602(3); § 42a-2-703. WHITE & SUMMERS, UNIFORM COMMERCIAL CODE (2d Ed) § 8-3, pp 314–15. Operationally, the substantive scope of the buyer's right to reject is limited, and his rejection therefore more likely to be wrongful, when the contract of sale is, as here, an installment contract. § 42a-2-612. Further exploration of these highways and byways must await another day.

112. [3] Under the provisions of General Statutes §§ 42a-2-326 and 42a-2-327, dealing with the sales on approval, it is, furthermore, doubtful whether the right to disapprove an otherwise conforming tender would have survived the protracted delay in its exercise.

on October 31st, but again it heard nothing. On February 27, 1974, again Bead Chain sent additional samples. It received no response until May 16, 1974, when Saxton's President wrote stating that after testing in Singapore, the part needed modification. This prompted unsuccessful negotiations, and Bead Chain sued.

2. *"Time is of the essence" clauses:* Lawyers often draft clauses that attempt to give their client the right to cancel a contract if there is any delay in performance. Consider a few examples used by major corporations:

(a) Buyers' Clauses

(i) A purchase order of Trane, a manufacturer of heating and air conditioning equipment provided:

DELIVERY DATE. Time is of the essence and if delivery of items or rendering of service is not completed by the time promised, the Buyer reserves the right without liability, in addition to its other rights and remedies to terminate this contract by notice effective when received by Seller, as to stated items not yet shipped or services not yet rendered, and to purchase substitute items or services elsewhere and charge the Seller with any loss incurred. Any provisions herein for delivery of articles or the rendering of services by installments shall not be construed as making the obligations of the Seller severable.

(ii) A purchase order of Allis-Chalmers, a manufacturer of heavy machinery, provided:

DELIVERY DATE. Shipment must be made to meet the required date specified. Time is of the essence. Production schedules established or commitments made to satisfy the required date must not contemplate production or procurement in advance of the current lead or procurement time required to meet such date, without the specific written approval of Buyer. On premature shipments, Buyer may return the goods at Seller's expense, and in any event payment will be withheld and any discount period will begin to run from the required date specified. Buyer, without waiving any other legal rights, reserves the right to cancel without charge or to postpone deliveries of any of the goods or services covered by this order which are not shipped in time to meet the required delivery date....

(b) Sellers' Clauses

The following clauses were used by the Xerox Corporation on some of their standard forms:

1. DELIVERY—Customer shall accept delivery of ... equipment at the installation address(es) indicated herein in accordance with the delivery schedule quoted by Xerox and in no event later than fifteen (15) days after notification by the appropriate Xerox branch that the Equipment is available for delivery. In case of multiple unit purchases, Xerox shall have the right to make separate deliveries. Xerox shall deliver the Equipment within 120 days of acceptance of this Agreement, provided that if Xerox fails to make timely delivery of any individual installation of Equipment, the Customer may treat this Agreement

as breached as to such individual installation only. If at the time of execution of this Agreement, Customer requests delivery more than thirty (30) days later than the delivery date quoted by Xerox, the Equipment Purchase Price shall be Xerox's Equipment price in effect at the time of actual delivery.

2. DEFAULT — Time is of the essence hereof and if Customer shall fail to pay when due any installment, or otherwise fail to observe, keep or perform any provisions of this Agreement required to be observed, kept or performed, or if Customer ceases doing business as a going concern, or if a petition is filed by or against Customer under any of the provisions or chapters of the Bankruptcy Act or any amendment thereto, or if Customer shall make an assignment for the benefit of creditors or call a general meeting of creditors, or attempts an informal arrangement or composition with creditors or if a receiver or any officer of a court be appointed to have control of any of the property or assets of Customer or if Customer makes or has made any misstatement or false statement of fact in connection with this transaction, or if any of the foregoing occurs with regards to any guarantor, the unpaid time balance hereunder shall become immediately due and payable at Xerox's option and without notice.

If any of the foregoing occurs, Xerox shall have all of the rights and remedies of a secured party upon default under the Uniform Commercial Code or any similar law as enacted in the state where the equipment is located.

To the extent permitted by law, Xerox may recover the balance of all amounts due hereunder, enter upon the premises where the Equipment may be and render the Equipment unusable and/or take possession thereof and hereunder. In addition, Customer agrees at Xerox's request to assemble the Equipment and make it available to Xerox at a place designated by Xerox.

All rights and remedies of Xerox shall be cumulative and may be exercised successively or concurrently without impairing Xerox's security interest in the Equipment. Customer agrees to pay to Xerox reasonable attorneys' fees and legal expenses in exercising any of its rights and remedies upon default up to 15 percent of the unpaid balance and if such percentage is not so permitted, such other percentage or amount as is permissible under law. All the foregoing is without limitation or waiver or any other rights or remedies available to Xerox according to law.

One might ask, to what extent do Trane, Allis-Chalmers, and Xerox Corporations gain greater rights by using these clauses than they would have if they said nothing about timely delivery or payment? To answer, one would begin by consulting UCC §§ 2-507, 2-503, 2-601, 2-602(1), 2-612; 2-508, 1-201(3), 2-309(1), 1-302(b), and 1-309. Xerox's rights as a secured creditor, and its rights in a bankruptcy or other insolvency proceeding are, of course, beyond the scope of this course.

The Restatement (Second) of Contracts deals with delayed performance in § 242. Two of the comments to that section suggest the Restatement's approach to common problems concerning delay that are found in the cases.

Substitute arrangements. It is often said that in commercial transactions, notably those for the sale of goods, prompt performance by a party is essential if he is to be allowed to require the other to perform or, as it is sometimes put, "time is of the essence." The importance of prompt delivery by a seller of goods generally derives from the circumstance that goods, as contrasted for example with land, are particularly likely to be subject to rapid fluctuations in market price. Therefore, even a relatively short delay in a rising market may adversely affect the buyer by causing a sharp increase in the cost of "cover." *See* Uniform Commercial Code §§ 2-712, 2-713. A less rigid standard applies to contracts for the sale of goods to be delivered in installments or to be specially manufactured for the buyer. On the other hand, considerable delay does not preclude enforcement of a contract for the sale of land if damages are adequate to compensate for the delay and there are no special circumstances indicating that prompt performance was essential and no express provisions requiring such performance....

Effect of agreement. The agreement of the parties often contains a provision for the time of performance or tender. It may simply provide for performance on a stated date. In that event, a material breach on that date entitles the injured party to withhold his performance and gives him a claim for damages for delay, but it does not of itself discharge the other party's remaining duties. Only if the circumstances, viewed as of the time of the breach, indicate that performance or tender on that day is of genuine importance are the injured party's remaining duties discharged immediately, with no period of time during which they are merely suspended. It is, of course, open to the parties to make performance or tender by a stated date a condition by their agreement, in which event, absent excuse ... delay beyond that date results in discharge ... Such stock phrases as "time is of the essence" do not necessarily have this effect, although ... they are to be considered along with other circumstances in determining the effect of delay....

C. "ANTICIPATORY BREACH" AND "REASONABLE GROUNDS FOR INSECURITY"

1. Repudiation and the Power to Walk Away from the Deal

EWANCHUK v. MITCHELL

Missouri Court of Appeals, Southern District
154 S.W.3d 476 (2005)

BATES, C.J.

Sharon Ewanchuk ("Ewanchuk") appeals from a judgment denying her claim for specific performance of an oral agreement to buy two rare Boston terrier puppies from Shelley Mitchell ("Mitchell"). The trial court denied relief because it concluded the oral agreement lacked the necessary definiteness to be enforced, in that there was "no meeting of the minds" between Ewanchuk and Mitchell concerning how the puppies were to be delivered. Ewanchuk claims the trial court should have granted her request for specific performance because all of the required elements of an enforceable contract were present, and Mitchell simply refused to deliver the puppies. We affirm because Ewanchuk's own testimony showed that Mitchell's decision not to deliver the puppies occurred after Ewanchuk repudiated the contract by insisting upon a mode of delivery to which she was not entitled, absent Mitchell's agreement.

I. Standard of Review

We must affirm the trial court's judgment unless it is not supported by substantial evidence, it is against the weight of the evidence, or it erroneously declares or applies the law....

II. Facts and Procedural History

Ewanchuk and Mitchell are both in the business of breeding and raising registered Boston terriers. Ewanchuk has been licensed in this business for twelve years and resides in Alberta, Canada. Mitchell has been licensed in this business for three years and operates a kennel in Cabool, Missouri. Mitchell sold only puppies, and she mainly marketed her animals to brokers that purchased animals for resale to pet stores.

On January 20, 2003, one of Mitchell's breeding females whelped two male Boston terrier puppies ("the puppies"). Rather than being the black and white color normally found in Boston terriers, the puppies were red and white in color. This made them very unique and desirable animals.

On February 20, 2003, Mitchell offered to sell the puppies by placing an ad on the Internet. That same day, Ewanchuk responded to the ad by leaving a message on Mitchell's answering machine. In the message, Ewanchuk expressed her interest in purchasing the puppies. She asked Mitchell to return the call, which Mitchell did. Ewanchuk and Mitchell had several more telephone conversations about the puppies, and Mitchell sent photographs of them to Ewanchuk. During these conversations, Ewanchuk did not commit to purchasing the puppies because they were still too young.

On March 21, 2003, Mitchell called Ewanchuk to inform her that the puppies were eight weeks old and were going to be sold to a broker the following Monday unless Ewanchuk agreed to buy them. The timing of the sale was very important to Mitchell because pet stores would not purchase puppies older than nine weeks of age, so she had to get them to a broker immediately if Ewanchuk did not buy them. Otherwise, the value of the puppies would decline because Mitchell would no longer be able to sell them to a broker or a pet store.

Mitchell initially priced the puppies at $350 each, but she agreed to sell the puppies for a total of $600 because Ewanchuk wanted to buy both of them. Ewanchuk provided Mitchell with a credit card number, which was used to charge the $600 payment.

Although Ewanchuk and Mitchell were able to agree on the puppies' price, they were unable to agree on when and how the puppies would be delivered to Ewanchuk. Because the puppies were only two months old, Ewanchuk wanted Mitchell to keep the puppies until they were three to four months old and fully vaccinated. Mitchell, however, insisted that Ewanchuk accept delivery by April 15, 2003.

Similarly, Ewanchuk and Mitchell were unable to reach any agreement concerning the mode of delivery to be used. Ewanchuk initially wanted both puppies shipped to her by air in one container, but Mitchell would not do so. She was concerned that the puppies might fight if they were shipped together. Ewanchuk said that she would try to get her husband or son, who were both truck drivers, to come pick the puppies up from Mitchell. Ewanchuk, however, was unable to make suitable arrangements to get this done. Ewanchuk also proposed that Mitchell bring the puppies to Ewanchuk in Oklahoma while she was on a trip to Texas to pick up some other dogs. Mitchell was willing to do so, but Ewanchuk provided no definite date as to when the trip would occur. Around April 1, 2003, Ewanchuk did travel from Canada to Texas to pick up the other dogs as planned. Because Ewanchuk failed to advise Mitchell the trip was underway, the planned delivery in Oklahoma did not occur.

After these events took place, Mitchell spoke to Ewanchuk by telephone. During the call, Ewanchuk said she wanted the puppies delivered by air on April 15, 2003. On that date, Ewanchuk telephoned Mitchell to discuss shipping arrangements. In this telephone call, Ewanchuk insisted Mitchell ship the puppies together in one crate. Ewanchuk testified that "I wanted the two puppies shipped together in one kennel, and they [Mitchell and her husband] refused to do that." Mitchell would not ship the three-month-old puppies together because she believed they "would fight and that it was not safe for the puppies to be in the same crate at that age." Mitchell was willing to send one puppy in one crate, but Ewanchuk wanted both delivered together. Ewanchuk testified that Mitchell "repudiated" the contract during that call and said she would refund Ewanchuk's money.

After April 15, 2003, Ewanchuk made no further arrangements to have the puppies delivered to her and had no further direct contact with Mitchell. Ewanchuk later hired an attorney, who filed suit on her behalf on May 16, 2003, seeking specific performance of the oral agreement and injunctive relief to prevent Mitchell from selling the puppies to someone else. After suit was filed but before Mitchell read the petition, she sold both puppies for $350 each to other buyers.[113] After Ewanchuk learned the puppies had been sold, she was granted leave to file an amended petition that added a count seeking actual and punitive damages from Mitchell. After hearing the foregoing evidence presented at trial on November 26, 2003, the trial court entered judgment for Mitchell and ordered that the $600 she had tendered into court be paid to Ewanchuk. The trial court found for Mitchell, in pertinent part, for the following reason:

There was no meeting of the minds as to one of the essential terms of the contract, namely when the puppies would be shipped to the Plaintiff in Canada, and how the shipment would be arranged.... Further, a dispute arose as to whether the puppies should be shipped in one crate or two crates. Therefore, the Court finds that all of

---

113. [7] Mitchell had tried to credit the $600 purchase price back to Ewanchuk's credit card, but Mitchell no longer had the credit card number. At trial, Mitchell tendered a cashier's check made out to Ewanchuk in the amount of $600, which the trial court accepted pending its resolution of the dispute.

the essential terms of the contract were not agreed upon and that the Agreement lacked a definiteness necessary for its enforcement.

Ewanchuk appealed.

III. Discussion and Decision

In Ewanchuk's single point on appeal, she claims the trial court should have granted specific performance because: (1) the required elements of an enforceable contract were present; and (2) Mitchell breached the contract by refusing to deliver the puppies. The oral agreement between Ewanchuk and Mitchell was a contract for the sale of goods within the meaning of Missouri's version of the Uniform Commercial Code ("UCC"). *See* § 400.2-105(1)....

In the first prong of Ewanchuk's bifurcated argument, she contends the trial court misapplied the law by concluding that the parties' failure to agree on the terms of delivery made their agreement too indefinite to be enforceable. We agree. We begin our analysis by noting that under the UCC, "even though one or more terms are left open a contract for sale does not fail for indefiniteness if the parties have intended to make a contract and there is a reasonably certain basis for giving an appropriate remedy." § 400.2-204(3).... Here, it is clear the parties did intend to make a contract because: (1) Mitchell admitted the contract's existence in her answer to the amended petition; and (2) she accepted full payment in advance for the puppies. *See* § 400.2-201(3)(b).... The manner and place of delivery was left unresolved by the parties' negotiation. Because the parties failed to agree upon the terms of delivery, the UCC cured this omission for them by specifying both the time and place of delivery. Section 400.2-309(1) required that the puppies be delivered within a reasonable time. Section 400.2-308(a) required that delivery take place at Mitchell's place of business in Cabool, Missouri.

The trial court misapplied the law by concluding that the parties' agreement "lacked a definiteness necessary for its enforcement." On appeal, however, we are "primarily concerned with the correctness of the trial court's result, not the route taken by the trial court to reach that result." *Business Men's Assur. Co. of America v. Graham*, 984 S.W.2d 501, 506 (Mo. *banc* 1999). "The judgment will be affirmed if cognizable under any theory, regardless of whether the reasons advanced by the trial court are wrong or not sufficient." *Id.*

The second prong of Ewanchuk's argument is that Mitchell breached the contract by refusing to deliver the puppies. We reject this aspect of Ewanchuk's argument. The trial court entered judgment for Mitchell after concluding the contract was unenforceable. This conclusion is correct, but for a different reason than the one upon which the trial court relied.

It is well-settled that a party is bound by his own testimony which is not corrected or explained.... At the trial, Ewanchuk testified unequivocally that she had always wanted the puppies shipped to her by air in the same container. She also testified unequivocally that, from the outset of the negotiation, Mitchell absolutely refused to do so because she believed the puppies would fight if they were shipped together. The issue about the mode of shipping came to a head during the telephone call on

April 15, 2003. Ewanchuk insisted the puppies be shipped to her in one crate, and Mitchell refused. Mitchell offered to ship one dog in one crate, but Ewanchuk was adamant that she wanted the puppies shipped together. At that point, Mitchell cancelled the contract and said she would refund Ewanchuk's money. Thereafter, Ewanchuk made no further arrangements to have the puppies delivered to her, and she never contacted Mitchell directly again.

As noted above, the parties failed to reach an agreement upon the manner and place of delivery during their negotiation. Therefore, the UCC supplied that term of the agreement by requiring Ewanchuk to pick up the puppies at Mitchell's place of business in Cabool. Ewanchuk did not pick up the puppies by April 15, 2003. Instead, on the date delivery was due to occur, Ewanchuk insisted that Mitchell ship both puppies by air in one crate to Alberta, Canada. It was this demand that caused Mitchell's refusal to deliver the puppies and consequent cancellation of the contract. Absent Mitchell's agreement, the UCC did not give Ewanchuk the right to receive delivery of the puppies in this fashion.

Both by decisional law and statute, Missouri recognizes the doctrine of anticipatory repudiation. *Missouri Public Service Co. v. Peabody Coal Co.*, 583 S.W.2d 721, 724 (Mo. App. 1979); § 400.2-610. A party repudiates a contract by manifesting a positive intention not to perform by words or conduct. *Gateway Aviation, Inc. v. Cessna Aircraft Co.*, 577 S.W.2d 860, 862 (Mo. App. 1978). Section 400.2-610 states in pertinent part that "when either party repudiates the contract with respect to a performance not yet due the loss of which will substantially impair the value of the contract to the other, the aggrieved party may ... (b) resort to any remedy for breach (§ 400.2-703 or § 400.2-711)...." Upon a buyer's repudiation of the contract, in whole or in part, one of the seller's available remedies is cancellation of the contract. § 400.2-703(f).

Here, Ewanchuk's own testimony demonstrated that she insisted upon a mode of delivery (both puppies in one crate) and a place of delivery (Alberta, Canada, via air transportation) to which Mitchell had not agreed and to which Ewanchuk was not entitled under the UCC. After making this impermissible demand, Ewanchuk also testified that she never contacted Mitchell directly again and made no further arrangements to have the puppies delivered to her.

Thus, Ewanchuk's trial testimony, by which she was bound, proved that she repudiated the contract on April 15, 2003. Since the puppies were then 12 weeks old, Ewanchuk's repudiation impaired the value of the contract to Mitchell because she could no longer sell the puppies to a broker or pet store. Based on this repudiation, Mitchell was authorized to cancel the contract, which she did....

... The judgment of the trial court is affirmed.

NOTES AND QUESTIONS

1. *The conceptual problem of anticipatory breach:* On January 2nd, Businessperson hires Interpreter to accompany her on an extended trip to various European countries. The trip is to begin on August 1st. On January 25th, Businessperson is promoted to

a new position and the trip is canceled. She immediately notifies Interpreter that their contract is canceled. Interpreter files suit on February 10th, alleging a breach of contract. Can he sue in February or must he wait until August 1st, when the contract was to begin? After all, Businessperson has only said that she will not perform in the future, and she might change her mind between February and the end of July. Reading the contract literally, Businessperson has promised to perform in August, and she cannot fail to perform in August until it *is* August. However, in *Hochster v. De La Tour*,[114] the English court allowed an immediate suit to be brought, and this rule is followed by almost all American jurisdictions. The Queen's Bench said that this rule would encourage employees to get other employment as soon as they could. However, the employee did not have to sue but could await the day of the employer's performance.

The Queen's Bench could have dealt with the problem without allowing a suit for "anticipatory breach" to be brought before performance was due. All the employee really needs in most instances is to be sure that he or she can take another job between January and August (in our example), without breaching the obligation to perform under the original contract. If Businessperson repudiates the contract before her performance is due, Interpreter is free to walk away from their contract at that point. In the language of Restatement (Second) of Contracts § 253(2): "Where performances are to be exchanged under an exchange of promises, one party's repudiation of a duty to render performance discharges the other party's remaining duties to render performance." Clearly, this kind of self-help to avoid or mitigate damages is important, and in many instances it is more important than the right to bring a lawsuit before the time for performance arises.

2. Anticipatory and present breaches distinguished: Suppose seller agrees to deliver one car on April 1st, ten on May 1st, and ten more on June 1st, and buyer promises to pay in specified installments for them. First, assume that on March 20th, seller tells buyer that the deal is off and that no cars will be delivered. This would be an anticipatory breach, since the repudiation came before the time specified for seller's performance. Second, assume there was no repudiation on March 20th, and seller delivered the first car on April 1st. However, seller fails to deliver the ten cars on May 1st and it is clear that seller will not deliver the ten cars due on June 1st. This would be a present breach of contract. (Anticipatory breaches are dealt with in UCC §§ 2-610 and 2-611, while present breaches of installment contracts are governed by § 2-612.)

Does the distinction between anticipatory and present breaches make a difference? For many purposes, a breach is a breach. The aggrieved party may sue or walk away free of obligation. However, there are a few distinctions. Suppose that the seller changes his or her mind and decides to perform the contract after repudiating it. Under § 2-611(1), the seller can reinstate the contract by retracting the anticipatory repudiation "unless the aggrieved party has since the repudiation canceled or materially changed his position

---

114. 2 El. & B. 678, 118 Eng. Rep. 922 (Q.B. 1853).

or otherwise indicated that he considers the repudiation final."[115] After a present breach of contract, however, seller can reinstate the deal only with buyer's agreement. Seller, acting alone, cannot withdraw the repudiation even in the absence of reliance.

3. *When does the statute of limitations start to run when there has been an anticipatory breach?* Section 2-725(1) states: "An action for breach of any contract of sale must be commenced within four years after the cause of action has accrued." A repudiation that is a present breach of contract starts the four-year period running. However, § 2-610 says that after an anticipatory repudiation the aggrieved party may "for a commercially reasonable time await performance by the repudiating party." Would the cause of action accrue to trigger the statute of limitations before "a commercially reasonable time"?

In *Romano v. Rockwell International, Inc.*,[116] on December 6, 1988, Romano's supervisor told him that he had to accept a one-year teaching fellowship and then retire when he was eligible for early retirement on May 31, 1991. From December 6th until Romano retired in 1991, he received his full salary. The Supreme Court of California said that if Romano established that his firing was wrongful, there would have been an anticipatory breach when Romano was told of the employer's plan. There would have been a present breach when Romano actually retired. When would the two-year statute of limitations begin to run? The court said that Romano had the power to await performance by his employer at the times set by his contract. The statute of limitations only began to run when Romano was forced to leave his employment. The court said:

> As Professor Corbin has explained: "For the purpose of determining when the period of limitation begins to run, the defendant's non-performance at the day specified may be regarded as a breach of duty as well as the anticipatory repudiation. The plaintiff should not be penalized for leaving to the defendant an opportunity to retract his wrongful repudiation; and he would be so penalized if the statutory period of limitation is held to begin to run against him immediately."[117]

4. *What is a repudiation?* Suppose the seller, before the time for delivery arrives, writes the buyer and says, "I doubt whether I shall be able to perform, and indeed, the way prices are going I doubt whether, if I am able, I shall care to do so." Restatement (Second) of Contracts § 250, Comment b, says that "mere expression of doubt as to his willingness or ability to perform is not enough to constitute a repudiation...."[118]

A more difficult issue is posed when one party insists on her rights under a contract as she sees them. Can a person repudiate a contract by insisting on an erroneous in-

---

115. Restatement (Second) of Contracts § 256 (1981) states a similar rule for contracts other than those involving transactions in goods.

116. 14 Cal. 4th 479, 926 P.2d 1114 (1996).

117. 4 CORBIN, CONTRACTS, § 989, p. 967.

118. However, the Restatement (Second) suggests that courts should expand UCC § 2-609 to all contracts and allow a party who has "reasonable grounds for insecurity ... with respect to the performance of" the other party to demand adequate assurance of performance and to suspend performance until it is received. We will turn to this section of the Code later in these materials.

terpretation of a contract? Suppose that she honestly believes that her interpretation is the correct one, but a court later finds that she is wrong. Suppose most lawyers would say that her interpretation was plausible. To the extent that you can breach by insisting on a mistaken understanding of a contract, how can you maintain your position and avoid repudiating the deal? Consider the following cases.

2. Insisting on My Interpretation of the Contract as a Form of Repudiation

BILL'S COAL CO., INC. v. BOARD OF PUBLIC UTILITIES OF SPRINGFIELD, MISSOURI

United States Court of Appeals, Tenth Circuit
682 F.2d 883 (1982)

LOGAN, J....

[Bill's Coal Company, Inc., had entered into a long-term contract in 1970 to supply all of the requirements of coal of the Board of Utilities of Springfield, Missouri ("Utility"). The contract provided for minimum and maximum amounts. The contract provided that before the end of each calendar year, Bill's Coal was to notify Utility as to the price for the next year, the price to take effect on April 1. The contract also contained an interesting termination clause. Utility was entitled to solicit bids from other coal companies. If Utility received a bid at least 25 percent under Bill's Coal's price, then Utility could terminate the contract effective March 31. If the bid was at least 15 percent less, then Utility could terminate, but not until the following March 31. The contract required Bill's Coal to quote its price F.O.B. its Garland, Kansas mine. Utility paid the cost of transportation from the mine to Springfield.

In March 1980 Utility notified Bill's Coal it was invoking the termination clause. Bill's Coal responded by bringing suit for breach of contract, and requesting both damages and injunctive relief. The trial court held that Bill's Coal had committed a bad faith breach by repeatedly urging an interpretation of the termination clause that it knew was contrary to the intentions of the parties. During discovery Bill's Coal had inadvertently given Utility a document that outlined an attorney's plan to assert that the contract required a comparison of the Bill's Coal price at its mine-head with the competitor's bid for coal delivered to Springfield. This interpretation would have given Bill's Coal a huge cost advantage with respect to other suppliers. The trial court had held that Bill's Coal had adopted this position in bad faith, and that such a position amounted to a repudiation of the contract because it manifested an intention not to be bound by the terms of the agreement. Bill's Coal argued (1) that Missouri would not recognize a claim grounded in a failure to abide by the UCC's good faith provision, (2) that Bill's Coal's interpretation was plausible and therefore could not be made in bad faith and, finally, (3) that even if the interpretation was made in bad faith, this did not interfere with any act of performance and so did not constitute a repudiation.]

... We do not address the first two arguments Bill's Coal makes since we agree that this type of bad faith behavior is not to be regarded as a contract breach or repudiation. In urging an interpretation of the termination clause it knew did not reflect the parties' intent, Bill's Coal did not affect either party's performance under the contract. A breach of a contract is a failure to provide the other party with the goods or services as the contract requires. *See* 20A Mo. Ann. Stat. §§ 400.2-601 to 608, 400.2-612; Restatement (Second) of Contracts §§ 235, 241, 243, 245 (1981). A repudiation is a party's manifestation that it is not going to provide those goods or services when they will be due at some future date. *See* 20A Mo. Ann. Stat. § 400.2-610; Restatement (Second) of Contracts § 250 (1981). The bad faith urging of a particular interpretation of a termination clause is neither a failure to perform contract obligations (breach) nor an indication those obligations will not be performed in the future (repudiation).

We can envision situations in which bad faith conduct might be actionable: for instance, if the Utility solicited bids from competing coal companies and Bill's Coal in some way coerced competitors into not submitting bids. That might constitute such a breach of Bill's Coal's good faith obligation as to allow the Utility to cancel the contract. But the mere urging of a particular interpretation is quite different. If a seller's interpretation of a termination clause is ludicrous, the buyer should ignore it; if the interpretation might prevail in a court of law, the seller has the right to urge it. If the party that wishes to invoke the termination clause is unsure of the merits of the other party's interpretation, it can either accept that interpretation, rely on its own interpretation, or obtain a declaratory judgment as to the meaning of the contract language....

Our review of the trial court's rulings has been restricted to the one issue treated in this opinion. We express no view on its other rulings in Phase I or II of the trial. The Utility raises questions in its motion for clarification and instructions concerning price to be paid and whether additional bond should be required. These should be addressed by the trial court after remand, in light of the conclusions in this opinion and the trial court's other rulings interpreting the contract.

The case is hereby remanded for further proceedings consistent with this opinion.

[BARRETT, J.'s dissenting opinion, published at 685 F.2d 360 (1982).]

It is my view that the District Court correctly concluded that Bill's Coal's demand for more than it was entitled under the contract with Utility constitutes a repudiation under § 2-610 of the Missouri Uniform Commercial Code (20A U.A.M.S. § 2-610), fully justifying the Court's January 29, 1982, order dissolving the injunction. Thus, I would affirm the District Court.

The main issue generating this litigation involves the "take-out" provision of the 1979 amendment to the coal contract. That provision states, *inter alia*, that if Utility can secure a bid ..."at a delivered price of at least 25 percent less than the price quoted by [Bill's Coal] (adjusted to eliminate the depreciation credit referred to in paragraph

6) ... [Utility] may by written notice cancel this agreement as of the end of the then current fiscal year."

Utility had until March of the year to exercise the take-out provision. At a meeting later in the same day that the 1979 amendment was drafted, an attorney representing Bill's Coal noted that the contract language could be viewed to require a comparison of Bill's Coal's quoted f.o.b. mine price to any competitor's delivered price. However, this attorney stated then that such was not the intention of the parties; rather, the parties agreed and intended that a comparison under the take-out clause would be delivery price versus delivery price.

In December 1979, Bill's Coal became aware that Utility was going to solicit bids and attempt to utilize the "take-out" provision. Bill's Coal then formulated a "plan" to block a take-out by insisting that Utility make a comparison of Bill's Coal's f.o.b. mine price to competitors' delivered price. When Bill's Coal supplied Utility with its f.o.b. mine price for 1980, it also "demanded" that Utility make the bid comparison in accordance with Bill's Coal's "plan." An agent of Utility vehemently rejected Bill's Coal's proposed comparison formula and informed Bill's Coal if it insisted on the formula that Utility would see Bill's Coal in court.

Inasmuch as Bill's Coal's mine is located substantially closer to Springfield's power plant than any of its competitors, a comparison between Bill's Coal's f.o.b. mine price to competitor's delivery price could hardly, if ever, result in a bid sufficient to trigger the take-out provision. Bill's Coal's f.o.b. mine price was substantially higher than any competitor's f.o.b. mine price.

Utility proceeded to solicit bids and to compare Bill's Coal's f.o.b. mine price to competitors' f.o.b. mine price. On March 27, 1980, Utility gave Bill's Coal notice of termination under the take-out clause. Utility thereafter filed a declaratory judgment action against Bill's Coal seeking a declaration of the relative rights and liabilities of the parties under the 1979 amendment. Bill's Coal filed a separate action against Utility for breach of contract. Bill's Coal's action was subsequently consolidated with Utility's action. In all of its pleadings, Bill's Coal held fast to its interpretation of the comparison language of the take-out clause.

The parties agreed that the litigation should be divided into three phases. Phase I involved the interpretation of the take-out clause. The Court concluded that the take-out provision called for a delivery price versus delivery price comparison. It was only after this court finding that Bill's Coal finally abandoned its interpretation of the take-out clause. *It amended its pleadings to assert that the contract language was ambiguous and that the parties had always intended a delivery versus delivery price comparison. In response, Utility amended its complaint to allege anticipatory repudiation and bad faith on Seller's part.*

Phase II was conducted to determine liability. The Court found anticipatory repudiation by virtue of Bill's Coal's demand that Utility use a different price comparison than that which the parties had agreed to. The District Court recognized that although this is an unusual case on its facts, for anticipatory repudiation, the law appears clear that if a party, in bad faith, demands performance of the other party beyond the terms of the contract, and the demanding party conditions his own performance on the injured parties' performance of the additional terms, then there is an anticipatory repudiation by the demanding party. The District Court thus found anticipatory repudiation. It specifically found that Bill's Coal's interpretation of the take-out provision was the result of bad faith in that it was not an honestly held interpretation because Bill's Coal had agreed to a different interpretation. The Court also found a separate cause of action for bad faith.

Based upon these conclusions, the District Court dissolved the injunction, and rendered detailed findings of fact and conclusions of law with which I agree. Specifically, the Court found that because Bill's Coal admitted that it knew at all times that the parties had in fact agreed to the delivery price versus delivery price interpretation of the "take-out" provision of the 1979 amendment, Bill's Coal did not entertain an honest mistake of contract interpretation when it insisted on its f.o.b. versus delivery price position. This, the Court concluded, was a bad faith contention. I agree.

When a party practices fraud, *i.e.*, assertion of a position it knows to be absolutely contrary to the agreement, it repudiates the contract if this false assertion, as here, impairs the value of the contract. This principle applies here inasmuch as the practical effect of Bill's Coal's false interpretation was to block any "take-out" and thus lock Utility into Bill's Coal's price. It follows that by forcing Utility to pay what may well be exorbitant prices under the contract, Bill's Coal impaired the value of the contract to Utility.

The majority opinion anchors its holding, it seems to me, on the proposition that Bill's Coal has "performed" under the contract because it has, at all times, delivered coal to Utility. This holding does not meet the issues addressed by the District Court relating to performance. What was the full performance promised? In terms of money values, it had to be Bill's Coal's promise to permit Utility to exercise the "take-out" provision in good faith by obtaining bona fide competitive bids based on delivery price versus delivery price. This plain intent was absolutely frustrated by the bad faith practiced by Bill's Coal. This bad faith could not be corrected. Accordingly, we are not here dealing with mere "deviations" from full performance that are inadvertent or unintentional. The "deviation" here is all pervasive and due to Bill's Coal's bad faith. It impaired the structure of the contract as a whole. It cannot be "repaired" and thus the contract must be terminated.

We have here an admitted, acknowledged manifestation on the part of Bill's Coal to frustrate the "termination" clause of the contract. The intention is unequivocal. Restatement of Contracts, (First), §§ 314, 315 and 318 (1932), as supplemented, states that in a bilateral contract, one who has failed, without justification, to perform all or any part of what is promised in a contract has breached it (here, Bill's Coal's refusal to recognize the right of Utility to receive proper competitive bids) and, further, that one who, like Bill's Coal, has prevented or hindered Utility from determining whether it is bound to the condition of further purchases of coal from Bill's Coal (performance of a return promise to purchase) is guilty of an anticipatory breach which constitutes a total breach of contract. Under § 318(a) it is stated that "... a positive statement to the promisee or other person having a right under the contract, indicating that the promisor will not or cannot substantially perform his contractual duties" constitutes an anticipatory breach.

UCC § 2-610, Comment 1, states that "anticipatory repudiation centers upon an overt communication of intention or an action which renders performance impossible or demonstrates a clear determination not to continue with performance." In *Neal-Cooper Grain Co. v. Texas Gulf Sulphur Co.*, 508 F.2d 283 (7th Cir. 1974), relied upon by the trial court, it was held that although a demand by a party to a contract for more than the contract calls for in the way of counter-performance is not in itself a repudiation, when a fair reading leads to the conclusion that it amounts to a statement of intention not to perform except on conditions which *go beyond the contract, it becomes a repudiation.* "In order to constitute an anticipatory breach of contract, there must be a definite and unequivocal manifestation of intention on the part of the repudiator that he will not render the promised performance *when the time fixed for it in the contract arrives.*" 4 Corbin on Contracts, § 973, p. 905. [Emphasis supplied.] And, "[w]here the two contracting parties differ as to the interpretation of a contract ... an offer to perform in accordance with his own interpretation ... [will] constitute such a breach, [if] the offer ... be accompanied by a clear manifestation of intention not to perform in accordance with any other interpretation." 4 Corbin on Contracts, § 973 at p. 911.

I would ... affirm the District Court.

NOTES AND QUESTIONS

1. *What is the law of Missouri?* Both the *Ewanchuk* and *Bill's Coal* cases purport to apply the law of Missouri. Are the cases consistent? A lawyer can assert to a court an interpretation of a contract that he knows is not what the parties intended, and this act has no legal consequences. A dog breeder asks for a delivery inconsistent with the default rules of Article 2, and this is an anticipatory breach. Is the answer that one of the two cases is just wrong?

In *Thunder Basin Coal Co. v. Tuco, Inc.*,[119] the court distinguished the *Bill's Coal* case:

[T]he decision is limited in its applicability to situations where the complaint for repudiation was based, in *and of itself* and *without more,* on the other party's urging of a particular interpretation but [if he] actually allows that interpretation to affect its performance, then the plaintiff has in fact stated *a claim* for contractual repudiation.

Does this reading limit the potential impact of the *Bill's Coal* decision? Why would a lawyer assert an interpretation of a contract that he knew did not reflect the intention of the parties?

---

119. 156 F.R.D. 665, 675 (D. Wyo. 1994).

2. *A demand for modification as an anticipatory breach:* In *Unique Systems, Inc. v. Zotos International, Inc.*,[120] Duane Lilja was the chief officer of Unique Systems, Inc., which held a patent on a multi-station hair spray system intended for use in beauty salons. However, Unique lacked the resources needed to manufacture and market the systems. Zotos International, Inc., was (and still is) a major manufacturer and distributor of shampoos, permanents, and setting lotions for the professional hair-dressing field.

Unique and Zotos entered a contract. Lilja was to develop, manufacture, and place in inventory hair spray systems. Zotos was to buy 15,000 systems over a two-year period, and it had an option to buy 7,500 systems a year for the following two years. The actual stocking and distribution of the systems would begin with what the contract called "month one," a "mutually agreed date in the year 1974."

During 1974, several unanticipated delays occurred, some of which were the fault of Lilja, some the fault of Zotos, and some the fault of third parties. By January of 1975, "month one" still had not been set. In early 1975, Lilja told Zotos that he was ready to receive an order. However, other firms had introduced similar systems, and Zotos feared that the market had softened. Zotos demanded that Lilja demonstrate that its system would work. In July of 1975, a test was held, and Zotos's officials agreed that the system complied with the warranties in the contract. However, they refused to put their approval in writing or set "month one" unless Lilja would agree to a test marketing of the systems. There were proposals and counterproposals, but Zotos insisted on conducting test marketing before it would place orders.

Lilja notified Zotos that the contract had been repudiated and sued. The trial court entered a judgment in favor of Lilja and Unique Systems for $398,760, and Zotos appealed. The judgment was affirmed. The court found there was a repudiation under UCC § 2-610. "If a party to a contract demands of the other party a performance to which he has no right under the contract and states definitely that, unless his demand is complied with, he will not render his promised performance, an anticipatory repudiation has been committed. When Zotos told Lilja ... that it would not proceed until market tests were performed with results subject to Zotos's approval, Zotos repudiated the contract and was in total breach. No market tests were required by the contract, a fact that Zotos admits that it knew."

3. *Anticipatory repudiation and the calculation of damages.* Suppose Buyer and Seller make a contract on November 1st for the sale of goods that are to be delivered several years later in installments. On December 1st, Buyer tells Seller that it will not perform the contract because the project for which the goods are to be purchased has been cancelled. Seller's officials are angry because they have invested engineering and selling effort in negotiating the deal and turned down other business opportunities. They seek to persuade Buyer's officials to reconsider and to reinstate

---

120. 622 F.2d 373 (8th Cir. 1980).

the contract. On March 1st of the next year, Buyer's representatives tell Seller that the deal is off and there is no chance of going forward with it. How would damages be calculated under the Uniform Commercial Code? Consider the following case.

COSDEN OIL & CHEMICAL CO. v. KARL O. HELM AKTIENGESELLSCHAFT

United States Court of Appeals, Fifth Circuit
736 F.2d 1064 (1984)

REAVLEY, J.

We must address one of the most difficult interpretive problems of the Uniform Commercial Code—the appropriate time to measure buyer's damages where the seller anticipatorily repudiates a contract and the buyer does not cover. The district court applied the Texas version of Article 2 and measured buyer's damages at a commercially reasonable time after seller's repudiation. We affirm, but remand for modification of damages on another point.

I. Case History

This contractual dispute arose out of events and transactions occurring in the first three months of 1979, when the market in polystyrene, a petroleum derivative used to make molded products, was steadily rising. During this time Iran, a major petroleum producer, was undergoing political turmoil. Karl O. Helm Aktiengesellschaft (Helm or Helm Hamburg), an international trading company based in Hamburg, West Germany, anticipated a tightening in the world petrochemical supply and decided to purchase a large amount of polystyrene. Acting on orders from Helm Hamburg, Helm Houston, a wholly-owned subsidiary, initiated negotiations with Cosden Oil & Chemical Company (Cosden), a Texas-based producer of chemical products, including polystyrene.

Rudi Scholtyssek, general manager of Helm Houston, contacted Ken Smith, Cosden's national sales coordinator, to inquire about the possibility of purchasing quantities of polystyrene. Negotiating over the telephone and by telex, the parties agreed to the purchase and sale of 1250 metric tons of high-impact polystyrene at $.2825 per pound and 250 metric tons of general purpose polystyrene at $.265 per pound. The parties also discussed options on each polystyrene type. On January 18, 1979, Scholtyssek met with Smith in Dallas, leaving behind two purchase confirmations. Purchase confirmation 04 contained the terms for high impact and 05 contained the terms for general purpose. Both confirmations contained the price and quantity terms listed above, and specified the same delivery and payment terms. The polystyrene was to be delivered during January and February in one or more lots, to be called for at Helm's instance. Confirmation 04 specified that Helm had an option for an additional 1000 metric tons of high impact, and confirmation 05 expressed a similar option for 500 metric tons of general purpose. The option amounts were subject to the same terms, except that delivery was to be during February and March. The options were to be declared, at the latest, by January 31, 1979.

On January 22, Helm called for the first shipment of high impact under order 04, to be delivered FAS at a New Jersey port to make a January 29 shipment date for a trans-Atlantic voyage. On January 23, Helm telexed Cosden to declare the options on purchase orders 04 and 05, designating the high impact option quantity as order 06 and the general purpose option quantity as order 07. After exercising the options, Helm sent purchase confirmations 06 and 07, which Cosden received on January 29. That same day Helm Houston received confirmations 04 and 05, which Smith had signed.

Cosden shipped 90,000 pounds of high impact polystyrene to Helm on or about January 26. Cosden then sent an invoice for that quantity to Helm Houston on or about January 31. The front of the invoice stated, "This order is subject to the terms and conditions shown on the reverse hereof." Among the "Conditions of Sale" listed on the back of the invoice was a *force majeure* provision. Helm paid for the first shipment in accordance with the agreement.

As Helm had expected, polystyrene prices began to rise in late January and continued upward during February and March. Cosden also experienced problems at two of its plants in late January. Normally, Cosden supplied its Calumet City, Illinois, production plant with styrene monomer, the "feed stock" or main ingredient of polystyrene, by barges that traveled from Louisiana up the Mississippi and Illinois Rivers to a canal that extended to Cosden's plant. Due to the extremely cold winter of 1978–79, however, the Illinois River and the canal froze, suspending barge traffic for a few weeks. A different problem beset Cosden's Windsor, New Jersey, production plant. A new reactor, used in the polystyrene manufacturing process, had recently been installed at the Windsor plant. A manufacturing defect soon became apparent, however, and Cosden returned the reactor to the manufacturer for repair, which took several weeks. At the time of the reactor breakdown, Cosden was manufacturing only general purpose at the Windsor plant. Cosden had planned on supplying Helm's high impact orders from the Calumet City plant.

Late in January Cosden notified Helm that it was experiencing problems at its production facilities and that the delivery under 04 might be delayed. On February 6, Smith telephoned Scholtyssek and informed him that Cosden was cancelling orders 05, 06, and 07 because two plants were "down" and it did not have sufficient product to fill the orders. Cosden, however, would continue to honor order 04. Smith confirmed the cancellation in a letter dated February 8, which Scholtyssek received on or about February 12. After Helm Hamburg learned of Cosden's cancellation, Wolfgang Gordian, a member of Helm's executive board, sent an internal memorandum to Helm Houston outlining a strategy. Helm would urge that Cosden continue to perform under 04 and, after receiving the high-impact polystyrene, would offset amounts owing under 04 against Helm's damages for nondelivery of the balance of polystyrene. Gordian also instructed Helm Houston to send a telex to Cosden. Following instructions, Scholtyssek then requested from Cosden "the relevant *force majeure* certificate" to pass on to Helm Hamburg. Helm also urged Cosden to deliver immediately several hundred metric tons of high impact to meet two February shipping dates for which Helm had booked shipping space.

In mid-February Cosden shipped approximately 1,260,000 pounds of high impact to Helm under order 04. This shipment's invoice, which also included the *force majeure* provision on the reverse side, specified that Helm owed $355,950, due by March 15 or 16. After this delivery Helm requested that Cosden deliver the balance under order 04 for shipment on a vessel departing March 16. Cosden informed Helm that a March 16 delivery was not possible. On March 15, citing production problems with the 04 balance, Cosden offered to sell 1000 metric tons of styrene monomer at $.41 per pound. Although Cosden later lowered the price on the styrene monomer, Helm refused the offer, insisting on delivery of the balance of 04 polystyrene by March 31 at the latest. Around the end of March, Cosden informed Scholtyssek by telephone that it was cancelling the balance of order 04.

Cosden sued Helm, seeking damages for Helm's failure to pay for delivered polystyrene. Helm counterclaimed for Cosden's failure to deliver polystyrene as agreed. The jury found on special verdict that Cosden had agreed to sell polystyrene to Helm under all four orders. The jury also found that Cosden anticipatorily repudiated orders 05, 06, and 07 and that Cosden cancelled order 04 before Helm's failure to pay for the second 04 delivery constituted a repudiation. The jury fixed the per-pound market prices for polystyrene under each of the four orders at three different times: when Helm learned of the cancellation, at a commercially reasonable time thereafter, and at the time for delivery.

The district court, viewing the four orders as representing one agreement, determined that Helm was entitled to recover $628,676 in damages representing the difference between the contract price and the market price at a commercially reasonable time after Cosden repudiated its polystyrene delivery obligations and that Cosden was entitled to an offset of $355,950 against those damages for polystyrene delivered, but not paid for, under order 04.

II. Time for Measuring Buyer's Damages

Both parties find fault with the time at which the district court measured Helm's damages for Cosden's anticipatory repudiation of orders 05, 06, and 07.[121] Cosden argues that damages should be measured when Helm learned of the repudiation. Helm contends that market price as of the last day for delivery—or the time of performance—should be used to compute its damages under the contract-market differential. We reject both views, and hold that the district court correctly measured damages at a commercially reasonable point after Cosden informed Helm that it was canceling the three orders.

Article 2 of the Code has generally been hailed as a success for its comprehensiveness, its deference to mercantile reality, and its clarity. Nevertheless, certain aspects

---

121. [5] The damages measurement problem does not apply to Cosden's breach of order 04, which was not anticipatorily repudiated. The time Helm learned of Cosden's intent to deliver no more polystyrene under 04 was the same time as the last date of performance, which had been extended to the end of March.

of the Code's overall scheme have proved troublesome in application. The interplay among §§ 2.610, 2.711, 2.712, 2.713, and 2.723, Tex. Bus. & Com. Code Ann. (Vernon 1968), represents one of those areas, and has been described as "an impossible legal thicket." J. White & R. Summers, Uniform Commercial Code § 6-7 at 242 (2d ed. 1980). The aggrieved buyer seeking damages for seller's anticipatory repudiation presents the most difficult interpretive problem.[122] Section 2.713 describes the buyer's damages remedy:

> Buyer's Damages for Non-Delivery or Repudiation
>
> (a) Subject to the provisions of this chapter with respect to proof of market price (§ 2.713), the measure of damages for non-delivery or repudiation by the seller is the difference between the market price *at the time when the buyer learned of the breach* and the contract price together with any incidental and consequential damages provided in this chapter (§ 2.715), but less expenses saved in consequence of the seller's breach (emphasis added [by the Fifth Circuit]).

Courts and commentators have identified three possible interpretations of the phrase "learned of the breach." If seller anticipatorily repudiates, buyer learns of the breach:

> (1) When he learns of the repudiation;
>
> (2) When he learns of the repudiation plus a commercially reasonable time; or
>
> (3) When performance is due under the contract.

… We would not be free to decide the question if there were a Texas case on point, bound as we are by *Erie* to follow state law in diversity cases. We find, however, that no Texas case has addressed the Code question of buyer's damages in an anticipatory repudiation context….

We do not doubt, and Texas law is clear, that market price at the time buyer learns of the breach is the appropriate measure of § 2.713 damages in cases where buyer learns of the breach at or after the time for performance. This will be the common case, for which § 2.713 was designed. *See* [Ellen] Peters, *Remedies for Breach of Contracts Relating to the Sale of Goods Under the Uniform Commercial Code: A Roadmap for Article Two*, 73 Yale L.J. 199, 264 (1963). In the relatively rare case where seller anticipatorily repudiates and buyer does not cover, … the specific provision for anticipatory repudiation cases, § 2.610, authorizes the aggrieved party to await performance for a commercially reasonable time before resorting to his remedies of cover or damages.

---

122. [6] The only area of unanimous agreement among those that have studied the Code provisions relevant to this problem is that they are not consistent, present problems in interpretation, and invite amendment.

In the anticipatory repudiation context, the buyer's specific right to wait for a commercially reasonable time before choosing his remedy must be read together with the general damages provision of § 2.713 to extend the time for measurement beyond when buyer learns of the breach. Comment 1 to § 2.610 states that if an aggrieved party "awaits performance beyond a commercially reasonable time he cannot recover resulting damages which he should have avoided." This suggests that an aggrieved buyer can recover damages where the market rises during the commercially reasonable time he awaits performance. To interpret 2.713's "learned of the breach" language to mean the time at which seller first communicates his anticipatory repudiation would undercut the time that 2.610 gives the aggrieved buyer to await performance.

The buyer's option to wait a commercially reasonable time also interacts with § 2.611, which allows the seller an opportunity to retract his repudiation. Thus, an aggrieved buyer "learns of the breach" a commercially reasonable time after he learns of the seller's anticipatory repudiation. The weight of scholarly commentary supports this interpretation. *See* J. Calamari & J. Perillo, Contracts § 14-20 (2d ed. 1977); [John A.] Sebert, *Remedies Under Article Two of the Uniform Commercial Code: An Agenda for Review*, 130 U. Pa. L. Rev. 360, 372–80 (1981); [George I.] Wallach, *Anticipatory Repudiation and the UCC*, 13 U.C.C. L.J. 48 (1980); Peters, *supra*, at 263–68.

Typically, our question will arise where parties to an executory contract are in the midst of a rising market. To the extent that market decisions are influenced by a damages rule, measuring market price at the time of seller's repudiation gives seller the ability to fix buyer's damages and may induce seller to repudiate, rather than abide by the contract. By contrast, measuring buyer's damages at the time of performance will tend to dissuade the buyer from covering, in hopes that market price will continue upward until performance time.

Allowing the aggrieved buyer a commercially reasonable time, however, provides him with an opportunity to investigate his cover possibilities in a rising market without fear that, if he is unsuccessful in obtaining cover, he will be relegated to a market-contract damage remedy measured at the time of repudiation. The Code supports this view. While cover is the preferred remedy, the Code clearly provides the option to seek damages. *See* § 2.712(c) & comment 3. If "[t]he buyer is always free to choose between cover and damages for non-delivery," and if 2.712 "is not intended to limit the time necessary for [buyer] to look around and decide as to how he may best effect cover," it would be anomalous, if the buyer chooses to seek damages, to fix his damages at a time before he investigated cover possibilities and before he elected his remedy. *See id.* comment 2 & 3....

Moreover, comment 1 to § 2.713 states: "The general baseline adopted in this section uses as a yardstick the market in which the buyer would have obtained cover had he sought that "relief." *See* § 2.610, comment 1. When a buyer chooses not to cover, but to seek damages, the market is measured at the time he could have covered—a reasonable time after repudiation. *See* §§ 2.711 and 2.713.

Persuasive arguments exist for interpreting "learned of the breach" to mean "time of performance," consistent with the pre-Code rule. *See* J. White & R. Summers, *supra*, §6-7.... If this was the intention of the Code's drafters, however, phrases in §§ 2.610 and 2.712 lose their meaning. If buyer is entitled to market-contract damages measured at the time of performance, it is difficult to explain why the anticipatory repudiation section limits him to a commercially reasonable time to await performance. *See* § 2.610, comment 1. Similarly, in a rising market, no reason would exist for requiring the buyer to act "without unreasonable delay" when he seeks to cover following an anticipatory repudiation. *See* § 2.712(a).

The interplay among the relevant Code sections does not permit, in this context, an interpretation that harmonizes all and leaves no loose ends. We therefore acknowledge that our interpretation fails to explain the language of § 2.723(a) insofar as it relates to aggrieved buyers. We note, however, that the section has limited applicability—cases that come to trial before the time of performance will be rare. Moreover, the comment to § 2.723 states that the "section is not intended to exclude the use of any other reasonable method of determining market price or of measuring damages...." In light of the Code's persistent theme of commercial reasonableness, the prominence of cover as a remedy, and the time given an aggrieved buyer to await performance and to investigate cover before selecting his remedy, we agree with the district court that "learned of the breach" incorporates § 2.610's commercially reasonable time.[123] ...

---

123. [11] We note that two circuits arrived at a similar conclusion by different routes. In Cargill, Inc. v. Stafford, 553 F.2d 1222 (10th Cir. 1977), the court began its discussion of damages by embracing the "time of performance" interpretation urged by Professors White and Summers. *Id.* at 1226. Indeed, the court stated that "damages normally should be measured from the time when performance is due and not from the time when the buyer learns of repudiation." *Id.* Nevertheless, the court conclude[d] that under § 4-2-713 a buyer may urge continued performance for a reasonable time. At the end of a reasonable period he should cover if substitute goods are readily available. If substitute goods are available and buyer does not cover within a reasonable time, damages should be based on the price at the end of that reasonable time rather than on the price when performance is due. *Id.* at 1227. The *Cargill* court would employ the time of performance measure only if buyer had a valid reason for not covering. In First Nat'l Bank of Chicago v. Jefferson Mortgage Co., 576 F.2d 479 (3d Cir. 1978), the court initially quoted with approval legislative history that supports a literal or "plain meaning" interpretation of New Jersey's § 2-713. Nevertheless, the court hedged by interpreting that section "to measure damages within a commercially reasonable time after learning of the repudiation." *Id.* at 492. In light of the unequivocal repudiation and because cover was "easily and immediately ... available ... in the well-organized and easily accessible market," *id.* at 493 (quoting Oloffson v. Coomer, 11 Ill. App. 3d 918, 296 N.E.2d 871 [1973]), a commercially reasonable time did not extend beyond the date of repudiation. We agree with the *First National* court that "the circumstances of the particular market involved should determine the duration of a 'commercially reasonable time.'" 576 F.2d at 492; *see* Tex. Bus. & Com. Code § 1.204(b). In this case, however, there was no showing that cover was easily and immediately available in an organized and accessible market and that a commercially reasonable time expired on the day of Cosden's cancellation. We recognize that § 2.610's "commercially reasonable time" and § 2.712's "without unreasonable delay" are distinct concepts. Often, however, the two time periods will overlap, since the buyer can investigate cover possibilities while he awaits performance. *See* Sebert, *supra*, at 376–77 & n.80. Although the jury in the present case did not fix the exact duration of a commercially reasonable time, we assume that the jury determined market

VI. "Cover" as a Ceiling

At trial Cosden argued that Helm's purchases of polystyrene from other sources in early February constituted cover. Helm argued that those purchases were not intended to substitute for polystyrene sales cancelled by Cosden. Helm, however, contended that it did cover by purchasing large amounts of high-impact polystyrene from other sources late in February and around the first of March. Cosden claimed that these purchases were not made reasonably and that they should not qualify as cover. The jury found that none of Helm's purchases of polystyrene from other sources were cover purchases.

Now Cosden argues that the prices of polystyrene for the purchases that Helm claimed were cover should act as a ceiling for fixing market price under §2.713. We refuse to accept this novel argument. Although a buyer who has truly covered may not be allowed to seek higher damages under §2.713 than he is granted by §2.712, *see* §2.713 comment 5; J. White & R. Summers, *supra*, §6-4 at 233–34, in this case the jury found that Helm did not cover. We cannot isolate a reason to explain the jury's finding: it might have concluded that Helm would have made the purchases regardless of Cosden's nonperformance or that the transactions did not qualify as cover for other reasons. Because of the jury's finding, we cannot use those other transactions to determine Helm's damages....

3. Uncertainty about the Other Side's Performance— The Code's Framework

AMF, INC. v. MCDONALD'S CORP.

United States Court of Appeals, Seventh Circuit
536 F.2d 1167 (1976)

CUMMINGS, J.

... AMF seeks damages for the alleged wrongful cancellation and repudiation of McDonald's Corporation's ("McDonald's") orders for sixteen computerized cash registers for installation in restaurants owned by wholly-owned subsidiaries of McDonald's and for seven such registers ordered by licensees of McDonald's for their restaurants. In July 1972, McDonald's of Elk Grove, Inc., sued AMF to recover the $20,385.28 purchase price paid for a prototype computerized cash register and losses sustained as a result of failure of the equipment to function satisfactorily.... [T]he district court rendered a memorandum opinion and order in both cases in favor of each defendant. The only appeal is from the eight judgment orders dismissing AMF's complaints against McDonald's and the seven licensees. We affirm....

In 1966, AMF began to market individual components of a completely automated restaurant system, including its model 72C computerized cash register involved here.

---

price at a time commercially reasonable under all the circumstances, in light of the absence of objection to the form of the special issue.

The 72C cash register then consisted of a central computer, one to four input stations, each with a keyboard and cathode ray tube display, plus the necessary cables and controls.

In 1967, McDonald's representatives visited AMF's plant in Springdale, Connecticut, to view a working "breadboard" model 72C to decide whether to use it in McDonald's restaurant system. Later that year, it was agreed that a 72C should be placed in a McDonald's restaurant for evaluation purposes.

In April 1968, a 72C unit accommodating six input stations was installed in McDonald's restaurant in Elk Grove, Illinois. This restaurant was a wholly-owned subsidiary of McDonald's and was its busiest restaurant. Besides functioning as a cash register, the 72C was intended to enable counter personnel to work faster and to assist in providing data for accounting reports and bookkeeping. McDonald's of Elk Grove, Inc., paid some $20,000 for this prototype register on January 3, 1969. AMF never gave McDonald's warranties governing reliability or performance standards for the prototype.

At a meeting in Chicago on August 29, 1968, McDonald's concluded to order sixteen 72Cs for its company-owned restaurants and to cooperate with AMF to obtain additional orders from its licensees. In December 1968, AMF accepted McDonald's purchase orders for those sixteen 72Cs. In late January 1969, AMF accepted seven additional orders for 72Cs from McDonald's licensees for their restaurants. Under the contract for the sale of all the units, there was a warranty for parts and service. AMF proposed to deliver the first unit in February 1969, with installation of the remaining twenty-two units in the first half of 1969. However, AMF established a new delivery schedule in February 1969, providing for deliveries to commence at the end of July 1969 and to be completed in January 1970, assuming that the first test unit being built at AMF's Vandalia, Ohio, plant was built and satisfactorily tested by the end of July 1969. This was never accomplished.

During the operation of the prototype 72C at McDonald's Elk Grove restaurant, many problems resulted, requiring frequent service calls by AMF and others. Because of its poor performance, McDonald's had AMF remove the prototype unit from its Elk Grove restaurant in late April 1969.

At a March 18, 1969, meeting, McDonald's and AMF personnel met to discuss the performance of the Elk Grove prototype. AMF agreed to formulate a set of performance and reliability standards for the future 72Cs, including "the number of failures permitted at various degrees of seriousness, total permitted downtime, maximum service hours, and cost." Pending mutual agreement on such standards, McDonald's personnel asked that production of the twenty-three units be held up and AMF agreed.

On May 1, 1969, AMF met with McDonald's personnel to provide them with performance and reliability standards. However, the parties never agreed upon such standards. At that time, AMF did not have a working machine and could not produce one within a reasonable time because its Vandalia, Ohio, personnel were too inexperienced. After the May 1st meeting, AMF concluded that McDonald's had cancelled all 72C orders. The reasons for the cancellation were the poor performance of the prototype; the lack of assurances that a workable machine was available; and the unsatisfactory conditions at AMF's Vandalia, Ohio, plant where the twenty-three 72Cs were to be built.

On July 29, 1969, McDonald's and AMF representatives met in New York. At this meeting it was mutually understood that the 72C orders were cancelled and that none would be delivered.

In its conclusions of law, the district court held that McDonald's and its licensees had entered into contracts for twenty-three 72C cash registers but that AMF was not able to perform its obligations under the contracts.... Citing § 2-610 of the Uniform Commercial Code (Ill. Rev. Stats. ch. 26, § 2-610 [1975]) and Comment 1 thereunder, the court concluded that on July 29, McDonald's justifiably repudiated the contracts to purchase all twenty-three 72Cs.

Relying on § 2-609 and 2-610 of the Uniform Commercial Code (Ill. Rev. Stat. ch. 26, §§ 2-609 and 2-610 [1975]), the court decided that McDonald's was warranted in repudiating the contracts and therefore had a right to cancel the orders by virtue of § 2-711 of the Uniform Commercial Code (Ill. Rev. Stats. ch. 26, § 2-711 [1975]). Accordingly, judgment was entered for McDonald's.

The findings of fact adopted by the district court were a mixture of the court's own findings and findings proposed by the parties, some of them modified by the court. AMF has assailed 10 of the 124 findings of fact, but our examination of the record satisfies us that all have adequate support in the record and support the conclusions of law.

Whether in a specific case a buyer has reasonable grounds for insecurity is a question of fact. Comment 3 to UCC § 2-609; ANDERSON, UNIFORM COMMERCIAL CODE, § 2-609 (2d ed. 1971). On this record, McDonald's clearly had "reasonable grounds for insecurity" with respect to AMF's performance. At the time of the March 18, 1969, meeting, the prototype unit had performed unsatisfactorily ever since its April 1968 installation. Although AMF had projected delivery of all twenty-three units by the first half of 1969, AMF later scheduled delivery from the end of July 1969 until January 1970. When McDonald's personnel visited AMF's Vandalia, Ohio, plant on March 4, 1969, they saw that none of the 72C systems was being assembled and learned that a pilot unit would not be ready until the end of July of that year. They were informed that the engineer assigned to the project was not to commence work until March 17th. AMF's own personnel were also troubled about the design of the 72C, causing them to attempt to reduce McDonald's order to five units. Therefore, under § 2-609 McDonald's was entitled to demand adequate assurance of performance by AMF.

However, AMF urges that § 2-609 of the UCC is inapplicable because McDonald's did not make a written demand of adequate assurance of due performance. In *Pittsburgh-Des Moines Steel Co. v. Brookhaven Manor Water Co.*, 532 F.2d 572, 581 (7th Cir. 1976), we noted that the Code should be liberally construed and therefore rejected such "a formalistic approach" to § 2-609. McDonald's failure to make a written demand was excusable because AMF's Mr. Dubosque's testimony and his April 2 and 18, 1969, memoranda about the March 18th meeting showed AMF's clear understanding that McDonald's had suspended performance until it should receive adequate assurance of due performance from AMF....

After the March 18th demand, AMF never repaired the Elk Grove unit satisfactorily nor replaced it. Similarly, it was unable to satisfy McDonald's that the twenty-three machines on order would work. At the May 1st meeting, AMF offered unsatisfactory assurances for only five units instead of twenty-three. The performance standards AMF tendered to McDonald's were unacceptable because they would have permitted the 72Cs not to function properly for 90 hours per year, permitting as much as one failure in every fifteen days in a busy McDonald's restaurant. Also, as the district court found, AMF's Vandalia, Ohio, personnel were too inexperienced to produce a proper machine. Since AMF did not provide adequate assurance of performance after McDonald's March 18th demand, UCC § 2-609(1) permitted McDonald's to suspend performance. When AMF did not furnish adequate assurance of due performance at the May 1st meeting, it thereby repudiated the contract under § 2-609(4). At that point, § 2-610(b) permitted McDonald's to cancel the orders pursuant to § 2-711, as it finally did on July 29, 1969....

... McDonald's could cancel the orders under §§ 2-610 and 2-711 because of AMF's failure to give adequate assurance of due performance under § 2-609....

Judgment Affirmed.

NOTES AND QUESTIONS

1. *Materials from the briefs of the parties:* AMF argued that McDonald's had no grounds for insecurity since the machine with the defects was a prototype model, McDonald's knew of all the defects when it placed its order for the machines, and then McDonald's decided it could buy more advanced technology for less money and so it looked for a way out. If it had made a written demand for assurances, AMF could have responded by giving appropriate assurances.

McDonald's cited an internal AMF memo that stated:

> On Tuesday, March 18, we had a meeting with McDonald's at which time they expressed their unhappiness with the last 2 months performance of the equipment and stated that they intended to cancel the order unless we could give them a warranty or assurance on the reliability of the production units, which reliability would have to be "considerably" better than the recent experience with the prototype.

What, if anything, would a formal written demand for assurances have added? Compare the approach of the court in *Eastern Air Lines v. McDonnell Douglas Corp., supra*.

2. *Does the demand have to be in writing?* The answer is most unclear; some cases read the statute literally, while others find no need for a writing when the one who is asked for assurances knows of the demand. In *Chronister Oil Co. v. Unocal Refining*

and Marketing Co.,[124] Judge Posner noted the conflict among just the Illinois cases (although he found that he did not have to decide whether a writing was required in the appeal before him because there was no right to demand assurances of future performance in any event):

> Chronister argues that if Unocal wanted assurances of performance it had to ask for them in writing, UCC § 2-609, and it did not. The only assurances sought were oral, and indeed implicit—Unocal informing Chronister of the failure of delivery and giving it a day to solve the problem, with the clear implication that if Chronister could not solve it within that time it would be in breach and Unocal would terminate. This was "demand" enough, but § 2-609 states that a party "may in writing demand" assurances. Although a number of cases, including Illinois cases and Seventh Circuit cases interpreting Illinois law, waive the requirement when the party on whom the demand is made knows that it has been made, *e.g., Toppert v. Bunge Corp.*, 60 Ill. App. 3d 607, 18 Ill. Dec. 171, 377 N.E.2d 324, 328–29 (Ill. App. 1978); *AMF, Inc. v. McDonald's Corp.*, 536 F.2d 1167, 1170–71 (7th Cir. 1976) (applying Illinois law); *Diskmakers, Inc. v. DeWitt Equipment Corp.*, 555 F.2d 1177, 1179–80 (3d Cir. 1977), the most recent Illinois cases insist on strict compliance with the terms of the section. *Bodine Sewer, Inc. v. Eastern Illinois Precast, Inc.*, 143 Ill. App. 3d 920, 97 Ill. Dec. 898, 493 N.E.2d 705, 712 (Ill. App. 1986); *Canteen Corp. v. Former Foods, Inc.*, 238 Ill. App. 3d 167, 179 Ill. Dec. 342, 606 N.E.2d 174, 184 (Ill. App. 1992).

Judge Posner's opinion was written in 1994. We have found no Illinois decision on point decided since then. Obviously, a lawyer advising a client will want to put demands in writing and avoid any issue if the situation turns into litigation. Why might a client not put a demand in writing? Why might a businessperson not want to do this?

3. *Section 2-609 as the all-purpose tool:* Professor James White[125] points out that the court used § 2-609 to avoid considering whether the failure to perform the installment contract met the tests for breach in § 2-612. "In effect, the court applied § 2-609 to one party's routine negotiating behavior and gave it significant legal consequence—namely, repudiation by the other."

In another case in which the court declined to require a written demand for assurance,[126] White says that the court used § 2-609 to magnify the importance of particular immaterial breaches and change them into material ones. "The analysis short-circuits the agonizing found in many common law cases in which a court attempts to determine whether a breach in one installment so affects the expectations or behavior for other installments as to constitute a material breach."

124. 34 F.3d 462, 464 (7th Cir. 1994).
125. James J. White, *Eight Cases and Section 251*, 67 Cornell L. Rev. 841 (1982).
126. ARB (American Research Bureau), Inc. v. E-Systems, Inc. 663 F.2d 189 (D.C. Cir. 1980).

In a third case,[127] a buyer of specialized industrial burners for an ammonia plant in Yugoslavia discovered that similar burners in use in Syria and Sri Lanka had developed problems in operation. The buyer, prior to installation of the burners, asked that the seller take the burners back—or failing that, to guarantee that they would operate properly, with the guarantee secured by a letter of credit. The seller refused, and the buyer was awarded a full refund of the purchase price. The court held that the seller had failed to provide meaningful assurances. Notice that by using UCC § 2-609, the buyer never had to prove that the burners would not have met the agreed specifications when they were installed in the Yugoslavian ammonia plant, which had yet to be completed and put into operation at the time of the hearing on the motion for summary judgment. Of course, it looks as if neither buyer nor seller thought the burners would have met specifications if they had been installed. The buyer did not have to deal with questions of whether it had accepted the burners and whether seller could still cure, or whether the buyer was entitled to revoke its acceptance because of a defect that substantially impaired the value of the burners to the buyer.

4. *The relation among UCC §§ 2-609, 2-610, and 2-611:* In the *AMF* case, the court said: "When AMF did not furnish adequate assurance of due performance at the May 1st meeting, it thereby repudiated the contract under § 2-609(4). At that point, § 2-610(b) ... permitted McDonald's to cancel the orders pursuant to § 2-711...."[128] If § 2-609(4) is applicable, must one also meet the requirements of and be subject to the qualifications in §§ 2-610 and 2-611? For example, could AMF have withdrawn its repudiation under § 2-611?

BRISBIN v. SUPERIOR VALVE CO.
United States Court of Appeals, Third Circuit
398 F.3d 279 (3d Cir. 2005)

AMBRO, C.J.

This dispute arises out of a long-term supply relationship gone bad. The plaintiff is Kirk Brisbin, an individual doing business as Specialty Manufacturing ("Specialty").[129] Superior Valve Company ("Superior"), one of the named defendants, was acquired by defendant Harsco Corporation in the fall of 1998. After a bench trial, judgment ultimately was entered in favor of Specialty in the amount of $746,675. On appeal, we review the Magistrate Judge's conclusions regarding adequate assurance and damage issues. We affirm in part, reverse in part, and remand for further proceedings.

I. Factual Background and Procedural History

In 1997 Brisbin and Superior began negotiating long-term supply contracts whereby Specialty would sell Superior certain industrial goods. The result was two separate

127. Creusot-Loire Int'l, Inc. v. Coppus Eng'g Corp., 585 F. Supp. 45 (S.D.N.Y. 1983).
128. AMF, Inc. v. McDonald's Corp., 536 F.2d 1167, 1171 (7th Cir. 1976).
129. [1] Thus this opinion refers to Brisbin and Specialty interchangeably.

contracts in May 1998. The first was for the sale of brass valves (hereinafter referred to as the "1065 valves"). The second contract was for the sale of two-inch, three-inch, four-inch, and five-inch brass shell castings (hereinafter referred to generally as "shells").

The performance of both contracts was subject to certain quality control standards. Before Specialty could manufacture either the 1065 valves or any of the shells on a full-time basis, it had to receive approval from Superior. The initial step in the approval process was known as First Article Inspection ("FAI"). Stated briefly, FAI would test whether the material and dimensions of the item met requirements. Upon FAI approval, Specialty would begin a trial production run of 100 pieces. Superior would then conduct tests to evaluate the consistency of the pieces. Only after Superior's approval of the samples from the trial production run could Specialty begin full-time production.

According to a memorandum written by Ed Wingenroth, Superior's director of quality assurance, Superior gave FAI approval to Specialty for the three-inch shells on January 25, 1999. Superior then ordered a 100-piece trial production run. Specialty completed the order in March. But because the shells were manufactured in South Korea,[130] Superior did not receive them until the beginning of June. Brisbin testified that Wingenroth tested the trial-production shells in April (in South Korea) prior to shipment. Superior, however, conducted additional testing in late July. Several Superior employees testified that this testing uncovered problems with the bronze alloy with which the shells were made.

For the 1065 valves, Wingenroth gave FAI approval in a letter written May 27, 1999. Superior claims that it never authorized Wingenroth to give FAI approval because the valve samples did not meet testing requirements. Yet Superior asked Specialty to begin the 100-piece trial production run for the 1065 valves in early June.

Specialty could not complete this trial production run. According to Brisbin, his South Korean manufacturers were unable to source six of the required component parts for the 1065 valves. In a June 21 letter, Brisbin formally requested that Superior supply these component parts. Superior previously had supplied a limited number of component parts, enabling Specialty to manufacture samples and thus facilitating the FAI approval process. Superior, however, decided not to supply the components for the trial production run. Specialty apparently was not informed of this decision.

Beginning in late June and continuing through July, Brisbin was frustrated with what he perceived as Superior's dilatory tactics.

> Well, I had spent over two years now of my time, considerable expense to my family, my business, and I was just not getting any direction.... At that point management clearly was not supporting the programs. I was having

---

130. [3] Specialty is not a manufacturing company. Its primary value consisted of Brisbin's relationship with several South Korean manufacturers. With Superior's express permission, Specialty subcontracted the actual production of the 1065 valves and the shells.

trouble having correspondence returned.... As of June, I will say late June, there was just starting to become a total collapse of effort and support in showing good faith toward the programs.

The one person at Superior with whom Brisbin corresponded was Joe Kilmer, the director of purchasing. But Brisbin testified that, while Kilmer was helpful in the sense that he actually returned calls, he did not facilitate Brisbin's repeated attempts to get feedback on the 1065 valves and three-inch shells projects.

At the end of July, Brisbin spoke with Kenneth Miller—vice president and general manager of a division of Harsco Corporation—concerning the projects' status. As a result, Brisbin and various Superior employees held a conference call on August 2. According to Brisbin, Superior told him for the first time that the FAI approvals for both the three-inch shells and the 1065 valves were either missing or did not exist. He was also informed that Superior would require additional testing. For the 1065 valves, a Superior engineer allegedly informed Brisbin on the call that the project was a low priority and would not receive any attention for several weeks. Despite Brisbin's repeated requests, Superior never supplied Specialty with any of the test results for either the 1065 valves or the shells demonstrating product nonconformance or the specific requirements Specialty would have to meet in order to be reapproved.

Brisbin memorialized his frustrations with Superior in an August 5 fax to Miller. It contained the following statements:

- Additionally, I am now hearing my programs have not passed First Article Inspections, when I have signed documents from your quality control manager at the time saying they [have].

- I cannot continue to pour my money into these programs, having never asked Superior Valve Company to pay one penny, if your employees are going to continue to deny, stall, fabricate, lose documents, lose samples, deny documents exist, issue incorrect purchase orders, change requirements, etc.

- I require these three invoices be paid to me, and that I receive this check of $112,868 in its entirety, before the close of business on Thursday, 19 August 1999, in my office in Texas.

- I want very much for these programs to go forward, but I must have, after two years, your company come forward and finally illustrate its good faith and pay the tooling and molding costs in as much [sic] as they continue to find reason to stall these programs.

- I would certainly expect ... some sort of preliminary agreement be signed by me agreeing with the reason the payment is being made, and to show clearly what my obligations are for this payment.

Brisbin received two responses to his August 5 fax. In an August 11 letter, Superior formally rescinded the FAI approvals given by Ed Wingenroth for the three-inch shells and the 1065 valves. The letter informed Brisbin that "a review of inspection documents shows that some required tests were not performed, and some dimensions were in nonconformance to engineering specifications." In an August 12 fax, Miller accused Brisbin of "attempting to establish a breach of contract" and denied that Superior was obligated to make any payments, but suggested that the parties arrange another conference call.

As a result, another conference call took place on August 17. In a fax that same day, Brisbin wrote:

- I am certainly interested in these programs and only wish they move forward as originally intended.

- However, understand Specialty Manufacturing believes, and has overwhelming documentation to support, our belief that our products have already been fully tested and approved.

- If additional testing and approvals are now required by Superior Valve Company—I understand. If this is the case, however, Specialty Manufacturing needs these new requirements in writing, and as soon as possible, and would expect Superior Valve Company to bear the additional costs incurred by Specialty Manufacturing in complying with these new conditions.

- In view of the delays in moving forward, I believe it is time for Superior Valve Company to now absorb these startup costs. As earlier stated to you, we request this immediately be discussed and agreed upon. I will discuss different options or arrangements than previously required, but this very importantly needs to be resolved, and soon.

Miller responded with a short fax to Brisbin disagreeing with his characterization of the phone conversation.

On September 1, Brisbin faxed to Miller a final attempt to reconcile the situation. After summarizing the past communications between the two companies, Brisbin stated:

> If Superior Valve ... has any last-minute ideas which would allow these programs to move forward, I would certainly listen, as I always have. Up to this point, however, I have not seen an expressed interest for these programs' forward movement by management.

The only response to this fax was a September 8 letter by Irene Ratajczak, a "Senior Administrative Assistant" at Superior, declaring its intention to refer "this matter over to our legal department."

Brisbin subsequently filed suit in the Western District of Pennsylvania seeking damages for breach of contract. Specifically, he requested lost profits from the two written contracts and the purported oral contract. With the consent of the parties, the matter was assigned to a magistrate judge for trial.

After conducting a bench trial, the district court's Chief Magistrate Judge entered judgment for Specialty in the amount of $758,875 (subsequently reduced to $746,675). He concluded that Specialty possessed reasonable grounds for insecurity under §2-609 of the Uniform Commercial Code and made reasonable requests for adequate assurance. The Magistrate Judge also held that Superior's failure to provide any assurance of future performance and its decision to disengage from the relationship materially breached the supply contracts.

For damages, the Magistrate Judge awarded Specialty its lost profits for the 1065 valves and shells contracts. He calculated profits for the 1065 valves on the basis of (1) three full years of production (2) at the original quantity estimate in the contract (3) at the profit rate of $2.15 per valve. He based profits for the shells contract on (1) five full years of production (2) for each model (*i.e.*, the two-inch shells, the three-inch shells, et al.) (3) at the quantities and prices listed in the attachment to the contract....

Both sides timely appealed....

II. Standard of Review

We review findings of fact for clear error and exercise plenary review over conclusions of law or the application of legal precepts to the facts. A factual finding is clearly erroneous when "the reviewing court on the entire evidence is left with the definite and firm conviction that a mistake has been committed" (citation omitted). "If the district court's account of the evidence is plausible in light of the record viewed in its entirety, the court of appeals may not reverse it even though convinced that had it been sitting as the trier of fact, it would have weighed the evidence differently" (citation omitted).

III. Analysis

Superior attacks the Magistrate Judge's conclusion that Specialty's grounds for insecurity and requests for adequate assurance were reasonable. It also challenges his damages calculation....

A. Insecurity and Adequate Assurance

1. Applicable Legal Standards

We have found no Pennsylvania cases discussing whether a trial court's conclusions on adequate assurance under 13 Pa. Cons. Stat. §2609 (UCC §2-609) are findings of fact or conclusions of law. Courts and commentary discussing §2-609 have concluded that these issues are generally questions of fact, but may sometimes be decided as a matter of law. *See* UCC §2-609, comments 3 and 4; *BAII Banking Corp. v. UPG, Inc.*, 985 F.2d 685, 702 (2d Cir. 1993) ("It is generally a question of fact whether a buyer has reasonable grounds for insecurity under §2-609. There are circumstances, however, where this issue may be resolved as a matter of law." (citations omitted)); *AMF v. McDonald's Corp.*, 536 F.2d 1167, 1170 (7th Cir. 1976) ("Whether in a specific case a buyer has reasonable grounds for insecurity is a question of fact ...").... For a court of appeals sitting in review of a district court, the inquiry of whether conduct was so egregious (or, conversely, so innocuous) as to allow a conclusion on adequate assurance as a matter of law is functionally the same as whether a district court's finding of fact was clearly erroneous. As the cases cited above suggest, we may not overturn the Magistrate Judge's conclusions unless the evidence reasonably supports only one conclusion.

Turning to the merits, Pennsylvania's Uniform Commercial Code provides that when "reasonable grounds for insecurity arise with respect to the performance of either party the other may in writing demand adequate assurance of due performance." 13 Pa. Cons. Stat. § 2609(a). Failure to provide such assurance within a "reasonable time not exceeding 30 days" constitutes repudiation of the contract. *Id.* § 2609(d).

What constitutes "reasonable" grounds and "adequate" assurance is to be defined by commercial, not legal, standards. *Id.* § 2609(b). Comment 3 to § 2-609 of the UCC provides that the grounds for insecurity "need not arise from or be directly related to the contract in question," and Comment 4 states that "repeated delinquencies must be viewed as cumulative." Further, Comment 4 indicates that what constitutes adequate assurance will vary depending on the circumstances and that the requested assurance need not be due under the contract. "What constitutes 'adequate assurance' is to be determined by factual conditions; [a party] must exercise good faith and observe commercial standards; his satisfaction must be based upon reason and must not be arbitrary or capricious." *Cinicola v. Scharffenberger*, 248 F.3d 110, 120 n. 10 (3d Cir. 2001) (quoting *Richmond Leasing Co. v. Capital Bank, N.A.*, 762 F.2d 1303, 1309–10 (5th Cir. 1985)).[131]

2. Analysis

On appeal, Superior challenges the Magistrate Judge's adequate assurance findings on three grounds: (1) Specialty could not be insecure because any project delays were its own fault, e.g., Specialty's inability to source the six internal components for the 1065 valves and the quality control problems with both the three-inch shells and the 1065 valves; (2) Specialty's request for payment of $112,868 was unreasonable because no contractual right to this payment existed; and (3) the Magistrate Judge erroneously interpreted internal Superior documents and improperly relied on this evidence in making his findings. The Magistrate Judge's findings, however, are fully supported by the factual record.

As to Superior's first challenge, we agree with the Magistrate Judge that Specialty's ability to manufacture the 1065 valves and shells in accordance with Superior's quality control standards is irrelevant. This inquiry pertains to the damages calculation, but it has no bearing on whether, in August 1999, Specialty had reasonable grounds to feel insecure about Superior's commitment to these projects.

As detailed above, a variety of evidence supports the Magistrate Judge's decision that Specialty had reasonable grounds to feel insecure. The 100-piece trial production run for the three-inch shells had been delivered to Superior by the late spring of 1999. Even assuming there were problems with the brass alloy used to manufacture the shells, the additional testing by Superior did not begin until a month and a half after their arrival. As for the 1065 valves, even assuming the FAI approval was unwarranted, the record indicates (and Superior does not dispute) that Wingenroth

---

131. [6] Although *Cinicola* involved the interpretation of a federal bankruptcy statute, 11 U.S.C. § 365(b), the language of the statute borrows the concept of UCC § 2-609.

had authority to give this approval. As such, Brisbin's reliance on Wingenroth's authority was reasonable. Superior's argument also ignores that it asked Specialty to start the 100-piece trial production run with knowledge that testing had not been completed. And while Superior may not have been obligated to supply the six component parts for the valve, it should have informed Specialty of its decision not to do so.

By June 1999, over a year had gone by since the contracts had been signed. Yet Specialty had not begun full-time production on any item. The record also indicates that, despite numerous attempts, Brisbin received little to no feedback on the status of these projects for at least a month and a half. When he finally received feedback during the August 2 conference call, he was told for the first time that Superior had either never given certain approvals, or had lost them and that it would require additional testing.[132] From Specialty's perspective, Superior reversed its position on the FAI approvals after two months of silence and without any explanation as to why. (Brisbin's repeated requests for the test results demonstrating noncompliance and the proper quality control protocols also went unanswered.) In this context, reasonable grounds existed for Specialty to feel insecure about Superior's commitment to the projects.

The record also supports the Magistrate Judge's finding that Specialty's requests for adequate assurance of Superior's performance were reasonable. Admittedly, the tone of Brisbin's August 5 fax was strident and Specialty had no right under the contract to recover the $112,868 Brisbin demanded as one means of assuring Superior's performance.[133] But we analyze a request for adequate assurance in a practical way, and such a request need not be tied to a contractual right. See U.C.C. § 2-609, comments 3 and 4. In light of Superior's dilatory behavior and its reversal of position, Specialty had good cause to doubt Superior's commitment to the projects. Further, Specialty was in a vulnerable position because it could not begin recouping startup costs until Superior had given all approvals. As such, we conclude Specialty's decision to ask for assurance of Superior's performance in this manner was reasonable, notwithstanding the lack of a contractual right to demand or receive the $112,868.[134]

Further, Brisbin's August 17 fax indicates a willingness to entertain alternative forms of assurance in lieu of immediate payment of the $112,868. Even his September 1 letter demonstrates a continued interest in reaching an amicable solution. Despite these entreaties, Superior neither presented a single counterproposal nor gave any

132. [7] It appears ironic that the August 2 conference call was initiated largely in response to Brisbin's repeated pleas for a status update on the projects. Absent his plea, we wonder when (or if) Superior would have informed Specialty of any problems.

133. [8] The contract was structured so that startup costs were incorporated into the unit price of the items.

134. [9] Superior argues that Specialty was requesting payment of the $112,868 without any corresponding price concession—i.e., to be paid twice for tooling and machinery costs. Brisbin's statements in the August 5 fax—that he "certainly" expected payment to be accompanied by an agreement detailing why "the payment is being made" and what his "obligations are for this payment"—indicate otherwise.

indication that it was willing and able to perform its obligations under the contract in good faith. Instead, Superior decided to cease all communications and referred the matter to its legal department.

[Discussion of the remaining issues, including damages, is omitted. The Third Circuit reversed the trial court on its damages award and remanded the case for further findings relating to damages.]

NOTES AND QUESTIONS

Does a demand for assurances rewrite the contract? Professor Larry T. Garvin[135] argues that a demand for assurances under § 2-609 may upset the allocation of risk in the contract. He says:

> Adequate assurance is a first cousin to contract modification. If the party demanding assurances actually gets them, it has in essence secured a change in the express terms. Even the promisor's unsupported promise that it will in fact perform goes beyond the bargain, in that the parties could have, but did not, arrange for periodic assurance. Any greater assurance—paying in advance or granting a security interest, or giving progress payments—gives the promisee more than it had when the contract was made. In essence, then, the promisee uses the mechanism of adequate assurance to secure a new contract, one that it had not bargained for and that, almost by definition, it could not get voluntarily from the promisor.

Does the decision in *Brisbin v. Superior Valve Co.* support Professor Garvin's observation? If so, is § 2-609 an unacceptable infringement on freedom of contract? Or is it a sensible recognition of the practicalities of performing under a long-term contract?

4. Uncertainty about Performance—At Common Law

Suppose a case does not involve a transaction in goods, and so Article 2 is inapplicable. Can a party who has "reasonable grounds for insecurity" suspend performance and demand assurances? The traditional common law position does not give a party any right to do so until the other party has done enough to constitute an anticipatory breach. Consider the following case.

MCNEAL v. LEBEL

New Hampshire Supreme Court
157 N.H. 458, 953 A.2d 396 (2008)

Hicks, J.

The plaintiffs, Jonathan and Paula McNeal, appeal an order of the Superior Court (McHugh, J.) in their action against the defendants, Pullman Modular Industries,

---

135. Larry T. Garvin, *Adequate Assurance of Performance: Of Risk, Duress, and Cognition*, 69 U. Colo. L. Rev. 71, 130 (1998).

Inc. (Pullman), and Robert M. Lebel d/b/a RML General Contractor (Lebel), arising out of the allegedly improper manufacture and/or construction of a modular home. We affirm in part, reverse in part, and remand.

The trial court found or the record supports the following facts. In April 2004, the plaintiffs contracted with Lebel for the construction of a modular home. The eventual contract price was $359,042. The plaintiffs and Lebel decided to purchase the home from Pullman. The home was to be constructed near the plaintiffs' existing home, allowing them to move into the new home and raze the old one upon completion.

Pullman manufactured the home and delivered it to the plaintiffs' property in August 2004. Mr. McNeal and Lebel noticed several problems, most prominently that the plaintiffs had expected different kitchen cabinets, the beam and joists for the attic did not allow for installation of a flat floor, and Pullman did not deliver any of the three sets of stairs it was to supply. Pullman eventually delivered, or built on-site, the stairs that it was responsible for supplying and Lebel built two sets of basement stairs as he had contracted to do. Once built, some of the sets of stairs failed to satisfy the applicable building code.

The terms of the plaintiffs' construction financing required the loan to be paid by September 30, 2004, but the home was not ready for occupancy by that date. In fact, by October 1, each of the parties had become, in the trial court's words, "somewhat disappointed and distrustful of one another." Lebel informed the plaintiffs that he would not continue construction unless he was assured payment for work done after October 1. He requested that funds be placed in escrow, but the plaintiffs were not willing to do so.

On October 4, 2004, the plaintiffs' attorney sent a letter to Lebel requesting that he prioritize his work to the exterior of the home. Lebel interpreted this letter to amount to his termination, and, as of October 7, 2004, stopped work on the home. The plaintiffs did not obtain a certificate of occupancy for the new home until July 2005.

The plaintiffs sued Lebel for breach of contract, and both defendants for negligence and violation of RSA 205-B:2 (2000) and RSA chapter 358-A (1995 & Supp. 2007). Lebel counterclaimed for amounts due under the contract and for unpaid work performed.

With respect to the common law theories, the court concluded that "none of the parties [is] without fault" and awarded damages as follows:

> [T]he Court awards the plaintiffs a verdict of $9,250.00 against defendant Lebel on their claims of breach of contract and negligence. The Court awards the plaintiffs a verdict of $9,250.00 against Pullman on their claim of negligence. The Court awards Lebel a verdict of $16,500.00 on his counterclaim against the plaintiffs as it finds that they breached their contract with him by not paying him for all the work that he did and by not allowing him to complete his work. Thus the plaintiffs owe Lebel $7,250.00 at present and Pullman owes the plaintiffs $9,250.00 at present.

On reconsideration, the court ruled that the plaintiffs were entitled to credit for $1,978.36 they paid Lebel for a change order, and reduced the damage award to Lebel by that amount. The trial court found that the evidence did not support the claimed statutory violations.

On appeal, the plaintiffs argue that the trial court erred in: (1) ruling that they breached the contract; (2) making certain factual findings; (3) determining damages; (4) ruling that the home contained no "substantial defects" as that phrase is used in RSA 205-B:2; and (5) ruling that neither defendant committed any unfair or deceptive trade practices as contemplated by RSA 358-A:2 (1995)....

The plaintiffs first challenge the trial court's determinations of contractual liability, asserting that Lebel materially breached and they committed no breach. They contend that Lebel breached the contract by leaving the job prior to completing his work after insisting upon conditions not contemplated in the contract; specifically, the placement of funds in escrow and assurance of end financing. They further contend that these were material breaches, relieving them of further contractual obligations.

The trial court found that on September 30, 2004, the plaintiffs' construction lender informed Lebel that it "would not be [disbursing] any more monies for the Plaintiff[s'] project because they were [two] months behind in [their] interest payments." The court also ruled that "Lebel performed his work in accordance with the contract until funding was withdrawn by the finance company" and that the plaintiffs' "unwillingness to escrow sufficient funds to enable Lebel to complete the project was unreasonable."

We read the court's order as implicitly ruling that the cessation of disbursements under the construction loan was an apparent anticipatory breach or repudiation of the plaintiffs' contractual obligations, entitling Lebel to seek assurance of payment before continuing his performance. "An anticipatory breach of contract occurs when a promising party repudiates his obligations either through words or by voluntarily disabling himself from performing them before the time for performance." *Syncom Indus. v. Wood*, 155 N.H. 73, 83–84, 920 A.2d 1178 (2007). Interestingly, as we noted in *Syncom*, the action constituting anticipatory breach in both of our leading cases on the subject, *LeTarte v. West Side Development Group, LLC*, 151 N.H. 291, 855 A.2d 505 (2004), and *Hoyt v. Horst*, 105 N.H. 380, 201 A.2d 118 (1964), was the failure to make payments under the contract. *Id.* at 84.

Our cases note that "[i]n instances of anticipatory breach, the non-breaching party has the option to treat the repudiation as an immediate breach and maintain an action at once for the damages." *LeTarte*, 151 N.H. at 294. As other courts have recognized, however, where the actions of the apparently repudiating party are equivocal or uncertain, this option presents the non-breaching party with a dilemma. *See Norcon Power v. Niagara Mohawk Power*, 92 N.Y.2d 458, 682 N.Y.S.2d 664, 705 N.E.2d 656, 659 (N.Y. 1998).

If the promisee regards the apparent repudiation as an anticipatory repudiation, terminates his or her own performance, and sues for breach, the promisee is placed in jeopardy of being found to have breached if the court determines that the apparent repudiation was not sufficiently clear and unequivocal to constitute an anticipatory repudiation justifying nonperformance. If, on the other hand, the promisee continues to perform after perceiving an apparent repudiation, and it is subsequently determined that an anticipatory repudiation took place, the promisee may be denied recovery for post-repudiation expenditures because of his or her failure to avoid those expenses as part of a reasonable effort to mitigate damages after the repudiation. *Id.*

In the case of contracts for the sale of goods, Article 2 of the Uniform Commercial Code (UCC) provides a means for dealing with this dilemma by providing a right to demand adequate assurance of due performance "[w]hen reasonable grounds for insecurity arise" and declaring a failure to provide such assurance within a reasonable time to be a repudiation of the contract. *See* RSA 382-A:2-609(1) (1994). This provision of the UCC "has been considered so effective in bridging the doctrinal, exceptional, and operational gap related to the doctrine of anticipatory breach that some States have imported the complementary regimen of demand for adequate assurance to common law categories of contract law, using UCC 2-609 as the synapse." *Norcon Power*, 705 N.E.2d at 660; *see also* Restatement (Second) of Contracts § 251 (1981).

Although a right to demand adequate assurance under general contract law has not previously been recognized in our case law, we conclude that the trial court correctly applied the doctrine here. The comment to § 251 of the Restatement (Second) of Contracts notes that that section is based upon a principle "closely related to the duty of good faith and fair dealing in the performance of the contract," Restatement (Second) of Contracts § 251, Comment a at 277, a duty that has long been an integral component of our common law of contracts; *see Centronics Corp. v. Genicom Corp.*, 132 N.H. 133, 139, 562 A.2d 187 (1989).

Because the record reveals sufficient grounds for Lebel to seek adequate assurance of future performance, which the plaintiffs did not supply, neither Lebel's request for the escrow of funds, nor his cessation of work pending such assurance, was a material breach relieving the plaintiffs of further obligation under the contract. *Cf. Kunian v. Development Corporation of America*, 165 Conn. 300, 334 A.2d 427, 433 (Conn. 1973) (where buyer under installment contract for piecemeal delivery of plumbing and heating material fell behind in payment, seller "had 'reasonable grounds for insecurity' and justifiably informed the [buyer] that it would deliver the balance of the material only if payment of the entire contract was guaranteed by the [buyer's] depositing sufficient cash in escrow to pay for the delivered materials"). We accordingly reject the plaintiffs' argument and uphold the trial court's rulings on this issue.

The plaintiffs also challenge a number of the trial court's factual findings, specifically contending that the court erred in finding: (1) that there was no real pressure or firm deadline for the plaintiffs to move into the new house; (2) that the plaintiffs' financing delays created unreasonable deadlines for completing construction; (3) that the plaintiffs' complaint was not with the quality of Lebel's work; and (4) that the plaintiffs deliberately waited to get their certificate of occupancy. We examine each challenged finding in turn.

The trial court stated: "Although the plaintiffs were anxious to get their new home constructed and move in, they were under no time constraints to do so because they could always continue to live in their existing house until the new house was ready." The court then observed that "[i]n hindsight it appears that it was the lack of any real pressure in terms of the plaintiffs not having a firm deadline to move into their new house that allowed the dispute between the parties to go unresolved for far longer than it reasonably should have."

The plaintiffs take issue with this language, arguing that they had a firm deadline of September 30, 2004, to pay off their construction loan. The trial court did not find to the contrary: the court explicitly noted in its order that "[t]he fact that the construction financing would run out on September 30, 2004 meant that there was some pressure on Lebel to have all of his work done by that date." We conclude that the court's background discussion regarding the plaintiffs' ability to remain in their old house indefinitely was not necessary to its legal rulings.

The plaintiffs next challenge the trial court's statement that "[t]he plaintiffs' delay in getting construction financing and ultimately converting that financing to a conventional mortgage created unreasonable deadlines for the completion of the construction that could not be met." They argue that, to the contrary, their construction financing was in place "as of June 1, in plenty of time to manufacture and set the house" and that it was mistakes by Pullman and Lebel that delayed conversion to a conventional mortgage.

The court's statement is not clearly erroneous nor does it appear to have affected the court's legal rulings to the plaintiffs' detriment. The court stated that "*[l]argely* because of the difficulty in obtaining construction financing, there was a delay in getting the plaintiffs' home built" (emphasis added), noting that "even though the contract that Lebel had with the plaintiffs was agreed upon in mid-April, production did not begin on the plaintiffs' house until mid-July." The plaintiffs do not dispute that their construction financing was not available until June 1, a month and a half after their mid-April agreement with Lebel. They assert that Lebel still delayed placing the order with Pullman until July 6, 2004, but we note that the court did not find Lebel blameless with respect to delays on the project. The court's order merely acknowledges that for various reasons, attributable in part to each of the parties, Lebel's time frame for completing the project shrank from five months (May through September) to slightly under two months (early August through September). We find no error.

The plaintiffs also contend that the trial court erred in finding that "[t]heir complaint was never with the quality of [Lebel's] work, just the fact that the construction had not been completed." They assert that the exhibits reveal repeated complaints to Lebel about the quality of his work. They also note that elsewhere in its order, the trial court stated that the plaintiffs "were dissatisfied with his failure to complete the project and with some of his work."

We conclude that the discrepancy on this issue is of no consequence. The challenged statement was made in the context of the court noting that the plaintiffs' end financing came through only a week after Lebel left the property. The court opined that it "ha[d] to wonder as to why the plaintiffs did not invite [Lebel] back to complete the job" when they now had the money to do so and had no complaint with the quality of Lebel's work. The reason the plaintiffs did not invite Lebel back, however, is immaterial.

"Only a breach that is sufficiently material and important to justify ending the whole transaction is a total breach that discharges the injured party's duties." *Fitz v. Coutinho*, 136 N.H. 721, 725, 622 A.2d 1220 (1993). Thus, the plaintiffs' subjective satisfaction, or lack thereof, with Lebel's work is legally irrelevant so long as any flaws in Lebel's performance did not amount to a material breach; absent material breach by Lebel, the plaintiffs were contractually obligated to allow him to finish the job.

The trial court found that Lebel performed in accordance with the contract until the construction lender stopped disbursing funds. This finding precludes a ruling that the flaws in Lebel's workmanship, if any, were material breaches of the contract. *Cf. id.* at 724 ("The trial court is in the best position to evaluate the evidence, and we will not reverse a finding on whether a party performed in a substandard manner, unless the finding lacks support in the record."). Accordingly, any finding regarding the plaintiffs' subjective satisfaction with Lebel's work is legally irrelevant, and we find no reversible error.

Finally, the plaintiffs challenge the trial court's finding that their "[w]aiting to obtain a Certificate of Occupancy until July of 2005 appears at least partially to have been calculated" and that they "elected not to get the stairs corrected, which was an item necessary for occupancy, until the following July." The trial court drew an inference from the facts, apparently not challenged, that when the plaintiffs obtained their permanent financing in October, they ordered new kitchen cabinets, an item not necessary for obtaining a certificate of occupancy, yet did not have the stairs repaired until July. We cannot say this inference was impermissible.

The plaintiffs also contend that the trial court erred in its calculation of damages....

[The appellate court found that the trial court had erred in some of its calculations.] Affirmed in part; reversed in part; and remanded.

NOTES AND QUESTIONS

1. *The common law view:* In *Louis Keppelon v. W.M. Ritter Flooring Corp.*,[136] a subcontractor refused to begin work. The general contractor sued, and the subcontractor asserted as a defense that the general's credit had become impaired and it had failed to meet other independent obligations. The trial court granted the general's motion to strike the claimed defense, and the appellate court affirmed. It said:

---

136. 97 N.J.L. 200, 205, 116 Atl. 491 (1922).

It has been held that mere doubts of the solvency of a party to a contract, or mere belief that he will be unable to perform when the time for his performance comes, will not excuse performance by the other party.... If contracts could be repudiated upon the mere allegation that the credit of the other party had become impaired, there would indeed be much consternation in the business world, for contracts are made in view of the fact that credit fluctuates, and it is common knowledge that contracts are frequently fully performed by those whose credit has become impaired.

It has also been held that the mere failure of a party to a contract to perform an independent contract will not excuse performance by the other party.... To adopt any other rule would result in the admission of so much extraneous matter as to make trials a hopeless procedure. It would involve in the trial of a single action evidence concerning every other contract between the same parties, to determine whether there was performance, or perchance cancellation, or rescission, or satisfaction, or a counterclaim, in order to determine whether there was, as a matter of fact, a breach of other obligations of the plaintiff.

Does the New Hampshire court in the *McNeal* case deal with these objections to the idea of § 2-609 of the UCC?

2. The Restatement (Second)'s attempt to expand the law: As the *McNeal* decision reports, the Restatement (Second) of Contracts § 251 provides:

(1) Where reasonable grounds arise to believe that the obligor will commit a breach by non-performance that would of itself give the obligee a claim for damages for total breach ... the obligee may demand adequate assurance of due performance and may, if reasonable, suspend any performance for which he has not already received the agreed exchange until he receives such assurance.

(2) The obligee may treat as a repudiation the obligor's failure to provide within a reasonable time such assurance of due performance as is adequate in the circumstances of the particular case.

The language of the Restatement (Second) § 251(1) differs from that of UCC § 2-609. Might anything turn on this difference?[137]

Will the courts take the Restatement's invitation to expand UCC § 2-609 to other-than-Code cases? In *C.L. Maddox, Inc. v. Coalfield Services, Inc.*,[138] the court said:

The principle of § 2-609 is generalized to all contracts in § 251 of the Restatement (Second) of Contracts (1981).... The Restatement, of course, is not law, and we cannot find any Illinois cases discussing § 251. But the principle strikes us as a sound one, and we have no reason to doubt that it would be so regarded by the courts of Illinois.

---

137. *See* Note, *A Right to Adequate Assurance of Performance in All Transactions: UCC § 2-609 Beyond Sales of Goods*, 48 S. Cal. L. Rev. 1358 (1975).

138. 51 F.3d 76, 80–81 (7th Cir. 1995).

The New York Court of Appeals was more cautious. In *Norcon Power Partners, L.P. v. Niagara Mohawk Power Corp.*,[139] it said that it would only decide that § 251 should apply "to the type of long-term commercial contract between corporate entities entered into by Norcon and Niagara Mohawk here, which is complex and not reasonably susceptible of all security features being anticipated, bargained for, and incorporated in the original contract." A lower New York court applied § 251 to a complex real estate contract in *David Peng v. Willets Point Asphalt Corp.*[140] It cited cases adopting the rule in real estate transactions decided in Connecticut, Maine, New Jersey, and Pennsylvania.

   3. *Contractual drafting to expand or make clear the rights granted by UCC § 2-609 and Restatement § 251:* A large manufacturing corporation uses the following clause on its purchase order:

> Buyer shall have the right to cancel and terminate this contract forthwith upon the happening of any one or more of the following events: (1) Seller's insolvency; (2) filing of a voluntary or involuntary petition in bankruptcy by or against the Seller; (3) the execution by the Seller of an assignment for the benefit of creditors; (4) appointment of a receiver or trustee for the Seller by any court of competent jurisdiction, or (5) if at any time, in the judgment of the Buyer, the Seller's financial condition shall be such as to endanger its performance hereunder. The acceptance of goods or performances after the occurrences of any of the above events shall not waive the right of the Buyer to cancel and terminate this contract, nor shall cancellation hereunder waive the Buyer's right to any damages to which the Buyer is otherwise entitled.

To what extent does the buyer gain greater rights under this clause than under UCC § 2-609? Are there limits to the extent to which one can use a contract term to alter the result reached by § 2-609?[141] What if, in a situation in which the preceding clause is contained in the agreement, the buyer makes an honest, but unreasonable, judgment about seller's financial condition?[142]

D. SELF-HELP IN THE FACE OF DEFAULT

   Often an aggrieved party facing a breach of contract will want to take some form of self-help rather than sue for breach of contract. If she can protect her interests without going to court, she is likely to come out better off. UCC § 2-702(1), for example, allows a seller who discovers that the buyer is insolvent to refuse to deliver

---

139. 92 N.Y.2d 458, 705 N.E.2d 656 (1998).

140. 27 Misc. 3d 1210A, 2010 N.Y. Misc. LEXIS 774 (S. Ct. Queens Co., Mar. 23, 2010).

141. *See* UCC §§ 1-103(b), 1-309.

142. *See generally* Harold Havighurst, *Clauses in Sales Contracts Protecting the Seller Against Impairment of the Buyer's Credit*, 20 Minn. L. Rev. 367 (1936). Although written long before the UCC was drafted or enacted, this article is still relevant if read in light of the changes made by the Code.

the goods "except for cash including payment for all goods theretofore delivered under the contract...." The *Wall Street Journal*[143] reported that a software developer had included a "drop-dead" function in a program. When the buyer refused to pay $40,000 that was due, the seller activated the function and blocked the buyer's access to vital data. The newspaper reported that a federal district judge in Tulsa, Oklahoma, ruled that this action was "abhorrent" and ordered that it not be used again. The article also discussed "time-bomb" functions in computer programs, which block use of the program unless they are deactivated. Arguably, a seller of computer software could include such functions in its programs if it provided for these rights in the contract, but the American Law Institute has taken a position against this practice in many instances and in any event disapproves of the use of disablement without a court order.[144]

What about buyers' rights to self-help? We will look at a buyer's right to deduct damages from what she or he owes a seller, checks "in full satisfaction of all claims," and a buyer's right to use the goods to avoid loss.

1. Deducting Damages from What Is Due

Section 2-717 gives a buyer a very limited right to deduct damages from what it owes a seller. First, the buyer can only deduct "damages resulting from any breach." This means that the buyer must determine the damages accurately. Second, the buyer may deduct damages only from "any part of the price still due under the same contract." Suppose the buyer has two contracts with the seller. The buyer has paid the price for goods that the buyer later discovers are defective. Nonetheless, the buyer may not deduct its damages under the first contract from what it owes on the second.[145] Third, the buyer must give the seller notice that it is deducting its damages from any part of the price still due.[146] You should see how § 2-609 can work with § 2-717 when buyer and seller have two or more contracts. The buyer cannot deduct damages for breach of contract number one from what is due on contract number two. However, the default on contract number one can give the buyer reasonable grounds for insecurity about whether it will receive the performance called for by contract number two. As the Official Comment to § 2-609 says: "[A] ground for insecurity need not arise from or be directly related to the contract in question."

---

143. May 8, 1989, at B1.

144. American Law Institute, Principles of the Law of Software Contracts § 4.03 (2010) (disapproving of "automated disablement" provisions in contracts with consumers or imposed by standard form in some instances and in any event calling for a court order before use of automated disablement against any type of customer). ALI uses "Principles" projects in areas of law that are less settled and more controversial than areas covered by Restatements.

145. There are a number of cases raising the two-contracts issue under § 2-717. We can wonder whether the statute is based on assumptions that are contrary to the practices of many or most businesspeople.

146. *See* William J. Geller, *The Problem of Withholding in Response to Breach: A Proposal to Minimize Risk in Continuing Contracts*, 62 FORDHAM L. REV. 163 (1993).

2. Checks in Full Satisfaction of All Claims

When buyer and seller dispute the quality of goods supplied or the amounts due, often buyer will send seller a check for an amount that the buyer asserts is all that is due. The check is restrictively endorsed and states that cashing it will constitute a full settlement of all claims. The common law rule was that a creditor could not cash the check and disown the condition upon which it was tendered.[147] However, UCC § 1-308 may change the common law rule and allow a creditor to cash the check if the creditor explicitly reserves her rights to do so. The courts are divided on this issue. For example, in *Flambeau Products Corp. v. Honeywell Information Systems, Inc.*,[148] where the Supreme Court of Wisconsin split four-to-three on the proper interpretation of UCC § 1-207 (now § 1-308, as revised in 2001), the majority found that a creditor cannot cash the check without accepting the debtor's offer of an accord and satisfaction. However, there must be consideration for the settlement of the claim. In *Kelly v. Kowalsky*,[149] the court held that merely retaining the checks did not settle the claim when the debtors failed to ask that the checks be returned.[150]

3. Using the Goods to Avoid Loss after Revocation of Acceptance

JOHANNSEN v. MINNESOTA VALLEY FORD TRACTOR CO., INC.

Minnesota Supreme Court
304 N.W.2d 654 (1981)

PETERSON, J.

The defendants, Ford Motor Co. and Minnesota Valley Ford (dealer), appeal from the judgment entered in favor of the plaintiff, Harvey Johannsen, the buyer of a defective tractor manufactured by Ford and sold to him by the dealer. After a trial in which the jury found that Johannsen had effectively revoked his acceptance of a Ford Model 9700 tractor (9700), the district court entered judgment for the plaintiff in the amount of the purchase price of the tractor less an offset for use and depreciation. Defendants appeal from the order denying post-trial motions for judgment notwithstanding the verdict or a new trial and also appeal from the judgment. We affirm.

… On July 13, 1977, plaintiff, together with his wife, went to the premises of the dealer to pick up his 1974 Ford Model 9600 tractor (9600), which had been taken to the dealer for repairs. Johannsen had experienced a number of problems with the

---

147. *See* Restatement (Second) of Contracts § 281.
148. 116 Wis. 2d 95, 341 N.W.2d 655 (1984).
149. 186 Conn. 618, 442 A.2d 1355 (1982).
150. *See* Albert J. Rosenthal, *Discord and Dissatisfaction: Section 1-207 of the Uniform Commercial Code*, 78 COLUM. L. REV. 48 (1978).

fourth gear and hydraulic system of his 9600. The tractor had jumped out of fourth gear on a number of occasions while Johannsen was plowing. Johannsen expressed his concern to Brian Gaard, one of the dealer's employees, that the 9600 would again jump out of gear.

Gaard told Johannsen that the transmission of the new 1977 Ford Model 9700 had been redesigned to avoid the transmission defects of the 9600 and that he could solve his tractor transmission problems by purchasing a new 9700 for $26,000. Gaard did not tell Johannsen that Ford had sent a letter to its tractor dealers in May of that year detailing transmission defects in the 9700. Dealers were informed that some 9700s jumped out of fourth and/or eighth gear. They were instructed to check all 9700s in stock for the defect and to sell defective tractors only if they would lose a sale. Johannsen purchased a 9700 from the dealer and traded in his 9600.

The dealer delivered the tractor to Johannsen's farm in late July. The tractor jumped out of fourth gear upon its first use, and at about the same time the frost plugs blew out of the engine, causing a loss of all the coolant. The dealer sent a repairman to plaintiff's farm on that day who told Johannsen to see the dealer about the transmission defect. On August 3, 1977, the tractor developed a fuel restriction problem and a hydraulic leak, which made it difficult to lower the implements into the soil. The dealer informed Johannsen that it could not fix the hydraulic defect until replacement parts became available in April 1978. Johannsen told every serviceman who called at his farm that he wanted to return the tractor.

On September 19, 1977, Johannsen, by his attorney, formally notified the dealer in writing of his revocation of acceptance due to transmission, hydraulic, and fuel line defects, and he directed the dealer to pick up the tractor immediately.

Johannsen continued to use the tractor after the written revocation and called the dealer on September 28 because the tractor continued to exhibit the same problems. The dealer made service calls on September 28, October 2, and October 9 in response to Johannsen's complaints. Ray Chaik, an employee of the dealer, told Johannsen that he could finish his fall work and bring the tractor in for winter servicing. Johannsen used the tractor for a total of 120 hours but was able to plow or disk only 150 acres of his farm with it. Approximately 90 of those hours were put on the tractor after the revocation letter of September 19. Johannsen put the tractor in storage in late October 1977.

The defendants contend that the plaintiff did not effectively revoke his acceptance of the 9700 tractor because ... the plaintiff continued to use the tractor after revocation of acceptance....

Defendants additionally contend that plaintiff's use of the tractor after he gave written notice of revocation of acceptance constitutes a second acceptance. Although the revoking buyer's continued use of defective goods may be wrongful under some circumstances, we think that there can be no blanket rule that prohibits such a buyer from continuing to use the goods. A blanket rule prohibiting a revoking buyer from continuing to use the goods would contravene the Code's rule of reasonableness and its underlying purpose of modernizing commercial transactions. We agree with those jurisdictions that have so held....

The reasonableness of the buyer's use of a defective good after revocation is a question of fact for the jury that is to be based on the facts and circumstances of each case. Several factors that the jury may consider include the seller's instructions to the buyer after revocation of acceptance; the degree of economic and other hardship that the buyer would suffer if he discontinued using the defective good; the reasonableness of the buyer's use after revocation as a method of mitigating damages; the degree of prejudice to the seller; and whether the seller acted in bad faith.

We hold, limited to the facts and circumstances of this case, that the jury could find that plaintiff's continued use of the 9700 tractor was reasonable and did not constitute a waiver of his revocation of acceptance. The defects in the 9700 tractor were major. Employees of the dealer knew that Johannsen specifically purchased the 9700 to avoid the transmission defect in the 9600, knew of the possibility of the identical defect in the 9700, and yet they led Johannsen to believe that buying the 9700 would solve all of his tractor transmission problems. In addition, evidence in the record tends to show that Johannsen used the tractor only to perform necessary tasks.

We note that the trial court, based upon expert testimony, allowed the defendants to setoff for use and depreciation of the tractor....

Defendants contend that the trial court improperly excluded for lack of foundation a warranty that limited a buyer's remedies to repair or replacement. Defendants asserted that plaintiff had been given a copy of Ford's standard warranty, but they were unable to produce an executed copy of the warranty. Plaintiff denied that he had executed any such warranty. We conclude that the trial court did not err in the exclusion of the alleged warranty.... Affirmed.

NOTES AND QUESTIONS

1. *Material from the briefs:* Johannsen argued:

In the present case, Johannsen's use of the tractor after revocation was reasonable. The 9700 tractor was the only tractor Johannsen had which was even capable of pulling much of Johannsen's equipment. Johannsen only used the tractor to finish out the 1977 crop season. However, because of the defects, he could not use the tractor for all the purposes that he wanted and as extensively as he would have liked.... To punish Johannsen for using the tractor for the remainder of the 1977 crop year when the sellers had his $26,000 in money and machinery and would not return them; when the only tractor that was capable of pulling much of his machinery was the new tractor is unreasonable. Offset is the reasonable appropriate remedy for Johannsen's use of the tractor rather than to invalidate his revocation of acceptance.

Ford responded:

Buyer in this case did more than simply continue using the tractor. His actions and words led Seller to believe he had changed his mind about revoking ac-

ceptance. Buyer requested additional service on the tractor ... allowed Ray
Chaik to field-test the tractor ... and agreed to allow Valley Ford to repair
the tractor during the winter.... [E]ach time Ray Chaik called him about
bringing the tractor in for repairs in November through January, Buyer indicated that it was too cold then to start the tractor or that he could not get
the tractor out because of the snow. In those conversations, Buyer did not,
however, inform Chaik that he never wanted the repairs made.... Had Sellers
realized that Buyer would later change his mind and file suit, they could have
made the necessary repairs immediately to avoid litigation, or they could
have removed the tractor before Buyer made further use of it. The Sellers,
not Buyer, would be punished for their good faith efforts to accommodate
a customer if Buyer is allowed to revoke his acceptance of the tractor. A buyer
should not escape the consequences of his continued use of goods following
a revocation of acceptance by arguing, after the fact, that this use constituted
mitigation of damages. Unless a buyer makes it clear to a seller at the time
of his continued use that this use is only for the purpose of mitigating damages
or is only because he has absolutely no other alternative, the seller is placed
in the awkward position of not knowing whether the buyer intends to revoke
acceptance or intends to honor his contract.

Compare the court's argument in the *Eastern Air Lines* case, *supra.*

2. *Another example of continued use:* In *Mitchell v. Backus Cadillac-Pontiac, Inc.,*[151]
the buyer purchased a two-year-old Cadillac Eldorado from a dealer. One of the
dealer's employees represented that the car had never been in an accident. Buyer met
the original owner of the car three weeks later and discovered that the car had been
in an accident. Moreover, the buyer found that the car had many mechanical problems,
and the dealer tried to fix them with little success. The buyer had a third party install
a sunroof. The buyer claimed that he had revoked his acceptance under §2-608 of
the UCC. The appellate court said that the buyer had continued to drive the car and
had a sunroof installed. These were acts inconsistent with ownership by the seller.
The court said that the buyer had reaccepted the goods after his purported revocation
of acceptance. How does this decision differ from that in the *Johannsen* case?

3. *Sections 2-608 and 2-508:* Ford argued that §2-608(3) of the UCC says that a
"buyer who so revokes has the same rights and duties with regard to the goods involved
as if he had rejected them." It continued by asserting that one of the duties imposed
upon *revoking* buyers by this statute is the duty to allow a seller to cure under §2-
508(2), which grants sellers this right in certain cases when a buyer *rejects* a nonconforming tender. The Supreme Court of Minnesota rejected this argument. It said
that "any right to cure should be limited to cases in which the defects are minor, and
we hold that the seller has no right to cure defects that substantially impair the good's
value." Is §2-508(2) by its terms limited to defects that do not substantially impair
the value of the goods?

151. 274 Ga. App. 330, 618 S.E.2d 87 (2005).

E. A CRITICAL REVIEW OF THE ISSUES

Arthur I. Rosett, *Contract Performance: Promises, Conditions, and the Obligation to Communicate*

22 UCLA L. Rev. 1083 (1975)[152]

Every morning the businessmen of America learn to their chagrin that their suppliers will not be delivering what they want when they want it. The goods will not arrive on time, they will be short count, and the only ones in stock are avocado green. If that were not bad enough, the same businessmen discover daily that their customers will not take and pay for what the businessmen think they ordered. Unfortunately, despite several centuries of effort by legal scholars and jurists, the businessman who has just learned that his order will be late or who did not receive exactly what he expected will not be given much useful advice by the common law as to what he should do next. Traditional contract law provides no comprehensive set of principles to supply clear answers to the central questions in most contract disputes: has there been performance; has there been a breach; has there been a discharge of obligation?

There are at least three reasons why the carefully tooled doctrines of Lord Mansfield, Williston, Corbin, and the notables of the American Law Institute have failed to help the very individuals whose experiences are the raw material for those doctrines. First, in formulating contract law, the lawmaker must fashion objective rules to govern what is essentially subjective — the expectations of the parties when they reached agreement. These expectations are rarely thought through, and inherent limitations on the process of drafting agreements make it certain that they will be incompletely and imperfectly expressed. Any effort to make rules to encompass the vagaries of agreement is inevitably unsuccessful. Unfortunately, too, the effort produces a varied and confusing vocabulary. A contract term may be a promise, a dependent or independent covenant, or a promissory condition; if it is a condition, it may be subsequent or precedent. A breach may be material or immaterial, or performance may be nonexistent, partial, or substantial. Consideration — whose adequacy the law never questions — may nonetheless fail partially or totally. Contracts may be unilateral or bilateral, express or implied in law or fact. It is no wonder that the businessman, faced with this formidable array of terms, does not keep treatises or the Restatement at his elbow, but instead considers contract law an incomprehensible lawyers' game. The confusion of overlapping sets of vocabulary could be dispelled if lawyers would settle on one set as the vehicle for expression and stick to it through more than one generation. This is unlikely, given the predilection of legal scholars for rejecting the sensible but somewhat imperfect work of those who have gone before. Even if a standard vocabulary did exist, the businessman's dilemma would not be solved, although at least he could discuss it intelligently.

---

152. Copyright © 1975, The Regents of the University of California. All Rights Reserved. Reprinted with permission.

A second and more important failure of traditional doctrine is that it has concentrated on helping a judge decide a breach of contract lawsuit at the expense of telling a businessman how to handle a breakdown in contract relations. Contract law is a common law system responsive to the needs of appellate courts. Even the most recent embodiment of contract doctrine—the tentative drafts of the Second Restatement—focuses on the time, probably some years after the businessman has received that first unsettling news, when the parties face one another in court.

The third shortcoming of traditional legal analysis is its tendency to treat unusual situations as prototypical and to underemphasize more usual transactions. In part this tendency may reflect the lawyer's inexperience with the business world, or it may simply be that the legal profession has been fascinated with the occasional exotic case or the professor's hypothetical. In any event, the result of this tendency is a distortion of the rules; they lavish attention on resolving far-fetched problems rather than providing simple solutions to common disputes.

The effects of these deficiencies are evident when we look at the way traditional doctrine deals with a basic contract dispute: [t]he parties have exchanged promises, committing themselves to future performance. But prior to or during performance one party finds its expectations are not being fulfilled: [t]he promised building is not completed or does not conform to plans; the goods delivered may not be quite what was expected or they are late, etc. The disappointed party will ask two questions: (1) shall I continue to perform my half of the contract or will the deal be terminated; and (2) how will I be compensated for the loss associated with my disappointment?

In answering these questions, traditional theory makes four inquiries. First, it asks whether one or both parties breached a promise; if so, the breaching party is liable to the other for damages. Second, it asks whether one or more of these breaches was material, that is, whether the breach was so serious that it justified the other side in suspending and ultimately terminating his own performance. Since most ruptures involve an interrelated set of failures on both sides, the answer to the last question is likely to require analysis of a third inquiry: the relationship between the promises the parties have exchanged. If it is concluded that the promise of performance of one was given in exchange for the performance of the other, then the failure of one performance affects the obligation to render the return performance. On the other hand, if the promises are deemed independent, any disappointment with performance does not relieve the obligation of counter-performance. The answers to the last two inquiries are likely to provide the resolution of the fourth—the determination of who committed the first material breach. That party is liable, not only for losses associated with the partial breach, but for damages measured by the value of the entire contract.

This brief description is unlikely to explain conventional contract law analysis to anyone not already familiar with it. However, it does make explicit the traditional approach, which is to sort out the conflicting claims that have arisen long after the contractual relationship has gone sour. From the standpoint of the businessman, this four-step analysis is likely to be of little use. It assumes that the crucial need is to advise judges and lawyers how to dispose of litigation. This assumption is misguided, for at the time of litigation courts are engaged in salvage operations at best, seeking to raise the hulk or to apportion blame for the sinking. At worst, courts serve a function analogous to that of the men with brooms who follow the passage of the circus parade.

This [excerpt] will suggest an expansion in the focus of contract rules to include the businessman's decisions during performance as well as the court's resolution of litigation. This widening of perspective is hardly a radical suggestion; it is implicit in the Restatement (Second) and more evident in the Uniform Commercial Code. In amplifying upon this suggestion, I must first look at the structure of contract terms and their contributions to problems of contract performance. Secondly, I will explore some of the reasons why contracts fail, emphasizing that there is an opportunity to cure most instances of defective performance, and that in virtually all cases the parties will be able to define the consequences of the failure to perform by communications between them. If this proposed expansion is accomplished, the ephemeral conceptual problems that have preoccupied legal scholars become more manageable.

I. Basic Contract Structure

In simplest terms, a contract demands that each party do what he promised. If a party fails to do what he promised, his failure is a breach; the universal consequence is that a court may require him to pay money damages sufficient to provide the non-breaching party with the financial equivalent of performance. However, not all promises are absolute; most obligations are limited by their terms. The promise is likely to be conditioned on an event, so that until the event occurs, the obligation to perform does not arise.

This simple framework can become complicated. The categories of promise and condition are not mutually exclusive. A performance event may be promised, it may be a condition to a promised performance, or it may be both. Both promises and conditions are defined in terms of the legal consequences which a breach of one or a failure of the other entails: [a] promise is that which produces damages for its breach; a condition is that which may require or may excuse or discharge further performance. The consequences of defining an event will therefore have quite different impact depending on which label is selected. Damages for breach of contract are generally conservative, and the burden on the breaching party is likely to be relatively light or at least bearable. In contrast, the result of finding a discharging condition is that one side will lose the entire benefit of the contract without any compensation whatsoever....

II. Causes of Contract Failure

In the preceding section we saw that inherent in the structure of contract is the potential for the creation of uncertainty. As a result, a party is unable accurately to predict whether his performance disappointment has terminated the contract and whether his damages will be measured on the basis of partial or total breach. Unfortunately ... conventional doctrine is of little help; in fact, it sometimes adds to the innocent party's anxiety by suggesting that he might be guilty of repudiation or failure to mitigate damages if his timing is poor. This portion of the article will discuss whether such uncertainty can be resolved by measures short of contract termination. In part this will depend on the causes of contract failure and the feasibility of communications between the parties and cure to enable the contract to continue in force.

A virtually infinite variety of contingencies may arise during contract performance to disturb the parties' expectations. It would be futile to attempt to catalog these disturbing events in detail, but in general, most performance difficulties are the product of:

(a) *Failure to perform.* One of the performing parties simply fails to act as he could have and should have acted;

(b) *External supervening event.* A party's ability to perform as promised is impaired by catastrophe, the unforeseen acts of individuals or governments, death, or the destruction of specific objects;

(c) *Market change.* A variation in the price or in supply makes the agreement much less attractive to one side than obtaining the same performance in the open market;

(d) *Agreement failure.* The process of agreement is defective because of mistake, ambiguity, incompleteness, or misunderstanding;

(e) *The bad marriage.* Some transactions degenerate into an interrelated series of escalating mutual breaches, each of which is quite minor viewed alone. The cause of the perturbation is less the troubling events themselves than the parties' responses to them. The deal is going sour, and that, rather than specific incidents, is the central problem.

Failure of performance, the situation in which the party could have performed but failed to do so without justification, is the clearest case for casting the burden of failure on the breaching party. However, the party in trouble is likely to be able to cure most failures of performance. If he cannot cure or cannot provide assurances of future performance, his material failure to perform is appropriately treated as a discharging event. The nonbreaching party is relieved from all further obligations of performance under the contract and is awarded damages measured by the total breach.

When the failure to perform, current or prospective, is the result of some *supervening event* outside the control of either party, the problem is not so easily handled by assigning fault or risk to one side. A strict application of conventional doctrine would leave the parties with all the risks they failed to avoid by expressly conditioning their promises. It would not necessarily matter that the cause of the trouble was beyond the party's control or even that performance as promised was literally impossible or illegal. One might not be able to perform, but one could almost always pay damages. However appealing this analysis may have been in an earlier, sterner age, it does not satisfy the expectations and realities of modern contract-making. Contract would not be a usable tool if the parties were required to state explicitly every assumption underlying their agreement and every conceivable contingency limiting it. When a person agrees to work for another he assumes he will be alive and well to perform; when specific goods are bought and sold it is assumed that they will remain in existence and that there will be money in circulation to pay for them. Ordinary people would think it strange, to say the least, if they were told that such assumptions must be expressed. When one of these basic assumptions of the contract has been weakened or destroyed it no longer makes sense to assign fault or impose on one side all the burdens associated with nonperformance. In an ongoing commercial relationship when such external event occurs, it is necessarily an excuse. The realistic choice is between modifying the agreement to conform to changed circumstances or relieving both sides of their obligations.

In contrast, because the possibility of *market change* is a primary and essential risk of all promise-making, when the failure of performance is traceable primarily to such change, the losses associated therewith should be left where they lie. It is likely that one party to almost any deal will feel that he sold too cheaply or bought too dearly. A judgment regarding the extent to which market change is an assumed contract risk must be made on the basis of the parties' agreement, trade usage, and community expectations. If the change is beyond assumed risk, the only practical choices are likely to be contract modification or discharge.

When there is *agreement failure*, it becomes apparent during the course of performance that the parties did not make the deal they thought they did. This failure may be the result of mistake, misunderstanding, ambiguity, erroneous information, or simply failure of the parties to think through and reach agreement on likely contingencies. Contract law is based on the premise that an agreement that results from the parties' intentional and consensual acts warrants enforcement since it is presumed to be serious, worthwhile, and socially desirable. If there has, in fact, been no agreement, this rationale for enforcement no longer applies. However, abandoning the contract altogether may work a real hardship on the parties. If the failure resulted from an honest mistake and not pettifogging, poor judgment, or fraud, some compromises may have to be made. It seems apparent that the parties are in a position to sort the problem out far superior to that of any court. Often the parties can cure their original agreement failure or can restate their deal in mutually satisfactory terms, while the best a court could hope to do is to impose some synthetic "reasonable" solution by "interpretation" of the agreement.

Bad contract marriages resemble the family disputes upon which the metaphor is based. Court efforts to untangle such situations on the basis of fault or risk are likely to prove futile or to create more problems than they solve. Again, the important point is that the parties are in a better position than a court to untangle the mess.

Conventional legal doctrine would deal with the parties in all the above-described situations as if they were strangers, isolated from one another. Too little weight is given the likelihood that most failures of performance are curable when, or soon after they occur. Breaches and failures become material in part because they are treated that way rather than promptly adjusted. When a party is faced with present or threatened failure of performance, the Restatement (Second) analyzes the issue in terms of whether this behavior is a breach and whether that breach is material. The party who is guilty of the first uncured material breach bears the loss. The Restatement emphasis is on characterizing the performance of the parties, not upon guiding them in determining whether to continue with the contract. Although the Restatement (Second) recognizes the possibility of communication, assurance, and cure, little emphasis is placed on whether the parties have tried to communicate to adjust the difficulties. No duty to communicate candidly is improved, nor are the parties bound by what they say if they do communicate. Not only are the parties not required to communicate, but there seems to be a real danger that candid communication advising the other side of the circumstances jeopardizing performance and requesting a modification to accommodate the changed circumstances, unless carefully phrased, will be interpreted as a repudiation—a material breach by the communicating party.

This traditional orientation is unrealistic, because most business transactions are part of an ongoing relationship between people who are or can easily be in direct communication. The first thing a contracting party in difficulty should do is contact the other party, explain the situation, and give assurances that the defect will be cured, or if that is not possible, seek to modify the agreement so that it can be performed, or else terminate it altogether....

... The point is that since the parties are in a better position than courts to determine what to do, they would best be served by rules that encourage them to solve the problem themselves. If they are unable to do so, and litigation results, the Court's resolution of the difficult question of excuse would be easier if it knew whether the injured party was willing to accept a modified or curing performance. Furthermore, by leaving primarily to the parties the characterization of the incident as one that terminates the agreement or merely suspends performance, any ultimate litigation will be limited to questions relating to damages or other forms of relief appropriate in cases of frustrated contracts.

Another possibility is that the communications following the insecurity-producing event are marked by disagreement, indefiniteness, equivocation, or avoidance. The breaching party may express his intention to perform and the hope that he will be able to, but at the same time he may express doubt whether he will be able to perform. Or, as in the classic case of *Norrington v. Wright*,[153] the lawyers may get into the act, supplanting the parties' attempts to communicate with evasive pettifogging. In *Norrington*, a British merchant sold scrap rails to a Philadelphia buyer through a local broker. The goods were to be delivered in monthly installments of a specified quantity, but the seller's early shipments were late and fell short. At the same time the market price declined sharply. The insecure buyer wanted out of the contract now made unattractive both by the market change and the imperfect installments. The communications that ensued between the lawyers for buyer and seller are models of equivocation, the flavor of which is conveyed by the following:

---

153. [23] 115 U.S. 188 (1885).

You ask us to determine whether we will or will not object to receive further shipments because of past defaults. We tell you we will if we are entitled to do so, and will not if we are not entitled to do so. We do not think you have the right to compel us to decide a disputed question of law to relieve you from the risk of deciding it yourself. You know quite well as we do what is the rule and its uncertainty of application.[154]

When, as here, both sides are intentionally evasive, it is hard to determine after the fact which side is responsible for the first uncured material breach or for making the other side insecure. If the law encouraged candid communications between parties, a court would be aided in evaluating the parties' competing claims. For example, the buyer in *Norrington* might simply have said that the falling market and the seller's failure to deliver timely and complete installments suggested to him that the seller was speculating on the falling market at the buyer's expense, and therefore the buyer wished to terminate the contract. Under the Restatement (Second), however, these statements by the buyer might be interpreted not as an attempt to resolve problems but as a repudiation and therefore as a material breach. This approach, however, discourages candid dispute settlement. The buyer should not be penalized without first examining the seller's response. The seller might have recognized the validity of the buyer's point and agreed to compensate him for market losses associated with the failure to deliver the full installments on time. It seems likely that the seller would try to keep the transaction alive because he had a profitable contract. However, if the seller were unable or unwilling to provide the buyer with substantial assurances of future performance or compensation for defaults, it would be easier for a court to find that these defaults were contract-terminating events....

III. Conclusion

In summary, when trouble arises during the life of a contract as a result of a present or threatened failure of performance, an insecure party should be justified in suspending his performance long enough to communicate with the other side to seek cure of past failures and to receive assurances of future compliance with the contract. A party who communicates candidly should not be considered to have repudiated unless he unequivocally refuses to perform or to give assurances of future performance. The quality of communications between the parties should be a major factor in the court's evaluation of their competing claims. Failure of a party to seek cure or assurances promptly creates a strong inference that the party did not regard the trouble a threat to the contract relationship. In such a case, the trouble would not condition either party's further performance; that is, it would not be a potential contract-terminating event. Of course, the aggrieved party would always be able to press a claim for damages measured by a partial breach.

In suggesting that contract law should place greater emphasis on advising the businessman in the course of performance, I am aware that there may be some who would

---

154. [24] *Id.* at 192.

question whether this is a proper task for the law to undertake. Some reassuring comments can be addressed to those who see this proposal as an unwarranted extension of present law.

First, the approach suggested is not a great departure from the substance of existing law embodied in statutes and cases. However, new emphasis is placed on the availability and importance of communication and cure when trouble arises in the course of contract performance. As suggested earlier, the requirement that parties communicate is implicit in current bodies of contract doctrine and is therefore hardly an unheard-of innovation. Second, the central assumption of contract law has always been that all interests are best served if the force of law is used to sanction the arrangements people make for themselves rather than to structure their relationships by externally imposed rules. Consequently, the law allows contracting parties to set limits on remedies for breach, to liquidate damages, and to opt out of the legal system's method of dispute resolution by arbitration. The same approach would support encouraging the parties to resolve their differences themselves by reinforcing the duties of communication and cure before turning to the institution of last resort, the courts.

Chapter 6

ADJUSTING TO CHANGED CIRCUMSTANCES: RISKS ASSUMED AND IMPOSED

A. HISTORY, CONFLICTING POSITIONS, AND UNACKNOWLEDGED LEGAL CHANGE

This chapter deals with risks that one party claims were not assumed by entering into a contract with the other party. Sometimes the party who wants out can point to language in a written contract, but often the document says nothing about the risk in question. People who enter contracts do not have perfect knowledge about the present state of the world. They also often find it extremely hard to predict the future. People make mistakes. Some mistakes are just the risks of the deal. For example, Seller, a used book dealer, sells an old book to Buyer for $5, and Buyer makes no misrepresentations. The book is a rare edition, worth $500. Or Buyer thinks the value of land or corporate securities will increase after their purchase, but their value falls sharply. The risk of some mistakes, however, is not implicit in the deal, and our sense of fairness may require intervention and adjustment. While situations at the extremes may not present too much difficulty, arguments can often be made that both a risk was assumed and that it was not.

Legal culture, at times, distinguishes mistakes concerning existing facts from assumptions and predictions about the future. Typically, the law of mistake focuses on errors about facts at or before the contract was made.[1] However, things may happen in the future that make it very difficult, impracticable, or virtually impossible to per-

---

1. RESTATEMENT (SECOND) OF CONTRACTS § 152 (1981) provides: "Where a mistake of both parties at the time a contract was made as to a basic assumption on which the contract was made has a material effect on the agreed exchange of performances, the contract is voidable by the adversely affected party unless he bears the risk of the mistake under the rule stated in § 154." Section 154 says that a party bears the risk if it "is allocated to him by agreement of the parties," or if he is "aware, at the time the contract is made, that he has only limited knowledge with respect to the facts to which the mistake relates but treats his limited knowledge as sufficient." It also says that a court may allocate a risk to a party "on the ground that it is reasonable in the circumstances to do so." Under Section 157, fault in failing to know or discover facts does not bar a party from relief for mistake unless it is "a failure to act in good faith and in accordance with reasonable standards of fair dealing."

form contractual duties. Lawyers often speak of this situation as one involving "impossibility."[2] However, I may be able to perform my duties under a contract without difficulty, but events may rob my performance of any value to you. In the classic *Krell v. Henry* situation, I rent to you a place from which you plan to watch an elaborate parade. The parade later is canceled. You can still stand or sit there and watch whatever passes by, but this right is far less valuable than what you assumed you were buying. Lawyers label this as a problem of "frustration of purpose."

There is much discussion of frustration of purpose in some quarters. However, Professor John Wladis surveyed the cases and concluded: "The *Krell* case [which established the frustration doctrine and involved the rental of space overlooking the planned parade to celebrate the coronation of King Edward VII] can be deleted or reduced to the status of a footnote case. For all the trouble it has caused generations of law students, and law professors, *Krell* has had virtually no influence upon the law."[3] This conclusion may be right in terms of the number of cases where a party raises the doctrine. Nonetheless, frustration of purpose is a resource that at least a few lawyers may be able to use, even if only in unusual situations.

UCC § 2-615 excuses *sellers* whose performance "has been made impracticable by the occurrence of a contingency the non-occurrence of which was a basic assumption on which the contract was made." You should notice that a great deal is hidden in this somewhat abstract statement. However, the text of the section says nothing about *buyers* whose purposes have been frustrated. Official Comment 9 suggests that when a seller knows that a buyer's order is based on a definite and specific venture "the reason of the present section may well apply and entitles the buyer to the exemption." Professor Wladis is right that there are few successful frustration defenses. We will see that the threat of international terrorism and financial crises may give new life to the old doctrine.[4]

While these distinctions—between impossibility and frustration, for example—can be drawn, as always we must ask whether the distinctions make any difference that matters. Many modern writers see mistake, impossibility, and frustration as involving essentially similar problems, although the doctrinal tests may be stated in different terms.

---

2. RESTATEMENT (SECOND) CONTRACTS § 261 (1981) provides: "Where, after a contract is made, a party's performance is made impracticable without his fault by the occurrence of an event the non-occurrence of which was a basic assumption on which the contract was made, his duty to render that performance is discharged, unless the language or the circumstances indicate to the contrary." One important difference between the two doctrines is the treatment of fault.

3. John D. Wladis, *Common Law and Uncommon Events: The Development of the Doctrine of Impossibility of Performance in English Common Law*, 75 GEO. L.J. 1575, 1630–31 (1988).

4. For a case in which the court applied the frustration of purpose doctrine, see Chase Precast Corp. v. Paonessa Company Inc., 566 N.E.2d 603 (Mass. 1991), where a subcontractor that had contracted to supply concrete median barriers to a highway construction contractor was denied a claim for lost profits when the state, acting in response to strong community protests, eliminated the use of median barriers on the project. The court characterized the frustration doctrine as a "companion rule" to the doctrine of impossibility.

Suppose, for example, Seller contracts with Buyer to deliver a machine built according to plans and specifications. Buyer is to pay on the date specified for delivery. The contract, however, says nothing about the effect of strikes, floods, fires, and the like that delay production. Assume:

(a) Seller needs a special type of steel to build the machine. Seller has a supplier whose employees strike, and this kind of steel cannot be obtained elsewhere in time so that Seller can perform; or

(b) Seller's own employees strike; or

(c) There is a flood in Seller's plant, stopping production.

Seller fails to deliver on time. Buyer sues Seller for breach of contract. Does Seller have a defense in any, all, or none of these situations?

Suppose, instead, Seller completes the machine a month after the delivery date. Seller's delay was caused by the strike or flood we've assumed. Seller then tenders the machine to Buyer. Buyer refuses to accept it. May Seller successfully sue Buyer for breach of contract or does Buyer have a defense? (These problems, of course, all raise issues of *impracticability* or *impossibility* since the seller cannot get the machine there on time.)

Suppose, finally, Seller could deliver on time, but Buyer is prevented from using the machine because of environmental protection regulations issued after the contract was made. The issue now is whether there is an excuse because of *frustration of purpose*.

1. The Paper versus the Real Deal: Formalism, Realism, and Changing Approaches

Consider the approaches taken by the common law in the 17th and 19th centuries and by the Uniform Commercial Code today. We can ask whether the legal system has gained any ground in 300 years. Whatever the reasons offered, we can see the spirit of the next case, *Paradine v. Jane*, in some decisions interpreting the Uniform Commercial Code or applying contract doctrine to other than transactions in goods. You will find that many of the rules in this area are very uncertain. It is an area where it is hard to argue that the rules alone determine the outcome of the cases. Nonetheless, lawyers must cope with the uncertainty and changes from one position to another and then back again over time.

a. A Deal Is a Deal — Enforce the Literal Text of the Written Contract

PARADINE v. JANE

King's Bench
Mich. 23 Car. Banco Regis.[5] Hil. 22 Car. Rot. 1178, & 1179

In debt the plaintiff declares upon a lease for years rendring rent at the four usual feasts; and for rent behind for three years, ending at the Feast of the Annunciation,

---

5. 23 Car. refers to 1647, the 23rd year of the reign of King Charles I.

21 Car. brings his action; the defendant pleads, that a certain German prince, by name Prince Rupert, an alien born, enemy to the King and kingdom, had invaded the realm with an hostile army of men; and with the same force did enter upon the defendant's possession, and him expelled, and held out of possession from the 19 of July 18 Car. till the Feast of the Annunciation, 21 Car. whereby he could not take the profits; whereupon the plaintiff demurred, and the plea was resolved insufficient....

It was resolved, that the matter of the plea was insufficient; for though the whole army had been alien enemies, yet he ought to pay his rent. And this difference was taken, that where the law creates a duty or charge, and the party is disabled to perform it without any default in him, and hath no remedy over, there the law will excuse him. As in the case of waste, if a house be destroyed by tempest, or by enemies, the lessee is excused. [S]o of an escape. So in 9 E. 3. 16. a supersedeas was awarded to the justices, that they should not proceed in a cessavit upon a cesser during the war, but when the party by his own contract creates a duty or charge upon himself, he is bound to make it good, if he may, notwithstanding any accident by inevitable necessity, because he might have provided against it by his contract. And therefore if the lessee covenant to repair a house, though it be burnt by lightning, or thrown down by enemies, yet he ought to repair it. Now the rent is a duty created by the parties upon the reservation, and had there been a covenant to pay it, there had been no question but the lessee must have made it good, notwithstanding the interruption by enemies, for the law would not protect him beyond his own agreement, no more than in the case of reparations; this reservation then being a covenant in law, and whereupon an action of covenant hath been maintained (as Roll said) it is all one as if there had been an actual covenant. Another reason was added, that as the lessee is to have the advantage of casual profits, so he must run the hazard of casual losses, and not lay the whole burthen of them upon his lessor; and Dyer 56. 6. was cited for this purpose, that though the land be surrounded, or gained by the sea, or made barren by wildfire, yet the lessor shall have his whole rent: and judgment was given for the plaintiff.

NOTES AND QUESTIONS

1. *Historical context:* Some very simplified history may help make the case more understandable. Who was Prince Rupert who invaded the land with an army and prompted this case? The phrase "an alien, and an enemy of the King" is misleading. King James I had several children. One was Charles I, the king at the time of the *Paradine* case. Charles's sister, Elizabeth, married Frederick, the Elector of the Palatine (then a state in central Europe). In 1619, Prince Rupert was born to Frederick and Elizabeth in Prague. Thus, Rupert was Charles's nephew.

In 1618, a revolt in Bohemia began the Thirty Years' War. In 1619, Frederick became King of Bohemia. The Bohemians were defeated in 1620, and Frederick, Elizabeth, and Rupert fled to Holland. James I attempted to aid his son-in-law by sending an army of 12,000 men to march to the Palatine, and it was landed in Holland. However, the army disintegrated because of sickness and lack of supplies. Frederick continued to fight in the Thirty Years' War, and Rupert joined him in battle when he was 14.

Paradine v. Jane is a product of the English Civil War that overthrew Charles I and brought Oliver Cromwell and the Parliamentarians to power. Several events produced this conflict. In 1603, James I asserted the absolute power to tax in order to finance his role in international affairs. Parliament resisted, asserting that only it could tax. Charles I became king in 1625. Soon he was involved in wars with Spain and France and needed money. In 1628, Parliament responded to Charles's actions with the Petition of Right, which asserted that the King's power to tax, imprison, and quarter soldiers was limited legally. Charles responded by dismissing Parliament in 1629.

Charles I also was involved in the religious battles of the time. Actions taken in his name drove the Puritans out of the Church of England to North America. In 1638, Charles tried to impose the Church of England on Scotland and prompted a revolt. The tensions between Catholics and Protestants were involved in the Thirty Years' War on the continent and in the conflicts in England as well.

Parliament met in 1640, where it attacked the King's policies and seized several of his ministers. The King came to Parliament and tried to arrest its leaders, but failed. The Civil War began in August of 1642. The King held the territory from Oxford to the North; the Parliament held London.

At the outbreak of the Civil War in 1642, Rupert came to England to join his cousin Charles at Nottingham. Although he offended various courtiers by "his rough manner and arrogance," he commanded the King's forces to a number of victories and proved himself one of the King's few able military leaders. He was named Earl of Holderness and Duke of Cumberland in 1644. In 1645, he became Governor of Bristol, but he surrendered it to Parliamentary forces. The King was angered by the surrender and banished Rupert, but Rupert brought about a reconciliation during that same year.

During most of the Civil War, neither side could win. Troops on both sides looted the estates of the nobility, a common practice of the time to pay armies and gain needed supplies. *Paradine v. Jane* involved one of the many minor actions in the war. Rupert's forces held the land from 1642 to 1645. Finally, in 1645, Cromwell organized what, for the time, was a professional army. Cromwell's army defeated the King's forces in a number of battles and, in 1646, the King surrendered. The Parliamentary forces captured Rupert when Oxford surrendered. He was ordered to leave the country. Charles I was beheaded in 1649. Cromwell took power and ruled until his death in 1657. Charles II gained power in 1660. Rupert returned with him. He fought in the wars against the Dutch, and he was First Lord of the Admiralty from 1673 to 1679. He died in 1682.[6]

2. *Grant Gilmore on* Paradine v. Jane: Professor Gilmore comments on the significance of the case:[7]

---

6. *See* Chris Cook & John Wroughton, English Historical Facts 1603–1688 (Rowman & Littlefield 1980).

7. Grant Gilmore, The Death of Contract 44–47 (1974). Copyright © 1974 by the Ohio State University Press. Reprinted by permission.

No legal system has ever carried into practice a theory of absolute contractual liability. Our own system, during the nineteenth century, may be the only one which has ever proclaimed such a theory. The proclamation ... at least in this country, was steadfastly adhered to, mostly as a matter of ritual incantation, throughout the century. The source of the absolute liability idea in English law was always confidently stated to be the seventeenth-century case of *Paradine v. Jane*. ... Two hundred years later we find Morton, J., for the Massachusetts court, explaining the "general rule" on excuse by reason of impossibility in this fashion:

... [W]here the party by his agreement voluntarily assumes or creates a duty or charge upon himself, he shall be bound by his contract, and the nonperformance of it will not be excused by accident or inevitable necessity; for if he desired any such exception, he should have provided for it in his contract.

This language was copied, almost word for word, from one of the seventeenth-century reports of *Paradine v. Jane*—a case which, in all probability, Judge Morton had never read and which he did not cite. ...

It would take us too far afield to inquire into the reasons for the success of such a theory; we might perhaps speculate that the Puritan ethic was somehow involved. ... Let me repeat a point I have already made: the absolute liability idea was often preached but rarely practiced. ... This comment makes the ideas themselves no less significant; it is always a matter of the highest interest when courts—like people generally—say one thing while doing its opposite. ...

Professor Gilmore invites us to speculate about the appeal of an absolute liability rule. In that spirit, we can ask: would the impact of such a rule be random or would it systematically benefit one group and disadvantage another?

Professor John Wladis reviews the history of the English law of impossibility. He says that law and history "are often incorrectly taught to law students. *Paradine*, for example, is usually cited for a proposition for which the case does not stand and which the judge had no intention of establishing." Wladis points to Aleyn's report, which says: "[W]hen the party by his own contract creates a duty or charge upon himself, he is bound to make it good, *if he may*, notwithstanding any accident by inevitable necessity, because he might have provided against it by his contract." The key phrase is "if he may." And "*Paradine* was not a case in which the defendant's dispossession made payment of the rent impossible."[8] Wladis continues, noting that "[f]ar from reflecting a general rule of the common law at the time, both the result and the reasoning in *Paradine* struggled for acceptance for some 150 years." He finds the first explicit recognition of the *Paradine* reasoning as a general principle in 1858,

---

8. John Wladis, *Common Law and Uncommon Events: The Development of the Doctrine of Impossibility of Performance in English Contract Law*, 75 GEO. L.J. 1575, 1576, 1583–84 (1987).

although he finds the decision used often in lease cases. Professor John Schlegel also looked at the history of the *Paradine* case. He noted that the case was "a symbolic representation of the attitude of the 19th century."[9]

3. *"A deal is a deal — the mistake parallel."* In *Wood v. Boynton*,[10] Ms. Wood sued to recover an uncut diamond alleged to be worth $1,000[11] from Samuel B. Boynton, who operated a jewelry store in Milwaukee. She had sold the stone, which was "about the size of a canary bird's egg" and straw-colored, to Boynton for $1. The trial court directed a verdict for Boynton, and the Supreme Court affirmed. "When this sale was made the value of the thing sold was open to investigation of both parties, neither knew its intrinsic value, and, so far as the evidence in this case shows, both supposed that the price paid was adequate." The facts that follow are taken from the record on appeal.

Ms. Wood made five trips to Boynton's store: (1) In September or October of 1883, she went to get a pin mended. While in the store, she showed Boynton the stone and asked what it was. "He took it in his hand and seemed some time looking at it. I told him I had been told it was a topaz and he said it might be." Boynton offered then to buy it "as a specimen" for $1, but she refused to sell. He asked where she found it, and she told him she found it in Eagle, Wisconsin.

(2) About December 28th, "I needed money pretty badly, and thought every dollar would help, and I took it back to Mr. Boynton and told him I had brought back the topaz, and he says, 'Well, yes; what did I offer you for it?' and I says, 'One dollar;' and he stepped to the change drawer and gave me the dollar, and I went out."

(3) She went into the store to get a clock repaired. Boynton questioned her about where she had found the stone. It came out of gravel thrown up when a well had been dug in Eagle, Wisconsin. Boynton then purchased the land where the stone was found.

(4) Boynton testified that "he sent word to her by her husband, that he wished to see her. She came to the store, and he told her, the stone he had purchased from her, proved to be of a good deal more value than he paid for it, and he intended to make her a nice present, not in jewelry, but in cash, when he got around to it. She said, 'Mr. Boynton, you do not owe me anything ... you gave me more for the stone than I could get anywhere else....'" He replied that he did not propose to be a hog, supposed that he did not owe her anything according to law, but was going to make it all right with her, because the stone proved to be worth more than he paid for it. Ms. Wood

---

9. John Henry Schlegel, *Of Nuts, and Ships, and Sealing Wax, Suez, and Frustrating Things — The Doctrine of Impossibility of Performance*, 23 RUTGERS L. REV. 419, 422 n.16 (1969).

10. 64 Wis. 265, 25 N.W. 42 (1885). Mystery lovers may want to read THE HEIRLOOM MURDERS by Kathleen Ernst (2011), which takes this case as its inspiration.

11. The Inflation Calculator tells us: "What cost $1000.00 in 1885 would cost $26,606.02 in 2015. "It also tells us, as we might expect, "What cost $1.00 in 1885 would cost $26.61 in 2015." *See* http://www.westegg.com/inflation.

denied that such an offer had been made and denied that she said he did not owe her anything.

(5) After an account of the diamond recovery appeared in the newspapers, she demanded return of the stone, tendering $1.10, which Boynton refused.

The day Boynton purchased the stone, he took a file and tried to cut it but could make no impression on it. He said to his son and partner, "Charlie, this is a diamond!" His son responded, "Pshaw!" His son then took it to several dealers who set diamonds, but they thought it was a sapphire. Boynton took it to Chicago and had it tested on a diamond wheel. Afterward he showed it to an expert from New York who said it was a diamond.

Ms. Wood's lawyer's brief to the Supreme Court of Wisconsin concludes:

> Clearly there was in the minds of the defendants no such uncertainty or speculation as will justify them in claiming that they bought a diamond or anything which might turn out to be a diamond. The uncertainty in their minds was limited to a narrow range of species of inferior crystals of values ranging from fifty cents to forty dollars. Their uncertainty or speculation did not in any event include a diamond of any value, and it is just as clear that this stone was bought and sold under a material misapprehension of an existing fact going to the very substance of the sale, as it would be if they had bought it supposing it to be a diamond and it had turned out to be a topaz, and the plaintiff's right to rescind is just as clear as theirs would have been in that case.[12]

Boynton's counsel struck a very different note:

> The effort of counsel [for Ms. Wood] to get this case before a jury is appreciated. Some of the phrases evidently conned for use before that body, are deftly fired at this court, on many pages of counsel's brief. Such as "the poor woman became pressed for money, so that even a dollar came to be regarded by her as an essential addition to her funds." "She felt too poor to purchase jewelry at any price;" "a woman in desperate want of money;' etc., etc. Is Ms. Wood, by reason of these conditions, entitled to any more remedies against the defendants, than Vanderbilt would have been, if he had sold us the stone? "A woman in desperate want of money," on one side, and two full-grown men on the other, with the disparity in value and price shown by this case, without a scintilla of proof of fraud, and without any mistake recognizable in the law, are the circumstances under which, counsel claims, that the case should have been submitted to the jury. The jury room has become the only legal refuge of the Commune in this country. Its jurisdiction ought not to

---

12. Ms. Wood's lawyer is making a "zone of risk" argument. We will see the argument again. Insofar as contract is claimed to rest on a true assumption of risk, isn't it likely an accurate claim on the facts of this case?

be extended. Balancing the scales of justice with an eye to a "desperate want of money" by one party, is no better practice than a verdict based on color, sex, or religion.[13]

4. *Possibly useful rhetoric from a famous judge:* The "deal is a deal" principle is a powerful one. Judge Jerome Frank, a famous judge who was a noted legal realist, invoked it in 1951 in *Guttman v. Illinois Central RR. Co.*[14] The dispute concerned the rights of preferred stockholders in the railroad to dividends. Between 1937 and 1947, the railroad had chosen not to declare any dividends, although it had had sufficient earnings so that it would have been possible for it to do so. In 1950, the company declared dividends for both the preferred and common stockholders. Preferred stockholders receive their dividends before common stockholders can be paid a dividend. Guttman, the holder of a stock designated as "non-cumulative preferred," sued to require that the preferred stockholders be paid all of the dividends that could have been paid to them from 1937 through 1947 before the common stockholders be paid any. The trial court dismissed the complaint, and Judge Frank, writing for the Second Circuit, affirmed:

> Here we are interpreting a contract into which uncoerced men entered. Nothing in the wording of the contract would suggest to an ordinary wayfaring person the existence of a contingent or inchoate right to arrears of dividends. The notion that such a right was promised is, rather, the invention of lawyers or other experts, a notion stemming from considerations of fairness, from a policy of protecting investors in those securities. But the preferred stockholders are not—like sailors or idiots or infants—wards of the judiciary. As courts on occasions have quoted or paraphrased ancient poets, it may not be inappropriate to paraphrase a modern poet, and to say that "a contract is a contract is a contract."[15] To be sure, it is an overstatement that the courts never do more than carry out the intentions of the parties: In the interest of fairness and justice, many a judge-made legal rule does impose, on one of the parties to a contract, obligations which neither party actually contemplated and to which the language of the contract is silent. But there are limits to the extent to which a court may go in so interpolating rights and obligations

---

13. Eds. note: The Eagle Diamond became part of the collection at the J.P. Morgan Hall of Gems and Minerals at the American Museum of Natural History. In the late evening of October 29th or the early morning of the 30th of 1964, 24 famous gems were stolen from the Museum. On January 8, 1965, nine of the gems were returned as part of a plea agreement with the robbers. Nine other stones had been sold to illegal gem dealers so that the robbers could pay for lawyers and bondsmen. The NEW YORK TIMES reported "authorities had virtually abandoned hope of recovering the 15.37-carat Eagle Diamond and four smaller stones." N.Y. TIMES, Jan. 13, 1965, at 74. The Eagle Diamond was never recovered, and it probably was cut into many smaller stones.

14. 189 F.2d 927, 930 (2d Cir. 1951).

15. Eds. note: The reference is to a line from Gertrude Stein's poem *Sacred Emily*: "Rose is a rose is a rose is a rose." Note that there are four roses, not just three, and no indefinite article to begin the line.

which were never in the parties' contemplation. In this case we consider those limits clear.

5. *Rule and counter-rule:* Whatever the force of the ideas associated with *Paradine v. Jane*, it was possible to fashion a counter-rule well within the traditions of the common law. A court could find that what appeared to be an absolute unqualified promise was in fact a promise subject to an implied condition. Consider the text of a British case reaching a different result but not formally overruling *Paradine v. Jane*.

b. What Was the Real Deal? Basic but Unspoken Assumptions
TAYLOR v. CALDWELL
King's Bench
3 B. & S. 826, 122 Eng. Rep. 309 (1863)

The declaration alleged that by an agreement ... the defendants agreed to let ... The Surrey Gardens and Music Hall, Newington, Surrey, for ... Monday the 17th June, 1861, Monday the 15th July, 1861, Monday the 5th August, 1861, and Monday the 19th August, 1861, for the purpose of giving a series of four grand concerts and day and night fetes, at the Gardens and Hall on those days respectively, at the rent or sum of 100£. for each of those days. It then averred the fulfilment of conditions &c., on the part of the plaintiffs; and breach by the defendants, that they did not nor would allow the plaintiffs to have the use of The Surrey Music Hall and Gardens according to the agreement, but wholly made default therein, &c.; whereby the plaintiffs lost divers moneys paid by them for printing advertisements of and in advertising the concerts, and also lost divers sums expended and expenses incurred by them in preparing for the concerts and otherwise in relation thereto, and on the faith of the performance by the defendants of the agreement on their part, and had been otherwise injured, &c....

[The defendants answered:] That at the time of the agreement there was a general custom of the trade and business of the plaintiffs and the defendants, with respect to which the agreement was made, known to the plaintiffs and the defendants, and with reference to which they agreed, and which was part of the agreement, that in the event of the Gardens and Music Hall being destroyed or so far damaged by accidental fire as to prevent the entertainments being given according to the intent of the agreement, between the time of making the agreement and the time appointed for the performance of the same, the agreement should be rescinded and at an end; and that the Gardens and Music Hall were destroyed and so far damaged by accidental fire as to prevent the entertainments, or any of them, being given, according to the intent of the agreement, between the time of making the agreement and the first of the times appointed for the performance of the same, and continued so destroyed and damaged until after the times appointed for the performance of the agreement had elapsed, without the default of the defendants or either of them.

On the trial, before BLACKBURN, J., at the London Sittings after Michaelmas Term, 1861, it appeared that the action was brought on the following agreement:—

"Royal Surrey Gardens,

"27th May, 1861.

"Agreement between Messrs. Caldwell & Bishop, of the one part, and Messrs. Taylor & Lewis of the other part, whereby the said Caldwell & Bishop agree to let, and the said Taylor & Lewis agree to take, on the terms hereinafter stated, The Surrey Gardens and Music Hall, Newington, Surrey, for the following days, viz.:—

"Monday, the	17th June, 1861,
"	15th July, 1861,
"	5th August, 1861,
"	19th August, 1861,

for the purpose of giving a series of four grand concerts and day and night fetes at the said Gardens and Hall on those days respectively at the rent or sum of 100£. for each of the said days. The said Caldwell & Bishop agree to find and provide at their own sole expense, on each of the aforesaid days, for the amusement of the public and persons then in the said Gardens and Hall, an efficient and organised military and quadrille band, the united bands to consist of from thirty-five to forty members; al fresco entertainments of various descriptions; coloured minstrels, fireworks, and full illuminations; a ballet or divertissement, if permitted, a wizard and Grecian statues; tight rope performances; rifle galleries; air gun shooting; Chinese and Parisian games; boats on the lake, and (weather permitting) aquatic sports, and all and every other entertainment as given nightly during the months and times above mentioned. And the said Caldwell & Bishop also agree that the before mentioned united bands shall be present and assist at each of the said concerts, from its commencement until 9 o'clock at night; that they will, one week at least previous to the above mentioned dates, underline in bold type in all their bills and advertisements that Mr. Sims Reeves and other artistes will sing at the said gardens on those dates respectively, and that the said Taylor & Lewis shall have the right of placing their boards, bills, and placards in such number and manner (but subject to the approval of the said Caldwell & Bishop) in and about the entrance to the said gardens, and in the said grounds, one week at least previous to each of the above mentioned days respectively, all bills so displayed being affixed on boards. And the said Caldwell & Bishop also agree to allow dancing on the new circular platform after 9 o'clock at night, but not before. And the said Caldwell & Bishop also agree not to allow the firework display to take place till a 1/4 past 11 o'clock at night. And, lastly, the said Caldwell & Bishop agree that the said Taylor & Lewis shall be entitled to and shall be at liberty to take and receive, as and for the sole use and property of them the said Taylor & Lewis, all moneys paid for entrance to the Gardens, Galleries and Music Hall and firework galleries, and that the said Taylor & Lewis may in their own discretion secure the patronage of any charitable institution in connection with the said concerts. And the said Taylor & Lewis agree to pay the aforesaid respective sum of 100£. in the evening of the said respective days by a crossed cheque, and also to find and provide, at their own sole cost, all the necessary artistes for the said concerts, including Mr. Sims Reeves, God's will permitting.

(Signed)   "J. Caldwell.

"Witness   "Chas. Bishop.

(Signed)   "S. Denis."

On the 11th June the Music Hall was destroyed by an accidental fire, so that it became impossible to give the concerts. Under these circumstances a verdict was returned for the plaintiff, with leave reserved to enter a verdict for the defendants on the second and third issues. . . .

H. Tindl Atkinson shewed cause [to enter a verdict for the plaintiffs]. — First. The agreement sued on does not shew a "letting" by the defendants to the plaintiffs of the Hall and Gardens, although it uses the word "let," and contains a stipulation that the plaintiffs are to be empowered to receive the money at the doors, and to have the use of the Hall, for which they are to pay 100£, and pocket the surplus; for the possession is to remain in the defendants, and the whole tenor of the instrument is against the notion of a letting. . . .

Secondly. The destruction of the premises by fire will not exonerate the defendants from performing their part of the agreement. In *Paradine v. Jane* (Al. 26) it is laid down that, where the law creates a duty or charge, and the party is disabled to perform it without any default in him, and hath no remedy over, there the law will excuse him; but when the party, by his own contract, creates a duty or charge upon himself, he is bound to make it good, if he may, notwithstanding any accident by inevitable necessity, because he might have provided against it by his contract. And there accordingly it was held no plea to an action for rent reserved by lease that the defendant was kept out of possession by an alien enemy whereby he could not take the profits.

Pearce, in support of the [defendant theater owner:]. — First. This instrument amounts to a demise. It uses the legal words for that purpose, and is treated in the declaration as a demise.

Secondly. The words "God's will permitting" override the whole agreement.

The judgment of the Court was now delivered by BLACKBURN, J. In this case the plaintiffs and defendants had, on the 27th May, 1861, entered into a contract by which the defendants agreed to let the plaintiffs have the use of The Surrey Gardens and Music Hall on four days then to come, viz., the 17th June, 15th July, 5th August, and 19th August, for the purpose of giving a series of four grand concerts, and day and night fetes at the Gardens and Hall on those days respectively; and the plaintiffs agreed to take the Gardens and Hall on those days, and pay 100£. for each day.

The parties inaccurately call this a "letting," and the money to be paid a "rent"; but the whole agreement is such as to shew that the defendants were to retain the possession of the Hall and Gardens so that there was to be no demise of them, and that the contract was merely to give the plaintiffs the use of them on those days. Nothing however, in our opinion, depends on this. The agreement then proceeds to set out various stipulations between the parties as to what each was to supply for these concerts and entertainments, and as to the manner in which they should be carried on. The effect of the whole is to show that the existence of the Music Hall in the Surrey Gardens in a state fit for a concert was essential for the fulfilment of the contract, — such entertainments as the parties contemplated in their agreement could not be given without it.

After the making of the agreement, and before the first day on which a concert was to be given, the Hall was destroyed by fire. This destruction, we must take it on the evidence, was without the fault of either party, and was so complete that in consequence the concerts could not be given as intended. And the question we have to decide is whether, under these circumstances, the loss which the plaintiffs have sustained is to fall upon the defendants. The parties when framing their agreement evidently had not present to their minds the possibility of such a disaster, and have made no express stipulation with reference to it, so that the answer to the question must depend upon the general rules of law applicable to such a contract.

There seems no doubt that where there is a positive contract to do a thing, not in itself unlawful, the contractor must perform it or pay damages for not doing it, although in consequence of unforeseen accidents, the performance of his contract has become unexpectedly burdensome or even impossible. The law is so laid down in 1 Roll. Abr. 450, Condition (G), and in the note (2) to *Walton v. Waterhouse* (2 Wms. Saund. 421 a. 6th ed.), and is recognized as the general rule by all the Judges in the much discussed case of *Hall v. Wright* (E. B. & E. 746). But this rule is only applicable when the contract is positive and absolute, and not subject to any condition either express or implied: and there are authorities which, as we think, establish the principle that where, from the nature of the contract, it appears that the parties must from the beginning have known that it could not be fulfilled unless when the time for the fulfillment of the contract arrived some particular specified thing continued to exist, so that, when entering into the contract, they must have contemplated such continuing existence as the foundation of what was to be done; there, in the absence of any express or implied warranty that the thing shall exist, the contract is not to be construed as a positive contract, but as subject to an implied condition that the parties shall be excused in case, before breach, performance becomes impossible from the perishing of the thing without default of the contractor.

There seems little doubt that this implication tends to further the great object of making the legal construction such as to fulfill the intention of those who entered into the contract. For in the course of affairs men in making such contracts in general would, if it were brought to their minds, say that there should be such a condition.

Accordingly, in the Civil law, such an exception is implied in every obligation of the class which they call *obligatio de certo corpore*. The rule is laid down in the Digest, lib. XLV., tit. 1, *de verborum obligationibus*, l. 33. "*Si Stichus certo die dari promissus, ante diem moriatur: non tenetur promissor."* The principle is more fully developed in l. 23. *"Si ex legati causa, aut ex stipulatu hominem certum mihi debeas: non aliter post mortem ejus tenearis mihi, quam si per te steterit, quominus vivo eo eum mihi dares: quod ita fit, si aut interpellatus non dedisti, aut occidisti eum."* The examples are of contracts respecting a slave, which was the common illustration of a certain subject used by the Roman lawyers, just as we are apt to take a horse; and no doubt the propriety, one might almost say necessity, of the implied condition is more obvious when the contract relates to a living animal, whether man or brute, than when it relates to some inanimate thing (such as in the present case a theatre) the existence of which is not so obviously precarious as that of the live animal, but the principle is adopted in the Civil law as applicable to every obligation of which the subject is a certain thing. The general subject is treated of by Pothier, who in his *Traite des Obligations*, partie 3, chap. 6, art. 3, § 668 states the result to be that the debtor *corporis certi* is freed from his obligation when the thing has perished, neither by his act, nor his neglect, and before he is in default, unless by some stipulation he has taken on himself the risk of the particular misfortune which has occurred.

Although the Civil law is not of itself authority in English Court, it affords great assistance in investigating the principles on which the law is grounded. And it seems to us that the common law authorities establish that in such a contract the same condition of the continued existence of the thing is implied by English law.

There is a class of contracts in which a person binds himself to do something which requires to be performed by him in person; and such promises, *e.g.* promises to marry, or promises to serve for a certain time, are never in practice qualified by an express exception of the death of the party; and therefore in such cases the contract is in terms broken if the promisor dies before fulfillment. Yet it was very early determined that, if the performance is personal, the executors are not liable; *Hyde v. The Dean of Windsor* (Cro. Eliz. 552, 553). *See* 2 Wms. Exors. 1560, 5th ed., where a very apt illustration is given. "Thus," says the learned author, "if an author undertakes to compose a work, and dies before completing it, his executors are discharged from this contract: for the undertaking is merely personal in its nature, and, by the intervention of the contractor's death, has become impossible to be performed." ... In *Hall v. Wright* (E. B. & E. 746, 749), Crompton J., in his judgment, puts another case. "Where a contract depends upon personal skill, and the act of God renders it impossible, as, for instance, in the case of a painter employed to paint a picture who is struck blind, it may be that the performance might be excused."

It seems that in those cases the only ground on which the parties or their executors can be excused from the consequences of the breach of the contract is, that from the nature of the contract there is an implied condition of the continued existence of the life of the contractor, and, perhaps in the case of the painter of his eyesight. In the instances just given, the person, the continued existence of whose life is necessary to the fulfillment of the contract, is himself the contractor, but that does not seem in itself to be necessary to the application of the principle; as is illustrated by the following example. In the ordinary form of an apprentice deed the apprentice binds himself in unqualified terms to "serve until the full end and term of seven years to be fully complete and ended," during which term it is covenanted that the apprentice his master "faithfully shall serve," and the father of the apprentice in equally unqualified terms binds himself for the performance by the apprentice of all and every covenant on his part.... It is undeniable that if the apprentice dies within the seven years, the covenant of the father that he shall perform his covenant to serve for seven years is not fulfilled, yet surely it cannot be that an action would lie against the father? Yet the only reason why it would not is that he is excused because of the apprentice's death.

These are instances where the implied condition is of the life of a human being, but there are others in which the same implication is made as to the continued existence of a thing. For example, where a contract of sale is made amounting to a bargain and sale, transferring presently the property in specific chattels, which are to be delivered by the vendor at a future day; there, if the chattels, without the fault of the vendor, perish in the interval, the purchaser must pay the price and the vendor is excused from performing his contract to deliver, which has thus become impossible.

That this is the rule of the English law is established by the case of *Rugg v. Minett* (11 East, 210), where the article that perished before delivery was turpentine, and it was decided that the vendor was bound to refund the price of all those lots in which the property had not passed; but was entitled to retain without deduction the price of those lots in which the property had passed, though they were not delivered, and though in the conditions of sale, which are set out in the report, there was no express qualification of the promise to deliver on payment. It seems in that case rather to have been taken for granted than decided that the destruction of the thing sold before delivery excused the vendor from fulfilling his contract to deliver on payment.

This also is the rule in the Civil law, and it is worth noticing that Pothier, in his celebrated *Traite du Contrat de Vente* (see Part. 4, § 307, &c.; and Part. 2, ch. 1, sect. 1, art. 4, § 1), treats this as merely an example of the more general rule that every obligation de certo corpore is extinguished when the thing ceases to exist. *See* Blackburn on the Contract of Sale, p. 173....

It may, we think, be safely asserted to be now English law, that in all contracts of loan of chattels or bailments if the performance of the promise of the borrower or bailee to return the things lent or bailed, becomes impossible because it has perished, this impossibility (if not arising from the fault of the borrower or bailee from some risk which he has taken upon himself) excuses the borrower or bailee from the performance of his promise to redeliver the chattel....

In none of these cases is the promise in words other than positive, nor is there any express stipulation that the destruction of the person or thing shall excuse the performance; but that excuse is by law implied, because from the nature of the contract it is apparent that the parties contracted on the basis of the continued existence of the particular person or chattel. In the present case, looking at the whole contract, we find that the parties contracted on the basis of the continued existence of the Music Hall at the time when the concerts were to be given; that being essential to their performance.

We think, therefore, that the Music Hall having ceased to exist, without fault of either party, both parties are excused, the plaintiffs from taking the gardens and paying the money, the defendants from performing their promise to give the use of the Hall and Gardens and other things. Consequently the rule must be absolute to enter the verdict for the defendants.

Rule absolute.

NOTES AND QUESTIONS

1. The court explains its decision by saying:

> [W]here, from the nature of the contract, it appears that the parties must from the beginning have known that it could not be fulfilled unless when the time for the fulfillment of the contract arrived some particular specified thing continued to exist, so that, when entering into the contract, they must have contemplated such continuing existence as the foundation of what was to be done; there, in the absence of any express or implied warranty that the thing shall exist, the contract is not to be construed as a positive contract, but as subject to an implied condition that the parties shall be excused in case, before breach, performance becomes impossible from the perishing of the thing without default of the contractor.
>
> There seems little doubt that this implication tends to further the great object of making the legal construction such as to fulfill the intention of those who entered into the contract. For in the course of affairs men in making such contracts in general would, if it were brought to their minds, say that there should be such a condition.

How do the judges know that people making contracts "would, if it were brought to their minds, say that there should be such a condition?" Is it likely that British judges in 1863 would know much about the practices of businesspeople in general or the assumptions of those promoting entertainment and renting theaters?

Could we argue that whatever the explanation given by the court, the case involves a kind of rough loss-splitting? As a result of the decision, the owner of the theater loses his building and future revenues from renting it until (if and when) it is rebuilt. The promoter loses the various reliance losses he spent promoting the entertainment events. In any event, the requirement of proof of damages with reasonable certainty often, if not usually, would block the promoter's recovery of lost anticipated profits lost because the theater burned.

Professor Schlegel reviewed the English cases provoked by the closing of the Suez Canal in 1956 as a result of a war between Britain, France, and Israel against Egypt. He was very critical of the way that the courts explained their decisions: "[N]o part of the law evokes the spirit of Alice more readily than the law of impossibility of performance."[16] He said:

---

16. John Henry Schlegel, *Of Nuts, and Ships, and Sealing Wax, Suez, and Frustrating Things — The Doctrine of Impossibility of Performance*, 23 RUTGERS L. REV. 419, 447 (1968).

It is time that English courts admit and approve the fact that courts can, do, and should make contracts for the parties. Contracts should be enforced only as long as, and to the point that, it is reasonable that they should be enforced....

A standard may serve where a rule may fail. To this end, I would like to suggest that, where an unusual event occurs and frustration is alleged, contracts should be enforced only when the contract in question is essentially similar to the archetypical contract situation: the contract between brokers, each essentially speculating on a narrowly fluctuating market. To the extent that the contract deviates from this model, it should be held frustrated and essential reliance damages—those resources consumed—as well as the cost of any partial performance, should be split between the parties. Thus, an event should be held frustrating when it is not one within that narrow range of events normally incidental to the average broker's or wholesaler's contract—slight delay and small market fluctuations.

As you work through the material that follows, consider whether you agree with Schlegel that the law makes no more sense than the conversation at the tea party in Alice in Wonderland. Consider, too, to what extent the courts seem to be carrying out the policy position that Schlegel advocated. Finally, throughout the course, we have reminded you that many scholars in the late 20th and early 21st century have argued that contract law should be clear, simple, and formal. How would they respond to Schlegel's proposal in light of the kinds of cases that we will consider in this chapter?

2. *The mistake parallel:* Compare the famous "cow" case, *Sherwood v. Walker*,[17] with *Wood v. Boynton*, the Wisconsin diamond case that we noted after *Paradine v. Jane*. They were decided within two years of each other. Sherwood, the buyer, sued for replevin of a cow and won in a Justice's Court. Walker, the seller, appealed. He argued that he was entitled to rescind because of a mutual mistake of fact. The judgment was reversed, with one judge dissenting. The majority opinion said that Sherwood, a banker, had called on Walker, a businessman,[18] seeking to buy some blooded cattle. "He was asked to go out and look at ... [some on Walker's Greenfield farm] ... with the statement at the time that they were probably barren, and would not breed." A few days later, Sherwood called on Walker to buy a cow known as Rose 2d of Aberlone. The price was set at $80. Walker told Graham, his employee, to deliver the cow at King's cattle yard. Graham then discovered that the cow was with calf, and Walker refused to deliver her. The cow had cost Walker $850, and if it were not barren, it would be worth between $750 and $1,000. The majority of the Michigan Supreme Court said that there had been a "mutual mistake of a material fact as to the substance of the thing bargained for." "[T]he mistake was not of the mere quality of the cow but

---

17. 66 Mich. 568, 33 N.W. 919 (1887).
18. We are told that this was Hiram Walker, a man whose business may be known to some readers.

went to the very nature of the thing. A barren cow is a substantially different creature than a breeding one." The cow was "evidently sold and purchased on the relation of her value for beef, unless the plaintiff had learned of her true condition, and concealed such knowledge from defendants." A new trial was ordered to consider whether the cow was sold upon the understanding of both parties that she was barren.

The dissenting judge said that there was nothing in the record indicating that the cow was sold as beef. The buyer was told by the seller that the cow was barren, but the buyer thought she could be made to breed. The mistake went only to the quality of the animal rather than to the substance of the contract. "As to the quality of the animal, and as to this each party took his chances. If this were not the law, there would be no safety in purchasing this kind of stock."

How, if at all, does the right to rescind for mutual mistake about a material fact differ from the defense of an implied condition excusing performance when there has been the destruction of a specific thing essential for that performance? One could say that the theater owner promised to have a theater available on certain dates and that Walker had promised to deliver Rose 2d of Aberlone; neither qualified his promise expressly. Yet both courts were willing to look to what they saw as the real deal behind the formal one.

Nonetheless, are there differences as to when each doctrine would apply? Presumably, Rose 2d of Aberlone was with calf when Walker sold her to Sherwood. The theater, however, was standing and available for performances when Caldwell agreed to let it to Taylor, with the fire occurring about 15 days later. Do we need different rules of law to cover these two situations or is the problem essentially the same? (Whatever your view on whether the difference as to when an event occurs makes a difference, you must recognize that, at least in form, mistake and impossibility are distinct doctrines.)

How do the cow and the diamond case differ? The buyer keeps the diamond, but the buyer does not get the cow. Is it possible that both cases reached the wrong conclusion? You should be able to fashion arguments for the seller and the buyer in each situation.

3. *The destruction of a specific thing necessary for performance of a contract:* Read UCC §§ 2-613 and 2-615. Often these sections are triggered when there has been a crop failure. In *ConAgra, Inc. v. Bartlett Partnership,*[19] a partnership entered four contracts for the sale of 300,000 bushels of corn in June 1992. The partnership had approximately 2,800 acres planted in corn. In 1992, the partnership undertook an extensive manure-spreading operation to improve the soil. To keep costs down, the partnership hauled corn to ConAgra's elevator in Grand Island and on the way back hauled manure from Hastings to the land the partnership farmed. This unusual arrangement prompted the partnership's interest in selling its corn to ConAgra, a fact known to ConAgra.

---

19. 248 Neb. 933, 540 N.W.2d 333 (1995).

On August 13, 1992, the partnership's crop was severely damaged by a hailstorm. One of the partners notified a ConAgra manager. The partnership delivered the corn it could salvage and bought some corn on the market, which it tendered to ConAgra. Nonetheless, it was some 61,500 bushels short of the quantity it had promised to deliver. ConAgra sued and recovered a directed verdict. The Supreme Court of Nebraska affirmed. If a farmer had made a contract to sell crops to be grown on designated land, and if they were destroyed without the farmer's fault, then he or she would be excused either because of the destruction of identified goods or because of the failure of a basic assumption of the contract. Here, however, the written contracts "did not identify the corn in any way other than by kind and amount. Nor did the contracts make any reference to corn grown or to be grown by the partnership on any identified acreage. The only limitation the contracts placed on the source of the corn was that it be grown in the continental United States." The language of the contracts was not ambiguous, and so they must be enforced according to their terms. Thus, the contract did not limit the partnership to corn grown on its land, and so neither § 2-613 nor § 2-615 applied. Although the court's opinion does not talk about the point, it seems likely that the contracts would be written on a ConAgra standard form. Would the partnership have known that it would get no relief if the corn was destroyed by a hailstorm? Does it seem likely that the partnership planned on delivering corn grown on its own land? Suppose the partnership regularly engaged in agricultural futures trading. Would this affect your judgment about the case?

4. *Destruction of a specific "thing"—the ability of the person who is to render personal services:* Restatement (Second) of Contracts § 262 provides that "[i]f the existence of a particular person is necessary for the performance of a duty, his death or such incapacity as makes performance impracticable is an event the non-occurrence of which was a basic assumption on which the contract was made." Such events excuse performance. However, what meaning should courts give to § 262's term *incapacity*?

HANDICAPPED CHILDREN'S EDUCATION BOARD OF SHEBOYGAN COUNTY v. LUKASZEWSKI

Wisconsin Supreme Court
112 Wis. 2d 197, 332 N.W.2d 774 (1983)

CALLOW, J.

This review arises out of an unpublished decision of the Court of Appeals that affirmed in part and reversed in part a judgment of the Ozaukee County Circuit Court, Judge Warren A. Grady.

In January of 1978 the Handicapped Children's Education Board (the Board) hired Elaine Lukaszewski to serve as a speech and language therapist for the spring term. Lukaszewski was assigned to the Lightfoot School in Sheboygan Falls, which was approximately 45 miles from her home in Mequon. Rather than move, she commuted to work each day. During the 1978 spring term, the Board offered Lukaszewski a contract to continue in her present position at Lightfoot School for the 1978–79 school year. The contract called for an annual salary of $10,760. Lukaszewski accepted.

In August of 1978, prior to the beginning of the school year, Lukaszewski was offered a position by the Wee Care Day Care Center, which was located not far from her home in Mequon. The job paid an annual salary of $13,000. After deciding to accept this offer, Lukaszewski notified Thomas Morrelle, the Board's director of special education, that she intended to resign from her position at the Lightfoot School. Morrelle told her to submit a letter of resignation for consideration by the Board. She did so, and the matter was discussed at a meeting of the Board on August 21, 1978. The Board refused to release Lukaszewski from her contract. On August 24, 1978, the Board's attorney sent a letter to Lukaszewski directing her to return to work. The attorney sent a second letter to the Wee Care Day Center stating that the Board would take legal action if the Center interfered with Lukaszewski's performance of her contractual obligations at the Lightfoot School. A copy of this letter was sent to the Department of Public Instruction.

Lukaszewski left the Wee Care Day Care Center and returned to Lightfoot School for the 1978 fall term. She resented the actions of the Board, however, and retained misgivings about her job. On September 8, 1978, she discussed her feelings with Morrelle. After this meeting Lukaszewski felt quite upset about the situation. She called her doctor to make an appointment for that afternoon and subsequently left the school.

Dr. Ashok Chatterjee examined Lukaszewski and found her blood pressure to be high. Lukaszewski asked Dr. Chatterjee to write a letter explaining his medical findings and the advice he had given her. In a letter dated September 11, 1978, Dr. Chatterjee indicated that Lukaszewski had a hypertension problem dating back to 1976. He reported that on the day he examined Lukaszewski she appeared agitated, nervous, and had blood pressure readings up to 180/100. It was his opinion that, although she took hypotensive drugs, her medical condition would not improve unless the situation that caused the problem was removed. He further opined that it would be dangerous for her to drive long distances in her agitated state.

Lukaszewski did not return to work after leaving on September 8, 1978. She submitted a letter of resignation dated September 13, 1978, in which she wrote:

> I enclose a copy of the doctor's statement concerning my health. On the basis of it, I must resign. I am unwilling to jeopardize my health and I am also unwilling to become involved in an accident. For these reasons, I tender my resignation.

A short time later, Lukaszewski reapplied for and obtained employment at the Wee Care Day Care Center.

After Lukaszewski left, the Board immediately began looking for a replacement. Only one qualified person applied for the position. Although this applicant had less of an educational background than Lukaszewski, she had more teaching experience. Under the salary schedule agreed upon by the Board and the teachers' union, this applicant would have to be paid $1,026.64 more per year than Lukaszewski. Having no alternative, the Board hired the applicant at the higher salary.

In December of 1978 the Board initiated an action against Lukaszewski for breach of contract. The Board alleged that, as a result of the breach, it suffered damage in the amount of the additional compensation it was required to pay Lukaszewski's replacement for the 1978–79 school year ($1,026.64). A trial was held before the Court. The trial court ruled that Lukaszewski had breached her contract and awarded the Board $1,249.14 in damages ($1,026.64 for breach of contract and $222.50 for costs).

Lukaszewski appealed. The Court of Appeals affirmed the circuit court's determination that Lukaszewski breached her contract. However, the appellate court reversed the circuit court's damage award, reasoning that, although the Board had to pay more for Lukaszewski's replacement, by its own standards it obtained a proportionately more valuable teacher. Therefore, the Court of Appeals held that the Board suffered no damage from the breach. We granted the Board's petition for review.

There are two issues presented on this review: (1) whether Lukaszewski breached her employment contract with the Board; and (2) if she did breach her contract, whether the Board suffered recoverable damages therefrom.

I. It is undisputed that Lukaszewski resigned before her contract with the Board expired. The only question is whether her resignation was somehow justified. Lukaszewski argues that, because she resigned for health reasons, the trial court erred in finding a breach of contract. According to Lukaszewski, the uncontroverted evidence at trial established that her employment with the Board endangered her health. Therefore, her failure to fulfill her obligation under the employment contract was excused.

We recognize that under certain conditions illness or health dangers may excuse nonperformance of a contract. This court held long ago that "where the act to be performed is one which the promisor alone is competent to do, the obligation is discharged if he is prevented by sickness or death from performing it." *Jennings v. Lyons*, 39 Wis. 553, 557 (1876). *See also* Restatement (Second) of Contracts § 262 (1981); 18 S. WILLISTON, A TREATISE ON THE LAW OF CONTRACTS § 1940 (3d ed. 1978). Even assuming this rule applies to Lukaszewski's failure to perform, we are not convinced that the trial court erred in finding a breach of contract.

A health danger will not excuse nonperformance of a contractual obligation when the danger is caused by the nonperforming party. *See Jennings v. Lyons*, 39 Wis. at 557–58. Nor will a health condition or danger that was foreseeable when the contract was entered into justify its breach. *Id.* It would be fundamentally unfair to allow a breaching party to escape liability because of a health danger that by his or her own fault has precluded performance.

In the instant case the trial court expressly found that the danger to Lukaszewski's health was self-induced. Lukaszewski testified that it was stressful for her to return to the Lightfoot School in the fall of 1978 because she did not want to work there and because she resented the Board's actions to compel her to do so. Citing this testimony, the court concluded: "The Court finds that the defendant's medical excuse was a result of the stress condition she had created by an attempted repudiation of her contract, and was not the product of any unsubstantiated, so-called, harrassment [sic] by the plaintiff's board." Lukaszewski further complained about the hazard of driving 45 miles to and from Sheboygan Falls each day. She alone, however, caused this commute by choosing to live in Mequon. The trial court pointed out in its decision from the bench that she could have eliminated this problem by simply moving to Sheboygan Falls. Thus the court clearly found that any health danger associated with performance of the employment contract was the fault of Lukaszewski, not the Board. This factual finding alone is enough to invalidate the medical excuse for Lukaszewski's breach.

The medical excuse is defective for a second reason. In order to excuse Lukaszewski's nonperformance, the trial court would have had to make a factual finding that she resigned for health reasons. The oral decision and supplemental written decision of the trial court indicate that it found otherwise. In its written decision the court stated:

> [Lukaszewski's] reasons for resignation were succinctly stated in her testimony, upon cross-examination . . . as follows: ". . . I had found a job that was closer in proximity to my home and it offered a different type of challenge . . . also that the pay was, was more, and I asked them if I could be released from my contract."

The trial court did not include the health danger. Indeed, the court appeared to doubt that Lukaszewski resigned for health reasons. The trial judge observed that Lukaszewski had a history of hypertension dating back at least five or six years. Her blood pressure would fluctuate at the slightest provocation. He further noted that she was able to commute between Sheboygan Falls and Mequon from January 1978 through the middle of the following summer. In short, the decisions indicate that the court believed Lukaszewski resigned for reasons other than her health.

These factual findings by the trial court invalidate Lukaszewski's medical excuse and thereby establish a breach. . . . We conclude that the trial court's findings of fact are not against the great weight and clear preponderance of the evidence and, therefore, must be upheld. Accordingly, we affirm that portion of the Court of Appeals' decision that affirmed the circuit court's determination that Lukaszewski breached her employment contract. . . .

By the Court. — The decision of the court of appeals is affirmed in part and reversed in part.

Day, J. *(dissenting).*

I dissent. The majority opinion correctly states, "The only question is whether her resignation is somehow justified." I would hold that it was.

Elaine Lukaszewski left her employment with the school board. She suffered from high blood pressure and had been treated for several years by her physician for the condition. She claimed her hypertension increased due to stress caused when the Board refused to cancel her teaching contract. Stress can cause a precipitous rise in blood pressure. High blood pressure can bring on damage to other organs of the body.

She was upset over what she perceived was the unreasonable attitude of her employer in refusing to cancel her contract. Following an unpleasant exchange with the Board's Director of Special Education, Mr. Morrelle, she went to her physician. He found her blood pressure to be 180 over 100, which he testified was very high. He advised her to rest and to get out of the situation that was causing her symptoms, which she properly interpreted to mean "quit the job." He also told her that her elevated blood pressure made it dangerous for her to drive the 90 miles round-trip each day, that commuting from her home in Mequon to Sheboygan Falls entailed.

The trial court and the majority of this court conclude she could have obviated the danger of driving by moving to Sheboygan Falls. But the fact is that would not have eliminated her illness nor the hazards to her health that her condition posed. There is not a shred of medical evidence that her blood pressure problems would be cured or appreciably alleviated if she moved from her home to Sheboygan Falls.

Once the dangerous hypertension is established, and here the only medical testimony did just that, it should follow that one should be relieved of a contractual obligation for services unless malingering is shown. In this case no one denies she has the condition. But, the trial court says, the condition was one "she had created," which the majority on this court refer to as "self-induced." The majority here seized on the rationale that illness that is "self-induced" is somehow less worthy of judicial consideration than illness caused by others, or by outside forces over which the patient has no control.

It seems clear from the trial judge's comments that if he had found her physical condition had been caused by the Board's "harassment," he would have let her out of the contract. This is the only logical conclusion from the statement by the trial judge that "The Court finds that the defendant's medical excuse was a result of the stress condition she had created by an attempted repudiation of her contract, and was not the product of any unsubstantiated, so-called, harrassment [sic] by the plaintiff's board."

In either instance, whether "caused" by the Board or "self induced" because of her gnawing feeling of being unfairly treated, the objective symptoms would be the same.

Either, in my opinion, should justify termination of the contract where the physical symptoms are medically certifiable as they admittedly are here.

The majority makes the following assertion: "It would be fundamentally unfair to allow a breaching party to escape liability because of a health danger which by his or her own fault has precluded performance."

Happily no authority is cited for this sweeping statement, which means that it will be easier to ignore it, gloss over it, "distinguish" it, or overrule it in the future. Under this new-found axiom, could a concert violinist under contract be sued to cover any added costs of his replacement if he lost an arm in an accident where he was found 100 percent negligent? Or could another party to a personal service contract be held liable if he was unable to perform because of a debilitating illness clearly caused by negligent health habits?

The majority cites a hundred-year-old case, *Jennings v. Lyons*, 39 Wis. 553 (1876), for two propositions:

> "A health danger will not excuse non-performance of a contractual obligation when the danger is caused by the nonperforming party. *See Jennings v. Lyons*, 39 Wis. at 557–58. Nor will a health condition or danger which was foreseeable when the contract was entered into justify its breach."

Jennings is cited by the majority to bolster its position. The case is not really in point. In that case a husband and wife contracted to work on a farm for one year for the sum of $300. He was to do outside work and she to do housework. After four and one-half months she had to leave to have a baby and the husband had to go with her. The employer refused to pay either of them anything and they brought suit to recover for the time they had worked. The trial court instructed the jury that if at the time the plaintiff and his wife quit working for defendant, the wife was sick and unable to do her part of the work, plaintiff was not bound to a further performance of the contract and was entitled to recover the value of his and his wife's services for the time they actually worked. The trial court found for the plaintiff.

This court reversed and held that the defendant did not have to pay them anything. The court held that the rule is that performance is excused:

> "... as where performance has been rendered impossible by an act of God, by the act of the law, or by the act of the other party ... the obligation is discharged if he is prevented by sickness or death from performing it ... sickness or death is generally recognized as an act of God in such a sense that it excuses the nonperformance, and a recovery is allowed upon a *quantum meruit....*"
> 39 Wis. at 557.

This court said that since the husband must have known his wife was four months pregnant when they took the job and that she would be unable to complete the year of work, therefore no recovery was allowed. This court said: "For when performance becomes impossible by reason of contingencies which should have been foreseen and provided against in the contract, the promisor is held answerable." 39 Wis. at 558. Nowhere did the *Jennings* court say "a health danger will not excuse nonperformance of a contractual obligation when the danger is caused by the nonperforming party."

The precedential value of *Jennings* is doubtful, but to the extent the rules stated may still be valid, it provides no support for the majority. Here there is an illness, "an act of God," there is nothing in the record to show that the severe increase in Elaine Lukaszewski's hypertension was foreseeable when she signed the contract. Thus, even under *Jennings*, the teacher should be excused from performance.

Hypertension is a health problem that when caused by stress, however induced, may require a job change. That is what occurred here.

But the majority has discovered what it apparently regards as a "fall back" position, that Elaine Lukaszewski really did not resign her teaching job for health reasons after all.

The majority says: "In short, the decisions [of the trial court] *indicate* that the court believed Lukaszewski resigned for reasons other than her health." (Emphasis added.)

The word *indicate* has picked up increasing popularity in the jargon of the legal profession in the past few years mostly, I believe, because it does not say anything one can pin down precisely. *Webster's Third New International Dictionary* (1961) gives a wide range of possible meanings to the word *indicate*. Among them are: "suggest, intimate, hint … *Indicate* signifies to serve as a sign or symptom pointing to (the inference or action), stressing only a general, unspecified connection between subject and object …"

"Indicate" seems to fall short on the definiteness required for a "finding of fact" by a trial court.

The first time the case came to the Court of Appeals they sent it back for further "findings" and it is the "original" remarks from the bench plus additional written comments by the judge on remand that form the bases for the appeal and this review.

What the trial court said was that the desire to take the better job brought on the physical symptoms when release from her contract by the Board was refused.

If the trial court had found that she quit merely for the better job and *not* because of her health problems brought on by the high blood pressure, this would be an entirely different case. However, that is *not* what the trial court found in my opinion. The trial court found her medical problems were self-induced and concluded they were therefore unworthy of consideration.

I would reverse the Court of Appeals decision that held she breached her contract....

NOTES AND QUESTIONS

1. *Contrasts and distinctions:* Suppose a Wisconsin promoter contracted with the representative of Count Basie[20] on March 20, 1984. The contract called for Basie and his orchestra to appear in Milwaukee on June 1, 1984. Assume that the contract was silent about the risk of Basie's death. Basie was born in 1904. Although he had suffered a serious heart attack and had been ill for about five years, Basie continued to perform with his band. Basie and his orchestra appeared in a concert in Hollywood on March 17, 1984. This was Basie's last appearance with his band. He died of cancer on April 26, 1984. You can assume that the promoter would not have to accept an appearance of Basie's band without Basie. Does the *Lukaszewski* decision suggest that the Mil-

---

20. Some readers may know little about Count Basie. Along with Duke Ellington, he is one of the important figures in big band jazz. We prescribe listening to a recording as you contemplate this hypothetical. You might also want to follow up this with a biography such as ALBERT MURRAY, GOOD MORNING BLUES: THE AUTOBIOGRAPHY OF COUNT BASIE (Random House 1985), which may change the way in which we hear the music—given its portrait of Basie's struggle, as a black musician, with the burdens of segregation. (Is this footnote irrelevant to a contracts student? Construct an argument that it is not.)

waukee promoter could sue Basie's estate successfully for the profits the promoter could prove it would have made from the band's Milwaukee appearance, or would Basie's death give his estate an impossibility excuse? Would the parties have to litigate Basie's personal habits to see if he were at fault for his death? Suppose, for example, as is likely, he had smoked cigarettes throughout the 1920s until sometime in the 1960s. Moreover, by playing in jazz clubs and dance halls during that period, he had been subject to a great deal of second-hand smoke. Would the promoter have to prove that Basie's smoking caused his death so that he could not perform in Milwaukee on June 1, 1984? Or would Basie's estate's lawyer have to prove that Basie was not responsible for his own death?[21] Would it matter that the majority of adult Americans smoked cigarettes during the 1930s through the 1960s? Wasn't it foreseeable to both the concert promoter and Basie's agents that there was a real risk that Basie would not be able to perform in Milwaukee on June 1st? If this is true, who assumed the risk of his health when the parties entered a written contract that said nothing about this risk? Would you want to know more about the customs and practices in the music performing business?

2. *Clear rules to avoid difficult questions of responsibility:* In *CNA International Reinsurance Co. v. Arlyn Phoenix*,[22] the actor River Phoenix had contracted to appear in two films. The agreement included a provision requiring Phoenix not to do anything that would deprive the film studio of the benefits of the contract. Phoenix took a large quantity of illegal drugs and died. As a result, one film had to be abandoned, while the other was completed with another actor playing Phoenix's part. The insurance company paid the film studio over $5.7 million. It was subrogated to the studio's rights, and it sued Phoenix's estate for breach of contract. The trial court dismissed the insurance company's complaint. The insurance company argued on appeal that Restatement (Second) of Contracts §§ 261 and 262, and *Handicapped Children's Education Board v. Lukaszewski*, bar an impossibility excuse when a person has destroyed his or her own health. "Appellants also suggest a policy basis for the ruling they advocate, arguing that in a society dealing with increasing problems created by illegal drug abuse, such conduct should not excuse the performance of the contract."

The Florida appellate court declined to follow the *Lukaszewski* decision. It said:

> ... [A]ny attempt to discern fault in a death case such as this one, or in a similar case, perhaps involving the use of tobacco or alcohol, would create another case-by-case and hard-to-interpret rule of law. Being mindful that there are already too many of these in existence, we are not persuaded by the

---

21. Our hypothetical case is an unlikely one. The written contracts used in the music business usually deal with situations where a performer cannot appear because of illness or death. You can never forget this problem when you draft a contract that calls for a service to be performed by a specific person. Indeed, you should also consider whether the services can be performed by anyone else and still satisfy the contract. For example, suppose the representative of Count Basie's estate tendered the services of the Count Basie Orchestra after Basie's death. Would the promoter have to accept this, or did the contract require Basie himself to appear directing the orchestra?

22. 678 So. 2d 378, 380 (Fla. Ct. App. 1996).

facts or the arguments presented to depart from the clear and unambiguous rule that death renders a personal services contract impossible to perform.

The court did say: "[W]e believe that the parties to the agreements could have provided specifically for the contingency of loss due to the use of illegal drugs...."

Suppose the exact facts of the *Lukaszewski* case arose in Florida today. Would you expect the Florida court to excuse the teacher from performing her original contract so that she could take the better offer? If film studios started using clauses providing "specifically for the contingency of loss due to the use of illegal drugs," won't courts have to make case-by-case decisions about the degree of fault of the actor and whether his or her drug use caused the inability to perform?

We are informed by an experienced entertainment lawyer that there is too much money at stake in a film production to risk a significant exclusion from cast insurance on a starring or featured performer. Every studio's actor's employment contract provides that cast insurance coverage at a non-rated premium is an absolute condition of employment. The lawyer tries to get a clause in the contract that permits his or her actor clients to meet the condition by paying the premium when a non-standard premium is demanded by the cast insurer. He did know of one instance where a production company had accepted an insurer's refusal to cover losses caused by a particular actor's inability to perform caused by drugs. This is a big risk, and those who finance pictures typically would not accept it. When an independent film company produces a picture, the producer typically must obtain a guarantee of completion from a bonding company so that the lenders will be assured that the picture will in fact be completed. A completion guarantor almost certainly would not issue such a bond without unqualified cast insurance.

2. Cleaning Up after the Unexpected: Allocations, Restitution, and Reliance Recovery

a. Allocations: Solutions with a High Potential for Dispute

A fire, strike, or flood may destroy part but not all of a supplier's productive capacity. The supplier is able to make some of its product but not enough to fill all of the claims on its supply. What can or must it do with what it has? Suppose, for example, a fire destroys part of a manufacturer's plant under circumstances that justify an impossibility excuse. It will be two months before the plant is back in full production. However, the manufacturer can still operate at exactly one-half of its former capacity — that is, before the fire it could produce 1,000 units a week but after the fire it can produce only 500 units. What can or must it do with the 500 units?

Before the fire, for example, the manufacturer had five contracts with five customers each calling for 100 units a week.

(1) One of these five contracts is legally unenforceable because of uncertainty as to price and quantity, but the parties have performed under it for six months before the fire.

(2) In addition to these five contract customers, the manufacturer had two regular customers who had purchased 100 units a week for five years but had no contract with the manufacturer at the time of the fire.

(3) Moreover, a division of the manufacturer's own company regularly took 100 units a week for use in its own operations.

(4) Shortly after the fire, the manufacturer received an order for 100 units a week from a large firm, but it has not yet accepted this order. The manufacturer had been trying to sell to this firm for years, and its business is more important to the manufacturer's continued success than that of any of its older customers.

(5) The manufacturer also received an order after the fire from a hospital that needs 100 units a week for purposes directly related to the treatment of seriously ill patients.

(6) One of the five customers that has a legally enforceable contract with the manufacturer for 100 units a week is a racetrack. Another customer with a contract has an inventory of these units large enough to supply its needs for at least three months. The units are not readily available on the market at the present time.

You are the manufacturer's general counsel. Which actual and potential customers get how many units per week?[23]

Some of the answers are fairly easy; many are not. Suppose that a manufacturer allocates its available goods in a manner that does not comply with § 2-615(b). A buyer who did not get enough sues. What is the consequence of the improper allocation? Does the manufacturer lose its entire impossibility excuse, or will the buyer be limited to damages based on the difference between its allocation and what it would have received had an improper allocation not been made? See § 2-615(a), granting an excuse in certain cases to a seller "who complies with paragraphs (b) and (c)." May we assume that a seller who fails to comply does not get the excuse granted by paragraph (a)?

Professor James J. White, of the University of Michigan Law School, studied contract administration in the chemical industry during a time of shortage.[24] There were widespread shortages and allocations in 1974 and 1975. White interviewed about 30 people at 10 chemical and pharmaceutical companies.

He found that no company had a written allocation plan or a fixed plan concerning all products. The predominant method of allocating production was on a *pro rata* basis in accordance with actual purchases over a historic period. This allowed allo-

---

23. *See* U.C.C. §§ 2-615(b)(c), 2-616, 2-615, Official Comment 11.

24. James J. White, *Contract Law in Modern Commercial Transaction, An Artifact of Twentieth Century Business Life?*, 22 WASHBURN L.J. 1 (1982).

cations to both contract and spot purchase customers. Some contracts had clever clauses, but businesspeople did not refer to them and often seemed not to know about them.

There were some deviations from *pro rata* allocations that seem justifiable. Some firms gave more product to military orders, to buyers who would otherwise have suffered extraordinary losses if all they received was their *pro rata* share, and to customers of a product not thought part of the pool such as a customer who had built a plant next door to the supplier's production facility.

There also were some deviations from *pro rata* allocations that seem unjustifiable. There were upstream diversions. The basic chemicals could be combined to produce a variety of products, but some firms found a product mix that produced the greatest yield for themselves. Often allocations were made only after all the internal needs were filled. One businessperson explained that he might be working next year for the president of the division that he had shorted this year, and he did not want to take this risk. Sales were made to new customers. "One should have a right to 'salt the market' because times of shortage were when one 'added to his market share.' We might serve new customers where in prior times we 'never got beyond the lobby.'" Extra allocations also were given to particularly good customers.

White concludes that "a large part of the behavior a lawyer might conceive as in response to the dictates of the law is in fact taken in ignorance or disregard of it." Lay agents of the seller ration subject to the sanctions within the corporations. Their decisions are largely based on immediate profitability and long-term relationships with buying companies. Furthermore, buyers are unlikely to discover or be able to prove that suppliers have not complied with the UCC allocation rules. Other buyers who got more than they should have are often competitors and are unwilling to share information. Even if a misallocation were discovered, fighting could be costly; buyers might hesitate to lose what relationship they do have with a seller.

b. Restitution after an Excuse

Impossibility or frustration may excuse performance, but a contract that has been stopped in mid-course will likely cause many reliance losses. Who should take these losses? How far can doctrines such as restitution be used to shift some or all of them? If one party to a contract confers a clear tangible benefit on the other before the contract is discharged for impossibility, most courts will allow its recovery in a restitution action. The one receiving the benefit has been unjustly enriched—something has been handed over on the assumption that it would be paid for when the contract was fully performed and now the contract will not go forward to completion. However, many writers find the case more difficult when the alleged benefit was itself destroyed by the event that provoked the impossible excuse. At best, the unjust enrichment was temporary.

Suppose, for example, a court decides that one who is to construct a machine or make repairs or alterations on another's building is excused because of, say, a fire that has destroyed the partially built machine or the structure on which the builder was to make alterations or repairs.[25] This means that the buyer cannot sue the seller for failure to perform. However, usually the seller's performance also will be a condition to the buyer's promise to pay, and so the seller will be unable to recover on the contract. But suppose the person trying to build the machine or make repairs has done a great deal of work trying to perform the contract before the fire. Can this seller of services or goods recover the value of that lost effort from the buyer? The answer is uncertain.

A seller whose duties were discharged by impossibility can recover for any benefits conferred in a restitution action.[26] As always, the difficult question is what courts will call a benefit and how they will value it. Comment b to § 377 states:

> Usually the measure of reasonable value is appropriate. A benefit may be found if it was conferred before the occurrence of the event even though the event later resulted in its destruction, and in that case recovery may be limited to the measure of increase in wealth prior to the event, if this is less than reasonable value.... A party cannot, however, recover his reliance interest under the rule stated in this Section, and his expenditures in reliance are not subtracted from what he has received in calculating benefit for which he is liable.... Furthermore, to the extent that the contract price can be roughly apportioned to the work done, recovery will not be allowed in excess of the appropriate amount of the price.

To what extent does this comment reflect the cases? More particularly, suppose Owner and Painter contract to have Painter paint three rooms in Owner's house. The house is destroyed by fire. Before the fire, Painter completed painting one room. He also masked woodwork in another room with plastic sheets and tape so that painting the walls would not damage the woodwork. He purchased the paint needed for the third room, and he tinted it so that it is the proper color for the job. Paint tinted in this manner cannot be sold to others. All of this paint remains in cans at Painter's place of business. Painter sues Owner for restitution of benefits conferred trying to perform the contract. For what items, if any, can he recover from the Owner? How will these items be valued?

The English common law view: In contracts discharged by impossibility, the English courts left all losses where they found them. Painter could recover nothing in restitution against Owner. A few early American cases also refused to allow either owner or contractor to recover for essential reliance expenditures that, arguably, had produced a benefit to the owner. Whether or not these old cases would be followed today in these states is uncertain.

---

25. Typically, a builder will not be excused if a partially constructed structure is destroyed by fire. The structure is under the builder's control, and placing the burden on builders gives them an incentive to insure or to insist that the owner buy insurance. Those repairing buildings, however, usually are excused if a building is destroyed, making it impracticable for them to do their job. Of course, builders can contract for excuses in case of fire and place the burden on owners to obtain insurance; indeed, this is commonly done.

26. *See* RESTATEMENT (SECOND) OF CONTRACTS § 377.

The American view: While many states have no cases dealing with the problem, a number have allowed restitutionary recovery after a contract is discharged by impossibility. Owners have been allowed to recover advance payments made to builders. However, courts have used the "entire" and "severable" concepts to divide the losses. If the contract is entire, the contractor is entitled to the contract price only when the job is done, and the installment payments do not reflect equivalents for the work to date. However, the contract might be severable—that is, several contracts in a single document. Then the contractor would earn an amount specified in the contract as each step was completed. Suppose, for example, there is a contract to paint a house. The owner, however, is to pay specified sums as each room is completed. The court might construe the contract so that, for example, Painter would be entitled to keep any installments paid as the price of painting each room he had completed before the fire.

Does Painter have a restitutionary claim for work done before the fire? Many are troubled by the idea that Owner has benefited by an attempt to perform the contract. Any benefit would seem to have gone up in smoke. Nonetheless, property concepts produce what some are willing to see as benefits. Suppose Painter finished the last room, doing the job perfectly. However, five minutes after Painter leaves with the money, the house burns to the ground. Painter is in no way responsible for the fire. The risk that the value of a coat of paint will be destroyed by fire, a leaking roof, or a falling tree that crashes into the house, are just part of the risk of owning property. Indeed, Painter handed over a tangible "thing." He left a thin layer of paint in the right places in the house, and this "thing" belongs to Owner. Thus, we can call it a benefit although it is destroyed immediately after the job is completed.

If we accept this property analysis, we can use it to tell us when a benefit has been conferred. When the paint is applied to the wall it becomes Owner's property, and thus he is benefited in a tangible way. Before the paint is applied, however, it still "belongs" to Painter, and thus the risk that it will be destroyed or rendered valueless is his. Painter could, for example, take paint purchased for Owner and sell it to a third party. On the other hand, Painter might take it to another job, add additional tinting pigments to modify the color, and apply it to the walls of another house. Thus, all these reliance expenditures by Painter will not become Owner's property until the paint is applied to the walls, and we could say that Owner will receive a benefit only at that point. A number of courts have taken just this approach.[27]

---

27. Carroll v. Bowersock, 100 Kan. 270, 164 P. 143 (1917), draws distinctions based on this theory. A builder sued to recover for part performance of a contract to tear out an old reinforced concrete floor in owner's warehouse and construct a new one. The warehouse was destroyed before the job was completed. The court allowed the builder to recover for tearing out the old floor and for new concrete footings that had been completed when the building was destroyed. However, the court refused recovery for wooden forms into which concrete was to have been poured, which were nailed in place, and for steel reinforcing rods that were wired in place and would have become a part of the structure when the concrete was poured. Both could have been removed by the builder. The court said that "the liability of the owner ... should be measured by the amount of the contract work done which, at the time of the destruction of the structure, had become so far identified with it as that but for the destruction it would have inured to him as contemplated by the contract."

Massachusetts and reliance: In *Young v. Chicopee*,[28] a contractor agreed to repair a wooden covered bridge by replacing timber wherever it had decayed. The contractor was to be paid compensation based on a sum per 1,000 feet of lumber actually used. However, so that public travel would not be stopped, the contract required that no work be begun until material for at least half the repairs was on the job site. The contractor stacked lumber on the bridge and on the riverbank. It was possible that some or much of this lumber would have never become part of the bridge. The bridge and all the lumber were destroyed by fire. The court held that the contractor could not recover for the timber which had not been "actually wrought into the bridge" at the time of the fire.

The law of Massachusetts seemed to follow the property notions we have described—as each board was nailed into the bridge, it became the bridge owner's property and at that point the risk of loss changed from the contractor to the bridge owner. However, the Supreme Judicial Court of Massachusetts reconsidered the matter in the 1950s, overturning a contract between John Bowen Co. and the Commonwealth of Massachusetts to build the Chronic Disease Hospital and Nurses Home in Boston. John Bowen Co., although in good faith, had failed to comply with the statutory procedure for bidding on public work.[29] However, the court's decision came after subcontracts had been awarded by John Bowen Co. and work had begun. All of these subcontractors were discharged since it became impossible to continue the work. The court said that John Bowen Co. was discharged since, although it caused the impossibility by its method of bidding, "it must appear ... that, except for the defendant's conduct, there would have been in existence valid and enforceable contracts" in order for the subcontractors to hold John Bowen Co. in breach. Had John Bowen Co. complied with the correct procedure, it would not have been the low bidder and could not have been awarded the general contract. Hence, Bowen's obligations under the subcontracts were excused by impossibility.[30] Are you impressed with this argument? Why do the subcontractors have to take the risk of John Bowen Co.'s command of bidding procedures?

Though relieved of liability for expectation damages suffered by subcontractors, John Bowen Co. soon found itself defendant in a series of suits seeking to recover for the work that had been done before the general contract was overturned in the *Gifford* case.

In *M. Ahern Co. v. John Bowen Co.*,[31] the plumbing subcontractor sued for labor and materials furnished before it was ordered to stop work. The court allowed recovery. The opinion, however, does not indicate whether the labor and materials had been "incorporated" into the structure, but the court did not seem to regard this as important. Bowen argued that it had received no "benefit" since it no longer held the general contract and would not be paid for this work by the Commonwealth. The

28. 186 Mass. 518, 72 N.E. 63 (1904).
29. *See* Gifford v. Comm'r of Pub. Health, 328 Mass. 608, 105 N.E.2d 476 (1952).
30. Boston Plate & Window Glass Co. v. John Bowen Co., 335 Mass. 697, 141 N.E.2d 715 (1957).
31. 334 Mass. 36, 133 N.E.2d 484 (1956).

court rejected the argument, saying that recovery in cases of excusable impossibility is *not* based "in the ultimate analysis on the principle of unjust enrichment … wherein recovery is limited to benefits received."

The court allowed recovery, explaining:

> [I]t is no longer necessary to find implications of a contract to support recovery. The implications are undoubtedly found in each case in accordance with what the court holds to be fair and just in the unanticipated circumstances and it is in order to proceed at once to that issue.

> This is not a case where the defendant stands fully apart, as the plaintiff does, from the circumstances which caused the unexpected destruction of the subject matter of the contract. The defendant did those things with respect to the subbids discussed in *Gifford v. Commissioner* … which caused its bid to appear the lowest, although in fact it was not. The *Gifford* decision has held that what the defendant did was not properly done. Even though we assume, as the defendant urges here, that it acted in good faith, and in respects as to which the prescribed course was not clear, the fact is that its actions, in a field where it had a choice, had a significant part in bringing about the subsequent critical events—the awarding to it of an apparent contract which turned out to be void and the ensuing decision of this court. In the circumstances it is plain that this is not a case of fully excusable impossibility. The defendant's part in the train of events is amply sufficient to offset the consideration that it has suffered uncompensable loss. Whatever might be said against the application of our established rule (and we do not intend any suggestion) to a case where the contract subject matter is destroyed by an event completely unconnected with either party and where both parties were equally interested in making the contract for mutual profit, and neither, by insurance or otherwise, could have provided against the risk of the unexpected loss and there is no final benefit, it is clearly fair and just to say in the instant case that "[i]t is enough that the defendant has actually received in part performance of the contract something for which when completed he had agreed to pay a price." WILLISTON, CONTRACTS (REV. ED.) § 1976, page 5551.[32]

The Massachusetts court squarely faced the question of recovery for reliance losses in preparation for performance in *Albre Marble and Tile Co. v. John Bowen Co.*[33] There, the subcontractor was allowed to recover for "preparation of samples, shop drawings, tests, and affidavits" that were required by the contract's provisions. John Bowen Co. relied on *Young v. Chicopee* and its requirement that work be "wrought into" the structure before recovery would be given. The court said that the "wrought into" test was merely a "variant" of the "inured to the benefit of the owner" requirement, and the term "benefit" could not be taken literally as was pointed out in the *M. Ahern* decision.

32. *Id.* at 40–41, 133 N.E.2d at 486–87.
33. 338 Mass. 394, 155 N.E.2d 437 (1959).

The court considered Fuller and Perdue, *The Reliance Interest in Contract Damages*.[34] It pointed out that John Bowen Co.'s responsibility for the impossibility was greater than the subcontractor's, although John Bowen Co.'s conduct was not so culpable as to render it liable for breach of contract. Later in its opinion, the court speaks of John Bowen Co.'s "fault."

The court noted that the efforts in preparation for performance involved in the case were not solely within the discretion and control of the subcontractor, as they were to be approved by John Bowen Co. These samples, shop drawings, and tests, by their very nature, could not be "wrought into" the structure. Under all these circumstances, the court was not disposed to "extend" the rule of *Young v. Chicopee* and deny recovery. The court concluded:

> A combination of factors peculiar to this case justifies such a holding without laying down the broader principle that in every case recovery may be had for payments made or obligations reasonably incurred in preparation for performance where further performance is rendered impossible without fault by either party.... [T]he damages to be assessed are limited solely to the fair value of those acts done in conformity with the specific request of the defendant as contained in the contract. Expenses incurred prior to the execution of the contract, such as those arising out of preparing the plaintiff's bid, are not to be considered.

The Supreme Judicial Court of Massachusetts returned to the problem of restitution and reliance in impossibility cases in *R. Zoppo Co., Inc. v. Commonwealth*.[35] Here, a construction company agreed to build a sewer for a sewage treatment plant in Boston. The contract called for a deep marine trench excavation, and the installation of "40 linear feet of 60-inch precast reinforced concrete subaqueous pressure diffuser pipe between designed stations on the outfall sewer line." The work involving this pipe was subcontracted to the Perini Corporation. The pipe was specially designed and required fabrication of special forms for its manufacture. It had no salvage value since its only possible use was in performance of the contract. Perini, following the requirements of the prime contract, submitted to the Metropolitan District Commission's engineer detailed drawings for the 60-inch pipe, and they were approved.

After the pipe was manufactured and delivered to the job site, tidal actions were discovered that in the opinion of the engineer required the final 24 linear feet of pipe to be deleted from the job. The Commission stored the deleted pipe.

The Massachusetts court found that performance in full was excused by impossibility. It then said:

> We hold that this case is governed by *Albre Marble & Tile Co., Inc. v. John Bowen Co., Inc.*.... There, as here, preliminary samples, shop drawings, and so forth, were prepared under a clause similar to that appearing in the contract

---

34. 46 YALE L.J. 52, 373 (1936–37).
35. 353 Mass. 401, 232 N.E.2d 346 (1967).

we discuss. There, as here, the labor and materials for which action was brought were not actually wrought into the structure but the preparatory efforts of the contractor were under the supervision of the defendant.... [I]t appears just, having regard to all the circumstances of the case ... that the petitioner here may recover for those expenditures that it made pursuant to the specific request of the Commission.

Is the *Zoppo* case just an application of the doctrine of *Albre Marble* or is it a major extension? Does it overrule whatever *Albre Marble* left of *Young v. Chicopee*?

Valuing the recovery under contracts discharged by impossibility: Suppose a court decides that impossibility excuses performance under a contract. It also decides that a party can recover for preparation or part performance under a reliance or benefit theory. How should it value the work? The Restatement (Second) of Contracts § 371 says that "as justice requires" a court may measure "benefit" either by what it would have cost to buy the performance elsewhere or by "the extent to which the other party's property has been increased in value or his other interests advanced."

Few cases deal with this issue. In a New Hampshire case,[36] the court awarded a portion of the contract price measured by a fraction comprised of the ratio of the costs of completing the work to the anticipated total cost. Is this a formula suggested by the Restatement (Second)? By contrast, in *R. Zoppo Co., Inc. v. Commonwealth*,[37] mentioned earlier, the court found that plaintiff, who had performed work in good faith that was rendered valueless by tidal action, to be entitled to the costs incurred in doing the work, including a reasonable profit.

Loss splitting as the solution: A number of writers have suggested that "benefit" and "reliance loss" are inappropriate concepts when a contract has been excused by impossibility. Losses should be shared in such cases.[38] The writer of a Comment in the *University of Chicago Law Review* gives the following example:

> Plaintiff has agreed to install an elevator in defendant's building. The contract price is $2,500. Nothing has been said about time or terms of payment. When the plaintiff has expended $800 in preparing to install the elevator, but before any part of the installation has been made, the building is destroyed by accidental fire. The preparations have consisted primarily of procuring and readying specialized materials that were to be used in the installation and which, because of their specialized nature and adaptation, have a present market value of only $100. While it is clear that further performance on the contract would be excused, under present loss distribution schemes ... the

---

36. Anderson v. Shattuck, 76 N.H. 240, 81 A. 781 (1911).

37. 353 Mass. 401, 232 N.E.2d 346 (1967).

38. *See* Comment, *Loss Splitting in Contract Litigation*, 18 U. Chi. L. Rev. 153, 157 (1951); Malcolm Sharp, *Promissory Liability II*, 7 U. Chi. L. Rev. 250, 269 (1940); Arthur Corbin, *Frustration of Contract in the United States of America*, 29 J. Comp. Legis. & Int'l L. (3rd Series, Part III–IV) 1, 8 (1947); Note, *Less Distribution in War-Time Impossibility of Performance*, 59 Yale L.J. 1511; Comment, *Quasi-Contract—Impossibility of Performance—Restitution of Money Paid or Benefits Conferred Where Further Performance Has Been Excused*, 46 Mich. L. Rev. 401, 421 (1948).

plaintiff would probably bear the complete loss for the materials purchased and work done. Under a principle of equal sharing of essential reliance losses, since the net loss is $700 [$800 expenditures less the $100 salvage], the plaintiff could recover $350 from the defendant.[39]

To what extent does this note on restitution actually offer a variety of loss-sharing schemes when a contract's value is destroyed by an unanticipated event? On the facts of the example in the University of Chicago Comment, why shouldn't the elevator contractor share some of the owner's loss from the fire that destroyed the building? Why should the elevator contractor be entitled to add to the loss suffered by the owner? From this perspective can we view the "wrought into" test as a kind of rough loss-sharing scheme that also has the virtue of some degree of certainty as compared to the Massachusetts recovery of some essential reliance loss in some cases?

A British solution to the problems: In *Fibrosa Spolka Akcyjna v. Fairbairn Lawson Combe Barbour, Ltd.,*[40] the House of Lords considered the impact of World War II on a commercial contract. In July 1939, Fairbairn, an English manufacturer of textile machinery, contracted to supply machinery to Fibrosa, a Polish textile manufacturer. Fairbairn was to build specially designed flax-hackling machines in England and install them in Gdynia in Poland. Fibrosa paid £1,000 as a down payment and was to pay £3,800 on delivery.

In August 1939, Germany invaded Poland, and Great Britain declared war against Germany. On September 7, 1939, Fibrosa's English representative asked for return of the £1,000 down payment since delivery of the hackling machines could not take place in Poland because of the German occupation and the English statutes prohibiting trading with the enemy. Fairbairn refused to return the down payment because considerable work had been done on the machines.

Fibrosa sued for the down payment. Fairbairn defended, asserting that performance of the contract was excused because it was frustrated by the German occupation of Gdynia. It said that Fibrosa had no right to the down payment because of several 1900 British decisions that said an excuse did not wipe out the contract retroactively, but only relieved the parties from further obligations. The Court of Appeal said that it hoped the House of Lords would overrule these earlier decisions and adopt "the more civilized rule of Roman and Scottish law." The Court of Appeal assumed that it would have to determine how much of the £1,000 Fairbairn should be allowed to retain to compensate it for its reliance losses and how much of the sum was "a pure windfall" and should be returned to Fibrosa.

The House of Lords did overrule the earlier cases, but awarded Fibrosa the entire £1,000. It said that the consideration had failed totally and, as a matter of quasi contract, Fairbairn had no claim to the money since its expenditures had not benefited Fibrosa at the time performance was excused. The House of Lords conceded that its position might work an injustice where there had been great reliance expenses that

39. 18 U. CHI. L. REV. 153, 157 (1951).
40. [1943] A.C. 32.

had not produced a benefit, but the common law did not furnish the court with a yardstick with which to apportion losses. "It must be for the legislature to decide whether provision should be made for an equitable apportionment of prepaid moneys...." However, we should note that Lord Roche mentioned that according to Fairbairn, the machines as far as completed were "realizable without loss."

Parliament reacted to the *Fibrosa* case by enacting The Reform [Frustrated Contracts] Act of 1943.[41] We can summarize a complicated statute as follows:

(1) The Act provides for recovery measured by benefits conferred (restitution) where there have been such benefits.

(2) The Act has no provision for equitably apportioning reliance losses if the seller has not received a down payment or if the buyer has not yet become liable to make payments.

(3) If there has been a down payment, the Act provides that a court "may, if it considers it just to do so having regard to all the circumstances of the case," apportion the losses following frustration or impossibility although these losses produce no increase in the assets (tangible benefit) to the other party.

(a) Little direction is given for the exercise of this discretion.

(b) The court is directed not to give weight to whether either party has secured insurance.

The classic case applying the Frustrated Contracts Act is *B.P. Exploration Ltd. v. Hunt.*[42] Nelson Bunker Hunt owned a concession giving him the right to drill for oil in Libya. He was required to start drilling by December 1960, but he lacked the resources and experience needed to explore and develop the concession. He entered an agreement under which B.P. Exploration Co., a wholly owned subsidiary of British Petroleum, would explore and develop the concession. The Court described the arrangement:

Obviously the expenditure incurred in the exploration and development of an oil field can be enormous. Under the agreement, however, up to the time when the field came on stream, all funds had to be advanced by B.P. Half such expenditure would be incurred for Mr. Hunt's account; but under the contract B.P. had no right of recoupment in respect of Mr. Hunt's share of the expenditure until the oil came on stream. All oil produced from the field belonged to both B.P. and Mr. Hunt, and was to be shared equally between them, subject to the provision that B.P. was entitled to take and receive a

---

41. 6 & 7 Geo. 6, c. 40. SWAN AND REITER, CONTRACTS 470–471 (3d ed. 1985), tell us that the Frustrated Contracts Act "was adopted by the Uniform Law Conference of Canada, and formed the basis for the legislation of all common law provinces except Nova Scotia, Saskatchewan, and British Columbia. The latter province has legislation that is special to it; the others have retained the common law. The model act was largely adopted in the other Canadian provinces." Swan and Reiter also note that the British Columbia Act differs principally in the definition of the term "benefit." The British Columbia statute defines it as something done under a contract, whether or not a benefit is received by the other party.

42. [1979] 1 W.L.R. 783, *aff'd* [1982] 1 All ER 925.

portion of Mr. Hunt's share of the oil, such proportion being called reimbursement oil, in order to recoup both the expenditure incurred by them for Mr. Hunt's account before the field came on stream ... plus 25 percent. Once the field came on stream, Mr. Hunt had to bear half the cost of production, and of further development of the field.

A large and very valuable oil field was discovered and developed at great expense. A large amount of oil was taken from the field, but Mr. Hunt's obligation to B.P. for exploration and development had not been covered. In 1969, a revolution overthrew the government of King Idris of Libya and substituted the government of the Revolutionary Command Council, led by Colonel Gaddafi. In 1971, the Libyan government expropriated B.P.'s assets, and in 1973, it expropriated Mr. Hunt's.

The court found that the work in exploration and development was a benefit to Mr. Hunt. It then awarded B.P. an amount which was "just." It considered Mr. Hunt's offsetting claims against B.P. B.P. was awarded a balance of $15,575,823 and £8,922,060 (the award was partly in dollars and partly in pounds sterling).

Justice Goff wrote a 68-page opinion. He noted:

> [I]n addition to difficult and novel questions of law, the case involves substantial questions of fact and of accounting procedure. The sums involved are enormous; B.P.'s claim was advanced in a number of alternative ways, the sum claimed varying from nearly $45,000,000 to nearly $230,000,000. Furthermore, allegations made by Mr. Hunt relating to the manner in which B.P. developed the oil field led to an investigation of almost the entire history of the exploration, appraisal, and development of the field, and the production of oil from the field. This investigation required a substantial body of evidence, much of it technical; and the documents before the court, which were very largely concerned with these allegations by Mr. Hunt, were very numerous—I was told that there were over 15,000 documents in court. Many of these were of a technical nature; and in any event they represented only the tip of the iceberg of documents disclosed on discovery. Only by reason of the good sense and restraint shown by counsel on both sides, and the efficiency of their instructing solicitors, was it possible for a so substantial piece of litigation to be kept under control and for the hearing to take no longer than 57 days.

In dealing with whether the statute authorized the court to take into account the time value of money, Justice Goff noted that the lawyers described the consequences as involving "only $10 million."

Justice Goff was very critical of the Act itself, saying:

> [A]ll these difficulties would have been avoided if the legislature had thought it right to treat the services themselves as the benefit. [That is, to allow compensation for essential reliance whether or not defendant ultimately gained from it.] In the opinion of many commentators, it would be more just to do so; after all, the services in question have been requested by the defendant,

who normally takes the risk that they may prove worthless, from whatever cause. In the example I have given of the building destroyed by fire, there is much to be said for the view that the builder should be paid for the work he has done, unless he has (for example by agreeing to insure the works) taken upon himself the risk of destruction by fire. But my task is to construe the Act as it stands. On the true construction of the Act, it is in my judgment clear that the defendant's benefit must, in an appropriate case, be identified as the end product of the plaintiff's services, despite the difficulties which this construction creates, difficulties which are met again when one comes to value the benefit.

How should losses caused by expropriation of a joint venture of this sort be allocated among the parties? Does the Frustrated Contracts Act give a court adequate guidance in solving the problem? Recall that one may look to essential reliance losses only when there has been a down payment or the buyer has become liable to pay a sum of money. In other cases, a court must find a benefit, value it, and then determine a "just" allocation of this amount among the parties. Beale, Bishop, and Furmston note:[43]

> As [Justice] Robert Goff points out, the Act does not enable the court to put the parties into the position they would have been in if the contract had been performed (*e.g.*, no recovery of lost profit), nor to restore them to their pre-contractual position. Thus the licensees in *Taylor v. Caldwell* would still get nothing for the wasted advertising.... Perhaps this is right: the court has already determined that neither party was better able to prevent the frustrating event, and maybe each is the best insurer of his own expenses, since he alone knows the amount of them.

Furthermore, we can ask whether courts have the capability to carry out the task given to them by the statute. Even concluding that Justice Goff did a splendid job, we must consider spending 57 days of court time plus all the lawyering that went into this process.[44] We may wonder about the impact of the case on contracts to develop oil concessions in the future. Should we expect parties to provide in their contracts ways to deal with the consequences of expropriation, or are answers to this possibility so complex that parties will tend to avoid them by using vague and general phrases about equitable adjustments?

Donald Harris, David Campbell, and Roger Halson[45] are very critical of the British Frustrated Contracts Act and the decision in the *B.P. Exploration* case. They comment:

---

43. BEALE, BISHOP & FURMSTON, CONTRACT: CASES AND MATERIALS 311 (London 1985).

44. Macaulay commented: "When we add what both parties paid lawyers and others to the cost of occupying the court for that amount of time, the case seems more like burning money ceremonially than dispute resolution." Stewart Macaulay, *Renegotiations and Settlements: Dr. Pangloss's Notes on the Margins of David Campbell's Papers*, 29 CARDOZO L. REV. 261, 283 (2007).

45. DONALD HARRIS, DAVID CAMPBELL & ROGER HALSON, REMEDIES IN CONTRACT AND TORT 253–254 (2002).

One might wonder why a position as unsatisfactory as that left by LR(FC)A[46] 1943 has been allowed to remain the law, and part at least of the answer has been that to a significant degree parties do not have recourse to the formal law to govern these aspects of economic action. Competent commercial parties, faced with the absurdity of the law of common mistake at common law or the weakness of the remedies for frustration, have included modification provisions in contracts of sufficient value and complexity to make this worthwhile. These clauses provide for non-binding alternative dispute resolution or arbitration … which give the parties far more flexibility to apportion loss than any conceivable restitutionary recasting of the frustration rules might do. Should provisions of this sort not prove adequate, such empirical evidence as is available shows that the parties ignore the terms of their contracts to reach superior outcomes than those contracts provide. The extremely limited scope of and the very inadequate remedies for common mistake and frustration provide a great incentive for parties to follow either or both of these courses, and the absolute paucity of cases on LR(FC)A 1943 would appear to be evidence that they are doing so.

How would cases such as *Fibrosa* and *B.P. Exploration* be decided in the United States? There is no clear answer. Indeed, Nelson Bunker Hunt argued that the contract in the *B.P. Exploration* case was governed by the law of Texas rather than the British statute.[47] If Texas law had no clear legal rules that were in point, why did Hunt's lawyers want the case moved to Texas?

Generally, American courts have looked for a tangible benefit conferred by performance before it was excused. However, outside of the area of building repair contracts, there is little authority. Nonetheless, in *Angus v. Scully*,[48] plaintiffs were to move a house from where it stood to another lot several blocks away. The house was moved about halfway and then left at the end of the workday. That night the house burned and was destroyed. The services rendered in moving the house part of the way to its new location were held to be a benefit to the owner, and plaintiffs recovered their fair-market value.

Official Comment 6 to § 2-615 of the UCC says: "In situations in which neither sense nor justice is served by either answer when the issue is posed in flat terms of 'excuse' or 'no excuse,' adjustment under the various provisions of this Article is necessary, especially the sections on good faith, on insecurity and assurance and on the reading of all provisions in light of their purposes, and the general policy of this Act to use equitable principles in furtherance of commercial standards and good faith." Could a court reach results similar to the British Frustrated Contracts Act under UCC § 2-615 and its official comments?

Notice that § 2-615 as such does not cover the typical frustration situation where delivery can be made on time but, because of changed circumstances, it has lost its

---

46. Law Reform (Frustrated Contracts) Act.
47. *See* [1976] 1 W.L.R. 788.
48. 176 Mass. 357, 57 N.E. 674 (1900).

value to the buyer. The text of § 2-615 speaks only of a seller's excuse. Official Comment 9, however, says:

> Even where notice is given by the buyer that the supplies are needed to fill a specific contract of a normal commercial kind, commercial understanding does not see such a supply contract as conditioned on the continuance of the buyer's further contract for outlet. On the other hand, where the buyer's contract is in reasonable commercial understanding conditioned on a definite and specific venture or assumption as, for instance, a war procurement subcontract known to be based on a prime contract which is subject to termination, or a supply contract for a particular construction venture, the reason of the present section may well apply and entitle the buyer to the exemption.

B. IMPRACTICABILITY, THE UCC, AND LEGAL REALISM, CHECKED BY DEMANDS FOR FORM AND CERTAINTY

1. "[M]ade Impracticable by the Occurrence of a Contingency the Non-Occurrence of Which Was a Basic Assumption on Which the Contract Was Made"

Students who remember the beginning of Volume I will see that the following case does not involve a transaction in goods but a contract for performing a service. Nonetheless, Judge Wright draws on Uniform Commercial Code § 2-615's approach. How does his analysis differ from that found in *Taylor v. Caldwell?*

TRANSATLANTIC FINANCING CORP. v. UNITED STATES

United States Court of Appeals, District of Columbia Circuit
363 F.2d 312 (1966)

J. SKELLY WRIGHT.

[On July 26, 1956, Egypt had taken over operation of the Suez Canal. On October 2, 1956, the U.S. contracted with Transatlantic Financing Corporation for the shipment of a full cargo of wheat aboard the S.S. Christos, a ship operated by Transatlantic, to a port in Iran. On October 27th, the S.S. Christos sailed from Galveston headed for Iran on a course that would have taken it through Gibraltar and the Suez Canal. On October 29 Israel invaded Egypt. On October 31, Great Britain and France invaded the Suez Canal Zone. On November 2, Egypt obstructed the Canal with sunken vessels and closed it to traffic. On November 7 a representative of Transatlantic contacted the U.S. and sought a promise that if the shipment of grain were shipped around the Cape of Good Hope that additional compensation would be paid to Transatlantic. The U.S. representative advised Transatlantic that they were expected to complete the charter, but that they should expect no additional compensation. Transatlantic made a claim against the U.S. for the additional costs it incurred when it proceeded to Iran via the Cape of Good Hope. The District Court dismissed the claim, and the D.C. Circuit affirmed.]

... Transatlantic's claim is based on the following train of argument. The charter was a contract for a voyage from the Gulf Port to Iran. Admiralty principles and practices, especially stemming from the doctrine of deviation, require us to imply into the contract the term that the voyage was to be performed by the "usual and customary" route. The usual and customary route from Texas to Iran was, at the time of contract, via Suez, so the contract was for a voyage from Texas to Iran via Suez. When Suez was closed this contract became impossible to perform. Consequently, appellant's argument continues, when Transatlantic delivered the cargo by going around the Cape of Good Hope, in compliance with the Government's demand under claim of right, it conferred a benefit upon the United States for which it should be paid in *quantum meruit*.

The doctrine of impossibility of performance has gradually been freed from the earlier fictional and unrealistic strictures of such tests as the "implied term" and the parties' "contemplation." Page, *The Development of the Doctrine of Impossibility of Performance*, 18 MICH. L. REV. 589, 596 (1920). *See generally* 6 CORBIN, CONTRACTS §§ 1320–1372 (rev. ed. 1962); 6 WILLISTON, CONTRACTS §§ 1931–1979 (rev. ed. 1938). It is now recognized that "'A thing is impossible in legal contemplation when it is not practicable; and a thing is impracticable when it can only be done at an excessive and unreasonable cost.'" *Mineral Park Land Co. v. Howard*, 172 Cal. 289, 293, 156 P. 458, L.R.A. 1916F, 1 (1916).... Uniform Commercial Code (U.L.A.) § 2-615, comment 3. The doctrine ultimately represents the ever-shifting line, drawn by courts hopefully responsive to commercial practices and mores, at which the community's interest in having contracts enforced according to their terms is outweighed by the commercial senselessness of requiring performance.[49] When the issue is raised, the court is asked to construct a condition of performance based on the changed circumstances, a process that involves at least three reasonably definable steps. First, a contingency— something unexpected—must have occurred. Second, the risk of the unexpected occurrence must not have been allocated either by agreement or by custom. Finally, occurrence of the contingency must have rendered performance commercially impracticable.[50] Unless the court finds these three requirements satisfied, the plea of impossibility must fail.

---

49. [1] While the impossibility issue rarely arises, as it has here, in a suit to recover the cost of an alternative method of performance, compare Annot., 84 A.L.R.2d 12, 19 (1962), there is nothing necessarily inconsistent in claiming commercial impracticability for the method of performance actually adopted; the concept of impracticability assumes performance was physically possible. Moreover, a rule making nonperformance a condition precedent to recovery would unjustifiably encourage disappointment of expectations.

50. [3] Compare Uniform Commercial Code § 2-615(a), which provides that, in the absence of an assumption of greater liability, delay or non-delivery by a seller is not a breach if performance as agreed is made "impracticable" by the occurrence of a "contingency" the non-occurrence of which was a "basic assumption on which the contract was made." To the extent this limits relief to "unforeseen"

The first requirement was met here. It seems reasonable, where no route is mentioned in a contract, to assume the parties expected performance by the usual and customary route at the time of contract. Since the usual and customary route from Texas to Iran at the time of contract was through Suez, closure of the Canal made impossible the expected method of performance. But this unexpected development raises rather than resolves the impossibility issue, which turns additionally on whether the risk of the contingency's occurrence had been allocated and, if not, whether performance by alternative routes was rendered impracticable.

Proof that the risk of a contingency's occurrence has been allocated may be expressed in or implied from the agreement. Such proof may also be found in the surrounding circumstances, including custom and usages of the trade. See 6 Corbin, *supra*, § 1339, at 394–397; 6 Williston, *supra*, § 1948, at 5457–5458. The contract in this case does not expressly condition performance upon availability of the Suez route. Nor does it specify "via Suez" or, on the other hand, "via Suez or Cape of Good Hope."[51] Nor are there provisions in the contract from which we may properly imply that the continued availability of Suez was a condition of performance. Nor is there anything in custom or trade usage, or in the surrounding circumstances generally, which would support our constructing a condition of performance. The numerous cases requiring performance around the Cape when Suez was closed, *see, e.g., Ocean Tramp Tankers Corp. v. V/O Sovfracht (The Eugenia)*, [1964] 2 Q.B. 226, and cases cited therein, indicate that the Cape route is generally regarded as an alternative means of performance. So the implied expectation that the route would be via Suez is hardly adequate proof of an allocation to the promisee of the risk of closure. In some cases,

---

circumstances, comment 1, see the discussion below, and compare Uniform Commercial Code § 2-614(1). There may be a point beyond which agreement cannot go, Uniform Commercial Code § 2-615, comment 8, presumably the point at which the obligation would be "manifestly unreasonable," § 1-102(3), in bad faith, § 1-203 [Eds.: *See* §§ 1-103b), 1-304 for the analogous provision in Article 1 as revised in 2001.], or unconscionable, § 2-302. For an application of these provisions, *see* Judge Friendly's opinion in United States v. Wegematic Corporation, 2d Cir., 360 F.2d 674 (1966).

51. [7] In Glidden Co. v. Hellenic Lines, Ltd., 2d Cir. 275 F.2d 253 (1960), the charter was for transportation of materials from India to America "via Suez Canal or Cape of Good Hope, or Panama Canal," and the court held performance was not "frustrated." In his discussion of this case, Professor Corbin states: "Except for the provision for an alternative route, the defendant would have been discharged, for the reason that the parties contemplated an open Suez Canal as a specific condition or means of performance." 6 CORBIN, *supra*, § 1339, at 399 n.57. Appellant claims this supports its argument, since the Suez route was contemplated as usual and customary. But there is obviously a difference, in deciding whether a contract allocates the risk of a contingency's occurrence, between a contract specifying no route and a contract specifying Suez. We think that when Professor Corbin said, "Except for the provision for an alternative route," he was referring, not to the entire *provision*— "via Suez Canal or Cape of Good Hope" etc.—but to the fact that *an alternative route* had been provided for. Moreover, in determining what Corbin meant when he said "the parties contemplated an open Suez Canal as a specific condition or means of performance," consideration must be given to the fact, recited by Corbin, that in *Glidden* the parties were specifically aware when the contract was made the Canal might be closed, and the promisee had refused to include a clause excusing performance in the event of closure. Corbin's statement, therefore, is most accurately read as referring to cases in which a route is specified after negotiations reflecting the parties' awareness that the usual and customary route might become unavailable. *Compare* Held v. Goldsmith, 153 La. 598, 96 So. 272 (1919).

even an express expectation may not amount to a condition of performance.[52] The doctrine of deviation supports our assumption that parties normally expect performance by the usual and customary route, but it adds nothing beyond this that is probative of an allocation of the risk.

If anything, the circumstances surrounding this contract indicate that the risk of the Canal's closure may be deemed to have been allocated to Transatlantic. We know or may safely assume that the parties were aware, as were most commercial men with interests affected by the Suez situation ... that the Canal might become a dangerous area. No doubt the tension affected freight rates, and it is arguable that the risk of closure became part of the dickered terms. Uniform Commercial Code § 2-615, comment 8. We do not deem the risk of closure so allocated, however. Foreseeability or even recognition of a risk does not necessarily prove its allocation. Compare Uniform Commercial Code § 2-615, Comment 1; Restatement, Contracts § 457 (1932). Parties to a contract are not always able to provide for all the possibilities of which they are aware, sometimes because they cannot agree, often simply because they are too busy. Moreover, that some abnormal risk was contemplated is probative but does not necessarily establish an allocation of the risk of the contingency which actually occurs. In this case, for example, nationalization by Egypt of the Canal Corporation and formation of the Suez Users Group did not necessarily indicate that the Canal would be blocked even if a confrontation resulted.[53] The surrounding circumstances do indicate, however, a willingness by Transatlantic to assume abnormal risks, and this fact should legitimately cause us to judge the impracticability of performance by an alternative route in stricter terms than we would were the contingency unforeseen.

We turn then to the question whether occurrence of the contingency rendered performance commercially impracticable under the circumstances of this case. The goods shipped were not subject to harm from the longer, less temperate Southern route. The vessel and crew were fit to proceed around the Cape.[54] Transatlantic was no less able than the United States to purchase insurance to cover the contingency's occurrence. If anything, it is more reasonable to expect owner-operators of vessels

---

52. [9] Uniform Commercial Code § 2-614(1) provides: "Where without fault of either party ... the *agreed* manner of delivery ... becomes commercially impracticable but a commercially reasonable substitute is available, such substitute performance must be tendered and accepted." (Emphasis added.).

53. [12] Sources cited in the briefs indicate formation of the Suez Canal Users Association on October 1, 1956, was viewed in some quarters as an implied threat of force. *See* N.Y. TIMES, Oct. 2, 1956, p. 1, col. 1, noting, on the day the charter in this case was executed, that "Britain has declared her freedom to use force as a last resort if peaceful methods fail to achieve a satisfactory settlement." Secretary of State Dulles was able, however, to view the statement as evidence of the canal users' "dedication to a just and peaceful solution." *The Suez Problem* 369–370 (Department of State Pub. 1956).

54. [13] The issue of impracticability should no doubt be "an objective determination of whether the promise can reasonably be performed rather than a subjective inquiry into the promisor's capability of performing as agreed." Symposium, *The Uniform Commercial Code and Contract Law: Some Selected Problems*, 105 U. PA. L. REV. 836, 880, 887 (1957). Dealers should not be excused because of less than normal capabilities. But if both parties are aware of a dealer's limited capabilities, no objective determination would be complete without taking into account this fact.

to insure against the hazards of war. They are in the best position to calculate the cost of performance by alternative routes (and therefore to estimate the amount of insurance required), and are undoubtedly sensitive to international troubles that uniquely affect the demand for and cost of their services. The only factor operating here in appellant's favor is the added expense, allegedly $43,972.00 above and beyond the contract price of $305,842.92, of extending a 10,000-mile voyage by approximately 3,000 miles. While it may be an overstatement to say that increased cost and difficulty of performance never constitute impracticability, to justify relief there must be more of a variation between expected cost and the cost of performing by an available alternative than is present in this case, where the promisor can legitimately be presumed to have accepted some degree of abnormal risk, and where impracticability is urged on the basis of added expense alone.[55]

We conclude, therefore, as have most other courts considering related issues arising out of the Suez closure, that performance of this contract was not rendered legally impossible. Even if we agreed with appellant, its theory of relief seems untenable. When performance of a contract is deemed impossible it is a nullity.... If the performance rendered has value, recovery in *quantum meruit* for the entire performance is proper. But here Transatlantic has collected its contract price, and now seeks *quantum meruit* relief for the additional expense of the trip around the Cape. If the contract is a nullity, Transatlantic's theory of relief should have been *quantum meruit* for the entire trip, rather than only for the extra expense. Transatlantic attempts to take its profit on the contract, and then force the Government to absorb the cost of the additional voyage.[56] When impracticability without fault occurs, the law seeks an equitable solution, see 6 Corbin, *supra*, § 1321, and *quantum meruit* is one of its potent devices to achieve this end. There is no interest in casting the entire burden of commercial disaster on one party in order to preserve the other's profit. Apparently the contract price in this case was advantageous enough to deter appellant from taking a stance on damages consistent with its theory of liability. In any event, there is no basis for relief. Affirmed.

NOTES AND QUESTIONS

1. *Impracticability and risk assumption:* Judge Wright tells us:

> We know or may safely assume that the parties were aware, as were most commercial men with interests affected by the Suez situation ... that the Canal

55. [15] See Uniform Commercial Code § 2-615, comment 4: "Increased cost alone does not excuse performance unless the rise in cost is due to some unforeseen contingency which alters the essential nature of the performance."

56. [17] The argument that the Uniform Commercial Code requires the buyer to pay the additional cost of performance by a commercially reasonable substitute was advanced and rejected in Symposium, *supra* note 13, 105 U. Pa. L. Rev. at 884 n.205. In Dillon v. United States, 156 F. Supp. 719, 140 Ct. Cl. 508 (1957), relief was afforded for some of the cost of delivering hay from a commercially unreasonable distance, but the suit was one in which the plaintiff had suffered losses far in excess of the relief given.

might become a dangerous area. No doubt the tension affected freight rates, and it is arguable that the risk of closure became part of the dickered terms.

Professor Schlegel tells us: "The seizure of the Canal sent rates up a bit more (index 70.5 to 72.5) and the freight shortage and conference rate increase in mid-September further raised rates (72 to 74.5). In late October, rates broke sharply upward to the point where the index reached 96 in early December."[57]

Would Judge Wright require the agent of Transatlantic Financing Corporation, who negotiated the charter of the ship, to actually know that the rates had increased because of the risk of the Canal closing, which would require the much longer voyage around Africa? Professor Eisenberg argues: "[I]t should be no defense to an individual seller who has received the risk premium that was impounded into her price, that she did not personally perceive that the event was foreshadowed."[58]

2. *The likely impact of UCC § 2-615:* If the *Transatlantic Financing Corp.* case reflects the way most courts will use § 2-615, is that statute likely to excuse performance very often? The late Professor Richard Speidel[59] argues that courts went from the formal approach found in cases such as *Taylor v. Caldwell* to § 2-615, which seems to call for a legal realist approach to these problems. Instead of looking for an "implied condition," courts take "at least three reasonably defined steps: First, a contingency—something unexpected—must have occurred. Second, the risk of the unexpected occurrence must not have been allocated either by agreement or by custom. Finally, the occurrence of the contingency must have rendered performance commercially impracticable." However, Speidel notes that the rise of law and economics and the interests many writers have today in certain clear rules to aid planning, has meant that courts today offer very little relief under § 2-615(a). Nonetheless, courts might change again to a more realist approach, and so subsection (a) might offer a potential resource for excuses being given in more cases in the future.

A seller may have a better chance of an excuse under the second part of § 2-615(a) when its performance has been made impracticable "by compliance in good faith with any applicable foreign or domestic governmental regulation or order whether or not it later proves to be invalid." Official Comment 10 notes, however, that "governmental interference cannot excuse unless it truly 'supervenes' in such a manner as to be beyond the seller's assumption of risk. And any action by the party claiming

---

57. John Henry Schlegel, *Of Nuts, and Ships, and Sealing Wax, Suez, and Frustrating Things—The Doctrine of Impossibility of Performance*, 23 RUTGERS L. REV. 419, 430 n.65 (1968).

58. Melvin A. Eisenberg, *Impossibility, Impracticability, and Frustration*, 218 J. LEGAL ANALYSIS 207 (2009). Professor Eisenberg cites Official Comment 8 to Section 2-615: "[T]he exemptions of this section do not apply when the contingency in question is sufficiently foreshadowed at the time of contracting to be included among the business risks which are fairly to be regarded as part of the dickered terms, either consciously or as a matter of reasonable, commercial interpretation from the circumstances."

59. RICHARD E. SPEIDEL, CONTRACTS IN CRISIS: EXCUSE DOCTRINE AND RETROSPECTIVE GOVERNMENT ACTS 14–17, 164 (2007).

excuse which causes or colludes in inducing the governmental action preventing his performance would be in breach of good faith and would destroy his exemption."

3. *The virtues of uniform and relatively certain law:* Is it important that the *Transatlantic Financing Corp.* case followed the British decisions denying relief based on the closing of the Suez Canal? Are there reasons in the international shipping area to have relatively certain uniform rules about such things as excuses?

4. *Industry response:* Victor Goldberg asserts: "Perusal of current shipping contracts indicates that the basic shipping form contracts were not altered after the *Suez* decisions. Closing of the canal is not an enumerated excuse in *force majeure* clauses. Hence, it would appear that the courts got it right."[60] Why does Goldberg say that this failure to change standard form contract clauses means that the "courts got it right"? What does he assume that courts should do when one party seeks an excuse because of an event such as the closing of the Suez Canal?

2. The Threat of Terrorism

7200 SCOTTSDALE ROAD GENERAL PARTNERS v. KUHN FARM MACHINERY, INC.

Arizona Court of Appeals
184 Ariz. 341, 909 P.2d 408 (1995)

Toci, J.

Kuhn Farm Machinery, Inc. ("Kuhn") contracted with 7200 Scottsdale Road General Partners, dba Scottsdale Plaza Resort (the "resort"), to use the resort's facilities for a convention at which Kuhn's European personnel were to present new products to Kuhn's dealers and employees. In this appeal from the granting of a summary judgment for Kuhn, we consider the following issue: did the risk to air travel to Scottsdale, Arizona, posed by the Gulf War and Saddam Hussein's threats of worldwide terrorism, substantially frustrate the purpose of the contract?

Reversing the trial court's grant of summary judgment for Kuhn, we hold as follows. First, the resort did not contract with the understanding that Kuhn's European personnel were crucial to the success of Kuhn's convention. Thus, even if the attendance of the Europeans at the Scottsdale convention was thwarted by the threat to international air travel, their nonattendance did not excuse Kuhn's performance under the contract. Neither did the risk to domestic air travel posed by the Gulf War entitle Kuhn to relief. Although that risk may have rendered the convention uneconomical for Kuhn, the threat to domestic air travel did not rise to the level of "substantial frustration." Finally, Kuhn's cancellation based on the perceived risk of terrorism was not an objectively reasonable response to an extraordinary and specific threat. Consequently, Kuhn is not entitled to relief on the theory of "apprehension of impossibility."

---

60. Victor Goldberg, *Impossibility and Related Excuses*, 144 J. Inst. Theoretical Econ. 100 (1988).

I. Facts and Procedural History

A. Background

On February 9, 1990, the resort and Kuhn signed a letter agreement providing that Kuhn would hold its North American dealers' convention at the resort. The agreement required the resort to reserve, at group rates, a block of 190 guest rooms and banquet and meeting rooms for the period from March 26, 1991, to March 30, 1991. Kuhn, in turn, guaranteed rental of a minimum number of guest rooms and food and beverage revenue of at least $8,000 from the use of the meeting and banquet rooms.

The agreement contained remedies protecting the resort if Kuhn canceled the meeting. Kuhn was required to pay liquidated damages for any decrease after January 25, 1991, of 10 percent or more in the reserved room block. Additionally, the resort agreed to accept individual room cancellations up to 72 hours prior to arrival without penalty so long as total attrition did not exceed 5 percent. The agreement also provided that, because the loss of food and beverage revenues and of room rentals resulting from cancellation were incapable of estimation, cancellation would result in assessment of liquidated damages.

Because Kuhn refused to hold its dealers' meeting at the resort at the time specified in the agreement, the resort sued for breach of contract, seeking the liquidated damages provided for in the agreement. The resort then moved for partial summary judgment to obtain a ruling in its favor on the issue of liability. Kuhn filed a cross-motion for summary judgment, alleging that its performance was discharged or suspended pursuant to the doctrines of impracticability of performance and frustration of purpose.

B. Additional Facts Established by Kuhn's Motion

In support of its motion for summary judgment, Kuhn offered the following facts. Kuhn S.A., the parent of Kuhn, is headquartered in France, where it manufactures farm machinery....

Kuhn and Kuhn S.A. planned to use the North American dealers' convention to introduce new products to Kuhn's salespeople and dealers, stimulate enthusiasm for the new products, and provide its salespeople and dealers with information to effectively market and sell the products. To accomplish these goals, Kuhn invited its top 200 independent dealers from the United States and Canada ("North Americans"), as well as some of its overseas suppliers, to attend the meeting. Approximately 25 Kuhn and Kuhn S.A. employees and suppliers from the United States, Europe, and Australia were to host the convention and present the new products.

Kuhn considered the overseas personnel ("Europeans") crucial to the presentation and success of the dealers' meeting. Of all of Kuhn's personnel, they were the most familiar with the design, manufacture, and production of the new products. Kuhn intended the Europeans to play the primary role in presenting the products and leading the discussions at the convention.

On August 2, 1990, Iraq invaded Kuwait. A few days later, the United States began sending troops to the Middle East. On January 16, 1991, the United States and allied forces, in Operation Desert Storm, engaged in war with Iraq. As a result, Saddam Hussein and other high-ranking Iraqi officials threatened terrorist acts against the countries that sought to prevent Iraq's takeover of Kuwait. Hussein stated: "Hundreds of thousands of volunteers ... [would become] missiles to be thrown against the enemy ..." and "the theater of operations would [include] every freedom fighter who can reach out to harm the aggressors in the whole world...."

Kuhn discovered that, apparently because of the war, convention attendance would not meet expectations. Many of Kuhn's employees who were to attend the meeting were concerned about the safety of air travel.... Because tentative registration was lower than Kuhn had anticipated when it signed the agreement, in late January—two months prior to the date of the planned convention—Kuhn reduced the reserved room block by more than 25 percent.

Interest in the proposed convention continued to wane. From February 4 to February 14, 1991, several of Kuhn's top dealerships who had won all-expense-paid trips to the convention canceled their plans to attend. By mid-February, 11 of the top 50 dealerships with expense-paid trips had either canceled their plans to send people to the convention or failed to sign up.

Kuhn S.A. wrote to the resort on February 14, 1991, requesting cooperation in rescheduling the meeting for a later date. Among other things, the letter stated that Kuhn was concerned with the safety of its people, that the dealers were reluctant to travel, and that attendance had decreased to a level making it uneconomical to hold the convention.

Without waiting for the resort's response, Kuhn decided to postpone the scheduled meeting. On February 18, 1991, Kuhn notified all potential convention participants that the dealers' meeting had been postponed. Although Kuhn and the resort did attempt to reschedule the meeting for the following year, the rescheduling negotiations broke down. The convention was never held at the resort.

C. The Resort's Response to Kuhn's Motion

The resort did not dispute Kuhn's description of the planned convention; rather, the resort contested the extent of the threat to air travel. Specifically, the resort noted that the articles cited by Kuhn indicated either that there was little risk or that the risk was primarily to overseas locations.

The resort also contested the inferences to be drawn from the facts presented by each party. The resort asserted that the facts did not establish that the threat of terrorism frustrated the ability of Kuhn associates to fly to Scottsdale. Although conceding that several dealers canceled because of fear of terrorism, the resort emphasized that nearly all of the approximately 150 dealers registered for the meeting signed up after the Operation Desert Storm attack on Iraq. In the resort's view, Kuhn's January 29, 1991, request for a reduction in the room block to 140 rooms impliedly reconfirmed the convention after the commencement of the war....

The trial court granted summary judgment to Kuhn, ruling that Kuhn proved both of its defenses.... The resort appeals from the summary judgment ruling....

II. Impracticability Distinguished from Frustration of Purpose

The trial court held that the contract was discharged under the doctrines of impracticability of performance and frustration of purpose. These are similar but distinct doctrines.... Impracticability of performance is ... utilized when certain events occurring after a contract is made constitute an impediment to performance by either party. *See* Restatement § 261. Traditionally, the doctrine has been applied to three categories of supervening events: death or incapacity of a person necessary for performance, destruction of a specific thing necessary for performance, and prohibition or prevention by law.

On the other hand, frustration of purpose deals with "the problem that arises when a change in circumstances makes one party's performance virtually worthless to the other...." Restatement § 265 cmt. a. "Performance remains possible but the expected value of performance to the party seeking to be excused has been destroyed by a fortuitous event, which supervenes to cause an actual but not literal failure of consideration." *Lloyd v. Murphy*, 25 Cal. 2d 48, 153 P.2d 47, 50 (Cal. 1944)....

Turning to the contract between Kuhn and the resort, Kuhn clearly has no claim for impossibility or impracticability.... Kuhn does not allege that it was impossible or impracticable to perform its contractual duty to make payment for the reserved facilities. Rather, it contends that the value of the resort's counterperformance — the furnishing of convention facilities — was rendered worthless because of the Gulf War's effect on convention attendance. This is a claim of frustration of purpose.

III. Frustration of Purpose

A. *Krell v. Henry*

The doctrine of frustration of purpose traces its roots to *Krell v. Henry*, [1903] 2 K.B. 740. There, the owner of a London apartment advertised it for rent to observe the King's coronation parade. Responding to the advertisement, the renter paid a deposit and agreed to rent the apartment for two days. When the coronation parade was postponed, the renter refused to pay the balance of the rent. The court held that the contract to rent the apartment was premised on an implied condition — the occurrence of the King's coronation parade.... Accordingly, when the parade was canceled, the renter's duty to perform was discharged by the frustration of his purpose in entering the contract. Several aspects of *Krell* are worth noting. First, the owner of the apartment was prepared to render the entire performance promised by him.... Second, the renter could have performed by simply paying the rental fee for the apartment. In other words, there was no impediment to the renter's performance of the contract. The renter's sole grievance was that his intended benefit from the contract had not been realized....

The complaint that a contracting party did not realize the benefit he intended to realize from the contract has been described as "frustration-in-fact." Frustration-in-fact results when, because of events subsequent to formation of a contract, the desirability of the performance for which a party contracted diminishes. The issue then becomes: should legal consequences flow from a contracting party's failure to realize the expected benefit from a contract?

B. Frustration of Purpose and The Equitable Doctrine of *Lloyd*

... [M]any authorities, including the courts of Arizona, extend limited relief for frustration-in-fact through an extraordinary legal remedy closely resembling relief in equity.... As Justice Traynor pointed out in his frequently cited opinion in *Lloyd*:

> The question in cases involving frustration is whether the equities of the case, considered in the light of sound public policy, require placing the risk of a disruption or complete destruction of the contract equilibrium on defendant or plaintiff under the circumstances of a given case, and the answer depends on whether an unanticipated circumstance, the risk of which should not be fairly thrown on the promisor, has made performance vitally different from what was reasonably to be expected. 153 P.2d at 50 (citations omitted).

...

D. Standard of Review

The trial court granted Kuhn's cross-motion for summary judgment on the theory that the purpose of Kuhn's contract with the resort was frustrated. In reviewing an order granting summary judgment, we must determine whether there is a genuine issue of disputed material fact.... Where the facts are not in dispute, we analyze the record to determine if the trial court correctly applied the law to the undisputed facts.... Here, the underlying facts are undisputed....

Whether a party to a contract is entitled to relief under the doctrine of frustration of purpose is generally treated as a question of law.... [F]rustration of purpose is essentially an equitable doctrine, and the power to grant relief under that doctrine is reserved to the court. Arizona courts have frequently followed this general rule. Thus, the issues to be considered here—principal purpose and substantial frustration— are questions of law for the court.

IV. Resolution of this Case

A. Requirements for Relief

Restatement § 265, cmt. a, lists four requirements that must exist before relief may be granted for frustration of purpose. First, "the purpose that is frustrated must have been a principal purpose of that party" and must have been so to the understanding of both parties.... Second, "the frustration must be substantial ...; [it] must be so severe that it is not to be regarded as within the risks assumed ... under the contract." Third, "the non-occurrence of the frustrating event must have been a basic assumption...." Finally, relief will not be granted if it may be inferred from either the language of the contract or the circumstances that the risk of the frustrating occurrence, or the loss caused thereby, should properly be placed on the party seeking relief....

Kuhn contends that the Gulf War with its attendant threats of terrorism was an "event the non-occurrence of which was a basic assumption" of the contract.... Here, because we find no substantial frustration of a principal purpose entitling Kuhn to relief, we need not decide if the nonoccurrence of the Gulf War and Saddam Hussein's threats of terrorism was a basic assumption of the parties.

B. Principal Purpose

1. A Forum for European Personnel

Kuhn contends that its principal purpose in scheduling the convention was to provide a forum for its European personnel to introduce new and innovative products to its North American dealers. The resort acknowledged that the primary threat of terrorist activity was to the United States' international interests rather than domestic targets. Even if we take this as an implied concession by the resort that it was too dangerous for Kuhn's European personnel to fly to Scottsdale, Kuhn is not entitled to relief for frustration of purpose on this ground.

For Kuhn to obtain relief based on the frustration of its plans for its European employees to introduce new products, those plans must have been understood by the resort as Kuhn's "principal purpose" in entering the contract, As the court noted in *Krell*, to establish that "the object of the contract was frustrated," it must be shown that the frustrated purpose was "the subject of the contract ... and was so to the knowledge of both parties." It is not enough that the promisor "had in mind some specific object without which he would not have made the contract," Restatement § 265 cmt. a.... In *Krell*, for example, the "coronation procession and the relative position of the rooms [was] the basis of the contract as much for the lessor as the hirer." [1903] 2 K.B at 751.

Here, Kuhn never established that both parties had a common understanding that Kuhn's principal purpose in entering the contract was a convention at which the European personnel would be present. First, the contract itself makes no mention of any particular purpose for the convention. Second, neither the deposition and affidavit of Timothy Harman (Kuhn's general sales manager responsible for scheduling the convention) nor the deposition of William Kilburg (the resort's vice president) raised any factual inference that the resort knew of Kuhn's plans concerning the European personnel. Harman's affidavit only related Kuhn's understanding of the purpose of the convention. The only other reference in the record to the purpose of the convention is Harman's deposition testimony that his role was to find a venue for a North American dealers' meeting....

2. Attendance of Most Invited Personnel

Nevertheless, Kuhn argues that the parties contracted with the idea that "all or most" of Kuhn's employees and dealers would come to Scottsdale for the meeting.... [N]othing in this record establishes that the resort contracted with the understanding that all or most of Kuhn's dealers and employees would attend the convention. Kuhn's degree of success was not of primary concern to the resort. To the contrary, the resort clearly contemplated that the convention might not meet Kuhn's expectations. Not only does the contract include a provision for attrition in attendance and outright cancellation, it assigns the risk of such events to Kuhn. Thus, as with the attendance of the European employees, the attendance of all or most of Kuhn's dealers and employees was not so completely the basis of the contract, as understood by the resort, that without such attendance the transaction would make little sense.

Kuhn did establish, however, that the resort contracted with knowledge that a principal purpose of Kuhn was a convention at which some of Kuhn's employees and dealers would attend. If that purpose was substantially frustrated by the Gulf War, Kuhn is entitled to relief. Consequently, we next consider whether the Gulf War and Saddam Hussein's threats of terrorism substantially frustrated a convention for some of Kuhn's employees and dealers.

C. Substantial Frustration

Kuhn argues that its purpose was effectively frustrated because air travel was unexpectedly rendered unreasonably dangerous. The resort, on the other hand, while essentially conceding that Kuhn's decision to cancel was made in good faith, contends that the general threat of terrorism was not sufficient to justify Kuhn's cancellation of the convention. We agree with the resort.

Preliminarily, as discussed above, Kuhn cannot rely on the absence of the Europeans as a basis for canceling the contract. Kuhn never established that both parties had a common understanding that Kuhn's principal purpose in entering the contract was a convention at which the European personnel would be present. Thus, in resolving this issue, we do not consider the threat posed to the European employees traveling internationally by air.

On the other hand, the threat to domestic air travel is a relevant consideration. Most of those invited to the convention resided in the United States and in Canada. Furthermore, the resort did not controvert Kuhn's assertion in its statement of facts that "the parties assumed that Kuhn personnel could and would travel to Scottsdale." Consequently, if the Gulf War effectively precluded domestic air travel, Kuhn could not have hosted a convention attended by even some of its dealers and employees. Under such circumstances, the resort's furnishing of its facilities would have been rendered valueless to Kuhn. We could then say that Kuhn's purpose in entering the contract was substantially frustrated. We conclude, however, that the contrary is true.

We begin our analysis on this point with the proposition that substantial frustration means frustration "so severe that it is not fairly to be regarded as within the risks ... assumed under the contract." Restatement § 265 cmt. a. Furthermore, "it is not enough that the transaction has become less profitable for the affected party or even that he will sustain a loss." *Id.* The value of the counterperformance to be rendered by the promisee must be "totally or nearly totally destroyed" by the occurrence of the event. *Lloyd,* 153 P.2d at 50.

Here, the conduct of Kuhn and its dealers clearly demonstrates that the value of the resort's counterperformance — the furnishing of its facilities for Kuhn's convention — was not totally or nearly totally destroyed by terrorist threats. In late January, after the United States attacked Iraq and when the threat of terrorism was at its highest level, Kuhn implicitly confirmed the convention date by reducing the reserved room block from 190 to 140. Furthermore, although several dealers canceled in early February, the uncontroverted record demonstrates that over one hundred dealers registered for the convention after the commencement of Operation Desert Storm on

6 · ADJUSTING TO CHANGED CIRCUMSTANCES

January 16, 1991. Thus, the frustration was not so severe that it cannot fairly be regarded as one of the risks assumed by Kuhn under the contract.

Kuhn argues, however, that even if the jointly understood purpose in holding the
convention was not substantially frustrated by the actual risk of terrorism, it was entitled to cancel the convention because of its perception of a serious risk to air travel.
For this proposition, Kuhn relies primarily on the wartime shipping cases.... The
wartime shipping cases essentially held that a ship captain is entitled to take reasonable
precautions, including abandoning the voyage, in the face of a reasonable apprehension
of danger. Read together, they establish that the promisor's decision not to perform
must be an objectively reasonable response to an extraordinary, specific, and identifiable threat.... The degree of danger is judged in light of the facts available at the
time, First Restatement § 465, cmt. b, but "mere good faith ... will not excuse" cancellation of performance.

... Even though Kuhn canceled the convention in good faith, ... Kuhn's cancellation
did not excuse its performance of the contract with the resort. Press reports in circulation at the time Kuhn canceled the convention indicated that the risk to domestic
air travel was slight. Moreover, the United States government announced that it was
taking measures to insure the safety of domestic air travel and that travelers should
not be put off by the threat of terrorist activity.

Furthermore, the record establishes that by the time Kuhn canceled the convention,
the risk of terrorism, if any, was diminishing. First, the danger, publicized since October 1990, had failed to materialize. Second, Kuhn itself recognized that even its
French employees could possibly travel as early as April. Finally, even after the commencement of Operation Desert Storm, more than one hundred of Kuhn's dealers
expressed their willingness to travel to Scottsdale. We conclude that Kuhn's cancellation
of the convention because of the perceived threat of terrorism was not an objectively
reasonable response to an extraordinary and specific threat. The slight risk to domestic
air travel by vague threats of terrorism does not equate with the actual and substantial
danger of running a naval blockade in time of war....

Finally, we consider whether Kuhn is entitled to relief on the ground that fear of
terrorist activities resulted in less than expected attendance, which in turn made the
convention uneconomical. Although economic return may be characterized as the
"principal purpose" of virtually all commercial contracts, mere economic impracticality
is no defense to performance of a contract.... Thus, although the Gulf War's effect
on the expected level of attendance may have rendered the convention uneconomical,
Kuhn was not on this ground relieved of its contractual obligation.

V. Procedural Disposition

The only issues raised by Kuhn in its response to the resort's motion for summary
judgment on liability were its claims for relief under the doctrines of impracticability
of performance and frustration of purpose. Because we conclude that Kuhn is not
entitled to relief under these doctrines, partial summary judgment must be granted
to the resort.

NOTES AND QUESTIONS

1. *What was the resort hotel selling to Kuhn Farm Machinery?* In *Krell v. Henry*, the person who owned an interest in the apartment was selling a place from which to watch a parade. It is very likely that he could not have sold seats from which people could look out the window of his apartment at the pigeons and people passing on the street absent a coronation parade. It is also likely that he was able to charge a premium price because of the happy coincidence that his apartment window faced the parade route. The Scottsdale Plaza Resort was selling a facility for a conference. It was not guaranteeing that Kuhn could run a successful conference; the contract put that burden on Kuhn. As far as we can tell, the Scottsdale Plaza Resort was ready to supply adequate conference facilities. Is this enough to distinguish the cases?

2. *Coming closer to* **Krell v. Henry?** A promoter of diving tours made a contract with 20 people for a tour that would allow participants to dive at Taveuni, one of the Fiji Islands in the Pacific. The tour was to be at Taveuni for a week that would include New Year's Eve at the end of 2000. The island lies on the 180-degree meridian line. Given the location of the island, it would be one of the very first places where the New Year would arrive and where dawn would come on January 1, 2001. Promoter's literature promoting the tour indicated that the members of the party would begin a dive at 11:30 P.M. on December 31 and surface 30 minutes into the New Year. Promoter made a contract with the Taveuni Island Resort to provide rooms for seven days for participants in his tour. The Resort's officials knew that the promoter was bringing people to their hotel who planned on diving at the reefs off the coast of Taveuni Island. These officials also knew of Promoter's plans to dive on New Year's Eve. All of the promotional literature published by the Resort featured stories about snorkeling and diving during the days and parties staged in the evenings. Local customs concerning New Year's Eve were described in this promotional literature, and they promised a grand party. While Taveuni Island is beautiful, it is sufficiently remote that relatively few people would travel there who were not interested in diving. The Resort's officials knew this.

On November 1, 2000, Ratu Glanville Lalabalavu, the paramount chief of the Cakaudrove Province (which included the island of Taveuni) died. Local custom dictated that a period of mourning be observed for 100 days, which began on November 4, 2000, and would end in mid-February 2001. During this period of mourning, custom established that there would be no parties and people would not dive near the many reefs around the islands in Cakaudrove Province. Ratu Tevita Vakalalabure, another chief, warned that he would use ancient rites to call up sharks to attack revelers. This threat had been used in the past as a way to keep both the local population and tourists from diving during the period of mourning.

Suppose Promoter sued the Taveuni Island Resort for his expectation and reliance losses caused by its breach of the contract it had made with him for his tour. The contract contains no express terms dealing with excuses for the performances promised by the Resort or by Promoter. Assume that the Fiji Islands once were a British colony, and its courts follow the common law. How likely is it that Promoter will recover for breach of the contract that he made with the resort? How would the Resort likely defend against Promoter's claim? What was the Resort selling to Promoter: hotel rooms from which you could do anything or rooms from which you could go diving?[61]

3. *Contract law and terrorism:* On September 11, 2001, terrorists destroyed the World Trade Center towers in New York and damaged the Pentagon in Washington, D.C., by hijacking three passenger aircraft loaded with fuel for a transcontinental trip and crashing them into these buildings. (A fourth plane was also hijacked, but did not reach its target.) The federal government closed the airline system. Planes did not come to the United States from abroad and all domestic flights were canceled. Suppose Kuhn Farm Machinery's convention in Scottsdale, Arizona, was scheduled to begin on September 13, 2001, during the period when all flights were canceled. The only Kuhn dealers who could get to the Scottsdale Plaza Resort were those who lived within driving distance from the resort.[62] Would the Arizona court now recognize a frustration of purpose defense to any claim that the resort tried to make against Kuhn? Would it be enough to say that the resort had promised to make available hotel and conference rooms on the specified dates, and it did exactly this? Absent a *force majeure* clause in the contract, why should we say that the resort assumed the risk of the loss of the United States airline system?

4. *What might we learn from World War II?* In *Mitchell v. Ceazan Tires, Ltd.*,[63] a lessee was a franchised dealer in new automobile tires. The original lease was made in 1937 for a three-year term, and it was renewed for another three-year term on March 21, 1940. The United States entered World War II after the Japanese bombed the American military bases and ships at Pearl Harbor on December 7, 1941. At the beginning of the war, the Japanese forces were very successful. They managed to take over what was then French Indo-China, which was the source of most of the world's supply of natural rubber. As a result, the United States faced a great shortage of rubber and automobile tires were rationed. Justice Roger Traynor, writing for the Supreme Court of California, rejected the lessee's claim that the war and tire rationing had frustrated the purpose of the lease. He said that the lessee had failed to prove that this risk was not reasonably foreseeable. Justice Traynor remarked that the entry of the United States into World War was the subject of much debate at the time the lease was renewed. Moreover, the California court imposed a second requirement for relief. The value of the lessor's performance to the lessee must have been "totally or nearly totally destroyed." Justice Traynor said that the lessee could change his business to meet the demand for recapped tires or he could sublease the building to someone running a different kind of business.

Professor Macaulay notes:

---

61. *See* Stuart Millar, *Shark Curse Threatens Party*, The Guardian (London), Dec. 6, 1999, at 1; 36 Condé Nast Traveler, Jan. 2001, at 76.

62. The media frequently reports on the estimated losses to the tourism industry following terrorist events, but rarely analyze the legal rights of the parties. *See* Doreen Carvajal, *Economic Fallout of Paris Attacks Hits Hotels Hard*, N.Y. Times, Nov. 20, 2015, at B1.

63. 25 Cal. 2d 44, 153 P.2d 53 (1944).

In 1944 [when Justice Traynor wrote his opinion] it was easy to say that a reasonable man should have seen a significant enough chance of war coming to this country when he considered the matter in 1940 so that he would make provision for it in his contracts. However, in early 1940 many believed war would not come or had little interest in the subject. Were they unreasonable to repress thoughts of disaster and carry on business as usual? ... Even if they should have foreseen war, should they have foreseen a war with Japan in which the Japanese would be so successful that they cut off American rubber supplies and created the need for rationing?[64]

Macaulay suggests that the *Mitchell* case can be explained on the basis of a policy concern apart from risk assumption or implied covenants:

Mitchell ... [was a] wartime case ... and governmental regulations disrupted many settled business practices then. An easily satisfied frustration doctrine would have overturned many contracts. It might have contributed to even further disruption of the civilian economy beyond that caused by shortages and regulations. Firms in the position of Ceazan Tires were encouraged, by Justice Traynor's position, to modify their businesses to ventures serving the national interest — here to replacement of needed consumer goods by a substitute. The case for an easy frustration doctrine, implicitly rejected by Justice Traynor, primarily turns on the policy of relieving hardship.[65]

Should courts considering whether to excuse performance of contracts due to war or natural disasters consider the broader consequences of making it easier to get out of contracts?

3. *Force Majeure* Clauses as the Solution?

A California lawyer said: "The pattern has always been that people address these things with general language ... and when some unexpected permutation occurs, they all rush to address that specifically." He expected more contract clauses to deal with terrorism explicitly as a result of the September 11 attacks in New York and Washington.[66] Some people did have contracts with clauses that they could argue governed the events of September 11th. In the same article, the managing partner of a large Los Angeles firm is quoted as saying:

We had booked rooms for a couple hundred lawyers [at a partners' meeting in Phoenix a week after the attacks].... We invoked our *force majeure* clause with the hotel [to avoid penalty fees], because no one could get there. If our meeting had been in December rather than September 18th, we would have

---

64. Stewart Macaulay, *Justice Traynor and the Law of Contracts*, 13 STANFORD L. REV. 812, 834 (1961).

65. *Id.* at 835–36.

66. Lisa Girion, *Businesses Seek a Legal Escape from Terrorism*, L.A. TIMES, Oct. 14, 2001, part 3, at 1.

had a different argument. The further you get away from this September 11 date, the harder it's going to be to make that claim.[67]

Typically, businesses use some type of "impossibility clause" on their contract forms if they use any legal provisions at all.[68] However, the common clause is very brief. By

---

67. The Excel Meetings and Events Newsletter for June of 2003 (www.excelmeetings.com) offers the following sample *force majeure* clause:

> The parties' performance under this Agreement is subject to acts of God, war, government regulation, threats or acts of terrorism or similar acts, governmental travel advisories, disaster, strikes (except those involving the Hotel's employees or agents), civil disorder, curtailment of transportation facilities, or any other cause beyond the parties' control, making it inadvisable, illegal, or impossible to perform their obligations under the Agreement. Either party may cancel the Agreement for any one or more of such reasons upon written notice to the other. In the event Group decides to hold its Meeting despite such circumstances, the Hotel shall waive any fees related to a reduced-size Meeting (including any room attrition fees, function space rental, food and beverage attrition fees) and shall offer the Group's guests any lower room rate offered to guests during the contractual dates.

On the other hand, the Monona Terrace Community and Convention Center in Madison, Wisconsin uses the following provision in its Facility Rental Agreement:

> Neither party shall be deemed to be in default in the performance of the terms of this agreement if either party is prevented from performing the terms of this agreement by causes beyond its control, including Acts of God; failure due to delay or performance by suppliers or contractors; any catastrophe resulting from earthquakes, flood, fire, explosion, or other cause beyond the control of the defaulting party; and strikes, lockouts, work stoppages, or other labor disputes. If any of the stated contingencies occur, the party delayed by *force majeure* shall immediately give the other party written notice of the cause of the delay. The party delayed by *force majeure* shall use reasonable diligence to correct the cause of delay, and if the condition that caused the delay is corrected, the party delayed shall notify the other party immediately and shall resume operations under the agreement.

You represent an academic association where the majority of members are professors at major universities. The association has made a contract with the Marx Hotel in a major city. The hotel is to be the location of the association's annual meeting. After the contract was made but before the meeting was to take place, the state agency charged with preventing discrimination against racial minorities found that the hotel had discriminated against its African-American employees on many occasions. Many members of the academic association reacted with anger, and they refuse to attend an annual meeting held at this hotel. Can the association cancel its contract with the hotel and move its meeting to another place? What problems do you see with each of the two *force majeure* clauses set out above? *See generally* Suzen M. Grieshop Corrada, *The Best Laid Plans: Force Majeure Clauses in Travel and Event Contracts*, 31 Nova L. Rev. 409 (2007); Lydia O'Connor, *Black Business Leaders Call for Boycott of San Francisco Tourism*, Huffington Post, Dec. 23, 2013.

68. Those drafting contracts often attempt to deal with the risks of various contingencies that could make their clients' performances more difficult or undercut the value of the other party's performance to their client. Some lawyers, particularly those drafting buyers' documents, use "cancellation for convenience" clauses. If events in the world change so that a buyer has ordered too much of an item, it can use its right to end the transaction. While this clause may solve many of the problems of dealing with changed circumstances, not all sellers will accept such a clause from all buyers. Sometimes the clause provides that the buyer will pay the seller's reliance losses if the right to cancel is used. Of course, there are other drafting devices to minimize or eliminate legal problems for one who does not want to perform a contract. For example, a remedy limitation can make the price of a breach relatively modest. Then, too, a party can act through a thinly capitalized corporation formed for only one transaction. The corporation may not be excused for its breach of contract, but the aggrieved party will have to try to execute any judgment against the limited assets invested. We have been told

far the most usual wording is no more than that the contract or order is "subject to" or "contingent on" certain specified events (such as "fire, strike, or other circumstances beyond our control"). This simple phrase is found on the business documents of both large and small firms. One businessperson told us that only a simple clause was needed. "If you tried to cover every possible contingency in a contract, you wouldn't have time to get any other work done."

Larger firms with legal staffs often attempt to spell out matters in much more detail. A major producer of metal uses a form providing:

> Seller will not be liable for any delay or failure in performance of this order or in the delivery or shipment of products hereunder, or for any damages suffered by Buyer by reason of such delay or failure, when such delay or failure is, directly or indirectly, caused by or in any manner arises from acts of God, or of public enemies, fires, floods, explosions, accidents, epidemics, quarantine restrictions, riots, mobilizations, war, rebellion, revolutions, blockades, hostilities, governmental regulations, requirements, restrictions, interference or embargoes, strikes, lockouts, differences with workmen, in-adequate transportation facilities, delays or interruptions in transportation, shortages of labor, fuel, raw materials, supplies or power, accidents to, break-downs to or mechanical failure of plant machinery or equipment arising from any cause whatsoever or any other cause or causes (whether or not sim-ilar in nature to any of those hereinbefore specified) beyond Seller's control. In no event will Seller be liable for any consequential damages for delay in or failure of performance, whether or not excused by the foregoing.

There are a number of questions to be raised in drafting and considering an elaborate excuse clause. Some of the many can be suggested by an outline:

(1) Who gets what excuse?

(a) Who is excused, the buyer, the seller or both?

(b) What excuse is given?

(i) If a party is "not liable" for delay or failure to perform, must the other accept a partial or delayed performance?

(ii) If a party is given an extension of time, is there any limit on how long the other must await performance?

(iii) If one party has an option to cancel, what happens to the other's reliance losses?

(2) How are the excusing events defined?

(a) Are they defined generally or in detail?

---

that motion pictures frequently are produced by such paper corporations. It is easy to catalog possible drafting devices to limit or avoid liability. Getting the other side to agree to such provisions may not be easy.

(b) Does the contract attempt to expand the "other causes" to include "similar or dissimilar" ones?

(3) What must the consequences of the event be in order to trigger an excuse? How serious an impact on the ability to perform? What about problems of multiple causation?

Realize also that courts may use their interpretive authority to avoid construing contracts that seem to undercut the spirit of the bargains the parties have made. That is, a court may strain to avoid literal application of a provision that allows a buyer to avoid risks that seemed inherent in the overall bargain the parties had made.[69] While we sometimes joke that "The large print giveth, and the small print taketh away," the courts, like all the rest of us, seek to avoid such consequences if it seems inconsistent with what reasonable parties likely expected and bargained for. We've been told by an experienced lawyer that many *force majeure* clauses give an excuse "if there is a cloud in the blue sky." Many are very broad. The following decision, however, suggests that *force majeure* clauses are not always a way out of burdensome obligations.

NISSHO-IWAI CO., LTD. v. OCCIDENTAL CRUDE SALES, INC.

United States Court of Appeals, Fifth Circuit
729 F.2d 1530 (1984)

GOLDBERG, C. J.

This diversity action involves a contract dispute between the Nissho-Iwai Company, Ltd. ("Nissho") and Occidental Crude Sales, Inc. ("Occidental"). Occidental appeals from a jury verdict awarding Nissho contract damages ... arising from Occidental's failure to perform a crude oil agreement. We hold that there was no reversible error in the finding that Occidental was liable for breach of contract. We reverse the damage award, however, and remand for a new trial limited to determining contract damages....

Facts

Nissho is a Japanese corporation that distributes oil to Japanese buyers. Occidental is an American corporation that explores for and produces oil. In 1965, Occidental obtained a number of "oil concessions" from the High Petroleum Council and the Council of Ministers of Libya. The concessions permitted Occidental to drill for oil in two separate blocks of property ("Concession 102" and "Concession 103"). The producing wells were managed by the Libyan Government, and Occidental was responsible for pipelines that transported oil from the wells to an export terminal in Zueitina. Each concession agreement provided for a royalty payment of 12.5 percent and a tax payment of 50 percent to the Government on each barrel of oil.

---

69. *See, e.g.,* Monolith Portland Cement Co. v. Douglas Oil Co., 303 F.2d 176 (9th Cir. 1962).

On September 1, 1969, a revolutionary government under Colonel Moammar Khadafy deposed the King of Libya and assumed control. In January 1970, Colonel Khadafy formed a committee to negotiate higher prices with Libyan oil producers, but the companies were unwilling to comply. Khadafy imposed a series of production restrictions, and in August 1973, he nationalized 51 percent of Occidental's concessions.

The Contract

Occidental had been under contract since 1971 to provide Nissho with "Zueitina Medium" crude oil produced from Concession 102. Zueitina Medium is a low-sulphur oil that is particularly useful to electric utility companies required to meet air pollution standards. After receiving the oil, Nissho would resell it to various Japanese power companies.

In 1973, Occidental, aware of the past difficulties with the Libyan Government, renegotiated its contract with Nissho. On October 4, 1973, Occidental and Nissho signed the new agreement, known as Contract 1038. Nissho agreed to purchase and Occidental agreed to supply 750,000 barrels of oil a month through December 31, 1978. The contract contains a "*force majeure*" clause excusing nonperformance caused by

> executive or administrative orders or acts [of the Libyan Government] ... or by breakdown or injury to ... producing ... or delivering facilities ... or by any other event, whether or not similar to the causes specified above ... which shall not reasonably be within the control of the party against whom the claim would otherwise be made [*i.e.* Occidental in this case].

The contract also provides that it is to be governed by the laws of California.

Events Leading up to Breach of Contract 1038

...

Actions of the Libyan Government

... [A]ctions of the Libyan Government affected Occidental's production. On February 7, 1974, the Government and Occidental entered into an Exploration and Production Sharing Agreement under which the Government received 81 percent of oil production. In the following months, the Government ordered increases or decreases in production from various wells. Occidental objected to some of the charges and negotiated remedial production quotas.

The parties reached an impasse in the summer of 1975, however. On July 31, the Government announced that Occidental's production exceeded the limits set in Petroleum Regulation Number 8 and that the wells in Concession 103 would be closed temporarily for testing. Then, on August 28, 1975, the Government issued a cutback order to become effective September 1, 1975. Occidental objected to the cutback, arguing that it violated the concession agreements and that Occidental would have "a right to look to the Government for reimbursement of all direct and consequential damages." In a separate letter, Occidental objected to the Government's failure to pay for certain oil exploration (as required by the Exploration and Production Sharing Agreement).

When the Government failed to restore production within seven days, Occidental sought arbitration of the claims. In addition, on September 30, Occidental withheld $117 million that it owed the Government, including $40 million for oil purchased from the Government and $77 million in back taxes and royalties.

The Government notified Occidental that if the payments were not made, the Government would prevent Occidental from exporting oil after October 1, 1975. Occidental refused to pay and the government placed an embargo on exports. Thus, Occidental was unable to perform its contract with Nissho that month.

The embargo on exports lasted until Occidental and the Government settled their disputes on December 3, 1975. Pursuant to the settlement agreement, the embargo order was lifted, the pending arbitrations were withdrawn, and the production of Occidental was restored to 300,000 barrels per day.

Pipeline Breakdowns

Breakdowns in the oil pipeline leading from Concession 102 to Zueitina also affected Occidental's ability to perform the contract with Nissho. Leaks appeared in early 1975, and Occidental shut down the pipeline for repairs from June 20 to July 10. The leaks persisted, however; and in October, Occidental began major repairs: the pipeline was pressure-tested, holes were dug, and a section of the pipeline was removed.

After the oil embargo ended in December 1975, Occidental attempted to reconnect the pipeline and repair any remaining leaks. Yet, when the pipeline was reattached, Occidental discovered sand in the line. To correct that problem, Occidental again had to remove a section of the line. Consequently, the pipeline was shut down from October 1975 through May 10, 1976, and no oil was produced from Concession 102 during that period.

Breach by Occidental

In sum, Occidental failed to supply Nissho with any oil during the last four months of 1975 and the first four months of 1976. The oil embargo prevented performance between October and December, 1975. Then, pipeline problems stopped the flow of oil until May 1976....

Negotiations Between Occidental and Nissho After Repair of Pipeline

After Occidental notified Nissho that the pipeline from Concession 102 was repaired, the parties met and exchanged letters concerning future performance. Because Nissho had lost Kansai as a customer, it proposed to suspend or cancel the contract with Occidental. In a letter dated May 12, 1976, Occidental replied that it would prefer to suspend the contract from October 1976 through March 1977, to give Nissho "time to persuade Kansai to honor its contract and resume lifting or alternatively find other Buyers for the crude oil." On May 27, Nissho wrote back to accept the proposal on the condition that any lifting requirements would be waived for calendar year 1976 and throughout the suspension period.... Nissho was unable to reestablish its contract with Kansai. It did make two "spot market" sales to Kansai in July 1976, and September 1976, but it has never obtained another long-term contract with Kansai....

Issues

... Occidental ... argues, first, that the judge erred in charging the jury about the *force majeure* clause. Occidental claims that the trial court should not have instructed the jury to consider whether an excusing event under the clause was within the reasonable control of Occidental. We hold that the instruction was proper. Moreover, we hold that Judge O'Conor properly refused a qualifying charge that Occidental had requested....

Discussion

...

Challenges to ... Force Majeure

Occidental raises several supposed errors ... as grounds for reversing that judgment. Occidental objects to the giving of one jury instruction and the failure to give another with regard to *force majeure*. At trial, Occidental attempted to defend its nonperformance on the ground that acts of the Libyan Government (in particular, the embargo) and pipeline breakdowns prevented Occidental from supplying oil. Both excuses come within specific provisions of the "Force Majeure" clause in Contract 1038, which provides in pertinent part:

> Neither party shall be liable for ... loss, damage, claims or demands of any nature whatsoever due to delays or defaults in performance ... caused by impairment in any manner of [Occidental's] crude oil supply, ... [by] executive or administrative orders or acts ... of any ... government, [by] breakdown or injury to ... producing ... or delivering facilities, ... [by] imposition of restrictions ... by any ... government, ... or by any other event, whether or not similar to the causes specified above ... which shall not be reasonably within the control of the party against whom the claim would otherwise be made.

Judge O'Conor instructed the jury that:

> [I]n order to find that Occidental's nonperformance was excused under the *force majeure* clause you must find from a preponderance of the evidence (1) that the excusing event or events relied upon by Occidental actually prevented Occidental's performance, and (2) that the excusing event or events were not reasonably within the control of Occidental or its supplier.

Occidental objects to the second element of the charge, which required the jury to consider whether pipeline difficulties and the Libyan oil embargo were within the reasonable control of Occidental. According to Occidental, the contract clause distinguishes between specifically enumerated events and the general category of "any other event"; only the latter must be beyond the reasonable control of the Seller. Occidental points out that in California, a limiting exception applies only to the last phrase preceding it, unless the context indicates otherwise. *See, e.g., In re Estate of*

Colyear, 17 Cal. App. 3d 173, 94 Cal. Rptr. 696, 702 (1971); *Grant v. Hipsher*, 257 Cal. App. 2d 375, 383, 64 Cal. Rptr. 892 (1967).

In this case, however, the California law of *force majeure* requires us to apply a reasonable control limitation to each specified event, regardless of what generalized contract interpretation rules would suggest. Thus, Judge O'Conor did not err in giving such an instruction. "*Force majeure*" has traditionally meant an event that is beyond the control of the contractor. *See* Squillante & Congalton, *Force Majeure*, 80 Com. L.J. 4, 5 (1979). The common law defense of impossibility due to Act of God requires the defendant to prove that an excusing event is beyond his control, *id.* at 5; and contractual *force majeure* provisions typically incorporate this requirement, *see Eastern Air Lines v. McDonnell Douglas*, 532 F.2d 957, 991 (5th Cir. 1976).

The term "reasonable control" has come to include two related notions. First, a party may not affirmatively cause the event that prevents his performance. The rationale behind this requirement is obvious. If a contractor were able to escape his responsibilities merely by causing an excusing event to occur, he would have no effective obligation to perform.... The second aspect of reasonable control is more subtle. Some courts will not allow a party to rely on an excusing event if he could have taken reasonable steps to prevent it.... *See Oosten v. Hay Haulers Dairy Employees & Helpers Union*, 45 Cal. 2d 784, 291 P.2d 17, 20–21 (1955); 6 Corbin on Contracts, § 1342, at 328 ... The rationale behind this requirement is that the *force majeure* did not actually prevent performance if a party could reasonably have prevented the event from occurring. The party has prevented performance and, again, breached his good faith obligation to perform by failing to exercise reasonable diligence.

The California Supreme Court has read into contractual *force majeure* provisions both aspects of "reasonable control"—good faith in not causing the excusing event and diligence in taking reasonable steps to ensure performance. In Oosten, *supra*, the parties had entered into a contract for the sale of milk. Clause 12 of the contract provided:

> In case of strike, lockout, or other labor trouble ... which shall render it impossible for [either party to perform], no liability for non-compliance with this agreement caused thereby ... shall exist or arise.... 291 P.2d at 19.

The clause did not explicitly refer to "reasonable control." Yet, the Court invoked the concept in describing the obligations of a party relying on a *force majeure* clause:

> In the instant case we construe clause 12, with respect to impossibility of performance, the same as it is construed generally in contract law with regard to whether performance has been made impossible. The only things the clause adds are that certain things—labor disputes, strikes—may excuse performance, when without it they might not, but the question remains whether those things have been made impossible. As has been said: "We cannot always be sure what causes are beyond the control of the contractor. Many fires can be prevented by the use of foresight and sufficient expenditure. Most strikes can be avoided by a judicious yielding or by an abject surrender

to demands. No contractor is excused under such an express provision unless he shows affirmatively that his failure to perform was proximately caused by a contingency within its terms; that, in spite of skill, diligence, and good faith on his part, performance became impossible or unreasonably expensive." *Id.* at 20–21.

To be sure, the facts in Oosten are distinguishable from our case. Nevertheless, the words of the California Court provide the most definitive statement of California law concerning the relationship between contractual *force majeure* clauses and the reasonable control limitation. The Court, in effect, requires proof that a party relying on a *force majeure* clause did not exercise reasonable control over the excusing event. California law supports Judge O'Conor's decision to apply the control limitation to each of the specified events in the *force majeure* clause of Contract 1038.[70]

The exemption envisioned by Occidental would certainly be broader than that provided in § 2-615. Although the statute does not contain an express "reasonable control" provision, virtually every court and commentator has read in such a limitation. *See, e.g., Eastern Air Lines, supra; Roth Steel Products v. Sharon Steel*, 705 F.2d 134, 149–50 (6th Cir. 1983); Hawkland, *The Energy Crisis and Section 2-615 of the Uniform Commercial Code*, 79 Com. L.J. 75, 79 (seller must have made reasonable efforts to perform). Moreover, Comment 10 to § 2-615 applies the equivalent of a reasonable control limitation in the context of interference by a government (notably one of the very excusing events relied upon by Occidental):

> Governmental interference cannot excuse unless it truly "supervenes" in such a manner as to be beyond the seller's assumption of risk. And any action by the party claiming excuse which causes or colludes in inducing the governmental action preventing his performance would be in breach of good faith and would destroy his exemption.

There is some dispute about whether § 2-615 provides specific boundaries to the breadth of *force majeure* clauses. Compare *Eastern Air Lines, supra* at 990 (only limit is "mercantile sense and reason") with Hawkland, *supra* at 79 (there are specific limits). In either event, the absence of a reasonable control provision would probably offend the Code. Professor Hawkland suggests that Comment 8 refers to two common law limitations, the second being that the occurrence of the

> excusing contingencies must have prevented or delayed the seller's performance in spite of his reasonable efforts to perform. These are the commercial

---

70. [19] Even apart from the California Supreme Court's interpretation of *force majeure* clauses, it is probable that UCC § 2-615 would require application of the "reasonable control" exception to each specified event in § XV of Contract 1038. Section 2-615, codified in California at Cal. Com. Code § 2-615, provides certain limitations on the breadth of exculpatory clauses. Comment 8 provides:

> Generally, express agreements as to exemptions designed to enlarge upon or supplant the provisions of this section are to be read in light of mercantile sense and reason, for this section itself sets up the commercial standard for normal and reasonable interpretation and provides a minimum beyond which agreements may not go.

standards reflecting mercantile sense and reason that have been established over the years, and these are the minimum beyond which American courts have not permitted the parties to contract.

As we have seen, the absence of a "reasonable control" limitation in our case would permit Occidental to rely on the *force majeure* clause without making reasonable efforts to ensure performance. Thus, if we adopted Professor Hawkland's standard, Comment 8 would probably require that the "reasonable control" phrase or its equivalent limit each of the excusing events in § XV [of Contract 1038].

Even if we adopted the looser standard (mercantile sense and reason) enunciated by this Circuit in *Eastern Air Lines*, a reasonable control limitation would probably be necessary. It is hard to imagine that any rational buyer would permit his seller to excuse performance because of an event over which the seller had control. As a matter of law, mercantile sense and reason would probably require that each excusing event be beyond the reasonable control of Occidental.

In sum, we conclude that Judge O'Conor was correct in requiring Occidental to prove that pipeline breakdowns or the acts of the Libyan Government were beyond its reasonable control.

Instruction on Legal Rights

Our reading of Oosten, *supra*, ... also convinces us that Occidental's second assignment of error concerning *force majeure* is incorrect. Occidental argues that even if the trial court was permitted to instruct on reasonable control, it should have given an additional clarifying instruction.

In its proposed instructions to the jury, Occidental requested the judge to charge:

> that parties may, in good faith, do or refrain from doing that which they have a lawful right to do even though they may anticipate that a foreign government may take some action in retaliation. If a party does or refrains from doing that which he has a lawful right to do, in good faith, it cannot be said that his action has caused or colluded in inducing governmental action, even though it may be anticipated that the government involved will take some step in retaliation.

The instruction does not mention "reasonable control," because it was originally requested in the context of a separate defense pursuant to UCC § 2-615. The statute would excuse Occidental's breach if performance had become "commercially impractical," quite apart from whether Occidental came within the protection of the contractual *force majeure* clause. The case, however, went to the jury not on the UCC defense, but only on the defense created by the contract clause. Therefore, the court did not give the requested charge concerning the meaning of UCC requirements.

After the judge had instructed the jury, however, Occidental did object

> with regard to the court's instructions to *force majeure* on the grounds that the court has not instructed the jury that a party is entitled to invoke its legal rights without losing its protection of a *force majeure* provision....

Assuming, however, that the issue was properly preserved for appeal, the requested instruction did not accurately reflect the law in California. The instruction would permit Occidental to rest on its legal rights and to refuse any demands by the Libyan Government that violated the contract between Libya and Occidental. When Libya imposed restrictions on Occidental's oil production in 1975, Occidental, acting on the advice of counsel, withheld $117 million in payments that were due. The Government retaliated by imposing an embargo. Under Occidental's proposed instruction, the embargo would not have been within Occidental's reasonable control even if Occidental knew in advance that it could prevent the embargo by paying the $117 million.

As we have seen, however, California law requires Occidental to take extra steps to prevent the embargo unless "extreme and unreasonable difficulty, expense, injury, or loss[es] are involved." Whether a third party violates a contract in demanding extra money from Occidental is certainly a factor in determining whether that expense is unreasonable. It is not dispositive, however. For example, if the Libyan Government had demanded that Occidental pay five extra dollars, the expense (though unlawful) would not be unreasonable in terms of Occidental's good faith obligation to perform its contract with Nissho. Therefore, Occidental's requested instruction was not accurate.

Nor was the trial court required to decide the issue of reasonable control as a matter of law. The issue is a classic jury question. Though we may disagree with the jury's result, we cannot reverse if there is substantial evidence to support the judgment.... If reasonable men could find that Occidental was able to prevent the embargo without incurring unreasonable expense, then we must affirm. A review of the record in this case reveals that there was sufficient evidence to support such a verdict.

It is clear Occidental was aware of the threatened embargo and could have prevented it by paying $117 million. This sum in itself was not unreasonable, since the entire figure represented back taxes, royalties, and oil costs that Occidental already owed the Libyan Government. Of course, even if Occidental had paid this sum and averted the embargo, it would still have faced production restrictions. A reasonable jury could have found, though, that Occidental would be able to recoup through arbitration or settlement any losses that might result from the restrictions. The company had already commenced arbitration proceedings against the Libyan Government; and, in December, it was able to reach a settlement. To be sure, the withheld payments and the resulting embargo were factors producing that settlement. That is not to say, however, that a settlement would not have been reached in the absence of an embargo. In the past, Occidental had been able to convince the Government to back down from production restrictions. A reasonable jury might have found that Occidental would again have been able to negotiate a reasonable settlement, particularly given the threat of the arbitration proceedings.

Similarly, there was sufficient evidence to support the view that Occidental had reasonable control over pipeline breakdowns. During 1975 and 1976, Occidental conducted numerous repairs on the pipeline leading from Concession 102 to Zueitina. In October 1975, Occidental began repairs and disconnected a section of the line.

The line remained severed until after the embargo ended in December. There was testimony that Occidental left the line disconnected because it did not want to spend money for repairs until after it had settled its dispute with Libya. When the line was reconnected, Occidental discovered that it was clogged with sand. A reasonable jury could have found that the blockage of the line or the failure to discover the blockage earlier was caused by Occidental's delay in repairing and reconnecting the line. The evidence supported a finding that the pipeline breakdown was within Occidental's reasonable control.

In sum, there was no reversible error in either the *force majeure* charge given by Judge O'Conor or the jury's result.

NOTES AND QUESTIONS

1. *What should Occidental have done to maintain its rights under the* force majeure *clause?* Suppose that Occidental's officials wanted to engage in aggressive negotiations with Libya. Could they risk a Libyan embargo and still have rights under the *force majeure* clause? To what extent is the court's "reasonable control" rule a regulation rather than a matter of seeking the likely reasonable expectations of the parties? Could Occidental's lawyers have drafted successfully around this problem so that it would be free to take negotiating positions in dealing with Libya that risked Libyan action that would interfere with Occidental's ability to deliver all of the oil called for under the contract with Nissho-Iwai Co.?

Cliffstar Corp. v. Riverbend Products, Inc.,[71] offers another example of the "reasonable control" limitation on impracticability excuses. Riverbend processed and sold tomato paste. Cliffstar ordered 3.2 million pounds of tomato paste on July 14, 1988. Riverbend had ordered tomatoes from growers sufficient to satisfy its projected needs in 1988. Riverbend began taking orders from customers based on its assumptions about the availability of tomatoes to process into tomato paste. Weather conditions caused a shortage of tomatoes in California and Arizona. Riverbend's contract growers delivered only about 56 percent of the tomatoes it had ordered. Riverbend allocated its available supply of tomato paste among its customers. Cliffstar moved for summary judgment, arguing that Riverbend's failure to deliver was not caused by the 1988 crop shortfall but by Riverbend's sale of too much tomato paste. That is, Riverbend made contracts to sell tomato paste when it should have known that it would not have sufficient tomatoes to produce enough tomato paste to fill all of those orders. The court denied summary judgment. Whether the tomato crop shortage had caused Riverbend to find performing its contracts impracticable was a question of fact. Was the shortage of tomatoes needed to fill its customers' orders something outside of Riverbend's control? We can imagine situations at the extremes where the answer to the question would be clear. However, how well will judges and juries be able to determine whether Riverbend's officials made reasonable judgments about the likely supply and the number of orders to take based on the knowledge they had at the time when they made these decisions?

71. 750 F. Supp. 81 (W.D.N.Y. 1990).

2. *"Reasonable control" and complying with the spirit of environmental protection regulations:* Compare *International Minerals & Chem. Corp. v. Llano, Inc.*,[72] where a buyer sought a declaratory judgment that it was excused from taking natural gas under the terms of a contract. The contract provided: "In the event … Buyer is unable to receive gas as provided in this contract for any reason beyond the reasonable control of the parties … an appropriate adjustment in the minimum purchase requirements … shall be made."

The New Mexico Environmental Improvement Board later issued a regulation requiring emissions from industrial plants to be reduced "as expeditiously as practicable." The buyer converted its plant to a chemical precipitation process that used about 50 to 60 percent less natural gas.

The trial court found that the buyer voluntarily complied with the regulation and had come into compliance earlier than required. Thus, there was no excuse. The court of appeals reversed and found the buyer excused. The regulation was an event beyond the reasonable control of the buyer that rendered it "unable" to receive its minimum amount of gas under the contract. The court said that "unable" was synonymous with "impracticable" as that term is used in UCC § 2-615. It concluded that as a matter of policy, those who cooperate with regulatory agencies and comply with the letter and spirit of legally proper regulations are to be encouraged. The court noted that the buyer's power was limited by the requirement of good faith. A buyer may not collude or induce a governmental agency to act so that the buyer can avoid a contract. However, cooperation to eliminate pollution "can hardly be termed improper collusion."

3. *UCC § 2-615 and* **force majeure** *clauses in contracts:* The introductory clause of Section 2-615 says that subsection (a) controls "[e]xcept so far as a seller may have assumed a greater obligation …." Does this mean that a seller cannot assume only a lesser obligation than it would have had there been no *force majeure* clause in the contract? *Eastern Air Lines, Inc. v. McDonnell Douglas Corp.*[73] interprets the statute as establishing that "if a promisor desires to broaden the protections available under the excuse doctrine, he should provide for the excusing contingencies with particularity and not in general language."

Whatever the merits of the *Eastern Air Lines* court's approach to construing a *force majeure* clause, a literal reading of the statute suggests that the drafters of Article 2 were trying to preserve free contract so that parties could allocate risk as they pleased. Suppose, for example, absent any provision in the contract, a court would find that if seller's plant burned down without any fault on seller's part, this would be the occurrence of a contingency, the non-occurrence of which was a basic assumption on which the contract was made. When the parties negotiated their deal, the buyer demands that the seller promise to deliver the goods whether or not seller's plant is destroyed. Buyer wants seller to assume the burden of finding substitute

---

72. 770 F.2d 879 (10th Cir. 1985).
73. 532 F.2d 957 (5th Cir. 1976).

goods on the market. Buyer agrees to a term in the written contract that says just this. Destruction of seller's plant no longer is the occurrence of a contingency, the non-occurrence of which was a basic assumption on which the contract was made. In the terms on the introductory section to § 2-615, the seller has "assumed a greater obligation" than the statute would have imposed had the written contract been silent on the point. And the introductory section says that the seller can assume such a greater obligation.

4. Coping with Changed Circumstances: Judicial Rewriting of Contracts

ALUMINUM CO. OF AMERICA v. ESSEX GROUP, INC.

United States District Court, Western District of Pennsylvania
499 F. Supp. 53 (1980)

TEITELBAUM, J.

Plaintiff, Aluminum Company of America (ALCOA), brought the instant action against defendant, Essex Group, Inc. (Essex), in three counts. The first count requests the Court to reform or equitably adjust an agreement entitled the Molten Metal Agreement entered into between ALCOA and Essex. The second count alleges that the Molten Metal Agreement was modified by oral amendment and that Essex has breached the amended agreement. The second count seeks a declaratory judgment that the alleged breach by Essex excuses ALCOA's further performance and seeks as well an award of damages caused by the alleged breach of Essex. The third count asks for a declaratory judgment that ALCOA's prior notice of termination of the Molten Metal Agreement was proper or, in the alternative, that ALCOA may terminate the Molten Metal Agreement if it be determined by this Court to be a contract for the sale of goods. Essex denies all of ALCOA's material allegations. Essex further counterclaims that ALCOA is liable to it for damages based on ALCOA's failure to deliver to Essex the amounts of molten metal ALCOA is contractually obligated to deliver under the Molten Metal Agreement and seeks entry of an order specifically enforcing its right to receive molten aluminum from ALCOA in the amounts requested.

Jurisdiction is based upon diversity of citizenship and amount in controversy and is one of the few issues in the case *sub judice* not in dispute.

In 1966 Essex made a policy decision to expand its participation in the manufacture of aluminum wire products. Thus, beginning in the spring of 1967, ALCOA and Essex negotiated with each other for the purpose of reaching an agreement whereby ALCOA would supply Essex with its long-term needs for aluminum that Essex could use in its manufacturing operations.

By December 26, 1967, the parties had entered into what they designated as a toll conversion service contract known as the Molten Metal Agreement, under which Essex would supply ALCOA with alumina, which ALCOA would convert by a smelting process into molten aluminum. Under the terms of the Molten Metal Agreement,

Essex delivers alumina to ALCOA which ALCOA smelts (or toll converts) into molten aluminum at its Warrick, Indiana, smelting facility. Essex then picks up the molten aluminum for further processing.

The price provisions of the contract contained an escalation formula that indicates that $.03 per pound of the original price escalates in accordance with changes in the Wholesale Price Index-Industrial Commodities (WPI) and $.03 per pound escalates in accordance with an index based on the average hourly labor rates paid to ALCOA employees at the Warrick plant. The portion of the pricing formula that is in issue in this case under counts one and two is the production charge that is escalated by the WPI. ALCOA contends that this charge was intended by the parties to reflect actual changes in the cost of the non-labor items utilized by ALCOA in the production of aluminum from alumina at its Warrick, Indiana, smelting plant. In count one of this suit ALCOA asserts that the WPI used in the Molten Metal Agreement was in fact incapable of reasonably reflecting changes in the non-labor costs at ALCOA's Warrick, Indiana, smelting plant and has in fact failed to so reflect such changes.

It is ALCOA's contention in count one of its complaint that the shared objectives of the parties with respect to the use of the WPI have been completely and totally frustrated, that both ALCOA and Essex made a mutual mistake of fact in agreeing to use the WPI to escalate non-labor costs at Warrick. ALCOA is seeking reformation or equitable adjustment of the Molten Metal Agreement so that pursuant to count one of its complaint, the pricing formula with respect to the non-labor portion of the production charge will be changed to eliminate the WPI and substitute the actual costs incurred by ALCOA for the non-labor items used at its Warrick, Indiana, smelting plant. Essex opposes relief under count one contending that: (1) ALCOA cannot obtain reformation of the Molten Metal Agreement on the grounds of mutual mistake since ALCOA has failed to establish any antecedent agreement on pricing not expressed in the Molten Metal Agreement; (2) ALCOA assumed the risk that its prediction as to future costs would be incorrect; (3) ALCOA has failed to prove that enforcement of the Molten Metal Agreement would be unconscionable....

Count One

ALCOA's first count seeks an equitable modification of the contract price for its services. The pleadings, arguments, and briefs frame the issue in several forms. ALCOA seeks reformation or modification of the price on the basis of mutual mistake of fact, unilateral mistake of fact, unconscionability, frustration of purpose, and commercial impracticability.

A.

The facts pertinent to count one are few and simple. In 1967 ALCOA and Essex entered into a written contract in which ALCOA promised to convert specified amounts of alumina supplied by Essex into aluminum for Essex. The service is to be performed at the ALCOA works at Warrick, Indiana. The contract is to run until the end of 1983. Essex has the option to extend it until the end of 1988. The price for each pound of aluminum converted is calculated by a complex formula that includes three variable components based on specific indices. The initial contract price was set at 15 cents per pound, computed as follows:

A: Demand Charge	$0.05/lb.
B: Production Charge	
(i) Fixed Component	.04/lb.
(ii) Non-labor production cost component	.03/lb.
(iii) Labor production cost component	.03/lb.
Total initial charge	$0.15/lb.

The demand charge is to vary from its initial base in direct proportion to periodic changes in the Engineering News Record Construction Cost—20 Cities Average Index published in the *Engineering News Record*. The Non-Labor Production Cost Component is to vary from its initial base in direct proportion to periodic changes in the Wholesale Price Index-Industrial Commodities (WPI-IC) published by the Bureau of Labor Statistics of the United States Department of Labor. The Labor Production Cost Component is to vary from its initial base in direct proportion to periodic changes in ALCOA's average hourly labor cost at the Warrick, Indiana, works. The adjusted price is subject to an overall "cap" price of 65 percent of the price of a specified type of aluminum sold on specified terms, as published in a trade journal, *American Metal Market*.

The indexing system was evolved by ALCOA.... ALCOA examined the non-labor production cost component to assure that the WPI-IC had not tended to deviate markedly from their non-labor cost experience in the years before the contract was executed. Essex agreed to the contract including the index provisions after an examination of the past record of the indices revealed an acceptable pattern of stability.

ALCOA sought, by the indexed price agreement, to achieve a stable net income of about 4 cents per pound of aluminum converted. This net income represented ALCOA's return (i) on its substantial capital investment devoted to the performance of the contracted services, (ii) on its management, and (iii) on the risks of shortfalls or losses it undertook over an extended period. The fact that the non-labor production cost component of ALCOA's costs was priced according to a surrogate, objective index opened the door to a foreseeable fluctuation of ALCOA's return due to deviations between ALCOA's costs and the performance of the WPI-IC. The range of foreseeable deviation was roughly three cents per pound. That is to say that in some years ALCOA's return might foreseeably (and did, in fact) rise to seven cents per pound, while in other years it might foreseeably (and did, in fact) fall to about one cent per pound. *See* Table I.

Essex sought to assure itself of a long-term supply of aluminum at a favorable price. Essex intended to and did manufacture a new line of aluminum wire products. The long-term supply of aluminum was important to assure Essex of the steady use of its expensive machinery. A steady production stream was vital to preserve the market position it sought to establish. The favorable price was important to allow

6 · ADJUSTING TO CHANGED CIRCUMSTANCES 663

TABLE I

YEAR	BASE WPI-IC[1]	WARRICK NON-LABOR PRODUCTION COSTS PER POUND[2]		PROFIT/ LOSS PER LB.	POUNDS DELIVERED	PROFIT/ LOSS
		CENTS	PERCENT			
1968	102.5	4.371	110.5	5.799	25,300,000	$1,467,147
1969	106.0	4.010	101.4	7.097	54,694,317	3,881,656
1970	110.0	4.397	111.1	6.517	84,370,265	5,498,410
1971	114.1	5.215	131.8	5.267	65,522,280	3,516,581
1972	117.9	5.309	134.2	5.721	83,128,209	4,755,765
1973	125.9	5.819	147.1	4.535	82,201,940	3,727,857
1974	153.9	9.009	227.1	2.070	86,234,310	1,785,050
1975	171.5	11.450	289.4	.189	76,688,530	144,941
1976	182.4	13.949	352.6	(.301)[3]	83,363,502	250,924
1977	195.1	17.806	450.1	(4.725)[3]	72,289,722	(3,415,689)
1978	209.4	22.717	574.2	(10.484)[3]	82,235,337	(8,620,504)

[1] The contract calls for a recomputation of the WPI-IC, so that the "Base Wholesale Price Index" equals 100 in 1967.

[2] Warrick Non-Labor Production Costs 1967 — 100%.

[3] The profit (loss) shown in years 1976 through 1978 was affected by a temporary surcharge agreement. Without the temporary surcharge the loss in cents per pound would have been as follows: 1967 (1.699); 1977 (6.725); 1978 (10.984). The loss each year would have been as follows: 1976 ($1,416,346); 1977 ($4,861,484); 1978 ($9,031,631).

Essex to compete with firms like ALCOA, which produced the aluminum and manufactured aluminum wire products in an efficient, integrated operation.

In the early years of the contract, the price formula yielded prices related, within the foreseeable range of deviation, to ALCOA's cost figures. Beginning in 1973, OPEC actions to increase oil prices and unanticipated pollution control costs greatly increased ALCOA's electricity costs. Electric power is the principal non-labor cost factor in aluminum conversion, and the electric power rates rose much more rapidly than did the WPI-IC. As a result, ALCOA's production costs rose greatly and unforeseeably beyond the indexed increase in the contract price. Table I illustrates the relation between the WPI-IC and ALCOA's costs over the years of the contract, and the resulting consequences of ALCOA.

During the most recent years, the market price of aluminum has increased even faster than the production costs. At the trial ALCOA introduced the deposition of Mr. Wilfred Jones, an Essex employee whose duties included the sale of surplus metal. Mr. Jones stated that Essex had resold some millions of pounds of aluminum that

ALCOA had refined. The cost of the aluminum to Essex (including the purchase price of the alumina and its transportation) was 36.35 cents per pound around June of 1979. Mr. Jones further stated that the resale price in June 1979, at one cent per pound under the market, was 73.313 cents per pound, yielding Essex a gross profit of 37.043 cents per pound. This margin of profit shows the tremendous advantage Essex enjoys under the contract as it is written and as both parties have performed it. A significant fraction of Essex's advantage is directly attributable to the corresponding out-of-pocket losses ALCOA suffers. ALCOA has sufficiently shown that without judicial relief or economic changes that are not presently foreseeable, it stands to lose in excess of $75,000,000 out of pocket during the remaining term of the contract.

B.

ALCOA's Warrick Works, located in Indiana, are the designated source of supply. The Essex plant, where the bulk of the aluminum is used, is also located in Indiana. Essex takes delivery at the Warrick Works.

The contract declares: "This Agreement shall be governed and interpreted in accordance with the laws of the State of Indiana." The parties surely have sufficient contacts with the State of Indiana and Pennsylvania courts would enforce their agreement respecting the application of Indiana law. Restatement 2d, Conflict of Laws § 187; *cf.* 13 Pa. C.S.A. § 1105(1) (UCC). This Court must enforce it as well....

This case presents many issues that are governed by common law principles. Most fall within the interstices of the reported decisions of Indiana courts. Some touch principles announced in hoary Indiana decisions. Where the Indiana law remains undeclared, or where the declaration is far from current, the obligation of this Court is to discern the most probable state of current Indiana law for "the outcome of the litigation in the federal court should be substantially the same, so far as legal rules determine the outcome of a litigation, as it would be if tried in a State court." *Guaranty Trust Co. v. York*, 326 U.S. 99, 65 S. Ct. 1464, 89 L. Ed. 2079 (1945).... In connection with these observations, the Court notes that the appellate courts of Indiana appear to join in the habits of thought and in the assessments of policy which have lately prevailed in most of the fine courts in this nation. The Indiana courts have joined the throng of state courts in (i) declaring that residential landlords are bound by an implied warranty of habitability. *Old Town Development v. Langford*, 349 N.E.2d 744 (Ind. App. 1976); (ii) adopting the rule of strict products liability from the Restatement 2d of Torts § 402A, *Perfection Paint & Color Co. v. Konduris*, 258 N.E.2d 681 (Ind. App. 1970); (iii) adopting the increasing prevalent view that harsh or unconscionable provisions in contracts of adhesion may be refused enforcement, *Weaver v. American Oil Co.*, 276 N.E.2d 144 (Ind. 1971).

C.

ALCOA initially argues that it is entitled to relief on the theory of mutual mistake. ALCOA contends that both parties were mistaken in their estimate of the suitability of the WPI-IC as an objective index of ALCOA's non-labor production costs, and that their mistake is legally sufficient to warrant modification or avoidance of ALCOA's promise. Essex appropriately raised several defenses to these claims. Essex first argues that the asserted mistake is legally insufficient because it is essentially a mistake as to future economic events rather than a mistake of fact. Essex next argues that ALCOA assumed or bore the risk of the mistake. Essex finally argues that the requested remedy of reformation is not available under Indiana law.

The late Professor Corbin wrote the best modern analysis of the doctrine of mutual mistake. Corbin took pains to show the great number and variety of factors that must be considered in resolving claims for relief founded on the doctrine of mistake, and to show the inappropriateness of any single verbal rule to govern the decision of mistake cases. CORBIN ON CONTRACTS § 597 at 582–83 (1960).

The present case involves a claimed mistake in the price indexing formula. This is clearly a mistake concerning a factor affecting the value of the agreed exchange. Of such mistakes Corbin concluded that the law must consider the character of the risks assumed by the parties. *Id.* at § 605. He further concluded:

> In these cases, the decision involves a judgment as to the materiality of the alleged factor, and as to whether the parties made a definite assumption that it existed and made their agreement in the belief that there was *no risk* with respect to it. Opinions are almost sure to differ on both of these matters, so that decisions must be, or appear to be, conflicting. The court's judgment on each of them is a judgment on a matter of fact, not a judgment as to law. No rule of thumb should be constructed for cases of this kind. 3 CORBIN ON CONTRACTS § 605 at p. 643 (1960).

The new Restatement 2d of Contracts follows a similar approach.[74] After defining "mistake" as "a belief not in accord with the facts," § 151, the Restatement declares:

§ 152. WHEN MISTAKE OF BOTH PARTIES MAKES A CONTRACT VOIDABLE.

(1) Where a mistake of both parties at the time a contract was made as to a basic assumption on which the contract was made has a material effect on the agreed exchange of performances the contract is voidable by the adversely affected party unless he bears the risk of the mistake under the rule stated in § 154.

(2) In determining whether the mistake has a material affect on the agreed exchange of performances, account is taken of any relief by way of reformation, restitution, or otherwise.

Both Professor Corbin and the Restatement emphasize the limited place of the doctrine of mistake in the law of contracts. They, along with most modern commentators, emphasize the importance of contracts as devices to allocate the risks of life's uncertainties, particularly economic uncertainties. Where parties to a contract de-

---

74. Eds. note: The court, in its opinion, often cites to the Restatement (Second) of Contracts. The citations were to a tentative draft, with different numbers than the final published version. We have changed the numbers so that they refer to the final published version.

liberately and expressly undertake to allocate the risk of loss attendant on those un-certainties between themselves or where they enter a contract of a customary kind which by common understanding, sense, and legal doctrine has the affect of allocating such risks, the commentators and the opinions are agreed that there is little room for judicial relief from resulting losses. CORBIN ON CONTRACTS § 598 and authorities there cited. The new Restatement agrees, § 154. This is, in part, the function of the doctrine of assumption of the risk as a limitation of the doctrine of mistake. Whether ALCOA assumed the risk it seeks relief from is at issue in this case. The doctrine of assumption of the risk is therefore considered below. The important point to note here is that the doctrine of assumption of the risk is not the only risk-allocating lim-itation on the doctrine of mistake. Other important risk-allocating limitations are inherent in the doctrine of mistake itself. They find expression in the cases and treatises in declarations that there has been no mistake, or no legally cognizable mistake, or a mistake of the wrong part.

ALCOA claims that there was a mutual mistake about the suitability of the WPI-IC as an index to accomplish the purposes of the parties. Essex replies that the mistake, if any, was not a mistake of *fact*, but it was rather a mistake in predicting future eco-nomic conditions. Essex asserts that such a mistake does not justify legal relief for ALCOA. The conflicting claims require the Court to resolve three questions: (1) Was the mistake one of "fact" as the cases and commentators use that word? (2) If so, was it of the sort of fact for which relief could be granted? (3) If the mistake was not one of "fact," is relief necessarily foreclosed?

The initial question requires the characterization, as a matter of fact rather than of law, of the claimed mistake. The cases and commentaries contain useful thoughts and analogous problems that aid in this characterization. But the characterization is itself a question of fact. That it may have ultimate legal significance, and that it requires the exercise of judgment does not distinguish this determination from other determinations of fact. The distinction between questions of law and questions of fact is old. Its resolution is often doubtful. No simple and mechanical verbal formula can capture the distinction and resolve the hard cases. Factors affecting the charac-terization of a question include its suitability for jury or other fact-finder determination and its analytical separability from the final determination of legal consequences. The separation of fact from things that are not fact—opinion, prediction, desire, and the like—is principally a question of common sense or epistemology rather than of law, even when the separation must be done by courts. So it is here. ALCOA calls the mistaken assumption that the index was suitable a factual assumption. Essex calls it a prediction. This is a dispute of facts, not law. Its resolution will affect the decision of this case as factual determinations usually do. The law must be applied to it to yield a result. Neither is this question beyond the usual function and capacity of a jury or other fact-finder.

The first Restatement of Contracts notes, and the published Tentative Draft No. 10 of the Restatement Second stresses, the distinction between "existing fact" and prediction. See Restatement of Contracts § 502, comment a; Restatement 2d of Contracts [Tentative Draft] §293 [§151 in the published version]. The approved final form ... modifies the emphasis by deleting the word "existing." The Reporter, Professor Farnsworth of the Columbia University School of Law, related the circumstances of that change to the Court when he appeared on behalf of ALCOA.

> ... My clear recollection is that following the discussion of misrepresentation, a number of people came up to me and later saw me in the hallway and said that they agreed with the speaker that "existing" should be dropped.
>
> It would be fair to say that there were probably as many reasons for dropping it given to me as there were people who had advanced the opinion.
>
> I would suppose at the end at least a dozen people had said they didn't like "existing," and nobody had defended it. *The reporter has the authority to change even the black letter when it is a matter of style, and since I did not bring it back to the Institute for a vote as a matter of substance, I think one would have to say that any change made was considered by the reporter to be a matter of style.*
>
> In any event, in response to the small but unanimous body of opinion that didn't like "existing," it was deleted in the draft that I finally sent off to the editor and it now reads "Belief that is not in accord with the facts."
>
> *I think that there is in the comment still a statement with respect to "existing," but the deletion from the black letter is at least a change that perhaps permits more flexibility with respect to the line between what is an existing fact or what is a fact and what is a pure presumption which is an extremely difficult line to draw in both cases.* Testimony of E. Allan Farnsworth 20–22 (emphasis added).

The Comment Professor Farnsworth mentioned declares:

> [T]he erroneous belief must relate to the facts as they exist at the time of the making of the contract. A party's prediction or judgment as to events to occur in the future, even if erroneous, is not a "mistake" as that word is defined here....

The Court finds the parties' mistake in this case to be one of fact rather than one of simple prediction of future events. Plainly the mistake is not wholly isolated from predictions of the future or from the searching illuminations of painful hindsight. But this is not the legal test. At the time the contract was made both parties were aware that the future was unknown, and their agreed contract was intended to bind them for many years to come. Both knew that Essex sought an objective pricing formula and that ALCOA sought a formula that would cover its out-of-pocket costs over the years and that would yield it a return of around four cents a pound. Both parties to the contract carefully examined the past performance of the WPI-IC before agreeing to its use. The testimony was clear that each assumed the Index was adequate to fulfill its purpose. This mistaken assumption was essentially a present actuarial error.

The parties took pains to avoid the full risk of future economic changes when they embarked on a 21-year contract involving services worth hundreds of millions of dollars. To this end they employed a customary business risk-limiting device—price indexing—with more than customary sophistication and care. They chose not a single index formula but a complex one with three separate indices.

… Here the practical necessities of the very long-term service contract demanded an agreed risk-limiting device. Both parties understood this and adopted one. The capacity of their selected device to achieve the known purposes of the parties was not simply a matter of acknowledged uncertainty like the … prediction. It was more in the nature of an actuarial prediction of the outside limits of variation in the relation between two variable figures—the WPI-IC and the non-labor production costs of ALCOA. Its capacity to work as the parties expected it to work was a matter of fact, existing at the time they made the contract.

This crucial fact was not known, and was scarcely knowable when the contract was made.[75] But this does not alter its status as an existing fact. The law of mistake has not distinguished between facts that are unknown but presently knowable, *e.g.*, *Raffles v. Wichelhaus*, 2 H. & C. 906 (1864), and facts that presently exist but are unknowable, *e.g.*, *Sherwood v. Walker*, 66 Mich. 568, 33 N.W. 919 (1887). Relief has been granted for mistakes of both kinds.

To conclude that the parties contracted upon a mistake of fact does not, by itself, justify an award of judicial relief to ALCOA. Relief can only follow if the mistake was mutual, if it related to a basic assumption underlying the contract, and if it caused a severe imbalance in the agreed exchange.

The doctrine of mistake has long distinguished claims of mutual mistake from claims of unilateral mistake. CORBIN ON CONTRACTS §608. The standards for judicial relief are higher where the proven mistake is unilateral than where it is mutual. Compare, *e.g.* Restatement 2d of Contracts §152 with §153.

Essex asserts that ALCOA's mistake was unilateral. Mr. O'Malley, chairman of the board of Essex Corporation, testified at trial that he had no particular concern for ALCOA's well-being and that in the negotiations of the contract he sought only Essex's best interests. Essex claims this testimony tends to rebut any possible mutual mistake of fact between the parties. The Court disagrees. …

The law of mutual mistake is not addressed primarily to motivation or to desire to have a good bargain, such as that credibly testified to by Mr. O'Malley. As Mr. O'Malley struck the bargain for Essex, he understood the function of the Wholesale Price Index, as part of the pricing formula, to be the protection of ALCOA from foreseeable economic fluctuations. He further had every reason to believe that the formula

---

75. [5] Clear hindsight suggests the flaw might have been anticipated and cured by a "floor" resembling the 65 percent "cap" that Essex wrote into the price formula. To the extent this possibility might be thought material to the case, the Court specifically finds that when the contract was made, even people of exceptional prudence and foresight would not have anticipated a need for this additional limitation to achieve the purpose of the parties.

was selected on the factual prediction that it would, within tolerable limits, serve its purpose. While he did not share the motive to protect ALCOA, he understood the functional purposes of the agreement. He therefore shared this mistake of fact. And his mistake was Essex's. The Court recognizes that Mr. O'Malley and Essex would cheerfully live with the benefit of their mistake, but the law provides otherwise. As a matter of law Mr. O'Malley's testimony of Essex's indifference concerning ALCOA's motivation for the use of the Wholesale Price Index as a gauge for tracking non-labor costs is immaterial.

Is it enough that one party is indifferent to avoid a mutual mistake? The Court thinks not. This situation resembles that in *Sherwood v. Walker, supra,* the celebrated case of Rose of Aberlone. There the owner of a prize breeding cow sold her for slaughter at the going rate for good slaughter cattle. The owner had unsuccessfully tried to breed her and had erroneously concluded she was sterile. In fact she was pregnant at the time of the sale and she was much more valuable for breeding than for slaughter. There as here, the buyer was indifferent to the unknown fact; he would have been pleased to keep the unexpected profit. But he understood the bargain rested on a presumed state of facts. The court let the seller avoid the contract because of mutual mistake of fact.

In *Sherwood,* the buyer didn't know the highly pedigreed Rose was with calf. He probably could not have discovered it at the time of the sale with due diligence. Here the parties could not possibly have known of the sudden inability of the Wholesale Price Index to reflect ALCOA's non-labor costs. If, over the previous 20 years, the Wholesale Price Index had tracked, within a 5 percent variation, pertinent costs to ALCOA, a 500 percent variation of costs to Index must be deemed to be unforeseeable, within any meaningful sense of the word.

Essex has not seriously argued that the mistake does not relate to an assumption that is basic to the contract. The relation is clear. The assumed capacity of the price formula in a long-term service contract to protect against vast windfall profits to one party and vast windfall losses to the other is so clearly basic to the agreement as to repel dispute. While the cases often assert that a mistake as to price or as to future market conditions will not justify relief, this is not because price assumptions are not basic to the contracts. Instead, relief is denied because the parties allocated the risk of present price uncertainties or of uncertain future market values by their contract. Where a "price mistake" derives from a mistake about the nature or quantity of an object sold, the courts have allowed a remedy; they have found no contractual allocation of that sort of risk of price error. Indiana cases hold that where land is sold as a tract for a set price, and it later appears that there was a material error in the parties' estimate of the quantity of land conveyed, the court will correct the error by adjusting the price, *McMahan v. Terkhorn,* 67 Ind. App. 501, 116 N.E. 327 (1917), or by allowing rescission, *Earl v. VaNatta,* 29 Ind. App. 532, 64 N.E. 901 (1902). See CORBIN ON CONTRACTS §§ 604–05. Similarly, many cases allow relief from unilateral price errors by construction contractors. An Indiana decision reached this result. *Board of School Comm'rs v. Bender,* 36 Ind. App. 164, 72 N.E. 154 (1904). *See* CORBIN

ON CONTRACTS § 609. Restatement 2d of Contracts § 153, cmt. a. These cases demonstrate that price assumptions may be basic to the contract.

Essex concedes that the result of the mistake has a material effect on the contract and that it has produced a severe imbalance in the bargain. *See* Restatement 2d of Contracts § 152, cmt. c. The most that Essex argues is this: ALCOA has not proved that enforcement of the contract would be *unconscionable.* Essex correctly points out that at the time of the trial ALCOA had shown a net profit of $9 million on the contract. Essex further argues that ALCOA has failed to prove that it ever will lose money on the contract, and that such proof would require expert testimony concerning future economic values and costs. These arguments are insufficient.

The evidence shows that during the last three years ALCOA has suffered increasingly large out-of-pocket losses.[76] If the contract were to expire today that net profit of $9 million would raise doubts concerning the materiality of the parties' mistake. But even on that supposition, the court would find the mistake to be material because it would leave ALCOA dramatically short of the minimum return of one cent per pound which the parties had contemplated.

But the contract will not expire today. Essex has the power to keep it in force until 1988. The Court rejects Essex's objection to the absence of expert testimony concerning future costs and prices. The objection is essentially based on the traditional refusal of courts to award speculative damages. But Essex presses the argument too far. The law often requires courts to make awards to redress anticipated losses. The reports are filled with tort and contract cases where such a awards are made without the benefit of expert testimony concerning future economic trends. Awards are commonly denied because they are too speculative where there is a claim for lost future profits and there is insufficient evidence of present profits to form a basis for protecting future profits.

Similarly, the courts often decline to speculate concerning future economic trends in calculating awards for lost future earnings. Many states refuse to consider any possibility of future inflation in calculating such awards despite the presence of expert testimony and the teachings of common experience.... This demonstrates the law's healthy skepticism concerning the reliability of expert predictions of economic trends. Where future predictions are necessary, the law commonly accepts and applies a prediction that the future economy will be much like the present (except that inflation will cease). Since some prediction of the future is inescapable in this case, that commonly accepted one will necessarily apply. On that prediction, ALCOA has proved that over the entire life of the contract it will lose, out of pocket, in excess of $60

---

76. [6] The Court recognizes that ALCOA has suffered even larger losses of potential profits that it might have earned, but for the contract, in the strong aluminum market in recent years. Essex, rather than ALCOA, has enjoyed those profits. But their existence is immaterial to the questions raised in this case.

million, and the whole of this loss will be matched by an equal windfall profit to Essex.[77] This proof clearly establishes that the mistake had the required material effect on the agreed exchange. Indeed, if this case required a determination of the conscionability of enforcing this contract in the current circumstances, the Court would not hesitate to hold it unconscionable.

Essex next argues that ALCOA may not be relieved of the consequences of the mistake because it assumed or bore the risk of the market....

The Restatements and these cases reveal four facets of risk assumption and risk allocation under the law of mistake. First, a party to a contract may expressly assume a risk....

Customary dealing in a trade or common understanding may lead a court to impose a risk on a party where the contract is silent. Often the result corresponds to the expectation of both parties, but this will not always be true. *See* Berman, *Excuse for Nonperformance in the Light of Contract Practices in International Trade*, 63 COLUM. L. REV. 1413, 1420–24 (1963). At times legal rules may form the basis for the inferred common understanding. Equity traditionally put the risk of casualty losses on the purchaser of land while the purchase contract remained executory. This allocation was derived from the doctrine of equitable conversion. "Equity regards as done that which ought to be done." The rule could always be modified by express agreement. It survives today—where it does survive—largely by reason of its acceptance as part of the common expectations of real estate traders and their advisors.

Third, where neither express words nor some particular common understanding or trade usage dictate a result, the court must allocate the risk in some reasoned way....

Fourth, where parties enter a contract in a state of conscious ignorance of the facts, they are deemed to risk the burden of having the facts turn out to be adverse, within very broad limits. Each party takes a calculated gamble in such a contract. Because information is often troublesome or costly to obtain, the law does not seek to discourage such contracts. Thus if parties agree to sell and purchase a stone that both know may be glass or diamond at a price that in some way reflects their uncertainty, the contract is enforceable whether the stone is in fact glass or diamond. If, by contrast, the parties both mistakenly believe it to be glass, the case is said not to

---

77. [8] The equivalence of ALCOA's loss and Essex's gain may distinguish this case from the concededly more difficult "Suez cases." Transatlantic Financing Corp. v. United States, 363 F.2d 312 (D.C. Cir. 1966); American Trading and Production Corp. v. Shell International Marine, 453 F.2d 939 (2d Cir. 1972); Glidden Co. v. Hellenic Lines, 275 F.2d 253 (2d Cir. 1960); Ocean Tramp Tankers Corp. v. V/U Sorracht (The Eugenia), [1964] 1 All E.R. 161 (C.A. 1963). In those cases an unexpected closing of the canal materially increased the cost of performing the contract, leaving the courts to determine the allocation of a loss not balanced by an equal profit. Those cases might also be distinguished in that they involved the doctrine of frustration of purpose rather than the doctrine of mistake. However, the similarity of these doctrines renders this distinction doubtful.

be one of conscious ignorance but one of mutual mistake. Consequently, the vendor may avoid the contract.

In this case Essex raises two arguments. First, it asserts that ALCOA expressly or by fair implication assumed the risk that the WPI-IC would not keep up with ALCOA's non-labor production costs. Second, it asserts that the parties made a calculated gamble with full awareness that the future was uncertain, so the contract should be enforced despite the mutual mistake. Both arguments are correct within limits, and within those limits they affect the relief ALCOA may receive. Both arguments fail as complete defenses to ALCOA's claim.

Essex first asserts that ALCOA expressly or implicitly assumed the risk that the WPI-IC would not track ALCOA's non-labor production costs. Essex asserts that ALCOA drafted the index provision; that it did so on the basis of its superior knowledge of its cost experience at the Warrick Works; and that ALCOA's officials knew of the inherent risk that the index would not reflect cost changes. Essex emphasized that, during the negotiation of the contract, it insisted on the inclusion of a protective "ceiling" on the indexed price of ALCOA's services at 65 percent of a specified published market price. Essex implies that ALCOA could have sought a corresponding "floor" provision to limit its risks.

Essex's arguments rely on two ancient and powerful principles of interpretation. The first is reflected in the maxim "*expressio unius est exclusio alterius*." The second is the principle that a contract is to be construed against its drafter. To agree to an indexed price term subject to a ceiling but without a floor is to make a deliberate choice, Essex argues. It is to choose one principle and to reject another. The argument is plausible but not sufficient. The maxim rules no farther than its reason, and its reason is simply this: often an expression of a rule couched in one form reflects with high probability the rejection of a contradictory rule. Less often it reflects a probable rejection of a supplementary rule. To know if this is true of a particular case requires a scrupulous examination of the thing expressed, the thing not expressed, and the context of the expression. The question here is precisely this: By omitting a floor provision did ALCOA accept the risk of any and every deviation of the selected index from its costs, no matter how great or how highly improbable? The course of dealing between the parties repels the idea. Essex and ALCOA are huge industrial enterprises. The management of each is highly trained and highly responsible. The corporate officers have access to and use professional personnel including lawyers, accountants, economists, and engineers. The contract was drafted by sophisticated, responsible businessmen who were intensely conscious of the risks inherent in long-term contracts and who plainly sought to limit the risks of their undertaking. The parties' laudable attention to risk limitation appears in many ways: in the complex price formula, in the 65 percent ceiling, in the "most favored customer" clause that Essex wrote into the contract, and in the elaborate "*force majeure*" clause favoring ALCOA. It appears as well in the care and in the expense of the negotiations and drafting process. Essex negotiated with several aluminum producers, seeking a long-term assured supply, before agreeing to the ALCOA contract. Its search for an assured long-term supply for its aluminum product plants itself bespeaks a motive of limiting risks. Essex settled on ALCOA's offer rather than a proffered joint venture on the basis of many considerations including the required capital, engineering, and management demands of the joint venture, the cost, and the comparative risks and burdens of the two arrangements. When ALCOA proposed the price formula that appears in the contract, Essex's management examined the past behavior of the indices for stability to assure they would not cause their final aluminum cost to deviate unacceptably from the going market rate. ALCOA's management was equally attentive to risk limitation.... They selected the WPI-IC as a pricing element for this long term contract only after they assured themselves that it had closely tracked ALCOA's non-labor production costs for many years in the past and was highly likely to continue to do so in the future. In the context of the formation of the contract, it is untenable to argue that ALCOA implicitly or expressly assumed a limitless, if highly improbable, risk. On this record, the absence of an express floor limitation can only be understood to imply that the parties deemed the risk too remote and their meaning too clear to trifle with additional negotiation and drafting.

The principle that a writing is to be construed against its maker will not aid Essex here. That principle once sounded as a clarion call to retrograde courts to pervert agreements if they could. Today it is happily domesticated as a rule with diverse uses. In cases involving issues of conscience or of strong policy, such as forfeiture cases, the principle complements the familiar doctrine of strict construction to favor lenient results. In other cases it serves as an aid in resolving otherwise intractable ambiguities. This case presents neither of these problems. The question of defining the risks ALCOA assumed is one of interpretation. It implicates no strong public policy. Neither does it present an intractable ambiguity.

Neither is this a case of "conscious ignorance," as Essex argues. Essex cites many cases that establish the general rule that mistaken assumptions about the future are not the sort of mistaken assumptions that lead to relief from contractual duties.... The general rule is in fact as Essex states it. but that rule has limited application. The new Restatement notes that the rule does not apply where both parties are unconscious of their ignorance — that is, where both mistakenly believe they know the vital facts. *See* § 154 Comment C....

This distinction is sufficient to settle many cases but it is framed too crudely for sensible application to cases like the present one. The distinction posits two polar positions: certain belief that a vital fact is true and certain recognition that a vital fact is unknown. Such certainties are seldom encountered in human affairs. They are particularly rare in the understanding of sophisticated businessmen....

The ... notion of a range of uncertainty is not unknown to Indiana law. In *McMahan v. Terkhorn, supra,* the parties contracted to purchase and to sell a tract of land which they thought to contain 133 acres for $15,000. Before the date for performance the purchaser had the land surveyed. The surveyor reported the tract contained 104.52 acres. The parties then adjusted the purchase price to $12,000 and completed the conveyance on that basis. Later the vendor learned the survey was wrong; the tract contained 129 acres. He then sued for and won the value of the "excess" land conveyed. The court distinguished between the normal range of survey error which parties are deemed to expect and to risk, and gross errors for which a remedy is available....

Once courts recognize that supposed specific values lie, and are commonly understood to lie, within a penumbra of uncertainty, and that the range of probability is subject to estimation, the principle of conscious uncertainty requires reformulation. The proper question is not simply whether the parties to a contract were conscious of uncertainty with respect to a vital fact, but whether they believed that uncertainty was effectively limited within a designated range so that they would deem outcomes beyond that range to be highly unlikely. In this case the answer is clear. Both parties knew that the use of an objective price index injected a limited range of uncertainty into their projected return on the contract. Both had every reason to predict that the likely range of variation would not exceed three cents per pound. That is to say both would have deemed deviations yielding ALCOA less of a return on its investment, work, and risk of less than one cent a pound or of more than seven cents a pound to be highly unlikely. Both consciously undertook a closely calculated risk rather than a limitless one. Their mistake concerning its calculation is thus fundamentally unlike the limitless conscious undertaking of an unknown risk, which Essex now posits.

What has been said to this point suffices to establish that ALCOA is entitled to some form of relief due to mutual mistake of fact. But the stakes in this case are large, and the chances of review by higher courts are high. Therefore the Court thinks it appropriate to rule on two other theories that ALCOA presented in support of its first count.

D.

ALCOA argues that it is entitled to relief on the grounds of impracticability and frustration of purpose. The Court agrees.

In broad outline the doctrines of impracticability and of frustration of purpose resemble the doctrine of mistake. All three doctrines discharge an obligor from his duty to perform a contract where a failure of a basic assumption of the parties produces a grave failure of the equivalence of value of the exchange to the parties. And all three are qualified by the same notions of risk assumption and allocation. The doctrine of mistake of fact requires that the mistake relate to a basic assumption on which the contract was made. The doctrine of impracticability requires that the non-occurrence of the "event," Restatement 2d of Contracts § 261, or the non-existence of the "fact," *id.* § 266, causing the impracticability, to be a basic assumption on which the contract is made. The doctrine of frustration of purpose similarly rests on the same "non-occurrence" or "non-existence," "basic assumption" equation. *Id.* §§ 265, 266.

The three doctrines further overlap in time. There may be some residual notion that the doctrine of frustration and impracticability relate to occurrences after the execution of the contract while the doctrine of mistake relates to facts as they stand at the time of execution. But that view has never won general acceptance. The first Restatement does not specifically limit the mistakes of fact for which relief may be granted to facts existing at the time of the contract. §§ 500, 502. Corbin and Williston do not suggest such a limitation. And the new Restatement equivocates on the point. Section 151 defines "mistake" as "a belief that is not in accord with the facts." The word "existing" modified the word "facts" in Tentative Draft Number 10 but was deleted by the Reporter. Comment a to the section does declare:

> [T]he erroneous belief must relate to the facts as they exist at the time of the making of the contract. A party's prediction or judgment as to events to occur in the future, even if erroneous, is not a "mistake" as the word is defined here.

This declaration is anomalous and unexplained. The Court believes the definition rather than the comment expresses the better rule. The denial of relief for mistakes of future facts is better understood to rest on policies of risk allocation discussed above than to rest on the definition of "mistake."

National Presto Industries, Inc. v. United States, 338 F.2d 99 (Ct. Cl. 1964), is a prime example of the application of the doctrine of mistake to developments after the execution of the contract. There the corporation contracted to produce artillery shells for the Army at a fixed price, using a new and only partially proven production method. The method was contrived to reduce wasted steel by eliminating the need for shaving excess metal from the shells. After the contract was signed, the corporation spent large sums of money in unsuccessful attempts to make the method work. Eventually it became clear that some shaving would be required. The corporation purchased the necessary equipment and paid for the materials and labor. Then it sought and obtained relief in the Court of Claims for its added expense. The court held that there had been an actionable mutual mistake of fact. The assumed capacity of the new method to produce shells without a shaving step proved to be mistaken.[78] The court based its decision solely on mistake of fact. It does not appear that frustration or impracticability were considered.

Conversely, the notion that the doctrines of frustration and impracticability apply only to events occurring after the execution of a contract appears to be drawn more from common experience with their application than from any inherent limitation of those doctrines. Nothing in the language of the first Restatement limits the doctrine to events occurring after the execution of the contract, though all three illustrations involve such supervening events. § 288. The new Restatement recognizes that circumstances existing at the execution of a contract may render performance impracticable or they may frustrate the purpose of one of the parties so as to excuse his performance. § 266.

Thus there is a substantial area of similarity between the three doctrines. Within that area, the findings and holdings with respect to the claim of mistake also apply

---

78. [14] The court further held that the corporation had not assumed the risk of the experiment by entering into an unconditional fixed price contract. The court found that the parties did not contemplate the hazard and did not assign its risk. 338 F.2d at 109–110. The court further found that the actual cost of testing and development in attempting to perfect the new method exceeded the testing expense implicitly risked by the corporation. 338 F.2d at 109.

to the claims of impracticability and frustration. It requires no further discussion to establish that the non-occurrence of an extreme deviation of the WPI-IC and ALCOA's non-labor production costs was a basic assumption on which the contract was made. And it is clear that ALCOA neither assumed nor bore the risk of the deviation beyond the foreseeable limits of risk.

The court must still consider those aspects of doctrines of frustration and impracticability that differ from the doctrine of mistake....

The focus of the doctrines of impracticability and of frustration is distinctly on hardship. Section 261 declares a party is discharged from performing a contract where a supervening event renders his performance impracticable. Comment d discusses the meaning of "impracticability." The comment states the word is taken from Uniform Commercial Code § 2-615(a). It declares that the word denotes an impediment to performance lying between "impossibility" and "impracticality."

> Performance may be impracticable because *extreme and unreasonable difficulty, expense, injury, or loss to one of the parties will be involved....*

A mere change in the degree of difficulty or expense due to such causes as increased wages, prices of raw materials, or costs of construction, unless well beyond the normal range, does not amount to impracticability since it is this sort of risk that a fixed-price contract is intended to cover. Restatement 2d Contracts, § 261 cmt. d.

Similarly, § 265 declares a party is discharged from performing his contract where his principal purpose is *substantially* frustrated by the occurrence of a supervening event. The extent of the necessary frustration is further described in comment a: "[T]he frustration must be substantial. It is not enough that the transaction has become less profitable for the affected party or even that he will sustain a loss. The frustration must be so severe that it is not fairly to be regarded as within the risks that he assumed under the contract."

Professor Corbin explained this requirement of a severe disappointment by relating this doctrine to the broad public policies that parties should generally be required to perform their contracts.

> Variations in the value of a promised performance, caused by the constantly varying factors that affect the bargaining appetites of men, are the rule rather than the exception. Bargainers know this and swallow their losses and disappointments, meantime keeping their promises. Such being the business mores, court decisions that are not in harmony with them will not make for satisfaction or prosperity. Relief from duty, outside of the bankruptcy court, can safely be granted on the ground of frustration of purpose by the rise or fall of values, only when the variation in value is very great and is caused by a supervening event that was not in fact contemplated by the parties and the risk of which was not allocated by them. CORBIN ON CONTRACTS § 1355.

This strict standard of severe disappointment is clearly met in the present case. ALCOA has sufficiently proved that it will lose well over $60 million dollars out of pocket over the life of the contract due to the extreme deviation of the WPI-IC from ALCOA's actual costs.[79]

Is this, then, a case of impracticability, of frustration, or both? The doctrine of impracticability and of frustration focus on different kinds of disappointment of a contracting party. Impracticability focuses on occurrences that greatly increase the costs, difficulty, or risk of the party's performance. Restatement 2d of Contracts, § 261.

The doctrine of frustration, on the other hand, focuses on a party's severe disappointment that is caused by circumstances that frustrate his principal purpose for entering the contract.[80] Restatement 2d of Contracts, § 265. The doctrine of frustration often applies to relieve a party of a contract that could be performed without impediment; relief is allowed because the performance would be of little value to the frustrated party. Illustration 1 of the new Restatement—abstracted from the Coronation Cases—typifies this aspect of the doctrine of frustration.

> A and B make a contract under which B is to pay A $1,000 and is to have the use of A's window on January 10 to view a parade that has been scheduled for that day. Because of the illness of an important official, the parade is cancelled. B refuses to use the window or pay the $1,000. B's duty to pay $1,000 is discharged, and B is not liable to A for breach of contract.

> Nothing impedes the full performance of this contract. B is able to pay $1,000 and to use the window despite the cancellation of the parade. But B's purpose—to observe the spectacle—has been frustrated.

In the present case ALCOA has satisfied the requirements of both doctrines. The impracticability of its performance is clear. The increase in its cost of performance is severe enough to warrant relief, and the other elements necessary for the granting of relief have been proven. Essex argues that the causes of ALCOA's losses are due to market price increases to which the doctrine of impracticability does not apply. The doctrine of impracticability of the new Restatement is one of recent evolution in the law. The first Restatement used the term as part of the definition of "impossibility." The interesting legal evolution from the strict standards of impossibility, evident at least by dictum in *Paradine v. Jane*, Aleyn, 26 (1647 K.B.), to modern standards of impracticability is traced in Professor Gilmore's *The Death of Contract* 35–90 (1974). The drafters of the Uniform Commercial Code adopted this line of development, particularly in § 2-615. The new Restatement expressly draws upon § 2-615 in defining

---

79. [15] The Court recognizes the additional requirement that the frustration or impracticability must not be the fault of the party who seeks relief. Restatement 2d of Contracts §§ 261, 265. Essex has not claimed or shown that ALCOA's dealings during the contract caused or contributed to ALCOA's losses. The record sufficiently proves that the great cost increases of some of the non-labor cost components (power, electrolytes, carbon) were beyond ALCOA's control....

80. [16] Professor Corbin primely observed: "A 'contract' never has a purpose or object. Only the contracting persons have purposes; and the purpose of any one of these persons is different from the purpose of any other. The hopes and purposes and objects of one of the parties may be frustrated by supervening events, although the purposes of the other party may not be at all affected by those events." CORBIN ON CONTRACTS § 1353.

the scope of the doctrine. § 261 comments reporter's notes. The official comment to § 2-615 lends strength to Essex's claim.

> 1. This section excuses a seller from timely delivery of goods contracted for, where his performance has become commercially impracticable because of unforeseen supervening circumstances not within the contemplation of the parties at the time of contracting....

However,

> 4. Increased cost alone does not excuse performance unless the rise in cost is due to some unforeseen contingency which alters the essential nature of the performance. Neither is a rise or a collapse in the market in itself a justification, for that is exactly the type of business risk which business contracts made at fixed prices are intended to cover. But a severe shortage of raw materials or supplies due to a contingency such as war, embargo, local crop failure, unforeseen shutdown of major sources of supply, or the like, which either causes a marked increase in cost or altogether prevents the seller from securing supplies necessary to his performance is within the contemplation of this section.

Several of the cases cited by Essex rely on comment 4 in denying claims for relief. [citations omitted] ... Each is distinguishable from the present case in the absolute extent of the loss and in the proportion of loss involved.

In *Publicker Industries v. Union Carbide Corp.*, 17 UCC Rep. Serv. 989 (E.D. Pa. 1975), the defendant Union Carbide had contracted in 1972 to sell ethanol in specified quantities over a three-year period to the plaintiff. The price was set by a formula, adjusted annually to reflect the seller's cost for raw materials, and subject to a ceiling on adjustment increases. The raw materials were derivatives of natural gas; their price soared beginning in 1973 as did ALCOA's energy costs. The seller's costs for ethanol rose from 21.2 cents a gallon in 1973 to 37.2 cents per gallon in mid-1974. The ceiling contract sales price was then 26.5 cents per gallon. The seller's loss of 10.7 cents per gallon led to a projected aggregate loss of $5.8 million. The court refused to relieve the seller. It found that the ceiling provision constituted an intentional allocation of the "risk of a substantial and unforeseen rise in cost" to the seller. It based this finding in part on the 25 percent rise in prices by OPEC in 1971, which made future cost increases highly foreseeable. The court addressed the degree of loss issue, declaring:

> We are not aware of any cases where something less than a 100 percent cost increase has been held to make a seller's performance "impracticable."

> ... "[T]here must be more of a variation between expected cost and the cost of performing by an available alternative than is present in this case, where the promisor can legitimately be presumed to have accepted some degree of abnormal risk, and where impracticability is urged on the basis of added expense alone."[81]

---

81. [17] Quoting Transatlantic Financing Corp. v. United States, 363 F.2d 312 (D.C. Cir. 1966).

Publicker Industries is clearly distinguishable from the present case respecting the degree of loss that the seller suffered in comparison to what it foresaw at the time of contracting. The fact that the Publicker contract was made after the substantial price increase of 1971 may justify the court's finding that the seller had assumed the risk of further large price increases. The contract in the present case antedated the 1971 price increase. There is no similar factual basis for finding that ALCOA assumed the risk of the full loss that it is experiencing.

Transatlantic Financing Corp. v. United States, supra, was one of the "Suez" cases. The carrier had contracted to transport a cargo from the United States to Iran for a specified price. The contract did not specify the route, but both parties knew the most direct route was by way of Suez. When the Canal was closed the carrier had to divert its ships around Cape Horn, adding three thousand miles to the expected ten-thousand-mile voyage, and adding an expense of about $44,000 to the contract price of about $306,000. Judge J. Skelly Wright, for a unanimous panel, found that "circumstances surrounding the contract indicate that the risk of the Canal's closure may be deemed to have been allocated to Transatlantic." But he found this conclusion doubtful enough to cause him to reject a direct application of the risk allocation rule. He went on:

> The surrounding circumstances do indicate, however, a willingness by Transatlantic to assume abnormal risks, and this fact should legitimately cause us to judge the impracticability of performance by an alternate route in stricter terms than we would were the contingency unforeseen. *Id.* at 318–19.

Judge Wright then held, in the passage quoted in *Publicker Industries, supra,* that there must be more than a 12 percent cost increase to constitute impracticability.

Here ALCOA's loss is more than a thousand times greater than the carrier's loss. And the circumstances surrounding the contract show a deliberate avoidance of abnormal risks....

Eastern Air Lines Inc. v. Gulf Oil Corp., 415 F. Supp. 429 (S.D. Fla. 1975), follows the pattern of these cases except in one detail. Gulf had contracted to furnish jet fuel to Eastern in designated cities from June 1972 until January 31, 1977. The price was tied to a specific trade journal report of posted prices for a specified type of domestic oil. During the contract the price of imported oil soared. Domestic oil was subjected to a complex and shifting body of regulations including a "two-tier" price control scheme regulating the price of "old oil" but not the price of "new oil." The specified trade journal reacted to the new system by publishing prices only for the regulated "old oil." Gulf sought to escape the burden of its contract and Eastern sued to compel Gulf to perform it.

The court required Gulf to perform the contract. It found that Gulf had failed to prove its defense. The "cost" figures in evidence included built-in intra-company profits such that the court could not "determine how much it costs Gulf to produce a gallon of jet fuel for sale to Eastern, whether Gulf loses money or makes a profit on its sale of jet fuel to Eastern, either now or at the inception of the contract, or at any time in between." *Id.* at 440. Thus Gulf failed to prove it had suffered losses on the contract.

In the course of the decision the court declared that relief was available under §2-615 for an *unforeseeable* failure of a pre-supposed condition. It inferred this requirement from Comment 8 to §2-615[82] and from the Suez cases. If it were generally adopted, this requirement would reduce the occasions for excusing performance under §2-615. Judge Wright rejected such a requirement in *Transatlantic Financing*, declaring:

> Foreseeability or even recognition of a risk does not necessarily prove its allocation.... Parties to a contract are not always able to provide for all the possibilities of which they are aware, sometimes because they cannot agree, often simply because they are too busy. Moreover, that some abnormal risk was contemplated is probative but does not necessarily establish an allocation of the risk of the contingency which actually occurs. 363 F.2d at 318.

The question is important in developing doctrine of impracticability. The Indiana cases are silent on it. The Court believes that Indiana courts would find Judge Wright's approach is more in keeping with the spirit and purpose of the Uniform Commercial Code than is the strict approach of Judge King in *Eastern Air Lines*. The Code, embodied in Title 26, Burns Ind. Stat. Ann. (1974) seeks to accommodate the law to sound commercial sense and practice. Courts must decide the point at which the community's interest in predictable contract enforcement shall yield to the fact that enforcement of a particular contract would be commercially senseless and unjust. The spirit of the Code is that such decisions cannot justly derive from legal abstractions. They must derive from courts sensitive to the mores, practices, and habits of thought in the respectable commercial world.

If it were important to the decision of this case, the Court would hold that the foreseeability of a variation between the WPI-IC and ALCOA's costs would not preclude relief under the doctrine of impracticability. But the need for such a holding is not clear, for the Court has found that the risk of a wide variation between these values was unforeseeable in a commercial sense and was not allocated to ALCOA in the contract.

The Court holds that ALCOA is entitled to relief under the doctrine of impracticability. The cases Essex relies on and the other cases discovered by the Court are all distinguishable with respect to the gravity of harm which the aggrieved contracting party was liable to suffer. Except for *Transatlantic Financing*, they are also distinguishable

---

82. [18] The provisions of this section are made subject to assumption of greater liability by agreement and such agreement is to be found not only in the expressed terms of the contract but in the circumstances surrounding the contracting, in trade usage and the like. Thus the exemptions of this section do not apply when the contingency in question is sufficiently foreshadowed at the time of contracting to be included among the business risks which are fairly to be regarded as part of the dickered terms, either consciously or as a matter of reasonable, commercial interpretation from the circumstances....

with respect to the question of allocation of the risk, inferred from the circumstances known to the parties at the time of the contract and from the contract terms.

ALCOA's claim of frustration requires more discussion. ALCOA's "principal purpose" in making the contract was to earn money. This purpose has plainly been severely disappointed. The gravity of ALCOA's loss is undisputably sufficient to meet the stern standard for relief. But the question remains whether the law will grant relief for the serious frustration of this kind of purpose, *i.e.*, for the conversion of an expected profit into a serious loss. All of the new Restatement illustrations center on purposes other than making a profit. However most of them bear on some stage of a profit-oriented activity....

In § 1360 Professor Corbin demonstrates that at times courts should treat loss avoidance as a principal purpose of a party. That section deals with frustration of purpose caused by inflationary depreciation of money. Corbin demonstrates that the decisions are not uniform on this subject, but he rejects as reprehensible the nominalist rule that a dollar's a dollar no matter how small. The injustice of the nominalist position was clearly recognized in the case of *Anderson v. Equitable Life Assurance Society*, 134 L.T. 557, 42 T.L.R. 302 (1926). The facts in *Anderson* were these: In 1887 an Englishman in Russia took out a 20-premium life insurance policy with premiums and benefits payable in German marks. The policy benefit was 60,000 marks. The premiums were paid from 1887 to 1907 and were converted, as both parties understood they would be, into pounds. Their value came to £2,377. The insured died in 1922 at the height of the German hyperinflation. At that time the value of 60,000 marks was less than an English penny. The insurer argued that it owed nothing on the contract, for it could not be required to pay a fraction of a cent. Astonishingly, the court agreed. Under English law the obligation to pay in foreign currency was absolute and unqualified by variations in exchange rates. The judges noted the harshness of the result and pressed upon the company its moral obligation to make some payment, which they held the law would not compel.

Happily, some American cases and the law of many foreign countries take a different view of the problem. The problem of serious, sustained inflation is not unique to modern America. During the Revolution and the Civil War, America witnessed serious inflation. And several other nations have recently experienced more severe inflation than America has. When the problem has arisen, here and abroad, courts and legislatures have repeatedly acted to relieve parties from great and unexpected losses. *See* MANN, THE LEGAL ASPECT OF MONEY (1938); CORBIN ON CONTRACTS § 1360 and cases there cited. The exact character of the relief granted is not important here. Neither is the exact explanation of the decisions found in the cases, because even the Civil War cases antedate the evolution of the distinct doctrine of frustration. What is important is this: first, the results of those decisions would be readily explained today in terms of frustration of purpose. Corbin discusses them in his chapter on Frustration of Purpose. And second, the frustration which they involved was a frustration of the purpose to earn money or to avoid losses. Thus it appears that there is no legitimate doctrinal problem that prevents relief for frustration of this sort.

There remain the customary strictures concerning risk allocation and gravity of injury. Those have been addressed above and need not be considered again here. The Court holds ALCOA is entitled to relief on its claim of frustration of purpose.

E.

This leaves the question of framing a remedy for ALCOA. Essex argues that reformation is not available. It cites many Indiana cases declaring that reformation is only available to correct writings that, through mistake, do not reflect the agreement of the parties. The declarations to that effect are clear....

But the point is immaterial here. This case does not fall within reformation as a traditional head of equity jurisprudence. It does fall within the more general rules of equitable restitution. Courts have traditionally applied three remedial rules in cases of mistake, frustration, and impracticability. In some cases courts declare that no contract ever arose because there was no true agreement between the parties, *Raffles v. Wichelhaus, supra,* or because the parties were ignorant of existing facts that frustrated the purpose of one party or made performance impracticable. Restatement 2d of Contracts, §266. In some other cases the courts hold that a contract is voidable on one of the three theories. In these cases the customary remedy is rescission. In both classes of cases where one or both parties have performed under the supposed contract, the courts award appropriate restitution in the light of the benefits the parties have conferred on each other. The aim is to prevent unjust enrichment. The courts in such cases often call this remedy "reformation" in the loose sense of "modification." *See* III PALMER, LAW OF RESTITUTION § 13.9 (1978). In *Schwaderer v. Huron-Clinton Metropolitan Authority*, 329 Mich. 258, 45 N.W.2d 279 (1951), the plaintiff contracted to clear a tract of land of trees and brush. The parties mistakenly believed the tract contained 239 acres, and on that belief the plaintiff bid $59,000 for the job. In fact the land contained 545 acres. The court "reformed" the contract to award the plaintiff the value of the extra work it had performed. Professor Palmer says this of *Schwaderer* and similar cases:

> [T]he judgment is aimed at carving out and leaving intact an exchange that approximates or is in substance the one the parties had in mind, and at the same time readjusting the contract or its consequences so as to prevent unjust enrichment.

> The cases ... demonstrate that many situations do not fit neatly into a general scheme of classification. There are many typical cases for which a standard remedy is appropriate; there are also cases for which the relief given should be responsible to the particular facts. III PALMER, LAW OF RESTITUTION § 13.9 at 61–62.

Indiana has accepted this remedial theory. In *McMahan v. Terkhorn, supra,* the parties had purchased and sold a tract of land at a price less than their contract price in reliance on a survey that erroneously showed there was less land in the tract than the parties had believed. After the sale and before the survey error was discovered the purchaser resold part of the land, making rescission inappropriate. The court "reformed" or modified the contract to require the purchaser to pay for the extra land that had been conveyed. There, in a fully executed contract, a price adjustment was necessary to protect the fair expectation of the parties and to prevent unjust enrichment.

The same ends can be achieved under a long-term executory contract by a similar remedy. To decree rescission in this case would be to grant ALCOA a windfall gain in the current aluminum market. It would at the same time deprive Essex of the assured long-term aluminum supply that it obtained under the contract and of the gains it legitimately may enforce within the scope of the risk ALCOA bears under the contract. A remedy that merely shifts the windfall gains and losses is neither required nor permitted by Indiana law.

To frame an equitable remedy where frustration, impracticability, or mistake prevent strict enforcement of a long-term executory contract requires a careful examination of the circumstances of the contract, the purposes of the parties, and the circumstances that upset the contract. For some long-term executory contracts rescission with or without restitution will be the only sensible remedy. Where developments make performance of the contract economically senseless or purposeless, to modify the contract and to enforce it as modified would be highly inappropriate. But in cases like the present one modification and enforcement may be the only proper remedy.[83] See *Parev Products Co. v. I. Rokeach and Sons, Inc.*, 124 F.2d 147 (2d Cir. 1941). In this case Essex sought an assured long-term supply of aluminum at a price that would let it earn a profit on its finished products. ALCOA, facing ordinary market risks in 1967, sought a long-term, limited-risk use for its Warrick Works. A remedy modifying the price term of the contract in light of the circumstances that upset the price formula will better preserve the purposes and expectations of the parties than any other remedy. Such a remedy is essential to avoid injustice in this case.

During the trial the parties agreed that a modification of the price term to require Essex to pay ALCOA the ceiling price specified in the contract would be an appropriate remedy if the Court held for ALCOA. The Court understands from the parties that ALCOA will continue to suffer a substantial but smaller out-of-pocket loss at this price level. But ALCOA has not argued that the ceiling price term is subject to the same basic assumptions about risk limitation as the indexed price term. Accordingly the Court adopts the ceiling price term as part of the remedy it grants to ALCOA.

The Court must recognize, though, that before the contract expires economic changes may make this remedy excessively favorable to ALCOA. To deal with that possibility, the Court must frame a remedy that is suitable to the expectation and to the original agreement of the parties. A price fixed at the contract ceiling could redound to ALCOA's great profit and to Essex's great loss in changed circumstances.

---

83. [21] The remedial provisions of the new Restatement agree. Section 272(2) declares that a court may frame a remedy by supplying a term that is reasonable in the circumstances to avoid injustice. The same provision appears in § 158(2).

Therefore the Court adopts the following remedial scheme. For the duration of the contract the price for each pound of aluminum converted by ALCOA shall be the lesser of the current Price A or Price B indicated below.

Price A shall be the contract ceiling price computed periodically as specified in the contract.

Price B shall be the greater of the current Price B1 or Price B2. *Price B1* shall be the price specified in the contract, computed according to the terms of the contract. *Price B2* shall be that price which yields ALCOA a profit of one cent per pound of aluminum converted. This will generally yield Essex the benefit of its favorable bargain, and it will reduce ALCOA's disappointment to the limit of risk the parties expected in making the contract. The profit shall be computed using the same accounting methods used for the production of plaintiff's exhibit 431. The profit and the resulting price shall be computed once each calendar quarter, as soon after the close of the quarter as the necessary information may be assembled. When Price B2 applies, ALCOA shall bill Essex periodically, as specified in the contract at the price specified at the last quarterly price computation. Essex shall pay those bills according to the payment terms previously observed by the parties. When the next quarterly price computation is completed, that price shall be applied retroactively to the aluminum converted during the previous quarter. ALCOA shall refund any surplus payment by Essex upon the computation of the price or shall bill Essex for any additional money due.

ALCOA shall keep detailed records of the pertinent costs, indices, and computations used to calculate Prices A, B1, and B2 and shall preserve them for two years beyond the termination of the contract. ALCOA shall send Essex, in the manner and at the times specified in the contract, the price information called for in the contract, as well as a quarterly statement of Price B2 whether or not that price then applies. The statement of Price B2 need not specify the elements from which it was calculated....

Conclusion

This case is novel. The sums of money involved are huge. The Court has been considerably aided by the thorough and commendable work of all of the counsel who have participated in the case. There remains a need for a few concluding remarks concerning the theory of count one of this case and its limitations.

One of the principal themes in the development of commercial contract doctrines since the 1920s has been the need for a body of law compatible with responsible commercial practices and understandings. The old spirit of the law manifest in *Paradine v. Jane, supra,* is gone. The new spirit of commercial law in Indiana and elsewhere appears in the Uniform Commercial Code, in new developments of implied covenants, and in the new Restatement.[84]

---

84. [34] The essential unity of the new spirit of commercial contract law appears in the recurring adoption of new statutory principles from the Code into the body of the common law by the Restatement and by the courts. *See* John Murray, *Intention Over Terms: An Exploration of UCC § 2-207 and New Section 60, Restatement of Contracts,* 37 FORDHAM L. REV. 317 (1969); John Murray, *Behaviorism*

At stake in this suit is the future of a commercially important device—the long-term contract. Such contracts are common in many fields of commerce. Mineral leases, building and ground leases, and long-term coal sales agreements are just three examples of such contracts. If the law refused an appropriate remedy when a prudently drafted long-term contract goes badly awry, the risks attending such contracts would increase. Prudent businesspeople would avoid using this sensible business tool. Or they would needlessly suffer the delay and expense of ever more detailed and sophisticated drafting in an attempt to approximate by agreement what the law could readily furnish by general rule....

Corporate managers are fiduciaries. Law, founded on good sense, requires them to act with care in the management of businesses owned by other people. Attention to risk limitation is essential to the fiduciary duty of corporate managers. Courts must consider the fiduciary duty of management and the established practice of risk limitation in interpreting contracts and in the application of contract doctrines such as mistake, frustration, and impracticability. Corporate managers should not gamble with corporate funds. Generally they do not. Courts should not presume that they do, nor should they frame rules founded on such a presumption. Instead, courts should be alert to indications that the parties to a commercial contract sought to limit their risks, and should interpret the contracts and frame remedies to protect that purpose.

Parev Products Co. v. I. Rokeach & Sons, Inc., supra, decided by Judges Clark, Frank, and Learned Hand, illustrated an aspect of this point. There Parev, the plaintiff, by contract gave the defendant the exclusive right to produce and to market its product, Nyafat, a cooking oil, for 50 years for a specified royalty. The defendant had the option to cancel the contract at any time for a fee. The plaintiff agreed not to market the product or any similar product during the contract, and the defendant agreed not to market the product or any similar product after the end of the contract. In 1939 competitors began to sell Crisco and Spry, white semi-solid cooking oils, which reduced the sales of the plaintiff's oil. The defendant responded to the falling sales by introducing a new product of its own, Kea, similar to Crisco and Spry. The plaintiff sued to enjoin this further competition with its product. Since the express negative covenants did not forbid this competition, the plaintiff argued that the court should imply a negative covenant to forbid it.

The court rejected the defendant's argument that only covenants intended by the parties may be implied. The court noted the then traditional "reluctance of courts to admit that they were to a considerable extent 'remaking' a contract in situations where it seemed necessary and appropriate to do so." 124 F.2d at 149. The court acknowledged that a discernible intent of the parties should control the case, but it found no sufficient indication of intent respecting this problem:

> Of course, where intent, though obscure, is nevertheless discernible, it must be followed; but a certain sophistication must be recognized—if we are to

---

Under the Uniform Commercial Code, 51 Or. L. Rev. 269, 272 (1972); Daniel E. Murray, *Under the Spreading Analogy of Article 2 of the Uniform Commercial Code,* 39 Fordham L. Rev. 447 (1971).

approach the matter frankly—where we are dealing with changed circumstances, 15 years later, with respect to a contract that does not touch this exact point and which has at most only points of departure for more or less pressing analogies. *Id.*

Thus the question of whether to imply some sort of covenant to protect the plaintiff did not rest on the parties' intent. It rested on the status, expectations, and needs of the parties to preserve the mutual benefit of the long-term contract under changed circumstances....

The court protected the "status" of both parties by implying a term requiring the defendant to compensate the plaintiff for royalties lost due to competition with the defendant's new product.

The court gave close attention to the legitimate business aims of the parties, to their purpose of avoiding the risks of great losses, and to the need to frame a remedy to preserve the essence of the agreement. To that extent the decision exemplifies the new spirit of contract law.

This attitude toward contract law and toward the work of the courts will disturb some people even at this late date. It strains against half-remembered truths and remembered half-truths from the venerated first-year course in Contract Law. The core of the trouble lies in the hoary maxim that the courts will not make a contract for the parties. The maxim requires three replies. First, courts today can indeed make contracts for the parties. Given certain minimal indicators of an intent to contract, the courts are today directed to impose on the parties the necessary specific provisions to complete the process. *See* UCC §§ 2-204, 2-207, 2-208; U.L.T.A. §§ 2-202 through 2-204. Second, a distinction has long been noted between judicial imposition of initial terms and judicial interpretations and implications of terms to resolve disputes concerning contracts the parties have made for themselves. The maxim bears less weight when it is applied to dispute resolution than it does when it is applied to questions of contract formation. This case is plainly one of dispute resolution. Third, the maxim rests on two sensible notions: (1) Liability under the law of contract rests on assent, not imposition; (2) Judges are seldom able businessmen; they seldom have the information, ability, or time to do a good job of contracting for the parties. Neither of these notions applies here. The parties have made their own contract. The Court's role here is limited to framing a remedy for a problem they did not foresee and provide for. And while the Court willingly concedes that the managements of ALCOA and Essex are better able to conduct their business than is the Court, in this dispute the court has information from hindsight far superior to that which the parties had when they made their contract. The parties may both be better served by an informed judicial decision based on the known circumstances than by a decision wrenched from words of the contract that were not chosen with a prevision of today's circumstances. The Court gladly concedes that the parties might today evolve a better working arrangement by negotiation than the Court can impose. But they have not done so, and a rule that the Court may not act would have the perverse effect of discouraging the parties from resolving this dispute or future disputes on their own. Only a rule that permits judicial action of the kind the Court has taken in this case will provide a desirable practical incentive for businessmen to negotiate their own resolution to problems that arise in the life of long-term contracts.[85]

Finally, the Court notes that this case presents a problem of the appropriate legal response to problems of inflation. There are many long-term contracts extant where inflation has upset the basic equivalence of the agreement. Courts will increasingly have to attend to problems like the present one....

The limitation of judicial relief to cases where the parties evidence a desire to limit their risks, where one party suffers severe out-of-pocket losses not adequately foreseen and provided for by the parties seems adequate to prevent a general disruption of commercial life by inflation. This limitation also seems generally compatible with the fair needs and understanding of responsible businessmen. Little more can be asked of the courts in the development of the law.

The foregoing shall constitute findings of fact and conclusions of law as required by Federal Rule of Civil Procedure 52(a). An appropriate Order will issue.

NOTES AND QUESTIONS

1. *Judge Teitelbaum's background:* Judge Teitelbaum graduated from the University of Pittsburgh Law School in 1940. He was an FBI Special Agent and United States Attorney for the Western District of Pennsylvania. When he wrote his opinion in the *ALCOA* case, he was an Adjunct Professor at the Duquesne University Law School in Pittsburgh and a member of the American Law Institute. Perhaps he was more ready than many federal judges to consider the innovations of the ALI's Restatement (Second) of Contracts.

2. *Essex's brief on appeal to the Third Circuit:* The case was appealed to the United States Court of Appeals for the Third Circuit. Lawyers for Essex Group argued:

> ... [T]he decision endangers the future of long-term contracts. It does this by replacing the escalated fixed price formula in a long-term contract involving in excess of $300,000,000 with a new formula drafted by the court and never discussed or intended by the parties, essentially converting the contract into a cost plus agreement....
>
> ... [Essex] contends that the trial court's decision is without precedent in American jurisprudence. It has charted a course which, unless reversed, will henceforth inextricably embroil courts in the constant supervision and administration of commercial contracts. For reasons hereinafter set forth, both the applicable law and the largely undisputed facts in this case require that the trial court's judgment be reversed and that judgment be entered for ... Essex Group, Inc.

---

85. [35] The Court is aware of the practical incentive to negotiation which lies in the delay, expense, and uncertainty of litigation. This case shows that at times these burdens are insufficient to prompt settlements.

Essex charged that the escalated fixed price formula used in the contract had been developed by ALCOA's Department of Economic Analysis and Planning. According to Essex, ALCOA used the formula because it believed that its costs at the Warrick, Indiana plant were under control and the wholesale price index would increase faster than ALCOA's actual costs of aluminum production. Thus, the formula selected provided an opportunity to increase profits in a way a cost plus contract could not. During the period from when the plant opened in 1960 to when the contract with the Essex Group was signed in 1967, the actual cost of producing aluminum at the Warrick facility had declined dramatically while the wholesale price index was increasing. Moreover, ALCOA did not want to use an escalator clause based on actual costs because then it would have to reveal its costs to Essex (both a customer and a competitor) and questions of cost accounting could lead to disputes.

First, consider the assertions Essex Group's lawyers made about the trial court's opinion. Do they describe fairly Judge Teitelbaum's opinion? Second, consider the brief as an exercise in rhetoric. Note the use of the term "rewrite" and the phrase "without precedent." The Restatement (Second) of Contracts provisions are ignored here. Why? How many strands of classic contract ideology can you identify? Notice, too, the phrase "embroil courts in the constant supervision and administration of commercial contracts," with its image of burdening the judiciary.

3. *ALCOA's brief on appeal to the Third Circuit:* ALCOA's lawyers, supporting Judge Teitelbaum's opinion, responded as follows:

> First, Alcoa proved a sufficient underlying agreement for reformation under Indiana law....
>
> Second, the fact situation here fits exactly with the Restatement 2d of Contracts definition of mutual mistake of fact (§ 152) for which the remedy of reformation (§§ 297 & 300) is provided. Professor Farnsworth, the Reporter of the Restatement 2d of Contracts, presented an oral brief at the trial, which brief is included in the transcript ... Professor Farnsworth testified:
>
> In my opinion, it is entirely possible that Alcoa could show at the trial that both parties at the time of contracting made a mistake as to the fact that the wholesale price index was then suitable for an escalation clause in an energy-intensive contract. An analogy by way of example would be to a mistake of two parties to a contract using specified equipment that the equipment was suitable to the task.
>
> Alcoa proved, and the trial court found, the facts to be as Professor Farnsworth suggested the evidence might show.
>
> If there is any difference between the provisions in the Restatement 2d of Contracts on mutual mistake of fact and the Indiana cases cited (Essex relies on the 1896 *Citizens National Bank* case), then certainly one would expect the Supreme Court of Indiana now to follow the Restatement as it has repeatedly done.

Third, the trial court cited Restatement 2d of Contracts, §300(2),[86] which allows a court to equitably adjust or supply a term that is reasonable in the circumstances to avoid injustice. As Professor Farnsworth stated in his oral brief, the Restatement has been liberalized to permit the formulation of a remedy to do justice and prevent an unconscionable result....

Restatement 2d of Contracts, §300(2), which is entitled "RELIEF IN-CLUDING RESTITUTION; SUPPLYING A TERM" states at page 306 of Tentative Draft No. 14:

In any case governed by the rules stated in this Chapter, if those rules together with the rules stated in prospective Chapter 16 will not avoid injustice, *the court may grant relief on such terms as justice requires* including protection of the parties' reliance interests. (Emphasis added).

Thus, Restatement 2d of Contracts §300(2) constitutes an alternative theory of law for the trial court's remedy, even if reformation were somehow ruled inappropriate.

ALCOA's lawyers also responded to Essex Group's charge concerning the reasons the formula was used by saying: "[T]he WPI was selected to meet Essex's desire for an objective and easily administered index to reflect ALCOA's Warrick non-labor costs, not to increase ALCOA's profits, and the trial court observing the testimony found it to be the fact."

Presumably, the *ALCOA* case was being tried under the law of Indiana as applied by federal courts. Whatever the merits of Judge Teitelbaum's opinion, did the ALCOA lawyers convince you that Indiana would adopt the new Restatement (Second) of Contracts approach? How would you argue this point for ALCOA or for Essex Group? As we have said several times in these materials, federal judges often develop state law dealing with contracts and statutes related to contracts problems. Federal judges must divine what a state court would do if it faced the problem. Yet diversity of citizenship jurisdiction keeps state courts from getting an opportunity to offer many modern clues.

4. *What was the real problem?* Under the contract, at one point, Essex was buying aluminum from ALCOA at about 36 cents a pound. It was then reselling this aluminum for about 73 cents per pound. This gave Essex a gross profit of 37 cents a pound. In footnote 6 of the court's opinion, the court says that ALCOA has suffered the loss of the profits that Essex made reselling the aluminum that was delivered to it by ALCOA. The court says that the existence of these profits "is immaterial to the questions raised in this case." We can speculate with some basis in the facts of the case that the purpose of this deal was to provide Essex with aluminum to use as a raw material in making products that it then would sell. ALCOA had little reason to take any risk that Essex would become a broker reselling aluminum in competition with ALCOA. The transaction between the parties could have been structured as a

---

86. This became §158 in the final version of the RESTATEMENT (SECOND).

requirements contract. Had the parties used this type of an arrangement, UCC § 2-306(1) provides that in a requirements contract "no quantity unreasonably dispro-portionate to any stated estimate or in the absence of a stated estimate to any normal or otherwise comparable prior ... requirements may be ... demanded." This provision probably would have blocked Essex from going into the business of selling unprocessed aluminum. Instead of a requirements contract, Essex bought bauxite from ALCOA and had it transported on ALCOA ships to the United States. It then paid ALCOA to convert the bauxite into aluminum. Essex built a factory near the ALCOA plant in Warrick, Indiana, and it took delivery of the aluminum there. Why did the parties structure the transaction this way? Might ALCOA, in substance, be selling aluminum to Essex at a lower price than ALCOA offered to its other customers?

5. *The outcome of the case:* The parties settled the case after oral argument to the United States Court of Appeals for the Third Circuit. Judge Arlin M. Adams, a member of the Third Circuit Court of Appeals, requested the parties to attend a conciliation session between the time briefs were filed and oral argument was scheduled, a relatively unusual procedure.

Following oral argument, ALCOA indicated an interest in settling the case. The parties conferred at length, with ALCOA giving ground in its demands. It appears that the case was settled on the basis that the original contract would continue in effect until December 31, 1981; that during the balance of the original time of the contract, ALCOA would sell at a more favorable price; and that ALCOA would extend the time of the contract for a period of five years on a favorable price basis, albeit not as favorable as during the contract period.

Judge Adams's settlement conference might not have promoted a settlement. Some-thing might have happened during oral argument to cause ALCOA to reevaluate its position, or it might have been waiting for what it thought was the right moment to strike a deal. There had been settlement discussions from time to time over a period of several years.

Why didn't the parties settle earlier and save all the investment in lawyering and judicial time? Did Judge Teitelbaum's opinion, work on the briefs, and the process before the Third Circuit serve some purpose?

6. *Scholarly criticism of the case:* The case provoked contracts scholars into print. The late Professor John Dawson was highly critical of the *ALCOA* decision. He said that the *ALCOA* approach "is the treatment that is now normally given frustrated contracts [in West Germany], a treatment described with the hope that our own courts can be dissuaded from a course so disastrous for the coherence and rationality of our law of contract."[87]

---

87. *See* John Dawson, *Judicial Revision of Frustrated Contracts: Germany*, 63 B.U. L. Rev. 1039 (1983); John Dawson, *Judicial Revision of Frustrated Contracts: The United States*, 64 B.U. L. Rev. 1 (1984).

Professor Sheldon Halpern[88] noted that courts have not followed the *ALCOA* decision. He argued that Judge Teitelbaum's decision did not rest on an accepted theory of contract law. While the court rejected the often fictional search for the parties' intentions, all it could point to was the need to relieve hardship. Judge Teitelbaum went too far, too soon, and with too little.

Judge, and formerly Professor, Richard Posner offered the following comments in *Northern Indiana Public Service Co. v. Carbon County Coal Co.*:[89]

> Since impossibility and related doctrines are devices for shifting risk in accordance with the parties' presumed intentions, which are to minimize the costs of contract performance, one of which is the disutility created by risk, they have no place when the contract explicitly assigns a particular risk to one party or the other.... *[A] fixed-price contract is an explicit assignment of the risk of market price increases to the seller and the risk of market price decreases to the buyer*, and the assignment of the latter risk to the buyer is even clearer where, as in this case, the contract places a floor under price but allows for escalation. If, as is also the case here, the buyer forecasts the market incorrectly and therefore finds himself locked into a disadvantageous contract, he has only himself to blame and so cannot shift the risk back to the seller by invoking impossibility or related doctrines. [Emphasis added.]

Judge Posner considered the *ALCOA* case in his article *The Law and Economics of Contract Interpretation*.[90] He said that he was unconvinced by Judge Teitelbaum's argument. He continues:

> ALCOA may not have invested enough care in drafting the price escalator clause. Borrowing from the economics of torts, we might ask who the "cheapest cost avoider" in the case was—that is, who could at least cost have minimized the transaction costs (broadly defined ... to include dispute-resolution and error costs) that ensued from the mismatch between the price escalator clause and the actual cost conditions of contract performance that gave rise to the litigation. In some cases it will be the court because the costs of drafting to avoid the mistake that later give rise to the litigation would have exceeded the expected benefits; if so, it would probably be better, that is cheaper, to allow the court to complete the contract if and when a dispute arises. But it seems pretty clear that ALCOA was the cheaper cost avoider; its mistake was careless in the economic, which is the legal, sense of a large gap between the lower costs of error avoidance and the higher costs of error.... ALCOA itself should have realized that the WPI did not track its own cost structure.

---

88. Sheldon Halpern, *Applicability of the Doctrine of Commercial Impracticability: Searching for "The Wisdom of Solomon,"* 135 U. PA. L. REV. 1123 (1987).

89. 799 F.2d 265, 278 (7th Cir. 1986).

90. Richard A. Posner, *The Law and Economics of Contract Interpretation*, 83 TEX. L. REV. 1581, 1602 (2005).

7. *Scholarly defense of adjustment:* Several other scholars have defended judicial adjustment of contracts. For example, Professor Leon Trakman argued: "The need for a functional category of remedial adjustments, however, becomes more pressing when an all-or-nothing principle of law governs nonperformance and produces neither fairness nor economic efficiency."[91]

Professor Robert A. Hillman argued that a supplier is entitled to adjustment of a contractual obligation in at least some situations.[92] Hillman has said the objective theory and interpretation seeking the reasonable expectations of the parties tells us whether there is a duty to adjust.[93] He pointed out that some contracts expressly provide for adjustment when the cost of performance is grossly inequitable. Such express provisions are common in some industries. Moreover, even if a supply contract contains no express agreement to adjust, the situation when the parties made the deal may show that they intended adjustments in light of changed circumstances. That they say nothing about adjustments in their written contract does not necessarily establish anything. Drafting a clause for what they see as unclear risks isn't worth the effort. Trade custom or the course of dealing or performance may establish a duty to adjust. Indeed, a party's duty of good faith may create an obligation to adjust a contract in light of changed circumstances.

Still, Professor Hillman recognized that not every contract raises a duty to adjust if something goes awry. Large one-time deals involving standardized commodities usually involve assumption of the risk of market shifts. The parties may see adjustment as a matter of comity rather than legal obligation. Buyer may adjust seller's obligation as a favor that seller will return in the future. The parties may bargain about rising prices and shortages, and this suggests that the written contract reflects their risk assumption. However, even when this is true, they may not intend their written provision to govern an extreme shift in the market. Hillman recognized that one of the most difficult questions is how much disruption triggers the duty to adjust.

Hillman also argued that parties may leave a gap in their agreement despite the appearance of settling their obligations in a formal writing. The evidence may not establish a duty to make adjustments, but a court may conclude that reasonable parties would not have expected the supplier to act as insurer. Courts could fill this gap in their agreement by finding a duty to adjust.

Are there any standards or must courts fly blind if they find a duty to adjust? Hillman argued there are standards. Courts may find that parties did not intend to allow a supplier to raise prices without a corresponding increase in its actual costs. They may find that parties did not intend buyers to be able to take advantage of a drastic

---

91. Leon Trakman, *Winner Take Some: Loss Sharing and Commercial Impracticability*, 69 MINN. L. REV. 471 (1985).

92. Robert A. Hillman, *Court Adjustment of Long-Term Contracts: An Analysis Under Modern Contract Law*, 1987 DUKE L.J. 1.

93. Contrast Professor Hillman's view with that of Judge Posner quoted above. Recall, too, the debates about the parol evidence rule. Do we read the words on paper or do we look at these words in full context seeking the parties' real deal?

market shift. Often they do not intend to allow buyers to raise their prices to third parties while insisting on seller's performance at a pre-inflationary price. Furthermore, courts can look to similar supply contracts made or adjusted under the changed conditions that provoked the problem. They can consider settlement offers. They can find large windfalls to be unjust enrichment. They can hold the supplier responsible to deliver at the old price only long enough to allow a buyer to cover its reliance losses based on this old price.

Professor Richard Speidel attempted to rationalize the approach, if not the result, of the court in the *ALCOA* case.[94]

> [C]an a case be made for imposing a duty on the advantaged party to accept a "fair and equitable" adjustment proposal made by the disadvantaged party? If so, what remedies are appropriate? Keeping the *ALCOA* facts in mind, a tentative case can be made that does not convert the law of contracts into a pervasive duty to be altruistic.
>
> First, the disadvantaged party must propose a modification that would be enforceable if accepted by the advantaged party. Under the Restatement (Second), [§ 89] this occurs if the disrupted contract is not "fully performed on either side" and if the modification is "fair and equitable in view of circumstances not anticipated by the parties when the contract was made." The changed circumstances are similar to but less than those required to discharge a contract for impracticability. This first requirement both neutralizes any opportunism by the disadvantaged party, *e.g.*, duress, and affirms that agreed adjustments are preferred — that contract is available to resolve the dilemma and has been employed by the disadvantaged party.
>
> Second, it must be clear that the disadvantaged party did not assume the risk of the unanticipated event by agreement, or under the test stated in the UCC in § 2-615(a), or otherwise. If the disadvantaged party did assume the risk, then the advantaged party has no duty to accept any proposed modification. The risk assumption question is complicated, and the answer will probably not be clear at the time that the adjustment is proposed. Why should the advantaged party be held to reject at his peril? Because it is in this precise situation — where there are substantial unbargained-for gains and losses caused by unanticipated events — that a case for the duty to rescue can be made. In this setting where the risk of changed circumstances has not been allocated to either party, a refusal to adjust by the advantaged party leaves all of the loss on the disadvantaged party and permits the advantaged party to salt away all of the gains. Short of discharging the contract and leaving the parties to restitution, a duty to adjust is necessary to avoid opportunism.

---

94. *See* Richard Speidel, *The New Spirit of Contract*, 2 J.L. & Com. 193, 206–208 (1982); Richard Speidel, *Court-Imposed Price Adjustments Under Long-Term Supply Contracts*, 76 Nw. U. L. Rev. 369 (1981). Reprinted with permission.

Thus, imposing the duty here is consistent with emerging notions of good faith performance and *ALCOA's* second peg in the "new" spirit, loss avoidance. More importantly, it is an imposition with little damage to the requirement of consent in contract law. . . .

Last, this conclusion is bolstered by what might be the imperatives of an emerging theory of relational contract law. In *ALCOA*, the parties, at the time of contracting, were unable adequately to deal with certain changed circumstances over the duration of a seventeen-year contract. Yet preserving the contract was important to the parties and to third parties dependent upon its performance but not represented in the litigation. Ian Macneil has argued that in situations such as this there are relational norms that the contract should be preserved and conflict harmonized by adjustment. These norms put a high premium upon developing mechanisms for adjustment over time and good faith efforts to adjust in the light of change. Thus, if in an ALCOA-type case, the court concludes that the disadvantaged party is entitled to "some relief" but not discharge, and the advantaged party has refused to accept a reasonable adjustment in light of risks that the disadvantaged party did not assume, relational theory also supports a court-imposed adjustment to preserve the contract, to adjust the price, and to avoid the twin devils of un-bargained for hardship and unjust enrichment.

In a tribute to Richard Speidel after his death,[95] Professor Hillman returned to the question of court adjustment of long-term contracts and concluded: "So we can say no more than *maybe* Dick Speidel was right about court adjustment." He looked at the goals of contract law as they applied to this approach:

[F]airness, efficiency, and autonomy . . . often point in the same direction remedially, but not always. For example, Posner asserts that court adjustment should depend on whether the court or the promisor is the cheapest cost avoider, and he suspects that ALCOA, the promisor, was that party. But fairness requires courts to avoid granting windfalls at the expense of a disadvantaged party, which suggests that the court should deny Essex at least some of the gain it would have realized by enforcing the contract. Finally, autonomy requires identifying whether the parties reasonably expected their counterpart to be flexible if things went awry, in which case Essex should have agreed to an adjustment without litigation.[96] Court adjustment under these circumstances is merely a form of specific performance. Even if contract law could identify the appropriate norm or norms to apply to court adjustment, each of the above conclusions about what the norm dictates is highly debatable, depends deeply on the context, and ultimately, may be impervious to empirical testing.

---

95. Robert A. Hillman, *Maybe Dick Speidel Was Right About Court Adjustment*, 46 San Diego L. Rev. 595, 604, 607 (2009).

96. Hillman noted: "Stewart Macaulay wrote that this remedy [the one reached by the court in the ALCOA case] was a compromise position in that it created 'a good price, but not the "you-can't-believe it" good price' that Essex had enjoyed under the contract's express terms." *Id.* at 597.

8. *The relational exchange approach to contracts:* The economist Victor Goldberg has written about price adjustment in long-term contracts.[97] He noted that business people often use "gross inequity" clauses in some long-term contracts. Under these clauses, parties leave the decision to adjust the contract or discharge the parties when performance would cause a gross inequity to an arbitrator or judge. Absent such clauses, courts will have to decide whether ever to grant any relief, what changes are sufficient to justify judicial action, and what relief they should grant.

Goldberg considered when parties might want a third party to make adjustments or award discharges. He said that the case for intervention is stronger "when the costs of a price dispute are high and the costs of settlement would be reduced by giving the disadvantaged party the right to call upon the court to revise the contract." There might be few such cases.

Goldberg pointed out that businesses have reason to use some form of price adjustment mechanism in their contracts. "Firms do not generally enter into multiyear contracts because of their concern for the future course of prices. Rather, they enter into the agreements to achieve the benefits of cooperation." Price adjustment clauses often are used when the contract calls for a complex product constantly redefined over the life of the contract. Adjustment also discourages the parties from wasting assets. Without adjustment, the below-market price of an input might cause a buyer to use too much of it. In addition, an adjustment clause reduces the likelihood that a party who had been a big loser on a contractual "bet" will try to recapture losses by minimal performance, retaliate by failing to cooperate, make threats to breach, or search for arguments to minimize the nature of the obligation.

Those who drafted the contract in *ALCOA v. Essex* used a price adjustment mechanism, but it didn't work. What kind of mistake was this, and should it warrant relief? Lawyers often find it hard to fashion an effective, acceptable price adjustment mechanism. Price indices are the easiest to use, but often in a long-term contract there is no unique external market price to use.

Goldberg noted that in the *ALCOA* case the failure of the price index to measure the change in fuel prices accounted for only about ten to twelve cents of the difference between the contract price and the market price for aluminum in 1979. The balance of the difference may have reflected demand-induced, rather than cost-driven, market price increases. The contract did not track changing demand conditions and the demand for aluminum was soaring in the late 1970s. Moreover, the contract was not designed to adjust to large changes in the overall price level. "Sixty percent of the initial contract price (the demand charge plus the fixed 'profit') was unadjusted for the life of the contract." Nonetheless, Goldberg says it is a close question whether ALCOA should have bargained to index the remaining 60 percent of costs. He says that parties do not necessarily confront the same external price, and this makes it hard to use a price index based on aluminum prices. It is as if they are dealing in two different, imperfectly connected, markets.

---

97. Victor Goldberg, *Price Adjustment in Long-Term Contracts*, 1985 Wis. L. Rev. 527.

> Alcoa's opportunity cost is the net price it could receive by using the Warrick capacity to produce ingot for export to other customers. Essex's opportunity cost is the price of delivered aluminum ingot. There is no *a priori* reason to believe that these will be close to each other. However, for an index to work it is not necessary that the prices be close, only that they move together over time. Whether these two opportunity costs (and the market price for aluminum ingot) move together over time is an empirical question which I intend to explore in a later paper.[98]

If we assume that the parties would have had difficulty finding an acceptable price adjustment mechanism, was the burden on ALCOA great enough to makes its performance impracticable? Goldberg argued that in the *ALCOA* case, the court assumed something about future costs and prices and concluded that ALCOA stood to lose about $75 million.

> What does Alcoa lose if it must fulfill the contract? It loses the chance to sell aluminum to someone else. That is the true measure of the loss, and in this case it is considerably greater than the figure cited by the judge. In the year the suit was brought the loss was over thirty cents per pound, over $20 million.

However, Goldberg said that we cannot define a magic number or percentage to allow us to judge whether relief should be granted. Even a very large difference between the market and contract prices for a standardized commodity might have little adverse effect on the expected value of the contract. On the other hand, at times a small difference might generate considerable joint costs and make revision valuable. However, if courts make relief too easy to get, it will generate additional joint costs, affecting performance and demands for renegotiations. Part of the problem is that when the opportunity costs of buyer and seller differ, it is not clear how an arbitrator should set a new price.

Professor Thomas Palay commented on Goldberg's article.[99] Palay praised Goldberg's approach to the problem, but Palay cautioned that we cannot focus on the written document to tell us whether the parties in a long-term contract could benefit from or expect price adjustments. "Parties who have, or anticipate, strong relational ties with their contracting opposites are not particularly worried about initial terms of agreement."

Palay then discussed Oliver Williamson's approach to transactional governance structures. Williamson argues that three variables determine structural characteristics: (1) the degree to which uncertainty is present; (2) the frequency of exchange; and

---

98. *Id.* at 540.

99. Thomas Palay, *A Contract Does Not a Contract Make*, 1985 Wis. L. Rev. 561. Copyright © 2010 by The Board of Regents of the University of Wisconsin System. Reprinted by permission of the Wisconsin Law Review.

(3) the extent to which exchanges are supported by idiosyncratic capital that cannot be devoted elsewhere easily.

Williamson's third variable is particularly important. Those in idiosyncratic exchanges can protect themselves by demanding a price that compensates them for marginal costs and includes an insurance component covering opportunistic behavior. They also can gain credible commitments not to act opportunistically. This is done by the mutual exchange of hostages—investments of capital assets that will be destroyed if the contract falls apart.

Palay looked at the problems in *ALCOA v. Essex*:[100]

> Alcoa's "hostage" was that portion of the Warrick capacity that was added for, or dedicated to, Essex. Alcoa might have believed that Essex had posted a similar hostage when it placed its fabricating facility near the Warrick smelter. The value of the fabricating facility, built specifically to receive aluminum from the Warrick plant, would diminish if the contractual relation failed. Alternatively, if Essex helped finance Alcoa's dedicated capacity, the arrangement could have led Alcoa to believe that Essex became tied to the aluminum manufacturer. After all, Essex could have lost its investment in Warrick if the contract failed.

> If these were the hostages Essex posted, imagining why they proved inadequate to force renegotiation of the contract is easy. Essex could receive aluminum from plenty of other sources if Alcoa were to breach, but any other source would entail additional transportation costs. This meant that as a hostage the plant was only worth the difference between its use in fabricating Warrick Aluminum and its use in fabricating aluminum that had to be transported from elsewhere. That is, as a hostage Essex's plant ranked right up there with giving the wicked king your lazy, shiftless third cousin. Using any of the financing aspects of the arrangement as a hostage would be similarly inadequate. Alcoa's pockets were simply too deep. Essex would know that Alcoa was never really in danger of defaulting on the "loan."

> Thus, under this scenario, Alcoa's problem was not so much a "mistake" concerning the price term, but rather a mistake about the importance that Essex would place on the preservation of the relationship. Admittedly, many of my observations are little more than speculation—but they are reasonable hypotheses that require the researcher to look beyond the formal documents for confirmation.

Assume Palay's speculation proved to be right. What significance would it have for our appraisal of Judge Teitelbaum's opinion? Would such a mistake fit into traditional notions of mistake or impossibility? Does it suggest what we should do?

---

100. *Id.* at 564.

9. *One economist offers a presumption as to the real deal:* Victor Goldberg argued:[101]

> Regardless of how the doctrine is labeled, courts, when considering a plea to excuse performance, should be constrained by the fundamental question: what would the parties have chosen? I will argue that, as a general rule, parties would not agree to excuse performance because of changed market conditions (neither supply nor demand shocks). The fact that market prices have doubled or tripled would be irrelevant. Parties are more likely to excuse performance if the supervening events adversely effect the costs of performing this particular contract for reasons that are essentially unrelated to overall market conditions....
>
> The crucial point is this. If the occurrence of a *force majeure* condition is not correlated with market conditions, the expected change in market price is zero, and therefore, the benefits anticipated at the contract formation stage from holding the promisor liable are likely to be low. However, if the seller refuses to perform because events subsequent to the formation of the contract have shown that the contract price is too low, the buyer does suffer. If the seller could perform, but would prefer not to, we can reasonably infer that the reason is that the contract price is too low; the seller could do better selling elsewhere. The changed conditions affect the market for the good or service involved. There is a widespread drought, the Suez Canal closes, etc. Discharging the contract in this instance carries a greater cost. If a seller could be excused simply because the contract price was below the market price, the substantial benefits from entering into a contract in a timely manner are sacrificed. While this sacrifice might be acceptable in some cases, it is clear that the costs of excusing a seller's performance when the contract price is too low are greater than excusing its performance in the event of a fire or other act of God.

Goldberg did note: "This is not to say that parties would never adjust the contract price. Price concessions in the face of changed market conditions are commonplace. But the grantor of the concession often expects a *quid pro quo,* either express (*e.g.,* an increase in the term of the contract) or implied (*e.g.,* enhanced good will). The grantor, that is, maintains the right to make (or not make) price concessions."[102]

Professor Eisenberg said[103] that "[o]ften a dramatic and unexpected increase in the promisor's cost of performance should support judicial relief even if the increase is not tied to a discrete event, because in many and perhaps most contracts, the parties do not expect that the promisor has undertaken an enormous financial risk."[104] Eisen-

---

101. Victor Goldberg, *Impossibility and Related Excuses,* J. Inst'l & Theoretical Econ. Vol. 144, 100–116 (1988).

102. *Id.* at n.3.

103. Melvin A. Eisenberg, *Impossibility, Impracticability, and Frustration,* 1 J. Legal Analysis 207 (2009).

104. *Id.* at 234.

berg proposed a special rule for such cases that he calls the *bounded-risk test.* In his words, "a promisor should be entitled to judicial relief if as a result of a dramatic and unexpected rise in costs, performance would result in a financial loss significantly greater than the risk of loss that the parties would reasonably have expected the promisor to have undertaken."

However, Eisenberg argued that the bounded-risk situation does not necessarily mean that the seller should be able to walk away from the contract without consequence. Eisenberg advocated awarding the buyer a limited form of consequential damages as the price for giving the seller relief. "[T]he buyer should be entitled to the expectation damages that would have been awarded if there had been a reasonably foreseeable increase in the seller's cost of performance and a corresponding increase in the market value of the commodity."[105] How would you expect Eisenberg's proposal to affect settlement negotiations?

10. *A note on the law and economics notes:* The previous notes both rely on the commentary of an economist and draw to some extent on the vocabulary of economics. This can be frustrating for those with little or no training in economics. A great deal of legal scholarship in recent decades has drawn on economic analysis. It is often controversial. Many reject the analysis and assert that it is not to be trusted because it contains concealed substantive or ideological biases. Others reject it by suggesting that it is untrustworthy because it is not complete, but is presented as if it were. One or both of these critiques may be right (or wrong). We offer this note to acknowledge the discomfort that the law and economics notes might cause some. As non-economists ourselves, we often share this discomfort. But we do need to be aware of, and take seriously, accounts that often seem to illuminate the issue, even if they are difficult and make us uncomfortable. Furthermore, the language of law and economics has become common among many judges and lawyers. Law and economics has incorporated more psychology, with one branch known as "behavioral law and economics" to acknowledge that humans' rationality is bounded, leading us to behave sometimes in surprising ways that simple models may not predict.[106]

11. *The role of jurists in the American system:* Professor E. Allan Farnsworth, a reporter for Restatement (Second) of Contracts, gave Judge Teitelbaum an oral brief that favored *ALCOA.* Interestingly, Professor John Dawson wrote in his article on the United States' approach to judicial revision of frustrated contracts, "counsel for Essex ... had requested me to comment on the briefs that were being prepared for the appeal by Essex. I had thus had considerably earlier an opportunity to form a highly adverse opinion of the trial court's decision." Dawson calls the *ALCOA* opinion a "bizarre solution." Had the appeal gone forward, the Third Circuit might have had to choose between the views of Farnsworth and the Restatement (Second) and Dawson. Dawson, then a professor at Boston University School of Law and an emeritus

---

105. *Id.* at 245.
106. *See* Cass R. Sunstein (Ed.), Behavioral Law and Economics (Cambridge Univ. Press 2000).

professor at Harvard Law School, was a recognized expert in contracts, comparative law, and legal history. Thus, each side could have pointed to a distinguished academic in its corner.

In what sense, if at all, are Professors Farnsworth, Dawson, Eisenberg, Hillman, Halpern, Schlegel, Speidel, Trakman, or the authors of *Contracts: Law in Action* "experts" on what contract law ought to be? Should there be some mechanism so courts could call on contracts professors for assistance in major cases, other than as experts hired by one party or the other? Do you see any problem with Professor Farnsworth giving an "oral brief" to the court but being sponsored by ALCOA or Professor Dawson consulting with the Essex Group lawyers on their briefs in the case?

12. *Is* ALCOA *the law or is it only a case to provoke law professors?* In *United States v. Southwestern Electric Cooperative*,[107] the court commented that the *ALCOA* decision had faded into obscurity. A party cannot get out of a contract because of an error in judgment about the construction costs of a project. However, in *Unihealth v. U.S. Healthcare, Inc.*,[108] the court placed great reliance on *ALCOA*. Health maintenance organizations had contracted with a hospital for services to their members. The contract called for discounts from the hospital's usual rates. However, the hospital sought to limit the amounts of these discounts. It provided: "If the overall discount for all Inpatients exceeds 40 percent during a calendar year, U.S. Healthcare will reimburse Meadowlands Hospital and Medical Center monies beyond the 40 percent discount." However, "the term 'discount,' specifically, the lodestar from which the discount should be assessed, is not referred to or defined anywhere in the Agreement." The contract was negotiated in 1991. The State of New Jersey had a regulatory scheme, the Diagnostic Related Groups (DRG) system, which had been in place since 1979. It required all hospitals to bill for inpatient services at prices set by the New Jersey Department of Health. The state repealed the DRG system, effective January 1, 1993. The hospital had provided services in 1992 and 1993, but the parties never were able to agree on how to calculate the limit on the amount of discounts once the DRG was repealed.

The court decided that the repeal of the DRG system frustrated the contract as written. This repeal was not a risk that was assumed by either party. The court relied on *Aluminum Corporation of America v. Essex Group* as showing its power to fashion a reasonable term to substitute for the one that the parties drafted that no longer could be applied. The court appointed a special master to act as a mediator. He was to try to help the parties reach an agreement about the compensation due. If agreement could not be reached, the master was to formulate a pricing system for medical services comparable to the former DRG system. Once this system was in place, then the discount clause could be applied.

---

107. 869 F.2d 310 (7th Cir. 1989).
108. 14 F. Supp. 2d 623 (D. N.J. 1998).

5. Coping with Changed Circumstances: "Coercive Mediation" by Judges to Push Parties to Rewrite the Contract

Westinghouse Electric Corporation sold nuclear reactors to 27 power companies in the '60s and early '70s. In order to persuade the utilities to buy the reactors, Westinghouse agreed to supply the uranium oxide that the reactors used as fuel. The contract price averaged $9.50 per pound. Westinghouse committed itself to supply 80 million pounds of fuel, although it owned at the time about 15 million pounds; it was confident that it could buy fuel on the market as the need arose. Much to the dismay of Westinghouse, the price of uranium oxide rose from about $6 per pound in 1972 to $44 per pound in 1978. It doesn't take a nuclear physicist to see that the financial implications of this to Westinghouse were significant, if not dire.

On September 8, 1975, Westinghouse shocked its utility customers, and others in the business community, by announcing that it would not honor its contracts to supply the nuclear fuel. It argued that it was excused from performance by §2-615(a) of the Uniform Commercial Code. That section provides a defense to an action for breach if the non-performance is "the occurrence of a contingency the non-occurrence of which was a basic assumption on which the contract was made." Westinghouse argued that the extreme and unforeseen change in the market for uranium oxide amounted to just such a contingency. The power companies responded by bringing suits that charged that Westinghouse was simply seeking to avoid responsibility for the risk it took when it promised to deliver fuel it didn't own, electing to rely on an inherently risky market. Their theory was that Westinghouse had made a business misjudgment by gambling on the market and was trying to avoid taking the consequences. The claims of the utilities aggregated approximately $2.6 billion. The net worth of Westinghouse was $2.3 billion at the end of 1977. Many of the utility suits were joined in a single suit in the federal court in Richmond, Virginia, presided over by Robert Merhige, Jr.

Question: How would you assess the strength of Westinghouse's §2-615 claim, acknowledging of course that you have only the sketchiest description of a very complicated story?

In 1976, documents surfaced in Australia that revealed an international uranium cartel, which had been organized in 1972 to control sales by producing governments, and so to raise prices. The United States producers apparently knew about the cartel, but had chosen not to participate. It was unclear whether or not such a cartel was legal under international law. Westinghouse argued that the cartel was the reason for the price run-up. A Canadian subsidiary of Gulf Oil was a participant in the cartel. Westinghouse brought suit in October 1976 against Gulf Oil and 29 uranium producers for price-fixing. It alleged that Gulf Oil's Canadian subsidiary provided the link between American uranium producers and the international cartel. Gulf Oil admitted the participation of its Canadian subsidiary, but said that the cartel had carefully excluded the American market from its plans. Gulf filed a countersuit in May 1978, alleging that Westinghouse itself had been seeking to monopolize markets for nuclear reactors, fabricated fuel, and uranium.

Question: What is the relevance, to the § 2-615 dispute, of the discovery of the international cartel?

From the very beginning, Federal Judge Merhige urged the parties to the suits between the utilities and Westinghouse to settle. Although the potential liability of Westinghouse exceeded $2 billion, most observers expected settlements in most, if not all, of the disputes. In addition to the risks associated with litigating and losing, the utilities had an interest in the survival of Westinghouse. Someone would have to continue to provide engineering for the reactor projects, as well as parts and service. In addition, the utility industry had a general interest in the survival of competition in the reactor and power-generation industry; Westinghouse was an important player in that market. At one point, after three months of trial hearings had been held, a Pittsburgh judge was asked about his efforts to convince the parties to settle:

> The fiscal well-being, possibly the survival, of one of the world's corporate giants is in jeopardy. Likewise, the future of thousands of jobs.
>
> Any decision I hand down will hurt somebody and because of that potential damage, I want to make it clear that it will happen only because certain captains of industry could not together work out their problems so that the hurt might have been held to a minimum....
>
> Solomon-like as I want to be, I can't cut this baby in half ...

There are also, of course, some pressures to proceed with the litigation. There is a chance that both parties overestimate their chances for winning the lawsuit, and so see the other side's position as unreasonable. One or both of the parties may in fact *be* unreasonable, making it more difficult to reach an agreement. And some reasons are more subtle. Professor Macaulay[109] has pointed out:

> [L]itigation may legitimate concessions in the eyes of outsiders who audit decisions. For example, the customers of Westinghouse are utilities whose rates are regulated. Without some strong justification, they could not negotiate a settlement with Westinghouse and then ask for approval of a rate increase to cover the balance of the loss. The chance that Westinghouse might win may serve to rationalize settlement, and the act of bringing suit might show the regulators that the utilities are not just giving money away. Consumer and antinuclear power organizations filed petitions in eleven states asking state utility regulators to scrutinize any out-of-court settlements that utilities may reach with Westinghouse. These groups assert that if utilities do not hold Westinghouse to its contracts, consumers will have to pay the extra fuel costs....

---

109. Stewart Macaulay, *Elegant Models, Empirical Pictures, and the Complexities of Contract*, 11 LAW & SOC'Y REV. 507 (1977). Reprinted with permission.

The *Wall Street Journal* ... points to ... [an] assertion of norms that are not coterminous with the law of contract, in the Westinghouse cases:

[T]he electric utilities have canceled and stretched out contracts for atomic power plants, putting a financial squeeze on such companies as Westinghouse.

"You and I know that in the real world of business there's going to be some horse-trading," an industry person says. "You can bet that Westinghouse is reminding companies like Con Edison that it has gone along with them in stretching contracts."

Conduct in prior transactions generally is legally irrelevant in contract law, which focuses on the particular contract under litigation. However, the claim of prior accommodation to the needs of the utilities was highly relevant if any settlement was to be reached.

Although it would be hard to prove, the contract litigation process may also exert an indirect influence on the behavior of the managers of industrial enterprises even where they devote little thought to it. Those making bargains may tacitly rely on the law to fill gaps and provide sanctions, in order to avoid the costs of negotiating about unlikely contingencies or constructing elaborate systems of security to ensure performance. Contract law may crystallize business customs and provide a normative vocabulary, affecting expectations about what is fair. Westinghouse, for example, did not repudiate its uranium oxide contracts in the name of pure self-interest but sought to cloak its actions in the language of the Uniform Commercial Code. Its positions, in that guise, may have been more palatable to some of its customers. It may be easier to negotiate with someone asserting a plausible claim of right than with an outlaw openly scorning those who had relied on its promise. (Perhaps the UCC served as a means of self-justification so that executives at Westinghouse felt better about not honoring the commitment their firm had made.) We can only speculate about the situation had the drafters of the Uniform Commercial Code adopted a more rigorous standard that rarely excused nonperformance based on the occurrence of an unforeseen contingency. Suppose the rule had been that one who makes a promise must perform, come hell or high water. Would Westinghouse have marched into bankruptcy trying to perform or would it have begged for mercy? Would the impact have been only on the amount of any settlement, since the likelihood of victory by Westinghouse would have been insignificant and thus worth little?

Ultimately, the cases brought by the utilities were settled. Judge Merhige, the federal judge presiding over most of the cases, pressed the parties to settle; the day the trial opened he told the assembled lawyers that "I don't ever expect to finish these cases.... I expect [them] to get settled."[110] There had been relatively little in the way of settlement negotiations up to that time. Lawyers for the utilities expressed surprise about this, but some who were following the case suggested that Westinghouse was digging up information about the international cartel and didn't want to discuss settlement until

---

110. Pappas, *Westinghouse, Utilities Under Pressure to Settle Uranium Suit Before Court Does* i, WALL STREET JOURNAL, June 2, 1978 at 32, cols. 1–3.

it had compiled that information. It was also noted that the utilities themselves had to be careful in reaching a settlement. If a rate-setting regulatory agency concluded that the utility had been too accommodating in reaching a settlement, they might refuse to allow the utility to pass along the extra fuel costs associated with settlement to customers. A Westinghouse representative said, "If these were industrial customers, we could have arrived at settlements months ago."[111]

As a way of increasing the likelihood of settlement, Merhige appointed a law school dean to serve as a special master to "be utilized for purposes of encouraging and assisting the parties in reaching an amicable adjustment of the respective claims in these cases." He also required the parties to file proposals for settlement. Something worked; the cases settled. In most cases the settlements were not cash settlements, but instead involved a combination of cash and services. In one case involving the Texas Utilities Services, Inc. the settlement (embodied in a 350-page settlement agreement!) was estimated to be worth $65 to $80 million to the utility, whereas Westinghouse estimated the settlement had cost it only $27 million. While it may be that the magnitude of the gap between the estimates reflects both sides' need to feel good about the settlement, it is quite plausible for a bargain to generate a substantial surplus of value. In fact, of course, every truly free bargain leaves both parties better off than they would have been with no bargain.

The antitrust suits that were brought against the 29 uranium producers, including perhaps most prominently Gulf Oil, were settled in the summer of 1981.

NOTES AND QUESTIONS

1. *The law firm's role:* James B. Stewart wrote a book about prominent American law firms.[112] Chapter 4 is devoted to the Chicago firm of Kirkland & Ellis, whose partner, William Jentes, was principal outside counsel for Westinghouse. Stewart's book contains an interesting account of some aspects of the litigation between Westinghouse and the utilities:[113]

> One of the Uniform Commercial Code's most controversial provisions is one which provides an escape for sellers who would otherwise be locked into their contracts under common law principles, and Jentes had mentioned it as a possibility at the first meeting with the Westinghouse lawyers.... [T]he provision had almost never been invoked or upheld in a court decision excusing non-performance. Undaunted, Jentes assigned some associates to scour the case law for some support should Westinghouse assert the commercial impracticability clause.
>
> Legal research, and the related preparation of a memorandum of law, are among the relatively few tasks mastered during the course of law school, and

---

111. *Id.*
112. James B. Stewart, The Partners: Inside America's Most Powerful Law Firms (Simon and Schuster 1983). Reprinted with permission.
113. *Id.* at 152.

part of that assignment at Kirkland & Ellis fell to James Goold, a law student at the University of Chicago who was working as a summer associate for the firm....

Eventually [Goold's] task of researching the question of impracticability would take a full year—he barely attended class at the University of Chicago in order to complete the research—and resulted in a 200-page memorandum....

There was considerable debate inside Kirkland & Ellis about whether the facts surrounding the Westinghouse uranium contracts satisfied [the] conditions [for relief under Section 2-615]....

As one general counsel for a major utility recalls, he found the Westinghouse default "almost unbelievable," given its scope; the legal opinion [of Kirkland & Ellis] he dismissed as "flimsy—obviously grasping at legal straws." The legal opinion may even have been a tactical error. Expected by Westinghouse to be interpreted by the utilities as an indication of how serious Westinghouse's plight had become, it was instead greeted as an audacious attempt by Westinghouse to wriggle out of the contracts rather than admit its own errors and ask the utilities to help restructure the deal. Jentes, however, doubts that the utilities would ever have expressed a conciliatory attitude. "They were not the least bit statesmanlike. They acted like we were repudiating the Bible." One by one, the utilities marched into courts across the country, all filing lawsuits against Westinghouse....

Meanwhile, another contingent of Kirkland & Ellis lawyers was assigned to shore up the legal positions. When he had been a student at the University of Chicago, Goold, who had now come to work full-time, had taken a class in contracts with Professor Soia Mentschikoff. Mentschikoff was the widow of Karl Llewellyn, the man who had actually drafted the Uniform Commercial Code, which formed the basis for Westinghouse's defense, and Mentschikoff had worked closely with him on the project. Goold hired her as a consultant on the case, and together they began to sift through Llewellyn's files for more clues about the meaning of the impracticability provision.

Eventually they found a bundle of handwritten notes, some of them nearly tattered beyond legibility, and after piecing them together, they derived some small encouragement for the position that a price increase, if it was the result of some unforeseeable event directly related to performance of the contract, might excuse performance....

As Judge Merhige had urged, by 1980 all of the utilities had reached out-of-court settlements with Westinghouse, [eliminating] the need for the planned trial on the damages issue.... [The settlements] were handled internally by Westinghouse executives and the company's legal staff—and though non-monetary aspects of the agreements make them difficult to value, it is estimated that they cost Westinghouse approximately $900 million, or about half of what the utilities had claimed. If Westinghouse and the utilities had simply split their differences in 1975, before resorting to litigation, the result would have been about the same.

In a review of Stewart's book, Peter W. Bernstein quotes this last paragraph about the final result in the Westinghouse cases.[114] He continues by saying:

> [Y]ou'd think that such details would spur some serious rethinking about the possibly excessive use of corporate lawyers. Ironically, the Westinghouse case seems to have had almost the opposite effect. Stewart reports that despite Kirkland & Ellis's setbacks, "it is the widespread perception among members of the corporate bar—and in the firm itself—that it was Kirkland & Ellis that saved Westinghouse." It would seem that lawyers can convince themselves of anything.

Does the final result of these cases show "excessive use of corporate lawyers"? Had the utilities and Westinghouse split their differences in 1975, the result would have been roughly the same as reached in 1980 after a large amount was paid in legal fees. But had Kirkland & Ellis not been called in and played the § 2-615 card, would the utilities and Westinghouse have split their differences?

2. *Anticipating unforeseen risks at the drafting stage:* We sometimes forget that there are different ways to proceed in the face of similar problems. Often the participants in different business cultures, or subcultures, react differently to trouble. In the *Westinghouse* cases we have just read about, the parties were reluctant to give up the gains they believed they had won by their bargain, and which they believed were embodied in their agreement; they chose to litigate the question of the contract's enforceability. Leon Trakman has written about the way that the multinational oil sellers respond, at the drafting stage, to the risks of unforeseen changes in oil supply and prices. Trakman sent questionnaires to the inside counsel of multinational oil sellers and buyers. He found that lawyers from the civil law tradition were much more likely to accept excuses for events beyond the control of a party than were lawyers from the common law tradition. He attributed this difference to "jurisprudential differences" between the two types of legal systems and the economic havoc that many civil law countries experienced after World War II.[115]

The standard contracts used in multinational oil transactions provided for the consequences of shocks that disrupted market prices as a result of political unrest.

> Nonperformance clauses in international crude oil contracts of sale were therefore the product of deliberate planning and compromise. As carefully formulated provisions, they constituted a means of avoiding deadlock and

---

114. FORTUNE, Apr. 4, 1983, at 189, 191.

115. Leon Trakman, *Nonperformance in Oil Contracts*, 29 OIL & GAS Q. 716 (1981). Copyright © 1981 by Matthew Bender & Co., Inc. and OIL AND GAS TAX QUARTERLY.

dissatisfaction over performance among oil companies. They summarized oil relations; and they embodied industry usages in their written terms. Most importantly, they ensured that crude oil transactors would not be left in doubt as to the nature and extent of their performance duties and as to their respective responsibilities in the event of nonperformance....

[A]fter each severe disruption in oil supply, international contracts for the sale of crude oil were revised to take specific account of fluctuating oil prices and severely impeded oil supplies. After each Middle Eastern War, inside legal counsel gave particular attention to the expanding role of governments in relation to crude oil contracts. They evaluated the effects upon performance of "royalty taxes," "new and changed government directions," and "increased government take." ...

Trakman reported that these inside lawyers for multinational oil sellers and buyers thought that those in this industry were incapable of foreseeing all categories of the risk of nonperformance. Moreover, they were unlikely to incorporate all types of nonperformance risks unambiguously into their contracts.

3. *Dealing with the problem by renegotiating the contract:* Another way in which the parties might respond to an unforeseen development, and again this may depend on the business culture in which the event occurs, is to renegotiate the agreement. Can such a response be successful? Doesn't renegotiation constitute a repudiation of the rationale for the contract itself? Jeswald Salacuse suggests that renegotiation is a common practice, at least in some international contexts.[116]

In recent years we have seen many examples of the phenomenon of renegotiations. Since the outbreak of the international debt crisis in 1982, Western commercial banks and their Third World borrowers have been engaged in a constant process of renegotiating loans that developing countries have been unable to repay, an exercise commonly known as "debt rescheduling." The dramatic fall in the price of oil and gas from the heights of the early 1980s has forced purchasers to seek renegotiation of long-term supply agreements that once seemed profitable but have now become ruinous. And the rapid decline in the value of the dollar, particularly against the Japanese yen, has since 1986 prompted attempts to renegotiate other long-term contractual relationships.

Renegotiation in international business is by no means peculiar to the 1980s. For decades, host country governments, often with the threat of nationalization in the background, have periodically sought to revise investment arrangements which they had previously made with foreign corporations

---

116. Jeswald W. Salacuse, *Renegotiations in International Business*, 4 Negotiation J. 347 (1988). Copyright © Negotiation Journal 1988. Reprinted with permission.

but later judged no longer advantageous.... These examples illustrate a traditional theme in international business circles: the lament over the "unstable contract," the profitable agreement that the other party refuses to respect. One common response to contractual instability is renegotiation....

Discussions of "renegotiation" apply the term to three fundamentally different situations, and it is important to distinguish each of them at the outset....

(1) Post-Deal Renegotiations

In this context, negotiations may take place at the expiration of a contract, when the parties, though legally free to go their own ways, nonetheless seek to renew their previous relationship....

(2) Intra-Deal Renegotiations

A second type of renegotiation occurs when the agreement itself provides that, during its life at specified times, the parties may renegotiate or at least review certain of its provisions. Here, renegotiation is anticipated as a legitimate activity in which both parties are to engage in good faith....

(3) Extra-Deal Renegotiations

The most difficult and emotional renegotiations are those undertaken in apparent violation of the agreement, or at least in the absence of a specific clause for redoing the deal. These renegotiations take place "extra-deal," for they occur outside the framework of the existing agreement. The renegotiations of the 1980s over Third World loans, petroleum prices, and currencies all fit within the category of extra-deal renegotiations, because in each case one of the participants was seeking relief from a legally binding obligation without any basis in the agreement itself for renegotiation....

Beyond mere disappointed expectations, extra-deal renegotiations, by their very nature, can create bad feeling and mistrust. One side sees itself as being asked to give up something to which it has a legal and moral right, and it views the other side as having gone back on its word, as having acted in bad faith by reneging on the deal. Indeed, the reluctant party may even feel it is being coerced into participating in extra-deal renegotiations, since a refusal to do so would result in losing the investment already made in the transaction or joint venture. Thus, it is very difficult for the parties to see renegotiations as anything more than a "zero-sum game," where one side wins and the other side loses.

The extra-deal renegotiation of an established arrangement may also have significant implications beyond the transaction in question. The party being asked to give up a contractual right may feel obliged to show various political constituencies, both inside and outside its own organization, that it is not "weak," and cannot be taken advantage of. Moreover, a party will usually fear that yielding to a demand for the renegotiation of one contract may encourage other parties to seek renegotiation of their agreements as well. This concern for the potential "ripple" effect from renegotiations clearly contributed to the reluctance of the international commercial banks to yield to demands by individual developing countries for a revision of loan terms. Concessions to Mexico would inevitably lead Argentina to demand equal treatment in its own renegotiation." ...

While a request for extra-deal renegotiations may provoke bad feeling in one party, an outright refusal to renegotiate may also create ill will on the other side since it will be seen as an attempt to force adherence to a bargain that has become unreasonable.

Ultimately, the basic conflict between the parties in an extra-deal renegotiation will be over the type of changed circumstances justifying the negotiations. Such circumstances may cover a broad spectrum, ranging from sudden changes in objective conditions over which neither of the parties has control, such as rising exchange rates or closed trade routes, to conditions determined subjectively by one side alone. With regard to the latter, for example, host country governments often reassess their relations with foreign investors based on the country's current need for the investor's capital and technology....

Today, most contracts explicitly or implicitly deny the possibility of change and therefore make no provision whatsoever for adjustments to meet changing circumstances. This assumption of contractual stability has proven false time and time again. For example, most mineral development agreements assume they will continue unchanged for periods of from 15 to 99 years, yet they rarely remain unmodified for more than a few years.... As Raymond Vernon ... has argued, with reference to mineral investment agreements, a bargain, once struck, will inevitably become obsolete and issues once agreed upon will be reopened at a later time as circumstances change. Indeed, to borrow Vernon's phrase, international business negotiations should probably assume that most long-term deals are "obsolescing bargains."

4. *Arbitration as an alternative:* We have seen that parties might deal with the unforeseeable by attempting to anticipate it in their drafting of the agreement, or by permitting renegotiation, or by resorting to judicial litigation. We must not forget private arbitration as another option. We offer an example which seems particularly apt, since it deals with the continued volatility of the uranium market after the changes that prompted Westinghouse to repudiate its duty to deliver fuel to the utilities.

According to a 1985 story in the *New York Times*,[117] "once again, uranium is making lawyers glow." In 1976, with uranium selling for $40 a pound, a Switzerland-based

---

117. N.Y. TIMES, Jan. 8, 1985, at 2, col. 1. Similarly, see Robert McGough, *Are Contracts Obsolete?* FORBES, Apr. 29, 1985, at 101 ("The plain fact is that for a number of companies, doing business by traditional contracts doesn't work anymore. More disturbing, courts are pressuring companies to compromise on contract claims or else are rewriting the contracts themselves."). *See also* Mary Williams Walsh & Jonathan Glater, *Contracts Now Seen as Being Rewritable*, N.Y. TIMES, Mar. 31, 2009, at 1

utility, Kernkraftwerk Graben A.G., contracted to purchase uranium oxide for a 12-year period from a New York Company, Freeport-McMoran, Inc. Over the next several years, the uranium contract price jumped up to $60 a pound. During the same time period, the market price plummeted to $17 a pound. To make matters worse, the Swiss government denied Kernkraftwerk a permit to build a nuclear power plant, thereby evaporating the utility's need for the uranium oxide.

Kernkraftwerk contended that the contract was no longer binding because of unforeseen circumstances. In 1982, the matter went to arbitration. Under a choice of laws agreement, the arbitrators applied New York contract law. Apparently, Kernkraftwerk had contractually agreed that it would not be excused from performing "on account of *force majeure* or any other reasons whatsoever." Yet, in August of 1984, the arbitrators agreed with Kernkraftwerk's argument that the purpose of the contract had been frustrated. In a decision that saved the utility $100 million, the arbitrators found that the dramatic price change, and the Swiss government's refusal to allow the nuclear power plant to be built, were events that the parties did not foresee and therefore the contract could not have been intended to cover these eventualities.

The *New York Times* reporter wrote that "the award illustrates the decline of the sanctity accorded to contracts since the heyday of laissez-faire in the last century." The reporter went on to suggest that courts in Britain and the United States modify contracts, construe terms contrary to the parties' intention, and help parties to evade duties and the like. Can you argue that the reporter did not understand what the arbitrators did? Would the arbitrators have to concede that they rewrote the contract in question here?

IN THE MATTER OF WESTINGHOUSE ELECTRIC CORP. URANIUM CONTRACTS LITIGATION, FLORIDA POWER & LIGHT CO. v. WESTINGHOUSE ELECTRIC CORP.

United States District Court, Eastern District of Virginia
517 F. Supp. 440 (1981)

MERHIGE, J.

The instant issue arises out of an alleged breach by the defendant Westinghouse Electric Corporation (Westinghouse) of a contract executed by the parties in May of 1966 with an effective date of November 15, 1965, for the long-term fueling of two nuclear steam supply systems manufactured by Westinghouse for ... [Florida Power and Light Company]. The contract in issue was entered into as a consequence of plaintiff having, in the same year, agreed to purchase from defendant two nuclear steam supply systems for the generation of electric power....

Florida seeks, in addition to monetary damages, an order requiring Westinghouse to comply with Section 27(a)(2) of the contract of May 1966 which reads as follows:

("The depth of the recession and the use of taxpayer dollars to bail out companies have made it politically acceptable for overseers to tinker with employment agreements.").

Section 27. Scope

(a) Westinghouse will: ...

(2) Remove the irradiated fuel from the plant site and dispose of it as Westinghouse sees fit....

On September 2, 1975, Westinghouse advised Florida by letter that it had no plans to remove the irradiated (spent) fuel from Florida's plant site, and this lawsuit followed.

The evidence reveals that in 1965 the nuclear industry was at an early stage in its evolution. In 1964 legislation had been enacted permitting, for the first time, private ownership of uranium, a necessary component of nuclear power. The sale of nuclear steam supply systems was in its infancy, and Westinghouse, a manufacturer of such systems, was most anxious to enter into a contract with Florida for its proposed plants designated as Turkey Point Units 3 and 4, located in Dade County, Florida. At the time, there were no nuclear plants operating in the south. Additionally, the opportunity was unique; for Florida contemplated the construction of two power plants at the same location. It was during a period when fossil fuels were relatively inexpensive, capital costs were down, and adequate gas, oil, and other fuels were available. While the potential for nuclear-powered plants for the production of electricity was considered bright, reactor sales were not abundant and few negotiations for nuclear power plants were in progress. Additionally, in the view of many, uncertainty existed during the period of 1965–66 as to whether nuclear power could compete economically in most areas of the country with fossil fuels.

The securing of a contract by Westinghouse with Florida for the sale of two pressurized water reactors was viewed by Westinghouse not only as a vote of confidence, but as an incentive for other utilities to seriously consider the use of nuclear power.

Florida, at the time, had no expertise in nuclear power, a fact well known to Westinghouse. Indeed, in March of 1965 Florida notified Westinghouse that it (Florida) lacked the manpower and knowledge needed to develop specifications and evaluate proposals for a nuclear plant. This lack of expertise resulted in Florida's continued insistence on the purchase of a complete package with a guaranteed maximum price. The evidence further reflects that Westinghouse actually encouraged Florida to rely on Westinghouse's professed nuclear knowledge and capability.

Ironically, Westinghouse was aided in inducing Florida to enter into the contracts by the fact that General Electric, a principal competitor, was also proposing that Florida convert to nuclear power, and in this effort provided much economic analysis tending to show its advantages. The competition between General Electric and Westinghouse was keen, and the form of Westinghouse's offer to Florida was influenced by its knowledge of General Electric's proposal. Westinghouse concluded that the form of its fuel offer, though not as it would have chosen in the absence of its knowledge of General Electric's position, was necessary in order to secure the contract. Coupled with this incentive was Westinghouse's knowledge that Florida's chief executive officer had expressed the view that the successful manufacturer of the contemplated units would have to assume responsibility for total fuel supply. He expressed the view most vividly in the following language:

> I do not want to buy a sheep to get a suit of clothes, and have the sheep sheared, dyed, treated, woven into cloth, cut, and sewn into a suit. I want to buy a suit, not go through all the procedures of having to acquire the wool that goes into the suit, nor the manufacture of the thread, nor the material or anything else. I want to buy a suit already made.

Florida's continued insistence on guaranteed fuel costs, for as long a period as possible, together with the extreme importance Westinghouse placed on obtaining the construction contracts, prompted Westinghouse's offer of a guaranteed ten-year fuel cycle cost. This, of course, included the cost of uranium and the purchase and disposal of the spent fuel as a part of the fuel cycle. In short, Florida expressed a consistent desire to look at a complete package.

The cost assumptions upon which Westinghouse predicated its proffered fuel contract were based on what one witness described as "very little knowledge." In its contract with Florida, Westinghouse agreed to a contract price fixed solely by reference to the amount of electricity generated by Florida, and independent of the cost to Westinghouse of the purchase or disposal of uranium. Joseph Rengel, who was principally responsible within the Westinghouse organization for developing the terms of Westinghouse's fuel proposal to Florida, quite candidly testified that under the mills per kilowatt hour formula used in the contract between the parties, the risks taken by Westinghouse encompassed "the reprocessing of the fuel at the end of the project." Mr. Rengel's explanation for Westinghouse's assumption of the risks inherent in a long-term, fixed-price fuel contract was that Westinghouse assumed "that the risks were not very significant." Indeed, the evidence reflects that it was not until after the contract had been executed that Westinghouse examined in detail the fuel cycle, consisting of enrichment, conversion, and reprocessing.[118]

Under the provisions of the contract, Florida had the right until "initial criticality" to elect one of three fuel purchase options. Initial criticality occurred at Turkey Point Unit 3 on October 20, 1972, and at Turkey Point Unit 4 on June 11, 1973. Under the option timely selected by Florida, option C, which includes the contested Section 27(a)(2), Westinghouse is required to furnish fuel until each plant goes off the line or "the first refueling after ten years from the date of initial criticality." Under that

---

118. [4] Irradiated, or spent fuel contains valuable fuel material. After the spent fuel has cooled for three or four months, it is loaded underwater into heavily shielded casks. These lead-lined casks are used to transport the fuel to a chemical reprocessing plant. At the reprocessing plant the fuel is unloaded into another underwater storage pool. The first step in reprocessing is to transfer the fuel from the storage pool to a cell where the assembly can be mechanically disassembled. After the end fittings have been removed, the fuel rods are sheared into short pieces. These pieces are placed in a dissolver where nitric acid selectively dissolves the fuel and leaves the cladding. The resultant fuel-bearing acid solution is treated by solvent extraction to separate the uranium and plutonium from the fission products. The uranium and plutonium are then subjected to further solvent extraction steps to purify them and remove nearly all of the fission products. Final products of the reprocessing are uranium and plutonium nitrate solutions.

option Florida's obligation to pay for the power generated by the fuel it received began with "initial criticality," which is defined as the first time self-sustaining chain reaction occurs in the core of a nuclear unit. It is a moment that may be determined with technical precision. It is an event that occurs only once in the life of a nuclear unit.

In its negotiations, Westinghouse endeavored, unsuccessfully, to convince Florida that its fuel cost would be lower if it undertook on its own to have the spent fuel reprocessed. Indeed, at one point Westinghouse offered to act as Florida's agent in obtaining reprocessing. Florida never seriously entered these suggestions, by virtue of its negotiator's insistence that it wished to purchase a complete package.

In view of the infancy of the commercial market in uranium at the time of the negotiations with Florida, Westinghouse had no way of determining whether the wholesale price index would be an accurate measure of increases in the price of uranium, yet it agreed to a specified price in reference to the cost to Florida for fuel based upon mills per kilowatt hour as a charge for the energy generated.

Westinghouse had full knowledge of Florida's hesitancy to use nuclear power but ultimately convinced Florida that the capital, fuel, and production costs of nuclear power would not exceed the costs that it was incurring for its fossil units, and would inure to the benefit of Florida's rate payers. Under the option that it exercised, if spent fuel were not reprocessed, Florida ran little risk, and though the parties contemplated that Westinghouse would remove the spent fuel and reprocess it, the contract by its terms requires Westinghouse to remove the spent fuel and "dispose of it as Westinghouse sees fit." Indeed, no witness for either party ever viewed Westinghouse's contractual obligation as encompassing a reprocessing of the irradiated (spent) fuel.

Reprocessing is, according to those knowledgeable in the nuclear power industry, the appropriate method of disposing of spent nuclear fuel. Absent reprocessing, spent fuel is not only valueless, but represents a financial burden.

It is obvious to the Court that Westinghouse took a calculated risk in providing the guarantees demanded by Florida. Included in those guarantees was Westinghouse's obligation to remove the spent fuel. To a great extent Westinghouse's willingness to accept the risks involved was premised on its understandable desire to enter into a contract for the building of Florida's nuclear reactors. Additionally, a not insignificant consideration was that Westinghouse anticipated that the reprocessing of the spent fuel, with its consequent recovery of uranium nitrate and plutonium nitrate, would result in a financial gain to it of between 16 and 19 million dollars, as the estimated value of reusable uranium and production of plutonium. While the given dollar value was simply an estimate on the part of Westinghouse, unsupported by hard evidence or reference to sources with a background of precise costs or values, the Court is satisfied that Westinghouse in its business judgment concluded that there was substantial value to it in reprocessing. Of necessity, the contract price also encompassed a charge to Florida for Westinghouse's anticipated service in removing the spent fuel.

The Court concludes that while both parties understood that Westinghouse intended to reprocess the spent fuel if it would inure to Westinghouse's benefit, that fact, excepting for its effect on the price Westinghouse offered to charge for the energy that Florida was purchasing, had no influence on Florida's executing the contract.

The only reference to reprocessing in the final contract is a provision permitting Westinghouse to use "plutonium and reprocessed or depleted uranium in fuel loadings subsequent to the initial fuel loading...."

Florida, unwilling to tie itself to reprocessing, was told by Westinghouse that as a consequence it was committing to pay a higher price for its fuel. In this regard, Westinghouse pointed out to Florida that it was its view that Florida's cost would be less if it would reprocess the spent fuel; for reprocessed fuel, which under the contract Westinghouse had the right to use in Florida's reloads, was contemplated to be less expensive than mined uranium. Nevertheless, Florida rejected a risk factor that Westinghouse was willing to take. The most logical conclusion in light of the nature of the negotiations is that Florida viewed Westinghouse's willingness to remove and dispose of the irradiated or spent fuel as inuring to Florida's benefit in the cost of energy and the completion of the "suit of clothes." That Westinghouse contemplated reprocessing, in light of its statements to Florida [that] reference the beneficial economics of same, was simply viewed by Florida as a factor to which Westinghouse gave more weight than Florida was willing to, especially in view of Florida's desire to have the limits of its responsibilities and concomitant costs precisely defined. As one [lawyer] suggested, Westinghouse was, at least as to any risk factors, simply "out-negotiated." The Court finds no evidence that would support a conclusion that the parties ever understood or intended that Westinghouse be contractually obligated to reprocess the spent fuel. One would be hard pressed to construe the phrase "... dispose of it as Westinghouse sees fit" as imposing a duty to reprocess.

Admittedly, although the possibility was present in the contract, Westinghouse, having offered three options to Florida, had no way of knowing until Florida selected option C in 1972 that it, Westinghouse, would in fact have responsibility for removal of the spent fuel.

Option A of the contract would have foreclosed any responsibility on the part of Westinghouse to remove the spent fuel—options B and C placed that responsibility on Westinghouse....

While, as the Court has concluded, both parties contemplated reprocessing, the fact remains that Westinghouse accepted the responsibility of removing the spent fuel and with that responsibility, to utilize that fuel as it saw fit. Its reliance on its own business judgment cannot in fairness impose on Florida greater burdens than it contracted for, absent what might be imposed by law, to which the Court addresses itself, *infra*.

That Westinghouse anticipated a monetary value is obvious. That Westinghouse took a calculated risk is just as obvious. No spent fuel had ever been commercially reprocessed as of the time of execution of the contract, and further, the first commercial reprocessing plant in the United States was not licensed until April 19, 1966, more than a year after negotiations between the parties had commenced. Additionally,

Westinghouse fully understood that its offer to Florida was premised on what it deemed to be a reasonable business risk that commercial reprocessing would come to pass and would be economically feasible, conditions that had not, at the time of execution of the contract, been demonstrated. Florida, on the other hand, had its "suit of clothes" and had no financial interest in the spent fuel.

In short, Westinghouse was, in its eagerness to construct the power plants, willing to accept the risks that Florida was not willing to take. That Westinghouse fully appreciated this fact is evidenced by a Westinghouse proposal of November 3, 1965, which would effectively have placed responsibility for spent fuel on Florida, as well as the fact that other written suggestions of Westinghouse making reference to "reprocessing" were not incorporated into option C of the final contract. Florida simply refused to tie its cost to what it deemed at the time to be uncertain technology.

Except for 18 spent fuel assemblies that Westinghouse arranged to be removed and which were sent to a governmental agency for experimental programs, Westinghouse has not removed the spent fuel, and as a consequence Florida at time of trial was storing 411 spent fuel assemblies.

The evidence discloses that over the life of the contract a total of 981 spent fuel assemblies will be generated. While no schedule for the removal of the spent fuel is set out in the contract, the Court finds that it was the intention of the parties that same be accomplished within six months to a year after the spent fuel is removed from the reactors, and as a consequence of Westinghouse's failure to remove same, Florida was compelled to expand its spent fuel storage pits to accommodate excess spent fuel.

Florida had, in anticipation of both temporarily storing spent fuel assemblies and in the event a problem occurred in the reactor vessel requiring an unloading of an entire core of fuel assemblies, caused to be constructed a storage pit for each reactor, each capable of holding 217 assemblies. The original expectation was that the pits would be sufficiently large enough to handle not only the anticipated annual discharge, but emergency unloadings as well. Each pit was intended for interim, temporary storage for the period between the time the fuel was taken out of the reactor and the time it was cool enough to be removed from the plant's site by Westinghouse. Had Florida not expanded its spent fuel storage pits, its operation of the nuclear units would have had to cease.

As a consequence of Westinghouse's refusal to remove the spent fuel assemblies, Florida has expended $9,473,242.04 in re-racking—that is, adding additional spent fuel storage racks at a closer center-to-center spacing, which permits each pit to have a larger capacity than contemplated in the original design. This of course has resulted in increased operating and maintenance costs, as well as potential environmental difficulties.

It is estimated that by the end of the year 1985 both storage pits will reach their potential capacity for storage. If such comes to pass, Florida's reactors will be forced to shut down with a consequent cost estimated to be approximately $500,000 per day, per unit, for replacement power.

While the government has announced plans to provide an interim storage facility during the 1980s, no capacity for a final disposal facility has been demonstrated, nor indeed is there any certainty that even the interim storage facility will come to pass.

Florida chose what it deemed to be a fixed-cost contract and as a part thereof, Westinghouse was to remove the spent fuel and dispose of it as Westinghouse saw fit. That conclusion, in the Court's view, is unassailable.

Finally in this regard, it can be said that the evidence reflects that Westinghouse's entry into the contract came about at a time when Westinghouse fully anticipated, despite the lack of a binding contract for reprocessing the spent fuel, to reprocess Florida's spent fuel with the hope of making its agreement with Florida under option C economically more profitable. Such anticipation was, however, just that—an anticipation fueled by its desire to secure the contract for the building of two nuclear steam supply systems and its own enthusiasm for its view of the merits and future of nuclear power.

Regardless of how one views the business judgment of Westinghouse in this regard, the fact is that, as early as 1957 the United States Atomic Energy Commission adopted a policy of assuring the nuclear power industry that the government would, in the event that commercial reprocessing services were not available at reasonable times and conditions when irradiated power reactor fuels were discharged from their reactors, make financial settlement for the materials contained in those fuel elements, and reprocess them. Indeed, in 1965 the Government was actively urging reprocessing of spent fuel, was accepting fuel for reprocessing, and to a limited extent was underwriting a portion of the financial burden associated therewith. Notably, however, at that period in time the uranium was leased by the government and was in fact government material.

As a consequence of this policy of encouragement, reiterated in January of 1968, a number of companies expressed interest, and at least one, National Fuel Services, Incorporated, built a plant that became operational in 1966 and operated until 1972.

It is to be noted, however, that the plant that became operational in 1966 was designed to operate at only about 300 tons per year. It is estimated that the Turkey Point plants will produce about 400 tons of spent fuel over the term of the contract with Westinghouse. Other companies, such as General Electric, which had expressed an interest in commercial reprocessing services, abandoned their plans.

Events occurring after formation of the contract, however, made Westinghouse's plans to reprocess—rather than merely remove—and dispose of Florida's spent fuel more difficult to accomplish than Westinghouse had anticipated. After the start of the small NFS reprocessing plant in 1966, no other commercial reprocessing concerns became operable. In 1970, four years after the execution of the contract, Westinghouse entered into a letter of intent with Allied-General Nuclear Services (AGNS), to contract with AGNS, subject to AGNS's receipt of a license, for the reprocessing of the Turkey Point spent fuel. At the time of the letter of intent, AGNS was not licensed to reprocess nuclear fuel; nor is it now. AGNS never executed a formal contract with Westinghouse, and in fact, in early 1974 AGNS advised Westinghouse that it was not prepared to execute a formal agreement. On September 2, 1975, Westinghouse notified Florida by letter that Westinghouse had no plans for removing the spent fuel from the Turkey Point site. Westinghouse assigned as its reason for not removing the spent fuel, the fact that the schedule for removing and reprocessing the discharged fuel was "of course, dependent on the Allied-General [Nuclear] Services' reprocessing schedule."

No stretch of the imagination nor the arguments of ingenious counsel could satisfy the Court that, regardless of whether reprocessing was an integral part of the contract, Florida ever agreed to condition Westinghouse's obligation to remove the spent fuel on "Allied-General Nuclear Services' (AGNS) reprocessing facility schedule."

In April 1977, two years after Westinghouse declared its unwillingness to fulfill the contract, President Carter, by Executive Order, precluded the development of domestic facilities for the commercial reprocessing of nuclear fuel and the exportation of nuclear fuel for reprocessing purposes. As a consequence of the presidential ban on reprocessing, licensing procedures for contemplated commercial reprocessing facilities have been terminated.

Two years after Westinghouse's breach, occurring because of its own failure to successfully negotiate a contract for the removal and storage of the spent fuel, or alternatively to have utilized the period between the date of Florida's exercise of Option C and its breach in 1975 to make other arrangements, the government's change of policy thwarted Westinghouse's hope for reprocessing. As a consequence of the ban on reprocessing, Westinghouse contends that it is faced with an effective bar to removal of the spent fuel.

Inexplicably, though Westinghouse introduced evidence to the effect that it and AGNS had reached a finalized agreement ... [for] the removal and reprocessing of the spent fuel as early as March 1973, no action was taken, nor has any since been taken, by Westinghouse, to enforce what it contends was its contract with AGNS. The Court concludes that no action has been taken in this regard because of Westinghouse's failure to expend millions of dollars in expanding its storage pits....

This, however, does not end the case. Florida seeks not only monetary damages as compensation for its having to expand its storage pits, but an order directing Westinghouse to remove the spent fuel.

The evidence does reflect that as a consequence of the presidential ban on reprocessing, licensing procedures for contemplated commercial reprocessing facilities have been terminated. There are, however, a number of facilities, including AGNS's Barnwell, South Carolina facility, where subject to appropriate licenses, spent fuel could be stored and perhaps ultimately reprocessed.

Finally in this regard, there are no commercial facilities, excepting for a few such as that of General Electric, which, because of the ban on reprocessing, has limited the use of its facility to taking spent fuel from its customers as an accommodation in lieu of being able to fulfill reprocessing commitments, that could be used for storage of spent fuel. Though there are eight government facilities with potential for storing spent fuel, which, theoretically, could store spent fuel produced beyond the year 2000, they would require extensive physical modifications to make them usable.

While there is now legislation pending to permit the U.S. Department of Energy to proceed to provide storage facilities, even if enacted, such facilities would not be available for a number of years.

It would appear that in the absence of a reversal of the government's policy against reprocessing or alternatively, facilities for the storage of spent fuel, if not presently available, becoming available, Florida's nuclear Turkey Point plants will be shut down by the year 1986 as to one plant, and 1988 as to the other.

Legal Issues

Westinghouse raises the following five defenses: (1) that its performance is excused by the common law doctrine of impossibility of performance; (2) that the government's change of policy concerning commercial reprocessing discharges its duty under the *force majeure* clause; (3) that performance by it has been rendered commercially impracticable under §2-615 of the Uniform Commercial Code; (4) that the non-availability of reprocessing has frustrated the purpose of the contract; and (5) that the parties' erroneous expectation that the spent fuel would be reprocessed discharges Westinghouse's obligation under the doctrine of mutual mistake.

Both in conceptual terms and in terms of the facts to which they relate there is considerable similarity among the defenses, particularly defenses 1, 3, 4, and 5. Commercial impracticability under the UCC is basically a codification of the common law doctrine of impossibility of performance, which, in turn, is grounded in the doctrines of mutual mistake and frustration of purpose. The purpose of each of the defenses is to

> ... discharge an obligor from his duty to perform a contract where a failure of a basic assumption of the parties produces a grave failure of the equivalence of value of the exchange to the parties. And all [of the defenses] are qualified by the same notions of risk assumption and allocation. *Aluminum Co. of America v. Essex Group, Inc.*, 499 F. Supp. 53, 70 (W.D. Penn. 1980).

> The burden of proving the elements of each of these defenses is on the party seeking to avoid performance. *Ocean Air Tradeways, Inc. v. Arkay Realty Corp.*, 480 F.2d 1112, 1117 (9th Cir. 1973).

The bulk of the Court's analysis will proceed under the two most similar of the claimed defenses, common law impossibility and commercial impracticability under the UCC....

I. Commercial Impracticability....

In the Court's view, Westinghouse's claim of commercial impracticability raises four issues: (1) Was performance as agreed rendered impracticable? (2) Did the claimed impracticability arise from an unforeseen contingency? (3) Was the non-occurrence of the contingency a basic assumption on which the contract was made? (4) Did the parties, explicitly or implicitly, allocate the risk that the contingency would occur?

There is nothing magical about these four questions: they are not, strictly speaking, elements of proof, or hurdles that Westinghouse must cross if it is to be excused for nonperformance. They merely provide, for purposes of the instant case, a useful method for structuring the inquiry.

It is further to be noted that the issues as framed are interrelated: the "answer" to each depends in part on the "answers" to the other three....

1. Was performance as agreed rendered impracticable?

Westinghouse contends that the reversal of the government's policy concerning reprocessing, and specifically the 1977 presidential order banning commercial reprocessing, has had the practical effect of rendering performance as contemplated impracticable. At the time the contract was executed, Westinghouse expected to recoup between 16 and 19 million dollars from the spent fuel. Now, however, the fuel is virtually valueless. Thus, Westinghouse's basic contention is that the government's actions have made commercial reprocessing unavailable, which in turn has massively increased the costs of removal of the spent fuel from Florida's plants....

The Court finds that the facts simply do not support the conclusion that Westinghouse's performance has been rendered impracticable. The short, albeit incomplete answer to Westinghouse's contentions is the plain language of the contract. The contract in unequivocal language requires Westinghouse to remove the spent fuel. It does not by any stretch of construction *require* Westinghouse to reprocess. The bargained-for performance was removal; reprocessing was merely an option given to Westinghouse....

In two very similar cases, *Transatlantic Financing Corp. v. U.S.*, 363 F.2d 312 (D.C. Cir. 1966) and *American Trading & Production Co. v. Shell International Marine, Ltd.*, 453 F.2d 939 (2d Cir. 1972), shipowners sought compensation for additional expenses incurred as a result of the fact that the Suez Canal was closed after they had begun their voyages. To reach their destinations the ships had to sail around the Cape of Good Hope, a much longer voyage than through the Suez. The shipowners claimed that the contemplated means of performance, *i.e.* passage through Suez, had been rendered impracticable. The courts rejected the shipowners' arguments: the fact that both parties to each of the contracts contemplated the Suez route "is not at all equivalent to an agreement that it be the exclusive method of performance." *American Trading*, 453 F.2d at 941. Because the promises to transport cargo from one point to another were unqualified, the shippers were not relieved of the obligation to perform by alternate means when the contemplated means became impracticable.

Thus, where the contract, explicitly or implicitly, provides for an exclusive means of performance, the impracticability of the specified means may release the promisor from his duty. Where, on the other hand, the promised performance is set forth in unqualified language, as was Westinghouse's promise to remove the spent fuel, the promisor may be required to perform by alternate means when the contemplated means become impracticable....

There can be no doubt that both Westinghouse and Florida contemplated that the spent fuel would be reprocessed. But there is no indication in the contract itself or in the history of its negotiation to indicate that reprocessing was viewed as the exclusive means of performance. Indeed, reprocessing was not in actuality the contemplated "means" of performance at all; it was the contemplated disposition of the spent fuel *after* performance. The means of performance, of removal, were left unspecified. Further, as will be hereinafter discussed, the evidence indicates that the unqualified nature of the promise was a consciously bargained-for term of the contract. Florida, in its negotiator's words, sought "a suit of clothes," without regard to the process necessary to achieve this.

Even if reprocessing could reasonably be viewed as an exclusive means of performance, or as an integral part of the exclusive means of performance, there is the additional question of whether the increased expense claimed by Westinghouse is sufficient to rise to the level of impracticability.

Promisors seeking to establish impracticability by reason of increased expense have not generally found a sympathetic ear in court.... Comment 4 to the Florida UCC section on impracticability provides that increased cost alone may constitute impracticability where the increase is due to an "unforeseen contingency which alters the essential nature of the performance." Generally, however, "the fact that performance has become economically burdensome or unattractive is not sufficient for performance to be excused.... We will not allow a party to a contract to escape a bad bargain merely because it is burdensome." *Neal-Cooper Grain Co. v. Texas Gulf Sulphur Co.*, 508 F.2d 283, 293–294 (7th Cir. 1974). The strictness of this rule is based on a number of considerations: the fact, for example, that the very purpose of a fixed-price agreement is to place the risk of increased costs on the promisor (and the risk of decreased costs on the promisee). Further, enforcing the bargain struck encourages parties to attempt to foresee cost variations, and to structure their agreements accordingly.

Without doubt, the sum that Westinghouse is precluded from recouping as a result of the unavailability of reprocessing is substantial. But impracticability by reason of additional expense is not to be determined by reference to the loss, or failure to profit, from one particular contract term in isolation. Rather, it is to be judged from the perspective of the entire undertaking. *Eastern Air Lines v. Gulf Oil Corp.*, 415 F. Supp. 429 (S.D. Fla. 1975); *United States v. Wegematic*, 360 F.2d 674 (2d Cir. 1966). There has been no showing that Westinghouse lost money on the entire "package deal" of plant and fuel contracts for Florida. Further, Westinghouse sought benefits beyond whatever profits it may have anticipated from the contracts: it clearly hoped that the Turkey Point plants would demonstrate the benefits of nuclear power, and would promote its own position in the industry.

Admittedly, the additional cost of removal itself might be sufficient to constitute impracticability in another context. As will be discussed *infra*, however, the Court believes that to the extent that Westinghouse was aware of the uncertainties of reprocessing, it assumed the risk that reprocessing would prove to be more expensive than anticipated, or not available at any price.

2. Did the claimed impracticability arise from an unforeseen contingency?

The success of a commercial impracticability defense often turns on whether the promisor foresaw, or should have foreseen, the contingency claimed to have made performance impracticable. Where the promisor had no reason to anticipate a supervening event which radically increases the difficulty of performance, or which renders performance impossible, it is manifestly unfair to hold him to the agreement. For instance, a seller of produce may be relieved because of a total crop failure. *Mitchell Canneries, Inc. v. United States*, 77 F. Supp. 498 (Ct. Cl. 1948). Conversely, where the contingency may reasonably be said to have been foreseeable, courts have generally taken the view that the promisor should not be released from his obligation. This rule is based on the notion that where the parties can reasonably anticipate events that may affect performance, the prudent course is to provide for such eventualities in their contract.

Because the future is by definition unknowable, a rule holding the obligor to performance only where he foresees, but fails to guard against, the *precise* event that renders performance more difficult, would be meaningless. As may be seen from the following cases, it may be enough that he is (or should be) aware of a certain trend, or that a given state of affairs is in flux, or that an assumption is more than usually uncertain.

In *Eastern Air Lines v. Gulf Oil Corp., supra*, the parties entered a requirements contract for jet fuel. They attempted to guard against price fluctuations through an escalator clause, which tied the price paid by Eastern for jet fuel to published prices of a certain type of domestic oil. In the year following the execution of the contract, the price of foreign oil rose substantially as a result of OPEC actions, including the 1973 embargo. In response, the United States government sought to control oil prices by implementing a "two-tier" pricing system. The indicator oil chosen by the parties was in the lower tier, and its price rose far less rapidly than did Gulf's oil costs.

The court held that Gulf's performance had not been rendered commercially impracticable. While Gulf could not reasonably have anticipated the embargo, the precise effect that OPEC's actions would have on worldwide oil prices, or the advent of the two-tier pricing system, it was aware of the volatility of affairs in the Middle East, of the constantly changing government price regulations, and of the general upward trend in oil prices. As one witness in that case stated, "The handwriting was on the wall." Therefore, even though the indicator chosen did not accomplish its intended purpose, in that it proved to be a very poor measure of Gulf's costs, the contract was enforced.

The analogies to the instant case are manifest. It is a fact that government policy favored reprocessing at the time the contract was negotiated; it is also a fact that, just as Gulf could not anticipate the two-tier pricing system, Westinghouse could not have anticipated in 1966 that 11 years later President Carter would ban commercial processing. But while Westinghouse could not have foreseen the precise eventuality claimed to excuse performance, its officers certainly knew that commercial reprocessing was, at best, a highly uncertain proposition. In fact, as a practical matter, there was no such thing as commercial reprocessing in 1966. Westinghouse's claim that the unavailability of reprocessing was an unforeseen contingency is belied by the fact that, even at the time the contract was executed, reprocessing for Florida's anticipated spent fuel was, for all practical purposes, unavailable.

Further, Westinghouse cannot, in the Court's view, rely on the 1977 presidential order banning commercial reprocessing as an excuse for its consistent refusal to perform beginning two years earlier. The unavailability of reprocessing or storage for Florida's spent fuel prior to 1977 is clearly attributable, at least in part, to Westinghouse's own less than zealous attempts to obtain a facility. Apart from the drawn-out, ultimately unsuccessful negotiations with AGNS, Westinghouse made no significant attempts to secure storage or reprocessing facilities, and gave little, if any, serious consideration to building its own facility, in spite of its knowledge that failure to remove the spent fuel could ultimately result in a shutdown of the plants.

3. Was the nonoccurrence of the contingency a basic assumption of the contract?

Westinghouse, pointing to the abundant evidence that both parties contemplated reprocessing, and to the fact that the price per kilowatt hour was calculated on the assumption that Westinghouse would obtain considerable value from the spent fuel, argues that the availability of reprocessing was a fundamental assumption of the contract, and therefore a condition of performance.

The Court finds, however, that notwithstanding the parties' expectation that reprocessing would occur, there is nothing in the evidence to evince any intention that Westinghouse was to be absolved from its responsibility to remove the spent fuel in the event that reprocessing would not be available. Indeed, it is difficult to discern how the availability of reprocessing could have been a basic assumption of the parties, given the fact that commercial reprocessing did not exist at the time the contract was executed, as well as the fact that the contract specifically calls for Westinghouse to do with the spent fuel as "it sees fit."

If there was a basic and mutual assumption in this regard, it was that Florida would have no involvement whatever with reprocessing, or with whatever alternate disposition Westinghouse might make of the spent fuel. Florida deemed reprocessing too speculative to undertake it. In light of Florida's rejection of formulas that tied its costs to reprocessing, it is inconceivable that Florida would have agreed to a term conditioning Westinghouse's performance on the availability of reprocessing.

Certainly, as the Court has found, the bargained-for price per kilowatt hour reflected the parties' anticipation that the fuel would be reprocessed. This, however, is not sufficient to transform an expectation into a basic assumption or a condition of performance. Arguments akin to that urged by Westinghouse in this regard were rejected in the Suez closing cases. In *American Trading and Pro. Co., supra,* the shipowner contended that because the shipping rate was based on a Suez passage, the availability of that route was a basic assumption of the contract. The court responded that "all that the ... rate establishes is that the parties obviously expected a Suez passage but there is no indication at all in the instrument or *dehors* that it was a condition of performance." 453 F.2d at 942. Here, not only is there an absence of evidence that reprocessing was a condition of performance, there are positive indications that the unqualified promise to remove the spent fuel was bargained for, and that reprocessing was a subject left entirely to Westinghouse. These facts are radically inconsistent with the contentions made by Westinghouse.

4. Did the parties, explicitly or implicitly, allocate the risk that the contingency would occur?

Generally, the risk of a contingency affecting performance is based on the promisor: "he is presumed, in the absence of evidence to the contrary, to have agreed to bear any loss occasioned by an event which was unforeseeable at the time of contracting." *Eastern Air Lines v. McDonnell Douglas Corp.*, 532 F.2d 957 (5th Cir. 1976). Comment 8 to Section 2-615 of the UCC explains that the defense of commercial impracticability is not available where the risk may be deemed to have been allocated to the promisor:

> The provisions of this section are made subject to assumption of greater liability by agreement and such agreement is to be found not only in the expressed terms of the contract but in the circumstances surrounding the contracting, in trade usage, and the like. Thus the exemptions of this section do not apply when the contingency in question is sufficiently foreshadowed at the time of contracting to be included among the business risks which are fairly to be regarded as part of the dickered terms, either consciously or as a matter of reasonable, commercial interpretation from the circumstances....

Thus, risk allocation is determined by the totality of the circumstances, including the comparative abilities of the parties to make informed judgments as to the extent of the risk; each party's interest in avoiding the risk; and the extent to which that interest was a factor in the negotiation of the contract. As indicated by the Comment, the foreseeability of the risk alone may well be sufficient for it to be regarded as implicitly assumed by the promisor.

Here, the record is replete with indications that Westinghouse, and not Florida, assumed the risk of any difficulties that might arise concerning reprocessing. As it made abundantly clear to Westinghouse throughout the negotiations, Florida, a public utility, had a strong interest in a low-risk, fixed-price contract. Indeed, "strong interest" is too mild an expression: Florida's position throughout was that it would not agree to anything other than its finished "suit of clothes." Florida required, and Westinghouse agreed, that the means by which the "suit of clothes" would be made was to be left entirely to Westinghouse. As noted earlier, Florida's rejection of options under which the price of the fuel would depend on reprocessing renders it inconceivable that it would have accepted a contract term under which Westinghouse's performance was contingent upon the availability of reprocessing.

Westinghouse, by contrast, was in an entirely different situation as it met Florida across the bargaining table. As a giant in the then-nascent nuclear industry, it had a powerful interest in promoting both the viability of nuclear power, and its own position in the industry. In light of Florida's requirements, and of Westinghouse's knowledge that General Electric was actively seeking the contract, Westinghouse's goals, as it perceived them then, could not be achieved without taking substantial risks — the availability and cost of reprocessing being just one of many. Westinghouse was certainly in a position to know of the uncertainties, both technological and commercial, of reprocessing. Indeed, at the time it entered the contract, Westinghouse had not yet conducted a detailed study of the fuel cycle.

Knowing full well Florida's requirements, and knowing that reprocessing, not being available even then as a practical matter, was highly uncertain, Westinghouse agreed to a contract term which in plain, unequivocal, unqualified language, required it to remove the spent fuel from Florida's plants. If this is not assumption of risk, the Court confesses itself unable to discern what would be. Whatever opinion one might hold as to Westinghouse's wisdom in agreeing to such a term, it did agree to it. There is nothing to indicate that the language of the term did not reflect the parties' intentions. On the contrary, all of the evidence, including the history of the negotiations and the parties' interests and goals in entering into the contract, indicate that the unqualified promise made by Westinghouse to remove the spent fuel was precisely the bargained-for performance.

II. Mutual Mistake

Westinghouse contends that the parties made two related assumptions: that reprocessing would be available, and that the spent fuel had value. These assumptions having proven to be erroneous, Westinghouse argues that its performance is excused under the doctrine of mutual mistake.

Section 152 of the Restatement of Contracts 2d provides as follows:

> (1) Where a mistake of both parties at the time the contract was made as to a basic assumption on which the contract was made has a material effect on the agreed exchange of performances, the contract is voidable by the adversely affected party unless he bears the risk of the mistake....

Section 151 defines "mistake" as a "belief not in accord with existing facts."

It is immediately apparent that the defense of mutual mistake includes two of the same elements as the doctrine of commercial impracticability: it requires the mistaken fact be as to a basic assumption, and it is qualified by the notion of risk allocation. The Court has already made findings as to these issues adverse to Westinghouse. However, in light of the magnitude of this dispute, the Court deems it appropriate to more fully address the issues as they arise under this defense.

The Court finds that the parties' anticipation that reprocessing of the spent fuel would occur was not a mutual mistake of fact, but rather an erroneous prediction. Indeed, Florida proved not to have been mistaken at all; it viewed reprocessing as too speculative a proposition to agree to any involvement in it, or to a contract under which either the price it would pay or Westinghouse's performance was in any way dependent upon it.

One recent case (decided after the parties' last briefing in this matter), *Aluminum Co. of America v. Essex Group, (Alcoa)*, 499 F. Supp. 53 (W.D. Penn. 1980), creates considerable tension in the distinction between a mistake as to a fact existing at the time the contract was executed, and an erroneous prediction of a future event. The Court addresses *Alcoa* not because it must distinguish it, but rather because its distinctions from the instant case are particularly enlightening.

In *Alcoa*, the parties entered a long-term contract in which Alcoa agreed to process alumina for Essex. After a careful study, the parties developed a complex pricing formula. One component of the formula was designed to reflect Alcoa's labor costs; another component, intended to reflect Alcoa's non-labor costs, was tied to the Wholesale Price Index (WPI). The non-labor component was arrived at on the basis of a study showing that for many years, there had been a close correlation between the WPI and Alcoa's non-labor costs. However, after the contract was executed, the price of electricity, a major component of Alcoa's non-labor costs, rose enormously, far outpacing the rise in the WPI; as a result, Alcoa suffered substantial losses. Essex, on the other hand, obtained considerable windfall benefits by selling the aluminum it manufactured from alumina processed by Alcoa, because the rise in the market price of aluminum also far outstripped the WPI.

The court held that the parties' belief, at the time the contract was executed, that the WPI would reflect Alcoa's non-labor costs was a mutual mistake of fact rather than an erroneous prediction of future events, and that therefore Alcoa was entitled to relief under the doctrine of mutual mistake.

While the Court has, most respectfully, some difficulty with the holding in *Alcoa*, it has no difficulty in finding that, even under that court's expansive reading of mutual mistake, Westinghouse's reliance on that defense is misplaced. As the *Alcoa* court noted, there is an important difference between conscious and unconscious ignorance of a material fact: "[W]here parties enter a contract in a state of conscious ignorance of the facts, they are deemed to risk the burden of having the facts turn out to be adverse, within very broad limits." 499 F. Supp. 53, 68. In the instant case, there can be no doubt that the parties entered the contract in a state of "conscious ignorance" as to the technology, costs, and even the availability of reprocessing for Florida's spent fuel, as indicated by the fact that commercial reprocessing was not then readily available, and by Westinghouse's candid admission that its price calculations were based on "very little knowledge."

A passage from *Alcoa* is particularly instructive as to the distinction between conscious and unconscious ignorance:

> [I]f parties agree to sell and purchase a stone that both know may be glass or diamond at a price that in some way reflects their uncertainty, the contract is enforceable whether the stone is in fact glass or diamond. If, by contrast, the parties both mistakenly believe it to be glass, the case is said not to be one of conscious ignorance but one of mutual mistake. 499 F. Supp. at 68.

The instant case falls in the first category; Judge Teitelbaum held that *Alcoa* fell in the second. While the Court is convinced that the price per kilowatt hour charged to Florida was lower than it would have been if Westinghouse had known that it would not be able to reprocess, the Court is equally certain that the price was higher than it would have been had there been no uncertainty about reprocessing. Expressed another way, Westinghouse was wagering that the stone would turn out to be a diamond. That it misjudged the odds does not release it from its bargain.

A related distinction is the manner in which the mistake, or the erroneous prediction, affects the contemplated performances or the equivalence of value. To the extent that *Alcoa* was disadvantaged by the mistake, Essex was enriched. Here, by contrast, while the unavailability of reprocessing has the effect of making performance by Westinghouse more expensive, it in no way enriches Florida, or gives Florida any benefit it did not bargain for.

Westinghouse's own poor judgment and mistakes cannot alone excuse its performance.

III. Force Majeure

Westinghouse claims that its nonperformance is excused by the terms of the contract's *force majeure* clause, which reads as follows:

Section 9. Force Majeure

Except as otherwise specifically provided in this contract, neither Westinghouse nor Florida shall be liable for loss, damage, detention, or delay resulting from causes beyond its reasonable control, including but not limited to, fire, work stoppage, civil or military authority, restrictions of the United States Government, or any department, branch or representative thereof, insurrection, or riot, embargoes, car shortages, wrecks or delays in transportation, or inability to obtain necessary labor or manufacturing facilities due to such causes.

Westinghouse points to other contract provisions, which give Florida responsibility for the fuel from the time that it is delivered until Westinghouse removes it. Read together, it is contended, these provisions indicate that Florida assumed the risk of having to store the spent fuel in the event that Westinghouse was unable to remove it as a result of one of the contingencies listed in the *force majeure* clause, and that therefore Westinghouse's performance is excused.

As noted earlier, the risk of a contingency that affects performance is presumed to rest on the promisor. However, the parties may agree to shift a particular risk to the promisee, or to allocate the various risks between them as they see fit.

For instance, in *Eastern Air Lines v. McDonnell Douglas*, 532 F.2d 957 (5th Cir. 1976), McDonnell Douglas urged both commercial impracticability and an "excusable delay" clause, exempting McDonnell Douglas from liability for delays beyond its control, in defense of Eastern's action for damages caused by late delivery. The late delivery was attributable to informal demands by the government that McDonnell Douglas accord priority to military aircraft for the Vietnam War. The court held that the excusable delay clause had the effect of broadening the protection afforded McDonnell Douglas under the UCC, and that the government's demands came within the terms of that clause.

Because of the same factors that compelled the Court to reject Westinghouse's defense of commercial impracticability, it is unable to view Westinghouse's obligation as discharged under the *force majeure* clause. To begin, Westinghouse's argument ignores the important fact that unlike the clause in *McDonnell Douglas*, which exempted only the seller, the *force majeure* clause at issue here *protects both Westinghouse and Florida*. To construe the clause as Westinghouse contends would, in effect, place the entire loss on Florida—a result not consonant with the clause itself, or with the parties' intentions concerning allocation of risk.

Further, the language of the clause is such that it is simply not applicable to the facts. The term reads "except as otherwise provided in the contract." Section 27 of the contract unequivocally places responsibility for removal of the spent fuel on Westinghouse. Westinghouse's contention that other contract terms place responsibility for the fuel on Florida until it is removed is not only misguided—it is cynical, in light of the fact that the fuel remains with Florida only because of Westinghouse's refusal to remove it. To adopt Westinghouse's construction of the phrase "until it is removed" as a valid defense to its failure to perform, in the context of the whole contract, would, in the Court's opinion, denude the law of reason.

Finally, the *force majeure* clause applies only to losses resulting from causes beyond the parties' reasonable control, including actions of the government. As noted in the discussion of commercial impracticability, the Court is unable to conclude that Westinghouse's failure to perform was in any meaningful way caused by the government's actions. Reprocessing, not removal from Florida's site, was rendered illegal by presidential order. No representative of the government has ever forbidden Westinghouse to transport spent nuclear fuel from Florida's spent fuel storage site to some other site; nor has any government stricture prevented Westinghouse from accepting responsibility for the spent fuel from Florida, as required by the contract. Further, the presidential order was not issued until two years after Westinghouse's initial refusal to remove the first spent fuel. Finally, in light of the fact that Westinghouse's attempts to obtain reprocessing facilities prior to the presidential order were less than aggressive at best, it has not been shown that Westinghouse's failure to obtain reprocessing during that period, much less its failure to remove the spent fuel, resulted from causes beyond its reasonable control.

IV. Frustration of Purpose

Westinghouse contends that, insofar as its purpose in promising to remove the spent fuel was to obtain value from it through reprocessing, that purpose has been completely frustrated by supervening events.

The defense of frustration of purpose, like commercial impracticability and mistake of fact, is limited by the parties' allocation of the risk that the supervening event will occur. *See* CORBIN, CONTRACTS, § 1354 (1964). Having found overwhelming evidence that Westinghouse assumed the risk of the uncertainties of reprocessing, the Court cannot find that frustration of purpose excuses its nonperformance.

Additionally, it is to be noted that while in the narrow sense, Westinghouse's purpose in agreeing to remove the spent fuel was to reprocess it, Westinghouse's broader purpose was to secure the Florida contract. The Court has found that Florida would not have agreed to a contract that required it to reprocess the fuel, or which gave it responsibility for the spent fuel after the "cooling off" period. Knowing this, Westinghouse agreed to remove the fuel; and by so doing, it did indeed achieve its larger purpose of obtaining the Florida contracts for the construction of two nuclear stream supply systems. That its accomplishment in this regard may now be viewed by it as a commercial tragedy is unfortunate, yet one cannot but conclude that Westinghouse is to a great extent the architect of its own misfortune.

V. Relief

As the Court has previously noted, Florida has already been financially damaged in an amount in excess of nine million dollars, and any relief must, of course, call for reimbursement, at least to that extent. There has been some evidence to the effect that other utilities have been considering the construction of interim spent fuel storage facilities. The estimates of the cost of such facilities, depending on the site and capacity, range from 20 million dollars to 44 million dollars. Estimates of the cost to construct a storage facility, if one can be constructed, at the Turkey Point site, are in excess of 33 million dollars, with a further annual cost of approximately one million dollars.

In addition to monetary damages for expenses incurred thus far in storing the spent fuel, Florida seeks an order requiring Westinghouse to specifically perform its promise to remove the spent fuel. Westinghouse contends that Florida is not entitled to a decree of specific performance under Florida law on the following grounds: (1) that Florida has not shown that monetary damages would be an inadequate remedy; (2) that Westinghouse cannot be ordered to remove the spent fuel because its performance necessarily depends on the cooperation and assent of third parties (specifically, government agencies that regulate the nuclear industry), and (3) specific performance is inappropriate in light of the difficulty of fashioning a specific and workable decree, and of monitoring the parties' compliance therewith over the long term.

Under Florida law, specific performance is often said to lie within the "sound discretion" of the Court. *Buck v. McNab*, 139 So. 2d 734 (Fla. App. 1962). It is discretionary in the sense that the Court may,—indeed, in many cases, must—make judgments based on equitable considerations. However, it is not "discretionary" in the sense that the Court's power is relatively unlimited:

> By saying that the exercise of discretion be "sound" and "judicial," the courts should be understood as meaning that there are reasonably well established working rules and standards by which they are governed in granting and refusing the remedy. CORBIN, CONTRACTS, § 1136.

Because the Court does not possess current information as to a number of crucial factors bearing on the appropriateness of a decree of specific performance, and, more importantly, because it wishes to provide the parties an opportunity to reach agreement as to how Westinghouse's duty may best be discharged, it does not now decide which of the remedies available to it should be applied here. The Court deems it appropriate, however, to discuss briefly the factors relevant to the selection of a remedy in the hope that the Court may assist the parties in reaching agreement, or, if such should prove necessary, that the parties may better assist the Court by providing evidence bearing on the matter as expeditiously as possible.

Specific performance may be warranted where the plaintiff cannot be adequately compensated by an award of damages. *City Stores Co. v. Ammerman*, 266 F. Supp. 766 (D.D.C. 1967). Here, there is considerable uncertainty as to Florida's future damages. Its estimate as to the expense it will have to incur should it be forced to shut down its plant in 1985 is just that—an estimate. Given the volatility of the price of all forms of energy, its actual expenses may vary considerably from this projection. Florida will, if the spent fuel is not removed, doubtlessly suffer very large future damages as a result of Westinghouse's breach. While this uncertainty would not be sufficient to defeat a damages claim, *Twyman v. Roell*, 123 Fla. 2, 166 So. 215 (1936), the uncertainty of the estimate is to be noted as one factor tending to militate in favor of specific performance. A further uncertainty arises from the probable difficulty of Florida obtaining from another party performance substantially similar to that promised by Westinghouse. The Court does not have information concerning the current availability of storage facilities or the present government regulations and policies concerning transportation of spent fuel. At trial, there was evidence that it would be extremely difficult, if not impossible, for Florida to obtain a contract for removal by another party. To the extent that this remains true, it may be viewed as another factor favoring specific performance.

By the same token, however, the very factors that might render it difficult for Florida to contract for removal with a third party would, obviously, make performance by Westinghouse difficult. While the Court has concluded that Westinghouse's nonperformance is not excused by commercial impracticability, this is not to be construed as precluding the Court from giving consideration to the hardship of performance in deciding the question of remedy. There are "[f]acts that are not sufficient to invalidate a contract and that may nevertheless be sufficient to induce the refusal of a decree for specific enforcement." CORBIN, CONTRACTS, § 1162.

Finally, while the court is fully cognizant of the difficulty of fashioning a sufficiently specific degree should the parties be unable to reach agreement, and should the Court conclude that specific enforcement is appropriate considering the various other factors, the Court believes that, with the assistance of the parties, a workable and appropriate decree would be achieved.

The Court, however, fervently hopes that it will not be called upon to draft a decree, not because it would be difficult, but rather because the Court is convinced that the parties themselves are in a far better position to find an equitable solution. The future of nuclear energy is a political question upon which the Court expresses no view. Resolution of the issue may or may not assist the parties in reaching an agreement. Regardless, however, of the government's present or future policies and actions vis-a-vis nuclear power, it is clear that, under the law, Westinghouse is liable to Florida for its breach of contract. It must pay damages, or perform, or some combination thereof, whether by agreement of the parties or by order of the Court. The former is, in the Court's view, far preferable in light of the parties' greater ability to discern the best interests of both Florida's rate payers and Westinghouse's shareholders, and their greater experience in solving complex practical problems.

The Court is not without some perspective as to the willingness and ability of the parties, with the assistance of the Court, to reach a fair agreement. Westinghouse has, in a series of cases which the multi-district panel transferred to this court along with the instant case, evidenced its good faith and willingness to work toward fair and equitable solutions of myriad complex problems. The agreements reached were, in the Court's view, beneficial to the parties and the public as well. Plaintiff, too, has shown its good faith as evidenced by the fair solution reached in another aspect of the instant case.

The solutions to which this court makes reference were reached after all parties, through their respective counsel, fairly, fully, and vigorously litigated the issue of liability. The court is satisfied that no less a result may be attained here. In the event, however, that the Court's hope in this regard does not reach fruition, then the parties may present further evidence on the issue of specific performance, as well as evidence in reference to a fair monetary award. As mentioned *supra*, there is considerable uncertainty in the present record as to Florida's future damages. Further evidence will be necessary, to the end that Westinghouse pay no more, and Florida receive no less, than is fair.

Therefore, the parties will be granted ninety (90) days within which to attempt to reach agreement as to the form of the decree to be entered in this matter. Should they wish additional time, the Court may be willing to grant it, upon a showing that additional time would be productive.

In the interim, the Court will meet and confer with counsel, in an effort to assist them in reaching agreement, and for the purpose of more fully apprising the parties as to the further information that the Court deems necessary to draft an appropriate decree in the event that the parties fail to reach an agreement. At such a meeting the parties should be prepared to render assistance in the selection of an expert for the purpose of assisting the Court, should the court conclude that such assistance is necessary, in ascertaining the various alternatives, if any, leading to the removal and storage of the spent fuel.

In view of the fact that the interests of both parties and the public would best be served by an expeditious and final resolution of this matter, both parties are urged to use the initial time period in an intensive attempt to reach agreement, rather than in preparing to further litigate the issue of remedy.

An appropriate order shall issue.

NOTES AND QUESTIONS

1. *Judge Merhige's background:* In the early 1970s, Judge Merhige ordered the Richmond, Virginia schools to integrate. In the mid-1980s, he heard around 350 of the Dalkon Shield contraceptive device claims against A.H. Robins Co. He helped about

140 of these cases settle out of court. He was also in charge of most of the Westing-house uranium litigation.

Emily Couric wrote about Judge Merhige in the *National Law Journal*:[119]

> U.S. District Judge Robert R. Merhige, Jr., of the Eastern District of Virginia tells a story: He privately brought together the two parties in a case before him. The case involved millions of dollars, and the trial, he predicted, would last at least six to eight weeks.
>
> "I sat the two of them down on a Sunday night in my [home's] sunroom," the judge recounts. "I pointed out to them the expense of the trial and the fact that it was a business decision they could make better than six people who know nothing about business."
>
> Then Judge Merhige left the room, and closed the door.
>
> "In 45 minutes they came out," he continues. "I was in my library. They thanked me for the effort. One said, 'We've tried, judge, but it's impossible.'"
>
> "For you to tell me it's impossible really frightens me," Judge Merhige recalls answering, "because I didn't think anything was impossible for American businessmen. I didn't think people got to be executive vice presidents by having 'impossible' in their vocabulary."
>
> One of the executives responded, "I guess that's not the right word. It's not impossible."
>
> "Why then, why don't you try again?" suggested Judge Merhige.
>
> The two men looked at each other, and retreated to the sunroom a second time.
>
> Fifteen minutes later they had reached a settlement....
>
> "Not infrequently, I will insist that the lawyers [in a case] bring their principals here because I want to satisfy myself that both principals recognize what [strong arguments] the other has," says the judge. "Even a pancake has two sides." ...
>
> Not everyone agrees that such an activist role in settling cases is appropriate for a judge....
>
> "Judges can't settle cases," says Judge Merhige. "I'm not worried about someone saying, 'He forced us to settle.' Good lawyers can't be forced to do anything."

2. *What happened next?* Despite Judge Merhige's efforts, the parties were unable to settle the case. The docket discloses that the parties filed joint reports of their efforts to resolve the dispute throughout 1981 and 1982. On October 10, 1983, there was a trial on the issue of damages that lasted almost six hours.

---

119. Emily Couric, *Judge Robert R. Merhige, Jr.*, THE NATIONAL LAW JOURNAL, Aug. 4, 1986, at 1, 20.

In *Florida Power and Light Co. v. Westinghouse Electric Co.*,[120] Judge Merhige reported: "The parties made a good faith effort to negotiate the remedy but failed." However, several things happened while the negotiations took place. The parties discovered that it was possible to "re-rack" the Turkey Point spent fuel storage pits a second time.[121] This provided sufficient on-site storage for all the spent fuel that the reactors would discharge over their useful life. As a result, the reactors did not have to shut down. FP & L did not have to spend a half-million dollars a day on substitute power. Westinghouse agreed to do the second re-racking at Turkey Point at no cost to FP & L.

Furthermore, the United States government passed the Nuclear Waste Policy Act of 1982.[122] The statute provides that the Department of Energy and the owners and generators of spent fuel are to enter into contracts. DOE takes title to the spent fuel and assumes full responsibility for it. The statute sets a timetable for the government to build a permanent storage facility. However, the permanent site to receive spent fuel was not scheduled to open until 1998 at the earliest, and was still not open as of 2010. The Act encourages interim storage at the reactor sites through the use of techniques such as re-racking. FP & L entered a contract with the DOE and agreed to pay a fee of $70 million.

FP & L argued that Westinghouse should pay the $70 million fee, roughly $13 million for the first re-racking, and roughly $12 million for the second re-racking. Judge Merhige found that the United States government had not acted in a timely fashion in honoring its implied commitment regarding spent fuel.[123] This was a contingency,

---

120. 597 F. Supp. 1456 (E.D. Va. 1984).

121. Prompted by the settlement negotiations, both Westinghouse and FP & L appointed panels of experts. They found that a second re-racking was the only practical option for dealing with the spent fuel.

122. 42 U.S.C. § 10101 *et seq.*

123. John L. Campbell, *The State and the Nuclear Waste Crisis: An Institutional Analysis of Policy Constraints*, 34 Soc. Probs. 18 (Feb. 1987), notes that the Atomic Energy Act of 1954 required the development of a private reprocessing industry. However, costs and environmental concerns made profitable operations extremely questionable. Some firms tried to enter the field, but those with superior technology could not get established. The Natural Resources Defense Council and the Sierra Club used their access to policy-makers to impose serious delays on the development of reprocessing. In 1976, President Ford imposed a three-year moratorium on reprocessing so that the risks associated with nuclear arms proliferation arising from the extraction of plutonium from spent fuel could be studied. In 1977, President Carter announced that reprocessing would be deferred indefinitely. Campbell notes that the French, for example, subsidize reprocessing as a necessary part of their nuclear energy policy.

As of 2016, the problem of what to do with nuclear waste is still unsolved. In August 2001, the United States Department of Energy made a favorable safety assessment of a plan to build an underground storage dump for radioactive spent fuel in Nevada's Yucca Mountain. The plan was opposed by both of Nevada's senators and the governor of the state. Environmental groups are also opposed to the proposal. Among other things, they point to the dangers involved in shipping the spent nuclear fuel from locations around the United States to Yucca Mountain, and they question the long-term safety of storing the fuel there. In February 2002, President George W. Bush said that "a 57-year accumulation of nuclear waste from power plants and weapons should be buried in the Nevada desert at Yucca Mountain, declaring that an end to the 40-year search for a place to isolate radioactive waste was necessary." N.Y. Times, Feb. 16, 2002, at A11. The *Times* commented: "What was seen in 1982

the non-occurrence of which was a basic assumption of the contract. It made performance of Westinghouse's implicit obligation to perform within a reasonable time impracticable under UCC § 2-615. "Both Florida and Westinghouse were aware that reprocessing might not be available, but neither of them anticipated that no alternative means of removal would be available until 1998 or after."

Judge Merhige said that an equitable allocation of the interim storage costs was in order. "In making the allocation, the Court must of necessity utilize its own sense of fairness." He said that there was "no reason to suspect that the costs of the permanent federal repository have been increased by the delays." As a result, he concluded that the $70 million DOE disposal fee should be borne entirely by Westinghouse. He then turned to the other costs caused by the delays. FP & L rate payers had benefited enormously from the use of nuclear power during the era of high oil prices. However, Westinghouse should not be rewarded for its lack of diligence during the early 1970s. Thus, Judge Merhige ordered the costs divided. "Without attempting mathematical precision, the allocation will divide the costs roughly as if Westinghouse were absorbing the costs of the first re-racking and Florida absorbing the costs of the second." He refused to award FP & L compensation for increased property taxes and insurance premiums. He concluded:

---

as a 16-year plan for finding a location and opening a repository is entering its 20th year and seems likely to last for at least 10 more." The Obama administration moved to abandon the Yucca Mountain waste facility in March of 2010.

In January 2010, the Obama administration created the Blue Ribbon Commission on America's Nuclear Future to assess the nuclear waste program. In TOO HOT TO TOUCH: THE PROBLEM OF HIGH-LEVEL NUCLEAR WASTE (2013), William M. Alley and Rosemarie Alley comment that the 2012 report "didn't come up with any new ideas because there are none. With no apparent sense of irony, the Commission called for 'prompt efforts to develop one or more geologic disposal facilities'" (314). The Commission members did not take a position on Yucca Mountain, nor did they identify any alternative sites. Though they conceded that interim storage was the only feasible solution in the short run, the March 2011 accident at the Fukushima Dai-ichi nuclear power plant in Japan, which happened during the Commission's deliberations, left them concerned about the concentration of nuclear waste at decommissioned reactor sites and in fuel pools at operating reactors. The states where this waste is stored (including South Carolina and Washington) brought a lawsuit to force the hand of the Obama administration. After warning the Nuclear Regulatory Commission (NRC) of its duty to make a decision about dealing with nuclear waste within the Congressionally mandated timetable in 2012, the D.C. Circuit Court issued a writ of mandamus against the NRC in In re Aiken County, 725 F.3d 255 (2013). The licensing process for Yucca Mountain resumed. Testifying before the Senate in March 2015, the NRC chairman estimated that completing this process would require at least an additional $330 million. The Alleys report that Sweden and Finland have moved forward toward licensing a site for spent nuclear fuel. Not surprisingly, the Fukushima accident acted as a death knell to such efforts in Japan.

Also as of 2016, there is no reprocessing of spent fuel in the United States. However, it is done in Europe by British Nuclear Fuels P.L.C., at its Sellafield plant in northwestern England. Irish and Scandanavian activists have campaigned to shut down spent-fuel reprocessing at Sellafield because of radioactive emissions into the Irish Sea and the atmosphere. In 1999, BNF bought the former Westinghouse nuclear energy operations. There are more than 400 nuclear plants worldwide, and Westinghouse designed four out of ten of them. Fuel reprocessing also takes place in France, Japan, Russia, and India.

The sums aforementioned are not intended to be precise. The Court is satisfied that the parties, who have worked so diligently toward settling their
differences, will not be unable to draft an appropriate decree in accord with
the Court's view as expressed herein.

3. *Criticism of Judge Merhige's approach:* Professor Richard W. Duesenberg[124]
argued that the significance of the *Florida Power and Light* case is "enormous." "It
takes its place in a growing line of decisions under § 2-615 in which the relief contemplated by the section has been denied. . . . [T]he language of the court is forbidding;
taking a 2-615 route out of a contract is not an easy journey." He also said that "[t]he
court's attitude on the *force majeure* provision contrasts remarkably from that of the
Fifth Circuit in *Eastern Air Lines v. McDonnell Douglas.*" Duesenberg has written a
great deal about the UCC. Are his assertions about the original *Florida Power and
Light* opinion correct? To the extent they are, why do the judges refuse to apply the
statute? Does Judge Merhige's second opinion suggest that Duesenberg might be hap-
pier with the final result of the case?

4. *The Court of Appeals neatens matters:* The parties appealed Judge Merhige's decisions. The United States Court of Appeals for the Fourth Circuit rejected much of
Judge Merhige's reasoning and reached a result more favorable to Westinghouse.[125]

First, the Fourth Circuit found that the situation was a classic case of impossibility.
Both parties had assumed that the spent fuel would be reprocessed, and both had
assumed that either commercial reprocessing would be available or the government
would provide this service. Westinghouse had not assumed the risk that neither reprocessing nor storage would be available. Moreover, there was no evidence that
Westinghouse could have mitigated any of the losses under the contract as no reprocessing facilities ever were available after Florida Power & Light exercised its option
to have Westinghouse remove the spent fuel.

Second, the court said that it must consider the equities of the parties after Westinghouse established that performance was impracticable. The parties had not challenged on appeal the District Court's allocation of the costs of re-racking the storage
facilities (though the Fourth circuit suggested it would have freed Westinghouse from
its share, if Westinghouse had appealed this issue). The Court of Appeals concluded
that the rate payers had enjoyed tremendous benefits (about $10 billion) because of
the much lower costs of nuclear power. Thus, it would be fair to charge them with
the entire cost of storing the spent fuel until the federal storage facility went into operation. Since the Florida Public Service Commission had given Florida Power &
Light the right to pass along these costs for the life of the Turkey Point facility, there
was no reason to charge any of the DOE disposal fees to Westinghouse.

To what extent, if at all, does the Fourth Circuit's decision differ from Judge Teitelbaum's approach in the *ALCOA* case? Is the Fourth Circuit writing the contract it

---

124. Richard W. Duesenberg, *Uniform Commercial Code Annual Survey: Sales and Bulk Transfers,*
37 Bus. Law. 949 (1982).

125. Florida Power & Light Co. v. Westinghouse Elec. Corp., 826 F.2d 239 (4th Cir. 1987).

thinks the parties should have written if they had known that nuclear power would produce great savings compared to oil but that reprocessing would not be available and storage would not be available until far into the future? Is the Fourth Circuit acting as an administrative agency seeking to balance the interests of power users, utilities, and equipment manufacturers? Were the interests of the rate payers adequately represented before the Fourth Circuit by FP & L's and Westinghouse's lawyers?[126]

Westinghouse and FP & L continued to do business. In 1989, they entered a risk-sharing contract under which Westinghouse provided certain maintenance items to the Turkey Point plant. If costs were below a fixed amount, Westinghouse earned a bonus; if they were above this amount, Westinghouse would be paid less. A factor that made it difficult to end the relationship was a Nuclear Regulatory Commission ruling that replacing items in the reactor with Westinghouse parts did not require a new license, while replacing items with a competitor's products would.

5. *The judge as mediator rather than as vindicator of rights:* Judge Merhige's solution to this Westinghouse problem was to (1) press the parties to settle; (2) find Westinghouse bound by the contract and not excused by changed circumstances; (3) ask the parties to agree on a settlement; and (4) limit the remedy so there was some sharing of the losses. In the *ALCOA* case, Judge Teitelbaum considered the purposes of the parties and drafted a new pricing clause in light of changed circumstances. However, Essex appealed, and the court of appeals pressed the parties to settle. Finally, Essex and ALCOA reworked their arrangement.

In both cases the parties gained a compromise settlement after one or more federal judges played the role of "coercive mediator." Judge Merhige made "suggestions" in a judicial opinion, and Judge Teitelbaum wrote an opinion that would stand if not overturned on appeal. The parties were pushed to work out matters rather than stand

---

126. Moreover, how broadly should we look into the relationship between FP & L and Westinghouse? In 1977, FP & L sued Westinghouse alleging defects in the design and construction of the Turkey Point nuclear plant. FP & L had to replace the tubes that carried the radioactive water to its six steam generators. The parties battled about whether FP & L could sue for negligent design or was confined to breach of warranty claims. The federal courts certified the question to the Supreme Court of Florida. It decided that where there was no personal injury all claims for defective products are limited to breach of warranty theories. *See* Florida Power & Light Co. v. Westinghouse Electric Corp. 785 F.2d 952 (11th Cir. 1986), 510 So. 2d 899 (S. Ct. Fla. 1987); 835 F.2d 817 (11th Cir. 1988). This decision would have brought all of the warranty disclaimers and remedy limitations in the contract into play. Moreover, it would have triggered the contract's provisions limiting the time within which FP & L must make claims.

Westinghouse's failure to remove the spent fuel may have influenced the decision of FP & L officials to bring this suit. Recall that one reason the Court of Appeals refused to charge Westinghouse for the costs of storing spent fuel was the great benefits power users in the Miami area enjoyed because of nuclear power. Expensive repairs to FP & L's Turkey Point plant could offset some of these benefits. Moreover, some of the losses suffered because of Westinghouse's inability to reprocess spent fuel might be recovered in the breach of warranty action if FP & L recovered a large sum that the jury did not calculate too precisely.

Westinghouse settled this suit, but the terms of the settlement were not made public. *See* 32 NU-CLEONICS WEEK, May 9, 1991, at 2.

on their rights. While ultimately Judge Merhige's effort was unsuccessful, the parties spent almost two years attempting to resolve the issue. Does this pressure to settle produce better solutions than the application of doctrinal contract law to produce decisions about breach and the amount of recoverable damages?

Judge Teitelbaum adjusted ALCOA's obligations and offered several options. Judge Merhige refused to excuse Westinghouse, but then used notions of foreseeability and fault to limit the remedy. The court of appeals found commercial impracticability, but then used its equitable powers to fashion a remedy it saw as fair. To what extent do these approaches differ in substance?

One important function of a mediator is to make a concrete proposal. The parties may accept it as a fair compromise. However, even when they do not accept it, often it moves along the process. Parties can offer variations on the mediator's solution. It serves as a new starting point. If the parties cannot find a better solution, they always can fall back on the mediator's compromise. How does a federal district judge's decision differ from that of a mediator? Remember that in both cases the trial judges' solutions were not final. The parties could and did appeal, and appellate courts could reverse these decisions. Moreover, at any time before the appellate courts acted, the parties could reach their own settlement.

6. *The rhetoric of the forum:* If Congress deals with a bad bargain (or a number of bad bargains) made by a major corporation, will the rhetoric and solutions reached differ from those used when courts try to cope with these problems? For example, in which forum would we expect negative views about nuclear power to play a role in dealing with contracts to build nuclear generating plants and dispose of the waste? Concern about the impact of a decision on the economy of Pittsburgh or another city? Concern about the jobs of airline employees who lost so much when senior executives of the corporation wrecked the airline?[127] What, if anything, does this say about the functions of contract doctrine? About the functions of various branches of the government? About politics?

6. The 2008 and Following Meltdown of the Economy

During the first decade of the 21st century, the financial system of much of the developed world fell into crisis. In testifying before Congress in October 2008, Alan Greenspan, the former Federal Reserve chairman, argued that "we are in the midst

---

127. In Northern Indiana Public Service Co. v. Carbon County Coal Co., 799 F.2d 265, 280 (7th Cir. 1986), Judge Posner considered arguments about the appropriate remedy after he found that a buyer was not excused from a contract to supply coal. The supplier sought specific performance. It asserted the interest of workers and merchants in Hanna, Wyoming, where the supplier's coal mine was located. Judge Posner said that the workers and merchants had no legal interest in the contract. "Moreover, the workers and merchants in Hanna assumed the risk that the coal mine would have to close down if it turned out to be uneconomical. The contract with NIPSCO did not guarantee that the mine would operate throughout the life of the contract but only protected the owners of Carbon County [the mining company] against the financial consequences of a breach."

of a once-in-a-century credit tsunami."[128] Individuals and businesses could not get loans, many people lost jobs or failed to get employment that they had expected, and individuals and firms went bankrupt. The federal government took many steps attempting to save the financial system as well as General Motors and Chrysler. At least some people tried to use impracticability and frustration of purpose as tools to deal with their disrupted expectations. How far, if at all, does contract doctrine offer solutions in the face of serious downturns in the economy?

HOOSIER ENERGY RURAL ELECTRIC CO-OP., INC. v. JOHN HANCOCK LIFE INS. CO.

United States District Court, Southern District of Indiana
588 F. Supp. 2d 919 (2008)

David F. Hamilton, United States District Judge.

Entry on Hoosier Energy's Motion for Preliminary Injunction

Introduction

This case provides a case study of some of the worst aspects of modern finance. The case arises from an elaborate transaction that combines the sometimes toxic intricacies of credit default swaps and investment derivatives with a blatantly abusive tax shelter. Investment bankers and lawyers made more than $12 million in fees for putting together the paper transaction known as a "sale in—lease out" or "SILO" transaction of an electrical generating plant. Although all parties have been making all payments required under the contracts, the transaction is now in crisis because credit rating agencies have downgraded the credit ratings of one of the parties.

At this stage of the case, plaintiff Hoosier Energy Rural Electric Cooperative, Inc., seeks a preliminary injunction to enjoin defendants (i) John Hancock Life Insurance Company, Merom Generation I, LLC, and OP Merom Generation I, LLC (collectively, "John Hancock"); and (ii) Ambac Assurance Corporation and Ambac Credit Products, LLC (collectively, "Ambac") from making any demand or any payment pursuant to any assertion that a default has occurred and enjoining John Hancock from asserting that a default has occurred. The court has received and considered the memoranda from both sides, including affidavits and supporting documents. The court has also heard and considered arguments presented at the hearing on Hoosier Energy's motion held on November 19, 2008. The court now states its findings of fact and conclusions of law pursuant to Rules 52 and 65 of the Federal Rules of Civil Procedure. As explained below, the court finds that the preliminary injunction should be granted, that further proceedings are needed on the issue of appropriate security for the injunction, and that discovery should proceed immediately.

As with any preliminary injunction matter, the court's findings of fact and conclusions of law are tentative because they are the result of an expedited process. That is true to an unusual degree in this case.... Because of the very short time frame that

---

128. Rick Newman, *Greenspan vs. Buffett*, U.S. News & World Report, Oct. 27, 2008.

resulted from the timing of the removal [from an Indiana state court to the federal court], the court emphasizes that these findings and conclusions are tentative and subject to further examination at the request of any party at any time if additional evidence becomes available or further argument would be fruitful.

Findings of Fact and Conclusions of Law

I. Structure of the Merom SILO Transaction

Plaintiff Hoosier Energy owns and operates an electrical generating plant in Merom, Indiana on the Wabash River. In 2002, Hoosier Energy and the other parties entered into a complex transaction known as a "sale in—lease out" or "SILO," in which Hoosier Energy leased certain assets at its Merom power plant to John Hancock for a term of 63 years (longer than its useful life) and then leased the same assets back for a term of 30 years. At the risk of oversimplifying a complex transaction, the court will try to summarize. John Hancock made an immediate one-time payment of $300 million for its 63-year lease. John Hancock then immediately leased these assets back to Hoosier Energy. Hoosier Energy kept about $20 million, and approximately $278 million was deposited with various Ambac entities, which in turn were required to make lease payments on Hoosier Energy's behalf to John Hancock. Hoosier Energy made payments into other funds controlled by Ambac with an eye toward the back end of the deal, when it would be virtually certain that Hoosier Energy would remain in control of the Merom plant.

The transaction was promoted and designed by lawyers and investment bankers (transaction costs were more than $12 million) with the hope that it would allow John Hancock to claim to be the "owner" of the Merom plant for tax purposes and thus enable it to claim tens of millions of dollars of tax deductions. Those deductions were of no use to Hoosier Energy as the plant owner because it simply does not earn significant profits. It is a cooperative made up of members that are rural electric cooperatives.

As part of the complex transaction (documented in approximately 4000 pages of fine print), Hoosier Energy was required to obtain a "credit default swap" from Ambac to give John Hancock further assurance that it would actually receive the promised lease payments. In general terms, the parties agreed that if Hoosier Energy defaulted on its obligations under the contracts, John Hancock could demand a "termination payment" from Ambac, and Ambac could turn to Hoosier Energy for payment under a closely parallel credit default swap contract between Ambac and Hoosier Energy. Ambac also provided a surety bond for the benefit of John Hancock.

As part of the terms of this credit protection for John Hancock, the parties agreed that if Ambac's credit rating dropped below a specific threshold, Hoosier Energy would have 60 days to find a new qualified swap provider. Hoosier Energy's failure to secure a new qualified swap provider would allow John Hancock to declare a default under the contracts, to terminate the entire transaction, and to demand an early termination payment from Ambac. In that event, Ambac would be able to demand very substantial payments from Hoosier Energy. The parties agreed to a schedule for the termination payment, depending on the date of the payment. The schedule was designed to give John Hancock, in the event of termination, the "Net Economic Return" it hoped to receive from the entire transaction, based on the assumption that it would be entitled to all of the hoped-for tax benefits. ("Termination Value" is "an amount intended to maintain the Net Economic Return of the Owner Participant [John Hancock] through the date in question.") ...

Because of the significant tax risk associated with the Merom SILO transaction, the deal's documents included a Tax Indemnity Agreement. Hoosier Energy insisted, and John Hancock agreed, that Hoosier Energy would not have liability for indemnification for loss resulting from, among other things, "a determination that the transactions contemplated by the Operative Documents are a sham, lack a valid business purpose or have a substance that is different from their form."

II. Rulings from the IRS and Subsequent Credit Crisis

Around the time these parties closed the Merom SILO transaction in 2002, the IRS began disallowing claimed income tax deductions from taxpayers who had participated in other SILOs. (IRS Notice 2005-13 regarding SILO transactions.) Courts have decided in favor of the IRS on transactions structured similarly to the Merom SILO transaction among these parties. [Citations omitted.] The IRS has gone so far as to offer earlier this year a form of tax amnesty for parties to similar SILO and LILO transactions, which the IRS deems abusive tax shelters. The IRS has announced that taxpayers involved in more than 80 percent of the SILO and LILO transactions have accepted the offer. John Hancock apparently has chosen not to take advantage of this offer, at least with respect to the Merom SILO transaction.[129]

At the time these parties entered into the Merom SILO transaction, they received opinions from several law firms to the effect that the transaction would produce legally valid and enforceable rights and obligations according to the terms of the agreements. The parties have not directed the court's attention to any opinion by counsel, even in 2002, to the effect that the transaction would be treated properly as a genuine sale and lease-back for federal income tax purposes so that John Hancock could be deemed a genuine owner of the Merom assets and thus entitled to the claimed tax benefits.

Hoosier Energy has filed an affidavit from Stanford Law School's Professor Alan Joseph Bankman, who is an expert in tax shelters. Professor Bankman has examined the Merom SILO transaction and has concluded: "The Merom Transaction was at its inception in 2002, and continues to be, an abusive tax shelter.... The IRS will certainly deny the tax benefits that Hancock is claiming." In the limited time the court has had to examine the issue, the court concludes that Professor Bankman is probably correct.

---

129. [1] Parallel to the Merom SILO transaction between John Hancock and Hoosier Energy, Hoosier Energy entered into a similar SILO deal with Bank of America for a smaller portion of the Merom assets. Bank of America apparently has decided to take advantage of the IRS amnesty program.

The complex flow of funds in the transaction has little or no economic substance and appears not to grant John Hancock the sorts of rights, risks, and responsibilities sufficient for it to be treated as an owner of the Merom generating facility. It appears highly likely that the intended tax benefits will not be allowed. The entire Merom SILO transaction appears to have been an abusive tax shelter, a sham with little or no economic substance.

Notwithstanding the tax problems, the IRS apparently has not yet examined the Merom deal or challenged John Hancock's claimed tax deductions, which appear to have been in the tens of millions of dollars so far. All parties to the transaction have made all payments required under the contracts, and John Hancock has received on time every penny it has been owed.

In June 2008, however, Ambac's published credit rating fell below the level specified in the contract documents. Hoosier Energy was notified of this change, recognized that the contract required it to find a new participant with comparably strong credit ratings, and began looking. It encountered extraordinary difficulty in doing so. Based on the limited information before the court, this year's credit "tsunami" appears to have been the primary reason that Ambac's credit rating fell. The credit crisis also appears to have made it impossible—or nearly impossible—for Hoosier Energy to find a substitute for Ambac with a sufficient rating, on time, and at any price.

"Nearly" impossible? The qualifier is important. In December 2007, nine of the thirteen financial guarantors tracked by Moody's and Standard & Poor's had ratings that satisfied the criteria of the Merom SILO agreements. In the summer and fall of 2008, credit markets experienced unparalleled adverse events. By June 2008, only three of those thirteen guarantors had the requisite ratings. The crisis was not anticipated by the most senior economists in the country. For example, former Federal Reserve Chairman Alan Greenspan testified before a Congressional committee on October 23, 2008:

> We are in the midst of a once-in-a-century credit tsunami. Central banks and governments are being required to take unprecedented measures.... This crisis ... has turned out to be much broader than anything I could have imagined. It has morphed from one gripped by liquidity constraints to one in which fears of insolvency are now paramount.... Those of us who have looked to the self-interest of lending institutions to protect shareholders' equity (myself especially) are in a state of shocked disbelief.

On June 19, 2008, Moody's downgraded Ambac to a rating of Aa3, which gave Hoosier Energy sixty days to replace Ambac in the credit default swap arrangements. Hoosier Energy immediately began trying to replace Ambac with a credit enhancement vehicle that would meet the credit conditions of the Merom SILO agreements....

Hoosier Energy informed John Hancock of these efforts by letter on June 20, 2008, but warned that it could take more than 60 days to secure a replacement because of the extraordinary state of the credit markets. Hoosier Energy also proposed potential solutions to the situation, including allowing Hoosier Energy more than the 60 days contemplated in the Agreement to secure a replacement, granting waiver of the Aa2 credit rating requirement, restructuring the transaction without credit enhancement requirements, and unwinding the transaction altogether. Hoosier Energy, John Hancock, Ambac, and CoBank conferred on July 10th, and John Hancock appeared to support Hoosier Energy's efforts in the face of the credit crisis. However, on July 21st, John Hancock rejected the proposals Hoosier Energy outlined in its June 20th letter, including permitting Hoosier Energy additional time to find a replacement for Ambac.

Hoosier Energy's efforts continued, and by August 6th it had made progress in negotiating with Bank of America and CoBank for letters of credit in amounts equal to the equity portion of the termination value. Hoosier Energy informed John Hancock of this development. John Hancock responded positively, stating that it would accept the proposed letters of credit but that it preferred to have Bank of America support the entire amount. John Hancock also stated that it would extend the replacement period until September 2nd, contingent on production of either signed term sheets or letters of intent from Bank of America and CoBank. However, Bank of America decided not to proceed with the credit enhancement for the Merom SILO transaction.

Hoosier Energy continued to seek a replacement for Ambac. On September 3rd, Hoosier Energy and John Hancock executed an agreement extending the replacement period another 30 days. On September 8th, Hoosier Energy received a proposal from Berkshire Hathaway that outlined alternative methods of providing credit replacement for Ambac. Negotiations began, and Hoosier Energy kept John Hancock apprised of its progress and the likelihood that it would need another extension of time to finalize the deal with Berkshire Hathaway.

On September 29th, John Hancock received a Summary of Terms and Conditions under which Berkshire Hathaway would issue a Lease Equity Surety Bond. The term sheet expressly contemplated a 90-day period between signing and closing, a provision required by Berkshire Hathaway. Hoosier Energy forwarded the term sheet to John Hancock and said that while it had found a suitable replacement for Ambac, it would need more time to close the deal.

On October 3rd, John Hancock agreed to extend the replacement period, but only by 20 days. Hoosier Energy attempted to accelerate the finalization of the Berkshire Hathaway deal. On October 13th, its board of directors voted to approve the term sheet, and the Berkshire Hathaway term sheet was executed. Hoosier Energy forwarded a copy of the executed term sheet to John Hancock. The replacement period was due to expire on October 22nd, and Hoosier Energy sent a draft Third Waiver Extension Agreement to John Hancock that would extend the replacement period by another 90 days. John Hancock did not respond. Also on October 22nd, Hoosier Energy was reassured that although Berkshire Hathaway senior management needed to approve the deal, Berkshire intended to close the deal. Hoosier Energy informed John Hancock of Berkshire's intent.

On October 23rd, however, the same day that Mr. Greenspan testified about the "credit tsunami," John Hancock pulled the plug on Hoosier Energy's effort to replace Ambac. John Hancock rejected Hoosier Energy's request for an additional extension and informed Hoosier Energy that an "Event of Default" had occurred under the contract. John Hancock advised Ambac that it would expect its termination payment of approximately $120 million on October 31, 2008. Such a payment would immediately trigger a duty on the part of Hoosier Energy to pay Ambac either the same sum of approximately $120 million immediately, or at least $26 million immediately, followed by installment payments over four years for total payments of approximately $160 million. Ambac has stated that it was and is ready, willing, and able to make the $120 million termination payment to John Hancock unless it is enjoined from doing so....

[Hoosier Energy asked for a temporary injunction that would give it more time to arrange a substitute for Ambac's participation in the deal.]

IV. Preliminary Injunction Requirements

"A plaintiff seeking a preliminary injunction must establish that he is likely to succeed on the merits, that he is likely to suffer irreparable harm in the absence of preliminary relief, that the balance of equities tips in his favor, and that an injunction is in the public interest." *Winter v. NRDC*, 555 U.S. 129, 129 S. Ct. 365, 172 L. Ed. 2d 249, 261 (2008).

A. Irreparable Harm

Hoosier Energy will likely suffer immediate and severe irreparable harm if preliminary injunctive relief is not granted. The record shows with sufficient clarity that if Ambac makes the $120 million termination payment to John Hancock tonight or tomorrow, Ambac will immediately be entitled to a payment of either the same $120 million from Hoosier Energy or at least $26 million (perhaps $40 million) immediately, followed by installment payments of approximately $40 million per year over the next four years. Hoosier Energy has been covering its operating expenses and debt service, but it would be impossible for Hoosier Energy to pay the termination payment either as a lump sum or in installments. The demand alone would make it impossible for Hoosier Energy to obtain any further credit to continue in business. In addition, Hoosier Energy would cross-default on hundreds of millions of dollars of other loans, lines of credit, and long-term supply contracts.

It is highly likely that Hoosier Energy would be forced to file very quickly for protection under Chapter 11 of the Bankruptcy Code. Where other requirements are also met, immediate exposure to bankruptcy "sufficiently meets the standards for granting interim relief, for otherwise a favorable final judgment might well be useless." *Doran v. Salem Inn, Inc.*, 422 U.S. 922, 932, 95 S. Ct. 2561, 45 L. Ed. 2d 648 (1975) (affirming preliminary injunction) ...

The court is not persuaded by John Hancock's argument that these harms are merely speculative or just "economic ripples" that the court should disregard. If the terms of the Merom SILO contracts are enforced as written, these consequences for Hoosier Energy will be imminent, direct, and foreseeable.

B. Likelihood of Success on the Merits

Hoosier Energy has shown a reasonable likelihood of success on the merits on two independent theories for relief: the essential illegality of the Merom SILO transaction, and temporary commercial impracticability. All of the contracts provide that New York substantive law governs them, though Indiana law might apply to whether the forum state's public policy has been violated by the contracts....

1. Illegality of the Entire Merom SILO Transaction

Hoosier Energy asserts that the entire Merom SILO Transaction is illegal and void as against public policy because it is no more than a paper transaction with no economic substance other than as an abusive tax shelter similar to that found unlawful in *AWG Leasing Trust v. United States*, 592 F. Supp. 2d 953, 2008 U.S. Dist. LEXIS 42761, 2008 WL 2230744 (N.D. Ohio, May 28, 2008). Professor Bankman's affidavit has detailed the similarities between the AWG tax shelter and the Merom SILO transaction at issue here. Defendants have not offered contrary evidence on this point. (Defense expert Dr. David Ellis, Ph.D., observed that the Merom SILO transaction is similar to other leveraged lease transactions with which he is familiar, but he did not express any opinions about the economic substance of the transaction or the viability of the tax strategy.) At this preliminary stage of the case, the court finds Professor Bankman's opinions persuasive on this issue. This deal was an attempt to create an appearance of a sale but without any real economic substance. Hoosier Energy retained essentially all of the benefits and burdens of ownership of the Merom plant. John Hancock did not take on sufficient benefits and burdens of ownership to be treated as an owner for federal tax purposes. Despite the reams of paper and the circular flows of hundreds of millions of dollars, the transaction appears to have been a sham, without economic substance.

The court is not persuaded by John Hancock's efforts to separate the legality of the John Hancock-Ambac credit default swap agreement from the rest of the entire Merom SILO transaction. All of the agreements that make up the entire transaction were conditioned upon the execution of all the other agreements. Without fitting every piece of the puzzle together, there would have been no transaction.[130]

The court also is not persuaded by John Hancock's attempt to separate the tax aspects of the transaction from its overall legitimacy. The Merom SILO transaction ... appears to have been a pure, abusive tax shelter, with no economic substance to the transaction at all, despite the elaborate and expensive window dressing. This deal was the attempted sale of tax deductions and no more than that; it appears to have been rotten to the core, so that the illegality affects every portion of the deal....

Assuming Hoosier Energy can prevail ultimately on this theory of illegality, what consequences should flow from a conclusion that the transaction is contrary to public policy and void? The long-term consequences would probably involve some form of unwinding or rescission of the transaction, using a court's equitable powers, and it

---

130. [2] ... Most important, the John Hancock-Ambac deal was part of an integrated whole that appears to have been abusive and illegal at its core.

is unlikely that a court would allow Hoosier Energy to keep the $20 million or so that it received from John Hancock at the front end of the transaction....

It may be that this theory of illegality should lead the court simply to deny relief to Hoosier Energy. After all, if no party is entitled to enforce the tainted contracts, why should a court step in and grant injunctive or declaratory relief to Hoosier Energy, which was itself a party to the transaction? That denial would leave Ambac free, if it were in fact willing to do so, to make a termination payment of $120 million to John Hancock, and then to take its own chances on whether it could recover any of the $120 million from Hoosier Energy. That course would probably maximize the prospects for an unjust result in the case, though the court assumes that Ambac might be reluctant to make the payment under those circumstances. Hoosier Energy has suggested, and the court believes, that the court may have the equitable power instead to "unwind" the illegal transaction (as the IRS is requiring in similar deals under the amnesty program) in a way that tries to minimize windfalls and unfair burdens for particular parties. Because of the public interest at stake ... an injunction that prevents irreparable harm and preserves the status quo while these difficult issues are explored further seems to be the more prudent and equitable course—one that also allows for the possibility that the court's conclusions may not be correct.

In reaching this tentative conclusion, the court is fully mindful of the long-honored principle that parties are free to order their affairs with an eye toward the tax consequences and to minimize the taxes they might legally owe. *See Superior Oil Co. v. Mississippi*, 280 U.S. 390, 395–96, 50 S. Ct. 169, 74 L. Ed. 504 (1930) ... That principle does not apply to the Merom SILO transaction, at least based on the record before this court at this point. For the reasons stated, the transaction appears to have had one motivating force: abusive and fraudulent use of tax deductions by a party who had no significant benefits or burdens of ownership of the property in question. The volume of paper used to dress up this central purpose does not affect its core illegality.

2. Temporary Commercial Impracticability

Even if the court is wrong about the essential illegality of the Merom SILO transaction, Hoosier Energy would also have a reasonable likelihood of succeeding on the merits on its theory of temporary commercial impracticability. Hoosier Energy does not argue that the credit crisis should forever excuse its obligation to replace Ambac as a credit swap partner. Hoosier Energy argues that, given the extraordinary but temporary circumstances presented by the credit crisis, it was entitled to a reasonable period of additional time to replace Ambac under the doctrine of temporary commercial impracticability.

While he still sat on the district court, Judge Smith of the Third Circuit addressed a similar defense and laid out some of the basic principles: "In the overwhelming majority of circumstances, contractual promises are to be performed, not avoided: *pacta sunt servanda*, or, as the Seventh Circuit loosely translated it, 'a deal's a deal.'" *Specialty Tires of America, Inc. v. CIT Group/ Equipment Financing, Inc.*, 82 F. Supp. 2d 434, 437 (W.D. Pa. 2000), quoting *Waukesha Foundry, Inc. v. Industrial Engineering,*

Inc., 91 F.3d 1002, 1010 (7th Cir. 1996), citing JOHN D. CALAMARI & JOSEPH M. PER-
ILLO, THE LAW OF CONTRACTS § 13.1, at 495 (4th ed. 1998). Judge Smith continued:
"Even so, courts have recognized, in an evolving line of cases from the common law
down to the present, that there are limited instances in which unexpectedly and radically changed conditions render the judicial enforcement of certain promises of little
or no utility. This has come to be known, for our purposes, as the doctrines of impossibility and impracticability." *Specialty Tires*, 82 F. Supp. 2d at 437. Given the importance of the principle that courts respect and enforce parties' valid and lawful
contracts, these are doctrines that must be employed with great caution, but they
retain a place in the law under sufficiently extreme circumstances.

To assert the affirmative defense of commercial impracticability, "the party must
show that the unforeseen event upon which excuse is predicated is due to factors beyond the party's control." *Cliffstar Corp. v. Riverbend Prod., Inc.*, 750 F. Supp. 81, 85
(W.D. N.Y. 1990), quoting *Roth Steel Prod. v. Sharon Steel Corp.*, 705 F.2d 134, 149–
50 (6th Cir. 1988). Temporary commercial impracticability excuses performance until
circumstances have changed, plus a reasonable time afterwards:

> Impracticability of performance or frustration of purpose that is only tem-
> porary suspends the obligor's duty to perform for the duration of the im-
> practicability or frustration; it does not discharge the ultimate duty or
> prevent it from arising. Thus, temporary impracticability only relieves the
> promisor of an obligation to perform for as long as the impracticability
> lasts plus a reasonable time afterwards. 30 WILLISTON ON CONTRACTS
> § 77:103 (4th ed. 2008); see also Restatement (Second) of Contracts § 269
> (1981).

… New York law recognizes the doctrine of temporary commercial impracticability.
See Bank of Boston Intl of Miami v. Arguello Tefel, 644 F. Supp. 1423, 1427 (E.D. N.Y.
1986) (recognizing doctrine but holding it did not apply after the obstacle to performance had been removed); *Bush v. Protravel Int'l, Inc.*, 192 Misc. 2d 743, 746
N.Y.S.2d 790, 797–98 (Civ. Ct. 2002) (applying doctrine based on interruptions in
communication following the September 11, 2001 terrorist attacks in New York).

John Hancock counters that an economic crisis cannot support a defense of impracticability, and that if that argument prevailed, "every debtor in a country suffering
economic distress could avoid its debts." … John Hancock … relies heavily on *Kel
Kim Corp. v. Central Markets, Inc.*, 70 N.Y.2d 900, 524 N.Y.S.2d 384, 519 N.E.2d 295
(N.Y. 1987), in which the court refused to excuse a tenant's failure to provide liability
insurance when, due to a liability insurance crisis, the tenant was unable to secure
the level of insurance required by the lease. The court found that the tenant's "inability
to procure and maintain requisite coverage could have been foreseen and guarded
against when it specifically undertook that obligation in the lease." *Id.* at 296. John
Hancock argues that it was not actually impossible for Hoosier Energy to find a replacement for Ambac, and that in any event, Hoosier Energy should have foreseen
and guarded against its inability to find a replacement.

If the nature and scope of the credit crisis were more limited or a mere economic downturn, John Hancock's argument that the crisis was foreseeable or that Hoosier Energy should have protected itself better might be more persuasive. However, the credit crisis facing the world's economies in recent months is unprecedented and was not foretold by the world's preeminent economic experts. The crisis certainly was not anticipated in 2002, when the deal between Hoosier Energy, Ambac, and John Hancock was being finalized. Retrospect will not assist John Hancock here, nor will an assertion that it was Hoosier Energy's responsibility to prepare for and guard against any imaginable commercial calamity. After all, "foreseeable" is different from "conceivable." *Specialty Tires*, 82 F. Supp. 2d at 439, quoting JOHN E. MURRAY, JR., MURRAY ON CONTRACTS § 112 at 641 (3d ed. 1990) ("If 'foreseeable' is equated with 'conceivable,' nothing is unforeseeable."). Hoosier Energy has come forward with evidence indicating that the obstacles it faced were not specific to Ambac but were the product of the credit crisis that effectively but temporarily froze the market for comparable credit products at any price. Those effects were not anticipated and could not have been guarded against.[131]

Unlike the defendants in the *Bank of New York* or *Kel Kim* cases, Hoosier Energy does not ask John Hancock to excuse its performance for an uncertain or unlimited period of time. In the midst of unprecedented economic tumult, Hoosier Energy had made significant headway in securing Ambac's replacement, even at what Hoosier Energy has described as a prohibitive price. But even after credit markets began to thaw, Hoosier Energy needed an additional 90 days to finalize the $120 million deal with Berkshire Hathaway, a deal that was already on the table. John Hancock points out that Hoosier Energy, by contract and with agreed extensions, had already had more than 120 days to replace Ambac. John Hancock contends that it was not obligated to grant Hoosier Energy unlimited extensions. Unlimited extensions, no. But reasonable extensions, in a time of economic crisis and under the doctrine of temporary commercial impracticability, yes. The Berkshire Hathaway deal, before John Hancock turned out the lights, was not theoretical or speculative. The preliminary terms had been executed and Berkshire Hathaway had indicated its intent to proceed. Under any circumstances, 90 days does not seem an unreasonable amount of time to finalize a complicated $120 million deal. Given the state of economic affairs on October 23rd, when John Hancock refused the extension, 90 days appears to have been a reasonable request. Hoosier Energy has shown a reasonable likelihood of success on the merits on its defense of temporary commercial impracticability.

---

131. [5] John Hancock points out that Hoosier Energy had been reluctant to accept terms offered by Berkshire Hathaway because the deal would have been ..."prohibitively expensive." Expensive does not mean impossible or impracticable. But the evidence shows that on October 13th, Hoosier Energy signed the term sheet for those "prohibitively expensive" terms, forwarded that information to John Hancock, and asked for time to close the deal. Thus, Hoosier Energy's temporary commercial impracticability argument seems to depend on the logistics of closing another complex deal, not on the expense of that deal.

C. Balance of Equities

The balance of equities favors Hoosier Energy. In applying this factor, the Seventh Circuit has often instructed district courts to try to minimize the risk of error, whether the error would be in granting or denying injunctive relief. *AM General Corp. v. DaimlerChrysler Com.*, 311 F.3d 796, 831 (7th Cir. 2002) ... If the court erroneously denies injunctive relief, Hoosier Energy will be forced into bankruptcy and into default on a host of other loans and supply contracts. The disruption of its business could not be remedied by a later award of money damages.

If the court erroneously grants injunctive relief, John Hancock will not receive immediately the termination payment to which the contractual documents entitle it. Instead, John Hancock would receive that payment later, presumably with interest. John Hancock argues that it faces serious credit risks, in that Ambac or Hoosier Energy or both could default on their obligations....

The character of the Merom SILO transaction as an abusive tax shelter also factors into the court's weighing of the equities. John Hancock understandably points out that Hoosier Energy happily entered into the transaction and received some $20 million in cash at the front end, and has not complained about the tax aspects of the transaction until now. John Hancock argues that the court should not interfere with Ambac's payment on its credit default swap with John Hancock and should defer consideration of Hoosier Energy's defenses to a later lawsuit between Ambac and Hoosier Energy. That approach would probably result in a great inequity if Hoosier Energy's challenge to the legality of the transaction is sound. John Hancock would walk away with the economic equivalent of the tax windfall it hoped to gain. Ambac would be left unable to collect from Hoosier Energy on the theory that the obligations of this entire transactions are void and that the courts should leave the parties where they find themselves. Yet John Hancock is the party who, in effect, tried to buy tax deductions it was not entitled to and who knowingly accepted the risk that the transaction might be deemed a sham and an abusive tax shelter.

The court has considered whether it should simply deny all relief on a theory of "unclean hands." After all, Hoosier Energy was itself a party to the transaction it claims is a sham. If the court reaches a final decision that the transaction was a sham, the court will face some challenging problems in crafting any appropriate remedies. But the court is satisfied that doing nothing now would almost surely produce an inequitable effect by letting John Hancock walk away with the windfall of fraudulent tax benefits. If the court is wrong about the illegality of the transaction but right about temporary commercial impracticability, a denial of all relief would still risk the irreparable harm described above. The more prudent, risk-minimizing course at this point is to grant injunctive relief to prevent irreparable harm and to sort out later the difficult terms of final equitable relief (such as addressing Hoosier Energy's $20 million in up-front benefits from the transaction).

D. Public Interest

A preliminary injunction to preserve the status quo will serve the public interest. The public interest is served by John Hancock not receiving a windfall in these circumstances. The public interest also is served by Hoosier Energy continuing to deliver power to its member cooperatives, which in turn provide power to Indiana homes, farms, businesses, and industries. If Hoosier Energy's ability to do so is imperiled, so may be its ability to fulfill its mission to the public. When denial of preliminary relief threatens irreparable harm to the plaintiff and to the public, the equities weigh heavily in favor of granting that relief....

John Hancock has argued that a decision calling into question the enforceability of its credit default swap with Ambac would be contrary to the public interest because such transactions have become so common and because so many businesses rely upon their validity. The point is a serious one, and it is certainly true that the public interest generally favors the enforcement of lawful contracts. In the context of this transaction, however, this argument has little force. As explained above, the record now before the court tends to show that the Merom SILO transaction was a blatantly abusive tax shelter from the beginning. The more general points about the sanctity of contracts do not apply to this elaborate effort to defraud other taxpayers....

Conclusion

For the reasons stated above, the court grants plaintiff Hoosier Energy's motion for a preliminary injunction and by separate order will continue in effect the injunctive relief already in place, pending a final judgment in this case or modification by order of this or any other court with jurisdiction.

So ordered.

HOOSIER ENERGY RURAL ELECTRIC CO-OP., INC. v. JOHN HANCOCK LIFE INS. CO.

United States Court of Appeals, Seventh Circuit
582 F.3d 721 (2009)

EASTERBROOK, C.J.

Hoosier Energy, a co-op, had depreciation deductions that it could not use. John Hancock Life Insurance Co. had income exceeding its available deductions. The two engaged in a transaction designed to move Hoosier Energy's deductions to John Hancock. They entered into a leveraged lease: John Hancock paid Hoosier Energy $300 million for a 63-year lease of an undivided two-thirds interest in Hoosier Energy's Merom generation plant. Hoosier Energy agreed to lease the plant back from John Hancock for 30 years, making periodic payments with a present value of $279 million. The $21 million difference, Hoosier Energy's profit, represents some of the value to John Hancock of the deductions that John Hancock could take as the long-term lessee of the power plant.

The transaction exposed John Hancock to several risks. The power station might become uneconomic before the parties' estimate of its remaining useful life (roughly 30 years). Or Hoosier Energy might encounter financial difficulties in its business as a whole. As a debtor in bankruptcy, Hoosier Energy would be entitled to repudiate the lease, leaving John Hancock with a power station that it had no interest in operating. Hoosier Energy's obligation as a repudiating debtor would be considerably less than the present value of the rentals. *See* 11 U.S.C. §502(b)(6). So Hoosier Energy agreed to provide John Hancock with additional security, in the form of both a credit-default swap and a surety bond. Ambac Assurance Corporation and three affiliates agreed to pay John Hancock approximately $120 million if certain events occurred. (For its part, Hoosier Energy posted substantial liquid assets to Ambac's credit, in order to protect Ambac should it be required to pay John Hancock; this was part of the transaction's swap feature.) A credit-default swap, like a letter of credit, is a means to assure payment when contingencies come to pass, without proof of loss (as a surety bond would require). One of the contingencies in this transaction is a reduction in Ambac's own credit rating. If that rating falls below a prescribed threshold, Hoosier Energy has 60 days to find a replacement that satisfies the contractual standards.

During 2008 Ambac's credit rating slipped below the threshold. John Hancock then demanded that Hoosier Energy find a replacement, and it extended the deadline from 60 days to more than 120 days when Hoosier Energy reported trouble. Whether replacing Ambac was "impossible" at the time, as Hoosier Energy maintains, or just would have cost Hoosier Energy more than it was willing to pay, as John Hancock believes, is a subject that remains in dispute. When the extended deadline arrived, Hoosier Energy told John Hancock that it was in negotiations with Berkshire Hathaway to replace Ambac. John Hancock concluded that "in negotiations" was not good enough (perhaps it suspected Hoosier Energy of stalling) and called on Ambac to perform. Ambac is ready, willing, and able to meet its obligations. But before Ambac could pay, Hoosier Energy filed this suit under the diversity jurisdiction, and the district court issued a temporary restraining order. The justification for that order, since replaced by a preliminary injunction, is that if Ambac pays, it will demand that Hoosier Energy cover the outlay, and that this will drive Hoosier Energy into bankruptcy—a step that the district court called an irreparable injury.

Irreparable injury is not enough to support equitable relief. There also must be a plausible claim on the merits, and the injunction must do more good than harm (which is to say that the "balance of equities" favors the plaintiff). *See Winter v. Natural Resources Defense Council, Inc.*, 129 S. Ct. 365, 172 L. Ed. 2d 249 (2008); *Illinois Bell Telephone Co. v. WorldCom Technologies, Inc.*, 157 F.3d 500 (7th Cir. 1998). How strong a claim on the merits is enough depends on the balance of harms: the more net harm an injunction can prevent, the weaker the plaintiff's claim on the merits can be while still supporting some preliminary relief. *See Cavel International, Inc. v. Madigan*, 500 F.3d 544 (7th Cir. 2007); *Girl Scouts of Manitou Council, Inc. v. Girl Scouts of the United States of America, Inc.*, 549 F.3d 1079 (7th Cir. 2008). The district court concluded that an injunction would have net benefits, because John Hancock would remain well secured in its absence (it remains the lessee of a power station that is essential to Hoosier Energy's business, so Hoosier Energy will not abandon the lease), and that Hoosier Energy's position on the merits is strong enough to support relief while litigation continues. 588 F. Supp. 2d 919 (S.D. Ind. 2008). The district court also directed Hoosier Energy to post $2 million in cash, a $20 million injunction bond with sureties, and an unsecured bond of $130 million, to ensure that John Hancock would be made whole should it prevail in the litigation.

As for the merits: The district court thought that Hoosier Energy has two arguments with enough punch to justify interlocutory relief. The first is that the transaction is an abusive tax shelter. The district court observed that the Internal Revenue Service has declined to allow similar transactions to transfer deductions from one corporation to another and concluded that this transaction probably should be unwound. The second is that, under New York law (which the parties agree supplies the rule of decision), "temporary commercial impracticability" permits Hoosier Energy to defer coming up with another swap partner until the economy has improved....

On the subject of irreparable injury, appellate review is deferential at the preliminary injunction stage, and we lack an adequate basis on which to disagree with the district court's assessment. That leaves the question whether Hoosier Energy has a plausible theory on the merits—not necessarily a winning one, but a claim strong enough to justify exposing John Hancock to financial risks until the district court can decide the merits. We do not agree with all of the district judge's reasoning, but we do not think that the court erred in thinking Hoosier Energy's claim sufficient for this limited purpose, given Ambac's continuing ability to perform and the injunction bonds posted under Fed. R. Civ. P. 65(c).

Let us start with the question whether the transaction is an illegal tax shelter that must be unwound rather than enforced. The district court's approach has two steps: First, the court concluded that the transaction lacks economic substance and therefore cannot be employed to transfer tax benefits from Hoosier Energy to John Hancock. Second, the court believed that a tax shelter that the Internal Revenue Code does not allow is "illegal" as a matter of contract law. The first of these steps may or may not be right; the tax treatment of leveraged leases, and related transactions such as the sale and leaseback, can be difficult. *See, e.g., Frank Lyon Co. v. United States*, 435 U.S. 561, 98 S. Ct. 1291, 55 L. Ed. 2d 550 (1978). The second is wrong. A leveraged lease is a perfectly enforceable contract. Whether or not the contract lawfully transfers tax benefits, there is nothing wrong with, or illegal about, the contract itself; only the claim of tax benefits from the contract would be problematic.

All questions about tax benefits to one side, a leveraged lease is simply a loan secured by a lease rather than a mortgage. John Hancock needs to make investments in order to have money available to pay the death benefits on its life insurance policies. Often it invests in real estate. The transaction with Hoosier Energy is one in which John Hancock invested $300 million in exchange for a promised stream of repayments that would last 30 years; it also obtained a security interest in the assets that Hoosier Energy would use to produce the funds for repayment. Neither New York nor Indiana would call such a transaction illegal, and the fact that a credit-default swap improved the lender's security does not create any additional problem.

Hoosier Energy has not cited, and we have not found, any decision holding a leveraged lease or sale-and-leaseback unenforceable as a matter of contract law, just because the main (or even the sole) reason for structuring the transaction that way, rather than as a loan, was tax benefits. "Economic purpose" is not a requirement for the enforceability of contracts. If the Green Bay Packers cut a player one day and then re-sign him the next, a court would not dream of canceling the new contract on the ground that a release and re-sign sequence lacks economic purpose. The Commissioner of Internal Revenue will address the question whether the leveraged-lease transaction provides John Hancock with the tax benefits it seeks. If the answer turns out to be no, Hoosier Energy still owes John Hancock the promised rental payments (and is entitled to keep the $21 million premium), while Ambac still provides security for those payments.

New York law is skeptical of contentions that irregular dealings between one contracting party and the government excuse the other contracting party's performance. For example, *John E. Rosasco Creameries, Inc. v. Cohen*, 276 N.Y. 274, 11 N.E.2d 908, 909 (N.Y. 1937), held that the dairy's customer must pay for goods received, even though the dairy lacked a license and thus should not have been in business.... John Hancock's taxes are a matter for it to resolve with the IRS; that John Hancock may have set out to take larger deductions than the law allows does not affect Hoosier Energy's contractual duties.

This leaves the doctrine of "temporary commercial impracticability." John Hancock's principal argument on this front is that New York law does not recognize any such doctrine. Like other states, New York recognizes the doctrine of impossibility—but even then only the kind of impossibility that the parties could not have anticipated. As John Hancock describes things, the parties anticipated the possibility that Hoosier Energy, Ambac, or both might get into financial distress and provided what was to happen: if Hoosier Energy did not come up with better security in 60 days, John Hancock could draw on the credit default swap to protect itself. When the economy turned sour, and the risk materialized, John Hancock tried to take advantage of this extra security. Yet the district court deemed the risk's coming to pass as a reason why John Hancock could not draw on the security. John Hancock sees this as perverse, an order that defeats the parties' bargained-for allocation of risks. The district court may have thought that economy-wide conditions justified this reallocation, but it is hard to see how an economic downturn can be alleviated by making contracts less reliable. Enforceable contracts are vital to economic productivity. *See* Simeon Djankov, et al., *Debt Enforcement around the World*, 116 J. POL. ECON. 1105 (2008); Thomas Cooley, Ramon Marimon & Vincenzo Quadrini, *Aggregate Consequences of Limited Contract Enforceability*, 112 J. POL. ECON. 817 (2004).

Whether Hoosier Energy's performance was "impossible" in the strong sense that contract law requires depends on what its obligations were. John Hancock urges on us the perspective that, when Ambac's credit rating slipped, Hoosier Energy had an option: find a new surety in 60 days, or pay Ambac the sums to which Ambac would become entitled once it paid John Hancock. The holder of an option may not be able to take advantage, but that differs from impossibility. Suppose that Hoosier Energy had an in-the-money option to purchase the Indianapolis Colts by the end of December 2008, and that as a result of the reduced availability of credit it was unable to find a lender to finance the transaction. That would not make performance "impossible" and extend the option's expiration, effectively giving Hoosier Energy a new option (for 2009) for free. Likewise if Hoosier Energy had borrowed $100 million and was obliged to pay the money back on October 1, 2008. That Hoosier Energy found itself unable to borrow money to roll over the loan would not excuse repayment; the "impossibility" doctrine never justifies failure to make a payment, because financial distress differs from impossibility. *See* Restatement (Second) of Contracts § 261 & cmt. d.

The uranium case illustrates these propositions. Westinghouse sold uranium on long-term requirements contracts at fixed prices, thus assuming the risk that market prices would rise (and it would lose money). Westinghouse anticipated that market prices would fall; its customers thought they would rise, or at least wanted protection against higher prices. And rise they did, partly as a result of a cartel. Westinghouse had neglected to protect its position in futures markets or through long-term forward contracts. Faced with large losses if it had to buy uranium on the spot market and resell to customers at lower prices, Westinghouse contended that the unanticipated spike in uranium prices made its performance impossible. The argument failed; the court observed that Westinghouse and its customers had negotiated over the risk of higher prices for uranium, and that the occurrence of the risk did not excuse one side's performance. Even if the losses drove Westinghouse into bankruptcy, that would not make performance "impossible"; it would just assure that all of Westinghouse's creditors received equal treatment. See *In re Westinghouse Electric Corp. Uranium Contracts Litigation*, 563 F.2d 992 (10th Cir. 1977); Richard A. Posner and Andrew M. Rosenfield, *Impossibility and Related Doctrines of Contract Law: An Economic Analysis*, 6 J. LEGAL STUD. 83 (1977).

Much the same can be said about Hoosier Energy. If keeping its promise to Ambac drives it into bankruptcy, this ensures equal treatment of its creditors. It is hard to see why Hoosier Energy should be able to stiff John Hancock or Ambac, while paying 100 cents on the dollar to all of its other trading partners, just because the very risk specified in the contracts between Hoosier Energy and John Hancock has occurred. Hoosier Energy did not expect an economic downturn, but Westinghouse did not expect an international uranium cartel. Downturns and cartels are types of things that happen, and against which contracts can be designed. When they do happen, the contractual risk allocation must be enforced rather than set aside. The district court called the credit crunch of 2008 a "once-in-a-century" event. That's an overstatement (the Great Depression occurred within the last 100 years, and the 20th century also saw financial crunches in 1973 and 1987), and also irrelevant. An insurer that sells hurricane or flood insurance against a "once in a century" catastrophe, or earthquake insurance in a city that rarely experiences tremblors, can't refuse to pay on the ground that, when a natural event devastates a city, its very improbability makes the contract unenforceable.

We postponed discussing New York law until the general points of contract doctrine had been set out. New York law is consistent with what we have said; indeed, New York takes a very dim view of "impossibility" defenses and has never suggested that, when an impossibility defense is unavailable, a "temporary commercial impracticability" defense might serve instead. New York courts refuse to excuse performance where difficulty "is occasioned only by financial difficulty or economic hardship, even to the extent of insolvency or bankruptcy." *407 East 61st Garage, Inc. v. Savoy Fifth Avenue Corp.*, 23 N.Y.2d 275, 296 N.Y.S.2d 338, 244 N.E.2d 37, 41 (N.Y. 1968). This applies to financial instruments—and, although impossibility might allow a party to suspend its obligations under a financial swap contract, this means more than a short-term inability to pay money. *General Electric Co. v. Metals Resources Group Ltd.*, 293 A.D.2d 417, 741 N.Y.S.2d 218 (App. Div. 2002). For its part, Hoosier Energy all but ignores New York law; its brief cites only a single decision, by a trial court; appellate decisions go unmentioned. And the trial-court decision that Hoosier Energy cites speaks of temporary impossibility, not "temporary commercial impracticability."

All of this assumes, however, that John Hancock is right to characterize Hoosier Energy as having an option to find a better surety. As Hoosier Energy understands the contract, however, it had a duty to find a better surety, and failure to perform this duty was the default allowing John Hancock to draw on the swap. Then it might be possible to make out a real impossibility defense, meaning that (a) all parties to the transaction assumed, when they negotiated the terms, that it would be possible to find some other intermediary with adequate credit standing, and (b) as a result of a financial crisis, no such intermediary existed in late 2008, no matter how much Hoosier Energy offered to post in liquid assets to secure its obligations.

Even this would be a difficult defense to make out under New York law. The leading New York case on impossibility, *Kel Kim Corp. v. Central Markets, Inc.*, 70 N.Y.2d 900, 524 N.Y.S.2d 384, 519 N.E.2d 295 (N.Y. 1987), says that the defense works only if some unexpected event upsets all parties' expectations; it is not enough that the unexpected event puts one side in a bind. The lessee of a roller-skating rink was required by contract to obtain liability insurance, which it got and maintained six years before the insurer declined to renew. When the policy expired, the lessor asserted default, and the lessee sought a declaration that performance was excused by impossibility, because no insurer would underwrite a liability policy for a roller rink at any price. Rejecting the lessee's argument, the Court of Appeals stated that impossibility can excuse performance only if the new event "could not have been foreseen or guarded against" in the contract. Financial distress could be and was foreseen; that's what the credit-default swap is all about. But if no one could have foreseen the extent of the credit crunch in 2008—and if it really made performance impossible, a subject on which the parties profoundly disagree—then the sort of argument that Hoosier Energy makes could satisfy the requirements of *Kel Kim*.

We have said enough to show that there is uncertainty about how this suit comes out under New York law. It is uncertain whether Hoosier Energy had a duty to replace Ambac, or just an option; the impossibility defense is unavailable if the option characterization is correct. (We have avoided quoting the documents; some portions of these lengthy contracts support each side's characterization of them.) It is uncertain whether the extent of the 2008 credit crunch, which extended into 2009, was foreseeable. It is uncertain whether Hoosier Energy could have replaced Ambac by offering more, or better, security to another intermediary. Hoosier Energy undermined its own position in the litigation by telling John Hancock that it was negotiating with Berkshire Hathaway and could strike a deal with just a little more time, which implies that replacing Ambac was not impossible, but John Hancock returned the favor by suggesting that this deal was just pie in the sky and that Hoosier Energy would not or could not ever replace Ambac—and, if "could not" is the right understanding, perhaps performance was impossible after all.

All of these uncertainties collectively support the district court's conclusion that Hoosier Energy has some prospect of prevailing on the merits. Because appellate review is deferential, the district court's understanding must prevail at the interlocutory stage.

But what was impossible in fall 2008 may well be possible in fall 2009. What is more, the longer this impasse continues, the more the balance of equities tilts in favor of John Hancock. Recall that the reason for the credit-default swap was concern that the Merom station would eventually become non-economic because of changes in the market for electricity, the regulation of emissions from coal-fired stations, or the advancing age of the plant. The more time passes, the more serious this risk—and the greater the risk that one or another problem may afflict Hoosier Energy as a firm. If, as Hoosier Energy asserts, meeting Ambac's demands under the swap contract will drive it into bankruptcy, then Hoosier Energy must be skating close to the edge, and the longer it skates there the greater the cumulative risk that it will fall over. Similarly, Ambac may become less desirable as a swap partner; while this appeal has been under advisement, Ambac's credit rating has been reduced twice.

John Hancock is entitled to the security it negotiated against these possible outcomes. The injunction bonds, at only $22 million in liquid security, do not cover John Hancock's exposure. The change in Ambac's credit rating, in particular, requires the district court to take a new look at the adequacy of the Rule 65(c) security promptly after receiving this court's mandate (which will be issued together with this opinion). So although we affirm the district court's preliminary injunction, we conclude that, if Hoosier Energy has not produced a replacement for Ambac by the end of 2009, the time will have arrived when the court must let John Hancock realize on its security. The district court itself stressed the word "temporary" in "temporary commercial impracticability"; we are confident that the court will not allow "temporary" to drag out in the direction of permanence.

AFFIRMED.

NOTES AND QUESTIONS

1. *What is each party getting out of the deal?* As explained in the opinions, Hoosier Energy was a tax-indifferent entity, which was unable to use the valuable tax benefits that the Merom plant could potentially provide. Babcock & Brown, a global investment

firm, approached Hoosier Energy about the deal and brought in Hancock as the equity investor. Hancock, in essence, would be purchasing the tax benefits of the Merom plant by putting the plant on its books and deducting the amount by which it depreciated in value each year. The two parties entered into a series of contracts that included, among others, a Head Lease, a Facility Lease, a Participation Agreement, and a Tax Indemnity Agreement.

Hancock was concerned that any one of a number of actions by Hoosier Energy, as well as exogenous market conditions, might destroy the value of the deal to Hancock. One of the measures it took to protect itself was to enter into several security agreements with Hoosier, which granted Hancock a mortgage and security interest in the Merom plant. In addition, Hancock included certain provisions in the contracts, any one of which would trigger an "Event of Default." Judge Easterbrook mentions one such possibility, namely Hoosier Energy's bankruptcy and subsequent rejection of the lease. Another trigger would be Ambac's credit rating falling below Aa2. If an Event of Default occurred, then Hancock and Hoosier had agreed that Hancock could terminate the agreement and receive a Termination Payment from Ambac (the mechanism for which was a credit default swap agreement between Hancock and Ambac). This Termination Payment would equal the balance Hoosier owed on its 30-year lease, as well as an "Equity Portion" equal to the present value of the Merom plant's tax benefits to Hancock. The amount of this Equity Portion would depend on the date of Hoosier's default. The parties had agreed to a payment schedule that listed the Equity Portion's value for each month of the 30-year lease. Since the amount of the Equity Portion varied according to the date of default, Hancock argued it was an enforceable liquidated damages clause.

While Hancock drafted the deal to protect its investment, Hoosier had bargained for an important protection for itself. This term in the agreement stipulated that Hoosier would not be liable to Hancock for the Equity Portion if the deal "[were] a sham, lacked a valid business purpose, or had a substance different from its form." The IRS had indeed labeled the deal an abusive tax shelter. Thus Hoosier argued that since the Equity Portion was only designed to compensate Hancock for the deal's *legal* tax benefits, which equaled $0 after the IRS finding, the Equity Portion was now an unenforceable liquidated damages clause.[132]

For this plan to be of benefit to Hancock, Hancock had to ensure that Hoosier's lease payments would be made timely and in full. Otherwise, the value of the Merom plant's tax benefits might be offset or canceled out by Hoosier's failure to make its lease payments. In addition to its mortgage and security interest in the Merom plant, Hancock further protected its equity investment by requiring insurance for Hoosier's ability to make its lease payments. As part of the agreements, Ambac entered into a credit default swap with Hancock and provided a surety bond relating to this swap agreement, which guaranteed payment by Ambac. Ambac entered into a separate

---

132. To read Hoosier Energy's more fully developed argument, see its Memorandum in Support of Its Motion for a Preliminary Injunction, 2008 U.S. Dist. Ct. Motions 1560.

credit default swap agreement with Hoosier in order to protect itself, which stated that in the event Ambac was required to make the Termination Payment, Hoosier Energy would owe Ambac the payment's Equity Portion. The Termination Payment that Hancock demanded from Ambac after it declared Hoosier in default was $413,129,634.43, the Equity Portion of which was $120,502,963.53.

For Ambac, the SILO agreement was a virtually risk-free infusion of capital. In exchange for making Hoosier's lease payments and guaranteeing a Termination Payment upon occurrence of an Event of Default (with a credit default swap and surety bond), Ambac received a $278 million deposit that it could use or invest at its discretion. In addition, as mentioned in the opinions, over $12 million in fees were generated during the course of structuring this transaction. Some of that $12 million presumably went to Ambac as origination and other service fees related to the credit default swap agreements, although the parties' motions do not confirm the details of these charges. The deal was relatively low-risk to Ambac, because if an Event of Default occurred, it had entered a separate swap agreement with Hoosier that ensured it would not be out-of-pocket for the Termination Payment demanded by Hancock.

This litigation arose from the fact that Hancock was attempting to realize gains from tax benefits that the IRS had labeled abusive. Hancock, its opponents argued, was simply using the drop in Ambac's credit rating as an excuse to make Hoosier foot the bill for abusive tax benefits. The drop in Ambac's credit rating was the result of what Alan Greenspan called a "credit tsunami," a contraction in the credit markets that few had anticipated. Ambac and Hoosier maintained that the drop in Ambac's rating did not affect its ability to abide by the terms of its credit default swap agreement with Hancock. In addition, Hoosier argued in its motions that the black letter law required Hancock to give Hoosier a "commercially reasonable" amount of time to find a new swap provider with a suitable credit rating. Hoosier argued that, in light of the "tsunami," the 60-day period in the original agreement was no longer commercially reasonable, and Hancock was using the mortgage crisis as an excuse to achieve a windfall (*i.e.*, the anticipated tax benefits that the IRS was disallowing). This windfall would be subsidized by the members of the Hoosier Energy cooperative and, ultimately, Midwestern electricity customers.

This transaction demonstrates both the potential advantages and the pitfalls of an increasingly complex and sophisticated financial system. On the one hand, companies like Hoosier Energy had the opportunity to turn "products" like tax deductions into cash (assuming such transactions pass muster with the IRS). However, in the event that such agreements go awry, the existence of complex financial instruments like credit default swaps place the burden of covering these transactions on parties without the resources to do so.

2. *Does the contrasting rhetoric affect judgments about impracticability?* Notice the contrasting rhetoric used by the trial and the appellate judges in their opinions. Judge Hamilton tells us: "This case provides a case study of some of the worst aspects of modern finance. The case arises from an elaborate transaction that combines the sometimes toxic intricacies of credit default swaps and investment derivatives with

a blatantly abusive tax shelter. Investment bankers and lawyers made more than $12 million in fees for putting together the paper transaction ...".[133] Judge Easterbrook differs: "[A] leveraged lease is simply a loan secured by a lease rather than a mortgage. John Hancock needs to make investments in order to have money available to pay the death benefits on its life insurance policies. Often it invests in real estate. The transaction with Hoosier Energy is one in which John Hancock invested $300 million in exchange for a promised stream of repayments that would last 30 years; it also obtained a security interest in the assets that Hoosier Energy would use to produce the funds for repayment."

3. *Rules of law or the outlook of the judges?* Who are the authors of these two opinions? Do their backgrounds suggest why they see the transaction so differently? At the time of the transaction involved in the case, David F. Hamilton was the Chief Judge of the Southern District of Indiana. He was born in Bloomington, Indiana in 1957, graduated from Yale Law School, practiced with a large law firm in Indianapolis, and served as legal counsel to Indiana Governor Evan Bayh. President Clinton appointed him as a judge on the United States District Court for the Southern District of Indiana. President Obama nominated Hamilton to be a judge of the United States Court of Appeals for the Seventh Circuit. Republican members of the United States Senate staged a filibuster to prevent a vote on the nomination. The Senate voted 70-29 to end the filibuster, and the Senate approved the nomination by a 59–39 vote on November 19, 2009. The *New York Times* called Judge Hamilton a "moderate."[134] The National Scene (thenationalscene.com), a conservative blog, objected to President Obama's appointment and called Hamilton "a radical judge." Among its many objections to the judge, the blog noted that he had served as a board member of the American Civil Liberties Union, a "far-left special interest group."

Frank Easterbrook sits on the United States Court of Appeals for the Seventh Circuit. He was born in Buffalo, New York in 1948, graduated from the University of Chicago Law School, and served as a Deputy Solicitor General in the 1970s during the Nixon Administration, arguing 20 cases before the Supreme Court of the United States. He became a faculty member at the University of Chicago Law School in 1978. In 1991, he published (with Daniel Fischel) *The Economic Structure of Corporate Law*. He was nominated to the Seventh Circuit by President Reagan in 1985. In 1981, Professors Easterbrook and Fischel wrote:

> [M]anagers do not have an ethical duty to obey economic regulatory laws just because the laws exist. They must determine the importance of these laws. The penalties Congress names for disobedience are a measure of how much it wants firms to sacrifice in order to adhere to the rules; the idea of

---

133. The *New York Times* agreed with Judge Hamilton: "Detailed in 4,000 pages of fine print, the SILO was a deal that only a Wall Street contortionist could love. Its components included a sale and leaseback, two credit-default swaps and a tax shelter similar to those that the Internal Revenue Service has since deemed abusive. In other words, a veritable trifecta of tortured finance." Gretchen Morgenson, *Just Call It Hoosier Baroque*, N.Y. Times, Dec. 21, 2008, at 1.

134. Neil A. Lewis, *Moderate is Reported to Be Pick for Court*, N.Y. Times, Mar. 17, 2009, at 14.

optimal sanctions is based on the supposition that managers not only may but also should violate the rules when it is profitable to do so.[135]

Do you think it likely that Judge Hamilton would agree with this passage? If the transaction collapsed, this was likely to drive Hoosier Energy into bankruptcy. It could have caused Hoosier Energy to default on millions of dollars of other loans, lines of credit, and long-term supply contracts. The company provides wholesale electric services to its member distribution cooperatives, who supply power to approximately 800,000 residents, businesses, industries, and farms. The costs of default were likely to be passed along to these people and businesses. From their opinions, would this potential increased cost trouble one of the judges more than the other?

4. *What happens in bankruptcy?* Both opinions refer to the possibility of corporate bankruptcy by Hoosier Energy, though in different contexts. Judge Hamilton bases his finding of irreparable injury (in the absence of a temporary injunction) on the risk of bankruptcy if Hoosier Energy is unable to meet its obligations to reimburse Ambac if it makes a termination payment, as demanded by John Hancock. Judge Easterbrook, on the other hand, seems to regard bankruptcy as just another way of continuing business. He says that "bankruptcy … ensures equal treatment of [Hoosier Energy's] creditors. It is hard to see why Hoosier Energy should be able to stiff John Hancock or Ambac, while paying 10 cents on the dollar to all of its other trading partners."[136]

What happens in bankruptcy? Both judges make a valid point, but neither provides a complete picture of the corporate bankruptcy process. Hoosier Energy is a rural electric cooperative, owned by 17 electric distribution cooperatives. Hoosier Energy produces electricity, which it then sells to its member/owners.[137] Cooperatives are treated as corporations in bankruptcy, and as a large corporation, Hoosier Energy would file bankruptcy under Chapter 11 of the Bankruptcy Code, a federal statute. If Hoosier Energy filed bankruptcy under this chapter, its obligation to reimburse Ambac (for the termination fee paid John Hancock) would be temporarily suspended, as would its obligations to other unsecured creditors for goods, services, or credit previously provided. The largest of these other creditors would likely be bondholders, if unsecured for loans previously provided to Hoosier Energy, and the sellers of coal

---

135. Frank H. Easterbrook & Daniel R. Fischel, *Antitrust Suits by Targets of Tender Offers*, 80 MICH. L. REV. 1155, 1177 n.57 (1982).

136. Martin J. McMahon, Jr., Ira B. Shepard & Daniel L. Simmons, *Recent Developments in Federal Income Taxation: The Year 2009*, 10 FLA. TAX REV. 79 (2010), charge: "Transactions underlying a tax shelter are just done for grins in the real world; you can take that to the bank, man! Hoosier homer judge grants injunctive relief to tax-indifferent party to a tax shelter contract without requiring the plaintiff to disgorge the $20 million it pocketed for entering into the tax shelter in the first place." Judge Hamilton was prominent in the Indiana Democratic Party before being appointed to the bench. The three tax professors note that in later proceedings Judge Hamilton did increase the bond required from Hoosier Energy and said that it might at some time in the future be required to give back the $20 million if the SILO arrangement was found to be an abusive tax shelter, but that there was no hurry about that.

137. For more detail on Hoosier Energy, see http://www.hepn.com.

to the Merom plant, which was the largest of Hoosier Energy's production facilities.[138] These creditors would not get paid until a "plan" was approved, and that plan would probably treat all unsecured creditors of Hoosier Energy "similarly," meaning that each would receive the same percentage of what they are owed. In corporate bankruptcies, it is commonly the case that this percentage is less than 100 percent. But when that is the case, then corporate bankruptcy normally alters the ownership structure of the corporate debtor. The underpaid creditors are given the ownership interest (or shares) in the post-bankruptcy entity, as a way of compensating them for the shortfall they received on the amounts they were owed by giving them a stake in any future profits of the corporation.

In Hoosier Energy's case, corporate bankruptcy would likely mean the electric distribution cooperatives would no longer be the owners of Hoosier Energy, though presumably they would remain its principal customers. The cooperatives might have to pay more in the future for their electricity, as the new owners (*i.e.*, former creditors) sought to make profits. Ambac would be treated similarly to other creditors, like coal suppliers, but the latter will receive less than they otherwise would. And since important suppliers are important to Hoosier Energy's future production, they might have to pay more for coal in the future just to maintain a regular supply of coal. This could be another reason that Hoosier Energy would charge more to its customers, the electric distribution companies, who could be expected in turn to pass on their extra costs to their customers, who include residential consumers.

In sum, corporate bankruptcy would mean that there are financial winners and losers. It would not mean, however, that Hoosier Energy would stop manufacturing electricity at its facility.[139] It is an important purpose of bankruptcy reorganization to allow the productive entities of an over-indebted corporation to remain in operation, providing they remain profitable.

In view of all this, do you think that the risk of bankruptcy presented by John Hancock's demand (of Ambac) for termination payments meant that there was a risk of "irreparable harm" to Hoosier Energy?

5. *What came next?* After Chief Judge Easterbrook's opinion, Judge Hamilton held a hearing and ordered Hoosier Energy to post a bond. On December 23, 2009, Hoosier Energy and John Hancock announced that the court had approved a settlement of the litigation. The terms were confidential. "'We are pleased to reach this agreement that meets the needs of both parties and appreciate the court's support in the mediation

---

138. If Hoosier Energy was not current on payments to a pension plan for its employees (we don't know if that is the case), they could be another important unsecured creditor in a bankruptcy proceeding.

139. Early in his opinion, Judge Easterbrook raises the possibility that in negotiating the original contract John Hancock was concerned that Hoosier Energy would file bankruptcy and reject its 30-year lease, which is something a corporate debtor can do in bankruptcy. But in rejecting that lease, Hoosier Energy would be giving up the Merom plant as a place it manufactured electricity. Since the Merom plant was by far Hoosier Energy's largest production facility, rejection of the lease was not a likely event.

efforts,' said Chris Tryba, Hoosier Energy's Communications Manager."[140] Notice the role taken by the trial judge after all of the formal legal proceedings.

6. *Article 2 of the UCC and temporary impossibility: See* § 2-616. Judge Hamilton seems very concerned about the balance between the burden on Hoosier Energy and the risks that John Hancock might face as a result of the delay. Of course, he is considering a request for an injunction. However, apart from the requirements of injunctive relief, to what extent, if at all, does § 2-616 direct a court to consider the burden on the one whose performance is subject to delay? Do not overlook the requirements of notice facing a seller who wants to claim an excuse because of a delay. *See* § 2-615(c).

7. *The post-2007 housing crisis plays its way into impracticability — do people assume the risk of the foreseeable but what they see as improbable?* In *Ner Tamid Congregation of North Town v. Krivoruchko*,[141] a real estate developer entered a contract on May 3, 2007, to purchase property that the seller owned on Rosemont Avenue in Chicago for about $3,500,000. There was no clause making the contract conditional on the developer's ability to obtain a mortgage on particular terms. Moreover, there was no *force majeure* clause in the document. The developer believed that he was credit-worthy, and he had not had problems in the past gaining financing from the lender with which he was dealing. He had closed over 250 units during the year before the contract was made, and many of these transactions were with the same lender. The closing of the transaction was set for October 31, 2007. However, the developer was unable to obtain the needed financing, and he was unable to close. Banks were increasingly rejecting loans from the late summer of 2007 to the end of the year that they would have accepted only a few months before. When the developer was unable to close on the property, the seller put the property back on the market but was unable to sell it at an acceptable price. The seller sued for breach of contract.

The developer asserted that he was excused because of impracticability. This was based on what the buyer said was the unforeseen downturn in the economy, which precluded him from obtaining the precise financing that he wanted. The court granted summary judgment in favor of the seller and against the buyer on the impracticability issue. The court found that the downturn in the American housing market had been the subject of public debate at least since 2005. It said that "if the event at issue might have been anticipated or guarded against in the contract, the parties shall be held to any unqualified undertaking in the contract." It concluded: "In short, the record shows conclusively that … [the developer] simply guessed wrong in assuming that financing would not be a problem." One who contracts to render a performance or to produce a result for which it is necessary to obtain the cooperation of third persons is not excused by the fact that they will not cooperate.

The court set out about two pages of citations and quotations showing that the risk of a collapse of the housing market was being discussed from 2005 onward. The

---

140. http://www.prnewswire.com/news-releases/john-hancock-and-hoosier-energy-settle-litigation-80007047.html (last visited June 24, 2010).

141. 2009 U.S. Dist. LEXIS 58318 (N.D. Ill., July 9, 2009).

court said: "Newspaper articles featured such headlines as 'Housing Bubble is Real, So Don't Get Hurt When It Finally Pops,' 'If Housing Bubble Pops, Look Out!' 'Hear a Pop? Watch Out,' 'Economists: Housing Boom Could Lead to Busts,' 'Four Out of 10 Americans Feel Real-Estate Bubble,' 'Efforts to Regulate Risky Mortgage Innovations Are So Far Ignored,' and 'Risky Lending Spurs Bubble.'" The court also devoted more than a paragraph to discussing the August 25, 2006, article in the *New York Times* by Paul Krugman. He said: "[W]hile the majority of business economists were predicting a soft landing for housing, this complacency looks increasingly like denial, as hard data … start to confirm anecdotal evidence that it is, indeed, a bust." The situation was not "unforeseeable," and the developer could have dealt with it by seeking a clause in the contract.

If Paul Krugman was right that the majority of business economists were predicting a soft landing for housing, was the developer so unreasonable when it continued to use a simple contract that made no attempt to deal with a housing crisis? Can we say that the court is engaging in 20-20 hindsight rather than looking at the risks as they would have been perceived by ordinary businesspeople in light of their experience?

Compare the experience of a famous real estate developer, Donald Trump. In 2001, Trump and the parent company of the *Chicago Sun-Times* formed a joint venture to build the Trump International Hotel & Tower Chicago. The Chicago Plan Commission approved plans for a 92-story skyscraper on the site of the existing seven-story Sun-Times building. The tower was substantially erected, but Trump failed to pay a $40 million guarantee that he made for the project. This guarantee was related to a $640 million construction loan taken out by Trump for the hotel and tower. Trump sued Deutsche Bank Trust Co. Americas and other lenders in November of 2006. He sought to extend the term of the construction loan for the tower. He said that the "unprecedented financial crisis in the credit markets" was a major event that should have prompted the lenders to ease their requirements. Deutsche Bank then sued Trump, and Trump countered by suing his lenders, claiming that they had injured his reputation.

Trump asserted that the *force majeure* clause in the lending agreement controlled. It allowed the borrower to delay finishing the tower if the delay were to be caused by riots, floods, or strikes. The clause also had a section covering "any other event or circumstance not within the reasonable control of the borrower." Trump argued that this provision gave him a defense. The *New York Times*[142] quoted Trump as saying: "Would you consider the biggest depression we have had in this country since 1929 to be such an event? I would … A depression is not within the control of the borrower." The reporter asked Trump if he would let remorseful condominium buyers in the Tower "walk away from contracts to buy apartments at predepression prices." He said that he would not: "They don't have a *force majeure* clause." Another reporter quoted Trump as saying in his lawsuit that "the global economic crisis was a 'once-in-a-

142. Floyd Norris, *Trump Sees Act of God in Recession*, N.Y. Times, Dec. 5, 2008, at 1.

lifetime credit tsunami' affecting his ability to sell units at the Tower and repay the loan."[143]

In early 2009, Trump and the group led by Deutsche Bank announced that they had suspended their lawsuits and would try to settle their differences and complete the Tower. Part of the reason was that they thought the dispute made it harder to sell condominium units in the Tower. At this point, about 75 percent of Trump's residential condos and 67 percent of its hotel condo units had been sold. Contracts had been signed on three units recently for prices ranging from $2.4 million to $3 million. A *New York Times* blog commented that Trump's claim that the global financial crisis came within the *force majeure* clause "was poppycock, but a private truce was apparently reached."[144]

In substance, how does Trump's situation differ from that of the real estate developer in the *Ner Tamid* case that we described at the beginning of this note? The developer there used a contract without a *force majeure* clause. Nonetheless, why should this difference make a difference in the legal result? Did Trump clearly place the risk of a global financial crisis on his lenders? Do you suppose that Trump and the group headed by Deutsche Bank negotiated about the provision on which Trump relies? Do you think that Deutsche Bank's lawyers ever read the clause and considered how it would apply to a "once-in-a-lifetime credit tsunami?" Is it enough that Trump had a plausible legal reading of the clause, the lenders had their own interest in having rich buyers purchase condominiums in the Tower, sales were relatively slow, and someone on one side or the other could fashion a deal that seemed better than continuing through the legal process? Whatever the merits of the settlement as viewed by each party, was the process more than an empty magic ritual? Don't the realities of legal procedure, trials, and appeals deter people from having their claims adjudicated by applying legal norms to the facts? Do you think that such settlements make the parties happy? Trump's settlement, which was provoked to some degree by his *force majeure* clause, was reported in a blog run by the *Chicago Tribune*. There were many individual responses to the article. Several expressed a highly negative reaction to Mr. Trump and his lawyers who had, in the view of those posting comments, evaded Trump's contractual obligations to Deutsche Bank. The "a deal is a deal" norm appears to be alive still in this small, not random sample of the public.

8. *Is the law inconsistent if not incoherent? What's the point of this chapter?* Consider the conclusions of Professors David Campbell and Stewart Macaulay.[145] Macaulay's article says:

> [Campbell] said provocatively: "Far from it being the function of the law of contract to (so far as possible) prevent breach, the function of that law is

---

143. Mary Ellen Podmolik, *Donald Trump, Deutsche Bank Reach Truce over Chicago Skyscraper's Finances*, CHI. TRIB., Mar. 4, 2009.

144. Dealbook, *Trump Sees Act of God in Recission*, Dec. 5, 2008, http://dealbook.blogs.nytimes.com/2008/12/05/trump-sees-act-of-god-in-recession.

145. Stewart Macaulay, *Renegotiations and Settlements: Dr. Pangloss's Notes on the Margins of David Campbell's Papers*, 29 CARDOZO L. REV. 261, 262, 265–66, 271, 279 (2007).

to make breach possible although on terms which the law regulates." In all but the exceptional case, he notes, the aggrieved party will be limited to the difference between the contract price and the market price as contracts damages. The limited remedies available provoke a sharing of losses in most cases....

Campbell objects to the idea that we always must keep our promises even though they have become almost impossible to carry out. We all know the folk norm that imposes a moral obligation to perform a promise. There are stories, for example, of people who were wiped out financially during the Great Depression of the 1930s, but who worked the rest of their lives trying to pay off their debts. The stories invite us to admire such people. Judge Richard Posner tells us that this also is the law:

[A] fixed price contract is an explicit assignment of the risk of market price increases to the seller and the risk of market price decreases to the buyer ... If ... the buyer forecasts the market incorrectly and therefore finds himself locked into a disadvantageous contract, he has only himself to blame and so cannot shift the risk back to the seller by invoking impossibility or related doctrines.[146]

Campbell objects to such statements in judicial opinions and legal writing about contracts. These statements, he says, may lead to extreme antagonism in commercial disputes because they influence the aggrieved party to see the matter as a moral issue. Campbell argues that such positions found in the law may radiate an influence on any attempted settlement and on any continuing relation....

He also tells us that, in all but a limited subset of cases, a seller who names a fixed price for a performance is only taking a zone of risk and not committing his or her firm to foolish, if heroic, measures to carry out the deal precisely as written.

My own empirical research supports Campbell's picture of commercial norms. For example, a general counsel of a maker of heating and air conditioning products said:

When we are purchasing, we often help a supplier in difficulty. We will not penalize him in monetary terms. We think a strike or fire is a justifiable impossibility excuse whether or not the courts would think so. Our suppliers work with us when we need to delay deliveries or cancel, and we work with them. You don't worry about legal niceties.

A purchasing agent of a major producer of agricultural machinery similarly noted:

---

146. [22] Northern Indiana Pub. Serv. Co. v. Carbon Co. Coal Co., 799 F.2d 265, 278 (7th Cir. 1986).

We have gone to great lengths to help our suppliers when they face situations beyond their control. A number of years ago there was a flood in the Connecticut Valley that put many electrical manufacturers out of business.... Our Boston works sent in people and equipment to help them clean up the mess so our suppliers could get back in operation.... You don't kick a man when he is down. Someday you may need help yourself.

Of course, we might expect a different approach in insurance contracts that specified particular risks, transactions on a commodities futures exchange, or wagers at a gambling casino. These deals are examples of the world of *pacta sunt servanda*. Moreover, there may be difficult borderline situations where the actual risk assumption is very unclear....

I think that there are two folk norms found in business. On one hand, people should perform their promises and not make excuses. "A deal is a deal." "You gave your word." On the other hand, those who would benefit from a promise that is extremely burdensome should help such promisors when they are not at fault and not seeking their own gain. As is true of most customary norms, they are uncertain at the margins, and the facts of each case are all-important. Contract law reflects both of these inconsistent ideas.[147] Typically, both the law of contract remedies and the law in action push for some loss sharing. However, it is always possible that the plaintiff might recover a large amount as consequential damages. This chance may keep defendants trying to perform at least a little harder than if they were totally free of this risk.

We have cited and quoted several scholars who advocate changing the law to provide more formal rules that could offer more certainty as to the outcome of litigation. A rule that rejected any excuse for unanticipated problems not covered by a *force majeure* clause — that is, a modern *Paradine v. Jane* — might provide some degree of greater certainty. Would any other rule offer any certainty?

---

147. Eds. note: Section 1-106(1) of the Uniform Commercial Code reflects the two ideas stressed by Campbell. It provides: "The remedies provided by this Act shall be liberally administered to the end that the aggrieved party may be put in as good a position as if the other party had fully performed but neither consequential or special nor penal damages may be had except as specifically provided in the Act or by other rule of law." See § 1-305 for the analogous provision in Article 1 as revised in 2001.

TABLE OF CASES

[References are to pages.]

765

TABLE OF STATUTES

[References are to pages.]

UCC § 1-205(4), 263, 265, 266
UCC § 1-207, 578
UCC § 1-301, 237
UCC § 1-302, 237
UCC § 1-303(e), 266
UCC § 1-305, 764
UCC § 1-308, 578
UCC § 1-309, 576
UCC § 2-101, 388
UCC § 2-102, 160, 164
UCC § 2-103, 129
UCC § 2-103(1)(b), 150
UCC § 2-104(1), 150
UCC § 2-106, 488
UCC § 2-201, 58, 59, 159, 160, 166,
    168, 169, 171, 242, 291
UCC § 2-201(1), 147, 168, 169
UCC § 2-201(3), 59
UCC § 2-202, 236, 293, 301, 306, 307,
    316
UCC § 2-202(a), 279
UCC § 2-204, 136, 218
UCC § 2-204(1), 171, 234
UCC § 2-204(3), 108, 136
UCC § 2-205, 38, 41, 58, 123
UCC § 2-206(1), 234
UCC § 2-207, 192, 193, 197, 198, 203,
    207, 208, 211, 214, 218, 219, 220,
    222, 223, 224, 225, 227, 228, 230,
    231, 232, 234, 235, 236, 241
UCC § 2-207(1), 198, 205, 206, 218,
    219, 222, 227
UCC § 2-207(2), 205, 219, 220, 223,
    224, 232
UCC § 2-207(2)(b), 220
UCC § 2-207(3), 206, 228, 229, 235
UCC § 2-208, 224, 401, 402, 405
UCC § 2-208(1), 260, 401, 404
UCC § 2-208(2), 266, 405
UCC § 2-208(3), 402, 404
UCC § 2-209, 388, 402
UCC § 2-209(1), 377, 385
UCC § 2-209(2), 387, 401, 402
UCC § 2-209(3), 391
UCC § 2-209(4), 391, 401, 402, 403,
    406

UCC § 2-209(5), 382, 402, 404
UCC § 2-305, 118, 120, 133, 135, 136
UCC § 2-305(2), 127, 131
UCC § 2-305(4), 108
UCC § 2-306, 146, 147, 148, 149, 151,
    152, 153, 157, 166, 167, 168, 169
UCC § 2-306(1), 148, 150, 154
UCC § 2-306(2), 157, 167
UCC § 2-307, 500
UCC § 2-311, 136, 151
UCC § 2-315, 224
UCC § 2-508, 495
UCC § 2-508(2), 499
UCC § 2-601, 495
UCC § 2-606(1)(a), 385
UCC § 2-607, 462, 470, 480, 483
UCC § 2-607(1), 495
UCC § 2-607(3), 482
UCC § 2-607(4), 497
UCC § 2-608, 484, 493, 496
UCC § 2-608(3), 495
UCC § 2-609, 399
UCC § 2-609, 399, 508, 544, 559, 561,
    562, 566, 567, 568, 575, 576
UCC § 2-609(1), 560
UCC § 2-610, 229, 543, 549, 550, 562
42 U.S.C. §§ 2-615, 734
UCC § 2-615, 136, 592, 618, 631, 733,
    734
UCC § 2-615(a), 618
UCC § 2-702(1), 576
UCC § 2-712, 229, 538
UCC § 2-713, 538
UCC § 2-714(2), 221
UCC § 2-714(3), 221
UCC § 2-715, 221
UCC § 2-715(2)(a), 221
UCC § 2-717, 410
UCC § 2-719, 19, 156, 222, 225
UCC § 2-719(2), 235, 498
UCC § 2-721, 364

Restatements of the Law

INDEX

[References are to sections.]

Parol evidence rule (See Parol
Evidence Rule)
UCC
Battle of the forms; Section 2-
207, 197, 230
Sales contracts, 170

Franchises
Enforcement, 153

Fraud
Parol evidence rule, 359, 366

G

Good Faith
Bargaining, 4
UCC requirement as to good faith
and fair dealing, 453

I

Impracticability
Commercial impracticability, 736
Economic downturn, effect of, 736
Excuse of contract, 591, 631

Indefiniteness
Conditions, contracts with, 238
Disaffirmation of contracts due to,
97
UCC gap-filling, 102

Installment Contracts
Partial performance, 500, 507
UCC remedies for nonperformance,
500, 507

Interpretation of Contracts
Generally, 251, 255, 412
Battle of the forms; UCC Section 2-
207, 197, 230
Conditions, examination of, 251
Construction and, 412
Literal terms of contract, 593
Market functioning policy approach,
4
Mistake in formation of contract, 20
Parol evidence rule (See Parol
Evidence Rule)
Transactional approach, 4

UCC, under, 4

L

Letters of Intent
Generally, 173

M

Mailbox Rule
E-mail communications, 33
Fax communications, 33
Offer and acceptance, 33

Mediation
Use of, 701

Mistake
Avoidance of contract, 31
Bids, 31
Careless use of language, 21
Formation of contract, 20
Latent ambiguity, 26
Mailbox rule, 33
Mutual mistake, 31
Patent ambiguity, 26
Reformation of contract, 660
Unilateral mistake, 73

Modification
Changed circumstances
Economic downturn, 736
Mediation, 701
Reformation of contract, 660
CISG, 386
Course of performance, 386
Sales contracts, 377
Statute of frauds, 386
UCC, 377, 386
"Written modifications only"
clauses, 386

N

Notice
UCC notice for breach or
nonconforming goods, 459

O

Objective Theory of Contract
Formation of contract, 4